Oracle Press™

Oracle Designer Generation

Kenneth Atkins
Paul Dirksen
Zikri Askin Ince

Osborne/**McGraw-Hill**

Berkeley New York St. Louis San Francisco
Auckland Bogotá Hamburg London Madrid
Mexico City Milan Montreal New Delhi Panama City
Paris São Paulo Singapore Sydney
Tokyo Toronto

Osborne/**McGraw-Hill**
2600 Tenth Street
Berkeley, California 94710
U.S.A.

For information on translations or book distributors outside the U.S.A., or to arrange bulk purchase discounts for sales promotions, premiums, or fund-raisers, please contact Osborne/**McGraw-Hill** at the above address.

Oracle Designer Generation

1234567890 DOC DOC 90198765432109

ISBN 0-07-882475-3

Publisher
Brandon A. Nordin

Associate Publisher and Editor-in-Chief
Scott Rogers

Acquisitions Editor
Jeremy Judson

Project Editor
Mark Karmendy

Editorial Assistant
Monika Faltiss

Technical Editor
Karen Foley

Copy Editor
Sally Engelfried

Proofreaders
Linda and Paul Medoff

Indexer
Jack Lewis

Computer Designers
Ann Sellers
Michelle Galicia
Gary Corrigan

Illustrators
Brian Wells
Beth Young
Robert Hansen

Series Design
Jani Beckwith

About the Authors...

Kenneth Atkins is a Senior Principal Consultant with ARIS Corporation. He has over 7 years' experience with Oracle Designer, and over 10 years' experience with the Oracle database and tools. He has written numerous articles for *Oracle Developer* and the ODTUG *Technical Journal*, and is a frequent presenter at Oracle conferences. He maintains an Oracle Tip Web site at http://www.arrowsent.com/oratip.

Paul Dirksen is a Consulting Manager with ARIS Corporation specializing in full life cycle Oracle CASE development. Functioning in technical lead and project managerial roles, Paul has successfully implemented CASE-generated applications for both Fortune 1000 and Public Sector organizations. Paul has been using Oracle's CASE tool since version 5.0 and has been a regular speaker at regional and international Oracle conferences, presenting on the generation aspects of the tool.

Zikri Askin Ince is a Principal Consultant with ARIS Corporation. He has more than 8 years' experience with Oracle and development tools, and has been using Oracle Designer since CASE version 5.0. Askin has led and managed many Oracle CASE projects. He has successfully used Oracle CASE through all aspects of system development. He has recently started presenting at Oracle conferences and publishing his work.

ARIS Corporation (NASDAQ: ARSC, www.aris.com) provides integrated information technology (IT) services. The company's consulting and training services enable organizations to quickly implement leading-edge technologies from Oracle, Microsoft, Sun Microsystems, and Lotus. ARIS also offers niche software products that enhance the productivity of IT professionals.

About the Authors

Contents

PART II
Server-Side Code Generation

PART III
Forms Generation

PART IV
Forms Generation Infrastructure

Acknowledgments

When we were first thinking about writing a book, many published authors warned us about how much pain and work were involved. We decided to write the book anyway, and now we know what they meant. Writing a technical book is a lot of work, especially when you are trying to work full time at the same time! Of course, we never could have done it without the help and support of many others.

First, we would like to thank the whole Oracle development community. We have learned so much from other Oracle Designer developers who have freely shared their knowledge and experience, both in person and on the ODTUG e-mail lists. Much of what we learned from you appears in this book.

There are a few people who greatly helped us produce this book, both by encouragement and example. We would like to thank Mark Kramm, who started this whole project. We are sorry you had to bow out. Thanks to Kent Graziano, who reviewed much of the material and gave us some great input (and made us do more work!). Thanks to Rick Hata, who as well as reviewing material, ghostwrote a chapter for us when we were up against a deadline. A special thanks to the book's DBA, "Dr." Bob Deszell, for keeping the Oracle software on our laptops up and running smoothly. We would also like to acknowledge David Wendelken and Carrie Anderson, from whose book, *Designer Generation Handbook* (ISBN 0-201-63445-7), we "borrowed" some layout and presentation ideas. And a very special thanks to Ian Fisher of Oracle Corporation who gave us a lot of support and always made sure we had the latest version of Designer available to work with.

We all would like to thank ARIS Corporation for supporting us in this project. We especially thank Rick Brauen who encouraged us to start the whole thing. Thanks to our management: Jan Gomez, Amy Spangler, and Kelly Williams, who supported this project even at some cost to the company. We would like to thank some of our peers at ARIS who put up with our constant dialog about the book, who reviewed some of the material, and who put up with our split priorities: Jeff Devitt, Jenifer Brauen, Bob Syslo-Seel, Jim Young, Pat Roach, Dean Aoyama, and Tamara Dull.

Thanks to all of the people at Osborne/McGraw-Hill who supported this project. Special thanks go to Scott Rogers, who originally supported our ideas for this book. Thanks to Jeremy Judson, who guided it through to its completion. Thanks to Mark Karmendy, who put up with our weird layout requirements and worked with us to make the book look good. Thank you Monika Faltiss for encouraging us to keep up to our schedule (we won't call it nagging). Thanks to Karen Foley for reviewing all of the material and giving us many valuable suggestions. Thanks to Sally Engelfried who took whatever it was we wrote, and turned it into English. And last, thanks to all of the other people at Osborne/McGraw-Hill who we know worked on the book, but were so good we did not know they were there.

Thanks to our clients: the IT department of the Washington State Department of Natural Resources, and the US Forest Service. They put up with weird hours and our divided attention while we were writing the book.

The Authors

I would like to thank my wife Janet, for putting up with hearing about "The Book" for such a long time, both before I started writing it and while I was writing. I especially thank her for putting up with all of the times I said, "I can't do that because I have to work on the book". Without her prayers and support, I would never have been able to do it. Thanks to my sons (David, Joshua, Sean, Samuel, Gabriel, Jared, and Noah) who had to share daddy with "The Book" for such a long time. Thanks to my parents (Raymond and Sonya) for raising me to work hard and to always try to do my best. Thanks to my friends and family who put up with my explanations of the writing process, and listening (with glazed eyes) as I tried to explain what the book was about. And my biggest thanks to God, without whom the universe we are modeling would not even exist.

Kenneth Atkins
Olympia, WA
March, 1999

My love and gratitude go to my wife Nicole, for putting up with my crazy schedule, mood swings, and overall attitude for the last 8 months. I couldn't have done this without you. I promise to leave the laptop off more on weekends. To my mother and father (Agnes and Don) thank you for teaching me not only to work hard, but how to work smart. I'd also like to thank my sister, in-laws, and friends for listening intently to the sagas of this project when I'm sure it was boring you to tears! To my coauthors Ken and Askin, thank you for your unwavering commitment to this project. Without your energy and vision this book never would have been created. Lastly, to my personal coauthor Lexie (our cat) thanks for keeping me company through the early mornings and late nights.

Paul Dirksen
Olympia, WA
March, 1999

I am not even sure if I can thank my wife and soul mate Pinar enough for supporting me in whatever I choose to do. Since the very first night when we, Ken, Paul, and yours truly, told her about this book (with big smiling faces), she had to put up with my long hours working on the book and my consulting project. I could not do it without her support. I would like to thank both Ken and Paul for their trust and constant support; you guys are the best! This has been a long and painful journey, but I enjoyed *almost* every moment of it. Finally, I'd like to dedicate my work to my wife, our soon-to-be-born child, and everyone who has inspired me to work hard, learn more, be tenacious, and search for perfection.

Zikri Askin Ince
Portland, OR
March, 1999

Introduction

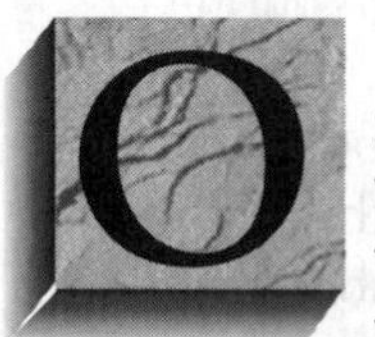

ne of the greatest strengths of Oracle Designer is its code generation capability. There are not too many CASE tools where all of the information that is collected and stored in the tool's repository can be readily used to generate most of the system. In spite of this apparent strength, however, many organizations using Oracle Designer decide *not* to use the code generators at all. Some organizations use Oracle Designer to perform the analysis and to produce the database schemas, but that's all. Other organizations use the generators to produce a default system, then make major changes after generation.

There are many reasons that the generators are not always used to their fullest capability. Some of the reasons are

- Lack of understanding of what the generators can do
- Dissatisfaction with the generated UI
- No experience with the generators
- Systems whose designs are difficult to generate

However, we think that these problems can be overcome for most systems. In our opinion, more organizations could (and should) use the generators more effectively.

We wrote this book to help those organizations that wish to use the Oracle Designer generators more effectively, especially the Oracle Developer generators (Forms and Reports). Based on our experience with these generators over many years and in multiple generated production systems, we will give you our suggestions and guidance about what does work and what does not.

Is This a Book for You?

To paraphrase an old saying, "A *book* can please some of the people all of the time, or all of the people some of the time, but it can't please all of the people all of the time!" And of course, that is also true about this book. It would be impossible to write one book that could cover all of the intricacies of the Oracle Designer product. And since there are other books that give a general overview about how to use the Oracle Designer product itself, we decided to focus on an area that has not received too much attention yet, generation.

We would be happy (and so would our publisher) if everyone who uses Oracle Designer decided to buy this book, but we know that this will not be the case. This introduction will summarize what this book is about, how it is designed, and who we expect will be using it. Reading through the introduction will also help people determine whether this is the right book to buy or recommend to someone. Therefore, if you have just picked up this book to thumb through at a bookstore or at a book table at an Oracle Conference, you can skim through the following pages to see if it's right for you (and we hope it is!).

What This Book Is Not

First, let's detail what this book is *not*. This book will not focus on *how* to use Oracle Designer, but rather on *what* to do with it. We will assume you are already familiar with the terminology used in Oracle Designer and know how to navigate around and use all of the tools. If you aren't already familiar with Oracle Designer, you should read the online documentation and go through the Oracle Designer tutorial, or perhaps you could attend some Oracle Designer training before using this book. Also, there are other Oracle

Designer books available that cover how to use the product. One such book is Koletzke and Dorsey's *Oracle Designer Handbook* published by Oracle Press.

This book will *not* detail the mechanics of performing system analysis and design. The focus, rather, is on the capabilities of the Oracle Designer generators. We may suggest that some designs are more easily generated than others. We will recommend steps that should be taken during analysis and design to increase the ease of generation. But it is up to you to use this information to perform the correct analysis and design for your application. Again, there are many good books available to assist you in this task.

We are only going to cover the Oracle Developer and server-side code generators. We are not covering the Visual Basic generator. Why? Partly because there have not been as many people using these generators for various reasons, but mainly because we do not have as much experience with these generators, and there is not as much we could tell you. We had originally planned to cover WebServer generation in this book. We decided to leave it out for a couple of reasons. First, we wanted to finish the book sometime in our lifetimes, and we had to narrow the scope somewhere. Second, there are many areas where the generation approach is vastly different when using WebServer, so we thought it might be better covered in a separate book. Hopefully, someone will write a WebServer generator book soon. Last, we are *not* going to cover the actual database (schema) generation.

However, the main reason that we are not covering some of these topics is that we needed to narrow the scope somewhere or we would have ended up with a 2000-page book. You might have liked that, but we would have ended up writing the book forever, which we (and our families) would not have appreciated.

What This Book Is

OK, so what *is* in this book? The primary focus is Generation, Generation, Generation! While we will talk about some general issues (like naming standards) and some analysis and design issues, everything will be geared toward how it affects generation. Also, this book will only focus on the following types of generation:

- Oracle Forms Generation
- Oracle Reports Generation

- Server-side PL/SQL generation (including the Table API)
- Microsoft Help Generation

Almost all of the client-server systems that are being generated out of Oracle Designer are based on Forms, Reports, and Server-side PL/SQL, so this focus makes sense. With the capability of deploying the generated forms and reports on the Web, these generators will probably still retain their dominance.

This book is designed to focus on Oracle Designer release 2, because that is the current production release. This material will also be applicable to release 6 of Designer scheduled for production shipping in the spring of 1999. The main purpose of release 6 is generation support for Developer 6, not the addition of new functionality. Sure, there will be a few discrepancies due to bug fixes, but the vast majority of this material contained in this book with still be valid.

We don't want to waste time just repeating what is in the current Oracle Designer documentation. Many things that are explained well in the Oracle Designer online documentation will be covered only briefly. We will refer you to the location of the relevant information in the online documentation. This in itself can be quite helpful since the online documentation has one major drawback: it can be quite difficult to find the help you need, even when it *is* there!

Target Audience

This book is intended for two different audiences:

- **The programmers or analysts who actually do the generation**

In some organizations it might be a functional analyst who does the generation, and in others it might be generation specialists or Oracle Developer programmers. No matter who is doing the generation, we are providing them with detailed information about how to achieve specific screen and report layouts, and specifics about including desired functionality.

- **The analysts or architects who are responsible for the system design**

For the analysts/architects, we will provide guidelines to assist them in creating system designs that *can* be generated. We will illustrate what can be easily generated and what cannot. The book includes screen shots of the types of layouts that can be generated. If these examples are used as guidelines during the design of the screen layout and functionality, designers can be sure that their designs will be easily generated. Programmers could then refer to the book to see how to generate each specific layout. Of course in smaller organizations, the same person might perform both of these functions.

Design of the Book

Next, we will detail some specifics about the book design that will help you use the book more effectively.

Pictures and Screen Shots

Since a picture is worth a thousand words, we are including *lots* of screen shots and diagrams. We want you to be able to find a screen shot of the layout you want, then easily see how to do it. Also, wherever possible, we will use diagrams to make points clear.

Tips and Notes

Sometimes there is a related issue that should be discussed in relation to a section of the book, but it is outside the flow of the current topic. In these cases, there will be a section with an icon like this:

NOTE
This note is just a test. Had this been a real tip, you would have been reading some really cool or useful information instead of this sappy sentence. The content could be a 'Tip', 'Note', or 'Caution', that would be useful at this point in the book.

These sections can give you useful tips and tricks, or explain a fine point in more detail.

Shaded Boxes

Throughout the book, there are shaded boxes that contain information that is relevant to the information presented in the chapter, but which is outside of the flow of the text. These topics were added to help share the authors' experiences with the topics provided, or to give detailed examples and techniques that will elaborate the chapter's content.

Troubleshooting Guides

Many of the detailed generation sections will include a Troubleshooting Guide, located at the end of the section in table form. This guide will list some common generation problems you might encounter when trying to generate the feature covered in that section. It will also give a solution to the problem (when there is one), or confirm that the problem is a bug with the generator.

CD Included

Also included with the book (as you may have noticed) is a CD. This CD will have all of the examples we use in the book, as well as some utilities, documentation templates, forms templates, and demos of third-party tools that we think will help you in your system generation efforts. You'll find a page near the CD at the back of the book explaining how to use the CD.

Example Application

We decided to base most of the examples in our book on one Example Application. This will give the book a little more cohesiveness, and the real-life type examples will be more useful to you (we hope). We decided to use an Issue Management system as the basis for our examples. We chose this type of system because the concepts involved (issues, bugs, database change requests, modules, etc.) should be something everyone who reads this book is familiar with. You should have a basic understanding of the need and purpose of this type of application without having to spend time trying to understand it. Appendix A contains a data diagram and an overview of this application. You can refer to this data diagram to help you understand the examples better.

Overview of the Book's Parts

The book's chapters are organized into parts. This is done to make it easier for you to find the chapters you are interested in. Following is an overview of all 5 parts.

Part I: System Generation with Oracle Designer

This part starts with an overview of the system generation process, then goes on to discuss the main goal of this book: highly generated systems. It concludes with a discussion of some of the things that are important to consider when approaching the development of a system using Oracle Designer. This part will give you a good understanding of what Oracle Designer system generation is, why you should be striving for highly generated systems, and how generation fits in the whole life cycle of your system.

Part II: Server-Side Code Generation

This part covers how to perform server-side code generation, including procedures, functions, packages, triggers, and the Table API. While the actual PL/SQL code for some of these components are not written by the Oracle Designer generators, there are many advantages to putting as much information about these programs into the repository, and then using this information to produce the SQL scripts to load the programs into the database. This part will detail how to enter the information into the repository in order to successfully produce the SQL to load the programs into the database.

Part III: Forms Generation

This part covers basic forms generation topics. You might call these the out-of-the-box generation techniques. The part starts with an overview of forms generation, including the sources for information that is used in generation, a description of the features of a generated form, and a list of the standard generated functionality. Part III continues with a chapter about tasks that should be performed before the modules are even created. Part III includes chapters on window, canvas, block, and item generation; GUI item generation, generation of standard functionality, LOV generation, navigation generation, and layout generation techniques. A special "Layout Generation Cookbook" chapter presents a series of screen shots along with the detailed generation techniques and preferences needed to produce them. This is a good section to read to get a general understanding about what can easily be generated, and how to do it.

Part IV: Forms Generation Infrastructure

This part covers more advanced forms generation topics that mostly relate to the infrastructure needed to generate the forms. The following advanced topics will be covered: template form and object library setup and usage, code sharing and reuse, application logic in the repository, help system generation, deployment considerations, and managing reference and code control tables. This is the part to read when you are ready to go beyond the standard out-of-the-box generation.

Part V: Reports Generation

This part starts with how to set up and use templates in reports generation, then continues with a chapter about how to define and generate a report. It continues with chapters about refining the data selection and refining the Where clause. It then goes on to detail some report generation techniques and how to generate some specific report styles and layouts. Part V concludes with an appendix that contains a data diagram for the example application system used throughout the book.

CD Contents and Information

A page providing you with a list of the contents of the CD and instructions about how to use it is found after the index at the back of the book.

Bon Appétit

Now that we have given you a summary of what is in the book, we hope you are ready to dive in and learn how to use Oracle Designer to generate user-friendly, quality, and easily supportable systems. This book has many chapters that can be read straight through to give you a better understanding of how to generate systems. There are also chapters that will be best used as references. However you use the book, it is our hope that you get a great benefit from it.

PART I

System Generation with Oracle Designer

CHAPTER 1

Overview of the System Generation Process

In this chapter, we are going to present a brief overview of the whole system generation process. Some of you may have no experience with Oracle Designer generation at all. Some of you may already be familiar with some aspects of Oracle Designer generation but may not understand the whole process. Others may be very familiar with the process but would like to see someone else's view of it. For all of these levels of experience, we thought a brief overview of the generation process would be helpful. When you are considering the topics we discuss in the rest of the book, you can refer to this chapter to see how they fit into the big picture.

This chapter can also be useful for another audience. Often people on a project team will not be directly involved in generation but would nevertheless benefit from an understanding of how Oracle Designer generation works. These people might be analysts, managers, user representatives, etc.; they can read this chapter to get a basic understanding of the whole process.

What Is Generation?

First, we want to come to an understanding of exactly what is meant by system generation. Let's consider the following definitions:

Oracle Designer *n.* A repository of information about or related to information systems.

System *n.* An assemblage or combination of things or parts forming a complex or unitary whole.[1]

Generation *n.* Production by natural or artificial processes.[1]

Using the definitions above, we might define system generation like this:

Oracle Designer System Generation *n.* The production and assembly of a combination of programs into a unitary whole by the use of a predefined process, based on the information stored in the Oracle Designer repository.

1 *Webster's Encyclopedic Unabridged Dictionary of the English Language.*

In Oracle Designer, system generation is the process that we use to take the information that we have laboriously stored in the repository and, from it, produce the actual application system. It is a way to leverage the analysis and design information that we have collected into the actual programs that are used to implement our design. Most of this book will talk about how to refine the information in the repository so that the generation process will produce the desired results. This chapter will talk about the process itself. Reading this chapter will help you fit the topics covered in the rest of the book into their correct positions in the whole process.

There are many good reasons to generate your Oracle application systems from Oracle Designer. There are also some difficulties that need to be overcome. In the next chapter, we will discuss why it is worthwhile to overcome these difficulties and use Oracle Designer to generate the system instead of just developing the system from scratch.

General Flow of Information in Oracle Designer

Before we look at the actual generation process, we are going to look at the general flow of information into and through Oracle Designer. This will help you understand some of the limitations of Oracle Designer and its generators. It will also help you understand when, where, and why you need to enter certain information into Oracle Designer.

Upper vs. Lower CASE (Computer-Aided Software Engineering)

It is very important to understand that the Oracle Designer repository and toolset is divided into two areas:

1. ANALYSIS (Upper CASE):
    a. Elements: entities, attributes, functions, dataflows, events, datastores, etc.
    b. Tools: Process Modeller, Entity Relationship Diagrammer, Function Hierarchy Diagrammer, Dataflow Diagrammer, Matrix Diagrammer.

2. DESIGN/BUILD (Lower CASE):
   a. Elements: tables, columns, views, snapshots, modules, etc.
   b. Tools: Design Editor (schema model, module data model, module logic model, etc.)

NOTE
In Release 1.3, instead of the integrated Design Editor, there was a multiplicity of editors: Data Diagrammer, Module Structure Diagrammer, Module Data Diagrammer, etc. In release 2.1 they were all merged into one, the Design Editor. However, the Upper CASE/Lower CASE division has always been a part of the tool.

These two areas are often referred to as Upper CASE (analysis) and Lower CASE (design/build). Oracle Designer is a computer-aided software engineering (CASE) tool and, before CASE became a bad word, Oracle Designer used to be called Oracle*CASE. With the perceived failure of many CASE approaches and tools, Oracle decided to rename their product to avoid the negative connotations. In the earlier versions of Oracle*CASE and in the RON (Repository Object Navigator), the analysis objects were generally placed above the design objects, probably because analysis comes before design and most people like to work in a top-down fashion. Because of this arrangement, and because of the play on words (upper- and lower-case text), the analysis part of the tool came to be called Upper CASE and the design area Lower CASE.

Why is there a distinction between the two areas? The distinction exists because there is a firm line between these two areas in the information flow and process of system development using Oracle Designer. After the analysis is completed, there is a transformation during which the analysis (Upper CASE) information is copied down into the design area (Lower CASE). The design elements are then refined to add additional information needed to actually generate the system. If changes are made to the design data elements (tables, columns, etc.), it is possible to use the retrofit capabilities in Oracle Designer to update the analysis elements (entities, attributes) with the changes. This capability can be used to keep the analysis and design data models in sync. However, there is no corresponding capability for the process elements (functions, data flows, etc.), so they have to be kept in sync manually. Because of this, the transformation often becomes a one-way transformation in which the design models are created from the analysis models and are then allowed to diverge as the system is actually designed. Therefore, it is usually a good idea to make sure your analysis models are as complete as possible before performing the transformations.

Sources of Information

In Figure 1-1 there are three sources of information that are indicated by text with ovals around the text. These sources indicate *very* general categories, because it is out of the scope of this book to discuss the exact methodologies used for gathering analysis and design information for your systems. These areas have been identified to illustrate the general flow of information in Oracle Designer. The three sources are

- Analysis information
- Design information
- Standards

Analysis Information

During the strategy and analysis phases of system development, much of the information about the system to be developed is collected and entered into the repository. This information is entered into the Upper CASE elements (entities, relationships, functions, etc.). Once the information is in place, various quality checks and further analysis can be done to ensure that the system is complete before the information is transformed into the design area.

Design Information

All of the information needed for the physical implementation of the tables and modules cannot be collected and stored in the repository during analysis. During the design phase, you must refine the elements that were

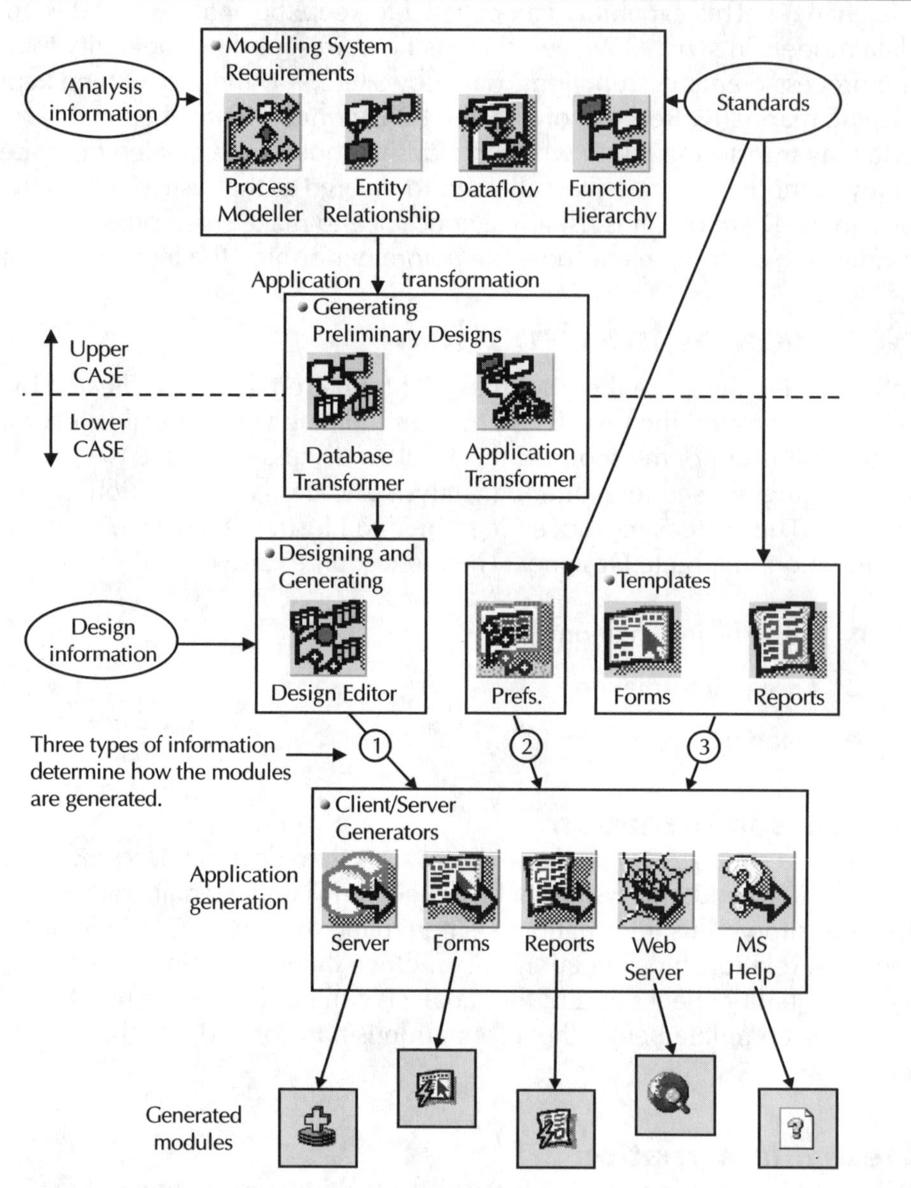

FIGURE 1-1. *Information flow in Oracle Designer*

created by the Application and Database Transformers. This will include such tasks as the following:

- Standardizing and refining the names of some of the tables and columns that are created by the Transformation Wizard
- Ensuring that the tables and modules conform to standards
- Refining the modules by adding information not available during analysis
- Setting preferences
- Building template forms and common libraries

Most of this book will be concerned with adding this type of information to the repository to help in your generation efforts.

Standards

Every development organization should develop a consistent and complete set of standards to guide the system development process. This set of standards can do much to increase the efficiency and consistency of the developed system. The standards will affect every area in the system development process, including the following:

- **Analysis** Domains and naming standards
- **Application Transformation** Guides design decisions made during transformation
- **Design** Naming standards, processing standards, GUI standards
- **Preferences** GUI standards, processing standards
- **Templates** GUI standards

A good set of standards can actually be considered a source of information that is used in the system development and generation process. This is because decisions about object naming, preference settings, normalization strategies, design strategies, etc., can be made once for an organization and won't have to be reinvented for every application. These decisions are the information that developers use to make the related design decisions.

The General Flow of Information

Now we will describe the flow of information in Figure 1-1.

The information for a particular system originates with the analysis performed for that application. This information is entered into the Upper CASE or analysis area of the repository using the analysis tools. The organization's standards are considered during the creation of the analysis elements (entities, functions, etc.), so the standards can be considered another source of information for analysis.

Once this information is entered and refined, the Database and Application Transformers are used to transform the analysis information into design information. This transformation takes the conceptual/logical model stored in Upper CASE and creates a physical model in Lower CASE.

NOTE
Many people like to produce separate functional and conceptual models during the analysis. Unfortunately, Oracle Designer does not support the concept of three model dimensions (conceptual, functional, and logical/physical) very well. It is possible to use Designer to do this, and there are various approaches, each with their own strengths and weaknesses. However, it is out of the scope of the book to discuss this.

The transformation may not be a one-step process. It can be advantageous to run the transformers multiple times with different sets of objects, using different transformation options each time. For instance, you may want to create surrogate keys for some objects and not others. You can run the Database Transformer once for the objects you want to create surrogate keys for and then again for the objects that do not need surrogate keys. You might also develop an application system in a series of parts, or phases, and only want to transform part of the system initially.

Once you are finished running the transformers for all of the relevant objects, the application is ready for design.

During the design phase, the elements produced by the wizards are refined when the developers add additional information about each object in the repository. This will include such design elements as the following:

- Table names and default titles
- Module types, languages, and titles
- Module component table usages, including the following:
  - Where clause restrictions
  - Usage alias
  - Links between table usages
  - Additional lookup usages
  - Help information
- Bound items, including the following:
  - Display length, format, and type
  - Display type
  - Sort order
  - Prompt
  - Help information
- The addition of unbound items
- Application logic
- Module network (menus)

Again, standards are an important input into this process. The names of the objects and elements need to conform to the standards, and the design and GUI standards will determine how each object's properties are set.

The support objects for the generation environment need to be developed at this point. These include the following:

- Forms Templates and object libraries
- Reports Templates
- Forms libraries

These templates and libraries will usually be refined and developed further during the system generation process, especially for the first few systems you develop.

Oracle Designer Sources for Generation

There are three major types of information that Oracle Designer uses to actually generate modules (see Figure 1-2):

1. **The Oracle Designer Repository**

   The repository contains the definitions of the tables, column, modules, etc., that define the structure and functionality of the generated modules. This is the primary source of information that is used by the generators to produce the module and is the source of information about *what* to generate.

2. **Oracle Designer Generation Preferences**

   The preferences are used by the generator to control the layout, GUI standards, and some of the functionality of the generated modules. While the preference settings are also stored in the Oracle Designer repository, they really are a different type of information. If the information in the rest of the repository tells the generators *what* to generate, then the preferences tell the generators *how* to generate it. The preferences are really generator directives that tell the generators how to lay out the modules and what standard functionality to include for the items.

3. **Oracle Developer Templates and Object Libraries**

   The templates are the base or container that the generators place the generated module into. The templates could be considered the canvas that the generators paint the modules onto! There can also be links to standardized code that is to be shared across many modules. The object libraries serve to set many of the properties of the generated items in a more flexible fashion than would be possible just using the templates and the preferences.

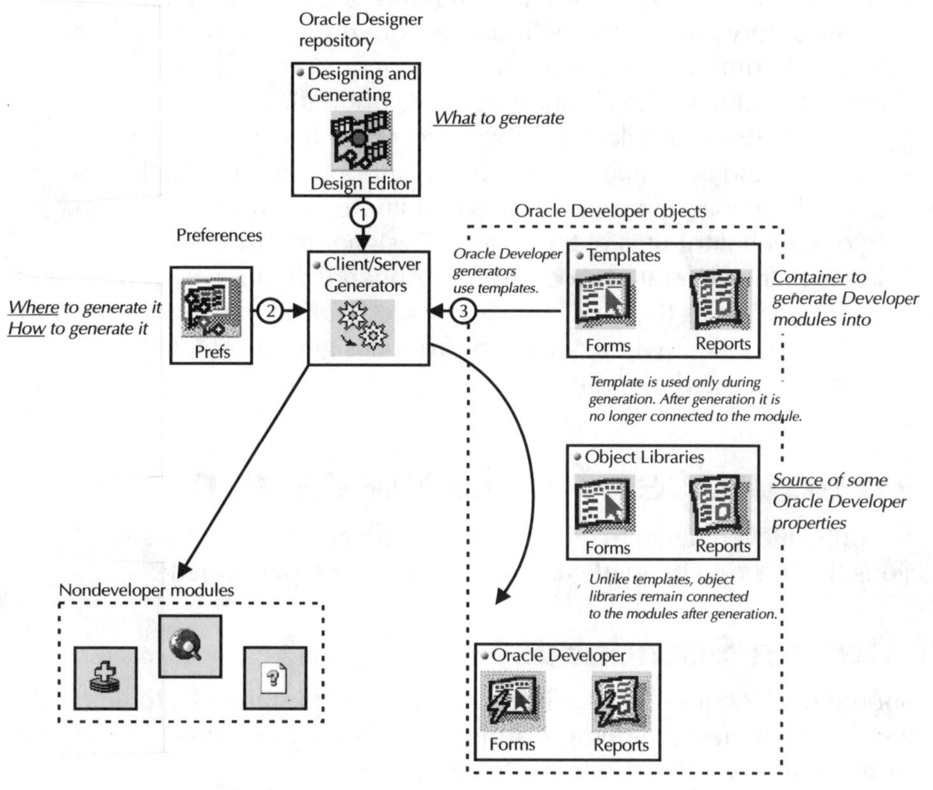

FIGURE 1-2. *Sources of information used in Oracle Designer*

NOTE

Forms Templates and Reports Templates were much more important in release 1.3. The templates often included standard code segments and links to standard libraries. The templates could be used to overcome some of the generator's limitations, such as the fact that the repository only allows a module to be directly linked to one library (via a preference). Many people also used the templates to add nongenerated code to modules by placing the code into a specific template for each module. Most of these methods of using the templates are no longer needed because of enhancements made in release 2.1.

The generators take the information that has been stored in the Oracle Designer repository and create the modules for your application system. Each piece of information is placed in a specific location (or locations) in the generated modules. The location depends upon the type of module being generated (for example, forms, reports, or Web server), the settings of the preferences, and the value of some of the attributes in the Oracle Designer repository. It is beyond the scope of this chapter to give an item-by-item mapping of which attributes in the Oracle Designer repository become which items in the generated modules; see Appendix D for a map of where attributes from analysis (Upper CASE) are placed during the application and data transformation and where attributes from design (Lower CASE) are placed in the generated modules.

Prerequisites for Generation

Before you can even begin to generate the application, there are some decisions that need to be made and some tasks to be performed.

UI Design Standards

You should develop a set of user interface (UI) design standards to help guide you during the development and generation of the system. These design standards should include the following:

- How windows will be used, choosing any of the following options:
    - One window for the whole application
    - Multiple windows displayed and active at the same time
    - Multiple windows used only in special cases
    - Whether the application should take over the screen or only display a small window
- How to use colors, line types, and fonts
- Whether or not to use list of values (LOV) buttons for each item with an LOV
- Toolbar design

- Navigation design, including any of the following:
    - Pull-down menus
    - Button navigation
    - Automatic query on navigation
- Multiblock layout (stubs, pop-ups, windows, etc.)

Application Preferences

Once you have developed your UI standards, you must implement them somehow. In Oracle Designer this is done primarily through setting the preferences. There are hundreds of preferences that affect the generation of the system, although most of them are usually the same for all of the modules in the application. When this is true, the preferences should be set at the application level; this will set the default for all of the modules in the application. The application-level preference settings can be used to enforce the UI standards and will ensure a greater consistency across all of the modules of the applications. In some cases, the application preference settings at the application level are just defaults and may be overridden for specific modules. In other cases, you will want to lock the preferences and not allow developers to change them for each module.

These application-level preferences should be set before you generate any of the modules for the system.

Preference Sets

Because there are so many preferences that can be difficult to manage, it is a good idea to define some preference sets as soon as you finalize your application's GUI standards. These sets will be used to generate specific types of modules. For instance, you may have a preference set defined for LOV-type modules, another for code maintenance modules, and another for standard modules. It is even a good idea to have a preference set for the application-level preferences that you used to define your UI standards. If you do this, the next time you develop an application with the same UI standards, you will only have to apply the preference set at the application level.

Preference sets may evolve over the life of your project. This is especially true for your first few Oracle Designer projects, because you may not know how you want to set all of the preferences before you generate your first application. Many of the preferences have layout and functionality repercussions that are not obvious without some experience. Although you will not know what the final setting for all of the preferences may be, you should still create the preference sets and set the preferences that you do know. You can refine these preference sets while you are developing your first few modules.

Preference sets will be discussed in more detail later in the book. There are also many example preference sets available on the CD that you can use as a starting place for your application's specific needs.

Templates, Object Libraries, and PL/SQL Libraries

You can generate working modules from Oracle Designer out of the box. That is, you can generate your modules using one of the standard templates that are provided with the tool. However, the capabilities and design of these templates may not fit into your organization's standards, nor meet the specific needs of your application. Because of this, most organizations will need to make modifications to the templates or develop new templates from scratch. Chapters 22 and 27 will cover in detail how to set up and use templates and object libraries in your generated forms and reports. Also, we have included some example templates and libraries on the CD to help you get started.

If you want a more robust set of templates than is available from Oracle or on the CD with this book, you can purchase some from various third-party template and library vendors. There are three template packages that we know are currently available:

- Uniscape's Design Assist (**www.seeristic.com**)
- UCC's Guidelines/2000 (**www.decade.nl**)
- Oracle's Head Start Templates (**www.oracle.com**)

They all have their own strengths and weaknesses, but any of them will help you develop robust, feature-rich applications from Oracle Designer. To help you evaluate them, we have included some marketing information and/or demos from each of them on the CD that comes with the book.

The Generation Process

The previous sections of this chapter presented the basic information flow in Oracle Designer generation and listed some of the prerequisites for generation. Next, we will detail the actual generation process itself. This will be a brief overview of the steps involved in just the generation aspect of system development in Oracle Designer.

Overview of Standard Generation Process

Figure 1-3 gives an overall picture of the flow of the module generation process. A description of each step in the process follows.

1. **Create the database definition in Oracle Designer.**

   Before the system can be generated, the database definition should be created using the Database Transformer. Once all of the table definitions have been created, you can start generating the modules. However, the default table definitions are not usually acceptable for generation. The physical design will need to be evaluated, and the column names and formats will need to be cleaned up. Auditing columns (if needed) can be added, views can be created to facilitate such activites as reporting and generation. Once you are happy with the basic physical database design, you can continue to the next step. This does not have to be the final physical design, and you will undoubtedly discover problems with the design during the creation of the modules. In these cases, the physical model will be changed, and any affected forms generated again.

2. **Create the physical database in Oracle.**

   Once the database design is correct, you can create the database in Oracle. You will need to have the database installed in a development instance before you can generate any of the modules. The tables have to exist physically in the database before the modules can compile.

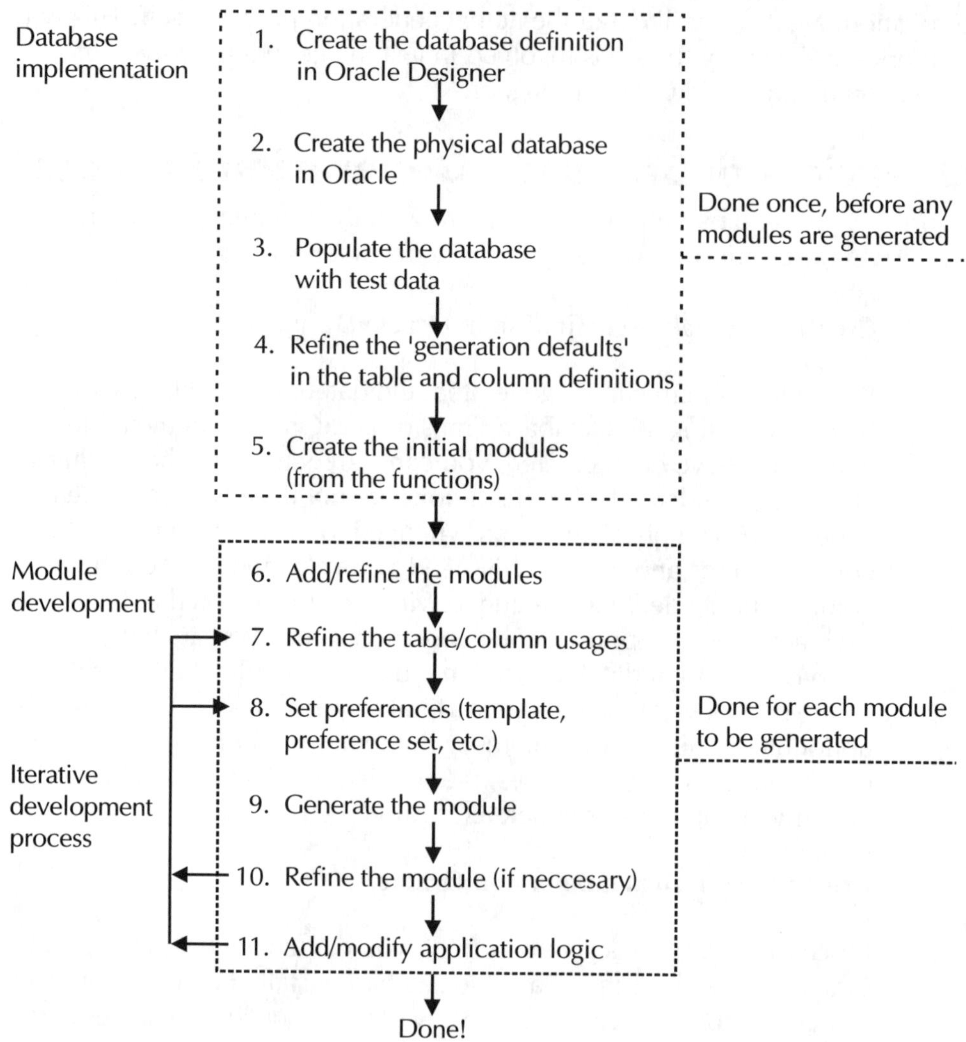

FIGURE 1-3. *Generation process flow*

NOTE
In Oracle Developer release 2.1 there are some terminology changes that may confuse experienced developers. In release 1.3 (and previous releases) the process of converting a Developer source file (.FMB, .MMB, .RDF) into an executable file (.FMX, .MMX, .REP) was given the title "generate." This caused much confusion between this function and the Oracle Designer generation function. In release 2.1, this process is named "compile."

3. **Populate the database with test data.**

   You cannot complete the generation of the forms without some sort of test data in the database. Otherwise, you cannot check to make sure you have included all of the desired functionality. For example, you cannot create any records in forms that have LOVs until you have put some data in the lookup tables. Similarly, you cannot test all of the query functionality until you have put some data into the tables. It is possible to use the application itself to enter the data (assuming you have included code table maintenance screens as part of the application), but this might not be the best way to populate the data. It is usually better to write some SQL scripts to populate the database with test data. This way, if you have to recreate the database (which is likely, especially if you are using a Rapid Application Development (RAD) or evolutionary prototype approach), you will just have to run the scripts again to populate the database with test data.

4. **Refine the generation defaults in the table and column definitions.**

   There are many properties in the table and column definitions that will be used as defaults for the modules' properties. Because of this, the table and column definitions should be refined before the modules are actually created. Some of the properties that should be verified and refined are outlined in the following table.

Table/Column Property	Module Property
Table: alias	DTU: usage alias
Table: display title	Module component: title
Column: display?	Bound item: display?
Column: display type	Bound item: display type
Column: prompt	Bound item: prompt

There are many more properties that need to be verified. The complete list will be covered in Chapter 11.

5. **Create the initial modules (from the functions).**

   Next, the Application Transformer is used to create the modules from the functions that were defined during analysis. Again, the Application Transformer is not perfect, so the modules will have to be refined.

NOTE
In release 1.3, the program that created modules in Lower CASE from the functions in Upper CASE was called the Application Wizard. It performed the same function as the Application Transformer does in release 2.

6. **Add/refine the modules.**

   This step, along with the next two, is really the core of this book. Most of this book will deal with these steps.

   The Application Transformer gives you the basic structure of many of the application's modules. However, the Application Transformer mainly gives you the module's data usages. Much work needs to be done to refine the modules so that they will generate with the desired design. Also, there may be many modules with no corresponding analysis function; these will have to be created from scratch. LOV modules and PL/SQL support modules are two examples of modules that often need to be created from scratch.

7. **Refine the table and column usages.**

   The primary task to perform for each module is to refine the detailed table and column usages. The detailed table usages will need to be placed in the correct order, the parent/child relationships established, the lookup usages defined, the titles and prompts set correctly, the item display format and sizes set, the window and canvas sizes set, etc. This is where most of the real work in module development will take place.

8. **Set preferences—template, preference set, etc.**

   Once you have determined what is going to be generated (by selecting the tables and columns, and adding unbound items, etc.), there remains one more task to perform before you can generate your module with the correct design: you have to modify the module's preferences. The module will have some default settings based either on the factory defaults for Oracle Designer or on any application defaults you set yourself (as mentioned previously). Now you will have to set some preferences specifically for the module. The first time you generate, you may want to accept the defaults and see what you get. Once you see what you have generated, modify some of the preferences and generate the module again. You will repeat (and repeat and repeat) this process many times until the module generates the way you want it to.

   As you work with the preferences, you will find that certain settings are being used for many of the modules. If they are being used for almost all of the modules, the preference default settings at the application level should be set. However, if certain preference settings are only used for a specific type of module (such as LOV modules, code maintenance modules, multirecord block with a scroll bar, etc.), you should put the preferences into a preference set. This preference set should then be attached to that module and any other modules of the same type. We will talk more about preference sets later in the book.

9. **Generate the module.**

   Now it's time to actually generate the module. The exact process for this depends on the target module type (reports, forms, Web server, for example), but it always involves entering some information in the generation dialogs, starting the generation, and watching it run. There will always be some warnings and sometimes errors. The errors are usually about problems with the data model (for example, a PK with no columns). The warnings are sometimes important and sometimes not. You will have to learn which warnings you need to deal with, and which you can take note of, then ignore.

10. **Refining the module again (and again, and again...).**

    Once the module is generated and the resultant program is evaluated, you will usually find that the generation was not perfect. You will have to go back into the module definition and the module's detailed table and column usages and change them to get the desired results. These steps (refine, generate, and evaluate) will be performed many times for each module (see the next section).

11. **Add the application logic for the module.**

    Wait until the basic layout and structure of your module is done before adding the application logic because the structure might change dramatically while you are trying to get the desired functionality. You might have to drop and re-create the table or column usages, change the base columns to views, or apply any number of basic structure changes before you get the desired result. If you have already added the application logic, you will have to cut it out and add it again to the new structure. Worse yet, you might forget about it until later and have to write it again! Once you have the module layout and structure that you need and you have generated as much functionality as is possible with the generators, you are ready to add the application logic. For some, the easiest way to add application logic may be to add it to the forms after generation, and then use the design recovery to get it back into the module definition. Even in this case you should wait until you are sure the module generation is complete before you add the application logic.

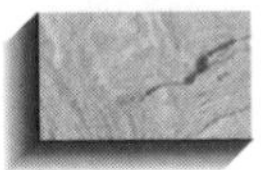

NOTE
Release 1.3 was not capable of generating the application logic into the module from information in the repository. Because of this, there were many postgeneration changes that had to be made to the modules. In release 1.3, it was always a good idea to wait until you were sure that the module's layout and structure were done before you added the postgeneration changes to the form. Even so, you still had to reapply the modifications five to ten times because of having to regenerate the module after the postgeneration changes were done!

Oracle Designer Generation Is an Iterative Process

The generation process is *very* iterative. You will be performing step 10 (which is actually steps 6 through 9) from the previous section many times in order to get the desired layout and functionality for the module (see Figure 1-3). This process will seem to take a long time at first. However, as you gain experience with the generators, you can get fairly close to the desired layout and functionality the first time, and you will not need too many iterations to get the exact design you want. So don't be too concerned if it seems to take forever to develop your first few modules—you'll get better with experience!

The process will always be iterative by nature, however, and it will always take a few iterations to get the module you want. This is not a problem though, because the whole system development process is iterative anyway, with or without Oracle Designer. We should already be accustomed to an iterative process.

Evolutionary Prototyping

In many projects it seems that the users are involved in the analysis (at least we hope analysts talk to them!), but then don't see the system again until the design and build are completed and they are supposed to start testing it! This approach can lead to systems that are not very well accepted by the users, because the systems do not really meet the users' needs. However, this approach is usually used because the programmers can't show the programs to the users until they are completed, and because the time, expense, and hassle of producing mock-ups is prohibitive.

One way to avoid this is to use an evolutionary prototype approach to system development. Because of the Form generators and Report generators, Oracle Designer really lends itself to this kind of approach. With an evolutionary prototype, the users will still be involved in the development process, even after the analysis is completed.

After the initial design is done, many of the screens and reports can be generated out of Oracle Designer and presented to the users as prototypes. The users can then give the development team feedback about missing requirements, the usability of the UI, and the completeness of the system. If the screens are presented to the users as early as possible, then any changes they request will have much less impact on the development of the system. When the first set of suggested changes is implemented, the screens can be presented to the users again for more suggestions. This is an iterative process where the final prototype becomes the actual module, hence the name *evolutionary prototyping*.

However, we would raise one caution about this approach. Sometimes it is difficult to get out of this iteration because this technique is susceptible to "scope creep," meaning that the users will not want to approve of the system until it is perfect. With the evolutionary prototype approach, it is best to give the user input phase a time limit, and then go on to the final development and testing phases just as in a regular development effort. During these final phases, the users can no longer make suggestions for the first release of the system. It is also usually a good idea to formalize the process for having the module signed off as complete.

The advantages of an evolutionary prototyping method are easily made use of in an Oracle Designer developed project, with a minimum of the disadvantages. For this reason, evolutionary prototyping it is a very good approach to take with Oracle Designer generation.

Conclusion

We hope this brief overview helped you understand the general flow of the system generation process. Since this was only a cursory treatment, many details were left out of the descriptions. These details will be provided in the remainder of the book.

This overview should help you understand where each task and technique discussed in the book fits in the whole process. Now you are ready to jump into the details of system generation with Oracle Designer.

CHAPTER 2

The GOAL—Highly Generated Systems

When Oracle promotes Oracle Designer as a tool, they usually talk about its generation capabilities. They often sell the tool by promoting the idea that it will generate most (if not all) of your system. Is this really possible or is this just hype? What do we have to sacrifice to achieve what Oracle claims? What exactly do people mean when they talk about 100 percent generation? We will attempt to answer these questions in this chapter.

It's a Philosophical Issue!

The first thing we need to realize is that the concept of highly generated systems is a philosophical issue! Some people are adamant about the fact that they can and do produce close to 100 percent generated systems using Oracle Designer. They will also claim that they do this without making nonacceptable sacrifices in the user interface of the system. Other people just as adamantly maintain that it's impossible to generate anything other than fancy default forms without major sacrifices to the system's user interface, data design, or both. How can these two groups of otherwise intelligent people hold to such diametrically opposed views?

It's because, from a philosophical perspective, each group places different value on different aspects of the generated system or the system development life cycle. Some people value the user interface over all other aspects, while others refuse to denormalize the data model for any reason. Some people want to ensure that the systems are automatically documented very well, while others don't think this is as important, or they trust the programmers to document the nongenerated aspects to an acceptable degree. What we need to realize is that neither group is necessarily wrong! They just have different views of what is important.

We Are Biased Toward Highly Generated Systems

Since this topic is so philosophical, you might want to know the philosophy of the authors of this book. As you probably surmised from the heading of this section, we are biased toward highly generated systems. We are convinced that there are many advantages of generating Oracle Developer applications out of Oracle Designer. We believe that in most cases, these advantages far outweigh the disadvantages. Therefore, the focus of this book is on what you *can* generate and how to get the most out of the generators.

The Goal Should Be Highly Generated Systems

When using Oracle Designer to develop your applications, you should strive to generate as much as possible. You should focus on learning the best generation techniques so that you can generate better systems. In our opinion, the capability to generate most, if not all, of your system is the greatest strength of Oracle Designer. In the rest of this chapter we will discuss the advantages (and disadvantages) of highly generated systems, and explore what exactly people mean by the term "100 percent generation."

What Is Meant by 100 Percent Generation?

The term "100 percent generation" is much discussed in the Oracle Designer development community. In their marketing information, Oracle claims that Oracle Designer release 2 will finally be able to achieve 100 percent generation. Many people have made presentations at conferences about how people have achieved 100 percent generation or gotten very close to it. Other authors and presenters say that we should not sacrifice our data model integrity, performance, or user interface in any way just to achieve 100 percent generation.

Before we can compare and evaluate the various claims about generation percentage, we will need to define the term. It does *not* mean the same thing to all people. There are two general definitions that people seem to adhere to:

- **100 percent generation = Total integration with the repository** This definition has also been called zero-gap generation. Using this definition, 100 percent generation means that the generated modules are not modified at all after generation. Even if there is a template and module-specific library attached to every generated module with a lot of custom nongenerated code, the module is still considered 100 percent generated.

- **100 percent generation = No custom code written for the module** In this definition, all of the functionality of the module has to come from the declarative definitions in the repository. All custom code must be created by a generator. Code stored in a module-specific library or template is not counted as generated. Even custom module-specific code that is stored in the Oracle Designer repository is not considered generated, because a programmer still had to write it!

Oracle's Definition

Oracle has always used the first definition ("Total integration with the repository") in its marketing of Oracle Designer, which is why they can claim that Oracle Designer release 2 can achieve 100 percent generation. Since the custom code can be stored in the repository as application logic, the generated forms are 100 percent integrated with the repository. While the Oracle marketing literature refers to this as 100 percent generation, we have seen some literature in which this definition is referred to as "round trip engineering." This is probably a more accurate term. However, because of its accepted use, this definition of 100 percent generation will be around for a while.

Some people take exception to this definition and say that it is misleading. They claim that it is not really 100 percent generation if you have to write custom tool–specific procedural code to get the desired functionality. However, there really is no problem with the definition if you understand what it means. If you agree with the premise that a very important function of Oracle Designer is to ensure adequate documentation of the system, then one of the primary goals is to ensure that the definition in the repository matches the generated code. If your system is 100 percent generated, you can be confident that your documentation is complete enough to perform accurate impact analysis and that you have more complete documentation than a nongenerated system. Using this definition, the 100 percent generation capability is still a good selling point for the tool.

"Real" Generation

There are problems with Oracle's definition of 100 percent generation. It can mislead people to think that if they use this tool they will not have to write any procedural programs. This especially can be true of managers who were sold on using Oracle Designer in part because it can generate 100 percent of the application. When this happens, the developers who actually use the tool have to either educate the management about the real meaning of Oracle's term, or limit the functionality or usability of the application.

In reality, you will always have to write some tool-specific procedural code in order to handle your more complex business rules—or even to handle simple business rules that are not supported by the generators. The application logic that is stored in the repository is just programming code, and this procedural logic still has to be written by a programmer. It is also specific to the target language. Application logic that is entered for an Oracle Forms module cannot be used if the module is changed to a Web Server module or a Visual Basic module. Because of this, it is not *real* generation. The portion of a module that is really generated is all of the code that is created by the generators to enforce the keys, perform lookups, present the GUI, etc. The fact that all of this code is generated by Oracle Designer is one of its great strengths. The programmers do not have to mess around with all of this basic and standard functionality and can focus on the code needed to implement the application logic.

Better Terminology

100 percent generation (by either definition) is a worthy goal and not one that we should devalue. However, we would prefer it if the industry adopted better terminology for these two types of 100 percent generation. Our suggestion is to use the following:

- **Repository integration = Total integration with the repository** This definition has also been called zero-gap generation. 100 percent repository integration means that all of the information needed to produce the working module is stored in the repository.
- **Declarative generation = No custom code written for the module** In this definition, all of the functionality of the module has to come from the declarative definitions in the repository. If a module is 100 percent generated, it cannot contain any custom code that was not really produced by the generator engine. Application logic in the repository would *not* count as generated even though you do not have to modify the generated programs directly.

Why Does It Matter?

You might ask, "Why does it matter?" It matters because when people are claiming to achieve 100 percent generation, you need to know what they mean in order to evaluate their claims. Some people have written thousands of lines of code for a system (stored in application logic or module libraries) and called it 100 percent generated. Other people have developed systems without writing *any* module-specific code, which is also called 100 percent generation. Saying that these two systems are both 100 percent generated does not mean that they are comparable.

What you mean is even more important if you are talking about *near* 100 percent generation. If you tell someone that your system was 90 percent generated, it has no meaning unless he or she has the same understanding of generation percentage that you do. We will discuss an objective way to define and measure the generation percentage later in this chapter.

What We Mean by 100 Percent Generation

In this book, we are going to use the "Better Terminology" mentioned above. When we are talking about the percentage of actual generation of the module from the declarative information in the repository, we will use *declarative generation.* When we are talking about a generated module's integration with the repository, we will use *repository integration.*

Both terms are important and useful in their own ways. In the rest of this chapter, when we are discussing the benefits and drawbacks of highly generated systems, we will try to indicate which type of generation we are discussing. This will give you an idea of the relative worth of each type in your environment.

Why Do We Want 100 Percent Generation, Anyway?

OK, now that we know what we are talking about when we say 100 percent generation, why do we want to focus on this, anyway? Because there are many advantages to highly generated systems, that's why. Some of these advantages are due to the fact that much of the code is actually created by the generators (declarative generation). Other advantages are due to the fact that the generated systems are usually much better documented (repository integration).

Now we will detail some of the advantages. We will also indicate which type of generation the advantage is attributed to.

1. More Complete and Accurate System Documentation (Repository Integration)

One of the big strengths of using Oracle Designer to generate applications is that you are almost guaranteed to have more complete system documentation than if you do not generate the system. In highly generated systems, you will know that the documentation in Oracle Designer will match the actual production code. This is very useful for any impact analysis you may do when you need to make changes to your system.

The level of detail of the documentation still depends on the discipline of the development team. While you know that all of the data usages are automatically documented in a generated system, you will still have to make sure that the descriptions, notes, etc., of the modules are complete. Even here, Oracle Designer helps you keep more complete and consistent documentation of the system by allowing you to run audit reports that check for the completeness of the documentation. If you don't like the canned reports that come with Oracle Designer, you can easily write your own reports against the repository.

Obviously, it is possible to have complete and accurate system documentation without generating the system from Oracle Designer. In order to do this, however, you must have very good procedures in place along with a very well- disciplined development staff. Quite often, when the system crunch time comes and you are up against a deadline, the system documentation is done in a very cursory fashion or postponed until after implementation. By the time you get around to it, you are out of money or on to your next project, and it is never fully completed. When this sort of thing happens, you will have much better documentation by default if you have a highly generated system using Oracle Designer. In fact, in our combined experience, we have found that the system documentation is much more complete for projects that use Oracle Designer than for those that do not.

2. Much Lower Defect Rate (Declarative Generation)

Another advantage of highly generated systems that many people do not think about is the fact that there is usually a much lower defect rate! This is because much of the code is generated and should not have any defects. A large part of the remainder of the code is probably shared (if the system is designed correctly). This also reduces the defect rate. Defects in the systems are very expensive, especially if they are not caught until the system is in production. The earlier in the process the defects are discovered, the less expensive it is to correct them. Figure 2-1 is a graph of the cost of defects versus the phase in the project that they are discovered. In Oracle Designer,

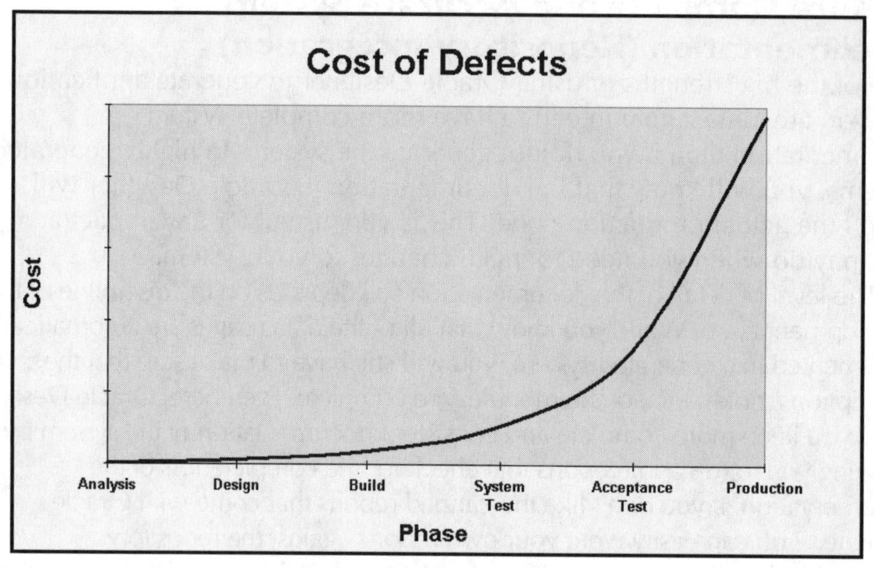

FIGURE 2-1. *Graph of defect cost versus phase*

you can quite often catch these defects earlier than in traditional projects, especially if you take full advantage of the quality and completeness reports that are available to you. Also, the actual code defects discovered in the production system are reduced because most of the code is generated.

3. Less Impact on the System When Major Changes Are Made to the Data Design (Declarative Generation)

Usually it is better to wait until the data design is complete before doing *any* work on the development of the modules. This is because changes in the data model can have a major impact on the design of the modules. If you start developing the applications screens and reports before the data model is stable, cardinality and relationship changes can cause you to have to throw away and redevelop much of the system at a very high cost.

Real World Example: Oracle CASE 5.0 Pilot Project

The first Oracle CASE 5.0 Project (an earlier version of Oracle Designer) that we worked on was a pilot project for a large development organization. Because it was a pilot, we benchmarked the defect rate against other non-CASE generated application systems. We found that the actual defect rate for the generated application was something like one-twentieth of the defect rate for the nongenerated system. We have also found the same reduced defect rate with systems generated using later versions of Oracle Designer.

This lower defect rate can be one of the greatest advantages of using Oracle Designer to generate your applications.We have also found the same reduced defect rate with systems generated using later versions of Oracle Designer.

However, this linear development approach can lead to some problems. If you wait until you have a bulletproof data model, you can end up with analysis-paralysis and never even get to the development stage (at least in your lifetime). Even if you are able to appease the data analysts and continue with development in reasonable time, this approach will increase the time (and money) it takes to develop the application.

In addition, you will almost *never* get the data model 100 percent correct until you have started to develop the application. When you actually start developing the modules, you will often uncover missing or incorrect relationships or cardinalities. Sometimes these are only discovered when you present the application to the users for the first system testing. Haven't we all had users tell us, "No, there are multiple X's for each Y. Didn't I tell you that?" Or, "Where do I enter the Z's?" (the Z's being a key part of the system that somehow got left out). These data model problems are sometimes so major that you have to scrap large parts of the application and start over. When this happens late in a standard application development process, it is very expensive.

However, if most of the application was generated from Oracle Designer, you can tell the user, "No big deal. We'll fix that." You can go back into Oracle Designer, fix the relationships, cardinality, or whatever, and then generate the application again. This capability has really saved projects for us that would have been terrible failures otherwise.

4. Less Oracle Developer Expertise Needed to Build and Maintain the System (Declarative Generation)

When you develop a system using just Oracle Developer (without using Oracle Designer for generation), you usually want your whole development staff to be as experienced as possible in using Oracle Developer. If the application is generated using Oracle Designer, however, you do not need your whole team to be highly experienced Oracle Developer programmers—some of them can be functional analysts and less experienced Oracle Developer programmers. Since most of the code will be generated from Oracle Designer, you can assign the development of the modules in Oracle Designer to the people with less Oracle Developer experience. You can have your very experienced Oracle Developer programmers handle the nongenerated PL/SQL logic and any other work that needs to be done in Oracle Developer.

5. More Consistent User Interface Across the Whole System (Both)

Generating your system from Oracle Designer can really help you ensure that the user interface is consistent across the whole system. There are three reasons for this:

- You are limited to the types of user interfaces that Oracle Designer can generate.
- All of the modules will use the same set of templates. When you develop the templates and their associated libraries, you will be establishing a standard user interface that will automatically be used by the generated modules.
- You can use the preferences to easily standardize the user interface for all of the modules. The preferences can be set at the application level or grouped into preference sets that are applied to the modules.

Of course, it is possible to get a consistent user interface without generating the system from Oracle Designer, but Oracle Designer really can help you implement and enforce the standards much easier.

6. Generation Encourages Code Sharing and Reuse (Declarative Generation)

It is better when a particular piece of functionality or business rule is only coded once in your whole system. If this can be done, it will increase the quality of your system. When a particular function is developed and debugged once, you will know that it will be error free when it is used again. If only one program unit implements a business rule, you know that it is being consistently enforced throughout the whole application. Code sharing will also reduce the development cost of your system, because you are not wasting time developing something that has already been developed.

There are many ways in which Oracle Designer makes it very easy to share much of the code that is needed to implement your system:

- All of the code that is inherited from the templates or object libraries (see Chapter 22) will be written once and used by many, if not all, of the modules in your system.
- All of the code that is produced by the generator (for example, the code needed to enforce referential integrity) is effectively shared, because it will be written in exactly the same fashion for all of the modules.
- Reusable module components (see Chapter 23) ensure that the same module component will be used by multiple modules to generate the same functionality.
- Oracle Designer facilitates the ability to tie code to enforce business rules directly to the tables to which they apply. This code can be placed in triggers (see Chapter 8) or generated into a table API for each table (see Chapter 9).

It is possible to implement procedures and policies that ensure code sharing and reuse without using a tool like Oracle Designer. It is also possible to produce redundant coding even if you do use Oracle Designer. However, we have found that projects that are generated with Oracle Designer generally do a much better job of this than projects that are not.

7. More Efficient Development (Declarative Generation)

In our opinion, generating your system from Oracle Designer can vastly improve the efficiency of your development efforts. This is especially true if you practice full life cycle development, meaning that you collect a lot of information during analysis and design. This information is stored in the Oracle Designer repository and is used to produce many of the definitions you need to generate your system. We have also found that once developers learn how the generators work, they are usually able to produce the modules much more quickly than if they were coded by hand. This may not apply on the first project, however, because it takes a little time to learn how to use Oracle Designer.

NOTE

Some organizations do not use a full life cycle development approach to develop their systems. For instance, one programmer might say to another, "We've got to start working on this new system. You go see what they want while I start coding." There are many problems with this approach to system development, and it is out of the scope of this book to discuss them. However, people who are not used to the full life cycle approach (strategy, analysis, design, build, test, and production) can often be daunted by the amount of information they need to place into Oracle Designer to generate a system. For these people, it will not seem more efficient to generate the system, because they are lumping all of the analysis and design they should have been doing into the work needed to generate the system.

8. Ease of Maintenance for Generated Systems (Both)

Systems generated out of Oracle Designer are usually much easier to maintain than systems developed directly in Oracle Developer. There are many reasons for this, some of which were also listed as other advantages. The two biggest reasons that highly generated systems are easier to maintain are

- Much better impact analysis capabilities
- The ability to regenerate modules affected by system changes

The Oracle Designer impact analysis capability lets you easily determine the effect of proposed changes and find all of the modules that need to be modified when the changes take place. This is usually much better than the standard method of searching through all of the code and hoping you find everything.

If you have a highly generated system, even after you have found the modules that need to be modified, you can make the changes much more easily. This is because, quite often, you will just have to regenerate the module! Even if you have to make some changes to the module, it is usually much easier than working with a nongenerated system.

Let's consider a couple of examples of how easy it is to maintain highly generated systems:

- **Column name changes** All you have to do is follow these steps:
  1. Run an impact analysis report to see which modules are affected by the change.
  2. Change the name of the column in the table definition.
  3. Generate all of the modules that were listed in step 1.
- **Key changes** System modifications that involve changes to the keys are also easy to maintain. This is because much of the code that handles the keys on the client side is generated. All you have to do is modify the keys and then regenerate your system.

While some modifications will not be as easy as these, there are many other that are just as easy to make, even in highly generated systems. We think that this is probably the greatest benefit of using Oracle Designer to generate your systems.

Drawbacks of Highly Generated Systems

It has been said, "There is no such thing as a free lunch." This is also true of systems generated using Oracle Designer. The benefits mentioned above come at some cost. It is up to you to determine if you think that the benefits outweigh the drawbacks. Below we will detail some of the drawbacks to help you make this determination.

1. The System Will Usually Have to Be Less Sophisticated

The tools in the Oracle Developer suite are a robust and feature-rich set of tools with which you can develop very sophisticated systems. The robustness of the toolset allows you to produce almost any user interface and functionality that you want.

Using the generators to generate your system limits you to only the user interfaces and functionality that the generators can produce. This is a limited subset of the possibilities you would have if you developed the application directly in the Oracle Developer builders. This is because, of course, it would not be possible for the generators to generate every single possible type of functionality or fancy user interface. You may or may not like the functionality that the developers of the tool decided to allow you to generate, but you should understand the reasons for the limitations.

With release 2 and the ability to add application logic to the generated modules, you will be able to overcome some of these limitations. However, the more custom programming you have to add using application logic, the higher the development and maintenance cost of the system, and the more you lose some of the other benefits of generation. It is usually better to stick to the capabilities of the generators as much as possible, and only add patches to the generation capabilities when it is really important for your system.

2. There Will Be Less Flexibility in the User Interface Design

The generators are designed to produce only certain user interfaces. There are preferences and generation techniques that can vary the user interface that can be produced, but this usually only allows variation within a certain type. For example, the designer generators cannot generate the following Oracle Developer user interfaces very easily:

- Mouse-aware items (e.g., drag-and-drop)
- Really compact layouts
- Some fancy GUI widgets (which might be available in Visual Basic)
- Greatly varying color, line, and font schemes

Again, it is possible to do some of these things, but it is not really native to the generators; and the more fancy the user interface that you add to your system, the higher the development and maintenance cost.

3. You May Be Tempted to "Mess Up" the Data Model

Certain data designs are easier to generate than others. For example, the generators do better with systems in which the screen design follows the data model. Therefore, some people will modify the data model away from the normalized model that we should produce from our analysis in order to generate specific required screen designs. This is not necessarily a bad idea. We denormalize and modify the physical model for many other reasons (like performance, legacy design, etc.). Striving for high generation is just another reason to modify the physical model. However, like any other denormalization, it should only be taken when the benefits outweigh the costs.

Many people think that the physical model should never be modified just to achieve high generation because the data will long outlive any particular application that uses it. Anything we do to mess up the model will have repercussions that will affect the organization long after the system you are generating is obsolete, so we need to take a long-range view about our data models.

It is not necessary to "mess up" the data model in order to generate your systems. Many generation techniques allow you to generate what you want without compromising the model. This is especially true in release 2 because of some of the enhancements to the tool. However, in organizations that emphasize high generation, there is always a temptation to modify the model to get the generation results we want; this is why we listed this as a drawback of highly generated systems.

4. Performance Issues?

Some of the techniques that are needed to achieve highly generated systems have some performance implications. The generators produce a lot of code using a very robust architecture. This can mean that there is unnecessary or redundant code in the module. The code is also very generic, which can lead to less efficient code. Another factor is that some of the techniques that are used to achieve a high generation percentage can lead to additional inefficiencies.

NOTE

Release 1.3: *Some of the drawbacks of highly generated systems are more applicable to systems generated under release 1.3.2 than release 2. Some of the capabilities available in release 2 allow us to keep the generation percentage high without sacrificing anything. This is especially true of the data model and performance drawbacks. We also have more user interface options with release 2.*

Designing for Generation

The most important thing that can be done to approach 100 percent generation is to design the system for generation. This means that the user interface and screen layout standards for the system must be something that Oracle Designer is capable of generating. There are also generation implications to various data design decisions you might make, and the impact of these decisions on generation must be considered.

Many times, users are willing to be flexible about the user interface design. Oracle Designer is capable of generating a user interface that, in most cases, is close to what people expect. It is a good idea to ask the users to accept a user interface that you know you can generate, and this is usually not a problem.

However, sometimes there is resistance to designing the system around what the generators are capable of producing. In these cases, it is advantageous to do a cost benefit analysis, comparing what the development cost of the system would be with a high generation percentage versus a system with a low generation percentage. Make sure to show the cost savings due to low defect rate, less experienced developers needed, ease of design changes, and modifications, etc. When the customer is shown that the total cost of a mostly generated system can be much less than a highly customized system, some of the resistance may be reduced.

Targeted Nondeclarative Modifications

It is not a good idea to get too dogmatic about 100 percent declarative generation, or the system ends up being user-hostile (as opposed to user-friendly). Most systems can be greatly enhanced by adding a little nondeclarative code in the right places (what used to be postgeneration modifications). This code can be added directly to the repository using the new application logic capability in Oracle Designer release 2, or it can be placed in module-specific libraries. There are also times when you might want to tweak the generated layout. However, you should be careful about doing this. While you sometimes need to add nondeclarative code to meet the requirements of an application, layout modifications are usually done for purely cosmetic reasons. You might please the users by tweaking the layout of an important form, but you need to be careful about opening the lid to Pandora's box. If the users start expecting any layout (instead of the layouts that are generatable), you will soon be spending a lot of time tweaking the layouts of *all* of your generated forms.

In our experience, the following is a good mix:

- About 50 percent of the forms are 100 percent declaratively generated (code forms and such).
- Another 40 percent of the forms have limited nondeclarative modifications (like 90–95 percent declaratively generated).
- Only 10 percent of the forms have heavy nondeclarative modifications.

Of course, if more of the system can be declaratively generated without sacrificing usability, that's even better!

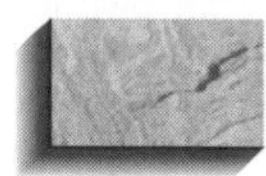

NOTE

Release 1.3: *What we are calling "nondeclarative code" is basically the same as what was called "postgeneration modifications" in release 1.3. In release 1.3, this code usually had to be added to the modules after generation or placed in module-specific libraries. Now this same code can be placed directly into the repository, if so desired.*

The forms with a large amount of nondeclarative modifications should always be the forms with which users spend most of their time. It is usually not worth the effort to make a lot of these modifications to forms that are used infrequently (like code maintenance forms). This time-consuming and costly work should be targeted to the areas in which it will be of the most benefit to the users.

Developing a Philosophy of Generation

Before you decide how far you want to go with code generation, you should develop a philosophy of generation for your application system. A consistent philosophy will guide the decision-making process during the development of the system and ensure that all of the developers understand what the goal is so that they can work together to achieve it. Below are a few possible philosophies:

1. **Use the Generation as a Default Layout.**

   Do not let the generation capabilities limit the user interface design. Customize the forms as much as needed to get the desired functionality and user interface. Do not even try to keep the repository in sync with the module after the changes are made.

2. **Generate as Much as Possible Using Standard Techniques.**

   Try to steer the user interface design into standards that are easily generated by Oracle Designer. Keep nondeclarative modifications to a minimum but allow them as needed. Attempt to keep the repository in sync by making sure all of the nondeclarative code is placed (or recovered) into the repository.

3. **Try to Get as Close to 100 Percent Declarative Generation as Possible.**

   Only allow user interface designs that can be generated by Oracle Designer. Use whatever techniques are feasible to allow functionality and business rules to be generated. Keep nondeclarative modifications to a minimum, and try to implement them in such a way that they can easily be applied again. All nongenerated code will be placed (or recovered) into the repository.

4. **Mandatory 100 Percent Declarative Generation.**

   Do not allow *any* nondeclarative modifications. Do not put any PL/SQL into the application logic in the repository.

In most cases, it is better to steer away from the two extremes. It is a tendency of some programmers, particularly people with much Forms experience, to resist putting much effort in trying to make the generators work for them. It seems easier for them to go ahead and make postgeneration modifications to the forms or to add nondeclarative code to the modules, even in cases in which it would be possible to generate the functionality.

Measuring Generation Percentage

Since we advocate trying to achieve a high generation percentage, we are always asked, "OK, so what was *really* the generation percentage for that application?" How should we answer this question? The usual seat-of-the-pants method most of us are probably using concerns us. When you start talking about "near" 100 percent generation, you have to start defining what you mean, or the percentages are meaningless. If I say my application was 90 percent generated, what does that mean? Ninety percent of the forms were 100 percent

Real World Example: The Effect of the Philosophy of Generation

One of the authors (Ken) was involved in one government project in which the goal was to reuse a similar existing system that was generated at another government site using CASE 5.0. The plan was to start with the existing application in the repository, make the necessary data and process changes, and generate a new version tailored to our site. When the existing system was analyzed, it was discovered that about 80 percent of the postgeneration modifications could have been generated, but the developers did not take the time to learn how to do it. They had obviously used the first philosophy listed earlier. This cost us (and them) much extra time.

generated? Ninety percent of the PL/SQL was generated? What about postgeneration layout changes done in the Forms designer?

Once you choose your generation philosophy, make sure your management and your whole development team understand and concur with it. You will also need to communicate your philosophy clearly to the development team.

Obviously, it's easy to know if a module is 100 percent generated. However, if you have made postgeneration modifications or nondeclarative code additions, your module is not 100 percent (declaratively) generated. In these cases, how do we really know how much of the module was generated? Most people can only guess about the generation percentage of the system: "Well, half the forms were 100 percent generated, most of the rest were probably 80 percent generated, and there were two that were maybe 50 percent generated; therefore, the system was 90 percent generated."

One big problem with this method is that it is very subjective. Two people can come up with very different estimates of the generation percentage, even for the same system. Unless you use some sort of objective measure, you really don't know what is meant by the percentage generation.

Oracle Developer is a 4GL, so standard objective metrics like number of lines of code do not really work because much of the work that has to be done to develop forms and reports has nothing to do with the lines of PL/SQL code in the module. The positioning of various GUI items and setting their attributes can encompass the largest part of programming the modules. Because of these concerns, we have developed a method to calculate a percentage generation metric for an application and for all of the forms in the application. We call this calculation a "metric" because it is not necessarily the real generation percentage in terms of lines of code or the amount of work that went into the module. Instead, it is just a consistent objective measure that can be used to give you an indication of the comparative generation percentage of different modules or application systems.

Why Do We Want to Use a Generation Percentage Metric?

There are many reasons why an analysis of the actual percentage of code generation is useful information for an organization that is using the Oracle Designer generators to produce applications. Some of the reasons are

- To determine performance against a goal (e.g., "If my goal was 90 percent generation, just how close did I actually come?")
- To compare Oracle Designer applications (e.g., "If application A achieved 90 percent generation, but application B only had 80 percent, what were the differences? Could the techniques used for application A be replicated?")
- To determine the value of generation in regard to maintenance costs (e.g., "Was a highly generated system actually cheaper to maintain? Is there a relationship between generation percentage and defects?")
- Marketing the tool (e.g., "We Oracle Designer bigots often claim the tool can generate much of an application. An analysis like this can give weight to this claim.")

Design of the Metric

In order to determine the real generation percentage for a module, you need to be able to measure how much of the module was generated and how much was not. To do this, you need to use an objective measure of the module size. For an application that was developed in C++, you could count the lines of code for each module, but in a 4GL like Oracle Developer, there is no easy number to use to determine the size of a module. The only direct equivalent in Oracle Developer is the PL/SQL code in the triggers and procedures, but in many modules this will be only a small percentage of the actual programming that is done for the module.

So how can we come up with a metric? The following pieces need to be in place to produce the metric:

- Determine a way to size the modules. Come up with something that would work like number-of-lines-of-code in a C++ program.
- Find a way to easily calculate this number from the source code of the modules.
- Determine how much of that number was generated and how much was added after generation.
- Define and calculate the generation percentage.

The source of an Oracle Developer Forms Module can be divided into two types:

- All of the PL/SQL in the triggers and procedures
- The stuff we do in the Designer to lay out the items, blocks, relations, LOVs, etc.

Calculating the Metric

For previous versions of forms, we had written a program that used the .FMT and .PLD files to perform the calculations needed to generate a percent generation metric. However, in the newest version of the tool, the PL/SQL is not longer carried as text in the .FMT and these scripts do not work.

Fortunately, there is a better way to perform these calculations now. Oracle has published an API for their developer tools which can be used to calculate a percent generation metric. We had not written such a program at the time this book was published, but when we do write a percent generation calculation program, we will make it available to you some way (on a Web site perhaps).

Conclusion

Whatever your opinion about the 100 percent generation question, most people agree that the generation capabilities of Oracle Designer are an important part of the tool. Whether you are a 100-percent-generation-or-die bigot or a die-hard postgeneration modifier, you should consider the generation capabilities and the benefits and drawbacks of highly generated systems so you can make an informed decision about how to approach generation. To put it another way, choose your philosophy of generation in a thought-out, informed fashion, and stick with it throughout the development of your application.

CHAPTER 3

Seven Keys to Successful System Generation

In the years we have been using Oracle Designer to generate Oracle Developer systems, we have learned that there are a few obstacles that can really hinder your development effort, but there are also some great opportunities to prepare the way for a very successful system development effort.

We have organized some of our experience into a series of important areas that you need to consider, which we call "The Seven Keys to Successful System Generation." They are

- Key 1: Management Support
- Key 2: Experienced Mentoring and/or Training
- Key 3: Infrastructure
- Key 4: Standards
- Key 5: Realistic Expectations
- Key 6: Designing for Generation
- Key 7: User Involvement

A perfect situation in every one of these areas is not needed to successfully generate a system, but they are all areas that you should consider as you try to improve your system development process. As you read about these keys, think about how your development organization approaches each of these areas. You may find areas in which you can improve the environment and therefore improve the chances that your system is developed successfully. You may also find problem areas that you cannot address at this time, but understanding your organization's weaknesses in each of these areas will help you reduce their impact on your development.

Key 1: Management Support

So you're convinced that Oracle Designer is the way to go. You want to develop quality systems and do good analysis before you start to build the application. You're convinced you can generate most of your application. It's time to talk to your manager about using the tool. "How much does the tool cost?" he asks. When you tell him, he exclaims, "But we've already spent all of that money for the other Oracle tools!" (strike 1). Next, you tell him that it is not easy to learn, and he will have to send all of his developers to at least two weeks of training. "I'm sorry, we don't have enough money in the training budget" (strike 2). Then you tell him that you will have to change the whole way you perform development to take advantage of the tool. "We've always done it this way, and it has worked so far! Who are you to tell me how to do system development!" (strike 3, you're out!*)*. There are also user interface limitations that might concern your management. While these concerns can be addressed easily, this is often the initial response to the suggestion of using Oracle Designer.

If yours is the lone voice (or one of a few) in your organization that is convinced that using Oracle Designer to generate your system is the way to go, you may have your work cut out for you. It usually takes some changes in the way your organization develops systems in order to use the Designer tool correctly, and this is very difficult to do without management support.

For instance, you will have to have support to justify the increased software and training cost of using Oracle Designer. It's the management's budget that will be impacted, and they will have to be convinced if they are to defend the request.

In addition, quite often, your development process will have to change significantly. For example, you will probably need more information earlier in the development process than you are used to. You will have to prevent developers from hacking the generated code instead of learning how to use the generators to the fullest capacity. It can be very difficult to get all of the developers to do this if the management is not supportive.

There are sometimes limitations to what you can generate with Oracle Designer. It is much better to accept the limitations and design your system to fit within them. However, quite often your customers will want to do something that you cannot generate but that is not really critical to the system. Your system will be more successful if your management supports the idea of near 100 percent generation. If your management is unwilling to hold a hard line on this, you may find yourself doing a lot of post-generation modifications, which can reduce the value of many of the benefits of using the generators. With release 2, the limitations are fewer than with release 1.3, but some limitations remain.

If your management is not already convinced that you should be using Oracle Designer, you will need to arm yourself with as many arguments as you can to convince them that using Oracle Designer is in your organization's best interest. You can use some of the advantages we detailed in Chapter 2 to help you come up with these arguments. There are also many people in the Oracle development community who have had great success using Oracle Designer and who will give you information that will help you justify using the tool. Ask these people to share their experiences with you. You can talk to these people at users group meetings or post questions in Oracle Designer e-mail lists.

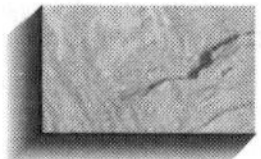

NOTE
The Oracle Development Tools User Group (ODTUG) e-mail lists are a great source for help in justifying the use of Oracle Designer. Many people who participate in the list will answer your specific questions as well as share their success (or failure) stories. These e-mail lists are also a great source for help with using the Oracle development tools. For information about becoming a member of ODTUG, check out their Web site at ***www.odtug.com****.*

Key 2: Experienced Mentoring and/or Training

Oracle Designer is a complicated tool. It is very difficult to use it without some sort of training or experienced mentoring. Usually, it is better to get both training and mentoring, but try to get at least one or the other.

Training

To get the development staff up to speed with Oracle Designer, everyone will need some training! It is possible to learn how to use the tool without specific classroom training (by using the tutorial or trial and error), but this is not the best way to get your staff quickly up to speed. Someone who learns how to use the tool without classroom training may not understand the whole process, and this can lead to a less efficient use of the tool. There are many ways to perform most of the development tasks using Oracle Designer, and the first way that someone figures out how to perform a particular task may not be the best way. You can learn many techniques and tricks in a class that are hard to figure out on your own.

The development staff should begin their Oracle Designer training as close as possible to the time when they are going to start using the tool (this is called just-in-time (JIT) training). If the staff is trained six months before they use the system, they will probably forget much of what they learned and will have to learn it all over again when they are ready to use it. On the other hand, getting the training after they have almost finished the development does not help very much either (we have seen this happen!).

If a development organization is large enough, the easiest way to get JIT training is to schedule on-site classes when they are needed. Oracle Education, many training/consulting companies (like the one we work for), and many independent consultants are available to come to your organization's site to do the training whenever it is needed. If an on-site class is out of the question, try to get the off-site training for the developers scheduled as close as possible to the time of the actual development.

Experienced Mentoring

Oracle Designer is a very complicated tool. There are many ramifications to decisions made about administration, design, standards, etc., that cannot be understood without some experience. Because of this, it is very important to get help with the first Oracle Designer project. An experienced Oracle Designer consultant can steer developers around some of the pitfalls and help the development team get up to speed on the tool much more quickly than they could otherwise.

An experienced consultant can do the following:

- Help you to gain management support for using Oracle Designer based on real world success and failure experiences. (Key 1).
- Set up the environment and infrastructure to support Oracle Designer development (Key 3).
- Help you develop and enforce standards (Key 4).
- Set realistic expectations based on their previous experience (Key 5).
- Help you design the system so that it can be easily generated (Key 6).
- Give specific help for the problems that are encountered during development.

As you can see, an experienced consultant can help you successfully implement many of the other keys to successful generation. Because of this, we feel that getting a consultant to help you with your first project is probably the best thing you can do to be successful.

However, the consultant should not be a permanent member of your staff. You should find a consultant who is a good mentor, someone who will train your staff adequately so you don't have to always rely on the consultant. Once an organization has a few Oracle Designer projects under its belt, a level of internal expertise should be developed that can be relied upon for future projects, and an outside consultant will no longer be needed.

Key 3: Infrastructure

The environment needed to support Oracle Designer is not a simple one. There are many complex management, environment, and infrastructure issues that need to be addressed correctly in order to generate systems successfully. The stability and robustness of the generation infrastructure is a factor that quite often separates successful system development efforts from unsuccessful ones. We will consider three major areas of infrastructure that need to be addressed:

- Repository installation and management
- Development environment
- Object libraries, templates, and template architecture

There are many separate but interrelated issues within each of these areas that need to be considered. They will be covered in the following sections.

Repository Installation and Management

Without a repository, you cannot use Oracle Designer at all! This may seem obvious, but quite often not enough emphasis is placed on making sure that the Oracle Designer repository is installed and managed correctly. An incorrectly managed repository can lead to performance problems with the tool, which can drastically reduce the efficiency of your developers. It can also lead to loss of data, which at best means that some development work will have to be redone; at worst it can introduce defects into your system. Your repository might become unavailable for a few days, which could have a major impact on your development schedule.

The Repository Should Be Considered a Production Installation

There is quite often a big difference between a development installation and a production installation of an Oracle instance. In a production instance, more care is taken to make sure that there are good regular backups. Usually the production instance will use archive logging or mirroring (or both) to ensure that there is no loss of data if there is a disk failure. The DBAs will monitor the instance more carefully, performing proactive maintenance on the instance to keep the performance acceptable and to ensure that the instance does not go down. This is not always the case for a development instance.

You should *always* consider the Oracle Designer repository instance as a *production* instance! It is running the production version of an important application that is used by many people. Quite often, your organization will lose as much money if it goes down as they would with many of the end-user production systems. Even if the rest of your environment is treated as a development environment with lower maintenance standards, you should make sure that the Oracle Designer repository instance is treated like a production instance.

As a production instance, the following should be in place:

1. The repository should be installed in an instance easily available to everyone on your development team. The connectivity between the server with the instance and the client machines that will use the tool should be stable.
2. There should be a regular backup of the repository. This can be done by having a regular backup of the whole instance or a backup of just the repository using the tools provided in Oracle Designer.
3. If possible, archive logging should be turned on, or the instance should be mirrored (either one or the other or both, at your DBA's discretion). This will prevent any loss of data in the case of a disk failure.
4. The DBA should monitor the instance for fragmentation and defragment the instance if it needs it.

Have an Experienced DBA

An experienced DBA should create the instance and install the repository. While most experienced Oracle developers can install the repository; they may not know enough about your organization's infrastructure to do the best installation possible. Oracle Designer allows you to split the repository up into multiple tablespaces according to how the tables in the repository are to be used. An experienced DBA will know how best to use this feature to improve the performance of the tool. They will also make sure that the instance and repository is set up in such a way that it can be easily recoverable in the event of a hardware failure or corruption of the repository.

Identify an Oracle Designer Repository Administrator

An Oracle Designer repository cannot be implemented in a turnkey, install-it-and-forget-about-it manner. It is a complicated database that will take some babysitting to keep it tuned and running well. The best way to do this is to identify someone in your organization to be the "official" Oracle Designer repository administrator. This administrator could be one of your DBAs or it could be someone on your development staff. The knowledge that is needed to administer the repository itself is very specialized and is not knowledge that a DBA already has, but any experienced developer or DBA should be able to learn to do this job.

The important task is to identify this person and *allocate time for this task*! You should make sure this person has time to do the job—don't just give them this task on top of their already 45+ hour/week workload. This person should be allowed to work on this task for approximately one hour per week for every full-time Oracle Designer user. For an organization with 30-40 people using Oracle Designer extensively, this should be a full-time position. If there are fewer people using Oracle Designer, the repository administrator will not need to be full time. For instance, if 15–20 people are using the repository, it might be need 50 percent of the administrator's time.

The repository administrator should be responsible for the following tasks:

1. Making sure the repository is backed up correctly (working with the DBAs)
2. Performing some cleanup and maintenance tasks that need to be performed from time to time

3. Monitoring the performance of the repository (for example, letting the DBAs know when the instance should be defragmented, making sure the appropriate procedures are pinned into memory, and any other tasks that would help improve the performance of Oracle Designer)
4. Planning and implementing repository upgrades
5. Coordinating the development and distribution of any custom repository utilities that are written
6. Designing and implementing an application partitioning and versioning standard across the organization
7. Loading data into the repository from any other sources (primarily other CASE tools that might be used by your organization) and helping export data from Designer for use in other applications or CASE tools

It is possible to distribute these tasks over the whole development team. However, it has been our experience that if there is not one person designated as being responsible, these tasks usually are not done at all or, if they are done, it is often in a haphazard fashion.

Development Environment

Setting up an environment to allow for a multiperson team to develop modules using Oracle Developer (and Designer) is fairly complicated. There are many details having to do with installation, file sharing, version control, and database access that need to be set up correctly so that your developers are not wasting their time and effort trying to get everything working instead of actually developing the modules.

A good development environment should include the following:

1. **Good Source Code Control**

   This may seem obvious, but we have worked for many organizations that did not really have adequate source code control. In these environments, there was not an easy way to see who was working on which module. There was also no way to keep previous versions of the programs in case you needed to roll back changes. This can easily lead to the loss of work and other inefficiencies in the development process.

You should make sure there is a good source code control system in place. Your source code control can be implemented using one of the following methods:

- A commercial software tool (like PVCS)
- Your own custom-developed system (if you consistently follow some established procedures)

2. A Standard for Module Versioning

You should also make sure you have a standard for keeping track of the versions of the modules. This is more important for maintenance releases than it is for your first production release. Nevertheless, it can be important for your initial development also, especially if any changes happen during system or acceptance testing.

This requirement is closely related to the first item in this list (source code control) and can often be handled by the same software system or procedure. However, since the modules will be generated out of Oracle Designer, the system or procedure needs to take into account the fact that the source really resides in the Oracle Designer Repository.

3. Change Control

Scope creep is a nemesis of almost all system development efforts. There are always missing requirements or enhancements that need to be made to the system, which are discovered during development or testing. While many of these changes really do need to be included in the system to make it successful, it is impossible to include all of the changes that are requested. If we tried to, we would never finish the development of the system.

This is why a good change control procedure or process is needed. This can be a manual process (though we do not recommend it), a commercial software package, or your own custom-developed system. A change control procedure will allow you to capture all of the change requests and problems, prioritize them, and make sure that they are eventually addressed (or at least scheduled for a future release).

For some reason, it seems that many organizations have not put a cohesive automated change control system in place. We have actually had to develop custom change control systems for many of our clients over the years to help remedy this problem. This is one of the reasons we chose an issue management (or change request) system as the example system for this book.

4. Separate Development, Test, and Production Environments and the Tools/Procedures to Manage Them

This is another standard and obvious infrastructure requirement. You will need to have separate environments for development, test, and production. Each of these environments should have their own database instances, source directories, and executable directories. You also need to have tools and/or procedures to migrate your programs and database changes between these environments. There are some commercial configuration management tools that can be used to manage the migration of your programs across these environments, and many of these tools will also take care of source code control and versioning.

Another capability that is needed and is not so readily available is the ability for the developers and testers to easily switch between these environments. These separate environments involve different Oracle Security IDs (SIDs) and different registry settings, and it is a good idea to make switching between the environments easy and consistent by providing programs to do this.

5. Stable Development Oracle Database Installation

Obviously, we cannot develop Oracle systems without having an Oracle database available. However, sometimes organizations can underestimate the importance of the development instance. While it is not a production Oracle instance, it is important that it be stable. If the development instance keeps going down, or if there is not adequate DBA support for it, it can severely hinder the developers' efficiency.

6. **Correct Developer and Designer Client Installations**

   The Oracle Developer and Oracle Designer client installations should be correctly and consistently installed on all of the developers' computers, as well as any computers you have set up for testing. You should not rely on the developers to install the tools themselves, although they are capable of doing it. If you do, you will not know if the installation is consistent for all of the developers. If different developers have different versions of the tools or have installed them differently, they may end up developing programs that work on their computer but do not work on the test or production computers.

   All of the developers should also be running the same versions of the tools, and they should all be upgraded to new releases of the tools in a well-planned fashion. Any upgrades should be done simultaneously, if possible, to ensure the correct interworking of the tools. Upgrades to new versions should be thoroughly tested to make sure they are compatible with the rest of the environment (Oracle versions, templates, object libraries, for example) before they are installed for all of the developers.

7. **Common Network Directory for Shared Objects**

   There are some files that need to be shared among all of the developers and should be placed on a network directory that is accessible to all of the developers. These files should also be protected from update by most of the developers. There will usually only be one or two people on a development team who are responsible for the development and maintenance of these objects. The following types of files usually need to be shared:

   - Shared PL/SQL libraries
   - Forms object libraries used during generation
   - Oracle Designer Forms and Reports Templates
   - Shared icon files (usually used in the templates)

   There also needs to be some sort of change control procedures implemented for these files, and the developers need to be notified when they change.

8. Correct Registry Setup

There are some registry variables that need to be set consistently on the developers' computers for the applications to work correctly. When the client tools (Oracle Developer and Designer) are installed on the developers' machines, these registry settings should be set correctly. The correct settings should also be documented and communicated to the developers, so that they can restore the correct settings if they modify their registry settings for any reason. Some of the registry settings that need to be setup correctly are

- FORMS50_PATH
- TK25_ICON
- REPORTS30_PATH
- REPORTS30_TMP
- SYSTEM_EDITOR
- ORACLE_SID

Object Libraries, Templates, and Template Architecture

Oracle Designer uses object libraries and templates to implement many design standards that should be consistent across your whole application. These objects need to be designed and developed early in the process and then made available to all of developers (see file sharing, mentioned earlier). The development of these templates and object libraries is a very important part of your development effort.

Using the templates, you can implement many features that are not normally available through the generators. The default templates that are provided with Oracle Designer are very simple and, in almost every case, the system will greatly benefit if some time is spent modifying and enhancing the templates.

We will discuss this topic more completely in Chapter 22.

Key 4: Standards

Standards are a greater factor in the success of system development efforts than many people might think. You can develop systems without many standards in place, but the systems will usually end up costing more in the long run. Standards can help make the development process more efficient by saving time in decision making. They can improve the efficiency of the developers and help make the system easier to maintain and document.

Naming Standards

Naming standards can have a profound effect on the overall quality of the system. They will help streamline the development process, actually improving the efficiency of the developers. They will greatly improve the maintainability of the system when it is complete. Naming standards will also make it much easier to connect and interface the various components of the system, as well as making it easier for external systems to interface into your system.

However, many developers feel that rigid naming standards are a hindrance to their development efforts. They complain that always having to worry about what they have to label something hinders their development efforts. While they are busy coding, someone is always fussing about the table, column, and parameter names they are using in their programs. While the naming standards might seem to be a hindrance at first, once the developers learn the standards, they will probably find that they help instead of hinder the development process. Try to convince the whole development team how important naming standards are and, even if you do not convince everyone, make sure that they are followed as much as possible, even by the reluctant developers.

Naming standards will never be perfect. There are many opinions about what naming standards should be, and you will never get the whole team to agree about every aspect of the standards. However, this should never prevent you from defining and using naming standards. Even standards that you do not like are better than no standards at all. We have yet to work at an organization where we agree with all of the standards, but this has not stopped us from using and supporting the use of those standards.

Design Standards

Design standards can also have a profound effect on your development effort. Each developer, designer, and system architect might have their own approach to solving design problems. However, these design problems should not be solved in a different fashion every time they are encountered in the system. If they are, you will end up with much more code to support (the same problem solved in many different ways). You will also have a system that is much more difficult to learn and support.

Each time a design question comes up, your development team should determine what the best design to use is and then use that design consistently across the whole system. Even if everyone does not agree that it is the best design, everyone should conform to the standard to improve the application's consistency. Some examples of design decisions that need to be made are

- Using surrogate keys or natural keys
- Using a three-tier or two-tier architecture
- Coding data-related business rules in the server instead of the client
- Whether or not to allow any denormalization
- Using module-specific libraries or placing custom code in the repository (application logic)

User Interface Standards

The user interface (UI) design standards should be determined for the system as early as possible. It is even a good idea to set these standards during analysis, before the design is even started. This is because an expectation about the UI design is usually developed during the early stages of analysis. Early in the design process, the designers are already trying to design the screens based on some sort of target UI that was proposed or just assumed during analysis. If this UI is not one that can be generated easily, the system will require more post-generation modifications and will therefore be much more time consuming to develop (this aspect will be discussed more fully in "Key 6: Designing for Generation").

The best way to prevent the expectation of a UI that is difficult to generate is to determine the UI design standards as early as possible, usually some time during the analysis phase. For generated systems, the best way to do this is to prototype the UI by actually generating a few screens. This is done by using the transformers to create a few prototype tables and modules from the analysis information. The entities and functions that are used do not have to be complete, because this is just a UI prototype. It does not matter if a few attributes are missing, or that the functions are not yet completely defined. However, the most complete entities and functions available at the time should be used because users are often sidetracked by missing requirements, even when it is explained to them that this is just a UI prototype.

After a few tables and modules have been created, some representative screens can be generated. Of course, this means that some work will have to be done on the object libraries and templates at this point. However, this is work that will have to be done sometime anyway, and the sooner it is done the better. Now approval can be sought for the UI that has been generated. If the generated UI is approved, this will ensure a much higher generation percentage than if the UI design was determined without even prototyping it. If it is not approved, a cost/benefit analysis can be done to show how much more expensive the desired UI could be. This will usually convince your customers to accept the UI that is easy to generate. Once the prototype is accepted, the UI standards can be documented and completely implemented in the object libraries, templates, and preferences.

Below is a list of some of the UI design decisions that need to be made:

- Single or multiple window application
- Toolbar design
- What colors, block decorations, and fonts to use
- Screen size (does it take over the PC or just open a small window?)
- Navigation types (pull-down menus, button navigation)
- Multiblock layout (stubs, pop-ups)
- Scope of screens or windows (a few large forms vs. many smaller forms)
- Whether to use tab canvases or stacked canvases

Commercially Available Standards

If you think the development of a comprehensive set of standards is going to be too difficult for your organization, you might want to consider adopting one of the commercially available standards. Here are a few of the commercially available packages that we know about:

- **Oracle CDM** Oracle has a product called Oracle Custom Development Methodology (CDM), which includes naming and development standards, documentation templates, and standardized procedures that will help you jumpstart your application development methodology. CDM also includes the use of the Oracle HeadStart templates, which can greatly enhance your generation. Contact your Oracle Sales Representative for more information.
- **UCC Guidelines/2000** A commercially available methodology that includes standards documentation, generation templates, and generator extensions that could help you get your standards implementation started. However, as of the writing of the book, we did not see any mention of release 2 support. For more information, look at their Web site at **www.decade.nl**.
- **DesignAssist** This is a template package that is available to help you implement your GUI standards. However, it does not address naming standards or development methodologies. For more information, look at their Web site at **www.seeristic.com**.

There are other commercial methodologies that are also available to help you with your standards development; however, most of them are not Oracle specific. We only detailed Oracle-specific commercial methodologies that we knew about.

Key 5: Realistic Expectations

Sometimes it seems like Oracle Designer is presented as the silver bullet that will cure all of your Oracle system development woes. It will perform wonders! It will allow you to use Very Rapid Application Development (VRAD) methodologies while maintaining the highest quality! Just complete your analysis; push a button and *voilà*! Your 100-percent-generated system is done! You will have automatic complete and accurate documentation of your system! It will leap tall buildings in a single bound!

Obviously, no one really expects quite that much from the tool. However, there seems to be many misconceptions about what Oracle Designer can and cannot do for your development effort. This lack of understanding of the capabilities and limitations of the tool has lead to the failure of many Oracle Designer projects. If you make an effort to set reasonable expectations early in the development process, you will have a better chance of having a successfully generated system.

Development Efficiency

One standard expectation that many organizations have is that the development will be more efficient using Oracle Designer. You might expect that you would not need as many people coding in Oracle Developer because much of the system is being generated. While this could easily be true after your team's third or fourth system developed using Oracle Designer, it is definitely not true for the first few systems.

Your first system developed using Oracle Designer will surely take as much time and effort as it would if was developed in Oracle Developer directly. In fact, for many organizations it will take more time! You will end up with a much higher quality system, but for the first system at least, it will not cost less, but more. This is primarily because of the relatively difficult learning curve usually involved with using Oracle Designer for the first time. In fact, your developers may be ramping up on up to four different learning curves at the same time:

- Learning the Oracle database and Oracle development environment (SQL, SQL*Plus, PL/SQL, Oracle Developer) if this is your first Oracle project
- Learning to use the Oracle Designer tool itself
- Learning a structured development methodology (if your shop has not really used one before)
- Learning how to generate the application from Oracle Designer

There is also a lot of work that needs to be done to get set up to generate the first application. Templates, object libraries, and shared PL/SQL libraries will need to be developed during your first project. You will have to get your development environment set up correctly. (See "Key 3: Infrastructure," earlier in the chapter).

However, these things (the learning curves and infrastructure setup) only apply to the first system developed using Oracle Designer. The templates, object libraries, and PL/SQL libraries can probably be used as is, or with minor modifications, in your subsequent systems. Your developers will have already learned much about how to use Oracle Designer effectively. Because of this, you should see a great increase in efficiency in your second and subsequent systems developed using mostly the same standards and the same development team. In fact, usually your second system will be developed more efficiently than it would have been without using Oracle Designer.

Using Oracle Designer for VRAD Development

Sometimes the Oracle Designer generation capability is touted as a method to develop systems easily using VRAD techniques. This claim may seem to be at odds with what we said above (that is, the first few systems will *not* be developed more efficiently), but it is not. Oracle Designer *can* be used very successfully to implement VRAD systems. However, using Oracle Designer for VRAD only makes sense when your development team is very experienced with the tool. Even when using VRAD techniques, it will take some time for the developers to gain enough experience to develop the applications really efficiently. However, once they gain this level of proficiency, Oracle Designer really does make an excellent VRAD tool. There are two reasons for this:

- Experienced Developers Can Generate the System *Much* More Rapidly

  Experienced Designer developers should be able to generate systems from Oracle Designer *much* faster than they could by writing the application directly in Oracle Developer. This is especially true if you keep the design of the system within the capabilities of Oracle Designer's declarative generation capabilities. For example, one of the authors has developed an 11-table, 2-screen (15 base blocks), and 4-report production application in under three man days. This system has been in production use for two years now and is still going strong.

- *Much* Better Documentation Than Typical VRAD Systems

  Another great advantage of using Oracle Designer for VRAD development is the fact that you will automatically get *much* better documentation than you would without using Designer. This documentation can be of great service when the application becomes successful and the users want to enhance it.

User Interface Expectations

There are limitations to the user interface (UI) that can be generated using Oracle Designer. If your management or the proposed users of the system you are developing have an expectation of the UI that cannot be easily generated; this can lead to one of two problems:

- The generated UI will not be acceptable to the users.

  If the users are expecting one user interface, and you generate another, they may reject the system, not because it does not meet the requirements, but because they don't like the UI. In many cases, if they had been prepared for the UI you generated from the beginning, they would have accepted the system.

- You will have to do many postgeneration customizations.

  If you end up doing many modifications of the system after it has been generated, you will lose many of the advantages of generating the system from Oracle Designer in the first place. This will make the system harder to support and more expensive to build.

Both of these problems can lead to a failed development effort. Therefore, the UI expectations should be set at the start of the development effort. For a more complete description of UI standards, read the "User Interface Standards" section, earlier in this chapter.

Oracle Designer Cannot Generate Everything

Another common expectation is that the whole system will be 100 percent generated. This was definitely not feasible in release 1, and though there have been great improvements in release 2, it's not really possible in that release either. While you will be able to store all of the customizations in the repository in release 2, thereby keeping the generated code 100 percent in sync with the repository, you will still have to code the modifications by hand. Whether the nongenerated code is added directly to the modules, entered into the repository as application logic, or placed in program units in PL/SQL libraries, it will still have to be written. (See Chapter 2 for more information about 100 percent generation.)

We have heard managers who were sold on the 100 percent generation capabilities of Oracle Designer complain about this fact. Some have even gone so far as to forbid the developers from doing any PL/SQL coding! In these cases, the system is either crippled by the limitations of the declarative generation capabilities, or the developers actually make the modifications anyway and mislead the management into thinking that they have not done any programming (this trick is easy to pull in release 2, where you can put the code directly in the repository).

It is better to let everyone know that they should expect there to be some custom coding needed to develop an effective system. The system will still be mostly generated and will achieve many benefits from that fact. If your management was been sold on the idea of Oracle Designer primarily because of its capability for 100 percent generation, you will have to convince them about the other benefits of using Oracle Designer.

Oracle Designer Is Not a Silver Bullet

Oracle Designer is just a tool. It will not solve all of your development and design problems. In fact, if the wrong approach is taken to using the tool it can even magnify the problems! It is possible to use Oracle Designer to develop a poorly designed system with incorrect analysis even faster and with more documentation than you could before.

However, Oracle Designer is a powerful tool for change. If you have identified problems with your development methodologies that you think you should address (for instance, lack of standards, lack of documentation, limited code sharing, or reuse) you can easily use Oracle Designer to help you fix the problems. You still have to identify the problems and determine a strategy to improve them in your organization, but using Oracle Designer will greatly help you implement the changes needed to address the problems.

People can expect that Oracle Designer will help them to implement a better development methodology and maybe even force them to use more structure in their development. Nevertheless, Oracle Designer cannot really identify the specific problems in your development methodology, nor can it be expected to fix them.

Key 6: Designing for Generation

You have many choices to make when you are designing an Oracle Developer system. Each of these choices will affect the outcome of your generation efforts. For each design decision, some options are easy to generate while others are more difficult. It is very important to the success of your system that, whenever possible, you choose the options that are easier to generate. While you might not always be able to choose the best option and still meet your application requirements, you should always consider the generation ramifications of each design decision.

In the following sections, we will discuss some of the different areas where design decisions need to be made and how these decisions might affect your generation efforts.

Data Model Design (Normalization)

There are many advantages to a highly normalized data design. For example, normalized designs are much more responsive to changing requirements and therefore much easier to maintain than nonnormalized designs. For this reason, many organizations try to ensure that the physical design is as normal as possible. However, a normal presentation of the data is not always intuitive for the users. The users will often ask for a nonnormal representation of the data in the screen design, because it makes more sense to them that way. Some examples of types of presentation denormalization that we have seen are

- Presentation of parent and child information all in the same row and all updateable.
- Allowing the same piece of information to be displayed and updated from two different tables in the system.
- Presenting a series of child data values in a single row, instead of a series of child rows.

While all of these denormalizations may make sense to the users, they can lead to problems for the developers. Therefore, for many systems there often seems to be a tension between data normalization and a more acceptable user presentation. This tension can be resolved in one of three ways:

- **Normalize the data; denormalize the presentation** Normalize the physical model, but modify the presentation so that it is more intuitive for the users.
- **Normalize the presentation** Keep the data model normalized. Present the screens to the users in a more normalized fashion. The screen design would closely match the data design.
- **Denormalized physical model** Denormalize the data in the physical design to match more closely what the users want the screens to look like.

Each of these approaches has its own strengths and weaknesses, and there will probably be times where you will need to use each of them. However, whenever you have a choice, you should make the design decision that is easiest to generate.

If the goal is to develop a highly generated, lower maintenance system, it is a good idea to avoid approach 1 (normalize the data, denormalize the presentation). When this approach is taken, it will always lead to more complicated code in order to denormalize the data for presentation and then renormalize it back into the normal data model. This will usually make the system more difficult to generate and will often lead to much more nongenerated code in your system.

The generators are capable of generating a certain amount of this presentation denormalization, especially with some of the enhancements in release 2. However, there will usually be some denormalizations that cannot be generated. Even if they can be generated, you will have to use much more complicated techniques that are more difficult to implement and maintain. For example, one technique that can be used to denormalize the presentation is to use an updatable view. While you can use the view to generate a denormalized presentation of the data, you now have another object to maintain. Whenever one of the underlying tables changes, the view will also have to be changed, which increases the amount of work.

Approach 3 (denormalized physical model) has the advantage of allowing for higher generation percentage of the presentation layer. To achieve this, however, more work will have to be done on the server side to maintain the denormalizations. While some people think it might be better to denormalize the physical model than to do excessive postgeneration modifications, there are many industry leaders who say that denormalizing the data will always cost more in the long run. With the advent of some of the improvements in release 2, especially the use of the Table API, it is now much easier to develop and maintain these denormalizations on the server side. Therefore, we might be able to use this approach a little more easily, especially for some of denormalization types (like carrying denormalized parent columns in child records). However, because of the cost of maintenance for this approach, it should be used sparingly.

We think that approach 2 (normalize the presentation) is the best approach to use whenever possible. This approach involves more user training, because users will often have to learn to understand some parent/child relationships in the data that they did not have to deal with before. The users will also have to be convinced why it is better to present the data in a normalized format, and this can be difficult. However, we think the benefits of an easily maintained, flexible system can often outweigh these concerns, and so we recommend this approach.

For a system with any amount of complexity, you will most likely use more than one of these approaches, and that is fine. Just make sure to consider the generation implications of each data design decision before it is made.

User Interface Design

In the "Key 4: Standards" section, we discussed the importance of establishing user interface (UI) design standards. The reason this is so important is to ensure that your UI design is easy to generate. If you use a UI design that is difficult to generate, you will end up doing large amount of post-generation modifications. This will increase the development cost for your system and substantially increase the cost of maintenance. The UI design includes all of the following aspects:

- The types and functionality of the GUI controls
- The screen and item layout standards
- Navigation between items, windows, and modules

A discussion of the generation considerations for each of these aspects follows.

Types and Functionality of GUI Controls

The Form generator can produce many of the standard GUI controls that we are used to seeing in Windows-based applications. However, there are some fairly common GUI controls that are not supported as native controls in Oracle Developer. It is possible to use OCX controls to implement controls that are not native to Oracle Developer; however, you should consider the costs carefully before you do this. Any time you try to integrate a third party control into Oracle Developer, you are going to add to the overall cost of the system. The native controls always work better and will have fewer problems, and they are much easier to generate from Designer. We are not saying that you can never use these nonnative controls, just that you should seriously consider the ramifications of going beyond the native functionality before deciding to do so. Even if you decide to use a nonnative control for a special situation, make sure to avoid making a nonnative control one of your standards.

Screen and Item Layout Standards

There are some screen and item layout standards that are difficult or impossible for Oracle Designer to generate. The Oracle Designer generators do not allow you to specify exactly where you want each item on the screen. Instead, they use a kind of rule-based layout approach, in which the properties and preferences of the blocks and items are used to determine the layout of the generated screen. To many people this is a very annoying limitation. However, if understood correctly it can be considered a strength.

Since the layout of the items is based upon a set of rules, you do not have to do the work of manually placing all of the items on the screen as you would if you coded the modules by hand. This can actually save you work. Once you understand how the generator will lay out the items, and once you learn how to manipulate the preferences correctly, you can get fairly precise control of the overall layout. However, there will be some layouts that you cannot generate. Therefore, it is important to make sure that the layout standards for your system are easy to generate. If you design your system to use layouts that are not easy to generate, you will have to do a lot of post-generation modifications just to tweak the layout of your generated modules. Even though the layout preservation capabilities of Oracle Designer have been enhanced in release 2, you should try to avoid doing the work in the first place.

Navigation Between Items, Windows, and Modules

The Oracle Designer generators will allow you to customize the navigation standards to a certain degree. For instance, you can connect blocks based on their generation order or parent/child relationships. You can connect the records in your blocks in various fashions and determine the scope of your window to window navigation. You can also easily generate buttons that connect various modules in your application. However, not every type of navigation standard can be generated easily. If you want to allow navigation that is not possible to generate declaratively, you will have to add the code yourself. This will increase the development and maintenance costs of your system.

For this reason, it is best to make sure you standardize on one of the generatable navigation possibilities. Only use custom navigation on a very limited basis, and only use it when it is very important to the success of the system.

The Definition and Implementation of Naming Standards

As we discussed earlier in this chapter, standards can be very important to the success of a system development effort. However, it can also be important *which* standards are implemented. For every standard that is to be implemented, you should consider its generation implications. Some standards are easy to implement and enforce using Oracle Designer, while others are difficult to enforce and may involve more manual effort or the development of API reports and utilities.

This consideration is obvious for the UI standards that were discussed in the preceding section. Nevertheless, the generation ramifications should be considered for naming standards, too. A good example of this is in the naming standards for the foreign keys and primary keys in your system. The Oracle Designer Database Transformer will implement a decent standard for the key names. It may not be perfect, but in our opinion, it's good enough.

However, it seems that many DBAs don't like the standard and want to implement a different one. While their standard might actually be better, is it really worth all of the manual effort involved to implement it? How important are the key names anyway? It will save a lot of work in the long run if you just accept the Oracle Designer key name standard as your own.

Learn Oracle Designer's Generation Capabilities Before Designing the System

In order to design a system that is easy to generate, you should learn all you can about Oracle Designer's generation capabilities before you actually design the system. If this is your first Oracle Designer system and you do not have the experience yet, you might want to get some help from an experienced consultant (as we mentioned in Key 1). The rest of this book will also tell you a lot about the Oracle Designer's generation capabilities. If you can't get other help, you can at least use the standards and techniques presented in this book to guide your system design.

Key 7: User Involvement

"Users? We would be able to develop *great* systems if it weren't for the users!"

While developers may not come right out and say it this way, this is often the attitude that they have at heart. It seems like the users are always nit-picking about what are, to us, unimportant problems with the system, or they are asking for changes to the system that will not be so easy to implement (at least this late in the process). Finally, they have the audacity to find bugs in *your* programs! It seems like there is always this tension between the development team and the users, but this does not have to be the case.

The system you are developing is *for* the users. They should have the greatest personal stake in helping the system to be a success. However, in order to foster an attitude of cooperation, you will have to make an effort to get the users involved in the process as early as possible and keep them involved during the whole process. From the start of the development effort, you should consider the users (or at least some key users) to be part of your team and get them involved in the development of the system.

Key Areas of User Involvement

Following is a list of some of the important areas to get the users involved in:

1. **Get the Users' Help with the Data and Process Design.**

   Your users may not understand data or process modeling, but they can help even after you have gathered requirements. Once you have developed your initial models, present them to some of the key users. If you need to, train them to understand the diagrams and show them the ERDs and the functional hierarchies. You will quite often uncover data relationships and missing processing that you would not have discovered until acceptance testing.

2. **Get Users' Input for the Proposed User Interface.**

   The acceptability of the user interface can be one of the greatest factors in affecting the overall acceptance of the system by the users. If the UI is cumbersome and difficult to use, the system may be a failure, even if it meets all of the requirements. The use of Oracle Designer does place some limitations on the user interface. Discuss these limitations with the users early on in the process, as well as the advantages of using a UI that is easy to generate, and you will have a much easier time getting the users to accept some compromises. You can show them the various options that are available and work with them to find options that are both acceptable and easy to generate. If you wait until acceptance testing to present the UI to the users, they may demand that you modify the system to meet their expectations even if it ends up taking a lot of time and makes the system more difficult to maintain.

NOTE

What do we mean by user interface (UI)? The UI refers to the overall design of how the system appears and functions for the user. It includes the colors and fonts used in the screens, whether one window or multiple windows are used in the application, and the design of the navigation between modules. It is determined in Oracle Designer generation by the design of the templates and object libraries, and by the default settings and management of the preferences used to generate the system.

3. **Use Evolutionary Prototyping.**

We like to use evolutionary prototyping to develop the important parts of the system. In evolutionary prototyping, the modules are generated and presented to the users for comment. They will test the modules and make suggestions for ways to improve the layout, functionality, and performance of the modules. They will also often find missed requirements or errors in the analysis. The developer will then make changes and present the modules to the users again. When the users and developers are both happy with the overall design of the module, it will then become the production module. This is called evolutionary because the prototype module evolves into the production module.

Using evolutionary prototyping is a very powerful way to involve the key users. They will really have some direct input into the design of system, making it a much better system and giving them a much greater sense of ownership. The most successful systems we have developed used this approach.

NOTE

One of the problems inherent in the evolutionary prototyping approach is its tendency to foster scope creep. There are a couple of ways to manage this. First, make sure that any change suggested by the users either fits into the accepted scope for the system or is absolutely necessary for the success of the system. If it is not in the scope or necessary, tell the users that it will be implemented in a future release of the system. It also helps to have a predetermined time frame for this phase of development. At the end of this time period, the evolutionary prototyping will cease, and the users will not see the module again until acceptance testing. Without this deadline, the module could get stuck in a perpetual prototyping phase.

4. **Make Sure to Perform User Acceptance Testing.**

   The users need to be involved in the testing of the system. Most systems cannot be adequately tested from just the information gathered during the requirements phase. We may be able to prove that the system meets what we documented as requirements but we cannot be sure it really meets the user's needs.

A Sense of Ownership

As you can see from the list above, we encourage you to get the users involved throughout the whole development process. When this is done, the users will have a sense of ownership of the application. They will feel that they were instrumental in the development and the success of the system, and they will be right!

VRAD Versus Full Life-Cycle Development

We think that a full life-cycle development approach is almost always better for the development of any system. However, we do understand that there are situations where a VRAD approach is the best option, and VRAD approaches are being used more and more frequently. How does the use of a VRAD approach affect the consideration of these keys?

We feel that these keys remain important even if you do not use a full life-cycle approach to development. Some of these keys may not be as critical if you are using a VRAD approach, but they are all areas that should still be considered. In addition, some of the keys are even *more* important for VRAD development. If you do not have a stable infrastructure (Key 3) in place before you start development, it can drastically slow down the development (there goes the "V"). If your users do not like the system (Keys 5 and 7), and do not accept it, does it matter how fast it was developed? If the system is not designed for generation (Key 6), then using Oracle Designer will actually slow you down. Therefore, the keys detailed in this chapter are still applicable for using Oracle Designer to development systems using VRAD techniques.

Conclusion

There are many, many factors that contribute to the success of a system development effort. These seven areas do not cover all of the possible factors, but they should help you think about some of the major concerns and issues that will have the greatest effect on the development of your system. While addressing these seven factors successfully may not guarantee a successful system, we have never had a system considered a failure that did address these issues adequately.

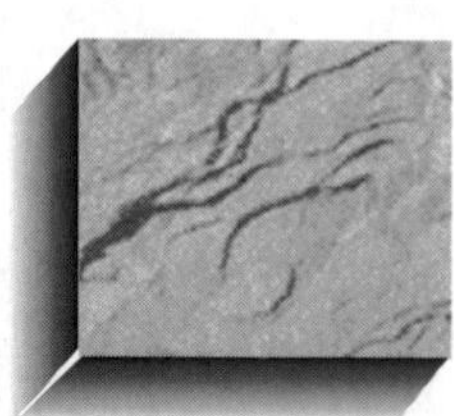

PART II

Server-Side Code Generation

CHAPTER 4

PL/SQL Definition Method

his chapter details the various methods of defining a PL/SQL definition within Designer. Release 2 of Oracle Designer has three methods for defining a PL/SQL definition. Each of these methods has specific advantages and disadvantages that you should be aware of. In this chapter we will

- Define what the PL/SQL definition method is
- Provide a detailed overview of each type of method
- Illustrate how to specify the method of a PL/SQL definition
- Discuss various PL/SQL program development approaches and how they integrate with the Oracle Designer PL/SQL definition method

In the chapters that follow in Part II, we will then present a series of step-by-step generation examples, which show all three methods in action.

Selecting a PL/SQL Definition Method

The second dialog of the PL/SQL Definition dialog appears in Figure 4-1.

The second item, *How the PL/SQL will be defined* is very important. We will call this the method used to create the PL/SQL definition. There are three settings for this value available in Designer 2.1:

- Operating System File
- Free Format
- Declarative

The method used to define a PL/SQL module tells the Server generator how to create the PL/SQL definition from the data stored in the repository. This can be as simple as generating an execution statement, which will execute a file on the operating system, or as complex as assembling the contents of individually defined repository elements to create the entire definition. Let's take a closer look at each method.

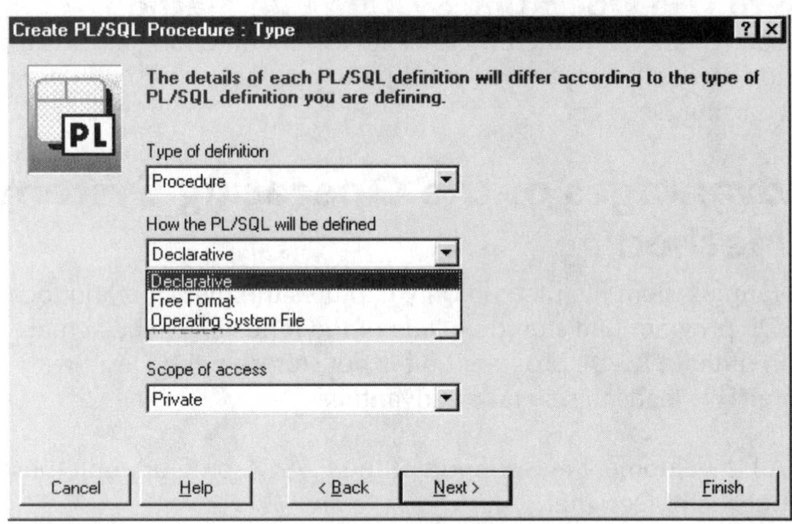

FIGURE 4-1. *PL/SQL Definition dialog*

Operating System File Method

As its name implies, PL/SQL definitions defined using the operating system file method contain the path and file location of the program unit definition. The entire program unit definition is stored outside the repository. The only thing stored in the repository is the name and location of the SQL file that is used to create it.

Advantages of the Operating System File Method

The operating system file method is useful for documenting existing PL/SQL definitions that were created outside of the Designer repository. This allows you to capture the structure of the PL/SQL program units in the repository without concerning yourself with administering the actual code. You can then associate these PL/SQL definitions to related application components defined within the repository. This activity increases the quality of impact analysis reporting.

When to Use Operating System File Method

The operating system file method is useful for documenting an existing production application system or third-party product, which will not be supported using Designer.

Disadvantages of the Operating System File Method

The operating system file method only captures the filename and location of the PL/SQL program unit stored outside of the repository. The actual definition of that PL/SQL program unit is not stored in the Designer repository. This leads to several disadvantages.

- All development and support of the PL/SQL program unit must occur outside of Designer.
- Code reuse is completely disabled within Designer.
- The majority of Designer's impact analysis capabilities are disabled.

When *Not* to Use the Operating System File Method

The operating system file method should be avoided in new application development using Designer or in applications targeted for support using Designer. In these instances, you should consider using one of the other two methods of defining a PL/SQL definition to pull more information into the repository.

Free Format Method

The free format method is one of two methods that stores all of the PL/SQL definitions' contents in the Designer repository. The header section of the PL/SQL program unit is generated through data entered when defining the PL/SQL definition. The body of the program unit remains your responsibility to define in the *PL/SQL Block* property of that PL/SQL definition.

Advantages of the Free Format Method

Using the free format method to define a PL/SQL definition has several advantages.

- It is easy to learn. The header of the program unit is the only part of the program unit not generated from data entered into the *PL/SQL Block* property of the PL/SQL definition. Experienced PL/SQL developers find this method to be the most intuitive of all methods because of this.
- The entire program unit is defined within the repository. This allows you to perform more complete impact analysis, increase the quality and quantity of documentation, and increase code reuse (although code reuse is only applicable to packages).
- You can more easily use advanced PL/SQL constructs. Examples of such constructs include overloaded functions/procedures and VARRAYS. Since you are responsible for defining the body of the program unit, you can use anything you wish and can rest assured that it will be generated.

When to Use the Free Format Method

There are two good uses of the free format method:

- When implementing advanced PL/SQL constructs. In most instances, developers can more quickly define and successfully generate complex PL/SQL constructs using this method.
- To increase productivity in cases where time is short and the team consists of experienced Oracle developers who have little or no knowledge of Designer.

Disadvantages of the Free Format Method

Limited code reuse is the main disadvantage of free format method. A PL/SQL definition defined using the free format method can be included in a declarative package. In this instance, the code initially provided to create the free format PL/SQL definition is reused. However, that is the extent of code reuse available using the free format method. A free format PL/SQL definition cannot include other PL/SQL definitions as subprogram units. The Server generator will ignore all subprogram specifications when creating DDL.

When *Not* to Use the Free Format Method

The least effective use of the free format method is in development of a package. Each of the individual program units defined within the package body cannot be reused by other PL/SQL definitions. Sure, you could copy and paste the code, but that's really not code reuse. Also, there is no direct visibility of, or documentation for, the package components.

Declarative Method

The declarative method is the other method that stores all of the PL/SQL definitions' contents in the Designer repository. When defining a PL/SQL definition using the declarative method, you will enter information that will be used to generate the header, declaration, and exception sections of the PL/SQL program unit. You are then responsible for entering the execution section in the PL/SQL block item property of that PL/SQL definition.

Advantages of the Declarative Method

The declarative method has two significant advantages:

- You can reuse code contained in other PL/SQL definitions. Package PL/SQL definitions use other PL/SQL definitions as subprogram units. These subprogram units are then generated into the package body by the Server generator. There is no coding, no copying and pasting; just code reuse.
- Increased quality and quantity of documentation of package components. Each package component is its own PL/SQL definition in the repository. As such, each PL/SQL definition has its own documentation and ability to be included in impact analysis.

When to Use the Declarative Method

You should always try to use the declarative method when defining a package. Doing this will help you reuse code and increase the quality of your documentation.

Disadvantages of the Declarative Method

PL/SQL definitions defined using the declarative method are more prone to encounter generation bugs than similar definitions using one of the other two methods. The troubleshooting guides located at the end of each of the upcoming Server Generator chapters contain the specifics. Examples include generating advanced PL/SQL constructs such as VARRYAS or overloaded

PL/SQL definitions and generation of the exception section of the program unit body.

When *Not* to Use the Declarative Method

The declarative method should be avoided when defining complex PL/SQL definitions. We are not saying that complex PL/SQL definition cannot be created using the declarative method but rather, that the time needed to successfully define and generate a complex PL/SQL definition is cost prohibitive, unless you have very experienced staff.

Setting the Method of a PL/SQL Definition

There are two ways you can specify the PL/SQL definition method:

- Using dialogs (reentrant wizards)
- Using the Properties palette

The difference between these two approaches is really quite simple. The dialogs present a step-by-step guide to defining a PL/SQL definition and show you only the necessary attributes of that PL/SQL definition. Conversely, the Properties palette shows all of the attributes of the PL/SQL definition with a basic sort order but without step-by-step presentation. In the following examples, we will illustrate how to specify the method each way.

Specifying Method Using the Dialogs

Follow these steps:

1. Create a new PL/SQL definition or view the properties of an existing module.
2. Complete the Name dialog and click Next.
3. Select the desired value for *How the PL/SQL will be defined* (refer to Figure 4-2).

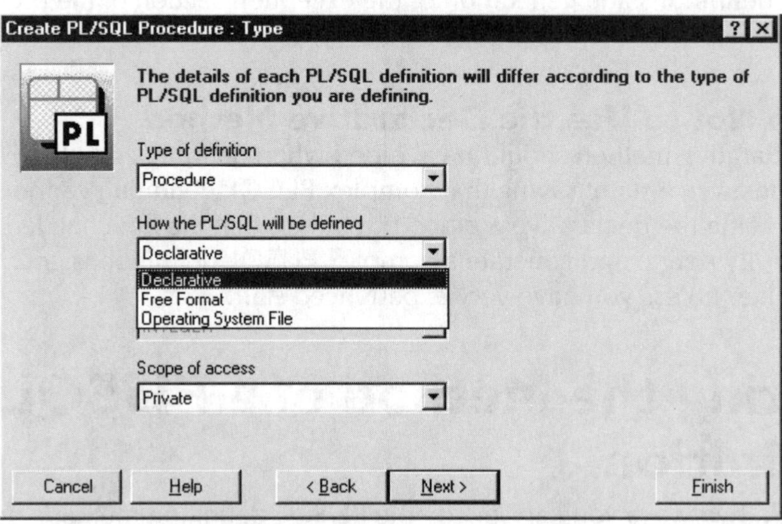

FIGURE 4-2. *Specifying method using the dialogs*

Specifying Method Using the Properties Palette

Specifying method using the Properties palette is slightly more challenging than using the dialogs in that there are two properties of a PL/SQL definition that control method. These properties are

- Free format declaration
- Source path

The following table illustrates of how to specify each method using the Properties palette.

Method	Free Format	Source Path	Screen Shot
Operating system file	Null or No	Path\filename	Declaration Free Format Declaration ? No Source Path C:\prc_os.sql
Free format	Yes	Null	Declaration Free Format Declaration ? Yes Source Path
Declarative	No	Null	Declaration Free Format Declaration ? No Source Path

PL/SQL Development Approach

It is out of the scope of this book to cover in detail how you should actually go about developing the PL/SQL server-side code that you will implement in your system. However, the approach you use to develop your code could have an influence over the Oracle Designer PL/SQL definition method you decide to use.

Using Oracle Designer, there are basically three approaches that you can use to develop PL/SQL that you want to implement. They each have their own strengths and weaknesses and work better with different PL/SQL definition methods. The three approaches are

- Define the PL/SQL directly in Oracle Designer
- Use a text editor to write the PL/SQL and compile and debug it in SQL*Plus
- Use a PL/SQL development tool like Procedure Builder

Next we will discuss how each of these approaches work, and detail their advantages and disadvantages. We will also indicate which PL/SQL definition method works the best with each approach.

Defining the PL/SQL Directly in Oracle Designer

Using this approach, you would add all of the information into Oracle Designer directly, then generate the scripts to install the programs into Oracle. If there were any bugs in your code, you would go back into Oracle Designer, update the definition, and generate and install it again.

- **Advantages** The main advantage of this approach is that you will ensure that you have good documentation and that your declarations will match the data definitions in your data model. This is also the only way you can use complete declarative PL/SQL definitions.
- **Disadvantages** It can be very difficult to write PL/SQL this way, especially if the declarative approach is used. The Logic Editor is not very helpful for developing the code because it does not have the capability to compile and debug the code. Debugging the code can

be very cumbersome because you have to add the time consuming step of actually generating the code into your debugging routine. A developer would have to be very experienced with PL/SQL and Oracle Designer before they could be efficient at using this approach.

- **Best PL/SQL Definition Method to Use** Declarative

NOTE

The Logic Editor *Oracle Designer has a tool called the Logic Editor that can help you define your PL/SQL definitions. In general, we have not found the user interface of the Logic Editor to be very friendly and do not often use it, preferring instead to use a text editor to enter the code into the PL/SQL definitions. Therefore, we will not go into detail about how to use the Logic Editor in the procedures detailed in the rest of this section. However, if you do want to use the Logic Editor after you have already created a definition, you can do this by selecting a PL/SQL definition, then pressing the Logic Editor button on the main toolbar,*

or by right-clicking and selecting Edit PL/SQL.

Using a Text Editor and SQL*Plus

Using this approach, you write the complete PL/SQL package by hand using a text editor. Then you install the program into Oracle using SQL*Plus and use the standard debugging available in SQL*Plus (SHOW ERRORS) to debug the program. Once it is debugged, load it into Oracle Designer. The program can be integrated with Oracle Designer in one of three ways:

- Install the program into an instance and use the design capture utility of Oracle Designer to load it into the repository (which will create the PL/SQL definition using the free format method).
- Place the content of your program into Oracle Designer by hand. This usually involves cutting and pasting pieces of the text file into various properties in Oracle Designer. This could be done for both the free format or declarative method.
- Use the Operating System File method, which means that the only thing you enter into Oracle Designer is the name of the SQL file that you wrote with the text editor.

The rest of the chapters in Part II detail where the information actually has to be placed in Oracle Designer.

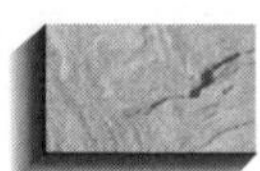

TIP

Use the ASCII Editor in Oracle Designer

When you are entering the large text pieces of the PL/SQL definitions (the PL/SQL Block and the package specification), you can edit the contents using the text editor of your choosing (it defaults to Notepad). This is done by highlighting the text property and pressing the ASCII Editor button,

in the Property palette. The advantage of this is that it is usually easier to cut and paste with an ASCII editor than with Oracle Designer's textpad.

- **Advantages** This is the easiest way to develop simple PL/SQL programs, especially for experienced developers. This approach makes it much easier to debug the PL/SQL than defining the programs directly in Oracle Designer.
- **Disadvantages** It is very difficult to implement the PL/SQL definitions using the declarative method using this approach, especially for packages. Therefore, this approach should probably not be used if you want to use declarative method.
- **Best PL/SQL Definition Method to Use** Operating System file or free format.

Using a PL/SQL Development Tool

This approach uses a PL/SQL Development tool to develop and debug the PL/SQL program and usually to install it into the Oracle database. You then load the program into Oracle Designer using one of the same techniques discussed in the previous section, "Using a Text Editor and SQL*Plus." However, when using some of the tools, you may have to export the text of the PL/SQL before you can get it into Oracle Designer. Some examples of PL/SQL Development tools are Oracle's Procedure builder, TOAD, and SQL*Navigator.

- **Advantages** For complicated programs, a PL/SQL development tool can really help the developer be more efficient in their development efforts. These tools also really help with debugging.
- **Disadvantages** Moving the source between the tool and Oracle Designer can be a cumbersome task and may discourage people from actually placing the code into Oracle Designer. For the most part, these tools are designed to maintain the code directly in the database and do not integrate with other tools such as Oracle Designer.
- **Best PL/SQL Definition Method to Use** Free format or Operating System file.

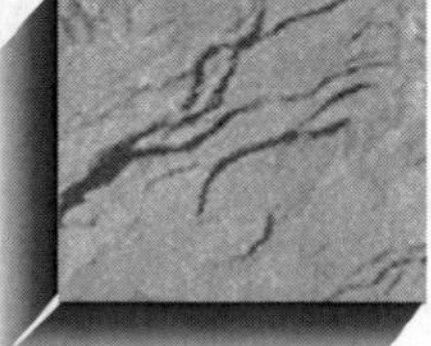

CHAPTER 5

Generating Procedures

This chapter is a detailed guide to help you generate procedures. In this chapter we will cover

- Generation of a sample procedure using each method of defining a PL/SQL definition and design capture
- The property settings used to generate each example
- Step-by-step instructions for creating the example using each method
- A troubleshooting guide to assist you with common generation problems

We think it's easier to understand the various methods if we use an example that at least looks like a real-world program. Therefore, we designed a sample procedure that performs a standard task that you might use in a real system.

NOTE

Example Description: *The example we are using in this chapter is a procedure that creates a record in a table (ACTIONS) for every occurrence of a record in another table (ISSUES) that has a particular status (PENDING) and FK ID (TAR_ID). The example is based on the example application provided with this book. The purpose of this particular procedure is to request that every issue that is affected by a TAR be retested when the TAR is resolved.*

The code shown in Figure 5-1 will be used in the sections that follow to show you a specific example of each method of creating a procedure. If you need additional background on each method presented, refer to Chapter 4.

```
CREATE OR REPLACE PROCEDURE TAR_ACTIONS (p_tar_id IN number) IS

/* Cursor Selects Issue and Issues Status related to given TAR */
CURSOR GET_ISS_STAT(p_dbcr_id IN NUMBER) IS
  select iss.id id, iss.istat_cd status
  from issues iss, issues_oracle_tars tar
  where iss.id = tar.iss_id
  and tar.tar_id = p_tar_id;

BEGIN
 FOR ISS_REC in GET_ISS_STAT(p_tar_id) LOOP
  BEGIN
   --  IF Pending Issues are found related to a closed TAR, create and
   --  action item to have the issue retested
   IF iss_rec.status = 'PENDING' THEN
    insert into actions
    (id
     , action_date
     , short_notes
     , iss_id
     , atyp_cd
     , per_id)
   VALUES
    (common_surrogate.nextval
     , sysdate
     , 'DBCR CLOSED, PLEASE RETEST TO VERIFY THAT PROBLEM HAS BEEN
RESOLVED.'
     , iss_rec.id
     , 'RETEST'
     , 4);  -- Assigned to my favorite DBA
   END IF;
  EXCEPTION
   WHEN OTHERS THEN RAISE_APPLICATION_ERROR
    (-21001, 'AUTOMATED ACTIONS PROCESS failed with: '||substr(SQLERRM,1,50));
  END;
 END LOOP;
END TAR_ACTIONS;
/
```

FIGURE 5-1. *Sample procedure*

Operating System File Method

The operating system file method is the only method that references definitions that are stored outside the repository. In order to use this method, you must place the source code for the program unit definition into an operating system file and specify the filename and path when you are creating the PL/SQL definition in the repository.

Generating the sample procedure using the operating system file method will create two files. In this example, the two files created are

- <file prefix>.SQL Executes the file <file prefix>.PRC
- <file prefix>.PRC Executes the true program unit definition, calling a specified path and filename that contain the DDL.

NOTE
<file prefix> is a name that you specify when generating server-side objects. This name will be given to all files created during that execution of the Server Generator.

Figure 5-2 is an annotated version of <file prefix>.PRC. The superscript numbers correspond to properties in the procedure definition, which created this file. See Table 5-1 for specific mapping of the generated code.

```
-- c:\aristmpl\application\ss\CH5_os.prc
--
-- Generated for Oracle 8 on Tue Jul 14  07:01:48 1998 by Server
Generator 2.1.19.5.0

PROMPT Creating [1]Procedure[1] [2]'TAR_ACTIONS'[2]
@[3]C:\ARISTMPL\Application\SS\proc\procedure.sql[3]
```

FIGURE 5-2. *Annotated generation example using the operating system file method*

Number	Feature	Source Using Dialogs	Source Using Properties Palette
1	PL/SQL definition type	TYPE TAB Field: Type of definition	PROCEDURE DEFINITION Property: Type
2	PL/SQL definition name	NAME TAB Field: Name	PROCEDURE DEFINITION Property: Implementation Name
3	Path and filename	FILE TAB Field: Path and filename of source	PROCEDURE DEFINITION Property: Source Path

TABLE 5-1. *Source of Generated Code Using the Operating System File Method*

Steps to Create This Procedure Using the Operating System File Method

Using the steps that follow, you will be able to re-create the sample procedure. Since there is more than one way to accomplish this task, we focus on defining steps that minimize the amount of time required to create the definition, while still taking advantage of the new features of release 2. We have chosen to use the dialogs for creating each definition and then to use the Properties Palette to enter the remaining information about the definition, which cannot be entered through the dialogs.

1. In the Design Editor (DE), click on the Server Model tab.
2. Create a new procedure definition (available under PL/SQL definitions). Do this by pressing the Create icon on the Design Editor toolbar. This will launch a set of dialogs that will gather all of the necessary information required for the procedure definition. The following steps detail the setting used for this example:

3. The Name dialog is the first dialog that will be displayed. Specify a short name for the procedure definition that will be used for naming generated files (*Short name of the PL/SQL definition* = **CH5_OS**). Next, specify a unique name for the procedure definition (*Name* = **CH5_OS**) and the purpose or short description of the procedure definition (*Purpose* = **Create an action to retest an issue when an associated TAR is resolved**). Last, specify the name you would like to use when implementing the procedure definition (*Implementation name* = **TAR_ACTIONS**). This name will be used in the header of the program unit. Figure 5-3 shows the Name dialog used for this example. When you have completed this dialog, click Next.
4. The Type dialog is the second dialog that will be displayed. Using this dialog you will be able to specify that you would like to define a procedure definition (*Type of definition* = **Procedure**). Next, specify that you would like to define the procedure using the operating system file method (*How the PL/SQL will be defined* = **Operating System File**). Last, specify that the scope of this procedure is private (*Scope of*

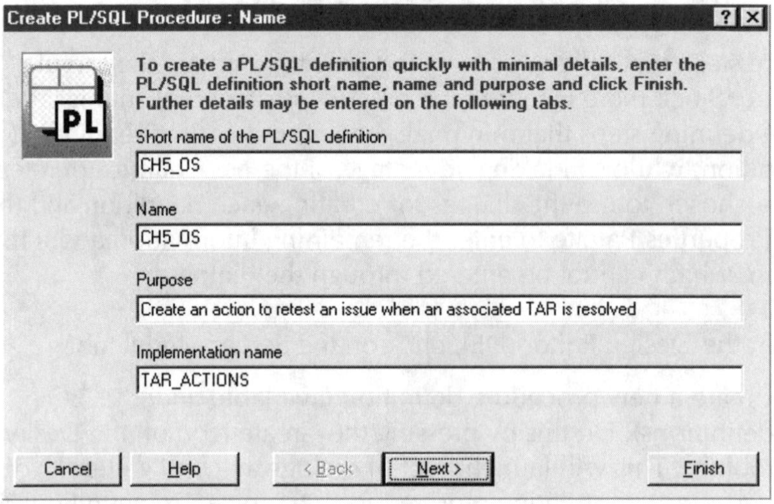

FIGURE 5-3. *Name dialog—operating system file example*

access = **Private**). Figure 5-4 shows the Type dialog used for this example. When you have completed this dialog, click Next.

5. The File dialog is the third dialog that will be displayed. Using this dialog, you will be able to specify the name of the file that contains the DDL for this procedure definition and its location (*Path and filename of source* = **C:\ARISTMPL\Application\SS\procedure.sql**). Figure 5-5 shows the File dialog used for this example. When you have completed this dialog, click Next.
6. The Goodbye dialog is the last dialog that will be displayed. This dialog provides you with three different ways that you can exit the dialogs you have just used to define the procedure definition. Since we have defined this example using the operating system file method, we have no additional information to enter. Option one, *Create the PL/SQL definition with the information provided,* is the only valid selection. Figure 5-6 shows the Goodbye dialog used for this example.

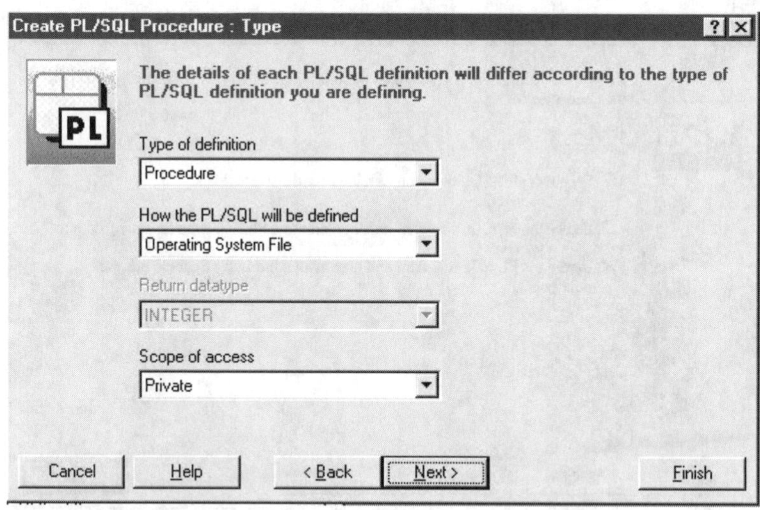

FIGURE 5-4. *Type dialog—operating system file example*

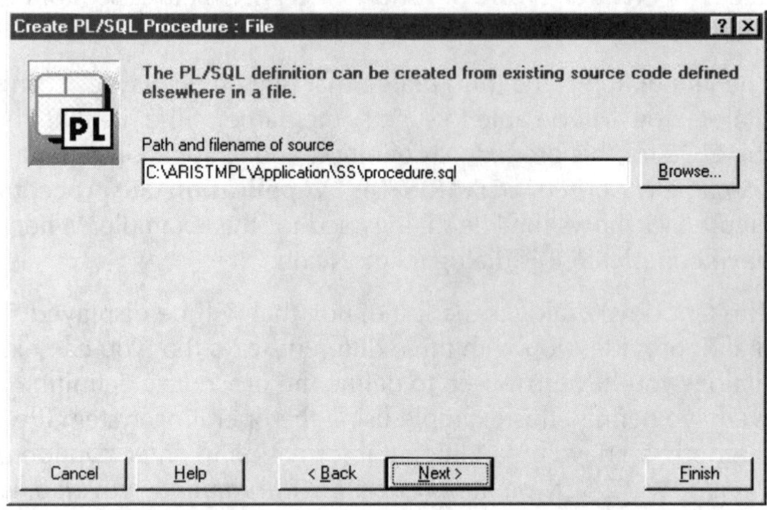

FIGURE 5-5. *File dialog—operating system file example*

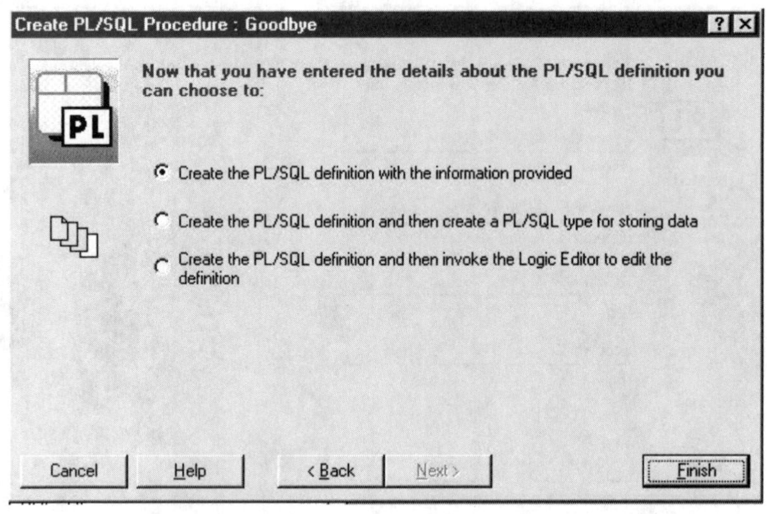

FIGURE 5-6. *Goodbye dialog—operating system file example*

7. We suggest that you create a PL/SQL implementation item for this procedure definition next. This is not a mandatory step, but it is very useful if you intend to manage database objects using databases and schema owner accounts defined within the Designer Repository. To do this, you will need to select the DB Admin tab and then navigate to the correct Oracle database and user under that database. Add this procedure to the procedure implementation schema objects for that user by pressing the Create icon in the Design Editor toolbar and then completing the dialogs.
8. Generate the procedure definition.

Free Format Method

The free format method is one of two methods of defining a PL/SQL definition in which the entire program unit is stored within the repository. When using this method, you need to decide how you would like to define and generate the declaration section of the program unit body. Declarations can be generated using the free format method in two ways:

- Using the *package specification* property
- Including the declarations in the *PL/SQL Block* property

These are the only two properties that will be used by the Server Generator to create the program unit body. If the *package specification* property is null, then the program unit body is created using the *PL/SQL Block* property only.

The procedure shown in Figure 5-7 makes use of the *package specification* property to create the declaration section of the program unit. Since the free format method is the only method that allows declarations in the *PL/SQL Block* property, it is good practice to remain consistent when defining PL/SQL definitions. For that reason, the *package specification* property is a better option for variable declaration than the *PL/SQL Block* property.

Generating the sample procedure using the free format method creates two files. In this example, the two files created are

- <file prefix>.SQL Executes the file <file prefix>.PRC
- <file prefix>.PRC Contains the generated program unit definition

```
-- c:\aristmpl\application\ss\proc\CH5_free.prc
--
-- Generated for Oracle 8 on Tue Jul 14  07:14:29 1998 by Server
Generator 2.1.19.5.0

PROMPT Creating 1Procedure1 2'TAR_ACTIONS'2
CREATE OR REPLACE 1PROCEDURE1 2TAR_ACTIONS2 (3P_TAR_ID3 4IN4 5NUMBER5 ) IS

--PL/SQL Specification
6/* Cursor Selects Issue and Issues Status related to given TAR */
CURSOR GET_ISS_STAT(p_dbcr_id IN NUMBER) IS
 select iss.id id, iss.istat_cd status
  from issues iss, issues_oracle_tars tar
  where iss.id = tar.iss_id
  and tar.tar_id = p_tar_id;6
-- PL/SQL Block
7BEGIN
 FOR ISS_REC in GET_ISS_STAT(p_tar_id) LOOP
  BEGIN
   --  IF Pending Issues are found related to a closed TAR, create an
   --    action item to have the issue retested
   IF iss_rec.status = 'PENDING' THEN
    insert into actions
    (id
     , action_date
     , short_notes
     , iss_id
     , atyp_cd
     , per_id)
   VALUES
    (common_surrogate.nextval
     , sysdate
     , 'DBCR CLOSED, PLEASE RETEST TO VERIFY THAT PROBLEM HAS BEEN
RESOLVED.'
     , iss_rec.id
     , 'RETEST'
     , 4);  -- Assigned to my favorite DBA
   END IF;
  EXCEPTION
   WHEN OTHERS THEN RAISE_APPLICATION_ERROR
    (-21001, 'AUTOMATED ACTIONS PROCESS failed with: '||substr(SQLERRM,1,50));
  END;
 END LOOP;
END TAR_ACTIONS;7
/
```

FIGURE 5-7. *Annotated generation example using the free format method*

NOTE
<file prefix> is a name that you specify when generating server-side objects. This name will be given to all files created during that execution of the Server Generator.

Figure 5-7 is an annotated version of <file prefix>.PRC. The superscript numbers correspond to properties in the procedure definition that created this file. See Table 5-2 for specific mapping of the generated code.

Number	Feature	Source Using Dialogs	Source Using Properties Palette
1	PL/SQL definition type	TYPE TAB Field: Type of definition	PROCEDURE DEFINITION Property: Type
2	PL/SQL definition name	NAME TAB Field: Name	PROCEDURE DEFINITION Property: Implementation Name
3	Argument name	ARGUMENT TAB Field: Arguments	ARGUMENT Property: Name
4	Argument type	ARGUMENT TAB Field: Argument type	ARGUMENT Property: Input Output
5	Argument datatype	ARGUMENT TAB Field: Datatype	ARGUMENT Property: Datatype
6	Declaration section of program unit body	NO SOURCE	PROCEDURE DEFINITION Property: Package Specification
7	Execution and exception sections of program unit body	NO SOURCE	PROCEDURE DEFINITION Property: PL/SQL Block

TABLE 5-2. *Source of Generated Code Using the Free Format Method*

Steps to Create This Procedure Using the Free Format Method

Using the steps that follow, you will be able to re-create the sample procedure. Since there is more than one way to accomplish this task, we focus on defining steps that minimize the amount of time required to create the definition, while still taking advantage of the new features of release 2. We have chosen to use the dialogs for creating each definition and then to use the Properties Palette to enter the remaining information about the definition, which cannot be entered through the dialogs.

1. In the Design Editor (DE) click the Server Model tab.
2. Create a new procedure definition (available under PL/SQL definitions). Do this by pressing the Create icon in the Design Editor toolbar. This will launch a set of dialogs that will gather all of the necessary information required for the procedure definition. The following steps detail the settings used for this example.
3. The Name dialog is the first dialog that will be displayed. Using this dialog you will be able to specify a short name for the procedure definition that will be used for naming generated files (*Short name of the PL/SQL definition* = **CH5_FREE**). Next, specify a unique name for the procedure definition (*Name* = **CH5_FREE**) and the purpose or short description of the procedure definition (*Purpose* = **Create an action to retest an issue when an associated TAR is resolved**). Last, specify the name you would like to use when creating the procedure definition (*Implementation name* = **TAR_ACTIONS**). This name will be used in the header of the program unit. Figure 5-8 shows the Name dialog used for this example. When you have completed this dialog, click Next.
4. The Type dialog is the second dialog that will be displayed. Using this dialog, you will be able to specify that you would like to define a procedure definition (*Type of definition* = **Procedure**). Next, specify that you would like to define the procedure using the free format method (*How the PL/SQL will be defined* = **Free Format**). Last, specify that the scope of this procedure is private (*Scope of access* = **Private**). Figure 5-9 shows the Type dialog used for this example. When you have completed this dialog, click next.

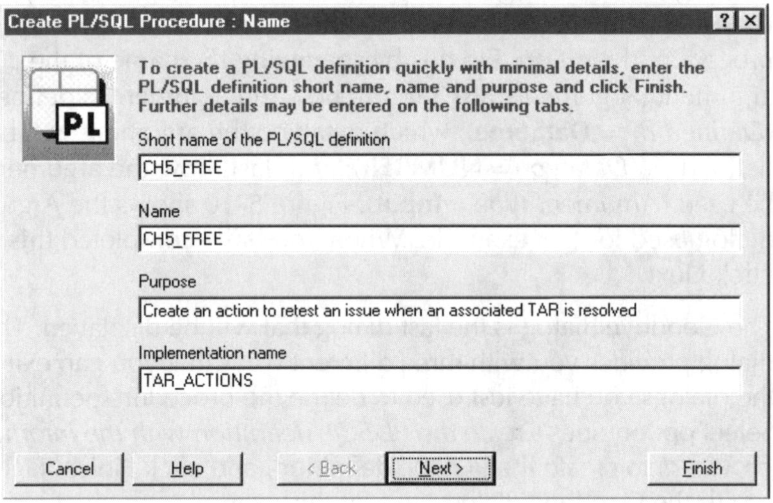

Create PL/SQL Procedure : Name

To create a PL/SQL definition quickly with minimal details, enter the PL/SQL definition short name, name and purpose and click Finish. Further details may be entered on the following tabs.

Short name of the PL/SQL definition: CH5_FREE

Name: CH5_FREE

Purpose: Create an action to retest an issue when an associated TAR is resolved

Implementation name: TAR_ACTIONS

Cancel | Help | < Back | Next > | Finish

FIGURE 5-8. *Name dialog—free format example*

Create PL/SQL Procedure : Type

The details of each PL/SQL definition will differ according to the type of PL/SQL definition you are defining.

Type of definition: Procedure

How the PL/SQL will be defined: Free Format

Return datatype: INTEGER

Scope of access: Private

Cancel | Help | < Back | Next > | Finish

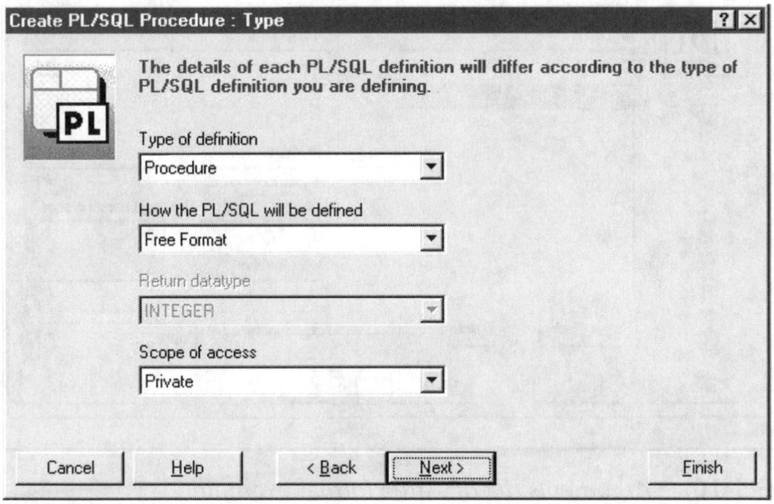

FIGURE 5-9. *Type dialog—free format example*

5. The Arguments dialog is the third dialog that will be displayed. Using this dialog, you can define the argument used by this procedure definition. Do this by specifying the name of the argument (*Arguments* = **p_tar_id**); how the argument is defined (*Defined By* = **Datatype**); which datatype the argument will be defined as (*Datatype* = **NUMBER**); and, last, how the argument will be used (*Argument type* = **Input**). Figure 5-10 shows the Arguments dialog used for this example. When you have completed this dialog, click Next.

6. The Goodbye dialog is the last dialog that will be displayed. This dialog provides you with three different ways that you can exit the dialogs you have just used to define the procedure definition. Select option one (*Create the PL/SQL definition with the information provided*) to create the PL/SQL definition, and click Finish. Figure 5-11 shows the Goodbye dialog used for this example.

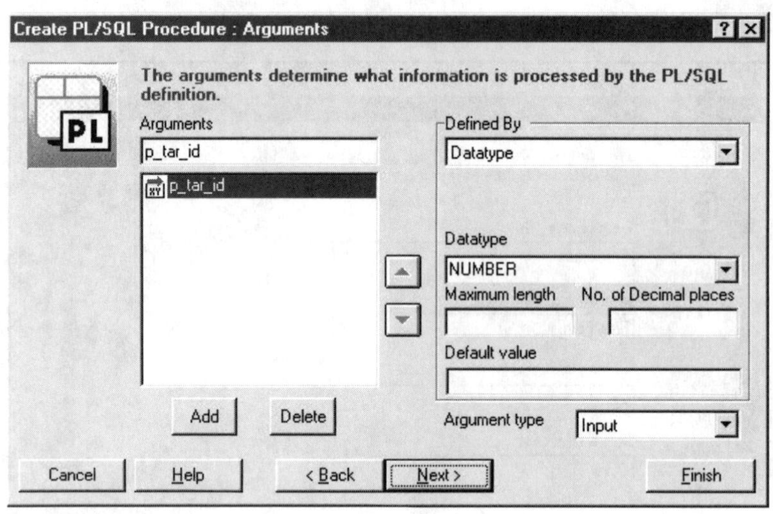

FIGURE 5-10. *Arguments dialog—free format example*

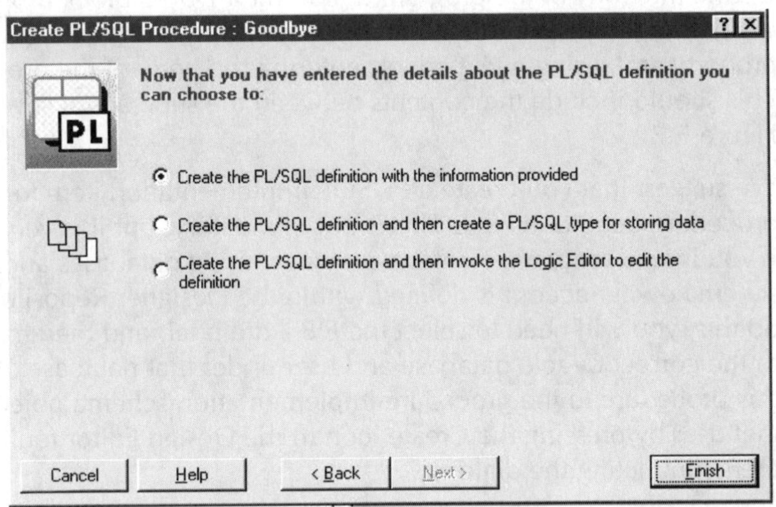

FIGURE 5-11. *Goodbye dialog—free format example*

NOTE
You could alternatively select option three (Create the PL/SQL definition and then invoke the Logic Editor to edit the definition)*. If you choose to define the procedure using this option, you can generate once you've finished defining the procedure using this editor.*

7. Switch to the Properties Palette from the dialogs by pressing the Property Dialogs/Palettes icon in the Design Editor toolbar.
8. Define the cursor program unit definition in the *package specification* property of the procedure definition. Do this by navigating to the *package specification* property and, using a text editor, entering the cursor program unit definition. This should include the contents between the superscript sixes in Figure 5-7.

9. Define the body of the program unit in the *PL/SQL Block* property of the procedure definition. Do this by navigating to the *PL/SQL Block* property and, using a text editor, entering the body of the procedure. This should include the contents between the superscript sevens in Figure 5-7.
10. We suggest that you create a PL/SQL implementation item for this procedure definition next. This is not mandatory, but it is very useful if you intend to manage database objects using databases and schema owner accounts defined within the Designer Repository. To do this, you will need to select the DB Admin tab and then navigate to the correct Oracle database and user under that database. Add this procedure to the procedure implementation schema objects for that user by pressing the Create icon in the Design Editor toolbar and then completing the dialogs.
11. Generate the procedure definition.

Declarative Method

The declarative method is the other method of defining a PL/SQL definition in which the entire program unit is stored within the repository. When using this method to generate our sample procedure, you will need to make the following decisions:

- How to generate the declaration section of the program unit
- How to generate the exception section of the program unit

The declaration section of the program unit body can be generated using the declarative method in three ways:

- Defining the desired declarations in the *package specification* property
- Defining each declaration as program data and/or subprogram units of the PL/SQL definition
- Mixing and matching the two methods above

Variable and constant declarations are simple to generate using any of the three methods just listed. The main difference between them is where the Server generator will get the information to create each declaration section of the program unit.

Cursor declarations are slightly more complicated. Prior to defining the cursor declaration, you should ask yourself, "Will I use this cursor in other PL/SQL definitions?" If the answer to this question is yes, then you should consider creating a separate cursor definition and including it as a sub-program unit. If, however, the answer to the question is no, then it is okay to use the *package specification* property of the PL/SQL definition.

The exception section of the program unit body can be generated using the declarative method in two ways:

- Defining the exception section immediately following the execution section of the program unit in the *PL/SQL Block* property.
- Defining each exception as program data of the PL/SQL definition. This will create user-defined exceptions that you then can reference throughout the program unit.

Exceptions are simple to generate using either of the two methods just listed. The main difference between them is where the Server generator will get the information to specify each declaration to be included in the exception section of the program unit.

The procedure shown in Figure 5-12 uses the package specification property to create the declaration section of the program unit. The exception section of the program unit was generated from the definition entered into the *PL/SQL Block* property. Each of these methods was chosen over the other alternatives because of problems encountered during generation. See the troubleshooting guide at the end of the chapter for the details.

Generating the sample procedure using the declarative method creates two files. In this example, the two files created are

- <file prefix>.SQL Executes the file <file prefix>.PRC
- <file prefix>.PRC Contains the generated program unit definition

NOTE
<file prefix> is a name that you specify when generating server-side objects. This name will be given to all files created during that execution of the Server Generator.

Figure 5-12 is an annotated version of <file prefix>.PRC. The superscript numbers correspond to properties in the procedure definition, which created this file. See Table 5-3 for specific mapping of the generated code.

```
-- c:\aristmpl\application\ss\proc\CH5_decl.prc
--
-- Generated for Oracle 8 on Tue Jul 14  07:34:15 1998 by Server
Generator 2.1.19.5.0

PROMPT Creating [1]Procedure[1] [2]'TAR_ACTIONS'[2]
CREATE OR REPLACE [1]PROCEDURE[1] [2]TAR_ACTIONS[2] ([3]P_TAR_ID[3] [4]IN[4] [5]NUMBER[5] ) IS
--PL/SQL Specification
[6]/* Cursor Selects Issue and Issues Status related to given TAR */
CURSOR GET_ISS_STAT(p_dbcr_id IN NUMBER) IS
 select iss.id id, iss.istat_cd, status
  from issues iss, issues_oracle_tars tar
  where iss.id = tar.iss_id
  and tar.tar_id = p_tar_id;[6]
-- PL/SQL Block
[7]BEGIN
 FOR ISS_REC in GET_ISS_STAT(p_tar_id) LOOP
  BEGIN
   --  IF Pending Issues are found related to a closed TAR, create an
   --     action item to have the issue retested
    IF iss_rec.status = 'PENDING' THEN
    insert into actions
    (id
     , action_date
     , short_notes
     , iss_id
     , atyp_cd
     , per_id)
```

FIGURE 5-12. *Annotated generation example using the declarative method*

```
   VALUES
    (common_surrogate.nextval
     , sysdate
     , 'DBCR CLOSED, PLEASE RETEST TO VERIFY THAT PROBLEM HAS BEEN
RESOLVED.'
     , iss_rec.id
     , 'RETEST'     , 4);  -- Assigned to my favorite DBA
   END IF;
  EXCEPTION
   WHEN OTHERS THEN RAISE_APPLICATION_ERROR
    (-21001, 'AUTOMATED ACTIONS PROCESS failed with: '||substr(SQLERRM,1,50));
  END;
 END LOOP;
END TAR_ACTIONS;7
/
```

FIGURE 5-12. *Annotated generation example using the declarative method* (continued)

Number	Feature	Source Using Dialogs	Source Using Properties Palette
1	PL/SQL definition type	TYPE TAB Field: Type of definition	PROCEDURE DEFINITION Property: Type
2	PL/SQL definition name	NAME TAB Field: Name	PROCEDURE DEFINITION Property: Implementation Name
3	Argument name	ARGUMENT TAB Field: Arguments	ARGUMENT Property: Name
4	Argument type	ARGUMENT TAB Field: Argument type	ARGUMENT Property: Input Output

TABLE 5-3. *Source of Generated Code Using the Declarative Method*

Number	Feature	Source Using Dialogs	Source Using Properties Palette
5	Argument datatype	ARGUMENT TAB Field: Datatype	ARGUMENT Property: Datatype
6	Declaration section of program unit body	NO SOURCE	PROCEDURE DEFINITION Property: Package Specification
7	Execution and exception sections of program unit body	NO SOURCE	PROCEDURE DEFINITION Property: PL/SQL Block

TABLE 5-3. *Source of Generated Code Using the Declarative Method* (continued)

Steps to Create This Procedure Using the Declarative Method

Using the steps that follow, you will be able to re-create the sample procedure. Since there is more than one way to accomplish this task, we focus on defining steps that minimize the amount of time required to create the definition, while still taking advantage of the new features of release 2. We have chosen to use the dialogs for creating each definition and then to use the Properties Palette to enter the remaining information about the definition, which cannot be entered through the dialogs.

1. In the Design Editor (DE), click on the Server Model tab.
2. Create a new procedure definition (available under PL/SQL definitions). Do this by pressing the Create icon in the Design Editor toolbar. This will launch a set of dialogs that will gather all of the necessary information required for the procedure definition. The following steps detail the settings used for this example.

3. The Name dialog is the first dialog that will be displayed. Using this dialog you will be able to specify a short name for the procedure definition that will be used for naming generated files (*Short name of the PL/SQL definition* = **CH5_DECL**). Next, specify a unique name for the procedure definition (*Name* = **CH5_DECL**) and the purpose or short description of the procedure definition (*Purpose* = **Create an action to retest an issue when an associated TAR is resolved**). Last, specify the name you would like to use when creating the procedure definition (*Implementation name* = **TAR_ACTIONS**). This name will be used in the header of the program unit. Figure 5-13 shows the Name dialog used for this example. When you have completed this dialog, click Next.

4. The Type dialog is the second dialog that will be displayed. Using this dialog you will be able to specify that you would like to define a procedure definition (*Type of definition* = **Procedure**). Next, specify that you would like to define the procedure using the declarative

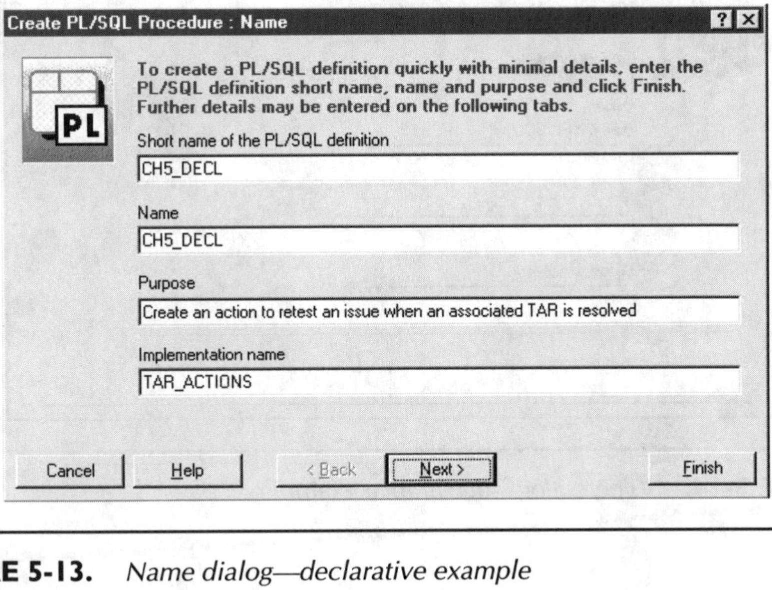

FIGURE 5-13. *Name dialog—declarative example*

method (*How the PL/SQL will be defined* = **Declarative**). Last, specify that the scope of this procedure is private (*Scope of access* = **Private**). Figure 5-14 shows the Type dialog used for this example. When you have completed this dialog, click Next.

5. The Arguments dialog is the third dialog that will be displayed. Using this dialog, you can define the argument used by this procedure definition. This is done by specifying the name of the argument (*Arguments* = **p_tar_id**); how the argument is defined (*Defined By* = **Datatype**); which datatype the argument will be defined as (*Datatype* = **NUMBER**); and, last, how the argument will be used (*Argument type* = **Input**). Figure 5-15 shows the Arguments dialog used for this example. When you have completed this dialog, click Next.

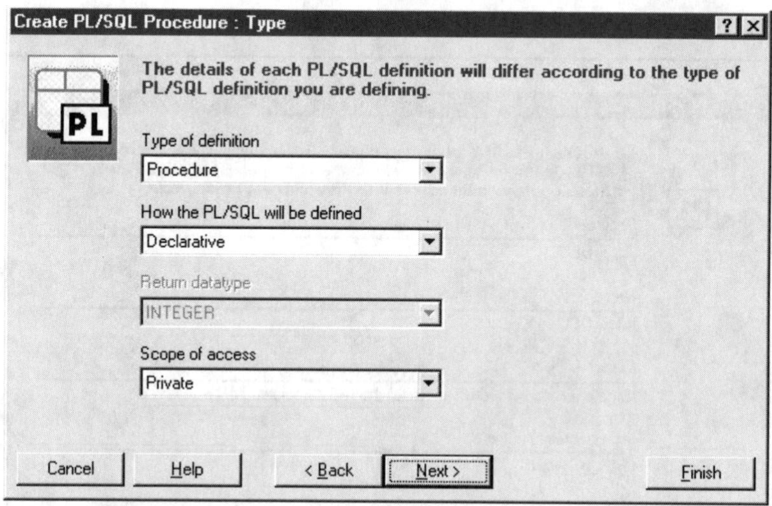

FIGURE 5-14. *Type dialog—declarative example*

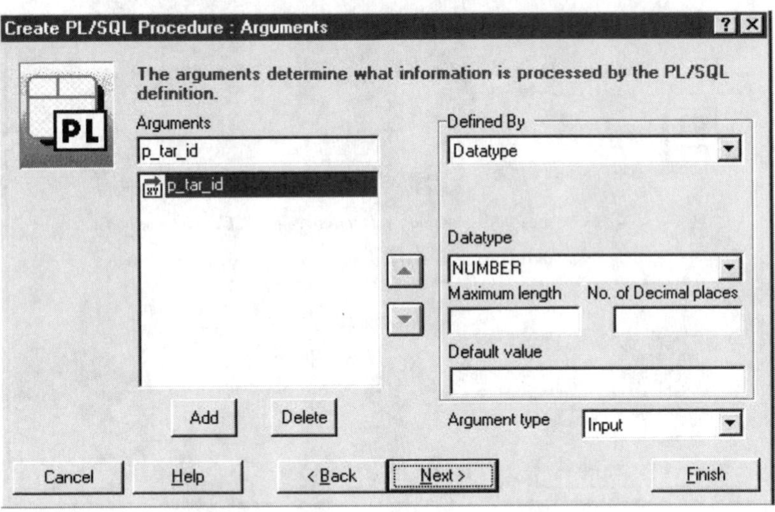

FIGURE 5-15. *Arguments dialog—declarative example*

6. The Exceptions dialog is the fourth dialog that will be displayed. We did not choose to define exceptions using this dialog in our example and instead define it using the *PL/SQL Block* property (see step 11). Click Next to skip this dialog.
7. The Data dialog is the fifth dialog that will be displayed. We did not have any variables or constants in our example. Click Next to skip this dialog.
8. The Goodbye dialog is the last dialog that will be displayed. This dialog provides you with three different ways that you can exit the dialogs you have just used to define the procedure definition. Select option one (*Create the PL/SQL definition with the information provided*) to create the PL/SQL definition and click Finish. Figure 5-16 shows the Goodbye dialog used for this example.

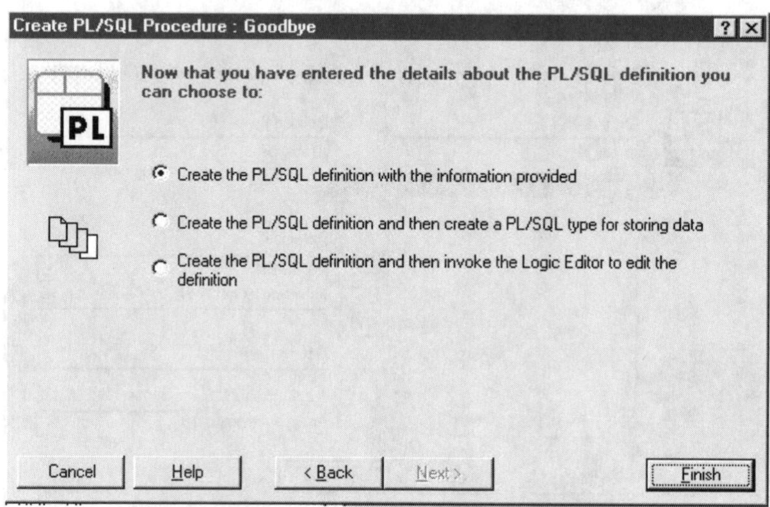

FIGURE 5-16. *Goodbye dialog—declarative example*

NOTE

*You could alternatively select option three (*Create the PL/SQL definition and then invoke the Logic Editor to edit the definition*). If you chose to define the procedure using this option, you can generate once you've finished defining the procedure using this editor.*

9. Switch to the Properties Palette from the dialogs. Do this by pressing the Property Dialogs/Palettes icon in the Design Editor toolbar.
10. Define the cursor program unit definition in the *package specification* property of the procedure definition. Do this by navigating to the *package specification* property and, using a text editor, entering the cursor program unit definition. This should include the contents between the superscript sixes in Figure 5-12.
11. Define the body of the program unit in the *PL/SQL Block* property of the procedure definition. Do this by navigating to the *PL/SQL Block*

property and, using a text editor, entering the body of the procedure. This should include the contents between the superscript sevens in Figure 5-12.

12. We suggest that you create a PL/SQL implementation item for this procedure definition next. This is not a mandatory step, but it is very useful if you intend to manage database objects using databases and schema owner accounts defined within the Designer Repository. To do this you will need to select the DB Admin tab and then navigate to the correct Oracle database and user under that database. Add this procedure to the procedure implementation schema objects for that user by pressing the Create icon in the Design Editor toolbar and then completing the dialogs.
13. Generate the procedure definition.

Design Capture

The Design Capture utility will create PL/SQL definitions in the repository based on program unit definitions located in one of two sources:

- Oracle database
- File system

Procedure definitions created in the repository using this utility are created using the free format method. In essence, the Design Capture utility reverses the generation process described in the "Free Format Method" section earlier in this chapter. Variable declarations are inserted into the *package specification* property, not the *PL/SQL Block* property. This is one of the reasons that it is better to use the *package specification* property for variable declaration when using either free format or declarative methods.

Figure 5-17 is an annotated version of the sample procedure provided in Figure 5-1. The superscript numbers correspond to properties in the procedure definition, which are populated by the Design Capture utility. See Table 5-4 for specific mapping of the properties populated by the Design Capture utility.

```
CREATE OR REPLACE [1]PROCEDURE[1] [2]TAR_ACTIONS[2] ([3]p_tar_id[3] [4]IN[4] [5]number[5]) IS
[6]/* Cursor Selects Issue and Issues Status related to given TAR */
CURSOR GET_ISS_STAT(p_dbcr_id IN NUMBER) IS
  select iss.id id, iss.istat_cd status
  from issues iss, issues_oracle_tars tar
  where iss.id = tar.iss_id
  and tar.tar_id = p_tar_id;[6]

[7]BEGIN
 FOR ISS_REC in GET_ISS_STAT(p_tar_id) LOOP
  BEGIN
   --  IF Pending Issues are found related to a closed TAR, create an
   --    action item to have the issue retested
  IF iss_rec.status = 'PENDING' THEN
    insert into actions
    (id
     , action_date
     , short_notes
     , iss_id
     , atyp_cd
     , per_id)
   VALUES
    (common_surrogate.nextval
     , sysdate
     , 'DBCR CLOSED, PLEASE RETEST TO VERIFY THAT PROBLEM HAS BEEN
RESOLVED.'
     , iss_rec.id
     , 'RETEST'
     , 4);  -- Assigned to my favorite DBA
   END IF;
  EXCEPTION
   WHEN OTHERS THEN RAISE_APPLICATION_ERROR
    (-21001, 'AUTOMATED ACTIONS PROCESS failed with: '||substr(SQLERRM,1,50));
  END;
 END LOOP;
END TAR_ACTIONS;[7]
/
```

FIGURE 5-17. *Annotated design capture example*

Number	Feature	Source Using Dialogs	Source Using Properties Palette
1	PL/SQL definition type	TYPE TAB Field: Type of definition	PROCEDURE DEFINITION Property: Type
2	PL/SQL definition name	NAME TAB Field: Name	PROCEDURE DEFINITION Property: Implementation Name
3	Argument name	ARGUMENT TAB Field: Arguments	ARGUMENT Property: Name
4	Argument type	ARGUMENT TAB Field: Argument type	ARGUMENT Property: Input Output
5	Argument datatype	ARGUMENT TAB Field: Datatype	ARGUMENT Property: Datatype
6	Declaration section of program unit body	NO SOURCE	PROCEDURE DEFINITION Property: Package Specification
7	Execution and exception sections of program unit body	NO SOURCE	PROCEDURE DEFINITION Property: PL/SQL Block

TABLE 5-4. *Properties Populated Using the Design Capture Utility*

Steps to Create a Repository Definition Using the Design Capture Utility

1. In the Design Editor menu navigate to Generate → Capture Design Of → Server Model from Database.

2. Select the source of the design capture:

   - *Database* captures definitions in an Oracle database.
   - *DDL file* captures the contents of a DDL file.

   If you select the Database option, you will need to fill in the *Username, Password,* and *Connect* properties. This information will be used to query the database to determine what objects this user can capture the design of. You will then need to click the Objects tab and select the procedure definition and move it into the *Capture* field.

   If you select the DDL file option, you will need to select *DDL File* and then specify the path/filename of the DDL file to be captured in the *Name* field and the type/version of database in the *Type* field.

3. Select the database/schema owner in which to create the definition. Do this by setting the *Capture Objects Into* property to the database schema owner in which you would like to create the procedure definition.
4. When satisfied with your selections, click Start.
5. Select how you would like to process the captured procedure definition:

   - *Save* commits the procedure definition to the repository.
   - *Revert* completes a rollback of the posted procedure definition.
   - *Browse/Edit* enables you to browse the posted procedure definition, make modifications, and then either commit or rollback.

 Generation Troubleshooting Guide

Problem	Methods	Solution
When I change the method of defining a PL/SQL definition from operating system file to either free format method or declarative method, it continues to generate the program unit definition using the operating system file method.	Free Format and Declarative	Remove the path\filename from the *source path* property. If this property is populated, the procedure will always be generated using the operating system file method, regardless of the value in the *free format declaration* property.
The variable declarations I defined in the *PL/SQL Block* property are not generating into the declaration section of the program unit body.	Declarative	You have two choices to eliminate this problem. Either define all the variable declarations in the *package specification* property, or create program data definitions for each variable you need to declare.
The cursor I included as a subprogram unit is being declared twice.	Declarative	This is a bug. Remove the errant cursor declaration from the generated code.
The cursor I included as a subprogram unit is not being declared at all.	Free Format	The Server Generator ignores subprogram units when using the free format method. Use declarative method if you would like to generate the cursor declaration as a subprogram unit.
The exceptions I entered as program data are generating into the declaration section of the program unit, not the exception section.	Declarative	The Server Generator is Generating the declaration of a user-defined exception. It will not use this information to create the exception section of the program unit.
I cannot specify a nonunique implementation name for procedure definitions.	Free Format and Declarative	This is a bug. Modify the generated code and rename the procedure to the desired name.

CHAPTER 6

Generating Functions

This chapter is a detailed guide to help you generate functions. In this chapter, we will cover

- Generation of a sample function using each method of defining a PL/SQL definition and design capture
- The property settings used to generate each example
- Step-by-step instructions for creating the example using each method
- A troubleshooting guide to assist you with common generation problems

We think it will be easier for you to understand the various methods if we use an example that at least looks like a real-world program. Therefore, we designed a sample function that performs a standard task that you might use in a real system.

NOTE

Example Description: *The example we are using in this chapter is a function that returns a character value given a numeric key. This example (based on the example application provided with this book) returns the name of the person who entered an issue into the system.*

The code shown in Figure 6-1 will be used in the sections that follow to show you a specific example of each method of creating a function. If you need additional background on each method presented, please refer to Chapter 4.

```
CREATE OR REPLACE FUNCTION GET_PERSON(p_id IN NUMBER)RETURN NUMBER IS

/* Cursor Selects Person Associated With Supplied Issue */
CURSOR GET_ID_CUR(p_id IN NUMBER) IS
  SELECT upper(per.first_name)||' '||upper(per.last_name) name, per.id
  FROM issues iss, people per
  WHERE p_id = iss.id
  AND iss.per_id = per.id;

/* Variable Holds Complete Name of Person */
v_name varchar2(50);

/* Variable Holds ID of Person */
v_id number;

BEGIN
 OPEN get_id_cur(p_id);
 FETCH get_id_cur into v_name, v_id;
 CLOSE get_id_cur;

/* If Bill Gates is encountered return zero */
 IF v_name = 'BILL GATES' THEN
  return('0');
 ELSE
  return(v_id);
 END IF;
EXCEPTION
 WHEN OTHERS THEN RAISE_APPLICATION ERROR
   (-21002, 'GET_PERSON_FUNCTION failed with: '||substr(SQLERRM,1,50));
END;
/
```

FIGURE 6-1. *Sample function*

Operating System File Method

The operating system file method is the only method that references definitions that are stored outside the repository. In order to use this method, you must place the source code for the program unit definition into an operating system file and specify the filename and path when you are creating the PL/SQL definition in the repository.

Generating the sample function using the operating system file method will create two files. In this example, the two files created are

- <file prefix>.SQL   Executes the file <file prefix>.FNC
- <file prefix>.FNC   Executes the true program unit definition, calling a specified path and filename that contain the DDL

NOTE
<file prefix> is a name that you specify when generating server-side objects. This name will be given to all files created during that execution of the Server Generator.

Figure 6-2 is an annotated version of <file prefix>.FNC. The superscript numbers correspond to properties in the function definition, which created this file. See Table 6-1 for specific mapping of the generated code.

```
-- c:\aristmpl\application\ss\CH6_os.fnc
--
-- Generated for Oracle 8 on Sun Jun 28  16:36:24 1998 by Server
Generator 2.1.19.5.0

PROMPT Creating ¹Function¹ ²'GET_PERSON'²
@³C:\ARISTMPL\Application\SS\func\function.sql³
```

FIGURE 6-2. *Annotated generation example using operating system file method*

Number	Feature	Source Using Dialogs	Source Using Properties Palette
1	PL/SQL definition type	TYPE TAB Field: Type of definition	FUNCTION DEFINITION Property: Type
2	PL/SQL definition name	NAME TAB Field: Name	FUNCTION DEFINITION Property: Implementation Name
3	Path and filename	FILE TAB Field: Path and filename of source	FUNCTION DEFINITION Property: Source Path

TABLE 6-1. *Source of Generated Code Using Operating System File Method*

Steps to Create This Function Using the Operating System File Method

Using the steps that follow, you will be able to re-create the sample function. Since there is more than one way to accomplish this task, we focus on defining steps that minimize the amount of time required to create the definition, while still taking advantage of the new features of release 2. We have chosen to use the dialogs for creating each definition and then use the Property Palette to enter remaining information about the definition that can not be entered through the dialogs.

1. In the Design Editor (DE), click the Server Model tab.
2. Create a new function definition (available under PL/SQL definitions). Do this by pressing the Create icon in the Design Editor toolbar. This will launch a set of dialogs that will gather all of the necessary information required for the function definition. The following steps detail the settings used for this example.

3. The Name dialog will be displayed first. Using this dialog, you will be able to specify a short name for the function definition that will be used for naming generated files (*Short name of PL/SQL definition* = **CH6_OS**). Next, specify a unique name for the function definition (*Name* = **CH6_OS**) and the purpose or short description of the function definition (*Purpose* = **Return the ID of the person associated with a supplied issue**). Last, specify the name you would like to use when creating the function definition (*Implementation name* = **GET_PERSON**). This name will be used in the header of the program unit. Figure 6-3 shows the Name dialog used for this example. When you have completed this dialog, click Next.

4. The Type dialog is the second dialog that will be displayed. Using this dialog, you will be able to specify that you would like to define a function definition (*Type of definition* = **Function**). Next, specify that you would like to define the function using the operating system file method (*How the PL/SQL will be defined* = **Operating System**

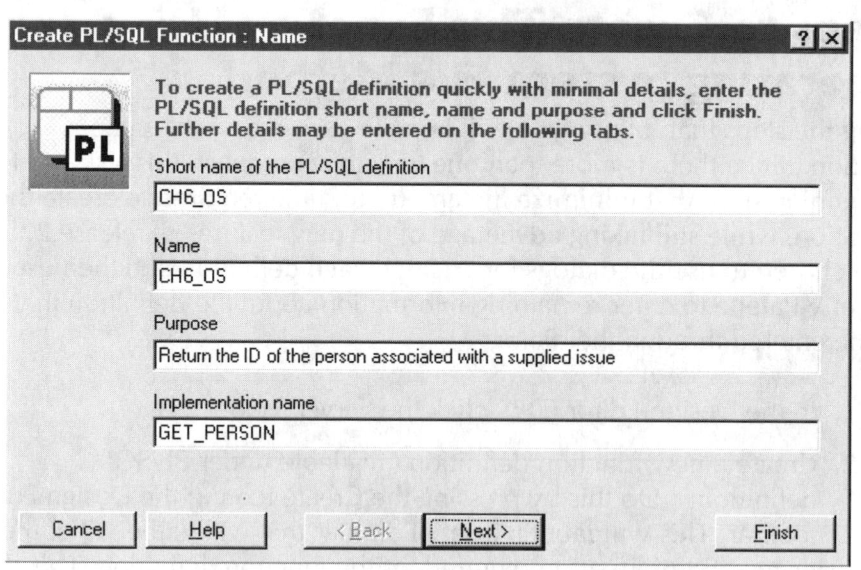

FIGURE 6-3. *Name dialog—operating system file example*

File), and that the function will return a number (*Return datatype* = **Number**). Last, specify that the scope of this function is private (*Scope of access* = **Private**). Figure 6-4 shows the Type dialog used for this example. When you have completed this dialog, click Next.

5. The File dialog is the third dialog that will be displayed. Using this dialog, you will be able to specify the name of the file that contains the DDL for this function definition and its location (*Path and filename of source* = **c:\ARISTMPL\Application\SS\function.sql**). Figure 6-5 shows the File dialog used for this example. When you have completed this dialog, click Next.

6. The Goodbye dialog is the last dialog that will be displayed. This dialog provides you with three different ways that you can exit the dialogs you have just used to define the function definition. Since we have defined this example using the operating system file method,

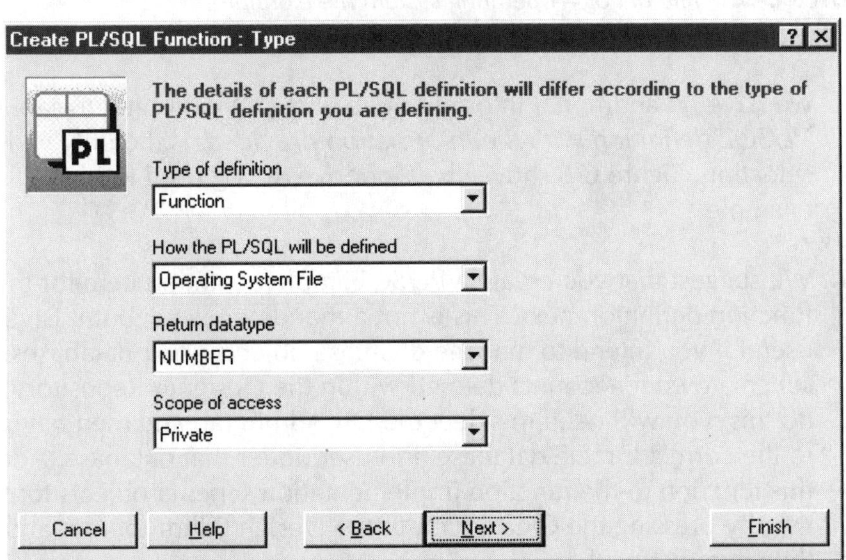

FIGURE 6-4. *Type dialog—operating system file example*

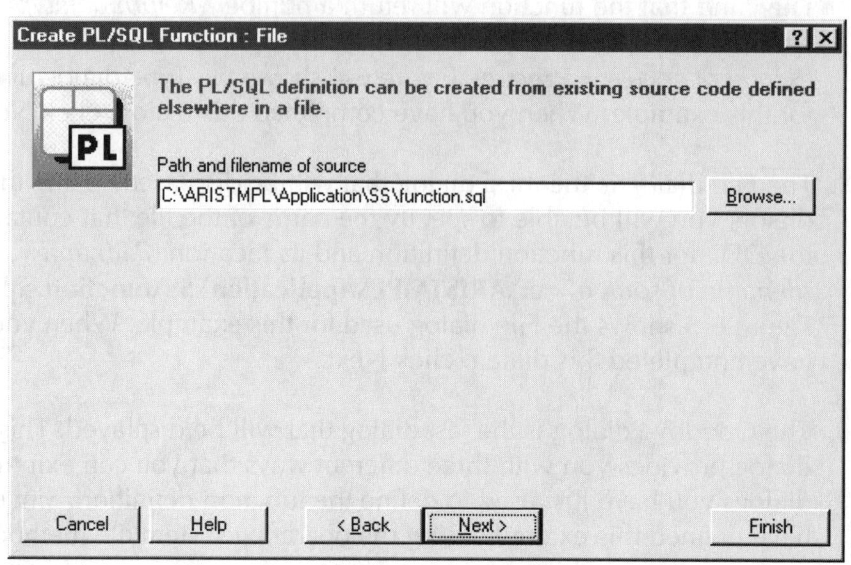

FIGURE 6-5. *File dialog—operating system file example*

we have no additional information to enter. Option one, *Create the PL/SQL definition with the information provided,* is the only valid selection. Figure 6-6 shows the Goodbye dialog used for this example.

7. We suggest that you create a PL/SQL implementation item for this function definition next. This is not a mandatory step, but it is very useful if you intend to manage database objects using databases and schema owner accounts defined within the Designer Repository. To do this, you will need to select the DB Admin tab and then navigate to the correct Oracle database and user under that database. Add this function to the function implementation schema objects for that user by pressing the Create icon in the Design Editor toolbar and then completing the dialogs.
8. Generate the function definition.

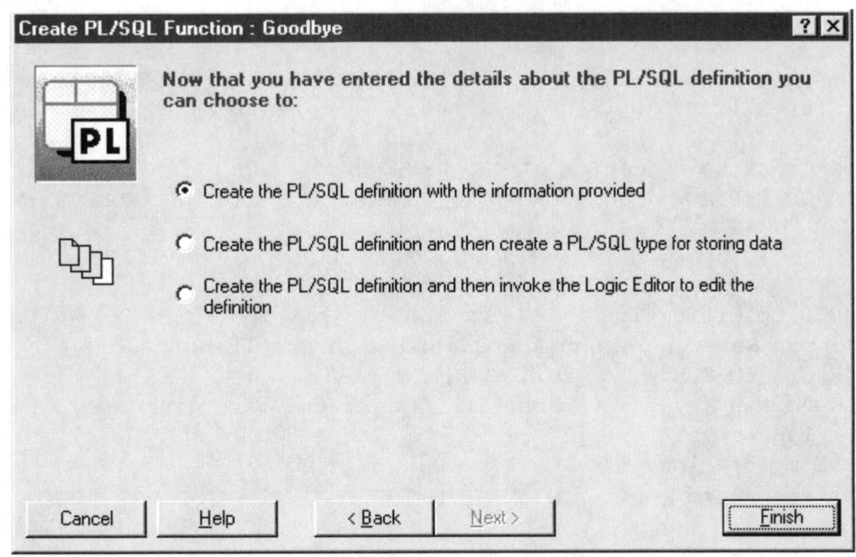

FIGURE 6-6. *Goodybe dialog—operating system file example*

Free Format Method

The free format method is one of two methods of defining a PL/SQL definition in which the entire program unit is stored within the repository. When using this method, you need to decide how you would like to define and generate the declaration section of the program unit body. Declarations can be generated using the free format method in two ways:

- Using the *package specification* property.
- Including the declarations in the *PL/SQL Block* property.

These are the only two properties that will be used by the Server Generator to create the program unit body. If the *package specification* property is null, then the program unit body is created using the *PL/SQL Block* property only.

The function shown in Figure 6-7 made use of the *package specification* property to create the declaration section of the program unit. Since the free

```
-- c:\aristmpl\application\ss\CH6_free.fnc
--
-- Generated for Oracle 8 on Sun Jun 28  16:50:46 1998 by Server
Generator 2.1.19.5.0

PROMPT Creating 1Function1 2'GET_PERSON'2
CREATE OR REPLACE 1FUNCTION1 2GET_PERSON2 (3P_ID3 4IN4 5NUMBER5 )
 RETURN 6NUMBER6 IS


--PL/SQL Specification
7/* Cursor Selects Person Associated With Supplied Issue */
CURSOR GET_ID_CUR(p_id IN NUMBER) IS
  SELECT upper(per.first_name)||' '||upper(per.last_name) name, per.id
  FROM issues iss,  people per
  WHERE p_id = iss.id
  AND iss.per_id = per.id;

/* Variable Holds Complete Name of Person */
v_name varchar2(50);

/* Variable Holds ID of Person */
v_id number;7

-- PL/SQL Block
8BEGIN
 OPEN get_id_cur(p_id);
 FETCH get_id_cur into v_name, v_id;
 CLOSE get_id_cur;

/* If Bill Gates is encountered return zero */
 IF v_name = 'BILL GATES' THEN
  return('0');
 ELSE  return('v_id');
 END IF;
EXCEPTION
 WHEN OTHERS THEN RAISE_APPLICATION ERROR
    (-21002, 'GET_PERSON_FUNCTION failed with: '||substr(SQLERRM,1,50));
 END GET_PERSON;8
/
```

FIGURE 6-7. *Annotated generation example using free format method*

format method is the only method that allows declarations in the *PL/SQL Block* property, it is good practice to remain consistent when defining PL/SQL definitions. For that reason, the *package specification* property is a better option for variable declaration than the *PL/SQL Block* property.

Generating the sample function using the free format method creates two files. In this example, the two files created are

- <file prefix>.SQL Executes the file <file prefix>.FNC
- <file prefix>.FNC Contains the generated program unit definition

NOTE
<file prefix> is a name that you specify when generating server-side objects. This name will be given to all files created during that execution of the Server Generator.

Figure 6-7 is an annotated version of <file prefix>.FNC. The superscript numbers correspond to properties in the function definition, which created this file. See Table 6-2 for specific mapping of the generated code.

Number	Feature	Source Using Dialogs	Source Using Properties Palette
1	PL/SQL definition type	TYPE TAB Field: Type of definition	FUNCTION DEFINITION Property: Type
2	PL/SQL definition name	NAME TAB Field: Name	FUNCTION DEFINITION Property: Implementation Name
3	argument name	ARGUMENT TAB Field: Arguments	ARGUMENT Property: Name

TABLE 6-2. *Source of Generated Code Using Free Format Method*

Number	Feature	Source Using Dialogs	Source Using Properties Palette
4	Argument type	ARGUMENT TAB Field: Argument type	ARGUMENT Property: Input Output
5	Argument datatype	ARGUMENT TAB Field: Datatype	ARGUMENT Property: Datatype
6	Function return type	TYPE TAB Field: Return datatype	FUNCTION DEFINITION Property: Return Type (Scalar)
7	Declaration section of program unit body	NO SOURCE	FUNCTION DEFINITION Property: Package Specification
8	Execution and exception sections of program unit body	NO SOURCE	FUNCTION DEFINITION Property: PL/SQL Block

TABLE 6-2. *Source of Generated Code Using Free Format Method* (continued)

Steps to Create This Function Using Free Format Method

Using the steps that follow, you will be able to re-create the sample function. Since there is more than one way to accomplish this task, we focus on defining steps that minimize the amount of time required to create the definition while still taking advantage of the new features of release 2. We have chosen to use the dialogs for creating each definition and then to use the Property Palette to enter the remaining information about the definition, which cannot be entered through the dialogs.

1. In the Design Editor (DE), click the Server Model tab.
2. Create a new function definition (available under PL/SQL definitions). Do this by pressing the Create icon in the Design Editor

toolbar. This will launch a set of dialogs that will gather all of the necessary information required for the function definition. The following steps detail the settings used for this example.

3. The Name dialog is the first dialog that will be displayed. Using this dialog, you will be able to specify a short name for the function definition that will be used for naming generated files (*Short name of the PL/SQL definition* = **CH6_FREE**) and a unique name for the function definition (*Name* = **CH6_FREE**). Next, specify the purpose or short description of the function definition (*Purpose* = **Return the ID of the person associated with a supplied issue**). Last, specify the name you would like to use when creating the function definition (*Implementation name* = **GET_PERSON**). This name will be used in the header of the program unit. Figure 6-8 shows the Name dialog used for this example. When you have completed this dialog, click Next.

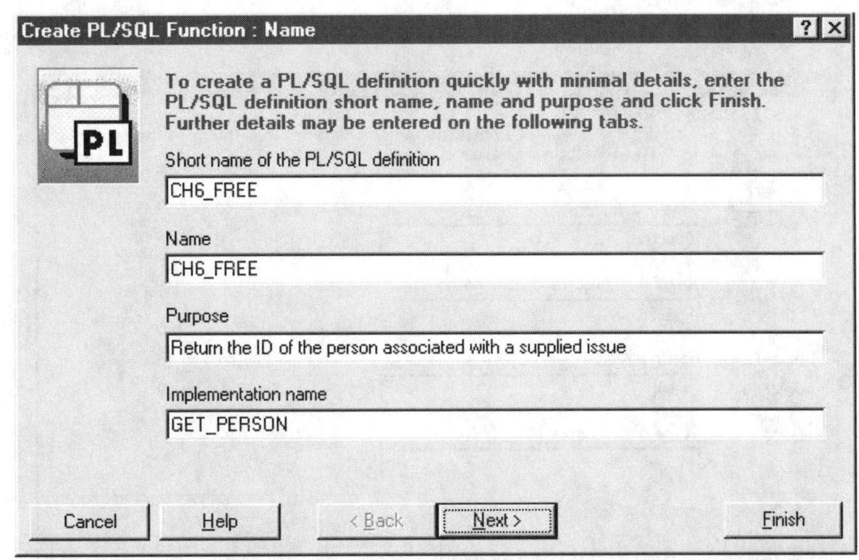

FIGURE 6-8. *Name dialog—free format example*

4. The Type dialog is the second dialog that will be displayed. Using this dialog, you will be able to specify that you would like to define a function definition (*Type of definition* = **Function**). Next, specify that you would like to define the function using the free format method (*How the PL/SQL will be defined* = **Free Format**) and that the function will return a number (*Return datatype* = **NUMBER**). Last, specify that the scope of this function is private (*Scope of access* = **Private**). Figure 6-9 shows the Type dialog used for this example. When you have completed this dialog, click Next.

5. The Arguments dialog is the third dialog that will be displayed. Using this dialog, you can define the argument used by this function definition. This is done by specifying the name of the argument (*Arguments* = **p_id**); how the argument is defined (*Defined By* = **Datatype**); which datatype the argument will be defined as (*Datatype* = **NUMBER**); and, finally, how the argument will be used (*Argument Type* = **Input**). Figure 6-10 shows the Arguments dialog used for this example. When you have completed this dialog, click Next.

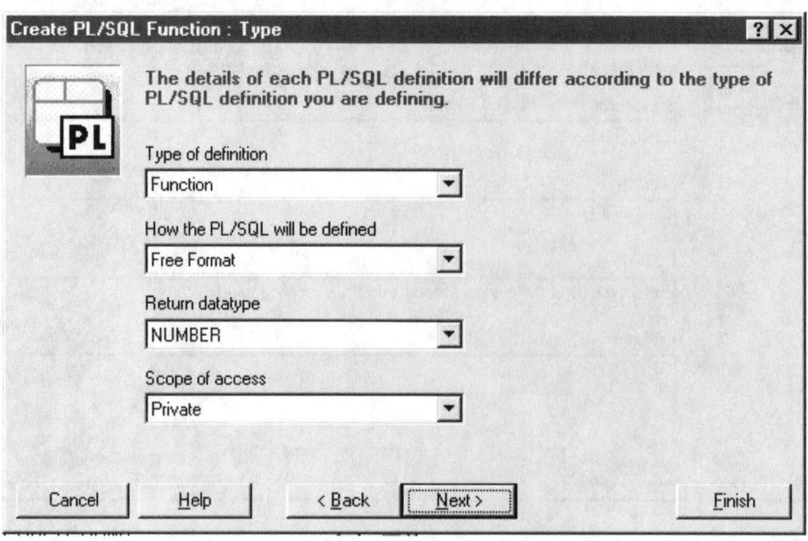

FIGURE 6-9. *Type dialog—free format example*

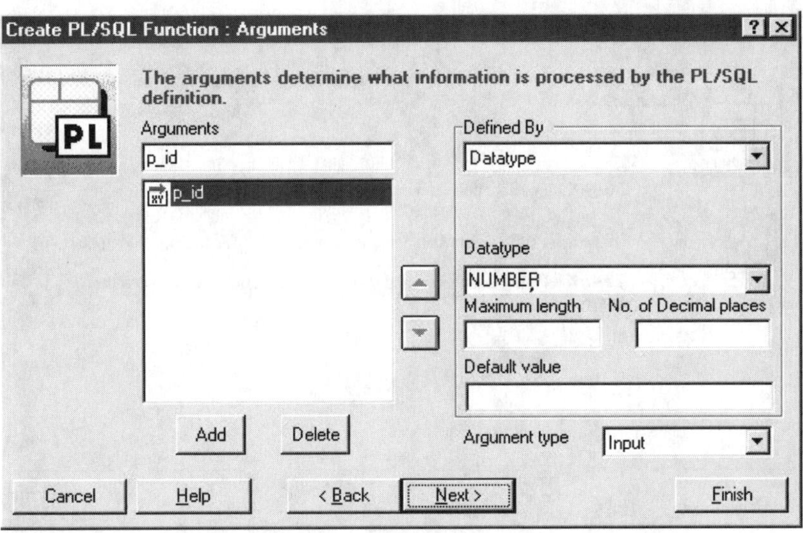

FIGURE 6-10. *Arguments dialog—free format example*

6. The Goodbye dialog is the last dialog that will be displayed. This dialog provides you with three different ways that you can exit the dialogs you have just used to define the function definition. Select option one (*Create the PL/SQL definition with the information provided*) to create the PL/SQL definition, and click Finish. Figure 6-11 shows the Goodbye dialog used for this example.

NOTE
*You could alternatively select option three (*Create the PL/SQL definition and then invoke the Logic Editor to edit the definition*). If you choose to define the function using this option, you can generate once you've completed defining the function using this editor.)*

7. Switch to the Properties Palette from the dialogs. Do this by pressing the Property Dialogs/Palettes icon in the Design Editor toolbar.

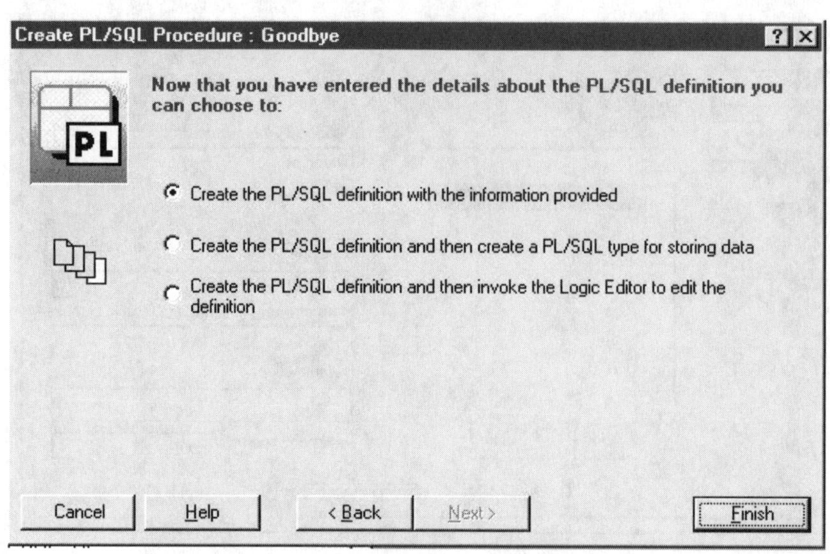

FIGURE 6-11. *Goodbye dialog—free format example*

8. Define the declaration section (cursor definition and variable declarations) of the program unit in the *package specification* property of the function definition. Do this by navigating to the *package specification* property and, using a text editor, entering the cursor program unit and variable declarations. This should include the contents between the superscript sevens in Figure 6-7.
9. Define the execution and exception sections of the program unit in the *PL/SQL Block* property of the function definition. Do this by navigating to the *PL/SQL Block* property and, using a text editor, entering the body of the function. This should include the contents between the superscript eights in Figure 6-7.
10. We suggest that you create a PL/SQL implementation item for this function definition next. This is not a mandatory step, but it is very useful if you intend to manage database objects using databases and schema owner accounts defined within the Designer Repository. To do this, you will need to select the DB Admin tab and then navigate

to the correct Oracle database and user under that database. Add this function to the function implementation schema objects for that user by pressing the Create icon in the Design Editor toolbar and then completing the dialogs.

11. Generate the function definition.

Declarative Method

The declarative method is the other method of defining a PL/SQL definition in which the entire program unit is stored within the repository. When using this method to generate our sample function, you will need to make the following decisions:

- How to generate the declaration section of the program unit
- How to generate the exception section of the program unit

The declaration section of the program unit body can be generated using the declarative method in three ways:

- Defining the desired declarations in the *package specification* property
- Defining each declaration as program data and/or sub program units of the PL/SQL definition
- Mixing and matching the two methods above

Variable and constant declarations are simple to generate using any of the three methods listed above. The main difference between them is where the Server Generator will get the information to create each declaration section of the program unit.

Cursor declarations are slightly more complicated. Prior to defining the cursor declaration, you should ask yourself, "Will I use this cursor in other PL/SQL definitions?" If the answer to this question is yes, you should consider creating a separate cursor definition and include it as a sub program unit. If, however, the answer to the question is no, then it is okay to use the *package specification* property of the PL/SQL definition.

The exception section of the program unit body can be generated using the declarative method in two ways:

- Defining the exception section immediately following the execution section of the program unit in the *PL/SQL Block* property
- Defining each exception as program data of the PL/SQL definition. This will create user-defined exceptions that you then can reference throughout the program unit.

Exceptions are simple to generate using either of the two methods listed above. The main difference between them is where the Server Generator will get the information to specify each declaration to be included in the exception section of the program unit.

The function shown in Figure 6-12 makes use of the mix and match method of creating the declaration section of the program unit. Variables are defined as program units and the cursor definition is defined using *package specification* property. The exception section of the program unit was generated from the definition entered into the *PL/SQL Block* property. Each of these methods was chosen over the other alternatives because of problems encountered during generation. See the troubleshooting guide at the end of the chapter for details.

Generating the sample function using the declarative method creates two files. In this example, the two files created are

- <file prefix>.SQL   Executes the file <file prefix>.FNC
- <file prefix>.FNC   Contains the generated program unit definition

NOTE
<file prefix> is a name that you specify when generating server-side objects. This name will be given to all files created during that execution of the Server Generator.

Figure 6-12 is an annotated version of <file prefix>.FNC. The superscript numbers correspond to properties in the function definition that created this file. See Table 6-3 for specific mapping of the generated code.

```
-- c:\aristmpl\application\ss\CH6_decl.fnc
--
-- Generated for Oracle 8 on Mon Jun 29  06:53:48 1998 by Server
Generator 2.1.19.5.0
PROMPT Creating [1]Function[1] [2]'GET_PERSON'[2]
CREATE OR REPLACE [1]FUNCTION[1] [2]GET_PERSON[2]
([3]P_ID[3] [4]IN[4] [5]NUMBER[5]
)
 RETURN [6]NUMBER[6]
IS


-- Program Data
[7]V_NAME[7] [8]VARCHAR2[8] [9](50)[9];
[7]V_ID[7] [8]NUMBER[8];



-- PL/SQL Specification
[9]CURSOR GET_ID_CUR(p_id IN NUMBER) IS
  SELECT upper(per.first_name)||' '||upper(per.last_name) name, per.id
  FROM issues iss, people per
  WHERE p_id = iss.id  AND iss.per_id = per.id;[9]

-- PL/SQL Block
BEGIN
 [10]OPEN get_id_cur(p_id);
 FETCH get_id_cur into v_name, v_id;
 CLOSE get_id_cur;

/* If Bill Gates is encountered return zero */
 IF v_name = 'BILL GATES' THEN
  return('0');
 ELSE
  return('v_id');
 END IF;
EXCEPTION
 WHEN OTHERS THEN RAISE_APPLICATION ERROR
   (-21002, 'GET_PERSON_FUNCTION failed with: '||substr(SQLERRM,1,50));[10]
END GET_PERSON;
/
```

FIGURE 6-12. *Annotated declarative method generation example*

Number	Feature	Source Using Dialogs	Source Using Properties Palette
1	PL/SQL definition type	TYPE TAB Field: Type of definition	FUNCTION DEFINITION Property: Type
2	PL/SQL definition name	NAME TAB Field: Name	FUNCTION DEFINITION Property: Implementation Name
3	Argument name	ARGUMENT TAB Field: Arguments	ARGUMENT Property: Name
4	Argument type	ARGUMENT TAB Field: Argument type	ARGUMENT Property: Input Output
5	Argument datatype	ARGUMENT TAB Field: Datatype	ARGUMENT Property: Datatype
6	Function return type	TYPE TAB Field: Return datatype	FUNCTION DEFINITION Property: Return Type (Scalar)
7	Program data name	DATA TAB Field: Declaration name	PROGRAM DATA Type: Variable Field: Name
8	Program datatype	DATA TAB Field: Datatype	PROGRAM DATA Type: Variable Field: Datatype
9	Declaration section of program unit body	NO SOURCE	FUNCTION DEFINITION Property: Package Specification
10	Execution and exception sections of program unit body	NO SOURCE	FUNCTION DEFINITION Property: PL/SQL Block

TABLE 6-3. *Source of Generated Code Using the Declarative Method*

Steps to Create This Function Using the Declarative Method

Using the steps that follow, you will be able to re-create the sample function. Since there is more than one way to accomplish this task, we focus on defining steps that minimize the amount of time required to create the definition, while still taking advantage of the new features of release 2. We have chosen to use the dialogs for creating each definition and then to use the Property Palette to enter the remaining information about the definition, which cannot be entered through the dialogs.

1. In the Design Editor (DE), click the Server Model tab.
2. Create a new function definition (available under PL/SQL definitions). Do this by pressing the Create icon in the Design Editor toolbar. This will launch a set of dialogs that will gather all of the necessary information required for the function definition. The following steps detail the settings used for this example.
3. The Name dialog is the first dialog that will be displayed. Using this dialog, you will be able to specify a short name for the function definition that will be used for naming generated files (*Short name of the PL/SQL definition* = **CH6_DECL**). Next, specify a unique name for the function definition (*Name* = **CH6_DECL**) and the purpose or short description of the function definition (*Purpose* = **Return the ID of the person associated with a supplied issue**). Last, specify the name you would like to use when creating the function definition (*Implementation name* = **GET_PERSON**). This name will be used in the header of the program unit. Figure 6-13 shows the Name dialog used for this example. When you have completed this dialog, click Next.
4. The Type dialog is the second dialog that will be displayed. Using this dialog, you will be able to specify that you would like to define a function definition (*Type of definition* = **Function**). Next, specify that you would like to define the function using the declarative method (*How the PL/SQL will be defined* = **Declarative**) and that the

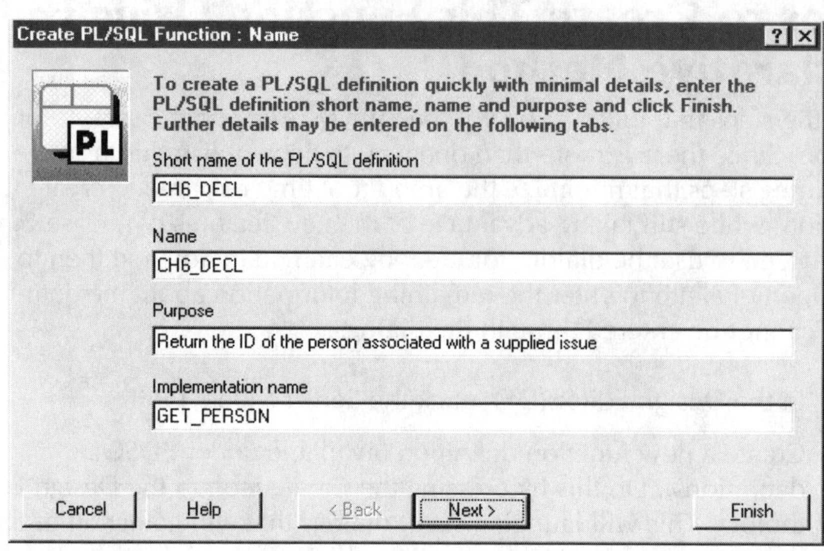

FIGURE 6-13. *Name dialog—declarative example*

function will return a number (*Return datatype* = **NUMBER**). Last, specify that the scope of this function is private (*Scope of access* = **Private**). Figure 6-14 shows the Type dialog used for this example. When you have completed this dialog, click Next.

5. The Arguments dialog is the third dialog that will be displayed. Using this dialog, you can define the argument used by this function definition. This is done by specifying the name of the argument (*Arguments* = **p_id**); how the argument is defined (*Defined By* = **Datatype**); which datatype the argument will be defined as (*Datatype* = **NUMBER**); and, last, how the argument will be used (*Argument type* = **Input**). Figure 6-15 shows the Arguments dialog used for this example. When you have completed this dialog, click Next.

6. The Exceptions dialog is the fourth dialog that will be displayed. We did not choose to define exceptions using this dialog and instead used the *PL/SQL Block* property covered in step 11. Click Next to skip this dialog.

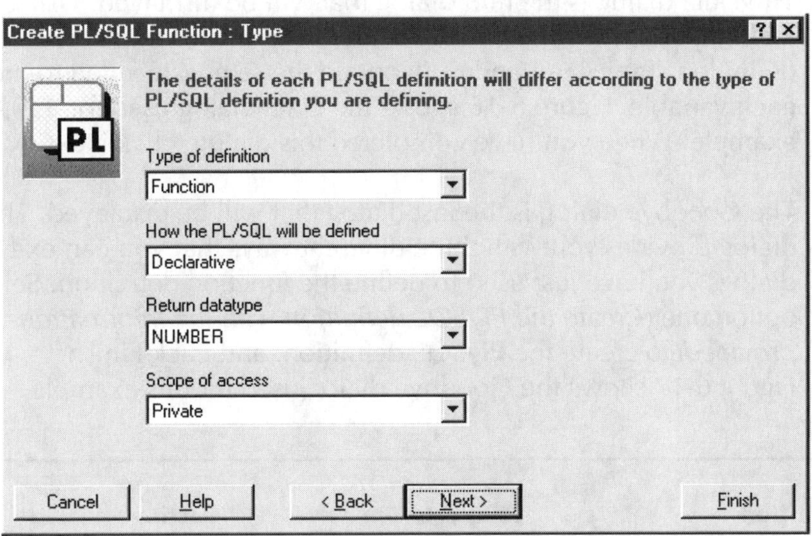

FIGURE 6-14. *Type dialog—declarative example*

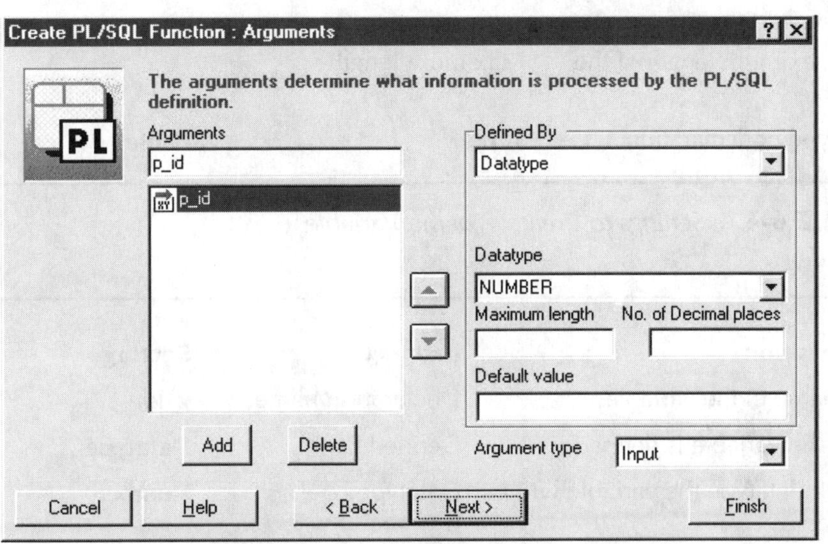

FIGURE 6-15. *Arguments dialog—declarative example*

7. The Data dialog is the fifth dialog that will be displayed. Using this dialog, you can define both variables used by this function definition. Tables 6-4 and 6-5 contain the settings needed to create each variable. Figure 6-16 shows the Data dialog used for this example. When you have completed this dialog, click Next.

8. The Goodbye dialog is the last dialog that will be displayed. This dialog provides you with three different ways that you can exit the dialogs you have just used to define the function definition. Select option one (*Create the PL/SQL definition with the information provided*) to create the PL/SQL definition, and click Finish. Figure 6-17 shows the Goodbye dialog used for this example.

Description	Property	Setting
The name of the variable	Declaration name	**v_name**
How the variable is defined	Defined By	**Datatype**
Which datatype the variable will be defined as	Datatype	**VARCHAR2**
The maximum length of the variable	Maximum length	**50**
The type of declaration	Type	**Variable**

TABLE 6-4. *Settings to Create v_name Variable*

Description	Property	Setting
The name of the variable	Declaration name	**v_id**
How the variable is defined	Defined By	**Datatype**
Which datatype the variable will be defined as	Datatype	**Number**
The type of declaration	Type	**Variable**

TABLE 6-5. *Settings to Create v_id Variable*

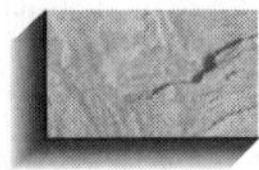

NOTE
*You could alternatively select option three (*Create the PL/SQL definition and then invoke the Logic Editor to edit the definition*). If you choose to define the function using this option, you can generate once you've completed defining the function using this editor.)*

9. Switch to the Properties Palette from the dialogs. Do this by pressing the Property Dialogs/Palettes icon in the Design Editor toolbar.
10. Define the declaration section (cursor definition only) in the *package specification* property of the function definition. Do this by navigating to the *package specification* property and, using a text editor, entering the cursor program unit definition. This should include the contents between the superscript nines in Figure 6-12.

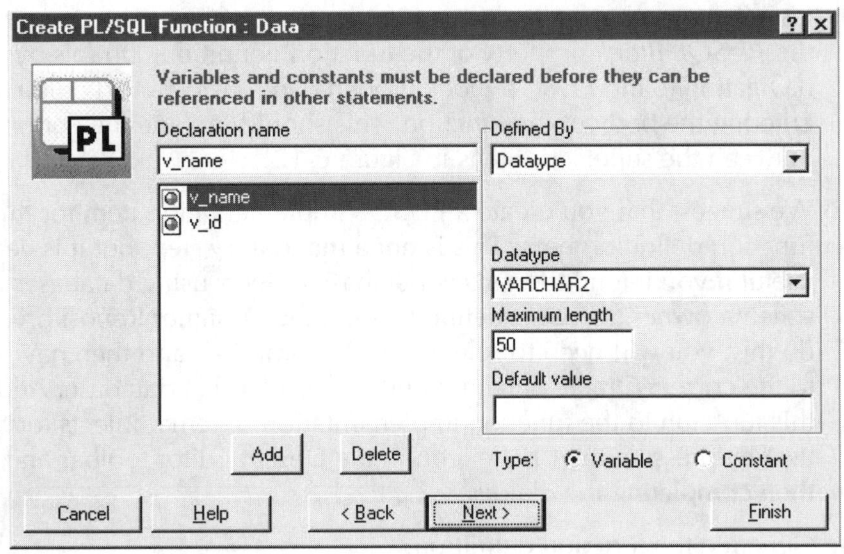

FIGURE 6-16. *Data dialog—declarative example*

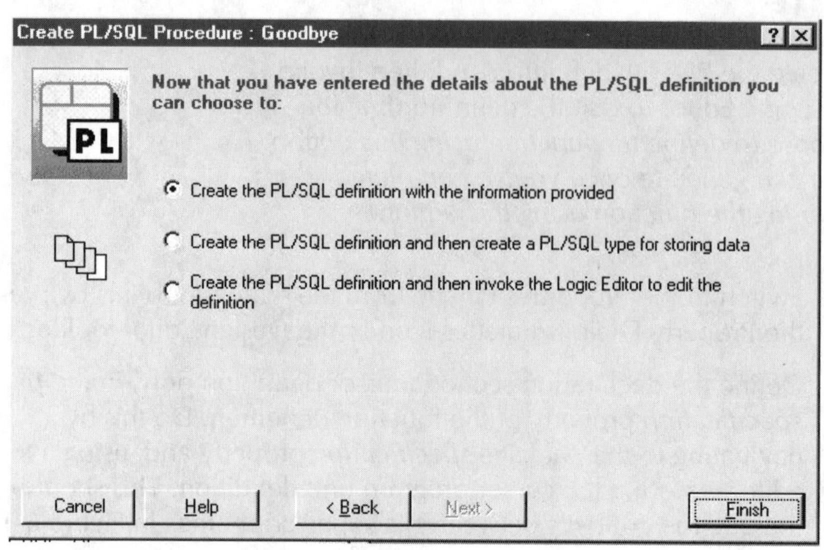

FIGURE 6-17. *Goodbye dialog—declarative example*

11. Define the execution and exception sections of the program unit in the *PL/SQL Block* property of the function definition. Do this by navigating to the *PL/SQL Block* property and, using a text editor, entering the body of the function. This should include the contents between the superscript tens in Figure 6-12.

12. We suggest that you create a PL/SQL implementation item for this function definition next. This is not a mandatory step, but it is very useful if you intend to manage database objects using databases and schema owner accounts defined within the Designer Repository. To do this, you will need to select the DB Admin tab and then navigate to the correct Oracle database and user under that database. Add this function to the function implementation schema objects for that user by pressing the Create icon in the Design Editor toolbar and then completing the dialogs.

13. Generate the function definition.

Design Capture

The Design Capture utility will create PL/SQL definitions in the repository based on program unit definitions located in one of two sources:

- Oracle database
- File system

Function definitions created in the repository using this utility are created using the free format method. In essence, the Design Capture utility reverses the generation process described in the free format method earlier in this chapter. Variable declarations are inserted into the *package specification* property, not the *PL/SQL Block* property. This is one of the reasons that it is better to use the *package specification* property for variable declarations when using either free format or declarative methods.

Figure 6-18 is an annotated version of the sample function provided in Figure 6-1. The superscript numbers correspond to properties in the function definition, which are populated by the Design Capture utility. See Table 6-6 for specific mapping of properties populated by the Design Capture utility.

Number	Feature	Source Using Dialogs	Source Using Properties Palette
1	PL/SQL Definition type	TYPE TAB Field: Type of definition	FUNCTION DEFINITION Property: Type
2	PL/SQL Definition name	NAME TAB Field: Name	FUNCTION DEFINITION Property: Implementation Name

TABLE 6-6. *Properties Populated Using the Design Capture Utility*

Number	Feature	Source Using Dialogs	Source Using Properties Palette
3	Argument name	ARGUMENT TAB Field: Arguments	ARGUMENT Property: Name
4	Argument type	ARGUMENT TAB Field: Argument type	ARGUMENT Property: Input Output
5	Argument datatype	ARGUMENT TAB Field: Datatype	ARGUMENT Property: Datatype
6	Function return type	TYPE TAB Field: Return datatype	FUNCTION DEFINITION Property: Return Type (Scalar)
7	Declaration section of program unit body	NO SOURCE	FUNCTION DEFINITION Property: Package Specification
8	Execution and exception sections of program unit body	NO SOURCE	FUNCTION DEFINITION Property: PL/SQL Block

TABLE 6-6. *Properties Populated Using the Design Capture Utility* (continued)

Steps to Create a Repository Definition Using the Design Capture Utility

1. In the Design Editor menu, navigate to Generate → Capture Design Of → Server Model from Database.
2. Select the source of the design capture:
   - Database captures definitions in an Oracle database.
   - DDL file captures the contents of a DDL file.

```
CREATE OR REPLACE 1FUNCTION1 2GET_PERSON2(3p_id3 4IN4 5NUMBER5)
 RETURN 6NUMBER6 IS

7/* Cursor Selects Person Associated With Supplied Issue */
CURSOR GET_ID_CUR(p_id IN NUMBER) IS
  SELECT upper(per.first_name)||' '||upper(per.last_name) name, per.id
  FROM issues iss, people per
  WHERE p_id = iss.id
  AND iss.per_id = per.id;

/* Variable Holds Complete Name of Person */
v_name varchar2(50);

/* Variable Holds ID of Person */
v_id number;7

8BEGIN
 OPEN get_id_cur(p_id);
 FETCH get_id_cur into v_name, v_id;
 CLOSE get_id_cur;

/* If Bill Gates is encountered return zero */
 IF v_name = 'BILL GATES' THEN
  return('0');
 ELSE
  return('v_id');
 END IF;
EXCEPTION
 WHEN OTHERS THEN RAISE_APPLICATION ERROR
   (-21002, 'GET_PERSON_FUNCTION failed with: '||substr(SQLERRM,1,50));
END;8
```

FIGURE 6-18. *Annotated Design Capture example*

If you select the database option, you will need to fill in the *Username, Password,* and *Connect* properties. These will be used to query to database objects to determine which objects this user can capture the design of. You will then need to click the Objects tab and select the function definition, and then move it into the *Capture* field.

If you select the DDL file option, you will need to select *DDL File* and then specify the path\filename of the DDL file to be captured in the *Name* field and the type\version of database in the *Type* field.

3. Select the database/schema owner in which to create the definition. Do this by setting the *Capture Objects Into* property to the database schema owner in which you would like to create the function definition.
4. When satisfied with your selections, click Start.
5. Select how you would like to process the captured function definition:

   - **Save** Commits the function definition to the repository
   - **Revert** Completes a rollback of the posted function definition
   - **Browse/Edit** Enables you to browse the posted function definition, make modifications, and then either commit or roll back

Generation Troubleshooting Guide

Problem	Methods	Solution
When I change the method of defining a PL/SQL definition from operating system file to either free format method or declarative method, it continues to generate the program unit definition using the operating system file method.	Free format and declarative	Remove the path\filename from the *source path* property. If this property is populated, the function will always be generated using the operating system file method, regardless of the value in the *free format declaration* property.
The variable declarations I defined in the *PL/SQL Block* property are not generating into the declaration section of the program unit body.	Declarative	To eliminate this problem, you have two choices: either define all the variable declarations in the *package specification* property, or create program data definitions for each variable you need to declare.

Problem	Methods	Solution
The cursor I included as a subprogram unit is being declared twice.	Declarative	This is a bug. Remove the errant cursor declaration from the generated code.
The cursor I included as a subprogram unit is not being declared at all.	Free format	The Server Generator ignores subprogram units when using the free format method. Use the declarative method if you would like to generate the cursor declaration as a subprogram unit.
The exceptions I entered as program data are generating into the declaration section of the program unit, not the exception section.	Declarative	The Server generator is generating the declaration of a user-defined exception. It will not use this information to create the exception section of the program unit.
I cannot specify a nonunique implementation name for function definitions.	Free format and declarative	This is a bug. Modify the generated code and rename the function to the desired name.

CHAPTER 7

Generating Packages

This chapter is a detailed guide to help you generate packages. In this chapter we will cover

- Generation of a sample package using each method of defining a PL/SQL definition and design capture
- The property settings used to generate each example
- Step-by-step instructions for creating the example using each method
- A troubleshooting guide to assist you with common generation problems

We think that it will be easier for you to understand the various methods if we use an example that at least looks like a real-world program. Therefore, we designed a sample package that performs a standard task that you might use in a real system.

NOTE
Example Description: *The example we are using in this chapter is a package that is designed to perform a cascade update of the status of related records when a parent record is changed. The example uses the DSTAT_CD in the DBCR table from the example application provided with this book. When this status code is updated, triggers will call the procedures in this package to perform the update.*

The code shown in Figure 7-1 will be used in the sections that follow to show you a specific example of each method of creating a package. If you need additional background on each method presented, please refer to Chapter 4.

Operating System File Method

The operating system file method is the only method that references definitions that are stored outside the repository. In order to use this method, you must place the source code for the program unit definition into an operating system file and specify the filename and path when you are creating the PL/SQL definition in the repository.

Generating the sample package using the operating system file method will create three files. In this example, the three files created are

- <file prefix>.SQL Executes the <file prefix>.PKS and <file prefix>.PKB files
- <file prefix>.PKS Executes the true program unit definition, calling a specified path and filename which contain the DDL
- <file prefix>.PKB This file does not contain any calls or DDL. When the operating system file method is used, this file will always be empty.

NOTE
<file prefix> is a Name that you specify when generating server-side objects. This name will be given to all files created during that execution of the Server Generator.

```
CREATE OR REPLACE PACKAGE dbcr_cascade AS
  PROCEDURE dbcr_row(P_ID IN NUMBER, p_CD IN VARCHAR2);
  PROCEDURE dbcr_transaction;
  PROCEDURE clear_pl_tbl;
  TYPE id_TabType IS TABLE OF dbcrs.id%TYPE INDEX BY BINARY_INTEGER;
  ptr_DBCR_ID     BINARY_INTEGER := 0;
  tab_DBCR_ID     id_TabType;
  tab_Empty       id_TabType; -- This table is used to clear the table
  TYPE cd_TabType IS TABLE OF dbcrs.dstat_cd%TYPE INDEX BY BINARY_INTEGER;
  tab_DSTAT_CD    cd_TabType;
  tab_UpdFlg      cd_TabType;

END dbcr_cascade;
/

CREATE OR REPLACE PACKAGE BODY dbcr_cascade AS
  c_Status_To_Cascade CONSTANT VARCHAR2(15) := 'CLOSED';
  PROCEDURE dbcr_row(P_ID IN NUMBER, P_CD IN VARCHAR2) IS
  BEGIN
    IF P_CD = v_Status_To_Cascade THEN
    ptr_DBCR_ID := ptr_DBCR_ID + 1;
    tab_DBCR_ID(ptr_DBCR_ID) := p_ID;
    tab_DSTAT_CD(ptr_DBCR_ID) := p_CD;
        tab_UpdFlg(ptr_DBCR_ID) := 'N';
    END IF;
  END dbcr_row;

  PROCEDURE dbcr_transaction IS
    CURSOR cur_rel_dbcr(pc_DBCR_ID IN NUMBER) IS
    SELECT child_dbcr_id, rel_type
      FROM DBCR_DBCRS
     WHERE parent_dbcr_id = pc_DBCR_ID;

  BEGIN
    FOR i IN 1..ptr_DBCR_ID LOOP
      FOR c IN cur_rel_dbcr(tab_DBCR_ID(i)) LOOP
```

FIGURE 7-1. *Sample package*

```
    IF c.rel_type = 'SUB' AND tab_UpdFlg(i) != 'Y' THEN
        tab_UpdFlg(i) := 'Y';
        UPDATE DBCRS SET DSTAT_CD = tab_DSTAT_CD(i)
         WHERE id = c.child_dbcr_id;
    END IF;
      END LOOP;
    END LOOP;
    clear_pl_tbl;
  END dbcr_transaction;

  PROCEDURE clear_pl_tbl IS
  BEGIN
    ptr_DBCR_ID := 0;
    tab_DBCR_ID := tab_Empty;
  END clear_pl_tbl;

END dbcr_cascade;
/
```

FIGURE 7-1. *Sample package* (continued)

Figure 7-2 is an annotated version of <file prefix>.PKS. The superscript numbers correspond to properties in the package definition, which created this file. See Table 7-1 for specific mapping of the generated code.

```
c:\aristmpl\application\ss\pack\CH7_os.pks
--
-- Generated for Oracle 8 on Wed Jul 22  06:32:17 1998 by Server
Generator 2

PROMPT Creating [1]Package[1] [2]'DBCR_CASCADE'[2]
@ [3]C:\ARISTMPL\Application\SS\Pack\package.sql[3]
```

FIGURE 7-2. *Annotated generation example using the operating system file method*

Number	Feature	Source Using Dialogs	Source Using Properties Palette
1	PL/SQL definition type	TYPE TAB Field: Type of definition	PACKAGE DEFINITION Property: Type
2	PL/SQL definition name	NAME TAB Field: Name	PACKAGE DEFINITION Property: Name
3	Path and filename	FILE TAB Field: Path and filename of source	PACKAGE DEFINITION Property: Source Path

TABLE 7-1. *Source of Generated Code Using the Operating System File Method*

Steps to Create This Package Using the Operating System File Method

Using the steps that follow, you will be able to re-create the sample package. Since there is more than one way to accomplish this task, we focused on defining steps that minimize the amount of time required to create the definition, while still taking advantage of the new features of release 2. We have chosen to use the dialogs for creating each definition and then to use the Properties Palette to enter the remaining information about the definition that cannot be entered through the dialogs.

1. In the Design Editor (DE), click on the Server Model tab.
2. Create a new package definition (available under PL/SQL definitions). Do this by pressing the Create icon on the Design Editor toolbar. This will launch a set of dialogs that will gather all of the necessary information required for the package definition. The following steps detail the settings used for this example.
3. The Name dialog is the dialog that will be displayed first. Using this dialog, you will be able to specify a short name for the package definition that will be used for naming generated files (*Short name of the PL/SQL definition* = **CH7_OS**). Next, you will specify a unique name for the package definition (*Name* = **CH7_OS**), then the

purpose or short description of the package definition (*Purpose* = **Performs cascade update when DBCR_CD is updated**). Last, specify the name you would like to use when creating the package definition (*Implementation name* = **DBCR_CASCADE**). This name will be used in the header of the program unit. Figure 7-3 shows the Name dialog used for this example. When you have completed this dialog, click Next.

4. The Type dialog is the second dialog that will be displayed. Using this dialog, you will be able to specify that you would like to define a package definition (*Type of definition* = **Package**). Also, you will specify that you would like to define the package using the operating system file method (*How the PL/SQL will be defined* = **Operating System File**). Figure 7-4 shows the Type dialog used for this example. When you have completed this dialog, click Next.
5. The File dialog is the third dialog that will be displayed. Using this dialog, you will be able to specify the name of the file that contains the DDL for this package definition and its location (*Path and filename of source* = **c:\ARISTMPL\Application\SS\package.sql**).

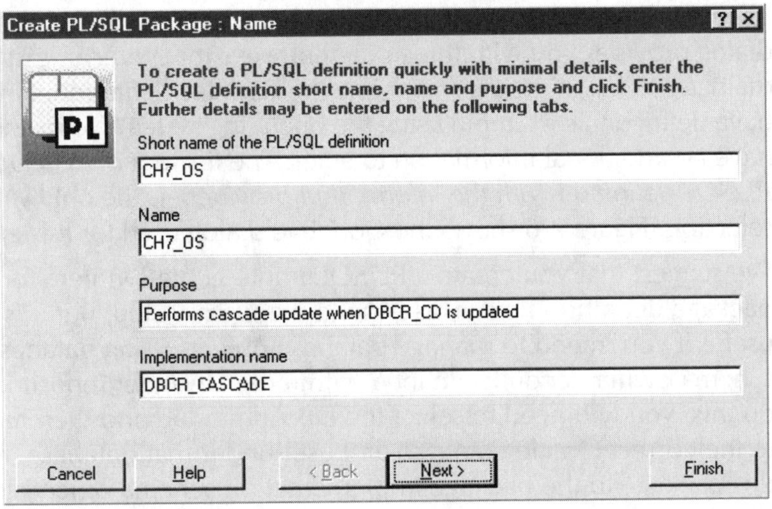

FIGURE 7-3. *Name dialog—operating system file example*

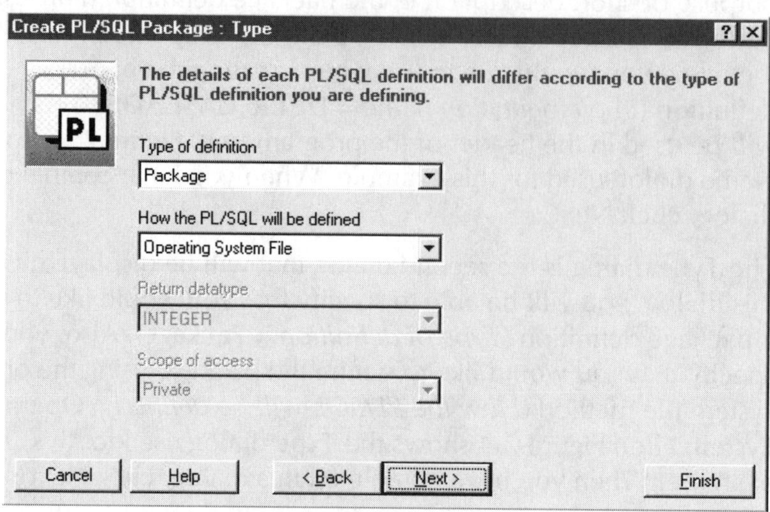

FIGURE 7-4. *Type dialog—operating system file example*

Figure 7-5 shows the File dialog used for this example. When you have completed this dialog, click Next.

6. The Goodbye dialog is the last dialog that will be displayed. This dialog provides you with three different ways that you can exit the dialogs you have just used to define the package definition. Since we have defined this example using the operating system file method, we have no additional information to enter. The first option, *Create the PL/SQL definition with the information provided,* is the only valid selection. Figure 7-6 shows the Goodbye dialog used for this example.
7. We suggest that you create a PL/SQL implementation item for this package definition next. This is not a mandatory step, but it is very useful if you intend to manage database objects using databases and schema owner accounts defined within the Designer repository. To do this, you will need to select the DB Admin tab and then navigate to the correct Oracle database and user under that database. Add this package to the package implementation schema objects for that user by pressing the Create icon in the Design Editor toolbar and then completing the dialogs.
8. Generate the package definition.

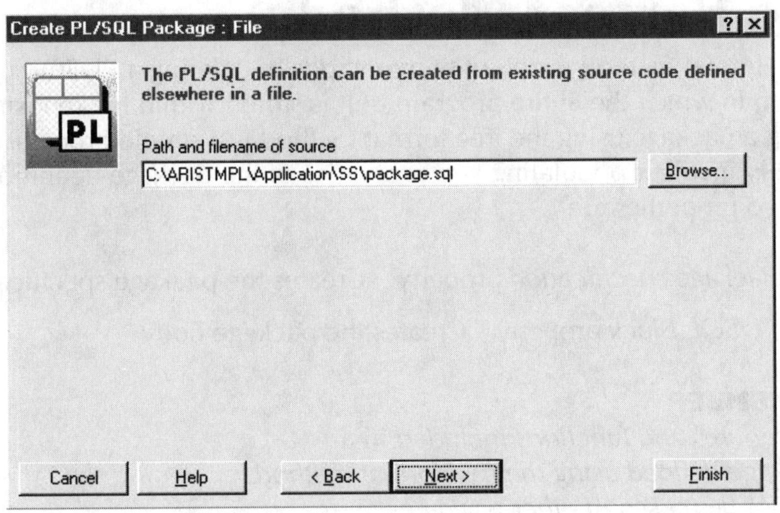

FIGURE 7-5. *File dialog—operating system file example*

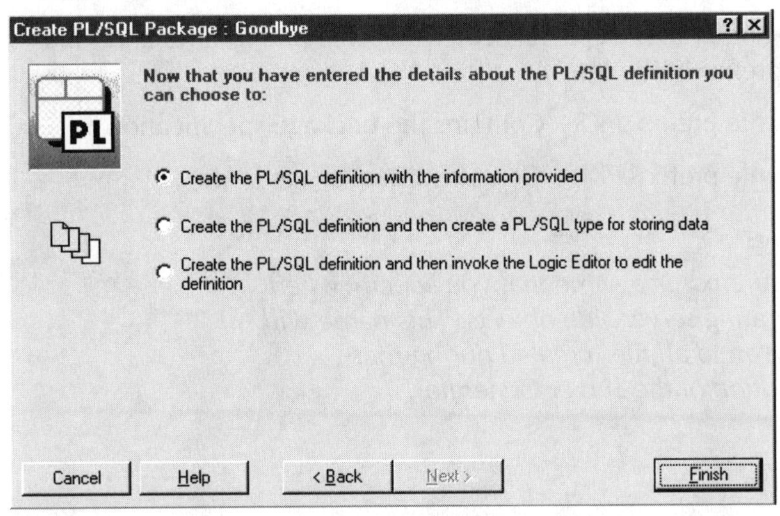

FIGURE 7-6. *Goodbye dialog—operating system file example*

Free Format Method

The free format method is one of two methods of defining a PL/SQL definition in which the entire program unit is stored within the repository. Defining a package using the free format method is a simple process, which essentially involves populating two properties of the package definition. These two properties are

- *Package specification* property Creates the package specification
- *PL/SQL Block* property Creates the package body

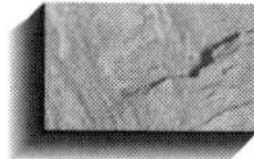

REMEMBER
Procedures and functions included in a package defined using the free format method cannot be reused in other packages or as separate PL/SQL definitions. If you want to reuse procedures and functions, you must use the declarative method of defining the package.

Generating the sample package using the free format method creates three files. In this example, the three files created are

- <file prefix>.SQL Executes the <file prefix>.PKS and <file prefix>.PKB files
- <file prefix>.PKS Contains the package specification
- <file prefix>.PKB Contains the package body

NOTE
<file prefix> is a name that you specify when generating server-side objects. This name will be given to all files created during that execution of the Server Generator.

Figure 7-7 displays the contents of the <file prefix>.PKS file. Figure 7-8 displays the contents of the <file prefix>.PKB file. The superscript numbers correspond to properties in the package definition, which created this file. See Table 7-2 for specific mapping of the generated code.

Steps to Create This Package Using the Free Format Method

Using the steps that follow, you will be able to re-create the sample package. Since there is more than one way to accomplish this task, we

```
-- c:\aristmpl\application\ss\pack\CH7_free.pks
--
-- Generated for Oracle 8 on Wed Jul 22  06:26:52 1998 by Server Generator
PROMPT Creating 1Package1 2'DBCR_CASCADE'2
CREATE OR REPLACE 1PACKAGE1 2DBCR_CASCADE2 IS
-- PL/SQL Specification
  3PROCEDURE dbcr_row(P_ID IN NUMBER, p_CD IN VARCHAR2);
  PROCEDURE dbcr_transaction;
  PROCEDURE clear_pl_tbl;

  TYPE id_TabType IS TABLE OF dbcrs.id%TYPE INDEX BY BINARY_INTEGER;
  ptr_DBCR_ID      BINARY_INTEGER := 0;
  tab_DBCR_ID      id_TabType;
  tab_Empty        id_TabType; -- This table is used to clear the table

  TYPE cd_TabType IS TABLE OF dbcrs.dstat_cd%TYPE INDEX BY BINARY_INTEGER;
  tab_DSTAT_CD    cd_TabType;
  tab_UpdFlg      cd_TabType;3

END DBCR_CASCADE;
/
```

FIGURE 7-7. *Annotated contents of <file prefix>.PKS file created using the free format method*

```
-- c:\aristmpl\application\ss\pack\CH7_free.pkb
--
-- Generated for Oracle 8 on Wed Jul 22  06:26:52 1998 by Server Generator

PROMPT Creating 1Package Body1 2'DBCR_CASCADE'2
CREATE OR REPLACE 1PACKAGE BODY1 2DBCR_CASCADE2 IS
4 c_Status_To_Cascade CONSTANT VARCHAR2(15) := 'CLOSED';
PROCEDURE dbcr_row(P_ID IN NUMBER, P_CD IN VARCHAR2) IS
  -- PL/SQL Block
BEGIN
    IF P_CD = c_Status_To_Cascade THEN
    ptr_DBCR_ID := ptr_DBCR_ID + 1;
tab_DBCR_ID(ptr_DBCR_ID) := p_ID;
    tab_DSTAT_CD(ptr_DBCR_ID) := p_CD;
        tab_UpdFlg(ptr_DBCR_ID) := 'N';
    END IF;
  END dbcr_row;

  PROCEDURE dbcr_transaction IS
    CURSOR cur_rel_dbcr(pc_DBCR_ID IN NUMBER) IS
    SELECT child_dbcr_id, rel_type
      FROM DBCR_DBCRS
     WHERE parent_dbcr_id = pc_DBCR_ID;
  BEGIN
    FOR i IN 1..ptr_DBCR_ID LOOP
      FOR c IN cur_rel_dbcr(tab_DBCR_ID(i)) LOOP
    IF c.rel_type = 'SUB' AND tab_UpdFlg(i) != 'Y' THEN
        tab_UpdFlg(i) := 'Y';
        UPDATE DBCRS SET DSTAT_CD = tab_DSTAT_CD(i)
         WHERE id = c.child_dbcr_id;
    END IF;
      END LOOP;
    END LOOP;
    clear_pl_tbl;
  END dbcr_transaction;
  PROCEDURE clear_pl_tbl IS
  BEGIN
    ptr_DBCR_ID := 0;
    tab_DBCR_ID := tab_Empty;
  END clear_pl_tbl;
END DBCR_CASCADE;4
/
```

FIGURE 7-8. *Annotated contents of <file prefix>.PKB file created using the free format method*

Number	Feature	Source Using Dialogs	Source Using Properties Palette
1	PL/SQL definition type	TYPE TAB Field: Type of definition	PACKAGE DEFINITION Property: Type
2	PL/SQL definition name	NAME TAB Field: Name	PACKAGE DEFINITION Property: Name
3	Declaration section of program unit body	SPECIFICATION TAB Field: Package specification	PACKAGE DEFINITION Property: Package Specification
4	Execution and exception sections of program unit body	NO SOURCE	PACKAGE DEFINITION Property: PL/SQL Block

TABLE 7-2. *Source of Generated Code Using the Free Format Method*

focused on defining steps that minimize the amount of time required to create the definition, while still taking advantage of the new features of release 2. We have chosen to use the dialogs for creating each definition and to then use the Properties Palette to enter the remaining information about the definition that cannot be entered through the dialogs.

1. In the Design Editor (DE), click on the Server Model tab.
2. Create a new package definition (available under PL/SQL definitions). Do this by pressing the Create icon in the Design Editor toolbar. This will launch a set of dialogs that will gather all of the necessary information required for the package definition. The following steps detail the settings used for this example.
3. The Name dialog is the dialog that will be displayed first. Using this dialog you will be able to specify a short name for the package definition that will be used for naming generated files (*Short name of the PL/SQL definition* = **CH7_FREE**), and a unique name for the package definition (*Name* = **CH7_FREE**). Next, you will specify the purpose or short description of the package (*Purpose* = **Performs**

cascade update when DBCR_CD is updated). Last, specify the name you would like to use when creating the package definition (*Implementation name* = **DBCR_CASCADE**). This name will be used in the header of the program unit. Figure 7-9 shows the Name dialog used for this example. When you have completed this dialog, click Next.

4. The Type dialog is the second dialog that will be displayed. Using this dialog, you will be able to specify that you would like to define a package definition (*Type of definition* = **Package**). Also, you will specify that you would like to define the package using the free format method (*How the PL/SQL will be defined* = **Free Format**. Figure 7-10 shows the Type dialog used for this example. When you have completed this dialog, click Next.

5. The Specification dialog is the third dialog that will be displayed. Using this dialog, you will be able to define the package specification for this example. Figure 7-11 shows the Specification dialog used for this example. Due to the size of the dialog, not all of the text is shown in this figure. This should include the contents

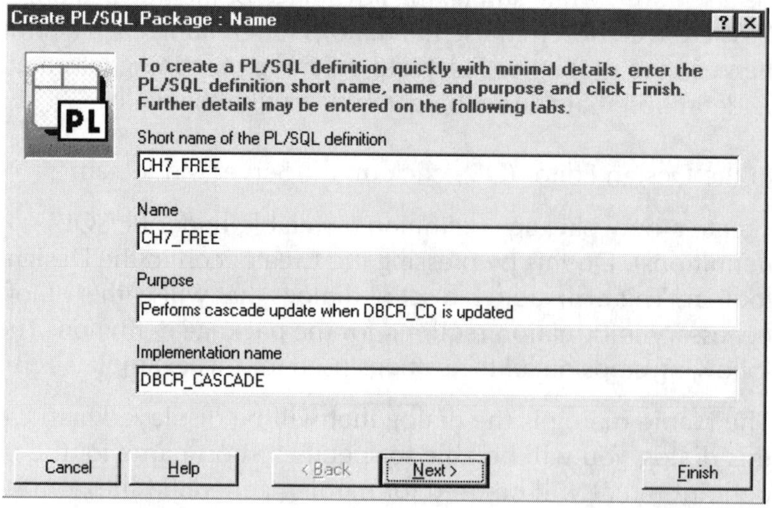

Create PL/SQL Package : Name

To create a PL/SQL definition quickly with minimal details, enter the PL/SQL definition short name, name and purpose and click Finish. Further details may be entered on the following tabs.

PL

Short name of the PL/SQL definition

CH7_FREE

Name

CH7_FREE

Purpose

Performs cascade update when DBCR_CD is updated

Implementation name

DBCR_CASCADE

Cancel | Help | < Back | Next > | Finish

FIGURE 7-9. *Name dialog—free format example*

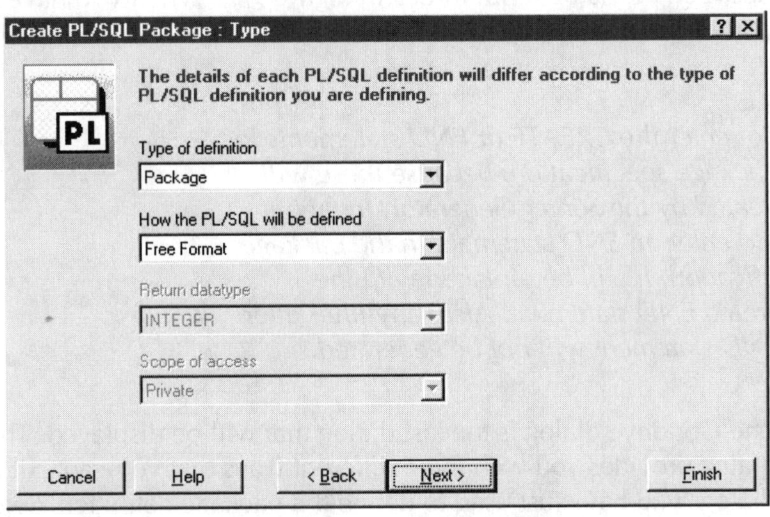

FIGURE 7-10. *Type dialog—free format example*

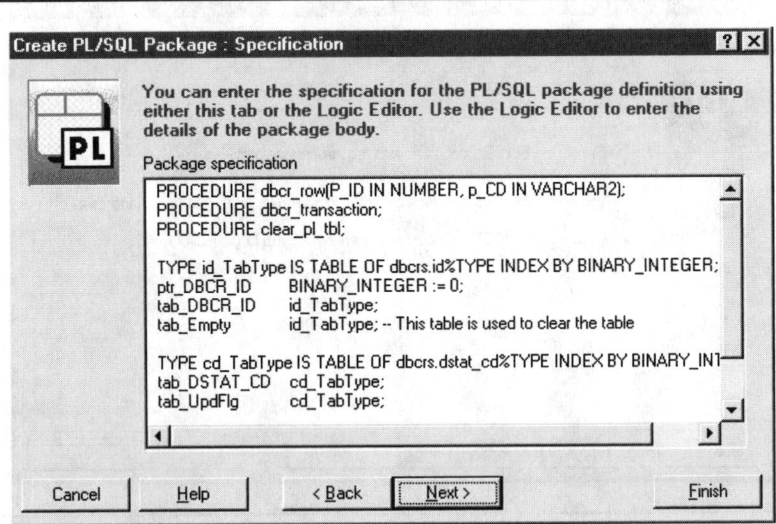

FIGURE 7-11. *Specification dialog—free format example*

between the superscript threes in Figure 7-7. When you have completed this dialog, click Next.

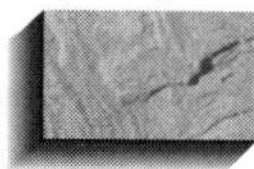

NOTE
Do not enter the CREATE or END statements for the package specification, because these will be created by the Server Generator. In fact, if you do enter an END statement in the package specification, it will be replaced with the generated END statement. Also, any lines after the END statement will not be generated.

6. The Goodbye dialog is the last dialog that will be displayed. This dialog provides you with three different ways that you can exit the dialogs you have just used to define the package definition. Select the first option (*Create the PL/SQL definition with the information provided*) to create the PL/SQL definition and click Finish. Figure 7-12 shows the Goodbye dialog used for this example.

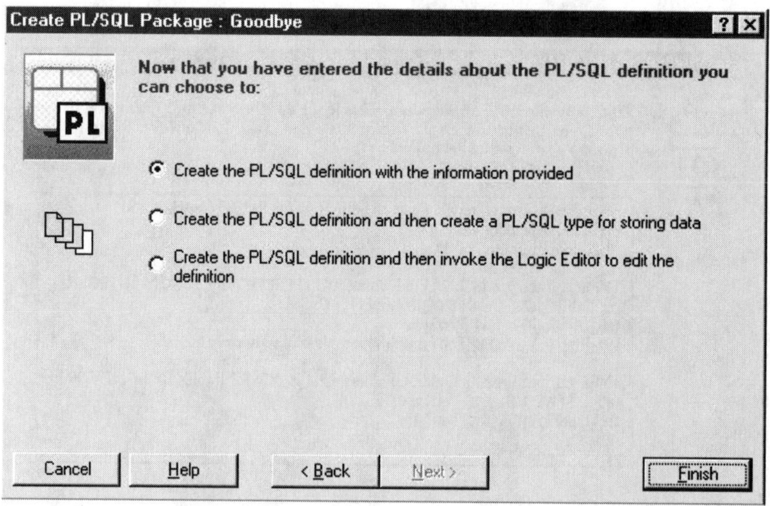

FIGURE 7-12. *Goodbye dialog—free format example*

NOTE
*You could alternatively select the third option (*Create the PL/SQL definition and then invoke the Logic Editor to edit the definition*). If you choose to define the package using this option, you can generate once you've completed defining the package using this editor.*

7. Switch to the Properties Palette from the dialogs. Do this by pressing the Property Dialogs/Palettes icon in the Design Editor toolbar.
8. Define the package body in the *PL/SQL Block* property of the package definition. Do this by navigating to the *PL/SQL Block* property and, using a text editor, entering the body of the program unit. This should include the contents between the superscript fours in Figure 7-8.
9. We suggest that you create a PL/SQL implementation item for this package definition next. This is not a mandatory step, but it is very useful if you intend to manage database objects using databases and schema owner accounts defined within the Designer Repository. To do this, you need to select the DB Admin tab and then navigate to the correct Oracle database and user under that database. Add this package to the package implementation schema objects for that user by pressing the Create icon in the Design Editor toolbar and then completing the dialogs.
10. Generate the package definition.

Declarative Method

The declarative method is the other method of defining a PL/SQL definition in which the entire program unit is stored within the repository. Before we go into the steps needed to create the examples, we will detail some important concepts and properties that will help you understand the steps that follow.

Sub program units are PL/SQL definitions referenced by a package definition that will be included in the package DDL when created by the

Server Generator. When using sub program units, you will want to pay particular attention to four things:

- The *called sequence* property of the sub program unit
- The *method of use* property of the sub program unit
- The *restrict references* properties of each PL/SQL definition included as a sub program unit
- The *scope* property of each of the PL/SQL definitions included as a sub program unit

The *called sequence* property communicates to the Server Generator the order in which it should place the PL/SQL definitions specified as sub program units into the package DDL. Values are read sequentially starting at 0, incrementing by 1.

The *method of use* property communicates to the Server Generator how to reference the sub program unit. To include the sub program unit in the generated DDL, set this property to **INCLUDE**.

NOTE

*You may want to set this property to **CALL** if you are making calls to a stand-alone procedure/function that you don't want to include in your package. This is very useful for documenting processing dependencies and will result in more complete impact analysis.*

The *restrict references* properties, located on each PL/SQL definition included as a sub program unit of the package, communicate to the Server Generator whether pragma restrictions should be created or not. The four *restrict references* properties that can be individually set are

- WNDS (Writes No Database State)
- WNPS (Writes No Package State)

- RNDS (Reads No Database State)
- RNPS (Reads No Package State)

The Server Generator only uses the *restrict references* properties of a PL/SQL definition when it is included in a declarative package. The settings for these properties are outlined in Table 7-3.

The *scope* property, located on each PL/SQL definition included as a sub program unit of the package, communicates to the Server Generator whether the PL/SQL definition should be included in the package DDL with private or public access. A package component generated with public access will be declared in the package specification and will be accessible to users who have been granted the execute privilege to the package. A package component generated with private access is created in the package body without a declaration in the package specification. Therefore, it is not available outside the scope of the current package. The Server Generator only uses the *scope* property of a PL/SQL definition when it is included in a declarative package; otherwise, it is ignored. The settings for these properties are outlined in Table 7-4.

We are going to present you with two approaches to using the declarative method, hybrid and pure. Each of these approaches has advantages and disadvantages. In the sections that follow, we will explore

Property Setting	**Action**
Default value	The generated DDL will *not* include pragma restrictions.
No	The generated DDL will *not* include pragma restrictions.
Yes	The generated DDL *will* include pragma restrictions.

TABLE 7-3. *Settings of* Restrict References *Properties*

Property Setting	Action
Private	The generated DDL will include only the definition of the package component in the package body.
Protected	The generated DDL will include only the definition of the package component in the package body.
Public	The generated DDL will include a declaration in the package specification and definition of the package component in the package body.

TABLE 7-4. *Settings of* Scope *Property*

these two approaches for using the declarative method and generate the sample package.

The Hybrid Declarative Approach

We are calling the first approach hybrid because it uses both declarative and free format methods to define the package. This approach focuses on maximizing the benefits of using the declarative method with the least amount of effort. Developers benefit from the ability of including procedure and function definitions to create the package body (code reuse), while maintaining the ability to quickly define and generate advanced public declarations without incurring generation problems. We believe this method to be a very practical implementation of the declarative method.

Defining a package using the hybrid declarative method involves populating two components of the package definition. These two components are

- The *package specification* property
- Sub program units

The *package specification* property allows you to generate declarations into the package specification. All declarations that you wish to make accessible outside the package should be specified here, with the exception of the procedures and/or functions contained within the package. These individual declarations will be created through their association as sub program units. Using this approach, we will define the package using the declarative method. The packaged procedures will be included as sub program units, and all other declarations will be made using the *package specification* property of the package definition. This is a very practical example of how to optimize usage of the declarative method of defining a package definition. Generating the sample package using the declarative method creates three files. In this example, the three files created are

- <file prefix>.SQL Executes the <file prefix>.PKS and <file prefix>.PKB files
- <file prefix>.PKS Contains the package specification
- <file prefix>.PKB Contains the package body

NOTE
<file prefix> is a name that you specify when generating server-side objects. This name will be given to all files created during that execution of the Server Generator.

Figure 7-13 displays the contents of the <file prefix>.PKS file. Figure 7-14 displays the contents of the <file prefix>.PKB file. The superscript numbers correspond to properties in the package definition, which created this file. See Table 7-5 for specific mapping of the generated code.

```
-- c:\aristmpl\application\ss\pack\CH7_hybrid_decl.pks
--
-- Generated for Oracle 8 on Thu Jul 23  14:22:27 1998 by Server Generator

PROMPT Creating [1]Package[1] [2]'DBCR_CASCADE'[2]
CREATE OR REPLACE [1]PACKAGE[1] [2]DBCR_CASCADE[2] IS
-- Sub-Program Unit Declarations
[3]/* Increments Binary Integer and Loads PL Table */[3]
[4]PROCEDURE[4] [5]DBCR_ROW[5]
 ([6]P_ID[6] [7]IN[7] [8]NUMBER[8]
 ,[6]P_CD[6] [7]IN[7] [8]VARCHAR2[8]
 );
[3]/* Updates DBCR table */[3]
[4]PROCEDURE[4] [5]DBCR_TRANSACTION;[5]
[3]/* Clears the PL Table and resets in Binary Integer */[3]
[4]PROCEDURE[4] [5]CLR_PL_TABLE;[5]

-- PL/SQL Specification
[9]TYPE id_TabType IS TABLE OF dbcrs.id%TYPE INDEX BY BINARY_INTEGER;
  ptr_DBCR_ID     BINARY_INTEGER := 0;
  tab_DBCR_ID     id_TabType;
  tab_Empty       id_TabType; -- This table is used to clear the table

  TYPE cd_TabType IS TABLE OF dbcrs.dstat_cd%TYPE INDEX BY BINARY_INTEGER;
  tab_DSTAT_CD    cd_TabType;
  tab_UpdFlg      cd_TabType;[9]
END DBCR_CASCADE;
/
```

FIGURE 7-13. *Annotated contents of <file prefix>.PKS file created using the hybrid declarative approach*

```
c:\aristmpl\application\ss\pack\CH7_hybrid_decl.pkb
--
-- Generated for Oracle 8 on Thu Jul 23  14:22:27 1998 by Server Generator

PROMPT Creating [1]Package Body[1] [2]'DBCR_CASCADE'[2]
CREATE OR REPLACE [1]PACKAGE BODY[1] [2]DBCR_CASCADE[2] IS
[10]c_Status_To_Cascade CONSTANT VARCHAR2(15) := 'CLOSED';[10]
-- Sub-Program Units
[3]/* Increments Binary Integer and Loads PL Table */[3]
[4]PROCEDURE[4] [5]DBCR_ROW[5]
([6]P_ID[6] [7]IN[7] [8]NUMBER[8]
,[6]P_CD[6] [7]IN[7] [8]VARCHAR2[8]
)
```

FIGURE 7-14. *Annotated contents of <file prefix>.PKB file created using the hybrid declarative approach*

```
 IS
-- PL/SQL Block
BEGIN
[11]IF P_CD = 'CLOSED' THEN
    ptr_DBCR_ID := ptr_DBCR_ID + 1;
    tab_DBCR_ID(ptr_DBCR_ID) := p_ID;
    tab_DSTAT_CD(ptr_DBCR_ID) := p_CD;
        tab_UpdFlg(ptr_DBCR_ID) := 'N';
    END IF;[11]
END DBCR_ROW;

[3]/* Updates DBCR table */[3]
[4]PROCEDURE[4] [5]DBCR_TRANSACTION[5]
IS
-- PL/SQL Specification
[12]CURSOR cur_rel_dbcr(pc_DBCR_ID IN NUMBER) IS
    SELECT child_dbcr_id, rel_type
      FROM DBCR_DBCRS
     WHERE parent_dbcr_id = pc_DBCR_ID;[12]
-- PL/SQL Block
BEGIN
[11]FOR i IN 1..ptr_DBCR_ID LOOP
      FOR c IN cur_rel_dbcr(tab_DBCR_ID(i)) LOOP
       IF c.rel_type = 'SUB' AND tab_UpdFlg(i) != 'Y' THEN
        tab_UpdFlg(i) := 'Y';
        UPDATE DBCRS SET DSTAT_CD = tab_DSTAT_CD(i)
         WHERE id = c.child_dbcr_id;
    END IF;
      END LOOP;
    END LOOP;
    clear_pl_tbl;[11]
END DBCR_TRANSACTION;

[3]/* Clears the PL Table and resets in Binary Integer */[3]
[4]PROCEDURE[4] [5]CLR_PL_TABLE[5]
IS
-- PL/SQL Block
[11]BEGIN
    ptr_DBCR_ID := 0;
    tab_DBCR_ID := tab_Empty;[11]
END CLR_PL_TABLE

-- PL/SQL Block

END DBCR_CASCADE;
/
```

FIGURE 7-14. *Annotated contents of <file prefix>.PKB file created using the hybrid declarative approach* (continued)

Number	Feature	Source Using Dialogs	Source Using Properties Palette
1	PL/SQL definition type	PACKAGE DEFINITION TYPE TAB Field: Type of definition	PACKAGE DEFINITION Property: Type
2	PL/SQL definition name	PACKAGE DEFINITION NAME TAB Field: Name	PACKAGE DEFINITION Property: Implementation Name
3	PL/SQL Purpose of sub program unit	PROCEDURE DEFINITON NAME TAB Field: Purpose	PROCEDURE DEFINITON Property: Purpose
4	Procedure sub program unit type	NO SOURCE	PROCEDURE DEFINTION Property: Type
5	Procedure sub program unit name	NO SOURCE	PROCEDURE DEFINTION Property: Implementation Name of the Sub Program Unit
6	Argument name	PROCEDURE DEFINITON ARGUMENT TAB Field: Arguments	PROCEDURE DEFINTION ARGUMENT Property: Name
7	Argument type	PROCEDURE DEFINITON ARGUMENT TAB Field: Argument type	PROCEDURE DEFINTION ARGUMENT Property: Input Output
8	Argument datatype	PROCEDURE DEFINITON ARGUMENT TAB Field: Datatype	PROCEDURE DEFINTION ARGUMENT Property: Datatype
9	PL/SQL table and variable declarations	NO SOURCE	PACKAGE DEFINITION Property: Package Specification

TABLE 7-5. *Source of Generated Code Using the Hybrid Declarative Approach*

Number	Feature	Source Using Dialogs	Source Using Properties Palette
10	Private package variables	NO SOURCE	PACKAGE DEFINITION Property: PL/SQL Block
11	Execution and exception sections of procedure sub program unit body	NO SOURCE	PROCEDURE DEFINITION Property: PL/SQL Block
12	Declaration section of procedure sub program unit body	NO SOURCE	PROCEDURE DEFINITION Property: Package Specification

TABLE 7-5. *Source of Generated Code Using the Hybrid Declarative Approach* (continued)

Steps to Create This Package Using the Hybrid Declarative Approach

Using the steps that follow, you will be able to re-create the sample package. Since there is more than one way to accomplish this task, we focused on defining steps that minimize the amount of time required to create the definition, while still taking advantage of the new features of release 2. We have chosen to use the dialogs for creating each definition and then to use the Properties Palette to enter the remaining information about the definition that cannot be entered through the dialogs.

1. Create individual procedure definitions for each of the procedures contained within the package. Refer to Chapter 5 for assistance with this task. In this example, each procedure was defined using the free format method. Be sure to set the *restrict reference* properties to **No** and the *scope* property to **Public** when completing each definition.

2. In the Design Editor (DE), click on the Server Model tab.

3. Create a new package definition (available under PL/SQL definitions) by pressing the Create icon in the Design Editor toolbar. This will launch a set of dialogs that will gather all of the necessary information required for the package definition. The following steps detail the settings used for this example.

4. The Name dialog is the dialog that will be displayed first. Using this dialog, you will be able to specify a short name for the package definition that will be used for naming generated files (*Short name of the PL/SQL definition* = **CH7_HYBRID_DECL**). Next, you can specify a unique name for the package definition (*Name* = **CH7_HYBRID_DECL**) and the purpose or short description of the package definition (*Purpose* = **Performs cascade update when DBCR_CD is updated**). Last, specify the name you would like to use when creating the package definition (*Implementation name* = **DBCR_CASCADE**). This name will be used in the header of the program unit. Figure 7-15 shows the Name dialog used for this example. When you have completed this dialog, click Next.

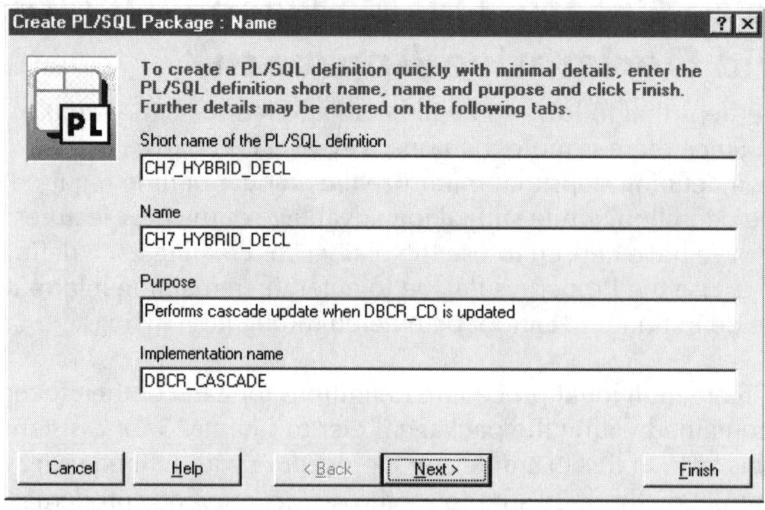

FIGURE 7-15. *Name dialog—hybrid declarative example*

5. The Type dialog is the second dialog that will be displayed. Using this dialog, you will be able to specify that you would like to define a package definition (*Type of definition* = **Package**). Also, you can specify that you would like to define the package using the declarative method (*How the PL/SQL will be defined* = **Declarative**). Figure 7-16 shows the Type dialog used for this example. When you have completed this dialog, click Next.
6. The Exceptions dialog is the third dialog that will be displayed. We did not have any exceptions in our example. Click Next to skip this dialog.
7. The Data dialog is the fourth dialog that will be displayed. We did not choose to define the variables using this dialog on our example and instead used the *package specification* property covered in step 10. Click Next to skip this dialog.
8. The Goodbye dialog is the last dialog that will be displayed. This dialog provides you with three different ways that you can exit the dialogs you have just used to define the package definition. Select

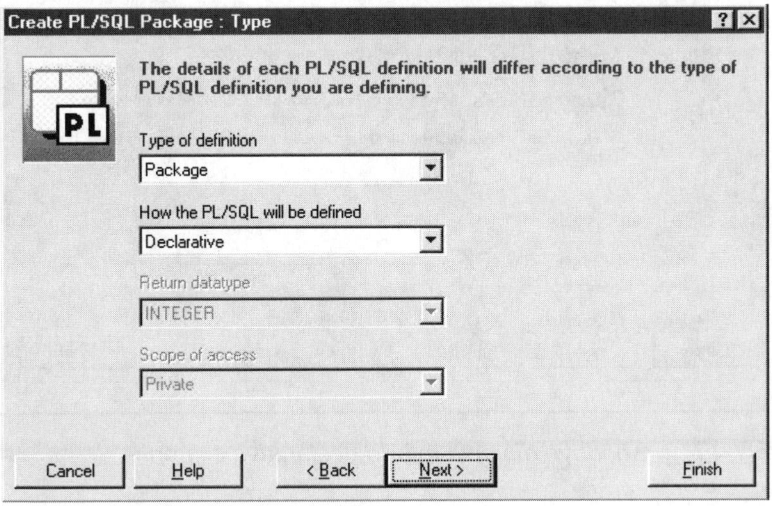

FIGURE 7-16. *Type dialog—hybrid declarative example*

option the first (*Create the PL/SQL definition from the information provided*) to create the PL/SQL definition and click Finish. Figure 7-17 shows the Goodbye dialog used for this example.

NOTE
*You could alternatively select the third option (*Create the PL/SQL definition and then invoke the Logic Editor to edit the definition*). If you choose to define the package using this option, you can generate once you've completed defining the package using this editor.*

9. Switch to Properties Palette from the dialogs. Do this by pressing the Property Dialogs/Palettes icon in the Design Editor toolbar.

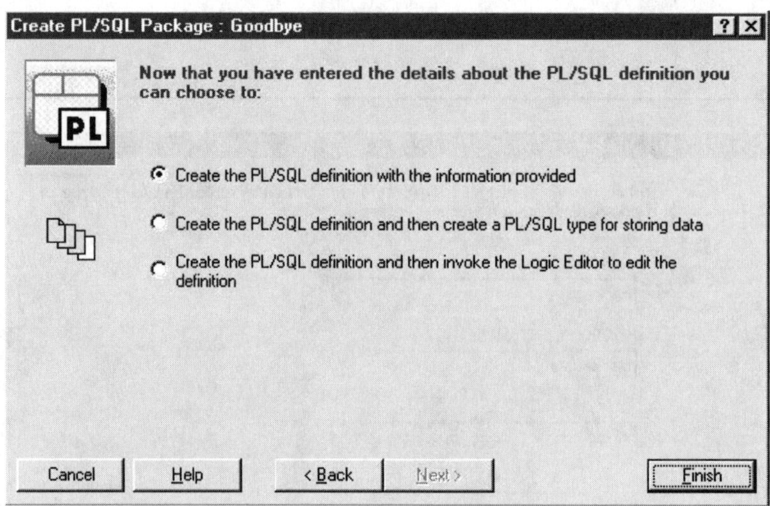

FIGURE 7-17. *Goodbye dialog—hybrid declarative example*

10. Define the package declarations in the *package specification* property of the package definition. Do this by navigating to the *package specification* property and, using a text editor, entering the package declarations. This should include the contents between the superscript nines in Figure 7-13.

11. Define the private package variable in the *PL/SQL Block* property of the package definition. Do this by navigating to the *PL/SQL Block* property and, using a text editor, entering the private package variable. This should include the contents between the superscript tens in Figure 7-14.

12. Include each of the procedures as sub program units. Do this by navigating to the sub program units of the package definition. Include each of the procedure definitions in the sub program units by pressing the Create icon in the Design Editor and then completing the dialog. Be sure to include the procedure definitions in the specific order you would like them to appear in the generated code. You can do this by using the dialog or by manually setting the *call sequence* property of each sub program unit definition. Also be sure that the *method of use* property of each sub program unit definition is set to **Include**. Figure 7-18 shows the Module Networks dialog used in this example.

13. We suggest that you create a PL/SQL implementation item for this package definition next. This is not a mandatory step, but it is very useful if you intend to manage database objects using databases and schema owner accounts defined within the Designer Repository. To do this, you will need to select the DB Admin tab and then navigate to the correct Oracle database and user under that database. Add this package to the package implementation schema objects for that user by pressing the Create icon in the Design Editor toolbar and then completing the dialogs.

14. Generate the package definition.

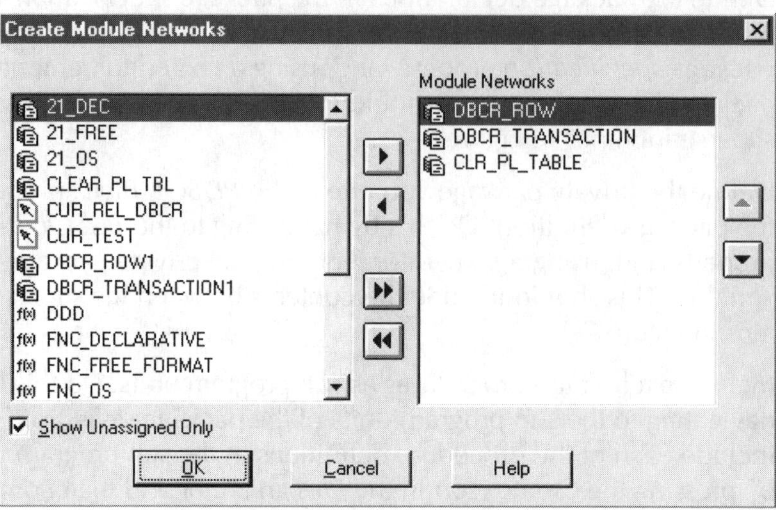

FIGURE 7-18. *Module Networks dialog*

The Pure Declarative Approach

We are calling the second approach pure because when using this approach, the goal is to define as much as possible in the declarative fashion. This includes

- Variables
- Constants
- PL/SQL tables
- PL/SQL records
- Cursors
- User exceptions
- Procedures/functions declarations and definitions

Developers benefit from using this approach by

- Increasing default documentation. Each repository definition has default documentation that can be enhanced by a developer.
- Increasing the opportunity to reuse code. PL/SQL tables, PL/SQL records, and cursors can be defined once and used by multiple PL/SQL definitions.
- Increasing the opportunity to perform customized impact analysis. Since each definition is stored in the Designer Repository, it can be accessed using an API utility to be included in custom impact analysis reporting.

These advantages do come at a cost. Typically, usage of the pure declarative approach requires increased development time, higher tolerance for dealing with generation problems and post-generation modifications, and increased maintenance time. These factors combined can offset an incremental benefit gained by using this method.

We used the pure declarative approach to generate the same sample package that we used previously. The package and all of its components were defined using the declarative method. With the release we had available at the time of this writing, we could not successfully create the package in the database without some post-generation modifications to clean up some generation problems. However, this example is useful for illustrating what can be produced from a pure implementation of the declarative method. We assume the problems we ran into will be fixed in a future release of Designer. Also, in order to show more complete examples of what can be declared, we have added a few additional constructs to the example that we have been using in this chapter.

Generating the sample package using the declarative method creates three files. In this example, the three files created are

- <file prefix>.SQL Executes the <file prefix>.PKS and <file prefix>.PKB files
- <file prefix>.PKS Contains the package specification

- <file prefix>.PKB Contains the package body

NOTE
<file prefix> is a name that you specify when generating server-side objects. This name will be given to all files created during that execution of the Server Generator.

Figure 7-19 displays the contents of the <file prefix>.PKS file. Figure 7-20 displays the contents of the <file prefix>.PKB file. The superscript numbers correspond to properties in the package definition, which created this file. See Table 7-6 for specific mapping of the generated code.

```
c:\aristmpl\application\ss\pack\CH7_pure_decl.pks
--
-- Generated for Oracle 8 on Fri Aug 14  15:23:49 1998 by Server
Generator
PROMPT Creating [1]Package[1] [2]'DBCR_CASCADE'[2]
CREATE OR REPLACE [1]PACKAGE[1] [2]DBCR_CASCADE[2] IS
-- Datastructure Definitions
TYPE [3]ID_TABTYPE[3] IS [4]TABLE[4] OF [5]DBCRS[5].[6]ID%TYPE[6] INDEX BY BINARY_INTEGER;
TYPE [3]CD_TABTYPE[3] IS [4]TABLE[4] OF [5]DBCRS[5].[6]DSTAT_CD%TYPE[6] INDEX BY BINARY_INTEGER;
TYPE [29]EXAMPLE_REC[29] IS [30]RECORD[30]
 ([32]KEEP_DATA_FLAG[32] [31]DBCRS[31].[33]KEEP_DATA_FLAG[33]%TYPE
 ,[32]REQUESTED_BY_PER_ID[32] [31]DBCRS[31].[33]REQUESTED_BY_PER_ID[33]%TYPE
 ,[32]D2K_UPD_FLAG[32] [31]DBCRS[31].[33]D2K_UPD_FLAG[33]%TYPE
 ,[32]APP_ID[32] [31]DBCRS[31].[33]APP_ID[33]%TYPE
 ,[32]DSTAT_CD[32] [31]DBCRS[31].[33]DSTAT_CD[33]%TYPE
 ,[32]NUM[32] [31]DBCRS[31].[33]NUM[33]%TYPE
```

FIGURE 7-19. *Annotated contents of <file prefix>.PKS file created using the pure declarative approach*

```
,[32]ASSIGNED_TO_PER_ID[32] [31]DBCRS[31].[33]ASSIGNED_TO_PER_ID[33]%TYPE
,[32]COMPLETED_DATE[32] [31]DBCRS[31].[33]COMPLETED_DATE[33]%TYPE
,[32]ID[32] [31]DBCRS[31].[33]ID[33]%TYPE
,[32]VER_ID[32] [31]DBCRS[31].[33]VER_ID[33]%TYPE
,[32]DBCR_DESC[32] [31]DBCRS[31].[33]DBCR_DESC[33]%TYPE
);

-- Program Data
[7]PTR_DBCR_ID[7] [8]BINARY_INTEGER[8] := [9]0[9];
[7]TAB_EMPTY[7] [10]PKG_DECL_PURE.ID_TABTYPE[10];
[7]TAB_DSTAT_CD[7] [10]PKG_DECL_PURE.CD_TABTYPE[10];
[7]TAB_UPDFLG[7] [10]PKG_DECL_PURE.CD_TABTYPE[10];
[7]TAB_DBCR_ID[7] [10]PKG_DECL_PURE.ID_TABTYPE[10];
[7]EXAMPLE_NUMBER[7] [8]NUMBER[8]([26]5[26], [40]2[40]);

-- Sub-Program Unit Declarations
[12]FUNCTION[12] [13]DBCRS_TO_CASCADE[13]
 ([14]P_DBCR_ID[14] [15]IN[15] [16]NUMBER[16]
 )
 [34]RETURN NUMBER[34];
[35]PRAGMA RESTRICT_REFERENCES[35] ([13]DBCRS_TO_CASCADE[13], [36]WNDS[36]);
[11]/* Increments Binary Integer and Loads PL Table */[11]
[12]PROCEDURE[12] [13]DBCR_ROW[13]
([14]P_ID[14] [15]IN[15] [16]NUMBER[16]
,[14]P_CD[14] [15]IN[15] [16]VARCHAR2[16]
);
[11]/* Updates DBCR table */[11]
[12]PROCEDURE[12] [13]DBCR_TRANSACTION;[13]
[11]/* Clears the PL Table and resets in Binary Integer */[11]
[12]PROCEDURE[12] [13]CLR_PL_TABLE[13];
END DBCR_CASCADE;
/
```

FIGURE 7-19. *Annotated contents of <file prefix>.PKS file created using the pure declarative approach* (continued)

```
--c:\aristmpl\application\ss\pack\CH7_pure_decl.pkb
--
-- Generated for Oracle 8 on Fri Aug 14  15:23:49 1998 by Server Generator

PROMPT Creating [1]Package Body[1] [2]'DBCR_CASCADE'[2]
CREATE OR REPLACE [1]PACKAGE BODY[1] [2]DBCR_CASCADE[2] IS
-- Program Data
[28] [7]c_Status_To_Cascade[7] [25]CONSTANT[25] [8]VARCHAR2[8]([26]15[26]) [27]:= 'CLOSED'[27];[28]-
-- Sub-Program Unit
[12]FUNCTION[12] [13]DBCRS_TO_CASCADE[13]
 ([14]P_DBCR_ID[14] [15]IN[15] [16]NUMBER[16]
 )
 [34]RETURN NUMBER[34]
 IS
-- Program Data
[37]V_RETURN[37] [38]NUMBER[38]([39]5[39]);

[17]-- PL/SQL Block
BEGIN
SELECT COUNT(*) INTO v_Return
  FROM DBCR_DBCRS
 WHERE parent_dbcr_id = p_DBCR_ID;
RETURN(v_Return); [17]
END [13]DBCRS_TO_CASCADE[13];

[11]/* Increments Binary Integer and Loads PL Table */[11]
[12]PROCEDURE[12] [13]DBCR_ROW[13]
([14]P_ID[14] [15]IN[15] [16]NUMBER[16]
,[14]P_CD[14] [15]IN[15] [16]VARCHAR2[16]
)
 IS
-- PL/SQL Block
[17]BEGIN
IF P_CD = c_Status_To_Cascade THEN
    ptr_DBCR_ID := ptr_DBCR_ID + 1;
    tab_DBCR_ID(ptr_DBCR_ID) := p_ID;
    tab_DSTAT_CD(ptr_DBCR_ID) := p_CD;
        tab_UpdFlg(ptr_DBCR_ID) := 'N';
    END IF;[17]
END DBCR_ROW;
/
```

FIGURE 7-20. *Annotated contents of <file prefix>.PKB file created using the pure declarative approach*

```
[11]/* Updates DBCR table */[11]
[12]PROCEDURE[12] [13]DBCR_TRANSACTION[13]
IS
-- Sub-Program Unit Declarations
[23]Cursor CUR_REL_DBCR
 (PC_DBCR IN NUMBER
 );[23]
--Sub-Program Units
[18]CURSOR[18] [19]CUR_REL_DBCR[19]
([20]PC_DBCR_ID[20] [21]IN[21] [22]NUMBER[22]
)
 IS
[24]SELECT child_dbcr_id, rel_type
 FROM DBCR_DBCRS
 WHERE parent_dbcr_id = pc_DBCR_ID;[24]
-- PL/SQL Block
[17]BEGIN
FOR i IN 1..ptr_DBCR_ID LOOP
      FOR c IN cur_rel_dbcr(tab_DBCR_ID(i)) LOOP
       IF c.rel_type = 'SUB' AND tab_UpdFlg(i) != 'Y' THEN
        tab_UpdFlg(i) := 'Y';
        UPDATE DBCRS SET DSTAT_CD = tab_DSTAT_CD(i)
         WHERE id = c.child_dbcr_id;
    END IF;
      END LOOP;
    END LOOP;
    clr_pl_table;[17]
END DBCR_TRANSACTION;

[11]/* Clears the PL Table and resets in Binary Integer */[11]
[12]PROCEDURE[12] [13]CLR_PL_TABLE[13]
IS
-- PL/SQL Block
[17]BEGIN
ptr_DBCR_ID := 0;
    tab_DBCR_ID := tab_Empty;[17]
END CLR_PL_TABLE;
-- PL/SQL Block
END DBCR_CASCADE;
/
```

FIGURE 7-20. *Annotated contents of <file prefix>.PKB file created using the pure declarative approach* (continued)

Number	Feature	Source Using Dialogs	Source Using Properties Palette
1	PL/SQL definition type	PACKAGE DEFINITION TYPE TAB Field: Type of definition	PACKAGE DEFINITION Property: Type
2	PL/SQL definition name	PACKAGE DEFINITION NAME TAB Field: Name	PACKAGE DEFINITION Property: Implementation Name
3	PL/SQL table name	PACKAGE DEFINITION PL/SQL TABLE Field: PL/SQL table name	PACKAGE DEFINITION DATASTRUCTURE Property: Name
4	PL/SQL table declaration	PACKAGE DEFINITION PL/SQL TYPE Field: Which PL/SQL type do you want to create?	PACKAGE DEFINITION DATASTRUCTURE Property: Type
5	Table reference	PACKAGE DEFINITION PL/SQL TABLE Field: Table	PACKAGE DEFINITION DATASTRUCTURE ITEM Property: Table
6	Column reference	PACKAGE DEFINITION PL/SQL TABLE Field: Column	PACKAGE DEFINITION DATASTRUCTURE ITEM Property: Column
7	Variable name	PACKAGE DEFINITION DATA TAB Field: Declaration name	PACKAGE DEFINITION PROGRAM DATA Property: Name

TABLE 7-6. *Source of Generated Code Using the Pure Declarative Approach*

Number	Feature	Source Using Dialogs	Source Using Properties Palette
8	Variable datatype	PACKAGE DEFINITION DATA TAB Field: Datatype Note: The Defined by field must be set to **datatype**	PACKAGE DEFINITION PROGRAM DATA Property: Datatype
9	Variable default value	PACKAGE DEFINITION DATA TAB Field: Default Value Note: The Defined by field must be set to **datatype**	PACKAGE DEFINITION PROGRAM DATA Property: Default Value
10	Variable declaration type	PACKAGE DEFINITION DATA TAB Field: Datastructure Note: The Defined by field must be set to **datastructure**	PACKAGE DEFINITION PROGRAM DATA Property: Datastructure
11	PL/SQL purpose of procedure sub program unit	PROCEDURE DEFINITION NAME TAB Field: Purpose	PROCEDURE DEFINITION Property: Purpose
12	Procedure sub program unit type	PROCEDURE DEFINITION TYPE TAB Field: Type of definition	PROCEDURE DEFINITION Property: Type
13	Procedure sub program unit name	PROCEDURE DEFINITION DATA TAB Field: Name	PROCEDURE DEFINITION Property: Implementation Name of the Sub Program Unit

TABLE 7-6. *Source of Generated Code Using the Pure Declarative Approach* (continued)

Number	Feature	Source Using Dialogs	Source Using Properties Palette
14	Procedure sub program unit argument name	PROCEDURE DEFINITION ARGUMENT TAB Field: Arguments	PROCEDURE DEFINITION ARGUMENT Property: Name
15	Procedure sub program unit argument type	PROCEDURE DEFINITION ARGUMENT TAB Field: Argument Type	PROCEDURE DEFINITION ARGUMENT Property: Input Output
16	Procedure sub program unit argument datatype	PROCEDURE DEFINITION ARGUMENT TAB Field: Datatype	PROCEDURE DEFINITION ARGUMENT Property: Datatype
17	Execution and exception sections of sub program unit body	NO SOURCE	PROCEDURE DEFINITION Property: PL/SQL Block
18	Cursor sub program unit declaration for procedure	CURSOR DEFINITION DATA TAB Field: Name	CURSOR DEFINITION Property: Type
19	Cursor sub program unit name	CURSOR DEFINITION ARGUMENT TAB Field: Arguments	CURSOR DEFINITION ARGUMENT Property: Implementation Name of the Sub Program Unit
20	Cursor sub program unit argument name	CURSOR DEFINITION ARGUMENT TAB Field: Arguments	CURSOR DEFINITION ARGUMENT Property: Name

TABLE 7-6. *Source of Generated Code Using the Pure Declarative Approach* (continued)

Number	Feature	Source Using Dialogs	Source Using Properties Palette
21	Cursor sub program unit argument type	CURSOR DEFINITION ARGUMENT TAB Field: Argument type	CURSOR DEFINITION ARGUMENT Property: Input Output
22	Cursor sub program unit argument datatype	CURSOR DEFINITION ARGUMENT TAB Field: Datatype	CURSOR DEFINITION ARGUMENT Property: Datatype
23	Invalid and unneeded cursor declaration. This needs to be removed by hand after generation. Generated into the package body when a cursor definition is added to the package. This happened in the version available when this book was written (v2.1.1). It may not be generated in future versions.		
24	Cursor sub program unit body	NO SOURCE	CURSOR DEFINITION Property: PL/SQL Block

TABLE 7-6. *Source of Generated Code Using the Pure Declarative Approach* (continued)

Number	Feature	Source Using Dialogs	Source Using Properties Palette
25	Constant variable indicator	PACKAGE DEFINITION DATA TAB Field: Type Radio Dial (Set to **Constant**)	PACKAGE DEFINITION PROGRAM DATA Property: Construct Type (Set to **Constant**)
26	Size of variable	PACKAGE DEFINITION DATA TAB Field: Maximum Length	PACKAGE DEFINITION PROGRAM DATA Property: Length
27	Variable default value	PACKAGE DEFINITION DATA TAB Field: Default	PACKAGE DEFINITION PROGRAM DATA Property: Default
28	Package variable declaration placed in body.	NO SOURCE	PACKAGE DEFINITION PROGRAM DATA Property: Scope (Set to **Private**)
29	Record type name	PACKAGE DEFINITION CREATE/EDIT DATASTRUCTURE DIALOG Field: Name of the PL/SQL record	PACKAGE DEFINITION DATASTRUCTURE Property: Name

TABLE 7-6. *Source of Generated Code Using the Pure Declarative Approach* (continued)

Number	Feature	Source Using Dialogs	Source Using Properties Palette
30	Datastructure type indicator	PACKAGE DEFINITION CREATE DATASTRUCTURE DIALOG Field: PL/SQL Type Radio group Selection	PACKAGE DEFINITION DATASTRUCTURE Property: Type (Set to **PL/SQL Record**)
31	Record type definition – table name	PACKAGE DEFINITION CREATE DATASTRUCTURE DIALOG Field: Table on which to base the PL/SQL record	PACKAGE DEFINITION DATASTRUCTURE ITEMS Property: Table
32	Record type definition – field name	PACKAGE DEFINITION CREATE DATASTRUCTURE DIALOG Field: Field Name	PACKAGE DEFINITION DATASTRUCTURE ITEMS Property: Name
33	Record type definition – column name	PACKAGE DEFINITION CREATE DATASTRUCTURE DIALOG Field: Column name	PACKAGE DEFINITION DATASTRUCTURE ITEMS Property: Column
34	Return declaration	FUCTION DEFINITION TYPE TAB Field: Return datatype	FUNCTION DEFINITION Property: Return Type

TABLE 7-6. *Source of Generated Code Using the Pure Declarative Approach* (continued)

Number	Feature	Source Using Dialogs	Source Using Properties Palette
35	Restrict references declaration	NO SOURCE	FUNCTION DEFINITION If any of the *restrict references* properties are set to **Yes**
36	WNDS parameter in the restrict references declaration (Note: this works the same for WNPS, RNDS, WNDS types, too.)	NO SOURCE	FUNCTION DEFINITION Property: WNDS? Set to **Yes**
37	Variable name	FUNCTION DEFINITION DATA TAB Field: Declaration name	FUNCTION DEFINITION PROGRAM DATA Property: Name
38	Variable datatype	FUNCTION DEFINITION DATA TAB Field: Datatype Note: The Defined by field must be set to **datatype**	FUNCTION DEFINITION PROGRAM DATA Property: Datatype
39	Size of variable (sub program unit variable)	FUNCTION DEFINITION DATA TAB Field: Maximum length	FUNCTION DEFINITION PROGRAM DATA Property: Length
40	Decimal places (Precision) for NUMBER variable declaration	PL/SQL DIALOG DATA TAB Field: No. of Decimal Places	PROGRAM DATA DEFINITION Property: Decimal Places

TABLE 7-6. *Source of Generated Code Using the Pure Declarative Approach* (continued)

Steps to Create This Package Using the Pure Declarative Approach

Using the steps that follow, you will be able to re-create the sample package. Since there is more than one way to accomplish this task, we focused on defining steps that minimize the amount of time required to create the definition, while still taking advantage of the new features of release 2. We have chosen to use the dialogs for creating each definition and then to use the Properties Palette to enter the remaining information about the definition that cannot be entered through the dialogs.

1. Create individual procedure definitions for each of the procedures contained within the package. Refer to Chapter 5 for assistance with this task. In this example, each procedure was defined using the declarative method. Be sure to set the *restrict reference* properties to **No** and the *scope* property to **Public** when completing each definition.
2. In the Design Editor (DE), click on the Server Model tab.
3. Create a new package definition (available under PL/SQL definitions).
4. The Name dialog is the dialog that will be displayed first. Using this dialog, you will be able to specify a short name for the package definition that will be used for naming generated files (*Short name of the PL/SQL definition* = **CH7_PURE_DECL**). Next, specify a unique name for the package definition (*Name* = **CH7_PURE_DECL**) and the purpose or short description of the package definition (*Purpose* = **Performs cascade update when DBCR_CD is updated**). Last, specify the name you would like to use when creating the package definition (*Implementation name* = **DBCR_CASCADE**). This name will be used in the header of the program unit. Figure 7-21 shows the Name dialog used for this example. When you have completed this dialog, click Next.
5. The Type dialog is the second dialog that will be displayed. Using this dialog you will be able to specify that you would like to define a package definition (*Type of definition* = **Package**). Also, you can specify that you would like to define the package using the declarative method (*How the PL/SQL will be defined* = **Declarative**). Figure 7-22 shows the Type dialog used for this example. When you have completed this dialog, click Next.

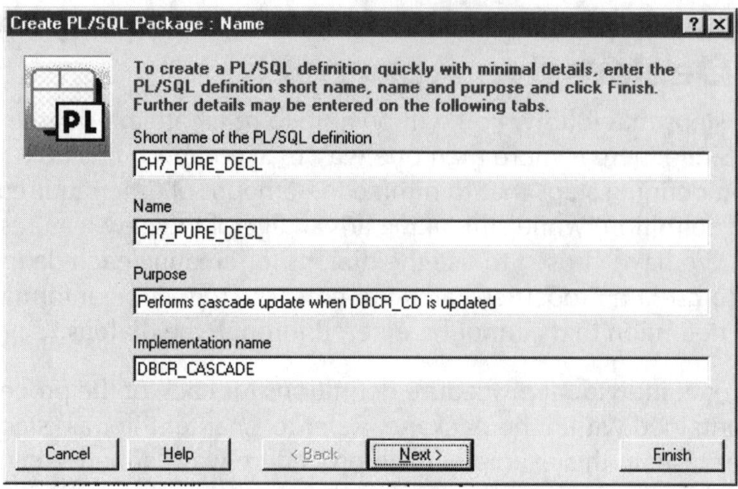

FIGURE 7-21. *Name dialog—pure declarative example*

6. The Exceptions dialog is the third dialog that will be displayed. We did not have any exceptions in our example. Click Next to skip this dialog.

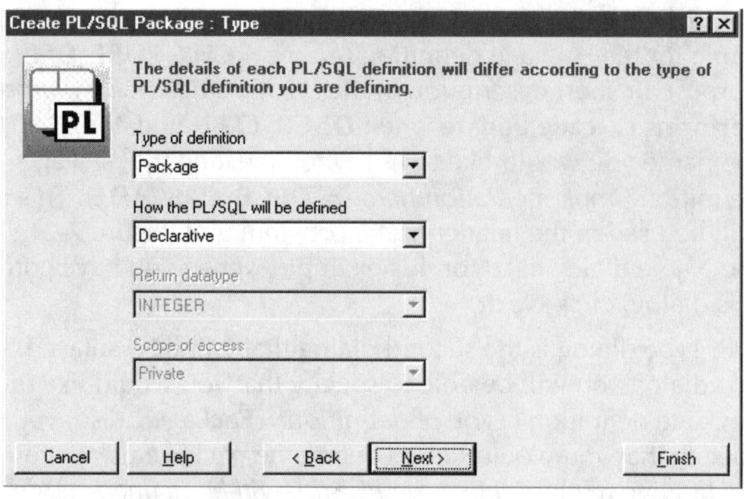

FIGURE 7-22. *Type dialog—pure declarative example*

7. The Data dialog is the fourth dialog that will be displayed. Use this dialog to create any variables that you want defined for the package. At this time, you can only create variables that are not based upon this package's datastructures because you have not created any datastructures for this package yet. After you have created the datastructures (in step 9), you will have to come back to this dialog to add any variables that are based on this package's datastructures. In the above example, we can create three variables at this time. Add these variables with the information in Table 7-7. Figure 7-23 shows the Data dialog used for this example. When you have completed this dialog, click Next.
8. The Goodbye dialog is the last dialog that will be displayed. This dialog provides you with three different ways that you can exit the dialogs you have just used to define the package definition. Select the first option (*Create the PL/SQL definition from the information provided*) to create the PL/SQL definition and click Finish. Figure 7-24 shows the Goodbye dialog used for this example.

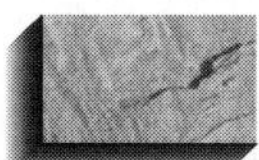

NOTE
*You could alternatively select the third option (*Create the PL/SQL definition and then invoke the Logic Editor to edit the definition*). If you choose to define the package using this option, you can generate once you've completed defining the package using this editor.*

Variable Name	Defined By	Datatype	Other Properties	Type
EXAMPLE_NUMBER	Datatype	NUMBER	*Length*: 5 *Dec. Places*: 2	Variable
ptr_DBCR_ID	Datatype	BINARY_INTEGER		Variable
C_Status_to_Cascade	Datatype	VARCHAR2	*Length*: 15 *Default*: CLOSED	Constant

TABLE 7-7. *Variable Property Settings for Pure Declarative Example*

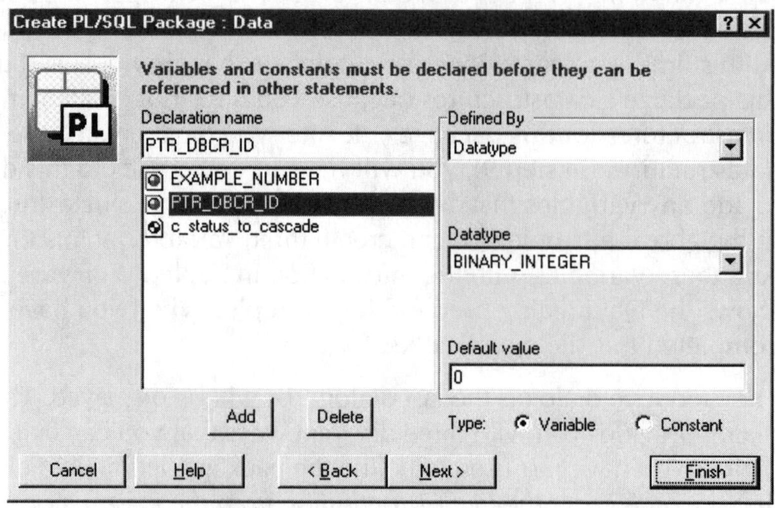

FIGURE 7-23. *Data dialog—pure declarative example*

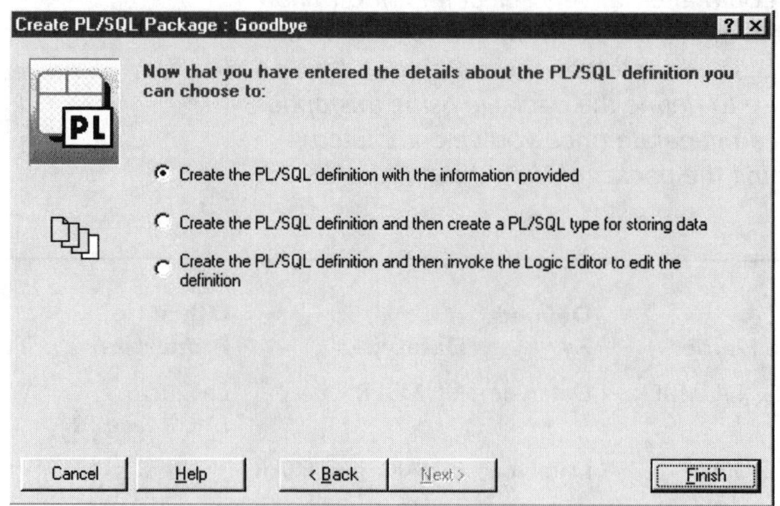

FIGURE 7-24. *Goodbye dialog—pure declarative example*

9. Next, create the PL/SQL table datastructures for the package. Navigate to the datastructure area of the package definition. Create a datastructure by pressing the Create icon in the Design Editor toolbar. The first dialog to be displayed is the Type dialog. Using this dialog you can specify that you would like to create a PL/SQL table datastructure. Select PL/SQL Table and click Next. Figure 7-25 shows the Type dialog used for this example.

10. The PL/SQL Table dialog is the second dialog that will be displayed. Using this dialog, you can enter the name of the PL/SQL table to be created (*PL/SQL table name* = **CD_TABTYPE**). Next, specify that the PL/SQL table will be defined using a column (*Defined By* = **Column**). Finally, specify the name of the table (*Table* = **DBCRS**) and column (*Column* = **DSTAT_CD**) that the PL/SQL table is to be based on. Figure 7-26 shows the PL/SQL Table dialog used for this example. When you have completed this dialog, click Finish.

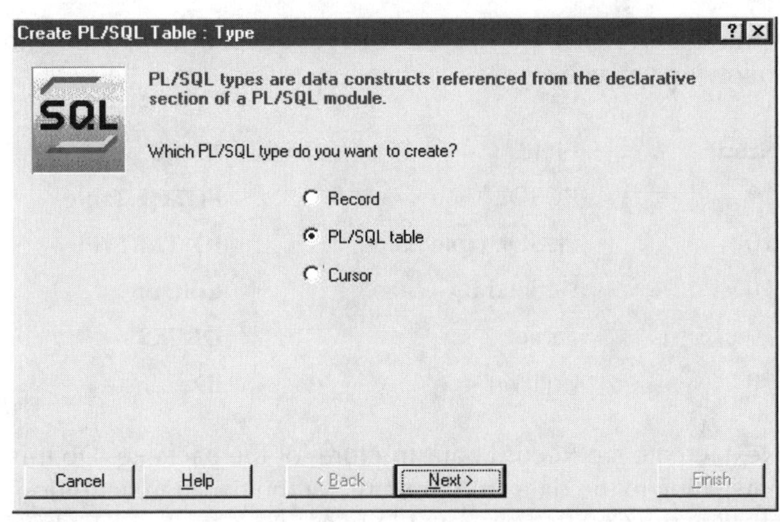

FIGURE 7-25. *PL/SQL datastructure: Type dialog—pure declarative example*

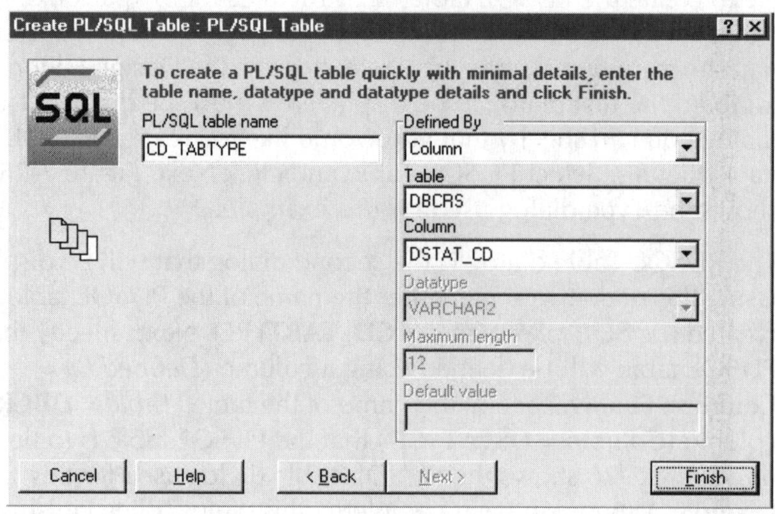

FIGURE 7-26. *PL/SQL Table dialog—pure declarative example*

11. For the above example, you will have to repeat steps 8–9 with the following values:

Step	Field	Value
9	PL/SQL Type	**PL/SQL Table**
10	PL/SQL table name	**ID_TABTYPE**
10	Defined By	**Column**
10	Table	**DBCRS**
10	Column	**ID**

12. Next, create the Record datastructure for the package. Do this by navigating to the data structure area of the package definition and clicking the Create icon in the Design Editor toolbar. The first dialog to be displayed is the Type dialog. Using this dialog, you can specify that you would like to create a Record datastructure. Select **Record** and click Next. Figure 7-27 shows the Type dialog used for this example.

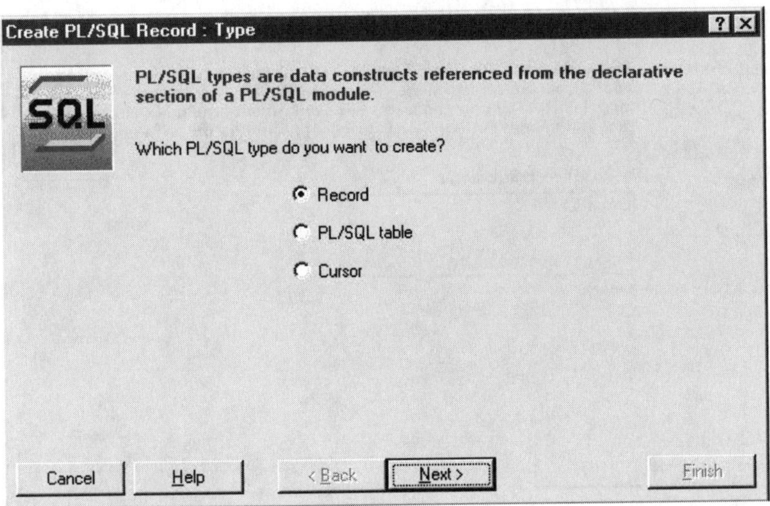

FIGURE 7-27. *PL/SQL Record: Type dialog—pure declarative example*

13. The PL/SQL Record: Name dialog is the second dialog that will be displayed. Using this dialog, you can enter the name of the PL/SQL record to be created (*Name of the PL/SQL record* = **EXAMPLE_REC**). Also, specify the table that you would like to base the record on (*Table on which to base the PL/SQL record* = **DBCRS**). Figure 7-28 shows the PL/SQL record dialog used for this example. When you have completed this dialog, click Next.

14. The PL/SQL Record: Fields dialog is the third dialog that will be displayed. Using this dialog, you can specify which columns in the table will be included in the PL/SQL record. In this example, we left all of the table's columns in the PL/SQL record. To do this, you just need to click Finish. Figure 7-29 shows the Fields dialog used for this example.

15. Now create the variables that will be based upon the datastructures you created in the above steps. In this example, we created four variables based upon the two PL/SQL table definitions. You can do this by reentering the Package dialogs and navigating to the Data tab

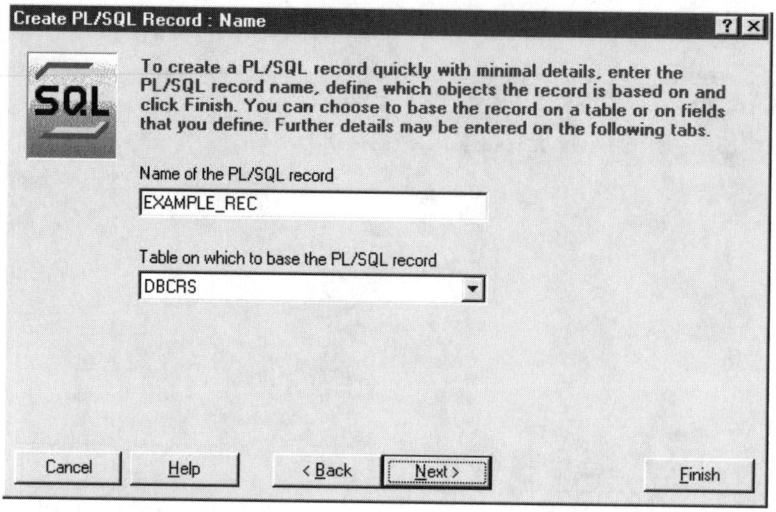

FIGURE 7-28. *PL/SQL Record: Name dialog—pure declarative example*

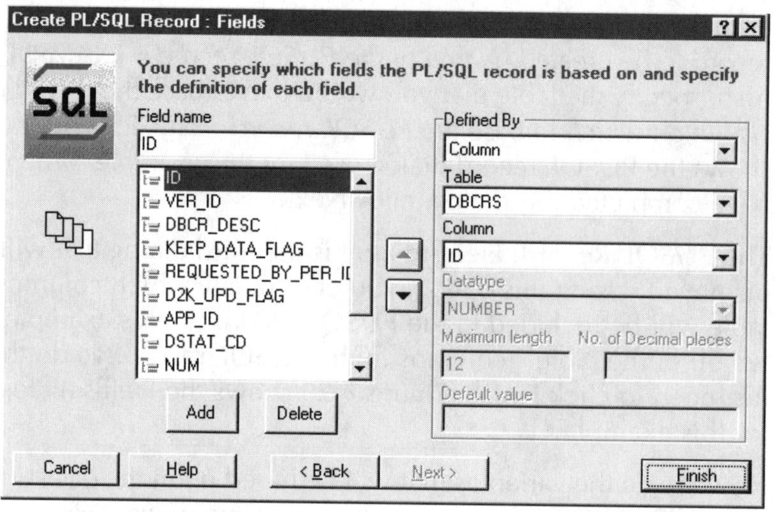

FIGURE 7-29. *PL/SQL Record: Fields dialog—pure declarative example*

(you saw this before in step 7). The settings needed to create these variables are outlined in Table 7-8.

16. Include each of the procedure definitions in the package as sub program units by navigating to the *Sub Program Units* for the package and pressing the Create icon in the Design Editor and then completing the dialog. Be sure to include the procedure definitions in the specific order that you would like them to appear in the generated code. You can do this by using the dialog or by manually setting the *call sequence* property of each sub program unit definition. Also, be sure that the *method of use* property of each sub program unit definition is set to **Include**. (See Figure 7-30.)

17. We suggest that you create a PL/SQL implementation item for this package definition next. This is not a mandatory step, but it is very useful if you intend to manage database objects using databases and schema owner accounts defined within the Designer repository. To do this, you will need to select the DB Admin tab and then navigate to the correct Oracle database and user under that database. Add this package to the package implementation schema objects for that user by pressing the Create icon in the Design Editor toolbar and then completing the dialogs.

18. Generate the package definition.

19. If you plan to implement the generated DDL in the database, you need to modify the generated DDL first. Refer to the troubleshooting guide at the end of this chapter for assistance with this step.

Declaration Name	Defined By	Datastructure	Type
TAB_EMPTY	Datastructure	ID_TAB_TYPE	Variable
TAB_DSTAT_CD	Datastructure	CD_TAB_TYPE	Variable
TAB_UPDFLG	Datastructure	CD_TAB_TYPE	Variable
TAB_DBCR_ID	Datastructure	ID_TAB_TYPE	Variable

TABLE 7-8. *Property Settings for Datastructure Variables*

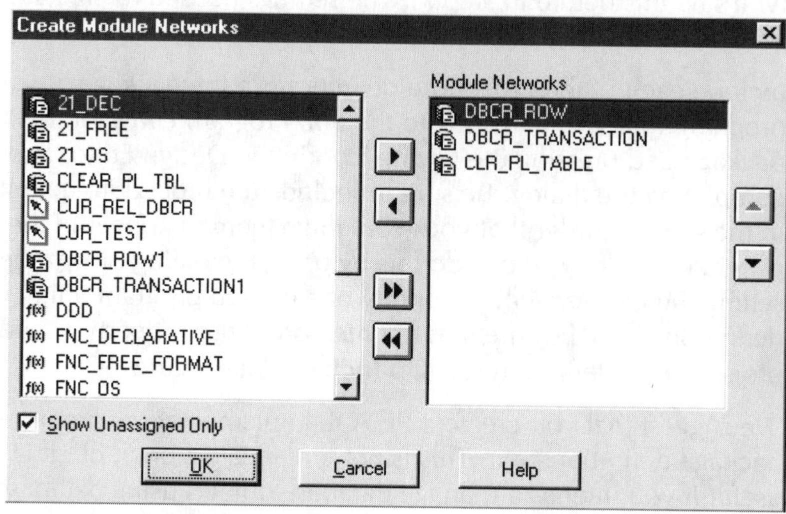

FIGURE 7-30. *Module network dialog—pure declarative example*

Program Data (Variables) Definition Sources

There are many ways that you can declare variables using declarative definitions in packages. The previous example only uses some of the possible techniques. Table 7-9 shows a list of the various declaration types, along with a brief description of each. The definition source can be set by the *defined by* property of the Data tab in the PL/SQL dialog or by one of the *defined by* or *definition* properties in the Program Data property sheet. Some of the sources (Table and Column) can only be set using the property sheet.

It is more straightforward to declare the variables directly using the definition properties. However, using some of the more sophisticated definition sources (domain, column, etc.) can save you time and trouble in the long run because you will know that the variable's declaration will match the definition of the column(s) in the database that it uses.

Definition Source	Description	Notes
Datatype	Uses the specified datatype (VARCHAR2, NUMBER, etc.)	
Domain	Uses the datatype of the specified domain to declare the variable.	When generated will look the same as a variable generated using the Datatype selection. However, the source of the definition is specified in the domain.
Datastructure	Creates a variable based on the specified custom data type (datastructure).	Used to create a PL/SQL table variable to be used with a table type declared as a datastructure.
Table	Declares a PL/SQL record type based on the specified table using the %ROWTYPE declaration.	Cannot be defined using the dialogs. You must use the property sheet to select this option.
Column	The variable declaration is based on a specified column using the %TYPE declaration.	Cannot be defined using the dialogs. You must use the property sheet to select this option.

TABLE 7-9. *Program Data (Variable) Definition Sources*

Design Capture

The Design Capture utility can create PL/SQL definitions in the repository based on program unit definitions located in one of two sources:

- Oracle database
- File system

Using the Design Capture utility for a package definition will create more than one PL/SQL definition in the Designer Repository. A PL/SQL definition will be created for the package, as well as each individual procedure and/or function contained within the package.

The package definition will be created using the declarative method. Each of the procedures and/or functions contained within the package body will be included as sub program units. Package declarations are inserted into the *package specification* property.

Each of the procedures and/or functions contained within the package body will be created using the free format method. Variable declarations are inserted into the *package specification* property of each procedure and/or function definition, not the *PL/SQL Block* property. This is one of the reasons that it is better to use the *package specification* property for variable declaration when using either free format or declarative methods.

Figure 7-31 is an annotated version of the sample package provided in Figure 7-1. The superscript numbers correspond to properties in the package definition, which are populated by the Design Capture utility. See Table 7-10 for specific mapping of the properties populated by the Design Capture utility.

```
CREATE OR REPLACE [1]PACKAGE[1] [2]dbcr_cascade[2] AS
  [3]PROCEDURE[3] [4]dbcr_row[4] ([5]P_ID[5] [6]IN[6] [7]NUMBER[7], [5]p_CD[5] [6]IN[6] [7]VARCHAR2[7]);
  [3]PROCEDURE[3] [4]dbcr_transaction[4];
  [3]PROCEDURE[3] [4]clear_pl_tbl[4];

  [8]TYPE id_TabType IS TABLE OF dbcrs.id%TYPE INDEX BY BINARY_INTEGER;
  ptr_DBCR_ID      BINARY_INTEGER := 0;
  tab_DBCR_ID      id_TabType;
  tab_Empty        id_TabType; -- This table is used to clear the table

  TYPE cd_TabType IS TABLE OF dbcrs.dstat_cd%TYPE INDEX BY BINARY_INTEGER;
  tab_DSTAT_CD     cd_TabType;
  tab_UpdFlg       cd_TabType;[8]

END dbcr_cascade;
/
CREATE OR REPLACE [1]PACKAGE BODY[1] [2]dbcr_cascade[2] AS
```

FIGURE 7-31. *Annotated Design Capture Example*

```
  [3]PROCEDURE[3] [4]dbcr_row[4]([5]P_ID[5] [6]IN[6] [7]NUMBER[7], [5]P_CD[5] [6]IN[6]
[7]VARCHAR2[7]) IS
  [9]BEGIN
    IF P_CD = 'CLOSED' THEN
    ptr_DBCR_ID := ptr_DBCR_ID + 1;
    tab_DBCR_ID(ptr_DBCR_ID) := p_ID;
    tab_DSTAT_CD(ptr_DBCR_ID) := p_CD;
        tab_UpdFlg(ptr_DBCR_ID) := 'N';
    END IF;[9]
END dbcr_row;

  [3]PROCEDURE[3] [4]dbcr_transaction[4] IS
    [10]CURSOR cur_rel_dbcr(pc_DBCR_ID IN NUMBER) IS
    SELECT child_dbcr_id, rel_type
      FROM DBCR_DBCRS
     WHERE parent_dbcr_id = pc_DBCR_ID;[10]

  [9]BEGIN
    FOR i IN 1..ptr_DBCR_ID LOOP
      FOR c IN cur_rel_dbcr(tab_DBCR_ID(i)) LOOP
    IF c.rel_type = 'SUB' AND tab_UpdFlg(i) != 'Y' THEN
        tab_UpdFlg(i) := 'Y';
        UPDATE DBCRS SET DSTAT_CD = tab_DSTAT_CD(i)
         WHERE id = c.child_dbcr_id;
    END IF;
      END LOOP;
    END LOOP;
    clear_pl_tbl;[9]
END dbcr_transaction;

  [3]PROCEDURE[3] [4]clear_pl_tbl[4] IS
  [9]BEGIN
    ptr_DBCR_ID := 0;
    tab_DBCR_ID := tab_Empty;[9]
  END clear_pl_tbl;

END dbcr_cascade;
/
```

FIGURE 7-31. *Annotated Design Capture Example* (continued)

Number	Feature	Source Using Dialogs	Source Using Properties Palette
1	PL/SQL definition type	PACKAGE DEFINITION TYPE TAB Field: Type of definition	PACKAGE DEFINITION Property: Type
2	PL/SQL definition name	PACKAGE DEFINITION NAME TAB Field: Name	PACKAGE DEFINITION Property: Implementation Name
3	Procedure sub program unit type	NO SOURCE	PROCEDURE DEFINTION Property: Type
4	Procedure sub program unit name	NO SOURCE	PROCEDURE DEFINTION Property: Implementation Name of the Sub Program Unit
5	Argument name	PROCEDURE DEFINITON ARGUMENT TAB Field: Arguments	PROCEDURE DEFINTION ARGUMENT Property: Name
6	Argument type	PROCEDURE DEFINITON ARGUMENT TAB Field: Argument type	PROCEDURE DEFINTION ARGUMENT Property: Input Output
7	Argument datatype	PROCEDURE DEFINITON ARGUMENT TAB Field: Datatype	PROCEDURE DEFINTION ARGUMENT Property: Datatype
8	PL/SQL table and variable declarations	NO SOURCE	PACKAGE DEFINITION Property: Package Specification

TABLE 7-10. *Properties Populated Using the Design Capture Utility*

Number	Feature	Source Using Dialogs	Source Using Properties Palette
9	Execution and exception sections of procedure sub program unit body	NO SOURCE	PROCEDURE DEFINITION Property: PL/SQL Block
10	Declaration section of procedure sub program unit body	NO SOURCE	PROCEDURE DEFINITION Property: Package Specification

TABLE 7-10. *Properties Populated Using the Design Capture Utility* (continued)

Steps to Create a Repository Definition Using the Design Capture Utility

1. In the Design Editor menu navigate to Generate → Capture Design Of → Server Model from Database.
2. Select the source of the design capture:
   - Database captures definitions in an Oracle database.
   - DDL file capture the contents of a DDL file.

   If you select the Database option, you will need to fill in the *username, password,* and *connect* properties. This will be used to query the database to determine what objects this user can capture the design of. You will then need to click the Objects tab and select the function definition and move it into the *Capture* field.

   If you select the DDL file option, you will need to select DDL File and then specify the path/filename of the DDL file to be captured in the *Name* field and the type/version of database in the *Type* field.
3. Select the database/schema owner in which to create the definition. Do this by setting the *capture objects into* property to the database schema owner you would like to create the package definition in.

4. When satisfied with your selections, click Start.
5. Select how you would like to process the captured package definition:
   - **Save** Commits the package definition to the repository
   - **Revert** Completes a rollback of the posted package definition
   - **Browse/Edit** Enables you to browse the posted package definition, make modifications, and then either commit or rollback

Generation Troubleshooting Guide

Problem	**Methods**	**Solution**
The PL/SQL definitions I included as sub program units are not showing in the package specification, only in the package body.	Declarative	Set the *scope* property on each PL/SQL definition you wish to reference in the package header to **PUBLIC**. The default setting for this property will include each PL/SQL definition as private to the package.
When I change the method of defining a PL/SQL definition from operating system file to either free format method or declarative method, it continues to generate the program unit definition using operating system file method.	Free Format and Declarative	Remove the path/filename from the *source path* property. If this property is populated, the package will always be generated using operating system file method, regardless of the value in the *free format declaration* property.
The cursor I included as a sub program unit to my package definition is not being declared at all.	Free Format	The Server generator ignores sub program units when using the free format method. Use the declarative method if you would like to generate the cursor declaration as a sub program unit.

Problem	Methods	Solution
The cursor I included as a sub program unit to a package component (procedure definition) is generating with two declarations.	Declarative	This is a bug. Remove the errant cursor declaration from the generated code.
The exceptions I entered as program data are generating at the beginning of the package body.	Declarative	The Server Generator is generating the declaration of a user defined exception. It will not use this information to create the exception section of the program unit.
When I try to add a variable in the Data Tab I am prompted to enter a default value for this constant when I try to save it. I don't want a default.	Declarative	Check the Variable button of the *Type* field at the lower right of the dialog. The default is Constant, so you always have to check this when you create a variable.

CHAPTER 8

Generating Triggers

This chapter is a detailed guide to help you generate triggers. In this chapter, we will cover

- How the Server Generator creates a trigger
- Generation and design capture of some example triggers
- The property settings used to generate each example
- Step-by-step instructions for creating the example using each method
- A troubleshooting guide to assist you with common generation problems

We think that it will be easier for you to understand the various methods if we use an example that at least looks like a real-world program. Therefore, we designed two example triggers that perform standard tasks that you might use in a real system.

NOTE
Example Description: *The triggers shown in this chapter call packaged procedures that perform a cascade update of the status of related records when a parent record is changed. The examples use DSTAT_CD in the DBCRS table from the example application provided with this book. When the status code is updated, the triggers call procedures in a package to perform the update (the package used is the same package that was used for an example in Chapter 7).*

These example triggers, shown in Figures 8-1 and 8-2, will be used in the sections that follow to show you a specific example of each method of creating a trigger.

```
CREATE OR REPLACE TRIGGER dbcr_stat_tran
AFTER UPDATE OF dstat_cd
ON dbcrs
DECLARE
BEGIN
  dbcr_cascade.dbcr_transaction;
END;
/
```

FIGURE 8-1. *Sample statement-level trigger*

```
CREATE OR REPLACE TRIGGER dbcr_stat_row
AFTER UPDATE OF dstat_cd
ON dbcrs
FOR EACH ROW
WHEN (dstat_cd <> 'NEW')
DECLARE
BEGIN
  dbcr_cascade.dbcr_row(:new.id, :new.dstat_cd);
END;
/
```

FIGURE 8-2. *Sample row-level trigger*

How the Server Generator Creates a Trigger

The process for generating a trigger differs slightly from the process for generating other server-side PL/SQL objects. Whereas other server-side

PL/SQL objects, such as a packages or procedures, are completely defined as PL/SQL definitions in the repository, triggers consist of two components:

- A relational table trigger definition
- A PL/SQL trigger definition

The relational table trigger definition creates the actual CREATE TRIGGER statement, including everything that is not in the body of the trigger. The PL/SQL trigger definition contains the trigger body of the trigger. Figure 8-3 illustrates how the Server Generator creates a trigger from definitions stored in the repository.

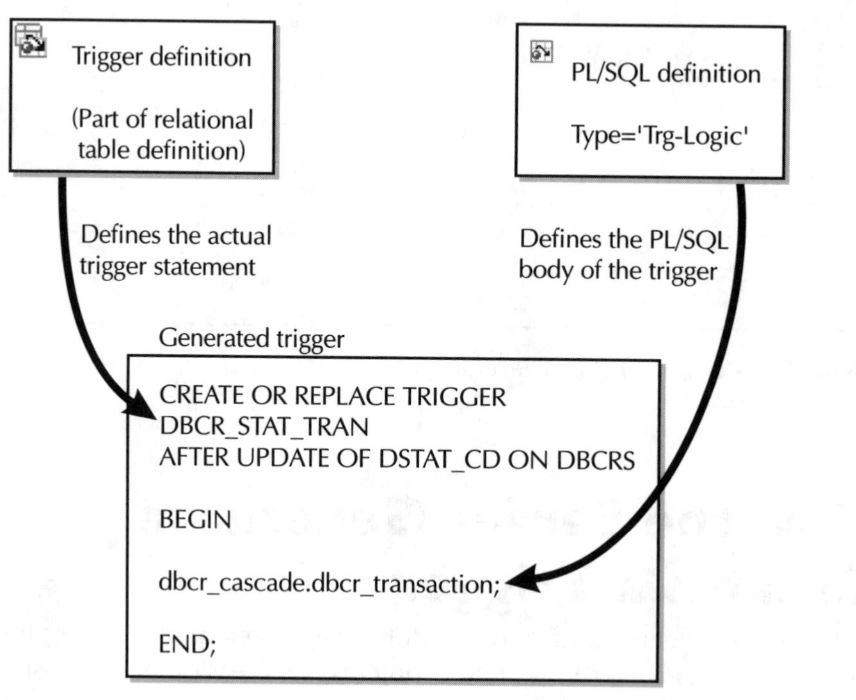

FIGURE 8-3. *How the Server Generator creates a trigger*

Statement-Level Trigger Generation Example

The only way to generate a trigger is to generate the relational table definition that it is associated with. In this example, the table is the DBCRS table from the example application. Generating the table will create numerous files, only two of which are important for trigger definitions:

- <file prefix>.SQL Executes the all of the files created when generating a table definition
- <file prefix>.TRG Contains the generated trigger definition(s)

NOTE
<file prefix> is a name that you specify when generating server-side objects. This name will be given to all files created during that execution of the Server Generator.

Figure 8-4 is an annotated version of the <file prefix>.TRG file. The superscript numbers correspond to properties in the trigger definition, which created this file. See Table 8-1 for specific mapping of the generated code.

```
PROMPT Creating 1Trigger1 2'DBCR_STAT_TRAN'2
CREATE OR REPLACE 1TRIGGER1 2DBCR_STAT_TRAN2 3AFTER3 4UPDATE4 OF
    5DSTAT_CD5ON 6DBCRS6
7BEGIN
dbcr_cascade.dbcr_transaction;
END;7
```

FIGURE 8-4. *Statement-level trigger generation example*

Number	Feature	Source Using Dialogs	Source Using Properties Palette
1	Trigger definition	NO SOURCE (Automatically generated for triggers)	NO SOURCE (Automatically generated for triggers)
2	Trigger name	NAME TAB Field: Name of the trigger	RELATIONAL TABLE TRIGGER DEFINITION Property: Name
3	When the trigger will fire	FIRES TAB Field: When the trigger will be fired?	RELATIONAL TABLE TRIGGER DEFINITION Property: Time
4	What actions will cause the trigger to fire	FIRES TAB Field: Which events will cause the trigger to fire?	RELATIONAL TABLE TRIGGER DEFINITION Property: Update
5	Triggering columns	COLUMNS TAB Field: Columns to fire trigger	RELATIONAL TABLE TRIGGER DEFINITION COLUMN Property: Column
6	Table name	NO SOURCE (Automatically populated)	RELATIONAL TABLE TRIGGER DEFINITION Property: Table (Automatically Populated)
7	Trigger logic	NAME TAB Field: Trigger logic – PL/SQL Definition	RELATIONAL TABLE TRIGGER DEFINITION TRIGGER LOGIC Property: PL/SQL Block or PL/SQL TRIGGER DEFINITION Property: PL/SQL Block

TABLE 8-1. *Source of Generated Code for Statement-Level Trigger Example*

Steps to Create This Trigger

Using the steps that follow, you will be able to recreate the sample trigger. Since there is more than one way to accomplish this task, we focused on defining steps that minimized the amount of time required to create the definition, while still taking advantage of the new features of release 2. We have chosen to use the dialogs for creating each definition and then use the Property Palette to enter the remaining information about the definition that cannot be entered through the dialogs.

1. In the Design Editor (DE), click on the Server Module tab.
2. Create a new relational table trigger definition for the DBCRS table. This is the actual trigger definition that will be created by the Server Generator. This relational table trigger definition will contain the triggering statement and will call (include) a PL/SQL trigger definition that contains the trigger body. Do this by pressing the Create icon in the Design Editor toolbar. This will launch a set of dialogs that will gather all of the necessary information required for this trigger definition. The following steps will detail the settings used for this example.
3. The Name dialog is the dialog that will be displayed first. Using this dialog, you will be able to specify a name for the relational table trigger definition (*Name of the trigger* = **DBCR_STAT_TRAN**). Next, you will enter a purpose or short description of the relational table definition (*Purpose of the trigger* = **Call dbcr_cascade.dbcr_transaction - cascade update**). Last, you will enter the name of the PL/SQL trigger definition that contains the logic to be executed when the trigger is fired. If you have previously created a PL/SQL trigger definition that contains the code you want executed in the trigger body, you can select its name from the drop-down list and skip steps 7 and 8. If you have not already created a PL/SQL trigger definition for this trigger, leave this field set to the default value (*Trigger Logic - PL/SQL Definition* = **<Create default trigger logic - PL/SQL Definition>**) and a PL/SQL trigger definition will be created by default when you complete step 6. Figure 8-5 shows the Name dialog used for this example. When you have completed this dialog, click Next.

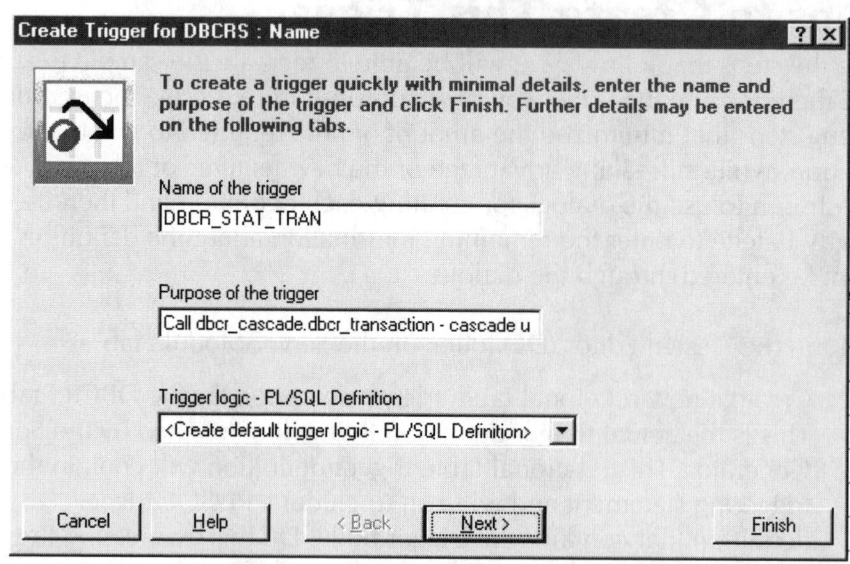

FIGURE 8-5. *Name dialog—statement-level trigger example*

4. The Fires dialog is the second dialog that will be displayed. Using this dialog, you will be able to specify that update statements will cause the trigger to fire (*Which events will cause the trigger to fire?* = **UPDATE Statement**). Next, you will specify that the trigger should fire after the statement is complete (*When will the trigger be fired?* = **After the statement**). Finally, specify that the trigger is a statement level trigger (*How many times is the trigger fired?* = **Once for the statement**). Figure 8-6 shows the Name dialog used for this example. When you have completed this dialog, click Next.

5. The Columns dialog is the third dialog that will be displayed. Using this dialog, you will be able to specify that the trigger should fire when the DSTAT_CD is updated (*Columns to fire trigger* = **DSTAT_CD**). Figure 8-7 shows the Columns dialog used for this example. When you have completed this dialog, click Next.

Create Trigger for DBCRS : Fires

You can determine when and how often a trigger is fired.

Which events will cause the trigger to fire?

INSERT statement

UPDATE statement

DELETE statement

When will the trigger be fired?

After the statement

How many times is the trigger fired?

Once for the statement

Once for each affected row

Cancel

Help

< Back

Next >

Finish

FIGURE 8-6. *Fires dialog—statement-level trigger example*

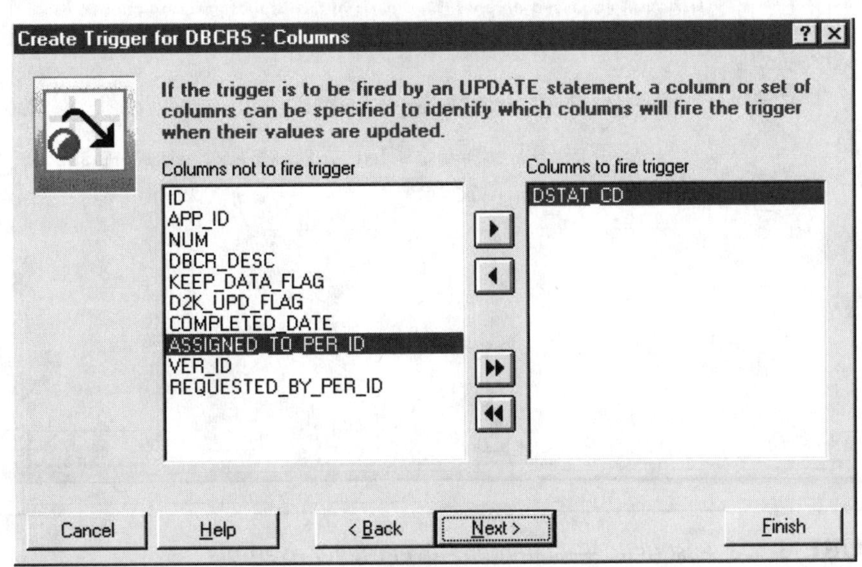

FIGURE 8-7. *Columns dialog—statement-level trigger example*

6. The Last dialog is, naturally, the last dialog that will be displayed. This dialog provides you with two different ways that you can exit the dialogs you have just used to define the relational table trigger definition. Select the first option (*Create the trigger with the information provided*) to create the trigger definition, and then click Finish. Figure 8-8 shows the Last dialog used for this example.

NOTE
*You could alternatively select the second option (*Create the trigger and then open the Logic Editor to edit the trigger's PL/SQL definition*). If you choose to define the trigger using this option, the Logic Editor will open the trigger body from the associated PL/SQL trigger definition. When you finish entering in the body of the trigger, you can then dismiss the Logic Editor and skip steps 7 and 8.*

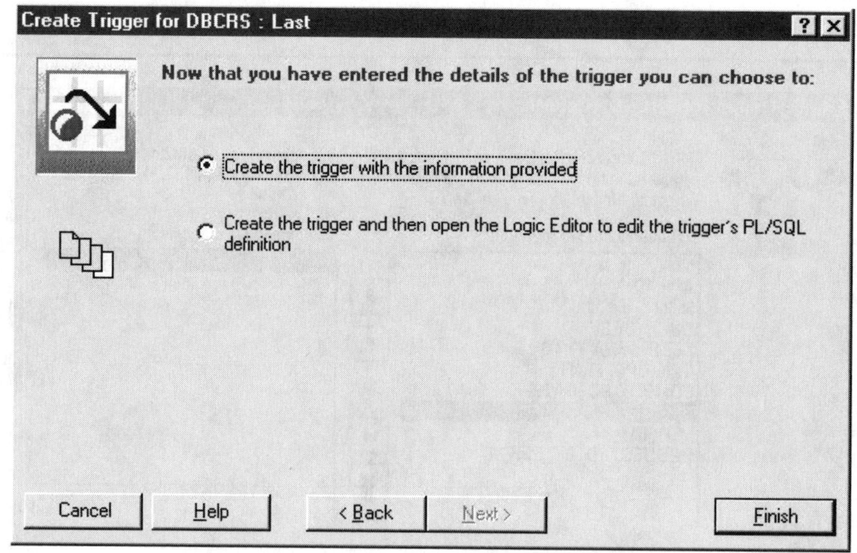

FIGURE 8-8. *Last dialog—statement-level trigger example*

7. Navigate to the PL/SQL trigger definition that is associated with the relational table trigger definition you just created. If you opted to let Designer create the PL/SQL trigger definition in step 3, there will be a PL/SQL trigger definition with the same name as the relational table trigger definition; otherwise, it will be the preexisting definition you specified using that dialog.

NOTE
A trigger logic definition that exists for a relational table trigger definition is the same thing as a PL/SQL trigger definition. Any changes made to one definition will be reflected in the other definition. The main difference between these two definitions is that a PL/SQL trigger definition can exist without a relational table trigger definition (meaning it's not yet connected), and a trigger logic definition cannot.

8. Define the body of the trigger in the *PL/SQL Block* property of the trigger definition PL/SQL definition. Do this by navigating to the *PL/SQL Block* property and, using a text editor, entering the body of the trigger. This should include the contents between the superscript sevens in Figure 8-4.

9. Next, We suggest that you verify that a table implementation has been defined for the relational table that this trigger has been defined against. This is not a mandatory step, but it is very useful if you intend to manage database objects using databases and schema owner accounts defined within the Designer Repository. To do this, you will need to select the DB Admin tab and then navigate to the correct Oracle database and user under that database. Look at the table implementations to see if the relational table is included in the list. If not, add the relational table definition to the table implementation schema objects for that user by pressing the Create icon in the Design Editor toolbar and then completing the dialogs.

10. Generate the relational table definition. The trigger that you just defined will be generated into the <file prefix>.TRG file.

Row-Level Trigger

The only way to generate a trigger is to generate the relational table definition that it is associated with. In this example, the table is the DBCRS table from the example application. Generating the table will create numerous files, only two of which are important for trigger definitions:

- <file prefix>.SQL Executes the all of the files created when generating a table definition
- <file prefix>.TRG Contains the generated trigger definition(s)

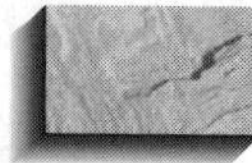

NOTE
<file prefix> is a name that you specify when generating server side objects. This name will be given to all files created during that execution of the Server Generator.

Figure 8-9 is an annotated version of the <file prefix>.TRG file. The superscript numbers correspond to properties in the trigger definition, which created this file. See Table 8-2 for specific mapping of the generated code.

```
PROMPT Creating ¹Trigger¹ ²'DBCR_STAT_ROW'²
CREATE OR REPLACE ¹TRIGGER¹ ²DBCR_STAT_ROW² ³AFTER³ ⁴UPDATE⁴ OF
    ⁵DSTAT_CD⁵ON ⁶DBCRS⁶
⁷FOR EACH ROW⁷
 ⁸WHEN (dstat_cd <> 'NEW')⁸
⁹BEGIN
dbcr_cascade.dbcr_row(:new.id, :new.dstat_cd);
END;⁹
/
```

FIGURE 8-9. *Row-level trigger generation example*

Number	Feature	Source Using Dialogs	Source Using Properties Palette
1	Trigger definition	NO SOURCE (Automatically generated for triggers)	NO SOURCE (Automatically generated for triggers)
2	Trigger name	NAME TAB Field: Name of the trigger	RELATIONAL TABLE TRIGGER DEFINITION Property: Name
3	When the trigger will fire	FIRES TAB Field: When will the trigger be fired?	RELATIONAL TABLE TRIGGER DEFINITION Property: Time
4	What actions will cause the trigger to fire	FIRES TAB Field: Which events will cause the trigger to fire?	RELATIONAL TABLE TRIGGER DEFINITION Property: Update
5	Triggering columns	COLUMNS TAB Field: Columns to fire trigger	RELATIONAL TABLE TRIGGER DEFINITION COLUMN Property: Column
6	Table name	NO SOURCE (Automatically populated)	RELATIONAL TABLE TRIGGER DEFINITION Property: Table (Automatically Populated)
7	Trigger level	FIRES TAB Field: How many times is the trigger fired?	RELATIONAL TABLE TRIGGER DEFINITION Property: Level
8	When condition	WHEN TAB Field: Restriction condition	RELATIONAL TABLE TRIGGER DEFINITION Property: Trigger When Condition
9	Trigger logic	NAME TAB Field: Trigger logic – PL/SQL Definition	RELATIONAL TABLE TRIGGER DEFINITION TRIGGER LOGIC Property: PL/SQL Block or PL/SQL TRIGGER DEFINITION Property: PL/SQL Block

TABLE 8-2. *Source of Generated Code for Row-Level Trigger Example*

Steps to Create This Trigger

Using the steps that follow, you will be able to recreate the sample trigger. Since there is more than one way to accomplish this task, we focused on defining steps that minimized the amount of time required to create the definition, while still taking advantage of the new features of release 2. We have chosen to use the dialogs for creating each definition and then use the Property Palette to enter the remaining information about the definition that cannot be entered through the dialogs.

1. In the Design Editor (DE), click on the Server Module tab.
2. Create a new relational table trigger definition for the DBCRS table. This is the actual trigger definition that will be created by the Server Generator. This relational table trigger definition will contain the triggering statement and will call (include) a PL/SQL trigger definition which contains the trigger body. Do this by pressing the Create icon in the Design Editor toolbar. This will launch a set of dialogs that will gather all of the necessary information required for this trigger definition. The following steps detail the settings used for this example.
3. The Name dialog is the dialog that will be displayed first. Using this dialog, you will be able to specify a name for the relational table trigger definition (*Name of the trigger* = **DBCR_STAT_ROW**). Next, you can enter the purpose or short description of the relational table definition (*Purpose of the trigger* = **Call dbcr_cascade.dbcr_row - cascade update**). Last, enter the name of the PL/SQL trigger definition that contains the logic to be executed when the trigger is fired. If you have previously created a PL/SQL trigger definition that contains the code you want executed in the trigger body, you can select its name from the drop-down list and skip steps 8 and 9. If you have not already created a PL/SQL trigger definition for this trigger, leave this field set to the default value (*Trigger Logic - PL/SQL Definition* = **<Create default trigger logic - PL/SQL Definition>**), and a PL/SQL trigger definition will be created by default when you complete step 7. Figure 8-10 shows the Name dialog used for this example. When you have completed this dialog, click Next.

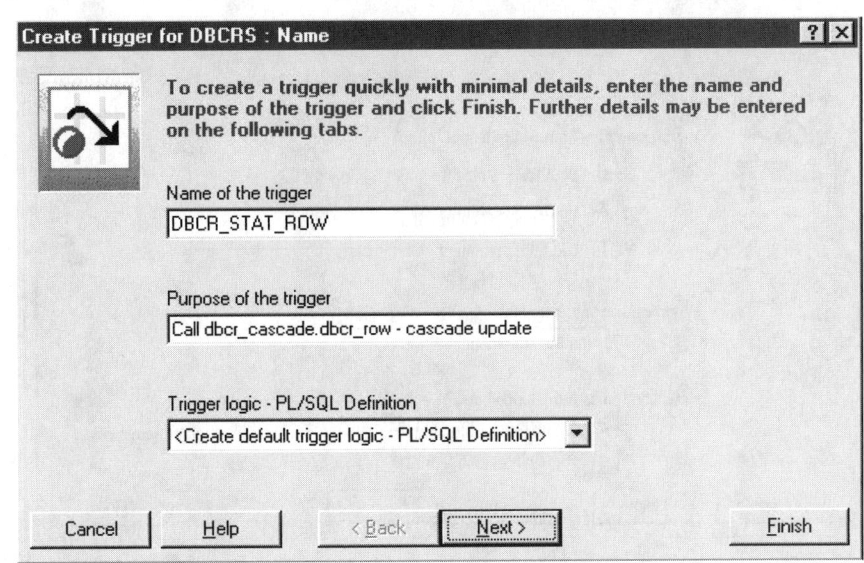

FIGURE 8-10. *Name dialog—row-level trigger example*

4. The Fires dialog is the second dialog that will be displayed. Using this dialog, you will be able to specify that update statements will cause the trigger to fire (*Which events will cause the trigger to fire?* = **UPDATE Statement**). Next, specify that the trigger should fire after the statement is complete (*When will the trigger be fired?* = **After the statement**). Finally, specify that the trigger is a row level trigger (*How many times is the trigger fired?* = **Once for each affected row**). Figure 8-11 shows the Fires dialog used for this example. When you have completed this dialog, click Next.

5. The Columns dialog is the third dialog that will be displayed. Using this dialog, you will be able to specify that the trigger should fire when the DSTAT_CD is updated (*Columns to fire trigger* = **DSTAT_CD**). Figure 8-12 shows the Columns dialog used for this example. When you have completed this dialog, click Next.

Create Trigger for DBCRS : Fires

You can determine when and how often a trigger is fired.

Which events will cause the trigger to fire?

INSERT statement

UPDATE statement

DELETE statement

When will the trigger be fired?

After the statement

How many times is the trigger fired?

Once for the statement

Once for each affected row

Cancel Help < Back Next > Finish

FIGURE 8-11. *Fires dialog—row-level trigger example*

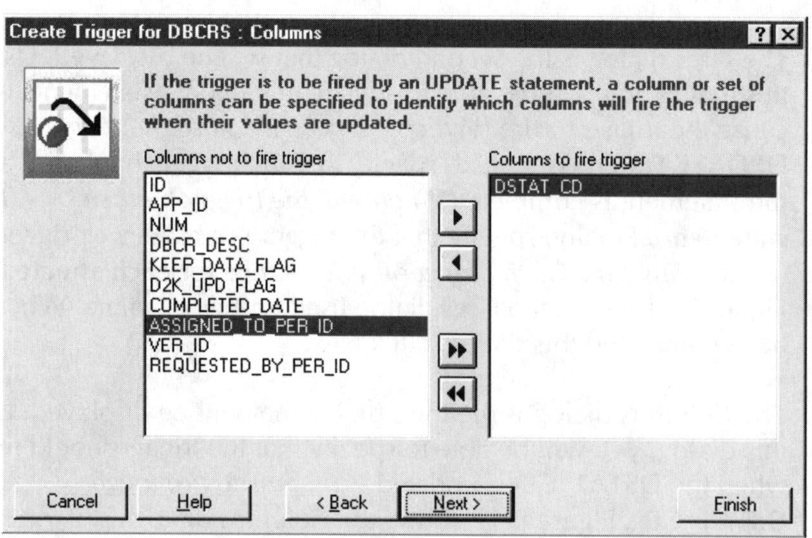

FIGURE 8-12. *Columns dialog—row-level trigger example*

6. The When dialog is the fourth dialog that will be displayed. Using this dialog, you will be able to specify the when condition of this trigger statement (*Restriction condition* = **dstat_cd <> 'NEW'**). Figure 8-13 shows the When dialog used for this example. When you have completed this dialog, click Next.

7. The Last dialog is, naturally, the last dialog that will be displayed. This dialog provides you with two different ways that you can exit the dialogs you have just used to define the relational table trigger definition. Select the first option (*Create the trigger with the information provided*) to create the trigger definition, and then click Finish. Figure 8-14 shows the Last dialog used for this example.

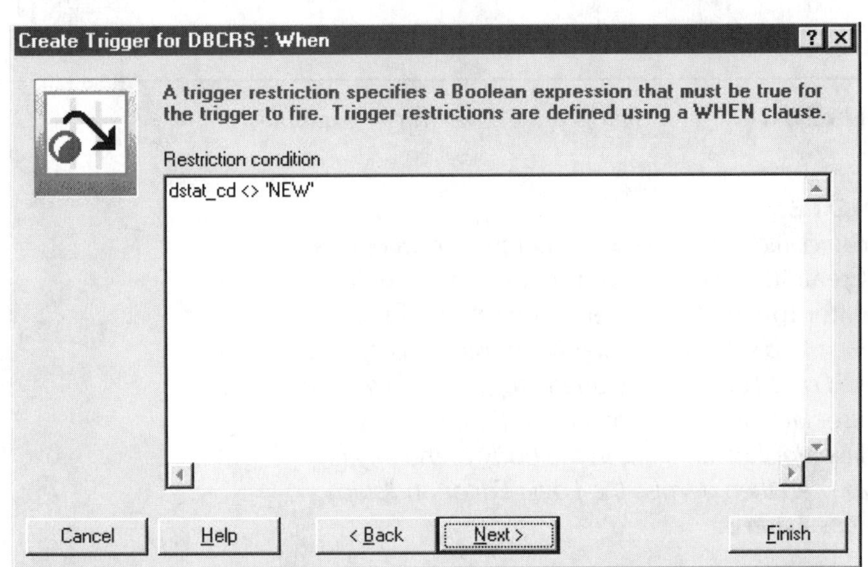

FIGURE 8-13. *When dialog—row-level trigger example*

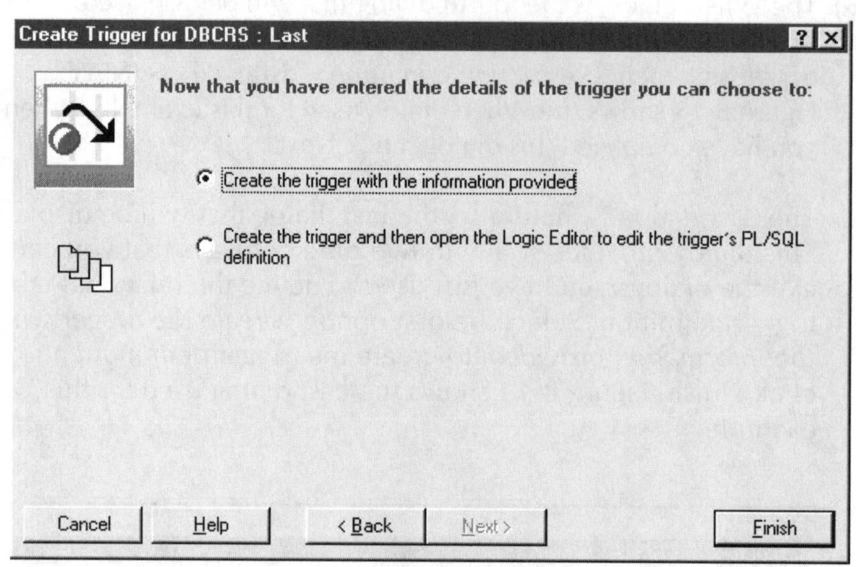

FIGURE 8-14. *Last dialog—row-level trigger example*

NOTE

*You could alternatively select the second option (*Create the trigger and then open the Logic Editor to edit the trigger's PL/SQL definition*). If you choose to define the trigger using this option, the Logic Editor will open the trigger body from the associated PL/SQL trigger definition. When you have finished entering in the body of the trigger, you can then dismiss the Logic Editor and skip steps 7 and 8.*

8. Navigate to the PL/SQL trigger definition that is associated with the relational table trigger definition you just created. If you opted to let Designer create the PL/SQL trigger definition in step 3, there will be a PL/SQL trigger definition with the same name as the relational table trigger definition; otherwise, it will be the preexisting definition you specified using that dialog.

NOTE
A trigger logic definition that exists for a relational table trigger definition is the same thing as a PL/SQL trigger definition. Any changes made to one definition will be reflected in the other definition. The main difference between these two definitions is that a PL/SQL trigger definition can exist without a relational table trigger definition (meaning it's not yet connected), and a trigger logic definition cannot.

9. Define the body of the trigger in the *PL/SQL Block* property of the trigger definition PL/SQL definition. Do this by navigating to the *PL/SQL Block* property and, using a text editor, entering the body of the trigger. This should include the contents between the superscript nines in Figure 8-9.

10. Next, We suggest that you verify that a table implementation has been defined for the relational table that this trigger has been defined against. This is not a mandatory step, but it is very useful if you intend to manage database objects using databases and schema owner accounts defined within the Designer Repository. To do this, you will need to select the DB Admin tab and then navigate to the correct Oracle database and user under that database. Look at the table implementations to see if the relational table is included in the list. If not, add the relational table definition to the table implementation schema objects for that user by pressing the Create icon in the Design Editor toolbar and then completing the dialogs.

11. Generate the relational table definition. The trigger that you just defined will be generated into the <file prefix>.TRG file.

Design Capture

The Design Capture utility will create trigger definitions in the repository based on program unit definitions located in one of two sources:

- Oracle database
- File system

Using the Design Capture utility for a database trigger will create more than one definition in the Designer Repository. A relational table trigger definition will be created and will contain the information from the triggering statement. A PL/SQL trigger definition will also be created and will contain the trigger body. This trigger definition is created in the repository using the declarative method of defining a PL/SQL definition.

Capturing the design of a database trigger, in essence, reverses the generation process described earlier in this chapter. Figures 8-15 and 8-16 are annotated versions of the sample triggers provided in Figures 8-1 and 8-2. The superscript numbers correspond to properties in the trigger definitions, which are populated by the Design Capture utility. See Tables 8-3 and 8-4 for specific mapping of properties populated by the Design Capture utility for each respective example.

```
CREATE OR REPLACE [1]TRIGGER[1] [2]DBCR_STAT_TRAN[2] [3]AFTER[3] [4]UPDATE[4] OF
    [5]DSTAT_CD[5] ON [6]DBCRS[6]
BEGIN
[7]dbcr_cascade.dbcr_transaction;
END;[7]
```

FIGURE 8-15. *Annotated statement trigger design capture example*

Number	Feature	Source Using Dialogs	Source Using Properties Palette
1	Trigger definition	NO SOURCE (Automatically generated for triggers)	NO SOURCE (Automatically generated for triggers)
2	Trigger name	NAME TAB Field: Name of the trigger	RELATIONAL TABLE TRIGGER DEFINITION Property: Name
3	When the trigger will fire	FIRES TAB Field: When the trigger will be fired?	RELATIONAL TABLE TRIGGER DEFINITION Property: Time
4	What actions will cause the trigger to fire	FIRES TAB Field: Which events will cause the trigger to fire?	RELATIONAL TABLE TRIGGER DEFINITION Property: Update
5	Triggering columns	COLUMNS TAB Field: Columns to fire trigger	RELATIONAL TABLE TRIGGER DEFINITION COLUMN Property: Column
6	Table name	NO SOURCE (Automatically populated)	RELATIONAL TABLE TRIGGER DEFINITION Property: Table (Automatically Populated)
7	Trigger logic	NAME TAB Field: Trigger logic – PL/SQL Definition	RELATIONAL TABLE TRIGGER DEFINITION TRIGGER LOGIC Property: PL/SQL Block or PL/SQL TRIGGER DEFINITION Property: PL/SQL Block

TABLE 8-3. *Properties Populated Using the Design Capture Utility—Statement-Level Trigger Example*

```
CREATE OR REPLACE [1]TRIGGER[1] [2]DBCR_STAT_ROW[2] [3]AFTER[3] [4]UPDATE[4] OF
    [5]DSTAT_CD[5] ON [6]DBCRS[6]
 [7]FOR EACH ROW[7]
 [8]WHEN (dstat_cd <> 'NEW')[8]
BEGIN
[9]dbcr_cascade.dbcr_row(:new.id, :new.dstat_cd);
END;[9]
/
```

FIGURE 8-16. *Annotated row-level trigger design capture example*

Number	Feature	Source Using Dialogs	Source Using Properties Palette
1	Trigger definition	NO SOURCE (Automatically generated for triggers)	NO SOURCE (Automatically generated for triggers)
2	Trigger name	NAME TAB Field: Name of the trigger	RELATIONAL TABLE TRIGGER DEFINITION Property: Name
3	When the trigger will fire	FIRES TAB Field: When will the trigger be fired?	RELATIONAL TABLE TRIGGER DEFINITION Property: Time
4	What actions will cause the trigger to fire	FIRES TAB Field: Which events will cause the trigger to fire?	RELATIONAL TABLE TRIGGER DEFINITION Property: Update
5	Triggering columns	COLUMNS TAB Field: Columns to fire trigger	RELATIONAL TABLE TRIGGER DEFINITION COLUMN Property: Column
6	Table name	NO SOURCE (Automatically populated)	RELATIONAL TABLE TRIGGER DEFINITION Property: Table (Automatically Populated)

TABLE 8-4. *Properties Populated Using the Design Capture Utility—Row-Level Trigger Example*

Number	Feature	Source Using Dialogs	Source Using Properties Palette
7	Trigger level	FIRES TAB Field: How many times is the trigger fired?	RELATIONAL TABLE TRIGGER DEFINITION Property: Level
8	When condition	WHEN TAB Field: Restriction condition	RELATIONAL TABLE TRIGGER DEFINITION Property: Trigger When Condition
9	Trigger logic	NAME TAB Field: Trigger logic – PL/SQL Definition	RELATIONAL TABLE TRIGGER DEFINITION TRIGGER LOGIC Property: PL/SQL Block OR PL/SQL TRIGGER DEFINITION Property: PL/SQL Block

TABLE 8-4. *Properties Populated Using the Design Capture Utility—Row-Level Trigger Example* (continued)

Steps to Create a Repository Definition Using the Design Capture Utility

1. In the Design Editor menu navigate to Generate → Capture Design Of → Server Model.
2. Select the source of the design capture:
   - Database captures definitions in an Oracle database.
   - DDL File captures the contents of a DDL file.

If you select the Database option, you will need to fill in the *username, password,* and *connect* properties. These will be used to query to database objects to determine what objects this user can capture the design of. You will then need to click the Objects tab and select the database trigger, and then move it into the *Capture* field.

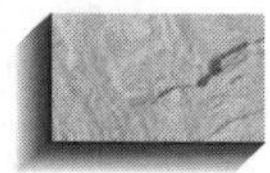

NOTE
Database triggers can be captured individually or as a group when the design of the relational table definition is captured using this utility. If you want to do the latter, check the Capture Triggers checkbox on the Source tab of Design Capture dialogs, select the table, and move it into the Capture field instead of the individual triggers.

If you select the DDL file option, you will need to select *DDL File* and then specify the path\filename of the DDL file to be captured in the *Name* field and the type\version of database in the *Type* field.

3. Select the database/schema owner in which to create the definition. Do this by setting the *capture objects into* property to the database schema owner you would like to create the function definition in.
4. When satisfied with your selections, click Start.
5. Select how you would like to process the captured Trigger definition.

- **Save** Commits the trigger definition to the repository
- **Revert** Completes a rollback of the posted trigger definition
- **Browse/Edit** Enables you to browse the posted trigger definition, make modifications, and then either commit or rollback

 Generation Troubleshooting Guide

Problem	Solution
I have to generate the relational table definition in order to generate the DDL for the trigger I created.	This currently is the only way to create the DDL for triggers associated with a table.
I can't generate my PL/SQL trigger definition.	You must create a relational table trigger definition and specify that you want it to use the PL/SQL trigger definition you have created. If you wish to generate the trigger, you must generate the relational table definition the trigger is associated with.

Problem	**Solution**
I can't specify which trigger definitions I want to generate.	Actually, you can. Each relational trigger definition has a *complete* property that has two settings, **YES** and **NO**. The default setting is **YES** so it appears as though you cannot generate subsets of trigger definitions for a particular table. However, if you do not wish to generate a particular trigger set the *complete* property to **NO**, and it will not generate.
The PL/SQL trigger definition I defined using the operating system file method is not created when I generate.	This feature does not currently work. Use either the declarative or free format methods for defining the PL/SQL definition that contains the trigger logic.

CHAPTER 9

Generating the Table API

This chapter is a detailed guide to help you generate the Table Application Programming Interface (API). In this chapter, we will cover

- An overview of the Table API
- Declarative functionality implemented using the Table API
- Advanced functionality implemented using the Table API
- A troubleshooting guide to assist you with common generation problems

What Is the Table API?

The Table API is a name for a set of generated server-side objects (triggers and packages) designed to enforce data rules on the server consistently, independent of the type of client application. The Table API is part of the overall Server API architecture that can be generated from Oracle Designer. The complete Server API architecture also includes the Module Component API, which can used by Oracle Developer Forms to interface to the Table API. The Module Component API will be covered in Chapter 24.

The Table API consists of the following components for each table that is specified to use the API:

- **One generated package** This package is referred to as a table handler. The table handler package contains many procedures designed to apply data rules and perform all DML for the table.
- **12 database triggers** These triggers are referred to as Table API triggers. The Table API triggers consist of one trigger for each possible trigger type for the table. These triggers call corresponding procedures in the table handler package. The procedures in the package perform the actual DML on the table.
- **One nongenerated package** There is one nongenerated package that is part of the Table API. It is called CG$ERRORS, and it is called by the generated table handler package to process errors.

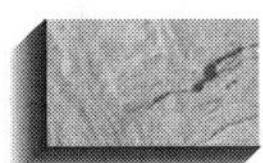

NOTE
The CG$ERRORS package must be installed, and permissions must be granted to the Table API schema owner prior to installing any generated table handler packages. The Server Generator will search for the package or a synonym when creating a table handler package. If nothing is found, it will create the CG$ERRORS package calling two scripts located in <oracle_home>\cgens70\sql named cdsaper.pks (creates the package specification) and cdsaper.pkb (creates the package body).

Figure 9-1 shows an example of the server-components that make up the Table API.

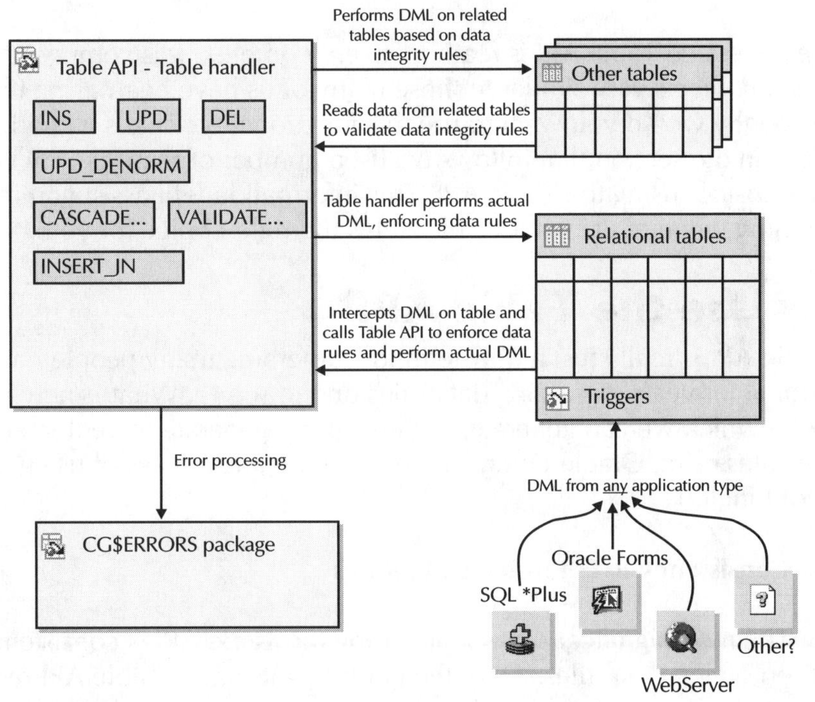

FIGURE 9-1. *High-level architecture of the Table API*

The Server Generator uses a consistent naming standard for all of the generated components of the Table API. This makes each component easily identifiable. The naming convention applied to these objects by the Server Generator is

- **Package** CG$<table_name>. An example of this would be CG$DBCRS.
- **Triggers** CG$<three letter trigger abbreviation>_<table_name>. Each of the three letters of the trigger abbreviation has a different meaning and domain of values. The first letter represents the timing that the trigger is fired. Valid values are "A" for After and "B" for Before. The second letter represents the event. Valid values are "I" for Insert, "D" for Delete, and "U" for Update. The third letter represents the scope or level of the trigger. Valid values are "R" for Row and "S" for Statement. Example names of the Table API trigger are CG$BIR_DBCRS and CG$AUS_DBCRS.

The generated Table API is really not very complex. It is composed of server-side objects very similar to those many of us have been using for years. So why would you want to use this functionality? That's a good question. In the section that follows we list a number of reasons why you should consider using the Table API. This information will assist you in determining whether using the Table API is the right choice for you.

Why Use the Table API?

The Table API is really just a new term for something many people have been doing for years: enforcing data rules on the server. What *is* new is the ease with which we can generate, modify, and regenerate the enforcement of such rules using Oracle Designer. Some of the advantages of using the Table API include

1. **Consistency in Enforcing Data Rules**

   The most significant reason for using the Table API is consistency in enforcing data rules. All of the components of the Table API reside on the server. Database triggers call the Table API table handler package for each DML request of the table. This allows data rule enforcement consistent, independent of how or where the request initiated. For example, you could have a standard Oracle Forms (client/server) application, an Oracle WebServer Application, a Visual Basic application, and even raw SQL, all updating and maintaining the same data, and you would be sure that the data rules are being enforced correctly.

2. **Robust Functionality**

   The Table API has very robust functionality. There are numerous types of functionality that can be easily generated without any coding at all. You simply use declarative definitions to implement these functions. You also have the ability to add customized, user-defined processing to handle more advanced data rules.

3. **Lower Development and Maintenance Costs**

   The Table API centralizes data business rule programming and places it in one location per table. This simplifies the process of developing server-side utilities in your application to enforce similar data rules. It also reduces the time you need to determine what rules have already been implemented by other applications. As rules change over time, simply update the Table API with the new rule, and all client applications will automatically begin using that new rule. This process can significantly reduce application maintenance costs.

4. **Repository Integration**

   The Table API is generated from table definitions in the Designer repository. This significantly increases your default system documentation. You will also benefit from the increased quality of your impact analysis reporting, and you will have better information to determine the cost of proposed changes.

The Table API has numerous advantages to its use. However, like all tools or techniques, it must be used properly to achieve the benefits. In the sections that follow, we will explain the different types of functionality that can be implemented simply by setting the properties of items in the Designer repository. We will also explain how to add your own user-defined processing to handle more advanced business rule requirements. This will also include a more detailed discussion of the Table API architecture.

Declarative Functionality Implemented Using the Table API

There are numerous declarative types of functionality that can be implemented using the Table API. This means that by setting values of repository properties of a table, column, or foreign key, for example, you can enable server-side enforcement of data rules using the Table API without doing any coding. The declarative types of functionality implemented by the Table API perform common tasks, routinely part of the application development process. The ease with which you can define and generate these features is one of the greatest benefits of using the Table API.

Table 9-1 provides a listing of all of the types of declarative features that can be implemented using the Table API. Included in the table is the location of the definition in the repository and the properties and settings required to implement each feature. Narrative descriptions of each feature, including step by step instructions for implementation, will follow later in this section.

Feature	Repository Definition	Property	Setting
Sequence populated columns*	Column	Sequence	***<sequence name>***
Default column values*	Column	Default Value	***<desired value>***
Audit columns	Column	Autogen Type Server Derived?	***<audit column name>*** **YES**
Forcing column values to uppercase*	Column	Uppercase	**YES**

TABLE 9-1. *Declarative Functionality Implemented Using the Table API*

Feature	Repository Definition	Property	Setting
Sequence within parent	Column	Autogen Type Server Derived?	**SEQ IN PARENT** **YES**
Domain validation*	Column	Domain	***<domain name>***
Nonupdateable unique key	Unique Key	Update Validate in	**NO** Either **SERVER** or **BOTH**
Foreign key cascade update	Foreign Key	Update Rule Validate in	**CASCADES** Either **SERVER** or **BOTH**
Foreign key nullifies update	Foreign Key	Update Rule Validate in	**NULLIFIES** Either **SERVER** or **BOTH**
Foreign key restricted update	Foreign Key	Update Rule Validate in	**RESTRICTED** Either **SERVER** or **BOTH**
Foreign key defaults update	Column Foreign Key	Default Value Update Rule Validate in	***<desired_value>*** **DEFAULTS** Either **SERVER** or **BOTH**
Foreign key cascade delete	Foreign Key	Delete Rule Validate in	**CASCADES** Either **SERVER** or **BOTH**
Foreign key nullifies delete	Foreign Key	Delete Rule Validate in	**NULLIFIES** Either **SERVER** or **BOTH**
Foreign key restricted delete	Foreign Key	Delete Rule Validate in	**RESTRICTED** Either **SERVER** or **BOTH**

TABLE 9-1. *Declarative Functionality Implemented Using the Table API* (continued)

Feature	Repository Definition	Property	Setting
Foreign key defaults delete	Column Foreign Key	Default Value Update Rule Validate in	***<desired_value>*** **DEFAULTS** Either **SERVER** or **BOTH**
Arc validation	Foreign Key	Arc Number Arc Mandatory	***<desired value>*** **YES**
Table journaling	Table	Journal	**YES**
Column derivations	Column	Derivation Expression Derivation Expression Type Server Derived?	***<desired expression>*** **SQL Expression** or **Function Call** **YES**
Denormalization: copy parent values to a child record	Column	From Column Via Foreign Key Server Derived?	***<desired column>*** ***<foreign key name>*** **YES**
Denormalization: aggregating child values into a parent record	Column	From Column Via Foreign Key Server Derived? Using Operator	***<desired column>*** ***<foreign key name>*** **YES** ***<desired operator>***

TABLE 9-1. *Declarative Functionality Implemented Using the Table API* (continued)

*Enforcement of this feature was generated into the Table API without setting the *Server Derived?* column property. New releases may later require this property. If you encounter problems, try setting the *Server Derived?* property to **Yes**.

Sequence-Populated Columns

Sequence-populated columns are widely used to implement surrogate keys for systems that are designed to use them. The sequence-populated column is typically the primary key of the table and is used to ensure the uniqueness of each record. Before Oracle Designer release 2, the implementation of these sequence-populated columns could only be generated into the client (Oracle Forms), which would allow data that was inserted by other tools (SQL*Plus or SQL*Loader, for example) to bypass the sequence.

To implement this feature:

1. Make sure that the sequence that you wish to use is defined in the repository. If it is not, create a sequence definition.
2. Navigate to the column definition that you wish to populate using a sequence.
3. Set the *Sequence* property to the desired sequence name.
4. Generate the Table API.

Default Values for Columns

Supplying a default value for a column is another feature that, before release 2, could only be generated into the client. Using the Table API to specify the defaults for a column ensures that the default is correctly set, even if the data is inserted outside of the client application.

To implement this feature:

1. Navigate to the column definition you wish to populate with a default value.
2. Set the *Default Value* property to the desired value.
3. Generate the Table API.

How to Generate the Table API for a Table

The following procedure can be used to generate the Table API for a table. This procedure is the same for all of the different types of functionality that are detailed in this chapter:

1. In the Design Editor, select the Server Model view in the navigator.
2. Select one or more relational table definitions (at least one must be selected).
3. Choose Generate → Generate Table API from the pull-down menu.
4. Select one of the generation targets (File or Oracle) and complete the rest of the properties for that type.
5. Enter the file prefix for the Table API generation script. This will be the name of the generated master SQL script that will install *all* of the table handlers for the tables you have selected. In addition to this master SQL script, there will be three SQL scripts generated for each table you select: <tablename>.PKB, <tablename>.PKS, and <tablename>.TRG. These scripts will be called by the master script.
6. To generate the database triggers that cause the Table API to always be used, make sure that the Generate Table API Triggers checkbox is selected.
7. Optionally, you can select and deselect tables to generate handlers for in the Objects tab.
8. Select Start to generate the scripts.

Audit Columns

Audit columns track when records in a table were created or modified and which Oracle user did the creation or update. They are very helpful in troubleshooting data-related problems. There are four types of audit columns that can be generated:

- Created By
- Date Created
- Modified By
- Date Modified

Each of the Create columns is populated by the generated code when a record is inserted into the table. Each of the Modified columns is populated by the generated code when a record in the table is updated. Before release 2, this feature could only be generated in the client, and any

Audit Columns Versus Table Journaling

Sometimes there is confusion between the functionality of the audit columns and table journaling (covered later in this chapter). Audit columns are columns that are added to the table to be audited, and therefore can only contain information about the insert and the most recent update of each record. Using audit columns, there is no information about any of the past updates of the record, nor is there any information about what actually changed. Using table journaling however, you can store a complete audit trail of every insert and update of the record, including the date updated, who updated it, and the actual changes that took place. For more information, see the section, "Table Journaling," later in the chapter.

data that was created or updated outside of the client would not have the audit data automataically.

To implement this feature:

1. Navigate to the table definition for which you want to define audit columns.
2. Define a new column definition for each audit column you would like to implement.
3. For each column definition you create in step 2, set the *Autogen Type* property to the desired audit column type.
4. Set the *Server Derived?* property to **Yes** for each column definition you create in step 2. This property cannot be set from the dialogs, only from the property sheet.
5. Generate the Table API.

Forcing Column Values to Uppercase

Forcing column values to uppercase is typically used for columns that store abbreviations, codes, or short names. This functionality is particularly useful to ensure that parameter-driven queries return accurate data without needing case conversion functions built into the SELECT statement. Before release 2, this feature could only be enforced on the client.

To implement this feature:

1. Navigate to the column definition that you want stored in uppercase.
2. Set the *Uppercase* property to **Yes**.
3. Generate the Table API.

Sequence Within Parent

If you need to generate and store the precise order that child records were created for a parent record, you should consider using the sequence within parent functionality. This feature automatically sets the value of the specified column in the child table to the sequence in which it was created within its parent. This would be useful when creating line items on an invoice or components that make up an assembly, for example. Before release 2, this feature could only be generated in the Forms client, and any data that was created or updated outside of the client did not automatically have the sequence within parent column updated.

To implement this feature:

1. Navigate to the column definition that you would like to populate using the sequence within parent functionality.
2. Set the *Autogen Type* property to **SEQ IN PARENT.**
3. Set the *Server Derived?* property to **Yes**. This property cannot be set from the dialogs, only from the property sheet.
4. Generate the Table API.

Domain Validation

In previous releases, we only had two options for domain validation, each with their own problems:

1. **Using Check Constraints** Check constraints can be used to validate the domains on the server. While this has the advantage of making sure that the column will always be within the domain, it can be difficult to maintain. This is especially true when domain values change often. Some of the problems with using check constraints are

   - In order to change a check constraint, you must have a DBA alter the constraint; it cannot be done from the application.
   - The system usually has to be brought down in order to change the check constraint.
   - The error message returned by the violation of the check constraint is not very user friendly.

2. **Client-side Validation Using the CG_REF_CODES Table** Client-side generation of domain validation against a standard domain table (CG_REF_CODES) can be generated. This has the advantage of allowing for easy changes to the domain without involving a DBA or having to have the system down, but the domain is only enforced for data entered using the client application. If data is entered directly using SQL, SQL*Loader, or another application the domain will not be validated.

Both of these methods are still available in release 2, but we now have a new option using the Table API. In release 2, the Table API can be used to enforce the domain validation on the server, while still using the CG_REF_CODES table. This is a nice improvement over the options for validating domains in prior releases, because it combines the benefits of both methods.

NOTE
By default, Oracle Designer will generate one reference code table, CG_REF_CODES, for all applications. Although it is possible for you to generate a separate reference code table for each application, for simplicity, we refer to the table as CG_REF_CODES. Chapter 27 details the creation and management of these tables.

To implement this feature:

1. Make sure that the domain that you wish to use is defined in the repository. If it is not, create a domain definition.
2. Navigate to the column definition that you would like to validate using a domain.
3. Set the *Domain* property to the desired domain name.
4. Generate the Table API.
5. Make sure that the reference code table is generated for the domain. If it is not generated, the functionality will not work. See Chapter 27 for instructions on how to do this.

Nonupdateable Unique Key

Sometimes tables are designed to have unique keys that are not updateable. Prior to release 2, this restriction could only be enforced in the client. Now, the Table API can be used to enforce this restriction, which means that it will always be enforced, even if the data is updated using SQL or a non-Developer application.

To implement this feature:

1. Navigate to the unique key definition that you would like to make nonupdateable.
2. Set the *Update Rule* property to **No**.
3. Set the *Validate in* property to **Server** or **Both**. Either setting will result in code generated into the Table API to enable the primary key to be updateable.
4. Generate the Table API.

Foreign Key—Update Validation

Update rules for foreign keys can be enforced using the Table API. Update rules specify what happens to the Foreign Key (FK) column in the child table when the referenced column in the parent table is updated. Each type of update rule is outlined next.

CAUTION

In order for the code to be generated to enforce the FK related rules detailed in this section, both the parent and the child tables of the FK relationship have to be generated at the same time! If you generate the tables separately, the code to enforce the rule will not be generated into the Table API. For this reason, it is usually a good idea to generate the Table API for all of the tables in the system at the same time.

Cascade Update

This option sets the FK column in the child table to the new value of the referenced column in the parent table whenever the referenced column is updated.

To implement this feature:

1. Navigate to the foreign key definition that you would like to implement using the cascade update rule.
2. Set the *Update Rule* property to **Cascades**.

3. Set the *Validate in* property to **Server** or **Both**. Either setting will result in code generated into the Table API, which will enforce the cascade update rule.
4. Generate the Table API of both the parent and child tables at the same time. The actual code to enforce the cascade update rule will be enforced by the parent table's Table API, even though the property settings are applied to the child table's foreign key definition.

Nullifies Update

This option sets the FK column in the child table to NULL whenever the value of the referenced column in the parent table is updated. This feature can only be used where the FK value is optional.

To implement this feature:

1. Navigate to the foreign key definition that you would like to implement using the nullifies update rule.
2. Set the *Update Rule* property to **Nullifies**.
3. Set the *Mandatory?* property to **No**.
4. Set the *Validate in* property to **Server** or **Both**. Either setting will result in code generated into the Table API, which will enforce the nullifies update rule.
5. Generate the Table API of both the parent and child tables at the same time. The actual code to enforce the nullifies update rule will be enforced by the parent table's Table API, even though the property settings are applied to the child table's foreign key definition.

Restricted Update

This option prevents the update of the referenced column in the parent table if there are any records in the child table that have the same value in the related FK column. This is the default rule for foreign key enforcement.

To implement this feature:

1. Navigate to the foreign key definition that you would like to implement using the restricted update rule.
2. Set the *Update Rule* property to **Restricted**.

3. Set the *Validate in* property to **Server** or **Both**. Either setting will result in code generated into the Table API, which will enforce the restricted update rule.
4. Generate the Table API of both the parent and child tables at the same time. The Oracle FK constraint that is generated for the table will actually be used to prevent the updates. All that is generated into the Table API is an error handling routine that is consistent with the other Table API error handlers.

Defaults Update

This option sets the value of the FK column in the child table to a predefined default value whenever the value of the referenced column in the parent table is updated.

To implement this feature:

1. Navigate to the foreign key definition that you would like to implement using the defaults update rule.
2. Set the *Update Rule* property to **Defaults**.
3. Set the *Validate in* property to **Server** or **Both**. Either setting will result in code generated into the Table API, which will enforce the defaults update rule.
4. Set the *Default Value* property of the FK column in the child table to the desired default value.
5. Generate the Table API of both the parent and child tables at the same time. The actual code to enforce the defaults update rule will be enforced by the parent table's Table API, even though the property settings are applied to the child table's foreign key definition.

Foreign Key—Delete Validation

Delete rules for foreign keys can be enforced using the Table API. Delete rules specify what happens to the related rows in the child table when the related row in the parent table is deleted. Each type of delete rule is outlined next.

CAUTION

In order for the code to be generated to enforce the FK related rules detailed in this section, both the parent and the child tables of the FK relationship have to be generated at the same time! If you generate the tables separately, the code to enforce the rule will not be generated into the Table API. For this reason, it is usually a good idea to generate the Table API for all of the tables in the system at the same time.

Cascade Delete

This option deletes all of the related rows from the child table whenever a record in the parent table is deleted. To implement this feature:

1. Navigate to the foreign key definition that you would like to implement using the cascade delete rule.
2. Set the *Delete Rule* property to **Cascades**.
3. Set the *Validate in* property to **Server** or **Both**. Either setting will result in code generated into the Table API, which will enforce the cascade delete rule.
4. Generate the Table API of both the parent and child table's at the same time. The actual code to enforce the cascade delete rule will be enforced by the parent table's Table API even though the property settings are applied to the child table's foreign key definition.

Nullifies Delete

This option sets the value of the FK column in the child table to NULL whenever the related record in the parent table is deleted. To implement this feature:

1. Navigate to the foreign key definition that you would like to implement using the nullifies delete rule.
2. Set the *Delete Rule* property to **Nullifies**.
3. Set the *Mandatory?* property to **No**.

4. Set the *Validate in* property to **Server** or **Both**. Either setting will result in code generated into the Table API, which will enforce the nullifies delete rule.
5. Generate the Table API of both the parent and child tables at the same time. The actual code to enforce the nullifies delete rule will be enforced by the parent table's Table API, even though the property settings are applied to the child table's foreign key definition.

Restricted Delete

This option prevents the deletion of a record in the parent table whenever related records exist in the child table. This is the default rule for foreign key enforcement.

To implement this feature:

1. Navigate to the foreign key definition that you would like to implement using the restricted delete rule.
2. Set the *Delete Rule* property to **Restricted**.
3. Set the *Validate in* property to **Server** or **Both**. Either setting will result in code generated into the Table API, which will enforce the restricted delete rule.
4. Generate the Table API of both the parent and child tables at the same time. The Oracle FK constraint that is generated for the table will actually be used to prevent the deletions. All that is generated into the Table API is an error handling routine that is consistent with the other Table API error handlers.

Defaults Delete

This option sets the value of the FK column in the child table to a predetermined default value whenever the related record in the parent table is deleted. To implement this feature:

1. Navigate to the foreign key definition that you wish to implement using the defaults delete rule.
2. Set the *Delete Rule* property to **Defaults**.
3. Set the *Validate in* property to **Server** or **Both**. Either setting will result in code generated into the Table API, which will enforce the defaults delete rule.

4. Set the *Default Value* property of the FK column in the child table to the desired default value.
5. Generate the Table API of both the parent and child tables at the same time. The actual code to enforce the defaults delete rule will be enforced by the parent table's Table API, even though the property settings are applied to the child table's foreign key definition.

Arc Validation

An arc is a set of mutually exclusive foreign keys from one to two or more FK tables. The Table API can be used to enforce arc FK validation. The following rules will be enforced:

- Values are entered for only one of the arc FK columns.
- Values are entered for at least one of the arc FK columns (if the arc is mandatory).

An exception is raised if these rules are violated. In previous releases, arcs could only be enforced on the client, which could lead to corruption of the arc if data were loaded using any tool other than Oracle Forms. Using the Table API ensures consistent enforcement of the arc rules.

To implement this feature:

1. Navigate to each of the foreign key definitions that you would like to implement using an arc relationship.
2. Set the *Arc Number* property to a numeric value. The value must be the same for all FKs that are to participate in the same arc. If you defined the arc relationship in the logical model and used the database transformer to create the tables and keys, the arc number will already be populated for you.
3. Set the *Arc Mandatory* property. If set to **Yes**, the Table API will ensure that at least one of the arc columns is entered. If set to **No**, the arc is optional, and records can be created without values in any of the arc columns.
4. Generate the Table API for the table that has the arc.

Explicit Versus Generic Arc Implementation

Two methods can be used to implement an arc relationship in your data model. The explicit method means that you have a separate column for every FK in the arc. Even if the arc is mandatory, each of these arc columns must be optional. This is because only one of the arc's columns can be populated at one time. In a generic arc implementation, there is only one mandatory arc column that is used to implement *all* of the FKs in the arc. In this case, there is usually a Type column used to specify which FK is being implemented, and the column can be made mandatory for mandatory arcs. The explicit method has a disadvantage because it is possible to corrupt the arc by either leaving all of the columns blank for a mandatory arc or by somehow getting a value in more than one column of the arc. In order to avoid this problem, many systems use the generic implementation, especially if surrogate keys (ID columns) are used in the data design (all of the FK columns have to have the same datatype for the generic implementation). The Table API only supports the explicit arc implementation declaratively. If you want to use the generic implementation, you will have to write the code to implement it yourself. However, since using the Table API eliminates the main weakness of the explicit implementation (because it will prevent the corruption of the data), there is no reason to use the generic implementation if you are generating your system from Oracle Designer and are planning on using the Table API.

Table Journaling

Table journaling is the best method for tracking activity on a given table over time. After each insert, update, or delete on the base table, a database trigger fires and inserts a record into a journal table. The journal table contains all of the information used to update the base table whenever a record is inserted, updated, or deleted. It also contains information in some special journal columns. These columns record the operation (insert, delete, update), date, user, application, session, and notes for the journaled operation.

To do this, the journal table will include the following information:

- **Inserts** A row is inserted into the journal table with all of the information in the insert. The JN_OPERATION column is set to INS.
- **Updates** A row is inserted in the journal table with just the columns that were updated. The JN_OPERATION column is set to UPD.
- **Deletes** A row is inserted in the journal table with just the key information. The JN_OPERATION column is set to DEL.

While table journaling is excellent for tracking changes, it does have resource demands. The journal table can get quite large, and you will need to put a process in place to manage it (for example, an archiving procedure). In addition, every insert, update, and delete will involve two database actions, therefore increasing the load on your database. Before release 2, Oracle Designer automatically created the journal table and generated the code to populate the journal table only into the Forms client. If the table were updated in SQL or from a nonforms application, no journaling would take place.

To implement this feature:

1. Navigate to the table definition.
2. Set the *Journal* property to **Server** or **Client Calls Server Procedure**.
3. Generate the Table API for the table.

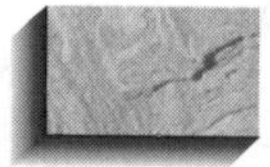

NOTE

*In the release available to us at the time of writing (2.1.2), there was no difference in the code generated in the Table API if the journal property was set to **Server** or **Client Calls Server Procedure**. Both settings generated the journaling code completely in the Table API. This may change in future releases.*

Column Derivations

The Table API can be used to automatically populate derived columns based on the values of other columns in the table. Some examples of uses for this would be

- **Storing precalculated numeric columns for performance or convenience** For instance, if the table had Width and Height columns, you could automatically derive and store an Area column.
- **Automatically storing derived text columns** For instance, you could store a person's name in separate columns (FIRST_NAME, LAST_NAME, MI) and also store a correctly formatted FULL_NAME column that is derived from the other columns.

To implement this feature:

1. Navigate to the table that you wish to add the derived column to.
2. Create a column to hold the derivation. Make sure the format and size of the column are correct for the derivation you wish to perform.
3. Select a *Derivation Expression Type* for the column. If this is left null, no derivation will be added to the Table API. Your options are **SQL Expression** or **Function Call**.
4. Enter a *Derivation Expression* for the column. (See the special section, "No Differences Between SQL Expression and Function Call," for limitations.)
5. Set the *Server Derived?* property to **Yes** for each column definition you create in step 2.
6. Generate the Table API.

No Differences Between SQL Expression and Function Call

In the current version of Designer (2.1.2), the derivation code seems to be generated in exactly the same way whether the Derivation Expression Type property is set to SQL Expression or Function Call. We expect that setting the type to SQL Expression would do something like a select from Dual, but it does not seem to. For both settings, the code that is generated is

```
:cg$rec.<derived column> := <derivation expression>;
```

This is what you would expect for the Function Call setting. This may be fixed in later releases. However, it is still possible to do simple column-based derivations without using a function. To do this, just refer to each column using the record that is used in the Table API. For instance, if you wanted to concatenate two columns (FIRST_NAME and LAST_NAME) to create a derived column called FULL_NAME, you could set its derivation expression to:

```
cg$rec.FIRST_NAME||' '||cg$rec.LAST_NAME
```

Then the generated code would look like this:

```
cg$rec.FULL_NAME := cg$rec.FIRST_NAME||' '||cg$rec.LAST_NAME;
```

which would give you the desired result.

Simple Denormalization—Copy Parent Values to a Child Record

The Table API can be used to perform some simple denormalization. One example of this is the ability to denormalize a column in a parent table into all of its child records. This might be used to populate a denormalized column in a child table with a frequently used descriptive value from the parent table. The generated code not only populates the denormalized column when the child records are created, it updates the denormalized column whenever the column in the parent table is updated! This is a very powerful way to consistently denormalize your data!

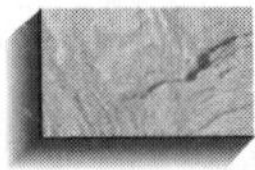

NOTE

Release 1.3.2 *Release 1.3.2 users may recognize the denormalization properties mentioned in this section (from column and via foreign key) because these properties have been available in Oracle Designer for a while. However, in previous releases, they were used for documentation purposes only. Now that they have come alive and actually perform a generation function, anyone who used them in an existing application will have to make sure that they really want the functionality that is now generated.*

To implement this feature:

1. Navigate to the column definition that you wish to denormalize into.
2. Set the *From Column* property of the column to denormalize into. You will be presented with a pull-down list of the columns that are related to the current table. Select the name of the column you wish to denormalize from. (See the special section, "Select Correct FKs for Parent Denormalization into Child Records.")
3. Set the *Via Foreign Key* property of the column to denormalize into. You will be presented with a pull-down list of the FKs that are related to the current table. Select the FK name of the FK that links to the parent table that has the column you selected in step 2. (See the special section, "Select Correct FKs for Parent Denormalization into Child Records.")
4. Set the *Server Derived* property of the column to denormalize into to **Yes**.

Select Correct FKs for Parent Denormalization into Child Records

For both the From Column and the Via Foreign Key properties, you will be presented with a list of *all* of the foreign keys that are related to the current table. Both the table's own FKs (where the current table is the many end) and any FKs that point *to* the current table (where it is the one end) will be presented. In order to denormalize a parent column into a child table, you should only select the FKs of the current table. The use of the other keys will be discussed in the next section.

5. Generate the Table API for both the denormalized into and denormalized from table at the same time. There will be code generated into the Table API for both tables to implement this functionality.

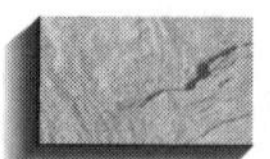

CAUTION

You need to make sure that the Table API for the table that is being denormalized from is generated at the same time as the table to denormalize into. If you do not do this, the code that updates the denormalized column when the source column is updated will not be generated!

Simple Denormalization—Aggregating Child Values into a Parent Record

Another example of a simple denormalization that can be implemented with the Table API is aggregating child values into a parent record. One example of using this feature is maintaining a denormalized column in the parent table with a precalculated sum of a column in the child table. Another useful option is maintaining the count of the children records. The operators that are provided are Average, Count, Maximum, Minimum, Standard Deviation, Sum, and Variance.

This capability can help improve the performance of queries by precalculating the aggregated value when the data is updated. However, there is a performance implication during updates because the aggregation has to be performed whenever the data is updated. Therefore, this option should probably only be used in situations where the data is queried much more frequently than it is updated.

To implement this feature:

1. Navigate to the column definition that you wish to denormalize into.
2. Set the *From Column* property of the column to denormalize into. You will be presented with a pull-down list of the columns that are related to the current table. Select the name of the column you wish to denormalize from. (See the special section, "Select Correct FKs for Aggregating Child Values into Parent Records.")
3. Set the Via Foreign Key property of the column to denormalize into. You will be presented with a pull-down list of the FKs that are related to the current table. Select the FK name of the FK that links to the parent table that has the column you selected in step 2. (See the special section, "Select Correct FKs for Aggregating Child Values into Parent Records.")

Select Correct FKs for Aggregating Child Values into Parent Records

For both the From Column and the Via Foreign Key properties you will be presented with a list of *all* of the foreign keys that are related to the current table. Both the table's own FKs (where the current table is the many end) and any FKs that point *to* the current table (where it is the one end) will be presented. In order to aggregate a child column into a parent table, you should not select one of the FKs of the current table, but only select an FK that points to the current table. The use of the other keys was discussed in the previous section.

4. Set the *Using Operator* property of the column to denormalize into to the desired value. If no operator is selected, the denormalization will not be performed.

5. Set the *Server Derived* property of the column to denormalize into to **Yes**.

6. Generate the Table API for both the denormalized into and denormalized from table at the same time.

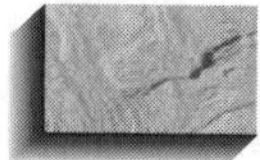

NOTE
In the release available to us at the time of writing (2.1.2), this feature was not fully supported. The code to populate the aggregate column when the parent record was updated was generated into the parent table's API. However, there was no code generated to update the aggregate column if the data in the child table changed. Because of this, you do not really need to generate the child Table API at the same time as the parent to implement this functionality. However, this may change in future releases, so you should get used to generating both of the Table APIs at the same time.

How to Find the Generated Code

Now that you have defined and generated declarative functionality, the next logical question is, "Where is it enforced?" This information is particularly useful once you begin to consider adding user-defined processing to the Table API, and you need to know how your custom code will interact with the generated code. It's also useful for debugging. Table 9-2 contains the listing of each feature and where in the generated Table API table handler package the source code is located. This will give you a starting place from which to examine the generated code.

Feature	Location
Sequence populated columns	Procedure UP_AUTOGEN_COLUMNS called from INS procedure
Default column values	Procedure INS
Audit columns	Procedure UP_AUTOGEN_COLUMNS called from INS and UPD procedures
Forcing column values to uppercase	Procedure UP_AUTOGEN_COLUMNS called from INS and UPD procedures
Sequence within parent	Procedure UP_AUTOGEN_COLUMNS Called from INS and UPD procedures
Domain validation	Procedure VALIDATE_DOMAIN called from CG$BIR and CG$BUR triggers
Nonupdateable unique key	Procedure UK_KEY_UPDATEABLE called from UPD procedure
Foreign key cascade update	Procedure CASCADE_UPDATE called from CG$AUS trigger
Foreign key nullifies update	Procedure CASCADE_UPDATE called from CG$AUS trigger
Foreign key restricted update	Procedure ERR_MSG called when update fails because of the database constraint
Foreign key defaults update	Procedure CASCADE_UPDATE called from CG$AUS trigger
Foreign key cascade delete	Procedure CASCADE_DELETE called from CG$ADS trigger
Foreign key nullifies delete	Procedure CASCADE_DELETE called from CG$ADS trigger

TABLE 9-2. *Location of Generated Code in the Table API Table Handler Package*

Feature	Location
Foreign key restricted delete	Procedure ERR_MSG called when the delete fails because of the database constraint
Foreign key defaults delete	Procedure CASCADE_DELETE called from CG$ADS trigger
Arc validation	Procedure VALIDATE_ARC called from CG$BIR and CG$BUR triggers
Table journaling	Procedure INSERT_JN called from INS, UPD, and DEL procedures
Column derivations	Procedure UP_AUTOGEN_COLUMNS called from INS and UPD procedures
Copy parent values to a child record	1. Procedure UPD_DENORM in the denormalized from (parent) table's API called from the UPD procedure 2. Procedure UPD_AUTOGEN_COLUMNS in the denormalized into (child) table's API called from INS and UPD procedures
Aggregating child values into a parent record	1. Procedure UPD_AUTOGEN_COLUMNS in the denormalized into (parent) table's API is called from INS and UPD procedures 2. It's likely that the procedure UPD_OPER_DENORM is supposed to be used for this function, but it does not seem to be working yet

TABLE 9-2. *Location of Generated Code in the Table API Table Handler Package* (continued)

Advanced Functionality Implemented Using the Table API

By advanced functionality we mean using the Table API to implement anything that cannot be defined using the declarative definitions detailed previously. This involves adding Table API/Trigger Logic to the table, and it means you will have to write your own code to implement the functionality. Some examples of the types of functionality you might want to add this way are

- Enforcement of data rules based on state relationships of data
- Denormalization of data that does not have a direct foreign key relationship
- Aggregation using operations not supported declaratively

Before you start writing the code to implement advanced functionality, it is a good idea to get a more detailed understanding of the Table API architecture, specifically the contents of the package and it's interrelationship with the database triggers. After you learn what is in the Table API package, the process for adding customized processing is quite simple.

Contents of the Table API Table Handler Package

The contents of the table handler package, CG$<table_name>, is a series of procedures that enforce data rules for a specific table. Based on the type of feature that you are trying to generate (declarative or advanced), a procedure may or may not contain logic, or for that matter, may or may not even exist! We should also point out that there are numerous PL/SQL constructs (PL/SQL tables, PL/SQL records, and so on) that assist in this process. Since we are just giving an overview of the Table API architecture, we will not be discussing these constructs in detail. Table 9-3 lists all of the procedures contained in the Table API table handler package. It also includes each procedure's accessibility outside of the package, a brief description of the procedure, and a list of the other Table API components that call the procedure. The information presented in this table was gathered after generating each type of declarative usage of the Table API but before adding any customizations. We chose to document its contents in this state because the probability is high that if you are reading this section, you have already implemented some declarative features of the Table API and now want to get more sophisticated. Therefore, the contents of the Table API you are working with will likely be similar to the one outlined in Table 9-3.

Procedure	**Scope**	**Brief Description**	**Called By**
Procedure INS	Public	Processes inserts into table	Trigger CG$BIR_<*Table*>
Procedure UPD	Public	Processes updates into table	Trigger CG$BUR_<*Table*>
Procedure DEL	Public	Processes deletes from table	Trigger CG$BDR_<*Table*>
Procedure LCK	Public	Processes row level locks for table	No Calls*
Procedure INSERT_JN	Public	Process journaling for table Note: Will only be in package if journaling option is enabled for table	Procedure INS Procedure UPD Procedure DEL
Procedure SLCT	Public	Selects values for a given record to be used in further processing	Procedure INS Procedure UPD
Procedure VALIDATE_ARC	Public	Performs arc validation (if applicable—super/sub relationships only)	Trigger CG$BIR_ <*Table*> Trigger CG$BUR_<*Table*>
Procedure VALIDATE_DOMAIN	Public	Performs domain validation for columns using values in CG$REF_CODES	Trigger CG$BIR_<*Table*> Trigger CG$BUR_<*Table*>

TABLE 9-3. *Procedures in the Table API Table Handler Package*

Procedure	Scope	Brief Description	Called By
Procedure CASCADE_UPDATE	Public	Performs cascade update functions in child records if the parent record in the table is deleted	Trigger CG$AUS_<*Table*>
Procedure CASCADE_DELETE	Public	Performs cascade delete function of child records if the parent record is deleted	Trigger CG$ADS_<*Table*>
Procedure UPD_DENORM	Public	Performs a copy of parent values into a child record to a child	Trigger CG$AUS_<*Table*> Procedure UPD
Procedure UPD_OPER_DENORM	Public	Probably supposed to aggregate the child values into a parent record—does not seem to be working yet	Trigger CG$AIS_<*Table*> Trigger CG$AUS_<*Table*> Trigger CG$ADS_<*Table*> Procedure INS Procedure UPD
Procedure VALIDATE_MANDATORY	Private	Processes optionality of columns	Procedure INS Procedure UPD
Procedure UP_AUTOGEN_COLUMNS	Private	Processes auto-generated column actions including sequences, uppercase and audit columns, and parts of the denormalization process	Procedure INS Procedure UPD

TABLE 9-3. *Procedures in the Table API Table Handler Package* (continued)

Procedure	Scope	Brief Description	Called By
Procedure ERR_MSG	Private	Processes errors for the package, calls CG$ERRORS package	Procedure INS Procedure UPD Procedure DEL
Procedure UK_KEY_UPDATEABLE	Private	Raises error when unique key is updated	Called from Procedure UPD when the UKs *Update?* property is set to **No**
Procedure FK_KEY_TRANSFERABLE	Private	Raises error if a foreign key is not transferable	Called from Procedure UPD when the FK's *Transferable?* property is set to **No**

TABLE 9-3. *Procedures in the Table API Table Handler Package* (continued)

*These procedures were not fully supported at the time this chapter was written.

With the knowledge of the contents of the table handler package behind us, we can now focus on the process of adding custom code into the Table API.

Adding Custom Code to the Table API

Adding custom code to the Table API is a simple process of creating a user-defined package that contains all of your customizations and then adding calls to your packaged procedures into the Table API structure.

TIP

We highly recommend placing all of your custom code in one user-defined package per table. This will significantly reduce the associated support effort. The alternative is individual PL/SQL definitions or worse yet, references to program units that do not exist in the repository. Both of these approaches have significant downsides and should be avoided if at all possible.

You have the option of generating code into either the individual triggers or the table handler package. Where you place your code is dependent upon when you would like it to be processed in relation to the generated code. The following table contains a listing of the timing choices and where in the Table API the code is placed.

Timing	Placement of Generated Code
Before <event>	Code is placed at the beginning of the Before <event> trigger.
After <event>	Code is placed at the beginning of the After <event> trigger.
Pre <event>	Code is placed at the beginning of <event> procedure in the table handler package.
Post <event>	Code is placed at the end of the <event> procedure in the table handler package.

We think that it will be easier to understand the process of generating custom code into the Table API if we use an example that at least looks like a real-world program. Therefore, we have designed a process that performs a standard task that looks like something you might use in a real system.

NOTE

Example Description: *The triggers and package shown in this example are designed to perform a cascade update of the status of related records when a parent record is changed. The examples use DSTAT_CD in the DBCRS table from the example application provided with this book. When the status code is updated, the triggers call procedures in a package to perform the update (the package used is the same package that was used for an example in Chapter 7, and the triggers used are the same triggers that were used as examples in Chapter 8).*

The example we are using is the same example we used in Chapters 7 and 8, with the only difference being that we will be integrating our code with the Table API's package and triggers instead of generating our own triggers. To avoid having you reference the other chapters to work through this example, the package is shown in Figure 9-2.

```
CREATE OR REPLACE PACKAGE dbcr_cascade AS
  PROCEDURE dbcr_row(P_ID IN NUMBER, p_CD IN VARCHAR2);
  PROCEDURE dbcr_transaction;
  PROCEDURE clear_pl_tbl;
  TYPE id_TabType IS TABLE OF dbcrs.id%TYPE INDEX BY
BINARY_INTEGER;
  ptr_DBCR_ID     BINARY_INTEGER := 0;
  tab_DBCR_ID     id_TabType;
  tab_Empty       id_TabType; -- This table is used to clear the
table
  TYPE cd_TabType IS TABLE OF dbcrs.dstat_cd%TYPE INDEX BY
BINARY_INTEGER;
  tab_DSTAT_CD    cd_TabType;
  tab_UpdFlg      cd_TabType;

END dbcr_cascade;
/
SHOW ERRORS;

CREATE OR REPLACE PACKAGE BODY dbcr_cascade AS
  PROCEDURE dbcr_row(P_ID IN NUMBER, P_CD IN VARCHAR2) IS
  BEGIN
    IF P_CD = 'CLOSED' THEN
    ptr_DBCR_ID := ptr_DBCR_ID + 1;
    tab_DBCR_ID(ptr_DBCR_ID) := p_ID;
    tab_DSTAT_CD(ptr_DBCR_ID) := p_CD;
        tab_UpdFlg(ptr_DBCR_ID) := 'N';
    END IF;
  END dbcr_row;

  PROCEDURE dbcr_transaction IS
    CURSOR cur_rel_dbcr(pc_DBCR_ID IN NUMBER) IS
    SELECT child_dbcr_id, rel_type
      FROM DBCR_DBCRS
     WHERE parent_dbcr_id = pc_DBCR_ID;
```

FIGURE 9-2. *Package example*

```
  BEGIN
    FOR i IN 1..ptr_DBCR_ID LOOP
      FOR c IN cur_rel_dbcr(tab_DBCR_ID(i)) LOOP
    IF c.rel_type = 'SUB' AND tab_UpdFlg(i) != 'Y' THEN
        tab_UpdFlg(i) := 'Y';
        UPDATE DBCRS SET DSTAT_CD = tab_DSTAT_CD(i)
         WHERE id = c.child_dbcr_id;
    END IF;
      END LOOP;
    END LOOP;
    clear_pl_tbl;
  END dbcr_transaction;

  PROCEDURE clear_pl_tbl IS
  BEGIN
    ptr_DBCR_ID := 0;
    tab_DBCR_ID := tab_Empty;
  END clear_pl_tbl;

END dbcr_cascade;
/
SHOW ERRORS
```

FIGURE 9-2. *Package example* (continued)

Steps for Generating Custom Code into the Table API

Here are the steps needed to implement this example:

1. Create the DBCR_CASCADE package PL/SQL definition with the above code. This is the package that contains the custom logic to be executed. For assistance with this step, please refer to Chapter 7, "Generating Packages."

2. Create a new Table API/Trigger Logic definition for the DBCRS relational table definition. Do this by pressing the Create icon in the Design Editor toolbar. This will launch a set of dialogs that will gather all of the necessary information required for the Table API/Trigger Logic definition. The following steps detail the settings used for this example.

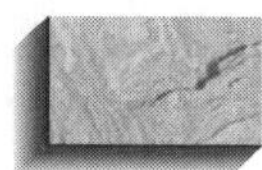

NOTE

You will need to define more than one Table API/Trigger Logic definition to complete the example. Each Table API/Trigger Logic definition is based on the event that triggers its action. You can specify more than one action to occur per event, but you cannot specify more than one event per definition. For instance, you could make multiple packaged procedure calls per ***After-Insert-row*** *event; however, you could not specify two different events on the same definition such as* ***After-Insert-row*** *and* ***After-Delete-row****. You will need to complete steps 2–6 twice to complete the example.*

3. The Events dialog is the will be displayed first. Using this dialog, you can specify that you would like to add user-defined processing to the **After-Update-row** event. The event selected from the list will determine the timing of when the logic will be executed, as well as where the code will be generated in the Table API architecture (trigger or package). Figure 9-3 shows the Events dialog used in this example. When you have completed this dialog, click Next.

4. The Logic dialog is the second dialog that will be displayed. Using this dialog, you can name the logic you are adding to this event (*Name* = **Cascade Status Update - Row**). This will give a label to the event logic you are adding to the Table API. This name is used by Designer to identify this custom code block in the Table API/Trigger Logic section of the Design Editor. You should always use a descriptive name so that you will be able to easily see what custom code has been added to the Table API. Figure 9-4 shows the Logic dialog used in this example. When you have completed this dialog, click Next.

5. The Last dialog is, naturally, the last dialog that will be displayed. This dialog provides you with two different ways in which you can exit the dialogs you have just used to define the relational table trigger definition. Select option two (*Create the Definition and open the Logic Editor to enter the logic code*) to create this definition, and then click Finish. Figure 9-5 shows the Last dialog used for this example.

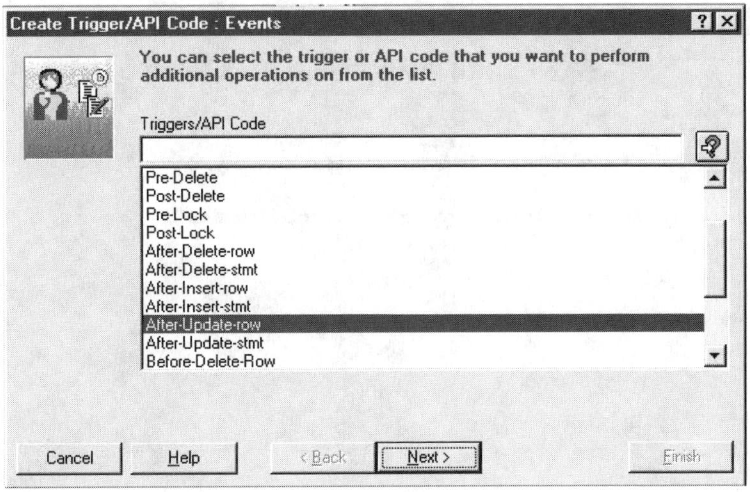

FIGURE 9-3. *Events dialog*

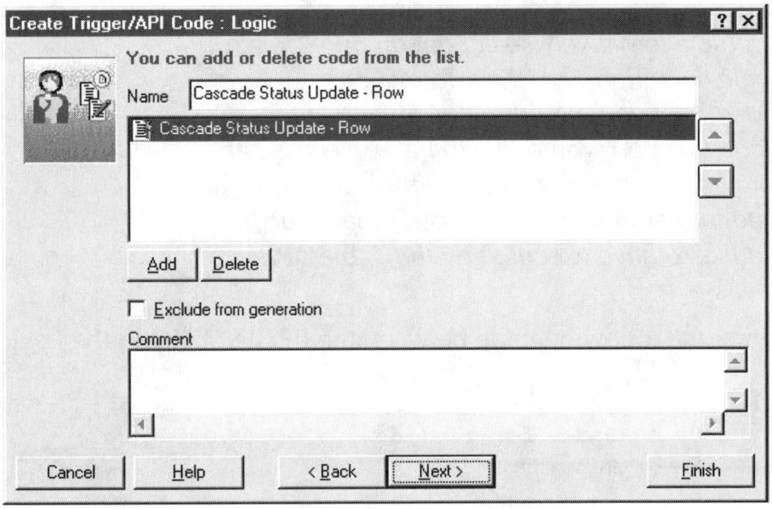

FIGURE 9-4. *Logic dialog*

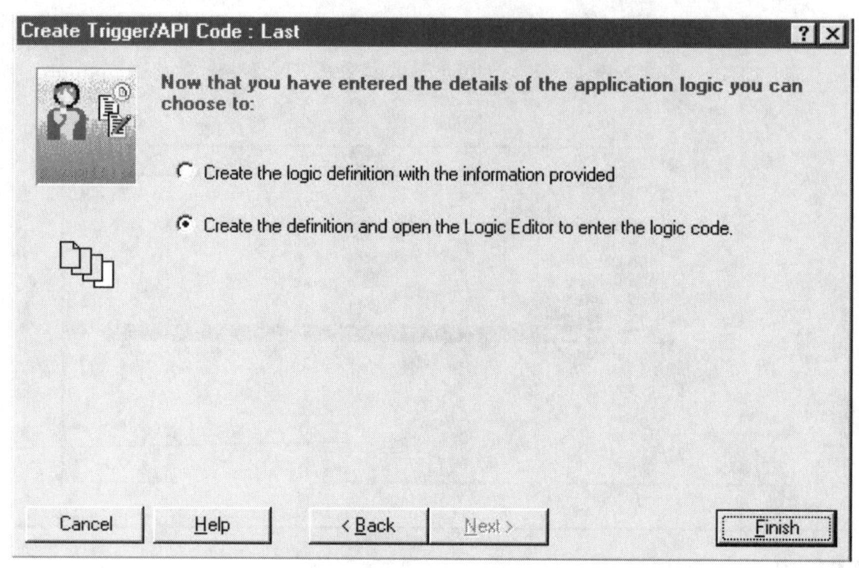

FIGURE 9-5. *Last dialog*

NOTE

You could alternatively select option one (Create the logic definition with the information provided), but you would not be able to enter the code that you would like to have executed at this time. Currently, the Logic Editor is the only method for defining the actual code that you would like to have executed by the Table API.

6. Enter the following code between the BEGIN..END in the Logic Editor:

```
IF new.dstat_cd <> old.dstat_cd AND new.dstat_cd  <> 'NEW' THEN
   dbcr_cascade.dbcr_row(:new.id, :new.dstat_cd);
END IF;
```

7. Click Save, then dismiss the Logic Editor.

8. Repeat steps 2–7, using the following information:

Step	Type	Value
3	Event	After-Update-stmt
4	Logic	Cascade Status Update - Statement
5	Finish	Select Create the Definition and Open the Logic Editor to Enter the Logic Code.
6	PL/SQL	`IF new.dstat_cd <> old.dstat_cd THEN dbcr_cascade.dbcr_transaction; END IF;`

9. Generate the Table API structure by navigating to Generate → Generate Table API. Generation of the Table API will create four files; those include

- <file prefix>.SQL Executes all of the files created when generating the Table API
- <file prefix>.PKS Contains the generated Table API package specification
- <file prefix>.PKB Contains the generated Table API package body
- <file prefix>.TRG Contains the generated Table API trigger definitions

NOTE
<file prefix> is a name that you specify when generating server-side objects. This name will be given to all files created during that execution of the Server Generator.

Figure 9-6 is an annotated version of the <file prefix>.TRG file. Since this file is quite large, we are only showing the trigger definitions that have our generated customizations included. To make finding our user-defined processing easier, they will appear in bold typeface and are surrounded by the number 1 in superscript, for example: [1]**a business rule**[1].

```
PROMPT Creating After Update Row Trigger on 'DBCRS'
CREATE OR REPLACE TRIGGER cg$AUR_DBCRS
AFTER UPDATE ON DBCRS FOR EACH ROW
BEGIN
--  Application_logic Pre-After.Update.Row <<Start>>
[1]BEGIN
 IF new.dstat_cd <> old.dstat_cd
     AND new.dstat_cd  <> 'NEW' THEN
  dbcr_cascade.dbcr_row(:new.id, :new.dstat_cd);
 END IF;
END;[1]
--  Application_logic Pre-After.Update.Row << End >>
    NULL;

--  Application_logic Post-After.Update.Row <<Start>>

--  Application_logic Post-After.Update.Row << End >>
END;
/

PROMPT Creating After Update Statement Trigger on 'DBCRS'
CREATE OR REPLACE TRIGGER cg$AUS_DBCRS
AFTER UPDATE ON DBCRS
DECLARE
    idx        BINARY_INTEGER := cg$DBCRS.cg$table.FIRST;
    cg$old_rec cg$DBCRS.cg$row_type;
    cg$rec     cg$DBCRS.cg$row_type;
    fk_check INTEGER;
BEGIN

--  Application_logic Pre-After.Update.Statement <<Start>>
[1]BEGIN
 IF new.dstat_cd <> old.dstat_cd THEN
 dbcr_cascade.dbcr_transaction;
 END IF;
END;[1]

--  Application_logic Pre-After.Update.Statement << End >>
    WHILE idx IS NOT NULL LOOP
        cg$old_rec.ID := cg$DBCRS.cg$table(idx).ID;
        cg$old_rec.APP_ID := cg$DBCRS.cg$table(idx).APP_ID;
        cg$old_rec.NUM := cg$DBCRS.cg$table(idx).NUM;
        cg$old_rec.DBCR_DESC := cg$DBCRS.cg$table(idx).DBCR_DESC;
        cg$old_rec.KEEP_DATA_FLAG := cg$DBCRS.cg$table(idx).KEEP_DATA_FLAG;
        cg$old_rec.D2K_UPD_FLAG := cg$DBCRS.cg$table(idx).D2K_UPD_FLAG;
```

FIGURE 9-6. *Generated Table API customization example*

```
        cg$old_rec.COMPLETED_DATE := cg$DBCRS.cg$table(idx).COMPLETED_DATE;
        cg$old_rec.DSTAT_CD := cg$DBCRS.cg$table(idx).DSTAT_CD;
        cg$old_rec.ASSIGNED_TO_PER_ID :=
cg$DBCRS.cg$table(idx).ASSIGNED_TO_PER_ID;
        cg$old_rec.VER_ID := cg$DBCRS.cg$table(idx).VER_ID;
        cg$old_rec.REQUESTED_BY_PER_ID :=
cg$DBCRS.cg$table(idx).REQUESTED_BY_PER_ID;

    IF NOT (cg$DBCRS.called_from_package) THEN
        idx := cg$DBCRS.cg$table.NEXT(idx);
        cg$rec.ID := cg$DBCRS.cg$table(idx).ID;
        cg$rec.APP_ID := cg$DBCRS.cg$table(idx).APP_ID;
        cg$rec.NUM := cg$DBCRS.cg$table(idx).NUM;
        cg$rec.DBCR_DESC := cg$DBCRS.cg$table(idx).DBCR_DESC;
        cg$rec.KEEP_DATA_FLAG := cg$DBCRS.cg$table(idx).KEEP_DATA_FLAG;
        cg$rec.D2K_UPD_FLAG := cg$DBCRS.cg$table(idx).D2K_UPD_FLAG;
        cg$rec.COMPLETED_DATE := cg$DBCRS.cg$table(idx).COMPLETED_DATE;
        cg$rec.DSTAT_CD := cg$DBCRS.cg$table(idx).DSTAT_CD;
        cg$rec.ASSIGNED_TO_PER_ID :=
cg$DBCRS.cg$table(idx).ASSIGNED_TO_PER_ID;
        cg$rec.VER_ID := cg$DBCRS.cg$table(idx).VER_ID;
        cg$rec.REQUESTED_BY_PER_ID :=
cg$DBCRS.cg$table(idx).REQUESTED_BY_PER_ID;

        cg$DBCRS.upd_denorm(cg$rec,
                              cg$DBCRS.cg$tableind(idx)
                             );
        cg$DBCRS.upd_oper_denorm(cg$rec,
                                 cg$old_rec,

                                 cg$DBCRS.cg$tableind(idx)
                                );
          cg$DBCRS.called_from_package := FALSE;
    END IF;

        cg$DBCRS.cascade_update(cg$rec, cg$old_rec);
        idx := cg$DBCRS.cg$table.NEXT(idx);
END LOOP;

    cg$DBCRS.cg$table.DELETE;

--  Application_logic Post-After.Update.Statement <<Start>>

--  Application_logic Post-After.Update.Statement << End >>
END;
/
```

FIGURE 9-6. *Generated Table API customization example* (continued)

Generation Troubleshooting Guide

Problem	**Solution**
When I generate the aggregation of a child value into the parent, the value gets aggregated when the parent record changes but is not updated if child records are deleted or updated.	This is a bug. It seems that only one side of this functionality is currently working. If you want this to work correctly, you will have to add the code yourself. This will probably be fixed in future versions.
The foreign key validation that I specified to be enforced using the Table API is not generating.	Make sure that you generate the Table API at the same time for both the parent and child tables that are related by the foreign key. This is the only way to generate enforcement of foreign key validation into the Table API.
I can't generate custom code at the end of a trigger. The code is always placed at the beginning of the trigger.	You are correct. Modify the <table_name>.TRG file and place the code you would like to have executed at the end of the desired trigger definition.
When I generate a simple denormalization for a parent value into the child, it populates the column when the child record is created but does not generate the code to update the denormalized column if the source is updated.	Make sure that you generate the Table API at the same time for both the parent and child tables that are related by the foreign key. The code needed to propagate changes to the source column is only generated if the Table API for both tables are generated at the same time.
I can't get the simple denormalization of a parent column into a child table to generate.	1. Make sure that you select a column and key that refers to a parent table. The table that the denormalized column is in has to be at the many end of the key you select. 2. Make sure that the denormalization - *Using Operator* property is **Null**.
I can't get the simple denormalization of an aggregation of child data into a parent column to generate.	1. Make sure that you select a column and key that refer to a child table. The table that the denormalized column is in has to be at the one end of the key you select. 2. Make sure that you enter a value for the denormalization - *Using Operator* property. If no operator is entered, the denormalization will not be generated.

Problem	Solution
When I try to compile the Table API with a derived column with a *Derivation Expression Type* of **SQL Expression**, I get compile errors.	In the release used for this book (2.1.2), the **SQL Expression** option is not working properly. The derivation expression is always generated as if it is a **Function Call**. To make the derived columns work in the Table API, always make sure the derivation expression works as a function (something that will work at the end of a :=) in the generated package. See the previous special section, "No Differences Between SQL Expression and Function Call," found in the "Column Derivations" section for a workaround.
There is no option to capture the design of the Table API.	You are right. The Table API is generated from the relational definition. If you are using the Table API, you should already have the all the definitions in the repository. You can create repository definitions for all of the components of the Table API using the Design Capture utility, but you would then need to map all of the functionality to the appropriate definitions to enable forward generation. This process is long and tedious and is not recommended.

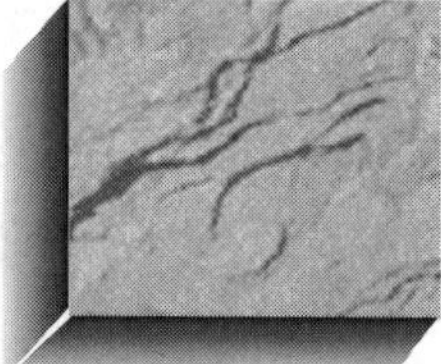

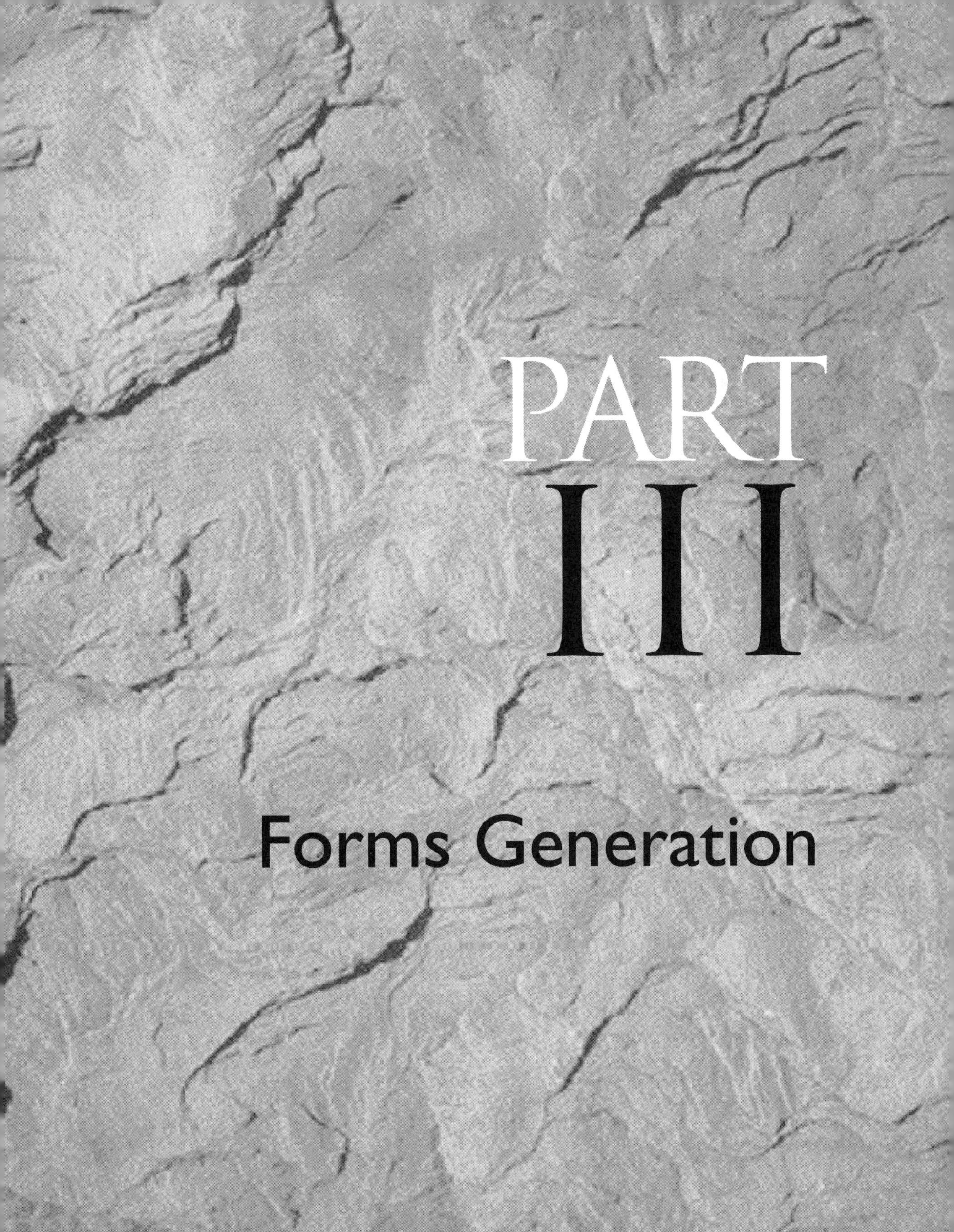

PART III

Forms Generation

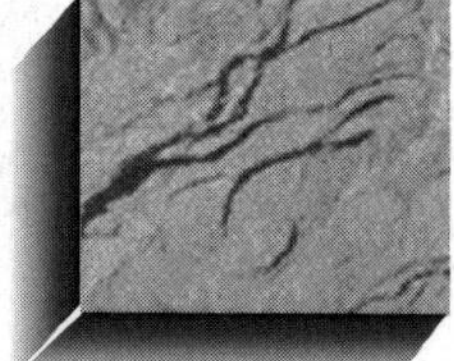

CHAPTER 10

Overview of Forms Generation

In Chapter 1, we presented a basic overview of the whole system generation process. In this chapter, we'll give a more detailed overview of Developer Forms generation. This chapter will cover the following topics:

- The basic layout of a generated form
- An overview of sources used for forms generation
- The source in Designer for the basic forms components.
- An overview of the basic features that can be generated
- An overview of some important design decisions you will need to make

Components and Layout of Generated Forms

Before we start showing you how to generate forms, we'll go over exactly what an Oracle Developer Form is. To do this, we'll give you an overview of the structure and layout of generated Oracle Developer Forms. Of course, if you already know all about Oracle Developer Forms, you can skip this section; but if you don't, or if you need a little refresher, this section may help you.

Layout of Generated Forms

We'll start with a couple of annotated examples of generated forms (Figure 10-1 and Figure 10-2). This will help you understand the forms generation nomenclature. Each of these examples has many of the forms features labeled and Tables 10-1 and 10-2 describe each of the features and indicate where they are covered in this book.

Mapping of Designer Objects to Developer Forms Components

Oracle Developer Forms consist primarily of the following four types of components: windows, canvases, blocks, and items. There are many other

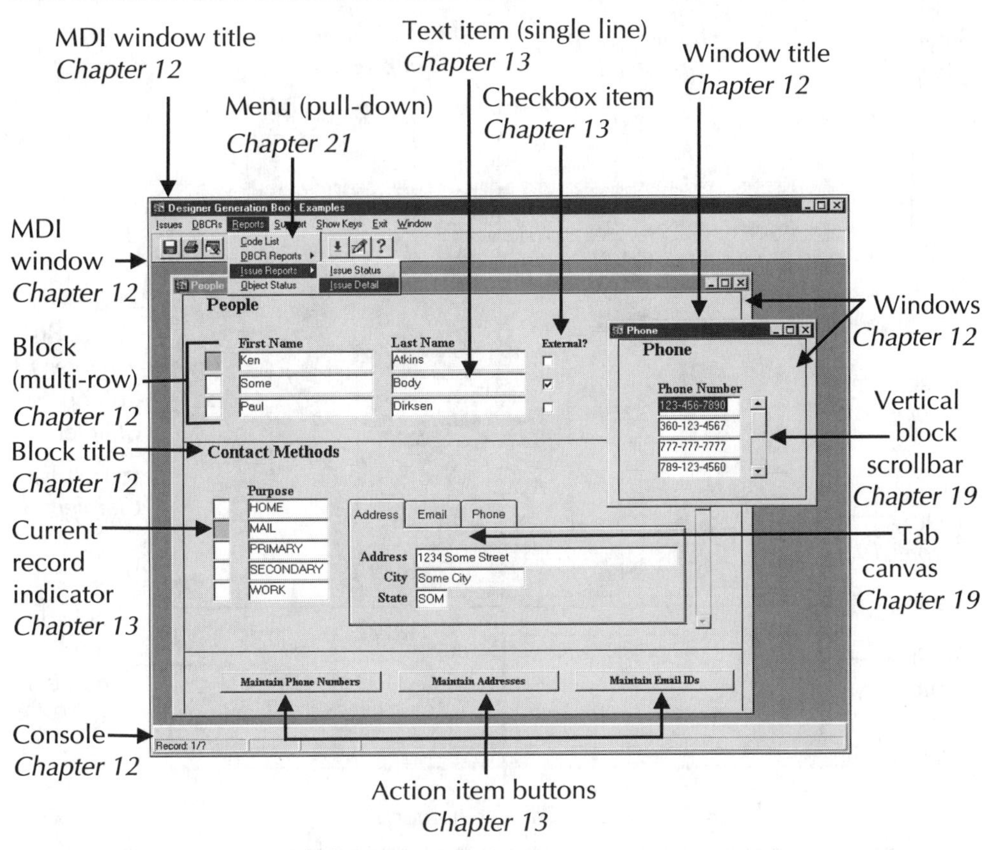

FIGURE 10-1. *Annotated example of a generated form (#1)*

component types, but they are mostly used to support these four basic types. These four component types are the foundation upon which the whole form is built. Table 10-3 lists these basic components and their source in Oracle Designer.

This only an overview of the mapping of Designer objects to Developer Form objects. It is intended to help give you a context for the discussions of forms generation in this book.

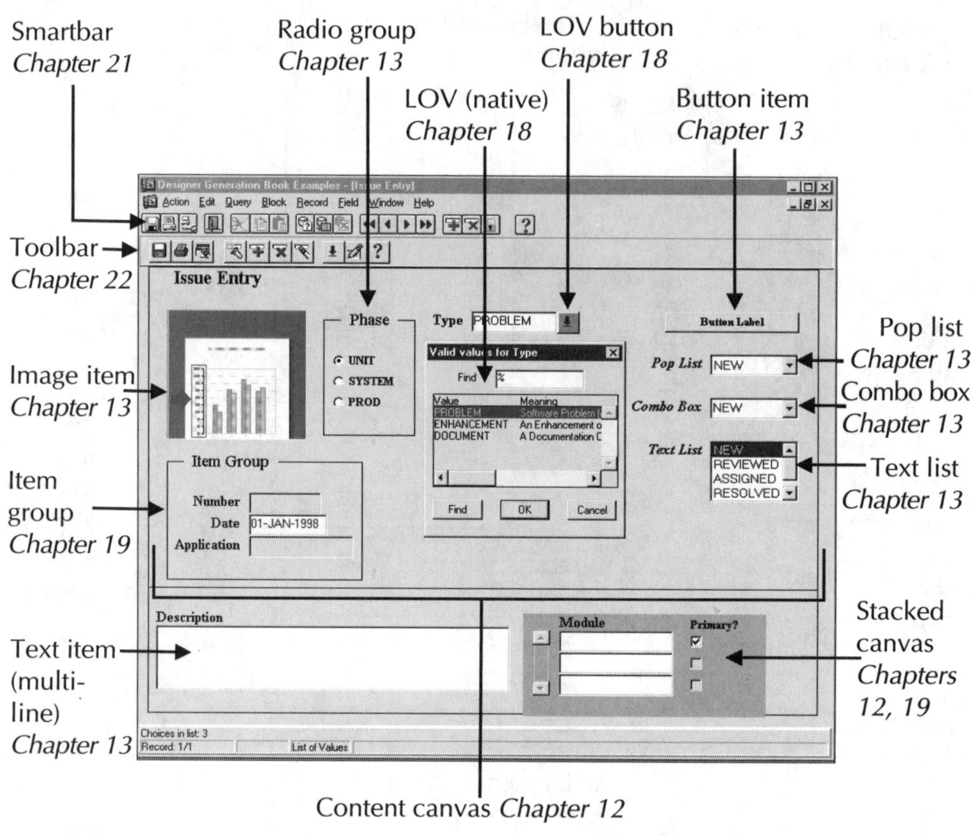

FIGURE 10-2. *Annotated example of a generated form (#2)*

Feature	Chapter	Description
Action item buttons	13	Action item buttons are buttons that can be easily generated to navigate between windows and forms.
Block (multi-row)	12	A block is a group of items that correspond to the same data source (table, query, procedure, or none). Each block in a generated form is produced by one module component.

TABLE 10-1. *Description of Features in Example Generated Form (#1)*

Feature	Chapter	Description
Block title	12	Each block can have a boilerplate text title.
Checkbox item	13	A GUI item that allows for two possible settings, one indicated by the box being checked and the other by the box being blank.
Console	12	An area at the bottom of the MDI window (or root window for non-MS deployment) that displays the form status and message area.
Current record indicator	13	A special text item that indicates the current record by having its background color changed when the cursor is on a record.
MDI window	12	In MS Windows, a special window that contains all of the other windows in the application. The MDI window has special significance in an MS environment.
MDI window title	12	The title of the MDI window becomes the title for the application, so it has special significance.
Menu (pull-down)	21	The standard method for navigating among all of the forms in your application system.
Tab canvas	19	A GUI control that is made up of one or more tab pages that can be used to group and display a subset of related information.
Text item (single line)	13	The most common item type. Allows for free format entry of textual information.
Vertical block scrollbar	19	Allows for scrolling through the records returned by a query when there are more records queried than can be shown on the screen.
Windows	12	A window is a rectangular area of the screen that contains an application. A window provides a frame through which all visual objects that make up a Form Module can be seen and interacted with.
Window title	12	Each window can have a title that appears on the shaded area at the top of the window.

TABLE 10-1. *Description of Features in Example Generated Form (#1)* (continued)

Feature	Chapter	Description
Button item	13	A button is used to initiate special functionality that has been written into the form.
Combo box	13	A combo box allows the user to select from a predefined list (like a pop list) or to enter a value that is not on the list.
Content canvas	12	The content canvas is the basic foundation upon which the items are placed.
Image item	13	An image item is used to display image and graphical data, for instance, a photograph or drawing.
Item group	19	Item groups are Designer objects that can be used to group sets of related items together on the screen layout. They can be used in many ways to control the generated layout.
LOV (native)	18	A native LOV is a standard method used to select the value of a text item from a predefined list. The list can be based on another table in the database (a lookup) or hard-coded into the form.
LOV button	18	A button can be generated next to items that use LOVs. Pressing this button brings up the LOV.
Pop list	13	A pop list allows the user to select values from a predefined list. The item's value can only be one of the values defined in the pop list. The user has to click the button next to the pop list to see all of the possible values.
Radio group	13	A radio group allows the user to select one value from a predefined list. All of the possible values are visible on the screen.
Smartbar	21	A smartbar is a special toolbar that is part of the menu form. It contains a set of icons that can be used to initiate standard functionality.
Stacked canvas	12, 19	A stacked canvas is a special canvas that can be defined to overlay an area of the underlying content canvas.

TABLE 10-2. *Description of Features in Example Generated Form (#2)*

Feature	Chapter	Description
Text item (multi-line)	13	Multiline text items allow for the entry of long textual data. They can be defined to automatically word wrap and can use scrollbars.
Text list	13	A text list allows the user to select values from a predefined list. The item's value can only be one of the values defined in the list. Two or more of the possible options can be displayed at all times.
Toolbar	22	A toolbar is a special canvas that is inherited from the template form used to generate the module. It consists of a set of icons that can be used to implement standard functionality.

TABLE 10-2. *Description of Features in Example Generated Form (#2)* (continued)

Designer Object	Forms Component	Comments
Module	Form	The form is the actual program that is generated. It contains all of the windows, canvases, blocks, and items.
Window	Window	Windows have a one-to-one mapping from the Designer Repository to the forms component.
Module component	Canvas	The canvas is the area that the items are placed upon. Canvases are created for module components, and all of the items in a module component will be placed on the canvas generated for that module component. However, two or more module components can be generated into the same canvas. There are many types of canvases: *Content* Contents are the main type of canvas. They are the basic foundation upon which all of the items are displayed. *Stacked* Canvases can be displayed on top of other canvases (stacked) and are used to generate advanced and dynamic layouts. *Tab* Canvases are used to implement the standard tab folder interface standard.

TABLE 10-3. *Mapping of Designer Objects to Developer Forms Components*

Designer Object	Forms Component	Comments
Module component	Block	A block will be generated for each module component. All of the items in that module component will be included in its generated block.
Bound item Unbound item	Item	There are two types of items in Oracle Designer: *Bound* items are connected to actual columns in the database. They are used to display, update, and insert data into these columns. *Unbound* items are not directly connected to any columns in the database. They are used for control and processing purposes in the generated forms.

TABLE 10-3. *Mapping of Designer Objects to Developer Forms Component* (continued)

Sources of Information for Forms Generation

In Chapter 1, we mentioned some of the basic sources of information that are used by the Oracle Designer Forms Generator to produce the forms. These basic sources are

- The Oracle Designer Repository
- Forms and Menu Templates
- Object libraries
- Preferences

Figure 10-3 gives you a graphical overview of these sources for generation. Not all of the sources are of equal significance in the generation of the form. For instance, as you would expect, most of the information comes from the Oracle Designer Repository, and, in the newest release of Designer, there is very little information that comes from the template forms.

Template Forms

Oracle Designer uses template forms as the "container" into which the form will be generated. The basic purposes of the template forms are to set up the following:

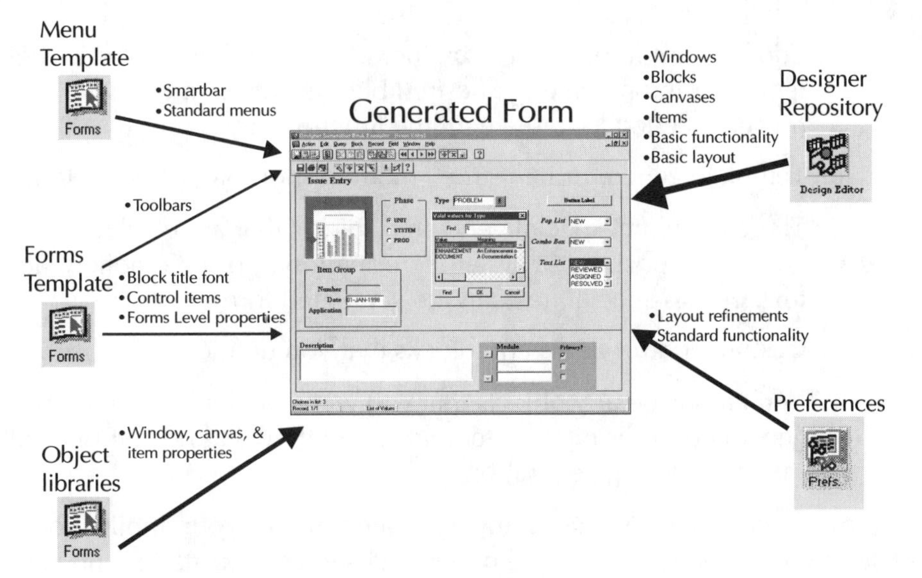

FIGURE 10-3. *Sources of information for form generation*

1. **The Source for Form-Level Properties**

   There are some form-level properties that are inherited from the template. Examples of these are *coordinate system* and *character cell width* and *height.*

2. **The Settings for Various Title and Decoration Properties**

   Most of the fonts and visual attributes for the generated items will be inherited from objects in the object libraries. However, in release 2.1, there are still some properties that are inherited only from template objects. These are mostly titles and decorations that are generated onto the form.

3. **Standard Objects to Include in the Forms**

   There are two types of objects that can be included in the templates. Custom user objects are copied into the generated form as is, and special generator objects direct the generators to create specific objects into the form. These objects are usually used to implement the following:

a. Toolbars

Toolbars are implemented by including a toolbar canvas in the template and placing the desired buttons into it, along with the triggers needed to implement the functionality.

b. Template generator items (i.e., module short name, user, etc.)

There are many special generator objects that are used to generate repository or system information into static boilerplate text, or into special items in the generated forms.

c. Custom control items and blocks that you define

You can place any objects that you want available in all of the generated forms into the template, and they will be automatically inherited during generation.

You will need to have at least one template form for your application. Oracle provides you with a couple of templates to get you started; however, you will probably end up customizing these templates to some extent. You can also develop many templates for your application, each designed for a particular type of form. For instance, you might have one standard template for your regular forms, another for parameter forms, and another for wizard forms.

As mentioned in Chapter 1, you can also purchase commercial templates that add a lot of value to your applications. See Chapter 1 for a list of the commercial template packages that are available. Some marketing information for these products is also included on the CD that comes with this book.

See Chapter 22 for more information about how to modify and use template forms.

Template Menus

Just like standard template forms, template menu forms are the containers into which the menus are generated. Template menus are Oracle Developer menus that serve the following purposes:

1. **Adding Standard Menus to Menu Modules**

   Any menus that you want to appear in all of your menus (for instance, a standard Help menu with Show keys, About, Help, etc.) can be placed into a menu template.

2. **Adding Iconic Menus (Smartbars) to Menu Modules**

   You can add smartbars (iconic menus) to your generated menu modules by defining them in menu templates.

Unlike with forms, you do not need to specify a menu template in order to generate menus. For more information about using menu templates, see Chapter 22.

Object Libraries

The use of object libraries is a new feature of Oracle Developer release 2, used by Oracle Designer. In previous releases, you could only generate specific forms properties that were defined to be used by the Forms Generator. If you wanted to set a property that was not used by the generator, you had to modify the form after it was generated. Using object libraries, however, you can now set almost *any* forms property either by modifying specially named objects in a standard object library, or by assigning designer objects to specific objects you have created in the object libraries. When you do this, the generated objects inherit all of the properties of the source object in the object library.

Oracle Designer Repository

Obviously, most of the information needed to generate the forms comes from the information you have entered into the repository. While the object libraries and preferences may define *how* an object will be generated, the information in the repository defines *what* will be generated. Nearly all of the rest of this book will deal with this topic, so we will not discuss it here.

Preferences

Preferences are generation directives that tell the generator how to generate the objects into the forms. They are used to implement UI design standards; refine the layout of the generated forms; and, in many cases, determine how the generated form will operate. Much of the details about how to generate specific layouts and functionality will be determined by the preferences. We will be discussing various preferences and their effects on generation throughout the rest of this book.

Overview of Standard Generated Functionality

An overview of the capabilities of the Forms Generator would be useful at this point. In the following chapters, we will be giving you detailed descriptions of how to generate this functionality; but this comprehensive overview of the generation possibilities will help give you a "big picture" understanding of generation.

Generated Functionality	Description
Referential integrity rules: PK constraints UK constraints FK constraints	Oracle Designer will generate all of the code needed to enforce your system's referential integrity. You can generate the code on the server, client, or both.
Canvas and window coordination	Oracle Designer will generate all of the code needed to coordinate the display and positioning of the forms, canvases, and windows. This includes functionality like the following: 1. The option of closing all dependent windows when the main window is closed. 2. The display and positioning of stacked header and footer canvases.
Block synchronization (for example, parent/child)	Oracle Designer will generate the code needed to synchronize the display of data blocks that are related by keys in the database. You can also generate code that will allow the user to decide how the synchronization will occur.
Navigation within a form Item navigation Keyboard shortcuts Action Items	The code needed to navigate between the items on the form can be generated. You can also generate shortcut keys that navigate to various places (blocks, item groups, etc.), as well as action items that can navigate between windows.
Item validation and lookups	Item validation using List of Values (LOV) forms or just generated triggers is generated for the appropriate items in your system.

Generated Functionality	Description
Form-to-form navigation Menu navigation Action items	Generated menus allow for easy navigation between forms, but that is not the only option. You can also easily generate buttons that will allow navigation between forms based on keys that are defined between the base tables in the two forms.
Error handling	Extensive error handling is generated into the forms. This error handling can be as simple as user-friendly static messages that will display when constraint violations occur, and as complex as a full-blown, table-based error message system.
Other functionality: Sequence numbers Journaling Audit columns Context items Derived items Summarizations	This list is just a sampling of the specific functionalities that can be generated into your system under certain circumstances.

Important Design Decisions

Before you start generating your system, there are some important design decisions that you need to make. We will be covering how to implement these decisions in Parts II and III of this book, as well as discussing some of the ramifications of various designs. However, an overview of some of the decisions you will need to make will be helpful.

Navigation Styles

There are many different navigation styles that can be generated into your system. Some examples are

- Relying exclusively on pull-down menu navigation and not using any form-to-form button navigation.
- Tying your whole system together with specific navigation buttons at the bottom of each form and only allowing navigation in context and when it makes sense.

- Including a system-specific navigation bar that allows for navigation between the modules by pressing the appropriate iconic buttons.
- Using a combination of all three of these!

When you make this decision, you should consider the development effort needed to initially produce and maintain the navigation. The pull-down menu navigation is probably the easiest to generate and maintain, but it is not very pretty, and the navigation can easily lose its context. For example, a user may ask, "What do I do now?" because the pull-down menus do not give them any visual clues for the next step. If you use navigation buttons at the bottom of the screen, however, the user will have an easy visual indication of what will most likely be the next screens they will need to use. This sort of navigation is more difficult to maintain, however, because the forms themselves have to be modified to alter the navigation.

Multiple/Single Window User Interface

One of the user interface design decisions you will need to make is whether you want to present the user with multiple movable windows, very few windows, or just a single window that displays the various screens when needed. The multiple window option conforms to the standard Microsoft Windows interface standard and, therefore, is probably used most often. However, if your user community is not very Windows-savvy, this type of interface can get them into a lot of trouble.

We find that it is often better to reduce the number of separate windows that are presented to the user. This can be as extreme as only having one full-screen window active at a time and toggling the various screens through it, or it can be a more moderate interface with one base window always displayed but allowing a few other subordinate windows.

Whatever you decide, you should consider this design carefully, taking into account your user base, the type of system, etc. Then you can make it a design standard and implement it consistently throughout the system.

Type of Help System

Oracle Designer can generate two types of help systems:

- A standard Microsoft Help system (MS Help)
- An Oracle Developer Forms-based help system.

If you are planning to deploy your system only on Microsoft-based systems (Windows, NT), then it's usually best to use MS Help system generation. The MS Help system is prettier, has more functionality, and is easier to maintain than the Forms-based system.

If your system is going to be deployed in a non-MS environment (for instance, using Web-based forms or in Motif), you should choose the Forms-based system. See Chapter 24 for more information about help system generation.

Domain Validation Method

Every system has columns that are restricted to a domain of distinct values. There are a couple of approaches that you can take to implement these domains using Oracle Designer:

- **Using the Case Generator Reference Code table**

  Using the Case Generator Reference Code table (CG_REF_CODES), you can implement all of these domains in a single, system-wide table. This table and the code needed to use it are generated easily from Oracle Designer. See Chapter 26 for more information about this approach. However, if many of your code tables have a lot of values, this table may get large and unwieldy.

- **Using Separate Code Tables for Each Domain**

  You can also choose to generate and maintain a separate code table for each domain in your system. Using these code tables is a little more intuitive, and you can more easily generate the code needed to maintain them. However, you will need many more tables in the database to implement this standard. This is a good option for domains with a lot of values.

- **Hard-Code the Domains into the Client and Server**

  You could choose not to store the code values in the database at all. You could use check constraints to enforce the code values on the server, and hard-code the distinct values in the forms. This option is almost always a bad idea. While this may be easy to generate and implement initially, it will end up costing you in maintenance, because you will have to modify the forms just to change the possible code values.

- **Use a Hybrid of These Approaches**

  You can also use a hybrid of all of these approaches. For most of your domains, in which there are only a few possible values (say, 5–20) that do not change too often, you could use the CG_REF_CODES approach. For larger domains that change frequently, you may want to implement a separate table for each domain. You could even make a case for using the hard-coded approach if the domain has only a few values, and you are *very* sure it will *never, never* change.

Layout Standards

There are many layout standard decisions that should be applied to the whole system. In most cases, you should strive for a consistent look and feel for the whole application. To do this, you should make these decisions once before the actual development is started and then use preferences, templates, object libraries, and written guidelines to enforce the standards. Some examples of layout decisions that need to be made are

- Where to place block scrollbars: Left or Right?
- Where to place the block title: Left, Center, or Right?
- Should you use LOV buttons?
- What font should be used for prompts and titles?

There are many more layout standard decisions that need to be made; and, in your first few applications you will probably continue to tweak your standards until you are satisfied. In the next section, we identify some of the many important preferences that you should set at the application level.

Important Preferences to Be Set at the Application Level

Before any generation is done for an application system, someone should review the whole list of preferences and decide what the settings should be for the application. Some of the preferences are used to implement the design decisions previously mentioned. Other preferences represent other design decisions you need to make.

To help you with this, Table 10-4 lists the preferences that are most often set at the application level for the whole system.

Preference	Purpose
Dba → Scope of online help table (HPTABL)	Determines if the generated Forms-based help system uses one table for all of the applications or a separate table for each application. Default: **Single Table**
End User Interface → Allow user to toggle block synchronization mode (BSCHMD)	Determines if user is allowed to toggle block synchronization. If set to **Yes**, you should also check the settings of the BSMON, BSMOFF, OFFFLD, and ONFLD preferences; you may want to change them from their defaults. Default: **Yes**
End User Interface → Block Sync – Co-ordination scope (BSCSCP)	Determines when the generated forms will synchronize the display of data in dependant blocks. Default: **any visible block on the current canvas**
End User Interface → Query block on entry to new canvas (BSQENP)	Determines whether the forms will automatically query the data when the user first enters a canvas. Default: **Yes**
End User Interface → Generate console window (CONWIN)	Determines if a console window is generated. If you don't want the console information displayed, you can suppress it with this preference. Default: **Yes**
End User Interface → Current Record Indicator Settings (CURREC)	Tells the generator to highlight the current record in a different color. Default: **No Blocks**
End User Interface → Warn user if delete will cascade to other tables (DELWRN)	Warns the user if a delete action will cascade to other tables. Default: **Warn if deletion cascades**

TABLE 10-4. *List of Preferences Most Often Set at the Application Level*

Preference	Purpose
End User Interface → Editor to use for CHAR text items (DFTCED)	Determines the editor that will be used to edit text items. If you modify this, you should also consider modifying the DFTLED preference for LONG items.
End User Interface → Automatically invoke field editor (EDITPP)	Causes the editor to automatically appear when the cursor is navigated into an empty text item for the first time. Default: **No**
End User Interface → Type of Help System used (HLPTYP)	Determines whether the MS help or Forms help systems are generated. If set to **MS Help**, make sure to set the HLPFRM preference also. Default: **MS Help**
End User Interface → Package used for messaging (MSGSFT)	Allows you to specify an alternative package to display error messages instead of the MESSAGE built-in.
End User Interface → National language for end-user text (NATLNG)	Sets the language for the generated error and warning messages. Default: **AMERICAN**
End User Interface → Add call to calendar window for date fields (USECAL)	Tells the generator to use a pop-up calendar window to set the date for date items. Default: **No**
Form/Menu Attachment → Name of menu module if not implicit menu generation (FMNDMN)	Specifies the name of the menu module if your application is to have one menu module as the master menu. Default: **<Null>**
Layout-Block → Block scrollbar position (BLKSBP)	Determines if the block scrollbars appear on the left or right of the blocks. The factory default for this preference is **Left justify**. However, most windows standards place the scrollbar on the right, so it should be changed to **Right justify**.

TABLE 10-4. *List of Preferences Most Often Set at the Application Level* (continued)

Preference	Purpose
Layout-Block → Title first block of form (BLKTFB)	Tells the generator if it should title the first block of a form. Since the first block title can often be redundant with the module title, setting this preference to **No** can save screen space. Default: **Yes**
Layout-Block → Block title justification (BLKTLJ)	Tells the generator where to place block titles. You should use the same setting for all blocks in your system for consistency. Default: **Left justification**
List of values → Use a button to indicate available list of values (LOVBUT)	Tells the generator if a special LOV button is to be placed next to every item that has an LOV available. Default: **No**
Menu-End User → Enable Use security flag (MNUEUS)	Determines if the role-based menu security is used. Set this to **No** if you do not want to use it. Default: **Yes**
Menu-Template → The name of the menu template (STMMMB)	Sets the default for the *Template Name* field of the Generate Form dialog for menu generation. This can be overridden during generation. You should enter the name of the most commonly used menu template here.
Standards → The name of the template form (STFFMB)	Sets the default for the *Template Name* field of the Generate Form dialog for form generation. This can be overridden during generation. You should enter the name of the most commonly used template here.
Standards → Name of Object Library for Generation (STOOLB)	Sets the default for the *Object Library Name* field of the Generate Form dialog for form generation. This can be overridden during generation. You should enter the name of the most commonly used object library here.

TABLE 10-4. *List of Preferences Most Often Set at the Application Level* (continued)

Many of the preferences that we did not include in this table are those that are usually set on a module-specific basis; this is especially true of the layout preferences. The other preferences that we did not cover are those that we have found are usually left at their factory defaults or those that are used for advanced features not covered in this book.

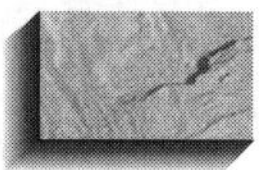

TIP

Instead of setting these preferences directly for the application, you should set them for a preference set and assign that preference set to the application. It is most likely that you will end up developing more than one application with the same design standard. Using a preference set will allow you to easily apply the preferences to other application systems in the future.

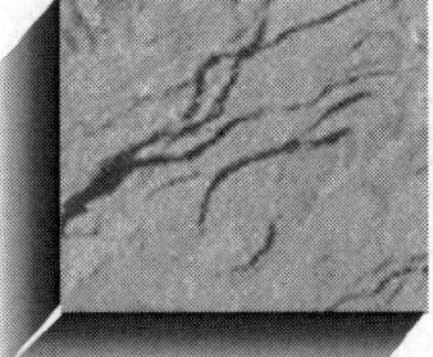

CHAPTER 11

Before You Create the Modules

ow that you understand what the Oracle Designer generators can do for you and the basic process of generating the application, it's time to get started generating modules, right? Not quite! There are some important tasks that should be done before you even create the modules in Oracle Designer. If you do not perform these tasks now, you will have to do a lot more work later before you can successfully generate the modules.

An overview of some of these tasks was given in Chapter 1 and we also discussed some of them in Chapter 3. In this chapter, we will give you a little more detail about some of these tasks. We are also reminding you that the best time to perform them is before the modules are created and generated. The tasks that we will discuss are outlined here.

1. Initial database creation.
   a. Create and refine the database definition in Oracle Designer.
   b. Create the physical database in an Oracle schema.
   c. Populate the physical database with test data.
2 Refine the database definition in Oracle Designer.
   a. Refine the generation defaults in the table and column definitions.
   b. Specify important PK, UK, and FK properties such as *Validate In* and *Error Message.*
3. Set up the generation infrastructure.
   a. Development environment.
   b. Templates and object libraries.

This chapter, especially the "Refine the Database Definition in Designer Repository" section, focuses mainly on forms generation, although some of the issues apply to reports generation as well.

Initial Database Creation

Obviously, before you can successfully generate any modules, you need to define and create a database. You cannot create the modules until the database definition is created in the repository. Once you create the modules, you usually cannot generate them until the physical database is created in a schema. Even if your database schema is created, it can be very difficult to develop the modules if there is no test data.

Because of these limitations, you need to pay attention to these steps and make sure they are done at the right time, even if you are not the DBA who actually creates the database.

Create and Refine the Database Definition in Oracle Designer

The first thing that needs to be done in order to create the database is to run the Database Transformer to create all of the Table Definitions. This can be a time-consuming task, and you may not even be the person who will do this. However, if it is not done, you will not be able to create your modules. Whoever does this will usually have some work to do to make sure that the tables and columns follow the naming standards for your organization.

NOTE

If you are using a Rapid Application Development (RAD) methodology, you might be creating the tables directly in the Design Editor without doing any analysis at all. In this case, you would not be using the Database Transformer, and some of these issues will not apply.

There is other work to do to refine the database before it is ready for generation. Although it is out of the scope of this book to cover these tasks in detail, we want to give you an idea of what usually needs to be done. The following list includes some of these tasks.

1. Add sequences for sequence-populated columns.
2. Add any necessary audit columns.
3. Add denormalized columns (if any).
4. Create views to implement your subtype/supertype designs.

The design that is created at this time does not have to be the final physical design. You will undoubtedly discover problems with the design during the creation of the modules. When this happens, you will change the physical model and generate the affected modules again.

TIP
When you do have to make changes to the physical model after you have generated your system, Oracle Designer provides some tools that will help you find the modules you have to regenerate. One tool you can use to do this is the Matrix Diagrammer. If you look at a matrix diagram of the modules against the tables, you can easily see which modules are affected by noting which table(s) changed. Another tool that you can use is one of the impact analysis repository reports that are available. For example, the Column Change Impact Analysis *report will list all of the modules that use a particular column.*

Create the Physical Database in an Oracle Schema

Once the database design is correct, it needs to be implemented physically in an Oracle instance. Even though you can define the modules in the Oracle Designer repository without actually creating the physical database, you will need to create the physical database before you can actually generate them. Because of this, it is usually easier to create the physical database as soon as the data design is complete. Then, when you create the modules and are ready to generate them, the physical environment is already in place. Creating the physical database after the design has the added advantage of giving you another QA check on your design. We have often discovered design problems by trying to physically create our data design.

Populate the Database with Test Data

You cannot complete the generation of the modules without some sort of test data in the database. If you do not have test data, it will not be possible to make sure you have included all of the desired functionality. For instance, if the code tables are not populated, you will not be able to tell if your LOVs are generated correctly. You also will not be able to create any records in forms that use these LOVs without the code data, nor will you be able to test all of the query functionality.

TIP

While it is possible to use the generated application (provided you generate the needed maintenance modules) to populate the data, it is usually better to write some SQL scripts to populate the database with test data. You will probably have to re-create the database at some point (for example, when you make a major design change), and you will probably have to populate the database in several instances (Development, Test, etc.). This will be much easier if you have SQL scripts that populate the data.

Another advantage of populating the database at this time is that it will help to ensure the quality of the data model itself because you will often uncover hidden problems with the data model while you are trying to populate it with a consistent data set.

A final advantage is that you can develop your modules in any order that makes sense for your project. If you plan to use the generated modules to populate the data, you will have to generate the modules in a particular order to make sure the necessary data is in place for the modules as you develop them. For instance, you will have to develop the code maintenance modules before you develop any modules that use the code tables, and you will have to develop the modules that support the fundamental data before you develop any modules that need the data. Populating the database before you actually generate your modules allows you to postpone the generation of less critical parts of the system (such as code table maintenance forms). You can then generate the most critical modules first, perhaps to use as prototypes.

Refine Database Definition in Designer Repository

Now that you have the database designed and created, it's time to get serious about generation. There are a lot of properties of the data definitions (*Tables, Columns, Keys)* that are not really used to create the physical database but are used by the module generators. Some of these properties are used as defaults for the module creation, and others are used during generation. This section focuses mainly on how the properties are used in forms generation. However, the mapping of the column and table properties to the module properties is the same for all types of modules (forms, reports, Web server, etc.).

Refine the Generation Defaults in the Table and Column Definitions

When the Application Transformer is used to create the modules from the functions, or even when the modules are created from scratch, many properties of the module are defaulted from the table and column definitions. Because of this, the table and column definitions should be refined before the modules are created.

Not doing this can lead to a lot of extra work, because multiple modules will use most of these properties. For instance, when a bound item is created, its *Prompt* property is initially set to the value from the *Prompt* property of the column that it is based on. This is true for many other column and table properties. It is much easier to enter the standard *Prompt* for a column once and have it automatically implemented in the ten forms and reports that use it than it is to enter the bound item *Prompt* ten times. Multiply this by all of the columns in the database and all of the modules in the system and you can see how much time this could save you.

Refining these properties before the modules are created will also give you a higher quality system. It is usually a better idea to make the *Prompt* for a column the same in every form and report that uses it. If you have defined the correct standard *Prompt* in the column definition before you create the modules, you will be more likely to have a consistent prompt for this column across the whole system. If you rely on each module's developer to do this, you may end up with inconsistencies.

Table Properties Used as Module Defaults

Table 11-1 is a list of the table properties that should be verified and refined before the modules are created. These properties can be set using either the Property Palette or the Edit Table dialog; however, the property names are slightly different between the two methods. The table below gives the property names from the Property Palette, but the names are similar enough for you to use this table even if you are using the Edit Table dialog. For more specific instructions about using the dialog, see the procedure in the next section.

Column Properties Used as Bound Item Defaults

Table 11-2 is a list of the column properties that should be verified and refined before the modules are created. These properties can be set using either the Property Palette or the dialog; however, the property names are slightly different between the two methods. The table gives the property names from the Property Palette, but the names are similar enough for you to use this table even if you are using the dialogs. For more specific instructions about using the dialogs, see the procedure in the next section.

Table Property	Becomes	Purpose in Generated Forms	Implementation Comments
Alias	*Table Usage: Usage Alias*	The Block name of the block generated from this module component.	Setting the *Alias* in the table automatically implements a block naming standard because all of the blocks based on the table will have the same name unless overridden in the module before generation.
Display Title	Module Component: *Title*	The title of the block that can be used as boilerplate text for the block based on this module component.	The Display Title in the table should be set to the most common title to be used for that table. This will ensure naming consistency across your application and will save having to do extra work. For the cases where the default title is not acceptable, the default can be overwritten in the module component.

TABLE 11-1. *Table Properties Used as Module Defaults*

Column Property	Bound Item Property	Purpose in Generated Forms Modules	Implementation Comments
Name	Name	The *Name* of the generated item.	Normally you will just leave the *Name* of a bound item the same as the column it is based on.
Optional? (Mandatory in the Dialog)	Optional?	If set to **No**, *the generated item will be mandatory (the Required property in the generated form will be set to* **Yes**).	The default in the modules will be based on the database requirements and, therefore, only the items based on mandatory columns in the database will be mandatory in the modules. If you want to make an item mandatory when that item is based on an optional column, you will have to override this property for the module.
Default Value	Default Value	Sets the *Initial Value property in the generated forms. This will be the value that the field will automatically have when new records are created.*	The table *Default Value* is used to set the standard default value for your whole system. You can override the *Default Value* for modules that will use a different default or no default.
Display?	Display?	Determines whether the item will be displayed in the generated form. If set to **No**, the generated item's *Visual* property is set to **Yes** and the *Canvas* is set to **<Null>**.	You will usually want to set the *Display?* Property to **No** for Surrogate Keys, Audit Columns, and any other columns that are not normally displayed. This will save you time when you implement table usages with these columns.

TABLE 11-2. *Column Properties Used as Bound Item Defaults*

Column Property	Bound Item Property	Purpose in Generated Forms Modules	Implementation Comments
Template/ Library Object	*Template/ Library Object*	Used to set the name of the object that the generated item is subclassed from.	You can use this to easily implement design standards by setting the *Template/Library Object* property for any columns for which you want to use a different display standard. For instance, if you would like the DBCRS.NUM column to always be displayed red, you could set this property to a "CUST$RED" object that you have created in the object library. Every module that displays this column will automatically inherit the object library setting.
Display Type	Display Type	This property determines the actual item type that will be generated (for example, **Text**, **Check box**, or **Pop List**).	Setting this property at the table level allows you to specify a default for the GUI item type you would like to use to implement a column (for example, setting the *Display Type* to **Check box** for Y/N flag columns).
Alignment	*Alignment*	Sets the *Justification* of the item in the generated form. The valid values are **Left**, **Right**, and **Center**.	Can be used to easily implement justification standards for specific columns. For instance, you can use this to implement the standard that the DBCRS.NUM column is always displayed Right Justified.

TABLE 11-2. *Column Properties Used as Module Defaults* (continued)

Column Property	Bound Item Property	Purpose in Generated Forms Modules	Implementation Comments
Display Length	Width	Sets the *Width* of the generated item after converting it into the correct units for the template form.	This is very useful for long columns for which you will not usually display the whole width of the column. For instance, if you have a VARCHAR(240) column, you might want to set the *Width* to 50 in order to implement a standard for that column across your whole application. There are preferences that will standardize a width for these lengthy columns, but these will usually be used to enforce a standard for the whole application.
Display Height	Height	Sets the *Height* of the generated item after converting it into the correct units for the template form.	This is very useful for longer textual columns that you want to use to display multiline text. By setting the *Height* at the column level, you will get a more consistent display standard for the column.
Uppercase	N/A	Sets the *Case Restriction* property on the generated item to **Upper**.	This column property is not actually copied to the bound item. However, it is used during generation to set the generated item property.

TABLE 11-2. *Column Properties Used as Module Defaults* (continued)

Column Property	Bound Item Property	Purpose in Generated Forms Modules	Implementation Comments
Display Sequence	Usage Sequence?	Determines the sequence the items will be placed in the generated form.	In many applications there is a logical sequence of columns that makes more sense to the users. In these cases, you should set the *Display Sequence* at the column level to save time and have a more consistent display standard across your whole application.
Format Mask	Format Mask	This property is copied directly into the *Format Mask* property for the item in the generated form.	If you want to specify a standard format mask for a particular column, you can use this column property to implement one. This can be used to override the default format (which is set by the appropriate object in the object library). However, a better way to do this might be to define a new object in your object library and use the *Template/Object Library Object* property to do this. That way, you can easily change the mask without regenerating the form.
Formatting	Formatting	Used by the Report and Web server Generators only. Specifies the highlighting (bold, underline, etc.) or special formatting for Web server (URL, MailTo, etc.).	.

TABLE 11-2. *Column Properties Used as Module Defaults* (continued)

Column Property	Bound Item Property	Purpose in Generated Forms Modules	Implementation Comments
Prompt	Prompt	This property is copied directly into the *Prompt* property for the item in the generated form.	This is probably the most important column display property to set. It cannot be derived from any other source, and if it is not entered for the column, the *Prompt* will be set to the column name, which is not very useful. If this happens, the developers will spend a lot of time entering user-friendly bound item *Prompt*s. Setting the *Prompt* at the column level will also give you a more consistent user interface.
Order By Sequence	Order By Sequence	This property will specify which columns are placed in the "ORDER BY" clause generated for the block and in which order they are placed there.	The users will often want the queried records to be displayed in a particular order for all (or most) of the forms in the system. In these cases, the *Order by Sequence* and *Sort Order* properties should be set at the table level. This will save time in module development and more consistently implement the specified standard.
Sort Order	Sort Order	This determines if each column is ordered **Ascending** or **Descending** in the order by clause.	See *Order By Sequence*.

TABLE 11-2. *Column Properties Used as Module Defaults* (continued)

Column Property	Bound Item Property	Purpose in Generated Forms Modules	Implementation Comments
Hint	Hint	This property is copied directly into the *Hint* property for the item in the generated form.	Just like the *Prompt* property, this property cannot be derived from any other source. If left blank, the generator creates a hint that looks like: "Enter Value for <Column Name>" which is not very useful. If the *Hint* is not specified at the column level, it will cause the developers to do a lot of work to enter meaningful *Hints*. Setting the *Hint* at the column level will also give you a more consistent user interface.

TABLE 11-2. *Column Properties Used as Module Defaults* (continued)

The properties that are set during the creation of the modules are only defaults and can be updated to any other setting during the design of the module. Therefore, you will usually set the table and column definition values to the values that are most common for your application system. For instance, if 80 percent of the modules have a standard prompt for a particular column, and the other 20 percent have a different prompt, you should set the *Prompt* in the column definition to the first value; then update it for the modules that need it.

Procedure for Setting the Table and Column Properties Used as Default

To set these properties, you can use the following procedure:

1. Edit each table definition in your application by selecting the table in the Design Editor Navigator and opening the Edit Table dialog.

2. The Name tab, with the module default table properties entered, is the first tab in this dialog, shown here.

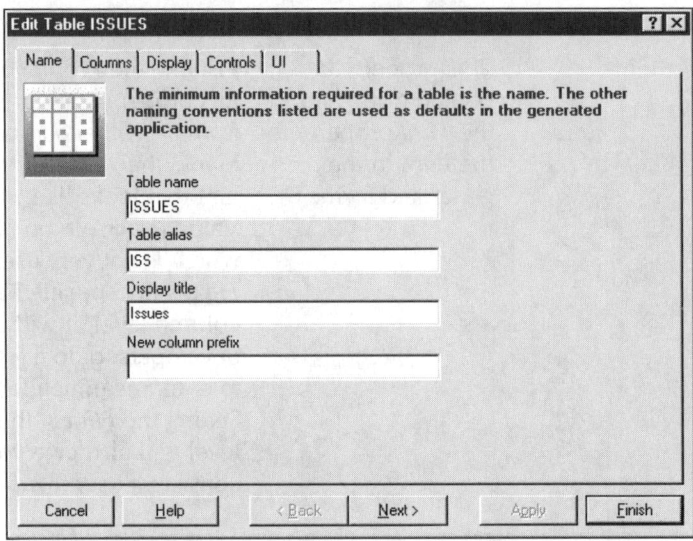

3. Click Next. This will show the Columns tab, shown here. The *Default value* and *Mandatory* (*Optional* in the Property Palette) properties are set here.

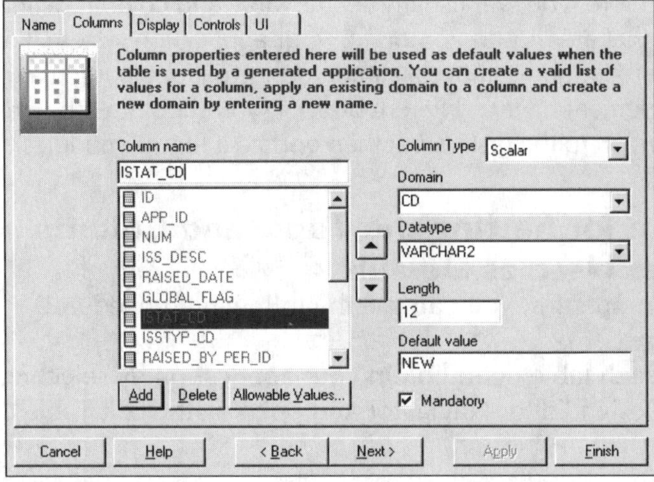

4. Click Next. This will show the Display tab, shown here. The *Display?* and *Display Sequence* properties are set here. The *Display?* property is

set by selecting columns from the Columns displayed box. The *Display Sequence* property is determined by the order the columns appear in the Columns displayed box. The arrow buttons between the Columns not displayed, and the Columns displayed boxes allow you to select and deselect the columns and change their order.

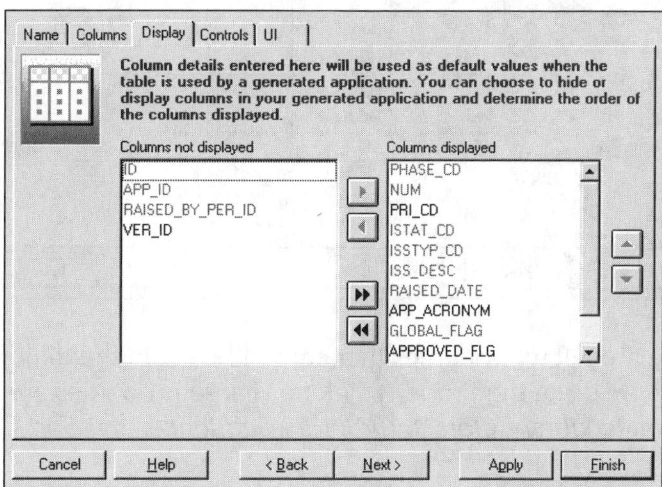

5. Most of the rest of the relevant properties are set using the Controls and UI tabs, shown here. You can use the Next button to navigate to these tabs, or just select them by clicking the tabs at the top.

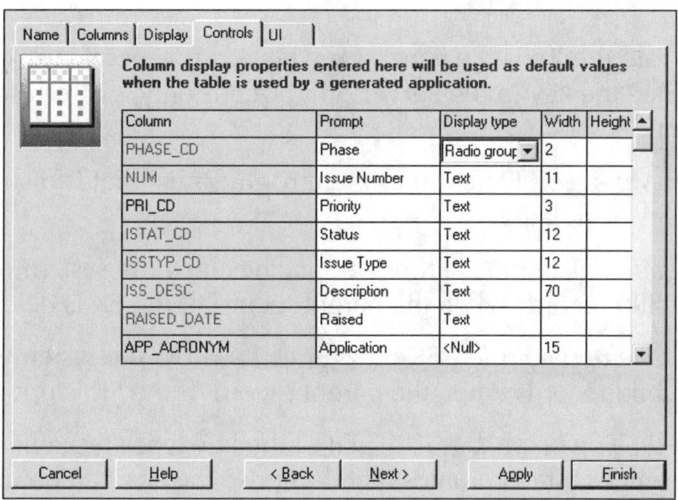

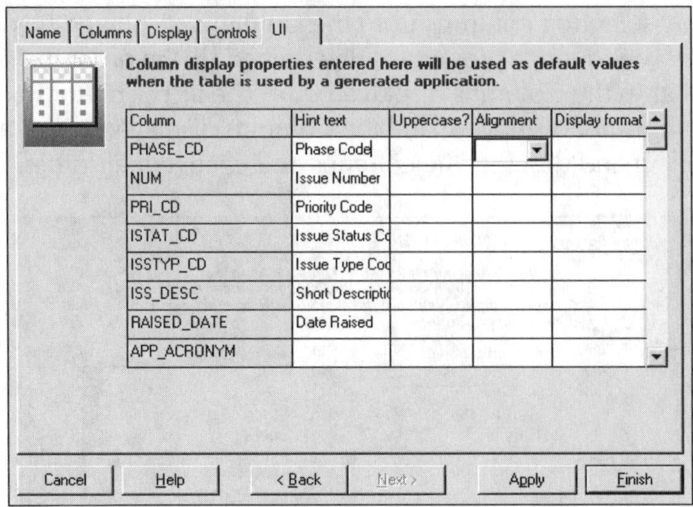

6. There are a few properties that cannot be set in the dialogs and must be set by using the Property Palette. These properties are *Template/Library Object, Order By Sequence,* and *Sort Order.*

Specify Important PK, UK, and FK Properties

There are some properties of the keys that are important to set before you generate your modules. These properties are

- *Validate in* Tells the generator whether to generate the code to validate the key in the **Server** only, **Client** only, or **Both** server and client.
- *Error Message* Determines the error message that is displayed when the key is violated.
- *Cascade delete rule* FK only. Specifies how the system will update the child records when the parent record of the FK is deleted.
- *Cascade update rule* FK only. Specifies how the system will update the child records when the parent record of the FK is updated.
- *Can the key be updated?* Each of the key types has a property that determines if the columns that comprise the key can be updated.

The first two properties can be set using the Validation tab that is available in each of the key dialogs (PK, UK, and FK).

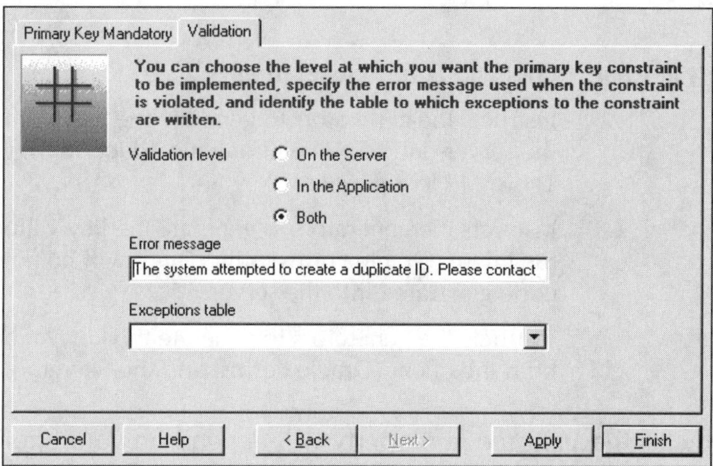

The cascade rules are only available in the Cascade Rules tab of the FK dialog:

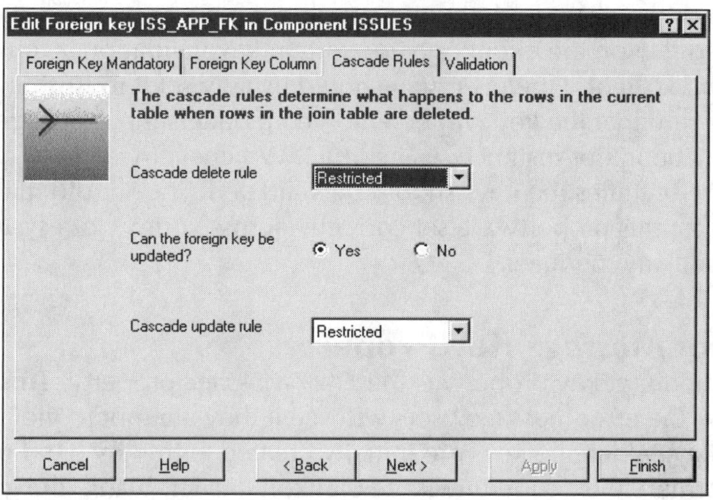

The *Validate in* Key Property

The *Validate in* property should be verified in the whole application system before any of the modules are generated. This is because this property will determine what type of key validation is generated into the modules. The following table lists the settings for this property and the effect on forms generation:

Validate in value	Effect on Forms Generation
Server	Instructs the generators to generate the key validation into the server only. Code will only be added to triggers or the Table API to enforce the key.
Client	Instructs the generators to generate the key validation into the client (Oracle Forms) only. There will be not validation code generated into the server.
Both	Instructs the generators to generate the key validation into both the client (Oracle Forms) and the Server.

How you set the *Validate in* property will depend on your application architecture. You do not need to set it exactly the same for all of the keys in your system. For example, if you use surrogate keys, you can set *Validate in* to **Server** for these PKs, because the surrogate keys will never be displayed to the user or the client and, therefore, will not need to be validated there. If you want to rely on the client only for certain key validations, you can set *Validate in* to **Client**. However, you should usually set it to **Both** in these cases to ensure that the key will be enforced if data is input outside of your client application (for instance, using SQL). Whichever way your application architecture specifies the keys should be validated, you should make sure the values for this property are set correctly across your whole system before you generate any modules.

The *Error Message* Key Property

Another important key property is the *Error Message* property. This property will specify the error message users will see if they attempt to violate the specified key. When the keys are initially created (either by hand or by using the transformer), this property will be blank. If it is left blank, the generated forms will have key violation messages that look like this:

Error: This <Column Name> does not exist.
Error: Row exists already with the same PK Col
Error: Row exists already with same UK Col

These error messages are not very user friendly. It's a good idea to enter more specific messages into the *Error Message* property to make it easier for your users to understand what they did wrong. For example, for a UK, you could enter a message like this:

The Issue Number you entered is already in use. Try another.

For a surrogate PK, you could enter

The system attempted to create a duplicate ID. Please contact support.

For an FK, you could enter

Invalid Status Code. Please use <LOV> to list valid codes.

Whatever message standard you decide upon, make sure that you verify the *Error Message* values for all of your keys before you generate the modules.

The *Cascade Delete Rule* Key Property

The *Cascade Delete Rule* tells the generated system what to do with child records in a Foreign Key relationship when their parent record is deleted. The settings of this property can have an effect on the generated client system. There are four possible values for this property, as shown in this table:

Property Setting	Action Taken	Where Enforced
Restricted	Prevents the deletion of the parent record if any child records exist.	Server, Client, or Both
Cascades	Deletes any related child records when the parent record is deleted.	Server, Client, or Both
Defaults	Sets the key column in the child records to a specified default value when the parent record is deleted.	Client only
Nullifies	Sets the key column in the child records to **Null** when the parent record is deleted.	Client only

If you select an option that is enforced only on the client, or if you set the *Validate in* property for a key to **Client** or **Both**, you will be generating code into the client forms to enforce the relationship. Because of this, you should make sure that the *Cascade Delete Rule* property is set correctly for every FK in your system before you generate any modules.

The *Cascade Update Rule* Key Property

The *Cascade Update Rule* tells the generated system what to do with the key column in the child records in a Foreign Key relationship when the key column in their parent record is updated. The settings of this property can have an effect on the generated client system. There are four possible values for this property, as shown in this table:

Property Setting	Action Taken	Where Enforced
Restricted	Prevents the update of the key column of the parent record if any child records exist.	Server, Client, or Both
Cascades	If the value of the parent key column is updated, will update the value of the FK column in any child records to match.	Client only
Defaults	If the value of the parent key column is updated, will set the FK column of the child records to a predefined default.	Client only
Nullifies	If the value of the parent key column is updated, will set the FK column of the child records to NULL.	Client only

If you select an option that is enforced only on the client, or if you set the *Validate in* property for a key to **Client** or **Both**, you will be generating code into the client forms to enforce the relationship. Because of this, you should make sure that the *Cascade Update Rule* property is set correctly for every FK in your system before you generate any modules.

The *Can the key be updated?* Property

Each of the keys has a property that determines whether the key can be updated. The setting for this property can effect the generated code, so it should be reviewed. For instance, you can have a mismatch between a key column property and the key it is a part of. You can also have an updateable column that is assigned to a nonupdateable key. If you define a column usage in a module to be updateable (which is allowed because the column is updateable), the generator will convert the usage to nonupdateable because of the nonupdateable key.

Set Up Your Generation Infrastructure

Earlier in this book (Chapters 1 and 3), we mentioned the generation infrastructure requirements that you need to meet in order to successfully generate systems using Oracle Designer. These issues are worth mentioning again because it is so important to fulfill these requirements before you generate your modules.

Development Environment

We covered the development environment requirements in fairly complete detail in Chapter 3 in the section entitled "Key 3: Infrastructure." Please refer to that chapter for suggestions regarding your development environment. Remember, if you do not address these issues before you start generating modules, you may end up adding a lot of work to your development efforts, especially if you have some problems in this area.

Templates and Object Libraries

In Chapter 1, we covered the basic flow of the generation process, and we mentioned that the Templates and Object Libraries need to be developed for your application before you can generate your production modules. This issue was also covered in the "Key 3" section of Chapter 3.

We would like to emphasize again that you should make sure to work on the templates and object libraries before you generate your application and even before you create most of the modules. This is important because, as you discover what it is possible to do with templates and object libraries, you might modify the values you place in the table display properties, or you might even modify your data model.

To develop your templates and object libraries, you will probably have to create a few modules and use them to test the display and functionality of forms generated using your custom templates and object libraries. When you finish developing them and have made any necessary changes to the data model and table and column properties, you will be ready to create your modules.

You do not have to get the templates perfect at this time. You can continue to refine them as you develop your application system. It is likely that you will create specialized versions for certain modules, or at least add objects to your object libraries. However, it is definitely beneficial to think about these issues before you even start.

Chapter 22 will cover template forms and object libraries in detail.

Now You Are Ready to Create Your Modules

Now you are really ready to create your modules. You will probably be using the Application Transformer to create the modules from the functions you defined during analysis. You will probably also be creating some of the modules directly in the Design Editor. No matter how you are creating your modules, however, if you make sure that you complete the tasks covered in this chapter, you will save time and generate a higher quality system.

CHAPTER 12

Window, Canvas, Block, and Item Generation

If you have ever built forms by hand, you know how tedious it is to deal with every little tiny bit and piece of a form to make sure that all works together smoothly. If you haven't, take our word for it: building a form by hand is a time-consuming and extremely error-prone process that includes creating the windows and canvases, building blocks and items, providing list of values and record groups for lookups, writing the code for business rule validations, and debugging errors. Multiply this with dozens, possibly hundreds, of forms that might be part of the front-end to your application, and imagine how monumental task it is to a build such a client interface for a system. If you think this is overwhelming, think about the standards that must be followed and enforced across the board among the hundreds of forms developed by an army of developers. It does not end here, either: remember that each such system must be maintained after it's built, with updates, enhancements, bug fixes, etc.

However, if you are using Oracle Designer, you can use Form Generator to automatically generate a significant amount of the functionality that is needed in your forms. With the enhancements and new features in release 2.1, Form Generator's ability to automatically generate very high percentages of form functionality makes it one of the best application development tools in the market. Using the data definitions, business rules and requirements, module definitions, standards recorded in the repository, and supporting templates and object libraries, Form Generator can generate systems with a few clicks of a mouse. Generating forms, windows, canvases, blocks, items, list-of-values, constraint validations, navigation, and standard application logic, etc., is pretty much standard and requires very minimal work to set the values of a few properties here and there. In addition, you get the bonus of forms with the same and look and feel, and the code generated will be predictable.

This chapter will show you how to generate windows, canvases, blocks, and items using the Form Generator in a step-by-step fashion. It will also highlight the limitations of the generator and provide you with guidelines and possible work-arounds for some of these limitations. Wherever applicable, a troubleshooting section will help you to solve some of the most common problems encountered in generating forms.

In this chapter, we will review the generation of standard functionality via the Form Generator. The following topics will be discussed:

- Window generation
- Canvas generation
- Block generation
- Item generation

This chapter covers some of the basic layout options, but a detailed presentation of all of the layout options would be very involved and might obscure your understanding of how to simply generate the form in the first place. Therefore, we will defer most of the discussion about layout options to Chapters 19 and 20.

Item generation is also very involved, and there are many layout and functionality options to cover. Therefore, we are only covering the basic creation of the items in this chapter. The item type and layout options are discussed in great detail in Chapter 13. Generating more complicated item functionality is covered in Chapter 14.

Window Generation

A window is a rectangular area of the screen that contains an application. A window provides a frame through which all visual objects that make up a form module can be seen and interacted with. Visual objects (text items, check boxes, radio groups, images, graphic texts, lines, boxes, etc.), are displayed on canvases that provide a background to display the visual objects in a window.

Each window has a title bar that helps to identify the window and window handles for sizing, moving and closing the window. Windows may also have scrollbars that can be used to view the parts of the background that do not fit in the window frame. Windows may look different on different platforms, depending on how the window manager on that platform renders them. Figure 12-1 shows a window in the Microsoft Windows environment.

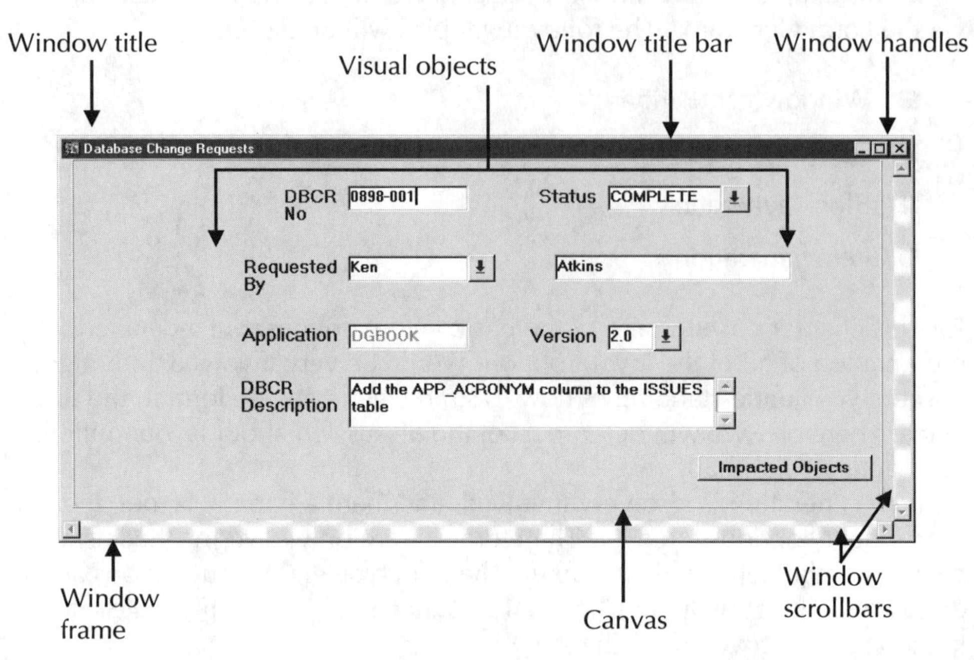

FIGURE 12-1. *A window in the Microsoft Windows environment*

Windows can be *modal* or *modeless.* A *modal* window requires the user to respond (enter data or press a button or a key) before continuing using the application. When positioned in a modal window, other parts of the form, including the menu and the toolbar, are not accessible. Modal windows are often used as dialog boxes when we want the user to complete a task before proceeding with other tasks. On the other hand, modeless windows do not have these restrictions; the user is free to interact with other parts of the form. Most of the windows used in applications are modeless windows.

There are also some special types of windows, such as the MDI window and the Root window. These special windows will also be reviewed later in this chapter. For more information about windows, window types, and restrictions that apply to each type, please refer to *Oracle Developer, Form Builder Online Help.*

Form Generator uses the Repository window definitions to generate windows. Window definitions are part of module definitions, and they are closely linked with the module component definitions. Form Generator can also create a window in the generated form if it sees a need to. For example, if you include a reusable module component into your module and don't change its display sequence or its *Window* property afterward, you end up with a module component without a window assignment. Form Generator creates a new window in the generated form and places that reusable module component in that window.

For a window definition to be included in the generated form, at least one module component must be assigned to the window, and the module component must contain at least one bound, unbound, or action item. Otherwise, empty windows are ignored by the Form Generator and are never generated into the form.

There are a few different ways to create a window definition in the Oracle Repository:

- In the Design Editor, a window definition is automatically created when a module component's *Placement* property is left blank or set to **New Content Canvas** during its creation. Figure 12-2 shows how this property can be set using the Edit Module Component dialog box.

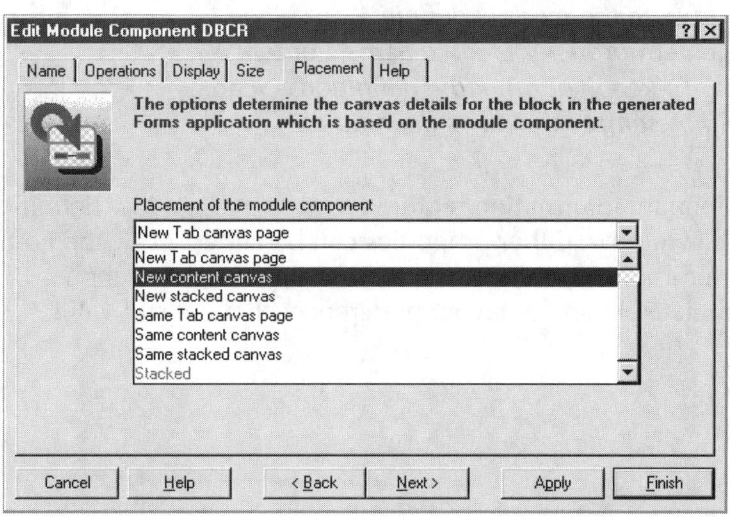

FIGURE 12-2. *Placement property of a module component*

Windows can also be created, modified, or deleted manually in the Design Editor using either the Module Diagram (under the display view only), or the Navigator (Property Palette or dialogs). Figure 12-3 shows a window definition on a module diagram representing the display view of a module. Window objects shown in the module diagram can be resized to include or exclude module components, or module components can be moved in or out of window objects via simple drag and drop operations. For further information about how to work with window definitions in module diagrams, please refer to *Oracle Designer Online Help → Creating window layout elements using Module Diagrams.*

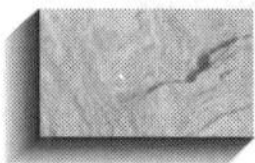

CAUTION

When you design form modules, it is possible to end up with window definitions that do not contain any items. One of the main reasons for this is that the window definition that is automatically created for a module component (when the Placement *property is left blank or set to* ***New Content Canvas****) is not deleted automatically when that module component is removed from the module definition, or when its* Placement *property is set to* ***Same Content Canvas****. To keep your module definitions clean, delete these empty windows definitions.*

The minimum information required to create a window definition is the name of the window. Other properties can be either set by the Form Generator or implicitly driven from other sources such as the source/template objects or layout preferences that are still valid.

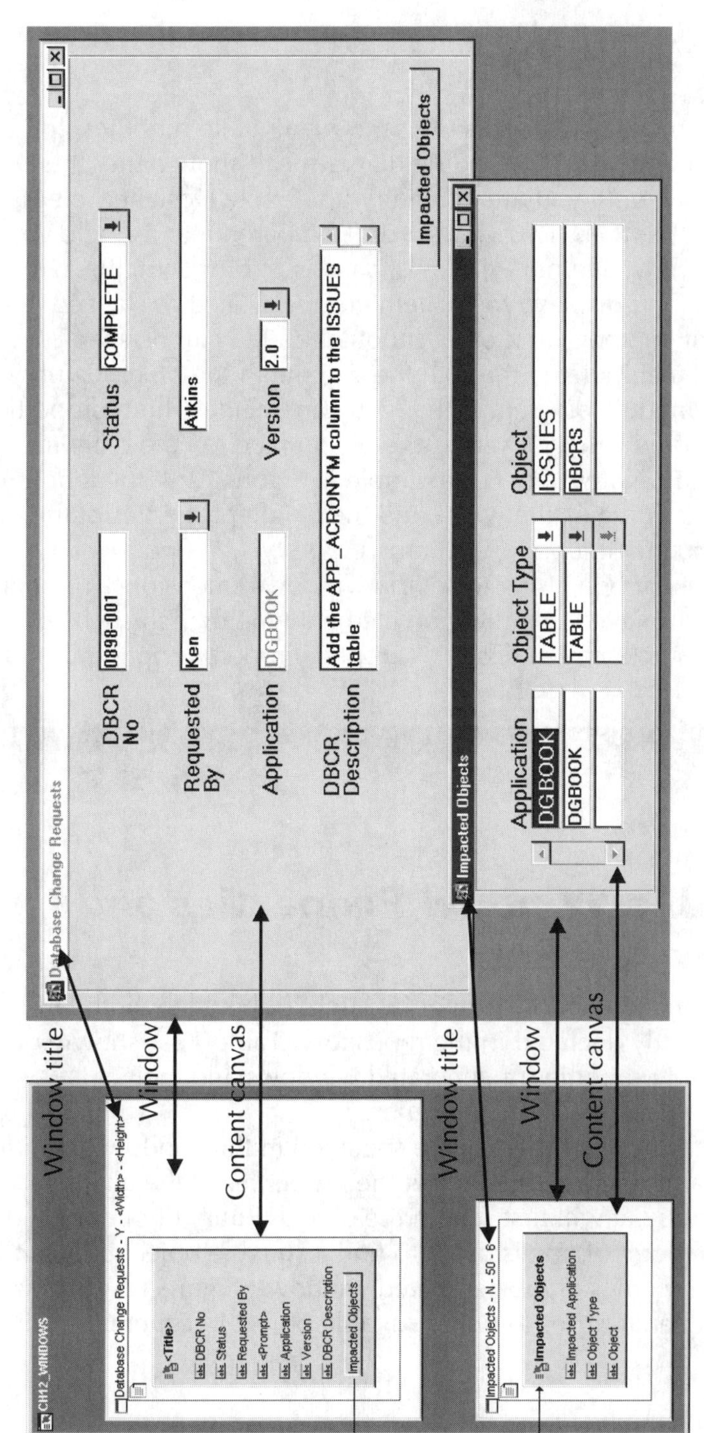

FIGURE 12-3. *Module diagram, Display view*

Module Diagrams

Module Diagrams are great tools to use to manipulate modules. In Oracle Designer release 2, a module diagram can show either the Data or the Display view. (If you are familiar with Oracle Designer release 1, you will remember these two views were combined into a single view.) In the Display view, all your windows, canvases, blocks, items (with icons showing their display types), item groups, nested or stacked item groups, navigation items, and other modules called can be seen pictorially and manipulated through the diagram. One other feature we like about the module diagram is that you can decide which properties of an object should be displayed as the object label on the diagram as well as on the navigator tree. For example in Figure 12-3, the label for window objects contains the width and the height properties of the window object, in addition to the name property. We find this extremely helpful when trying to set the window dimensions. To change the properties displayed, highlight an element type branch such as Modules, right-click, and choose the Display Properties option from the pop-up menu.

Generatable Window Properties and How They Are Set

Many of the generated window properties such as the title, width, and height can be directly declared in the repository. Table 12-1 shows some of the most important properties of generated windows and their corresponding sources in Oracle Designer.

If the values for these properties are specified in the window definition, the Form Generator will use them to set the properties of the generated windows. Otherwise, it will first search the object library (if one is used) and then the template form (if one is used) to find a suitable object that can be used to set the properties of the generated windows. Figure 12-4 shows the process Form Generator uses to find a suitable object to generate a window.

Window Property	Source in Oracle Designer
Name	*Name* property of the window.
Title	*Title* property of the window.
Scrollable	*Scrollable* property of the window.
Subclassed From	*Template/Library Object* property of the window.
Width & Height	*Width & Height* properties of the window, source/template object in the object library, template window in the template form, or layout preferences.
X & Y Position	*X & Y Position* properties of the window, source/template object in the object library, template window in the template form, or layout preferences.

TABLE 12-1. *Summary of Generatable Window Properties*

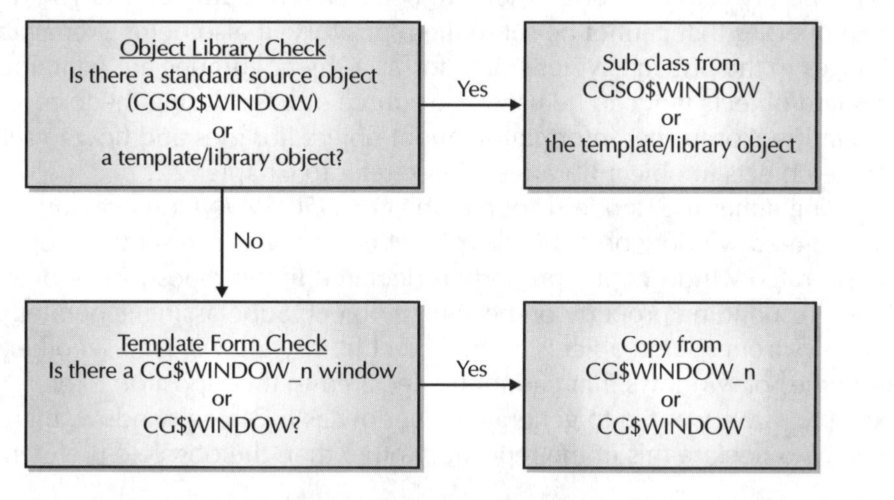

FIGURE 12-4. *Finding a suitable object for window generation*

As you can see from Figure 12-4, in addition to reading the properties that are declared in the repository, Form Generator also searches the object library, the template form, and the *Layout – Window* preferences to set the other properties that cannot be directly declared in the repository.

CAUTION

Release 1.3 *In the earlier versions of Oracle Designer, there was no such thing as an object library. Template forms and preferences were the only ways of setting all of the window properties. These preferences are still available in release 2 in order for the generators to be backward compatible, but their use is strongly discouraged. These preferences are obsolete and will be removed in a future version.*

There are some obsolete preferences that are still available to set some of the same properties that can be set by subclassing (see the Release 1.3 Note), but subclassing windows (or any other object for this matter) from an object library is the preferred method, because it not only allows you define the properties that cannot be set in the repository, it also helps propagate changes in the previously generated forms. Object libraries are containers of standard objects that can be used as a source or base during the form generation. For further information about object libraries and how to set up source objects in object libraries, please refer to Chapter 22.

Using either the standard source object *CGSO$WINDOW* or any other user-defined window object in the object library, you can set the properties of generated windows. If a property is declared in the repository, it overrides the corresponding property of the source object. Subclassing generated windows from source objects in the object library allows us to set other properties of windows that cannot be declared in the repository. For example, if we wanted to generate a window as a Dialog window, there is no way to declare this in the repository other than the obsolete preference

Layout – Window → Window is a dialog (WINDLG). Since this preference is obsolete, the best way to generate a dialog window is to create a source/template window object in the object library, set its *Window Style* property to **Dialog**, and then specify this source object in the window's *Template/Library Object* property.

NOTE
For further information about the obsolete preferences, please refer to Oracle Designer Online Help → Alphabetical list of obsolete preferences and the equivalent object library properties. *If you are familiar with the earlier versions of Oracle Designer, you might have used these preferences to set other properties of windows that cannot be declared in the repository. In Oracle Designer release 2, these properties are driven from the template/source objects in the object library.*

Setting the Window Title

Form Generator uses the value specified for the *Title* property of a window definition to set the window title when it generates a window. If the *Title* property is left **Null** (as it would when a window definition is automatically created when module component is placed on a new content canvas), the Form Generator uses the algorithm shown in Figure 12-5 to determine the title of the window.

As you can see from Figure 12-5, Form Generator might assign window titles like "Issue Types:Window 0," if a window *Title* is not defined in the repository and the module component title is blank. You will usually want better titles than this. Therefore, it is important to define the standards for your own window titles and make sure that window titles are specified before generating the form.

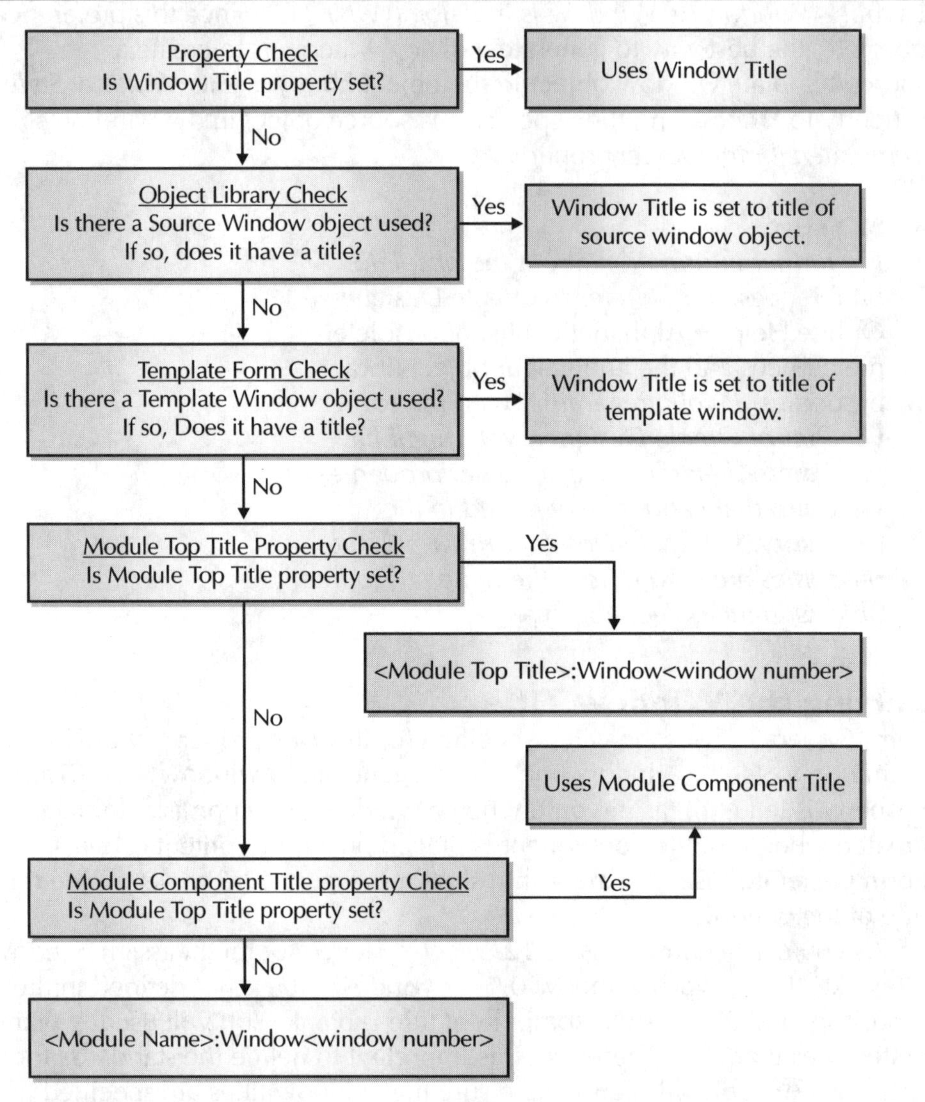

FIGURE 12-5. *How Form Generator sets the window title*

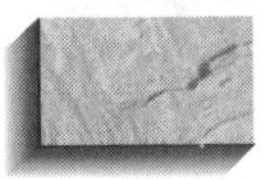

TIP

Dynamic window titles *Window titles can also be made dynamic to reflect the current context. This is pretty much standard in MS Windows-style user interfaces. For example, a window title like "Employee Maintenance: Department(10)-Finance" may be used to indicate that editing of employee records will be limited to only those employees who work for the finance department (department code=10). Such window titles help you save some screen real estate (because you don't need a block title then) and generate more "windowish" forms. To change window titles dynamically at run time, you can use the Set_Window_Property Form Builder built-in.*

Specifying the Size and the Position of the Window

Form Generator uses the values specified for the *Width, Height, X Position,* and *Y Position* properties of the Repository Window definition when it generates a window. However, these properties only serve as a guideline when determining the actual values. The dimensions of a window are closely related to the size of canvases that will be displayed in that window and whether scrollbars are allowed or not. Figure 12-6 shows the algorithm Form Generator uses to determine the size and the position of a generated window.

Again, using source objects in the object library is the preferred method to set the window size and positions. You can also use template windows such as CG$WINDOW or CG$WINDOW_1 (template for the first window), CG$WINDOW_2 (template for the second window), etc., defined in the template form, but this is not recommended, since it does not provide any advantage over the subclassing method.

During generation, Form Generator may override the dimensions of windows if one of the content canvases assigned to the window does not fit

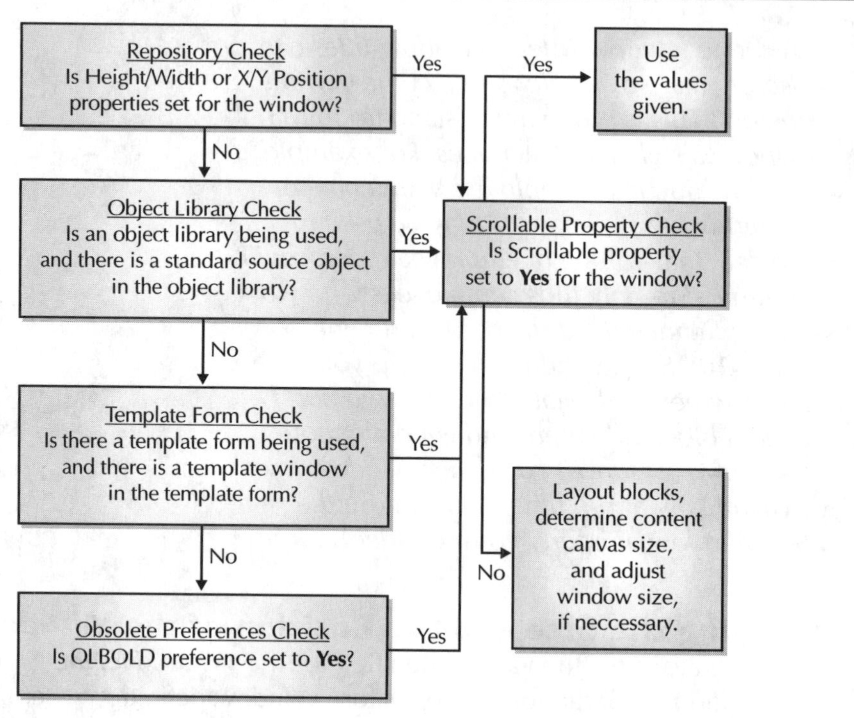

FIGURE 12-6. *How Form Generator sets the size and position of the window*

in the window. For example, if a content canvas dimension is set to 50 x 8 and the window it's assigned to is 40 x 6 (smaller than the content canvas), and the *Scrollable* property of the window is set to **No**, Form Generator will increase the window width and height to make sure that the whole content canvas is visible.

The size and position properties defined in the repository are in terms of the *Average Character Cell Size* (a form property) of the template form used in generation. For example, if the average character cell width is .25 inches and the height is .1 inches, a window width of 20 and height of 10 units is converted to 5 inches (20 x .25) and 1 inch (10 x .1) respectively. If a template form is not specified, Form Generator uses the Form Builder default values listed in the following table:

Window Property	Default Value
Coordinate System	Real
Real Unit	Inches
Character Cell Width	0.069
Character Cell Height	0.194

The most important consideration when setting the window dimensions is to maintain consistency among all of the windows in an application. Each application should have guidelines and standards for generated windows. These standards should clearly state how big the windows should be, where they should be positioned, etc. Some applications have a fixed size for all the windows, and some don't. This is one of the design decisions you should make early in your generation efforts. For more information about the things that you should consider before generating modules, please refer to Chapter 10.

Special Windows

In Form Builder, there are certain types of windows that have some unique characteristics, such as MDI and Root windows.

The MDI Window

The MS Windows-specific term MDI is an acronym for "Multiple Document Interface." In MS Windows, the MDI window can be seen as the parent window or the application window. All of the other windows of a form are displayed within the MDI window. If these other windows are document windows, they cannot be moved outside of the MDI window. More than one document window can be displayed in an MDI window, and these windows can be tiled, cascaded, or moved by hand to any location within the MDI window. A document window's display size is limited by the size of the MDI window. If the document window is bigger than the MDI window, it is clipped, but scrollbars on the MDI window can be used to move the MDI window's view around to see the rest of the document window.

Dialog windows, on the other hand, are free-floating, and can be moved outside of the MDI window. In addition, the MDI window does not appear in the list of windows in the window pull-down menu. Figure 12-7 shows an example of an MDI window. For further information about MDI windows, please refer to *Oracle Developer, Form Builder Online Help.*

LIMITATIONS/PROBLEMS The MDI window, like any other window, has window properties such as the title, position, and size. However, an MDI window is not a regular window object that can be manipulated in Form Builder, and it cannot be defined in the repository. The MDI window

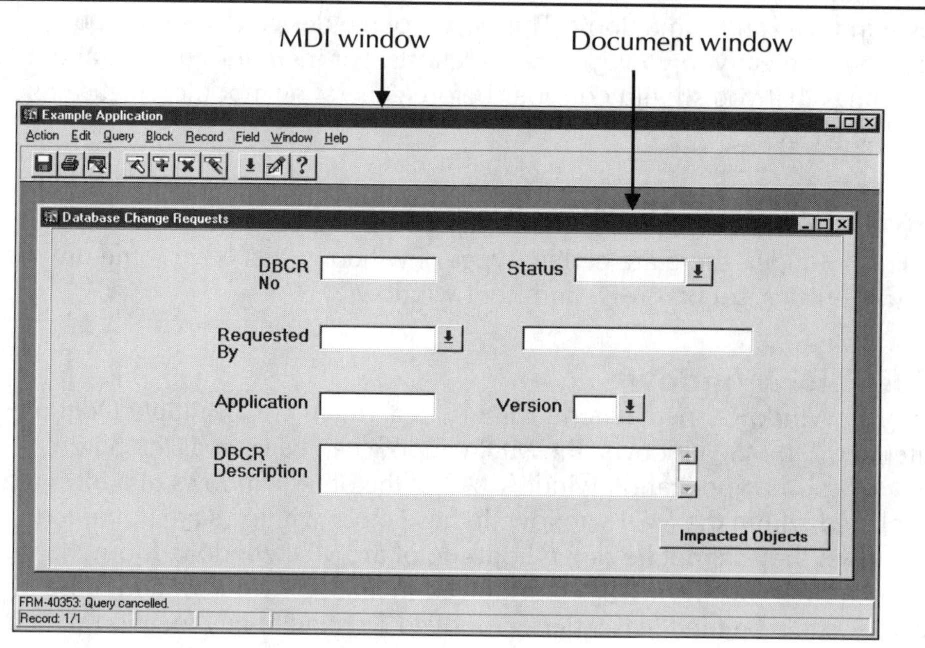

FIGURE 12-7. *MDI window*

properties are derived from the form-level properties of the template form (if one is used in generation). The MDI window properties can also be set by the Form Builder API. For example, the horizontal and vertical toolbar properties of the MDI window are derived from the template form. The way that Form Builder supports MDI windows is rather odd: an MDI window is not a separate window object in Form Builder, but some of its properties (e.g., horizontal/vertical toolbars) can be set through the *Form* properties. There are also other MDI window properties (such as the MDI Window Title) that cannot be set using Form Builder.

SETTING THE MDI WINDOW TITLE The default title for an MDI window in an Oracle Developer Form application is "Developer/2000 Forms Runtime for Windows 95/NT." This title is useless, because the only thing it does is to state the fact that we are running an Oracle Developer form in a Windows95 or NT environment. Usually we want the MDI title to display more meaningful information, such as the name of the application that is running.

The technique for setting the MDI title is not very obvious. First, the MDI window title cannot be set directly using Form Builder. It needs to be set programmatically during run time using the *Set_Window_Property(FORMS_MDI_WINDOW, title, 'MDI Title Here')* Form Builder built-in. FORMS_MDI_WINDOW is a special handle that refers to the MDI window, and it is valid only on MS Windows platforms.

The following sample code is taken from the PRE-FORM trigger in the OFGPC1T.FMB standard template form shipped with Oracle Designer (located in <oracle_home>\cgenf50\admin). This code sets the MDI window title to the title of the repository application system from which the form module is generated. The application system title is generated into the form using a special generator object CG$AT. For more information about special generator objects, please refer to Chapter 22.

```
/* CGAP$TES_SEQUENCE_AFTER */
  -- The following lines of code sets the window title for the
  -- MDI window to the Application display title.
  set_window_property(FORMS_MDI_WINDOW,TITLE,
        get_item_property('CG$CTRL.CG$AT',HINT_TEXT));
```

Sample code from Standard Form template that sets MDI title

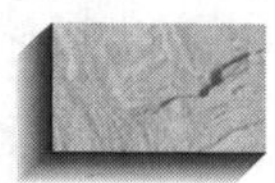

TIP

Restrictions to the use of FORMS_MDI_WINDOW handle *If you are going to deploy forms in platforms other than MS Windows, then you should consider portability issues, for example, the MDI window does not exist in the Unix MOTIF environment. To avoid a run time error message, you should check what the current platform is before attempting to set the MDI window title. This can be done by using Get_Application_Propety (Operationg_System) built-in. For further information, please refer to the Oracle Developer, Form Builder Online Help.*

TIP

D2KWUTIL library *This utility library contains many other routines for commonly used Windows functions such as Open File Dialog, Choose Printer Dialog, etc. Moreover, the same library can be used from Reports and Graphics as well. The PL/SQL library also provides a very good example for creating your own DLL calls. For more information about the windows API functions, ORA_FFI package, and the FFI_GEN utility, please refer to* Form Builder Online Help *about how to use windows API functions from forms.*

Setting the MDI Window Icon

MDI Window Icon is the icon that appears on the desktop when the application is minimized. A smaller size version of this icon also shows up on the title bar. The default icon for an MDI window in an Oracle Developer form application is the icon associated with the forms runtime program (F50RUN32.EXE in Oracle Developer release 2). Changing the MDI window icon is a little bit more challenging because it requires us to use some low-level MS Windows API routines. To access these low-level system routines, you have to use the *Oracle Foreign Function Interface* (ORA_FFI). However, the Oracle Developer suite contains a sample PL/SQL library as part of the Oracle Developer demo (<Oracle_Home>\Tools\Devdemo20\Demo\Forms\D2KWUTIL.PLL). This PL/SQL library contains many routines for the most frequently done tasks in the MS Windows environment, such as getting a filename.

To change the MDI Window Icon:

1. Attach the D2KWUTIL.PLL library to your application launch form. If you don't have a launch form, attach it to your template form or make sure that this library is attached to the form.
2. Create a PRE-FORM trigger in the template form, if it does not exist.
3. Add the following line to the PRE-FORM trigger:

```
Win_Api_Session.Change_MDI_Icon(Win_Api_Utility.Get_Active_Window,
'C:\MY_APP\ICONS\MY_APP.ICO');
```

In general, most applications have at least one main launch form that does the security check and initial environment setup, and presents the application menu. It makes sense to set the MDI Window properties once in this application if they are not going to change throughout the session. However, if you don't have a launch form, you can add the code to the PRE-FORM trigger (or WHEN-NEW-FORM-INSTANCE) in your template form, or you can define the application logic in the repository.

Root Window

A Form Builder root window is a window that can be useful in multiple-form applications. The root window can be used to

- Display the console (the status and message line displayed at the bottom of the window) for the currently active form (on platforms other than MS Windows)
- Display the content canvas assigned to the root window of the currently active form

Having a root window is useful when running multiple-form, multiple-window applications in an environment other than MS Windows (such as Motif or Web Forms). This is because when there is a root window, the console can be displayed in this common window rather than a specific window that may be minimized or covered by other windows or forms. Root windows are especially useful for displaying a toolbar and a console on platforms other than MS Windows. On MS Windows, the console is always displayed on the MDI window.

The root window has special characteristics, and some of its properties have fixed settings. For example, the root window cannot have scrollbars, nor can it be set to a fixed size. Figure 12-8 shows a root window. For more information about root windows, refer to *Form Builder Online Help*.

You can generate root windows by

- Including a window named ROOT_WINDOW in the template form
- Setting the *Name* property of a window definition to ROOT_WINDOW

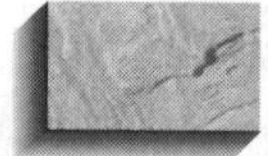

TIP

Root windows and Web forms *When a form is run in a Java applet, there is no MDI window to display the console or the toolbar. Instead, the root window can be used to display the toolbar and the console.*

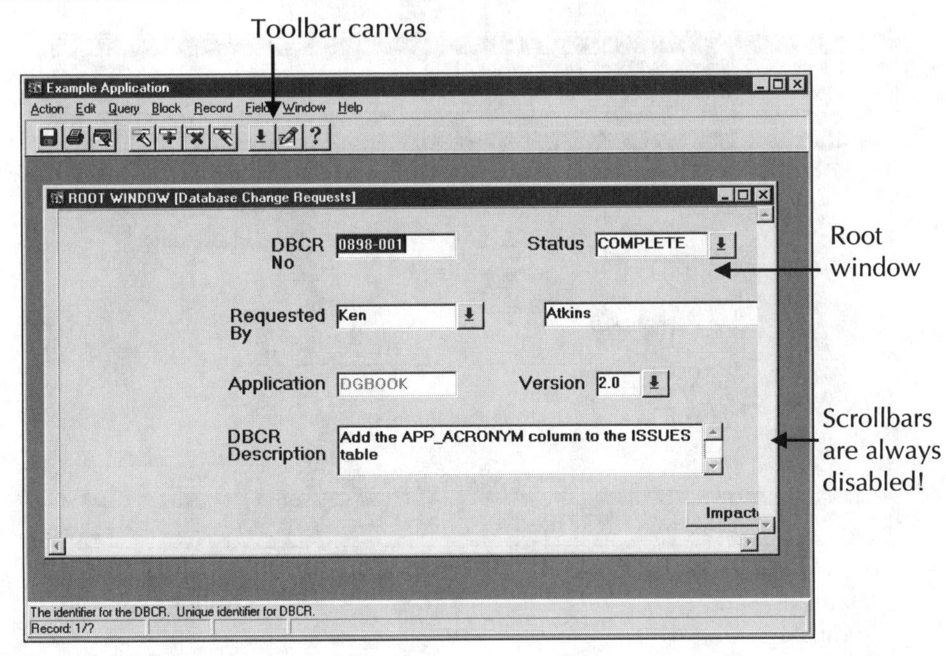

FIGURE 12-8. *Root window*

Form Builder Console

The Form Builder console is the area at the bottom of a window that displays the current status of the form (query mode or normal), the current record number, whether the current item has a list-of-values associated, a brief hint text for the current item, and any messages raised when running a form. Figure 12-9 shows an example of the Form Builder console. On MS Windows, the console is always displayed on the MDI window, unless the form-level *Console Window* property is set to **Null**. On platforms other than MS Windows, it may be advantageous to have the console appear on the root window (a window common to all forms running at the same time), since there can be only one console, and the console can be attached to one and only one window.

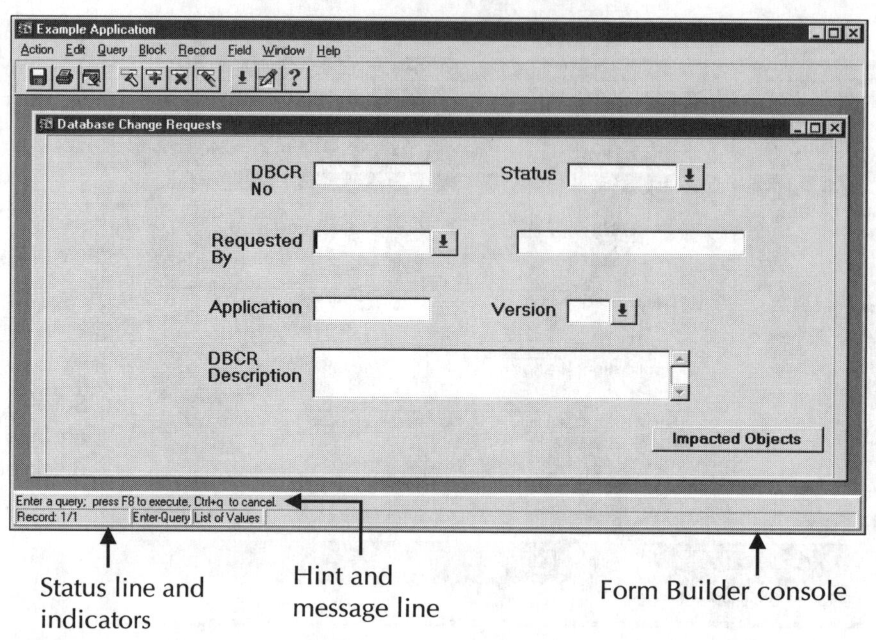

FIGURE 12-9. *Form Builder console*

The *Console Window* property, which is meaningful only for platforms other than MS Windows, cannot be set in the repository, nor can it be changed dynamically at run time. It has to be set in the template form. If the forms in your system will ever need to be run on a platform other than MS Windows, the Console feature is one that you should seriously consider using for its portability advantages. For multiwindow applications, set the console property to the root window; for single window applications, set the console property to the window.

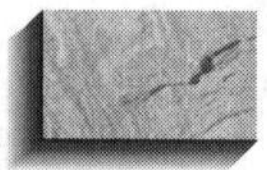

CAUTION

If you set the Console Window *property to* ***Null****, the error/warning messages that are normally displayed on the console window will not be displayed unless you trap these messages and provide some other facilities to display them (such as alerts and display-only items). Unless you are absolutely sure how to handle these side effects, you should never set the* Console Window *property to* ***Null****.*

Window Generation Troubleshooting Guide

Problem	Resolution
I am unable to specify a window size in the repository. No matter what I enter, the generated window is always the same size.	This is a very frustrating situation. If the *Scrollable* property of the window is set to **No**, and the window size is not large enough for the largest canvas assigned to the window, Form Generator adjusts these properties automatically, whether the source object allows scrollbars or not.
I am trying to set the size and location of the window, and I'm getting some unexpected results.	The units of measure for dimension and location properties are determined by the average character cell size. Check your template form and find out what the average character cell width and height are.
I cannot get the scroll bars to appear in my window. I have already checked, and the *Scrollable* property is set to **Yes**.	Check the source object for your window and make sure that *Show Horizontal and Vertical Toolbar* properties for this window object are also set to **Yes**. Please refer to Chapter 22 for further information.
I am getting the warning message, "CGEN-00052 Expanding width of window: WINDOW to fit canvases," and I have not defined the width of any of my canvases or windows.	This is a warning message. At least one of the content canvases assigned to the window is wider than the window, and the window is not scrollable. Either allow the window to be scrollable, or make sure that the content canvases assigned to the window are not wider than the window itself.
I am getting the message, "CGEN-00037 The scrollable window: MAIN_WINDOW does not allow vertical scrollbars." I have checked the *Scrollable* property of my repository window definition, and it is set to **Yes**.	Check the *Show Vertical Scrollbar* property of the source window object (CGSO$WINDOW if you are using the standard object library) in the object library. If this is set to **No**, the generated window will not have the vertical scrollbar. Note that the same comments apply to horizontal scrolling.

The Difference Between Canvases and Windows

Many people get confused about the difference between *windows* and *canvases* in Oracle Forms. We would like to try to clarify the difference a little bit. First, we will describe the differences; then we will go on to use a metaphor to help you grasp the difference.

The Forms *windows* are the "containers" that hold all of the form objects in the context of the window manager (e.g., MS Windows or Motif). The location, functionality, and display of all of the other objects that make up a form are managed within the *window*. For instance, no object can be designed to be displayed outside the window that contains it. Windows also give the user methods to manipulate an area of the form. They can be minimized and maximized, scrolled, resized, and iconified using the standard methods appropriate for the window manager (MS Windows, Motif, etc.)

Canvases on the other hand, are the "surfaces" that the GUI display items and decorations are placed upon. They could also be considered to be the "background" against which the actual GUI display items and decorations are placed, and in fact, the background color you see on the forms comes from the *canvas* color. Canvases are not usually used to manipulate an area of the screen. For instance, they cannot be minimized, maximized, iconified, or resized (although they can be scrolled in certain cases).

All *canvases* have to be assigned to a *window*, and a window can have many canvases assigned to it. The canvases assigned to a window can be set up to be displayed one at a time or overlaid. GUI display items and decorations cannot ever be assigned directly to a *window*; they must be assigned to a *canvas*, and the *canvas* is then assigned to the *window*.

To help you understand this, let's borrow the metaphor that was used to name the canvases. Consider an oil-on-canvas painting framed by a wooden frame. The frame represents Oracle Forms' *windows*. It is the *container* that holds the picture together, but the painting is not placed *on* the frame. The canvas that the picture is painted upon represents (of course) an Oracle Forms *canvas*. Just as the canvas is stretched into the frame, an Oracle Forms *canvas* is "stretched" into a Forms *window*. The picture painted on the canvas represents the actual GUI display items and decorations in Forms. The figures, scenery, and decorations that make up the picture are painted upon the canvas just as the GUI display items are "painted" onto the Forms canvas.

We hope this little illustration will help you keep the difference straight as we continue to discuss how to generate windows and canvases.

Canvas Generation

In Oracle Forms, there are four different types of canvases, shown in Figure 12-10. A description of each of these types is listed here:

Canvas Type	Description
Content canvas	The most common canvas type. Occupies the entire window. At least one content canvas is required for each window. More than one content canvas can be shown in the same window, but only one content canvas can be visible at any time.
Stacked canvas	Displayed on top of a content canvas displayed in a window, hence the term stacked. More than one stacked canvas can be displayed in the same window at the same time. The whole stacked canvas is visible to the user when the cursor is placed in any item on the canvas.
Tab canvas	Tab canvases are similar to stacked canvases. They are made up of a set of tabs (or tab pages) shown in the same area of the screen. The are used to save space when displaying large amounts of information. Each tab shows one group of information.
Toolbar canvas	A toolbar is usually a collection of user iconic buttons that execute functions. A toolbar canvas is special canvas aligned horizontally along the top or vertically down the side of a window. Toolbar canvases are dynamically sized when the window they are assigned to is resized.

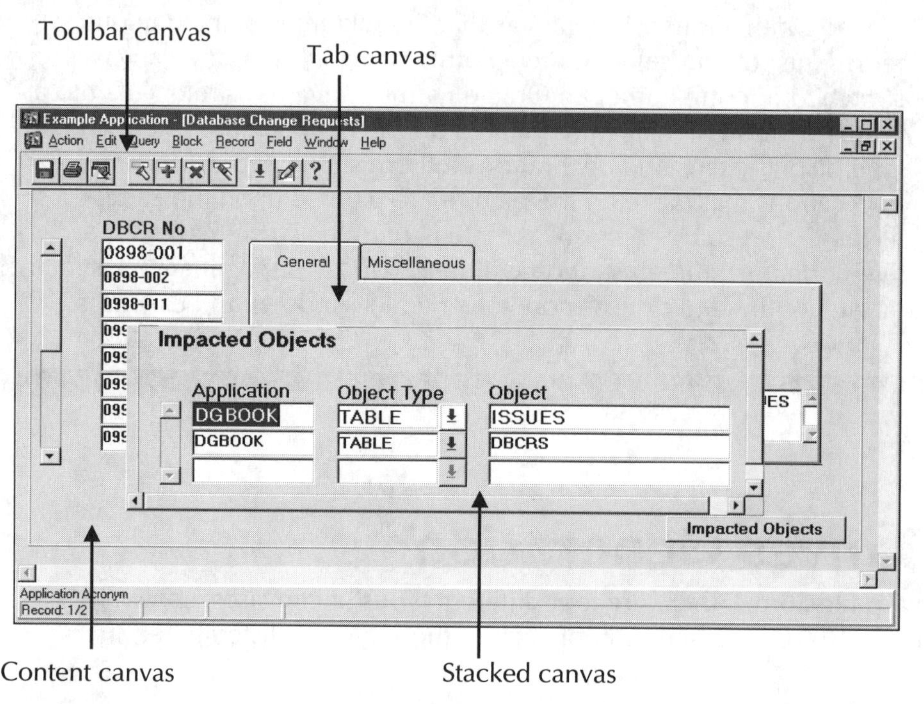

FIGURE 12-10. *Different canvas types used in a form*

Form Generator can generate all of these canvas types but the toolbar canvases. Toolbar canvases cannot be defined in the repository module definitions. To implement a toolbar canvas, you must include it in a template form. When a form is generated, the toolbar canvases from template forms are copied into the generated form (if they are referenced from another reference form, they will still stay referenced after being copied into the generated form).

Content Canvases

Content canvases are automatically generated when a module component's *Placement* property is left blank or set to **New content canvas** (see Figure 12-11). Since content canvases are the most commonly used canvases, the default value for this property is also **New content canvas**.

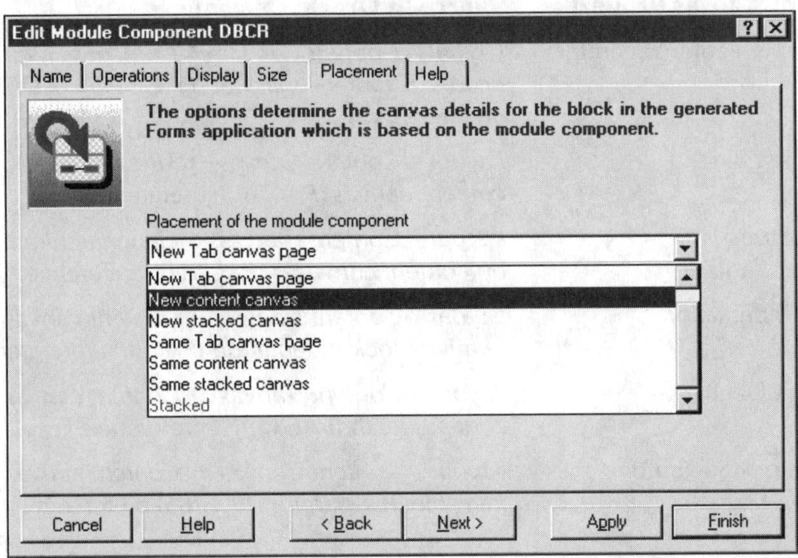

FIGURE 12-11. *Module component* Placement *property*

The following table shows a summary list of canvas properties that can be generated:

Content Canvas Property	Source in Oracle Designer
Window	*Window* property of the first module component displayed on the content canvas.
Width & Height	*Canvas Width & Height* properties of the first module component displayed on the content canvas, *Template/Library* object property, template form, and user preferences. See the *"Specifying the Size of the Content Canvas" section later in this chapter.*
*Left and Right Margins	*Layout – Content Canvas → Content canvas margin (PAGMAR)* preference.
*Header & Footer	Template form.

Content Canvas Property	Source in Oracle Designer
*Header & Footer Separator	*Layout – Content Canvas → Content canvas header & footer separator (PAGHDS, PAGFTS)* preferences.
*Title First Block	*Layout – Content Canvas → Title first block on content canvas (PAGTFB)* preference.
*Block Stubs	*Layout – Content Canvas → Generate block stubs on content canvases (PAGSTB)* preference.
*Block Indentation	*Layout – Content Canvas → Content canvas relative block indentation (PAGBIN)* preference.
*Context Depth	*Layout – Content Canvas → Content canvas context depth (PAGCON)* preference.
*Inter-Block Separator	*Layout – Content Canvas → Content canvas inter-block separator (PAGIBS)* preference.

*These properties do not correspond to any of the canvas object properties in Form Builder. These are layout related unique features generated by the Form Generator. For further information about these features, please refer to Chapters 19 and 20, which cover layout issues in great detail. Figure 12-12 shows some of these content canvas properties.

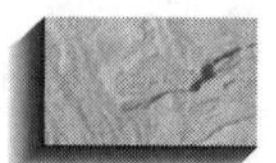

NOTE

Terminology Change *In earlier versions of Oracle Designer, content canvases were known as "pages" (that's why the user preference names are prefixed with PAG).*

How to Generate a Content Canvas

To generate a content canvas follow these steps:

1. Create a module first, if you have not done so.
2. Create a module component, and set its *Placement* property to **New content canvas**.
3. Use the layout preferences (i.e., preferences from *Layout – Content Canvas, Layout – Stacked Canvas* categories) to specify other properties, such as the page margins, etc. Set these preferences at the module level, or better yet, define and use Preference Sets.

4. Optionally, set the width and height of the canvas using the module component's *Canvas Width* and *Canvas Height* properties. However, this is a strategic decision about the user-interface design. If you were trying to have standard canvas sizes, you would not want to set the canvas size here. Instead, you would use either layout preferences or template canvases. If you are going to allow different canvas sizes, then you can go ahead and specify the *Canvas Height* and the *Canvas Width*. For further information about how to specify content canvas size, refer to the next section.

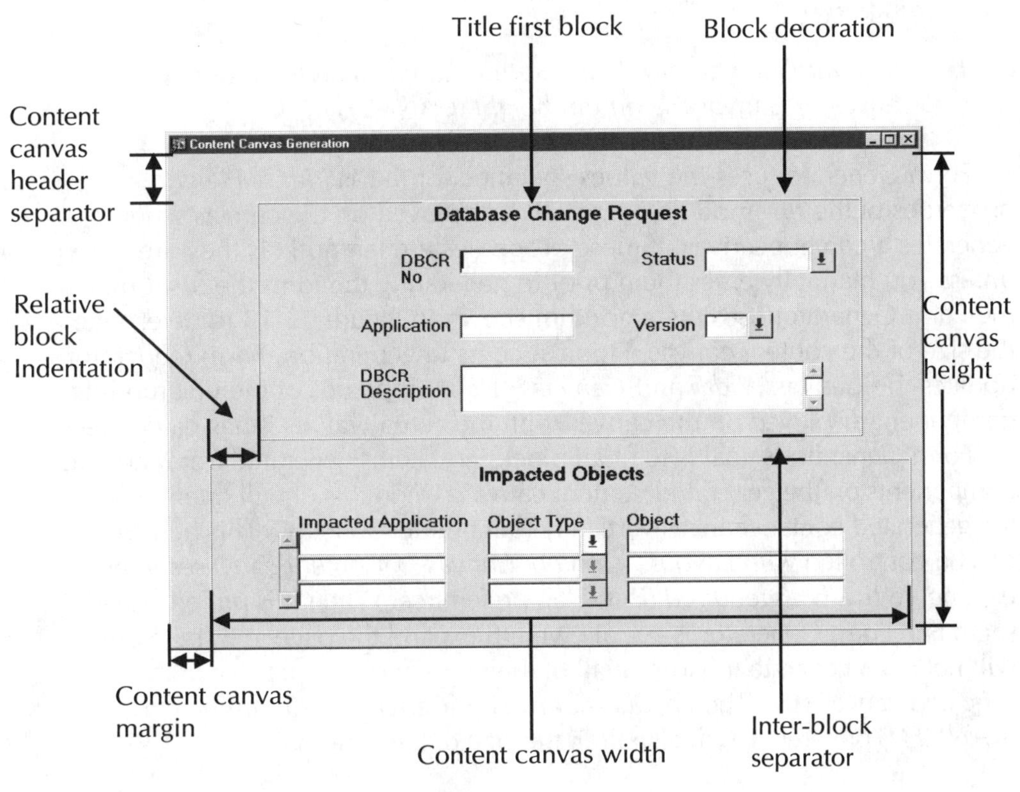

FIGURE 12-12. *Content canvas properties*

Specifying the Size of the Content Canvas

When determining the size of a content canvas, the following factors are important:

- *Width & Height* properties of the module component(s). A content canvas can be used to display one or more module components!
- Number of rows displayed in each module component and the layout styles chosen for the module component(s).
- *Content Canvas Expansion Allowed* preference *Layout – Content Canvas → Content canvases may expand vertically as required (PAGEXP).*
- *Maximum Height for all Generated Canvases* preference *Layout – Canvas → Canvas maximum height (CANMHT).*

Form Generator uses the values specified for the *Width & Height* properties of the *first* module component displayed on the canvas when it generates a content canvas. If these properties are left null (as they are unless you manually enter them prior to generating the form the first time), the Form Generator uses the algorithm shown in Figure 12-13 to determine the size of the content canvas. Upon successful generation, Form Generator updates the *Canvas Width* and *Canvas Height* properties of the first module component displayed on the canvas with the actual values it has calculated.

Form Generator's goal is to fit all blocks and items generated from module components on the generated content canvas. To do this, it will often expand the generated content canvas vertically (but not horizontally). This behavior can be controlled with *Layout – Content Canvas → Content canvases may expand vertically as required (PAGEXP)* preference. When this preference is set to **No**, Form Generator is not allowed to expand the page and therefore will not even generate the form if all of the items and rows cannot fit in the specified canvas size. The *Layout – Canvas → Canvas maximum height (CANMHT)* preference will also limit the size of the canvas.

Stacked Canvases

Stacked canvases are automatically generated when a module component's *Placement* property is set to **New stacked canvas**. There is one major

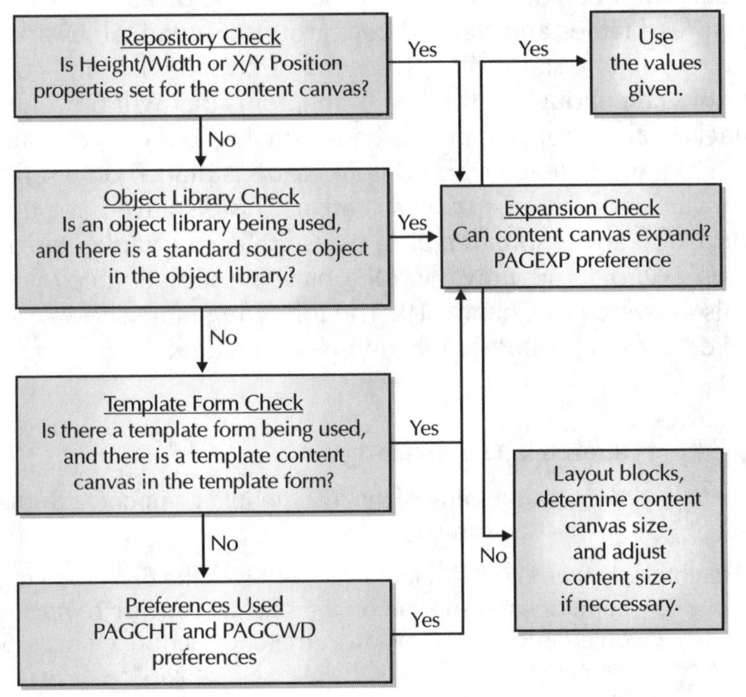

FIGURE 12-13. *How Form Generator sets the size of a content canvas*

restriction for stacked canvas usage: the very first module component of a form cannot be placed on a stacked canvas.

NOTE

Release 1.3 *In earlier versions of Oracle Designer, stacked canvases were known as pop-up pages. However, they were still called stacked canvases in Oracle Developer Forms, and this difference in terminology confused some of the experienced forms developers. The change to a consistent terminology between the two tools (Developer and Designer) is a great improvement in release 2.*

Form Generator can also generate a special type of stacked canvases for scrollable spread tables and stacked item groups. Spread tables are horizontally scrollable stacked canvases that are used when the content canvas is not wide enough to hold all of the items that will be generated onto it. Stacked item groups can also cause stacked canvas generation to save screen real estate (each stacked item group is placed on a separate stacked canvas, and only one of these canvases is displayed at a time). For more information about spread tables, please refer to *Oracle Designer Online Help → Block overflow* control topic. The spread table overflow option is also covered in Chapter 19. The following table shows a summary list of stacked canvas properties that can be generated:

Stacked Canvas Property	Source in Oracle Designer
Window	*Window* property of the first module component displayed on the stacked canvas
Width & Height	*Canvas Width & Height* properties of the first module component displayed on the stacked canvas, *Template/Library* object property, template form, and user preferences. See the "Specifying the Size of the Stacked Canvas" section later in this chapter.
View Width & Height	*View Width & Height* properties of the first module component displayed on the stacked canvas, *Template/Library* object property, template form, and user preferences. See the "Specifying the Size of the Stacked Canvas" section later in this chapter.
View X & Y Position	*X & Y Position* properties of the first module component displayed on the stacked canvas, *Template/Library* object property, template form, and user preferences. See the "Specifying the Size of the Stacked Canvas" section later in this chapter.
Horizontal & Vertical Scrollbars	*Show Horizontal & Vertical Scrollbar* properties of the source object (CGSO$CANVAS_POPUP) in the object library, *Template/Library* object property, template form, and user preferences.
Bevel	*Bevel* property of the source object (CGSO$CANVAS _POPUP) in the object library, *Template/Library* object property, template form, and user preferences.

Stacked Canvas Property	Source in Oracle Designer
Left and Right Margins	*Layout – Stacked Canvas → Stacked canvas margin (POPMAR)* preference.
Header & Footer	Template Form.
Header & Footer Separator	*Layout – Stacked Canvas → Stacked canvas header & footer separator (POPHDS, POPFTS)* preferences.
Title First Block	*Layout – Stacked Canvas → Title first block on stacked canvas (POPTFB)* preference.
Block Stubs	*Layout – Stacked Canvas → Generate block stubs on stacked canvases (POPSTB)* preference.
Block Indentation	*Layout – Stacked Canvas → Stacked canvas relative block indentation (POPBIN)* preference.
Context Depth	*Layout – Stacked Canvas → Stacked canvas stacked depth (POPCON)* preference.
Inter-Block Separator	*Layout – Stacked Canvas → Stacked canvas inter-block separator (POPIBS)* preference.

For further information about *Layout – Stacked Canvas* preferences, please refer to *Oracle Designer Online Help → Layout preferences - stacked canvas* topic. Figure 12-14 shows some of these properties of a stacked canvas.

NOTE
In earlier versions of Oracle Designer, stacked canvases were known as "pop-up pages." This is why the user preference names are prefixed with "POP".

How to Generate a Stacked Canvas

To generate a stacked canvas, follow these steps:

1. Create a module first, if you have not done so.
2. Create a module component and set its *Placement* property to **New stacked canvas**. Make sure that there is at least one other module component sequenced before the new module component: the very first module component cannot be generated onto a stacked canvas.

3. Use the layout preferences (i.e., preferences from *Layout – Stacked Canvas* category*)* to specify other properties such as the stacked canvas margins, etc.
4. Optionally, set the width and height of the stacked canvas using the module component's *Canvas Width, Canvas Height, View Width,* and View *Height* properties. Stacked canvases in the template form and stacked canvas properties provide default values for the width and height, but you can override them. For further information about how to specify stacked canvas size, please refer to the next section.

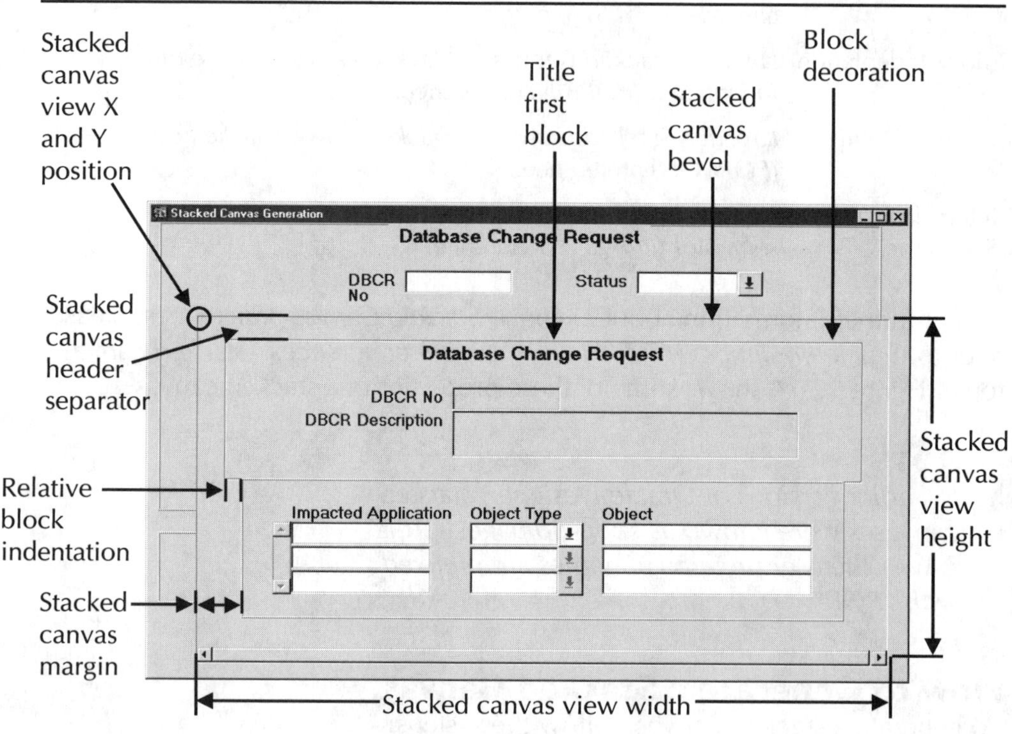

FIGURE 12-14. *Stacked canvas properties*

Specifying the Size of the Stacked Canvas

When determining the size of a stacked canvas, the following factors are important:

- *Width & Height* properties of the module component(s). A stacked canvas can be used to display one or more module components!
- Number of rows displayed in each module component and the layout styles chosen for the module component(s).
- *Stacked Canvas Expansion Allowed* preference *Layout – Stacked Canvas → Stacked canvases may expand vertically as required (POPEXP).*
- *Maximum Height for all Generated Canvases* preference *Layout – Canvas → Canvas maximum height (CANMHT).*

Form Generator uses the values specified for the *Width & Height* properties of the *first* module component displayed on the stacked canvas when it generates a stacked canvas. Note that you can specify width and height for the stacked canvas and the view separately. View width and height are dimensions that will affect how much of the stacked canvas can be seen through the view. If the view width and height is smaller than the stacked canvas, then scroll bars might be needed to view the other parts of that stacked canvas. If these properties are left null (which would normally be the case unless you manually enter them prior to generating the form the first time), the Form Generator uses the algorithm shown in Figure 12-15 to determine the size of the stacked canvas. Upon successful generation, Form Generator updates the *Width & Height* properties of the first module component displayed on the stacked canvas with the actual values it has calculated.

Form Generator's goal is to fit all blocks and items generated from module components on the generated stacked canvas. To do this, it will often expand the canvas vertically (but not horizontally). This behavior can be controlled with the *Layout – Stacked Canvas → Stacked canvases may expand vertically as required (POPEXP)* preference. When this preference is set to **No**, Form Generator will not expand the stacked canvas and does not even generate the form if all of the items cannot fit on the canvas. There is also another preference (*Layout – Canvas → Canvas maximum height (CANMHT))* that controls how much the Form Generator can expand the stacked canvas.

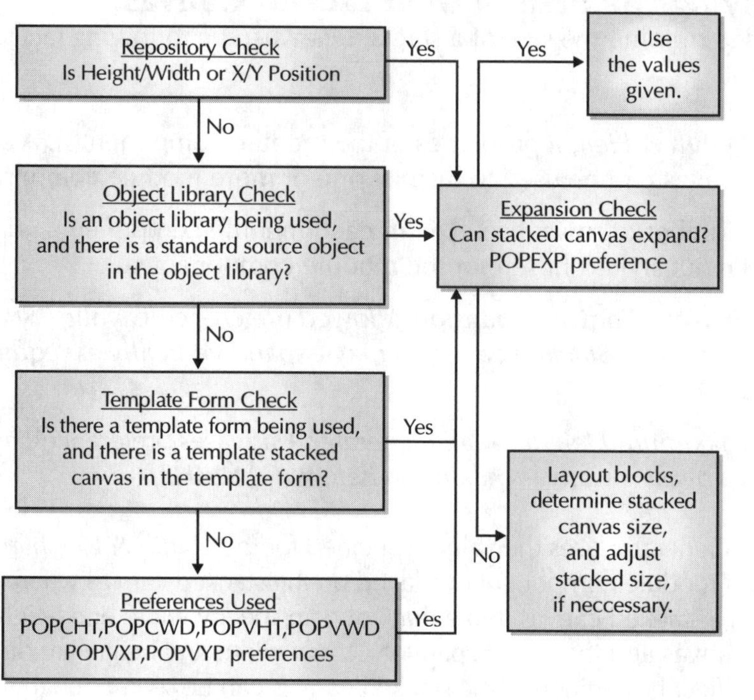

FIGURE 12-15. *How Form Generator sets the size of a stacked canvas*

Generating Tab Canvases

Tab canvas is a new implementation method for stacked item groups. Tab canvases are generated when two or more item groups are stacked together (*Stacked* property set to **Yes**), and tab canvas generation preference *Layout – Canvas → Native tab canvases (CANNTC)* is set to **Yes**. Figure 12-16 shows an example of tab canvas. Starting with release 2.1.2, Form Generator allows generation of blocks onto tab canvases by setting the *Placement* property to **New Tab canvas page** or **Same Tab canvas page**. For more information about tab canvases, please refer to Chapter19. Some examples of tab canvases can also be found in Chapter 20.

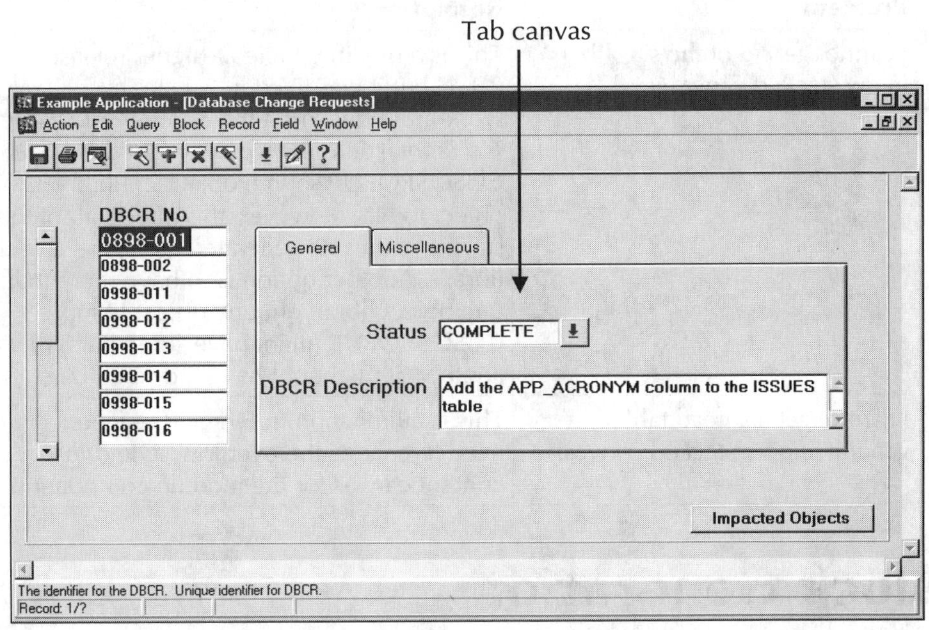

FIGURE 12-16. *Tab canvas*

Canvas Generation Troubleshooting Guide

Problem	Resolution
When I set the *Placement* property to **New content canvas**, I cannot navigate to my module component.	This was a bug in Oracle Designer release 2.1.1, but it was fixed in 2.1.2. The generated stacked canvas's width is set to zero. That is why you cannot navigate to your stacked canvas.
I cannot get the stacked canvas width and height set properly.	This is a bug in Oracle Designer release 2.1.1, but it was fixed in 2.1.2. The work-around is to specify a template/library object.

Problem	Resolution
I cannot get rid of the scrollbars in my stacked canvases.	This is a bug in Oracle Designer release 2.1.1, but it was fixed in 2.1.2. The work-around is to set the *Show Vertical and Horizontal Scrollbars* property of the CGSO$POPUP source object in library object to **No**. However, this affects all of the stacked canvases generated using the object library. Another option is to have more than one object library. In one object library, CGSO$POPUP might have scroll bars; in another, it might not have the scroll bars.
I cannot get a spread table generated on a stacked canvas.	This is a limitation in Oracle Designer. You need to change the overflow style or use a content canvas for the module component.

Block Generation

A block is a container for items (the interface elements the users interact with). Items in a form must belong to a block. Blocks are not displayed on a form, but the items contained in the blocks are. Blocks can be either data or control blocks:

Block Type	Description
Data block or base table block	Provides a link to a data source. Enables users to view and access data stored in the data source. Data sources can be database tables, views, snapshots, procedures, etc. Items in a data block may or may not correspond to a data source element.
Control block	Not associated with a data source. Also known as non-base table blocks. Provides miscellaneous user interface items.

Figure 12-17 shows examples of blocks. Blocks can be either single record (showing one row of data at a time) or multirecord (showing more than one row of data at once). Blocks enable us to group related items together. Although blocks are logical objects and not displayed on a form, Form Generator can create a border surrounding the items belonging to a block and place a title on the block to help users identify different units of information. Block decoration and layout options are discussed in Chapters 19 and 20.

Both data and control blocks are generated from module components defined in the repository.

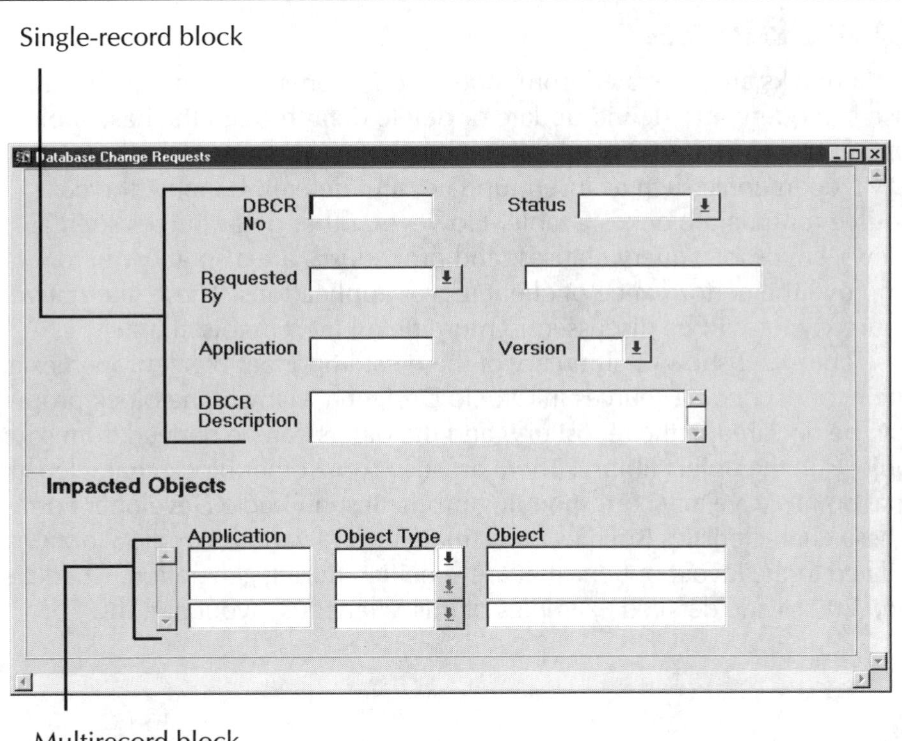

FIGURE 12-17. *Examples of blocks*

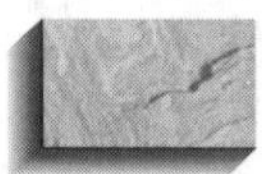

NOTE

Control block generation is a new feature in release 2 of Oracle Designer. This long-awaited feature eliminates the need for creating dummy tables in the repository and making post-generation changes or creating new templates with control blocks just to have a control block in the generated forms. If you are upgrading from earlier versions of Oracle Designer, you should consider taking advantage of this new feature.

Data Blocks

Data blocks are generated from module component definitions that allow users to query, insert, and update or delete data through the base table usage. Data blocks need to be linked with data sources for both query and DML operations (such as insert, update, and delete). Usually, the data source for a data block is a table. However, other data sources such as views, snapshots, query clauses, and procedures are also allowed to improve the performance of client/server applications. These alternative data source types will be discussed in more detail later in this chapter.

Table 12-2 shows a summary of the most important block properties and their corresponding sources in Oracle Designer. Many of the block properties can be declared in the repository, and the others can be derived from source objects in the object library. There are also some other block characteristics that do not have any corresponding properties in Oracle Developer Forms. These characteristics (such as block margins and various overflow options) are related to the layout options that are specified during generation. Chapters 19 and 20 provide detailed examples of miscellaneous layout options.

Block Property	**Source in Oracle Designer**
Name	*Name* property of the module component.
Subclass Information	*Default Source Object in the Object Library or Template/Library Object* property of the module component, if an object library is used and subclassing from the object library.
Previous/Next Navigation Block	*Module Component Sequence* and *the Navigation* preferences. Block and item navigation is discussed in more detail in Chapter 14.
Query Data Source Type	*Data Source Type* property of the module component.
Query Data Source Name	*Name* property of the base table usage specified for the module component if the *Data Source Type* property is set to **Table**. For more information about other data source types please refer to the "Generating Blocks Based on Alternative Data Sources" section later in this chapter.
DML Data Target Type	*Data Target Type* property of the module component.
DML Data Target Name	*Name* property of the base table usage specified for the module component if the *Data Target Type* property is set to **Table**. For more information about other data source types please refer to the "Generating Blocks Based on Alternative Data Sources" section later in this section.
Query Allowed	*Query?* property of the module component.
Insert Allowed	*Insert?* property of the module component.

TABLE 12-2. *Generatable Block Properties and Their Corresponding Sources in Oracle Designer*

Block Property	Source in Oracle Designer
Update Allowed	*Update?* property of the module component.
Delete Allowed	*Delete?* property of the module component.
Number of Records Displayed	*Rows Displayed* property of the module component.
Number of Records Buffered	Computed from *Rows Displayed* property of the module component. The minimum is 4.
Record Orientation	Vertical.
Where Clause	*Where Clause of Query?* property of the base table usage specified for the module component.
Order By Clause	*Order By Sequence* and *Sort Order* properties of bound items. (Can also be set in the *Where Clause of Query?* property of the base table usage specified for the module component if order by sequence properties are not set!)
Show Scroll Bar	*Show Scroll Bar* property of the *Default Source Object or Template/Library Object* in the object library, or *Sort Order* properties of bound items.

TABLE 12-2. *Generatable Block Properties and Their Corresponding Sources in Oracle Designer* (continued)

CAUTION

Block names *In earlier versions of Oracle Designer, there used to be a Form Generator preference* Coding Style → Naming Convention for block names (BLKNME) *for specifying how the generated blocks are named. This preference is obsolete in release 2 and may cause some potential problems if you are upgrading from an earlier version and used the BNN convention for naming blocks, where generated block names were B1, B2, B3, etc.*

How to Generate a Data Block

Data blocks can be generated based on many different types of data sources, including tables, views, subqueries, and procedures. Data blocks based on tables and views are the most common, and that is what we will focus on in this section. Generating other types of data blocks is not much different than generating data blocks based on tables or view. However, some special considerations have to be taken into account when using these data sources. We will discuss these alternative data sources later in this chapter.

The following steps outline the process of generating a data block based on a table or view:

1. Create a module definition in the Design Editor, if you have not done so.
2. Create a module component. There are two ways of creating module components:

   - **Using dialogs** Dialogs provide a very user-friendly interface and will walk you step-by-step through this process. For less experienced users, dialogs provide a fail-safe interface because they do not allow you to set properties that are not valid in a particular context. The process starts with the selection of the base table or view and the lookup table or views used in the module component, and it continues by defining the operations users are allowed to do in this module component (or block). Dialogs will also walk you through the selection of bound items and how to set their display properties. Dialogs are very intuitive and easy to use.
   - **Using property palettes** Unlike dialogs, property palettes do not walk you through this process at all. They are simply data-entry tools for more experienced users. If you do not have a good understanding of the properties of repository elements, you should use the dialogs instead of using the property palettes. If you are using property palettes, you need to start with the base table usage, and then add any other lookup table usages that you might need. Then you can add the bound items to the table usages. Create other module components as outlined in the previous step.

3. Display the module on a module diagram. Review the data and display views to verify the data usage(s) (base and lookup items, key-links, etc.) and display properties (windows, canvases, titles, item groups, display sequences, etc.). Make changes as required.
4. Generate the module.

Data Block Generation Techniques

There is more to data block generation than simply creating a few module components and a few bound items. The following sections will discuss some of the important issues in data block generation.

HOW TO GENERATE MASTER-DETAIL RELATIONSHIPS All but very simple forms have master-detail relationships. In a master-detail relationship, there may be one or more detail records for each master record. A master block can have many detail blocks. A detail block can have at most two masters. A detail block can also be a master for another detail block. Master and detail blocks do not need to be displayed on the same canvas or even in the same window.

The master-detail relation between two blocks (module components) in the same module is defined as a *key-based link* between the two base table/view usages of the two module components. A key-based link is based on the foreign key relationship between the two tables/views. This type of link is also known as a *master-detail link.* Figure 12-18 shows a master-detail link in a module diagram.

There are several different ways to create a master-detail link. One way is to have them automatically created when a detail module component is created via the dialogs. Master-detail links can also be added later, through either the module diagram or the Property Palette. Make sure that the diagram is in the Data view mode; otherwise the Designer's iconic toolbar does not show the buttons needed to create key based-links. If you are using the Property Palette, find the key-based links branch under the master table usage, and create the link under the master, not the detail.

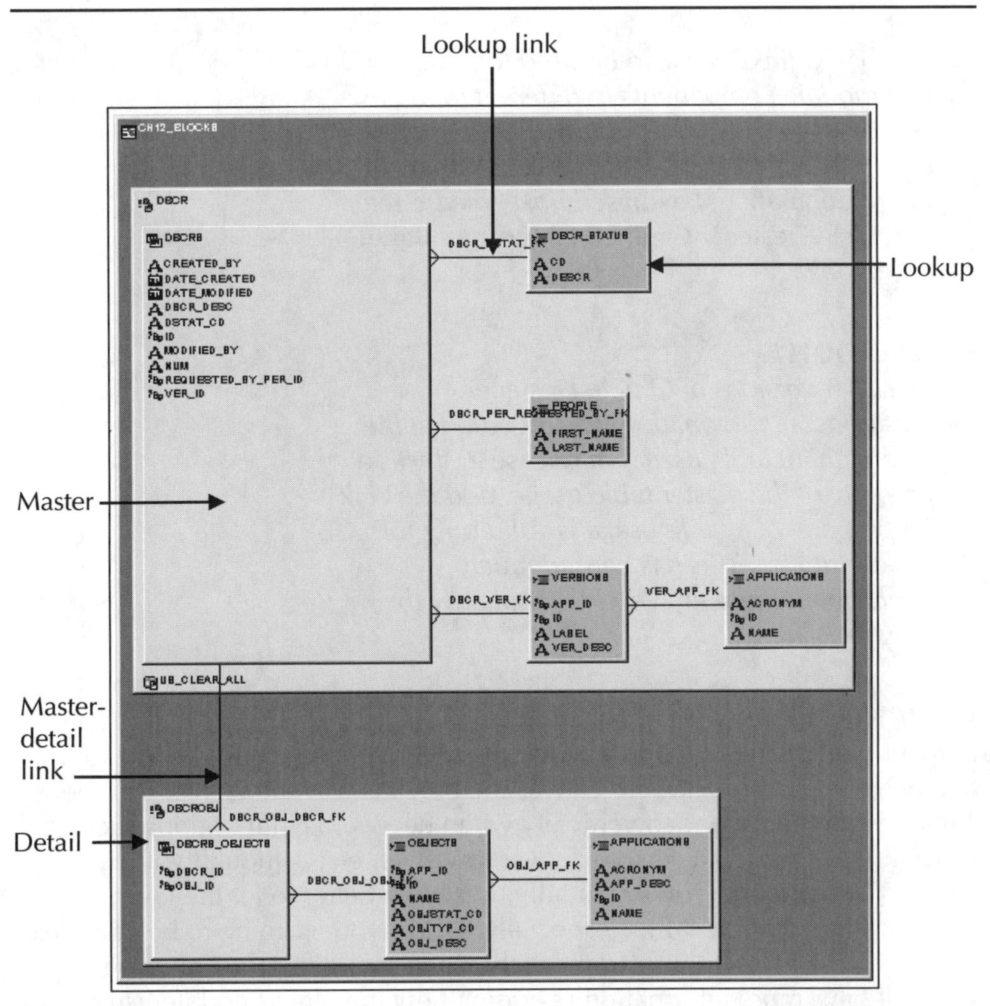

FIGURE 12-18. *Master-detail link*

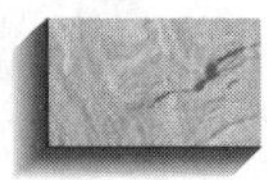

TIP

Key-based links can also be used for linking two module components in different modules, as well as for lookup links, inverted master-detail links, and same-table links. For more information about key-based links, please refer to Oracle Designer Online Help → Key Based Links *topic.*

CAUTION

In earlier versions of Oracle Designer, master-detail information was recorded at the detail (child) table usage. In release 2, this is a property of the master table usage, and the Link To *property of a table usage is valid only for lookup usages. This has caused much confusion for people who are familiar with release 1.*

HOW TO SPECIFY THE NUMBER OF ROWS DISPLAYED The number of rows displayed in a block depends on many factors: the width and height of content/stacked canvas the block is placed on, whether the canvases can be expanded vertically when needed, layout options such as separators between blocks, block overflow style, etc. Although you can specify the number of rows manually, it is often better to let the Form Generator to compute it first, especially if the layout is going to be complex and if you are going to display more than one row. After the first generation, you will have more information regarding how the blocks and items are laid out. To let the Form Generator to compute the number of rows to display you must do the following:

- **Using dialogs** Set the *Number of rows displayed* to **Maximum**.
- **Using Property Palette** Set the *Rows displayed* property to **0** or leave it blank.

Whether you specify the *Number of rows displayed* or let the Form Generator compute it, Form Generator always calculates the following two figures during the generation:

- Maximum number of rows that can be displayed without expanding the canvas (content or stacked)
- Maximum number of rows that can be displayed when the canvas (content or stacked) is expanded to the maximum size

Before setting the number of rows displayed, Form Generator compares these two figures with the *Number of rows displayed* property of the module component. The flowchart in Figure 12-19 shows the algorithm Form Generator uses to set the number of rows displayed.

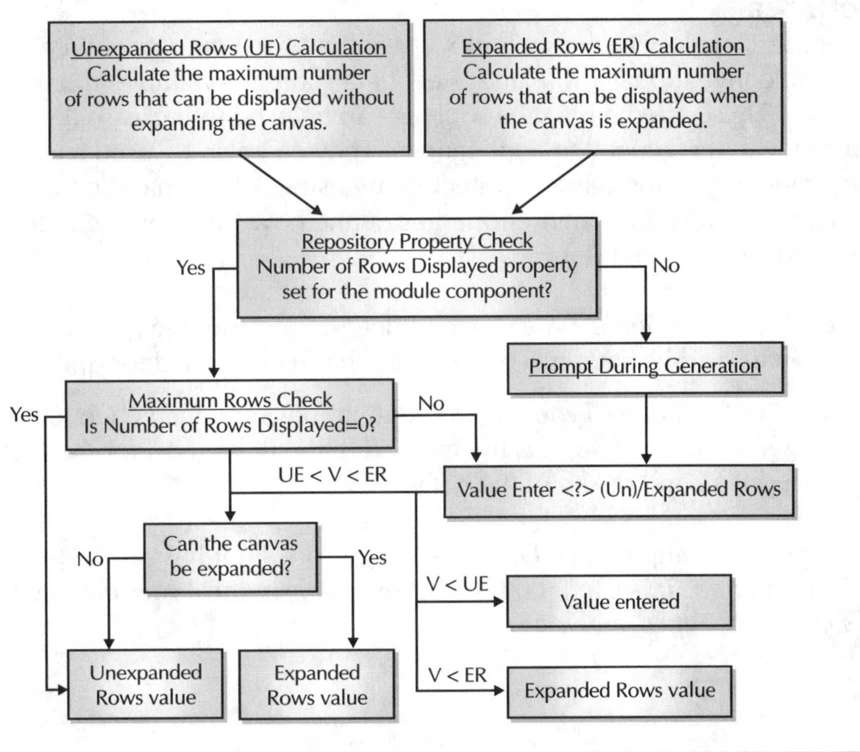

FIGURE 12-19. *How Form Generator sets the number of rows displayed*

HOW TO PREVENT INSERT, UPDATE, DELETE, AND QUERY OPERATIONS ON A DATA BLOCK Insert, Update, Delete, and Query operations are valid only for the data blocks. If you want to prevent any one of these operations on a data block, just set the corresponding *Insert?*, *Update?*, *Delete?*, or *Query* properties of the module component to **No**.

The Oracle Designer Online Help is a little misleading about how this is implemented. It seems to state that Form Generator creates code into the corresponding key triggers (KEY-CREREC, and KEY-DELREC), and the before event triggers (PRE-INSERT, PRE-DELETE, and PRE-UPDATE) to prevent the action. However, this is not exactly true. The Form Generator just sets the corresponding Oracle Developer Forms properties (*Insert Allowed, Update Allowed,* and *Delete Allowed)* to **No**. This has the effect of disabling the appropriate triggers without actually generating any code.

Generating Data Blocks Based on Alternative Data Sources

In Oracle Developer release 2, blocks can be based on data sources other than the conventional Table and View data sources available in previous releases. These alternative data sources can be used to increase the network efficiency of the generated applications. They can also be used to implement a true three-tier architecture by using APIs to handle transactions.

Two module component properties define how the generated blocks will save and retrieve their data:

- The *Datasource Type* property determines how the generated block will read its data. It is the method that will be used for querying data.
- The *Datatarget Type* property determines how the generated block will write its data. It is the method that will be used for the insert, update, and delete of the data.

A module component's *Datasource Type* does not have to be the same as its *Datatarget Type*. In fact, some of the *Datasource Types* cannot be used as *Datatarget Types,* and vice versa.

A Better Method to Display Block DML Capabilities to the User

When the create, update, and delete functionality is disabled by setting the appropriate property (*Insert, Update, or Delete*) to **No**, the user does not know that these operations are disabled until he or she tries to perform the function. Only then, a message would appear in the console area (or in an alert box) that says something like "Record cannot be deleted." While there is nothing wrong with this, from a functionality perspective this is not very user friendly.

A better approach would be to use a When-New-Block-Instance trigger and automatically disable menu options or toolbar icons if any one of these operations were not allowed. This can be done by adding some standard code to your template that reads the block properties of the generated block and sets the display of the menu items or toolbar icons accordingly. The following code sample, taken from a When-New-Block-Instance trigger, shows how to check if the delete operation is allowed. It then disables/enables the menu option and the toolbar button if deletions are not allowed:

```
. . . . . . .
If get_block_property(name_in('system.trigger_block'),
    delete_allowed) = 'FALSE'
Then
    Disable_Menu_Option('DELETE_RECORD');
    Disable_Toolbar_Button('DELETE_RECORD');
    Enable_Menu_Option('DELETE_RECORD');
    Enable_Toolbar_Button('DELETE_RECORD');
End If;. . . . . . .
```

The procedure calls above (i.e., "Disable_Menu_Option" and "Enable_Toolbar_Button") are not Form Builder built-ins. They are custom procedures that use the built-ins to manipulate the buttons and menu items. This example is intended to show you how to determine the DML operations allowed for a block, not provide the complete code needed to implement this functionality.

Data Source and Target Property Names and Values in Oracle Developer Forms

In the generated Oracle Developer Forms, the data source and target properties and values have slightly different names. The names of these properties in the two tools are compared here:

Designer Property Name	Developer Forms Property Name
Datasource Type	*Query Data Source Type*
Datatarget Type	*DML Data Target Type*

The values that these properties are set are also different between Designer and Forms. This table compares the values used in the two tools:

Designer Property Value	Developer Forms Property Value
Table	Table
View	Table
Query	FROM clause query
PL/SQL Procedure	Procedure
Transactional Triggers	Transactional Triggers

When the forms are generated, these values are copied from Designer to Developer Forms with the above name changes. The generator also sets the other Forms attributes needed to implement the specified data source/target.

If you want more information about how Oracle Developer Forms implements these alternate data sources, please refer to *Oracle Developer Forms Online Help*.

The following table shows a list of possible data source/target types and whether they can be defined as the *Datasource Type* or the *Datatarget Type*:

Data Source/Target Type Value	Allowable Datasource Type?	Allowable Datatarget Type?
Table Data source is a table or a view definition in the repository specified by the base table usage.	Yes	Yes
View Data source is a view that needs to be generated via the Generate Module Component API utility. The view generated contains all the bound items.	Yes	Yes
Transactional Trigger Data source for DML operations is a set of triggers ON-INSERT/UPDATE/DELETE that uses the Table API procedures.	No	Yes
Query Data source is a select statement generated by the Form Generator based on the table usages specified for the module component.	Yes	No
PL/SQL Procedure Data source is the Module Component & Table API procedures that need to be generated with the Generate Module & Table API utilities.	Yes	Yes

To generate data blocks based on one of these data sources, create a module component as you normally would, and set the *Datasource Type* and *Datatarget Type* properties accordingly. If you select **PL/SQL Procedure** as your source or target, you will have to make sure that the Module Component API and Table API are generated before you generate and run your module. The following section will explain how the various data sources/targets can be used in generating data blocks. We will also provide some guidelines for choosing the right data source and targets for your needs.

HOW TO GENERATE BLOCKS BASED ON TABLES We have already explained the steps that need to be taken to generate a data block based on a table earlier in this chapter. Using a table for both the data source and data target is the most common method used in generating blocks, and it is the easiest to implement because it requires minimal maintenance and setup work.

HOW TO GENERATE BLOCKS BASED ON VIEWS You might think that generating data blocks based on views means generating data blocks based on the views that you defined in your application. However, this is not what it means. If you want to base a block on an existing view, you should set the *Datasource Type* property to **Table** and select the view as the *Base Table Usage.*

When the *Query Data Source Type* property of a module component is set to **View**, the generator will actually base the generated block on a special view that is created specifically for that module component. To do this, you do not have to select a view as your base table usage for that module component. Instead, you can just select an existing table as the base table and proceed as if you are generating a data block based on a table data source, adding lookup usages, etc. However, before you generate the module, you will need to generate the Module Component API.

Array Processing with a Table Data Source/Target

One of the main disadvantages of using tables as the data source and targets is the higher network traffic generated (as compared to some of the other data source/target types). However, the network traffic can be reduced through array processing by allowing the Form Runtime engine to process groups of records at a time instead of processing one record at a time. This is done by setting the *Query Array Size* and *DML Array Size* properties of a block and specifying a run-time parameter called *Array Processing* to enable array processing. Although these properties cannot be declared in the repository, they can be defined for the source/template objects (CGSO$BLOCK and any other user-defined block object) in the object library, and any generated blocks based on these source blocks will inherit these properties.

TIP

Generating the Module Component API *First, in the Design Editor select the module component for which to generate the API. Second, choose the* Generate → Module Component API *option from the menu. If you choose to generate to a file, don't forget to execute the file before trying to generate the module.*

When the Module Component API is generated, a view that combines all of the bound items from the base table and its lookup usages will be created for that module component. The name of this generated view will be

CGV$<module_short_name>_<module_component_name>

The name may be truncated to 21 characters. This view will be created with all of the lookups implemented as joins. This will often give you better performance and reduce the network traffic because the lookup information is retrieved and joined to the base table on the server, then sent to the client as a single record. (Normally, the generated forms will retrieve columns from each lookup usage using a separate query to the server in the POST-QUERY trigger.)

Joins in Module Component API Views

By default, the Server Generator joins lookup table usages using the equi-join method. However, this causes the view not to return rows if any of the foreign key items are left null. To fix this problem, set the *Outer Join?* property of lookup table usages to **Yes**. The generated view will use the outer-join method to join lookups with the base table, and all rows from the base table will be returned, whether foreign keys are null or not.

HOW TO GENERATE BLOCKS BASED ON TRANSACTIONAL TRIGGERS Typically, transactional triggers are used when running Oracle Forms against non-Oracle data sources. Transactional triggers (ON-INSERT, ON-UPDATE, ON-DELETE, ON-SELECT, and ON-LOCK) replace the default Form Builder functionality for query, lock, insert, update, and delete operations.

However, transactional triggers can be used against Oracle data sources as well. When running against Oracle data sources, transactional triggers can be used to overcome some of the update restrictions with complex join-views where the updates were not allowed on some or all of the view columns. In Oracle Designer release 2.1.2, transactional triggers are only allowed as *Datatarget Types*.

NOTE
Form Builder allows a transactional trigger data source for both query and DML operations. It is a restriction in the current release of Oracle Designer that these cannot be used as query data sources.

Generating a block based on a transactional trigger data source is no different than generating a block based on a table data source: First, create the module component and set the *Datatarget Type* property of the module component to **Transactional Triggers**. Second, add the table usages for both the base and the lookups, and add the items as needed.

When the form generates, all of the necessary transactional triggers are automatically created by the Form Generator. For example, if inserts are allowed but updates and deletes are not allowed, then Form Generator generates only the ON-INSERT trigger.

Transactional triggers generated against Oracle data sources make use of the Table API for the DML operations. Therefore, the Table API must be generated before you generate and run the form. Table API is a package generated for a table/view that contains procedures such as select, insert, update, delete, lock, etc., that allow us to handle the table via a standard interface layer on the server.

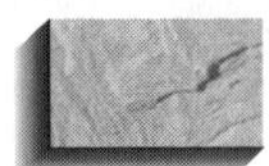

TIP
Generating the Table API *First, in the Design Editor select the table/view for which to generate the API. Second, choose the* Generate → Table API *option from the menu. You have the option of generating the Table API and saving in the database immediately, or you can save it to an operating system file. If you choose to generate to a file, don't forget to execute the file before trying to generate the module. For further information about the Table API, refer to Chapter 9.*

HOW TO GENERATE BLOCKS BASED ON SUBQUERIES (FROM CLAUSE) One of the nice features introduced with Oracle7.3 Server was the ability to nest another SELECT statement in the FROM clause of a SELECT statement. The subquery placed in the FROM clause is also known as a *Pseudo Table* or an *In-line View*. Subqueries can be used as data sources for query operations only. In a sense, using a subquery as a block data source is almost similar to using an updateable join view, except that there is no view defined in the database.

Generating a block based on a subquery data source is no different than generating a block based on a table data source: First, create the module component and set *Datasource Type* property to **Query**. Second, add the table usages (both base and lookup) and items as needed; then generate the module.

When the form is generated, it will contain a select statement in its *Query Data Source Name* property. This select statement will select all the bound items from all the table usages defined for that module component. The select statement generated is identical to the Module Component API view generated when the data source type is set to **View**.

HOW TO GENERATE BLOCKS BASED ON STORED PROCEDURES The last but the most advanced option for generating data blocks based on alternative data sources is to use stored procedures for the data sources and targets. Stored procedures can be used as both *Datasource Types* and *Datatarget Types.* In Oracle Developer Forms, a stored procedure can return the data to a data block by using either a "table of records" or a "ref cursor." Oracle Designer release 2.1.2 generates stored procedures that use a table of records and does not use the ref cursor method. This is because ref cursors can only be used as Query Data Source for a block and cannot be used as the data target.

NOTE
There are other differences between using a table of records and using a ref cursor, but it is out of the scope of this book to discuss these differences. For more information about ref cursors and PL/SQL table of records, please refer to PL/SQL documentation.

When using stored procedures as Query Data Source, you must generate the Module Component API before you can generate the form. To generate the Module Component API, highlight the module component first and then run *Generate → Module Component API* from the menu. The generated Module Component API is a PL/SQL package and contains procedures to handle query, insert, update, and delete operations on the module component. The package name is set to

CGC$<module_short_name>_<module_component_name>

The package name may be truncated if the module or component name is too long. If a stored procedure is used as *Datatarget Type* you must also generate the Table API for the base table specified for the module component before you can generate the form.

WHY GENERATE BLOCKS BASED ON DATA SOURCES OTHER THAN TABLES There are many advantages to using alternative data sources. Some of the advantages follow.

1. Reduce network traffic.

One of the main reasons you would want to use alternative data sources is to increase the network efficiency. When a table is used as a data source, Form Generator creates a post-query trigger to populate the lookup items. As the records are retrieved from the database, the post-query trigger fires for each record queried. The post-query trigger in turn queries the database for each lookup item separately. These individual lookups can cause a lot of network traffic. If these lookups can be prevented, the total number of network trips to query a row of data with all of its lookups will be faster, and the overall performance of the network will be better. That is why these other data sources were created. They are methods that can be used to process the lookups and complex calculations on the server where the data is.

2. **Improve the query performance of your generated forms.**

   The query performance can also be improved for the same reasons specified in the first advantage.

3. **Allow multiple tables to be queried and updated seamlessly.**

   Updating more than one table from a single-block generated from Oracle Designer is not possible because a module component can only have one base table usage; however, using alternative data sources makes it possible.

4. **Hide some of the complexities.**

   When alternative data sources are used, some of the complexities and data rules of the data model are hidden by encapsulations and automatically handled by the Form Generator.

5. **Reuse generated Module Component and Table APIs.**

   Using the Module Component and Table APIs provides an interface layer between the actual database tables and application programs. Using these APIs for multiple forms allows you to place data rules in *one* place for the whole application.

6. **Offer better security.**

   Alternative data sources may offer better security. Generated table or module component API packages can be enhanced by adding custom event codes for tighter security checks (checks that cannot be implemented with simple role and object grant assignments).

GUIDELINES FOR CHOOSING THE DATASOURCE AND DATATARGET TYPES Choosing the right *Datasource Type* and *Datatarget Type* for a module component can be tricky. The first thing you should do is to list your data access requirements:

- Will the block be query only?
- Will it allow the DML (insert/update/delete) operations?
- Will the users want to be able to query by example (i.e., enter query criteria in the same block where they edit the data)?
- Is the amount of network traffic important?

Once you have the answers to these questions, you can compare them to the capabilities of each *Datasource* and *Datatarget Type*, along with the considerations in the previous section, and make your decision. To help you with this, Tables 12-3, 12-4, and 12-5 present a summary comparison of each option.

Data Source	Allows Query	Allows DML	Allows Query by Example	Allows Array Processing
Table	Yes	Yes	Yes	Yes
View	Yes	No[1]	Yes	Yes
Query	Yes	No	No	Yes[3]
PL/SQL Procedure	Yes	No[2]	No	No[4]
Transactional Triggers	Yes	Yes	No	No[4]

TABLE 12-3. *Comparison of Data Source Options*

[1]With an exception of certain join-updateable views.
[2]If REF CURSOR variables were used, DML is allowed.
[3]Only for the queried records.
[4]If TABLE of RECORDS was used, array processing is allowed.

Data Source	Advantages	Disadvantages
Table	Generated code easy to read. No LONG data type restrictions. Array processing possible	Increased network traffic due to extensive lookup processing in post-query.
View	More efficient than table lookups done on the server. Array processing available.	A different database object may be required for DML operations.
Subquery	Less database maintenance than a view.	A different database object is required for DML operations. Query By Example not supported.
Procedure	Improved network traffic, entire block is returned from the server in a PL/SQL table of records	Complex code. Query By Example not supported.

TABLE 12-4. *Advantages and Disadvantages of Data Source Options*

Data Target	Advantages	Disadvantages
Table	Generated code easy to read. No LONG data type restrictions. Array processing possible.	Bad network performance.
PL/SQL Procedure	Improved network traffic, entire block is returned from the server in a PL/SQL table of records. Uses standard API to enter data.	Large sets of data could impact network performance, derived columns are not automatically requeried.
Transactional Triggers	Uses Standard Table API to enter data. Array processing allowed.	Fires for each created or updated record.

TABLE 12-5. *Advantages and Disadvantages of Data Target Options*

Control Blocks

A control block is an Oracle Developer Forms block that is not associated with any data source at all. Items contained in a control block are not associated with data elements, either. These types of items, items that do not correspond to columns in a data source, are referred to as *control items.*

NOTE
In previous versions of Oracle Developer Forms, there was only one option for the data source: Table. Since both the control blocks and control items were not based on tables, they are also known as non-base table blocks and non-base table items.

Control items do not have to be hidden; they can be displayed and manipulated just like any other item. For example, the toolbar iconic buttons are all control items, and they all are displayed (they have to be!). Control items do not have to be placed in control blocks, either.

In Oracle Designer Repository, a module component with no table usage corresponds to a control block in Oracle Forms. Similarly, unbound items in a module component, regardless of whether they are in a data block or not, correspond to control items. For example, navigation action items, summary items, and formula items, are all control items.

Control blocks can be used for various reasons:

- To group all control items together under a single block container and provide a logical collection of items. This keeps the form organized better and provides a standard place to look for control items.
- To provide standard interface elements that are not related to any other module component in a form: e.g., the standard toolbar in a number of forms.

How to Generate a Control Block

Although it was possible to generate control blocks in earlier versions of Oracle Designer, it was not very straightforward, and it was not possible to *directly* generate control blocks. Control block generation is a new and long awaited feature in Oracle Designer release 2. Control blocks are generated from module components that do not have any table usages. A module component with no table usage can only have unbound (or control) items.

Control blocks can be created specifically for a module or built as reusable module components to be used in any number of modules. If you have already defined some control blocks as reusable module components, you could simply include them in other modules. For more information about reusable module components, please refer to Chapter 23.

To generate a control block specific to a single module:

1. In the Design Editor, create a module component with no table usages. If you are using dialogs, do not select a table for the base table property; instead click the Finish button to create the module component without the table usages. If you are using Property Palette, do not create table usages after creating the module component.
2. Create the unbound items for the module component as necessary. When creating an unbound item, there are some decisions that you have to make besides choosing the display data type or the width and the height of the item. The most important property is the *Item Type* or *Unbound Type*. For further information about unbound items, please refer to Chapter 15.
3. Generate the form module.

How to Include a Control Block in the Generated Form Without Defining It in the Repository

To generate a control block without creating a module component, you must create the block in the template form as a user block. When the form is generated, all of the user objects in the template form are copied into the generated form without a change. For more information about the user object in templates, please refer to Chapter 22.

The prime example of a control block included in generated forms without being defined in the repository is the toolbar block in the standard template form OFGPC1T.fmb (<oracle_home>\cgenf50\admin) shipped with Oracle Designer. In a form, there is no limitation on the number of control blocks. You can have as many control blocks as you want, but it is best to keep them to a minimum number to facilitate their organization and management.

Where to Define the Control Blocks: in the Repository or the Template Form

Control blocks can be generated either from the repository module components (both specific and reusable) or from the control blocks created in the template form. Given these options, how do we decide where to define the control blocks: in the template forms or the repository? When making this decision you should consider the following:

- If the same control block is needed in large number of forms (e.g., the toolbar is needed in all forms), then create it as a packaged object group in the object library and subclass in the template form. You could also define this as a reusable module component, but the layout design may be more challenging.
- If the control block will be specific to a single module, create it as a module component in that module.
- If the control block is to be used for a few forms but not the whole application, it might not be worth maintaining another template form, so you could use a reusable component.
- When a control block is defined in the repository, it is very well documented. This might be more important to you.

Block Generation Troubleshooting Guide

Problem	**Resolution**
I have decided to use **View** as the query data source type for my module component. The form generated OK, but I am getting the message, "Table or view does not exist," when I run the form.	You must generate the Module Component API before you can run your form. In Design Editor, select the module component first and choose *Generate → Module Component API* from the menu. This will create the view required to query this module component.
I have decided to use **Transactional Triggers** as DML data target type for my module component. But the Form Generator is unable to compile the form.	You must generate the Table API before you can generate your form. In the Design Editor, select the table/view first, and choose *Generate → Table API* from the menu. This will create the table handlers required by the transactional triggers.

Problem	Resolution
I have decided to use **Transactional Triggers** as DML data target type for my module component. Even after generating the Table API, I still cannot compile the form.	This is a bug in Form Builder version 5.0.6.8. If you test the generated transactional triggers in SQL*Plus (or a similar environment), they DO work!
I have decided to use **Procedure** both for Query data source and DML data target types. However, the Form Generator is unable to compile the form.	You must generate the Module API if your Query data source type is set to **Procedure**. You must generate both the Table and the Module Component API if your DML data target source type is **Procedure**.
I am unable to query the records that I want.	If your Query Data Source Type is **Sub-Query** or **Procedure**, you are not going to be able to take advantage of the query-by-example feature of Developer2000 Forms.
I have added a new bound item to my module component, and my form does not generate or run any more.	Remember to regenerate the Module Component API after adding/deleting bound items to your module component.
I am using a **View** datasource type. I have generated both the Module Component API and the module successfully, but the query does not return some of my records.	Make sure that the *Outer Join?* property of your lookup table usages is set to **Yes**. The default is **No**, and this causes the view to do an equi-join. Also check your *WHERE Clause of Query?* and *Lookup Validation WHERE clause* properties to make sure that there is not any condition that may be filtering out those records.
How can I generate blocks with horizontal record orientation?	You cannot. This needs to be done in post generation.

Item Generation

Items are interface elements that allow users to interact with a form. They display information and allow users to query and edit data stored in the database. Items can also be used to initiate action or perform functions. Items are drawn on canvases (background objects displayed in windows) and displayed within windows (frames that provide a viewport for the form). Items are logically grouped together under the block objects. An item can be either a data item or a control item. The following table summarizes properties of data and control items:

Data item	An item in a data block that corresponds to a column in the data source/target defined for the block. Also known as *base table item*.
Control item	An item in any block that does not corresponds to a column in the data source/target defined for the block. Also known as *non-base table item*. They can be used to display lookup values, summary, and other derived information. They can also be used to obtain input from the user, execute an action or a command, indicate the current record, etc. For further information about control items, please refer to Chapter 15.

In a graphical user interface environment, items may appear and behave differently based on their GUI or display type. Possible display types for items include Text Item, Display Item, List Item, Check Box, Radio Group, Image Item, Chart Item, Push Button, and OLE Container. For further information about GUI or display types, refer to Chapter13.

Both data and control items can be generated from repository item definitions recorded for module components. There are two different types of repository item definitions:

- **Bound items** that correspond to a single column in a table or view stored in the database. Bound items can be defined either for base table or lookup table usages.
- **Unbound items** that do not correspond to a single column in a table or view stored in the database. Unbound items are defined directly for module components, not for table usages on module components.

Data items (base table items) can only be generated from bound items that are defined as part of the base table usage on a module component. There can be only one base table usage for a single module component. Control items can be generated from either unbound items or action items defined in the repository module definitions. They can also be generated automatically by the Form Generator for different reasons (such as providing context information). During generation, Form Generator may also create additional control items to support the functionality wanted. Figure 12-20 shows bound and unbound items in the data view of a module data diagram.

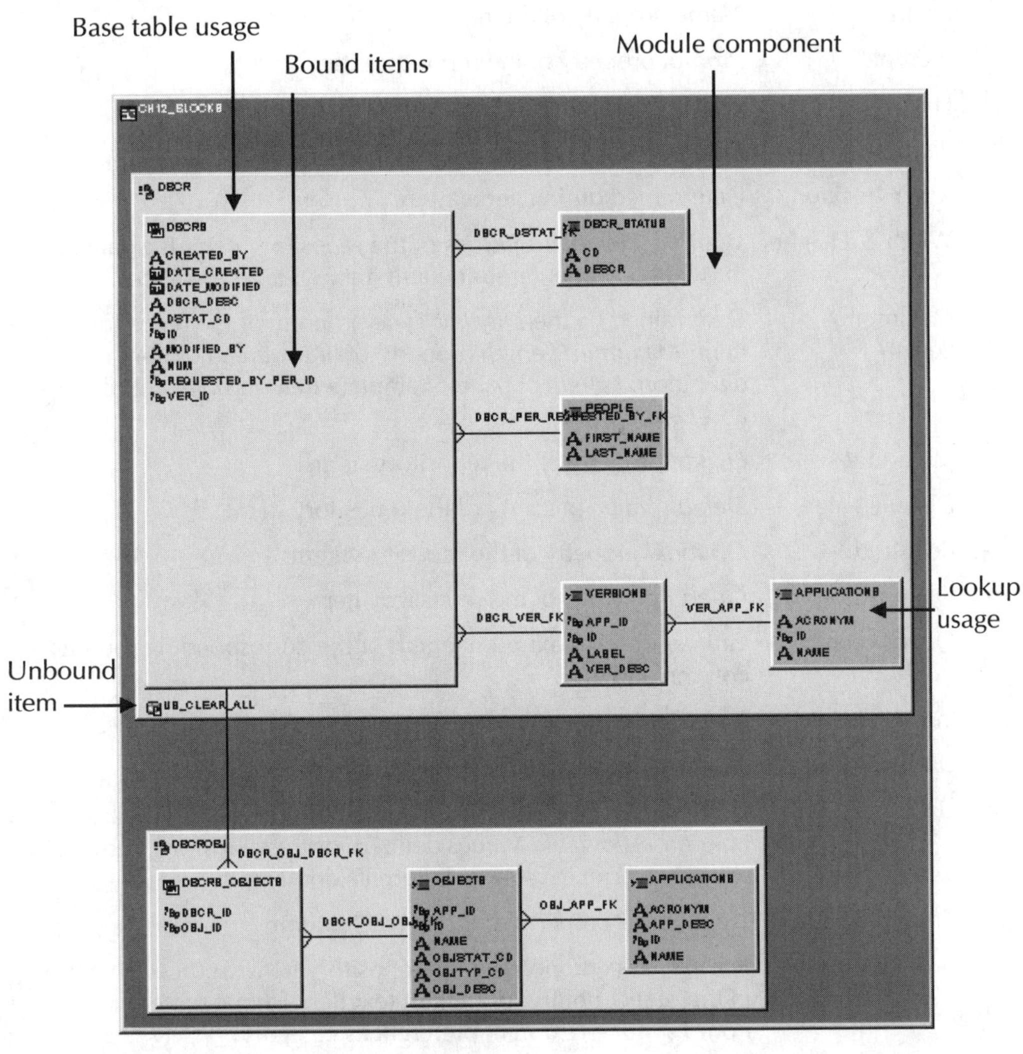

FIGURE 12-20. *Bound and unbound items*

There are many properties of both data and control items that can be declared in the repository. The following table shows a summary of generated item properties and their sources in Oracle Designer:

Generated Item Property	Source in Oracle Designer
Name	*Name* property of the repository item.
Prompt	*Prompt* property of the repository item.
Hint	*Hint* property of the repository item.
Item Type	*Display Type* property of the repository item.
X & Y Position	Determined during generation.
Width & Height	*Width & Height* properties of the repository item. If a value for width is not entered, default item width preferences.
Maximum Length	Determined by the *Display Type* property of the repository item, *Maximum Length* property of the source column definition, *Length* of source/template item in object library, and *User Preferences.*
Multi-Line	*Height* property of the repository item.
Default Value	*Default Value* property of the repository item.
Required	*Optional* property of the repository item.
Query Allowed	*Query?* property of the repository item.
Query Length	Greater of the maximum length of the corresponding source column and 225.
Insert Allowed	*Insert?* property of the repository item.
Update Allowed	*Update?* property of the repository item.
List of Values	Determined by whether the source column is a foreign key column, *Allowable Values* defined for the repository item, its source column, or source column's domains.
Case Restriction	*Uppercase?* property of the source column.
Format Mask	*Format Mask* property of the repository item, *Source Object(s)* in the object library, or default text item format preferences from *Layout - Text Item* preferences category.

Generated Item Property	Source in Oracle Designer
Item Font and Visual Attribute	*Source Object(s)* from the template/object library and *Template/Library Object* property of the item.
Keyboard Navigable	*Insert/Update Allowed* properties of the repository item.
Copy Value from item	Corresponding reference item in the parent table usage.
Synchronize item	Corresponding item in the parent table usage.

There are also other properties of items that you cannot declare in the repository but that can be subclassed from source/template object(s) in the object library. In addition, you can use item preferences to affect the generated items. When Form Generator generates an item, it uses

- Bound and unbound item definitions recorded in module components
- Table/view column definitions corresponding to bound items
- Source/template object(s) in the object library
- User preferences

For more information about the specific settings for all of these sources of information, refer to Chapters 13 and 15.

How to Generate Data (Base Table) Items

Data Items can be generated from bound items. To generate a data item:

1. Create a module definition first, if you have not done so.
2. Create a module component definition that corresponds to a data source or target. The data source/target can be either a table or view, a subquery statement, or a stored procedure. For further information about data source types, please refer to the "*Generating Blocks Based on Alternative Data Sources*" section, earlier in this chapter.

3. Create the base table usage for the module component.
4. Create bound item(s) for the base table usage and set the relevant item properties properly. Setting these properties depends heavily on the display type of the bound item. For further information about how to define properties for different GUI types, please refer to Chapter 13.
5. Generate the module.

How to Generate Control (Non-Base Table) Items

Control items can be generated from both unbound and action items. To generate a control item:

1. Create a module definition first, if you have not done so.
2. Create a module component definition.
3. Create unbound items or action items in the module component. Set their properties properly. For further information about unbound and action items, please refer to Chapter 15.
4. Generate the module.

Item Generation Troubleshooting Guide

Item generation is covered in detail in Chapters 13 and 15. For more information about troubleshooting item generation, please refer to these chapters.

CHAPTER 13

GUI Item Generation

racle Designer allows you to generate many of the GUI item types that are available in Oracle Developer Forms. The following GUI item types are discussed in this chapter:

Text items
Checkboxes
Radio groups
Pop lists
Combo boxes
Text lists
Image items
Push buttons
Action items
Current record indicators

Each of the GUI item types has its own method of generation and presents you with unique problems and opportunities. The following sections will guide you through the generation of each of these item types. Each section, corresponding to one GUI item type, will include the following information in order to help you with the generation of that item type:

- An example of what that type looks like
- A listing of the important preferences and attributes that affect that type
- A step-by-step procedure describing how to generate that type
- A troubleshooting guide to help you diagnose any problems you may have
- Examples of some of the various layout options available for that type

Text Items

A *text item* is a GUI control that displays text in either a single- or a multiline display area. A shorter single-line text item is usually used for standard field entry, while longer multiline text items are used for long free format text entry. A text item is the most basic GUI control available, and it is the one most frequently used. In a text item, the user simply enters the text in the area provided. Figure 13-1 shows examples of both single- and multiline text items.

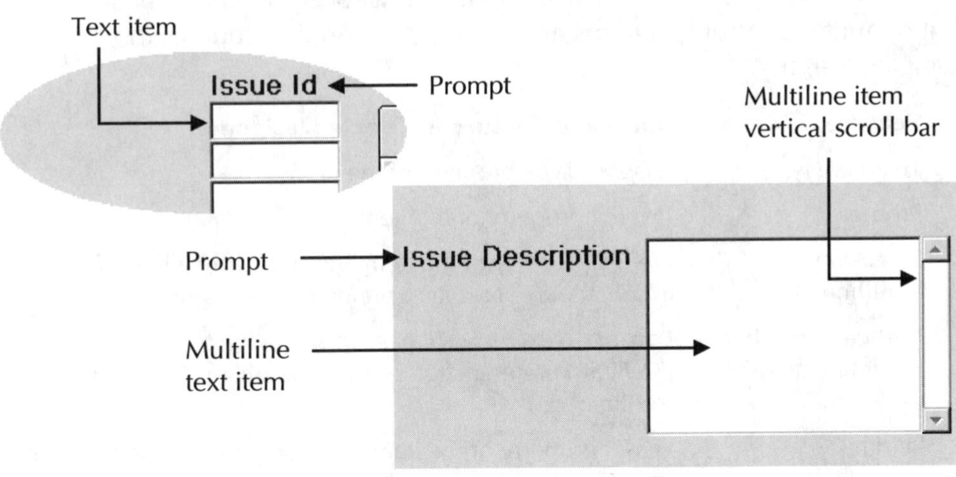

FIGURE 13-1. *Text item examples*

Another variation of a text item is called a *display item*. A display item is a display-only text item that does not allow users to enter or edit text. Display items are normally dimmed to indicate that they are unavailable for data entry. Oracle Designer generates display items from lookup items only. However, a text item can be marked as noninsertable and nonupdateable to provide similar functionality. This is important because it is difficult to read the dimmed (or grayed out) fields, and using a noninsertable and nonupdateable text item eliminates this problem.

TIP
Display Items may be hard to read since they are dimmed or grayed out. However, you can dynamically change the visual attributes of display-only items at run time to make them more readable.

The following table shows a summarized list of some of the most important features of text items and their corresponding sources in Oracle Designer.

Feature	Source of Feature in Oracle Designer
Text item type	*Display Type* property of the item
Prompt	*Prompt* property of the item
Single versus multiline	*Height* property of the item and default height preferences from *Layout – Text Item* preferences category
Vertical scroll bar (multiline items)	*Layout – Text → Scrollbar for multi-line text items (TXTVSB)* preference. **Yes** = add scrollbar, **No** = no scrollbar
Width	*Width* property of the item and default width preferences from *Layout – Text Item* preferences category
Format	*Display Format* property of the item, default text item format preferences from *Layout – Text Item* preferences category, and *Source Object(s)* from the template/object library
Item font	*Source Object(s)* from the template/object library and *Template/Library Object* property of the item

How to Generate a Text Item

You can generate text items from either bound or unbound items. In order to generate a text item, you must do the following:

1. Create either a bound or an unbound item.
2. Set the *Displayed* property of the item to **True**.

NOTE
How to Set the* Displayed *Property. *For the bound items, the* Displayed *property can be set against either the item or the column upon which the item is based. Because all of the properties of a bound item are defaulted from the source column definition when it's first created, it is highly recommended that you set the* Displayed *property against the source column. See Chapter 11 for a full discussion of this suggestion.*

3. Set the *Display Type* property of the item to **Text**.

TIP

Display Type = GUI Type. *The* Display Type *property of an item determines its* GUI Type. *Each generator (Forms, Reports, Web, etc.) has its own list of* GUI Types *that it can generate.*

4. If you are generating a text item from an unbound item, make sure that the *Data Type* property is set. *Data Type* can be set to any value, including **image**. Make sure that the *Unbound Type* property is set to **Custom**, if you are not generating a derived item. Unbound items are covered in more detail in Chapter 16.

NOTE

How to Set the* Unbound Type *Property*.** *If you choose an* Unbound Type *property other than* **Custom**, *the generated item will be a display item, and you will not be allowed to insert or update values through it. You will also have to enter some other properties related to that unbound item type. For example, if you set the* Unbound Type *to* ***SQL-Expression, *then the* Derivation Text *property needs to be defined; otherwise, you will receive a warning message during generation, and the unbound item type will default to* ***Custom***.

5. If applicable, define the format and the justification of the item. There are a few ways of doing this: you can use item properties, source object properties from an object library, or layout preferences. You should use the repository item properties to set the format and justification, but you can also use object libraries if you want to. You should avoid using layout preferences as much as possible, because most of these preferences are becoming obsolete in Oracle Designer and will not be supported in future releases.

6. If applicable, define the *Allowable Values* for the item, or attach the item to a domain that has allowable values. For bound items, domains must be attached to the source column. Domains can be directly attached to unbound items.

7. Set the other properties of the item appropriately. The item properties that are most critical for text items are shown in the following table:

Item Property	**Important, Because...**
Display Width	If left blank, the width of the text item will be derived from *Layout – Text Item* preferences. Using these preferences, you can define the default width for items with different datatypes as well. For example, the default width for a number text item could be different from the width of a date text item.
Display Height	This will help determine whether the text item can be displayed as a multiline item or not. For multiline items, set the display height at least **2** or more. The value entered must be an integer.
Template/Library Object	This will help subclass the text item from an object library. By subclassing, you can define many of the properties of the text item, including the font, alignment, etc. If left blank and the item height is set to **1** (i.e., single-line item), the *CGSO$CHAR* source object defined in the object library will be used for deriving these other properties. For multiline text items, the default source object is *CGSO$CHAR_MLINE*.

TIP

Standard Source Object Hierarchy. *There is a predefined hierarchy of standard source objects. For example,* CGSO$CHAR_MR *source object is used for single-line text items in multirow blocks, and* CGSO$CHAR_DO *is used for display-only, single-line text items. See Chapter 23 for a full discussion of source objects.*

8. Set the *Layout Preferences* for the item to control the layout details. Although many preferences have become obsolete in Oracle Designer, there are still some that are very important. Some of the

most important preferences for text items are shown in the following table (all of the preferences are in the *Layout – Text Item* category).

Preference	Tips for Preference Settings
Multi-line text items (TXTMLI)	If the item height is greater than one, should it be generated as a multiline text item? The default setting for this preference is **Yes**.
Scroll bar for multi-line text items (TXTVSB)	Should multiline text items have a vertical scroll bar? The default setting for this preference is **Yes**.

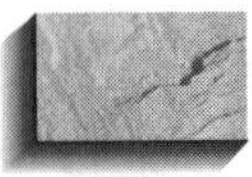

NOTE

How to Set Form Generator Preferences. *Form Generator preferences can be set at different levels (e.g., application system, module component, bound item, table, column, etc.). In order to maintain standards and to have consistent look and feel in your applications, set these preferences at the highest level possible, that is, set them at the application system level, so that they can be inherited at lower levels. You can always override these preferences and change them at lower levels such as module or module component. In addition, try using Preference Sets to reduce the amount of preference maintenance work.*

Obsolete Preferences

Try to use preferences sparingly and avoid obsolete preferences unless they are your only choice. Instead, use source objects in object libraries to set properties that cannot be declared in the repository. Many of the preferences have become obsolete in Oracle Designer, and many others might become obsolete in a future release. For further information about obsolete preferences, please refer to Oracle Designer Online Help (*What's New in This Release →Form Generator →What's new in Form Generator in Designer/2000 Release 2.1? →Alphabetical list of obsolete preferences and equivalent object library properties*).

Examples of Text Item Layout Options

There are not many layout options for text items except the vertical scrollbar option for multiline text items. Figure 13-2 shows two multiline items, one with a vertical scrollbar and one without. The only difference between these two items is the setting of *Layout – Text Item → Scrollbar for multi-line text items (TXTVSB)* preference.

When to Use Text Items

As we've already stated, text items are the most commonly used GUI controls. In fact, when the *Display Type* property is left blank, Form Generator sets it to **Text Item**. Text items must be used whenever the data to be entered is free format. Almost all of the other GUI types require that the entry be restricted to a limited set of allowable values. While you can limit the values that are allowed in the text items using LOVs or ranges of values, they generally allow much more freedom of entry than the other GUI types. Text items also do not take up as much screen space as many of the other GUI types.

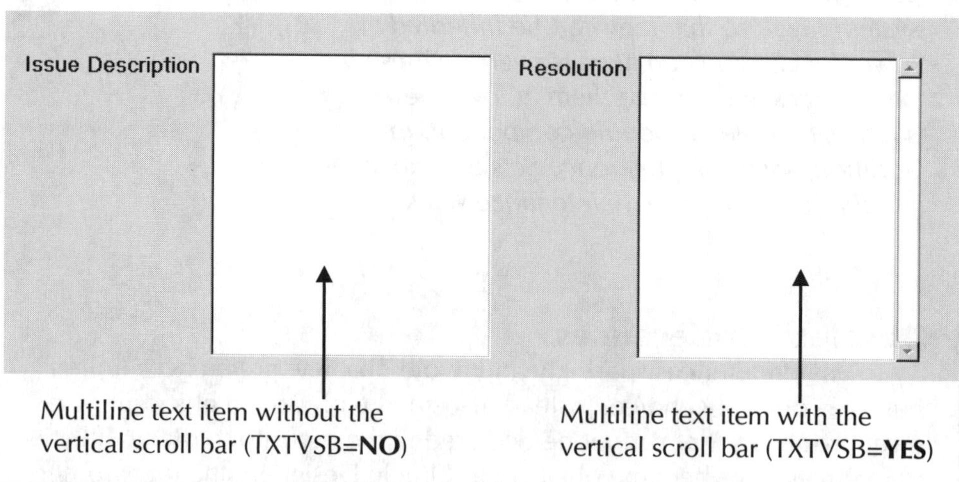

FIGURE 13-2. *Text item layout example: vertical scrollbar option for multiline text items*

Multiline text items are especially useful when displaying relatively long descriptions. Using multiline text items allows you to display more than one line of text at once and scroll through the remaining text. The only drawback of multiline text items is that they take up more screen space.

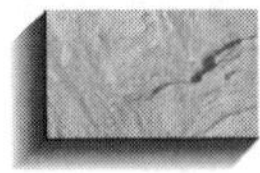

NOTE
Fixed in Developer/2000 Release 2.1. *If you have used one of the earlier versions of Developer/2000 Forms, you have probably encountered the problem with TAB and ENTER keys in multiline text items. These keys are used to navigate to the next item; however, in multiline text items, the TAB key inserted a TAB character, and the ENTER key inserted a CR/LF character rather than moving to the next item. In Developer/2000 release 2.1, this annoying feature has been eliminated, and both the TAB and the ENTER keys do the next item function even in multiline text items.*

Text Item Generation Troubleshooting Guide

Problem	Solution
I have set the height of my text item to four lines. Although I get my multiline text item, it does not wrap the text as it is supposed to.	Make sure that the *Layout – Text Item → Multi-line text items (TXTMLI)* preference is set to **Yes**. Also, if you want a vertical scrollbar for this multiline item, make sure the *Layout – Text Item → Scrollbar for multi-line text items (TXTVSB)* preference is set to **Yes**.

Problem	Solution
Although I have set the *Layout – Text Item → Scrollbar for multi-line text items (TXTVSB)* preference to **No,** the generated item still has the vertical scrollbar.	This seems to be a problem in release 2.1.2. Try subclassing from a source object in the object library. Make sure that the *Vertical Scrollbar?* property of the source object is set to **No**.
When I generate a multiline item from an unbound item, it does not allow me to enter long text.	Although you can generate multiline text items from unbound items, they work a little differently. Since the unbound items do not have the maximum width property, the display width becomes the maximum length. Although the item may be displayed as a multiline item, you don't get the wrapping and scrolling effects.

Checkboxes

A *checkbox* is a GUI control that allows two possible values that can be interpreted as on versus off or true versus false. You can toggle the control to **on** (the checked state) and **off** (the unchecked state) simply by clicking the checkbox indicator. A checkbox field can only have two values: one value will correspond to the checked state, and the other value will correspond to the unchecked state. Here's an example of a checkbox:

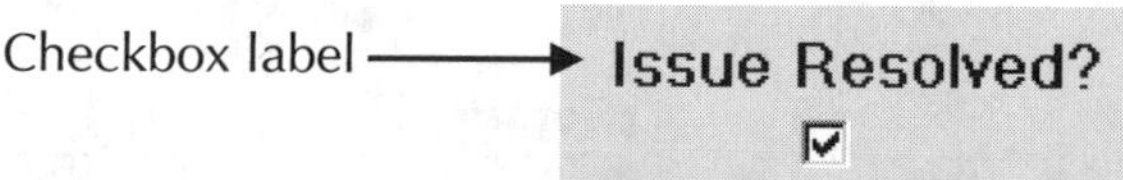

The following table shows a summarized list of some of the most important features of checkboxes and their corresponding sources in Oracle Designer.

Feature	Source of Feature in Oracle Designer
Checkbox item type	*Display Type* of the item.
Checkbox label	*Prompt* of the item.
Checked and unchecked values	*Allowable Value(s)* for the item.

Feature	Source of Feature in Oracle Designer
Width of prompt	*Width* property of the item.
Initial state (checked or unchecked)	*Default* property of the item. The state is determined by which allowable value the *Default* is set to.
Checkbox font	*Source Object(s)* from the template/object library, and *Template/Library Object* property of the item.

How to Generate a Checkbox

You can generate checkboxes from either bound or unbound items. In order to generate a checkbox, you must do the following:

1. Create either a bound or an unbound item.
2. Set the *Displayed* property of the item to **True**. See the "How to Set the *Displayed* Property" note earlier in this chapter, in the "How to Generate a Text Item" section.
3. Set the *Display Type* property of the item to **Checkbox**.
4. If you are generating a checkbox from an unbound item, make sure that the *Data Type* property is set. Also, make sure that the *Unbound Type* is set. If you are not generating a derived item, then choose **Custom** for the unbound type. See the "How to Set the *Unbound Type* Property" note earlier in this chapter in the "How to Generate a Text Item" section for more information.
5. Define the *Checked/Unchecked Values* for the checkbox. The *Checked Value* is the value that will be stored in the database when the checkbox is in the checked state. *Checked/Unchecked Values* are defined using the allowable values.

   The following rules apply when you are defining the *Checked/ Unchecked Values* for checkboxes:

   - Value ranges cannot be used to define the *Checked/ Unchecked Values.*
   - If the checkbox is for a mandatory item, there must be exactly two allowable values. The first in sequence will become the checked value, and the second will become the unchecked value.

- If the checkbox is for an optional item, there must be exactly one allowable value. The value entered will become the *Checked Value*, and the unchecked value will be null.

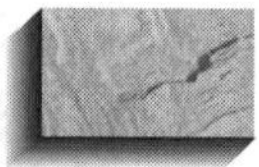

TIP

Sequencing Allowable Values. *Oracle Designer Online Help states an algorithm that Form Generator uses to assign the checked value. However, this algorithm is not totally correct. During our tests, we observed inconsistent results when we did not specify a sequence number for both of the allowable values. Therefore, we recommend that you make sure that each allowable value has a sequence number.*

Mapping of Other Values in Checkbox Items

Developer/2000 Form Builder allows you to specify how any fetched value that is different than checked/unchecked values should be interpreted using the *Checkbox Mapping of Other Values* property. There are three possible settings for this property: **Checked**, **Unchecked**, and **Not allowed**. If the item is required, this property is set to *Not allowed*: i.e., if a queried record contains a value different from the checked/unchecked values, the record is rejected and no error is raised. If the item is optional, this property is set to **Unchecked**. Unfortunately, there is no property in the repository that will allow you to set this Developer/2000 Form property directly. If you need to change the default behavior, you can use the generator's ability to subclass from an object library. To do this, set the *Checkbox Mapping of Other Values* property of an item in an object library, then use the *Template/Library* property of the item to subclass the generated item.

6. Set the *Optionality* property of the checkbox. The setting must be appropriate for the number of allowable values for the item. If there is only one allowable value, the item must be optional (Optional?=**Yes**), and the item will be null when the item is unchecked. If there are two allowable values, the item must be mandatory (Optional?=**No**).

7. Set the other properties of the item appropriately. The item properties that are most critical for checkboxes are shown in the following table:

Item Property	Important, Because...
Prompt	This will become the *Checkbox Label.*
Display Width	This will determine the width of the checkbox. The width should allow room for the prompt and the checkbox indicator. If the width is not large enough, the generator will increase the width so that at least the checkbox indicator can be displayed. See the box "How to Set Display Dimensions."

How to Set Display Dimensions

Sometimes it may be difficult to determine the width of a generated item. The space required to display each GUI control depends on the width of the average character, whether all uppercase or lowercase characters are used, and some other GUI control indicators such as the scroll bar or checkbox indicator. You may easily forget to consider these factors when you specify the display length for an item. Therefore, you might want Form Generator to compute the display width and height. The *Layout – Item → Override Display Dimensions (ITMODD)* preference directs Form Generator to ignore the dimensions provided for the item and compute the proper values. For further information about this preference, please refer to Oracle Designer Online Help (*Generating Form Builder Applications → Using Form Generator preferences → Form Generator preferences – organized alphabetically → ITMODD*).

Item Property	Important, Because...
Default Value	This will determine the initial state of the checkbox (checked versus unchecked) for new records. It must be one of the allowable values for the item, or you will get an error message when the generated form is compiled.
Template/Library Object	This will help to subclass the checkbox from an object library. By subclassing, you can define miscellaneous properties (including the font, alignment, etc.) of the checkbox. If left blank, the *CGSO$CHECK_BOX* source object defined in the object library will be used for deriving these other properties.

8. Set the *Layout Preferences* to control the layout details. The most important layout preference for checkboxes is shown in the following table:

Preference	Tips for Preference Settings
Layout – Checkbox → Allow label above check indicator in a multi-row block (CBXALM)	In multirow blocks, it is important to specify the position of each checkbox label. The default setting for this preference is **Yes**, meaning the label will be displayed above the checkbox item. If you wish to display the label to the side of the checkbox, set this preference to **No**. This preference can be set at application, module, or module component level. Therefore, all checkboxes in a multirow block will have the same style label.

CAUTION

Allowable Value Quality Check. *Oracle Designer does not validate allowable values against the domain, attribute, or column definitions until you generate a form.*

Examples of Checkbox Layout Options

There are not many layout options for checkboxes except the position of the label in multirow blocks. The following is an example of how you can control the positioning of checkbox labels:

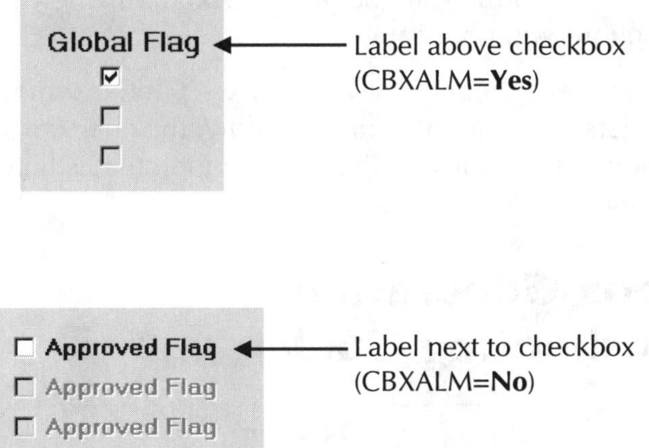

In this illustration, there are two examples of checkboxes in multirow blocks. In one, the label is placed above the checkbox. This is done by setting the *Layout – Checkbox → Allow label above check indicator in a multi-row block (CBXALM)* preference to **Yes.** In the other, each instance of the checkbox has a label because the same preference is set to **No**. Please note that the lowest level you can set this preference is at the module component level! When the label is displayed above the checkbox, it then becomes the prompt for the item and will have the properties of the item prompt rather than the item itself.

When to Use Checkboxes

Checkboxes should only be used when there are only one or two possible values for an item. Checkboxes are most commonly used for flag items that have two possible values, usually **Yes** and **No** (or **True** and **False**). One advantage of checkboxes is that they use less screen real estate than other GUI controls. However, checkboxes have a couple of drawbacks:

- The checked and unchecked values are hard-coded into the form. This means that if you want to change these values, you will have to generate the form again. So, use checkboxes when you are sure that the options will not change.
- Checkboxes are not displayed very well under some Windows managers. For example, in X-Window, the checked state of a checkbox is indicated with a sunk-in look that is hard to distinguish for some people.

Checkbox Generation Troubleshooting Guide

Problem	Solution
I am getting the "CGEN-03255 – Not enough valid values defined for checkbox item" message when generating the form.	Add a second valid value, or make the checkbox item optional. If the source of the checkbox item is required, you must have two allowable values for the item.
I am getting the "CGEN-03253 – Too many valid values defined for checkbox item" message when generating the form.	If the item that the checkbox is based on is mandatory, make sure that you have exactly two valid values. If it is optional, then make sure that you have only one allowable value for the item.
I am getting the "CGEN-01339 - Unable to generate checkbox; ranges exist in the valid values" message when generating the form.	Ranges are not allowed as valid values for a checkbox. Clear the *High Value* property from all of the allowable values before generating.

Problem	Solution
The generated checkbox is not storing the correct values in the database.	Resequence the allowable values for the item so that the value that you want to be stored in the database when the item is checked is the value that is sequenced first. Make sure that each allowable value has a sequence number. Otherwise, Form Generator uses an internal algorithm to determine the checked value. For more information about this algorithm, please refer to Oracle Designer Online Help (*Generating Form Builder Applications → Form Generation → About generated checkbox items*).
I get the "FRM-30361: Invalid initial value for checkbox" message when compiling the generated forms.	Make sure that the *Default Value* for the item matches one of the *Allowable Values* for itself. This message happens when the item's default is not a valid value for itself.
I want the label to show up above the item, not next to each checkbox indicator.	In a single-row block, the checkbox label is always displayed next to the checkbox indicator. If the generated checkbox is in a multirow block, make sure the *Layout – Checkbox → Allow label above check indicator in a multirow block (CBXALM)* preference is set to **Yes**.

Radio Groups

A *radio group* is a GUI control that displays a fixed number of mutually exclusive options. Each option is presented as an individual radio button. You can select any option by clicking on the radio button that represents the option you want. A radio group can include any number of radio buttons, but there are some practical limits due to screen real-estate restrictions. Here's an example of a radio group:

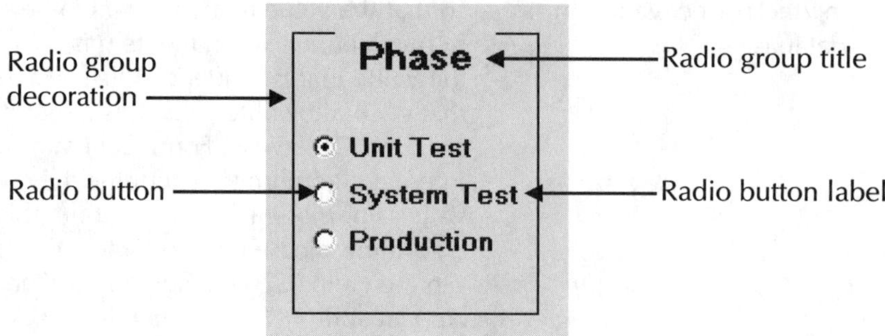

The following shows a summarized list of some of the most important features of radio groups and their corresponding sources in Oracle Designer.

Feature	**Source of Feature in Oracle Designer**
Radio group type	*Display Type* property of the item.
Radio group title	*Prompt* property of the item.
Radio group title font	*CG$RADIO_TITLE* visual attribute in the form template.
Radio group decoration	*Layout – Radio Group → Radio Group Decoration (RADDEC)* preference.
Radio group decoration style	*Layout – Radio Group → Radio Group Dash Style (RADDST)* preference.
Radio buttons	*Allowable Values* for the item.
Radio button label	*Value, Abbreviation,* or *Meaning* of allowable values for the item. *Show Meaning* property of the item determines which one of these will be displayed as button labels.
Width of radio buttons	*Width* property of the item.
Initial setting of radio group	*Default* property of the item. The *Default* value must be one of the valid allowable values defined for the radio group.
Radio button label font	*Source Object(s)* from the template/object library, and *Template/Library Object* property of the item.

How to Generate a Radio Group

You can generate radio groups from either bound or unbound items. In order to generate a radio group, you must do the following:

1. Create either a bound or an unbound item.
2. Set the *Displayed* property of the item to **True**. See the "How to Set the *Displayed* Property" note earlier in this chapter in the "How to Generate a Text Item" section.
3. Set the *Display Type* property of the item to **Radio Group**.
4. If you are generating a radio group from an unbound item, make sure that the *Data Type* property is set. Also, make sure that the *Unbound Type* property is set. If you are not generating a derived item, then choose **Custom** for the unbound type. See the "How to Set the *Unbound Type* Property" note in this chapter in the "How to Generate a Text Item" section.
5. Set the *Optional* property of the item to **No**. If you leave the item optional, your radio group will include another radio button with no label, which corresponds to the null value. A radio button with no label may be confusing for the users so, generally, it may be better to use radio groups only for mandatory items.
6. Define the *Allowable Values* for the item, as well as its *Default Value.* Each allowable value will become a radio button. If you set the *Default Value,* it will be initially displayed as the selected button. When setting the default value, make sure that it matches one of the allowable values. If the radio group is for a mandatory item, you should provide a default value for it. Otherwise, a warning message is issued when the generated form is compiled.

   Below are some rules that need to be followed when you are defining the *Allowable Values* for radio groups.

   - At least one *allowable value* must be defined.
   - Value ranges cannot be used to define the *Allowable Values.*
   - If the radio group is for a mandatory item, a default value must be provided. Otherwise, a warning message is issued when the generated form is compiled.

7. Select the *Show Meaning* property for the item. This property will determine how the radio button labels are generated. See the "The Effect of the *Show Meaning* Property on GUI Items" section later in this chapter for more information. You can also look at the layout examples, later in this chapter, for a better understanding of how the various settings affect radio groups.

8. Set the other properties of the item appropriately. The item properties that are most critical for radio groups are shown in the following table.

Item Property	Important, Because...
Prompt	This will become the radio group title.
Default Value	This will determine which radio button (if any) will be initially chosen for the new records. It must match one of the allowable values for the item or you will encounter errors when compiling the form.
Display Width	This will determine the width of the radio buttons. Each radio button will have the same width. Therefore, it is very important that you choose a width that will not cause button label truncations. Depending on how the *Show Meaning* property is set up, calculate the maximum length of code, abbreviation, or meaning of allowable values defined for the item. Alternatively, let the generator determine the space required and override any display dimensions that might be held against the item. You can accomplish this by setting the *Layout – Item → Override display dimensions (ITMODD)* preference to **GUI** or **RADIO GROUP**.
Template/Library Object	This will help to subclass the radio group from an object library. By subclassing, you can define miscellaneous properties (including the font, alignment, etc.) of the radio group. If left blank, the *CGSO$RADIO* source object defined in the object library will be used for deriving these other properties.

9. Set the *Layout Preferences* for the item to control the layout details. Since Form Generator generates radio groups similar to item groups, most of the item group preferences are available for radio groups as

well. Some of the most important layout preferences for radio groups are shown in the following table (all of the preferences are in the *Layout – Radio Group* category).

Preference	Tips for Preference Settings
Radio group decoration (RADDEC)	This preference determines what kind of decoration (line, rectangle, raised, lowered, etc.) should be used for the radio group. If this preference is set to **Do not decorate the object (NONE)**, the radio group will not have any decoration.
Radio group brush width (RADBWD)	The thickness of the lines, if the radio group has decorations. Thinnest lines look best on most GUI platforms.
Radio group dash style (RADDST)	This preference determines the type of line that will be used in displaying the corresponding lines.
Radio group title position (RADTLP)	Where should the radio group title be displayed? Choices include inside the decoration, outside the decoration, not at all, etc.
Radio group title justification (RADTLJ)	The justification of the radio group title.
Radio group header separator (RADHDS)	Should there be a header separator and, if so, how many lines?
Radio group footer separator (RADFTS)	Same as the header separator but applies the footer of the radio group.
Radio group orientation within group (RADOWG)	This preference determines whether the radio buttons are laid out horizontally or vertically within a radio group.
Radio group multi-line format (RADMLF)	If the radio group orientation (*RADOWG*) is set to **Horizontal layout**, how many buttons can be laid across on the same line? Choices include one, two, as many as can fit, etc.

Example of the Effect of the *Show Meaning* Property

The following example will show the effect of the *Show Meaning* property setting on the generated radio groups. For this example, consider the following list of allowable values:

Value	Abbreviation	Meaning
UT	Unit	Unit Test
SY	Sys	System Test
PR	Prod	Production

Figure 13-3 shows radio groups with different *Show Meaning* property settings.

Examples of Radio Group Layout Options

There are many layout options available for radio groups. Form Generator preferences, listed under the *Layout – Radio Group* category, can be used to change the following:

- The orientation of the radio buttons in the radio group
- The type of decoration that is used around the radio group

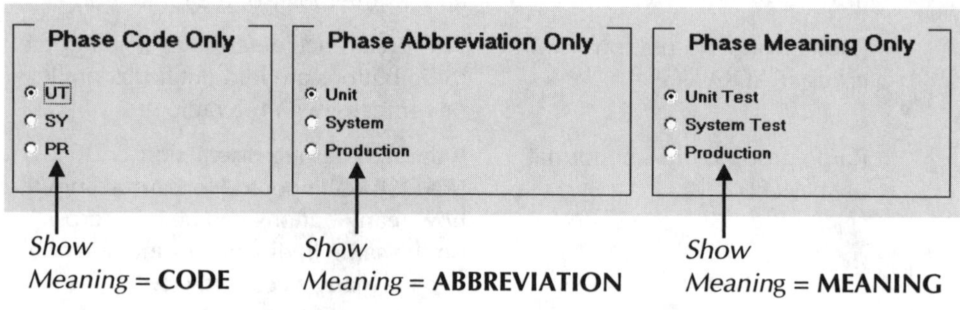

FIGURE 13-3. *Effect of the* Show Meaning *property setting*

- Whether the radio group title is displayed or not, and its position
- The margins around the radio buttons

In the following sections are some examples of layout options for radio groups. For further information, refer to Oracle Designer Online Help *(Generating Form Builder Applications → Form generation → Generating windows, canvases, blocks, and items → Radio group and radio button generation*).

Radio Group Layout Example 1

In this example (shown in the following illustration), the radio group decoration is set to have a rectangular decoration. The decoration has a raised bevel. The radio group title is centered and placed inside the decoration. The layout is set to be horizontal, which means that the radio buttons are placed in a horizontal line. The radio buttons will be placed on the same horizontal line until there is no more space and will then be wrapped to the next line.

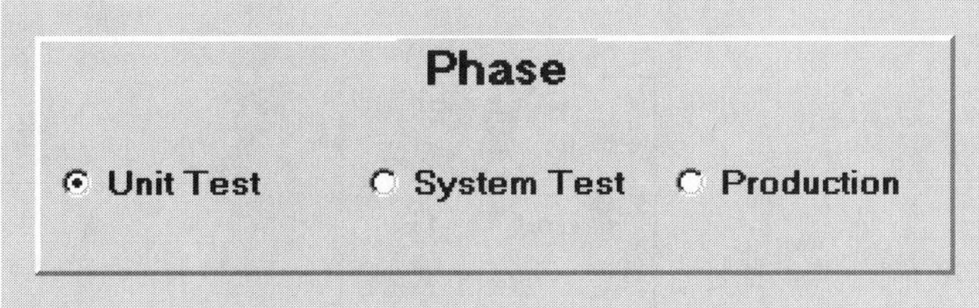

The preferences and their settings to produce this example are shown in the following table (all of these preferences are in the *Layout – Radio Group* category).

Preference	Setting
Radio group brush width (RADBWD)	Thinnest line available (0)
Radio group decoration (RADDEC)	Draw a rectangle around the object with raised bevel
Radio group dash style (RADDST)	SOLID
Radio group header separator (RADHDS)	1

Preference	Setting
Radio group footer separator (RADFTS)	1
Radio group title justification (RADTLJ)	Centered
Radio group title position (RADTLP)	Title inside any decoration
Radio group orientation within group (RADOWG)	Horizontal layout
Radio group multi-line format (RADMLF)	Keep adding fields as long as they fit (WRAP)

Radio Group Layout Example 2

In this example (shown in the following illustration) the radio group decoration is changed to have no bevel. The radio button orientation is set to be vertical, which means that the radio buttons are placed in a column, with each radio button under the previous one.

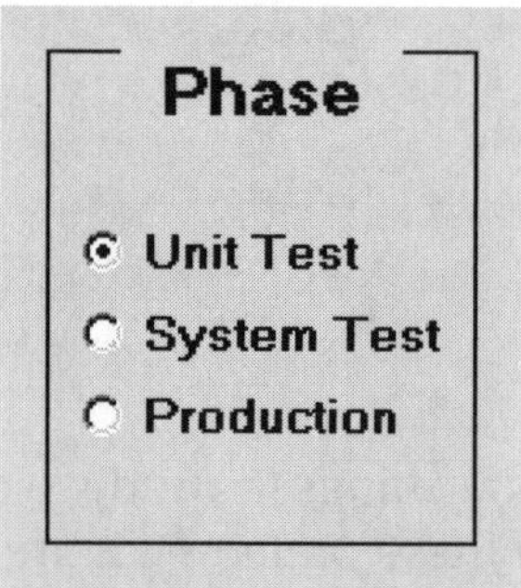

The preferences that differ from those used to produce Example 1 are shown in the following table (all of these preferences are in the *Layout – Radio Group* category).

Preference	Setting
Radio group decoration (RADDEC)	Draw a rectangle around the object
Radio group orientation within group. (RADOWG)	Vertical layout

Radio Group Layout Example 3

The decoration and title of a radio group are optional. In this example (shown in the following illustration), the radio group decoration and radio group title are both set to **NONE**.

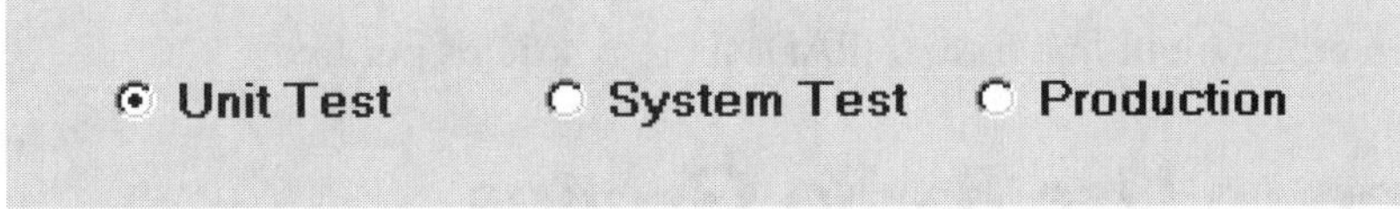

The preferences different from those used to produce Example 1 are shown in the following table:

Preference	Setting
Radio group decoration (RADDEC)	Do not decorate the object (NONE)
Radio group title position (RADTLP)	Do not title (NONE)

Radio Group Layout Example 4

If you have many radio buttons to be displayed in a horizontal radio group, they will not fit in one row and must be wrapped. The *Layout Radio Group → Radio group multi-line format (RADMLF)* preference lets you set the number of radio buttons that are placed in one line. In this example (shown in the following illustration) the RADMLF preference is set to **4**. The radio group title is left justified and placed on the decoration. The width of the decoration lines has also been increased to **2**.

Phase

Prototype Testing   Unit Test   System Test   Distirbuted Testing
Alpha Testing   Beta Testing   Production

The preferences different from those used to produce Example 1 are shown in the following table (all of the preferences are in the *Layout – Item Group* category).

Preference	Setting
Radio groupbrush width (RADBWD)	2
Radio group title justification (RADTLJ)	Left justification
Radio group title position (RADTLP)	Title is placed on any decoration
Radio group multi-line format (RADMLF)	4 fields per line

When to Use Radio Groups

Radio groups are useful when you want to show the users all of the possible options for an item at a glance. Radio groups show all options on the screen at all times, as opposed to other GUI controls, such as pop lists and combo lists, where the user has to pull down and scroll through a list of options to see all of the possible values. However, radio groups have a couple of drawbacks:

- Radio groups take up a lot of screen space. They should only be used when you have just a few options to present or plenty of room on the canvas.
- The list of options are hard-coded onto the page. This means that if you want to change the options, you have to generate the form again; so you should only use radio groups when you are sure that the list of options will not change.

Radio Group Generation Troubleshooting Guide

Problem	Solution
I keep getting an extra radio button without a label that I do not want in my radio group.	Make the item that the radio group is based on mandatory. If the source of the radio group is optional, the generator creates an additional button to represent a null value for the item.
I get the "Invalid Default?" message when compiling the generated forms.	Make sure that the *Default Value* for the item matches one of the *Allowable Values* for the item. This message happens when the item's default is not a valid value for the item.

Problem	Solution
The labels of radio buttons are being truncated.	The width of the label of each radio button is based on the *Width* property of the item, so increase the *Width* property of the item that the radio group is based on. Recompute the width, or let the generator calculate the display dimensions (*Layout – Item → Override Display Dimensions (ITMODD)* preference).
I am able to change the font of the radio button label by changing the font for the *CGSO$RADIO_GROUP* object in the object library, but it does not change the radio group title.	Set the font of the *CG$RADIO_TITLE* visual attribute in the template form. The radio group title font is not inherited from the *CGSO$RADIO* object in Oracle Designer.
The buttons in my horizontal radio group all have the same width. How can I set the width of each button individually?	Use the *Layout – Item → Override Display Dimensions (ITMODD)* preference to generate variable width radio buttons. See the box "How to Set Display Dimensions" in the section "How to Generate a Checkbox," earlier in this chapter.

Pop Lists

A *pop list* is a GUI control that displays a list of mutually exclusive options. It appears initially as a single field with a list icon beside it. When the user selects the list icon, a list of available options appears. The user can select an option by clicking on the list icon and highlighting the desired option. Only one of the values from the list may be selected at any time. The options are also known as list elements. A pop list can include any number of options (list elements). Here's an example of a pop list:

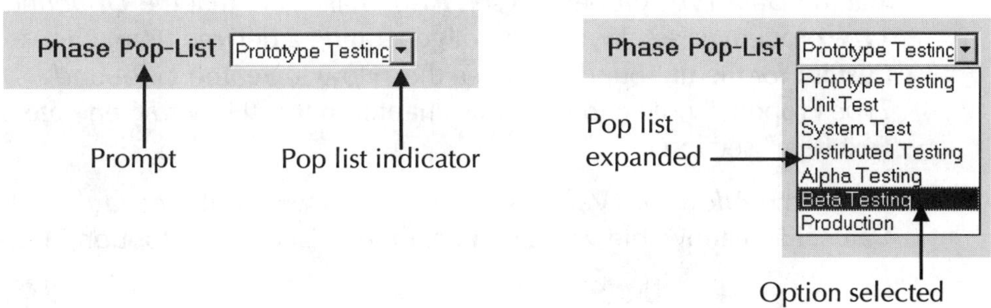

The following table shows a summarized list of some of the most important features of pop lists and their corresponding sources in Oracle Designer.

Feature	Source of Feature in Oracle Designer
Pop list type	*Display Type* property of the item
Pop list label	*Prompt* of property of the item
Pop list elements	*Allowable Values* for the item
Dynamic list (soft list)	*Dynamic List* property of the item
Pop list element display value	*Show Meaning* property of the item
Width	*Width* property of the item
Initial value of pop list	*Default* property of the item
Pop list element font	*Source Object(s)* from the template/object library and *Template/Library Object* property of the item

How to Generate a Pop List

You can generate pop lists from either bound or unbound items. In order to generate a pop list, you must do the following:

1. Create either a bound or an unbound item.
2. Set the *Displayed* property of the item to **True**. See the "How to Set the *Displayed* Property" note earlier in this chapter in the "How to Generate a Text Item" section for more information.
3. Set the *Display Type* property of the item to **Pop list**.
4. If you are generating a pop list from an unbound item, make sure that the *Data Type* property is set. Also, make sure that the *Unbound Type* property is set. If you are not generating a derived item, choose **Custom** for the unbound type. See the "How to Set the *Unbound Type* Property" note earlier in this chapter in the "How to Generate a Text Item" section.
5. Define the *Allowable Values* for the item, as well as the *Default Value*. Each allowable value will become a list element (option). If

you set the *Default Value,* it will be initially displayed as the selected option. When setting the default value, make sure that it matches one of the allowable values.

Below are some rules you should follow when defining the *Allowable Values* for pop lists.

- At least one *Allowable Value* must be defined.
- Value ranges cannot be used to define the *Allowable Values.*
- If the pop list is for a mandatory item, a default value must be provided. Otherwise, a warning message is issued when the generated form is compiled.

6. Select the *Show Meaning* property for the item. This property will determine which pop list labels are generated. See the "The Effect of the *Show Meaning* Property on GUI Items" section, later in this chapter, for more information.
7. Set the other properties of the item appropriately. The item properties that are most critical for radio groups are shown in the following table.

Item Property	Important, Because...
Prompt	This will become the pop list label.
Dynamic List	This will determine whether the pop list options are hard-coded into the generated item or dynamically built during run time (soft list). Set this property to **True** if you want to avoid hard-coding of the values. When dynamic or soft lists are used, the list values are kept in the Reference Codes table and dynamically queried from this table. For further information about how to maintain and deploy these reference code tables, refer to Chapter 26.
Default Value	This will determine which list element (if any) will be initially displayed as selected for the new records. It must match one of the allowable values for the item or the form will give errors when it compiles.

Item Property	Important, Because...
Width	This will determine the width of the pop list. If the width is not large, the generator will increase the length so that at least the pop list indicator can be displayed.
Template/Library Object	This will help subclass the pop list from an object library. By subclassing, you can define miscellaneous properties (including the font, alignment, etc.) of the pop list. If left blank, the *CGSO$POP* source object defined in the object library will be used for deriving these other properties.

8. Set the *Layout Preferences* for the item to control the layout details. There are only a few preferences that can be set for pop lists. Some of the most important layout preferences for pop lists are shown in the following table (all of the preferences are in the *Layout – Pop Lists* category).

Preference Name	Tips for Preference Settings
Pop list indicator width (PLSIWD)	This preference can be used to specify the space allocated for the pop list indicator icon. It does not specify the size of this icon. Normally, you do not need to change this preference at all. However, if your target environment is other than MS Windows and you experience layout problems, you may want to adjust this preference.
Maximum number of values in a pop list (PLSMAX)	If the number of allowable values for a pop list item is more than this, Form Generator issues a warning. If this preference is not set, no check is made on the number of values. If the item is optional, the null value will always be included in the pop list. Therefore, the actual threshold for optional pop lists is one less than this value. This can be used to implement a GUI standard that would limit the number of items that appear in a pop list.

When to Use Pop Lists

Refer to "How to Choose the Right List Item Type" section, later in this chapter, for information about when to use pop lists.

Pop List Generation Troubleshooting Guide

Problem	**Solution**
I get the following warning message, "CGEN-03259 WARNING List item display type 'POP LIST' chosen, but no list of allowed values," and generation fails.	This is actually an error message. Form Generator requires you to have at least one allowable value-defined pop list item. Make sure that the source column has an attached domain that has allowable values, or the column has its own allowable values.
I get the "Invalid Default?" message when compiling the generated forms.	Make sure that the *Default Value* for the item matches one of the *Allowable Values* for the item. This message happens when the item's default is not a valid value for the item.
The labels of pop list options are being truncated.	Increase the *Width* property of the item. Recompute the width based on the allowable values and the *Show Meaning* property, or let the generator calculate the display dimensions using the *Layout – Item → Override Display Dimensions (ITMODD)* preference.
I get "FRM-30188: No initial value given, and other values are not allowed" after the form is compiled.	Make the item optional or provide a default value.
I keep getting the "CGEN-03353 - Multiple ranges, or combination of ranges and discrete values not supported" message.	Ranges in allowable values are not supported. Redefine the Domain (or list of *Allowed Values* against the element) as a list of discrete values (with no ranges) or as a single range. If a combination of ranges and discrete values is required, this can be validated using application logic.

Problem	Solution
I want both the code and the meaning of my allowable values to show up in my pop list.	Currently, this option is available only for text lists. However, as a work-around, you may manually add the code to the meaning.

Combo Boxes

A *combo box* is a GUI control that displays a *suggested* list of options. A combo box initially appears as a single field with a list icon beside it. When the user selects the list icon, a list of available options appears, and the user can select an option by clicking it or can enter a different value that is not in the list. A combo box can include any number of options (list elements). Here's an example of a combo box:

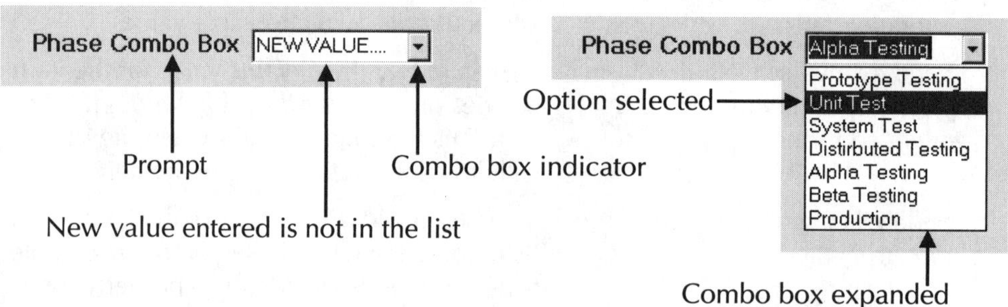

Combo boxes are very much like pop lists. The following table shows a summarized list of some of the most important features of combo boxes and their corresponding sources in Oracle Designer.

Feature	Source of Feature in Oracle Designer
Combo box type	*Display Type* and *Suggestion List* properties of the item
Combo box label	*Prompt* of property of the item
Combo box elements	*Allowable Values* for the item
Dynamic list	*Dynamic List* property of the item
Combo box element display value	*Show Meaning* property of the item
Width	*Width* property of the item

Feature	Source of Feature in Oracle Designer
Initial value of combo box	*Default* property of the item
Combo box element font	*Source Object(s)* from the template/object library and *Template/Library Object* property of the item

How to Generate a Combo Box

You can generate a combo box from either bound or unbound items. Since combo boxes are very similar to pop lists, the steps to generate a combo box are almost identical to those for generating a pop list.

1. Create either a bound or an unbound item.
2. Set the *Displayed* property of the item to **True**. See the "How to Set the *Displayed* Property" note earlier in this chapter in the "How to Generate a Text Item" section.
3. Set the *Display Type* property of the item to **Combo Box**.
4. If you are generating a combo box from an unbound item, make sure that the *Data Type* property is set. Also, make sure that the *Unbound Type* property is set. If you are not generating a derived item, then choose **Custom** for the unbound type. (Also, see the note "How to Set the *Unbound Type* Property," earlier in this chapter in the "How to Generate a Text Item" section.
5. Define the *Allowable Values* for the item, as well as its *Default Value*. Each allowable value will become a list element (option). If you set the *Default Value,* it will be initially displayed as the selected option. When setting the default value, make sure that it matches one of the allowable values.

   Below are some rules that need to be followed when you are defining the *Allowable Values* for combo boxes.

   - At least one value must be defined.
   - Value ranges cannot be used to define the *Allowable Values.*
   - If the combo box is for a mandatory item, a default value must be provided for it. Otherwise, a warning message is issued when the generated form is compiled.

6. Select the *Show Meaning* property for the item. This property will determine how radio button labels are generated. See the "The Effect of the *Show Meaning* Property on GUI Items" section, later in this chapter, for more information.

7. If generating a combo box based on a bound item, set the *Suggestion List* property of the source column to **True**.

8. Set the other properties of the item appropriately. The item properties that are most critical for combo boxes are shown in the following table.

Item Property	Important, Because...
Prompt	This will become the combo box label.
Dynamic List	This will determine whether the combo box options are hard-coded into the generated item or dynamically built during run time. Set this property to **True** if you want to avoid hard-coding of the values.
Default Value	This will determine which list element (if any) will be initially displayed as selected for the new records. It must match one of the allowable values for the item or the form will give errors when it compiles.
Width	This will determine the width of the combo box. If the width is not large, the generator will increase the length so that at least the combo box indicator can be displayed.
Template/Library Object	This will help subclass the pop list from an object library. By subclassing, you can define miscellaneous properties (including the font, alignment, etc.) of the pop list. If left blank, the *CGSO$COMBO* source object defined in the object library will be used for deriving these other properties.

9. Set the *Layout Preferences* for the item to control the layout details. These are similar to pop lists in that there are only a few preferences that you can set. Some of these important layout preferences for combo boxes are shown in the following table (all of these preferences are in the *Layout – Combo Box* category).

Preference Name	Tips for Preference Settings
Combo box indicator width (CLSIWD)	This preference can be used to specify the space allocated for the combo box indicator icon. It does not specify the size of this icon. Normally, you do not need to change this preference at all. However, if your target environment is other than MS Windows and you experience layout problems, you may want to adjust this preference.
Maximum number of items in a combo box (CLSMAX)	Form Generator issues a warning if you have more suggestive values than what is specified by this preference. If this preference is not set, no check is made on the number of values. This can be used to implement a GUI standard that limits the number of items that appear in a combo box.

When to Use Combo Boxes

Refer to "How to Choose the Right List Item Type" section, later in this chapter, for information about when you should use combo boxes.

Combo Box Generation Troubleshooting Guide

Problem	**Solution**
The labels of combo box options are being truncated.	Increase the *Width* property of the item. Recompute the width based on the allowable values and the *Show Meaning* property, or let the generator calculate the display dimensions (*Layout – Item → Override Display Dimensions (ITMODD)* preference).
I am getting the "CGEN-03353 - Multiple ranges, or combination of ranges and discrete values not supported" message.	Ranges in allowable values are not supported. Redefine the Domain (or list of *Allowed Values* against the element) as a list of discrete values (with no ranges) or as a single range. If a combination of ranges and discrete values is required, application logic can be used for complex validations.

Problem	Solution
I want both the code and the meaning of my allowable values to show up in my combo box.	Currently, this option is available only for text lists. However, as a work-around, you may include the code in the meaning and choose *Meaning Only* option.

Text Lists

A *text list* is a GUI control that displays a list of mutually exclusive options and looks like a multiline item that displays a fixed number of possible values. When a text list contains more possible values than it can display, a vertical scroll bar is automatically activated that allows users to view and select other values. A text list can include any number of options (list elements). Only one of the values from the list may be selected at any time. Here's an example of a text list:

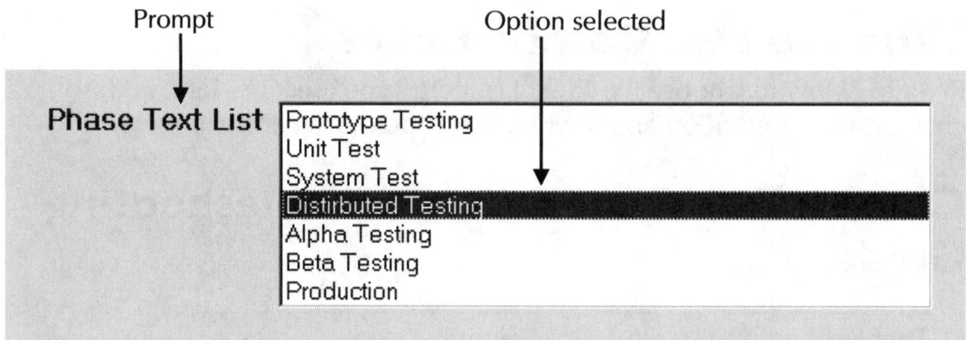

Text lists are very much like pop lists except that the allowable values are displayed without user intervention. The following table shows a summarized list of some of the most important features of text lists that distinguish them from pop lists and their corresponding sources in Oracle Designer.

Feature	Source of Feature in Oracle Designer
Text list type	*Display Type* of the repository
Text list label	*Prompt* of property of the item

Feature	Source of Feature in Oracle Designer
Text list elements	*Allowable Values* for the item
Dynamic list	*Dynamic List* property of the item
Text list element display value	*Show Meaning* property of the item
Width	*Width* property of the item
Height	*Height* of the item
Initial value of text list	*Default* property of the item
Text list element font	*Source Object(s)* from the template/object library and *Template/Library Object* property of the item

How to Generate a Text List

You can generate a text list from either bound or unbound items. Since text lists are very similar to pop lists, the steps to generate a text list are almost identical to those for generating a pop list.

1. Create either a bound or an unbound item.
2. Set the *Displayed* property of the item to **True**. See the "How to Set the *Displayed* Property" note, earlier in this chapter, in the "How to Generate a Text Item" section.
3. Set the *Display Type* property of the item to **Text List**.
4. If you are generating a text list from an unbound item, make sure that the *Data Type* property is set. Also, make sure that the *Unbound Type* property is set. If you are not generating a derived item, choose **Custom** for the unbound type. See the "How to Set the *Unbound Type* Property" note earlier in this chapter in the "How to Generate a Text Item" section.
5. Define the *Allowable Values* for the item, as well as the *Default Value*. Each allowable value will become a list element (option). If you set the *Default Value,* it will be initially displayed as the selected option. When setting the default value, make sure that it matches one of the allowable values.

Below are some rules that need to be followed when you are defining the *Allowable Values* for text lists.

- At least one *Allowable Value* must be defined.
- Value ranges cannot be used to define the *Allowable Values.*
- If the text list is for a mandatory item, a default value must be provided for it. Otherwise, a warning message is issued when the generated form is compiled.

6. Select the *Show Meaning* property for the item. This property will determine how radio button labels are generated. If you wish to display both the code and the meaning in the text list, set the *Show Meaning* property to **Meaning Alongside Code**. See the "The Effect of the *Show Meaning* Property on GUI Items" section, later in this chapter, for more information.
7. Set the other properties of the item appropriately. The item properties that are most critical for radio groups are shown in the following table.

Item Property	**Important, Because...**
Prompt	This will become the pop list label.
Dynamic List	This will determine whether the pop list options are hard coded into the generated item or dynamically built during runtime. Set this property to **True** if you want to avoid hard coding of the values. When dynamic or soft lists are used, the list values are kept in the Reference Codes table and dynamically queried from this table. For further information about how to maintain and deploy these reference code tables please refer to Chapter 26.
Default Value	This will determine which list element (if any) will be initially displayed as selected for the new records. It must match one of the allowable values for the item, or the form will give errors when it compiles.

Item Property	Important, Because...
Width	This will determine the width of the text list.
Template/Library Object	This will help subclass the text list from an object library. By subclassing, you can define miscellaneous properties (including the font, alignment, etc.) of the text list. If left blank, the *CGSO$TEXT_LIST* source object defined in the object library will be used for deriving these other properties.

8. Set the *Layout Preferences* for the item to control the layout details. As with pop lists, there are only a few preferences you can set. Some of these important layout preferences for text lists are shown in the following table (these preferences are all in the *Layout – Text List* category).

Preference Name	Tips for Preference Settings
Maximum number of items in a text list (TLSMAX)	Form Generator issues a warning if you have more values than specified by this preference. If this preference is not set, no check is made on the number of values. This can be used to implement a GUI standard that limits the number of items that appear in a text list.
Text list horizontal scrollbar height (TLSSBH) and Text list vertical scrollbar width (TLSSBW)	These preferences can be used to adjust the height and width of the scroll bars attached to the text lists. Text list scroll bars will only appear if the list cannot fit into display size.

When to Use Text Lists

Refer to "How to Choose the Right List Item Type," later in this chapter, for information about when you should use text lists.

Text List Generation Troubleshooting Guide

Problem	Solution
I get the warning message "CGEN-03259 WARNING List item display type 'TEXT-LIST' chosen, but no list of allowed values," and generation fails.	This is actually an error message. Form Generator requires you to have at least one allowable value defined text list items. Check the column, or domain it uses to make sure that there are allowable values.
I get the "Invalid Default?" message when compiling the generated forms.	Make sure that the *Default Value* for the item matches one of the *Allowable Values* for the item. This message happens when the item's default is not a valid value for the item.
The labels of text list options are being truncated.	Increase the *Width* property of the item. Recompute the width based on the allowable values and the *Show Meaning* property, or let the generator calculate the display dimensions (*Layout – Item → Override Display Dimensions (ITMODD)* preference).
I get the "FRM-30188: No initial value given, and other values are not allowed" message after the form is compiled.	Make the item optional, or provide a default value.
I keep getting the "CGEN-03353 - Multiple ranges, or combination of ranges and discrete values not supported" message.	Ranges in allowable values are not supported. Redefine the Domain (or list of *Allowed Values* against the element) as a list of discrete values (with no ranges) or as a single range. If a combination of ranges and discrete values is required, this could be validated using application logic.

Image Items

An *image item* is a GUI control that can be used to display images. Images may be stored either directly in the database or in external operating system

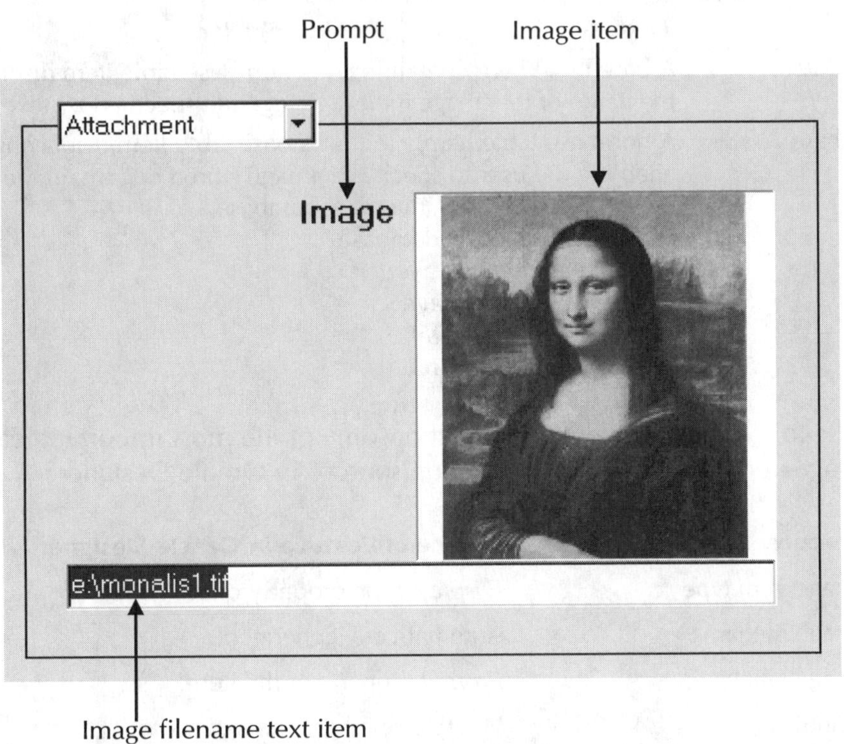

FIGURE 13-4. *Image items*

files. In order to store images in the database, RAW or LONG RAW type columns must be used. When images are stored in external operating system files, only the name of the file containing the image is stored in the database. Figure 13-4 shows an example of an image item.

When generating an image item, Form Generator may create a text item associated with the image item. This text item is used to specify the filename associated with the image, and it is needed to load the image into the database. Creation of the image filename text item is controlled via the *Layout – Image → Display image filename item (IMGDFI)* preference. The following table shows the list of items created by Form Generator for an image item.

Image Location	Generated Items	
	Text Item	**Image Item**
File system	A base table item containing the name of the image file.	A non-base table item displaying image file specified by text item.
Database	A non-base table item, enabling the user to specify filenames so that the images can be read into the database item. Created if the *Layout – Image → Display image filename item (IMGDFI)* preference is set to **True**.	A base table item displaying the image stored directly in the database.

The following is a summarized list of some of the most important features of image items and their corresponding sources in Oracle Designer.

Feature	Source of Feature in Oracle Designer
Image item type	*Display Type* property of the item.
Image filename	Automatically generated.
Image label	*Prompt* property of the item.
Width	*Width* property of the item.
Height	*Height* property of the item.
Image quality options	*Source Object(s)* from the template/object library and *Template/Library Object* property of the item. In earlier versions of Oracle Designer, image quality options were controlled via the *Layout – Image* preferences.

How to Generate an Image Item

You can generate an image item from both bound and unbound items. In order to generate an image item, you must do the following.

1. Create either a bound or an unbound item.
2. Set the *Displayed* property of the item to **True**. See the "How to Set the *Displayed* Property" note earlier in this chapter in the "How to Generate a Text Item" section.

3. Set the *Display Type* property of the item to **Image**.

4. Set the *Data Type* property of the item to specify where the image is stored (either in the database or in an external operating system file). Form Generator uses the *Data Type* property to determine the storage location of the image. If generating an image item from an unbound item, make sure that the *Data Type* property is set to **CHAR**. Also, make sure that the *Unbound Type* is set to **Custom**.

Image Location	Allowable Item Type	Data Type Property Setting
File system	Bound or unbound	VARCHAR2
Database	Bound only	LONG RAW

5. Set the other properties of the item appropriately. The item properties that are most critical for image items are shown in the following table:

Item Property	Important, Because...
Display Width & Height	This will determine the width and height of the image item.
Template/Library Object	This will help subclass the image item from an object library. By subclassing, you can define miscellaneous properties (including the font, alignment, etc.) of the image item. If left blank, the *CGSO$IMAGE* source object defined in the object library will be used for deriving these other properties.

6. Set the *Layout Preferences* for the item to control the layout details. Some of the most important preferences for image items are shown in the following table. There are other image item preferences, such as image item bevel, image quality etc., but many of these have become obsolete in Oracle Designer. Instead, source object property settings can be used to set some of these layout properties. Some of the preferences shown in the table are not specific to image items but apply to all two-dimensional GUI controls like multiline text

items, chart items, etc. These preferences can be used to specify how the rest of the items in a block should be laid out when there is a two-dimensional GUI control.

Preference	Tips for Preference Settings
Layout – Image → Display image filename item (IMGDFI)	If the image is stored in the database, use this preference to specify whether an additional text item is generated to enter a filename before the image is read and stored in the database. The default setting for this preference is **Yes**, meaning a text item will always be generated. If you don't generate the filename text item, you will need to manually write the code for reading the image into the image item.
Layout – Image → Image file prefix (IMGIFP)	If there is a certain operating system directory where the image files are stored, *Image file prefix* can be used to specify this path name. The value for this preference must include the directory separator ("\" in MS Windows, "/" in a Unix environment) at the end of the path, as the filename is simply appended to this value.
Layout – Image → Image filename item width (IMGFIW)	The width of the filename text item that is displayed with an image. If this preference is not set, the image filename text item is the same width as the image.
Layout – Single Area → Enable creation of single areas for multi-row blocks (SARENB)	If the rows in a multirow block do not wrap, images as well as other large two-dimensional items can waste a lot of space on the canvas. In order to reduce the amount of space wasted, only one instance of the image is created. The default setting is **Yes**, meaning reserve space. (See Example 3 later in this chapter.)
Layout – Single Area → Limit rows within highest single area (SARLIM)	If you choose to generate single areas, you can also choose to restrict the number of rows displayed in the block with the height of the single area. The default setting is **Yes**, meaning the number of rows displayed will be recalculated based on the highest two-dimensional object. (See Example 4 later in this chapter.)

Preference	Tips for Preference Settings
Layout – Single Area → Single area cutoff height (SARCHT)	When generating single areas for image items, as well as other two-dimensional objects, you could use this preference to specify a criterion for the selection of items that will be placed into the single area. For an item to be included in the single area, its height must be greater than or equal to the height specified by this preference.

Examples Image Item Layout Options

In earlier versions of Oracle Designer, there were many layout preferences to control such image items as image bevel, dimensions, display quality, sizing style, and scrollbars, that are now obsolete in release 2.1. Instead, the settings for these particular properties of image items in release 2.1 are determined by object libraries. There are many combinations of property settings you can use to generate various layouts so, in order to help you see some of the options that are available, a few examples of some of the generation possibilities are presented in the following sections. For further information, please refer to Oracle Designer Online Help.

Image Item Layout Example 1

In the example shown in Figure 13-5, some of the image item properties of the source object in the object library have been modified from their default values. For example, the *Sizing Style* property is set to **CROP**. The image item is set to have both a horizontal and a vertical scroll bar to allow users to scroll and see other parts of the image. Also, the *Show Palette* property is set to **Yes** to display an image-manipulation palette that allows users to zoom, pan, and rotate the image item. These properties and their settings to produce this example are shown in the following table.

Property Name	Property Setting	Property Setting Description
Sizing Style	**CROP**	Display only the portion of the full image that fits in the display rectangle.

Property Name	Property Setting	Property Setting Description
Show Palette	**Yes**	Display an image-manipulation palette, which allows users to zoom, pan, and rotate the image, adjacent to the image item.
Show Horizontal Vertical Scroll Bar	**Yes**	Display horizontal/vertical scroll bar to scroll and see the parts of the image that do not fit in the display rectangle.
Image Quality	**Medium**	Displays the image with medium quality, using fewer resources.

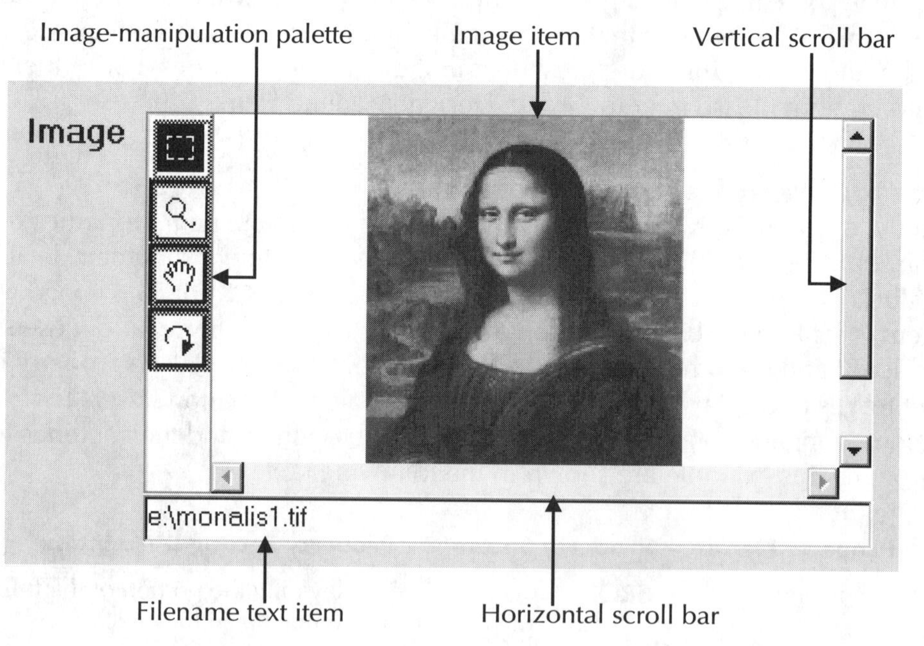

FIGURE 13-5. *Image item layout example*

Image Item Layout Example 2

The example shown in Figure 13-6 illustrates how single areas can be generated to save some screen real estate. Only one instance of the image (or any two-dimensional item) is displayed. The image displayed belongs to the current record. The number of rows displayed property for this module component was set to 15 initially. However, Form Generator reduced it to 13, which is equal to the height of the image item displayed in a tab canvas. The preferences and their settings to produce this example are shown in the following table (these preferences are in the *Layout – Single Area* category).

Preference	Setting
Enable creation of single areas for multi-row blocks (SARENB)	Yes
Limit rows within highest single area (SARLIM)	Yes

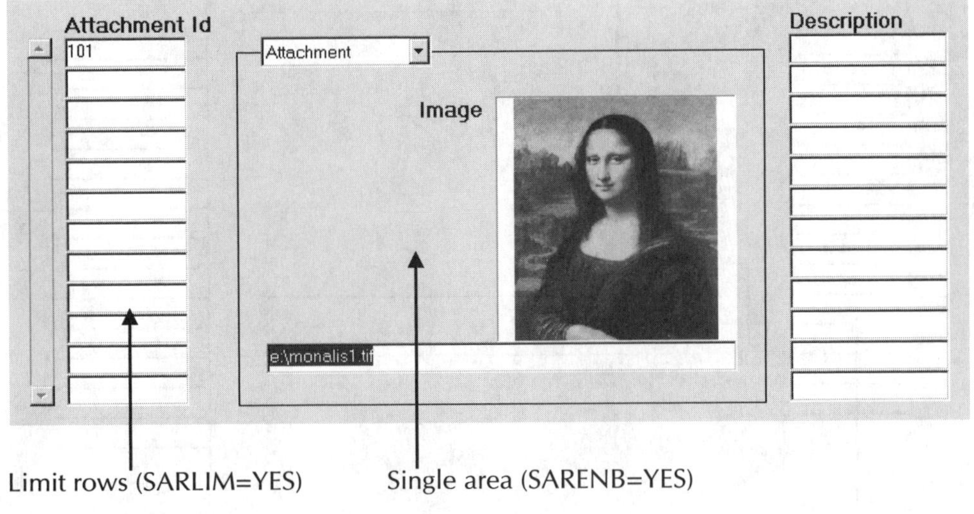

FIGURE 13-6. *Single area*

Image Item Layout Example 3

The example shown in Figure 13-7 illustrates the effect of *Layout – Single Area → Limit rows within highest single area (SARLIM)* preference. This preference determines whether the rows displayed should be limited to the height of the image item. In this example, the number of rows displayed is set to 15, and the height of the image item is set to 11. The preferences and their settings to produce this example are shown in the following table (these preferences are in the *Layout – Single Area* category).

Preference	**Setting**
Enable creation of single areas for multi-row blocks (SARENB)	**Yes**
Limit rows within highest single area (SARLIM)	**No**

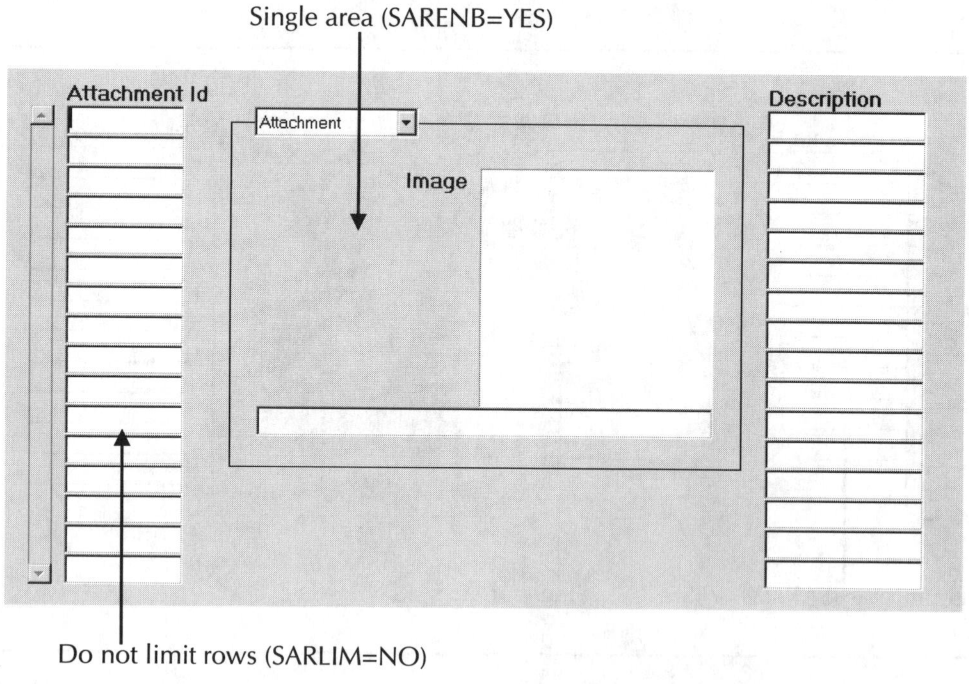

FIGURE 13-7. *Rows not limited within highest single area*

Image Item Layout Example 4

This is the first example of two that show the effect of the *Layout – Single Area → Single area cutoff height (SARCHT)* preference. This preference determines which items should be included in the single area. In Figure 13-8, the SARCHT was set to **2**. Since the height of the description is 2, which is equal to the height specified by this preference, the item is included in the single area. The preferences and their settings to produce this example are shown in the following table (these preferences are in the *Layout – Single Area* category).

Preference	Setting
Enable creation of single areas for multi-row blocks. (SARENB)	**Yes**
Limit rows within highest single area. (SARLIM)	**Yes**
Single area cutoff height. (SARCHT)	**2**

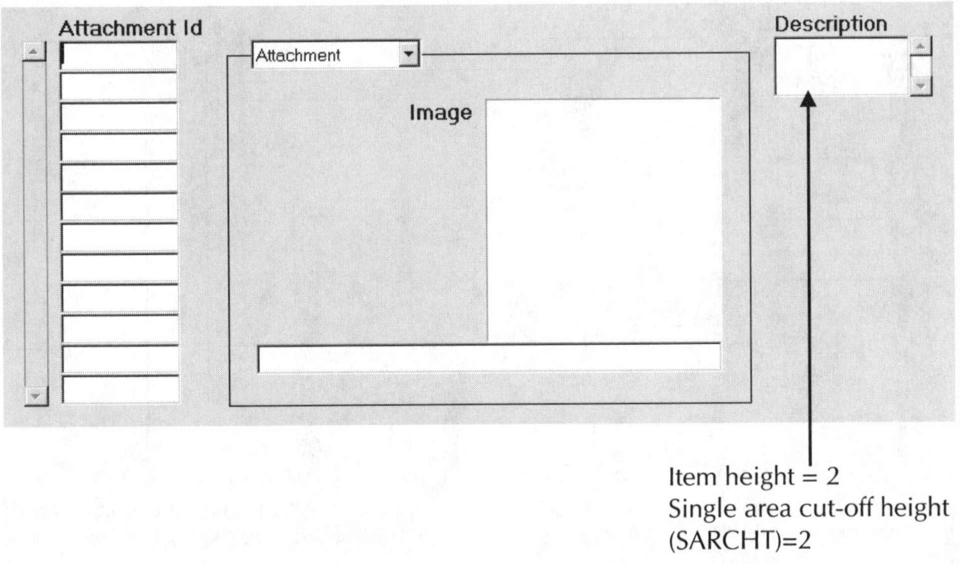

FIGURE 13-8. *Single area cut-off height (1 of 2)*

Image Item Layout Example 5

This is the second of two examples that show the effect of the *Layout – Single Area → Single area cutoff height (SARCHT)* preference. This preference determines which items should be included in the single area. In Figure 13-9, the SARCHT is set to **3**. Since the height of the description is 2, which is less than the height specified by this preference, the item is not included in the single area. The preferences and their settings to produce this example are shown in the following table (these preferences are in the *Layout – Single Area* category).

Preference	**Setting**
Enable creation of single areas for multi-row blocks (SARENB)	**Yes**
Limit rows within highest single area (SARLIM)	**Yes**
Single area cutoff height (SARCHT)	**3**

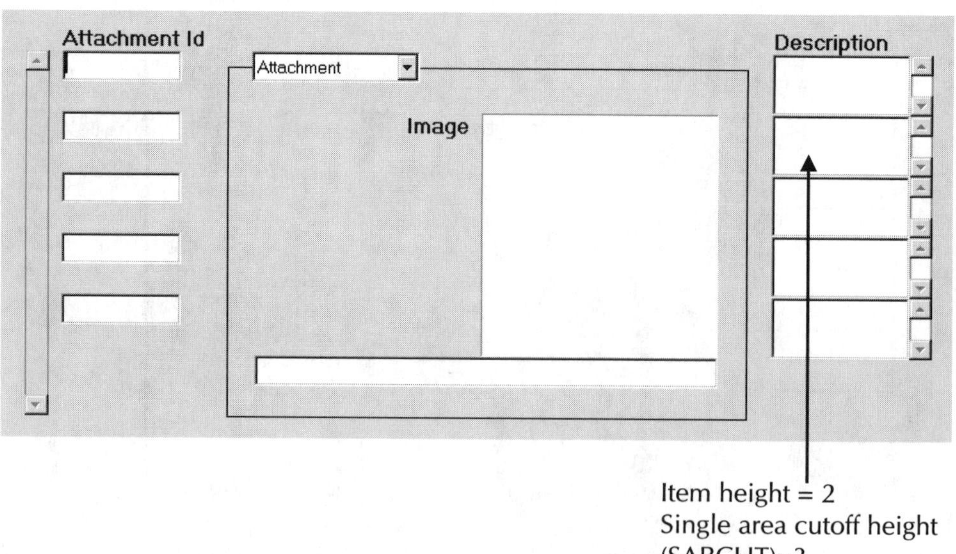

FIGURE 13-9. *Single area cutoff height (2 of 2)*

When to Use Image Items

Image items can be used whenever you need to display an image or graphic. Some examples of possible uses of image items are pictures of items sold, technical drawings, pictures of employees, etc. You can also use image items creatively to increase the appeal of your screens. For example, images can be used to generate splash screens.

Images can be stored either directly in the database using the internal Oracle format, or in external operating system files. Form Generator generates all the necessary items and the code to read and display images. A new feature in Developer/2000 Form Builder is the ability to present an image-manipulation tool that allows users to zoom in or out or rotate the image. Although there is no property to generate this new feature, it can be generated by subclassing from a source image item with the proper setting in the object library.

Unfortunately, image items tend to take up a lot of screen real estate. However, the single area preferences, as well as layout overflow properties, can be used to reduce some of these problems.

Image Item Generation Troubleshooting Guide

Problem	**Solution**
I get the "CGEN-03465 ERROR: Item can only be displayed as IMAGE or OLE CONTAINER" message.	If you are storing images in the database, you must have defined a **LONG RAW** column for the image. Make sure that the *Display Type* property is set to **IMAGE** for this column.
I get the "CGEN-03299 WARNING: Item Column Data Type 'IMAGE' unsuitable for use in Query WHERE clause" message.	You cannot query an image item that is stored in the database. Make sure that Query flag for the item is set to **No**.
The text item generated to enter the image filename is not large enough.	Use the *Layout – Image → Image filename item width (IMGFIW)* preference to specify the width of the filename text item. If you leave this preference blank, the width will be the same as the width of the image item.

Problem	Solution
How can I specify the prompt for the image filename text item?	You cannot. We have tried setting this through the source object properties, but we were unable to position the prompt properly.
I have set the IMGIFP preference to the directory where I keep all of my images, but when I run my form, I don't see this path name in the image filename text item.	The value entered for the *Layout – Image → Image prefix (IMGIFP)* preference is not displayed on the screen. When you enter an image filename, the form will search that image starting from the directory that is specified in this preference.
My image item is cropped and I want it to be fully displayed in the area I have defined.	Set the *Sizing* property of the source object in the template/source object library to **Adjust**.
I have checked to make sure that the IMGHSB and IMGVSB preferences (horizontal and vertical scrollbars) are both set to **Yes**, but I am not getting any scrollbars for my image item.	These preferences are obsolete and should not be used. However, if you have to use them, you should also set the *Layout – Standards → Object library keep old preferences (OLBOLD)* preference to **Yes**.
Image Item is generated as enabled and navigable, and I don't want it to be.	Modify corresponding properties of the source object in template/source object library.

Current Record Indicators

A *current record indicator* is a special text item that can be generated next to the items in multirow blocks. A current record indicator acts as a marker to visually identify the currently selected record. The generated form has the indicator item highlighted in a different color to identify the current record. When the cursor is on a record, the visual attribute of the indicator item in that record changes to the visual attribute specified by the item's *Current Record Visual Attribute Group* property. When the user navigates to a different record, the indicator item returns to its previous state.

Current record indicators can also be generated with the ability to allow navigation to a detail block for the current record. In this case, the item is called a current record drill-down indicator. These items are displayed exactly like the regular current record indicators; but, when the user double-clicks on the item, the form navigates to the detail block and queries the detail records for the current item. If there is no detail block, this functionality is ignored, and a current record indicator is generated. Here's an example of a current record and/or drill-down indicator:

Current record and/or drill-down indicator

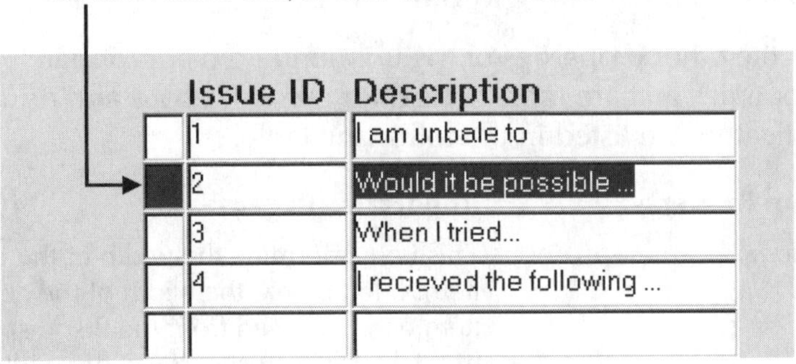

The following table shows a summarized list of some of the most important features of current record and drill-down indicators and their corresponding sources in Oracle Designer.

Feature	**Source of Feature in Oracle Designer**
Current record indicator	*Display Type* property of the item
Current record drill-down indicator	*Display Type* property of the item
Width	Width of the item
Height	Height of the repository
Color and the other properties	*Source Object(s)* from the template/object library and *Template/Library Object* property of the item

How to Generate a Create Current Record and Drill-Down Indicators

Both current record indicators and drill-down indicators can only be generated from unbound items. In order to generate a current record indicator or a drill-down indicator, you must do the following:

1. Create an unbound item.
2. Set the *Displayed* property of the unbound item to **True**.

3. Set the *Display Type* property of the unbound item to **Current Record Indicator** or **Drill-down Current Record**.
4. Set the *Data Type* property to **CHAR**.
5. Set the *Unbound Type* to **Custom**.
6. Set the other properties of the unbound item appropriately. The item properties that are most critical for current record and drill-down indicators are listed in the following table.

Item Property	Important, Because...
Width	This will determine the width of the indicator item. If left blank, the width of the generated item will be driven from the first displayed item in the block. You should set the width to the minimum value so that the indicators don't take up too much space.
Template/Library Object	The name of the template/object library object that will be used as a source when generating some of the other features of the current record indicator object that cannot be set or generated directly by Form Generator. If left blank, the *CGSO$CUR_ REC_IND* (for current record indicator) and *CGSO$DRILL_IND* (for drill-down record indicator) source object hierarchies defined in the object library will be used during generation.

Current Record Indication Using Visual Attributes

Oracle Designer provides another alternative for giving a visual indicator of the current record. It is possible to generate the forms so that the whole current record is highlighted with a different foreground and/or background color.

This is done by using the *Current Record Visual Attribute* property in Oracle Developer Form Builder. Using this property, a special visual attribute (which includes foreground and background color as well as font information) can be specified to be used for the current record. Then, at run time, the current record will use this visual attribute, while the rest of the records will use the regular visual attribute. In order to take advantage of this feature, you should set the current record visual attribute for the source block object in your object library. The standard object libraries shipped with Oracle Designer do not have this feature, so you will have to either modify the source block object(s) in the standard object library or add your own source block objects. In addition to the object library settings, the *End User Interface Preferences → Current record attribute property settings (CURREC)* preference can be used. If CURREC were set to **NONE**, the current record would not be highlighted. Setting this preference to **ALL** causes all of the displayed items to be highlighted, and setting it to **MULTI** causes only those items that are displayed more than once to be highlighted.

When to Use Current Record and Drill-Down Indicators

Multirow blocks in Oracle Forms should have some sort of visual indicator to identify which row is the current row since it can be very difficult for users to identify which row is the current when the cursor is not in that block. In addition, if more than one block is displayed on the same page, it would be even more difficult to know which record is current. Since it is a necessity to have a current indication, what remains is the choice between using the current record visual attribute or generating a current record indicator.

Both current record indicators and the current record attribute have advantages and disadvantages. Some of the advantages and disadvantages of each method are listed in the following tables.

Using current record indicator items:

Advantages	Disadvantages
Clearer indication of the current record	More work because you have to add an unbound item to every module component.
More visible for people who have visual problems (like color blindness)	The item takes up some screen space. This can be a problem if you have a lot of items to place in a multirow block.
Ability to allow drill-down navigation	

Using current record visual attributes:

Advantages	Disadvantages
Less work because you just have to modify the template and all of the forms will inherit the feature.	Can be less visible, especially for people with color blindness
Does not use any screen space.	Does not allow drill-down navigation
Some people may like the presentation better than the indicator item.	

Current Record and Drill-Down Indicator Generation Troubleshooting Guide

Problem	Solution
The width of the current record indicator item is too long.	Make sure to specify a width for the unbound item. If the width is left null, the width of the first displayed item in the block will be used.
I am getting a prompt for my current record indicator item.	Remove the prompt from the unbound item.
I can't get CURREC=MULTI to work, and instead of only the context being displayed, the whole record is.	Make sure that the *CG$CURRENT_RECORD* visual attribute is included in the template.
I am getting the "CGEN-01425 WARNING: The Data Type CHAR is not suitable in an Oracle 7 database" message.	This harmless warning message is actually a bug with unbound item definitions. Although Form Generator wants this item to be a VARCHAR2, the list of values for unbound item data types does not include VARCHAR2. You can choose another Data Type (e.g., number) if you don't want to get this message.

Problem	Solution
I am getting the "CGEN-01029 WARNING: Visual Attribute CG$OTHER_RECORD not found in template form" message.	Make sure that you have both the *CG$OTHER_RECORD* visual attribute and the *CG$CURRENT_RECORD* visual attribute. The standard templates shipped with the product do not include these visual attributes, so you need to add them manually.
I am getting the "CGEN-01046 WARNING: Drill-down generated as current record indicator" message.	This harmless warning message is pointing to the fact that there are no detail blocks to the block where you have used the drill-down indicator item.
I don't want the gap between the current record indicator and the first field in my block.	Set *Layout – Item → Prompt/item gap (ITMPIG)* and *Layout – Item → Item/prompt gap (ITMIPG)* preferences to control the spacing of items. You could also try to use an item group to have better control of the layout.
I have created more than one current record indicator.	Oracle Designer allows you to have more than one current record indicator item. If you need only one, remove the ones that you don't need.

Push Buttons

A *push button* is a GUI control that can be used to execute commands, initiate actions, or perform navigation. Some possible uses for push buttons are

- Displaying lists of values
- Navigation to other windows, forms, or reports
- Executing some user application logic (e.g., a PL/SQL program unit) to perform a task

Here's an example of push buttons:

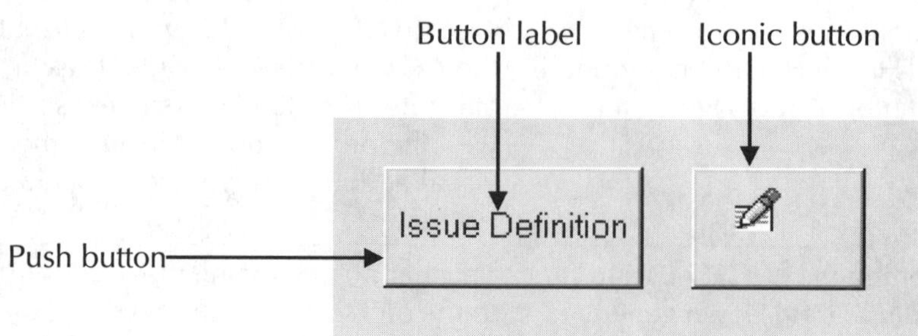

The following table shows a summarized list of some of the most important features of push buttons and their corresponding sources in Oracle Designer.

Feature	**Source of Feature in Oracle Designer**
Push button	*Unbound Item* with a *Display Type* of *Button*
Button label	*Prompt* property of the unbound item
Icon name	*Iconic* and *Icon Filename* properties of the source object
Display width and height	*Width* and *Height* properties of the unbound item
User defined logic to perform a task	*PL/SQL Block* property and *Application Logic* of the defined for unbound item
Other properties	*Source Object(s)* from the template/object library and *Template/Library Object* property of the item

How to Generate a Push Button

You can generate a push button only from an unbound item. In order to generate a push button, you must do the following:

1. Create an unbound item.
2. Set the *Unbound Type* property. Select **Client Side Function** from the list if the PL/SQL routine you wish to execute is defined on the client side, or **Server Side Function** if it is stored in the database. You can select **Custom** for all other types.

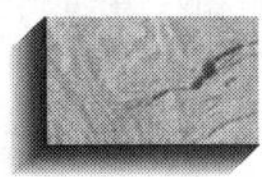

CAUTION
Client Side Function *or* ***Server Side Function*** *selections may be misleading because the word "function" in this context does not refer to a PL/SQL function, it refers to a PL/SQL procedure.*

3. Set the *Displayed* property of the unbound item to **True**.
4. Set the *Display Type* property of the unbound item to **Button**.
5. Specify what the PL/SQL code to be executed when push button is pressed. There are two ways to specify this:
   - **PL/SQL Text** Enter the name of the client- or server-side procedure to run.
   - **Application Logic** Enter either the name of a client- or server-side procedure, or the PL/SQL code to run for the WHEN-BUTTON-PRESSED event.
6. Set the other properties of the unbound item appropriately. The item properties that are most critical for push buttons are shown in the following table.

Item Property	Important, Because...
Prompt	This will be the label of the push button.
Width and Height	This will determine the width and height of the push button.
Template/Library Object	The name of the template/object library object that will be used as a source when generating some of the other features of the push button object that cannot be set or generated directly by Form Generator. If left blank, the source object hierarchy *CGSO$BUTTON*, defined in the object library, is used during generation.

When to Use Push Buttons

Refer to "How to Choose the Right Button Type,"later in this chapter, for information about when you should use push buttons.

Push Button Generation Troubleshooting Guide

Problem	Solution
I looked at both the Property Palette and Property dialogs, but I cannot find the *Icon Name* property for button items.	*Icon Name* is not a property for button items. In order to generate an iconic button, you must create a new template/library source object in the object library, and specify *Icon Filename* for this source object.
I cannot find where I can specify the color of the button.	Unfortunately, there is no way to do this in the MS Windows environment. Buttons inherit their color from windows attributes defined for your desktop. However, buttons in the Motif environment can be colored using the *CGSO$BUTTON* source object.
I get the "CGEN-01195 ERROR: Module: Failed to create .FMX file for form module" message. The form is created, but I cannot run it.	Make sure that the PL/SQL text or the application logic you have specified is correct. If you have specified a PL/SQL text, make sure that it is a procedure not a function and that it exists.
Although I have specified an icon filename for my push button, I am not seeing the icon. Instead, I get a colored button.	Make sure that the filename specified for the *Icon Filename* property of the template/library source object does not have a file extension.

Action Items

Action items, which are a new feature in Oracle Designer release 2, are a special type of push button. Like push buttons, action items can be used for navigation or executing user-defined logic. Action items can be displayed as iconic buttons with graphic images or buttons with text labels. Action items are different from regular push buttons because Oracle Designer allows you to easily add navigation using action items without having to do any programming. Action items are also displayed differently in the module diagram display view. Here's an example of an action item:

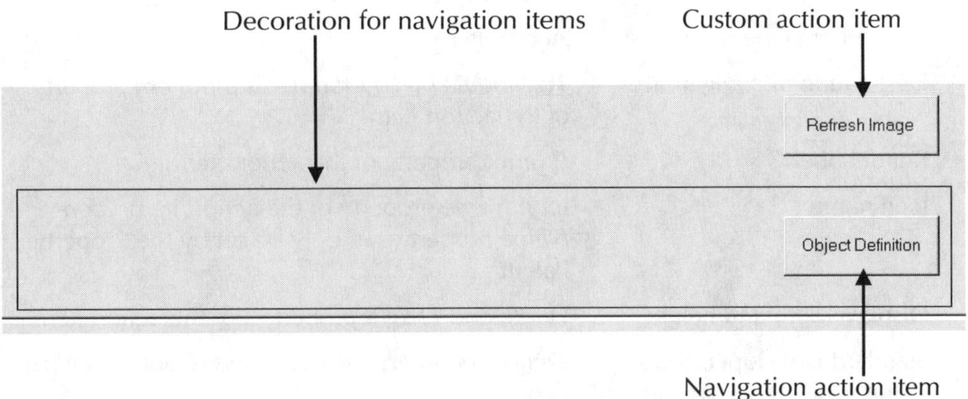

There are three types of action items: navigation action items, custom action items, and generator action items. However, the generator action items can only be used with Visual Basic applications. This table shows a brief description of action item types.

Action Item Type	**Description**
Navigation action items	Used to navigate within the same generated application or to another generated application. These can be defined for module components and windows. Each navigation action item must have a target destination.
Custom action items	Used to execute a specific piece of user-defined code from a generated application.
Generator action items	Used to execute a piece of standard generator functionality, e.g., Commit or Next Block, in Visual Basic applications only.

This table shows a summarized list of some of the most important features of action items and their corresponding sources in Oracle Designer.

Feature	Source of Feature in Oracle Designer
Action item type	*Action Item.*
Destination of navigation	*To Module* or *To Module Component* property of the action item.
Button label	*Prompt* property of the action item.
Icon name	*Icon Name* property of the action item. *Icon Name* property can only be set by the Property Palette.
Display width and height	*Width* and *Height* properties of the action item.
Standard Developer/2000 Forms function to execute	*Template/Library Object* property of the action item.
User defined logic to perform a task	*Application Logic* property of the action item.
Other properties	*Source Object(s)* from the template/object library and *Template/Library Object* property of the item.

How to Generate an Action Item

In order to generate an action item, you must do the following:

1. Create an action item.
2. Specify the type of action item to create. The action item types and generation purposes are shown in the following table.

Action Item Type	Action to Generate...
Navigation	Navigate to another form, report, etc., or to another block within the same form. Specify a target module for the *Navigate to Module* property if you wish the action item to initiate navigation to another form, report, etc. *Navigate to Module Component* can also be specified if the target destination is another module component within the same form.

Action Item Type	Action to Generate...
Custom	Create the application logic for those events that you wish to handle or specify the name of the standard source object in the template/object library that would provide the standard functionality you want. For example, if you want to create a button to go to the next page, set the *Template/Library Object* property to *CGAI$NEXT_PAGE*.

3. Set the other properties of the action item appropriately. The item properties that are most critical for action items are shown in the following table.

Item Property	Important, Because...
Prompt	This will be the label of the action item.
Icon Name	This will determine the graphic image displayed for an iconic action item. When entering the icon name, you should not include the file extension. This property can only be set by the Property Palette.
Width and Height	This will determine the width and height of the action item.
Template/Library Object	The name of the template/object library object that will be used as a source when generating some of the other features of the action item object that cannot be set or generated directly by Form Generator. If left blank, the *CGSO$BUTTON* source object hierarchy defined in the object library is used during generation.

4. Set the *Layout Preferences* for the action item to control the layout details. Some of the most important preferences for action items are shown in the following table (these preferences are all in the *Layout – Action Item* category).

Preference	Tips for Preference Settings
Action item button width (AIBBWD)	In conjunction with the *Width* property of an action item, this preference will determine the width of the generated buttons. If it's set to **NONE**, the width property of the action item will be used. If it's set to **LONGEST TEXT**, the width of each button will be equal to the width of the button with the longest text. Another setting for this property is **INDIVIDUAL TEXT**, meaning each button will be wide enough to display its label. You can also specify a numeric value to set all buttons to a specific size determined by the preference.
Generate default action item button (AIBDEF)	This preference is used to mark the first action item button as the default button. If you set this preference to **Yes**, the first action item in a module component will be the default button. Users then can execute the action item by simply pressing the ENTER key. Once created, you can always resequence action items.

When to Use Action Item Buttons

Refer to "How to Choose the Right Button Types" later in this chapter, for information about when you should use action items.

Action Item Generation Troubleshooting Guide

Problem	Solution
After adding a new action item, I could not generate my form again.	Make sure that the events that you have attached to the action item have application logic defined.

Problem	Solution
Although I did not create any navigation action items, a navigation item is generated automatically. Why?	Form Generator automatically creates a navigation action item if two module components in the same module are linked together via a key based link and the module components do not appear in the same window. Similarly, if a module network link is created between two modules, a navigation action item is created automatically. If you do not want these automatically created action items, you will have to delete them.

Considerations That Cross Multiple GUI Types

This section will give you some information that applies to multiple GUI types. The first subsection details information about the effects of certain GUI properties that are used similarly by multiple GUI types. The remaining sections give you some information that will help you select between some of the similar GUI types.

The Effect of the *Show Meaning* Property on GUI Items

The options displayed for the following GUI features are affected by the value of the *Show Meaning* property:

- Radio groups
- Pop lists
- Combo boxes
- Text lists

The *Show Meaning* property effects how the allowable values defined for a column or unbound item will be used to display the item on the screen. Allowable values can be defined at the following levels:

- **For a column** In this case, any bound items that use the column will inherit the list of allowable values defined against that column. You must navigate to the column definition to enter or modify the allowable values.
- **For an unbound item** In this case, the allowable values are defined specifically for each unbound item. The allowable values can be entered and modified directly from the unbound item definition.
- **For a domain** Allowable values can also be defined for a domain. Any column or unbound item that is attached to that domain (by setting the *Domain* property) will inherit the allowable values for that domain.

The *Allowable Values* properties are used to display the option labels for the GUI items listed at the start of this section. The *Value* property of the allowable values is matched to the actual value of the item to determine which *Allowable Value* property is used to generate the labels. The options for the *Show Meaning* property and the effect on the generated GUI items are shown in the following table.

Show Meaning Property	Source of the Label Feature for the Items Options
<null>	The actual code. Uses minimal screen real estate but should be used only when the codes are intuitive or well known.
Abbreviation Only	The *Abbreviation* property of the allowable value for the item. Again, useful only when the abbreviations are intuitive or well known to the end users.
Meaning Only	The *Meaning* property of the allowable value for the item. Very intuitive for the end users but can take a lot of screen real estate.
Meaning Alongside Code	This option is valid only for text lists. When this option is selected, both the code and the meaning are displayed in the text list. This option could be used for training users with new codes.

How to Choose the Right List Item Type

Three of the GUI controls that were presented in this chapter behave in a very similar fashion:

- Pop lists
- Text lists
- Combo boxes

In this section, we will help you decide when you should use one of these GUI controls, and which one of them should be used.

In general, these GUI controls can be used when you want to present the user with a list of mutually exclusive options and you want to conserve screen space. These controls present the possible values in a fashion that is easier for the user to access than LOVs without taking up the screen space that a radio group would.

Although these GUI controls are very similar, each control has some unique features that will help you determine when each should be used. The following table lists some of the distinguishing features, and indicates which lists control which elements. Use this table to help you decide which type to use.

Feature	Pop Lists	Combo Boxes	Text Lists
(1) Restricts selection to predefined list only.	Y		Y
(2) Only takes up one line of screen space	Y	Y	
(3) User can see all of the options without clicking.			Y
(4) Optionally displays code and meaning.			Y
(5) Allows custom entry not in predefined list.		Y	

The descriptions of these features are detailed in the following list.

(1) Restricts selection to predefined list only. The user can only enter predefined selections for the control. This feature is important if you need to ensure that the value is *only* one of the predefined ones.

(2) Only takes up one line of screen space. The control is displayed using only one line. The user will have to click the indicator icon to see all of the possible values. This feature is important when screen space is limited. It is also important for multirow blocks, because you usually do not want an item to take more than one line to display for each row. You should only use text lists (which can take more than one line) in multirow blocks if they are placed in an overflow area.

(3) User can see all of the options without clicking. All of the possible values are visible on the screen at the same time. The current value is highlighted, and the user can change the selection by clicking the desired value. This feature is important if you want to make sure the users easily see all of the possible values so they can more readily make the correct selection. Doing this takes more screen space, however, so you should only use text lists when there are not many possible values.

(4) Optionally displays code and meaning. All of these controls can optionally display the code value, abbreviation, or meaning. For the text list control only, the item can be generated to show both the code and the meaning. This is useful when the code has some inherent meaning but you still want to add more explanation of each code's meaning. This can be important when some users are familiar with the codes (usually from a legacy system), and you want to present new users with full descriptions of the codes.

(5) Allows custom entry not in predefined list. The combo box control allows users to enter a value that is not one of the predefined values in the list. This is useful when most of the possible values are known ahead of time, but you need to allow the users to enter custom values. By presenting a list of possible values, you can standardize the input and reduce entry errors without preventing the users from entering new values. However, the new values will not automatically appear on the list. If you need this functionality, you will have to add it to the item yourself.

As a general rule of thumb, pop lists should be used when you want to show a moderate number of options to the user and the user doesn't have to see all of the options at a glance. Text lists make a better choice when more than one option needs to be displayed at once. Combo boxes should be used when you want to allow the user to enter values that are not in the predefined list.

CAUTION

Dynamic Lists*. If the* Dynamic List *property of an item or a domain is set to* **No***, the list of options are hard-coded onto the form. This means that if you want to change the options, you will have to generate the form again. Therefore, you will usually want to make sure that the* Dynamic List *property is set to* ***Yes****.*

How to Choose the Right Button Type

Push buttons and action items should be used whenever you want to present the user with the option of performing some specific function in the context of the current location on the form. Buttons have an advantage over other forms of navigation (such as menu selections) because they can be placed near the data that is to be acted upon. This makes the context of the action readily apparent to the user. Some examples of functionality that can be implemented using push buttons or action items are

- Navigation to another block in the current form
- Navigation to another form in the application
- Running a report using the current context
- Executing a database procedure that manipulates the data using the current context
- Executing a client-side procedure to act on the data currently displayed on the form

Both regular push buttons and action items can be used to implement functionality like this. In fact, action items are generated as push buttons.

However, there are some differences between how push buttons and action items are defined and generated. The following are some of these differences:

- Navigation action items are generated as buttons at the bottom of a block or window. Form Generator creates a separate block for each window or block that has navigation action items. Push buttons are generated within a block along with other bound and unbound items. So are custom action items.
- Navigation action items cannot be accessed via the keyboard.
- PL/SQL code for navigation action items is automatically generated and cannot be customized. PL/SQL code for push buttons must be manually defined, but it can be totally customized by entering the application logic for the button item.

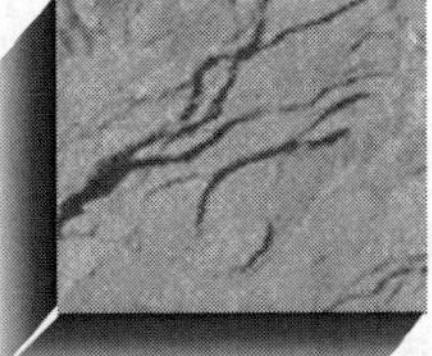

CHAPTER 14

Item Navigation Functionality

s we have pointed out in previous chapters, not only can the Forms Generator produce objects in forms, it can also automatically generate a lot of the functionality your forms need. This chapter will begin to detail how you can generate specific functionality into your forms, starting with item navigation generation. The next three chapters will continue this theme with unbound item functionality in Chapter 15, error handling in Chapter 16, and other miscellaneous functionality in Chapter 17.

In this chapter, we will show you how you can generate some of the standard navigation functionality supported by the Forms Generator, in a step-by-step fashion. We will highlight the current limitations of the Forms Generator in this area and possible workarounds for these limitations. Wherever applicable, we will also provide a troubleshooting section, which will help you solve some of the most common problems encountered when implementing the standard functionality.

Introduction to Navigation Generation

One of the most important characteristics of a form is how the navigation within that form is handled. The navigation within a form is very important, because you want users to be able to accomplish their tasks as smoothly as possible. The form should assist users when they are performing their tasks, especially if they are going to navigate to the other parts of the form. That is why the flow or navigation in a form is so important. The users should be comfortable using the form, and the form should provide all the assistance it can offer to the users who run that form to do their jobs. Figure 14-1 shows examples of different types of navigation that might occur in a form.

The navigation in a form may occur at different levels, and may include some or all of the following navigation features:

- Form startup navigation
- Block navigation
- Record and item navigation
- Window navigation
- Using keyboard shortcuts for navigation

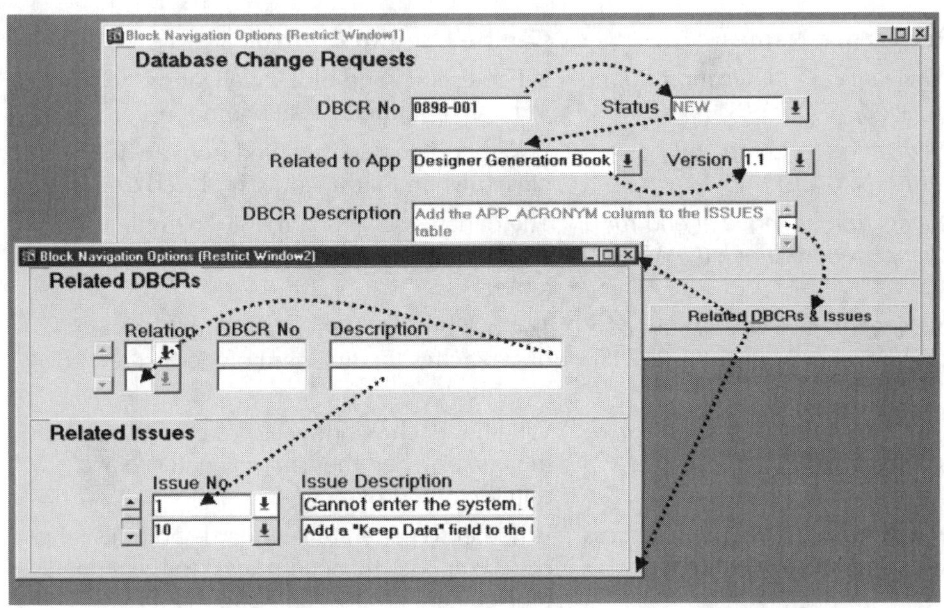

FIGURE 14-1. *Form navigation*

In Oracle Designer release 2, the Forms Generator provides many options for generating all kinds of navigation types within a form. As usual, the Forms Generator uses the repository property settings and the user preference values to implement this functionality. In fact, there is even a new Forms Generator preference category in release 2 called *Navigation*. Table 14-1 shows a summary of Forms Generator preferences that control navigation between items, records, blocks, and windows.

TIP

Oracle Designer release 1 users *Almost all of the new navigational features in release 2 are controlled via the preferences in the Navigation category.*

Navigation is not limited to the confines of a single form. In many systems, there are tens or even hundreds of forms that are very tightly integrated. In most cases, when a user runs a form, they will move to another form to complete other parts of their tasks. This very important topic

Preference Name	**Can Be Used to Control**
Navigation → Navigation bound by window (NAVBWN)	Whether item and block navigation within the form are confined to each window
Navigation → Close child forms (NAVCCF)	Whether other forms called from a window are closed when that window is closed
Navigation → Move at end for change record block (NAVCRE)	The behavior of [Next Item] when the user reaches the last item of the last record of a block
Navigation → Move at start of a change record block (NAVCRS)	The behavior of [Previous Item] when the user reaches the first item of the first record of a block
Navigation → Navigation cursor management (NAVCUR)	Whether each window stores the location of the cursor when the user navigates to a different window
Navigation → Mnemonic access key generation (NAVKEY)	Whether to generate keyboard shortcuts (also called mnemonic access keys) for generated blocks, item groups, and buttons
Navigation → Navigation next/previous block (NAVNPB)	Whether the *Next Navigation Block* and *Previous Navigation Block* properties are set for each generated block
Navigation → Navigation restrict block navigation (NAVRBN)	Whether block navigation is restricted to navigation between master-detail blocks only
Navigation → Navigation window management (NAVWND)	Whether closing a window within a form will close all of its child windows if a master detail relationship exists between blocks displayed in the two windows
Navigation → Navigation wrap (NAVWRP)	Whether the item navigation and block navigation should wrap around when the last item or last block is reached
Navigation → Use primary key recall (USEPKR)	Whether the form should perform a query upon startup (Startup Query Mode)
End user Interface → Maximum number of rows to auto-query (MAXQRY)	Whether the query should be automatically performed when using *Navigation → Use primary key recall (USEPKR)* to control the default startup query mode of a generated form

TABLE 14-1. *Summary of Preferences that Control Navigation Between Items, Blocks, and Windows*

of navigating among multiple forms will be covered and discussed in more detail later in Chapter 21.

Form Startup Navigation

The very first navigational event that happens when a form is run is the form startup. When you run a form, by default (if there is no overriding program code), the cursor will be placed in one of the following places:

- The first enterable item in the first enterable block
- The first enterable item in the first navigation block specified by the *First Navigable Block* property of the form

However, this default behavior may not be sufficient for your requirements. It may even cause problems in some of your forms. For example, if the first block in a form is a control block that contains the toolbar, you probably do not want the cursor to start in this block. Instead, you probably want the cursor placed in the first block that you have defined in module definition. In addition, you may want the form to query the records automatically when it starts up.

Forms Generator allows you to control the form startup process by allowing you to specify

- Which block the user navigates to when they start a form
- The form startup query mode

TIP

The functionality covered in this section is the functionality that can be ***declaratively*** *generated from Oracle Designer. Simply by setting a few property and preference values, you can generate a lot of functionality. However, you may have some requirements that cannot be generated declaratively by the current version of the Forms Generator. In this case, you can use the application logic and object libraries to generate the kind of functionality you need in your forms without making any post-generation changes.*

Which Block Users Navigate to When They Start a Form

When the Forms Generator generates a form, it creates blocks from module components defined in the repository module definition and from blocks defined in the template form. Blocks in a generated form can be grouped in two categories:

Block Type	Description
Generated Blocks	Blocks generated from module components and their table usages defined in the repository.
User Blocks	Blocks generated from user blocks defined in the template form, for example, the toolbar block. A user-defined block is simply copied into the generated form. For more information about user-defined blocks, please refer to Chapter 22.

By default, Forms Generator positions user blocks (copied from template form) before all of the generated blocks, but it sets the *First Navigation Data Block* property of the form to the first block generated from the first module component. Setting the following preferences can control this behavior of Forms Generator:

1. Set the *End User Interface → Navigate to first block on startup (GENNAV)* preference to
   - **Yes**, if you want the cursor positioned in the first generated block derived from a repository module component. This is the default value for this preference.
   - **No**, if you want the cursor positioned in the first block that has at least one enterable field, whether the block is derived from a repository module component table usage or copied from the template form.
2. Set the *Standards → Order template blocks at end (OTBAEN)* preference to
   - **No**, if you want to position the blocks from the template form before the generated blocks. This is the default value for this

preference. We recommend that you change this preference to **Yes** at the application system level.

- **Yes**, if you want to always position the generated blocks before the user blocks copied from the template form.

CAUTION
The End User Interface → Navigate to first block on startup (GENNAV) *and* Standards → Order template blocks at end (OTBAEN) *preferences are very interdependent. In order to get the best results, make sure that both of these preferences are set correctly.*

Controlling Startup Query Mode

In addition to allowing you to control the positioning of generated blocks and the block the cursor is placed in when the users start a form, the Forms Generator also allows you to control the *startup query mode* of the form. The startup query mode determines whether a query needs to be performed when the form starts up. You can decide if you want a form to start in enter query mode, to automatically execute a query, or to start in the normal entry mode. The startup query mode allows you to restrict the type of data users can enter or query by providing the values for module arguments. Module arguments then can be used as dynamic default values for the bound and unbound items in a form.

A few factors affect the startup query mode. First, whether the form is run stand-alone or is called from another form. If the form is run stand-alone, the startup query mode is referred to as *default query startup mode.* There is a distinction between these two factors because their implementation methods are slightly different.

Controlling Startup Query Mode—When a Form Is Run Stand-Alone

We can control the default startup query mode of a form when it is run stand-alone by

- Setting the CG$STARTUP_MODE parameter
- Setting the *Navigation → Use primary key recall (USEPKR)* preference

Specifying the Default Startup Query Mode Using CG$STARTUP_MODE

New in Oracle Designer release 2, CG$STARTUP_MODE is a special module argument that specifies the default startup query mode. An argument generates a parameter that allows you to pass data to a form or a report. The Forms Generator creates a parameter for each argument specified in a module definition. Arguments can also be associated with bound item usages of the first module component, or with unbound item usages in any module component in a module definition.

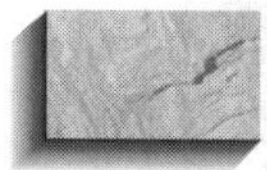

TIP

If you want to pass values to items in second, third, ...nth module component, define the module arguments and add the necessary application logic in the called form to provide the functionality you want.

CG$STARTUP_MODE determines the query mode of a generated form. It also determines whether the parameter values passed to the form are assigned to items in the first navigable, generated block of the form. The values passed with parameters can then be used as default values for query purposes as well as for entering new records.

The following procedure shows how you can control the default startup query mode using CG$STARTUP_MODE:

1. In the Design Editor, navigate to the *Arguments* line for the module and create an argument by pressing the Create icon. This will open the Property Palette to create a new argument.
2. Enter **CG$STARTUP_MODE** as the argument *Name.*
3. Set the *Default Value* property of the CG$STARTUP_MODE argument to one of the valid values shown in Table 14-2.

   As you can see from Table 14-2, the RESTRICTED modes enable you to limit permanently the records users can query or enter in the block. For example, if you have defined an argument called ARG_ISS_STATUS, specified a default value of OPEN, and set CG$STARTUP_MODE to RESTRICTED AUTO QUERY, the form will automatically query open issues and limit users to entering or querying only the open issues.

Value of the CG$STARTUP_MODE	Description and Comments
NORMAL	Default form functionality. No restriction on the data users can query or enter. Parameters passed to the form are not assigned to items.
NEW	Same as NORMAL, but allows parameter values to be passed to the generated form. The parameters passed are used as default values (both in query mode and for new records) for bound items that they are passed, and users can modify them.
RESTRICTED NEW	Same as NEW, but users cannot modify the passed values.
ENTER QUERY	Upon startup, form will be in query mode. Parameter values passed to the form will be used as default values for the items generated from bound items in the first navigable block.
RESTRICTED ENTER QUERY	Same as ENTER QUERY, but users cannot modify the passed values.
AUTO QUERY	Upon form startup, the first generated block will be automatically queried. Parameter values passed to the form will be used as default values for the items generated from bound items in the first navigable block.
RESTRICTED AUTO QUERY	Same as AUTO QUERY, but users cannot modify the passed values.

TABLE 14-2. *Valid Values for the CG$STARTUP_MODE Parameter*

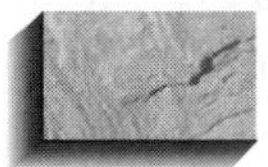

TIP
You can create a STARTUP_MODE domain and specify the allowable values (all in uppercase) for the domain. You can then use this domain to automatically set the data type, length, etc., for the CG$STARTUP_MODE arguments.

4. Define any other arguments you need to, and assign them to bound and unbound items in the first module component in your module.

Do not forget to set the *Default* property of an argument, if the argument is assigned to a required item and the CG$STARTUP_MODE is set to one of the RESTRICTED modes.

5. Generate the form.

TIP

The first module component *In the Design Editor Navigator, module components are sorted by their Name property, rather than their Usage Sequence property. This can be very confusing. In order to change the sort order of module components in the Navigator, right-click on the module components branch and choose Sort from the pop-up menu.*

NOTE

Parameter values passed to the form are always assigned to items generated from unbound items with their corresponding argument usages, regardless of the startup query mode. The restriction for assigning passed parameter values to items does not apply to unbound items.

Specifying the Default Startup Query Mode Using USEPKR Preference

The *Navigation → Use primary key recall (USEPKR)* preference controls whether a query should be performed when the form starts. It also controls whether the query should be automatically executed upon entry to the form. In previous versions of Oracle Designer, this was the only method available to control the startup query mode declaratively. The Forms Generator creates a POST-FORM trigger to save the primary key column values in each generated block to Form Builder global variables. It then uses these globals to query the same rows in subsequently called forms. This feature is also known as remembering the primary key.

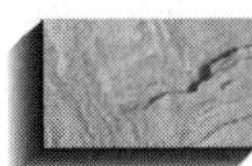

CAUTION
Although saving primary key values in global variables works in many cases, the way these globals are named might cause problems. Global variables must have unique names, but what if there are multiple keys with the same name? If you use this capability, you should make sure that each key column in your system is uniquely named.

Use the following procedure to specify the default startup query mode using the USEPKR preference:

1. Set the *Navigation → Use primary key recall (USEPKR)* preference to specify when to perform the query:

Preference Setting	Behavior
Query Only (QUERY)	Query is performed if the first block is query only.
All Forms (ALL)	Always perform the query.
No Storage (NONE)	Do not ever perform the query.

2. Set the *End User Interface → Maximum number of rows to auto-query (MAXQRY)* preference to specify when to execute the query automatically during the form startup. The Forms Generator compares the value entered for this preference with the value specified for the *End Rows* property of the base table usage defined in the first module component, and determines whether the first block should be queried automatically or not.

Preference Setting	Behavior
(*End Rows* <= MAXQRY) and *End Rows* > 0	Query is automatically executed upon entry to the form.
(*End Rows* > MAXQRY) or *End Rows* = 0	Form stays in the query mode upon entry to the form.

TIP
It is always a good programming practice to be consistent when building systems. We recommend that you choose either the CG$STARTUP_MODE or the USEPKR method to control the form startup mode for all of your modules. Adopting this as a standard will reduce the possibility of confusion among developers.

You can set these preferences either at the application or the module level. This allows you to have an application-wide GUI standard and to handle special requirements of individual modules.

Controlling Startup Query Mode—When a Form Is Called from Another Generated Form

We can control the startup query mode of a form that is called from another generated form by

- Setting the STARTUP MODE named passed value
- Setting the *Navigation → Use primary key recall (USEPKR)* preference

Specifying the Startup Query Mode Using STARTUP MODE Named Passed Value

STARTUP MODE named passed value works like the CG$STARTUP_MODE argument. In fact, STARTUP MODE named passed value is used to set the CG$STARTUP_MODE parameter in the called form.

When passing values from a module to another, we can use

- *Argument passed values* to pass user-defined arguments
- *Named passed values* to pass predefined (or standard) arguments

For example, CALL METHOD and SWITCH MENU are some of the standard arguments used in calling forms.

The Forms Generator creates a CG$STARTUP_MODE parameter in every form generated whether you have defined it or not. In order to control the startup query mode of a called form, you need to pass a value to this parameter as follows:

1. If you have not done so already, create two modules and build a module network between the two modules by calling one (called module) from the other (calling module). If you use navigation action items, the module network is automatically built. Otherwise, you can manually create module networks.
2. In the calling module, create a new named passed value and set its *Name* property to STARTUP MODE from the pop-up list. Besides the startup mode, there are a few other standard parameters that you may specify when calling other forms, such as CALL METHOD and SWITCH MENU.
3. Set the value of the STARTUP MODE named passed value to one of the following values: NORMAL, NEW, RESTRICTED NEW, ENTER QUERY, RESTRICTED ENTER QUERY, AUTO QUERY, RESTRICTED AUTO QUERY. Please refer to Table 14-2 for brief descriptions of each option.
4. In the called module, create the necessary module arguments against bound items in the first navigable block.
5. In the calling module, specify the argument passed values that will be passed to arguments in the called module.
6. Set the *Navigation → Use primary key recall (USEPKR)* preference to **NONE**.
7. Generate the form.

Form Startup Navigation Troubleshooting Guide

Problem	Resolution
I am trying to set the value of *End User Interface → Navigate to first block on startup (GENNAV)* preference, but I cannot see this preference in my Generator Preferences window.	Make sure that the Generator Preferences window is in the *Show Descriptions* and the *Show All Values* mode. Also, make sure that you are looking at the module or application level preferences.
I am getting the following message: "FRM-40360: Cannot query records here."	Check your GENNAV and OTBAEN preferences to make sure that the first navigable block is a generated block. If you want to navigate to a user block, make sure that the block is queryable, or change your startup query mode.
I set the CG$STARTUP_MODE argument to Auto Query, but the form does not automatically query my records.	If you are using a version prior to release 2.1.2, the CG$STARTUP_MODE argument or parameter is case sensitive. Make sure that its value is uppercase.
I created a named passed value to call another form in restricted auto-query mode, but it does not auto-query.	If you are using a version prior to release 2.1.2, the STARTUP MODE named passed value is also case sensitive. Make sure that you select its name from the pop-up list (it will be uppercase). Also, make sure that its value is uppercase.
I am trying to use the *Navigation → Use primary key recall (USEPKR)* preference to control the startup query mode. My block is query only, but the form does not perform query when it starts.	Make sure that CG$STARTUP_MODE argument doesn't have a conflicting setting that is overriding the preference setting. If it doesn't, check the *End Rows* property on your base table and the *End User Interface → Maximum number of rows to auto-query (MAXQRY)* preference.

Block Navigation

All but the simplest forms have more than one block, and users move from block to block within a form by using [Next Block] and [Previous Block] keys, or the mouse. By default, the sequence of blocks is determined by the order of module components.

One of the new features in Oracle Designer release 2 is its ability to control the block navigation. In earlier versions of Oracle Designer, we either had to write complex PL/SQL code in event libraries or make post-generation changes to enhance block navigation. In release 2, the Forms Generator expands upon the default block navigation paradigm and gives us options to

- Restrict the navigation between blocks within relationships (master-detail)
- Restrict the navigation between blocks within windows
- Specify the behavior when last block or first block is reached

NOTE
The [Next Block] and [Previous Block] functions can be performed with function keys, menu options, or with PL/SQL code via the Forms Builder PREVIOUS_BLOCK and NEXT_BLOCK built-ins. From this point on, when we say [Next Block], we are referring to the next block function, whether it's initiated with a key, a menu option, or a built-in.

Controlling Next Block/Previous Block Functionality

You can use the following procedure to control the behavior of block navigation in generated forms.

1. First, assign the module components to the correct windows and arrange them in the order you want. The easiest way to do this is to use the module diagram in the Design Editor. Use the Display view to easily reorder the module components, create windows and canvases, and place module components in these canvases and windows.
2. Set the following *Navigation* preferences, as required:

- *Navigation → Restrict block navigation (NAVRBN)* to specify whether block navigation is restricted to navigation between blocks within relationships. If set to **Yes**, navigation will never be allowed between unrelated blocks (that is, no parent-child relationship between blocks). If set to **No,** the block navigation behavior is determined by the other preferences.
- *Navigation → Navigation wrap (NAVWRP)* to specify how block navigation behaves when the last block or first block is reached. If set to **Yes**, when the next item (or block) function is pressed from the last item of the last block, the cursor will go to the first item of the first block. If set to **No**, navigation will stop at the last item of the last block.
- *Navigation → Navigation bound by window (NAVBWN)* to specify whether block navigation is restricted to navigation between blocks within the same window. If set to **Yes,** pressing Next Item from the last item in a window will *not* move to the next window (assuming that next block is in another window). If set to **No,** pressing Next Item *will* navigate to the next window.
- *Navigation → Navigation next/previous block (NAVNPB)* to specify whether the *Next Navigation Block* and *Previous Navigation Block* properties are set for every generated block. If set to **Yes,** the next/previous navigation block properties are set for each generated block. If set to **No,** they are only set when necessary to implement the navigation determined by the other preferences.

3. Generate the form.

NOTE

Setting navigation preferences *These preferences can be set at the application system or the module level only. You should decide how the majority of forms in your system should implement the block navigation, and set the application-level preferences accordingly. You can set the preferences for forms that need to behave differently at the module level to override the values inherited from the application level.*

Restrict Within Relationship

By default, the Forms Generator does not restrict navigation between generated blocks. However, sometimes you may not want users to navigate freely from block to block. Instead, you may want to restrict the navigation to blocks that are connected together with a master/detail relationship. Alternatively, you may want to effectively disable [Next Block] and [Previous Block], because there is no logical sequence among the blocks. In this case, you can set the *Navigation → Navigation restrict block navigation (NAVRBN)* preference to **Yes**. When this preference is set to **Yes**, the Next Navigation Block and Previous Navigation Block properties for a block are set to the current block name, for blocks that do not have any master/detail relationships. This prevents the user from navigating to the next or previous block via [Next Block] or [Previous Block] keys. For blocks with a master/detail relationship, the following settings are used:

- If the block has a master block, its *Previous Navigation Block* property is set to the master block.
- If the block has one or more child blocks, its *Next Navigation Block* property is set to the first child block. This is quite important, because if we don't provide an alternative way (buttons, keyboard shortcuts, etc.) to navigate to other detail blocks, users can never visit them.
- If the first detail block is in another window, and navigation is restricted to blocks within a window (see below), [Next Block] will not work.

NOTE

*Setting this preference to **Yes** will override both the NAVWRP and NAVNPB preferences. This means that [NextBlock] in the last block will not navigate to the first block, and Next/Previous Navigation Block properties will be set for every generated block.*

Navigation Preference Coordination Examples

The navigation preferences are very interrelated. When you change the setting of one, it can affect how the other preferences work. Navigation preferences can be very confusing. To help you understand this, we are going to use some examples of various combinations of settings. We cannot cover all of the possible combinations, of course, but we will use the examples to detail some useful combinations and to help explain how they work. The first example will show you how to restrict navigation to be within relationships.

Example 1: Block Navigation Restricted to Blocks Within Relationships

In this example, we have three module components linked together, as seen here:

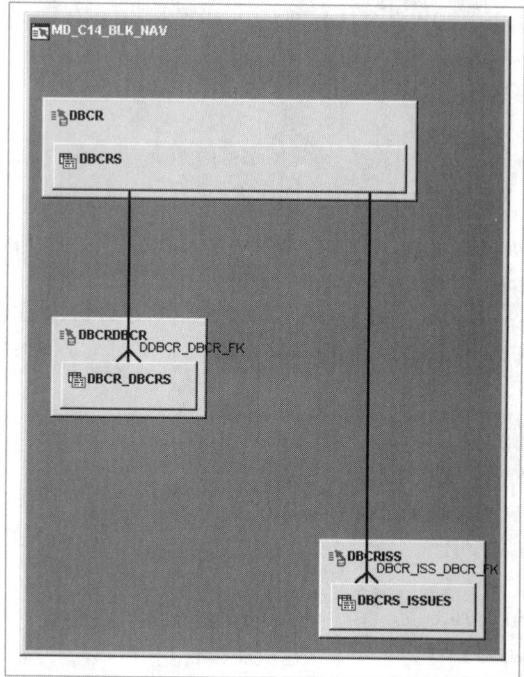

All three module components are placed on the same content canvas. Figure 14-2 shows the generated form.

By default, block navigation is not restricted in generated forms. However, in this example we want to limit the block navigation to the blocks that are connected with master/detail relationships by setting the *Navigation → Navigation restrict block navigation (NAVRBN)* preference to **Yes**.

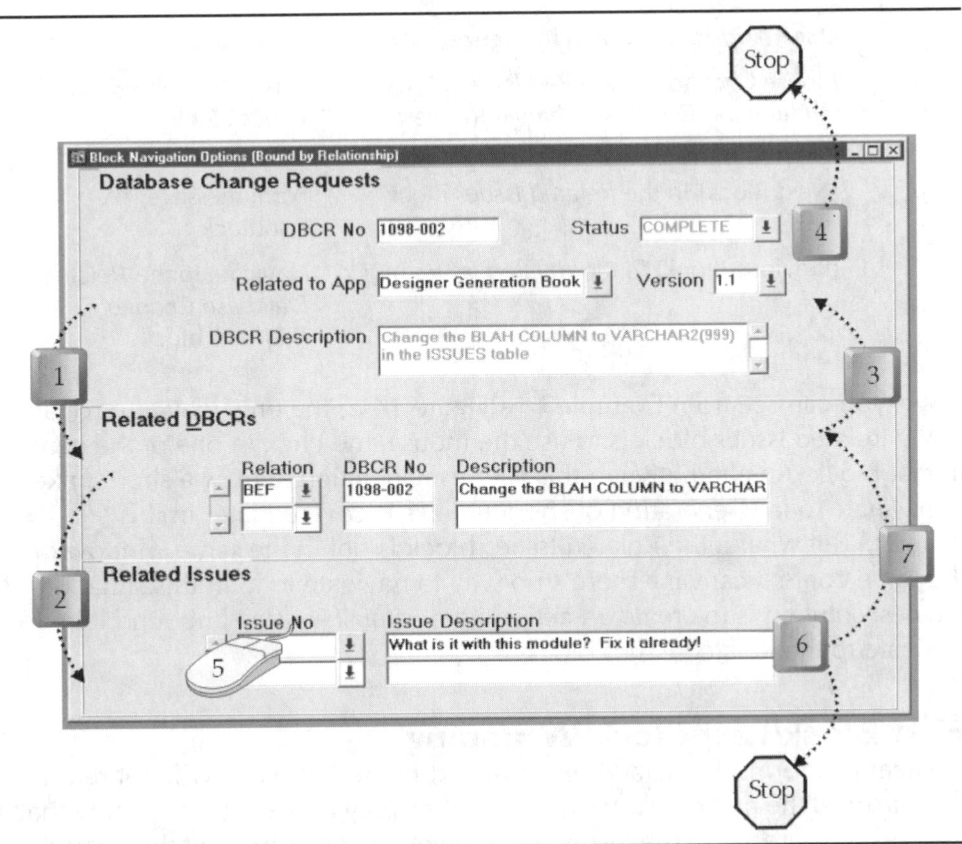

FIGURE 14-2. *Block navigation is restricted within linked blocks*

The following table summarizes the behavior of the generated form when the block navigation is set to restrict between blocks in relationship:

	User Action as Shown in Figure 14-2	Form Behavior
1	[Next Block] in the *Database Change Requests* block	Navigate to the *Related DBCRs* block
2	[Next Block] in the *Related DBCRs* block	Form message, "At last block."
3	[Previous Block] in the *Related DBCRs* block	Navigate to the *Database Change Requests* block.
4	[Previous Block] in the *Database Change Requests* block	Form message, "At first block."

	User Action as Shown in Figure 14-2	Form Behavior
5	Mouse Click to the *Related Issues* block while in the *Database Change Requests* block	Navigate to the *Related Issues* block.
6	[Next Block] in the *Related Issues* block	Form message, "At last block."
7	[Previous Block] in the *Related Issues* block	Navigate to the *Related Database Change Requests* block.

As you can see from Example 1 in Figure 14-2, the only way to navigate to the Related Issues block is to use the mouse and click in one of the items in that block. An alternative to this is to use an action item or a shortcut key to navigate to it. (Generation of shortcut keys is covered later in this chapter.) But what if the Related Issues block is not in the same window or the same content canvas? There's no way to navigate to it. In this situation, the best solution is to create an action item or *push-button* unbound item to navigate to the Related Issues block.

First Block/Last Block Wrapping

In generated forms, by default [Next Block] in the last block will not return the cursor to the first block. Instead, it will display a message indicating that the cursor is already in the last block. However, you may want the cursor to navigate to the first block. This behavior is known as *block wrapping*.

In order to allow block wrapping in generated forms, you need to set the *Navigation → Navigation wrap (NAVWRP)* preference to **Yes**. When this preference is set to Yes, [Next Block] in the last block will move to the first block, and [Previous Block] in the first block will move to the last block.

NOTE
*If the Navigation → Navigation restrict block navigation (NAVRBN) preference is set to **Yes**, it overrides the block wrapping.*

Example 2: First Block/Last Block Wrapping

In this example, we continue using the module described in the first example. Sometimes, you may want to block navigation to wrap when the last of the first block is reached. This navigation style, shown in Figure 14-3, can be easily generated by setting the following preferences:

Navigation Preferences (Module Level)	**Setting**
Navigation → Navigation wrap (NAVWRP)	**Yes**
Navigation → Navigation restrict block navigation (NAVRBN)	**No**

Remember, if *Navigation → Navigation restrict block navigation (NAVRBN)* is set to **Yes**, it overrides the block wrapping preference.

Table 14-3 summarizes the behavior of the generated form when block wrapping is allowed.

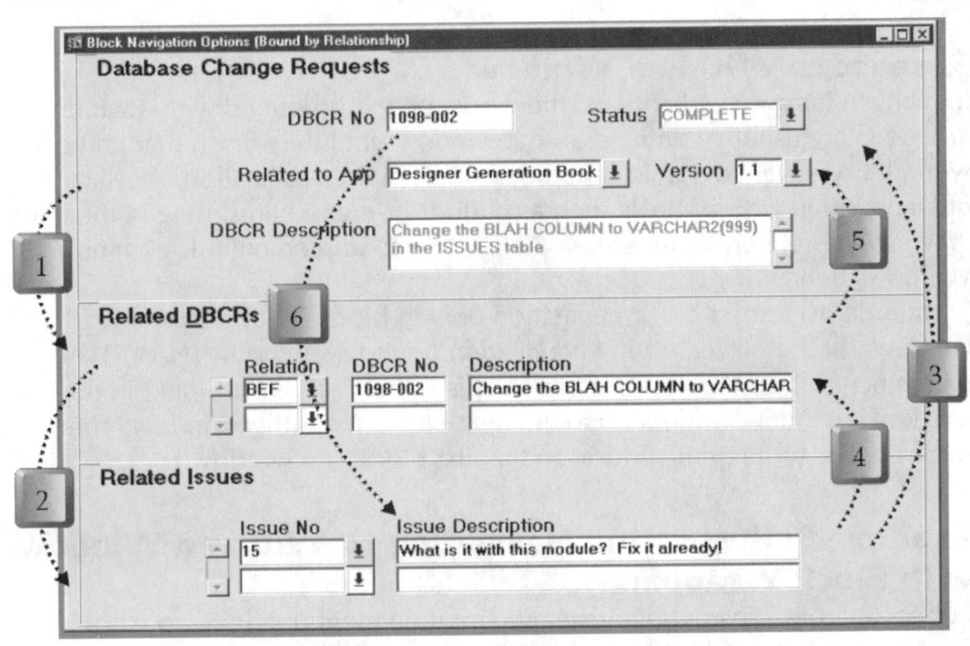

FIGURE 14-3. *Block wrapping*

	User Action as Shown in Figure 14-3	Form Behavior
1	[Next Block] in the *Database Change Requests* block	Navigate to the *Related DBCRs* block.
2	[Next Block] in the *Related DBCRs* block	Navigate to the *Related Issues* block.
3	[Next Block] in the *Related Issues* block	Navigate to the *Related DBCRs* block.
4	[Previous Block] in the *Related Issues* block	Navigate to the *Related DBCRs* block.
5	[Previous Block] in the *Related DBCRs* block	Navigate to the *Database Change Requests* block.
6	[Previous Block] in the *Database Change Requests* block	Navigate to the *Related Issues* block.

TABLE 14-3. *Summary of Form Behavior Used in Example 14-2*

Restrict to Within a Window

In many Windows applications, the work context is defined with a window, and users are usually confined to that window until they finish that unit of work. If users want to navigate to other areas of the application, they are often provided with controls such as buttons or menu items. One of the new *Navigation* preferences in release 2 allows us to implement this common Windows behavior.

In order to restrict block navigation only to blocks within the same window, set the *Navigation → Navigation bound by window (NAVBWN)* preference to **Yes**. When this preference is set to **Yes**, [Next Block] in the last block of a window will not go to the next block in another window. The same applies to [Previous Block] in the first block of a window.

Example 3: Restricting Navigation to Within a Window with Block Wrapping

In this example, we continue using the module mentioned previously, but this time the Related DBCRs and Related Issues module components will be placed on a new window. By default, block navigation is not restricted in generated forms. However, in this example, we want to limit the block navigation to the confines of each window. This navigation style, shown in Figure 14-4, can be easily generated by setting the following preferences:

Navigation Preferences (Module Level)	Setting
Navigation → Navigation bound by window (NAVBWN)	**Yes**
Navigation → Navigation wrap (NAVWRP)	**Yes**
Navigation → Navigation restrict block navigation (NAVRBN)	**No**

Remember, if *Navigation → Navigation restrict block navigation (NAVRBN)* is set to **Yes**, it overrides the restricted to window preference.

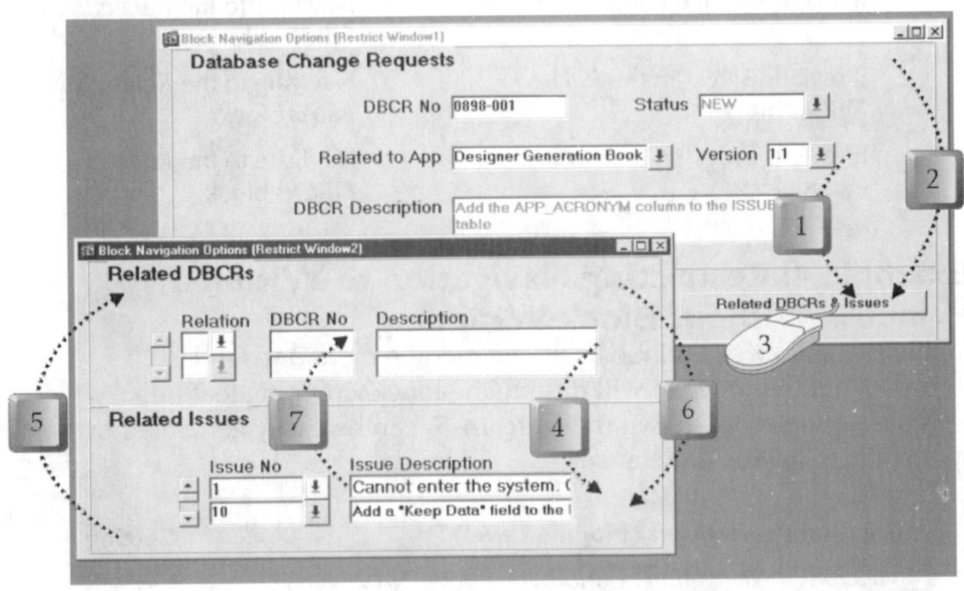

FIGURE 14-4. *Navigation bound by window with block wrapping allowed*

The following table summarizes the behavior of the generated form when the block navigation is restricted to being within a window and block wrapping is allowed:

	User Action as Shown in Figure 14-4	**Form Behavior**
1	[Next Block] in the *Database Change Requests* block	Navigate to the *Related DBCRs & Issues* action item button that is placed in another block sequenced right after this block.
2	[Previous Block] in the *Database Change Requests* block	Navigate to the *Related DBCRs & Issues* action item button.
3	[Mouse Click] on the *Related DBCRs & Issues* action item button.	Navigate to the *Related DBCRs* block.
4	[Next Block] in the *Related DBCRs* block	Navigate to the *Related Issues* block.
5	[Next Block] in the *Related Issues* block	Navigate to the *Related DBCRs* block.
6	[Previous Block] in the *Related DBCRs* block	Navigate to the *Related Issues* block.
7	[Previous Block] in the *Related Issues* block	Navigate to the *Related DBCRs* block.

Example 4: Restricting Navigation to Within a Window Without Block Wrapping

In this example, we continue using the module mentioned in last example, but this time we will disable the block wrapping feature. This navigation style, shown in Figure 14-5, can be easily generated by setting the following preferences:

Navigation Preferences (Module Level)	**Setting**
Navigation → Navigation bound by window (NAVBWN)	**Yes**
Navigation → Navigation wrap (NAVWRP)	**No**
Navigation → Navigation restrict block navigation (NAVRBN)	**No**

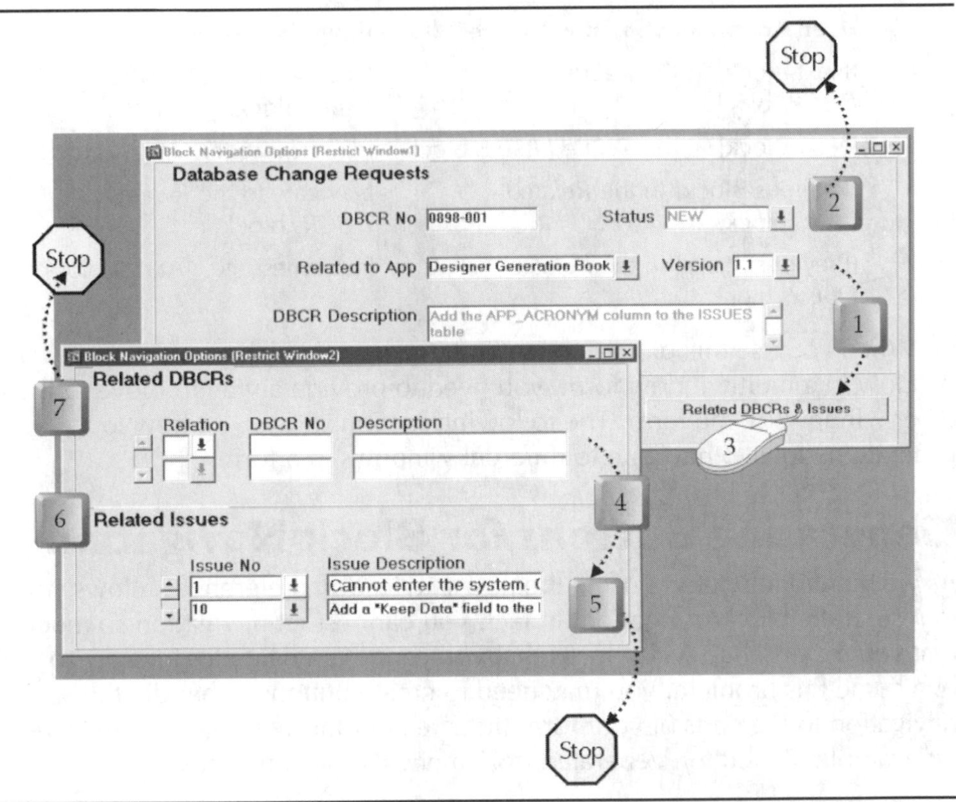

FIGURE 14-5. *Navigation bound by window with block wrapping not allowed*

The following table summarizes the behavior of the generated form when block navigation is restricted to being within a window and block wrapping is disabled:

	User Action as Shown in Figure 14-5	Form Behavior
1	[Next Block] in the *Database Change Requests* block	Navigate to *the Related DBCRs & Issues* action item button that is placed in another block sequenced right after this block.
2	[Previous Block] in the *Database Change Requests* block	Form message, "At first block."
3	[Mouse Click] on the *Related DBCRs & Issues* action item button.	Navigate to the *Related DBCRs* block.

	User Action as Shown in Figure 14-5	Form Behavior
4	[Next Block] in the *Related DBCRs* block	Navigate to the *Related Issues* block.
5	[Next Block] in the *Related Issues* block	Form message, "At last block."
6	[Previous Block] in the *Related Issues* block	Navigate to the *Related DBCRs* block.
7	[Previous Block] in the *Related DBCRs* block	Form message, "At first block."

When you use this preference to limit navigation to the confines of each window in a multiwindow form, you need to provide a way to move to the other windows of the form. The following section shows you how to generate buttons to navigate to different windows in a form.

Generating Buttons for Block Navigation

As we mentioned before, using the new *Navigation* preferences allows you to restrict the block navigation. In fact, you can restrict navigation so much that you may end up with blocks that you cannot navigate to. In order to overcome this problem, you may need to create buttons to handle the navigation to the parts of your form that are not otherwise navigable. Here is an example of a button generated from a navigation action item:

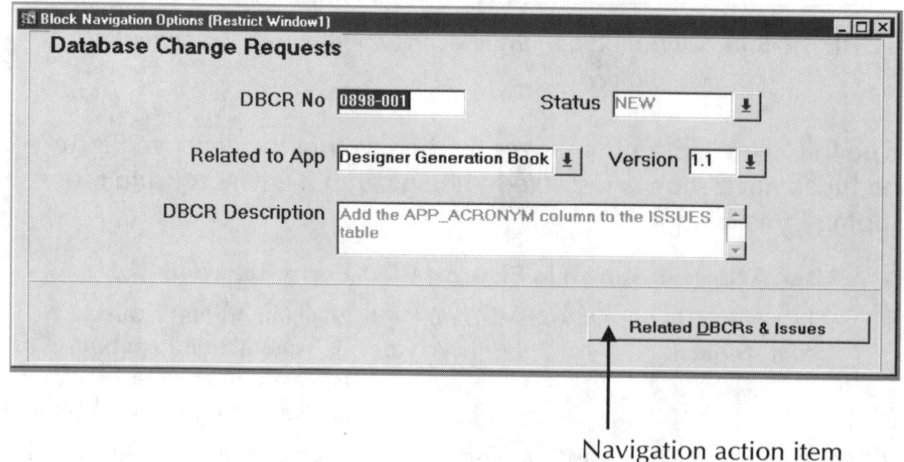

Please refer to Chapter 13 for more information about how to create an action item or a pushbutton.

Block Navigation Guideline

The following table outlines the advantages and disadvantages of each block navigation option presented in this section.

Block Navigation	Advantages	Disadvantages
Restrict within relationship	Better navigational control, because navigation is limited to logical context.	May require you to build action items to navigate to other blocks, even if they're in the same window.
Restrict within window	Better navigational control, because navigation is limited to each window.	May require you to build action items to navigate to other blocks in other windows.
Block wrapping	Easy navigation to the first block from the last block.	Does not work with the restrict within relationship.

In addition to the navigation options we have mentioned so far, we would like to point out that the control of flow in forms should be considered very seriously. Although the Forms Generator can automatically generate a lot of the functionality for you, it may still not be sufficient. For example, consider the action items generated for block navigation. Although the action items make it easier to generate buttons for navigation, they do not check the current context before executing the navigation logic. For example, if you do not want users to navigate to another window until they finish entering certain information in the current window, you are going to have to choose a different approach for navigation.

Block Navigation Troubleshooting Guide

Problem	Resolution
I have a master and a detail block. My detail block is in another window, and I cannot navigate to it via [Next Block].	Make sure that [NAVBWN] Navigation bound by window preference is not set to **Yes**.

Problem	Resolution
I have a master and two detail blocks. [Next Block] in my first detail block does not navigate to my second detail block. I have checked the block wrapping preference, and it's set to **Yes**.	This is the normal generated behavior if the *Navigation → Navigation restrict block navigation (NAVRBN)* preference is set to **Yes**.
The [Next Block] in my master block does not navigate to the detail block in another window.	This is the normal generated behavior if the *Navigation → Navigation bound by window (NAVBWN)* preference is set to **Yes**.
The [Next Block] in my master block does not navigate to the detail block in another window. How can I go to next block?	Assuming that the *Navigation → Navigation bound by window (NAVBWN)* preference is set to **Yes**, you are going to need to create a button item for navigation or enable to the keyboard shortcut generation (this process is explained later in this chapter).

Record and Item Navigation

What is record and item navigation and what is unique about it? If you consider moving from record to record or item to item via [Next Record/Item] and [Previous Record/Item], there is nothing special about it, because that's the default and ordinary behavior of a form. However, if you consider changing records or even blocks via [Next Item] and [Previous Item], that is different. Imagine a data entry person doing heads-down data entry by entering a value and pressing the [Next Item] key, and again entering a value and pressing the [Next Item] key to go to the following item, repeating this for pages and pages of data. If the cursor did not move to the next record when the user finished entering the last item on a record, he or she would have to either press [Next Record] or use the mouse to navigate to the next record, losing valuable time. Item navigation is very important because it can have an extremely positive impact on the productivity of users.

If you are familiar with Oracle Developer, you should know that one of the properties that control item navigation is the *Navigation Style* property of a block. The *Navigation Style* property of a block defines what should happen when the [Previous Item] or [Next Item] function is performed on the first or last enterable item of a record in that block. Table 14-4 shows a list of valid values for the *Navigation Style* property of a block, as well as brief description of how the form behaves.

Changing records and blocks as part of the item navigation has been available in Oracle Forms since Oracle Developer release 1. However, Oracle Designer did not support declarative generation of this feature until release 2. In prior versions we had to write complex PL/SQL code in libraries and form triggers to implement this feature. Finally, the Forms Generator in Oracle Designer release 2 allows us to take advantage of the navigation style property by using

- Source objects in object libraries
- Forms Generator preferences

Navigation Style	Description
Same Record	Pressing [Next Item] at the last item of the current record in a block moves to the first item of the same record. Pressing [Previous Item] at the first item of the current record in a block moves to the last item of the same record. This is the default setting.
Change Record	Pressing [Next Item] at the last item of the current record in a block moves to the first item of the next record. Pressing [Previous Item] at the first item of the current record in a block moves to the last item of the previous record.
Change Block	Pressing [Next Item] at the last item of the current record in a block moves to the first item of the next block, if there is one. Pressing [Previous Item] at the first item of the current record in a block moves to the last item of the previous block, if there is one.

TABLE 14-4. *Valid Values for the* Navigation Style *Property of a Block*

NOTE
The [Next Item] and [Previous Item] functions can be performed with function keys, menu options, or Form Builder PREVIOUS_ITEM and NEXT_ITEM built-ins. From this point on, when we say [Next Item], we mean the next item function performed, whether it's performed with a key, a menu option, or a built-in.

Controlling Item Navigation

You can use the following procedure to control the behavior of item navigation in generated forms:

1. Arrange the module components and displayed items in your module in the order you prefer. The easiest way to do this is to use the Display View of the module diagrammer in the Design Editor.
2. Set the *Navigation Style* property of the standard source block object named **CGSO$BLOCK** in the object library. This is required to control the way [Next Item] and [Previous Item] behave when the user of the generated form reaches the last item or first item in the block. Use Table 14-4 as a reference for the valid options for the *Navigation Style* property. For more information about object libraries, please refer to Chapter 22.

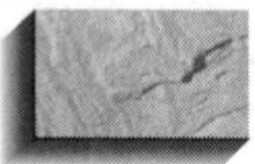

NOTE
The CGSO$BLOCK object is also used as a standard source object for multirecord blocks in the absence of CGSO$BLOCK_MR object. If you want item navigation to behave differently when navigating within a multirecord block versus within a single-record block, set the Navigation Style property of the multirecord block object CGSO$BLOCK_MR in the object library as required.

3. If you set the *Navigation Style* of the source object used for the block (CGSO$BLOCK and/or CGSO$BLOCK_MR) to **Change Record,** you may also set the following *Navigation* preferences:

   - *Navigation → Move at end for change record block (NAVCRE)* to specify how item navigation behaves when the last item of the last record of a block is reached.
   - *Navigation → Move at start of a change record block (NAVCRS)* to specify how item navigation behaves when the first item of the first record of a block is reached.

   Both of these preferences can have the following settings:

Value	Effect
All blocks (ALL)	For all blocks, the cursor will move to the next/previous block when the last (or first) item in the last (or first) record is reached.
Multirecordblock (MULTI)	The cursor will only move to the next/previous block for multirecord blocks. In single-record blocks, pressing [Next Item] or [Previous Item] will do nothing (or, if allowed, it will create a record).
Single-record block (SINGLE)	The cursor will only move to the next/previous block for single-record blocks. In multirecord blocks, pressing [Next Item] or [Previous Item] will do nothing (or, if allowed, it will create a record).
<Null>	When [Next Item] or [Previous Item] item is pressed from the first (or last) item, nothing will happen (or, if allowed, a new record will be created).

4. In addition to setting the above item navigation preferences, set the following block navigation preferences to refine the block and item navigation:

   - *Navigation → Navigation wrap (NAVWRP)* to specify how item navigation behaves when the last item of the last block or the first item of the first block is reached. If set to **Yes** then when the next item (or block) function is pressed from the last item of the last block, the cursor will go to the first item of the first block. If set to **No**, navigation will stop at the last item of the last block.

- *Navigation → Navigation bound by window (NAVBWN)* to specify whether item navigation only occurs within a window or whether the user can use [Next Item] and [Previous Item] to navigate to items in different windows.

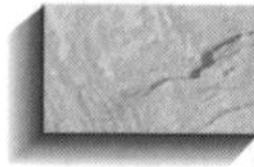

NOTE
Both the Navigation → Move at end for change record block (NAVCRE) *and the* Move at start of a change record block (NAVCRS) *preferences are only applicable if the Navigation Style of the source object used for the block (CGSO$BLOCK and/or CGSO$BLOCK_MR) is* ***Change Record****.*

5. In order to control whether buttons generated are navigable or not, set the *Keyboard Navigable* and *Mouse Navigable* properties of the CGSO$BUTTON standard source object in the object library. By default, buttons will be keyboard navigable and [Next Item] and/or [Previous Item] will navigate to buttons.
6. Generate the form.

Now, to help you understand how these preferences work, we will give you some examples.

Example 5: Block Navigation Style = Change Block

In this example, we have a master/detail relationship between two module components: Database Change Requests and Related Issues. We want the cursor to move to the next block when the [Next Item] key is pressed in the last enterable item of a record, as shown in Figure 14-6. In order to accomplish this:

1. Set the *Navigation Style* property of CGSO$BLOCK source object to **Change Block**. For more information about how to modify object libraries, please refer to Chapter 22.
2. Set the following preferences:

Navigation Preferences (Module Level)	Setting
Navigation → Navigation wrap (NAVWRP)	**Yes**
Navigation → Navigation restrict block navigation (NAVRBN)	**No**

NOTE
Remember if Navigation → Navigation restrict block navigation (NAVRBN) *is set to* ***Yes****, it limits the navigation to be within the master and its first child block.*

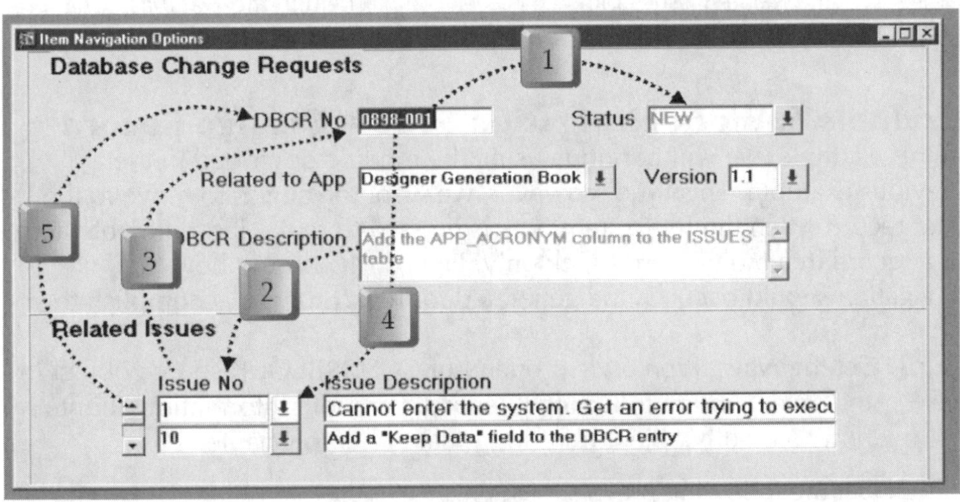

FIGURE 14-6. *Item navigation as explained in Example 5*

The following table summarizes the behavior of the generated form when the navigation style is set to change block via the source object in the object library:

	User Action as Shown in Figure 14-6	Form Behavior
1	[Next Item] in the *DBCR No* item in the *Database Change Requests* block	Navigate to the next item in the same block.
2	[Next Item] in the *DBCR Description* item (last enterable item) in the *Database Change Requests* block	Navigate to the *Issue No* item in the *Related Issues* block.
3	[Next Item] in the *Issue No* item (the one and only enterable item) in the *Related Issues* block.	Navigate to the *DBCR No* item in the *Database Change Requests* block
4	[Previous Item] in the *DBCR No* item in the *Database Change Requests* block	Navigate to the *Issue No* item in the *Related Issues* block.
5	[Previous Item] in the *Issue No* item in the *Related Issues* block.	Navigate to the *DBCR No* item in the *Database Change Requests* block

Example 6: Block Navigation Style = Change Record

In this example, we will continue using the module described in the previous example. This time, however, we want the cursor to move to the next record when the [Next Item] key is pressed from the last enterable item of a record in a multirecord block only. Figure 14-7 shows how the navigation should occur in the generated form. In order to accomplish this:

1. Set the *Navigation Style* property of CGSO$BLOCK source object in the object library to **Change Record**. For more information about how to modify object libraries, please refer to Chapter 22.
2. Set the following preferences:

Navigation Preferences (Module Level)	Setting
Navigation → Move at end for change record block (NAVCRE)	**Multi-record block**
Navigation → Move at start for change record block (NAVCRS)	**Multi-record block**

Navigation Preferences (Module Level)	Setting
Navigation → Navigation wrap (NAVWRP)	**Yes**
Navigation → Navigation restrict block navigation (NAVRBN)	**No**

The following table summarizes the behavior of the generated form when the navigation style is set to change record via the source object in the object library:

	User Action as Shown in Figure 14-7	Form Behavior
1	[Next Item] in the *DBCR No* item in the *Database Change Requests* block	Navigate to the next item in the same block.
2	[Next Item] in the *DBCR Description* item (last enterable item) in the *Database Change Requests* block	Navigate to the *DBCR No* item in the first enterable item in the same block.
3	[Mouse Click] in the *Issue No* item in the *Related Issues* block	Navigate to the *Issue No* item in the *Related Issues* block.

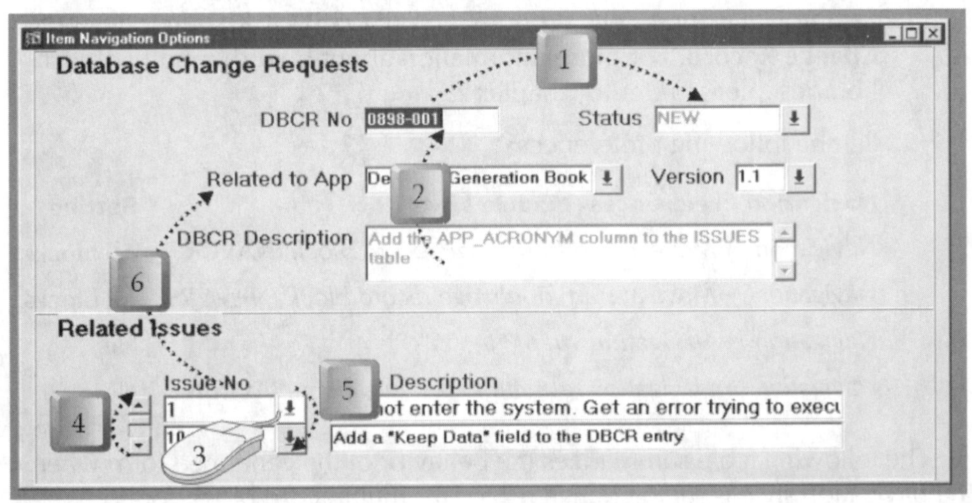

FIGURE 14-7. *Item navigation as explained in Example 6*

	User Action as Shown in Figure 14-7	Form Behavior
4	[Next Item] in the *Issue No* item (the one and only enterable item) in the *Related Issues* block	Navigate to the next record in the same block.
5	[Previous Item] in the *Issue No* item (the one and only enterable item) in the *Related Issues* block	Navigate to the previous record in the same block.
6	[Previous Item] in the *Issue No* item in the one first record of the *Related Issues* block	Navigate to the previous block, *Database Change Requests.*
7	[Next Item] in the *Issue No* item in the one last record of the *Related Issues* block	Navigate to the next block, *Database Change Requests.*

Example 7: Block Navigation Style = Change Record and NAVWRP = No

In this example, we want to show you what happens when block wrapping is not allowed under the conditions specified in the previous example. Figure 14-8 shows how the navigation should occur in the generated form. In order to accomplish this:

1. Set the *Navigation Style* property of CGSO$BLOCK source object to **Change Record**. For more information about how to modify object libraries, please refer to Chapter 22.
2. Set the following preferences:

Navigation Preferences (Module Level)	Setting
Navigation → Move at end for change record block (NAVCRE)	**All blocks**
Navigation → Move at start for change record block (NAVCRS)	**All blocks**
Navigation → Navigation wrap (NAVWRP)	**No**
Navigation → Navigation restrict block navigation (NAVRBN)	**No**

The following table summarizes the behavior of the generated form when the navigation style is set to change record for multirecord blocks only:

	User Action as Shown in Figure 14-8	Form Behavior
1	[Next Item] in the *DBCR Description* item (last enterable item) in the *Database Change Requests* block	Form message, "At first block."
2	[Mouse Click] in the *Issue No* in the Related Issues block	Navigate to the *Issue No* item in the *Related Issues* block.
3	[Previous Item] in the *Issue No* item in the first record of the *Related Issues* block	Navigate to the previous block, *Database Change Requests.*
4	[Next Item] in the *Issue No* item in the last record of the *Related Issues* block	Form message, "At last block."

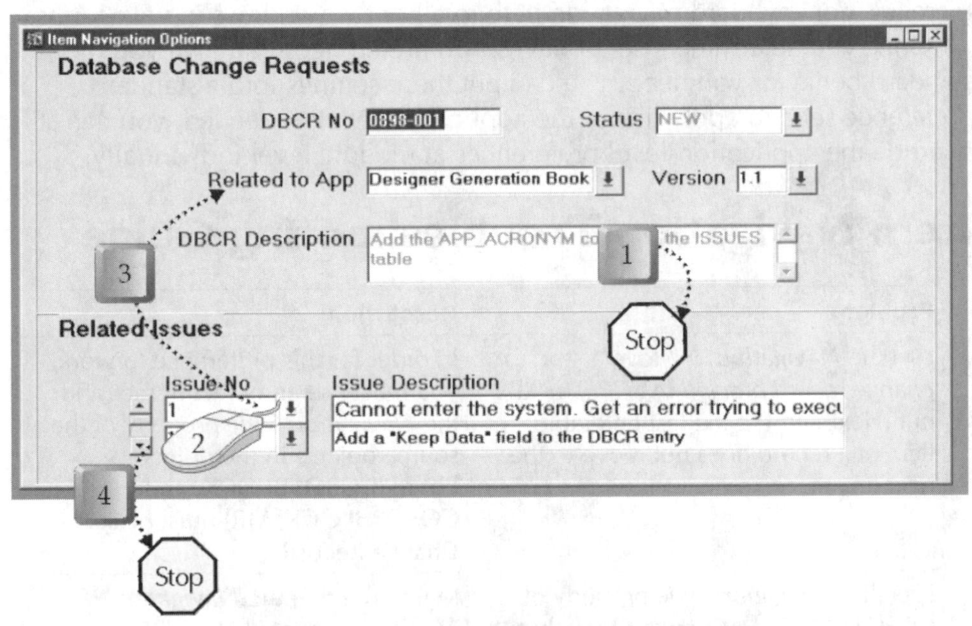

FIGURE 14-8. *Item navigation as explained in Example 7*

Coordinating Block Navigation and Item Navigation

When implementing the item navigation rules, keep in mind that whenever the item navigation causes a "block navigation," it is subject to the block navigation rules. For example, if the *Navigation Style* is set to **Change Block** in order for [Next Item] to move to the next block, the next block should be navigable in that context. If the block navigation is limited to within the confines of a window and the next block is another window, [Next Item] will attempt to move to the next block, but it will fail without giving any error messages!

Therefore, you should make sure that your set of navigation standards is consistent at the item and the block navigation levels. You should also make sure that the navigation standards are consistent with the layout standards and application design. For example, if your navigation standard is to restrict keyboard navigation to within windows, then you should make sure that there is a nonkeyboard navigation path to all of the windows in your forms.

Once you determine a set of navigation preferences that give you the standard behavior you need, you can put these settings into a standard preference set and apply that at the application level. If needed, you can still override the application-level preferences at module level individually.

Item Navigation Troubleshooting Guide

Problem	Resolution
I set the *Navigation → Move at end for change record block (NAVCRE)* to **All**, but [Next Item] at the last enterable item of a record does not move to the next record.	In order for this preference to work, you must use an object library and the *Navigation Style* property of the source objects in the object library(CGSO$BLOCK, and CGSO$BLOCK_MR) must be set to **Change Record**.
I set the *Navigation Style* property of CGSO$BLOCK to **Change Block**, but when I press [Next Item] in the last enterable item of the last block on a page, it does not move to the first block.	Make sure that the *Navigation → Navigation wrap (NAVWRP)* preference is not set to **No**.

Problem	Resolution
General: Unexpected navigational behavior.	Check the following preferences first: *Navigation → Navigation wrap (NAVWRP), Navigation → Navigation restrict block navigation (NAVRBN), and Navigation → Navigation bound by window (NAVBWN)* preferences.

Window Navigation

In multiwindow applications, users can move from window to window within the application. There are a few aspects of window navigation that you must consider when you are generating multiwindow forms:

- Navigation to a window in the same form
- Navigation to a window in another form
- Management of cursor location when navigating between windows
- Management of child windows and forms

Navigation to Windows in the Same Form

By default, the Forms Generator does not prevent users from navigating between blocks in the same form, but you can limit block navigation to the confines of each window by setting the *Navigation → Navigation bound by window (NAVBWN)* preference to **Yes**. This type of window navigation behavior is very common in standard Windows applications. However, when you choose to limit navigation to current window, you may need to create action items or push buttons to go to the other windows in the same form.

You can use the following procedure to generate code for navigation between windows in the same module:

1. Set the *Navigation → Navigation bound by window (NAVBWN)* preference to
    - **Yes**, to limit item and block navigation to within the confines of the current window.

- **No**, to allow users navigate to other windows via [Next Block], [Next Item], etc. This is the default setting for this preference. For more information about navigating to other windows via [Next Item] or [Previous Item], please refer to the "Record and Item Navigation" section earlier in this chapter.

2. If you set the *Navigation → Navigation bound by window (NAVBWN)* preference to **Yes**, and there is more than one window in your form:

    a. Create navigation action items to navigate to other windows within the module as necessary.

    b. Create unbound items of type push button to navigate to other windows within the module as necessary.

TIP

Navigation Action Items and Push Buttons

For more information about generating navigation action items and pushbuttons for navigation, please refer to Chapter 13.

For an example of how to limit navigation within the confines of a window, please refer to the examples given under the "Restrict to Within a Window" topic covered in "Block Navigation."

Navigation to Windows in Other Forms

Many systems are comprised of tens, or even hundreds, of tightly integrated forms. In such systems, it is common to have a need for navigating from form to form. This very important topic deserves more in-depth discussion, and that is exactly why Chapter 21 is dedicated solely to navigation among modules. However, in this chapter, we will outline the basic steps of the process for you.

You can use the following procedure to generate code for navigation to windows in other forms:

1. Create the modules as necessary.
2. Create a navigation action item in the calling module, and specify the module to navigate to (called module). For more information about navigation action items, please refer to Chapter 13.

3. In the calling module, create a new *named passed value* and set its *Name* property to **STARTUP MODE** from the pop-up list. Besides the startup mode, there are a few other standard parameters that you may specify when calling other forms, such as CALL METHOD and SWITCH MENU.
4. Set the value of the **STARTUP MODE** named passed value to one of the following values: NORMAL, NEW, RESTRICTED NEW, ENTER QUERY, RESTRICTED ENTER QUERY, AUTO QUERY, RESTRICTED AUTO QUERY. Please refer to Table 14-2 for brief descriptions of each option.
5. In the called module, create the necessary module arguments against bound items in the first navigable block.
6. In the calling module, specify the argument passed values that will be passed to arguments in the called module.
7. Generate the form.

Management of Cursor Location When Navigating Between Windows

A common feature in standard Windows applications is that each window stores the location of the cursor when the user navigates to a different window. On reactivation of the original window, the cursor is displayed in the stored location, unless the user clicks on another item. This is called *cursor management,* and it determines where the cursor is displayed when the user navigates from one window to another.

By default, Oracle Developer Forms does not store the location of the cursor in each window. If you were building forms by hand (e.g., not generating them from Oracle Designer), you would need to write complex PL/SQL code to implement this functionality in forms. However, the Forms Generator in Oracle Designer release 2 allows you to implement this standard Windows functionality declaratively via new navigation preference called *Navigation → Navigation cursor management (NAVCUR).*

If the *Navigation → Navigation cursor management (NAVCUR)* preference is set to **Yes**, the location of the cursor is stored when the user leaves a window. When the user navigates back to the window by clicking the window title or any part of the window, the cursor will be displayed in the stored location unless

- The user clicks on another item in the window
- The user uses [Previous/Next Block] or [Previous/Next Item] to navigate to a specific item

Example 8: Window Navigation Cursor Management

In order to show this feature in an example, we need a form with at least two windows. Figure 14-9 shows a form with two windows.

The following table summarizes the behavior of the generated form under different cursor management options:

	User Action as Shown in Figure 14-9	Form Behavior
1	[Mouse Click] in the *Version* item in the *Database Change Requests* block	Navigate to the *Version* item in the *Database Change Requests* block.

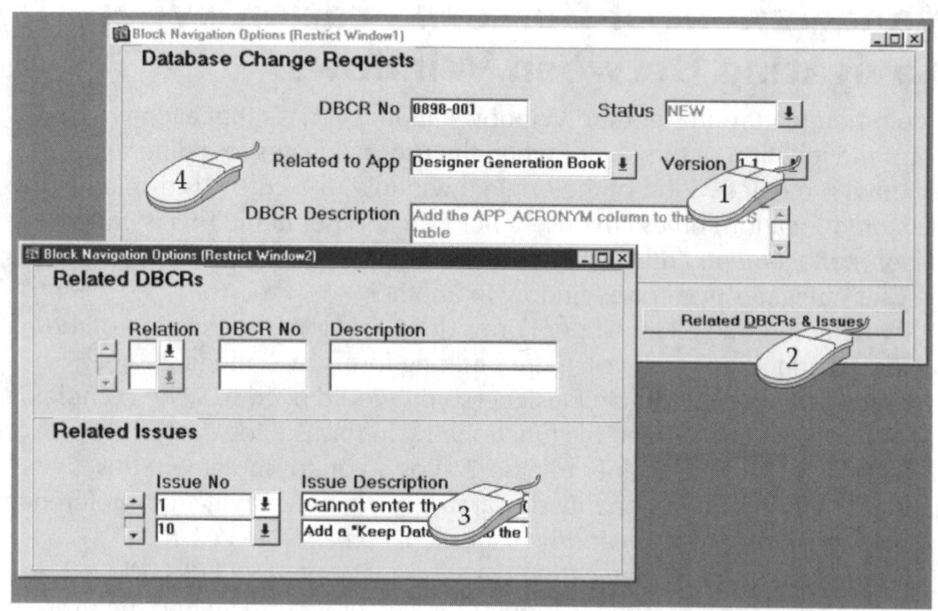

FIGURE 14-9. *Cursor management as explained in Example 8*

	User Action as Shown in Figure 14-9	Form Behavior
2	[Mouse Click] on the *Related DBCRs & Issues* button in the Database Change Requests block	Navigate to the *Relation* item in the *Related DBCRs* block.
3	[Mouse Click] in the *Issue Description* item in the *Related Issues* block	Navigate to the *Issue Description* item in the *Related Issues* block.
4	[Mouse Click] on the canvas displayed in the first window but not in any item	If the *Navigation → Navigation cursor management (NAVCUR)* preference is set to **No** (default setting), the cursor is placed in the *DBCR No* item in the *Database Change Requests* block (Form Builder default). If the *Navigation → Navigation cursor management (NAVCUR)* preference is set to **Yes**, the cursor is placed back in the *Version* item in the *Database Change Requests* block, where it was last positioned before moving out of this window.

Management of Child Windows and Forms

Another standard behavior seen in many Windows applications is that all of the child windows (windows opened from a window) are automatically closed when the parent window is closed. In other words, users do not have to close other windows they have opened, one by one. However, this is not a standard feature in Form Builder, and if you were building forms by hand you would need to write PL/SQL code to implement this functionality.

New in Oracle Designer release 2, the Forms Generator supports the generation of code to close child windows automatically via new navigation preference called *Navigation → Navigation window management (NAVWND)*. Use this preference to specify whether closing a window within a form will close all of its child windows. In this context, a window is considered to be the child of another window if a master/detail relationship exists between blocks displayed in the two windows. The window containing the detail block is considered the child of the window containing the master block.

If the *Navigation → Navigation window management (NAVWND)* preference is set to **Yes**, the Forms Generator will create the necessary code to automatically close all of the child windows when a parent window is closed. The definition of child window in Forms Generator terminology is a little bit different than the standard Windows terminology. When there is a master/detail relationship between two blocks displayed in two different windows, the window that displays the detail block is considered to be the *child window* of the window displaying the master block. So, the generated code may not close all of the windows opened from a window. If there is no master/detail relationship between the blocks in two windows, closing one window will not close the other. Figure 14-10 shows the module diagram of a module that has a parent and a child window, as well as a child form.

The *Navigation → Navigation window management (NAVWND)* preference also generates code to enable users to close windows using the standard window handles. If a window is closeable (the *Close Allowed?* property of the source object for the window CGSO$WINDOW or another user-defined source object is set to True in the object library), then the user can close a window by using

- The Windows System menu
- The top-left button in a window's title bar (Windows 3.1)
- The X iconic button in a window's title bar (Windows95/98)

Another new feature in release 2 is that the Forms Generator can now generate code to automatically close other forms that have been called from a button (generated from an action item) at block level or window level in the calling form. This behavior is controlled by the new *Navigation → Close child forms (NAVCCF)* preference. If this preference is set to **Yes**, any child forms called from the parent window are also closed when a parent window is closed.

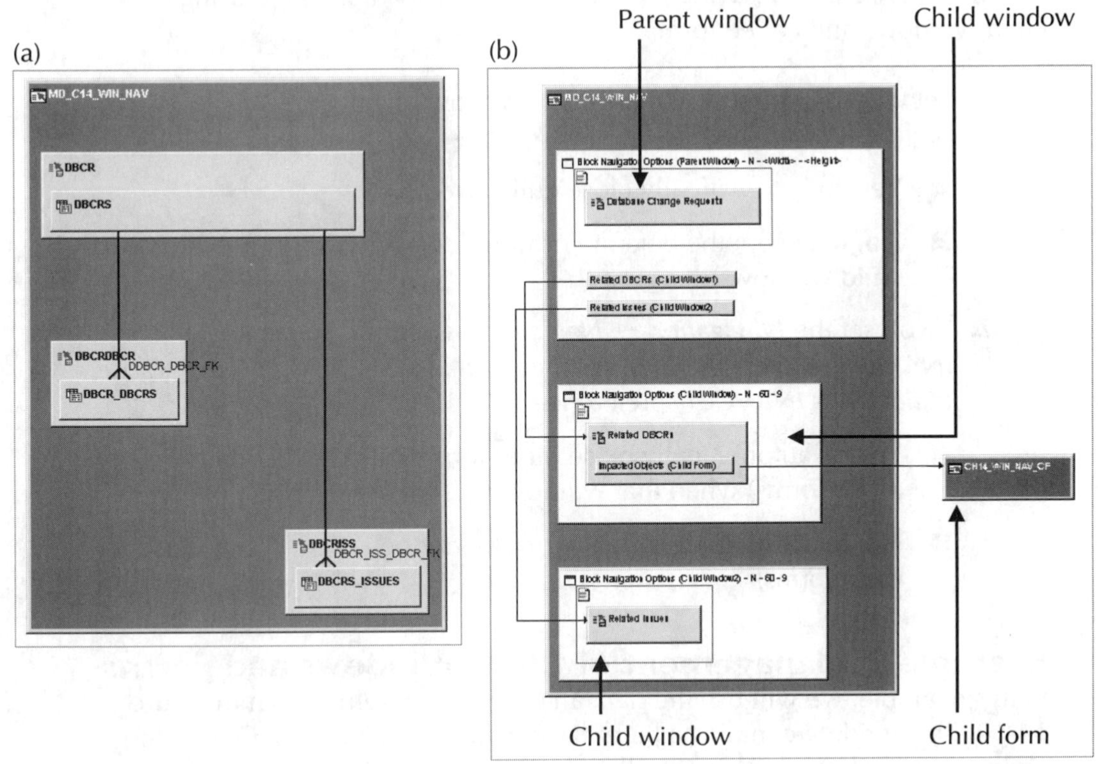

FIGURE 14-10. *Parent and child windows and a child form*

TIP

The Forms Generator implements this functionality by setting a global called CGNV$NAV_CLOSE_FORMS in the generated form to ***True*** *or* ***False****. You can change the run-time behavior of generated forms by entering application logic, which sets this global programmatically.*

You can use the following procedure to control automatic closing of child windows and called forms:

1. Set the *Navigation → Navigation window management (NAVWND)* preference to
   - **Yes**, to automatically close child windows
   - **No**, to accept the default Form Builder behavior (not to close child windows)
2. If you set the *Navigation → Navigation window management (NAVWND)* preference to **Yes**, you can also set *Navigation → Close child forms (NAVCCF)* preference to
   - **Yes**, to automatically close other forms called by a window (child forms) when that window is closed
   - **No**, to accept the default Form Builder behavior (not to close child forms)

Example 9: Management of Child Windows and Forms

In this example, we will use the data and layout diagram shown in Figure 14-10. This module contains a parent and two child windows. One of the child windows has a button to call a child form. Figure 14-11 shows the window management functionality the Forms Generator can generate in release 2.

The following table summarizes the behavior of the generated form under different cursor management options:

	User Action as Shown in Figure 14-11	**Form Behavior**
1	[Mouse Click] on the *Related DBCRs* button in the *Database Change Requests* block	Navigate to the *Related DBCRs* block in the first child window.
2	[Mouse Click] on the *Related Issues* button in the *Database Change Requests* block	Navigate to the *Related Issues* block in the second child window.

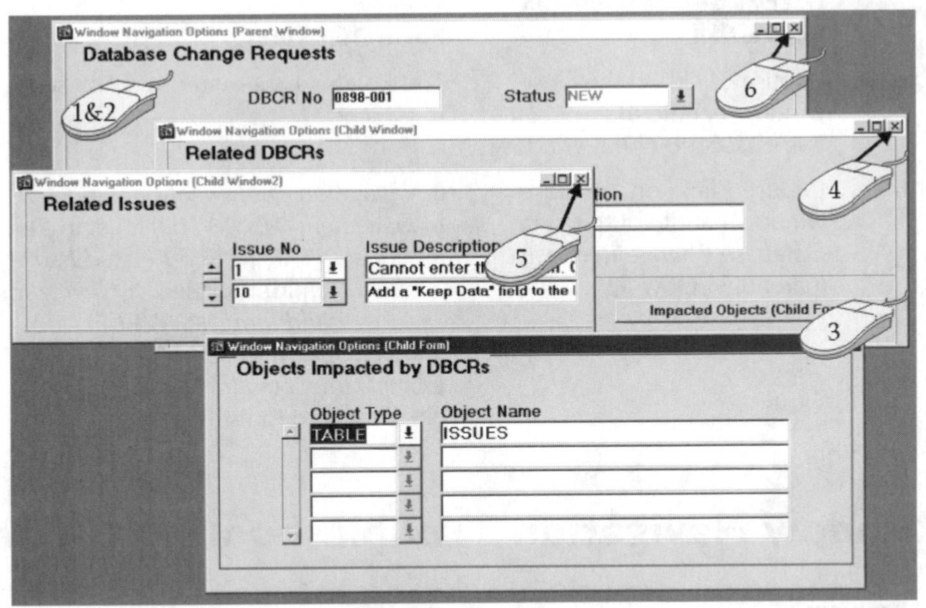

FIGURE 14-11. *Management of child windows and forms, as explained in Example 9*

	User Action as Shown in Figure 14-11	Form Behavior
3	[Mouse Click] on the *Impacted Objects* button in the *Related DBCRs* block.	OPEN[1] Objects Impacted form.
4	[Mouse Click] on the close window handle of the *Related DBCRs* (first child) window	If *Navigation → Navigation window management (NAVWND)* is set to **Yes**, the *Related DBCRs* window is closed. If *Navigation → Close child forms (NAVCCF)* preferences is also set to **Yes**, the *Objects Impacted* form is also closed.

[1] In this example, the *Impacted Objects* (Child Form) button on the first child window opens the *Impacted Objects* form, rather than calling it. If the *Impacted Objects* form were *called* instead of *opened*, we would not be able to activate the *Database Change Requests* form until we closed the called form (the *Impacted Objects* form).

	User Action as Shown in Figure 14-11	Form Behavior
5	[Mouse Click] on the close window handle of the *Related Issues* (second child) window	The *Related Issues* window is closed.
6	[Mouse Click] on the close window handle of the *Database Change Requests* (parent) window	If *Navigation → Navigation window management (NAVWND)* is set to **Yes**, the *Related DBCRs* and *Related Issues* windows (child) is closed. If *Navigation → Close child forms (NAVCCF)* preferences is also set to **Yes**, the *Objects Impacted* form is also closed. Finally, the form itself is closed.

Window Navigation Troubleshooting Guide

Problem	Resolution
I set the *Navigation → Close child forms (NAVCCF)* preference to **Yes** to automatically close the forms called, but it does not seem to be working.	This preference only has an effect if *Navigation → Navigation window management (NAVWND)* is set to **Yes**.

Using Keyboard Shortcuts for Navigation

A keyboard shortcut is a keyboard key or key combination such as CTRL-S or ALT-N that invokes a particular command or navigates to particular area of the screen. Also known as *mnemonic access keys*, keyboard shortcuts are fairly standard in Windows applications.

In the Form Builder, shortcut keys are combinations of a control key (such as the ALT key in MS Windows) and another letter (access key). These keys can be defined for menu items, push buttons, radio buttons, and check boxes. The access key (shortcut character) is underlined in the title or label of the corresponding object. Figure 14-12 shows a sample form with different types of keyboard shortcuts.

Although the Form Builder has supported this feature for quite a long time now, it was not until release 2 of Oracle Designer that the Oracle Designer Forms Generator started generating keyboard shortcuts. The Forms

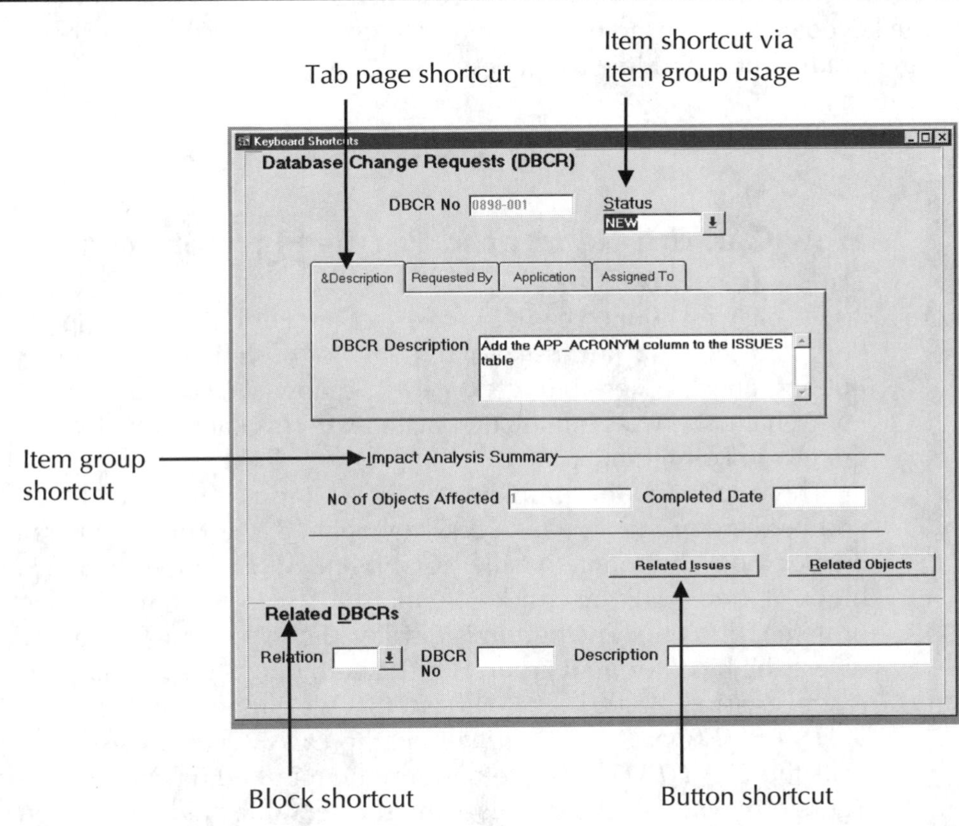

FIGURE 14-12. *Keyboard shortcuts*

Generator can now create keyboard shortcuts from the *Title* and *Prompt* properties of module components, item groups, action items, and unbound items of type pushbutton. Generated keyboard shortcut keys can be used to

- Navigate to the first navigable item in a generated block
- Navigate to the first navigable item in a generated item group
- Activate a generated button

However, the Forms Generator in release 2.1.2 and earlier does not create keyboard shortcuts to navigate either to items (even if they are check boxes or radio buttons) or the tab pages of tab canvases.

How Can the Generated Forms Have Shortcuts to Boilerplate Text?

As we have mentioned earlier in this section, Form Builder supports keyboard shortcuts (access keys) but only for push buttons, radio buttons, check boxes, and menu items. So how can the generated Forms have shortcuts to the boilerplate text? This cannot be done directly in Form Builder.

The solution to this problem is a little bit tricky. For each block and item group that has an access key defined, the Forms Generator creates a pushbutton item called *CGNV$NAVKEY* in the *CG$CTRL* block. It then sets its access key to the shortcut defined in the block or item group title. The button is displayed on the same canvas where the block or item group is displayed, but its display size is set very small (0.001 x 0.001″), so that we cannot see it. The *WHEN-BUTTON-PRESSED* trigger on the *CGNV$NAVKEY* item calls the *GO_ITEM* built-in to perform the required navigation. Therefore, when the user presses the shortcut, the "hidden" button is pressed, and the navigation occurs. Kudos to the Oracle Designer Forms Generator team for this clever solution!

Why Create Keyboard Shortcuts?

We want to generate keyboard shortcuts because they enable users to

- Navigate quickly to a particular block or item in the generated form without using the mouse. This is especially useful for data entry persons who have very good keyboard skills and do not want to lift their hands away from the keyboard.
- Navigate to areas in the generated form that cannot be accessed in any other way. For example, if the navigation is restricted to blocks within relationships, the only way to go to unrelated blocks is by using action items, pushbuttons, or keyboard shortcuts.

How to Generate Keyboard Shortcuts

You can use the following procedure to generate a keyboard shortcut:

1. Set the *Navigation → Mnemonic access key generation (NAVKEY)* preference to **Yes** to enable the keyboard shortcut generation.
2. Insert an ampersand (**&**) immediately in front of the character you want to use as the shortcut in any of the following properties.
   - A module component's Title property (becomes the block title)
   - An item group's Prompt property (becomes the item group title)
   - The Prompt property of an action item or unbound item (becomes button label)

If you want to include an "&" in a generated block title, item group title, or button label, follow the "&" with a space, because the Forms Generator removes ampersands unless they are followed by a space. The following table shows you the label and shortcut key that is actually generated for various combinations of "&" usage and NAVKEY preference settings:

NAVKEY	Text of Repository Prompt or Title	Generated As	Keyboard Shortcut
Yes	Related &Issues	Related Issues	i
Yes	Related DBCRs & Issues	Related DBCRs & Issues	none

NAVKEY	Text of Repository Prompt or Title	Generated As	Keyboard Shortcut
Yes	Related DBCRs & &Issues	Related DBCRs & Issues	i
No	Related &Issues	Related Issues	none
No	Related DBCRs & &Issues	Related DBCRs & Issues	none

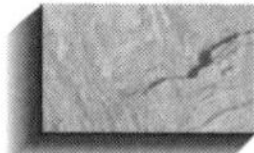

TIP

Remember that menu items have access keys as well. For example, the default menu ALT-A *has an access key for the Action menu, and the menu access keys have a precedence over other access keys. So, when you specify a keyboard shortcut for a block, item group, or a button, make sure the shortcut character that you have picked is not already used by menu items or other objects.*

Restrictions for Generating Keyboard Shortcuts

The Forms Generator does not generate keyboard shortcuts for

- Items
- Iconic buttons (because they do not have a label)
- Tab pages on a tab canvas (maybe in a future release?)

Keyboard Shortcut Generation Troubleshooting Guide

Problem	Resolution
How can I generate a shortcut for the pages of a tab canvas?	The short answer is, you cannot. Instead, you can use buttons or item group labels inside the tab pages and define shortcuts for navigation. However, the tab title will not have a character underlined.
I set the *Navigation → Mnemonic access key generation (NAVKEY)* preference to **Yes** and specified a shortcut key for a button, but when I press ALT-B, I get the block menu instead.	Before you choose a shortcut key for an object, you must remember that the menu items may be already using some of the access keys such as (B) for Block menu, or (A) for Action menu.

CHAPTER 15

Unbound Item and Lookup Item Functionality

hen you generate a form, you will often want to include some items that are not based on columns of a base table. For example, a push button to perform an action, an item that displays some sort of summary information, or a description field for a foreign key. Such items are referred to as unbound items in release 2 of Oracle Designer.

These types of generated items often go by other names. In previous releases of Designer, they were implemented using what was called "Secondary Column Usages." In the generated forms, they are often called non-base table items. In this book, we will always refer to them by the name given them in Designer, "unbound items."

In this chapter, we will show you how you can generate some of the unbound item functionality supported by the Forms Generator, in a step-by-step fashion. We will also highlight some of the current limitations of the Forms Generator and possible workarounds for these limitations. Wherever applicable, we will also provide a troubleshooting section, which will help you solve some of the most common problems encountered when implementing the standard functionality. We will cover the generation of the following unbound items, as well as the necessary code associated with them:

- Lookup items (which are not really unbound items, but have similar generated functionality)
- Calculated items
- Button items
- Current record indicator items
- Empty unbound items (for which you can enter appropriate code after generation)

Lookup Items

Lookup items are not really unbound items at all. In Oracle Designer they are bound to a lookup usage bound item. (See Figure 15-1.) They do have a source column in a lookup (or reference) table. However, since they produce similar results in the generated forms (like unbound items they are populated by generated code), we decided to cover them here.

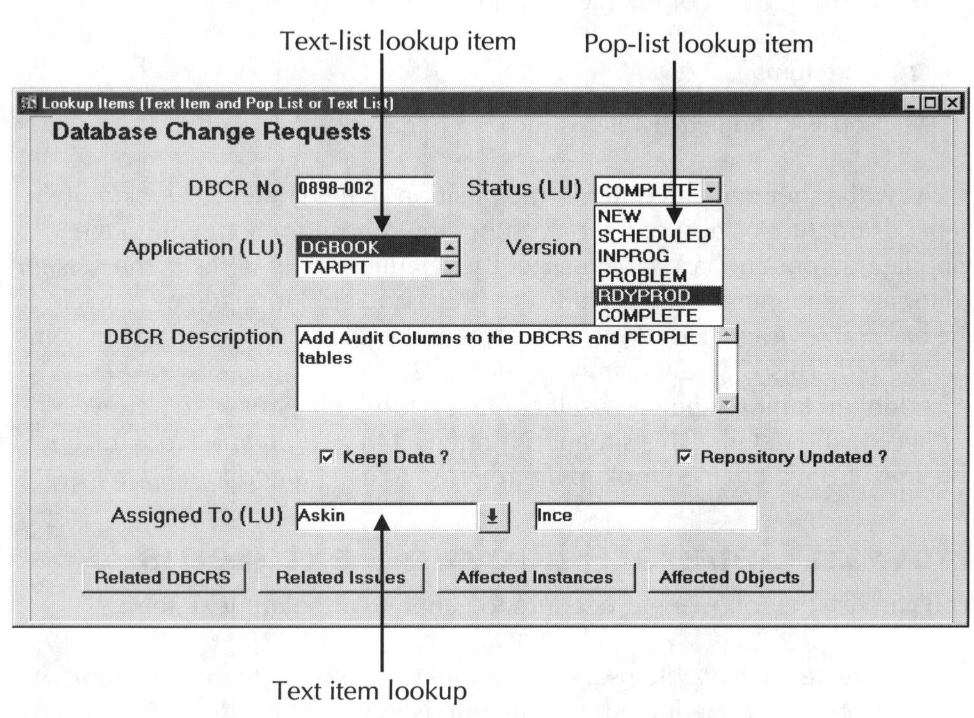

FIGURE 15-1. *Lookup item generation options*

A lookup item is an item in a base table block that contains a value from a table other than the base table of that block. They are called lookup items because the form needs to query, or *look up*, a value for the item whenever a query is executed in the block, whenever the current record changes, or whenever the value of the item, which the lookup is based upon, changes.

The Forms Generator creates lookup items from repository items in lookup table usages linked to the base table usage. The link between a base table usage and a lookup table usage is derived from the relationship between a foreign key in the base table usage and a primary key in the lookup table usage.

The Forms Generator enables you to generate lookup items as

- Text items
- Pop-list and text-list items (new in release 2)

As with other generated items, the position of the generated lookup item depends on the position of the corresponding repository item within the module component base table usage. By default, lookup items in the Design Editor are sequenced immediately after the associated foreign key items in the base table usage. However, you can change the position of lookup items as required. This is a new feature in release 2.

A lookup table usage can itself contain a foreign key used to retrieve further lookup details. This situation is referred to as a *chained lookup*, and the items from a chained lookup are referred to as *chained lookup items*.

How to Generate Lookup Text Items

You can use the following procedure to generate a lookup text item:

1. Create a base table usage and a lookup table usage for each table from which the lookup information is to be retrieved.
2. In the lookup table usage, create a bound item for each lookup item you want to be generated into the form.
3. Set the *Display Type* property of each of the lookup items to **Text**.
4. Set the *Display* property to **Yes**, if you want to display the generated item.
5. Decide whether the users can enter values via the lookup items or not. Often times lookup items are display only, and the users do not have enter values using them. However, if the foreign keys are system generated/maintained id numbers that would not make much sense to an end user then the users should be able to enter data via the lookup items. To allow lookup items for data entry, use a combination of the repository items' *Display* properties and the lookup table usage's *Enter FK Via Descriptor* property. The *Enter FK Via Descriptor* property of the lookup table usage enables you to generate a lookup item that allows input.

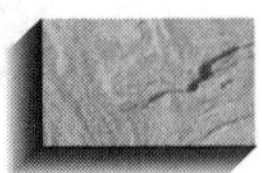

NOTE

Intelligent versus nonintelligent keys *This is a very controversial issue in database design. An intelligent key has values that are meaningful to the users. For example, customer code "Northwest Cargo," or company code "ARIS Consulting." A non-intelligent key is usually a system-generated value that serves as a pointer to a more meaningful code. For example, "35" for "Northwest Cargo," or "1" for "ARIS Consulting." It is out of scope of this book to discuss the pros and cons of both.*

How to Generate Lookup Pop-List and Lookup Text-List Items

Follow these steps:

1. Create a base table usage.
2. Create a lookup table usage for each table from which lookup information is to be retrieved.
3. Create items in the table usages as required, making sure to include
   - All foreign key items in the base table usage that form the relationship with the lookup table usage.
   - All primary key items in the lookup table usage.
   - The item to be generated as a pop list or text list in the lookup table usage. (If the base table and the lookup table are joined by a multiple column foreign key constraint, the lookup item must be based on the only column in a unique key.)
4. Set the *Display* property of the foreign key item(s) in the base table usage to **No**.
5. Set the *Display* property of the lookup item you want displayed as a pop list or text list to **Yes**, and set the *Display* property to **No** for all

other items in the lookup table usage. You can have only one item displayed for each lookup.

6. Set the *Display Type* property of the lookup item to **Pop list** or **Text list**.
7. Now you can set other properties for the generated pop-list or text-list item. Some of the properties of the generated item are based on the properties of the base table item, and some properties are based on the lookup table item. The following table indicates which properties must be set for the base item and which must be set for the lookup table item.

Property	Base Table Item	Lookup Table Item
Insert?	X	
Update?	X	
Query?	X	
Create Lookup Item	n/a	n/a
Display in LOV?	n/a	n/a
Display?		X
Template/Library Object		X
Prompt		X
Display Type		X
Show Meaning		X
Width		X
Height		X
Alignment		X
Format Mask		X
Item Group	X	
Context?	X	
Datatype	X	
Default Value	X	
Optional	X	

Property	Base Table Item	Lookup Table Item
Order By Sequence	X	
Sort Order	X	
Hint		X
User/Help Text		X
Comment		X

If the foreign key between a base table and a lookup table includes multiple columns, the Forms Generator determines

- *Display* properties of the generated pop-list or text-list item from the lookup item in the lookup table usage (the column in the lookup table from which the pop-list/text-list item is generated must be the only column in a unique key).
- *Data* properties of the generated pop-list or text-list item from the first foreign key item in the base table usage.

8. Generate the form.

NOTE

In release 1, lookup items had to be placed after the item they were based upon. In release 2, this restriction has been removed. You can place lookup items before their base item by simply resequencing them in the display view of the module diagram.

Restrictions to Generation of Lookup Pop-List or Lookup Text-List Items

Although we can generate pop-list or text-list items for the lookups, there are some restrictions:

- The *Where clause of Query* property of lookup table usages is ignored. This is a very big restriction that limits the use of pop-list or text-list lookups. A possible work-around is to define a view based on the lookup table, place the Where clause in the view text, and use that view as a lookup, but this requires creating a dummy foreign key relationship between the table and the view, so that the view can be used for the lookup.

- The *Order By* properties of columns in the lookup table usage are ignored, so the list will be unsorted. However, this can be remedied using *ordered indexes*.
- Only one item in the lookup table usage (i.e., the pop-list or text-list item) can have its *Display* property set to **Yes**, and all items in subsequent (i.e., chained) lookups linked to the first lookup table usage must have their *Display* properties set to **No**. Moreover, this item must be either the primary key or one of the unique keys.
- If allowable values have been defined for a lookup column definition in the repository, generated lookup pop-list or text-list items will be populated with these allowable values, rather than the values from the lookup table.
- The lookup values will be populated when the form starts, and will not be repopulated while the form is running. So, any new values added to the lookup table will not be seen in the pop list or text list until the form is restarted.
- For long lists, i.e., lookups that have a lot of values, the performance will not be good, and the users will not have the option to reduce the list.

In conclusion, pop-list or text-list lookups are perfect for very simple lookups that are pretty much static, globally applicable (do not need a Where clause), and contain only a few options.

Calculated Item Generation

A calculated item is a display-only unbound item that is calculated from one or more variable values. For example, consider a change management system. In such a system, you might want to display the total number of database change requests entered for a particular object, along with the number of open issues for the same object. This can be easily done with a calculated item generated by the Forms Generator.

A calculated item can have one of two calculation modes: **Summary** or **Formula.**

Summary Items

A summary item is a calculated item that performs a *single summary* calculation on the values of a *single item* (the summarized item) over all the rows in a block (see Figure 15-2). For example, you might want to display the number of database change requests that are still open for a particular object by applying the COUNT summary function to the DBCR No item.

A summary item can be based on one of the following summary functions: COUNT, MIN, MAX, AVG, SUM, VARIANCE, or STDDEV.

A summary item is marked for recalculation whenever any value of its summarized item is inserted, modified, or deleted. However, recalculation

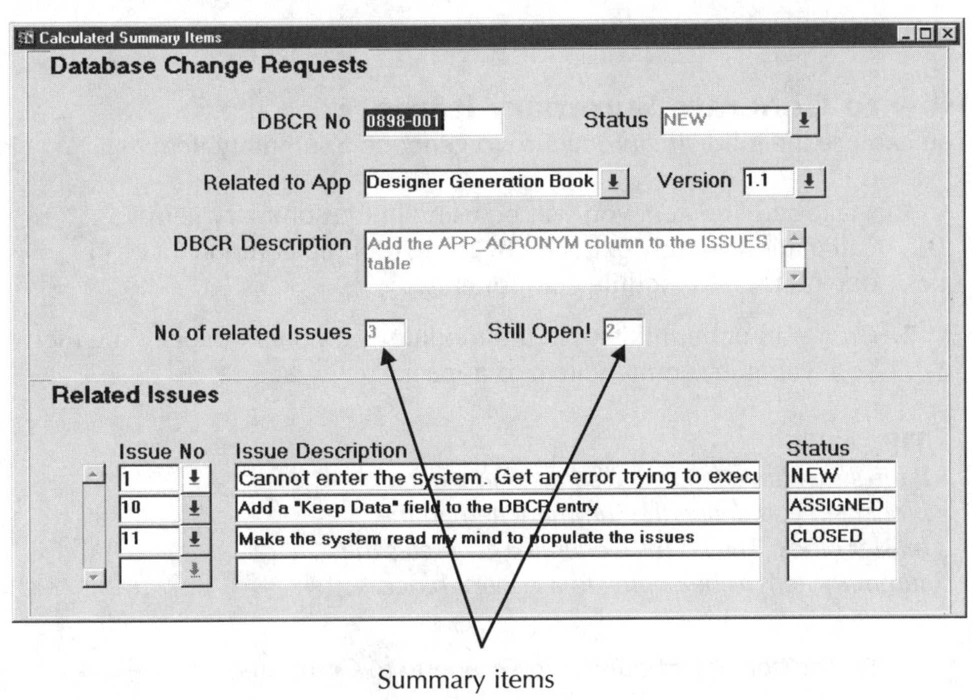

FIGURE 15-2. *Summary items*

does not occur immediately. The item is marked for recalculation to ensure that it is recalculated before the new value is referenced or displayed to the user of the form. You should not write any code that depends upon the recalculation occurring at a specific time.

The Forms Generator generates a summary item for any unbound item of type **Computed**. The value of the summary item is derived from the calculation specified in the *Derivation Text* property of the unbound item. The unbound item used to define the summary item must be capable of storing a value. Therefore, the *Display Type* of the unbound item must be one of the following: **Display Item**, **Check box**, **Radio Group**, **List Item**, or **Text Item**. The *Display Type* cannot be either a **button** or an **image**.

The repository item to be summarized must be in the same module component as the summary item, or it should one of the following:

- A bound item
- An unbound item of types *SQL Expression, Client Side Function,* or *Server Side Function*

How to Generate Summary Items

You can use the following procedure to generate a summary item:

1. Make sure the item you will be using in the summary item calculation already exists in the same module component or in one of its child module components.
2. Create an unbound item in the module component (block) in which you want the summary item to appear.

TIP
If the summarized item is displayed in a detail block and you define the summary item in the master block, The Forms Generator generates the summary item as belonging to a control block.

3. Set the item's *Unbound Type* property to **Computed**.

4. Specify the item's *Datatype* property based on the summary function you are going to use:

Summary Function	Data Type
SUM, COUNT, AVG, STDDEV, VARIANCE	Any numeric data type.
MAX, MIN	Same as the data type of the summarized item. For example, a summary item that displays the most recent (i.e., maximum) date in date column must have a data type of DATE.

5. Specify the summary calculation in the item's *Derivation Text* property, for example, COUNT(iss.iss_id) or MAX(iss.raised_date). There are special rules for entering SQL and PL/SQL expressions in the repository. These rules are detailed in the "Using PL/SQL to Add Functionality to Unbound Items" section later in this chapter.

TIP

Design Editor Dialogs *If you are using the dialogs to edit repository properties, you are not going to be able to select a source item from any of the detail module components. The Item Used pop list in the Edit Unbound Item dialog (in the Computed tab when item type is set to Computed) shows only items from the same module component. You will have to use the Property Palette to enter the summarized item name if it is in one of the detail module components.*

6. Use the *End User Interface → Display summary on query of master (DSMOQM)* preference to specify whether the value of the summary item is to be displayed when the master record is queried or when a query is performed on the detail block:

   - **Yes** to display the summary values when the master record is queried

- **No** to display the summary values after the detail records are queried

7. Generate the form.

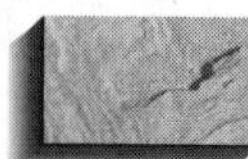

NOTE
If the user enters a restrictive query in the summarized block, the value displayed in the summary item may not be accurate. For this reason, The Forms Generator creates a PRE-QUERY trigger in the summarized block to display a warning message indicating the fact that the summary value may not be accurate.

The following table shows a list of properties set for the generated summary items.

Generated Summary Item Properties	Derived from or Set To
Calculation Mode	Summary
Summary Function	The summary function used in the repository item's *Derivation Text* property
Summarized Block	The block to which the summarized item belongs
Summarized Item	The item enclosed in parentheses in the repository item's *Derivation Text* property
Insert Allowed	No
Update Allowed	No
Query Allowed	No
Mouse Navigable	No
Keyboard Navigable	No
Required	No
Update Only if NULL	No
Visible	The repository item's *Display* property

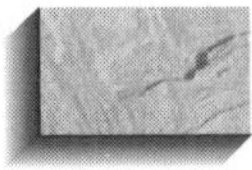

CAUTION
The Forms Generator sets the Query All Records *property of the summarized block to* ***True****, so that all the records matching the query criteria should be fetched into the data block when a query is executed. However, if you have a lot of records to query it may take a while!*

Summary Item Examples

In this example, we will use the module shown in Figure 15-2. This module contains a parent, *Database Change Requests*, and a child block, *Related Issues*. For a given database change request, it would be nice to know how many issues are related, and how many of these issues are still open.

In order to create a summary item that shows the total number of related issues logged against a particular database change request:

1. Create an unbound item in the *Database Change Requests* table usage.
2. Set the following properties:

Property	Setting
Unbound Type	Computed
Derivation Text	count(dbcriss.iss_id)
Name	TOTAL_RELATED_ISSUES
Prompt	Number of Related Issues
Displayed	Yes
Display Width	5

3. Generate the form.

Creating a summary item that shows the total number of related issues that are still open is a little bit more difficult. Follow this procedure:

1. Create another unbound item in the *Database Change Requests* table usage.
2. Set the following properties:

Property	**Setting**
Unbound Type	Computed
Derivation Text	sum(decode(dbcriss.istat_cd, 'CLOSED', 0, 1))
Name	TOTAL_OPEN_ISSUES
Prompt	Still Open!
Displayed	Yes
Display Width	5

   Let's try a simple decode statement with a sum function and see if will give us what we want.

3. Attempt to generate the form. The form generation does not complete; instead we receive a rather generic error message: "CGEN-01061 ERROR: Item DBCR.TOTAL_OPEN_ISSUES: Invalid derivation expression 'SUM(decode(dbcriss.istat_cd, 'CLOSED', 0, 1))' for this item's type." From this message, it is obvious that we cannot use a DECODE function within the SUM function in summary item derivations. However, there is another way to do the same thing.
4. Create another unbound item in the Related Issues table usage.
5. Set the following properties:

Property	**Setting**
Unbound Type	SQL Expression
Derivation Text	decode(dbcriss.istat_cd, 'CLOSED', 0, 1)
Name	NB_OPEN_OR_NOT
Displayed	False

6. Change the derivation expression of the summary item created in step 1:

Property	Setting
Derivation Text	sum(dbcriss.nb_open_or_not)
Name	TOTAL_OPEN_ISSUES
Prompt	Still Open!

7. Generate the form again; it will work this time.

Summary Item Restrictions

There are some restrictions for the summary item usages:

- You cannot have summary items in control blocks.
- You cannot have summary items over summarized items if the two module components are not linked.
- Summary functions are limited to those supported by Oracle Designer. This is actually a restriction imposed by the Oracle Developer forms!
- You cannot use functions like DECODE in the *Derivation Expression* text. However, there are ways to work around this limitation (see "Summary Item Examples," earlier in the chapter).

Formula Items

A formula item is a calculated item that displays values derived from a calculation involving *one or more* items, parameters, global variables, system variables, or constants. For example, you might want to display an employee's total income, which is calculated from the salary and commission of that employee. Formula items can also call functions held on the server or the client. Figure 15-3 shows an example of formula item.

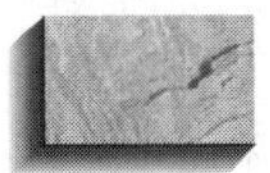

NOTE
Formula items were called "derived items" in earlier versions of Oracle Designer.

A formula item is marked for recalculation whenever a change occurs to any item, parameter, or global variable that appears in the calculation.

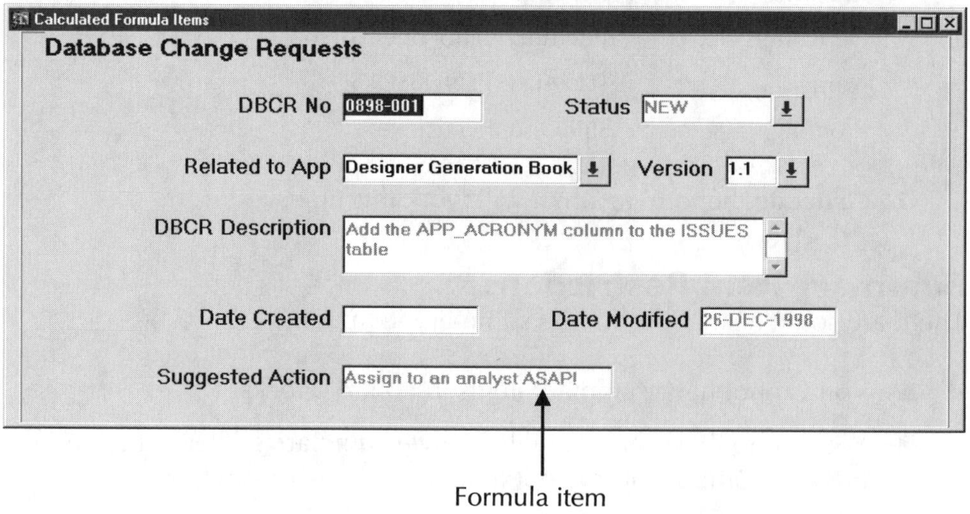

FIGURE 15-3. *Formula items*

However, recalculation does not occur immediately. The item is marked for recalculation to ensure that it is recalculated before the new value is referenced or displayed to the user of the form. You should not write any code that depends upon the recalculation occurring at a specific time.

The Forms Generator generates a formula item for any unbound item of the following types:

- SQL expression
- Client Side Function
- Server Side Function

The value of the formula item is derived from the calculation specified in the *Derivation Text* property of the unbound item. The unbound item used to define the formula item must be capable of storing a value. Therefore, the *Display Type* of the unbound item must be one of the following: **text item**,

display item, **check box**, **list item**, and **radio group**. However, the *Display Type* cannot be a **button** or an **image** item.

How to Generate Formula Items

You can use the following procedure to generate a formula item:

1. Create an unbound item in the module component (block) in which you want the formula item to appear.
2. Set the item's *Unbound Type* property to
   - **SQL Expression** If the calculation is a simple expression
   - **Client Side Function** If the calculation contains a call to a function that resides on the client (i.e., in the form itself, in the template form, in a library attached to the template form, or in a library attached to the form)
   - **Server Side Function** If the calculation contains a call to a function that resides on the server
3. Enter the SQL expression or function call that defines the calculation in the *Derivation Text* property. For example: emp.sal + nvl(emp.comm,0) or calc_sal(emp.sal,emp.comm).

TIP

If the expression contains a decode statement such as decode(some_flag,0, 'FALSE', 'TRUE'), The Forms Generator creates a function to perform the decode statement. A call to the generated function will be used in the formula text instead of the decode statement.

Restrictions for Formula Item Derivation Text

1. Do not include any of the following in the formula item's *derivation text*, because they will cause errors during compilation of a generated form:
   - References to restricted built-in subprograms

- Data Manipulation Language (DML) statements
- Circular dependencies (referencing the formula column itself)

2. Avoid using built-ins such as COPY, NAME_IN, DO_KEY, and EXECUTE_TRIGGER. Although these built-ins will not produce errors at compile time, the Form Builder might be unable to accurately recalculate the formula item at run time.
3. Do not include comments in the *Derivation Text* property (even in the format /*comment */). If you want to include a comment, do so in the item's *Description* property or *Notes* property. In the earlier versions of release 2, this caused error messages, but this has been fixed in release 2.1.2.

Properties of Generated Formula Items

The following table lists some of the most important properties of a generated formula item, and the source in Oracle Designer if applicable:

Generated Properties	Derived from or Set To
Calculation Mode	Formula
Formula	The repository item's *Derived Text* property
Insert Allowed	No
Update Allowed	No
Query Allowed	No
Mouse Navigable	No
Keyboard Navigable	No
Required	No
Update Only if NULL	No
Visible	The repository item's *Display* property

Formula Item Example

In the following example, we will create a formula item that shows the suggested action for a database change request.

1. Create an unbound item in the Database Change Requests table usage.
2. Set the following properties:

Property	Setting
Unbound Type	Client Side Function
Derivation Text	Suggest_Action(dbcr.status_cd, dbcr.modified_date)
Name	SUGGESTED_ACTION
Prompt	Suggested Action!
Displayed	YES
Display Width	30

3. Create a function named SUGGEST_ACTION that returns a suggested action based on the status code and the last modification date. You can create this function using module application logic. You can also create it in the template form or in a library that will be attached to the form.
4. Generate the form.

Calculated Item Troubleshooting Guide

Problem	Resolution
I am getting the message, "CGEN-01061 ERROR: Invalid derivation expression for this item's type." for my summary item.	Remove any DECODEs you might have in the *Derivation Text*. (See the "Summary Item Examples" section earlier in the chapter for a possible work-around.)
I have created a summary block to place all my summary items in, but I keep getting the message, "CGEN-01061," and the Forms Generator does not create my summary items.	As of release 2.1.2, you cannot have summary items is control block. Try to use data blocks that are linked to summarized blocks, or use Formula Items.

Problem	Resolution
I am getting the message, "CGEN-01195 ERROR: Failed to create .FMX."	Check your *Derivation Expression Text* defined against summary or formula items. If you are using functions (client or server), make sure that the number of arguments and their types match with your function calls.
I have a formula item generated in my form. The form generated OK, but when I run it, I get an FRM-0 message.	Make sure that the values returned by your derivation expression are compatible with the data type of your summary/formula item. Check data type and maximum length properties.

Button Items

Button items are covered in detail in Chapter 13, "GUI Item Generation." Various types of buttons (e.g., buttons generated from unbound items, buttons generated from action items, and buttons generated from navigation action items), button generation techniques, and troubleshooting button are discussed in Chapter 13.

Empty Items

An *empty item* is an unbound item with an unbound type of **Custom**. Empty items are generated just like any other unbound item; however, The Forms Generator does not create any special code for these items. You must enter the code using application logic in the repository or by entering it manually in the Form Builder after generation. In the earlier versions of Oracle Designer, we could not specify the logic for the empty item in the repository and we had to resort to post-generation changes. Creating these items using Oracle Designer instead of just creating them directly in the form after it has been generated from Oracle Designer, has the following benefits:

- Better documentation of the form.

- Allows the Forms Generator to take the empty item into consideration when it is laying out the form. This allows you to generate the item anywhere you want within the generated layout.
- Reduces the chance of losing the item when the form is generated again.

How to Generate Empty Items

You can use the following procedure to create an empty item:

1. In the Design Editor, create an unbound item.
2. Set the unbound item's *Unbound Type* property to **Custom**.
3. Leave the unbound item's *Derivation Text* property empty, and make sure that the *Display Type* property is *not* set to **Button**.
4. Optionally, enter some or all of the application logic to the unbound item.
5. Generate the form.
6. Optionally, open the generated form in the Form Builder to edit the properties of the empty item and add necessary code to meet your needs.

   The generated item will have the following properties:

Generated Item Property	Source in Oracle Designer
Name	CGNBT_<ITEM_NAME><UNIQUE_NUMBER>
Display Type	The *Display Type* property of the repository item
Navigable	False
Enabled	False
Prompt	The *Prompt* property of the repository item
Dimensions	The *Width* and *Height* properties of the repository item
Hint	The *Hint* property of the repository item

Using PL/SQL to Add Functionality to Unbound Items

When you generate unbound items, you can also add functionality by entering some PL/SQL code. When entering SQL or PL/SQL expressions for items, there are certain rules you have to follow. Before we continue with the unbound item generation techniques, we will explain how you can use PL/SQL in Oracle Designer to add more functionality to your generated forms.

PL/SQL is Oracle's procedural extension to the SQL database language. It combines the data manipulation and transaction processing capabilities of SQL with programmatic constructs such as variable and constant declarations, assignments, looping, and conditional branching, which are typically found in procedural programming languages. PL/SQL is the main language used in Oracle development tools such as forms, reports, and graphics.

You can use PL/SQL to enhance and modify the default functionality that is generated by the Forms Generator. However, you need to be familiar with PL/SQL concepts and syntax. In a form module, you write PL/SQL code when you create

- Triggers
- User-named subprograms
- PL/SQL packages
- PL/SQL-type menu items
- Menu startup code

You can also use PL/SQL in the repository module definitions where the language is set to an Oracle Developer Tool (e.g., Forms, Reports, Common Library) or Oracle WebServer. PL/SQL code can be defined against the following elements in the repository:

- The *PL/SQL Block* multiline text property of bound and unbound items
- The *Derivation Text* property of unbound items
- The *Derivation Expression* property of column definitions
- The Application Logic

Rules for Using PL/SQL

There are some rules that the Forms Generator enforces when you enter PL/SQL code against repository elements. Table 15-1 summarizes the rules you need to follow when calling PL/SQL functions and procedures from repository elements.

When you enter PL/SQL code against a repository module, you often make references to the items or columns used in the module definition. Table 15-2 shows a summary of different syntax options you can follow in referring to these items. In a repository definition, you can have the same column usage in different module components or in different lookup table usages within the same module component. You can avoid ambiguous references to column usages by referencing them by their *Name* property, since the repository item names must be unique within a repository module. The "Ability to Ensure Uniqueness" column in Table 15-2 shows the ranking of different syntax options, where 1 is highest rank.

The syntax to be used when referring to repository elements when entering PL/SQL for these elements also depends on the repository property it is defined against. For example, when you enter the *PL/SQL Block Text* property for a button, you should refer to repository items by their names in the module definition. However, when you enter the *Derivation Text* property for an unbound item, you should use the <Module_Component_Name>.<repository_item_name> format. Table 15-3 shows a repository item property/supported syntax matrix.

Rule No.	Description
1	If a parameter is passed to a function or procedure, it must be one of the following: A literal A bound item in the same module component (either in the base table usage or a lookup table usage linked to the base table usage) (field derivation only) A global variable. A column from the same table (column derivation only)
2	To ensure uniqueness when referencing columns in calls to functions and procedures, you should use the name of the repository item. However, other methods of identifying columns in procedure and function calls are also supported.
3	If you use a called function or procedure it must exist in one of the following places: In a stored program on the server In the template form used to generate the module In a library attached to the template form In a library attached to the generated form In the form itself (as user-named routine added under the module Application Logic)
4	The function or procedure may contain any valid PL/SQL, including Form Builder built-ins and references to valid tables and columns. Any values returned by a function must be appropriate for the *Display Type* of the column or the repository item. **Note:** Formula items must not reference restricted built-ins, e.g., GO_BLOCK (for more information about restricted built-ins refer to the Form Builder Help System).
5	You can enter a call to a Form Builder built-in for an unbound item with a *Display Type* of button, provided that any parameters required by the built-in meet the rules above for passing parameters. For example, the GO_BLOCK built-in accepts a literal as a parameter, so the following procedure call would be valid: GO_BLOCK ('EMPLOYEES') However, the following call is invalid because the parameters passed to the **FORMS_MDI_WINDOW** parameter violates Rule #1: SET_WINDOW_PROPERTY(**FORMS_MDI_WINDOW**,POSITION,5,10);

TABLE 15-1. *Rules for Entering PL/SQL Code for the Repository Elements*

Rule No.	Description
6	When a procedure (e.g., the NAME_IN Form Builder built-in) requires the name of a generated item in the form, enclose the item name in quotes. For example, NAME_IN ('ename')
7	Enter and call PL/SQL procedures as the PL/SQL Block multiline text property of bound and unbound items, but do not use more than one line. Enter and call PL/SQL functions that return a value as the *Derivation Text* property of unbound items or the *Derivation Expression* property of column definitions.
8	Do not include function calls in SQL expressions. For example, the following SQL expression is invalid because it includes a call to the my_func function: empno > my_func(100) Note that this rule also applies when setting the *Where/Validation Condition* property of check constraints that you want to be validated on the client.
9	Do not attempt to call multiple functions (also known as nesting functions) in *Derivation Expressions* or *Where/Validation conditions*. Create a single function that contains the multiple function calls, and call that function instead.
10	Do not prefix the function calls with "COMPLEX:". This was the standard in previous releases of Designer, and many people who are used to using the earlier version might be tempted do this.

TABLE 15-1. *Rules for Entering PL/SQL Code for the Repository Elements* (continued)

Syntax	Ability to Ensure Uniqueness	Example
<Repository_item_name>	1	Mydeptno
<Table_usage_alias>.<column_name>	2	Myempalias.deptno
<Column_name>	3	Deptno

TABLE 15-2. *Syntax to Make References to Repository Item Usages*

Repository Property	Supported Syntax
PL/SQL Block Text property of unbound items where *Display Type* is set to Button	<repository_item_name> e.g., mydeptno
Derivation Text property of unbound items where *Unbound Type* is set to Computed	<module_comp_name>.<repository_item_name> e.g., empmc.mydeptno
Derivation Expression property of columns	<column_name> e.g., deptno

TABLE 15-3. *Syntax Supported by the Repository Property*

CHAPTER 16

Error-Handling Functionality

In this chapter, we will show you, step-by-step, how you can generate some of the standard error-handling functionality supported by the Forms Generator. We will also highlight the current limitations of the Forms Generator and possible workarounds for these limitations. Wherever applicable, we will also provide a troubleshooting section, which will help you solve some of the most common problems encountered when implementing the standard functionality.

Generating Error-Handling Code

The Forms Generator creates the code and objects needed to display and handle error and warning messages raised when the business rules declared in the repository are violated. Figure 16-1 shows the error-handling process.

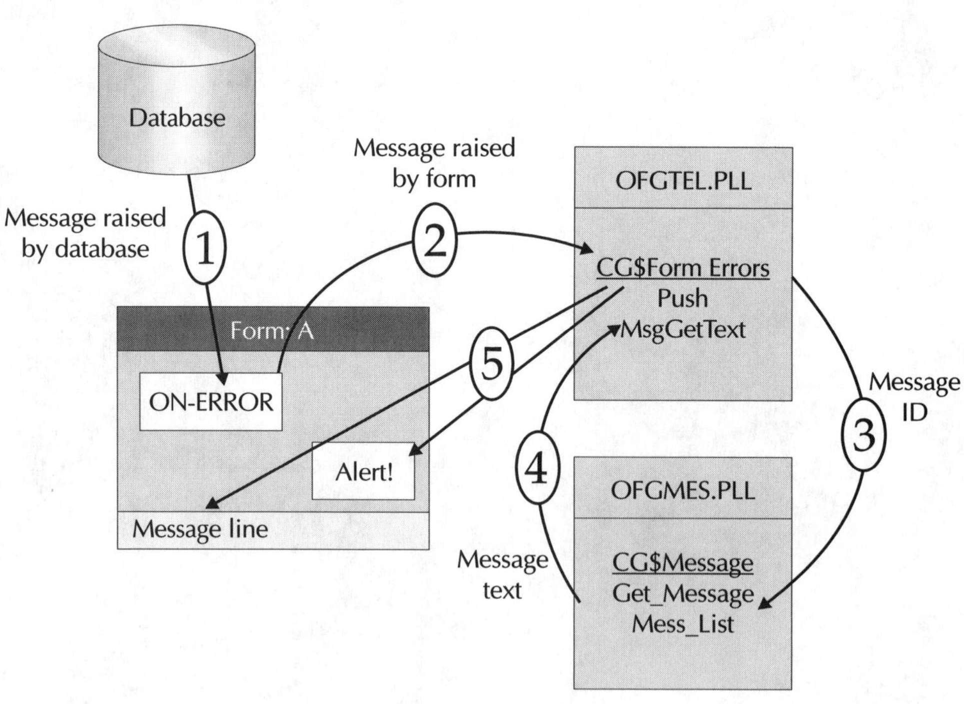

FIGURE 16-1. *Error handling in generated forms*

Error messages may originate from either the database or the form. Regardless of how they are propagated, error messages can be grouped into two categories:

Message Categories	Description
Standard Generator Messages	Generic error messages defined either in a message source file (MSB) or PL/SQL library file (OFGMES.PLL) that are shipped with Oracle Designer. For example: "Error: Cannot delete while dependent records exist." The messages can be standard text strings, or they may contain tokens to be replaced with other values during runtime.
User Messages	These are the error messages defined against the business rules (constraints), which can be directly declared in the repository—for example, primary key, unique key, foreign key, and check constraints. When you define a constraint in the repository, you can specify the error message to be displayed when the constraint is violated. For example: "Error: Category Code you have entered already exists in database. Please enter a different code, or query to edit existing record." You can also specify validation conditions and messages to be displayed when they are violated at the column level. For more information about constraints and validation of constraints, please refer to Chapter 18.

NOTE

MSB files are language specific, but the OFGMES.PLL is not. For example, CFXUS.MSB is the binary source file for generator messages in U.S. English. These files are binary files and cannot be edited. MSB files are located in the <oracle_home>\cgenf50\admin directory.

Error-Handling Options

Besides the default functionality provided by the Forms Generator, there are several different options for customizing how messages are handled:

- Forms Generator default
- Displaying messages in alert boxes
- Externalizing messages in PL/SQL libraries
- Externalizing messages in database table(s)

The following sections will discuss the implementation details and highlight the advantages and disadvantages of each option.

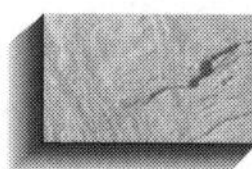

NOTE
In earlier versions of Oracle Designer, Forms Generator could use a form (OFG4ERRM) to display error and warning messages. You could set End User Interface → Form Level Procedure for Messaging (MSGFLP) to MSG_POPUP, and copy the MSG_POPUP message from OFG4LIBF template into your template form to call a form (OFG4ERRM) for displaying the error and warning messages. The MSGFLP preference is removed in Oracle Designer release 2, and its functionality is replaced with a new preference: End User Interface → Package used for messaging (MSGSFT). If you are upgrading from an earlier version of Oracle Designer and still want to use a form to display error messages, you are going to need to migrate your old message-handling routine to the new format.

Error-Handling Options: Forms Generator Default

By default, both the user and the generator messages are hard-coded into the triggers and program units in generated forms. During generation, Forms Generator reads user messages from the repository and the generator messages from an MSB file (a binary message source file) and uses the Forms Builder MESSAGE built-in to display both the user and the generator messages on the message line. Here is an example of an error message displayed on the message line:

Error-Handling Options: Displaying Messages in Alert Boxes

One problem with the default method reviewed in the previous section is that when the MESSAGE built-in is used, the messages appear in the console (the bottom part of a designated window for displaying messages and the status line). This area is fairly small and unobtrusive and may not get the user's attention very effectively. A better way to display messages is to display them in pop-up windows called alert boxes. When an alert box is displayed, the user must acknowledge the message, so you can be sure that the message has been seen. Alert boxes also allow you to specify an icon representing the severity level of the message displayed. For example, if the message is an error message, and the processing will stop after the message is displayed, a stop sign could be displayed in the alert box. The standard templates shipped with Oracle Designer contains four alert boxes to handle different types of messages (Fatal, Error, Warning, and Informative), all predefined for you. Here is an example of an error message displayed in an alert box:

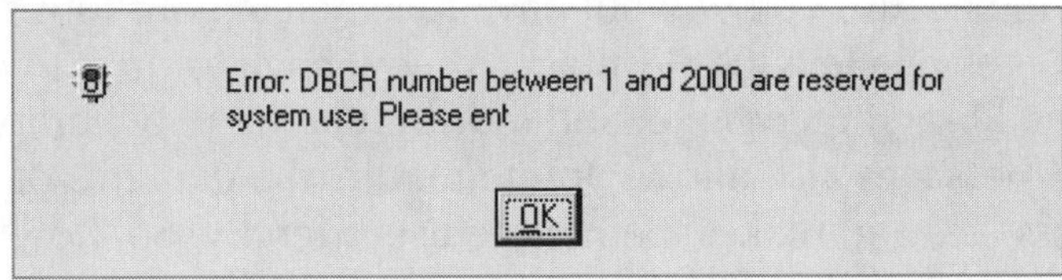

To display error messages in alert boxes, follow these steps:

1. If you are using a customized template, make sure that your template contains the alerts Forms Generator uses. These alerts (CFG_INFORMATION, CFG_WARNING_A, CFG_ERROR, CFG_SYSTEM_ERROR) can be found in templates shipped with Oracle Designer.
2. Set the *End User Interface → Package used for messaging (MSGSFT)* preference to **CG$FORM_ERRORS**. CG$FORM_ERRORS is a package supplied with Forms Generator in the OFGTEL.PLL library. This package includes a procedure called PUSH to display messages using corresponding alerts. The CG$FORM_ERRORS package offers a lot more than the ability to display messages in alert boxes; these other features will be discussed in more detail later in this chapter.
3. Generate and run the form.

Error-Handling Options: Externalizing Messages in PL/SQL Libraries

It is nice to display error and warning messages in alert boxes, but there is still one problem with the default error-handling method. The user messages are hard-coded in the triggers and program units of the generated forms. If you had to change the message text after the forms were generated, you would have to either generate them again or edit the forms by hand. In order to avoid such a big and costly maintenance headache, Oracle Designer provides you with a very flexible facility to customize and externalize messages: a totally customizable error-handling package.

Externalizing error messages prevents Forms Generator from hard-coding messages in generated forms and provides message-handling services through PL/SQL procedures and packages in PL/SQL libraries. When message contents are not hard-coded in generated forms, it is much easier to maintain them, because you will not have to generate your forms again just to update the message text they contain. All you have to do is to correct the message in the library, recompile, and redistribute the new library. Externalizing messages also allows you to modify the contents of standard generator messages and makes them more user friendly. So, how can you take advantage of this great feature?

How to Externalize Message Handling

The first step in externalizing messages is to specify a package to handle messages. The OFGTEL.PLL standard library shipped with Oracle Designer contains a sample package called CG$FORM_ERRORS. This is the same package you used for displaying messages in alert boxes. In order to specify the error-handling package, set the *End User Interface → Package used for messaging (MSGSFT)* preference to **CG$FORM_ERRORS**. The listing that follows shows the code Forms Generator creates to handle messages.

```
IF (name_in('DBCR.L_PER_FIRST_NAME') IS NOT NULL OR
    name_in('DBCR.L_PER_LAST_NAME') IS NOT NULL) THEN
      BEGIN
        CGFK$LKP_DBCR_DBCR_PER_FK(TRUE ,:DBCR.ASSIGNED_TO_PER_ID);
      EXCEPTION
        WHEN NO_DATA_FOUND THEN
          CG$FORM_ERRORS.PUSH(CG$FORM_ERRORS.MSGGETTEXT(13,
            'This <p1> does not exist', 'Assigned To,Last Name' )
            , 'E', 'OFG', 13);
           CG$FORM_ERRORS.RAISE_FAILURE;
         WHEN OTHERS THEN
          CGTE$OTHER_EXCEPTIONS
      END;
  ELSE
      CG$FORM_ERRORS.PUSH(CG$FORM_ERRORS.MSGGETTEXT(78,
        '<p1> must bentered', 'Assigned To,L_PER_LAST_NAME' )
        , 'E', 'OFG', 78);
       CG$FORM_ERRORS.RAISE_FAILURE;
END IF;
```

As you can see from this listing, when messages are externalized, triggers and PL/SQL program units in the generated forms will call the PUSH and MSGGETTEXT procedures from the CG$FORM_ERRORS package in the OFGTEL library rather than calling the standard Oracle Forms MESSAGE built-in. The MSGGETTEXT procedure then calls the GET_MESSAGE procedure in the CG$MESSAGE package in the OFGMES library to read the message text from another procedure (MESS_LIST) in the same CG$MESSAGE package. For a complete list of error-handling packages mentioned above, please refer to the OFGTEL.PLL library.

By simply specifying the error-handling package name via the *End User Interface → Package used for messaging (MSGSFT)* preference, you have externalized the standard generator error messages. The standard error messages are not going to be hard-coded into the generated forms anymore;

instead, they will be dynamically read from the MESS_LIST procedure in the OFGMES.PLL library.

```
procedure mess_list(msgno  in  varchar2,str    out varchar2) IS
BEGIN
  if (msgno =  '3') then
    str := 'No row in table %s';
  elsif (msgno = '4') then
    str := 'Cannot update %s while dependent %s exists';
  elsif (msgno =  '5') then
    str := 'Cannot delete %s while dependent %s exists';
  elsif (msgno =  '6') then
    str := 'Row exists already with same %s';
  elsif (msgno = '10') then
    str := 'Invalid value for %s';
. . . . . .
. . . . . .
  elsif (msgno = '84') then
    str := 'Validation failed on constraint %s';
  else
    str := null;
  end if;
END; /* mess_list */
```

NOTE

Even when messages are externalized into PLL libraries, messages will still be generated into forms. Although the generated code contains the generator message text, this text is not used if there is a match found in the message list procedure. So, even though it may look like the generator messages are still hard-coded, in fact they are not! These "hard-coded" messages are just used to display standard messages if, for some reason, the procedure cannot find the externalized message.

How about the user messages? How can you externalize the user messages (sometimes referred to as "Application Messages") and still take full advantage of externalized messaging? Externalizing user messages is a little bit more involved, but it's really not difficult at all. It requires a few strategic decisions and a few standards, that's all. First, the user messages are always hard-coded into the generated forms, regardless of the setting of the MSGSFT preference. However, you can still externalize them by using message identifiers (or labels) instead of actual messages! The listing that follows shows an example of how Forms Generator creates the code to handle the validation of a check constraint (i.e., DBCR.NUM must be greater than 2000). In this example, the label "DBCR-0001" was defined as the error message text in the repository for this constraint (you will see why we used this message later).

```
/* CGCC$CHK_CONS_ON_INS */
BEGIN
  IF (name_in('DBCR.NUM') IS NOT NULL) THEN
    IF (:DBCR.NUM > 2000) THEN
      NULL;
    ELSE
      CG$FORM_ERRORS.PUSH('DBCR-0001', 'E', 'OFG', 0);
      CG$FORM_ERRORS.RAISE_FAILURE;
    END IF;
  END IF;
END;
```

As you can see from this listing, Forms Generator copies the contents of the error message text directly into the generated PL/SQL. Although hard-coding the message contents into the generated forms is not normally a good idea, you can use it to your advantage by assigning a unique identification label to each error message and storing the label only, but not the message text, in the repository. For example, if the error message for a constraint was "DBCR Numbers between 1 and 2000 are reserved for system use. Please re-enter," you could assign an identification label such as "DBCR-0001" to this message. The generated code would then contain only this identifier, not the actual message text. By using a unique message identifier, you have externalized the user error messages, and the message text is not hard-coded into the generated form anymore. However, in order to display the message text, you have to modify the error-handling packages and add your own code to handle your own messages. Otherwise, users will see a message like "Error: DBCR-0001," which is not user friendly at all.

CAUTION

If you externalize messages as suggested here, you have to consider the side effects on the Table API. Error messages are also hard-coded in the Table API, and other client tools may receive messages like "Error: DBCR-0001." Please refer to Chapter 9 for more information about error handling in the Table API.

How to Customize Error-Handling Packages

Both the CG$FORM_ERRORS and CG$MESSAGE packages which are the standard error-handling packages provided with Oracle Designer, can be totally customized (following certain rules set by the Forms Generator, of course). You may wish to customize the error-handling packages:

- To modify some or all of the generator messages.
- To add support for the user messages.
- To override how messages are handled and displayed. For example, you may want to provide a "Cause/Action" option for users to learn more about the error and how to correct it.
- To add support for messages in multiple languages.

There are many different ways to customize these packages, depending on your level of expertise with Oracle Developer Forms and PL/SQL. However, the following steps outline how we customized the example application that is provided on the companion CD-ROM:

1. Set *End User Interface → Package used for messaging (MSGSFT)* preference to **CUSTOM$FORM_ERRORS** to use a custom package for error handling. Note that you can rename your own error-handling message differently!
2. Specify a unique identification label as message text in the repository for each of the user messages you want to externalize. The message label does not have to be a number. If you do choose to use numbers, do not use numbers between 1 and 100, because they are reserved for Forms Generator messages.

TIP

Naming Conventions for User Messages *We recommend that you group and categorize your messages and choose a unique message prefix for each category. For example, in the example application, we chose DBCR as the prefix for messages about Database Change Requests.*

3. Create a new PL/SQL library for error handling. We don't recommend directly modifying the packages in the standard shipped libraries.

TIP

You can create and generate PL/SQL libraries from Oracle Designer in release 2. You can even attach them to modules via the module network. Try the new Library Generator, you'll like it! For more information, refer to Chapter 23.

4. Copy the CG$FORM_ERRORS package from OFGTEL.PLL and the CG$MESSAGE package from OFGMES.PLL library into the new library.
5. Rename CG$FORM_ERRORS to CUSTOM$FORM_ERRORS and CG$MESSAGE to CUSTOM$MESSAGE.
6. Replace references to CG$MESSAGE in CG$FORM_ERRORS with references to CUSTOM$MESSAGE. However, do not change the names or declarations (arguments, argument data types, etc.) of the PUSH procedure and MSGGETTEXT function, because Forms Generator creates the code to run with these standard definitions. If you modify the arguments, you may get unexpected results.
7. If needed, modify the CUSTOM$FORM_ERRORS and CUSTOM$MESSAGE packages to customize the handling of user error messages. (The example in the section following this procedure shows exactly how to do this.)

8. If you want to modify the text of the standard generator messages, edit the MESS_LIST procedure in the CUSTOM$MESSAGE package. (The example in the section following this procedure shows exactly how to do this).

9. If you want to add other functionality, such as providing Cause/Action options, edit the CUSTOM$FORM_ERRORS procedure. However, do not the change the definitions of the PUSH and MSGGETTEXT routines, because Forms Generator creates code to run with these standard definitions.

10. Attach this new PL/SQL library to your template form.

11. Generate and run the form.

As you can tell from the example, you are not restricted to only using the standard CG$FORM_ERRORS package to handle errors. You can build your own custom package and specify that package instead of the CG$FORM_ERRORS. However, your custom package must contain a procedure named PUSH and a function named MSGGETTEXT with similar functionality. You must also follow the naming conventions and parameter requirements (as defined in the standard CG$FORM_ERRORS package) when building your customized package.

Example of Adding User Message Handling

If you want to add the handling of user messages to your standard error-handling routine, you have two choices:

- Modify the PUSH procedure in the CUSTOM$FORM_ERRORS package (copied from the standard CG$FORM_ERRORS package) to add code to handle user error messages.
- Modify the GET_MESSAGE procedure in the CUSTOM$MESSAGE package (copied from the standard CG$MESSAGE package) to append the user messages to the list of generator messages.

We will show you examples of each method.

In the following listing, we modified the PUSH procedure to handle the custom errors:

```
procedure push(msg      in varchar2,
               error    in varchar2 default 'I',
               msg_type in varchar2 default '',
               msgid    in integer  default 0,
               loc      in varchar2 default '')
is
  msg_string   varchar2(1000) := msg;
  . . . .
begin
-- Customized Code Start
if msgid = '0' then
   if msg = 'DBCR-0001' then
      msg_string = 'DBCR Numbers between 1 and 2000 are reserved
      for system use. Please re-enter, or query to edit.;
   elsif msg = 'DBCR-0002' then
     . . . .
   else
    null;
   end if;
-- Customized Code End
/* select the alert to use from the template form */
/* according to the value in errt                 */
if (error  = 'F')
then
  alert_is   := find_alert('CFG_SYSTEM_ERROR');
  msg_string := 'Fatal Error: '||msg_string;
elsif (error  = 'E')
then
  alert_is := find_alert('CFG_ERROR');
  msg_string := 'Error: '||msg_string;
elsif (error = 'W')
then
  alert_is := find_alert('CFG_WARNING_A');
  msg_string := 'Warning: '||msg_string;
elsif (error  = 'I')
then
  alert_is := find_alert('CFG_INFORMATION');
  msg_string := 'Information: '||msg_string;
end if;

if (error IN ('F','E','W','I'))
and (not id_null(alert_is))
then
  set_alert_property(alert_is, ALERT_MESSAGE_TEXT, msg_string );
```

```
  alert_button := show_alert(alert_is);
else
  message(msg_string);
end if;
end;
```

In the next example, we modified the GET_MESSAGE procedure instead of the PUSH procedure:

```
procedure get_message
(msgno  in     varchar2
,msg    in out varchar2
,param1 in     varchar2 default ''
,param2 in     varchar2 default '
,param3 in     varchar2 default ''
,param4 in     varchar2 default '')
IS
  . . . . .
BEGIN

-- Standard Code
-- mess_list(msgno, msg);
-- Customized Code Start
if msgno = '0' then
   if msg = 'DBCR-0001' then
      msg = 'DBCR Numbers between 1 and 2000 are reserved for
system use. Please re-enter, or query to edit.;
   elsif msg = 'DBCR-0002' then
     . . . .
   else
     null;
   end if;
-- Customized Code End
. . . . . .
. . . . . .
END; /* get_message */
```

As we mentioned above, there are quite a few different ways to customize message-handling routines and you are not limited to the examples we have given. For example, you can even create your own GET_MESSAGE procedure.

Example of Customizing the Standard Message Text

The following listing shows how to modify the standard message that is used by the generators and replace it with your own custom message.

```
procedure mess_list(msgno  in  varchar2,str    out varchar2) IS
BEGIN
  if (msgno =  '3') then
      -- OLD MESSAGE str := 'No row in table %s';
      -- NEW MESSAGE
      str := 'Unable to find a row in the lookup table %s';
  elsif (msgno = '4') then
  . . . . . .
  . . . . . .
end if;
END; /* mess_list */
```

Error-Handling Options: Externalizing Messages in Database Tables

Although externalizing messages in PL/SQL libraries is great improvement over hard-coded messages in generated forms, there is still a minor problem: when messages change (adding new messages, modifying the message text to correct a typo, etc.), you need to modify the *libraries* and redistribute them. Modifying a library even for a small typo does not sound very efficient.

However, there is yet another way to handle messages: storing messages in database tables. Rather than hard-coding messages in library routines, messages can be stored in a message table and dynamically read from the table. There can even be a user-friendly front-end to maintain messages.

The following example shows you how you can externalize messages in database tables:

1. First, create a table APPLICATION_MESSAGES to store messages. The table must have at least two columns: MESSAGE_ID and MESSAGE_TEXT. However, you can add more columns such as MESSAGE_SEVERITY, MESSAGE_CAUSE, and ACTION_TO_TAKE. Messages will be uniquely identified by the MESSAGE_ID (or message label).

NOTE

You are not limited to a single table to build your messaging system. You can design a very sophisticated system with several tables if your needs dictate so. The idea is to read messages from the database rather than hard-coding in PLL libraries.

2. Create necessary module(s) to maintain messages in the message table.
3. Insert messages into the message table. Make sure that the message id matches what you have entered in the repository.
4. Modify the error-message handling routines (PUSH and/or GET_MESSAGE procedures in the CG$FORM_ERRORS package) to read the messages from the message table. The following is an example of how you can customize the MESSAGE procedure. In this example, we have used a custom function CUSTOM$GET_MESSAGE_DB to read the messages from the database table:

```
procedure get_message
(msgno  in     varchar2
,msg    in out varchar2
,param1 in     varchar2 default ''
,param2 in     varchar2 default '
,param3 in     varchar2 default ''
,param4 in     varchar2 default '')
IS
  . . . . .
BEGIN

-- Standard Code
-- mess_list(msgno, msg);
-- Customized Code Start
if msgno = '0' then
   msg = CUSTOM$GET_MESSAGE_DB(msg);
end if;
-- Customized Code End
. . . . . .
. . . . . .
END; /* get_message */

function CUSTOM$GET_MESSAGE_DB (pin_message_id in varchar2)
return varchar2 is
  cursor c_msg (pin_msg_id varchar2)
  select MESSAGE_TEXT
    from APPLICATION_MESSAGES
   where MESSAGE_ID = pin_msg_id;
  cr_msg c_msg%rowtype;
BEGIN
  open  c_msg(pin_message_id);
  Fetch c_msg into cr_msg;
```

```
    If c_msg%notfound then
      return('Unable to find the message (ID =
'||pin_message_id||').');
    else
      return(cr_msg.MESSAGE_TEXT);
  end if;
  END; /* CUSTOM$GET_MESSAGE_DB */
```

As you can see from the example, storing messages in database offers you a lot of flexibility. On the other hand, there is a cost associated with it: every time a message needs to be displayed, the message needs to be read from the database!

Comparison of Error-Handling Options

As we have discussed, there are many different ways of handling error and warning messages raised by a system. The following table compares these different options and highlights the advantages and the disadvantages of each option:

Error-Handling Method	Advantages	Disadvantages
Forms Generator Default (displaying messages in message area)	An easy-to-use method.	Messages are hard to read due to the small font used; they don't draw attention. Messages are hard-coded in forms. If the error message changes, the forms have to be either generated again or manually edited. Error message text length is limited to 70 characters in the repository. Generator messages cannot be modified.

Error-Handling Method	Advantages	Disadvantages
Displaying messages as alerts	Messages are displayed in alert boxes and are easier to read. An icon representing the level of severity of the message can also be displayed along with the message text. Users can interact with alert boxes and choose one of the available actions.	Messages are hard-coded in forms. If the error message changes, the forms have to be either generated again or manually edited. Error message text length is limited to 70 characters in the repository. Generator messages cannot be modified.
Externalizing messages in PL/SQL libraries	Messages are not hard-coded in forms. Forms don't have to be generated again when error messages change. Generator messages can be modified. Multilingual messages can be supported.	When error messages change, new libraries must be distributed. Generator messages can be modified. If messages are displayed using alert boxes, a maximum of 200 characters can be displayed at a time.
Externalizing messages in database table(s)	The most flexible method. Maintenance of messages is very easy, and there's no need to distribute new libraries. There is no limit on the message text length, and the possible cause(s), and action(s) can be displayed along with the error text.	Complex. Messages must be read from the database, and this may cause some performance problems. May require a custom form to display error messages providing additional information about messages, and include links to the user documentation.

Error-Handling Troubleshooting Guide

Problem	Resolution
I have externalized error messages, but when I run the form I am getting messages like "Error: 125."	You have probably not completed the process. You need to add the message texts that correspond to your message number into the error-handling routine. Please refer to step 7 in the "How to Customize Error-Handling Packages" section
I have externalized error messages, but my messages are being truncated.	There is a limit of 1,000 characters for the message string in the PUSH procedure. Increase it to 2,000, which is the maximum that can be handled in alerts, or try using a custom form.

CHAPTER 17

Other Standard Functionality

In this chapter, we will show you how you can generate some of the standard functionality supported by the Forms Generator that was not covered in the previous three chapters. We will also highlight some of the current limitations of the Forms Generator and possible workarounds for these limitations. In addition, wherever applicable, we will provide a troubleshooting section that will help you solve some of the most common problems encountered when implementing the standard functionality.

The following topics will be covered in this chapter:

- Block synchronization
- Change history columns
- Table journaling
- Autogenerated sequence numbers
- Sequence within parent columns
- Derived columns

Block Synchronization

Block synchronization is the coordination of master and detail blocks in forms so that they display consistent data. In a master/detail relationship, you want the detail block to display records for the current record in the master block.

Block synchronization seems very simple. However, both Oracle Developer and Oracle Designer give us a few options to customize the behavior of master/detail block synchronization. These options are tightly related, and they can be confusing at times. In this section, we will cover the block synchronization features in Oracle Designer in detail, and hopefully clear some of the issues that can confuse people.

Block Synchronization in Oracle Developer Forms

When a master/detail form is generated from Oracle Designer, the links between master and detail module components become relation objects in the generated form. In Form Builder, each relation object has two important properties:

- *Deferred* Specifies whether the coordination should be immediate or deferred
- *Automatic Query* Specifies whether the detail block(s) should be queried automatically

Table 17-1 shows the valid settings for the *Deferred* and *Automatic Query* properties of a master/detail relationship object in Form Builder.

A coordination-causing event is any event that causes the current record in a master block to change. It could be a next or previous record operation, an enter query, or a clear record operation in the master block. Once the current record in master block changes, detail blocks have to be refreshed to display consistent data.

Block Synchronization in Oracle Designer

In Oracle Designer, block synchronization is controlled by some template objects as well as by some Form Generator preferences. When a form is

Deferred	Automatic Query	Description
No	Ignored	The default setting. When a coordination-causing event occurs in the master block, the detail records are fetched immediately.
Yes	Yes	When a coordination-causing event occurs, Form Builder defers fetching the associated detail records until the operator navigates to the detail block.
Yes	No	When a coordination-causing event occurs, Form Builder defers fetching the associated detail records until the operator navigates to the detail block and explicitly executes a query.

TABLE 17-1. *Master/Detail Block Coordination in Oracle Developer Forms*

generated from Oracle Designer, the block synchronization between master/detail blocks will be immediate and automatic, that is, the detail blocks are queried immediately and automatically (Form Builder default). However, this may be less than desirable in some situations. For example, if the detail block is not on the same page or pop-up as the master block, there is no reason to query detail records and incur the extra network traffic. It would be much more efficient if the query of details on separate pages could be deferred until the user navigated to it. An even better solution would be if the user could control it.

Block Synchronization Modes

Before we discuss the block synchronization features, we have to look at some of the block synchronization modes supported by the Form Generator. Table 17-2 lists the block synchronization modes that can be generated from Oracle Designer.

Mode	Description
A	**Always query details when the master changes.** When the record displayed in any given block is changed, all its detail blocks are automatically cleared. Those detail blocks that are currently displayed and within the query scope are requeried. When a block is cleared, all its detail blocks are also cleared.
E	**Query details on entry to the detail block.** Upon initial entry to a block that is a detail of another block, a query is automatically performed. However, if no rows are returned and the block is navigated to again, the query is not repeated (i.e., users must manually requery the detail blocks).
N	**Never query details automatically.** When the record displayed in any given block is changed, all its detail blocks are automatically cleared but not requeried (users must manually query the detail blocks).

TABLE 17-2. *Block Synchronization Modes*

By default, Form Generator creates code to always query detail blocks when the master record changes (Mode A).

Allowing User to Toggle Synchronization Mode

The *End User Interface → Allow user to toggle block synchronization mode (BSCHMD)* preference allows users to change block synchronization mode when they are running the form. If this preference is set to **Yes**, Form Generator creates code that allows the user to switch between two distinct block synchronization modes by using the [Block Menu] function either via the keyboard, the menu, or the toolbar (block synchronization toggle).

You can even define which block synchronization modes are to be used when the toggle is in the ON or OFF position by setting the following preferences:

- *End User Interface → Type of block synchronization when ON (BSMON).* This preference specifies the block synchronization mode when the block synchronization toggle is in the ON position. This preference can be set to any of the valid block synchronization modes listed in Table 17-2.
- *End User Interface → Type of block synchronization when OFF (BSMOFF).* This preference specifies the block synchronization mode when the block synchronization toggle is in the OFF position. This preference can be set to any of the valid block synchronization modes listed in Table 17-2.

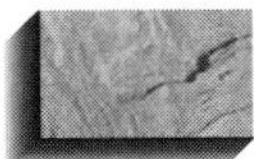

CAUTION

It is possible to set both of these preferences to the same synchronization mode. However, if you do, the block synchronization toggle does not do anything at all and is, therefore, useless. You should always make sure that the two preferences are set to different values in order to achieve the toggle effect.

The initial block synchronization mode upon entry to the form is also specified by the *End User Interface → Type of block synchronization when*

ON (BSMON) preference. However, when a form is called by another form, the initial mode is inherited from the calling form.

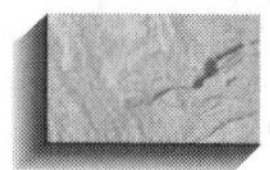

CAUTION

Allowing users to change the query mode is a controversial issue. *Some people think that controlling the synchronization mode is a complex task that end users don't need. Others say that power users like being in control of how the coordination occurs. Your decision of whether to allow users to change the block synchronization mode should be based on how much data is processed through your application and the sophistication of your user population.*

Options for Displaying Block Synchronization Mode

If you are going to allow users to change the block synchronization mode at run time, you should also include some sort of an indicator to help identify the current block synchronization mode. Form Generator provides us with a few options to display the current block synchronization mode and to indicate when it changes:

- Explicitly, by displaying text in a generated text item to indicate the current synchronization mode
- Explicitly, by displaying a message text to indicate changes of synchronization mode
- Implicitly, by relying on the appearance of the item that users use (e.g., a checkbox) to toggle between modes

The Query-Mode Indicator Generator Item: CG$QI

Form Generator recognizes a special generator item in your template forms called CG$QI. Although CG$QI may be referred to as a query-mode indicator, it can be an indicator or a toggle or both, depending on the GUI type of the CG$QI item. If the CG$QI is a text item, the generated item would be a query-mode indicator displaying the current block synchronization mode (ON or OFF position). If the CG$QI is a pushbutton, the generated item would be a query-mode toggle to switch the block synchronization mode from ON position to OFF position. If the CG$QI is a checkbox, the generated item acts as both a toggle and an indicator.

You can have all three of these block synchronization toggles/indicators (a text item, a checkbox, and a button) in your forms if you want to (though a checkbox seems to be the best choice). Figure 17-1 shows a form with examples of all three block synchronization toggles/indicators.

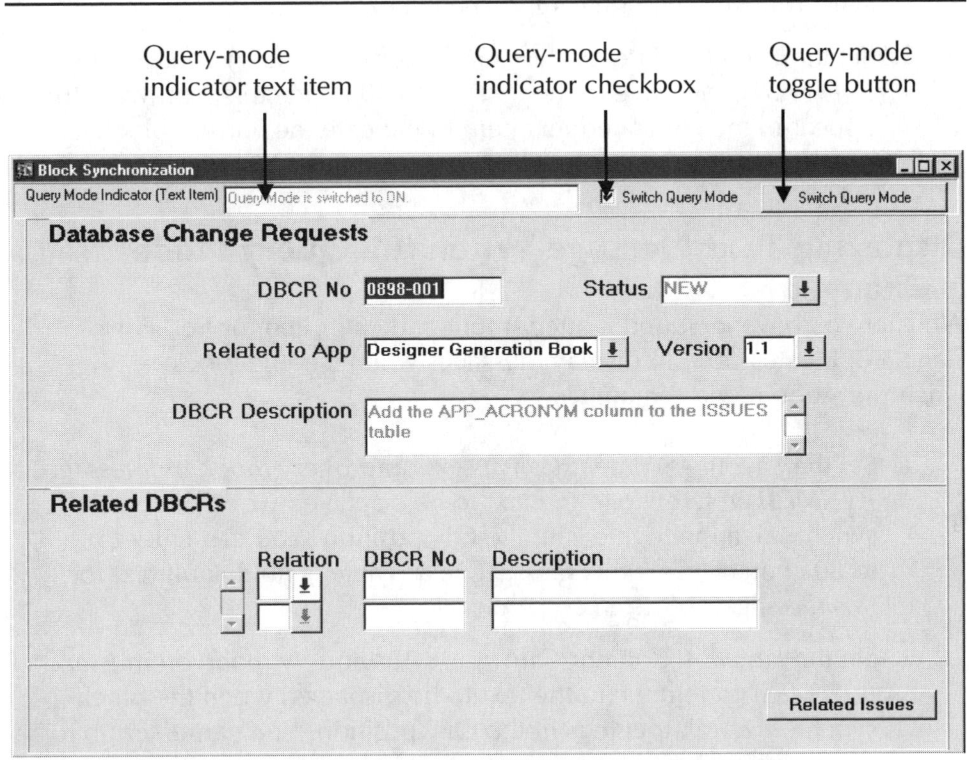

FIGURE 17-1. *Block synchronization mode toggles and indicators*

Displaying Query Mode in a Text Item

You can use the following procedure to generate a text item to display block synchronization mode:

1. Create a text item on a header or footer canvas (e.g., CG$HEADER) in the template form, and name the item CG$QI. This has to be a text item, not a display item. For more information about customizing template forms, please refer to Chapter 22.
2. Set the *End User Interface → ON message in query-mode field (ONFLD)* preference to the text (up to 80 characters) you want to appear in the generated text item to indicate the current block synchronization mode is ON. The default is "**-AQ-**".
3. Set the *End User Interface → OFF message in query-mode field (OFFFLD)* preference to the text (up to 80 characters) you want to appear in the generated text item to indicate the current block synchronization mode is ON. The default is "**- -**".

Displaying Text Message When the Query Mode Is Changed

Whether you have included a query-mode indicator item or not, Form Generator creates code to display messages whenever the block synchronization mode is changed:

1. Set the *Layout – Content Canvas → Auto-query mode on message (ONMES)* preference to the text to be displayed when the block synchronization toggle is in the ON position. You can enter up to 80 characters for this message text. There is no default text for this message.
2. Set the *Layout – Content Canvas → Auto-query mode off message (OFFMES)* preference to the text to be displayed when the block synchronization toggle is in the OFF position. You can enter up to 80 characters for this message text. The default text for this message is "Auto-query mode off."

Generating a Toggle to Allow Users to Switch Between Block Synchronization Modes

You can use the following procedure to generate a GUI item to toggle block synchronization mode:

1. Create a generator item of type Button or Checkbox on a header or footer canvas (e.g., CG$HEADER) in the template form, and name the item CG$QI. If you are going to create both, name the second item CG$QI2. For more information about customizing the template forms, please refer to Chapter 22.

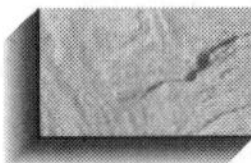

TIP
Unfortunately the standard object library does not contain a suitable source object for CG$QI. But a few examples of CG$QI items are included in the expert template OFGEXPT.FMB (<oracle_home>\cgenf50\admin). You may need to resize the CG$QI object after you copy it, due to the differences in the character cell sizes of the OFGEXPT.FMB and your template form. This template form contains many other examples of generator items, some of which may not be recommended for use in release 2. Please refer to Chapter 22 for more information.

2. Set the *End User Interface* → *Allow user to toggle block synchronization mode (BSCHMD)* preference to **Yes**.
3. Set the *End User Interface* → *Type of block synchronization when ON (BSMON)* preference to specify the mode when the block synchronization toggle is in the ON position. Table 17-2 shows a list of valid values and their descriptions.
4. Set the *End User Interface* → *Type of block synchronization when OFF (BSMOFF)* preference to specify the mode when the block synchronization toggle is in the OFF position. Make sure that the

OFF mode is different from the ON mode setting, otherwise you will not get the toggle effect. Table 17-2 shows a list of valid values and their descriptions.

5. Generate the form.

Changing the Appearance of a Block Synchronization Toggle GUI Item

When a checkbox is used as a query-mode toggle, it also acts like a query-mode indicator item. Users check it on or off to switch between the two distinct query modes, and the checkbox always indicates the current query-mode. For example, when the checkbox is checked, it means that the toggle is ON position.

NOTE
If block synchronization is not required in the generated form, block synchronization has been turned off, or the End User Interface → Allow user to toggle block synchronization mode (BSCHMD) *preference is set to* ***No****, the query mode items are still generated in the application, but they will be disabled (dimmed or grayed-out) during runtime.*

Specifying the Query Scope

When the current block synchronization mode is set to **Always Query Details**, detail blocks are requeried whenever the master changes. However, this may be less than desirable in some situations. For example, if the detail block is not on the same page or pop-up as the master block, there is no reason to query detail records and incur extra network traffic. It would be much better if the query of details on separate pages could be deferred until they are navigated to.

The *End User Interface → Block synchronization - co-ordination scope (BSCSCP)* preference allows you to specify the scope of the query operation for displayed detail blocks. The scope of the query operation can be the entire form, or it can be limited to blocks in the current window or on the current canvas:

(BSCSCP) Preference Setting	Description of Query Scope
P	Blocks displayed on the current canvas (best performance)
W	Blocks displayed in the current window
F	Blocks displayed in the current form (default behavior)

However, this is only applicable when the form is running in auto-query mode, because this preference specifies which blocks will be queried immediately. If the block synchronization is always deferred (Block synchronization mode = N), then the detail blocks will not be queried, even if they are on the same window or canvas.

Query Blocks on Entry to New Canvas

When the current block synchronization mode is Always Query Details and the query scope is Current Canvas or Current Window (e.g., *End User Interface → Block synchronization - co-ordination scope (BSCSCP)* preference is set to P or W), you can specify whether a block on a new canvas is queried on entry to that canvas using the *End User Interface → Query block on entry to new canvas (BSQENP)* preference. If this preference is set to **Yes**, an automatic query is performed when the cursor enters a detail block on a new canvas.

Block Synchronization Example

In this example, we will use the module shown in Figure 17-2. This module contains a parent and two child blocks, and one of the child blocks is on a stacked canvas. In addition, a query-mode indicator/toggle is available through the template form to allow users control the block synchronization mode.

By default, block synchronization is not immediate and automatic (detail blocks are not immediately and automatically queried) in generated forms.

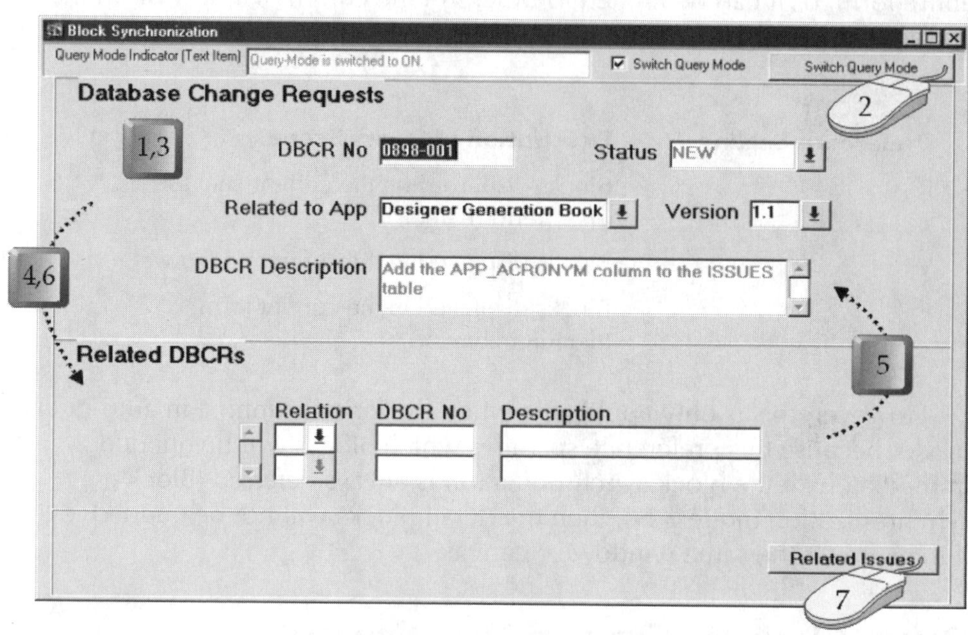

FIGURE 17-2. *Module diagram for the module used in block synchronization example*

However, in this example, we want to show you how you can control the master/detail synchronization in generated forms by setting the following preferences:

Navigation Preferences (Module Level)	Setting
End User Interface → Allow user to toggle block synchronization mode (BSCHMD)	**Yes.**
End User Interface → Type of block synchronization when ON (BSMON)	Always query details when the master changes.
End User Interface → Type of block synchronization when OFF (BSMOFF)	Query details on entry to the detail.

Navigation Preferences (Module Level)	Setting
End User Interface → ON message in query-mode field (ONFLD)	Auto-query mode is switched ON.
End User Interface → OFF message in query-mode field (OFFFLD)	Auto-query mode is switched OFF.
End User Interface → Block synchronization - co-ordination scope (BSCSCP)	Current Canvas.
End User Interface → Query block on entry to new canvas (BSQENP)	**Yes**.

The following table summarizes the behavior of the generated form under different cursor management options:

	User Action	Form Behavior
1	[Execute Query] in the *Database Change Requests* block.	Both the *Database Change Requests* and the *Related DBCR* blocks are queried, because the ON mode is set to always query and query scope in current canvas. The *Related Issues* block, on a separate canvas, is not queried yet.
2	[Mouse Click] on the Switch Query Mode checkbox to switch the block synchronization mode to OFF.	Auto-query mode off message is displayed on the message line. The Switch Query Mode checkbox is checked off, and Query Mode is switched to OFF. Text is displayed in the Query Mode Indicator (Text Item).
3	[Execute Query] in the *Database Change Requests* block.	The *Database Change Requests* block is queried. The *Related DBCR* block is not queried, because the synchronization mode is set to OFF. The *Related Issues* block, on a separate canvas is not queried yet.
4	[Next Block] in the *Database Change Requests* block and [Execute Query] in the *Related DBCRs* block.	The *Related DBCRs* block is manually queried and displays detail records for the first master record.

	User Action	Form Behavior
5	[Previous Block] in the *Related DBCRs block* and [Next Record] in the *Database Change Requests* block.	Navigates to the master block and fetches the second master record. The *Related DBCRs* block is not refreshed and still displays the child records for the first master record.
6	[Next Block] in the *Database Change Requests* block.	Navigates to the *Related DBCRs* block and execute query immediately to refresh the block to synchronize with master because the OFF mode is set to Query details on entry to the detail block.
7	[Mouse Click] on the *Related Issues* button.	Navigates to the *Related Issues* block on another stacked canvas, and executes query immediately to synchronize with master because the *End User Interface → Query block on entry to new canvas (BSQENP)* preference is set to **Yes**.

Block Synchronization Troubleshooting Guide

Problem	Resolution
I have set the *End User Interface → Query block on entry to new canvas (BSQENP)* preference to **Yes**, but it does not seem to be working.	Make sure that the *End User Interface → Allow user to toggle block synchronization mode (BSCHMD)* is set to **Yes** and your current block synchronization mode is set to Always Query Details before you navigate to a new canvas.

Other Generated Functionality

This section will cover other types of functionality that Forms Generator can generate from the repository definitions. Just by setting a few properties in the repository, Forms Generator can create the code to handle many different types of common requirements. Some of the functionality that is easy to generate is

- Change history columns
- Table journaling
- Sequence columns
- Sequence within parent columns
- Derived columns

Client-Side Versus Server-Side Implementation

All of the functionality listed above can be generated in two ways:

- On the client side, the code to implement the functionality is included inside the client applications.
- On the server side, the code to implement the functionality is included on the server side. This is the preferred method, because it is not limited to a certain set of client application. The details of server-side implementations are discussed in great detail in Chapter 9.

In this chapter, we will show you how to implement this functionality in the client applications. Before we start reviewing the details of each functionality, we should consider what happens if the functionality is implemented on the server side as well as the client side.

Coordination of Display of Results Generated on Server Side

The functionality listed at the beginning of this section (with an exception of table journaling) are very similar in nature: a column's value is automatically assigned by the code created by Oracle Designer generators (Form and Server). These columns are also known as *derived columns*. When a derived column's *Server Derived* property is set to **Yes**, the column is to be populated by code in the server. When generating an item based on a server-derived column, Form Generator creates

- A display-only base table item, so that the users can not change it.
- Triggers to requery the database and populate the base table item with the value returned from the derived column. If the module component allows inserts, then a POST-INSERT trigger will be created at the block level. The same applies to an update operation where a POST-UPDATE trigger will be created. There is one restriction, though: the block should not be based on a procedure!

The Form Generator primarily uses the *Server Derived* property of the source column to decide if it should create the code just mentioned. If this property is not set and the column's value is still derived in the server, then the values stored in the database may end up being different than the values that were entered in the client application (form). This will happen if the logic on the server overrides the values coming in from the client (see Figure 17-3). When this does happen, Form Generator displays error messages indicating that another user has changed the record! Although there is still a slim chance that some other user really did change the record, it is usually the server-side logic that has actually changed the record. Therefore, it is crucial to set this property to **Yes** for all the columns derived in the server.

Generating Change History Columns

Change history columns are columns that allow you to record some information about certain operations performed against a row in a table. For example, a column named CREATED_BY_USER can be used to record the user who created the record. Oracle Designer can automatically generate the code required to populate the following four types of change history columns:

- **Date Created** The date on which the record was created
- **Created By** The Oracle username of the user who created the record

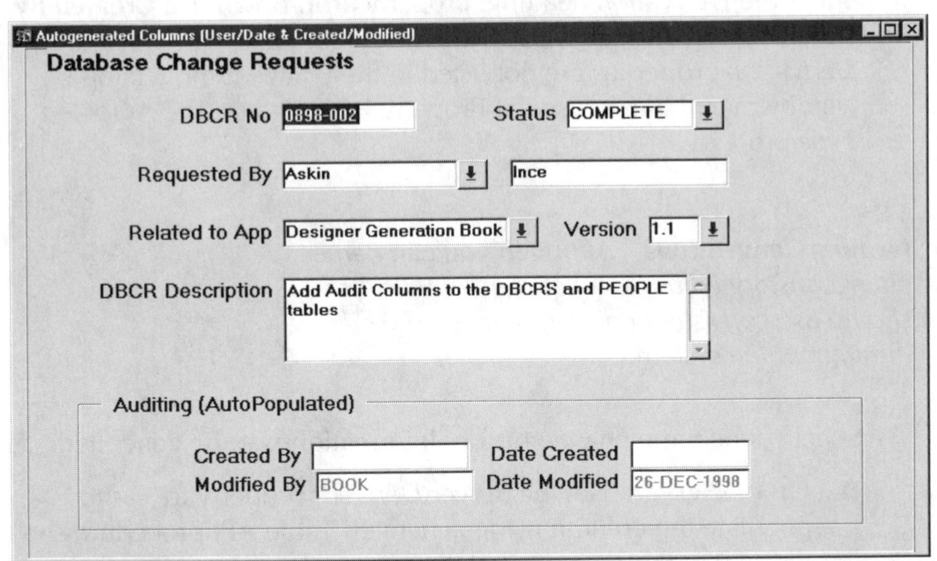

FIGURE 17-3. *Coordination of server-assigned values in forms*

- **Date Modified** The date on which the record was modified
- **Modified By** The Oracle username of the user who modified the record

These change history columns can be populated either on the server or on the client side. Populating these columns on the server is the preferred method, and this can be done by generating the database triggers for a table via the Table API Generator. Please refer to Chapter 9 for detailed information about how to generate Table API.

You can use the following procedure to generate change history columns for a table:

1. In the Design Editor (or Repository Object Navigator), create a new column in which to record change history information. You don't have to create a new item if you have one created already.
2. Specify the type of change information you want to be recorded in the column. Select the proper type from the *AutoGen Type* (listed

under the *Derivation* heading) property drop-down list: **Created By, Date Created, Modified By, Date Modified**. Please note that the *Derivation* properties are not listed in the Edit Column Dialog window; you have to use the Property Palette to set the *AutoGen Type* property.

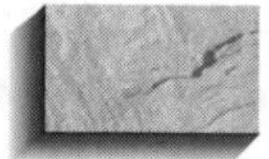

TIP
Naming Conventions *Although you can name change history columns whatever you like, you should use consistent column names throughout the system.*

3. Specify where the change history information is to be generated:
   - **On the Server** Set the *Server Derived?* property to **Yes** to populate the column using generated Table API procedures on the server. For more information about the Table API, please refer to Chapter 9.
   - **On the Client** Set the *Server Derived?* property to **No** if the column is to be populated on the client via PRE-INSERT and PRE-UPDATE triggers, wherever applicable. For example, if the module component allows inserts but not updates, only the PRE-INSERT trigger will be created, and it will include the code to set Date Created and User Created columns.
4. If the *AutoGen Type* property is set to **Modified By** or **Date Modified**, make sure that the *Optional?* property is set to **Yes**, because when a row is created these columns will be null. Similarly, if the *AutoGen Type* property is set to **Created By** or **Date Created**, make sure that the *Optional?* property is set to **No**.
5. Specify whether the generated code should record the time portion of the date information when setting *Date Created* or *Date Modified* columns. In Design Editor, select *Options→Generator Options→General* from the menu to launch the Edit window (shown in Figure 17-4), and check the *Record Time on Change History Columns* checkbox. Note that you will have to do this only once for each application system on each client machine.

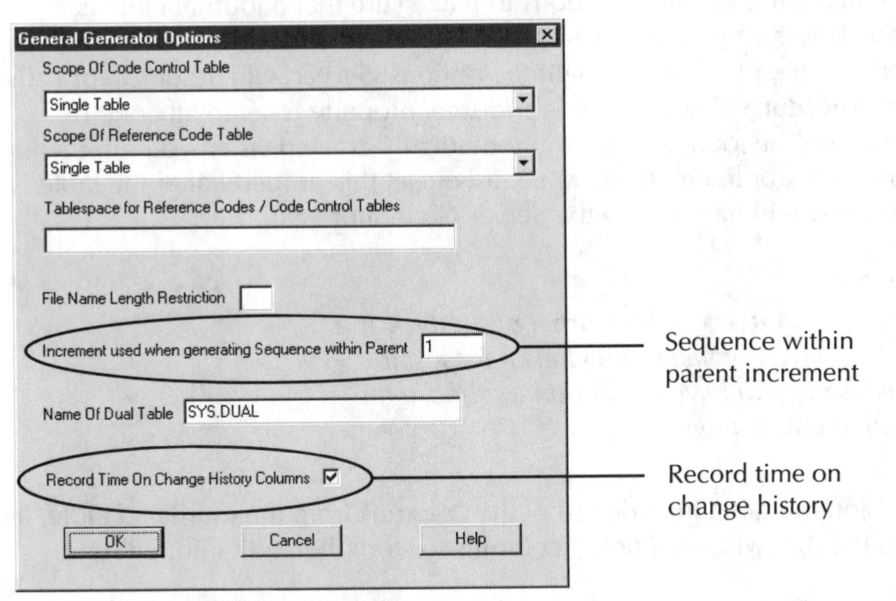

FIGURE 17-4. *General Generator Options Window (Option → Generator Options → General)*

6. Repeat step 1 for each type of change history information you want to record.
7. If the *Server Derived?* Property is set to **Yes**, you must generate the Table API and triggers. If you don't do this, these values will not be derived at all! Because the Form Generator does not create the code to derive them on the client side. For more information about how to generate the Table API, please refer to Chapter 9.

Generating Table Journaling

Table journaling is keeping a log of operations performed on the rows of a database table in another table called a *journal table*. For security and auditing purposes, you may wish to record the name of the user who made the change and what changes were made to the record. Oracle Designer can generate all the code needed to implement this functionality.

The first thing you need to do is to make sure that a journal table is created. This is very easy to do—all you have to do is set the table's *Journal* property to one of the following three options: **Server**, **Client**, or **Client calls server procedure**. Once the table's *Journal* property is set to any one of these values, the journal table is automatically created when you run the Server Generator to create the table. If you set this property after the table is created, you will have to run the Server Generator again.

NOTE
Release 1.3 users *The Journal property was a YES/NO type of flag in previous releases. In Release 2, you have the option to choose the implementation type.*

The journal table includes all of the columns from the journaled table, as well as the following additional columns to store the audit information:

Column Name	Data Type	Notes
JN_OPERATION	CHAR(3) NOT NULL	INS, UPD, DEL
JN_ORACLE_USER	VARCHAR2(30) NOT NULL	Oracle Userid of the person who made the change
JN_DATETIME	DATE NOT NULL	Date and time of the change
JN_NOTES	VARCHAR2(240)	Reason for the change
JN_APPLN	VARCHAR2(30)	Application Name
JN_SESSION	NUMBER(38)	Oracle Session Id

CAUTION
Any table being journaled in this way should have a nonupdateable primary key. Also, be aware that use of the journaling feature has an impact on the performance of the generated form and the sizing of your database.

How to Generate Table Journaling

Oracle Designer offers a few options to implement table journaling:

Journaling Option	Description
Server	Database triggers on the journaled table, and the table API will automatically populate the journal table.
Client	Client-side code maintains the journal table.
Client calls server procedures	Client-side code calls the table API procedures to maintain the journal table.

In order to implement table journaling in the *server,* all you have to do is set the table's *Journal* property to **Server**, and run the Server Generator to create the table and the Table API.

In order to implement table journaling in the *client,* all you have to do is set the table's *Journal* property to **Client** and generate the form.

You can also use the following procedure to implement table journaling using a third option:

1. Set the table's *Journal* property to **Client calls server procedure**.
2. Run the Server Generator to create the table and the Table API.
3. Set the *Journaling → Which operations require note field entry (JNNTRQ)* preference to specify the operations (Insert, Update, Delete) for which users will be able enter comments. For example, if you wish to record journaling only when a record is changed or deleted, set this preference to **UD** (U for update and D for delete). In this case, Form Generator will automatically create a nonbase table item to allow users enter a reason for change (limited to 240 characters).
4. If you have set the *Journaling → Which operations require note field entry (JNNTRQ)* preference, you can decide for which operations users must enter journaling notes. Set the *Journaling → In which operations is note field mandatory (JNNTMD)* preference to one or more of the operations listed in the JNNTRQ preference. This will force users to enter a reason for the change.
5. Set the *Journaling → Record userenv('sessionid') on journal rows (JNSSID)* preference to record auditing session identifiers in the JN_SESSION column of the journal table.
6. Generate the form.

When a table is journaled, the following information is recorded in the journal table:

Operation on Journaled Table	Information Recorded in Journal Table
Create a row	Primary key of the new row and all column values
Update a row	Primary key of the updated row and all column values
Delete a row	Primary key of the deleted row

Generating Sequence-Derived Columns

Sometimes you may want the values of a column to be automatically generated with unique sequence numbers. This functionality is often used to implement surrogate keys for tables. These *auto-generated sequence columns* are usually defined as primary or unique keys or as part of the primary or unique keys. The data type for these columns must be "number."

Oracle Designer can generate unique sequence numbers for columns in one of the following two ways:

- **From an Oracle sequence** When sequence numbers are generated from an Oracle Sequence, there is a possibility that the numbers can be buffered but not used, and this can cause gaps in the sequence of numbers.
- **From a code control sequence** The code control sequences are stored in a table referred to as the code control table, which is created and maintained by Server Generator. Code control sequences guarantee unique numbers that are also sequential. During the table generation, Server Generator creates the code control table and inserts a row in the table to store details about the code control sequence. Each row in the code control table records the sequence name, the next value to be automatically generated during an insert operation, the increment value, and any comment recorded about the sequence in the Repository. For more information, please refer to Chapter 26.

Autogenerated sequence columns can be populated either on the server or on the client. Populating these columns on the server is the preferred method and can be done by generating the database triggers for a table via the Server Generator. However, you can also generate the code to populate these columns in the client by using the following procedure:

1. Create the sequence definition, if you have not done so yet. You can do this by navigating to the Sequence Definition area in the Design Editor (under the Server Model tab).
2. Specify the type of sequence. Set the *Code Control?* property to **Oracle Sequence** or **Code Control Sequence**.
3. Select the DB Admin tab to complete the details of the sequence definition. Edit the sequence definition to define the start value, increment value, maximum value, etc. If this is an Oracle sequence, make sure that proper grants are given to the proper roles and users.

CAUTION

Seek DBA help before creating database objects. *If you are not responsible for creating and maintaining schemas, seek help from your DBA. Do not create any database objects without checking with your DBA first.*

4. Create the autogenerated sequence column, if you have not done so yet.
5. Edit the autogenerated sequence column to specify the sequence Oracle Designer should use when generating values for the column. Select the sequence you created in step 1 from the list for the *Sequence* property.
6. Specify where the sequence values will be generated by setting the *Server derived?* property:
   - **On the server** Set the *Server Derived?* property to **Yes** to populate the column using generated Table API procedures on the server if a value is not provided by the calling application (if the column value is not set in the form).
   - **On the client** Set the *Server Derived?* property to **No** if the column is to be populated on the client. In order for the Form

Generator to create the code to generate the sequence value for the autogenerated column, there must be a bound item in module definition based on that column.

When the Sequence Numbers Are Fetched

If an Oracle Sequence is used, the generated code depends on the value of the *Generate Options → Apply sequence values at commit time (SEQCMT)* preference. If this preference is set to **Yes**, values are assigned on PRE-INSERT; otherwise, the next sequence value is used as the default value for the field. To do this, the item's default value will be set to :SEQUENCE.<sequence_name>.NEXTVAL. The preferred setting is **Yes**, because if the record is not committed, a fetched sequence number will be lost. Note, however, that buffered sequence numbers will be used, even if they are assigned at commit time when the validation fails and the user rolls back the transaction by clearing the record.

Generating Sequence Within Parent Columns

Generating sequence within parent columns is best explained by an example. Say that you have two tables, one named Message Categories, whose primary key column is MSGCAT_CD, and another named Messages. The Messages table is a child to the Message Categories table, and we want the message numbers to be unique within each message category (the composite primary key is composed of two columns: MSGCAT _CD and MESSAGE_NO). In this example, we want the MESSAGE_NO column to be auto-populated with the next unique number within its parent MSGCAT _CD. The idea is that all of the messages that belong to the same category will have the same message category code, and they will have different sequential message numbers. In Oracle Designer terminology, this is known as *sequence within parent.* Figure 17-5 shows an example of a sequence within parent item.

Sequence within parent columns can be populated either on the server or on the client side. Populating these columns on the server is the preferred method, and can be done by generating the database triggers for a table via

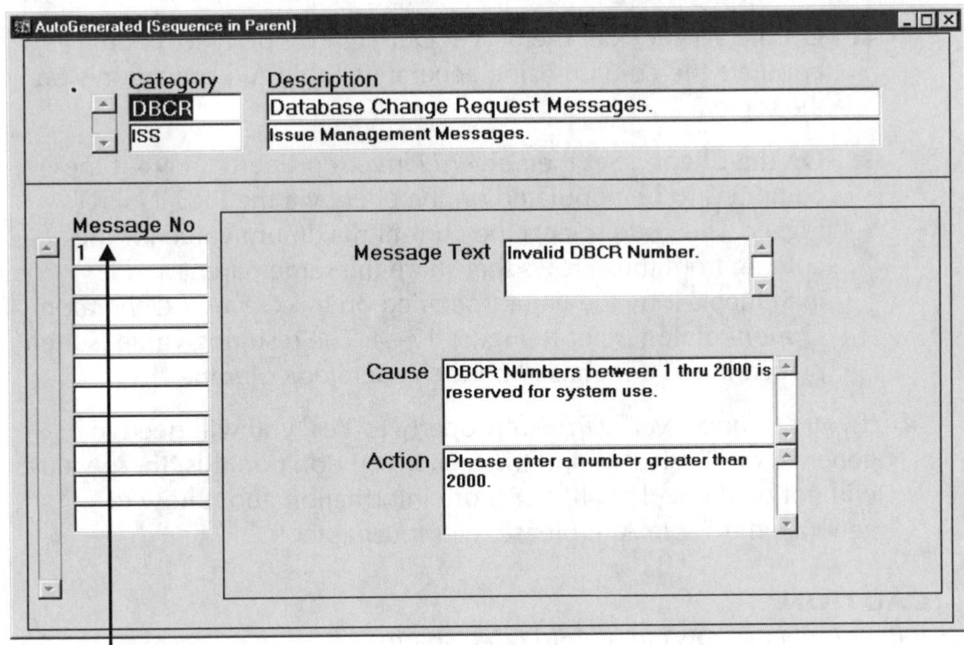

FIGURE 17-5. *Sequence within parent column*

the Server Generator. You can also generate the code to populate sequence within parent columns on the client by using the following procedure:

1. In the Design Editor (or Repository Object Navigator), create a column to hold the generated sequence number, if you have not done so yet. Make sure that the data type is numeric, and that it is part of one of the primary or unique keys.
2. Set the *AutoGen Type* (listed under the *Derivation* heading) property to **Seq In Parent**. The *Derivation* properties are not listed in any of the tabs of the Edit Column Dialog window; you have to use the Property Palette.

3. Specify where the sequence number is to be generated:

   - **On the Server** Set the *Server Derived?* property to **Yes** to populate the column using generated Table API procedures on the server.
   - **On the Client** Set the *Server Derived?* property to **No** if the column is to be populated on the client via the PRE-INSERT trigger. The code selects the current maximum value for the column from those rows that share the same parent and increments it by the value specified on the *General Generator Options* dialog (refer to Figure 17-4). The resulting value is then placed in the item based on the generated column.

4. If you set the *Server Derived?* property to **Yes**, you will need to generate the Table API and triggers. If you don't do this, these values will not be derived at all! For more information about how to generate the Table API, please refer to Chapter 9.

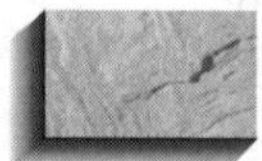

CAUTION

If the number of rows in a child table sharing the same parent increases to hundreds or thousands of rows, you may experience performance problems because the code queries the child table for the maximum number used. Properly built indexes should reduce this problem.

Generating Derived Columns

A derived column is a column whose value is derived from a calculation involving other columns in the same table. To define a derived column in the Repository, enter a SQL expression or PL/SQL function call as the column definition's *Derivation Expression* property.

For example, you might want a column called TOTAL_SALARY in the EMP table to contain an employee's total salary, including commission. To achieve this, you might set the column definition's *Derivation Expression* property to **emp.sal + NVL(emp.comm,0)**. You can also include literals in the expression, for example, **emp.sal + emp.sal * 0.35**.

Derived columns can be populated either on the server or on the client. Populating these columns on the server is the preferred method, and can be done by generating the table API and database triggers for a table via the Server Generator. When derived columns are populated on the client, the derivation calculation is performed in the client application (the form).

You can use the following procedure to generate derived columns into your forms:

1. In the Design Editor (or Repository Object Navigator), create a new column definition for the derived column, if you have not done so yet.
2. Set the column's *Derivation Expression* property to the SQL expression or PL/SQL function call that will populate the column. Table 17-3 summarizes the list of rules to follow when entering column derivation expressions.

Rule	Description
1	Only literals, columns from the same table, and SQL or PL/SQL functions are allowed in the derivation expression. PL/SQL procedures cannot be used in column derivation expressions.
2	If the *Server Derived?* property is set to **Yes**, functions used in the derivation expression must exist in the server. Otherwise functions used in the derivation expression may exist in the server, a template form, a library attached to the template form, or a library attached to the generated form.
3	Do not nest function calls in derivation expressions (e.g., foo1(foo2(foo3()))). Instead, create a single function that contains the multiple function calls, and call that function.
4	Do not include function calls in SQL expressions. For example, the following SQL expression is invalid because it includes a call to the foo function: empno > foo(100).
5	Use Y2K-compliant date formats for date/character string conversions.
6	For those of you who are familiar with earlier versions of Designer/2000, do not prefix calls to PL/SQL functions and procedures using the **COMPLEX**: notation.

TABLE 17-3. *Rules for Entering Column Derivation Expressions*

NOTE
Using Oracle Developer Forms globals in derivation expressions. *You should not use globals in column derivation expressions because Form Generator creates a WHEN-VALIDATE-ITEM trigger to derive the column's value. This type of trigger fires only when a base table item changes. If you use global variables in the derivation expression, the value of the column derivation may not be updated when the global value is changed, and it will then be inaccurate.*

3. Specify the type of derivation expression to be used to derive the column's value by setting its *Derivation Expression Type* property:
   - If the derivation expression is a simple SQL expression, set the *Derivation Expression Type* property to **SQL Expression**.
   - If the derivation expression is a call to a PL/SQL function on the client or the server, set the *Derivation Expression Type* property to **Function Call**.
4. Specify where the derivation is to be performed:
   - **On the Server** Set the *Server Derived?* property to **Yes**, to populate the column using generated Table API procedures on the server, if no value is provided by the calling application.
   - **On the Client** Set the *Server Derived?* property to **No** if the column is to be populated on the client using generated client-side code. Also make sure that the following is true:
     a. The column's *Server Defaulted?* property is set to **No**.
     b. The column does not have a default value.
     c. The column is not of type **LONG RAW**.
     d. The column's *Derivation Expression* does not refer to the column itself.

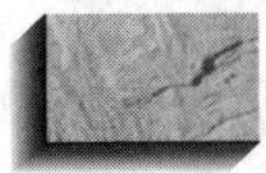

NOTE
You can also enter derivation text against unbound items to define functionality for non-base table items.

5. If you set the *Server Derived* property to **Yes**, make sure to run the Server Generator to create the table API procedures to populate the derived column.

Other Generated Functionality Troubleshooting Guide

Problem	Resolution
When I run my form, I am getting a warning message that says, "Invalid data in derived column."	If a client-derived column's value is changed in the database, you will get this message when the form recalculates the derived value. Make sure that the derived column values are recalculated and updated in the server.
I have changed a column to be server derived but the server is not deriving values.	You need to regenerate the Table API and triggers.
I could not generate a client-derived column.	This is a problem in release 2.1.2. If you don't specify the height for the derived column, the generated item will have a height of 0.001", making it pretty darn difficult to see! Set the *Height* property to 1".
I could not generate my form after enabling the journaling.	Make sure that the journal table(s) are created. If necessary, rerun the Server Generator.

CHAPTER 18

Item Validation and LOV Generation

very business system has some business rules that impose restrictions on the values stored in columns of database tables. These business rules may be enforced in different ways:

- Using the referential integrity rules between tables
- Using check constraints defined against tables
- Using static or dynamic lists of allowable values defined in the client
- In more complex situations, using database triggers

Oracle Designer supports all of these and usually offers more than one alternative for implementing them: in the database server, in the client applications, or in both places.

When these business rules are being validated and enforced, the user interface should help the user by showing the list of values that they can enter. As in the implementation of business rules, there are different ways of providing these lists of values.

In this chapter, we will show you how item and constraint validation works and how you can influence the Form Generator to optimize the validations. We will also show you how to generate lists of values for lookups. We will highlight the limitations and provide you with guidelines and possible workarounds for some of the limitations. Wherever applicable, a troubleshooting section will help you to solve some of the most common problems encountered in generating the functionality mentioned above.

In this chapter, we will review the generation of standard validation code and the lookup generation. The following topics will be discussed:

- Item validation
- Constraint validation
- List of values generation

Item Validation

The business rules that define how a generated system should function also impose restrictions on the values users can enter in the generated items. Although there may be some free-format entry fields in your systems (fields that are not validated or descriptions, for example), many if not most of the items in your system will allow only certain values.

There are many different ways to restrict the values of an item. Sometimes these restrictions might be based on primary, unique, foreign keys, and check constraints. Alternatively, a list of allowable values defined for the column, the domain it uses, or for the module item itself (if it is an unbound item) might restrict the values.

The method used to validate generated items depends on the source of the validation information:

- A list of allowable values
- A single or a list of allowable value ranges
- A constraint (primary, unique, foreign key, or a check constraint)

Again, regardless of the business rule, the validation can be done in the client applications (generated forms), in the database server, or both in the client and the server. In this section, we will focus only on the client-side validation that occurs in the generated forms. For more information about how to enforce business rules in the database, please refer to Part II (including Chapter 9).

NOTE

Constraint terminology *Check constraints defined against table definitions are also known as* table-level check constraints, *because they are defined for the table definitions in the repository. To be consistent with Oracle Designer terminology, we are going to stick to the term* check constraint *rather than* table-level check constraint.

Validating an Item Against a List of Allowable Values

When a list of allowable values is defined against a column (either directly or via domain) or an unbound item, the validation of that item can be done in the following ways:

- Using a GUI item and the default validation rules of Form Builder
- Using a Form Builder LOV associated with the item
- Using a Form Builder trigger

Using a GUI Item and the Default Validation Rules of Form Builder

Some of the GUI item types in Form Builder offer very simple validation options for items validated against a list of values by limiting what the users can enter into the items. For example, a checkbox can be used to force exactly two distinct values against an item (either two non-null values, or a null and a non-null value), as shown in the following illustration. When an item is displayed as a radio group, a pop list, or a text list, users can only enter values that are allowed by the GUI item. They can't even attempt to enter an invalid value, because the GUI item simply will not allow it.

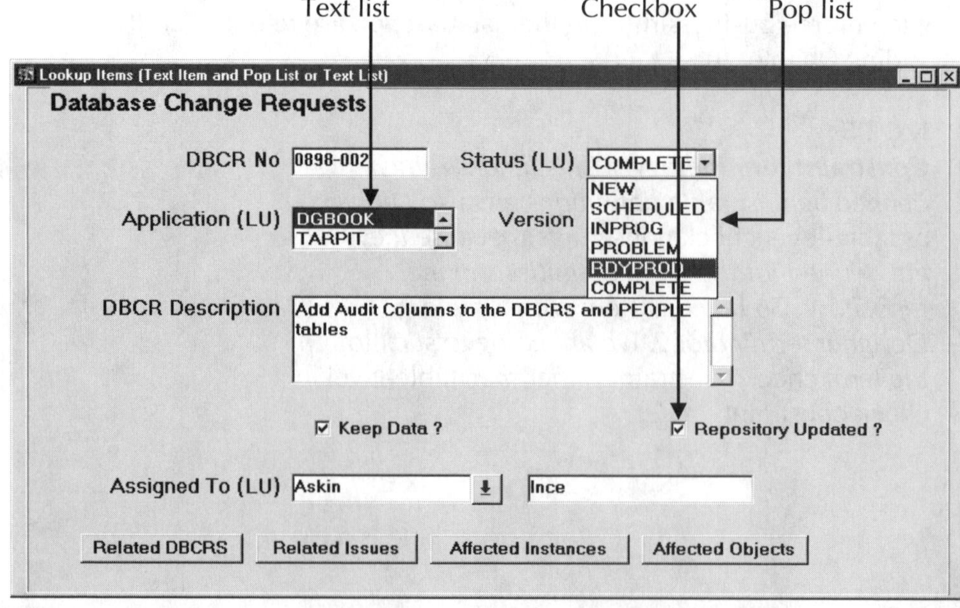

In order to take advantage of the GUI item validations in Form Builder, you have to set the *Display Type* property of the repository item properly.

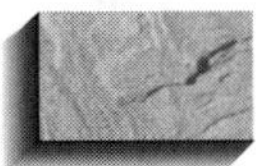

CAUTION
You should only use radio groups or checkboxes for items when the list of valid values will never change. This is because the allowable values for these item display types are physically hard-coded into the forms. If you have to change the allowable values, you will have to generate the form again.

For more information about the GUI item types and for guidelines for using different GUI items, please refer to Chapter 13.

Using a Form Builder LOV to Validate the Item

Another very common method to validate items against a list of allowable values is to use a Form Builder List of Values (LOVs). A Form Builder LOV is a scrollable pop-up window that allows users to select a single value from a list of values. This illustration shows a sample Form Builder LOV.

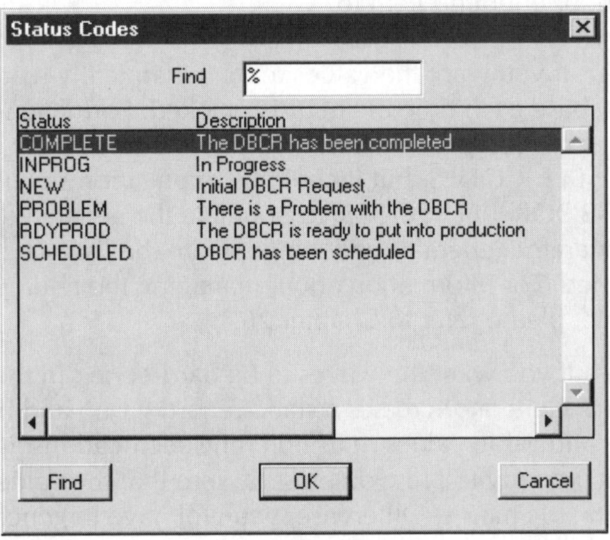

Form Generator can easily generate an LOV for an item and use the generated LOV for validating the item if there is a list of allowable values defined against the item (a source column for a bound item, an associated domain, or an unbound item).

In order to generate and use an LOV for item validation, follow these steps:

1. Create the allowable values for the source column, an associated domain, or an unbound item, if you have not done so. Be sure to check the following:

   - Do not forget to enter the meanings and abbreviations for the allowable values, because they might be displayed in the LOV.
   - Make sure that the allowable values do not include ranges. You can use the Property Palette to view the *Low* and *High* properties of each allowable value.

TIP

Dialogs in Design Editor do not allow you to define ranges for allowable values! You must use the property sheet to do this.

2. Set the *Dynamic List?* property of the source column, associated domain, or unbound item to

   - **Yes** If you want the values to be dynamically read from the database each time the LOV is invoked. Form Generator creates a query-record group based on the reference code table (usually CG_REF_CODES, but it could be application specific, such as DGBOOK_REF_CODES) to populate the generated LOV. Form Generator generates code to populate the lists when the form is started. For information about managing the reference code table, please refer to Chapter 26.
   - **No** If you want the values to be hard-coded in the form. Form Generator creates a static-record group and hard-codes the allowable values in its column specifications. If you set this property to **No**, you must be sure that the values are never going to change. Otherwise, you will have to generate client modules again.

TIP

The Auto-Refresh *property of an LOV object controls when the query to populate the LOV should be re-executed. The default value for* Auto-Refresh *is* ***Yes*** *so that the query is executed each time the LOV is invoked. This ensures that the user sees the latest changes made to lookup codes. However, this will make the LOV run slower. If the codes do not change very often, you may want to set this to* ***No*** *to make the LOV run faster.*

3. Set the *List of Values → Display domain abbreviation in LOV (LOVDAB)* preference to **Yes**, if you want to display abbreviations of the allowable values in the LOV (assuming you have already defined the abbreviations when specifying the allowable values).
4. Set the *List of Values → Display domain meaning in LOV (LOVDMN)* preference to **Yes**, if you want to display meanings of the allowable values in the LOV. You should have defined the meanings when specifying the allowable values.

NOTE

Many of the List of Values preferences are defined at the module or the application system level, with the exception of LOV size and location preferences. Therefore, they affect the entire list of values generated in a form, and all of the LOVs in a form will have to work similarly.

5. If the item you are trying to generate an LOV for is a bound item, set the *Display in LOV?* Property to **Yes** if you want to display the values in the LOV, along with abbreviations and meanings as described in the previous steps.

NOTE
If you don't set the Display in LOV? *property to* ***Yes*** *and don't display the meaning or the abbreviation, Form Generator still generates an LOV object, but it sets LOV column widths to zero and the LOV is not displayed at run time.*

6. Decide whether the generated item is to display the meaning of the allowable value. Set the *Show Meaning* property to

   - **Meaning only** To generate a text item to enter and display the meaning of the allowable value instead of its value. The real item value will be populated into a nondisplayed item. This illustration shows an example in which the data entry is done via the meaning item:

   - **Meaning alongside code** To generate a display-only text item with no prompt and display the meaning of the allowable value beside the generated text item used for entering/displaying the value. Form Generator automatically calculates the width of the generated item based on the longest of meanings defined for the list of allowable values. This illustration shows an example in which the meaning is displayed next to the code value:

   - You may leave this property blank, if you don't want the meaning of the allowable value displayed on the screen.

CAUTION

In release 2.1.2, we have come across a problem. When we set the Show Meaning? *property to* **Meaning Only**, *Form Generator created an item with a height of 0.001 inches. In addition, the generated LOV indicator buttons were too big. As a workaround for this problem, add code to the form startup that sets the height of the item to .25 inches. An even better fix is to add code to your templates that always automatically find and fix these items.*

7. Set the *List of Values → Validate item in LOV (LOVVAL)* preference to **Yes** to use the generated LOV to validate the generated item. Form Generator will set the *Validate from list* property of the generated item to **Yes**, and it will not create validation triggers for the generated item.
8. Set the *List of Values → Use a button to indicate available list of values (LOVBUT)* preference to **Yes** if you want Form Generator to create a push button next to the item to indicate and invoke the LOV. These LOV buttons help to visually identify which items have a list of valid values, but they also use screen real estate.

TIP

Using standard source objects in object libraries and objects in templates, you can influence the generated properties of the LOV indicator buttons. For example, you can change the icon of the LOV buttons. LOV generation is covered in detail later in this chapter in the section "List of Values (LOV) Generation."

9. When generating the LOV functionality, Form Generator creates a native Form Builder LOV object. However, if you wish to call

another form to display the allowable values, you can set the *List of Values → Name of form to display valid values (DVLOVF)* preference to the name of the form that will display the list of values. You may use the standard LOV form OFGLOVF shipped with Oracle Designer or make a copy of the standard and customize it for your specific needs. The following illustration shows an example of the LOV form.

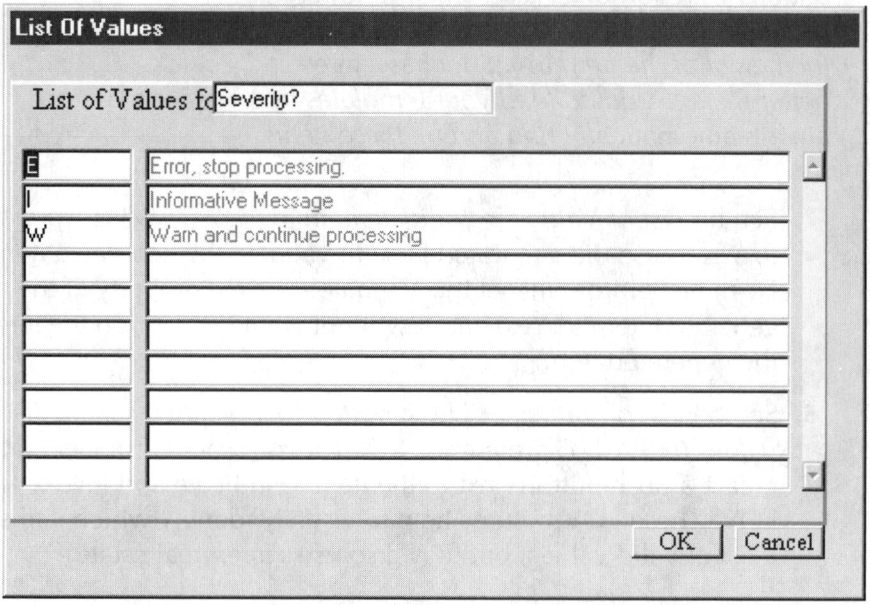

10. Generate the form.

Restrictions When Using an LOV Form to Display Allowable Values

We don't recommend using an LOV form to display allowable values because of the following problems:

- The native Form Builder LOV objects are easier to use.
- The code generated to call LOV forms is less than perfect in release 2.1.2. If you click the Cancel button after the LOV form pops up, you get a forms error message indicating CG$REF_MEANING global does not exist. If you make any changes in the form, you will have to save them before the LOV form is called, and this can be very annoying!

- If you are using *application-specific* reference codes tables, (each application may have its own reference code table), you cannot use the standard LOV form OFGLOVF.FMB. You will have to customize it before using it, because it queries allowable values from the generic CG_REF_CODES table.
- There is no explicit ordering of values in the OFGLOVF.FMB; however, values will be ordered by their *Low Value* property in the native LOVs.
- The LOV form cannot be used for item validation, and Form Generator has to create additional triggers and PL/SQL code.

Validation Using a Form Trigger

Instead of using a GUI item or an LOV to validate generated items, you may want Form Generator to create a WHEN-VALIDATE-ITEM trigger. To do this, set the *List of Values → Validate item in LOV (LOVVAL)* preference to **No**. Form Generator will still generate LOVs, but they will not be used to validate the item. In addition to the WHEN-VALIDATE-ITEM trigger, Form Generator uses the CGDV$REF_CODES package from the OFGTEL library to perform the validation.

Validating an Item Against a List of Allowable Value Ranges

Sometimes an item may need to be validated against a list of allowable value ranges. For example, you could use a range to validate a column that stores percentage values between 0 and 100. It would not be practical to list all the numbers between 0 and 100, and it would not even work if the column allowed decimal values. In cases like this, it is better to use ranges in item validations.

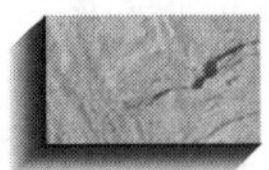

NOTE
Although you can define either single or multiple value ranges (using the Property Palette; dialogs do not allow this) against a column, a domain, or an unbound item usage, Form Generator cannot generate multiple value ranges.

You can decide how item value ranges are validated by setting the *List of Values → Implement single range using field attributes (DVHILO)* preference to one of the following:

- **Yes** To validate the item using the *Low* and *High* properties of the generated item. This is the simplest method, since it does not require any PL/SQL code. However, the values are hard-coded into the form and you will have to generate the form again (or update it by hand) if the ranges change.
- **No** To validate the item using the reference codes table. Furthermore, you can either use a native LOV object or call an LOV form. Form Generator is shipped with a sample LOV form, OFGHLVF, that can be used for valid range lookup. For additional information about using LOV forms to display allowable values, see "Restrictions When Using an LOV Form to Display Allowable Values," earlier in this chapter.

Validating an Item Against a Constraint

An item may also be validated against a constraint (primary, unique, foreign key, or check constraint). Constraints often include multiple columns, and therefore the validation of items against constraints is more involved. In fact, due to its complexity, the constraint validation will be covered more thoroughly in the following section.

Item Validation Generation Troubleshooting Guideline

Problem	Resolution
I cannot define a range for validation using the Edit dialogs.	Use the Property Palette to enter the high value. Once defined, ranges can be edited via dialogs.
I am getting the message, "CGEN-03353 ERROR: Item MSGCAT.NO_OF_MSGS: Multiple ranges, or combination of ranges and discrete values not supported."	Form Generator cannot generate multiple range validations. Moreover, it does not support the combination of a range and discrete values.

Problem	Resolution
How can I control the size of meaning displayed alongside the code?	You cannot. Forms Generator creates an item called MEAN_<base_item_name> during generation and sets its width to the longest of all meanings defined for the item.
Although the item hint indicates that there is an LOV, nothing happens when I press the [List Values] key.	If you are not displaying either the meaning or the abbreviation, make sure that the *Display in LOV?* property of the item is set to **Yes**.
I have changed my allowable values, added new codes, and removed some; but, when I run my form, I don't see any change.	Make sure that the values were not hard-coded in the forms. Check the *Soft List?* property of the source column (it should be set to **Yes** for dynamic lookups), and check the *Display Type?* property of bound/unbound items (it should be set to **Text** for dynamic lookups). In addition, make sure that the reference code table is updated. If needed, regenerate the form.

Constraint Validation

Constraints are the rules that govern the data stored in columns and tables in a database. In Oracle RDBMS, there are four types of constraints:

- Primary key constraints
- Unique key constraints
- Foreign key constraints
- Check constraints

NOTE
In addition to the constraint objects in the database, there may be additional, and usually more complex, business rules validated and buried under the database triggers and procedures/functions called from database triggers.

In addition to the four constraint types listed here, Oracle Designer offers another type of check constraint that can be defined against a column. Using the *Where/Validation Condition* property of a column, you can enter a validation condition to be validated against the column value. This condition is always validated in the client application. The Server Generator does not create a check constraint for this in the database; however, the Table API (called from database triggers) includes code to perform the validation.

Once a constraint is defined in the repository, the next thing to do is to decide *how* and *where* it is going to be enforced. Using the *Validate In* property (*Validation Level* radio group in the Edit Constraint dialog) of a constraint, you can specify where the constraint should be enforced. The following table lists the possible settings for this property:

Setting	Effect
Client only	The code required to perform the validation is created in the client application (form) only. The client application verifies whether the constraint is satisfied before sending the data to the database server. The data is not sent to the server until it passes all validations. Constraint is not validated in the database, leaving a door open for invalid codes.
Server only	The code required to perform the validation is created in the server. The data is validated in the database server without being validated in the client first. If the validation fails, the database server raises an error message to the client. The constraint is not validated until the changes are committed. The validation in the server can be done either declaratively or via database triggers using Table API (see Chapter 9).
Both Client and Server	The code required to perform the validation is created both in the client application and the server side. This means that the validation is done twice: first the client validates the data, and if the data satisfies the constraint, it is sent over to the server. The server then validates it again. This double effort may seem redundant, but it can produce a more user-friendly interface because the user gets immediate feedback. The validation on the server is still required to enforce the validation if the data is entered or updated directly in the database.

Setting	Effect
None	This option is valid only for foreign keys. It can be used to specify that the constraint is not validated either in the client or in the server. This allows you to define foreign keys that can be used only for linking master/detail and master/lookup table usages in module designs. Sometimes, these foreign keys are referred to as *pseudo* or *dummy* foreign keys.

TIP
This is yet another area where you should consider implementing standards. It is usually better to have a consistent method for handling constraints across the whole system in the client, in the server, or both, declaratively or using database triggers.

The *Validate In?* property of constraints can also be overridden by yet another Form Generator preference: The *Generate Options → Where to enforce data integrity (WEDI)* preference can be used to enforce *all* the constraints used in a module either in the (**C**)lient or the (**S**)erver only. The default setting for this preference is **D**, indicating that data integrity rules must be enforced as defined in the *Validate In?* property of each constraint. This preference can only be set at the application or the module level. The main purpose is to support rapid application development by simplifying the process of specifying where each constraint should be validated. If you want to make sure that constraints are always validated in the client, set this preference to **Client**.

When to Validate Constraints

As previously mentioned, there are three possible options for specifying where the constraint validation occurs. Another important consideration is *when* the constraints are validated in the client applications. Form Generator can generate code to validate constraints at the following times:

When to Validate	Effect and Comments
At the item level	Validation occurs as soon as user enters the data. This gives immediate feedback to the user if the constraint is violated.
At the commit time	Validation occurs when the data is committed, before it is sent to the database. This may be more network efficient because all of the validation occurs at once in the client.
Both the item and commit time	This may seem redundant; but, due to the complex interdependencies among items and constraints, a constraint that was satisfied during the item-level validation might become violated after additional data is entered. Otherwise, bad data may be sent to the database in some cases.
None	The constraint is not validated in the form, and all validation is done in the server. This option is not user friendly. Database errors must be trapped properly by the client application.

For each constraint type (primary key, unique key, foreign key, and check constraint), Forms Generator uses a different preference to specify when the validation should be done in the client application. The following table shows a list of these preferences. Each preference allows the same values: (**B**)oth at field and commit level, (**C**)ommit time only, (**F**)ield level only, and (**N**)ever. Each one of these preferences can be set at all possible levels: Application, Table, Constraint, Module Component, and Constraint Usage.

Constraint Type	Form Generator Preference
Primary Key	*Generate Options → When to validate primary keys (VLDTPK)*
Unique Key	*Generate Options → When to validate foreign keys (VLDTUK)*
Foreign Key	*Generate Options → When to validate unique keys (VLDTFK)*
Check Constraint	*Generate Options → When to validate table-level check constraints (VLDTTC)*

By default, validation of constraints with multiple columns will be done when all values are entered for all columns in the constraint. The main reason the validation is deferred until all pieces are entered is to avoid extra network trips to the database. However, if you don't like this behavior, you can set the *Generate Options → Optimize constraint validation (VLDOPT)* preference to **No** so that the generated triggers always check the constraint, regardless of whether all the values have been entered or not. If you decide not to optimize the validation, then you should also decide how to handle the null values in constraints.

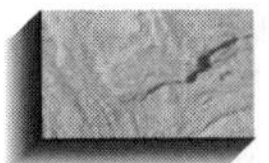

NOTE
The Defer Status property of a constraint specifies whether the validation of the constraint to be deferred in the database server until the transaction is completed. It does not affect the client code generation.

Constraints and Null Values

Many times, a constraint is based on multiple column values, and some of these columns may be null when the constraint is validated in the client application. Regardless of when the constraint is validated, Form Generator needs to know how to treat the null values in constraint validations. Form Generator handles null values for all the *Key Constraints* (primary, unique, and foreign) similarly, but it takes a different approach for the check constraints.

Key Constraints and Null Values

Form Generator uses the *Generate Options → Null is a valid value in key constraints (NIVVKC)* preference to determine how to handle null values in key constraints. An exception to this is the way nulls are handled in the primary keys; since the primary key columns are always mandatory, null values are not allowed in primary keys. This preference specifies whether the Form Generator should treat a null value in any column of the constraint as a valid or an invalid value. The following table summarizes how this preference affects the validation behavior in generated forms:

Setting of NIVVKC	Optionality of Key Constraint	How Null Values Are Treated in Unique and Foreign Key Constraints
Yes. Null is a valid value.	Mandatory	Null is treated as a valid value, but at least one column in the key must be non-null.

Setting of NIVVKC	Optionality of Key Constraint	How Null Values Are Treated in Unique and Foreign Key Constraints
Yes. Null is a valid value.	Optional	Null is treated as a valid value. Alternatively, all columns in the key can be set to null, in which case no validation is performed.
No. Null is not a valid value!	Mandatory	Validation code requires all key columns to be non-null.
	Optional	Validation code requires key columns to be either all null or all non-null.

Check Constraints and Null Values

Forms Generator uses the *Enforce when Null?* property of the check constraint to determine whether a null in any column of the constraint is a valid value or an invalid value. If this preference is set to

- **Yes** The constraint will always be validated as long as at least one of the columns in the constraint is not null. This is the default value.
- **No** The constraint will not be validated if any column of the constraint is null.

How Constraint Validation Works

In order to validate constraints, Form Generator creates triggers and program units in generated forms. Form Generator may also generate code to trap any constraint violation errors, which might be raised by the database server. However, before the Form Generator creates a single line of code, it checks for the existence of certain conditions.

Conditions for Generating Code to Support Primary Key Constraints

To enforce a primary key constraint in the generated form, Form Generator requires at least one of the following conditions to be true:

- The *Validate In* property of the constraint is set to **Client** or **Both**.
- The *Insert?* and/or *Update?* properties of the module component are set to **Yes**.

- The *Insert?* and/or *Update?* properties of at least one of the items in the constraint are set to **Yes**.
- There is an item based on every column in the primary key.

However, there are some exceptions:

- **Exception 1** If a primary key constraint includes an automatically assigned column (such as a column based on a sequence or sequence in parent columns), the Form Generator does not generate the code to validate it, because the generated item will not be enterable.
- **Exception 2** If the module component is updateable but not insertable, Form Generator does not generate the code for validation unless one or more of the items in the primary key are updateable. For more information about updateable primary keys, please refer to the *Referential Integrity Rules* topic in the online help.
- **Exception 3** Form Generator will generate PL/SQL code to trap the server-side errors, if the *Insert?* and/or *Update?* properties of the module component are set to **Yes**.

Details of Primary Key Constraint Validation by Form

Form Generator creates a procedure for each primary key constraint it validates to check the uniqueness of the primary key columns. The name of the procedure will be in the format of CGUV$CHK_<primary_key_constraint_name>, and the name will be truncated to 30 characters.

The primary key validation procedure is then called from the item- and/or block-level triggers. Assuming that the *Validate In* property of the primary key constraint is set to **Client** or **Both Client and Server**, Form Generator may create the PL/SQL code for primary key validation in the following triggers:

Trigger	Generated If...
WHEN-VALIDATE-ITEM (item)	1. The primary key is validated at item level, *Generate Options → When to validate primary keys (VLDTPK)* is set to **F** or **B**. 2. The item's *Insert?* property is set to **Yes**. The generated trigger will call the primary key validation procedure.

Trigger	Generated If...
PRE-INSERT (block)	1. The primary key is validated at commit time, *Generate Options → When to validate primary keys (VLDTPK)* is set to **C** or **B**. 2. The module component's *Insert?* property is set to **Yes**. The generated trigger will call the primary key validation procedure.
PRE-UPDATE (block)	1. The primary key is validated at commit time, *Generate Options → When to validate primary keys (VLDTPK)* is set to **C** or **B**. 2. The module component's *Update?* property is set to **Yes**. 3. The *Update?* properties of the constraint, the module component, and one of the key items are set to **Yes**. There are, however, some referential integrity issues. A primary key can only be updated if there are no child rows in referencing tables, or if the foreign key constraints on these tables are validated in the client and their *Update Rule?* properties are set to **Cascades** or **Defaults** or **Nullifies**. The generated trigger will call the primary key validation procedure to check for uniqueness and another procedure to do the cascade update of the child rows.
PRE-DELETE (block)	1. The primary key is validated at commit time, *Generate Options → When to validate primary keys (VLDTPK)* is set to **C** or **B**. 2. The module component's *Delete?* property is set to **Yes**. There are, however, some referential integrity issues. A row can only be deleted if there are no child rows in referencing tables, or if the foreign key constraints on these tables are validated in the client and their *Delete Rule?* properties are set to **Cascades** or **Defaults** or **Nullifies**. The generated trigger will call a procedure to cascade delete the child rows.
KEY-DELREC (block)	Same rules listed for the PRE-DELETE (block) trigger. Generated trigger will check to see if there are any child rows and either error out if there are any, or cascade delete the child rows depending on how the deletes are handled by the referencing foreign key constraints. Additional code will be generated to warn the user before cascading the delete if the *End User Interface → Warn user if delete will cascade to other tables (DELWRN)* preference is set to **Always** or **Cascades**.
ON-ERROR (block)	This trigger is always generated to trap and display errors returned from server-side validation.

Code Group Labels

Form Generator creates the PL/SQL code as code groups or code segments and properly labels them with comments. For example, the label "/* CGUV$CHK_KEYS_ON_INSERT */" in a PRE-INSERT trigger indicates that the code that follows the trigger is to check the row if it is unique according to tables constraints. In Oracle Designer Online Help you can find more information about the code groups generated by searching the help system (Help → Find) for **Form Generator code groups** (see the following illustrations for examples). There is even an alphabetical list of all code groups.

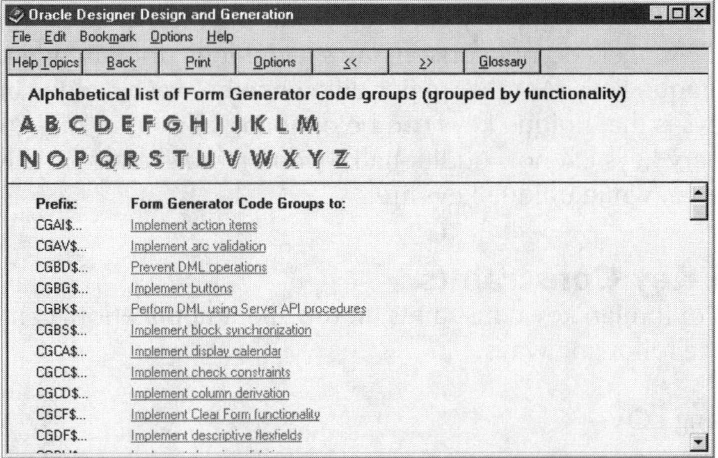

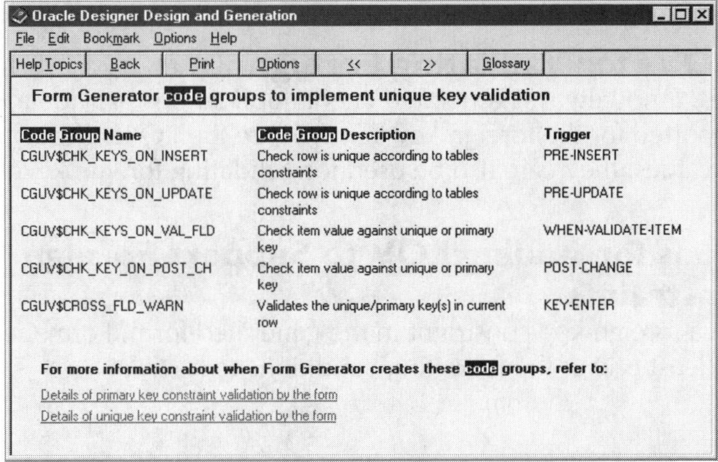

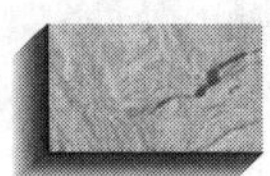

NOTE
The Oracle Designer Online Help → Referential Integrity Rules *topic is an excellent source of information about referential integrity in general.*

Unique Key Constraints

Unique keys are almost identical to primary keys, as far as uniqueness validations are concerned. They are subject to same conditions for adding code as the primary keys are, and the generated triggers are almost identical. The exceptions are the referential integrity related features. For example, the primary keys may be involved in relationships with other columns in other tables, but the unique keys may not be. Therefore the KEY-DELREC (block) is never created for a unique key constraint, and the PRE-UPDATE and/or PRE-DELETE triggers do not contain any special logic for cascade update/ delete of unique keys. Another major difference between unique and primary keys is that unique keys can be optional (all or part of a composite), while primary keys cannot. Additionally, primary keys are normally nonupdatable, while unique keys are.

Foreign Key Constraints

Validation of foreign key constraints (in the client application) can be done in one of the following ways:

- Using LOVs
- Using Form Builder triggers

Using LOVs for Validating Foreign Keys

Many times, if not always, generated client applications provide a list of values supported for the foreign key items. Since the LOVs display only the allowable values, they can also be used for validating foreign keys.

Conditions for Adding LOV to Support Foreign Key Constraints

To enforce a foreign key constraint in the generated form, Form Generator requires at least one of the following conditions to be true:

- The *Validate In* property of the constraint is set to **Client** or **Both**.
- The *Select?, Insert?,* or *Update?* properties of at least one of the items in the constraint is set to **Yes**.
- If there is no lookup table usage, then the *Display in LOV?* property of at least one of the foreign key item(s) in the base table usage must be set to **Yes**.
- If there is a lookup table usage, then the *Display in LOV?* property of at least one of the foreign key item(s) in the base table usage or one of the lookup items in the lookup table usage must be set to **Yes**.

However, there are some exceptions:

- **Exception 1** If the module component is updateable but not insertable, Form Generator does not generate the code for validation unless one or more of the items in the foreign key are updateable.
- **Exception 2** Form Generator will also generate PL/SQL code to trap the server-side errors, if the *Insert?* and/or *Update?* properties of the module component are set to **Yes**.

How to Generate LOVs for Foreign Key Items

You can use the following procedure to generate LOVs for foreign key items:

1. Create the module component and decide whether you are going to have lookup table usages for the foreign keys. Create a lookup table usage if you want to
    - Enter values via the items in the lookup table usage.
    - Display descriptive information (such as code description), etc. for the foreign key item.
    - Restrict the values displayed in LOV with additional criteria.
    - Narrow down the LOV before it's displayed if it contains a long list.
2. If you are not going to have a lookup table usage for a foreign key, set the *Display in LOV?* property of the foreign key items in the base

table usage to **Yes**. Form Generator will create an LOV to display the values of all the primary key columns. However, you will have very little control over the generated LOV. For example, you are not going to be able to specify which columns you want to be displayed, their display order, the sorting order for the values, or any additional restriction criteria for the displayed rows. In this case, skip to step 7.

3. You must be using a lookup table if you are at this step. Select the items you want displayed from the lookup table usage. Set the *Display?* property to **Yes** for these items.

4. Set the *LOV Title* property of the lookup table usage to specify the title of the LOV. If you don't, the Form Generator will set it to Valid values for <display title of the lookup table> or, if the display title is null, to Valid values for <item prompt>.

5. Set the *Enter FK via Descriptor* property of the lookup table usage to **Yes**, if you want to enter the values via the generated lookup items. For example, rather than entering the Department Number (base table item) you might want to enter the Department Name (lookup item).

6. Set the *Lookup Validation WHERE clause* property of the lookup table usage to restrict the values from a lookup table. For example, when choosing the person to assign a task to, you may want to limit the list of values to those who still work for the company and in a certain department. We will discuss this in more detail later in this chapter in "List of Values (LOV) Generation."

7. Set the *List of Values → Validate item in LOV (LOVVAL)* preference to **Yes** to use the generated LOV for validating the foreign key item.

8. Set the *List of Values → Use a button to indicate available list of values (LOVBUT)* preference to **Yes** if you want Form Generator to create a push button next to the item to indicate and invoke the LOV.

9. Optionally, set the following preferences to change physical appearance of the LOV:

   List of Values → List of values - X co-ordinate (LOVXCO)

   List of Values → Horizontal position of LOV (LOVHPN)

List of Values → List of values - co-ordinate (LOVYCO)

List of Values → Vertical position of LOV (LOVVPN)

List of Values → List of values height (LOVMHT)

List of Values → Maximum width of LOV (LOVMWD)

10. When generating the LOV functionality, Form Generator creates a native Form Builder LOV object. However, if you wish to call another form, you can set the *List of Values → For LOV on foreign key, use Form Builder LOV SQL text (FKLOVT)* preference to call an LOV form to display the list of values. For more information about how to use LOV forms, refer the "List of Values (LOV) Generation," later in this chapter.
11. Generate the form.

Using Form Builder Trigger for Validating Foreign Keys

To enforce a foreign key constraint in the generated form, Form Generator requires at least one of the following conditions to be true:

- The *Validate In* property of the constraint is set to **Client** or **Both**.
- The *Select?, Insert?,* or *Update?* properties of at least one of the items in the constraint is set to **Yes**.

Conditions for Adding Code to Support Foreign Key Constraints

Form Generator creates the necessary PL/SQL code to validate foreign keys if the following conditions are true:

- The LOVs are not used for validation, i.e., the *List of Values → Validate item in LOV (LOVVAL)* preference is set to **No**.
- The LOVs are not used for validation, i.e., the *List of Values → Validate item in LOV (LOVVAL)* preference is set to **Yes**, but foreign key is entered via the lookup items.
- There is an LOV form used to display allowable values, i.e., the *List of Values → For LOV on foreign key, use Form Builder LOV SQL text*

(FKLOVT) preference is set to **Call form** or **Call form if exists, otherwise use SQL text** and there is an LOV form attached to the calling form.

However, there are some exceptions:

- **Exception 1** If the module component is updateable but not insertable, then Forms Generator does not generate the code for validation unless one or more of the items in the foreign key are updateable.
- **Exception 2** If the *Insert?* and/or *Update?* properties of the module component are set to **Yes**, Form Generator will also generate PL/SQL code to trap the server-side errors.

Details of Foreign Key Constraint Validation by the Form

Form Generator might create the following procedures for each foreign key constraint:

1. **CGFK$CHK_<foreign_key_constraint_name>** (will be truncated to 30 characters) to check if the values entered in the foreign key columns are valid.
2. **CGFK$LKP_<foreign_key_constraint_name>** (will be truncated to 30 characters) to look up values for the lookup items included in the generated form when inserting or updating.
3. **CGFK$QRY_<foreign_key_constraint_name>** (will be truncated to 30 characters) to look up values for the lookup items included in the generated form when querying.
4. **CGSF$CLR_<foreign_key_constraint_name>** (will be truncated to 30 characters) to clear dependent lookup items.

Assuming that the *Validate In* property of the foreign key constraint is set to **Client** or **Both Client and Server**, Form Generator may create the PL/SQL code for foreign key validation in the following triggers.

Trigger	Generated If...
WHEN-VALIDATE-ITEM (item)	1. The foreign key is validated at item level, *Generate Options → When to validate foreign keys (VLDTFK)* is set to **F** or **B**. 2. The item's *Insert?* property is set to **Yes**. 3. There is no LOV to perform the validation, or the foreign key is entered via lookup items. The generated trigger will call the primary key validation procedure.
PRE-INSERT (block)	1. The foreign key is validated at commit time, *Generate Options → When to validate foreign keys (VLDTFK)* is set to **C** or **B**. 2. The module component's *Insert?* property is set to **Yes**. The generated trigger will call the foreign key validation procedure.
PRE-UPDATE (block)	1. The primary key is validated at commit time, *Generate Options → When to validate foreign keys (VLDTFK)* is set to **C** or **B**. 2. The module component's *Update?* property is set to **Yes**. 3. The *Update?* properties of the constraint, the module component, and one of the key items are set to **Yes**. The generated trigger will call the foreign key validation procedure.

Conditions for Adding Code to Support Table-Level Check Constraints:

To enforce a table-level check constraint in the generated form, Form Generator requires at least one of the following conditions to be true:

- The *Validate In* property of the constraint is set to **Client** or **Both**.
- The *Insert?* and/or *Update?* properties of the module component are set to **Yes**.
- The *Insert?* and/or *Update?* properties of at least one of the items in the constraint is set to **Yes**.
- There is a module item displayed based on the columns in the check constraint.

Form Generator will also generate PL/SQL code to trap the server-side errors, if the *Insert?* and/or *Update?* properties of the module component are set to **Yes**.

Details of Check Constraint Validation by the Form

Form Generator does not create a procedure for each check constraint it validates. Instead, it embeds the validation code into the triggers it generates.

Assuming that the *Validate In* property of the foreign key constraint is set to **Client** or **Both Client and Server**, Form Generator may create the PL/SQL code for check constraint validation in the following triggers.

Trigger	Generated If...
WHEN-VALIDATE-ITEM (item)	1. The check constraint is validated at item level, *Generate Options → When to validate table-level check constraint (VLDTTC)* is set to **F** or **B**. 2. The item's *Insert?* or *Update?* property is set to **Yes**.
PRE-INSERT (block)	1. The check constraint is validated at commit level, *Generate Options → When to validate table-level check constraint (VLDTTC)* is set to **C** or **B**. 2. The module component's *Insert?* property is set to **Yes**.
PRE-UPDATE (block)	1. The check constraint is validated at commit level, *Generate Options → When to validate table-level check constraint (VLDTTC)* is set to **C** or **B**. 2. The module component's *Update?* property is set to **Yes**.

When a check constraint refers to more than one column, the above mentioned WHEN-VALIDATE-ITEM trigger code is created on each item that is part of the check constraint.

List of Values (LOV) Generation

When the business rules are being validated and enforced in an application, the user interface is expected to help the user by showing the list of values that can be entered in the generated items. Whether it is for a list of allowable values defined against a repository element or table lookups that reference the values in other tables, Form Generator allows us to generate a list of values in many different ways:

- With or without lookup buttons
- Using native Form Builder LOV objects
- Using LOV forms
- As row LOVs

Displaying Lookup Buttons by the Items in the Calling Form

It is definitely nice to have the LOVs for generated items, but there is one thing missing: we cannot tell which items have LOVs attached until we navigate to them and pay close attention to the indicators written in tiny characters on the status line of the form. Form Generator offers a very nice solution to this problem. It can create a pushbutton beside each item that has an LOV available. When the user clicks this button, the corresponding LOV is activated. The following illustration shows what the default LOV button looks like:

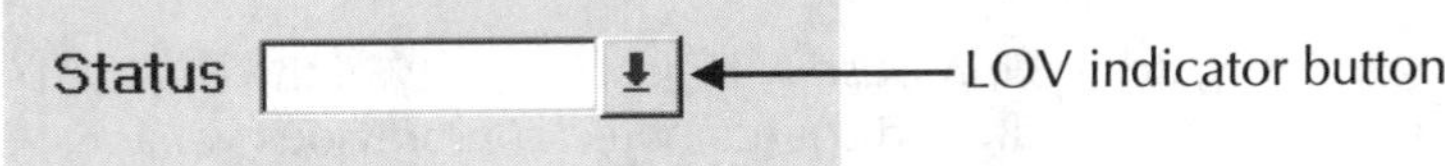

How to Generate List of Values Indicator Buttons

1. Set the *List of Values → Use a button to indicate available list of values (LOVBUT)* preference to **Yes** to specify that a push button should be created adjacent to each item that has an LOV attached.
2. Set the *List of Values Preferences* to control the following layout features:

Preference Category	Preference Name	Preference Description Tips for Preference Settings
List of Values	LOVITG	List of Values, item gap. Used for setting the gap between the item and its LOV button. Default is **1** character, but we recommend you set this preference to **0** and save some screen real estate.
List of Values	LOVBAL	List of values button alignment. Used to specify the vertical alignment of an item and its LOV button. The default value is **Center**. Other options are **Top** and **Bottom**.

3. Optionally, modify the CGSO$LOV_BUT standard LOV source object to customize the other properties of the LOV indicator button:

LOV Button Property	Source of the Property
Keyboard Navigable	The *Keyboard Navigable* property of the CGSO$LOV_BUT standard source object. (In previous versions, this was controlled with a now obsolete preference, LOVNAV.)
Mouse Navigate	The *Mouse Navigate* property of the CGSO$LOV_BUT standard source object. (In previous versions, this was controlled with custom PL/SQL code in templates and/or libraries.)
Long List	The *Filter Before Display?* property of the lookup table usage.
Dimensions	The CGSO$LOV_BUT standard source object in the object library, or the CG$LB item in the template form.
Icon	The CGSO$LOV_BUT standard source object in the object library, or the CG$LB item in the template form.
Visual Attribute	The CGSO$LOV_BUT standard source object in the object library, or the CG$LB item in the template form.

4. Generate the form.

Using a Custom Icon for the LOV Indicator Buttons

If you want to use a custom icon for the LOV indicator buttons, you can modify either the CGSO$LOV_BUT standard source object in the object library, or the CG$LB item in the template form. Set the *Icon File* property to the name of the icon file you wish to use. When entering the icon filename, do not enter the path name or file extension. Make sure that the directory in which the icon file is stored is on the search path. If needed, modify your TK25_ICON registry variable to include the directory in which your icon files are kept. The following illustration shows an example of a custom icon:

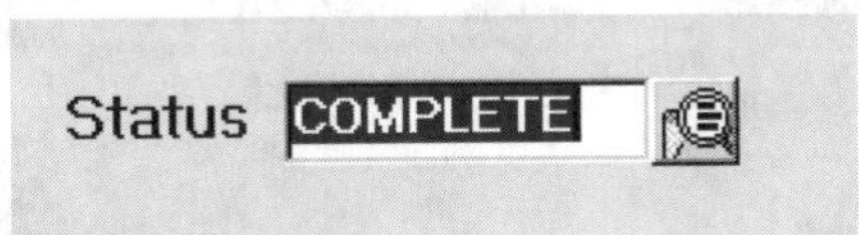

Controlling the Appearance and Functionality of Native Form Builder LOV Objects

The native LOV object in Oracle Developer Forms is the default method Forms Generator uses to provide list of values functionality for the generated items. Generating native Form Builder LOVs are explained in detail earlier in this chapter in "Using a Form Builder LOV to Validate the Item" and "Using LOVs for Validating Foreign Keys," earlier in this chapter.

However, many people are confused about how to control the appearance and functionality of the generated LOV objects. It can be difficult to know which properties need to be set where to get the desired results. This section should help you understand how to correctly generate your LOVs. We will start with an example of a native LOV (Figure 18-1). Many of the settings were discussed above; this figure is just intended as a visual reference for some of the settings.

To help you get a better understanding of how to generate LOVs, we decided to use some realistic examples. We will detail the appearance and functionality of various LOV options and tell you what property settings are

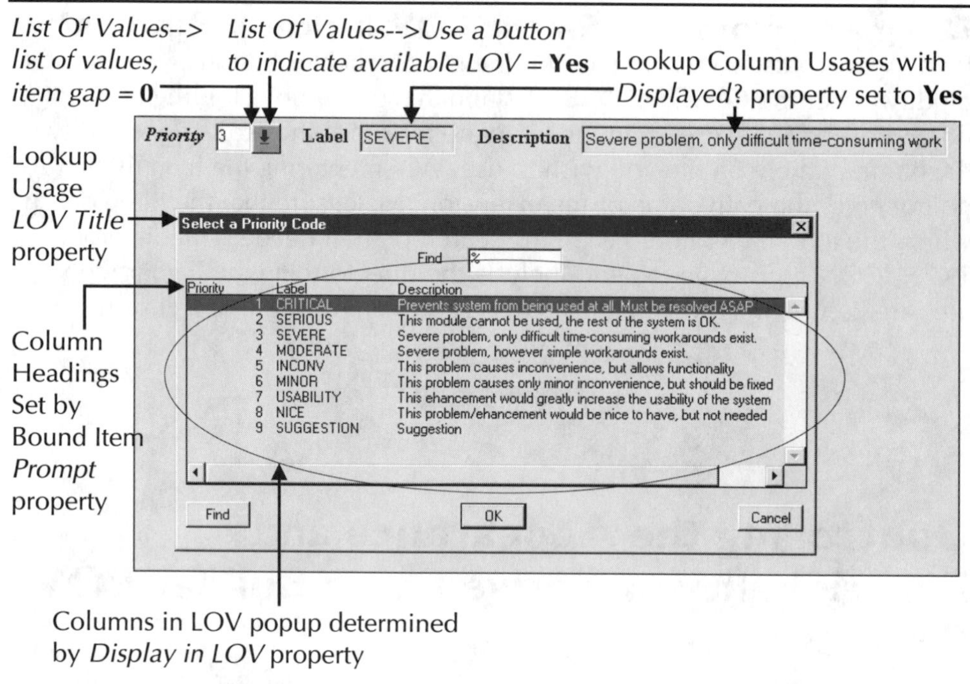

FIGURE 18-1. *Sources of LOV and lookup features*

needed to produce them. The first four examples will use the following module data diagram.

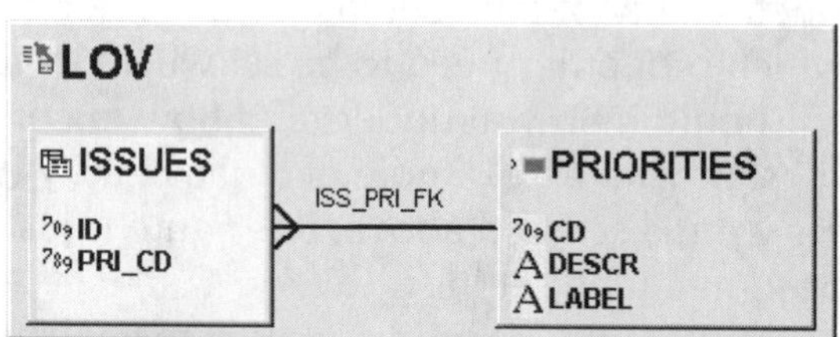

LOV Example 1: FK Column Displayed and Enterable, Lookup Column Shown in LOV

In this example, we will show how to generate the simplest LOV, a single displayed column with an FK to a table with a list of allowable values. The

LOV pop-up will show the key column as well as a descriptor column. This example is shown here.

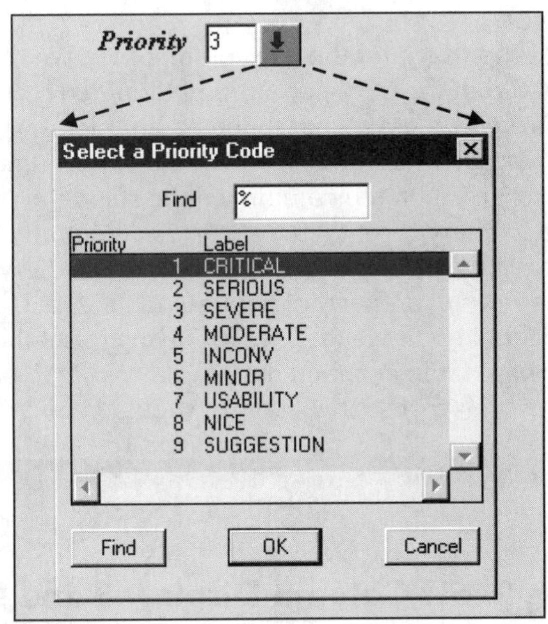

The lookup table usage *Enter FK Via Descriptor* property is set to **No** for this example. The following item properties need to be set to produce this layout and functionality:

Item	**Prompt**	**Insert**	**Update**	**Display**	**Display in LOV?**
PRI_CD	Priority	Yes	Yes	Yes	n/a
CD	n/a	No	No	n/a	Yes
LABEL	Label	No	No	No	Yes
DESCR	n/a	No	No	No	No

This example is available in the application on the CD as CH18_ENT_FK_NDIS_LKP.

Setting *Display* and *Prompt* Properties in the Correct Place

If you have a lookup usage for the key column, then whether the column is displayed in the LOV pop-up is determined by the properties of the item in the lookup usage, not in the base table usage. For instance, if the *Display in LOV?* property of the CD column in these examples is set to **Yes**, then the column will be shown in the pop-up, no matter what the property is set to in the PRI_CD column. However, the column label that appears above an FK column in the LOV pop-up is derived from the *Prompt* property of the base table item usage (e.g., PRI_CD), not the lookup usage (e.g., CD). Having to set the *Prompt* property for the base table item and the *Display in LOV?* property on the lookup usage is kind of strange, so you should keep this in mind.

LOV Example 2: FK Column Displayed and Enterable, Lookup Column Displayed but Not Enterable

In this example, we will show how to generate an LOV that shows a lookup column on the form but still uses the key column to enter the value. This example is shown here:

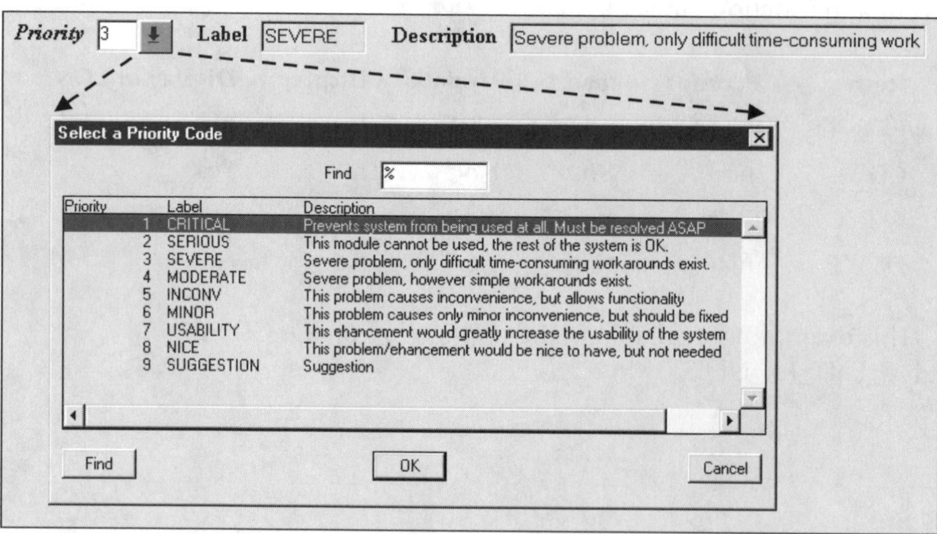

The lookup table usage *Enter FK Via Descriptor* property is set to **No** for this example. The following item properties need to be set to produce this layout and functionality:

Item	Prompt	Insert	Update	Display	Display in LOV?
PRI_CD	Priority	Yes	Yes	Yes	Yes
CD	n/a	No	No	n/a	Yes
LABEL	Label	No	No	Yes	Yes
DESCR	Description	No	No	Yes	Yes

This example is available in the application on the CD as CH18_ENT_FK_DIS_LKP.

LOV Example 3: FK Column Not Displayed, Lookup Column Displayed and Enterable

In this example, we will show how to generate an LOV that only shows a lookup column on the form and uses the LOV to return the FK column into a hidden item that is saved to the database. This is a very common LOV method, especially when surrogate keys are used in your database design. This example is shown here:

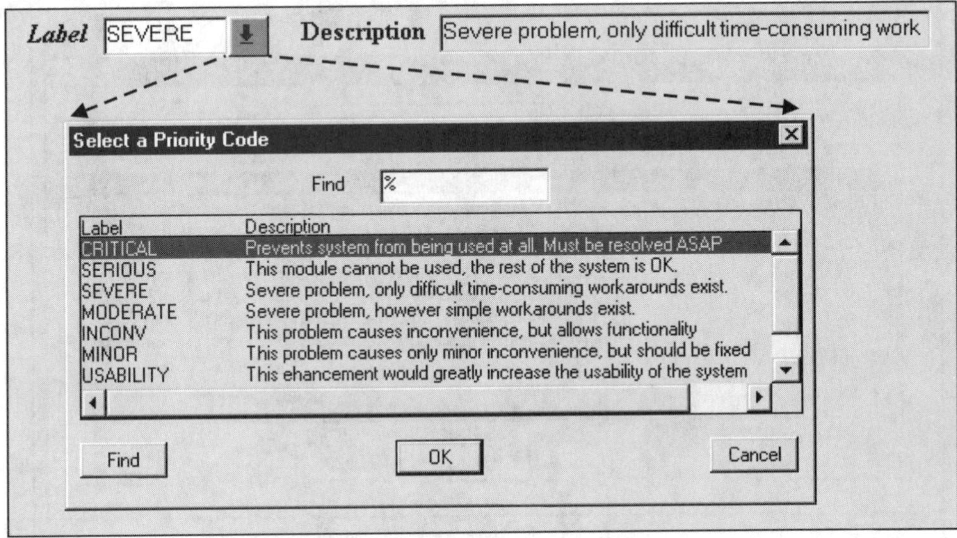

The lookup table usage *Enter FK Via Descriptor* property is set to **Yes** for this example. The following item properties need to be set to produce this layout and functionality:

Item	Prompt	Insert	Update	Display	Display in LOV?
PRI_CD	Priority	Yes	Yes	No	No
CD	n/a	No	No	n/a	No
LABEL	Label	No	No	Yes	Yes
DESCR	Description	No	No	Yes	Yes

This example is available in the application on the CD as CH18_NDIS_FK_ENT_LKP.

LOV Example 4: FK Column Displayed but Not Enterable, Lookup Column Displayed and Enterable

In this example, we will show how to generate an LOV that shows both the FK column and a lookup column on the form, but only allows entry on the FK. This example is shown here:

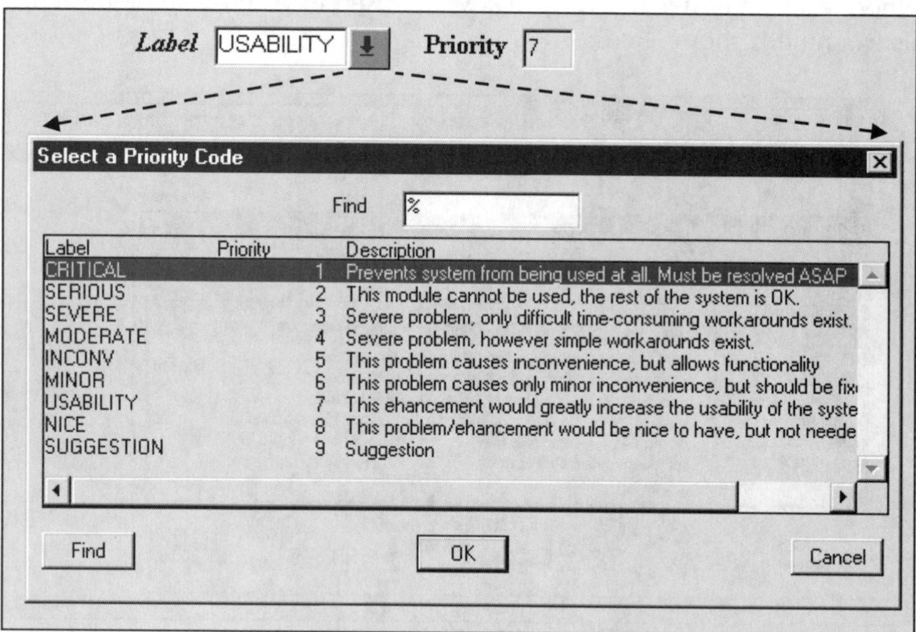

The lookup table usage *Enter FK Via Descriptor* property is set to **Yes** for this example. The following item properties need to be set to produce this layout and functionality:

Item	Prompt	Insert	Update	Display	Display in LOV?
PRI_CD	Priority	Yes	Yes	Yes	Yes
CD	n/a	No	No	n/a	Yes
LABEL	Label	No	No	Yes	Yes
DESCR	Description	No	No	No	Yes

This example is available in the application on the CD as CH18_DIS_FK_ENT_LKP.

Incorrect Source Objects Used for Generated Lookup Items

One annoyance about the way the lookup items are generated (at least in release 2.1.2) is that the lookup items are *always* sourced from the display-only source objects (e.g., CGSO$CHAR_DO) in the object library. This is true even if they are used to enter the value (in which case they are not really display only). This can cause a problem with your display standards if you use a different font or background for display-only items (which we did in those examples in which the display-only items had a gray background). However, you can easily overcome this problem using the item's *Template/Library Object* property. If you want one of the generated lookup items to be displayed using the enterable item standards, you can set this property accordingly. For example, we set the *Template/Library Object* property to CGSO$CHAR for the LABEL item in Example 3 to give it a white background. The same problem occurs with the FK column in the base table usage when it is set up to be nonenterable. It will still use the standard source object, not the display-only object. Example 4 in this section had this problem. The FK column (Priority) was set up to be display only, but by default it used the standard source object (CGSO$CHAR). In order to give this column a gray background, we had to set its *Template/Library Object* property to CHSO$CHAR_DO.

LOV Example 5: Chained Lookup

In this example, we will show how you can chain two FKs together to generate a chained lookup. Consider the following module data diagram:

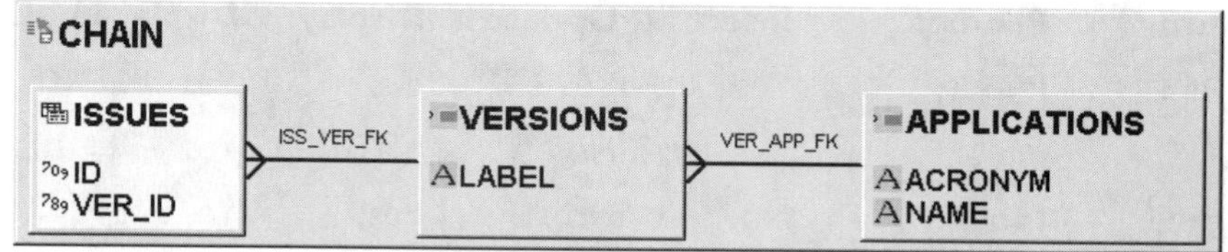

You can generate an LOV from the *Issues* table that shows the columns in the *Applications* table even though it is not related directly to the *Issues* table. You do this by "chaining" the lookups as in this diagram. This can be done using the module data diagrammer, or by adding lookup usages as children of other lookup usages in the Design Editor Navigator. An example of a chained lookup is shown here:

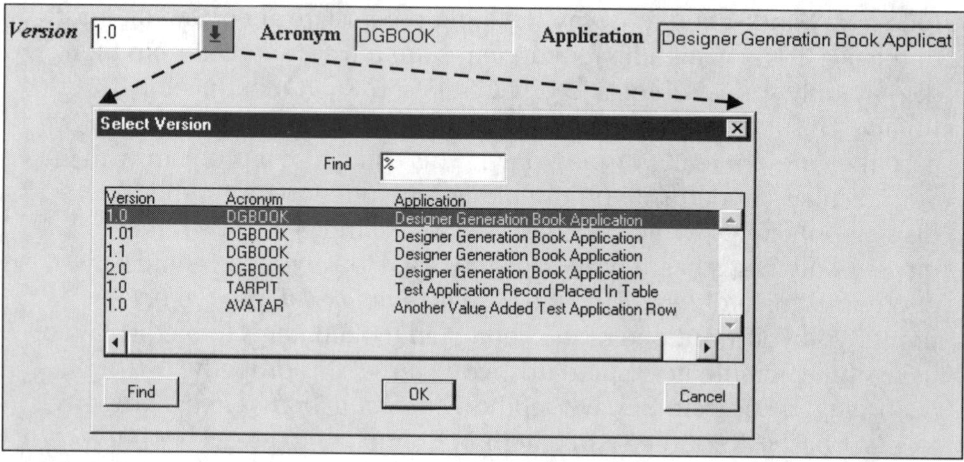

The lookup table usage *Enter FK Via Descriptor* property is set to **Yes** for this example. The following item properties need to be set to produce this layout and functionality:

Item	Prompt	Insert	Update	Display	Display in LOV?
VER_ID	n/a	Yes	Yes	No	No
LABEL	Version	No	No	Yes	Yes
ACRONYM	Acronym	No	No	Yes	Yes
NAME	Application	No	No	Yes	Yes

This example is available in the application on the CD as CH18_CHAINED_LKP.

Using LOV Forms

As we have mentioned before, the Form Generator creates native Form Builder LOV objects to display the list of values for foreign key items and items that have a list of allowable values. Although the native Form Builder LOV object works very well with small sets of data, it has a few restrictions:

- **Limited Find functionality** You can enter only one value for the first column displayed in the LOV to find a specific record, or you must narrow down your list. It also does not support query-by-example.
- **Limited Display Style options** Since they are always in spreadsheet format, users need to scroll to see long descriptions or other columns.
- **Poor performance with large lists** Especially if the *Filter Before Display?* (long list) property of the lookup table usage is not set to **Yes**.

In order to overcome the deficiencies of native Form Builder LOV objects, Form Generator can generate code to call another form (LOV form) to perform the lookups. LOV forms are form modules defined in the repository that have a special *Layout Format* type of LOV. Other than their unique layout format type, LOV forms are regular query-only forms that can be run stand-alone or called for lookup purposes.

NOTE
In fact, the only restriction for an LOV module is that the first module component needs to be query-only; subsequent module components can allow inserts or updates. However, when an LOV form is called from another form for list of values purposes, the call mode is set to query-only. So even if you have an LOV form that allows updates, you will not be able to perform the updates when the form is called as an LOV.

How to Use LOV Forms

In order to use an LOV form, first generate an LOV form and then call the LOV form from the calling module.

1. Create a module with your base table and foreign key lookup table usages as usual.
2. Choose a foreign key for which you want to call an LOV form when users perform the lookup.
3. Create another module to be the LOV form for the foreign key selected.
4. Set the *Layout Format* property of the LOV form to **LOV**.
5. Create a query-only module component in the LOV form.
   - Specify the lookup table you have chosen in step 2 as the base table for the first module componenet
   - Set the module component's *Query?* property to **Yes** and its *Insert?*, *Update?*, and *Delete?* properties to **No**.
6. Create other table (base or lookup) and item (bound, unbound, or action) usages in the LOV form as needed.

7. Generate the LOV module. Now, you have an LOV form to call.
8. Add the LOV module you have created in step 3 in the module network of the calling form. In release 2.1.2, after you add a module in the called modules (module network) Oracle Designer automatically creates an action item to call that module. This is not needed, so you should delete it.
9. Set the *List of Values → For LOV on foreign key, use Form Builder LOV SQL text (FKLOVT)* preference to one of the following:
   - **Call form (F)** To use an LOV form for the lookup. If Form Generator cannot find the LOV form, list of values functionality is not generated for the foreign key item.
   - **Call form if exists, otherwise use SQL text (B)** To use either an LOV form or a native Form Builder LOV for the lookup. If Form Generator cannot find the LOV form, the native Form Builder LOV object is generated for the foreign key item.
10. Generate the module.

Row LOVs

A row LOV is an alternative to the default Query By Example method used in forms. In Oracle Developer forms, by default, users press the Enter Query key, enter some query criteria (for example, users may enter A% in the department name field to query departments whose name starts with A), and press the Execute Query key to query records. The user can also simply execute the query without defining any query criteria to perform a raw query.

The row LOV gives you an alternative method for selecting existing records, usually for a single record block. A row LOV is a generated native Form Builder LOV that displays all the available records for a queryable block. When the current block is queryable, the selection of a menu option (or some other mechanism) displays a Form Builder LOV. The LOV contains values from columns in the base table for each available record. When the user of the generated form selects a record from the LOV, that record is queried into the block. The LOV cannot contain any information from the lookup tables. Row LOVs are a common feature in Oracle Applications forms. Here is an example of a row LOV:

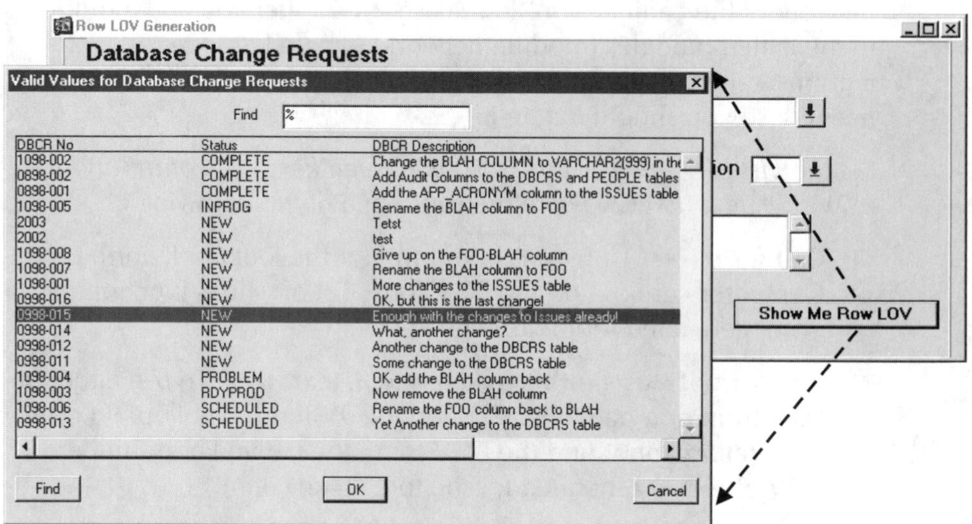

How to Generate a Row LOV

1. Set the *End User Interface → Implement row LOV functionality (ROWLOV)* preference to **Yes**. Form Generator will create a native Form Builder row LOV for any queryable block. The LOV displays all the records in the table on which the block is based.

2. Set the *Display in LOV?* property of the bound items (from the base table usage) you want to display in the LOV.

3. Form Generator creates a trigger called QUERY_FIND to display the row LOV, but it does not provide any method to execute this trigger. You will need to provide the user with a way to launch the row LOV: either a menu option or a toolbar button. To launch the row LOV, use a statement like

   execute_trigger('QUERY_FIND').

4. The generated QUERY_FIND trigger calls the CG$QUERY_FIND procedure. This procedure must exist in one of the following places: in the template form, in the libraries attached to template, in the

libraries attached to the generated form, or as application logic in the generated form. The OFGTEL.PLL standard library shipped with Oracle Designer contains a sample CG$QUERY_FIND procedure.

5. Generate the form.

NOTE
The row LOV does not disable the default query-by-example method of forms. It is an extra functionality that you can provide in your forms.

The Query Where Clause Versus the Lookup Validation Where Clause

You will often want to use different criteria for querying the foreign key lookup items than you do for validating them. This requirement is often needed because of obsolete codes. It is quite frequently the case that the list of valid values for certain codes will change over the life of a system because of changing business needs. When this happens, you are left with a dilemma. If you delete these obsolete codes from the code tables, then any records that have these codes will raise errors when they are queried (If you are using FK constraints to enforce referential integrity, you will not even be able to delete them anyway). If you reset these codes to some other code, then you lose historical information and introduce errors into the data. However, if you leave the obsolete codes in the tables, there is nothing to prevent users from continuing to use them. What you need to be able to do is validate the old codes for existing records while not allowing the user to enter them for new records.

In the previous versions of Oracle Designer, you had to write some tricky Where clauses to support this functionality. But in release 2, you are given a property to specify a query Where clause separately from a lookup validation Where clause:

- **Lookup validation Where clause** Used to restrict the list of allowable values from a lookup table when entering new data or editing existing data. For example, you can add a CURRENT_FLG column to your lookup tables then and add the following validation Where clause:

CURRENT_FLG = 'Y'

- **Where Clause of Query** Used to restrict the list of allowable values when querying the existing data.

LOV Validation Generation Troubleshooting Guideline

Problem	**Resolution**
How can I sort records in an LOV?	Specify the *Order By Sequence* and *Sort Order* properties of repository items.
I have created an LOV form, but the form still pops up the native LOV.	Make sure that the LOV module is included in the module network and that the *List of Values → For LOV on foreign key, use Form Builder LOV SQL text (FKLOVT)* preference is set to Call form if exists; otherwise, use SQL text or Call form.
LOV indicator buttons are not created for items calling LOV forms.	This seems to be a bug in release 2.1.2.
When I call an LOV form for a list of allowable values (e.g., domain values), the generated buttons are huge.	This seems to be a bug in release 2.1.2.
When I set the *Show Meaning* to Meaning Only, my text item is not displayed.	This seems to be a bug in release 2.1.2. Try using a pop list instead of a text item.

Problem	Resolution
The Lookup validation Where clause is not passed to the LOV forms.	This is the way LOV forms work. If you want to restrict what users can query in the LOV form, pass parameters between modules.
When I press the LOV button, it takes a long time before the LOV window pops up.	If you are using a native Form Builder LOV object, LOV tries to query all of the records at once. If you have a large list, this may take a while. Either set the *Long List?* property of the lookup table usage to **Yes** to further restrict values before the query is executed, or use an LOV form.

CHAPTER 19

Layout Generation Techniques

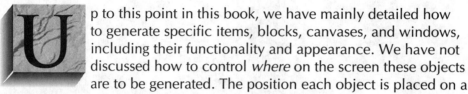

Up to this point in this book, we have mainly detailed how to generate specific items, blocks, canvases, and windows, including their functionality and appearance. We have not discussed how to control *where* on the screen these objects are to be generated. The position each object is placed on a screen, both in relation to the screen itself and to other objects, is called the screen's *Layout*. In this chapter (and the next) we will be discussing various techniques you can use to control the layout of your generated screens. In this chapter we will cover

- How to conserve screen space (real estate)
- Single-record block layout techniques
- Multiple-record block layout techniques
- Other layout topics, including item prompt formatting and smaller character cells

In this chapter, we will primarily cover how to position items within a block. In the next chapter, we will cover how to control the layout of the whole form.

Conserving Screen Real Estate

Before we get into the specific layout techniques, we thought it would be a good idea to give you some guidelines about the utilization of your screen *real estate*. By screen real estate, we are referring to the space that is available to place your GUI items into. Screen real estate is the Forms Developer's most precious commodity, so conservation of screen real estate is extremely important. The best way to minimize wasted screen space is to plan your layout standards carefully, and select standards that do not waste screen space. Every feature that you generate takes room, and you should be sure that each feature is important to your system before you include it in your layout standards.

Below is a list of suggestions for making the best use of your screen real estate. Some of the suggestions refer to the block layouts (which are covered in this chapter), and other suggestions refer to the selection and layout of the items themselves.

Suggestions to Conserve Screen Real Estate

1. Do not put titles on screens; use the window titles instead.

By default, the generator will place the module component *Title* property into the generated window title (the text in the shaded bar at the top of the window). While this title can be less obvious than having a title on the screen itself, it saves a lot of space to use it as a standard rather than putting the module title on the screen itself.

2. Make the items appear adjacent in multirow blocks.

In order to fit as many items as possible on your screen without having to use the overflow options, set the item spacing to 0. This will make the items appear adjacent in multirow blocks.

3. Only use multirow blocks when needed.

It is important to decide how many rows are realistically needed for multirow blocks. If the user will be looking at a large table, it is useful to get as many records on the screen as possible. However, if you have a child block in which 90 percent of the parent records will only have one child record, and the rest have at most two child records, then giving the child block five rows is wasting a lot of space!

4. Fit as much as possible on each screen.

If there is a lot of information, try to let the user see as much as possible on one screen. A crowded screen is often easier to use than having to scroll through multiple screens.

5. Use overflows for long text fields.

For records with a long text field (e.g., note, comment, or description), you should not try to display the long text field in every row or you will waste a lot of screen space. Instead, make the long text field into a multirow text field and place it in an overflow area.

6. Size buttons appropriately.

Buttons shouldn't be any bigger than necessary. They need only to display the button label with a few extra pixels on each side. Also, all of the buttons in a row of buttons do not need to be the same size.

7. Do not repeat buttons in multirow blocks.

You should not repeat buttons multiple times in multirow blocks. If you have a button that is one of the items of a multirow block, either place it in an overflow below so that it's placed at the bottom of the block, or place it in an overflow right so that it's placed at the right of the block.

8. Use pop lists instead of radio groups or text lists.

Pop lists are major space saving devices. Unlike radio groups or text lists, pop lists only show the currently selected value and, therefore, only take up one row. The pop list will still show the user the complete list of allowable values but only when they navigate to it and select the list.

9. Avoid logos.

In general, logos and fancy graphics are usually unnecessary. They take up a lot of space and are not very useful. Logos are especially not needed for internal forms within organizations. Employees don't need to see the company logo on every form. For forms going to those outside the company, graphics and logos can be placed on just the welcome screen rather than eating up memory, functionality, and space by placing them on the working forms.

10. Decrease the *Width* of long text items.

You can often get away with decreasing the width of long text items (like descriptions or names), because the database column size is usually set to handle the longest possible value. If 95 percent of your data is much narrower than the column width, then decreasing the item's *Width* will usually show you all of the data and will take up less room. Users will still be able to enter and view longer values by scrolling the text in the field.

Single-Record Block Layout Techniques

First, we are going to cover some layout techniques that are usually used for single-record blocks. In a single-record block, the items from only a single base record are visible on the screen at one time. Single-record blocks are usually used when there are too many items to fit into one row or when the form design does not allow for enough vertical space for more than one record.

A single-record block is generated when you set the *Number of rows displayed* property on a module component to **1**. The layout algorithm and techniques used to control the layout are different for single-row blocks and multiple-row blocks. In this section, we will cover some techniques that will allow you to control the layout generation for single-row blocks.

The Basics of Single-Record Block Layout

The algorithm used by the generator to control the layout of the generated forms is fairly simple. The generator starts in the upper left of the designated area of a canvas and places items (including prompts and decorations) across the area from left to right until no more items fit. Then the generator moves to the next line and continues placing items from left to right on the second line. The generator continues adding lines until all of the items in the block have been placed. There are preferences that control the amount of space to place between items, the amount of blank lines to include between each line of items, and how the items are justified (right, left, or center) in the layout area.

The layout that is generated for single-record blocks is primarily controlled by the following factors:

- **The display order (*Usage Sequence*) of the items.** The most important factor in determining layout is the display order of the items. This order is set by the items' *Usage Sequence* property. It is most easily viewed and modified using the display view of the module diagrammer, especially if there are lookup usages and item groups. You will use the display order to control how the items are grouped and placed on the canvas.

- **The display size of the items (*Width* & *Height*).** These properties determine how much room each item will take on the canvas and, therefore, the number of items that fit on each line. You can use the size of an item to control the layout. For example, sometimes you can decrease the size of a wide text item by a couple of characters to allow more items to fit on a single line, which could give you a better layout. (You could also increase the display width of an item for the same reason.)
- **Key layout preferences.** There are some key layout preferences that control single-record block layout. These will be detailed in the next section.

How Block Layout Regions Are Used in Layout Generation

The layout algorithm uses a concept of a block *region* in order to control the layout generation. A region is the area of the generated layout that is defined by the width of the longest line that is generated. Here is an example of a region:

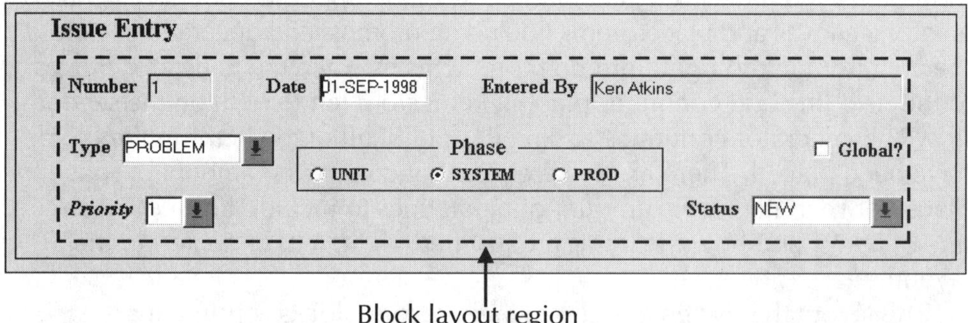

The important thing to understand about layout regions is that some of the preferences are used to control the position of the whole region in relation to the rest of the form, and other preferences control how the items are positioned within the region.

Important Preferences for Single-Record Block Layout Control

There are some important preferences that control how the Forms Generator creates the layout of single-record blocks. To help you understand how they work, we have identified their effect in the two examples of generated layouts shown in Figures 19-1 and 19-2.

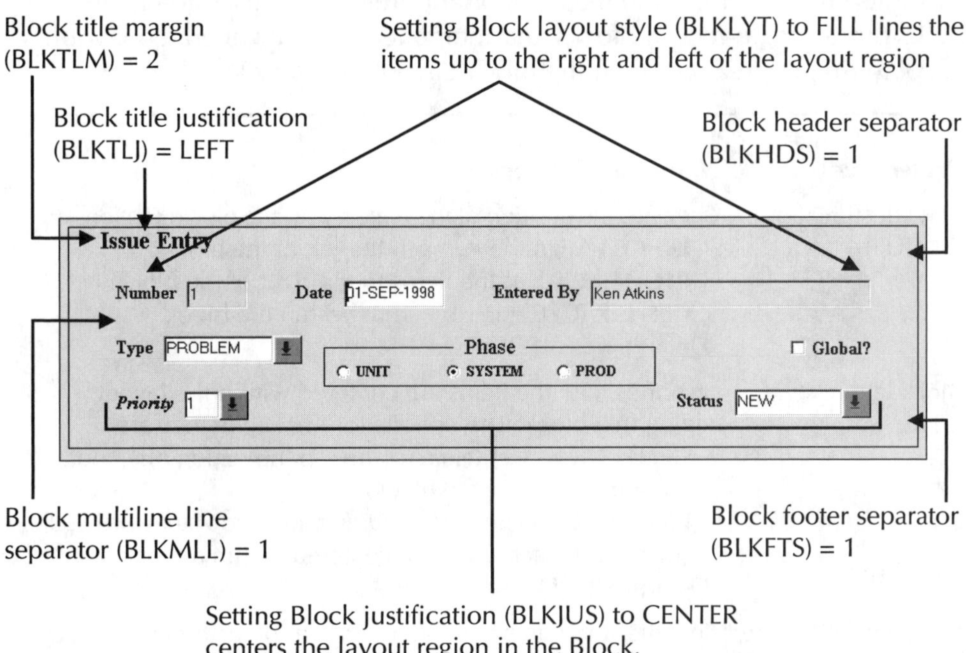

FIGURE 19-1. *Key preferences for single-record block layout control #1*

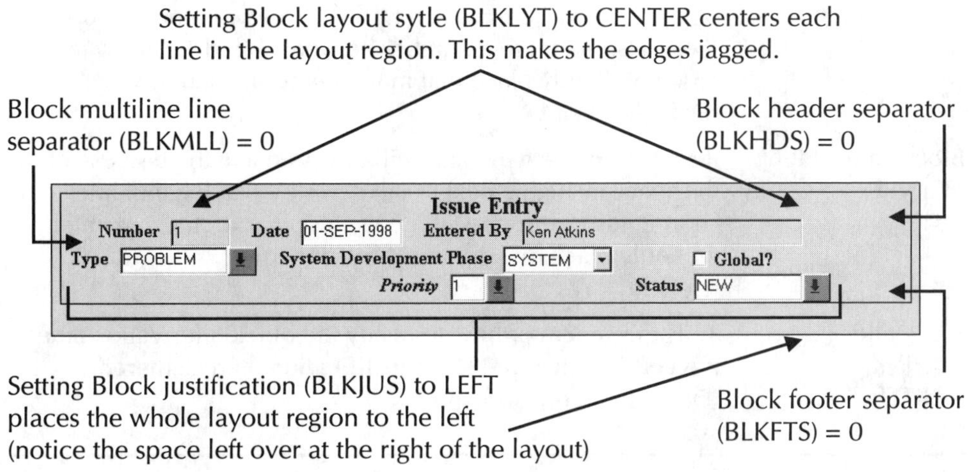

FIGURE 19-2. *Key preferences for single-record block layout control #2*

Table 19-1 is a list of the most important preferences used to create the layout of single-record blocks and their effect on the generated layout. (All of these preferences are in the Block-Layout category.)

Preference	Values and Effect
Block Justification (BLKJUS)	Specifies the position of the region with the block. Options are **LEFT** (L) Align the items to the left of the block. **RIGHT** (R) Align the items to the right of the block. **CENTER** (C) Center the items within the block. (Default = **CENTER**)
Block layout style (BLKLYS)	Specifies how the items are centered within the layout region in a block. The options for this preference are **CENTER** (C) Centers each line in the region (the width of the longest line in the block). **FILL** (F) Each line is left- and right-justified within the block. **(no value)** Items are not centered within a block at all. (Default = **FILL**)
Block multiline line separator (BLKMLL)	Specifies the number of blank lines to place between each row of items when a single-record spans multiple rows. (Default = **1**)
Block multiline format (BLKMLF)	Specifies the number of items that are placed in each row when a single record spans multiple rows. If it is set to **Keep adding fields as long as they fit (WRAP)**, the generator will place as many items as can fit on each row before wrapping. It can also be set to a number between 1 and 10, in which case it will only place that many items on each row. (Default = **WRAP**)
Block vertical fill (BLKVFL)	If set to **Yes**, the generator will always make the best use of the space available next to tall items by placing multiple short items next to the tall items. If set to **No**, the generator will only place one item next to tall items. (Default = **Yes**)
Block title justification (BLKTLJ)	Tells the generator how to justify the block title. Valid values are **Left justification**, **Right justification**, and **Centered**. (Default = **Left justification**)

TABLE 19-1. *Important Single-Record Block Layout Preferences*

Single-Record Block Layout Troubleshooting Guide

Problem	**Solution**
The items are not lining up correctly on each line. Some of the items are placed in the area that should be the space between lines.	Some of the GUI-based item types (such as radio groups and, multiline text boxes) can cause this problem. The layout generator treats them like they were single-line items even though they take up more than one line. This causes some of the rows to be uneven. There are a few things you can do to fix this: 1. Order the items so that all of the two-line items are on the same row. 2. Place the two-row items to the right of any multirow text items. 3. Use item groups to group items together to get a better layout.
I have a multiline text item, and the generator is only placing one row if there are items to its right. This wastes a lot of space.	Make sure the *Block vertical fill (BLKVFL)* property is set to **Yes**. This will usually cause the generator to place multiple rows of items to the right of a multiline item. However, sometimes the layout generator does not take full advantage of this space. In those cases, you might want to place the items in an item group and place the item group next to the multiline text item.
My two word prompts are wrapping, and I would like them not to wrap.	Set the *Item - layout → Allow split prompts (ITMASP)* preference to **No, never do it (N)**. When the *Allow split prompts* preference is set to **Yes, always do it (Y)** the generator will often split two word prompts in order to fit more items on each row.
It looks to me like there is room for another item on a line, but the generator is wrapping the line anyway.	The generator needs to take into account the inter-item spacing and margins defined by the preferences, so sometimes items don't fit when they look like they should. Check the values of the *Item/prompt gap, Prompt/item gap,* and *Block margin* preferences, and reset them if needed. If this does not help, decrease the *Width* of the items until they fit.

Now that we have covered the basics of single-record block layout, we can go into some of the more complicated single-record layout techniques.

Using Nonstacked Item Groups for Layout Control

Item groups can be used in Oracle Designer to group related items together for display purposes. When you create an item group and assign items to it, the layout generator treats it like a single item. The whole item group can be sequenced within a series of items (or other item groups), and all of the items in the item group will stay together and have the same layout in relation to each other.

Creating Item Groups

There are two ways to create item groups. You can create them easily if you use the Module Creation Wizard to create your module. However, since you will often not know which item groups you will need when you first create your modules, you can also create them later using the Create Item Group dialog. Refer to the online help for information about how to create item groups.

Important Preferences for Item Group Layout

There are many preferences that can be used to control the layout of the items within the item groups. In order to help you understand how these preferences effect the Item Group Layout, we have identified their effect on three different item group examples in Figure 19-3.

Table 19-2 is a list of the most important preferences used to create the layout of single-record blocks and the effect of these preferences on the generated layout. (These preferences are all in the *Layout - Item Group* category.)

Using Item Groups to Group Logically Related Items

The most straightforward use of item groups is to organize the display of a block that has a lot of items by grouping logically related items together and giving them a special label and layout. If the items have some sort of hierarchy, you can even nest the item groups by placing item groups within other item groups.

Using Item Groups for Layout Control Only

You can also use item groups to group together items that are not really related to each other in order to get better control of the generated layout.

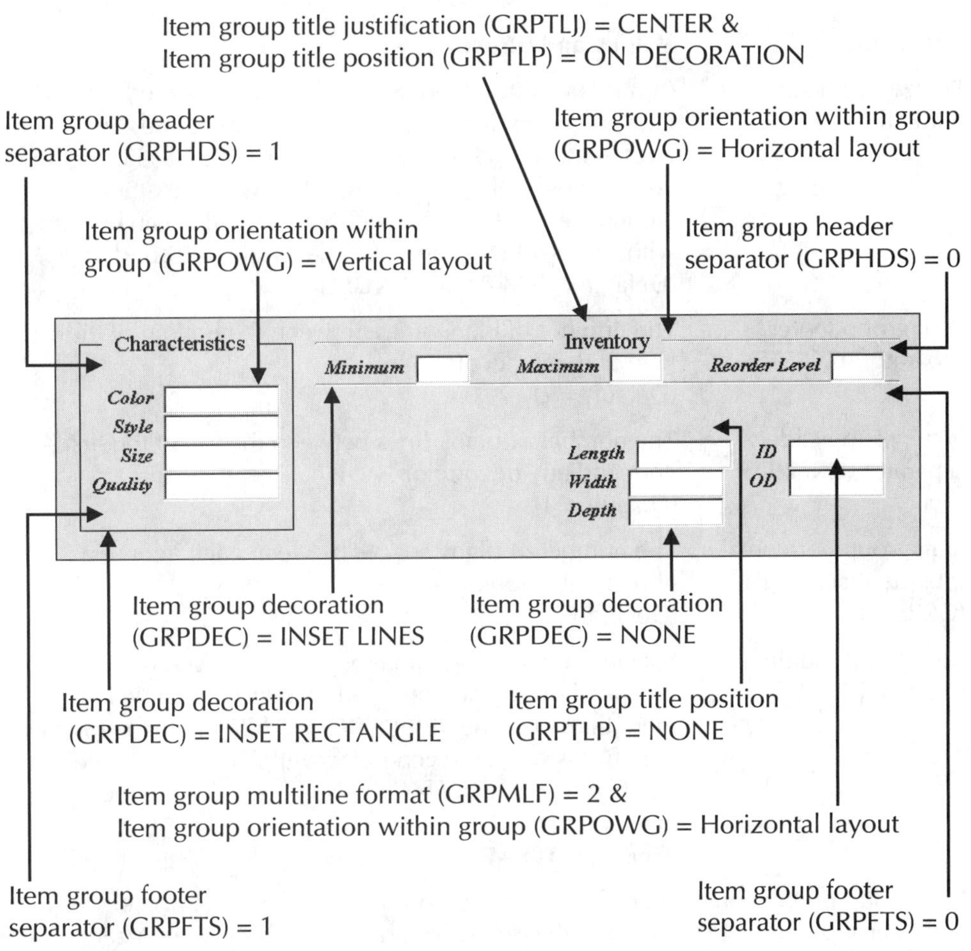

FIGURE 19-3. *Item Group Layout preferences*

When you create an item group with no decoration and add some items to it, the generator will lay out these items as if they were one big item. You can use the item group layout preferences (including header, footer, horizontal and vertical inter-item spacing, and tab stops) in order to get these items positioned correctly in respect to each other. Then you can use the standard item and block layout preferences to position this group of items in relation to other items (and item groups) in the block. There are some examples that use this technique in the next chapter.

Preference	Values and Effect
Item group decoration (GRPDEC)	Controls whether there is any decoration placed around the item group. It can be set to **Do not decorate the object (NONE)** to suppress any decoration. It can also be set to generate either lines above and below or a rectangle around the whole item group. The decoration can be drawn with an inset bevel, an outset bevel, or with solid lines. (Default = **INSET RECTANGLE**)
Item group footer separator (GRPFTS)	The number of blank lines between the bottom of the last item and any decoration. (Default = **1**)
Item group header separator (GRPHDS)	The number of blank lines between the top of the first item and any decoration. (Default = **1**)
Item group horizontal inter-item spacing (GRPHIS)	The number of blank spaces between each item in a horizontal layout. (Default = **2**)
Item group multiline format (GRPMLF)	Specifies the number of items that are placed on each line in a horizontally oriented item group that wraps to more than one line. If set to **Keep adding fields as long as they fit (WRAP)**, the generator will place as many fields on each line as will fit. Can also be set to a number between **1** and **10**. (Default = **WRAP**)
Item group orientation within group (GRPOWG)	Specifies the orientation of the item group, or the direction that the fields are placed in relation to each other. The two options are **Vertical layout** Each item is placed directly below the previous item, and there is always one item per line. **Horizontal layout** Each item is placed to the right of the previous item. The number of items per line is specified by the GRPMLF preference. (Default = **Vertical layout**)

TABLE 19-2. *Important Item Group Layout Preferences*

Preference	Values and Effect
Item group title justification (GRPTLJ)	Specifies the justification of the item group title. This preference can be set to **LEFT**, **RIGHT**, or **CENTER**.
Item group title position (GRPTLP)	Specifies how the title is placed in relation to the decoration. It has one of the following four values: **Do not title (NONE)** **Title inside any decoration (INSIDE)** **Title is placed on any decoration (ON DECORATION)** **Title outside any decoration (OUTSIDE)**

TABLE 19-2. *Important Item Group Layout Preferences* (continued)

Nonstacked Item Group Layout Troubleshooting Guide

Problem	Solution
I would like the items in a vertical item group to be aligned by the start of the items, but the generated item group is aligning by the end of the items, which causes the start of the items to be staggered.	Yes, it seems that by default the items in a vertical item group are left aligned by the end of the items. This is an annoying default. There are two methods to remedy this: 1. Set the *Width* of all of the items in the item group the same. This usually means that you will have to make some of the items wider than the column width. This is not a problem. The generated forms will still not let the user enter data wider than the column. This also gives you a very appealing item group appearance. 2. Use the item group tabulation preferences to align the start of the items. Do this by setting the *Layout - Item Group → Use group tabulation table (GRPUTT)* to **Use tabs to align start of the display (SD)**. The default tab settings in the *Group tabulation table* preference are often fine, but you may want to tweak the tab stops. See "Using Tab Stops to Control Layout," later in this chapter, for more information about using tab stops.

Problem	Solution
I want to place the prompts above the items in an item group, but the generator seems to ignore the *Allow prompts above in a single-row block* preference.	You are right, the preference is ignored. This is a limitation of the generator in the current version (and in previous versions, for that matter). The prompts in item groups will always be placed to the left of the items.

Tab Canvas Item Groups

Tab canvases are a new feature in Oracle Developer Forms release 2. A *tab canvas* is a GUI control that is made up of one or more tab pages that can be used to group and display a subset of related information. Tab canvases look like folders in a regular filing cabinet. Each tab page corresponds to a folder and has a labeled tab used for accessing it. When the users click the labeled tab, the page corresponding to that page moves to the front. Each tab page takes up the same amount of space, and only one tab page can be seen at a time. The illustration shown here is an example of a tab canvas.

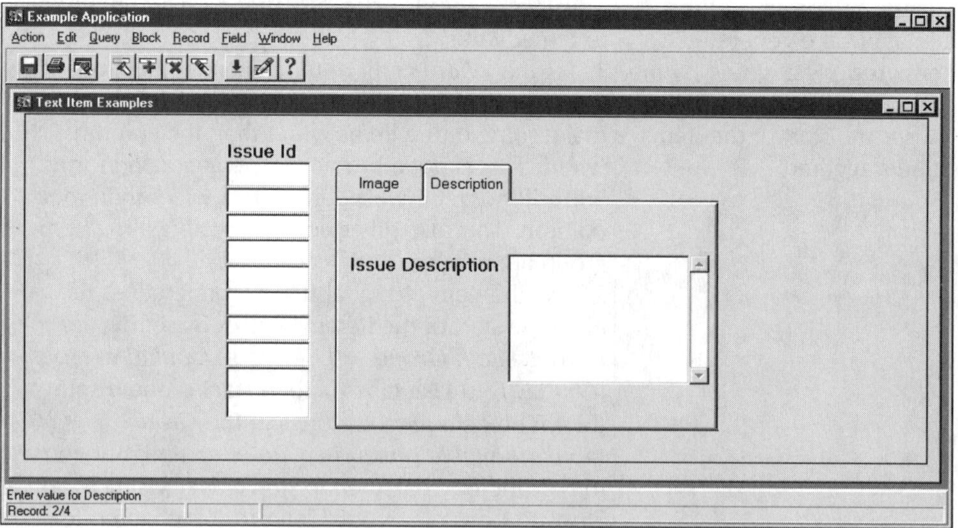

This table shows a summarized list of some of the most important features of tab canvases and their corresponding sources in Oracle Designer.

Feature	Source of Feature in Oracle Designer
Tab canvas	*Layout – Canvas → Native tab canvases (CANNTC)* preference category and stacked item groups
Tab pages	*Stacked Item Groups*
Tab labels	*Item Group Prompt* property of item groups
Other properties	*Source Object(s)* from the template/object library and *Template/Library Object* property of the item

How to Generate a Tab Canvas

You can generate a tab canvas from one or more item groups. In order to generate a tab canvas, you must do the following:

1. Create one or more item groups and set the *Stacked* property to **Yes**.
2. Set the other properties of the item groups appropriately. The item properties that are most critical for tab canvases are shown in the following table.

Item Group Property	Important, Because...
Prompt	This will be the label of the corresponding tab page (i.e., the text that appears in the tab).
Template/Library Object	For the tab canvas, defaults to those of the *CGSO$CANVAS_TAB* source object defined in the object library used for generation. However, you can specify another source object via the *Template/Library Object* property of the item. For the pages of a tab canvas, *CGSO$TAB_PAGE* source object is used to derive other properties of the generated tab pages. Currently, there is no place to specify a template/library object for the pages of a tab canvas.

3. Set the Layout Preferences for the tab canvas and the item groups to control the layout details. Some of the most important preferences for tab canvases are shown in the following table.

Preference Category	Tips for Preference Settings
Layout - Canvas → Native Tabbed Canvases (CANNTC)	Native tab canvases. This preference is used to specify how stacked item groups are displayed. If the preference is set to **Yes**, Forms Generator creates a native tab canvas and creates a tab page for each stacked item group. If it is set to **No**, Forms Generator creates a stacked canvas for each stacked item group, displays them in the same area of the screen, and provides a pop list. This control is also for easy navigation among these stacked canvases. Release 1.3.2 also had this capability.
Layout - Item Group (All of the preferences)	Several item group preferences can be used to control how items on the tab pages are laid out.

When to Use Tab Canvases

Tab canvases should be used when there is a lot of information to be displayed and the users do not need to see all that information at once. Related items can then be grouped together and displayed on a single tab. At run time, only one tab page will be displayed at a time. The user can then click on the labeled tab to navigate to the corresponding page. Tab canvases are very intuitive and easy to use, which is why they are so prevalent in many windows-based applications. They also help you save a lot of screen space since they reuse the same area of the screen.

However, there are also some limitations to tab canvases:

- Only one set of tab canvases can be generated per block (or module component).
- Tab canvases cannot be generated onto other stacked canvases such as spreadtables and stacked pages.
- In master-detail block implementations, if the detail block contains a tab canvas that includes items from the master block (e.g., context items), the End User Interface *Preferences → Block synchronization - coordination scope* (*BSCSCP*) preference needs to be set up as Window or Form.

- If all of the items in a detail block are on a tab canvas, Forms Generator creates a block context area above the tab canvas for any context items from the master block.
- Only one row of tabs is displayed. However, previous and next tab controls are activated if there are more tabs than what can be displayed in one row of tabs.

Stacked Item Group Canvases

Similar functionality can also be generated via the stacked item group canvases. Indeed, this was the only implementation supported prior to Oracle Designer release 2.1. To provide this functionality, Forms Generator creates a stacked canvas for each stacked item group and displays them in the same area of the form. At run time, users can navigate to these canvases by either navigating through the items or via the canvas selector pop list. The canvas selector is a pop list item that has the list of stacked canvases. When the user selects an option from the list, the cursor will navigate to the selected stacked canvas. The illustration here shows an example of stacked item group canvases.

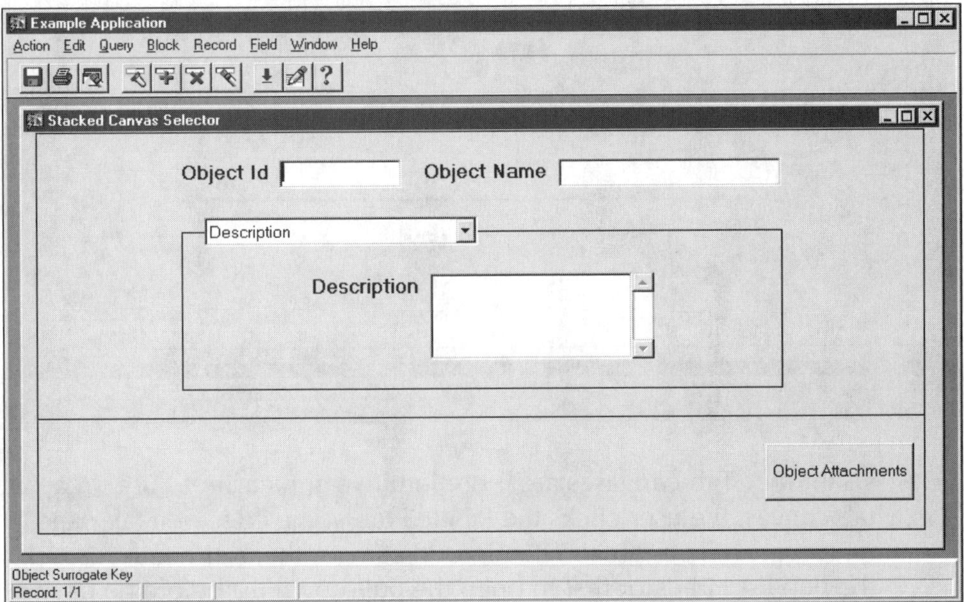

How to Choose Layout Style for Stacked Item Groups

Both tab canvases and stacked item group canvases can be used to implement stacked item groups. However, there are some differences between the two options:

- **Appearance** Tab canvases look nicer than stacked item group canvases. However, if you have long labels for tabs or too many tabs, Forms Generator will add a series of buttons at the upper-right corner of the tab canvas. Using these buttons, called *tab navigation controls*, you can navigate to the previous, next, first, or last tab. This illustration shows a tab canvas with these tab navigation controls activated.

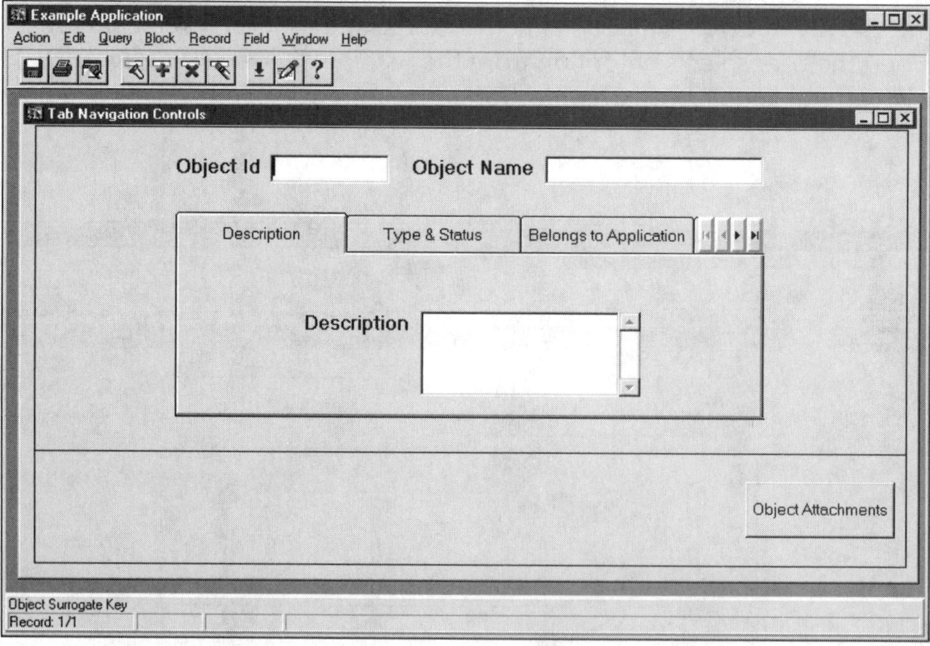

- **Usability** Tab canvases are more intuitive and easier to use. In a tab canvas, the user clicks the labeled tab at the edge of a tab page to activate it. In a stacked item group canvas, the user needs to click the pop list indicator first to open the pull-down list before he or she can choose the canvas to activate it.

One last word about stacked item group implementations: we can only have one layout style, either tab canvases or stacked canvases, for all of the stacked item groups in a form. In other words, we cannot have tab canvases in one block and stacked item group canvases in another. This is mainly because the *Layout - Canvas → Native tab canvases (CANNTC)* preference is set either at module or application system level. This shouldn't be a problem, because you want to be consistent anyway and use only one implementation style throughout your application. Indeed, this preference promotes a standard look and feel and consistency in generated applications.

Tab Canvas Generation Troubleshooting Guide

Problem	Solution
I cannot get a tab canvas (or stacked item group canvas) generated into a spreadtable area.	This is a current limitation with tab canvases and stacked canvases, and the same limitation also applies to context areas. In general, stacked canvases cannot be generated onto other stacked canvases in Oracle Designer.
I have defined two stacked item groups, but I am not getting the native tab canvas generated.	Make sure that the item groups are stacked. If one item group is marked as stacked and the other is not, the generator cannot generate a single-tab canvas. Also, make sure that the *Layout - Canvas → Native tab canvases (CANNTC)* preference is set to **Yes** at either module or application level.
How can I include items from multiple blocks in a tab canvas item group?	You cannot. However, there is a workaround for this: First, create a view that joins the multiple tables. Then use this view definition as your base table usage for that module component. This method works very well with query-only screens. If you need insert, update, or delete capabilities, you will need to use view API.

Using Tab Stops to Control Layout

Another option that you have to control the item layout is the use of tab stops. Tab stops allow you to specify tab positions that the generator uses to line up the items in the generated layout. There are two preferences at the block level that control the use of tab stops for block layout. These two preferences (available in the *Layout-block* area of the preference navigator) are

- ***Use block tabulation table (BLKTAB)*** This preference controls whether a tabulation table is used at all and how it is used. There are many different ways that the tab stops can be used to align the items; these options will be covered in the next section.
- ***Block tabulation table (BLKUTT)*** This preference contains a list of the tab stops to use separated by a period (.). For example, the default is 2.20.42.60, which places tab stops at 2, 20, 42, and 60 characters, respectively.

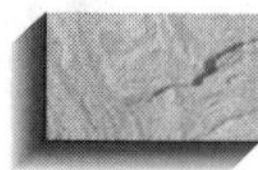

NOTE
Tab stops are available for item groups also. They work identically to tab stops used for block layout, the only difference being that the tab stops are measured from the edge of the item group instead of the block layout region.

Tab Stops Measured from Block Layout Region

The tab stops used for block layout are measured not from the left edge of the canvas that the block is placed in, but from the left edge of the block layout region. See "How Block Layout Region Is Used in Layout Generation," earlier in this chapter, for a discussion of block layout regions. Figure 19-4 shows how this works for a block that has its *Block justification* preference set to **Centered** (which is the default).

Since the tab stops are measured from the edge of the block region, it can be difficult to get the items lined up exactly where you want them if the *Block justification* is set to **Centered** like in this example. If you change the order of the items or add or remove items, the apparent position of the tab stops will change. It will even get worse if you are trying to use tab stops to line up items from more than one block, because each block's layout region will be different!

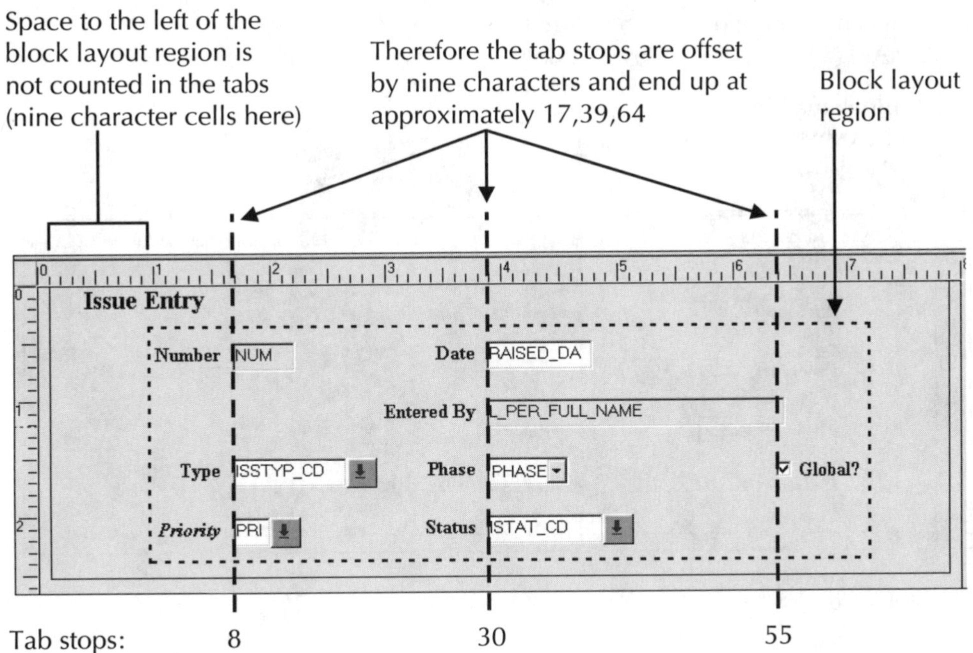

Block tabulation table (BLKTAB) = 8.30.55
Use block tabulation table = Use tabs to align the start of the display
Block justification = Centered

FIGURE 19-4. *Tab stops within block layout region—centered block*

SETTING PREFERENCE WHEN USING TAB STOPS The solution to this problem is to always set the *Block justification* preference to **Left justification** whenever you are using tab stops. When you do this, the tab stops will be consistent even when you reorder or add or remove items, because the starting position of the block layout region will not change. The tab stops are still not measured from the left of the canvas, because the block layout region still starts to the right of the decoration and the block margin. Figure 19-5 shows how the tab stops line up for a block that has its *Block justification* preference set to **Left justified**.

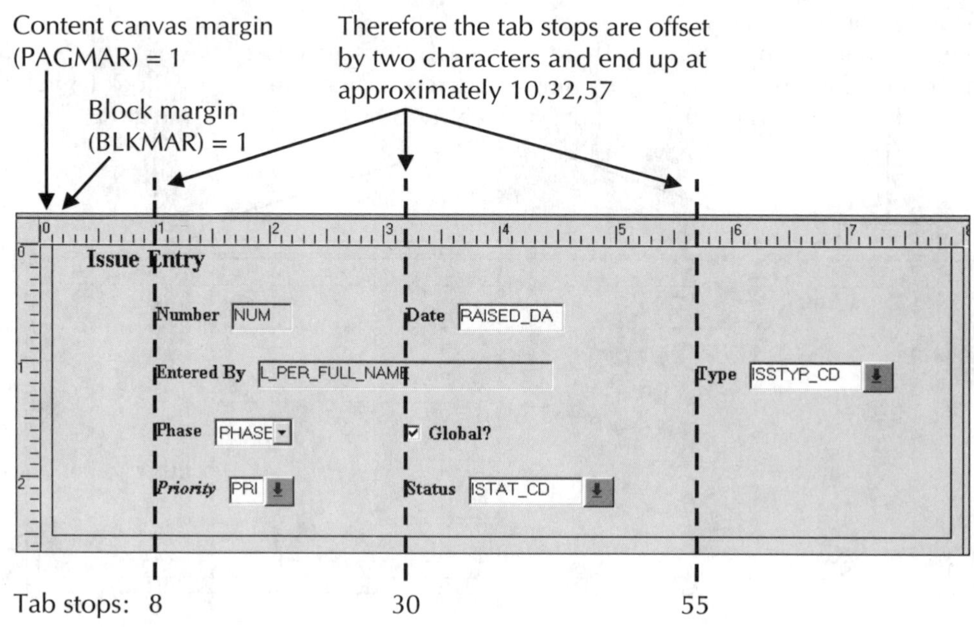

FIGURE 19-5. *Tab stops within the block layout region—left justified block*

Effect of *Use block tabulation table* Preference Settings

The terminology used to describe the settings of this preference is somewhat confusing. These descriptions use the term *display,* and it is not obvious what this refers to. The term *display* refers to the actual position of the item. Therefore, "Use tabs to align the start of the display" means that the start of the items will be aligned. The following table details the effects of the various settings for this preference:

Setting	Effect
Use tabs to align the end of the display (ED)	The tab stops are used to align the end of the items.
Use tabs to align the end of the post prompts (EP)	The tab stops are used to align the end of the post-prompts (if there is no post-prompt, then the effect is the same as for ED).
Use tabs to align the start of the display (SD)	The tab stops are used to align the start of the items.
Use tabs to align the start of prompts (SP)	The tab stops are used to align the start of the prompts.
Align start of prompt and start of display (SS)	The tab stops are used to align the start of the prompts and align the start of the items.
Align end of prompt and end of display (EE)	The tab stops are used to align the end of the prompts and align the end of the items.
Align start of prompt and end of display, save space (SE1 & SE2)	The tab stops are used to align the start of the prompts and align the end of the items. The SE1 and SE2 settings have the same effect.

TABLE 19-3. *Effect of* ***Use block tabulation table*** *Preference Settings*

Examples of the Effect of the *Use block tabulation table* Preference

Figure 19-4 showed an example of setting *Use block tabulation table* to **Use tabs to align the start of the display**. Figure 19-5 showed an example of setting *Use block tabulation table* to **Use tabs to align start of prompts**. In our last example, Figure 19-6 shows the effect of setting the *Use block tabulation table* preference to **Align start of prompt and start of display**.

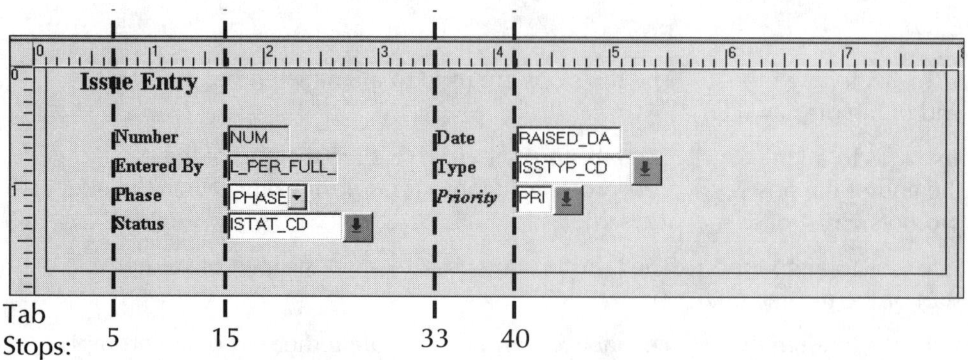

Block tabulation table (BLKTAB) = 5.15.33.40
Use block tabulation table = Align start of prompt and start of display
Block justification = Left justification

FIGURE 19-6. *Tab stops aligning both prompts and items*

Multiple-Record Blocks Layout Techniques

The other major type of block layout is called a multiple-record block. In a multiple-record block, the items from many base records are visible on the screen at one time. Multiple-record blocks are usually used when all of the items to be shown will fit into one or two rows, and you want to show the user many rows at the same time.

A multiple-record block is generated when you set the *Number of rows displayed* property on a module component to **<null>**, **0**, or any other number greater than 1. If the property is set to **<null>** or **0**, the generator will determine the number of rows to be displayed based upon the amount of room left on the canvas. If the property is set to any number greater than 1, that number of rows will be displayed.

The layout algorithm and techniques used to control the layout are different for single-row blocks and multiple-row blocks. In this section, we will cover some techniques that will allow you to control the layout generation for multiple-row blocks.

The Basics of Multiple-Record Block Layout

The algorithm used by the generator to control the layout of multiple-record blocks is a little more complicated than the one for single-row blocks. The generator starts at the left of the canvas and places items from left to right, leaving preference-specified gaps between the items, until no more items fit. The prompts are by default placed above the items. However, there are a few little twists to the layout algorithm. The first is that the layout needs to make room for the width of the prompts for each item. If a prompt is longer than the item, the layout will move the next item over in order to make room for the prompts. The second twist is that if some of the prompts are multiword prompts, the generator will try wrapping the prompt onto two lines and try to fit more items that way. If they fit, the prompts will be wrapped. However, if the items don't fit even with the prompts wrapped, the prompts may be left on single lines, and the line will be overflowed or wrapped.

There are preferences that control the amount of space to place between items, the amount of blank lines to include between each record if the record wraps, and whether to wrap the record or overflow the record if all of the items do not fit on one line.

The layout that is generated for multiple-record blocks is primarily controlled by the following factors:

- **The *Width* of the items** The *Width* property determines how much room each item will take on the canvas and, therefore, the number of items that fit on the line. You can use the size of the item to determine which items will get moved into the overflow area (or will be wrapped onto another line). For example, sometimes you can increase the size of a text item by a couple of characters to push another item into the next line.
- **The length (number of characters) in the prompts** The width of the item prompts is also important for multiple-record layout generation. The generated layout needs to have room for the prompts as well as the items themselves.
- **The *Item/Prompt gap* preference** This preference determines the space between the items in each row. If set to **0**, the items will be

placed adjacent to each other, giving the layout a spreadsheet-like look. If set to a number greater than 0, that number of spaces are placed between each item.

- **Other Key Layout Preferences** There are some key layout preferences that control single-record block layout. These will be detailed in the next section.

Important Preferences for Multiple-Record Block Layout Control

There are some important preferences that control how the Forms Generator creates the layout of multiple-record blocks. To help you understand how they work, we have identified the effects of some of them in the following two examples of generated layouts. Figure 19-7 shows an example of a multiple-record block where all of the items fit onto a single line. Figure 19-8 shows an example of a multiple-record block in which the record wrapped to multiple lines.

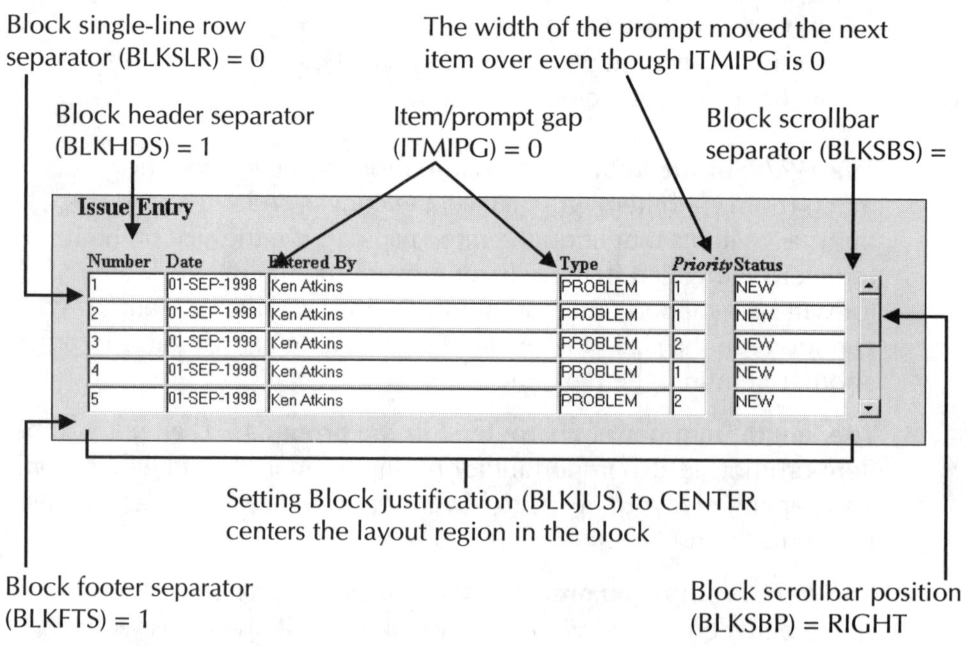

FIGURE 19-7. *Key preferences for multiple-record block layout control #1*

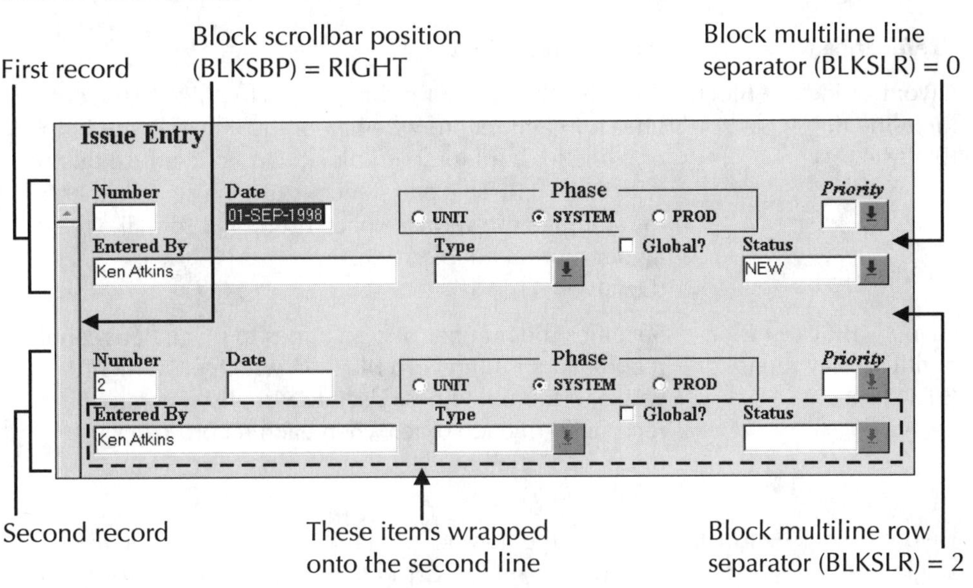

FIGURE 19-8. *Key preferences for multiple-record block layout control #2*

Table 19-4 is a list of the most important block layout preferences used to create the layout of multiple-record blocks and their effects on the generated layout.

Preference	Values and Effect
Layout - Block → Block Justification (BLKJUS)	Specifies the position of the region with the block. Options are **LEFT** (L) Align the items to the left of the block. **RIGHT** (R) Align the items to the right of the block. **CENTER** (C) Center the items within the block.

TABLE 19-4. *Important Single-Record Block Layout Preferences*

Preference	Values and Effect
Layout - Block → Block multiline line separator (BLKMLL)	Specifies the number of blank lines to place between the lines for each record when all of the items do not fit in one line for a multirecord block. Do not confuse this with BLKMLR. This preference is usually set to either **0**, to minimize the vertical space used, or **1** to make the layout more readable. (Default = **1**)
Layout - Block → Block multiline row separator (BLKMLR)	Specifies the number of blank lines to place between the records in a multirecord block in which each record wraps to multiple lines. Used to visually separate the records from each other when each record takes up more than one line. (Default = **1**)
Layout - Block → Block single-line row separator (BLKSLR)	Specifies the number of blank lines to place between the records in a multirecord block in which the records do *not* wrap to multiple lines. Having a separate BLKMLR and BLKSLR allows you to keep the records together for single-line records (as in Figure 19-7), while placing spaces between the records for multiple-line records (as in Figure 19-8). (Default = **0**)
Layout - Block → Block scrollbar position (BLKSBP)	Specifies the position of the vertical scroll bar in the block. Valid values are **Left justify** **Right justify** To specify whether the scroll bar is even shown for the block, you need to set the *Show scrollbar* property in the block's source object to **Yes**. (Default = **Left justify**)

TABLE 19-4. *Important Single-Record Block Layout Preferences* (continued)

Preference	Values and Effect
Layout - Item → Allow split prompts (ITMASP)	Specifies if the generator can split prompts if the specified layout will not fit on one line. There are three valid values: **Yes, always do it.** This setting allows the generator to split the prompts if it needs to. It does not *force* the generator to split the prompts, however. If you want to force the prompt split, use ITMFPS. **Never do it.** This setting prevents the generator from ever splitting the prompts. **Do it for multirow blocks.** This setting works like **Yes** for multiple-row blocks and **No** for single-row blocks. (Default = **Yes, always do it)**
Layout - Item → Marker to force prompt splitting (ITMFPS)	Specifies a character that can be used to force the prompts to split at a certain location. For example, if this preference is set to "|" and a particular prompt is set to "Issue|Number", then the prompt will be split between "Issue" and "Number", no matter how much room is available for the prompt. (Default = **<no value>**)
Layout - Item → Item/prompt gap (ITMIPG)	Specifies the number of blank spaces to place between the end of one field and the start of the prompt of the next field. If set to **0** in multirecord blocks (with the prompts above the items), the items will be placed adjacent to each other with no spaces between them. This will produce a spreadsheet-like layout. (Default = **2**)
Layout - Item → Item split prompt marker (ITMSPM)	Specifies a character that can be used to specify the location to split a prompt if the generator determines that it needs to be split. Using this character will *not* force the prompt to split and will only give the generator a suggested location to split the prompt if it needs to. (Default = **<no value>**)

TABLE 19-4. *Important Single-Record Block Layout Preferences* (continued)

Multiple-Record Block Layout Troubleshooting Guide

Problem	**Solution**
I set ITMIPG to 0, but some of my items are not appearing adjacent to each other.	This is probably because you have prompts that are wider than your items. You can solve this by 1. Reducing the width of the prompts (use abbreviations). 2. Increasing the *Width* of the items until they are wider than the number of characters used by the *prompt.* You can make the items wider than the column that they are based on without any problems because the generated form still limits the entry to the column width. 3. If you have multiple-word prompts, you can use the ITMFPS preference to force the prompt to split.
I have prompts that are the same size as the items, and this is causing my prompts to run into each other because ITMIGP is set to 0.	Use the same techniques as in the previous problem.
My two-word prompts are not wrapping, and this is taking up too much room.	Unless you use the ITMFPS preference, the prompts will not necessarily split where you want them to. If you want to force a split at a particular place, use ITMFPS.
I want all of the items to be on one line, but the generator keeps wrapping some of the items to the next line.	Try the following approaches: 1. Make sure that the *Width* of all of the items will fit into one line. You can reduce the *Width* to be less than the actual column size and allow users to scroll to see the whole text. 2. Reduce the size of the prompts so that they are narrower than the item widths. 3. Use ITMFPS to force any multiword prompts to split onto two lines.

Now that we have covered the basics of multiple-record block layout, we can go into some more complicated multiple-record layout techniques.

Overflow Options

In a multirecord block when all of the items do not fit onto one line, the remaining items will overflow into another area. There are four different overflow styles that are available:

Overflow Style	Description
Wrap line	The items that don't fit on a single line will be wrapped onto another line. This is the default setting. Figure 19-8 is an example of this.
Overflow area right	The block will be split vertically into two areas, a multirecord context area on the left, and a multiple-line (one record at a time) overflow area on the right. The amount of space in each area is determined by preferences. The items in the overflow area will display the values for the record that the cursor is on.
Overflow area below	The items that don't fit on a single line will be moved into an overflow area below the main multirecord area (the context area). The items in the overflow area will display the values for the record that the cursor is on.
Spreadtable	The block is split vertically into a context and overflow region like in the Overflow Right style. One or more rows of context items are laid out in a one-line-per-row multirow format in the context area at the left. A *spreadtable* (a stacked canvas with a horizontal scrollbar) that contains the overflow items on a single line is at the right. Because the spreadtable is a scrollable stacked canvas, its width is not restricted by the width of the content canvas.

TABLE 19-5. *Multirecord Block Overflow Options*

The overflow options are determined by the value of the module component's *Overflow style* property, which is available in the Display tab of the Edit Module Component dialog.

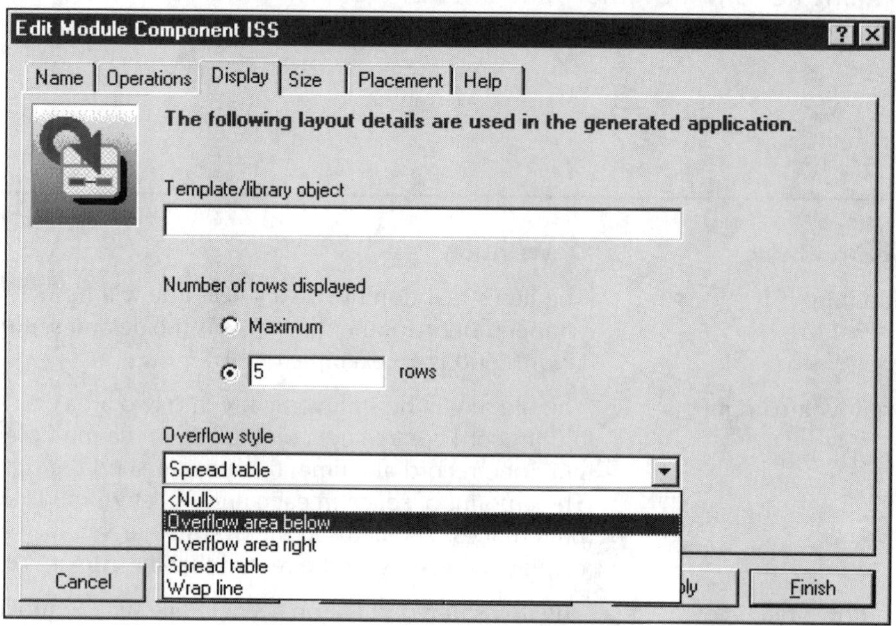

The overflow style also can be set using the *Overflow* property of the module component's Property Palette. In the following sections, we will present examples of each type of overflow.

Overflow Right Example

Figure 19-9 is an example of a generated Overflow Right block. The effects of some of the important Overflow Area preferences are identified in the figure.

Table 19-6 is a list of the important preferences that control Overflow Right layout.

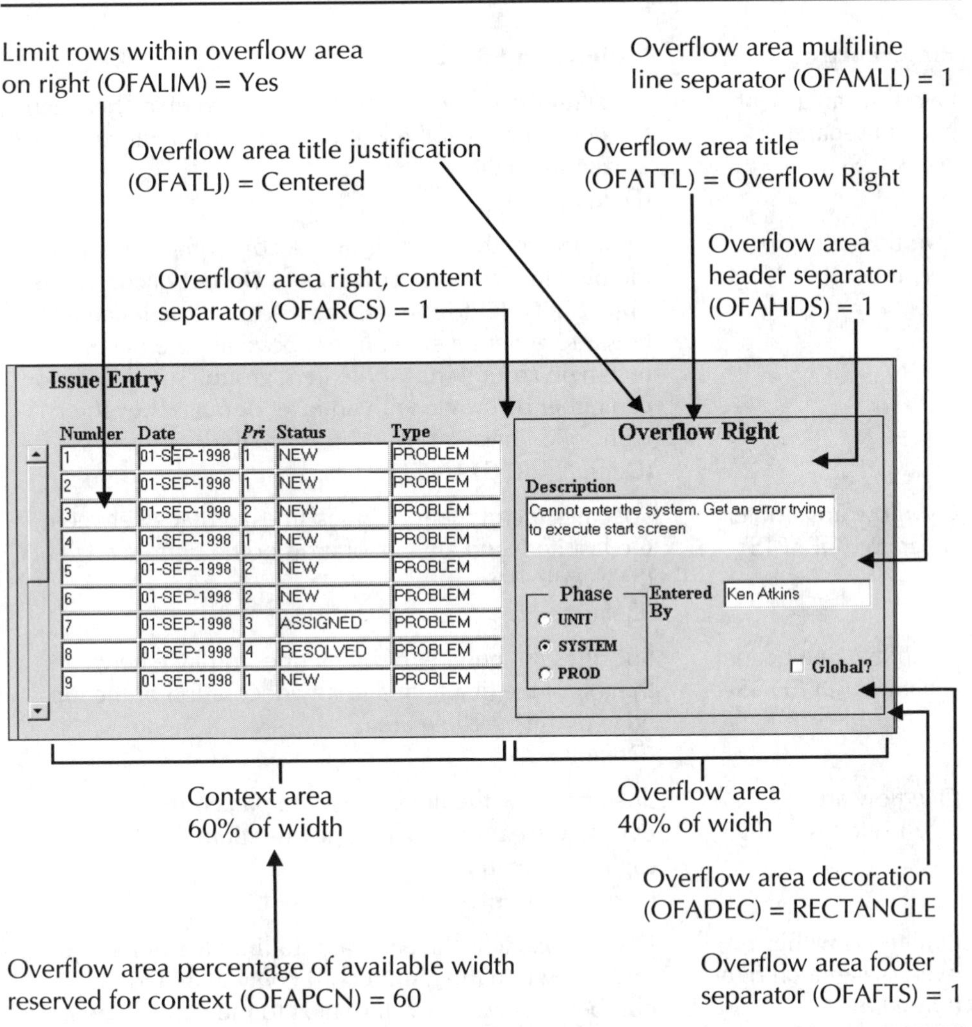

FIGURE 19-9. *Overflow Right example*

Preference	Values and Effect
Overflow area right, content separator (ORARCS)	Specifies the number of blank spaces to place between the context area at the left and the spreadtable overflow area at the right. (Default = **1**)
Overflow area decoration (OFADEC)	Controls whether there is any decoration placed around the overflow area. It can be set to **Do not decorate the object (NONE)** to suppress any decoration. It can also be set to generate either lines above and below or a rectangle around the whole item group. The decoration can either be drawn with an inset or outset bevel, or with solid lines. (Default = **RECTANGLE**)
Overflow area footer separator (OFAFTS)	Specifies the number of blank lines to place between the last item and any decoration or the bottom edge of the overflow area. (Default = **1**)
Overflow area header separator (OFAHDS)	Specifies the number of blank lines to place between the top of the first item and any decoration or the top edge of the overflow area. (Default = **1**)
Overflow area justification (OFAJUS)	Specifies how the items are to be placed in the overflow area. Values: **Left justification**, **Centered**, **Right justification**. (Default = **Centered**)
Limit rows within overflow area on right (OFALIM)	If set to **Yes**, tells the generator to limit the number of rows shown in the multirecord context area to the number of rows that will fit next to the context area. Setting this preference to **Yes** makes it easy to even up the context area and the overflow area, no matter how high the overflow area ends up. If set to **No**, the number of records will be based on the *Rows displayed* property as usual. (Default = **Yes**)

TABLE 19-6. *Important Overflow Right Preferences*

Preference	Values and Effect
Overflow area multiline line separator (OFAMLL)	Specifies the number of blank lines to place between each row of items in the overflow area. (Default = **1**)
Overflow area percentage of available width reserved for context (OFAPCN)	For overflow right, this is probably the most important preference for layout control, because it tells the generator how to divide the block between the context area at the left and the overflow area at the right. It specifies the percentage of the available area to reserve at the left for the context area. The default is **50**, which splits the block evenly between the context area and the overflow area
Overflow area title justification (OFATLJ)	Tells the generator how to justify the title that is placed over the overflow area. (Default = **Left justification)**
Overflow area title (OFATTL)	Unlike blocks or item groups, there is no property in the repository that can be used to specify the title in an overflow area. Instead, the overflow title is specified using this preference. If you want to title your overflow areas, you will have to specify this preference separately for each block in your form that has an overflow. This preference has no value by default and, if left empty, there will be no title generated.

TABLE 19-6. *Important Overflow Right Preferences* (continued)

Overflow Below Example

Figure 19-10 is an example of a generated Overflow Below block with the effect of some of the important Overflow Area preferences identified in the figure.

Most of the oveflow layout preferences work essentially the same for the Overflow Below region as they do for the Overflow Right region. Refer to Table 19-6 for a description of how the overflow layout preferences work.

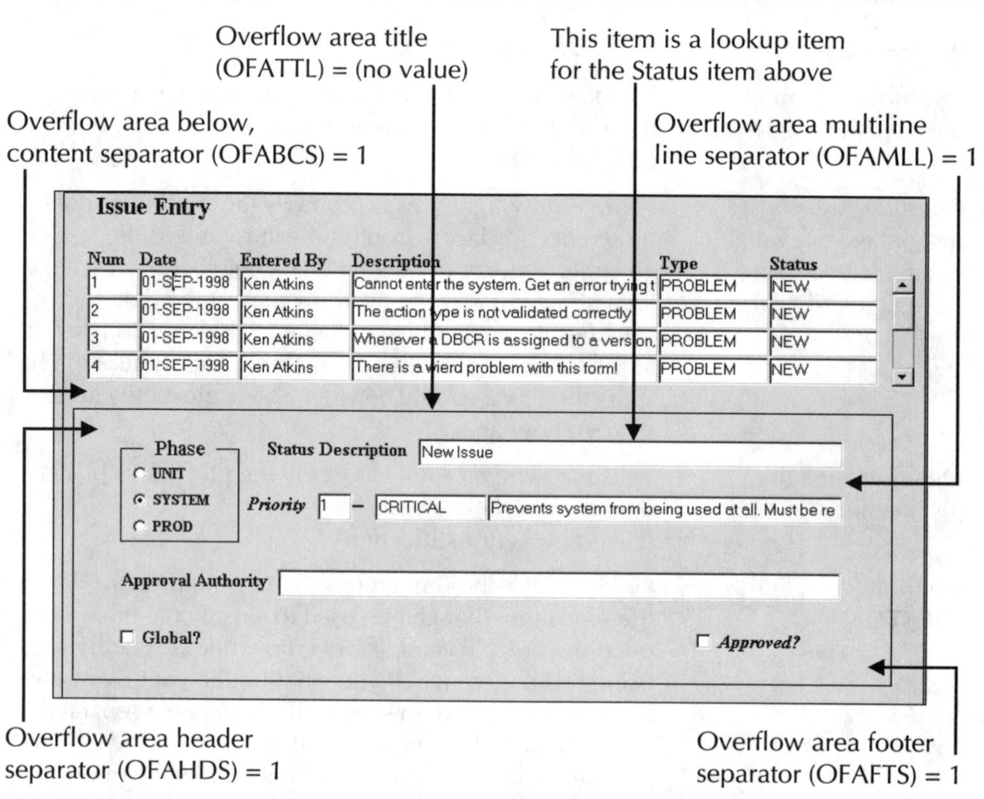

FIGURE 19-10. *Overflow Below example*

The following preference is specific to Overflow Below:

Preference	**Values and Effect**
Overflow area below, content separator (OFABCS)	Specifies the number of blank lines to place between the bottom of the context area and the start of the overflow area. (Default = **1**)

Spreadtable Overflow Example

Figure 19-11 is an example of a generated Spreadtable Overflow block with the effect of some of the important Overflow Area preferences identified in the figure.

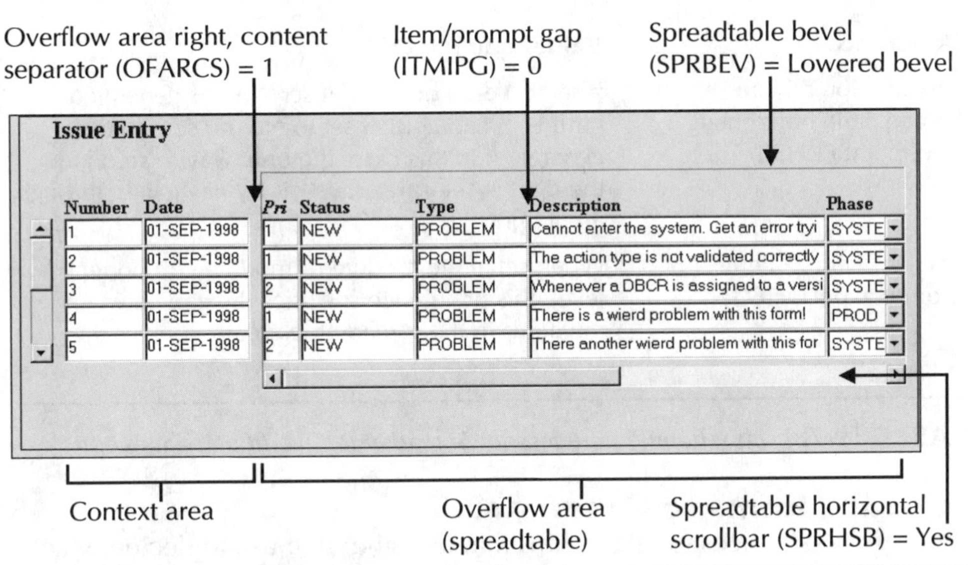

FIGURE 19-11. *Spreadtable Overflow example*

Table 19-7 is a list of the important preferences that control Spreadtable Overflow layout.

Preference	Values and Effect
Layout - Overflow → Overflow area right, content separator (ORARCS)	Specifies the number of blank spaces to place between the context area at the left and the spreadtable overflow area at the right. (Default = **1**)
Layout - Spread Tab → Spread table bevel (SPRBEV)	Specifies the beveling of the spreadtable. Valid options are **Lowered bevel** (Default) **Raised bevel** **No bevel**

TABLE 19-7. *Important Preferences for Spreadtable Overflow*

Preference	Values and Effect
Layout - Spread Tab → Spread table horizontal scrollbar (SPRHSB)	If set to **Yes**, a horizontal scrollbar is generated for the spreadtable. If set to **No**, no scrollbar is generated. In this case, the only way to scroll to the right in the spreadtable is by navigating through the items.
Layout - Item → Item/ prompt gap (ITMIPG)	When set at the module or module component level, this preference specifies the gap between the items in the spreadtable area as well as the context area.

TABLE 19-7. *Important Preferences for Spreadtable Overflow* (continued)

Selecting Items to Overflow

There are two choices for algorithms that Designer will use to decide which items to place into the overflow area. It uses the same algorithms for all of the overflow types, with a few differences. The algorithm chosen is determined by the *Overflow area table uses default context items (OFADFT)* preference, which has the effect shown in Table 19-8.

OFADFT Setting / First Item Type	Algorithm Used to Select Context Items
Yes / PK or Descriptor	If the first displayed item in the module component is either a PK or a descriptor, then the following algorithm is used: Forms Generator puts the first item into the context area, and then keeps adding items to the context area in the order they are set to be displayed, until either. There is no room in the context area, *or* The next item is not a PK or descriptor item. All remaining Repository items (regardless of the *Context* property or whether they are part of the primary key or are descriptors) are put in the overflow area. (Note that a descriptor item is an item that is based on a column that has a value in its *Descriptor sequence* property.)

TABLE 19-8. *Effect of the* overflow area table uses default context items (OFADFT) *Preference*

OFADFT Setting / First Item Type	Algorithm Used to Select Context Items
Yes / Not PK or Descriptor	If the first item is not a PK or descriptor column, the first item is placed in the overflow and all of the rest of the items (regardless of *Context* property or whether they are part of the primary key or are descriptors) are put in the overflow.
No Context	Setting this preference to **No** allows you to specify the overflow items specifically by using the item's *Context* property. If the first item has its *Context* property set to **Yes**, the generator will place it in the context area and keep adding items to the context area in the sequence they were entered until either There is no room in the context area, *or* The next item has its *Context* property set to **No** or is null. We have found this setting to be the most useful. It allows you to easily specify which items go into the context area and which are to overflow.
No Not Context	If the first item has its *Context* property set to **No**, the first item is placed in the overflow, and all of the rest of the items (regardless of the *Context* property, or whether they are part of the primary key or are descriptors) are put in the overflow.

TABLE 19-8. *Effect of the* overflow area table uses default context items (OFADFT) *Preference* (continued)

Block Overflow Troubleshooting Guide

Problem	Solution
Even though I identified the item as a context item, it still overflowed right.	Check the setting of the OFAPCN preference. If there is not room in the available context percentage, items will be placed in the overflow even if they are identified as context items.
Some of my items are not overflowing even though they have their *Context* property set to **Yes**.	All of the context items need to be sequenced together. When the generator reaches a noncontext item, that item will be placed in the overflow and so will the rest of the items, no matter what their *Context* property is set to.

Problem	Solution
When I set the ITMIPG preference to 0 to save space in the multirecord context area, it also eliminates space between items and prompts in the overflow area, which I don't want.	Yes, this is the way it works. Many of the layout settings apply equally to the context items and the overflow items, and you cannot use different settings for each. You have three options to get around this problem: 1. Work with the item layout in the overflow to reduce the effect of this (i.e., place only one item in each row). 2. Set ITMIPG to 1 or 2. 3. Add the items to vertical item groups, and use item group settings to space them correctly.
I only get one item in the context area and the rest are placed in the overflow, no matter how I set the items' *Context* properties.	Check the properties of that first item. The problem will be one of the following: 1. If using the context method (OFADFT=N), then the first item probably does not have its *Context* property set to **Yes**. 2. If using the PK/Descriptor method (OFADFT=Y), then the first item is neither a PK nor a descriptor. Fix the settings of the first item, or reorder the items so the first item has the correct settings.
I tried to use the tab stop preferences to format my overflow area and it is not working.	The tab preferences do not work for overflow areas. Sorry.

Using Item Groups in Multirecord Blocks

You can use item groups in multirecord blocks, but the effect is a little different than in single-record blocks. As well as being used to add decorations to a group of items, they can be used to effectively implement an "overflow within" option. The layout control and selection of items work the same for multirow blocks as they do for single-record blocks, so for these topics refer to "Using Nonstacked Item Groups for Layout Control," earlier in the chapter.

Effect of *Layout Style* Property on Item Group Layout

The *Layout Style* property of item groups, along with a few preferences, determines how the item group will be generated in multirecord blocks. There are basically three different styles, which we will detail in the following examples.

Item Groups in Multirecord Blocks: Standard Layout

This option repeats the item group for each record. The item group layout is much the same as in a single-record block. The following illustration shows how this looks.

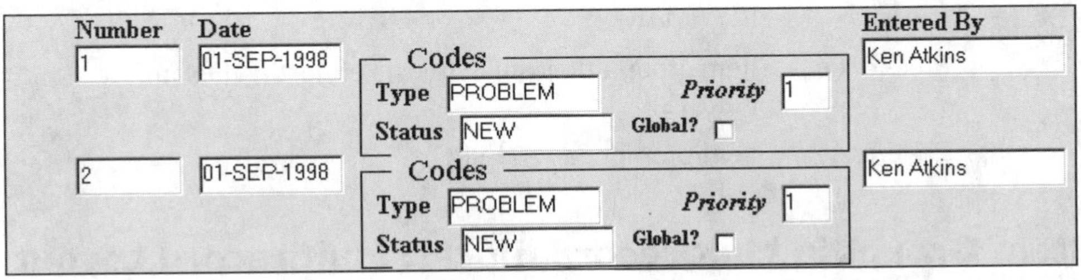

The following property settings and preferences were used to produce the layout in this illustration. The Key preferences that make the item group use this style are listed first and are marked. The other preferences were used to get this particular layout.

Key	Type	Property/Preference	Setting
Yes	Preference	Enable creation of single areas for multirow blocks (SARENB)	No
Yes	Property	Item Group *Layout Style*	Standard
Yes	Property	Item Group *Stacked?*	No
	Property	Item Group *Prompt*	Codes
	Preference	Item group orientation within group (GRPOWG)	Horizontal

Key	Type	Property/Preference	Setting
	Preference	Item group decoration (GRPDEC)	Rectangle
	Preference	Item group footer separator (GRPFTS)	0
	Preference	Item group header separator (GRPHDS)	0
	Preference	Item group horizontal inter-item spacing (GRPHIS)	1
	Preference	Item group margin (GRPMAR)	1 (Default)
	Preference	Item group title justification (GRPTLJ)	Left justify (Default)
	Preference	Item/prompt gap (ITMIPG)	1

Item Groups in Multirecord Blocks: Multirecord Layout

This option displays the items in the item group in a multirecord layout just like the rest of the items. The effect of this is to group items together for decoration purposes. You can easily use this setting to label a group of items as in the following illustration:

Number	Date	Codes: Type	Codes: *Priority*	Codes: Status	Entered By	Global?
1	01-SEP-1998	PROBLEM	1	NEW	Ken Atkins	☐
2	01-SEP-1998	PROBLEM	1	NEW	Ken Atkins	☐
3	01-SEP-1998	PROBLEM	2	NEW	Ken Atkins	☐
4	01-SEP-1998	PROBLEM	1	NEW	Ken Atkins	☐
5	01-SEP-1998	PROBLEM	2	NEW	Ken Atkins	☐

The following property settings and preferences were used to produce the layout in this illustration. The Key preferences that make the item group use this style are listed first and marked. The other preferences were used to get this particular layout.

Key	Type	Property/Preference	Setting
Yes	Preference	Item group orientation within group (GRPOWG)	Horizontal
Yes	Property	Item Group *Layout Style*	Multirecord
Yes	Property	Item Group *Stacked?*	No
	Property	Item Group *Prompt*	Code
	Preference	Item group decoration (GRPDEC)	Rectangle
	Preference	Item group footer separator (GRPFTS)	1 (Default)
	Preference	Item group header separator (GRPHDS)	0
	Preference	Item group horizontal inter-item spacing (GRPHIS)	1
	Preference	Item group margin (GRPMAR)	1 (Default)
	Preference	Item group title justification (GRPTLJ)	Centered
	Preference	Item/prompt gap (ITMIPG)	1

Item Groups in a Single Area in a Multirecord Block

This option displays only one occurrence of the item group and displays the values for the current record in the item group fields. This functions like an overflow, but the item group can be placed between the multirecord items. You might call it an *overflow within* layout. Here is an example of what it looks like:

Number	Date	Codes	Entered By
1	01-SEP-1998	Type PROBLEM Priority 2	Ken Atkins
2	01-SEP-1998	Status NEW Global? ☐	Ken Atkins
3	01-SEP-1998		Ken Atkins

The following property settings and preferences were used to produce the layout in the illustration just shown. The Key preferences that make the item group use this style are listed first and marked. The other preferences were used to get this particular layout.

Key	Type	Property/Preference	Setting
Yes	Preference	Enable creation of single areas for multirow blocks (SARENB)	Yes
Yes	Property	Item Group *Layout Style*	Multirecord
Yes	Property	Item Group *Stacked?*	No
	Property	Item Group *Prompt*	Code
	Preference	Item group decoration (GRPDEC)	Rectangle
	Preference	Item group footer separator (GRPFTS)	1 (Default)
	Preference	Item group header separator (GRPHDS)	0
	Preference	Item group multiline format (GRPMLF)	2
	Preference	Item group orientation withing group (GRPOWG)	Horizontal
	Preference	Item group horizontal inter-item spacing (GRPHIS)	1
	Preference	Item group margin (GRPMAR)	1 (Default)
	Preference	Item group title justification (GRPTLJ)	Left (Default)
	Preference	Item/prompt gap (ITMIPG)	1

Single Areas in Multirecord Blocks

Another layout feature that can be very useful is called *single areas*. Using single areas, you can specify that two-dimensional items like images and multiline text areas can be displayed once for a multirecord block. As the current record changes, the value of the single area item changes accordingly. Here is an example of a layout that uses a single area:

Number	Date	Type	Description	*Priority*	Status
1	01-SEP-1998	PROBLEM	Cannot enter the system. Get an error trying to execute start screen	1	NEW
2	01-SEP-1998	PROBLEM		1	NEW
3	01-SEP-1998	PROBLEM		2	NEW
4	01-SEP-1998	PROBLEM		1	NEW

You can also use item groups to place multiple items in a single area, as was detailed in the previous section. Single area generation is controlled by the following preferences (all of these preferences are in the *Layout – Single Area* category):

Preference	Values and Effect
Single area cutoff height (SARCHT)	The minimum height an item can be to become a single area item. (Default = **2**)
Enable creation of single area for multirow blocks (SAREN)	Tells the generator whether or not to create single areas. If set to **No**, single areas are never created. If set to **Yes**, single areas are created for items that meet the other criteria. (Default = **Yes**)
Limit rows within highest single area (SARLIM)	If set to **Yes**, tells the generator to limit the number of rows in the block to the number of rows that will fit next to the single area. If set to **No**, the number of records will be based on the *Rows displayed* property as usual.

Item Prompt Formatting

Even though we have covered many prompt-related issues in the previous sections, there are a few prompt topics that we thought we should cover specifically.

Forcing Prompts to Split

By default, the generator will split two prompts to fit the items in the layout. However, sometimes we want the prompts to always split, no matter what the layout. You might want to do this so that *all* of the prompts are split in a layout. There is a generator preference that allows you to do this. If you set the *Layout - item → Marker to Force Prompt Splitting* (*ITMFPS*) preference to a character, then you can insert that character into the prompt, and the generator will always split the prompt there. For example, if you set the following,

- *Marker to Force Prompt Splitting (ITMFPS)* = ">"
- *Item Prompt* = "Issue>Description"

you will get the following prompt layout, even if there is room above the item to display the prompt without splitting it.

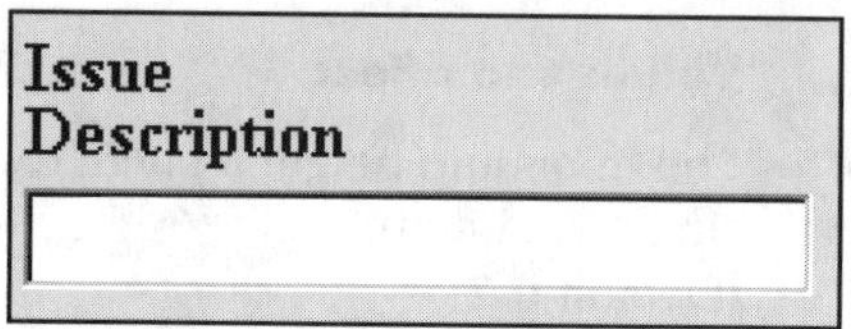

TIP

Forcing prompts to split on a multirecord block in which the prompts are above the items causes a slight problem. The prompts are all aligned at the top, so the unsplit prompts are not immediately above the items. This space between the items and the prompts is not very appealing. We detail a way to fix this problem in the next chapter (refer to the second tip in Recipe 4).

This preference should not be confused with another very similar preference: *Layout - Item → Item split prompt marker (ITMSPM)*. That preference is used to give the generator a suggested place to split the prompt if it needs to, but it does not force the split.

Split Prompts on Single-Record Blocks

For single-record blocks, the prompts are usually placed to the left of the item and they are not split. However, if the generator cannot fit more items in a smaller space, it will split the prompts at the left as in the following example:

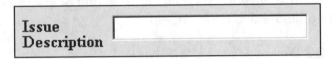

Issue
Description

This behavior is controlled by the *Layout - Item → Allow split prompts (ITMASP)* preference, which has the following possible values:

- **Yes, always do it.** (Default) Tells the generator that it can split the prompts whenever it can save room by doing so.
- **No, never do it.** Tells the generator that it can never split the prompts.
- **Do it for multirow blocks.** Tells the generator that it can split the prompts in multirecord blocks (in which the prompts are above) but not for single row blocks (in which the prompts are to the left).

Prompts Above on Single-Record Blocks

Normally, the generator places the prompts to the left of the items in single-record blocks. However, sometimes you might like to place the prompts *above* the items in a single-record block. You can use the *Layout - Item → Allow prompts above in a single-row block (ITMPAS)* preference to force this to happen. The default for this preference is **No**, which will place the prompts to the left. If you set it to **Yes**, the prompts will be generated above the items just like for multiple-record blocks. There is an example of this in the next chapter.

Post Prompts

Most of the time you will only need prompts to the left or above an item. Sometimes, however, you might like to place some static prompts immediately to the right of an item. For example, you might want to place a measurement unit to the right of an item. You can use a special character specified by the *Layout - Item → Item post prompt marker (ITMPPM)* to enter a post prompt (text displayed immediately after the item) into the *Prompt* property of an item along with the standard prompt. For example, if you set the following properties and preferences,

- *Item Post Prompt Marker (ITMPPM)* = "|"
- *Item Prompt* = "Diameter|Inches"

then you would generate an item that looked like this:

Controlling Layout Using Smaller Character Cells

All of the spacing preferences and size properties in Oracle Designer refer to the character cell identified in the *Character cell Width* and *Height* properties in the template form used to generate the forms. If the *Layout - Block → Block footer separator (BLKFTS)* is set to **1**, this means that there will be one character cell between the bottom of the items and the decoration. In the templates provided by Oracle, the character cell size is .1 inches by .25 inches. Therefore, there will be .25 inches between the bottom of the items and the decoration. All of the examples in this chapter and the next are using the default character cell size of .1 inches wide by .25 inches high.

However, the character cell size is customizable. You can edit the template forms and set the character cell to any size you want, but you need to consider carefully the effect that changing the character cell size will have on the preference settings you use. If you make large changes to the character cell size, the factory settings may no longer be reasonable. For instance, if you make the character cell only .01 inches wide, the factory setting for *Layout - Item → Prompt/Item separator* of 1 would place the prompts right next to the items, which does not look good.

One problem with the default character cell sizes is that they are too granular. Consider the block header and footer spacing. If we set the *Block footer separator (BLKFTS)* and the *Block header separator (BLKHDS)* to 0 to save space, the items end up being placed right against the block decoration, which does not look good. If we leave these preferences at their factory settings of 1, we have wasted .5 inches of our screen real estate.

There is a solution to this problem that has been used very effectively for years. If you set the character cell size very small, and then set the layout preferences to settings that make sense with the new character cell size, you can get much more precise control of the layout. One trick is to set the template's *Real Unit* property to **Pixel** and set the character cell to something like 5 x 4 pixels. Then you can update all of the preferences to make sense with this character cell size. Since the standard character cell is 10 x 24 pixels, you need to multiply the factory setting of every vertical spacing preference by 6 and the factory setting of every horizontal spacing preference by 2. You must do this for every setting to make sure you get consistent layout results. Then from this starting place, you can modify the settings to save space. For example, the pixel equivalent for the factory setting of the *Layout - Block → Block footer separator* would be 6. You could probably set this preference and the header equivalent to 3, thereby saving .25 inches in your layout. You would also have to update all of your item display widths by the same multiplier in order get the correct item widths.

This approach seems like a lot of work, so you might wonder if it is worth the effort. However, if you create a standard preference set with all of the factory equivalents, you can always apply the preference set at the application level whenever you create a new application so that every module inherits the correct preferences. You could also set the *Display width* and *height* settings for all of the columns so that when the items are added to the modules, they will automatically have the correct widths. Or, you could write an API routine that would automatically set the *Display width* and *height* for the columns, using each column's width and multiplying it by the correct factor.

CHAPTER 20

A Layout Generation Cookbook

In this chapter, we are going to present you with a series of example screens that can be generated from Oracle Designer and show you how to generate them. Instead of giving you detailed step-by-step generation techniques for each example, we are just going to detail what property and preferences settings were needed to generate the layouts. Our goal in this chapter is not to show you *how* to navigate and enter data in the tool, but rather *what* to enter in order to achieve the desired results. In the sections that follow, each of which represents a screen example, we will include the following:

- A screenshot of the example
- A list of the layout features implemented in the example, along with some comments about each feature
- Tables showing the key property settings that were used to produce the example
- Tables showing the key preference settings used to produce the example
- Where appropriate, a "Layout Generation Tips" section with tips, techniques, and warnings about generating the example.

A Layout Generation Cookbook

You might want to consider this chapter a kind of generation "cookbook," with each section below a recipe. Each recipe starts with a picture of the finished "dish" (a screenshot), gives you an ingredient list (tables of property and preference settings), and describes the dish (navigation and functionality). Just like most recipes that assume you know the basics of cooking, we will assume you know the basics of using the Design Editor, and so we will not go into detail about how to create the module. Obviously, this cannot be an exhaustive list of all possible layouts. We have tried to pick some layouts that will be the most common or most useful. In order to get the most out of each example, we will cover multiple layout techniques with each one. This does not mean you have to use the exact combinations that we use. You can often mix and match different techniques to produce the layouts you need.

We are not going to present an exhaustive list of all of the properties and preferences needed to produce the layouts. We will include *all* of the preference settings that were modified from the factory defaults, as well as some of the default preference settings that are very important to the specified layout. However, we will only include property settings that are important to the specified layout.

Using Preference Sets

We have defined many of the preferences used to produce these layouts as preference sets that are available on the CD that comes with this book. In the title of each table of preferences defined, we have indicated the name of the preference set in parentheses. If you want to implement some of these design standards, you can load the preference sets into your own applications and use them as they are or as a starting place for developing your own.

Using preference sets instead of setting the preferences directly on the objects does not make a difference in the generated layouts. However, using preference sets is a much better and easier way to manage the hundreds of preferences that you have to deal with in Oracle Designer.

Another point you will notice is that we have used some naming conventions when we named these preference sets. We have reserved the first two characters of the name to identify what level the preference set is defined for. For example, if a preference set name starts with "IG_," we know it is a preference set that is intended to be applied to an item group. Similarly, "MC_" applies to module components, "MD_" applies to modules, "AP_" applies to applications, etc. For the rest of the names, we have tried to be descriptive by naming the settings for some of the more important preferences in the set. For example, "IG_H_2_REC_LEFT" indicates that this is a preference set to implement a horizontal item group, allowing two items per row, with a rectangle decoration, and a left justified title. We cannot name every preference in the set, nor would we want to. We just want to make it a little easier to find the preference set we're looking for.

Single Block Layouts

We will start with some single block layouts. These layouts can also be used for blocks placed in multiple block layouts, but these styles are generally used for blocks that have many items that take up a lot of space.

NOTE

For the single block examples (Recipes 1–3), we are going to depart from our standard application for a bit and use a different table. This example and the ones that follow will use a table called WIDGETS that contains category, characteristic, dimension, and inventory information about widgets. All of these areas have three or four items in them, and they are usually grouped into corresponding item groups.

This section will include the following recipes:

- **Recipe 1: Grouping Logically Related Items Using Nested Item Groups** This example shows how item groups can be used to group items together. It also shows how item groups can be nested, both for layout control and for labeling.
- **ecipe 2: No Space Between Lines, Using Tab Stops to Align Items** This example shows what a single record block layout with no space between the lines looks like. It also shows how you can use tab stops to align items into columns.
- **Recipe 3: Single Block Tab Canvas, Zero Space Item Group** This example shows you how to use a single block tab canvas (item group tab canvas) to fit many items into the same page. It also details how to use "zero space" item groups to help control layout.

Recipe 1: Grouping Logically Related Items Using Nested Item Groups

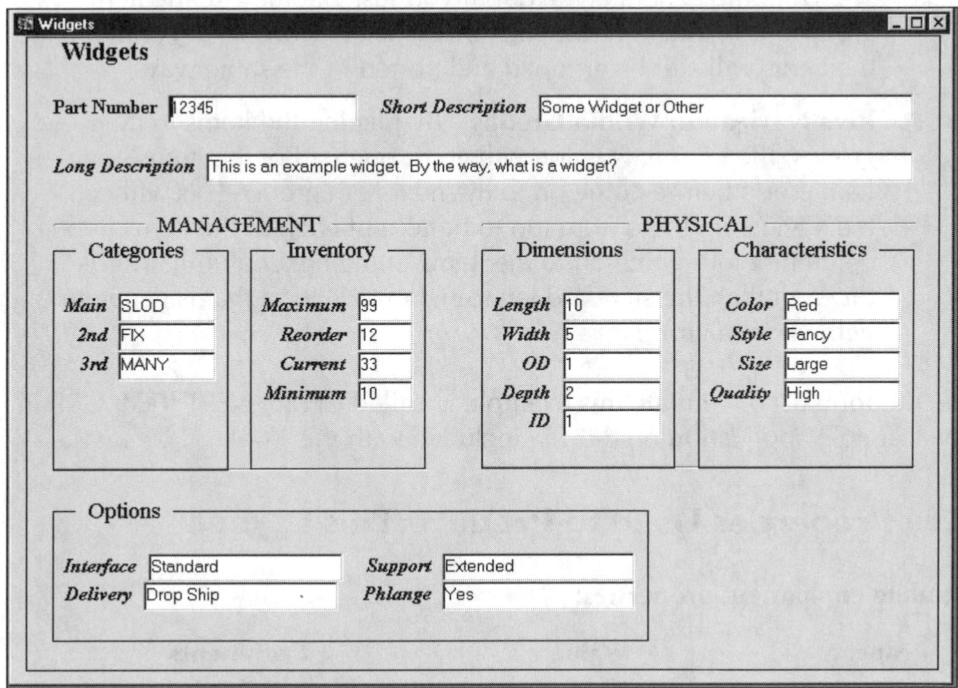

Features of This Layout

- **Single Block / Single Record Layout** Since there were so many items in this block, only one record from one table is shown at a time.
- **Related Items Grouped into Item Groups** This table has many items that are logically related to each other. This layout places each group of logically related items in item groups so that they will be displayed together.
- **Item Groups Are Nested** Since some of the item groups are also logically related, some of the item groups were placed in other parent item groups. These are called *nested* item groups.

- **Item Groups Are Decorated** In this example, the item groups are decorated with rectangles and, for the parent item groups, horizontal lines. These decorations were used mainly to help identify the item groups in the generated layout. If you just want to use the item groups for layout control, you can dispense with the decoration, and the items will still be grouped and nested in the same way.
- **Item Navigation Within Groups** By placing the items in item groups, the item navigation will go through all of the items in an item group before going on to the next item group. This will cause the navigation to go from top to bottom of each of the items in one column before going on to the items in the next column. This is different than the standard left to right navigation that is generated without item groups.

The form used to create this example is called CH20_NEST_ITM_GRP in the example application on the CD included with this book.

Key Properties Used to Produce This Layout

Module component properties:

Property	Value	Comments
Rows Displayed	1	Only displays one row.
Placement	New content canvas	Creates a new content canvas for the parent.
Title	Widgets	

Item group properties:

Item Group	Property	Setting
<All Item Groups>	Stacked?	No
MANAGEMENT	Prompt	MANAGEMENT
CAT	Prompt	Categories
INV	Prompt	Inventory
PHYSICAL	Prompt	PHYSICAL

Item Group	Property	Setting
DIM	Prompt	Dimensions
CHARC	Prompt	Characteristics
OPT	Prompt	Options

Preferences Used

The descriptions of the preferences are shown first, with the names in parentheses. Factory default settings are identified with an asterisk (*).

Module/module component preferences used:

This module used the factory default settings for all of the preferences at the module level. However, we are still going to list the major preference settings that affected the layout. These settings can be set at the module for all of the blocks in the module or at the module component level for just one block.

Preference	Setting
*Layout-Block → Block decoration (BLKDEC)	Draw a rectangle around the object.
*Layout-Block → Block dash style (BLKDST)	SOLID
*Layout-Block Block header separator (BLKFTS)	1
*Layout-Block → Block footer separator (BLKHDS)	1
*Layout-Block → Block justification (BLKJUS)	Centered.
*Layout-Block → Block Layout Style (BLKLYS)	FILL
*Layout-Block → Block multiline format (BLKMLF)	Keep adding fields as long as they fit.
*Layout-Block → Title first block of form (BLKTFB)	Yes
*Layout-Block → Block title justification (BLKTLJ)	Left justify.
*Layout-Item → Item/prompt gap (ITMIPG)	2
*Layout-Item → Allow prompts above items in a single-row block (ITMPAS)	No
*Layout-Item → Prompt/item gap (ITMPIG)	1

* Factory Default Setting

TIP

Even though these preferences were all set at the factory default, we included them in a preference set. Doing this allows us to set preferences at the application or module level and then to apply this preference set at the module component level to override higher levels and get back to the factory defaults.

Parent item group preferences used:

Different preferences were used for the parent item groups (MANAGEMENT & PHYSICAL) than were used for the children, and for the non-nested item group (Options).

Preference	Setting
Item group decoration (GRPDEC)	Draw lines at top and bottom with inset bevel.
*Item group dash style (GRPDST)	SOLID
Item group footer separator (GRPFTS)	0
Item group header separator (GRPHDS)	0
*Item group horizontal inter-item spacing (GRPHIS)	2
Item group margin (GRPMAR)	0
*Item group multi-line format (GRPMLF)	Keep adding fields as long as they fit.
Item group orientation within group (GRPOWG)	Horizontal layout.
Item group title justification (GRPTLJ)	Centered.
*Item group title position (GRPTLP)	Title is placed on any decoration.

Child item group preferences used:

Preference	Setting
*Item group decoration (GRPDEC)	Draw a rectangle around the object.
*Item group dash style (GRPDST)	SOLID

* Factory Default Setting

*Item group footer separator (GRPFTS)	1
*Item group header separator (GRPHDS)	1
*Item group horizontal inter-item spacing (GRPHIS)	2
*Item group margin (GRPMAR)	1
*Item group orientation within group (GRPOWG)	Vertical layout.
*Item group title justification (GRPTLJ)	Left justify.
*Item group title position (GRPTLP)	Title is placed on any decoration.

"Options" item group preferences used:

Preference	Setting
*Item group decoration (GRPDEC)	Draw a rectangle around the object.
*Item group dash style (GRPDST)	SOLID
*Item group footer separator (GRPFTS)	1
*Item group header separator (GRPHDS)	1
*Item group horizontal inter-item spacing (GRPHIS)	2
*Item group margin (GRPMAR)	1
Item group multiline format (GRPMLF)	2 fields per line.
Item group orientation within group (GRPOWG)	Horizontal layout.
*Item group title justification (GRPTLJ)	Left justify.
*Item group title position (GRPTLP)	Title is placed on any decoration.

In order to get the item groups to line up correctly, we overrode the setting of the *Item group footer separator (GRPFTS)* preference for the following item groups (see Tip 2 on "Layout Generation Tips," following, for a discussion of this):

Item Group	Setting
CAT (Categories)	3
INV (Inventory)	2
CHARC (Characteristics)	2

* Factory Default Setting

Layout Generation Tips

Tip 1: Placing the Items in Item Groups and Ordering the Items and Item Groups

There are two methods that can be used to easily add items to item groups and to order the items and item groups in your display.

1. The easiest method is probably the display view of the module diagram. You can easily see which items are in which item groups and what their display order is. You can drag and drop the items into the order and groups that you want them to be in.
2. If you don't want to bother opening the module diagram, you can use the *Displayed Items and Groups* area of the navigator to do the same thing. While it does not give you a graphical representation, you can still drag and drop items into the correct locations.

Tip 2: Using Headers and Footers to Align Item Groups

You will notice in the layout that for the first four item groups the decorations (rectangles) all have the same height. This was accomplished by setting the *Item group footer separator (GRPFTS)* preference higher for the item groups with fewer items. This setting moves the bottom of each decoration down so that they all lined up, which we think looks better.

Tip 3: Using Item Sizes to Line Up Items in Item Groups

By default, the items in vertical item groups are aligned to the right. If the items are of different sizes, it will cause the left edges of the items to be jagged, which does not look good. In order to prevent this, we made all of the items in each item group have the same display *Width* property. This does not mean that they have to have the same size in the database. The generated form will still correctly enforce the column width defined in the database. If you make the display width wider than the column width, there will be some leftover space at the right of the field. Another option for lining up the items in an item group is using tabs.

Recipe 2: No Space Between Lines, Using Tab Stops to Align

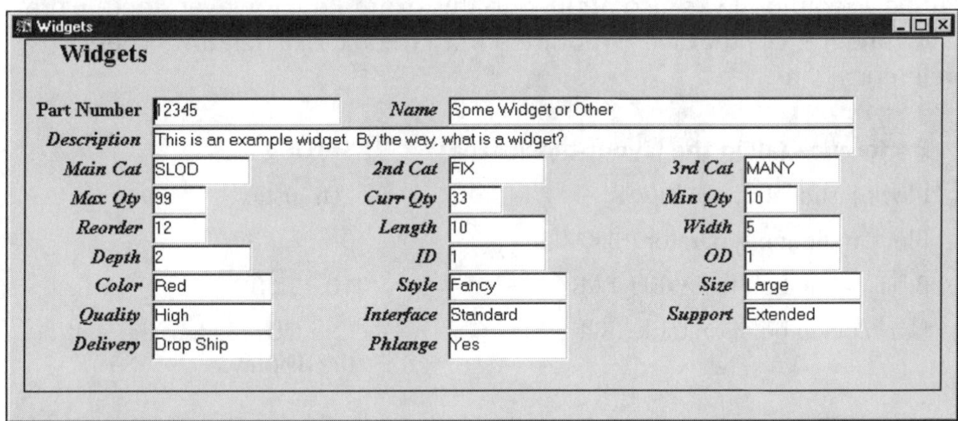

Features of This Layout

- **The Items Are Arranged into Multiple Columns Aligned by the Item Start** This layout uses tab stops to align the items into three columns. The items are aligned by the start of the actual item, which leaves the start of the prompts jagged at the left in each column.

The form used to create this example is called CH20_TAB_STOPS in the example application on the CD included with this book.

Key Properties Used to Produce This Layout

Module component properties:

Property	**Value**	**Comments**
Rows Displayed	1	Only displays one row.
Placement	New content canvas	Creates a new content canvas for the parent.
Title	Widgets	

Preferences Used

Most of the module component level preferences were left at their factory defaults. Therefore, the same preference set that was defined for the Recipe 1 example was also applied to this example. However, there were a few preferences that were modified from the factory defaults. These preferences are

Preference (all in the layout-block area)	Setting
Block justification (BLKJUS)	Left justify.
Block multiline separator (BLKMLL)	0
Block tabulation table (BLKTAB)	10.35.60
Use block tabulation table (BLKUTT)	Use tabs to align the start of the display.

Layout Generation Tips

Tip 1: Determining Tab Stops to Use

There are a few different methods that can be used to determine the tab stops you need to generate a tab layout:

- **Guess and Refine** The most straightforward method to determine the tab stops you need is to make an initial guess and then generate the form and see what you get. After you see the layout, you will have to change the preferences and try again. After a few iterations, you should get what you want.
- **Generate and Measure** Another method is to make your best guess and generate your module. Then open the module in Form Builder and use the ruler at the top of the design area to determine where you will need to set your tab stops. Chapter 19 discusses how the tab stops in Designer map to the ruler.
- **Use a Utility** There is at least one product (Design*Assist) that has a utility that will help you specify tab stops for a generated module. Others may be released in the future.

Tip 2: Using Left Block justification Only

If you want to get consistent placement of your items based on the tab stops you define, you should always set the *Layout-Block → Block justification* to **Left justification**. When you do this, the tab stops are always measured consistently from the left of the layout area. If this preference is set to **Right** or **Center**, the block layout region changes and the tab stops end up in different places on the screen when there are changes to the item sizes or placements.

Tip 3: Using Similar Prompt and Item Display Widths

The layout and positioning of the items is very sensitive to the overall width of the item display area (the width of the item and prompt together). It is much easier to achieve a columnar layout if the prompts and icons are close to the same size. If there are big differences in the sizes, it can be very difficult to get things to line up.

Recipe 3: Single Block Tab Canvas, Zero Space Item Group

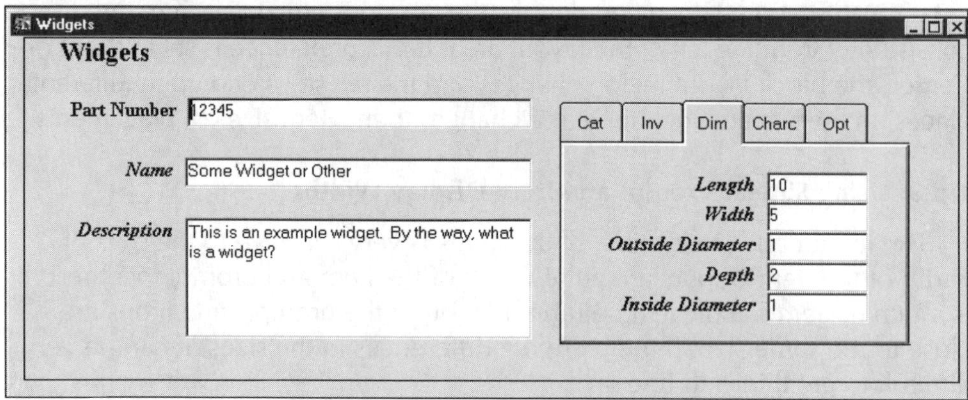

Features of This Layout

- **Tab Canvas Is Used to Display Groups of Related Items** In order to save room, the items in the different categories were placed in stacked tabbed canvases at the right of the layout. This allows five sets of items to be displayed in the same area. The disadvantage of doing this is that all of the item groups cannot all be seen at the same time. However, if that is not a concern, this layout can save you a lot of space.

- **A Zero Space Item Group Is Used to Position Items at Left** The three items at the left of the layout were placed in a *zero space* item group. By this we mean an item group that has its header, footer, and margin set to 0, with no decoration or title. This allows us to use the item group purely for grouping and positioning the items. In this case, it allows us to easily place the three items to the left of the tab canvases.

The form used to create this example is called CH20_SNGL_BLK_TABS in the example application on the CD included with this book.

Key Properties Used to Produce This Layout

The module component level properties for this example are the same as in the first example (Recipe 1).

Item group properties:

Item Group	Property	Setting
<All Item Groups>	Stacked?	Yes
CAT	Prompt	Cat
INV	Prompt	Inv
DIM	Prompt	Dim
CHARC	Prompt	Charc
OPT	Prompt	Opt

Preferences Used

Most of the module component level preferences were left at their factory defaults. Therefore, the same preference set that was defined for the Recipe 1 example was also applied to this example, MC_REC_CENTER_FILL. However, there is one preference that needs to be set correctly at the *Module* level:

Module Preference	Setting
*Layout-Canvas → Native Tabbed Canvases (CANNTC)	Yes

Item group preferences:

The items are laid out in the tab canvas item groups just as they are in a nonstacked item group. The tab canvas item group preferences were all set to the standard set of preferences identified for the child item groups in Recipe 1. However, there was one item group preference modified specifically for all of the stacked item groups in this example:

Preference	Setting
Item group header separator (GRPHDS)	0

* Factory Default Settings

This layout also featured a zero space item group that was used purely to position the three items at the left. The preference settings for this item group were as follows:

Preference	Setting
Item group decoration	Do not decorate the object.
Item group footer separator	0
Item group header separator	0
Item group margin	0
*Item group orientation within group	Vertical layout
Item group vertical inter-item spacing	1

* Factory Default Settings

Layout Generation Tips

Tip 1: Manipulating Tab Canvas Area Width and Label Width

There is no way to specify the width of the tab canvas area directly. It is determined by the width of the widest item group layout within the set of tabs. In the same way, the width of each tab is determined by the widest prompt. Because of this, you have to be careful about interactions between the width of the item group prompts and the overall width of the tab canvas area.

If your item group layouts all are narrow and you have many wide tabs, they will not all fit in the tab canvas area. In this case, the generator displays only the tabs that fit and places some tab navigation controls at the right of the tabs to allow you to scroll through the tabs (see Chapter 19 for an illustration of this). However, this is not really a good user interface. One of the advantages of tabs is that users can see all of the areas or tabs at the same time and select the one they want. You should always try to select tab *Prompts* that are narrow enough so that all of the tabs can fit in the tab canvas' width. You can also modify the item group layouts so that the tab canvas area ends up larger.

Tip 2: Positioning the Tab Canvas Area

The tab canvas area is treated by the generator like one large multiline item. It will place items before and after it and will even place multiple rows of items next to it (if the preferences are set correctly).

Tip 3: Using Item Layout Within Tab Canvases

You don't have to use the same layout preferences for each stacked item group. You can make some of the item groups vertical and others horizontal. You can change their headers and footers, etc., in order to get the layout within each tab that you need.

Tip 4: Using Zero Space Item Groups

Besides the tab canvases, this layout example used another technique, which we are calling *zero space* item groups. This is an undecorated item group that has its header, footer, and margin all set to 0. By placing the Part Number, Name, and Description items in this item group, we were able to easily place them in a vertical column to the left of the tab canvas area.

Tip 5: Correctly Ordering Item Groups

You need to make sure all of the item groups that will be part of the tab canvas set are sequenced together in the layout of your module. If there are any other items or item groups placed between the stacked item groups, you will end up generating two tab canvases! The easiest way to do this is to use the display view of the module diagrammer. You can also use the *Displayed Items and Groups* branch in the Design Editor object navigator.

Multiple Block Layouts

The recipes in this section show various ways that multiple blocks can be brought together into a single layout. For the multiple block layouts, we are returning to examples from the example application.

The recipes included in this section are

- **Recipe 4: Child with Indented Rectangle Decoration, Adjacent Items, Prompts Above, Prompts Split** This example shows a clean and simple parent/child block layout with rectangle decoration that is indented for the child block. It shows items placed adjacent to each other with split prompts above. It also shows a single record block with split prompts above.
- **Recipe 5: Overflow Below and Multiple Block Tab Canvas** This example shows a very compact layout with adjacent items and split

prompts above. It has a multirecord parent block with multiple child blocks implemented as tabs on a tab canvas in the same window.

- **Recipe 6: Multiple Windows Using Action Items, Single Area Tab Canvas** This example has an item group tab canvas implemented as a single area in a multirow block. It also shows how action items can be used to link to multiple child windows.
- **Recipe 7: Control Block, Adjacent Stacked Canvases** This example shows a control block that controls the scope of query of the main block in the form. It also shows how stacked canvases can be used to implement multiple child blocks side-by-side.

Recipe 4: Child with Indented Rectangle Decoration, Adjacent Items, Prompts Above, Prompts Split

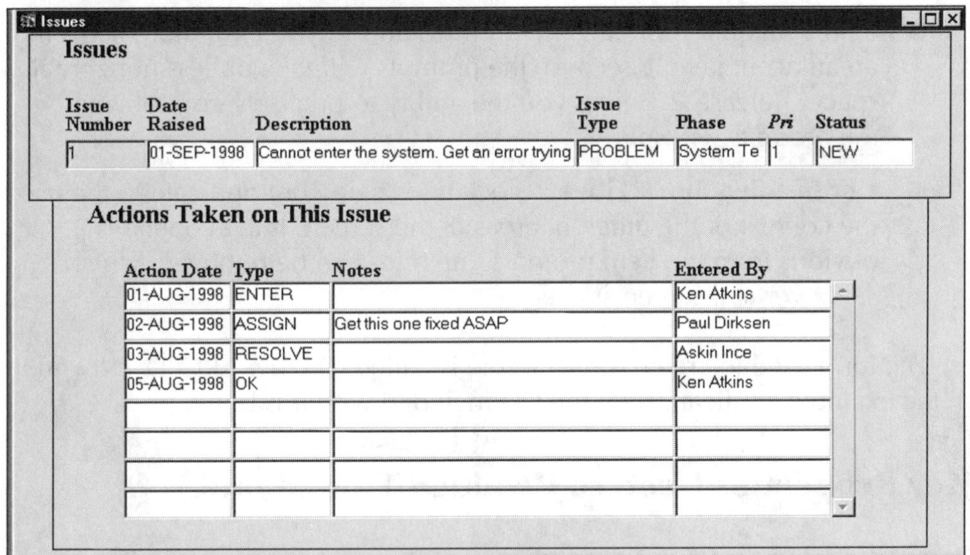

Features of This Layout

- **Parent and Child in Same Window** It is quite often easier for users to have both the parent and child block in the same window than to have the child in a separate window.
- **Block Decoration Is Solid Rectangle with Child Indented** The indentation gives the users a visual indication of the parent/child relationship between the two blocks.
- **Adjacent Items (0 Gap Between Items)** Adjacent items give you more room to add items to the layout without having to use overflow areas. It also gives the form a spreadsheet-like look that is familiar to most people.
- **Prompts Above in Single Row Block** Placing the prompts above a single row block can often give you a layout that fits all of the items onto a single row. This type of layout can take up less screen space

than a layout that has the prompts to the left, which will force the line to wrap (often into three or more lines). The visual similarity between the parent and child block in the previous illustration is also visually appealing and will often be easier for the users to navigate with.

- **Split Prompts** Splitting the prompts allows you to fit more items in an adjacent layout because the prompts will take up less horizontal space. Release 2.1 gives you the ability to precisely control where the prompts will split.
- **Left Justified Block Titles** Block titles help communicate to the user the context of the different areas of the screen. If the context is obvious from the item prompts, the titles can be removed, which saves vertical screen space.

The form used to create this example is called CH20_PARCLD_IND_ADJ in the example application on the CD included with this book.

Key Properties Used to Produce This Layout

Parent module component properties:

Property	Value	Comments
Rows Displayed	1	Only displays one row.
Placement	New content canvas	Creates a new content canvas for the parent.
Title	Issues	

Child module component properties:

Property	Value	Comments
Rows Displayed	0 or <null> (Maximum)	Entering 0 or <Null> (maximum from the dialog) tells the generator to fit as many rows as possible into the standard window size.
Placement	Same content canvas	This will place the child block in the same canvas as the parent.

Property	Value	Comments
Window	<Same window as Parent>	It does not matter what the name of the window is, as long as it is the same window as the parent.
Title	Actions Taken on This Activity	

Bound item properties:

Item Type	Property	Setting
Items with two line prompts	Prompt	First Line<Second Line (Example: "Item<Num")
Items in first block with single line prompts (see Tip 2 in the upcoming section "Layout Generation Tips."	Prompt	" "<Prompt (Example: " <Description")

Preferences Used

Module component preferences (MC_IND_ADJ_ITM_RT_SCR):

Preference	Setting
*Layout-Block → Block decoration (BLKDEC)	Draw a rectangle around the object (RECTANGLE)
*Layout-Block → Block dash style (BLKDST)	SOLID
*Layout-Block → Block header separator (BLKFTS)	1
*Layout-Block → Block footer separator (BLKHDS)	1
*Layout-Block → Block justification (BLKJUS)	Centered (CENTER)
*Layout-Block → Block Layout Style (BLKLYS)	FILL
*Layout-Block → Block multiline format (BLKMLF)	Keep adding fields as long as they fit (WRAP)
*Layout-Block → Block scrollbar position (BLKSBP)	Right justify (RIGHT)

*Factory Default Setting

Preference	Setting
Layout-Block → Block scrollbar separator (BLKSLR)	0
*Layout-Block → Title first block of form (BLKTFB)	Yes (Y)
*Layout-Block → Block title justification (BLKTLJ)	Left justify (LEFT)
Layout-Content Can → Content canvas relative block indentation (PAGBIN)	-2
*Layout-Item → Allow split prompts (ITMASP)	Yes, always do it (Y)
Layout-Item → Marker to Force Prompt Splitting ITMFPS)	<
Layout-Item → Item/prompt gap (ITMIPG)	0
Layout-Item → Allow prompts above items in a single-row block (ITMPAS)	Always (A)
Layout-Item → Prompt/item gap (ITMPIG)	0

* Factory Default Setting

These preferences have been defined in the MC_IND_ADJ_ITM_RT_SCR preference set that is defined in the example application that is on the CD provided with this book.

Layout Generation Tips

Tip 1: Determining the Width Settings Needed to Fill the Block with Adjacent Items

When you have a lot of items that you need to place in a single line, you will often have to reduce the width of some of the items to fit (as we did above). When you do this, you will want to make the items as wide as possible while still fitting them on one line. This can be difficult and time consuming to do. One quick method for this is to do the following:

1. Make your best guess at the width of all of the items in the block.
2. Reduce one of the wider items (like a description) to just a few characters. This should ensure that all of the items will be generated onto one line (assuming your estimates are anywhere close to correct).

3. Generate the form.
4. Open the form in the Developer Form Builder and open the generated canvas (CG$PAGE_1 for the first content canvas). You should be able to determine how many characters you have left by dividing the space left by the character cell width of your template (which is .1 inches/character in the standard template).
5. Increase the width of the item you reduced in step 2 by the number of characters you calculated in step 4.
6. Generate the form again. If the record wraps, reduce the width by one character and try again. Repeat this until the record does not wrap.

Tip 2: Aligning Split and Nonsplit Prompts Correctly

This screen standard includes allowing split prompts above the items. You can force the prompts to split where and when you want them to by setting the ITMPFS (Item Force Prompt Split) preference to a specific character (<), and including that character in the prompts where you want them to split. Using this technique can lead to a layout problem. If you have a single-line row with some prompts you want to split and others that you do not, the fields will not line up evenly. This is because the top of the prompts are aligned vertically, not the top of the field! In order to get around this, you need to split *every* prompt. For prompts that you do not want to split, enter a space, then enter the split character and then the prompt (for example, " <Description"). This will split the prompt, placing a blank in the first line, and the real prompt in the second line. One caution: If you leave out the leading space, not only will the prompt fail to split, it will disappear altogether (at least in release 2.1.2).

Tip 3: Remembering to Reset the *Rows Displayed* After Major Layout Changes

When the generation is successfully completed for a module component that had its *Rows Displayed* set to <null> or 0, the generator will set the *Rows Displayed* to the actual number of rows that fit into the generated form. If you make some other layout changes that might allow more rows to fit, you might want to reset the *Rows Displayed* back to <null> before generating again. This will let the generator determine how many rows should fit with the new layout.

Recipe 5: Overflow Below and Multiple Block Tab Canvas

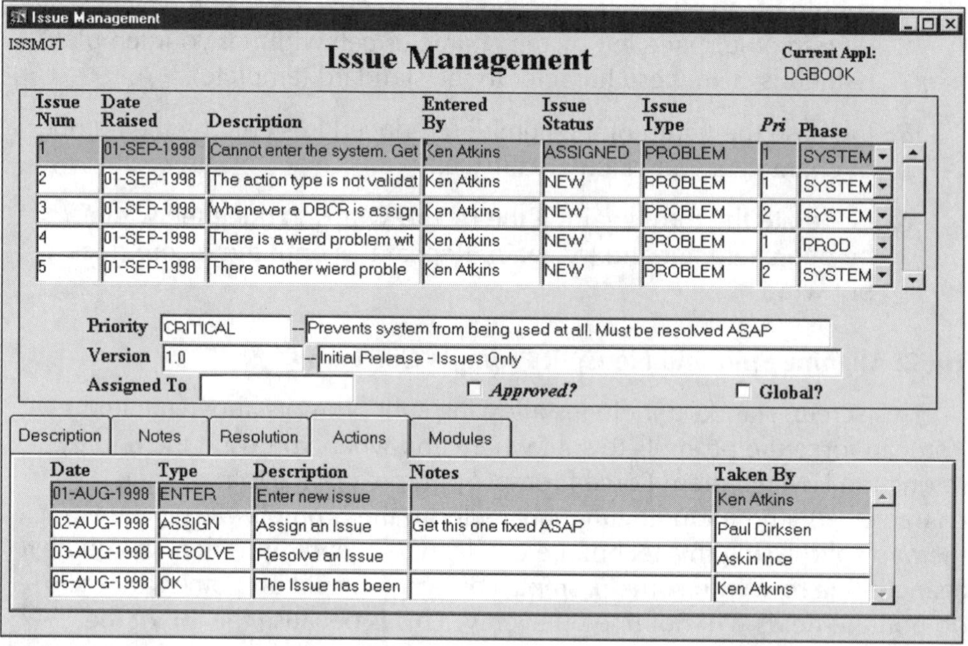

Features of This Layout

- **Multiple Child Blocks as Tab Canvas** An area at the bottom of the screen has a tab canvas with information from multiple children shown, one in each tab. The user can select the child that they want to see by selecting the tab, and that child's information will be shown for each record as they scroll through the records in the parent block.
- **Overflow Below** This recipe used an overflow below to show some items that did not fit in the multirecord layout. The values in these items will correspond to the current record in the context area.
- **0 Space Item Groups Used to Group Item and Descriptor** In the overflow area, there are some items and their descriptors that are grouped together using a zero space item group (for example,

"Version"). This prevents the line from wrapping between the item and its descriptor and saves horizontal space.

- **No Block Titles** There are no block titles in this layout. The module title functions as the block title for the parent block, and the tabs function as titles for the child blocks.
- **Module Title and Context Items from Template Form** This example also uses a different template form than the previous ones. The template form used for this example has the module title centered at the top and includes the module name at the left and a context item at the right. Chapter 22 covers how to use template forms.
- **Overflow Below of Descriptive Items** Overflow below can be used to effectively show descriptive columns for key columns in the context area. For example, the "Pri" column in the context area has two descriptive columns in the overflow area (after the "Priority" prompt).

The form used to create this example is called CH20_MULT_BLK_TAB in the example application on the CD included with this book.

Key Properties Used to Produce This Layout

Module properties:

Property	Value	Comments
Top Title	People Maintenance	Used to determine the title placed at the top of the module (see Chapter 22 for more on template usage).

Parent module component properties:

Property	Value	Comments
Rows Displayed	5	Displays five rows.
Placement	New content canvas	Creates a new content canvas for the parent.
Overflow	Overflow area below	When items do not fit in the multirecord context area, they will be placed below.

Tab canvas (child) module component properties:

Property	Value	Comments
Rows Displayed	Various (4 in the tab displayed in the preceding illustration)	Set this value to 1 to show single record child blocks, and set it to the same value for all of the multirecord child blocks.
Placement	New Tab canvas page	Places each child block in a separate tab canvas page.
Window	<Same window as Parent>	It does not matter what the name of the window is, as long as it is the same window as the parent.
Title	Text you want to appear in the tab	The title determines the text that will appear in the tab at the top of each tab canvas. In the example screenshot, the title of the module component for the selected tab is Actions.

Important item properties:

Item Name	Property	Value	Notes
L_VER.L_VER_VER_LABEL	Prompt	Version|--	The | is used to make the -- a post prompt.
L_PRI.L_PRI_LABEL	Prompt	Priority|--	See above.
All items with two line prompts. Example: ISS.RAISED_DATE	Prompt	Line1>Line2 Example: Date>Raised	The > forces the prompt split.
All items in context area with single line prompts. Example: ISS.DESCRIPTION	Prompt	{sp}>Prompt Example: >Description	See Tip 2 of Recipe 4.
All items that appear in the multirecord context area.	Context?	Yes	Setting this property to **Yes** tells the generator to leave the item in the context area.

Preferences Used

Parent module component preferences:

Module Preference	Setting
*Layout-Block → Block decoration (BLKDEC)	Draw a rectangle around the object.
Layout-Block → Block footer separator (BLKFTS)	0
Layout-Block → Block header separator (BLKHDS)	0
*Layout-Block → Block justification (BLKJUS)	Centered
*Layout-Block → Block layout style (BLKLYS)	FILL
*Layout-Block → Block margin (BLKMAR)	1
*Layout-Block → Block multi-line format (BLKMLF)	Keep adding fields as long as they fit.
Layout-Block → Block scrollbar position (BLKSBP)	Right justify.
Layout-Block → Block scrollbar separator (BLKSBS)	0
Layout-Block → Block single-line row separator (BLKSLR)	0
Layout-Block → Title first block of form (BLKTFB)	No
Layout-Item → Marker to Force Prompt Splitting (ITMFPS)	>
Layout-Item → Item/prompt gap (ITMIPG)	0
Layout-Overflow → Overflow area decoration (OFADEC)	Do not decorate the object.
Layout-Overflow → Overflow area table uses default context items (OFADFT)	No
Layout-Overflow → Overflow area footer separator (OFAFTS)	0
Layout-Overflow → Overflow area header separator (OFAHDS)	0
Layout-Overflow → Overflow area multi-line separator (OFAMLL)	0

* Factory Default Setting

These preferences have been defined in the MC_OVER_BELOW preference set that is defined in the example application that is on the CD provided with this book.

Child (tab canvas) module component preferences:

Preference	Setting
Layout-Block → Block decoration (BLKDEC)	Do not decorate the object.
Layout-Block → Block footer separator (BLKFTS)	0
Layout-Block → Block header separator (BLKHDS)	0
Layout-Block → Block scrollbar position (BLKSBP)	Right justify.
Layout-Block → Block scrollbar separator (BLKSBS)	0
Layout-Item → Item/prompt gap (ITMIPG)	0
Layout-Stacked Can → Title first block on stacked canvas (POPTFB)	No

These preferences have been defined in the MC_TAB_CANV_MR preference set that is defined in the example application that is on the CD provided with this book.

Layout Generation Tips

Tip 1: Using the *Context?* Property to Control Overflow

We find that it is much easier to set the *Layout-Overflow → Overflow area table uses default context items (OFADFT)* preference to **No** and use the items' *Context?* property to determine which items should remain in the context. If this preference is left as its default, the generator uses the key items and items identified at the table level as descriptor items to determine which items to leave in the context area. Since you will often want different context items in different layouts of the same data, you cannot use the descriptor columns to give you what you want in a consistent fashion.

Tip 2: Setting Headers and Footers to 0

Many times, if you set the headers and footers of the blocks and overflow areas to 0, you will end up with an unappealing layout. However, in this example, we were able to get away with it because of how they interacted with other design decisions. For example, since we did not title the blocks, we were able to set the block header to 0 and place the prompts right up against the decoration and still have it look OK. The same thing worked for the layout within the tab canvases.

Tip 3: Let the Generator Determine Canvas Sizes

Leave the width and height of the canvases blank. The generator will fit the canvases into the available area and, if the preferences identified above are used, everything will fit on one page.

Tip 4: Current Record Visual Attribute

When multiple record layouts are used, there needs to be a visual indication of which record the cursor is on. In this recipe (and the ones that follow) the current record visual attribute method was used. See the "Current Record Indication Using Visual Attributes" section of Chapter 13 for information about how to do this.

Recipe 6: Multiple Windows Using Action Items, Single Area Tab Canvas

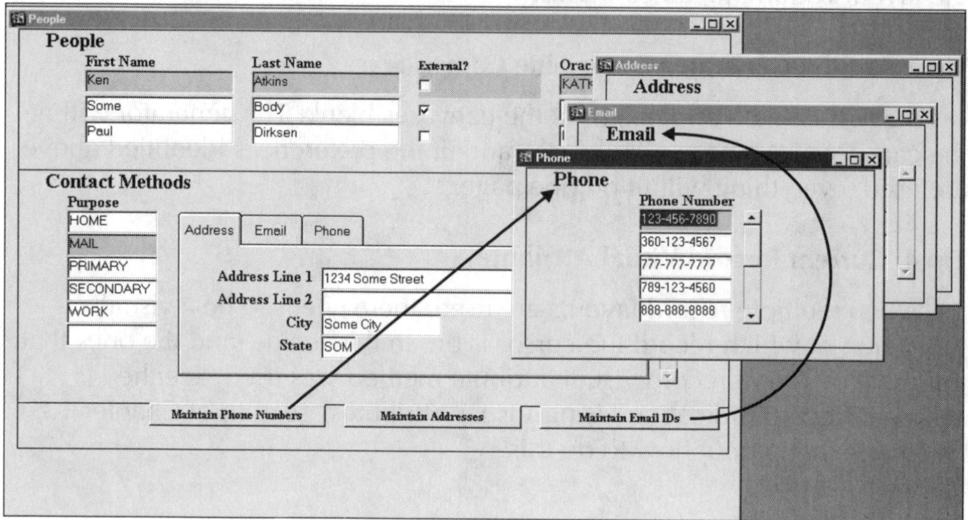

Features of This Layout

- **Action Items That Navigate to Windows** This layout uses action items at the bottom of the screen to navigate to separate windows that are used to maintain child data of the main block.
- **Nonindented Block Decoration** In this example, there was no indentation in the block decoration.
- **Tab Canvas in Single Area** In the second block, all of the items except for one are placed in an item group tab canvas. This whole item group is treated like a single area and placed as a single occurrence to the right of the single item in the context area. See the "Single Areas in Multirecord Blocks" section of Chapter 19 for more information about this.

The form used to create this example is called CH20_MULT_WINDOW in the example application on the CD included with this book.

Key Properties Used to Produce This Layout

Top (parent) module component properties:

Property	Value	Comments
Rows Displayed	3	Displays 3 rows.
Placement	New content canvas	Creates a new content canvas for the parent.
Title	People	Specifies block title.

Bottom (child) module component properties:

Property	Value	Comments
Rows Displayed	6	Displays 6 rows.
Placement	Same content canvas	Places the block on the same content canvas as the previous one.
Title	Contact Methods	Specifies block title.
Window	(Same as parent)	The window property has to be set the same as the parent for the block to appear in the same window.

Windowed child module component properties:

Property	Value	Comments
Rows Displayed	Various (5 in the Phone window)	Displays 5 rows.
Placement	New content canvas	Creates a new content canvas for the parent.
Title	Various: Phone, E-mail, Address	Specifies block title.
Window	(Various)	Each of three blocks (Phone, E-mail, Address) has its own window.
Canvas Width	40	Specifies the width of the layout area for the block.
Canvas Height	11	Specifies the height of the layout area for the block.

Window properties:

Property	Value	Comments
Title	Various: Phone, E-mail, Address	Specifies the title that appears in the shaded window bar at the top of the window.
Scrollable?	No	Windows will not be scrollable.
Width & Height	<null>	Leaving these as <null> will set the window size based on the canvas sizes.
X Position & Y Position	50 5	Specifies the position the window will initially appear on the screen. The user can move the window after it appears.

Item group properties:

Property	Value	Comments
Title	Various: Phone, E-mail, Address	Specifies the title that appears in the tab of the tab canvases.
Layout	Standard	
Stacked?	Yes	Creates stacked canvases. By default these will be tab canvases.

Preferences Used

Most of the block layout preferences were left at their factory settings for this example. However, the following preferences were set to nonfactory settings. They were set at the module level so they would be used by all of the module components in the module.

Preference	Setting
Layout-Block → Block header separator (BLKHDS)	0
Layout-Block → Block scrollbar position (BLKSBP)	Right justify.
Layout-Block → Block scrollbar separator (BLKSBS)	0
Layout-Item Group → Use group tabulation table (GRPUTT)	Use tabs to align the start of the display.
Layout-Item Group → Group tabulation table (GRPTAB)	20
*Layout-Single Area → Enable creation of single areas for multirow blocks (SARENB)	Yes (Default)

* Factory Default Setting

These preferences (except for the item group preferences) have been defined in the MC_REC_CENTER_FILL_0H preference set that is defined in the example application that is on the CD provided with this book.

Layout Generation Tips

Tip 1: Using Item Group Tab Stops to Line Up Start of Items in an Item Group

By default, the items in an item group are lined up by the end of the item, not the start of the item. This leaves the items jagged on the left, which does not look very good. In this example, the start of the items in the "Address" item group were lined up by using tab stops.

Tip 2: Cleaning Up Unneeded Windows and Action Items

When you create new module components using the wizards, Oracle Designer automatically creates a new window for each module component. If you are implementing layouts that only use one window, you will have to reset the window property of the module components to all use the same window, then delete the windows that you do not need.

Also, when you create key-based links between module components, the wizards automatically place action items in the parent window to navigate to the child windows. If you move the child module components into the same window as the parent, you do not need these action items and they will have to be deleted. If they are not deleted, you will end up with buttons on the form that you do not want.

Recipe 7: Control Block, Adjacent Stacked Canvases

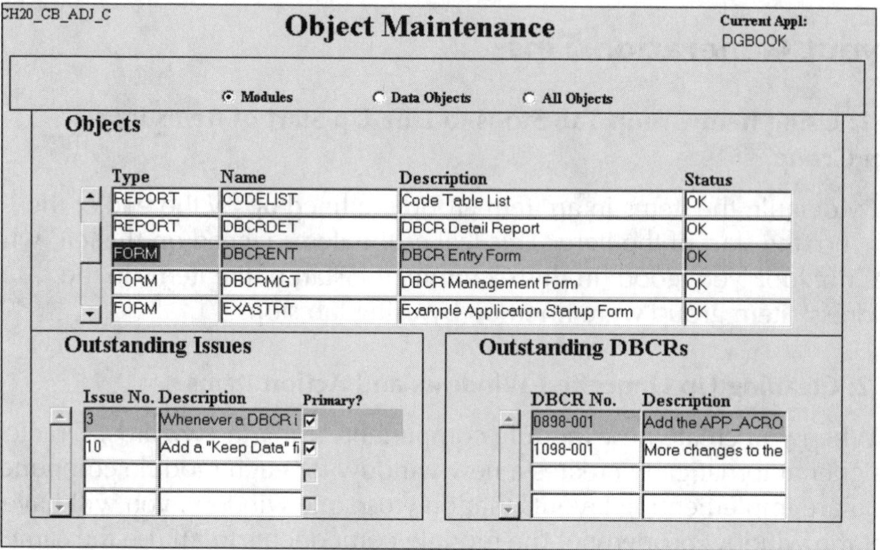

Features of This Layout

- **A Control Block at the Top of the Form That Limits the Query** A radio group is placed in a control block at the top of this example. This control block is used to limit the records returned in the Objects block to either Modules only, Data Objects only, or All Objects. When the user changes the value on the radio group, the form is automatically requeried.
- **Block Scrollbars on the Left** The block scroll bars are at the left, which is the factory default.
- **Two Children Blocks Appear Side-by-Side** There are two children blocks (Outstanding Issues and Outstanding DBCRs) that appear side-by-side in this layout. This is not a normal layout, and is achieved by using a special technique. See Tip 1 in the upcoming "Layout Generation Tips" for a discussion of this.

The form used to create this example is called CH20_CB_ADJ_CANV in the example application on the CD included with this book.

Key Properties Used to Produce This Layout

Module properties:

Property	Value	Comments
Top Title	Object Maintenance	Used to determine the title placed at the top of the module. (Chapter 22 covers template usage.)

Top (control block) module component properties:

Property	Value	Comments
Rows Displayed	1	Displays 1 row.
Placement	New content canvas	Creates the initial content canvas for the form.
Insert, Delete, Update	No	Control blocks do not update the database directly.
Canvas Width	80	The standard screen width of 80 character cell units. When you create the module component, you can usually leave this (and the *Height* property) blank, and the values will be defaulted from preferences that are used to set your standards.
Canvas Height	22	The standard screen width of 22 character cell units.

Second (parent) module component properties:

Property	Value	Comments
Rows Displayed	5	Displays 5 rows.
Placement	Same content canvas	Places the Objects block on the same content canvas as the control block.
Title	Objects	Specifies block title.
Window	(Same as first block)	The window property has to be set the same as the first block for this block to appear in the same window.

Child module component properties:

Property	Value	Comments
Window	(Same as first block)	The window property has to be set the same as the first block for this block to appear in the same window.
Placement	New stacked canvas	Places the block on a new stacked canvas.
X Position	Left Block: 2	The left module component is set to 2 so that its left decoration edge lines up with the indented decoration of the parent block.
	Right Block: 40	The right module component is set to start at the middle of the whole width of 80.
Y Position	12	Is set the same for both module components so that the two stacked canvases appear side-by-side.
Title	Left: Outstanding Issues Right: Outstanding DBCRs	Specifies block title.
Rows Displayed	4	In this example, it is the same for both child blocks, but it does not have to be.
Canvas Width	38	Determines the area available for the generator to create the layout within. In this example, the children split the width evenly, so for both of them it is set to half of the parent width of 80, minus 2 characters for the indentation.
Canvas Height	10	Determines the initial height available for the layout.
View Width	38	Determines the width of the area that will actually be shown on the screen. For nonscrollable stacked canvases, it should always be set to the same as the canvas width.

Property	Value	Comments
View Height	10	Determines the height of the area that will actually be shown on the screen.

Radio group control item properties:

Property	Value	Comments
Unbound Type	Custom	Custom unbound items have no standard functionality generated for them. You will add the functionality yourself.
Insert? & Update?	Yes	Allow the user to change the value.
Prompt	<null>	No prompt for this item.
Display Type	Radio group	Makes the unbound item a radio group.
Show Meaning	Meaning only	The allowable value *Meaning* will be shown for each button in the group.
Width	15	Specifies the width of each button in the radio group.
Height	1	
Datatype	CHAR	
Default	ALL	Determines which radio group button is initially selected. Must equal one of the allowable values *Value*.

Allowable values for radio group control item:

Value	Abbreviation	Meaning
MODULE	Mod	Module
DATA	Data	Data Objects
ALL	All	All Objects

Preferences Used

The block layout for this recipe is very similar to Recipe 4, and the preference settings are set at the module level to the same settings as those in the module component preferences table, with the exceptions listed next.

Module preferences:

Preference	Setting
Layout-Block → Block footer separator (BLKFTS)	0
*Layout-Block → Block scrollbar position (BLKSBP)	Left justify.
Layout-Block → Block scrollbar separator (BLKSBS)	0
End User Interface → Block Sync – Co-ordination scope (BSCSCP)	Any visible block in the current window.

* Factory Default Setting

These preferences have been defined in the MC_IND_ADJ_ITM_LT_SCR_0F preference set that is defined in the example application that is on the CD provided with this book.

Stacked module component preferences:

Preference	Setting
Layout-Stacked Can → Stacked canvas bevel (POPBEV)	No bevel.
Layout-Stacked Can → Stacked canvas horizontal scrollbar (POPHSB)	No
Layout-Stacked Can → Stacked canvas vertical scrollbar (POPVSB)	No

These preferences were also set at the module level so that both of the stacked canvases could inherit them.

Radio group item preferences:

Preference	Setting
Layout-Radio Group → Radio group decoration (RADDEC)	No
Layout-Radio Group → Radio group footer separator (RADFTS)	0
Layout-Radio Group → Radio group header separator (RADHDS)	0
*Layout-Radio Group → Radio group horizontal inter-item spacing (RADHIS)	2

Preference	Setting
Layout-Radio Group → Radio group multi-line format (RADMLF)	Keep adding fields as long as they fit.
Layout-Radio Group → Radio group orientation within group (RADOWG)	Horizontal layout.

* Factory Default Setting

These preferences were applied directly to the radio group item using a preference set. They have also been defined in the IT_RG_NODEC_H preference set that is defined in the example application that is on the CD provided with this book.

Layout Generation Tips

Tip 1: Implementing Adjacent Stacked Canvases

There are two children blocks (*Outstanding Issues* and *Outstanding DBCRs*) that appear side-by-side in this layout. This is not a normal layout, and it is achieved by using a special technique. These two blocks are generated as stacked canvases, with settings for their *X, Y, Width,* and *Height* properties that place them as shown in the preceding illustration.

Stacked canvases are not normally visible over the content canvas. You either have to navigate to one of the items on the stacked canvas or use triggers to make them visible. Then when you navigate back to the content canvas, the stacked canvas will disappear. This normally makes them difficult to use for layout control.

The best way to make stacked canvases useable for layout control is to place a WHEN-NEW-RECORD-INSTANCE event on all of the blocks in the content canvas with the following code:

```
SHOW_VIEW('CG$POPUP_1');
SHOW_VIEW('CG$POPUP_2');
```

These commands will make sure that the first two stacked canvases are displayed whenever the cursor enters a record in one of the blocks on the content canvas. SHOW_VIEW is a Forms built-in that makes the specified stacked canvas visible. Oracle Designer always names the stacked canvas CG$POPUP_ followed by a sequential number that corresponds to the order the canvases are displayed (as determined by the *Usage sequence* property). Therefore, adding these commands will make sure that the first two stacked canvases are still visible when the cursor navigates back to the content canvas.

While you could add this code to other events, we have found that the WHEN-NEW-RECORD-INSTANCE event works best for this functionality.

Tip 2: Adding Functionality to Control Radio Group

This example shows how to create a control block with a radio group control item. However, without any functionality the control item is useless. In this example, we are using the radio group to limit the scope of the query in the Objects block. To do this, follow these steps.

1. **Adding a Where Clause to the Query Block** The control item can be used in the Where clause of a block by adding an appropriate Where clause to the *WHERE Clause of Query* property of the module component. In this example, we added the following Where clause:

```
WHERE (:TYPESEL.OBJTYPE = 'ALL'
    OR :TYPESEL.OBJTYPE = DECODE(OBJTYP_CD,'FORM','MODULE'
          ,'REPORT','MODULE','WEBSERVER','MODULE'
          ,'TABLE','DATA','VIEW','DATA'
          ,'SNAPSHOT','DATA','PL/SQL','MODULE'
          ,'TAPI','MODULE','ALL')
      )
```

2. **Adding a WHEN-RADIO-CHANGED Event to the Control Item** We added a WHEN-RADIO-CHANGED event to the radio group control item in order to make the data block requery automatically whenever its value changes. The following code was added to this event:

```
GO_BLOCK('OBJ');
EXECUTE_QUERY;
```

This example code is very simple. You would probably have to implement much more complicated code in order to do things like preserving the previous query criteria.

Special Forms Layouts

All of the previous examples were for standard data input or display forms. However, most applications also need some forms with special layouts and functionality that is not based primarily on data entry. These forms may be used to start the application, select special information, or perform special navigation. While it's not possible to include every possible special form layout, we cover some of the more common types here. Hopefully, this will give you ideas about how you can generate the other special layouts that you need.

The special layout forms we are including are

- **Recipe 8: Startup Form (Splash Screen)** Most applications need a form to start with. Often this form will have very little functionality because the user needs to select where in the application to start. This kind of startup form is sometimes called a *splash screen.*
- **Recipe 9: Record Selection Form** There are often times when you will need the user to select a context or other setting when first entering the application. This is often done by displaying some records and allowing the user to highlight and select one.
- **Recipe 10: Wizard Style Form** You should be familiar with this style, since you have been using wizard dialogs to create the modules you are generating! This is an example of a generated wizard form with tab canvases that works in a very similar fashion.

Recipe 8: Startup Form (Splash Screen)

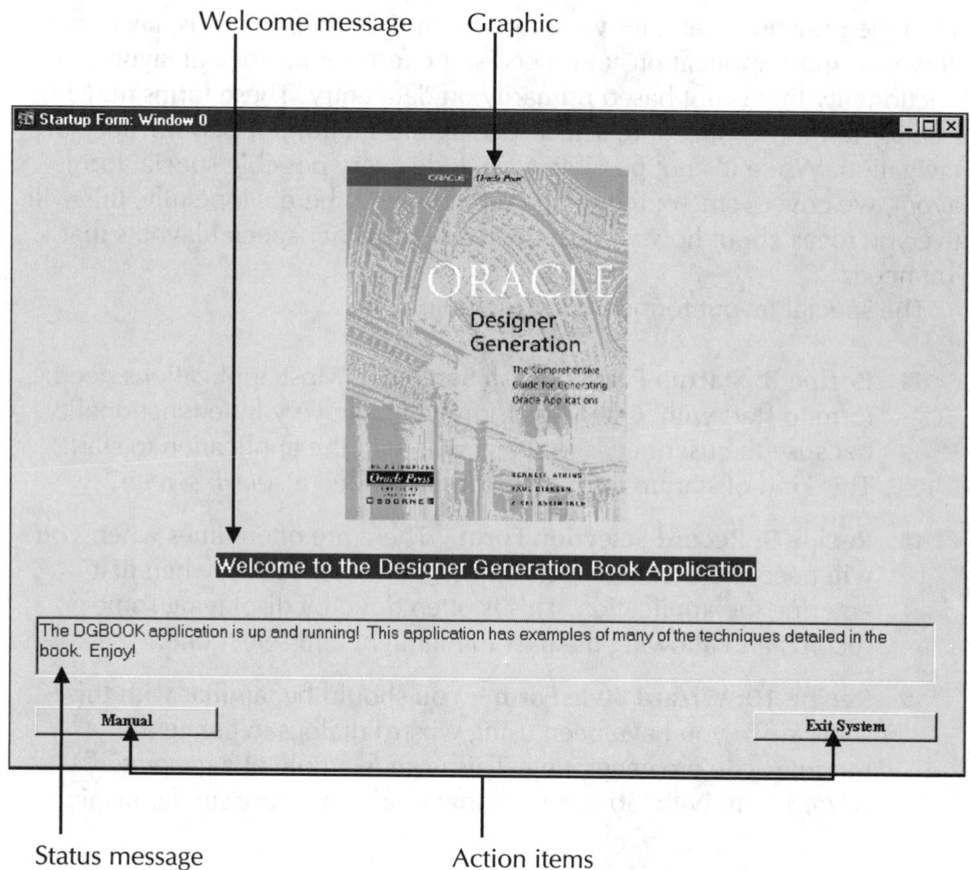

Features of This Layout

- **Displays Graphic** A large area on the display is reserved to display a graphic file. This can be used to display a logo for the corporation or department or a special graphic that represents the application system.
- **Displays System Message** An area is reserved for the display of a system status message. This can be used to communicate easily with the users when the system will have scheduled downtime, upgrades, or whatever.

- **Buttons for Special Functionality** There are some buttons that can be used to implement special functionality. This should be used to make it easy for new users to learn how to use the system.
- **No Toolbar** Since there are no standard database functions that need to be done on this screen, it was generated with a template that did not use a toolbar. (We used the DGBKTMP3 template provided on the CD.)

The form used to create this example is called CH20_STARTUP in the example application on the CD included with this book.

Recipe 8: Module Design

This module consists of one query-only module component against a table that has the system status message. The table has records for more than one application, so the module has a Where clause that limits the query to just the one application. The module includes the following unbound items:

- **Image Item** The image is produced using a custom unbound item with a *Display Type* of **Image**. This will produce an image item and an image filename item. The image filename item is populated during the form startup, which will cause the image to be displayed.
- **Welcome Message** The welcome message is also a custom unbound item. Its value will also be populated during startup.
- **Manual Button** This is implemented as a button unbound item with a when-button-pressed event that calls an online manual.
- **Exit Button** This is implemented as a button unbound item with a when-button-pressed event that exits the system.

In order to display the image and welcome message, a POST-QUERY event was added to the module component that copies a filename into the image filename item and copies the welcome message into the welcome message item. A WHEN-NEW-FORM-INSTANCE event is added to perform any application startup functionality that you need for your application. Also, a CG$STARTUP_FORM argument was added to make the form automatically query upon startup.

Key Properties Used to Produce This Layout

Module component properties:

Property	Value	Comments
Rows Displayed	1	Displays 1 row.
Placement	New content canvas	Creates the content canvas for the form.
Insert, Delete, Update	No	This form is not used to create, delete, or update data.
Canvas Width	80	The standard screen width of 80 character cell units. When you create the module component, you can usually leave this (and the *Height* property) blank, and the values will be defaulted from preferences that are used to set your standards.
Canvas Height	22	The standard screen width of 22 character cell units.

Image item properties:

Property	Value	Comments
Item Type	Custom	We will handle the item's functionality.
Insert? & Update?	No	Do not allow user to modify item.
Template/Library Object	TM$START_IMG	An object library object was used to set some of the item properties for the image item. This included the following: *Bevel:* None *Scrollbars:* No *Sizing Style:* Adjust *Keyboard Navigable:* No
Display Type	Image	Makes the item an image.

Property	Value	Comments
Width	120	Sets the width of the image item.
Height	10	Sets the height of the image item.
Alignment	Center	Centers the image in the item.
Datatype	CHAR	Specifies the data type of the filename item that will be generated.

Welcome message item properties:

Property	Value	Comments
Unbound Type	Custom	We will handle the item's functionality.
Insert? & Update?	No	Do not allow user to modify item.
Template/Library Object	TM$CANVAS_BLD	An object library object was used to set some of the item properties for the image item. This included the following: Bold, Larger Font, No Bevel Background same color as canvas
Display Type	Text	Makes the item a text item.
Width	100	Sets the width of the item.
Height	1	Sets the height of the item.
Alignment	Center	Centers the image in the item.
Datatype	CHAR	Specifies the data type of the filename item that will be generated.

Button item properties:

Property	Value	Comments
Unbound Type	Custom	We will handle the item's functionality.
Prompt	Left: Manual Right: Exit	Sets the label of the button.
Display Type	Button	Makes the item a button.

Property	Value	Comments
Width	20	Sets the width of the button.
Height	1	Sets the height of the button.
PL/SQL Block	Left: APLB$MANUAL; Right: APLB$EXITSYS;	Implements the button's functionality. The actual code is in these procedures in an attached library.

Status message item properties:

Property	Value	Comments
Column	MESSAGE	This is the column in the table that the status is queried from for our example.
Insert? & Update?	No	Do not allow user to modify item.
Display Type	Text	Makes the item a text item.
Width	120	Sets the width of the item.
Height	3	Sets the height of the item.
Wrap Style	Wrap	Allows long text items to wrap within the item's area.

CG$STARTUP_MODE argument properties:

Property	Value	Comments
Name	CG$STARTUP_ MODE	Adding an argument with this name will allow you to specify the startup query mode.
Datatype	VARCHAR2	
Default	AUTO QUERY	Defaulting the argument to this value causes the form to perform a query upon startup.

Preferences Used

All of the preferences were left at their factory default except for the following. These preferences were simply set at the module level.

Module Preference	Setting
Layout - Image → Display image filename item (IMGDFI)	No
Standards → The name of the template form (STFFMB)	Dgbktmp3.fmb

Generation Tips

Tip 1: Adding Application Logic

You will need to add the following events in order to implement the message functionality:

- **Module POST-QUERY** Add code to populate the image and welcome message areas. For example:

```
COPY('dgbook.bmp','START.GRAPHIC');
COPY('Welcome to the '||NAME_IN('START.NAME'),
     'START.WELCOME_MESSAGE');
```

- **Module WHEN-NEW-FORM-INSTANCE** Add code to perform any specific application startup routines you need. For example, security checks, context selection, etc.

Look at the example module that is included on the CD to see how a fully functional form with this functionality would work.

Recipe 9: Record Selection Form

Many applications need to have the user select a *context* that will be used in the application as default values or to restrict the queries and data entry. An example of this would be a department or agency selection, or maybe a region. In our example application, we have the user select the context application that they are to work with. This is very similar to Oracle Designer itself! When you first enter Designer, you are asked to select the application to work with. This recipe shows one method that can be used to generate a context or record selection form. The generated form looks and works very much like the application selection dialog in Oracle Designer:

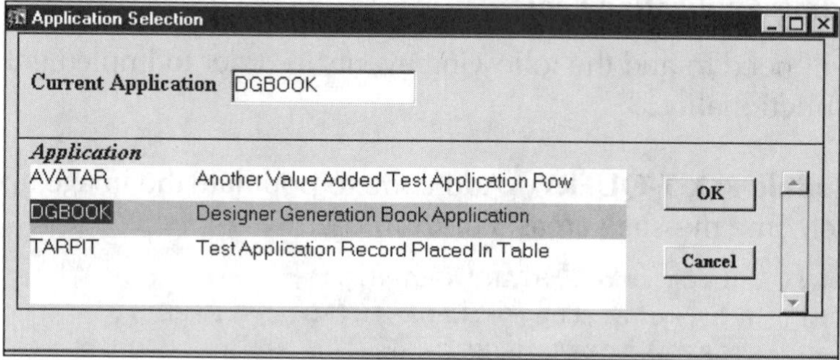

Features of This Layout

- **Control Block with Current Application Selection Displayed** There is a control block at the top of the form that shows the currently selected application. It is set to the value for the record that is highlighted in the bottom block.
- **Buttons at Right Allow Selection or Cancel** There are two buttons at the right that allow the user either to accept a new application selection or to cancel the window, leaving the selection as is.
- **Whole Current Record Highlighted** The whole current record is highlighted to show which record is to be selected.
- **Items Displayed Without Bevels** There are multiple items displayed without bevels to make it look like a single selection.

The form used to create this example is called CH20_REC_SEL in the example application on the CD included with this book.

Recipe 9: Module Design

This module consists of a control block at the top that displays the currently selected application and an application list block at the bottom that lists all of the available applications. There is a WHEN-NEW-FORM-INSTANCE event that executes a query on the application block and then navigates to the record for the currently selected application (if there is one), which is read from a global variable. The application module component has a WHEN-NEW-RECORD-INSTANCE trigger that copies the current records value into the control item at the top of the form. If the OK button is pressed, the current selection is saved in a global variable. If the CANCEL button is pressed, the form exits without setting a global.

Key Properties Used to Produce This Layout

Window properties:

Property	Value	Comments
Title	Application Selection	Sets the window title, which appears in the shaded area at the top of the window.
Width	60	Determines the width of the window that is generated.
Height	9	Determines the height of the window.
X Position	20	Determines the initial horizontal position of the upper-left corner of the window.
Y Position	3	Determines the initial vertical position of the upper-left corner of the window.

Control block (top) module component properties:

Property	Value	Comments
Rows Displayed	1	Displays 1 row.
Placement	New content canvas	Creates the content canvas for the form.
Insert, Delete, Update	No	This form is not used to create, delete, or update data.

Property	Value	Comments
Canvas Width	60 (same as window *Width)*	Sets the canvas width used to determine the layout area.
Canvas Height	9 (same as window *Height*)	Sets the canvas height used to determine the layout area.

"Current application" unbound item properties:

Property	Value	Comments
Unbound Type	Custom	No special generated code will be created for the item.
Insert? & Update?	No	This item is not enterable.
Prompt	Current Application	Sets the item prompt.
Display Type	Text	This is a text item.
Width	20	Sets the width of the item.

"Application" block (bottom) module component properties:

Property	Value	Comments
Rows Displayed	4	Displays 4 rows.
Placement	Same content canvas	Adds the block to the same canvas as the control block.
Insert, Delete, Update	No	This form is not used to create, delete, or update data.
Window	<Same as first module component>	This module component must be in the same window as the first module component.
Overflow	Overflow area right	Will allow the buttons to be overflowed to the right.

Key bound item properties in application block:

Property	Value	Comments
Template/Library Object	TM$NOBEVEL	An object library object was used to set some of the item properties for the items.

Property	Value	Comments
Context?	Yes	Keeps these items in the multirecord context area of the block.

Key button item properties in application block:

Property	Value	Comments
Unbound Type	Custom	No special generated code will be created for the item.
Prompt	Top: OK Bottom: Cancel	Sets the label of the buttons.
Width	8	The width of the buttons (same for both).
Height	1	The height of the buttons.
Context	No	Places the buttons in the overflow area.
PL/SQL Block	Top: APLB$APPSEL_OK; Bottom: APLB$APPSEL_CANC;	Implements the button's functionality. The actual code is in these procedures in an attached library.

Preferences Used

Most of the preferences were left at the factory default for this layout. The preferences that were modified from the factory default are shown here.

Module preferences:

Module Preference	Setting
Layout-Block → Title first block of form (BLKTFB)	No
Layout-Content Can → Content canvas relative block indentation (PAGBIN)	0
Standards → The name of the template form (STFFMB)	dgbktmp3.fmb

Control block module component preferences:

Preference	Setting
Layout-Block → Block justification (BLKJUS)	Left justify.

Application block module component preferences:

Preference	Setting
Layout-Block → Block footer separator (BLKFTS)	0
Layout-Block → Block header separator (BLKHDS)	0
Layout-Block → Block scrollbar position (BLKSBP)	Right justify.
Layout-Overflow → Overflow area decoration (OFADEC)	Do not decorate the object.
Layout-Overflow → Overflow area used default context items (OFADFT)	No
Layout-Overflow → Overflow area percentage of available width reserved for context (OFAPCN)	85

Generation Tips

Tip 1: Adding Application Logic

You will need to add the following events to implement the functionality in this example:

- **Module WHEN-NEW-FORM-INSTANCE** Add code to query the block and navigate to current context. For example:

```
GO_BLOCK('APP');
EXECUTE_QUERY;
WHILE bContinue LOOP
  IF NAME_IN('APP.ACRONYM') = NAME_IN('GLOBAL.CURR_APP') THEN
    bContinue := False;
  ELSE
    NEXT_RECORD;
  END IF;
  IF NAME_IN('SYSTEM.LAST_RECORD') = 'TRUE' THEN
```

```
      bContinue := False;
    END IF;
  END LOOP;
```

- **Application Block WHEN-NEW-RECORD-INSTANCE** Add code to set the Current Application control item to the value for the current record. For example:

```
COPY(NAME_IN('APP.ACRONYM'),'CURRAPP.CURRENT_APP');
```

- ***PL/SQL Block* of OK Button** Add code to save the selected application in a global and then exit the form. For example:

```
COPY(NAME_IN('CURRAPP.CURRENT_APP'),'GLOBAL.CURR_APP');
EXIT_FORM;
```

- ***PL/SQL Block* of Cancel Button** Add code to exit the form. For example:

```
EXIT_FORM;
```

Recipe 10: Wizard Style Form

As you probably know, one of the user interface standards in the MS Windows world is called a *wizard*. A wizard guides the user through a series of screens in which information is entered in an ordered, step-by-step sequence. Users navigate between the pages using Next and Previous buttons at the bottom of the screen. Typically, a wizard will also include an OK or Finish button to complete the process and a Cancel button to abort the entry. Wizard-style dialogs are often implemented as tab pages, which give the user another method for navigating between the various pages. In fact, many of the dialogs in Oracle Designer itself (for example the Module and Module Component Creation Wizards) use this standard.

The wizard-style interface is familiar to many users and is very useful when the user needs to be guided through a process step-by-step, when each step depends on information in the previous step:

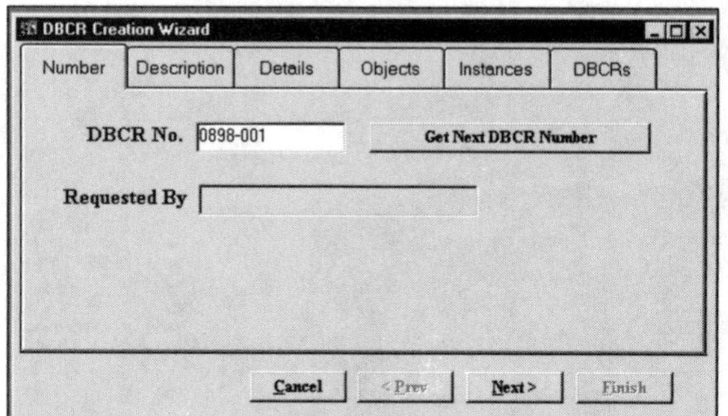

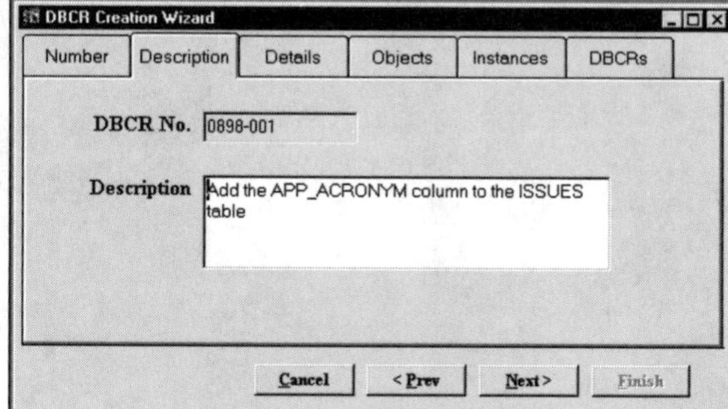

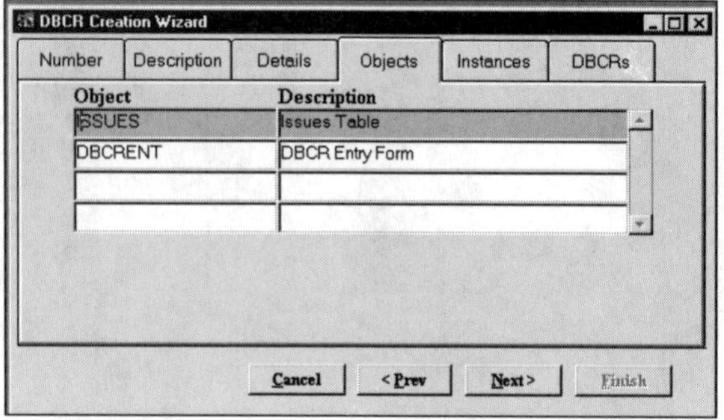

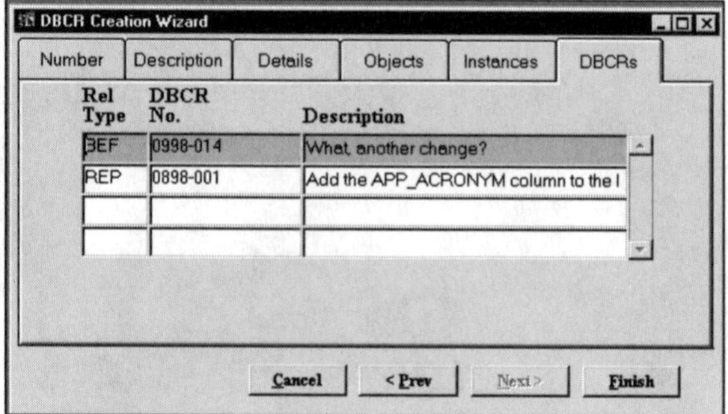

Features of This Layout

- **Tabs at Top of Screen Allow Users Easy Access to Each Page** The form consists of tab canvases *only*. This places the tabs at the very top of the page, which makes it look like a standard wizard.
- **Buttons at the Bottom of the Screen Navigate Between Pages** Navigation buttons appear at the bottom of the pages, allowing the user to navigate forward or backward through the pages, as well as to finish or cancel from the wizard.
- **Buttons Can Be Activated and Deactivated as User Navigates** The navigation buttons can be activated or deactivated to enforce the necessary requirements (for example, you can deactivate the Next button until all items are entered).
- **No Block Titles or Decoration** There are no block titles or decorations. The tab titles and the standard tab graphics are enough to set off each block.
- **No Toolbar or Module Title** Since there are no standard database functions that need to be done on this screen, it was generated with a template that did not use a toolbar or module title. (We used the DGBKTMP3 template provided on the CD.)

The form used to create this example is called CH20_WIZARD in the example application on the CD included with this book.

Recipe 10: Module Design

This module consists only of a series of tab canvas blocks. Each block normally references a different base table. The navigation buttons are custom action items added to the window. We used a package in an attached library to handle all of the wizard functionality. We added the following events to implement some of the wizard functionality:

- **Module WHEN-BUTTON-PRESSED** Handles the navigation button functionality. It uses the item name of the button that is pressed to determine what function to perform (this is very similar to the way the toolbar works in the templates provided with Designer).

- **Module POST-BLOCK** Saves the block context in a package variable, which is used by the block navigation implemented with the buttons.
- **Module WHEN-NEW-BLOCK-INSTANCE** Handles the activation and deactivation of the navigation buttons.
- **Module WHEN-NEW-FORM-INSTANCE** Handles some initialization processing, including making sure the navigation buttons are visible.

This is probably not an exhaustive list of what you would have to add to make a fully functional wizard available for your application. It is just intended to give you an idea about how to implement the functionality. A fully functional wizard form is included in the example application on the CD that comes with this book. You can look at the code for that example to see how these events were implemented.

Also, there are several different methods that can be used to implement the navigation button functionality. We are just detailing one possibility here. Some other possible designs are

- Using items on a template form to implement the navigation buttons (instead of action items)
- Using a parameter or control item to store the tab canvas context (instead of a package variable)
- Using item group tab canvases to implement a wizard for a single table

NOTE
The Designer online help actually has a procedure to generate wizard forms. It is available at Generating Oracle Developer Form Builder applications → Form generation → Generating windows, canvases, blocks, and items → Block generation → More about blocks → Generating blocks onto native Form Builder canvases → Generating Wizard style forms.

Key Properties Used to Produce This Layout

We are only going to detail the properties used to produce the tab canvases and navigation items. You can use the standard layout techniques detailed in the rest of this chapter and in Chapter 19 to produce the layout you want within each tab.

Wizard tab module component properties:

Property	Value	Comments
Window	Same for All	All of the tab canvases must use the same window.
Placement	New Tab canvas page	
Title	Various. For example, the first one is "Number"	The module component title appears as the text in the tab created for that module component.
Canvas Width	55	Specifies the layout width for the tab canvases. Should be the same for all of the module components. Should also match the window width.
Canvas Height	12	Specifies the layout height for the tab canvases. Should be the same for all of the module components. Should also match the window height.
View Width & Height	55,12	Set to the same as the canvas *Width & Height.*

Window properties:

Property	Value	Comments
Title	DBCR Creation Wizard	Specifies the title that appears in the shaded window bar at the top of the window.
Scrollable?	No	Windows will not be scrollable.
Width	55	Determines the width of the wizard window.

Property	Value	Comments
Height	12	Determines the height of the wizard window.
X Position	15	Specifies the position the window will initially appear on the screen. The user can move the window after it appears.
Y Position	5	

Action item properties:

Property	Value	Comments
Window	Same window as module components	Specifies the window the action items will appear at the bottom of.
Prompt	Various: "&Cancel" "< &Prev" "&Next >" "&Finish"	Sets the label of the action item buttons. The "&" will be used to set the mnemonic key access for the button.
Button Height	<null>	The height is determined by standard objects in the object library.
Button Width	<null>	The width is determined by longest text of all of the action items (AIBBWD=LONGEST TEXT).

Preferences Used

The following preferences were set at the module level so that they would apply to all of the module components in the form. The rest of the preferences were left at the factory default for the module components. We are only detailing the preferences that are important for the creation and layout of the tab canvases and navigation items. You can set other preferences at the module component or item level to control the layout within each tab.

Module preferences:

Module Preference	Setting
*Action Item → Action Item Button Width	LONGEST TEXT
Layout-Block → Block decoration (BLKDEC)	Do not decorate the object.
Layout-Block → Block scrollbar position (BLKSBP)	Right justify.
Layout-Block → Block scrollbar separator (BLKSBS)	0
Layout-Block → Title first block of form (BLKTFB)	No
Layout-Content Can → Title first block on content canvas (PAGTFB)	No
Layout-Item → Marker to Force Prompt Splitting (ITMFPS)	>
Layout-Item → Item/prompt gap (ITMIPG)	1
Layout-Stacked Can → Title first block on stacked canvas (POPTFB)	No
Navigation → Mnemonic Access Key Generation (NAVKEY)	Yes
Standards → The name of the template form (STFFMB)	dgbktmp3.fmb

* Factory Default Setting

These preferences have been defined in the MD_WIZARD preference set that is defined in the example application that is on the CD provided with this book.

Generation Tips

Tip 1: Adding Application Logic

You will need to add some application logic in order to make the wizard work correctly. Refer to "Recipe 10: Module Design," earlier, to see what type of events you might need to add.

CHAPTER 21

Navigation Module Generation

One of the most important issues in a multimodule application is the navigation between the generated modules. Such an application may include forms, reports, graphic displays, Web modules, etc. The navigation between these modules should be easy and seamless. However, it is very likely that there will be some navigation security restrictions and that some users (or a group of users) will not be allowed to access certain modules.

Form Generator offers at least two methods for navigation generation: using menus and using navigation action items. Each has its own advantages and disadvantages. For example, there is no security information generated for navigation action items. On the other hand, it is much easier to pass data from module to module using navigation items.

In this chapter, we will review the techniques for generating navigation code. Menu generation will be discussed in depth, and navigation action items will be reviewed. Wherever applicable, a troubleshooting section will help you solve some of the most common problems related to navigation module generation. The following topics will be discussed in this chapter:

- Generating menu modules
- Customizing menu generation
- Generating menu security
- Using navigation action items for navigation between modules
- Application startup navigation

Generating Menu Modules

A menu module is a collection of related menus and menu items. Menus allow the user to navigate between different modules (a form, report, graphic display, or a Web document) in an application or to execute actions (commands executing PL/SQL code) by selecting menu items from menus. Menus usually have a hierarchical structure: a top-level menu (also called main menu) contains one or more submenus (a group of menu items), which in turn include other submenus or menu items. The following illustration shows a typical menu.

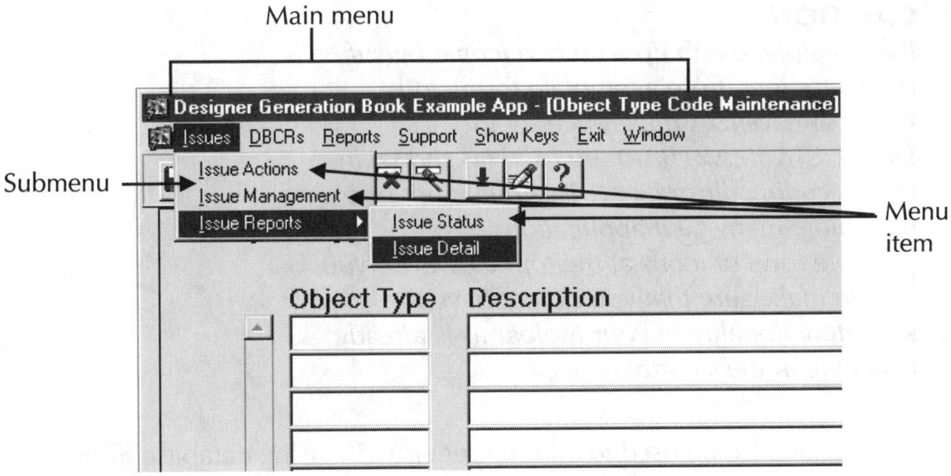

The standard style for menus in most GUI applications is pull-down menus. However, it is also possible to generate full-screen modules for character-based applications.

One of the new features in Oracle Developer release 2 is the standard menu toolbar (also called a smartbar). The *smartbar* is a toolbar attached to a window (horizontal, vertical, or both) that displays a set of buttons. Each button on the smartbar corresponds to a menu item (not a submenu). You can control which menu item will be displayed on the horizontal smartbar by setting the *Display in Horizontal Menu Toolbar* property to **Yes**; the same applies to a vertical smartbar as well.

CAUTION

It is possible to end up with two iconic bars if both a toolbar (from a template form) and a smartbar (FMNDA preference set to DEFAULT&SMARTBAR) are used (as shown in the preceding illustration). This might not be a bad thing; many GUI applications have multiple rows of icons at the top. However, you should make sure that you do not have the same functionality in your toolbar as is already available in the smartbar.

Menus can also be used to enforce security. By using database roles, access to a menu item (or a submenu) can be restricted. Each menu item can specify a list of database roles that are allowed access to it, and only those users who are granted those roles can select that menu item.

A menu module cannot be run by itself; it has to be attached to a form module. On the other hand, a form module can be run without any menu module. By default, a form module uses the default form menu that allows the user to perform standard form functions such as enter query, delete record, clear block, etc. However, you can set the *Menu Module* property of a form module to a null value not to attach any menu. It is also possible to attach a custom menu to a form module.

In a multiform application, it is very common to see the following types of menus:

- **Application menus** Application menus are shared among many forms in an application, with each form having the same standard application menu. The standard application menu may contain items for navigating to other modules in the application, as well as menu items that correspond to standard form functions.

- **Single form menus** Unique to a particular form, a single form menu contains menu items that are specific to a single form. For example, it could include special navigation or calculation functionality that is only applicable to that one form.
- **Combination of application and single form menus** It is possible to combine Application Menus within a single form menu. One of the many different ways to implement this is to dynamically enable/disable menu items based on the current context.

Defining Menu Modules

Menu modules are generated from menu modules using the module networks in Designer. A menu module is an Oracle Developer Forms module (language property) with a *Module Type* of **Menu**. Although it is possible to generate menus from modules of **Default** type, it is best to set the module type to **Menu**. Module networks describe relationships between modules in an application system:

- The modules called by a particular module (child modules)
- The modules calling a particular module (parent modules)

The following illustration is an example of a generated Menu Module.

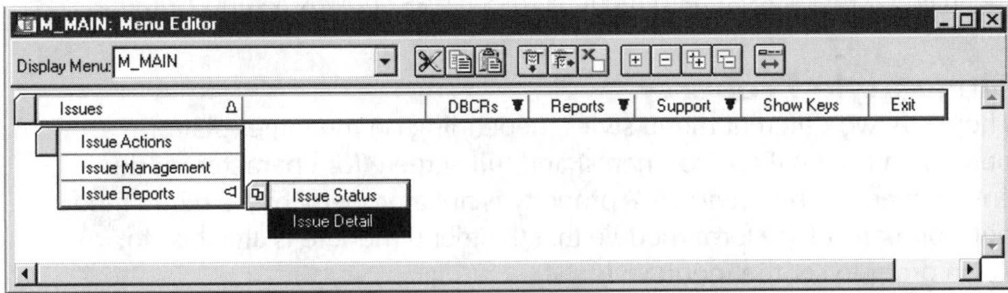

TIP
Module networks can be transformed from Function Hierarchy Diagrams. Use the Application Design Transform Wizard to convert function hierarchy diagrams to module networks. However, many people find the module networks created this way are not very useful because of the way the generated module network is organized (by business unit). Therefore, most of the time, you will want to create the module network by hand.

Module networks can be easily maintained via the Navigator in Design Editor. Simply click to open the **Module Networks** node for adding, deleting, or moving components of module networks. Figure 21-1 shows a module network in two different view modes: horizontal and vertical. The default view mode is vertical, but you can view module networks horizontally as well (make sure that the Navigator window is active and set *View → Display Network Horizontally*). Module networks can also be maintained at the module level. For each module, you can specify a list of modules that it calls.

At the top of the menu structure is the root menu. Its *Implementation Name* will become the menu name. Menu modules called by the root menu become submenus. The other subordinate modules become menu items in the generated menus.

Form Generator can be used to generate a menu module on its own, or it can generate the menu along with a form that it is attached to. (See "Attaching the Generated Menu to Your Forms," later in this chapter, to see how menus are attached to forms). When generating a menu module, you can also specify the scope of generation: the entire module network or a subsection starting at a specified point.

Form Generator can also merge generated menus with those from a template menu and add other standard menu items such as *Show Keys* and *Exit*.

Menu Style Property

There are two different menu styles, depending on the target platform: pull-down (for GUI environments) and full-screen (for character mode environments). The *Menu Style* property is not a property of the menu module but a property of the form module that the menu module is attached to.

In order to set the menu style:

1. If you are generating the menu module alone, use the *Form/Menu Attachment → Menu style if not implicit menu generation (FMNDST)* preference to set the *module type* property to **FULL-SCREEN** or **PULL-DOWN**.

2. If you are generating the form module and its menu simultaneously, use the *Menu – Full Screen → Menu style used during generation (MNUSTY)* preference to set the *module type* property to **FULL-SCREEN** or **PULL-DOWN**.

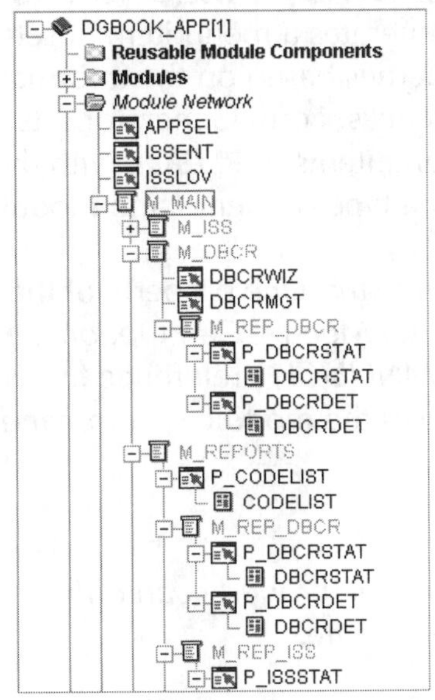

Vertical view

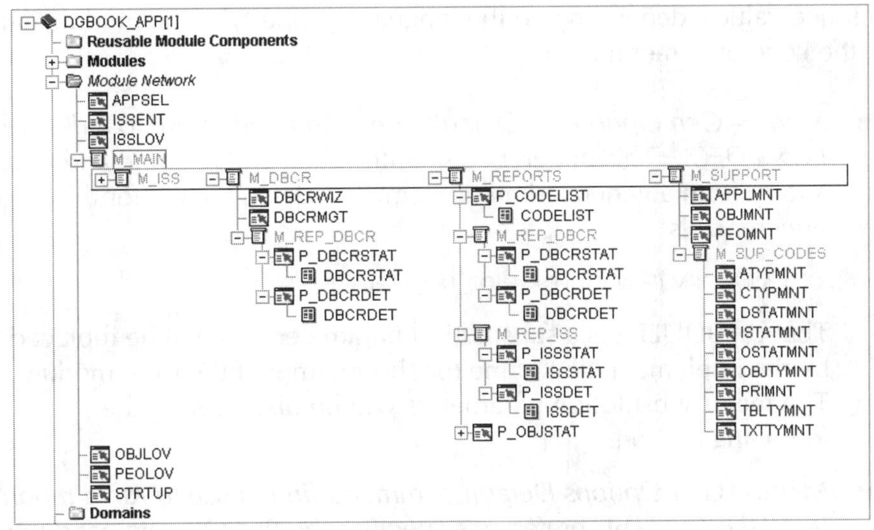

Horizontal view

FIGURE 21-1. *Module networks (horizontal and vertical views)*

Command Lines Used by Menu Items

When Form Generator generates a menu item, it sets the *Command Type* and *Command Line* properties based on the information stored in the repository and the preferences. Form Generator sets the *Command Type* property of generated menu items to **PL/SQL** with the exception of submenus (modules with a type of Menu) and modules with no language specified.

In order to set the *Command Line* property of the generated menu item, Form Generator looks at the *Menu – Gen Options → Use command line from module definition (MNUUCL)* preference first. If this preference is set to **Yes**, Form Generator uses the module's *Command Line* property (if it has been set).

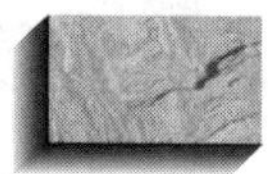

TIP
A module's Command Line property can only be set via the Property Palette.

Otherwise (if the MNUUCL preference is set to **No**), Form Generator ignores the module's *Command Line* property and uses one of the following preference values, depending on the language property of the module called from the generated menu item:

- *Menu – Gen Options → Default command line to use to call a form (MNUDFC)* This preference specifies the PL/SQL command to call a form from a generated menu item. The default value for this preference is

  ```
  CALL_FORM ('<MODULE>', HIDE, DO_REPLACE);
  ```

  The <MODULE> is a substitution parameter and will be replaced by the implementation name (or short name) of the form module. The menu substitution parameters will be discussed in the following section.

- *Menu – Gen Options Default command line to use to run a report (MNUDRC)* This preference specifies the PL/SQL command to call a report from a generated menu item. The default value for this preference is

  ```
  RUN_PRODUCT (REPORTS, '<MODULE>', SYNCHRONOUS, RUNTIME, FILESYSTEM,' ','');
  ```

- *Menu – Gen Options → Default command line to use to run a Graphics module (MNUDGC)* This preference specifies the PL/SQL command to call a graphics module from a generated menu item. The default value for this preference is

  ```
  RUN_PRODUCT (GRAPHICS,'<MODULE>',SYNCHRONOUS,RUNTIME,FILESYSTEM,'','');
  ```

- *Menu – Gen Options → Default command line to use to invoke a HOST command (MNUDHC)* This preference specifies the PL/SQL code to invoke a HOST (operating system) command from a generated menu item. The default value for this preference is

  ```
  HOST('<CMDLINE>');.
  ```

- *Menu – Gen Options → Default command line to use to invoke SQL*Plus (MNUDSC)* This preference specifies the PL/SQL code to invoke a SQL*Plus command file from a generated menu item. The default value for this preference is

  ```
  HOST('SQLPLUS <UN>/<PW> @<MODULE>');.
  ```

  The <UN>, <PW>, <MODULE> are menu substitution parameters and will be replaced by the username, password, and the name of the SQL*Plus module called from the menu.

These default command line preferences can be set at the application system or the module level; and they allow up to 240 characters.

COMMAND LINE SUBSTITUTION STRINGS The *Command Line* property of a module and the *Default Command Line* preferences can include substitution strings placed inside angle brackets, e.g., <MODULE> or <UN>. Table 21-1 is a list of the substitution strings and how they are set.

For an explanation of how substitution strings and menu parameters work, let us consider the following example. There is a module that calls a program called FOO and passes it the module name, username, and password. The command line to call this module could be

```
HOST('foo <module> <UN> <PW>')
```

If the module was called "PROCESS_ISSUES," and the username password was "scott/tiger," the actual command line issued would be

```
HOST('foo PROCESS_ISSUES scott tiger').
```

Substitution String	Replaced With
<MODULE>	The *Implementation Name* (if set) or *Short Name* property of the repository module. Note this substitution parameter is case sensitive and has to be entered in uppercase.
<CMDLINE>	The *Command Line* property of the repository module. Note this substitution parameter is case sensitive and has to be entered in uppercase.
<UN>	The current Oracle username. Note: This substitution string and the ones that follow will simply be replaced by standard Form Builder menu substitution parameters. For example, <UN> will be replaced with &UN and will be automatically set by the Form Builder at run time without user intervention.
<PW>	The Oracle password used to connect to the current user.
<SO>	The current menu item (selected option).
<TT>	The terminal type.
<AD>	The menu file location (application directory).
<LN>	The language preference (specified by the NLS_LANG environment variable).

TABLE 21-1. *Command Line Substitution Strings*

Besides the standard substitution strings listed above, Form Generator can generate other menu parameters from the module arguments. Module arguments are parameters passed between modules. If a module argument's *Substitution String* property is set, then its value can be included in the *Command Line* property of the module. For example, if the substitution string property of a module argument is set to DBCR_NO, then the command line can include <DBCR_NO>. Form Generator then converts these substitution strings to menu substitution parameters and, if necessary, can derive the name of the substitution parameter. When the user selects a menu item that includes such a menu substitution parameter, Form Builder prompts the user to enter a value for the parameter. However, in order to pass this parameter to other modules, you need to create a parameter list and add this parameter to the list.

Menu Substitution Parameters

Menu substitution parameters are two-letter variables. The variables UN, PW, SO, TT, AD, and LN are predefined in Form Builder. As mentioned earlier, Form Generator can generate menu substitution parameters from module arguments. However, module argument names or the substitution strings specified for module arguments are usually longer than two letters so that their names are more meaningful. In this case, Form Generator can automatically assign unique names (from A0 to Z9) if the *Menu - Gen Options → Generate unique parameter strings (MNUUPS)* preference is set to **Yes**. This is recommended; otherwise, you have to make sure that the substitution strings defined for module arguments are suitable, i.e., two-letter and unique within a module.

CUSTOMIZING COMMAND LINES As mentioned above, the command lines are generated from either the *Command Line* property of the modules or the *Default Command Line* preferences. The command line property is not defaulted, and the default values for the relevant preferences are simple CALL_FORM or RUN_PRODUCT commands.

However, you might have more complex requirements for navigating between modules. For example, you might have tighter security and audit control that requires you to check the user's privileges (beyond his/her database role assignments) and log an audit record in a journal. In this case, rather than using a simple CALL_FORM or RUN_PRODUCT command, you may want to use a custom routine to control navigation. Form Generator allows you to customize the command lines and provide your own routines to call other modules.

You can use one of the following two methods to modify a command line to use a custom routine (or any other command line change):

- Modify the *Default Command Line* preferences at the module or application system level. We recommend setting the defaults at the application system level and overriding them at the module level wherever needed. For example, you might want to launch all forms and reports through a custom library procedure called

LAUNCH_SECURE_APPS. First, you set the *Menu – Gen Options → Default command line to use to call a form (MNUDFC)* preference to something like LAUNCH_SECURE_APPS(<module>, 'F');. The second argument indicates the module type **Form**. You then set other default command line preferences (MNUDRC, MNUDGC, and MNUDHC) similarly. Finally, you create the LAUNCH_SECURE_APPS routine in one of the libraries attached to forms. When the menu is generated, the menu items generated then call the routine from the library. The customized command line and the custom procedure created in a library allow you to modify the method for calling other modules without ever generating the menu again.

- Modify the *Command Line* property of each module. However, this method is not recommended unless there are only a few modules affected due to heavy maintenance. Even so, for consistency, it is better to use preferences because they provide a better solution overall.

How to Include Standard Menu Items in Your Generated Menu

Form Generator can automatically add certain standard menu items in your generated menus. The standard menu items are *Show Keys* and *Exit* (there is also a third one, Previous Menu, but this is applicable only when generating character mode menus).

Generating *Show Keys* Menu Items

In order to generate the *Show Keys* standard menu item, set the *Menu – Gen Options → Include show keys option on generated menus (MNUSKY)* preference to one of the following settings:

- **TOP** Includes it in the top-level menu only
- **ALL** Includes it in all menus
- **NONE** Does not include it in any menu, including the top-level one

Generating *Exit* Menu Items

In order to generate the *Exit* standard menu item, set the *Menu – Gen Options → Include Exit option on generated menus (MNUEXI)* preference to one of the same possible settings identified for the *Show Keys* menu item in the previous section. The standard menu items are sequenced after all the other menu items, and *Show Keys* comes before *Exit* menu item.

How to Generate Separator Items

Menu separator items are horizontal lines that are used to visually separate logically related groups of menu items that are displayed on the same menu.

In order to generate a menu separator item:

1. Create a new module and set its *Language* property to **Null**. If you are using dialogs, select a language first to create the module and then, using the Property Palette, set the module's *Language* property to **Null**.
2. Include the module in the module network where you need a separator item. You can include the same module in the module network as many times as you want. So, if you need two separators, include the same separator module twice in appropriate locations in the module network.
3. Generate the menu.

How to Generate Menu Access Keys

Menu access keys are keyboard shortcuts for selecting menu items. Menu access keys are indicated by an underlined character. For example, in many GUI applications, *"S"* is the menu access key for the Save menu item. Menu access keys can be invoked with a platform-specific key combination. For example, in the MS Windows environment, the Save menu can be accessed when the ALT and S keys are pressed simultaneously.

In order to generate menu access keys:

1. Set the *Menu – End User → Unique letter or capital letter as menu access key (MNUULC)* preference to

- **Yes** If you want the Form Generator to find and underline a unique letter in each menu item.
- **No** If you want to control which access key is generated. The default Form Builder functionality is to underline the first uppercase letter or the character preceded by an ampersand in the generated menu item's label (derived from the module short title or short name properties). Make sure that you specify user-friendly short titles for your modules and that you specify an access key by placing an ampersand before it.

Map of Generated Menu Properties to Repository Properties

The following table is a summary of some of the important menu module properties and their source in Oracle Designer:

Menu Module Property	Source in Oracle Designer
Name	The *Implementation Name* or *Short Name* property of the repository module
Main Menu	The *Short Name* property of the repository module
Menu Directory	The *Destination* location as specified on Menu Option tab of the Form Generator Options dialog
Menu Filename	The *Implementation Name* or *Short Name* property of the repository module
Use Security	The *Menu – End User → Enable Use security flag (MNUEUS)* preference
Module Roles	All of the roles assigned to individual menu items

The following table is a summary of some of the important menu item properties and their source in Oracle Designer:

Menu Item Property	Source in Oracle Designer
Name	The *Short Title* or *Short Name* property of the called module
Label	The *Short Title* or *Short Name* property of the called module
Menu Item Type	Either *Plain* or *Separator*
Command Type	PL/SQL (for called modules), menu (for submenus), or null (for separators)
Menu Item Code	The *Command Line* property of the called module or the relevant *Default Command Line* preference (depending on the module language and type)
Item Roles	Database roles granted access to the called module
Hint	The *Short Name* property of the called module

How Generated Menus Are Merged with Template Menus

Similar to template forms, you can also use template menus during menu generation. A template menu is a menu module that is used as a shell into which your menus are generated. The purpose of the template menu module is to provide a standard look and feel for all of the generated menus by including standard menu items that you want to appear in all of your menus.

Template menus either can be generated from the repository just like any other menu module, or they can be manually built using Form Builder. Form Generator is already shipped with a standard template menu module called OFGMNUT.FMB (located in <ORACLE_HOME>\cgenf50\admin directory). The standard template menu module is almost identical to the Form Builder default menu module.

In order to use a template menu module:

1. Decide which template menu you want to use. If you want to create a custom template menu, create one either using Form Builder or by generating one from Oracle Designer.
2. Decide whether the template menu will be used in all the generated menus or only for selected menus. Set the *Standards → The name of the menu template (STMMMB)* preference at the application system level to ensure the same menu template is used for all the menus. The preference can also be specified at the module level. If you are testing a template menu, use the *Template Name* field on the Generate Form dialog window to specify the name of the template menu to be used during a particular generation session.
3. Specify the location of the template menu module by selecting the *Standard* tab of the Form Generator Options dialog box.
4. Set the *Menu – Gen Options → Sequence generated menu items after template items (MNUSGA)* preference to
   - **Yes** If you want the generated menu items placed after the items coming from the template menu (applies to top-level menus only)
   - **No** If you want the generated menu items placed before the items coming from the template menu (applies to top-level menus only)
5. You must decide the level of security for menu items copied from the template menu if there is no security already defined for them. To do this, set the *Menu – Roles → Grant all roles access to generated template items with no security (MNUADR)* preference to **Yes** if you don't want to restrict access to these menu items.

Attaching the Generated Menu to Your Forms

There are two ways to attach a menu to a form:

1. **Preference** You can use the *Form/Menu Attachment → Name of menu module if not implicit menu generation (FMNDMA)* preference to determine the name of the menu module that is attached to a form. This preference can be set either at the application system level (which provides a default for all form modules) or at the module level. The default value for this preference is DEFAULT, which will use the Form Builder default menu. You can also specify the name of the starting menu within the attached menu module via the *Form/Menu Attachment → Name of the start menu if not implicit menu generation (FMNDMN)* preference.
2. **Module network** You can also specify the name of the menu module to attach to a form using the module network. If you add a menu module to a form's module network, that menu module will be attached to the form. This will take precedence over the FMNDMA preference setting.

Using the preference method is much easier when you want to specify an application-level menu that is to be attached to all of the forms in your system. If you need to override this default for any specific menu, you can use the module network method. This will give you better impact analysis for custom menu modules that are only used by a few forms.

Menu Security

Form Generator allows us to specify security options for the generated menu items. In a Form Builder menu module, security can be enforced at the menu item level. Access to each menu item can be granted to one or more database roles. The menu-level *Use Security* property controls whether the security is enforced or not.

Since menu items are generated from module networks, the security needs to be defined at the module level. For each repository module, you can specify the user(s) and the role(s) that are allowed to access the module. If you want everybody to access a module from a generated menu, you can grant it to public. Before you assign the users and roles to modules, you need to create them.

How to Generate Menu Security

In order to generate the menu security:

1. Create users and database roles first, if you have not done so.
2. After you have created the modules, assign users and database roles to them. If you want to allow all roles and users to access a repository module, assign the standard PUBLIC role to the module. Also, if you are not sure which roles or users will be allowed access to some of the modules, you can create a default database role and specify that Forms Generator should automatically assign this role to modules with no security information. Use the *Menu - Roles → Name for the default role (MNUDRN)* preference to specify the database role to be used as a default role for all generated menu items, including the ones copied from the template menu.
3. Create the module networks needed to create your menu.
4. Set the *Menu – Roles → Generate Menu Security (MNUSEC)* preference to **Yes** (Default) to have Form Generator create the menu security information. If this preference is set to **No**, Form Generator does not create any menu security.

5. Set the *Menu – End User → Enable Use Security flag (MNUEUS)* preference to **Yes** (Default) to enforce the menu security information generated into the menu. If it is set to **No**, the security will not be activated in the generated menu even though the security role assignments are generated, and all users will have access to all menu items.
6. If you are using a template menu, specify the security information in the template menu. Otherwise, the default role will be assigned to them upon generation.
7. Generate the menu.

TIP
*If you are having problems with your security generation, or you do not have the roles created in the database yet, set the Menu – End User → Enable Use Security flag (MNUEUS) preferences to **No.** This will allow you to generate and use the menu until you get the security problem solved or until the database roles are generated. At that time, you can reset this preference to **Yes** and generate the menu again to implement full security.*

Suppressing All Security in the Menus

If your application does not call for any security at all, you can suppress the generation of all forms of security in the modules by setting the *Menu Roles → Generate Menu Security (MNUSEC)* preference to **No**. This will suppress the generation of any role or role assignment in the generated menus and will set the *Use Security* property in the generated form to **No**.

Security in Generated Menus

The security in the generated forms menus is based on database roles. However, there are a few setup and management issues you should be aware of:

Make sure to create the FRM50_ENABLED_ROLES view.

The menu security uses a special view named FRM50_ENABLED_ROLES to implement the role-based security. In order for the menu security to work, you will need to make sure this view is installed correctly in your instance. This view is automatically created as part of the Form Builder installation if you choose the **Create database tables** option. If you did not choose that option, you or your DBA must log on as SYSTEM and run the SQL script FRM50SEC.SQL. If you selected the **Create database tables** option, this script is located in the Form Builder SQL directory. If you did not choose this option, you will need to find the script on the computer that had it installed, or go ahead and install the database tables on your computer. We have included this script on the CD that comes with this book in case you have problems finding it.

Module roles

The generated form will include a list of *Module Roles* available from the *Module Roles* property of the menu module itself. This property includes a list of roles that can be used in the rest of the module. Before a role can be assigned to any item in the menu, it must be listed here. Also, these roles must exactly match the database roles that are used to implement the actual security. Therefore, if you ever modify these roles directly, you need to make sure that these roles match the database roles.

One great advantage of generating the menus and database roles from Designer is that the names will always match, since they come from the same source object. You will find that all of the roles that you have assigned to any of the module nodes that are included in the generated menu will be listed in the *Module Roles* property, as well as having the roles specifically assigned to the menu items.

Menu Generation Troubleshooting Guideline

Problem	**Resolution**
My menu labels are not user friendly; they are all set to the module name!	Make sure that you have entered a *Short Title* property for your modules. Module Short Title becomes the menu item label. If this is not set, Form Generator uses the module short name.
I have tried to customize the command line property, but I cannot get the module name included in the command line.	The substitution string <MODULE> is case sensitive, and has to be entered in uppercase. The same applies to <CMDLINE>.
I cannot get the Form Generator to create menu parameters from my module arguments.	This seems to be a bug in release 2.1.2.
I have set default command line preferences at application system level and then overridden them at a specific module. However, Form Generator ignored it.	This seems to be a bug in release 2.1.2.
I cannot get a module argument generated as a menu parameter.	The preference *Menu – Gen Options → Generate unique parameter strings (MNUUPS)* does not seem to be working in release 2.1.2. Make sure that the substitution strings you have specified for module arguments are two-letter only.
Even after, using two-letter substitution strings, I still cannot get a menu parameter generated.	The generated code includes the parameter in QUERY_PARAMETER dialog, but no parameter is created for it!
I could not figure out how to generate a menu item that calls a HOST (operating system) command.	You need to create a module and set the *Language* property to a language like C, C++, COBOL, etc. Also, do not forget to enter a command line. For example, in order to call a program called FOO, enter FOO in the command line.

Problem	Resolution
How can I generate a radio button or checkbox menu item?	You cannot. Form Generator always sets the *Menu Item Type* property to **Plain**. You need to manually change the GUI type after the menu is generated.
How can I generate the menu startup code?	Define the startup code in a template menu.
I have created a menu separator and included it in the module network, but I don't see it!	Menu separators are applicable only in submenus.
The *Menu Directory* property of the generated MMB file is being hard coded to the location where the MMX file is created.	Although hard coding of path names is very bad for portability, this property is applicable only when the menu source files are stored in the database.
When I set the Generate Associated Menus flag while I am generating a forms module, the menu is always generated with the same name as the forms module, even if the associated module has a different name.	It seems that in this release, the associated menu always has the same name as the form it is generated with. This is a problem if you want to use the same menu for more than one form. Therefore, you should never generate the menu along with the module unless the menu is only to be used for that module and you don't mind that it has the same name. This is actually a useful standard, but we think it's a bug to force it this way.
I can't find out where to assign a role to a menu module Design Editor.	Unfortunately, the release 2.1.2 Design Editor Navigator does not display the security branch for menu modules and, therefore, you cannot use it to assign roles or users to menu modules (we think this is a bug). You can assign a role or user to a menu module in two ways: 1. Use the Repository Object Navigator (RON). It does show the security branch. 2. Temporarily set the module's *Module Type* property to **Default**. Assign the roles and users to the module, then set the *Module Type* back to **Menu**.

Problem	Resolution
The *Use Security* property on my generated menu form is not set to **Yes** even though I have set the preferences correctly.	This seems to be a bug in release 2.1.2. You will have to set this property to **Yes** manually in the generated form.
When I try to run a menu with security enabled, I get the message "FRM10256: User is not authorized to run Form Builder Menu," even when I know I have the correct roles granted to the user.	Make sure the FRM50_ENABLED_ROLES view is created correctly. (See the box, "Security in Generated Menus," earlier in this chapter.)

Navigation Between Modules

As mentioned in Chapters 13 and 15, it is also possible to generate action items to navigate between modules. When navigation action items are used, Form Generator creates buttons and generates code to pass any parameters to the called module. See these chapters for a detailed description of how to create the action items.

Defining Module Arguments (Forms Parameters)

Module arguments are used to pass data between modules. Each module argument becomes a form parameter in the generated form. Module arguments can then be used to provide default values for queries or data entry as well as restricting queries and data entries. For example, when an employee maintenance form is called from a department maintenance form, you might restrict the employees queried or entered to those who work in the department viewed in the department maintenance form.

Creating module arguments is very easy. Click the module arguments node and select the create option from the menu. Once a module argument is created, it can be associated with an item (bound/unbound) usage. However, there are some restrictions that apply to the bound items associated with module arguments: for example, module arguments can only be associated with bound items in the first navigable block; otherwise, they will be ignored by the Form Generator.

Specifying Arguments for Navigation Action Items

When you create the navigation action items, you can specify a value to be passed to the argument in the called module. The value passed can be a static value or it may be passed from a source item in the calling module.

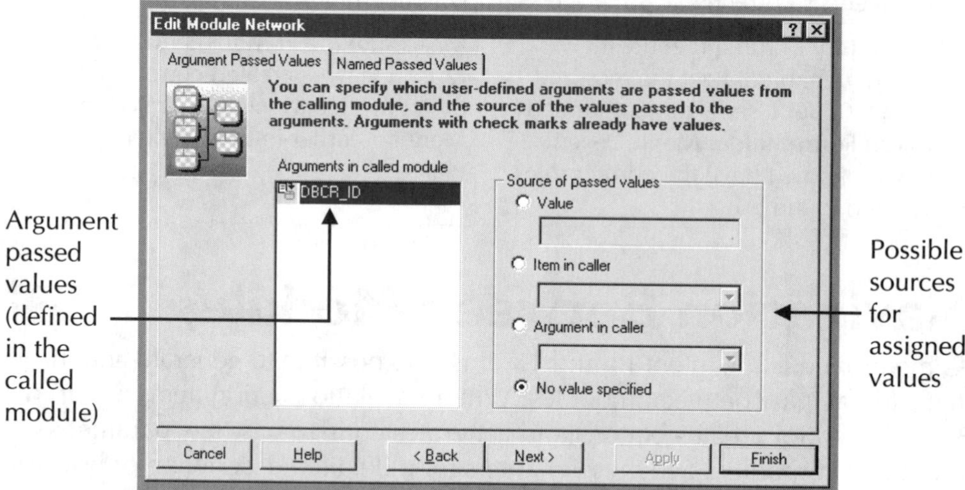

Specifying Named Passed Values

Named passed values are the standard parameters created in every form, and they are not shown in the Design Editor. The following illustration shows the dialog to set these values. One of the most important named passed values is the STARTUP_MODE.

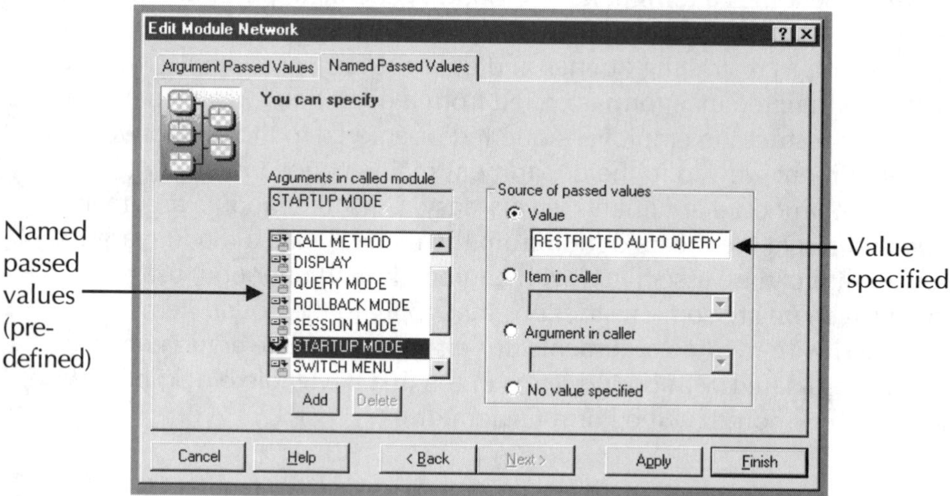

The CG$STARTUP_MODE Argument

The CG$STARTUP_MODE argument is used to control the startup query mode of a generated form. It also determines whether the parameter values passed to the form are assigned to items in the first navigable block of the form. (The first navigable block needs to be generated from a module component [i.e., not copied from a template form], and there are some bound items associated with module arguments.) The values passed with parameters can then be used as default values for query purposes, as well as for entering new records. The CG$STARTUP_MODE named passed value can be set to many different values with varying effect. The following table shows a list of valid values and a brief description of their effect:

STARTUP_MODE	Description
NORMAL	Default form functionality. No restriction on the data users can query or enter. Parameters passed to the form are not assigned to items generated from bound items in the first navigable block.
NEW	Same as NORMAL, but allows parameter values to be passed to the generated form. The parameters passed are used as default values (both in query mode and for new records) for bound items that they are passed, and users can modify them.
RESTRICTED NEW	Same as NEW, but users cannot modify the passed values.
ENTER QUERY	Upon startup form, will be in query mode. Parameter values passed to the form will be used as default values for the items generated from bound items in the first navigable block.
RESTRICTED ENTER QUERY	Same as ENTER QUERY, but users cannot modify the passed values.
AUTO QUERY	Upon startup form, the first generated block will be automatically queried. Parameter values passed to the form will be used as default values for the items generated from bound items in the first navigable block.

STARTUP_MODE	Description
RESTRICTED AUTO QUERY	Same as AUTO QUERY, but users cannot modify the passed values.

As you can see from the table, the RESTRICTED modes enable you to permanently limit the records users can query or enter in the block. For example, if you have defined an argument called ARG_ISS_STATUS, specified a default value of OPEN, and set CG$STARTUP_MODE to RESTRICTED AUTO QUERY, the form will automatically query open issues and limit users to enter or query only the open issues.

Tips on Using the CG$STARTUP_MODE Parameter

Here are some tips that will help you use the CG$STARTUP_MODE parameter:

Use a Domain You can create a STARTUP_MODE domain and specify the allowable values (all in uppercase) for the domain. You can use this domain to automatically set the data type, length, etc. for the CG$STARTUP_MODE arguments.

Set the *Default* property If the argument is assigned to a required item and the CG$STARTUP_MODE is set to one of the RESTRICTED modes, do not forget to set the *Default* property of an argument.

The first module component In Design Editor Navigator, module components are sorted by their *Name* property rather than their *Usage Sequence* property, and this can be very confusing. In order to change the sort order of module components in the Navigator, right-click the module components branch and choose *Sort* from the pop-up menu to correct this.

Parameters Assigned to Unbound Items Parameter values passed to the form are always assigned to items generated from unbound items with their corresponding argument usages, regardless of the startup query mode.

Calling Other Module Types

Calling other module types (reports, graphics, Web modules, etc.) is no different than calling form modules. Follow the same steps as outlined above for other module types.

Navigation Between Modules Troubleshooting Guideline

Problem	Resolution
I have created a named passed value to call another form in restricted auto-query mode, but it does not auto-query.	STARTUP MODE named passed value is case sensitive. Make sure that you select its name from the pop list. Also, make sure that its value is uppercase as well.

Application Startup Navigation

When you are designing your application, you need to consider how your application will start up. In essence, this is a special type of navigation in which you are navigating **into** the application. We are calling this the *application startup navigation.* For most applications, you will need to have a special application startup form that is used to initialize variables, enforce security, etc. If you are primarily using menus for application navigation, you need this form to hang the menu on for the initial navigation (you can't run a menu stand-alone).

Application Startup Form

In order to implement the application startup navigation, you usually have to develop an application startup form. You have many options of how you want to develop this form. It can be custom built in Form Builder, or it can be generated. You can create a separate form for each application, or you can develop one form that can handle many applications (provided they have the same basic architecture). However you decide to develop it, there are two basic aspects to consider:

- Appearance
- Functionality

Application Startup Form Appearance

There are many different ways you can design the appearance of the application startup form. If you want to include a company logo or other graphic in your application, this is a great place to do it. You can also place fancy navigation buttons or graphics, as well as system welcome or status messages, on this screen. In fact, since the initial view of an application often greatly affects new users' perception of the application, it is a good idea to make this form look very good. This is why the startup screen is often called the "splash screen." It is the screen that creates the initial splash when the application is started. For an example of a simple splash screen that can be easily generated from Oracle Designer, look at Recipe 8 in Chapter 20.

Application Startup Form Functionality

Once you have the layout of your startup form specified, you will need to add the startup functionality. You should consider adding the following types of functionality to your startup form.

- Application menu presentation
- Application startup security
- Startup context (if applicable)
- Additional navigation (buttons or clickable images)
- System messaging

This functionality will be implemented using various techniques. The best way to add some of the functionality is to add a WHEN-NEW-FORM-STARTUP event to the application startup form. However, the code should not be added directly to the form itself. Instead, you should add a call to a procedure in an attached library. When you do this, you can change the form startup functionality without having to generate the form again. Some of the functionality will be implemented with buttons on the startup form, and the application main menu is attached to this form just like any other.

It is out of the scope of this book to give you precise techniques for implementing these functions, especially since there are many ways to implement each one and we cannot cover each option. However, all of these ideas are easily generatable, and this list will help you decide what you do want to include in your startup form. We have also included each of these capabilities in the example application that is included on the CD that comes with this book.

APPLICATION MENU PRESENTATION Since you will not usually know where the user wants to start in your system, the first thing you generally want to present to them is a menu. However, Oracle Forms Menus cannot be displayed unless they are attached to a form. Therefore, the primary purpose of the application startup form is to present the user with the application menu. This is easy to do using the standard preference: *Form/Menu attachment → Name of menu module if not implicit (FMNDMA)*. If you set this preference to the name of the application's main menu, the generated application startup form will display this menu. In fact, since you will usually set this preference at the application level, you will not even have to change it for the application startup form. You can also use the module network to specifically set the menu to be used for the form.

APPLICATION STARTUP SECURITY Most applications have some sort of security requirements above and beyond the standard Oracle security your users will use to connect to the database. Implementing security within an application using menus was discussed earlier in this chapter. However, you will often have multiple applications running from the same instance, and you will want to prevent unauthorized users from accessing your application at all. This is best done by preventing the user from even entering the application using the application startup form.

The simple way to do this is to create an application security table and have the application startup form check to see if the current user is in that table. If not, an error message, "You are not authorized to use this application," can be displayed in an alert, and the application can exit. Starting from this simple design, you can enhance the startup processing to add additional features like expiration dates, application passwords, access logging, etc.

This functionality is usually implemented using the WHEN-NEW-FORM-STARTUP event of the application startup form. The example application provided on the CD includes an example of this type of functionality.

STARTUP CONTEXT Many applications include the concept of an application "context." This is usually a certain master parent value that is used by a major portion of the system. All of the data queried and entered for the system automatically inherits the current context. The user usually has a certain default context, but there are users who can enter data for multiple contexts. There might be a function in the system that allows a user to specify the context. One example of this type of functionality is Oracle Designer itself! When you start Oracle Designer up, you have to select an application. This application is your current context. Some examples of data that is often given as a context field are Department, Region, Contract, Account, etc.

Another thing that the startup form will have to do is to default or allow the user to specify the context for the application. This will usually involve a selection form that is called from the WHEN-NEW-FORM-STARTUP event. The example application provided on the CD includes an example of this type of functionality. There is also an example of a context selection form in Chapter 20.

ADDITIONAL NAVIGATION In addition to the main application menu, you may want to present the user with some additional navigation in the startup screen. This navigation is usually presented as buttons that the user can press. It could be used to present the following types of options:

- **An exit system button** Although there will usually be an exit item on the menu and you may leave the window exit capability activated, you might want to present the user with an obvious way to exit the system. This would be a way for novice users and people who accidentally start the system to easily leave the system without having to be familiar with the regular forms usage and navigation.
- **A help or manual button** Again, this function will probably also be on the menu. However, having an obvious button can be very helpful for users who start up the application and have no idea where to go from there. The help you start from this button can be targeted at just such novice users.
- **Shortcuts to key screens** If you have some key screens that the users usually start with, you can save them some hassle by placing easy navigation shortcut buttons on the startup screen. You can even get very fancy and make these buttons dynamic and present keys based on the user's role (if you have a way to keep that information in your system).

This type of functionality can easily be added to the startup form using custom unbound items, with calls to library procedures that actually implement the functionality specified by the buttons. See Chapters 13 and 15 for more information about generating buttons into the form. The example application provided on the CD includes an example of this type of functionality.

SYSTEM MESSAGING Yet another very useful capability to add to your application startup form is application system messaging. There are always useful messages and notifications that you would like to easily distribute to all of the users of your application. For example, you can warn users of upcoming downtime, announce new releases, etc. One of the easiest ways of doing this is to include the capability to display a system message when the user logs in to your application system.

There are two basic ways to add this capability to your startup form:

1. Add a module component that has a query-only data usage for a table in your application system. This table would contain the system message for your application (you could share this table across many applications by adding an application key that is used by the startup form to query the correct application). Then just add the CG$STARTUP_MODE parameter to the form to have it automatically query upon startup. (See Chapter 14 for details on how to do this.)
2. Create a control block by adding a module component with no data usages. Add a text unbound item to the module component to display the system message. Then add a call to a procedure to populate this item in the WHEN-NEW-FORM-INSTANCE event of the module. This procedure could query a table, read a text file, or retrieve a message in any way you want and have it displayed on the screen.

The example application provided on the CD includes an example of using the first method to implement this type of functionality. There is also an example of a startup form layout that includes a system message in Chapter 20.

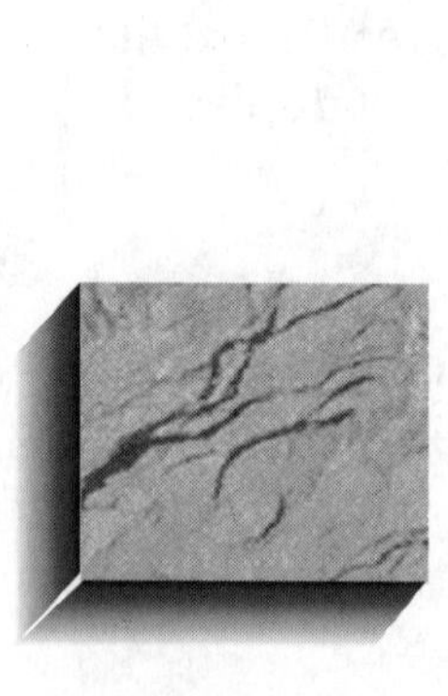

PART IV

Forms Generation Infrastructure

CHAPTER 22

Using Templates and Object Libraries

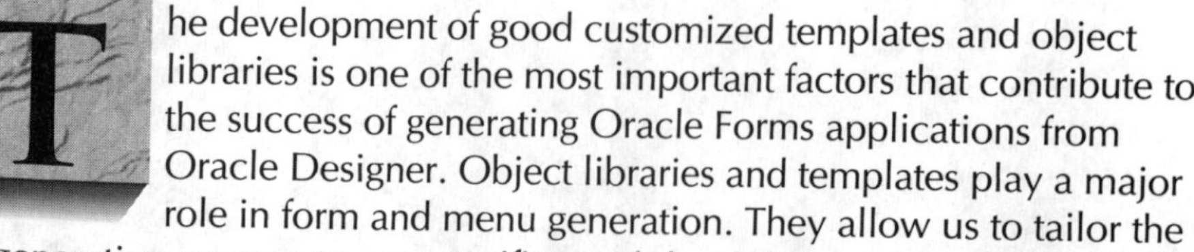

The development of good customized templates and object libraries is one of the most important factors that contribute to the success of generating Oracle Forms applications from Oracle Designer. Object libraries and templates play a major role in form and menu generation. They allow us to tailor the form generation process to our specific needs by defining and enforcing our own user-interface and coding standards. They also allow us to take advantage of object and code reuse features. Although it is possible to generate forms and menus without using custom templates or object libraries, most systems of at least average complexity will need to make customizations.

This chapter will help you understand the purpose of templates and object libraries and will detail their roles in the form generation process. This chapter will also show you how to customize standard templates and object libraries and how to create new ones in order to meet your specific needs. A more advanced discussion of how to define an architecture for templates and object libraries is also included in this chapter.

In this chapter, we will cover the following topics:

- What are the template forms and object libraries?
- Why do we need template forms and object libraries?
- Characteristics of templates and object libraries shipped with Oracle Designer
- How to customize templates and object libraries
- How to create new templates and object libraries
- Object libraries and earlier versions of Oracle Designer
- How to define an architecture for templates and object libraries
- A guide for troubleshooting templates and object libraries

Introduction to Templates and Object Libraries

The generation of forms and menus from Oracle Designer is a complicated process with many steps, and it involves a lot of information about what to generate and how to generate it. Figure 22-1 shows the components that have an effect on the form generation process.

A module definition, stored in the repository, defines the structure of a module. A module definition specifies *what to generate*: windows, canvases, blocks, items, etc. On the other hand, templates and object libraries tell the Form Generator *how to generate* a module: how the items and blocks should be laid out and decorated, or how the properties should be set or the validations should be performed. Figure 22-2 shows the form generation process and how templates and object libraries are used during generation. For further information about the form generation process, please refer to Chapter 10.

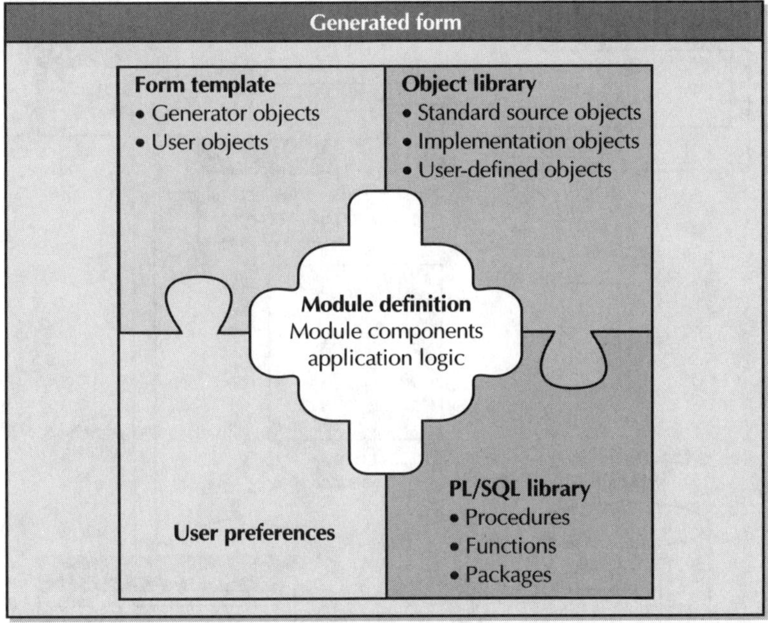

FIGURE 22-1. *Inputs to form generation process*

As you can see from Figure 22-2, templates and object libraries play a major role in the form generation process. Form Generator uses templates and libraries to

- Determine the properties of form objects that cannot be derived from the repository
- Provide a standard and a consistent user interface for generated forms
- Reuse standards and objects that may be common to many forms

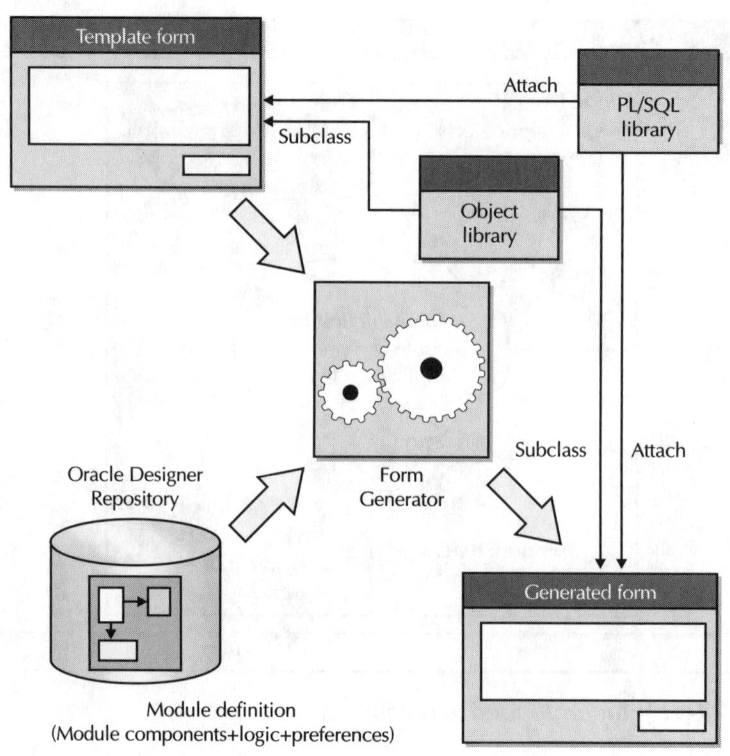

FIGURE 22-2. *Form generation process*

Templates provide a foundation upon which Form Generator can build new forms. When generating a form, Form Generator may copy objects from the template into the generated form without any modification, or it may use objects from the template as directives for creating new objects in the generated form. Templates might also contain common objects and code shared among many forms, such as toolbars and code for advanced security features.

Object libraries are essentially libraries of miscellaneous form objects. They are merely containers of standards and reusable objects. Form Generator uses these standard objects to set the properties of generated objects. These are some examples of the ways object libraries can be used.

- **Setting item properties** If you want to display certain text items in a bold red font, you could define a text item in the object library (named, say, UG$RED) and use it as the source object for certain items.
- **Adding standard code** If you want to do some fancy date validation to allow your users to enter dates in any format and have them validated, you can create a date item in the object library (named something like UG$DATE), add a validation trigger to it, and make it the standard source object for all of the date items in your system.
- **Implementing window standards** If you want to make some of the windows in your system a certain size, or if you want to set some window properties that cannot be derived from the repository, you can create a window object in the library and make it the source object of the windows.

Templates and object libraries help Form Generator generate applications that have a consistent look and feel. A good set of templates and libraries can really give a big boost to system generation efforts. In fact, templates and libraries are so crucial to forms generation that there are some commercially available template packages. These template packages provide a lot more features than the standard templates and object libraries. For a list of available commercial template packages, refer to the "Prerequisites for Generation" section of Chapter 1. We have also included some information about the commercial template packages on the CD that is included with the book.

What Are the Template Forms?

Template forms are Oracle Developer forms that Form Generator uses as a base for building new forms. Template forms are used to define

- Form-level properties that cannot be defined in the repository
- Some layout details (page headers and footers)
- Objects and code that may be common to many forms (user objects)

While many of the form-level properties can be specified directly in Oracle Designer, there are some that cannot be defined in the repository. These properties must be set using the template form. For example, there is no place in Oracle Designer to define the *coordinate system* and the *character cell width* and *height* size of a generated form. Therefore, if you want to use a nondefault coordinate system or a character cell size, you have to set these properties in a template form.

In addition to providing form-level properties, template forms may contain other form objects that may be common to many forms throughout a generated system, such as windows, canvases, blocks, items, alerts, record groups, triggers, procedures, and visual attributes. For example, if you are going to have the same standard header, footer, and toolbar in all of the forms in your system, you can place these in a template form and have the Form Generator automatically generate them into the generated forms.

Types of Objects in Template Forms

In general, objects in template forms can be divided into two main groups, based on how the Form Generator uses them:

- User objects
- Generator objects

Form Generator determines the type of an object based on its name. If an object's name does not start with the CG$ prefix, Form Generator considers the object to be a user object. On the other hand, a generator object's name must start with CG$, and include a special keyword recognized by the Form Generator (see "Generator Objects," later in this chapter, for a detailed description of the CG$ item naming standard). Form Generator treats these two types of objects totally differently. Figure 22-3 shows how the Form Generator uses generator and user objects from template forms.

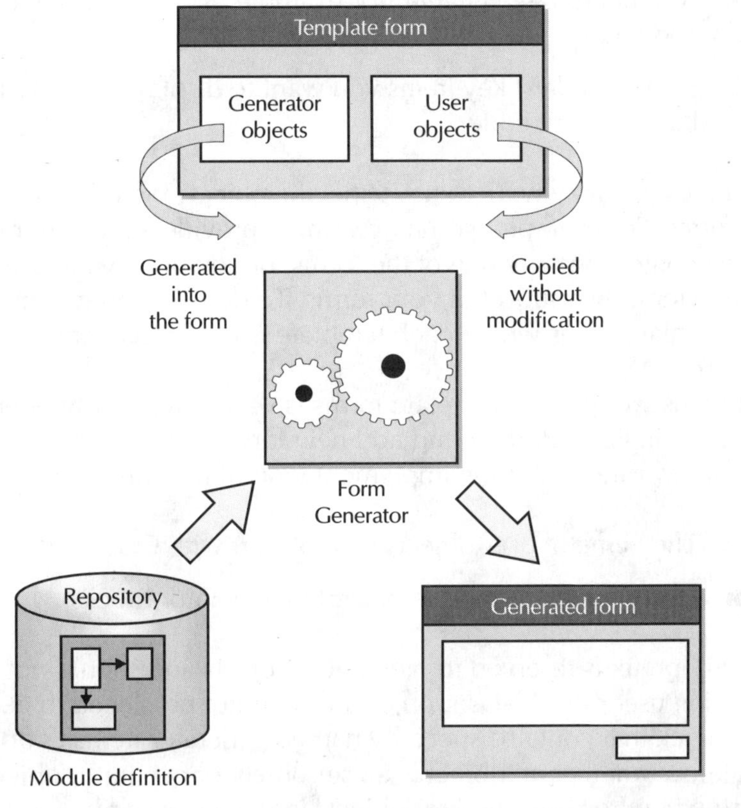

FIGURE 22-3. *How Form Generator uses objects from template forms*

User Objects

Form Generator copies user objects from the template form into the generated form without any change. Examples of user objects may be windows, canvases, blocks, items, record groups, list-of-values, visual attributes, alerts, property classes, triggers, program units, attached libraries, etc. For example, a user-defined toolbar might be composed of the block, many items, property classes, and triggers that are needed to implement the toolbar. User objects allow us to extend the standard functionality provided by Oracle Designer. In general, user objects are common to many forms throughout a generated system. Some examples are

- A standard toolbar that you want on every form
- A standard page header (for example, with the form name and date)
- Some standard key items you want to display on every form (like business unit code)

Sometimes you may want to have specific objects included in only one or a few forms. For example, you may want to provide a navigator control (a.k.a., tree control) in only one of the forms, or you may want to use a wizard style for only a subset of your forms. To do this, you can develop multiple template forms where each template is used to generate a different style of form.

Creating user objects in template forms is very easy: simply open a template form in Form Builder and add new form objects to it. There are, however, a few rules about the implementation of user objects:

- The name of user objects cannot start with CG$
- User objects cannot be placed in generator blocks

The CG$ prefix is reserved for generator objects and should not be used when naming user objects. User objects should not be placed in generator blocks (a block that contains specially named generator items). Form Builder does not know whether an object is a user object or generator object, and it will not stop you from putting user objects into a generator block. However, Form Generator will simply ignore any user objects placed in a generator block. It won't even give you a warning message, making it more difficult to figure out why a user object that you have just added to the template form is not being generated into your form. Therefore, it is best to be careful and keep user objects separate from generator objects.

User Objects and Reusable Module Components

In Oracle Designer release 2, templates and object libraries are not the only way to share an object among many forms. It is now possible to place some shareable objects into the repository. Oracle Designer release 2 allows us to define control blocks (blocks that are not based on any data source) as module components. These can be created as reusable module components, which can be shared among many module definitions. Now, you may ask, "How do I know where to put my user objects: in template forms or reusable module components?"

The most obvious benefit of using reusable module components for user objects is better documentation and impact analysis. In a repository-driven development environment, this is very important. However, even if you use reusable module components, you may end up creating some custom implementation objects in the object library in order to control the properties of these generated shared user objects. It may be easier to maintain the shared objects if they are placed in templates only so that they are only maintained in one place. It is still possible to document the shared objects by creating module definitions for each template with components and data usages that match the template, however. These modules will allow the templates to be included in any impact analysis you may perform. Also, remember that you have the ultimate flexibility in Form Builder—you can design the layout of these objects as you wish; whereas if you use reusable module components, you will be restricted by the generator's limitations.

As you can see, there are pros and cons to each option. As a general rule of thumb, place those user objects that are common to all or most of the generated forms in template forms, and create reusable module components for those that are common to only a few.

Maintenance of User Objects in Template and Generated Forms

Form Generator copies user objects from the template form into the generated forms without any change. This sounds great, because we can easily add our custom objects to templates. However, the fact that these user objects are just copied into the generated forms may cause a big maintenance problem. Upon generation, the generated user objects are simply copies of the user objects in template forms, and they are not linked to template objects at all. Once a form is generated, any changes made in the template form (for enhancements, bug fixes, etc.) will not be reflected in the generated form. In order to apply the changes in templates to the previously generated forms, you must do one of the following:

- Generate the forms again
- Manually make the changes in *all* of the generated forms

Both of these options are very time consuming; and, considering that there will be many changes to template forms at different times, you can imagine the maintenance nightmare this might represent.

Although we can put user objects directly into the template forms, a better approach is to place them in object groups in an object library and subclass these object groups in template forms, as shown in Figure 22-4.

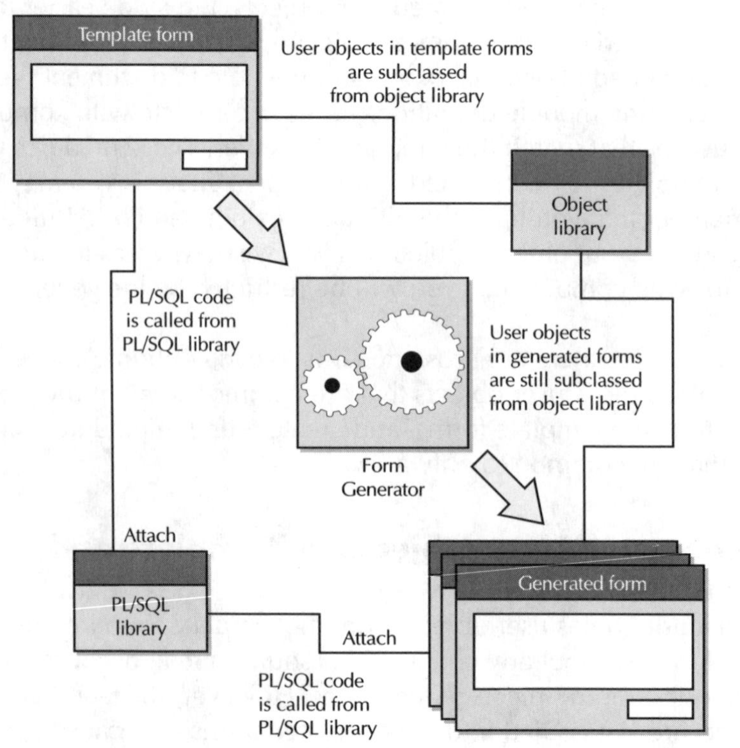

FIGURE 22-4. *User Objects in template forms and subclassing*

Because Form Generator copies the user objects into generated forms just as they are, the user objects will remain as subclassed from object libraries.

The advantage to this method is that user objects in object libraries can be easily modified without having to generate the previously generated forms or manually make these changes in each individual form. The changes made to user objects in object libraries will be reflected in the previously generated forms when they are recompiled and generated from Oracle Developer. Recompiling forms is very easy and can be automated using either a script or Project Builder. Therefore, this method makes it very easy to synchronize the previously generated forms with the changes in template forms.

Generally, user objects should be defined as packaged object groups in object libraries and subclassed from the object libraries.

Defining PL/SQL Code in Template Forms

In the previous section, we detailed some of the benefits of referencing form objects. The same comments can be applied to PL/SQL code placed in template forms. Although the PL/SQL program units can be defined in template forms, a better approach is to place the PL/SQL code in PLL libraries and attach these PLL libraries to template forms. By using PLL libraries, shared PL/SOL code can be modified very easily. You only have to modify the code

Object Libraries Versus Reference Forms

Object libraries were not available in previous releases of Oracle Developer Forms. However, there is another technique that is very similar to subclassing from object libraries. It is called "Referencing" objects from "Reference Forms." This technique was available in Forms 4.5, and is still available in the current version of Forms. Even though this method is still available, it is not the best method to use. Whenever possible, you should use subclassing from object libraries. When you use reference forms, it is an all-or-nothing proposition. You have to reference *all* of the properties of an object. With subclassing you can modify some of the properties on the subclassed object, and still have the other properties subclassed from the object library. Object libraries also allow you to define the objects in a hierarchy of subclassed objects, which makes it easier to implement and maintain standards.

in the PLL library and then compile it, and the updates will automatically be reflected in all of the forms that use the library. When shared PL/SQL code is put in a PLL library, the forms that use the code don't have to be generated from Oracle Designer or compiled from Oracle Developer again.

However, there are some differences in the way you write your PL/SQL code if it is to be placed directly into the template or placed in PLL libraries. The main difference is that the standard **:** notation for referencing form objects cannot be used in PLL libraries. Instead of referencing form objects directly with the **:** notation, you have to use the NAME_IN and COPY built-ins. For example, instead of using ':Toolbar.Button_Help' to refer to the Button_Help item in the Toolbar block, we have to use NAME_IN ('Toolbar.Button_Help'). This restriction is not only for Form items, but also for any global and system variables. The NAME_IN forms built-in can be used to get the value of an item, system variable, or a global variable. Similarly, the COPY built-in can be used to assign a value to an item, system variable, or a global variable. The following listings show an example of the difference between coding directly in the template form and in PL/SQL libraries.

Code in template form:

```
BLK_HTBAR.TOOLTIP := get_item_property(:system.mouse_item,label);
```

Code in PL/SQL library (PLL):

```
COPY(get_item_property(name_in('system.mouse_item'), label),'BLK_HTBAR.TOOLTIP');
```

Another difference between writing PL/SQL code for forms and for PLL libraries is that PLL libraries are a little more difficult to debug. This is because any mistakes in object names cannot be caught during the compilation time. Since the objects are referenced indirectly through the COPY and NAME_IN built-ins, they are not validated during compilation. The only way to find these types of errors is to run the forms and have the PLL library code executed. This means that the only way to make sure that you do not have any bugs is to make sure every single line of code that contains a COPY or NAME_IN is executed.

Generally, all of the PL/SQL code should be placed in PLL libraries. All of the triggers and other program units defined in template forms should call the code stored in these PLL libraries. This would allow a more object-oriented architecture.

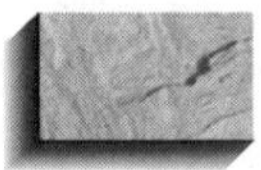

TIP

Design capturing of template objects *When you capture design of a form, by default, template objects are not captured into the repository. This is because Form Generator adds a directive string* ***CG$IGNORE_ON_DESIGN_CAPTURE*** *in the comment property of objects during generation, instructing not to capture user objects during design capture. Normally, you don't need to capture these user objects back into the repository; however, if you ever want to do this, simply open the form in Form Builder and remove these comments from user objects before you run the Design Capture utility.*

Generator Objects

Generator Objects are specially named objects defined in templates, and they receive special treatment by the Form Generator. Unlike user objects, these objects are not copied directly into the generated forms. Instead, they are used as the basis for the generation of new objects, and their properties are used to set the properties of these new objects. Generator objects can be used to

- Derive the properties of generated objects
- Create both static and dynamic text from information stored in the repository
- Generate special functionality, such as calling other modules

For example, the CG$BLOCK_TITLE visual attribute can be used to define the font, size, and pattern for block titles. Similarly, the CG$USER generator object can be used to create an item to display the name of the user running the form, and the CG$PM generator object can be used to create the "Page 1 of 3" style static graphic text in page headers or footers.

In the Oracle Developer template forms, generator objects are just regular form objects and can be defined and maintained very easily using Form Builder. The only feature that distinguishes them as generator objects is their name. The name of a generator object must be in the format

CG$<keyword>_<seq>

where

CG$ =	Indicates to the Form Generator that this is a Generator Object.
<keyword> =	Is a keyword recognized by the Form Generator. The list of these keywords will be given in the following sections.
<seq> =	The sequence number in generator object's name is optional and is only needed when more than one instance of the same object is included. For example, CG$STACKED_HEADER_1 is the stacked header for the first generated page, and CG$STACKED_HEADER_2 is the stacked header for the second generated page.

If an object name starts with CG$ but does not include a valid keyword, it is ignored by Form Generator without any warning or error message displayed. Therefore, you must be careful to enter the keywords correctly, or you will not get the objects you want to be generated, and you will not know why. Generator objects can be windows, canvases, items, or visual attributes.

Obsolete Generator Objects in Oracle Designer Release 2

The support for object libraries, and subclassing, has drastically decreased the role of generator objects in templates. Many of the generator objects have become obsolete, because object libraries offer solutions that are more flexible. For backward compatibility, these obsolete generator objects are still supported in release 2, but you should avoid using them because they will be eliminated in future releases. However, there are a few generator objects that are not obsolete, and we will still need to use these particular generator objects in release 2 because there are no alternatives to them.

Generator Objects—Windows and Canvases

Template windows and canvases can be defined in template forms to influence the layout generation. For example, the CG$HEADER canvas can be used to create a header area that will be merged with generated pages. In earlier versions of Oracle Designer, Form Generator used CG$ window and canvas objects to derive the properties of generated windows and canvases (for example, the size of the window, whether it can be minimized or maximized, etc.). However, support for object libraries and subclassing objects from object libraries has superceded this functionality.

The following table shows a list of generator objects used for window and canvas generations.

Generator Object Name	Purpose
CG$WINDOW	To set properties of a generated window
CG$PAGE	To set properties of a generated page (content canvas)
CG$POPUP	To set properties of a generated pop-up (stacked canvas)
CG$HEADER	To set properties of a header area included in a generated page
CG$FOOTER	To set properties of a footer area included in a generated page
CG$STACKED_HEADER	To set properties of a header area assigned to a generated window
CG$STACKED_FOOTER	To set properties of a footer area assigned to a generated window
CG$HORIZONTAL_TOOLBAR	To set properties of a horizontal toolbar canvas assigned to a generated window
CG$VERTICAL_TOOLBAR	To set properties of a vertical toolbar canvas assigned to a generated window

The use of most of the window and canvas generator objects has been superceded by the use of object libraries. However, the header and footer objects are still required in order to define the headers and footers in the template. When a form is generated, CG$HEADER and CG$FOOTER canvases are merged with the generated pages' CG$STACKED_HEADER and CG$STACKED_FOOTER canvases. However, they are generated as separate stacked canvases that float on top of the headers and footers (see Figure 22-5).

Generator Objects—Items

Template forms may also include some specially named form items known as generator items. Generator items are placed in the generator blocks, which contain only CG$ generator objects. Generator items can be used for the following purposes:

- To include information from the repository (generated as graphic text and hint properties of generated items)
- To implement certain Oracle Developer Forms functionality via buttons

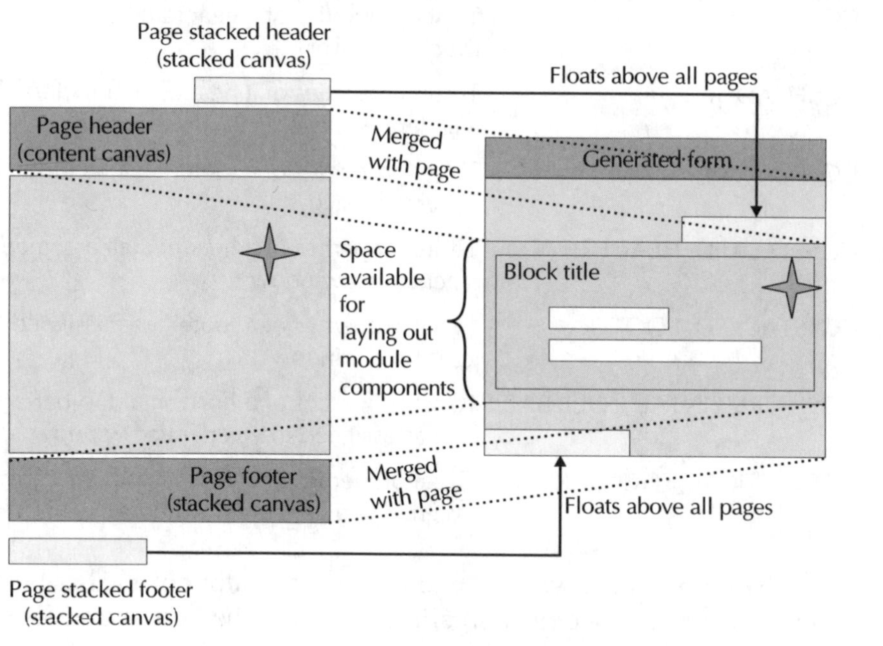

FIGURE 22-5. *Interaction of headers and footers with page*

Generator items can be used to include some repository information in generated forms. Some examples of the information that can be generated into the forms are

- The name or title of the form
- The project code or task code for the module
- The name of the application system and its version
- The "company name" for the application

Some of the information generated by these items can also be defined as static graphic text in template forms or source objects in object libraries. However, objects that are generated by some of the generator items cannot be generated in any other way. For example, we may want to display the name of the form as graphic text in the header of each generated form. If we used a graphic text hard-coded into the template, we would have to change the template for each module we generate because each module has a different name. Instead, by using the CG$MN generator item, we can cause the generator to create a static graphic text in generated forms to display the name of the module as it is defined in the repository. The following table shows a list of CG$ generator items that can be used to include some repository information in generated forms.

CG$ Generator Item Name	Template Item Type	Source of Information
CG$AN	Text Item	*Name* property of the application system
CG$AV	Text Item	*Version* property of the application system
CG$AT	Text Item	*Title* property of the application system
CG$CN	Text Item	Value specified by *the Field Layout → Company Name (CONAME)* preference
CG$MB	Text Item	*Bottom Title* property of the module
CG$MI	Text Item	*Implementation Name* property of the module
CG$MJ	Text Item	*Project Code* property of the module

CG$ Generator Item Name	Template Item Type	Source of Information
CG$MK	Text Item	*Task Code* property of the module
CG$MN	Text Item	*Name* property of the module
CG$M1	Text Item	*First part of module's Top Title* property that precedes a I character (e.g., if module's *Top Title* property is Employee I Details, Employee is used)
CG$M2	Text Item	*Second part of module's Top Title* property that follows a I character (e.g., if module's *Top Title* property is Employee I Details, Details is used)
CG$MP	Text Item	*Purpose* property of the module
CG$MS	Text Item	*Short Name* property of the module

If these generator items are displayed on a canvas in the template forms, Form Generator converts them to static graphic text. Otherwise, a non-displayed text item is generated and the repository information is placed into the hint property of the generated item. These non-displayed items can be used to programmatically retrieve the desired information.

Some of the other CG$ generator items can only be generated as static graphic text. The following table shows a list of the CG$ generator items to use to generate page number information as graphic text.

CG$ Generator Item Name	Template Item Type	Purpose
CG$PN	Text Item	Show the *Current Page Number* (content canvases).
CG$PT	Text Item	Show the *Total Number of Pages* (content canvases).
CG$PM	Text Item	Show "Page *n* of m" text, where *n* is current page (content canvas) number and *m* is total number of pages in the form.

The page number may be redundant when most of your forms have only one page. In addition, just showing the text, "Page 1 of 5" doesn't mean

Using Page Numbers

Displaying page numbers on screens was common in older style character-based user interfaces in which users had to use keystrokes to navigate between multiple pages of information. With the advent of GUI interfaces, page numbers are really no longer needed; so you should consider your standards carefully before using this capability. Of course, if you are unfortunate enough to have to generate a character-based application (which is still possible with the current tools), you might want to use page numbers.

much if there are no controls to navigate to those other pages. This is exactly why the CG$NP (next page) and CG$PP (previous page) push-button items (or preferably, the CGAI$NEXT_PAGE and CGAI$PREV_PAGE source objects) should be used when CG$PM exists in page headers or footers.

There are also other CG$ items that can be used to implement special features. The following table shows a list of miscellaneous CG$ generator items. Form Generator uses these items to generate similar items with the necessary logic to provide the functionality.

CG$ Item	Item Type	Purpose
CG$DT	Text Item	Show *Current Date.*
CG$FF	Pop List	Display *List of Modules* that can be called from the current form.
CG$FF	Text List	Display *List of Modules* that can be called from the current form.
CG$NP	Button	Navigate to *Next Page.*
CG$PP	Button	Navigate to *Previous Page.*
CG$QI	Button	Toggle *Block Synchronization Mode* on and off, i.e., whether the query of detail blocks should be deferred (on) or not (off).

CG$ Item	Item Type	Purpose
CG$QI	Check Box	Display and toggle *Block Synchronization Mode* on and off, i.e., whether the query of detail blocks should be deferred (on) or not (off).
CG$QI	Text Item	Display *Block Synchronization Mode.*
CG$US	Text Item	Show *Current User* of the form.

TIP

Expert Template *Examples of all of these objects are included in the expert template OFG4EXPT.FMB shipped with the product and available in the <ORACLE_HOME>\cgenf50\admin directory.*

Generator Objects—Visual Attributes

Generator objects can also be used to define visual attributes of generated objects. For example, the font, size, and pattern for checkbox items can be derived from a CG$CHECKBOX named visual attribute.

Obsolete Visual Attributes

Most of the Visual Attribute generator objects (*a.k.a., Release 1.x Style Generator Named Visual Attributes*) should *not* be used in release 2 generation. This is because by using standard source or implementation objects in object libraries, we can set *any* property of a generated object; we are not limited to only the font, color, and pattern properties that are available using visual attributes. Also, the support for CG$ visual attributes stored in template forms is obsolete and will be phased out in a future release of Oracle Designer. They are available in release 2 only for backward compatibility.

Although CG$ visual attributes are being phased out (see the preceding special box, "Obsolete Visual Attributes"), there are still a few that have not been replaced by standard source objects in object libraries. The CG$ visual attributes for titles and decorations are still being used. For example, the CG$BLOCK_TITLE visual attribute is the only way to set the font, size, and color of block titles. The following table shows a list of the visual attributes that still must be defined in the template forms.

Visual Attribute	Purpose/Comment
CG$BLOCK_DECORATION	Used for block decorations
CG$BLOCK_TITLE	Used for block titles
CG$CONTEXT_DECORATION	Used for context area decorations
CG$CONTEXT_TITLE	Used for context area titles
CG$DECORATION	Used for any decorations in the absence of specific visual attributes
CG$GROUP_DECORATION	Used for item group decorations
CG$GROUP_TITLE	Used for item group titles
CG$RADIO_DECORATION	Used for radio group decorations
CG$RADIO_TITLE	Used for radio group titles
CG$STUB_DECORATION	Used for block stub decorations
CG$STUB_TITLE	Used for block stub titles
CG$TEMPLATE_TEXT	Used for static graphic texts
CG$TITLE	Used for any titles in the absence of specific visual attributes

The best way to implement these visual attributes is to define them in object libraries and subclass them back into the templates. This approach will allow you to share the visual attributes among multiple templates if you need to. However, subclassing the visual attributes will not make much difference in the generated form. This is because the graphic text objects (decorations and titles) that are actually generated into the forms cannot use visual attributes. Therefore, the graphic text is created with its attributes hard-coded into the generated form. Since there is no link to an object library or reference form, these objects cannot be updated except by editing the generated form directly.

Maintenance of Generator Objects in Template and Generated Forms

We discussed using subclassing user objects from object libraries earlier in this chapter. You may automatically think that the same would apply to the generator objects. However, Form Generator treats generator objects very differently from other objects in the template. It does not simply copy them over from template forms into the generated forms. For the most part, it creates new objects and, therefore, does not carry over the subclassing.

Visual attributes, however, are an exception to this rule. Visual attributes in templates, whether they are user named or CG$ named, are copied into the generated forms without a change. Therefore, the subclassing or referencing technique that we mentioned earlier in this chapter in "Maintenance of User Objects in Template and Generated Forms" can only be applied to CG$ visual attributes. Remember, subclassing and referencing information on other generator objects is not inherited.

Templates in Earlier Versions of Oracle Designer

In earlier versions of Oracle Designer, templates played a much more important role in the form generation process. Prior to release 2, object libraries did not even exist. Templates and user preferences were the only means available for tailoring the generated forms. Form templates were used to implement various features for everything from generating control blocks to placing the hooks for standard form event triggers. They were also used to implement module-specific customizations, in which case there was a separate template for each module (which rather defeats the purpose of templates!). Even the visual properties of generated objects were completely driven from visual attributes stored in templates. Even the visual properties of generated objects were completely driven from visual attributes stored in templates. Other properties of generated objects were driven from the user preferences. In earlier versions of Oracle Designer, template forms could contain the following generator objects:

- **Generator objects** To set properties of generated objects
- **CG$ template button items** To provide default Form Builder functionality
- **Generator named visual attributes** To set properties of generated objects

However, the use of object libraries, the ability to store and customize the application logic right in the repository, and the ability to generate PLL libraries and attach them via the module network definitions (again, right in the repository) has significantly diminished the role of template forms. Nevertheless, template forms still play an important role in form generation. For example, page header and footers (both content and stacked), standard graphic text generated based on the repository information (the name of a module, the name and the version of an application system, etc.), background images embedded in canvases, and titles and decoration visual properties are still defined in templates. For further information, please refer to *Oracle Designer Online Help → Release 1.x style template functionality superseded by object library.*

Object Libraries

An object library in Oracle Developer is a container for reusable objects, user-interface guidelines, and standards. Object libraries enable you to

- Apply standards to existing objects
- Reuse standards and objects in many forms

Form Generator uses objects in object libraries to derive the properties of objects in generated forms. For example, when an object is generated, its visual properties (e.g., font size, color, and pattern), sizes, and even triggers can be derived from an object in the object library. When the same standard object is used for some object definitions in Designer, all of the generated objects will look and behave similarly in all the generated forms.

Some of the object properties can be derived from both the module definitions in the repository and the source objects in the object library. If a property is defined in the repository, it overrides the value defined for the source object in the object library. For example, if a checkbox item defined in the repository has two possible values **A** and **B**, and the source object has two possible values **Value1** and **Value2**, values **A** and **B** are used from the repository definition. However, if the source object's *Mapping of Other Values* property is set, Form Generator uses this property from the source object because this property cannot be defined in the repository object.

Subclassing Versus Copying

Generated objects can either be copied or subclassed from object libraries. The *Standards → Object Library Subclass or Copy (OLBSOC)* preference can be used to specify whether the generated objects are copied or subclassed from source objects in the object library, which is specified by another preference, *Standards → Name of the Object Library (STOOLB)*. If the OLBSOC preference is set to **Copy**, Form Generator will create an object in the generated form as a copy of the source object; otherwise, the generated object will be a subclass of the source object. The preferred method is to subclass objects from object libraries, because the changes made to a source object in an object library can be propagated to any object subclassed from that object by recompiling the appropriate forms.

When an object is subclassed, the subclassed object maintains its link to the source object, and it automatically inherits any changes made to the source object once the forms are recompiled from Oracle Developer. If you change a source object, you won't even have to generate it again from Oracle Designer. A simple compilation and generation from Oracle Developer is all that's needed to synchronize the previously generated forms with the changes in the object libraries.

However, when an object is copied, the copied object does not maintain its link to the source object. The changes made in the source object can only be reflected in objects copied from this object by either generating from Oracle Designer again or manually making the same changes that were made in the source objects. This can lead to maintenance problems, because these source objects often need to be modified either for an enhancement or a bug fix. It is very time consuming to generate all of the forms again (and again and again) whenever a change is made in source objects. This is especially true if there are any post-generation changes made in generated forms. In addition, manually making changes is even more troublesome; it is more time consuming and error prone. Copying objects from object libraries is not a good idea, and it defeats the main purpose of using object libraries in the first place!

Moreover, the fact that subclassing is maintained at the property level and not at the object level makes it more flexible. For example, after a text item is subclassed from a source object in the library, if its prompt is changed, other properties, such as its bevel, font, triggers, etc., still stay subclassed. This gives you the ultimate flexibility.

Types of Objects in Object Libraries

In general, objects in object libraries can be divided into two main groups, based on how the Form Generator uses them:

- Standard source objects
- Implementation source objects

Form Generator determines the type of an object on the basis of its name. If an object's name does not start with the CGSO$ prefix, Form Generator considers the object to be an implementation object. On the other hand, a standard generator source object's name must start with CGSO$, and it must include a special keyword recognized by the form. The naming standard for the standard generator source objects is

CGSO$<object_type>_<suffix>

where <object_type> is an object type tag that is recognized by the generator and <suffix> is a recognized suffix that usually relates to how the item is used.

An example of a standard generator source object name is

CGSO$CHAR_DO

Standard Source Objects

Form Generator uses standard source objects when creating a specific type of generated object. The names of standard source objects are prefixed with CGSO$ and are followed by a keyword that indicates the type of form object that can be used as a source. For example, the CGSO$CHECK_BOX standard source object is the source object for generated checkboxes.

The standard source objects must follow the predefined hierarchy. Figure 22-6 shows part of the source object hierarchy for item objects. Form Generator first searches for a specific source object. In the absence of this specific source object, it searches the object library for the parent of this object and uses that instead. Form Generator keeps searching the object library to find an appropriate parent. If it cannot find one (for instance the CGSO$DEFAULT_ITEM is not in the object library), it defaults to internal default values.

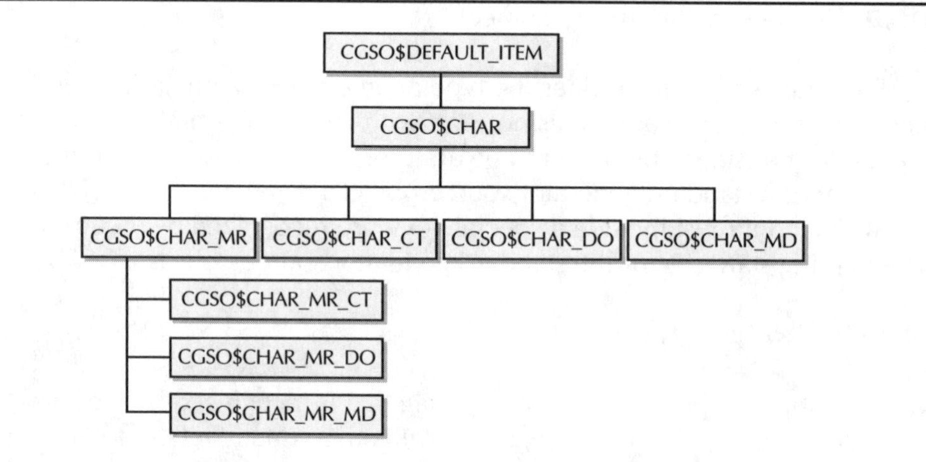

FIGURE 22-6. *Hierarchy of standard source objects*

The following table shows a list of standard source objects and their hierarchy.

Parent Source Object Name	Source Object Name	Possible Suffixes	Source Object Type	Type of Generated Item
(none)	CGSO$BLOCK	MR, CT	Block	-
(none)	CGSO$CANVAS	-	Canvas	-
(none)	CGSO$CANVAS_HTOOL	-	Canvas	-
(none)	CGSO$CANVAS_POPLIST	-	Canvas	-
(none)	CGSO$CANVAS_POPUP	-	Canvas	-
(none)	CGSO$CANVAS_SPREAD	-	Canvas	-
(none)	CGSO$CANVAS_TAB	-	Canvas	-
(none)	CGSO$CANVAS_VTOOL	-	Canvas	-
(none)	CGSO$DEFAULT_ITEM	MR, CT, DO, MD	Item	-
(none)	CGSO$LOV	-	LOV	-
(none)	CGSO$LOV_BUT	MR, CT	Item	Button
(none)	CGSO$TAB_PAGE	-	Tab Page	-
(none)	CGSO$WINDOW	-	Window	-
CGSO$BUTTON	CGSO$AIBUTTON	CT	Item	Button
CGSO$CHAR "	CGSO$ALPHA	MR, CT, DO, MD	Item	Alpha
"	CGSO$CHAR_MLINE	MR, CT, DO, MD	Item	Char
"	CGSO$DATE	MR, CT, DO, MD	Item	Date
"	CGSO$DATETIME	MR, CT, DO, MD	Item	Datetime
"	CGSO$NUMBER	MR, CT, DO, MD	Item	Number

Parent Source Object Name	Source Object Name	Possible Suffixes	Source Object Type	Type of Generated Item
CGO$CHAR	CGSO$TIME	MR, CT, DO, MD	Item	Time
CGSO$DEFAULT_ ITEM	CGSO$BUTTON	MR, CT	Item	Button
"	CGSO$CHAR	MR, CT, DO, MD	Item	Char
"	CGSO$CHART	MR, CT, DO, MD	Item	Chart
"	CGSO$CHECK_BOX	MR, CT, DO, MD	Item	Checkbox
"	CGSO$COMBO	MR, CT, DO, MD	Item	Combo box
"	CGSO$CONTEXT	MR, CT, DO, MD	Item	Char
"	CGSO$CUR_REC_IND	MR, CT, DO, MD	Item	Char
"	CGSO$DESC_FLEX	MR, CT, DO, MD	Item	Char
"	CGSO$DRILL_IND	MR, CT, DO, MD	Item	Char
"	CGSO$IMAGE	MR, CT, DO, MD	Item	Image
"	CGSO$LONG	MR, CT, DO, MD	Item	Long
"	CGSO$OCX	MR, CT, DO, MD	Item	OCX control
"	CGSO$OLE	MR, CT, DO, MD	Item	OLE container
"	CGSO$POP	MR, CT, DO, MD	Item	Pop list
"	CGSO$RADIO	MR, CT, DO, MD	Item	Radio group

Parent Source Object Name	Source Object Name	Possible Suffixes	Source Object Type	Type of Generated Item
CGSO$Default	CGSO$RADIO_BUTTON	MR, CT, DO, MD	Item	Radio button
"	CGSO$SOUND	MR, CT, DO, MD	Item	Sound
"	CGSO$TEXT_LIST	MR, CT, DO, MD	Item	Text list
CGSO$NUMBER	CGSO$INTEGER	MR, CT, DO, MD	Item	Integer
"	CGSO$MONEY	MR, CT, DO, MD	Item	Money

STANDARD SOURCE OBJECT SUFFIXES Standard source object names can include one or more suffixes. These suffixes allow us to further refine the context in which the standard source objects can be used. The following table shows a list of valid suffixes that can be appended to the standard source object names.

Order	Suffix	Use if generated object will be a
1	MR	Multirecord block, or an item in a multirecord block
2	CT	Control block, or an item in a control block
3	DO	Display-only item
4	MD	Mandatory item

For example, CGSO$CHECK_BOX is the standard source object used for all of the checkboxes. However, if we want to specify different properties for mandatory checkboxes, then we create a new source object, add the **MD** (mandatory item) suffix to its name, and call it CGSO$CHECK_BOX_MD.

When using more than one suffix, there is a precedence that must be followed. The *Order* column in the table refers to this precedence.

If the suffix or the order in which the suffixes are appended is not valid, Form Generator ignores that standard source object. For example, the **MR** suffix has a higher precedence than **MD. CGSO$CHECK_BOX_MR_DO** is a valid name of a standard source object that can be used to generate a display-only checkbox in a multirecord block. However, an object named **CGSO$CHAR_MD_DO** would never be used, because suffix **DO** has higher precedence than **MD** suffix. The correct name should be **CGSO$CHAR_DO_MD**. During generation, Form Generator first looks for a standard source object whose name contains all of the applicable suffixes. If it cannot find one, Form Generator searches the object library for the standard source object whose name contains the greatest number of appropriate suffixes. For example, if Form Generator is generating a display-only checkbox item in a single-record block, the only appropriate suffix is **DO**. If there is more than one standard source object with the same number of appropriate suffixes, Form Generator checks the precedence of suffixes and uses the one whose name contains the suffix that has the highest precedence. For example, say there are three standard source objects, CGSO$CHAR, CGSO$CHAR_DO, and CGSO$CHAR_MR, defined in the object library, and we are generating a display-only character item in a multirecord block. Form Generator would use the CGSO$CHAR_MR standard source object because the **MR** has a higher precedence than the **DO** suffix or no suffix at all.

The standard source object suffix concept can be a little bit confusing at first. Figure 22-7 shows a flowchart of how Form Generator determines which standard source object to use.

Determining Which Object Was Actually Subclassed

The hierarchy of standard source objects can be confusing. Sometimes you won't be sure which source object will be used in your generated module. If you want to find out which standard source object was used for a generated object, open the generated form in Form Builder. Find the object and check the *Subclass Information* property under the *General* heading. This will display the name of the object and the module that contains it. Figure 22-8 shows an example of this. Please note that this does not work if objects were copied.

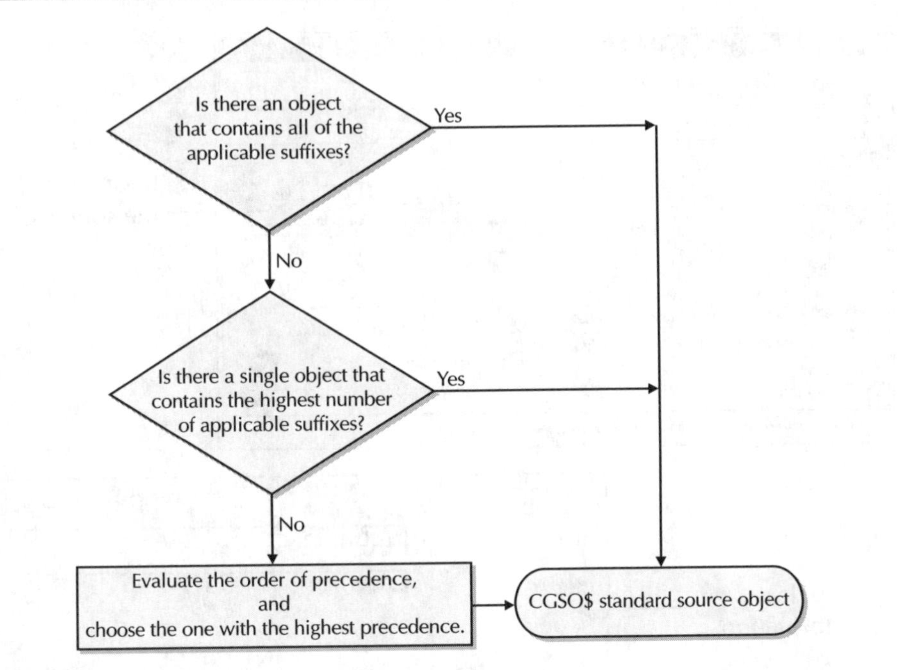

FIGURE 22-7. *How Form Generator uses standard source object suffixes*

Implementation Source Objects

Implementation source objects provide an alternative to using objects in object libraries. Implementation source objects can be used to explicitly specify which object in the object library Form Generator should use when generating a particular object. Using implementation source objects is a method for overriding the standard source objects. Implementation source objects are almost identical to standard source objects except

- They can be named freely. There are no complex rules or hierarchies to worry about.
- The *Template/Library Object* property must be used to specify the implementation source object Form Generator should use when creating a particular object; otherwise, Form Generator ignores them. Figure 22-9 shows how you can set the *Template/Library Object* property.

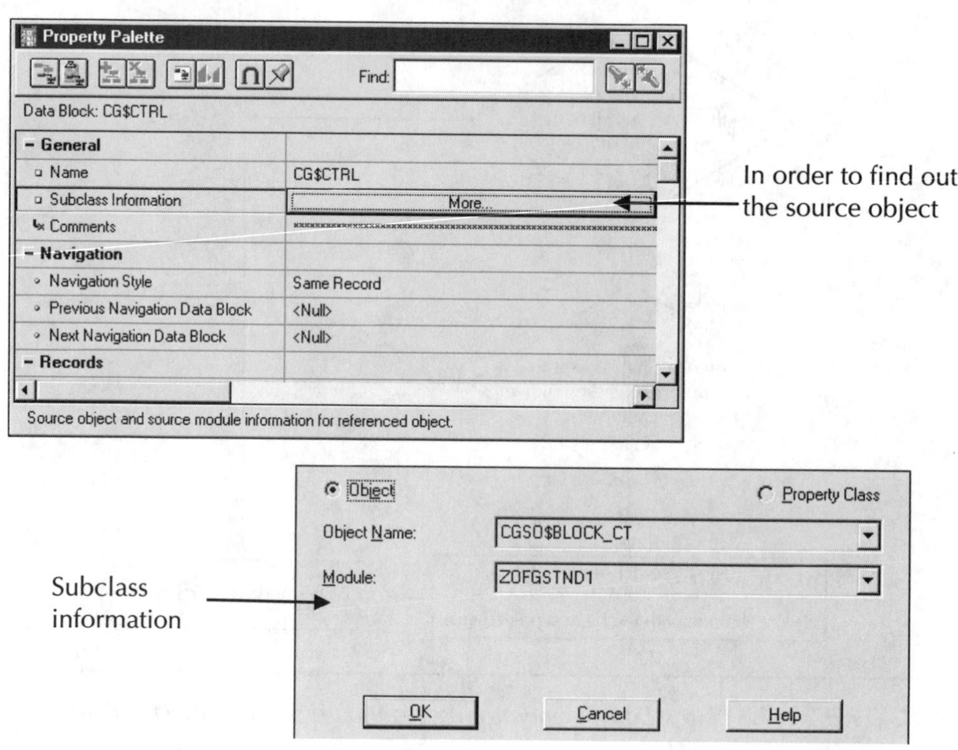

FIGURE 22-8. *Subclass information*

The following table shows a list of repository elements in which an implementation source object can be used. These are the repository elements that have the *Template/Library Object* property.

Repository Element
Window
Module component
Item
Action item

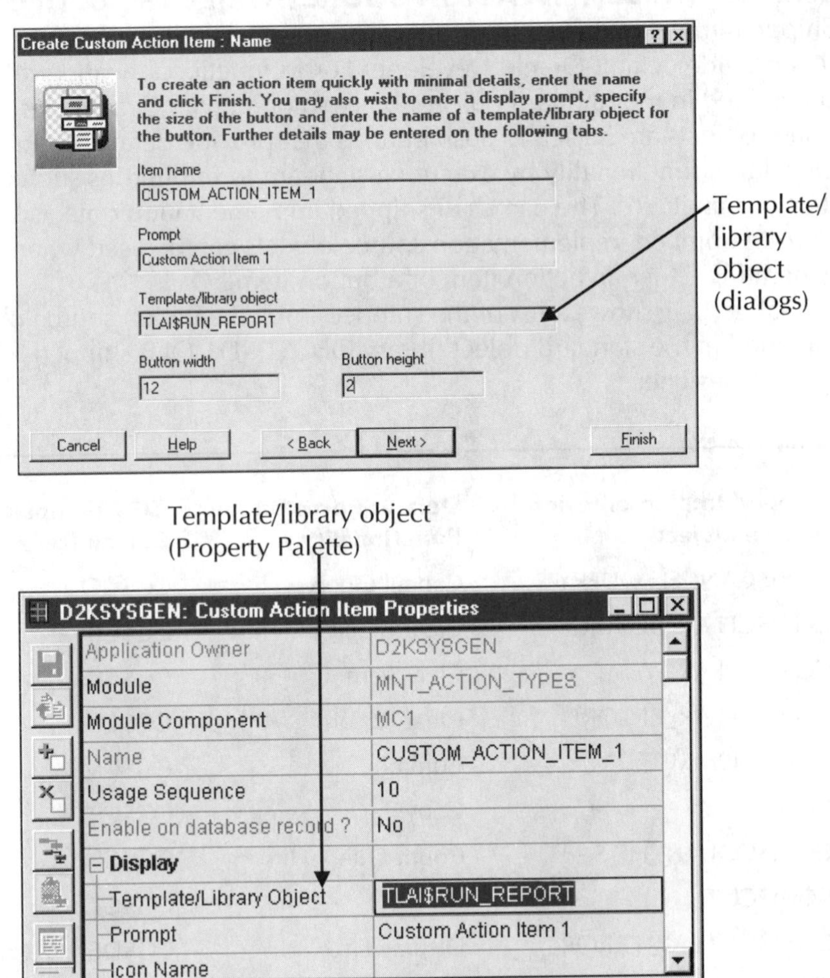

FIGURE 22-9. *Specifying template/library objects*

There are basically two types of implementation source object:

- Shipped implementation source objects
- User-defined implementation source objects

SHIPPED IMPLEMENTATION SOURCE OBJECTS (ACTION ITEMS)

Shipped implementation source objects are special types of source objects that provide default Oracle Developer Forms functionality and are predefined in the standard object library shipped with Oracle Designer. These objects are basically push buttons that provide default Oracle Developer functionality by executing standard form built-ins such as clear item, commit, etc. The names of shipped implementation objects start with CGAI$. Shipped implementation source objects can be used when generating either an action item or a button item.

Table 22-1 shows a list of the shipped implementation source objects included in the standard object library OFGSTND1.OLB shipped with Oracle Designer.

Shipped Implementation Source Object	Default Form Builder Functionality	CG$ Template Button Item
CGAI$CANCEL_QUERY	Cancel Query	CG$CQ
CGAI$CLEAR_BLOCK	Clear Block	CG$CB
CGAI$CLEAR_ITEM	Clear Item	CG$CF
CGAI$CLEAR_RECORD	Clear Record	CG$CR
CGAI$COMMIT	Commit	CG$CM
CGAI$COPY	Copy	CG$CP
CGAI$COUNT_HITS	Count Query Hits	CG$CH
CGAI$CUT	Cut	CG$CT
CGAI$DISPLAY_ERROR	Display Error	CG$DE
CGAI$DUPL_ITEM	Duplicate Item	CG$DF
CGAI$DUPLICATE_RECORD	Duplicate Record	CG$DR
CGAI$EDIT	Edit Item	CG$ED
CGAI$ENTER_QUERY	Enter Query Mode	CG$EQ
CGAI$EXECUTE_QUERY	Execute Query	CG$XQ

TABLE 22-1. *Implementation Source Objects Included in OFGSTND1.OLB*

Shipped Implementation Source Object	Default Form Builder Functionality	CG$ Template Button Item
CGAI$EXIT	Exit	CG$EX
CGAI$FETCH_NEXT_SET	Fetch Next Set	CG$FN
CGAI$HELP	Help	CG$HP
CGAI$INSERT_RECORD	Insert Record	CG$IR
CGAI$KEYS	Keys	CG$KY
CGAI$LAST_CRITERIA	Last Criteria	CG$LQ
CGAI$LOCK_RECORD	Lock Record	CG$LR
CGAI$LOV	List of Values	CG$LV
CGAI$NEXT_BLOCK	Next Block	CG$NB
CGAI$NEXT_ITEM	Next Item	CG$NF
CGAI$NEXT_PAGE	Next Page	CG$NP
CGAI$NEXT_RECORD	Next Record	CG$NR
CGAI$PASTE	Paste	CG$PA
CGAI$PREV_BLOCK	Previous Block	CG$PB
CGAI$PREV_ITEM	Previous Item	CG$PF
CGAI$PREV_PAGE	Previous Page	CG$PP
CGAI$PREV_RECORD	Previous Record	CG$PR
CGAI$PRINT	Print	CG$OP
CGAI$REFRESH	Refresh	CG$RF
CGAI$REMOVE_RECORD	Remove Record	CG$RR
CGAI$ROLLBACK	Rollback	CG$RB
CGAI$SCROLL_DOWN	Scroll Down	CG$SD
CGAI$SCROLL_UP	Scroll Up	CG$SU

TABLE 22-1. *Implementation Source Objects Included in OFGSTND1.OLB* (continued)

CAUTION

CGAI$ implementation source objects are almost identical to CG$ button items specified in template forms. Although the CG$ button items are still supported in release 2 of Oracle Designer, we strongly recommend that CGAI$ implementation source objects be used instead of CG$ buttons in template forms. The support for CG$ button items will be discontinued in future releases.

USER-DEFINED IMPLEMENTATION SOURCE OBJECTS

User-defined implementation source objects are the objects that you create in the object libraries. They allow you to control how a particular item is generated by explicitly specifying which object in the object library Form Generator should use for subclassing or copying. For example, you might want to generate a particular window in a particular form as a dialog window and not allow users to change its size. Since the standard window object in our object library cannot be used for this very specific window, we create a new window object (user-defined implementation object) in the object library and specify it in the *Template/Object Library* property of the window definition in the repository.

User-defined implementation source objects do not have to be buttons. They can be of any type: a window, a canvas, a block, a radio group, etc.

User-Defined Source Object Naming Conventions

Object libraries promote standards. If we are using object libraries, we must value these standards. One more area for standards is the naming of user-defined implementation source objects. You should come up with your own naming standards for your user-defined implementation source objects. For example, you could use UDSO$ as a prefix to stand for User Defined Source Object.

However, there is one very simple rule to follow: when naming user-defined implementation objects, do not use any names or prefixes reserved for Form Generator's use. These prefixes include CG$, CGAI$, and CGSO$.

Templates Shipped with Designer

Oracle Designer is shipped with a number of templates that can be used just as they are. These templates are also known as Standard Template Forms and can serve as a good starting place for the development of your own templates. Standard template forms can be found in the <ORACLE_HOME>\cgenf50\admin directory. Table 22-2 shows a list of standard template forms shipped with Oracle Designer release 2 and a summary of the characteristics of each template.

Template Name	Characteristic
OFGPC1T	Default template form. Designed for Microsoft Windows 32-bit environment. Features an iconic toolbar.
OFG4PC1T	Included for backward compatibility. Release 1.*x* version of OFGPC1T. Oracle does not recommend using this template.
OFGWEB1T	Supposed to be a copy of OFGPC1T with necessary modifications for deployment on the Web using Oracle Developer Web cartridge. The current version includes alerts only.
OFGPC2T	Included for backward compatibility. Same as OFGPC1T. Designed for Microsoft Windows 32-bit environment. Features an iconic toolbar. Has functionality for implementing buttons for interform navigation; however, this functionality has been superceded by the new action item support. **Note:** This template can only be used to generate a form module that has child modules specified in the module network diagram.
OFG4PC2T	Included for backward compatibility. Release 1.*x* version of OFGPC2T. Oracle does not recommend using this template.

TABLE 22-2. *Standard Template Forms Shipped with Oracle Designer Release 2.1*

Template Name	Characteristic
OFGWEB2T	Supposed to be a copy of OFGPC2T with necessary modifications for deployment on the Web using Oracle Developer Web cartridge. The current version includes alerts only.
OFGCHRT	Designed for character mode. Coordinates in character cells.
OFGMF1T	Similar to OFGPC1T. Designed for Motif environment.
OFGLOVT	Template form for generating list of values forms from repository module definitions.
OFG4GUIT	The very first version of GUI template. Obsolete!

TABLE 22-2. *Standard Template Forms Shipped with Oracle Designer Release 2.1* (continued)

The main features of the OFGPC1T.FMB and OFGPC2T.FMB standard templates are

- A toolbar with iconic buttons and tool tips
- Visual attributes (font selection, etc.) for the Microsoft Windows environment
- Code to set the application title bar
- Use of real coordinates
- Use of a pop list together with buttons to navigate to other modules (OFGPC2T)

TIP
We have also included the templates we used to generate the book's examples on the CD that comes with the book. These are not robust, production-worthy templates, but they do illustrate some of the issues that are mentioned in this chapter.

Other Forms Shipped with Oracle Designer

In addition to the standard templates just described, Oracle Designer release 2 is shipped with utility forms. The following table shows a list of these standard template forms and a summary of characteristics of each template.

Form Name	Comments
OFGHLPF.FMB	Default help form displays context sensitive help from the help table. **Note:** If the *DBA → Scope of online help table (HPTABL)* preference is set to **APPSYS** application specific help table, any references to CG_FORM_HELP table in this form must be replaced with the name of the new help table created for the application system: <application_system_name>_ FORM_HELP.
OFGHLVF.FMB	LOV form to display allowable ranges for an item instead of the default Form Builder LOV. **Note:** The *List of Values → Name of form to display valid ranges (DVHLVF)* preference must be set to **OFGHLVF** to use this LOV form.
OFGLOVF.FMB	LOV form to display allowable values for an item instead of the default Form Builder LOV. **Note:** The *List of Values → Name of form to display valid values (DVLOVF)* preference must be set to **OFGLOVF** to use this LOV form.
OFGCALT.FMB	Contains a calendar object, which can be copied into a template form and used as a LOV for date items. Requires the **OFGCALL.PLL** library. For further information, refer to *Oracle Designer Online Help → Calendar Windows for Date Items.*
OFGEXPT.FMB	Known as the expert template, it is included only for backward compatibility. It contains a number of CG$ generator items that could be copied into template forms. However, since CG$ generator item functionality is superceded by implementation source objects in the object libraries, Oracle does not recommend using this form. **Note:** This form is not a template form and cannot be used in the generation of a form.

Customizing Template Forms

Oracle Designer is shipped with some ready-to-use templates and object libraries. The out-of-the-box functionality provided with these templates and libraries is good enough for a quick start, especially for your first-time prototyping. However, these standard templates and object libraries may not meet some or all of the requirements you have for sophisticated user interfaces. In those cases, you can either customize the default templates and object libraries or build new ones from scratch.

For example, the toolbar in the standard template form (OFGPC1T.FMB) does not have a button for exiting the form, and your standards may force you to have an exit button. You can add one by modifying the standard template form (after making a copy of it first, of course).

The main reason for customizing standard templates and object libraries is to reduce the amount of post-generation changes (changes made to forms after they are generated from Oracle Designer) you might have to make.

Customizing templates and libraries is not difficult, but it requires an in-depth understanding of what templates and libraries are and how they affect the generated forms. Templates and object libraries are regular Oracle Forms Modules and can be easily modified using Form Builder. Although modifying the templates requires that you have some experience with Form Builder, it is more important that you have an understanding of how the Form Generator uses template forms.

When customizing templates, it is very important to remember to subclass user objects from object libraries. As we mentioned earlier in this chapter in "Maintenance of User Objects in Template and Generated Forms," subclassing user objects from object libraries or referencing them from reference forms drastically reduces the amount of maintenance that might be required later. Therefore, you should make sure that the user objects are either subclassed from object libraries or referenced from reference forms. Also, for the same reason, remember to place all of the PL/SQL code in PLL libraries.

In order to help you understand the process of modifying the templates, we have detailed a couple of example modifications that you might want to make to the standard template forms.

CAUTION

Before you start customizing, remember to make a copy of the standard template; only modify the copy. If you do not do this, you may corrupt the standard template and end up not being able to generate anything.

Example 1: Customizing Form-Level Properties

The standard template form (OFGPC1T.FMB) has a real coordinate system and a character cell size of width=0.1" and height=0.25". The selection of coordinate system and character cell size depends on the target deployment environment, the desired font sizes, and the screen resolution under which the forms will run. The character cell size in this standard template form is chosen for deploying forms in the MS Windows95/NT environment, running on an SVGA at medium to high screen resolutions, with MS Sans Serif used as a base font. However, your standards may require that you use a different font, bigger font sizes, and a lower screen resolution. In order to do this, you may have to change the average character cell size property at the form level. This can be done very easily by following these steps:

1. Make a copy of the standard template form, if you have not done so yet.
2. Open the new template form in Form Builder.
3. Open the Property Palette for the form itself.
4. Navigate to the *Coordinate System* property in the *Physical* area of the form-level Property Palette, as shown here:

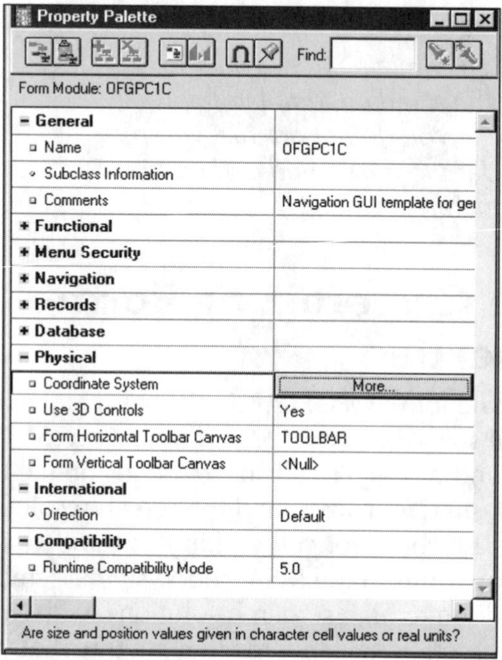

5. Press the **More** button that appears when the cursor is on the *Coordinate System* property. You will see the Coordinate Info dialog:

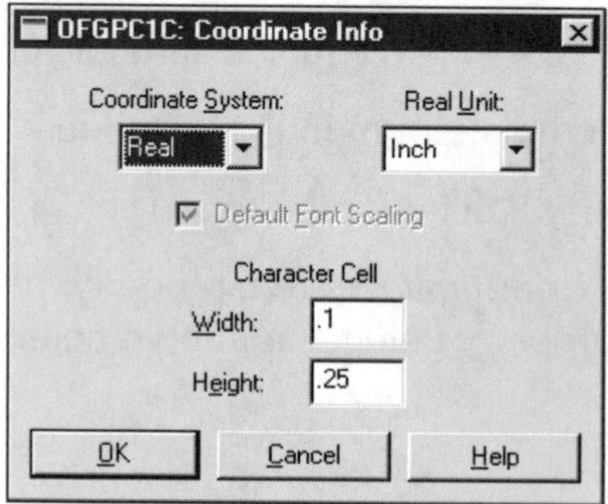

6. Change the form-level *Character Cell Size* property, then press the OK button to close the dialog.
7. Save your changes to the template. Make sure to document the changes and purpose for the new template.

NOTE

Documenting changes *It is always good programming practice to document changes, including changes made to the templates. Each organization should have rules and guidelines for documenting these changes, version control, and change management.*

Example 2: Customizing Title Fonts and Appearance

Although the majority of the visual properties of generated objects are defined through source/implementation objects defined in the object libraries, there are still a few visual attributes used from the template forms. Form Generator in Oracle Designer release 2 continues to use named visual attributes from template forms for setting the font, size, and style of generated graphic text and decorations for various objects including blocks, item groups, context areas, etc. Examples of these are the CG$TITLE and CG$DECORATION visual attributes.

The standard template forms contain some standard visual attributes for titles and decorations. However, you may have different standards for static graphic text (boilerplate text) in your forms. For example, you may choose to use a different font, size, or color for different types of titles. Your block titles may be larger than item prompts, and they may also be italicized. In order to implement these changes, you would modify the CG$ named visual attributes in the template form.

Changing the named visual attributes in template forms is very easy:

1. Make a copy of the standard template form, if you have not done so yet.
2. Open the new template form in Form Builder.

3. Navigate to the *Visual Attributes* area of the object navigator and open up the list of visual attributes:

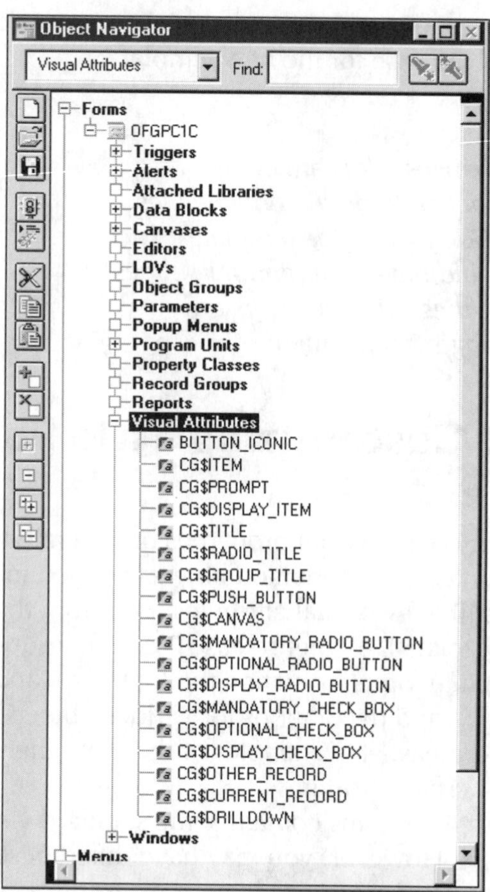

4. If the visual attribute you want to change is included in the template form, you can modify its properties by selecting it and opening its Property Palette. You can also create a new visual attribute, but you need to make sure its name is recognized by the form generator (for a list of visual attribute names, refer to the *Oracle Designer Online Documentation*).

5. Use the Property Palette to change the font properties for the visual attribute:

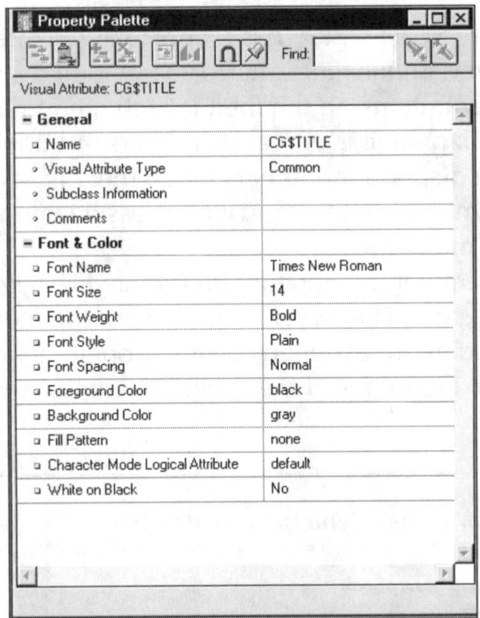

6. Save your changes to the template. Make sure to document the changes and purpose for the new template.

The visual attributes used by the standard template forms are designed to complement one another. When modifying one of them, consider whether any of the others need changing. For example, if you change the CG$GROUP_TITLE visual attribute used for item group titles, you may want to consider changing the CG$RADIO_TITLE visual attribute used for radio group titles.

Example 3: Iconic Toolbar Versus Smartbar (Iconic Menu Bar)

In Oracle Developer release 2, there is a new feature called *iconic menu bar* or *smartbar*. Iconic menu bars and smartbars are toolbars with a list of icons corresponding to menu items on the menu. Each menu item can be displayed on the horizontal or vertical menu bars or both of them. Oracle Forms automatically displays menu bars when there is at least one menu item assigned to them. Menu items must have associated icons in order to be displayed on the menu bars.

Standard menu templates shipped with Oracle Designer release 2 are also taking advantage of this new feature. Some of the menu items in the standard template menu are assigned to a horizontal menu bar. Figure 22-10 shows the horizontal menu bar in the standard template menu module.

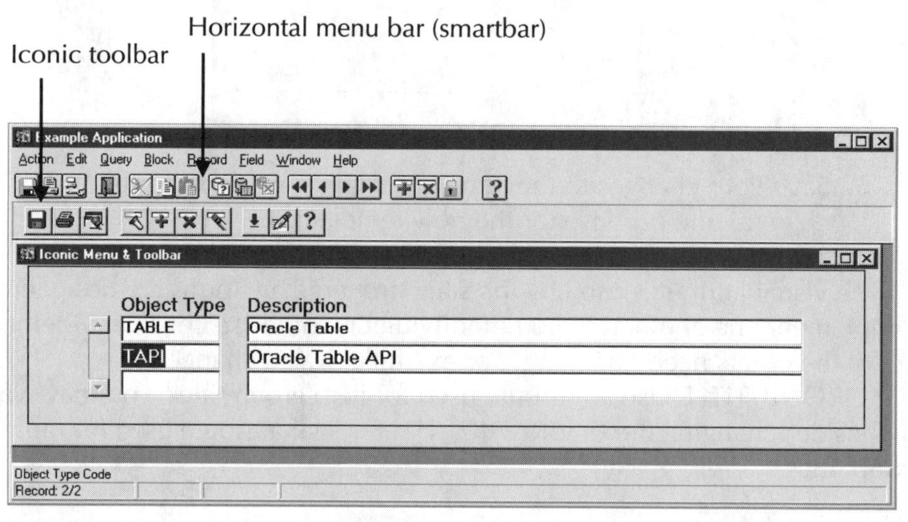

FIGURE 22-10. *Smartbar and iconic toolbar*

In earlier versions of Oracle Forms when there was not a smartbar feature, it was very common to develop an iconic toolbar made up of some iconic push buttons and timer-based bubble help (or a pop-up tool tip). In fact, the standard template form (OFGPC1T.FMB) includes such an iconic toolbar with buttons corresponding to some of the common tasks users perform when running a form, such as entering and executing queries, committing changes, clearing changes, etc.

As is always the case when there is increased flexibility, there is also increased complexity. Now you have to make a decision about how you want to implement an iconic toolbar. You have the following three options:

1. Use the iconic toolbar from the template only.
2. Use the smartbar only.
3. Use both the smartbar and the iconic toolbar from the template.

If you choose option 2 (smartbar only), you will have to completely remove the template toolbar. If you choose option 3 (both smartbar and template toolbar), you will have to modify the template toolbar and remove the buttons that are duplicated on the smartbar. If you choose either option 2 or 3, you will have to modify the template.

For the first part of this example, let's assume that you choose option 2 (smartbar only) because you think the smartbar is easier to maintain in comparison to the old-style iconic toolbar. To use the smartbar, set the *Form/Menu attachment → Name of menu module if not implicit menu generation (FMNDMA)* preference to **DEFAULT&SMARTBAR**, and generate the form. Once the form is generated, you'll see that there are two horizontal toolbars with similar buttons. Now you have to get rid of the iconic toolbar.

In order to remove (or modify) the iconic toolbar, you need to understand its architecture. The toolbar object is composed of the following components:

- Toolbar buttons are defined in the toolbar block.
- Each toolbar button has an icon associated with it.
- Button labels are displayed as tool tips.

- The TOOLBAR_ACTIONS program unit controls what happens when a button is pressed.
- The BUTTON_HELP program unit controls how the bubble help (tool tip) is displayed for a toolbar button.

Removing buttons from the toolbar is very easy:

1. Make a copy of the standard template form, if you have not done so yet.
2. Open the template form in Form Builder.
3. Delete the following objects from the template:
    - TOOLBAR block
    - Form-level WHEN-TIMER-EXPIRED trigger
    - TOOLBAR canvas
    - TOOLBAR_ACTIONS program unit
    - BUTTON_HELP program unit
    - DELETE_TIMER program units
4. As always, document and save your changes.
5. Make sure that the *Form/Menu attachment → Name of menu module if not implicit menu generation (FMNDMA)* preference is set to **DEFAULT&SMARTBAR**.

For the second part of this example, let's assume that you choose option 1, to use the iconic toolbar. However, you want to add a few more buttons, delete some, and rearrange some. Adding new buttons to the toolbar is little bit more difficult:

1. Make a copy of the standard template form, if you have not done so yet.
2. Open the template form in Form Builder.

3. To create a new button, copy an existing button and change its name, label, and icon name. Rearrange buttons using the Layout Editor. The label will be displayed as the tool tip, and the icon name will define the icon displayed on the button. There are a number of useful standard icons supplied under <ORACLE_HOME>\cgenf50\icons\pc.
4. Add the logic for the new button to the TOOLBAR_ACTIONS program unit. This program unit contains a very simple IF...ELSIF construct that tests the name property of the button. Add a new ELSIF statement followed by the code that you want to be executed when the new button is pressed. As we recommended earlier in this chapter in "Maintenance of Template Forms" section, it is best to put the actual code in a PL/SQL library and call it from the TOOLBAR_ACTIONS program unit. As a matter of fact, you can do this for all of the program units that are part of the toolbar object.

TIP

PL/SQL programming in PLL libraries *In PLL libraries, the standard : notation for referencing form objects cannot be used. Instead of referencing form objects directly with the : notation, we have to use NAME_IN and COPY built-ins. For example, instead of :System.Mouse_Item and :Block.Item, use NAME_IN('System.Mouse_Item') and NAME_IN('Block.Item').*

5. Remove buttons that you don't want. Don't forget to also remove the logic assigned to these buttons from the TOOLBAR_ACTION program unit.
6. Rearrange the button layout as desired.
7. Document and save your changes.
8. Make sure that the *Form/Menu attachment → Name of menu module if not implicit menu generation (FMNDMA)* preference is set to **DEFAULT**.

It is also possible to use both the smartbar and the iconic toolbar, but you should make sure that there are not any redundancies between these two bars. Also, instead of having a horizontal smartbar, you might want a vertical smartbar. All of these are very strategic decisions that may affect the whole system.

Example 4: Adding Standard Application Code

Let us assume that you have very tight security requirements, and you want to keep unauthorized users out of your system and keep track of who is accessing your system. The standard template form (OFGPC1T.FMB) does not include any special logic for form security, and the default functionality of using roles may not be secure enough for your system. Therefore, you need to generate some application logic (code to handle events and provide functionality) into the forms.

In earlier versions of Oracle Designer, this could only be done using form-level triggers in template forms. However, in Oracle Designer release 2, you have more options as to where your custom code can be placed. They can be

- Created as triggers for objects in object libraries
- Entered into the repository as new events
- Entered into the repository as event code segments for existing events before, after, or between different segments in generated functionality
- Entered as triggers in the templates

Therefore, it may not be very clear where the code should be placed: template forms, object libraries, or the repository. At the end of this chapter, there is a discussion of this complex issue. For the sake of this example, we will add the application logic to the template form. Therefore, we have to customize the template form again.

There are quite a few different ways of implementing this security requirement; we will try to accomplish this by adding logic to the PRE-FORM trigger to authenticate the user and keep a log of user accesses.

Note that we could have defined the PRE-FORM trigger in the repository using application logic, but then we would have to repeat this for every single module.

1. Make a copy of the standard template form, if you have not done so yet.
2. Open the template form in Form Builder.
3. Create the form-level PRE-FORM trigger and add the necessary logic to enforce security and audit requirements. There are a number of different ways to add the PL/SQL code to the template forms. One way is to put the code directly into the triggers. However, if you ever need to change the code (in the case of a bug fix or an enhancement, for example) after generating forms, you would have to either generate the forms again or manually make the same change in each form. This would be a maintenance nightmare. The better approach is to put the PL/SQL code either in the database or in the libraries and have the triggers in the template form call these routines. This allows you to make changes in the PL/SQL code without worrying about the forms. If the PL/SQL code is placed in a library, then you need to attach the library to the generated form either by attaching the library to the template form specifying that the library be attached via user preferences, or through using the module network.
4. Document and save your changes.

Adding application code to template forms may be far more complex than what is shown in this example. The trigger used in this example, PRE-FORM, was a form-level trigger that is not generated by the Form Generator. However, triggers like WHEN-NEW-FORM-INSTANCE, WHEN-NEW-BLOCK-INSTANCE, KEY-ENTRY, etc., are generated by the Form Generator. It is far more difficult to add these types of triggers to template forms because of the interaction between your code and the generated code.

Example 5: Adding New User Objects

A user object is any object in the template form with a name that does not start with the CG$ prefix. The toolbar is a user object or a group of user objects such as the toolbar block, the items, and the triggers program units associated with it. For example, a generic *Multi-Select* tool can be added to template forms to augment the default functionality provided by the standard template forms.

As we mentioned earlier in this chapter, Form Generator simply copies user objects into the generated forms without making a change. However, Form Generator treats different types of user objects in different ways. The following table summarizes these differences.

User Object	Form Generator Behavior
Window	User windows should be associated with user canvases.
Canvas	User canvases should be associated with user windows. Any user items that appear on the canvas are also copied, but the CG$ generator items are not.
Block	When Form Generator copies user blocks into the generated form, it also copies the user items belonging to the user block, as well as any block-level or item-level triggers associated with the user block. CG$ generator items belonging to the user block are either converted into graphic text or reassigned to the CG$CTRL control block.
Item	The rules for a user item object to be copied into the generated form are 1. The user item belongs to a user block 2. The user item is placed on a user canvas, a header or footer canvas, or a toolbar canvas. 3. The user item does not appear either partially or totally off its template canvas. 4. Any objects the user item is dependent on (e.g., its item-level triggers) or subordinate to are also included in the generated form. A user item is only included once in the generated form. For example, if a header is applied to content canvases 1 and 2 in the generated form, any user items in the header are only included on content canvas 1.

To add user objects to the template form:

1. Make a copy of the standard template form, if you have not done so yet.
2. Open the template form in Form Builder.
3. Create user blocks, windows, canvases, items, triggers, etc. as needed.
4. Document and save your changes.

How to Create a New Template Form

Template forms are regular Oracle Forms modules and can be easily created using Form Builder. In order to create a new template form:

1. Use Form Builder either to copy one of the standard template forms shipped with Oracle Designer or to create a new form. If you think that you can use some of the objects defined in one of the standard template forms, use it as a starting point to save some time. However, you may want to start from scratch and gradually build a new template if you think you have enough experience with templates.
2. Define any form-level properties you want generated forms to have as form-level properties of the template form. These may include the coordinate system, character cell size, navigation, etc.
3. Include in the template form the user objects you want to appear in all forms generated with the template. When creating user objects, remember the guidelines that were presented earlier in this chapter in the "User Objects in Template Forms" section.
4. Try to package objects you created into object groups. Object groups allow you to reduce the number of objects to deal with and to manipulate objects at a more abstract level. For example, the toolbar object should be defined as an object group with elements such as the canvas, the block, the items, their triggers, etc.

5. Document changes and save the template form.
6. Subclass the objects (especially the user objects) in template forms from object libraries. This is very important, because it will make the maintenance of these objects much easier down the road. For further information, refer to "Maintenance of User Objects in Template and Generated Forms," earlier in this chapter. In order to subclass objects, you have to
   a. Save a copy of the template. In case something goes wrong with the following steps, you can always revert back to the saved copy of your template.
   b. Copy the objects from the template form into the object library first. We strongly recommend organizing objects in object libraries. Object Library tabs can be used for keeping related objects or object groups together under the same heading.
   c. Document changes and save the object library.
   d. Remove the objects from the template form so that you can subclass them back from the object library.
   e. Subclass them back from the object library. Simply drag-and-drop objects (or object groups) from the object library into the template form. Object groups are very handy in these situations, and with a single drag-and-drop operation you can subclass many objects at the same time. Due to the dependencies among form objects before an object is subclassed, its parents must be subclassed; otherwise, the linkage between the child and the parent is lost.
   f. Check to make sure you have subclassed everything successfully and there are no pieces missing.
7. Save the template form.

How to Specify the Template Form to Use During Generation

In order to specify the template form the Form Generator should use during form generation:

1. Use the *Template Name* field on the Generate Form dialog, shown next, to specify the name and extension of the template form. The default value in this field is specified by *Standards* → *The name of the template form (STFFMB)* preference. The STFFMB preference can hold values of up to 240 characters, and the factory default value is set to **ofgpc1t**. The STFFMB preference can be set at either application or module level.

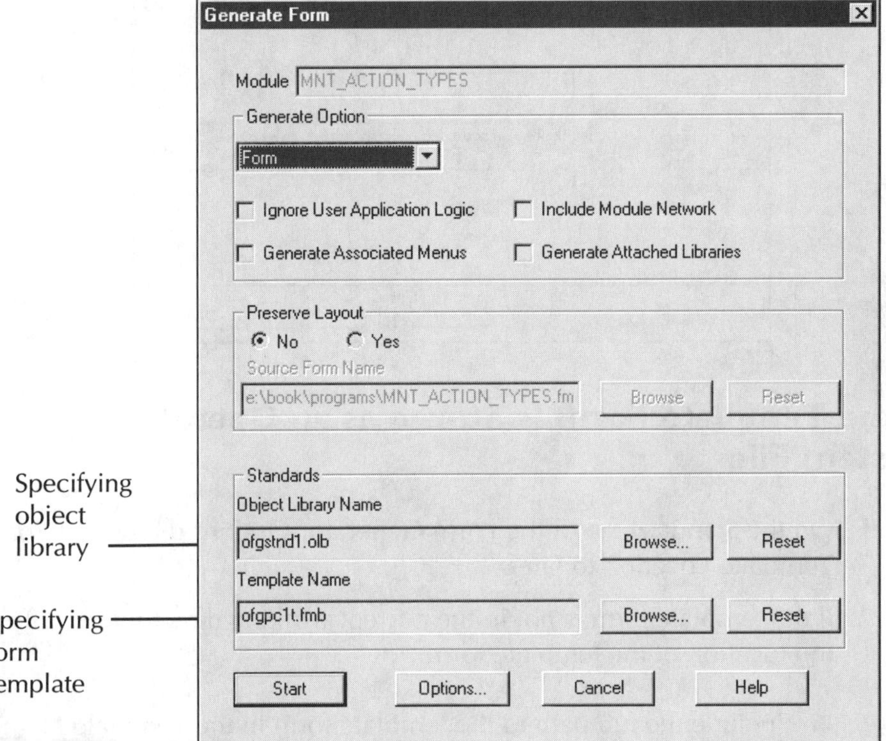

2. If a path to locate the template is not specified in the Template Name field, use the Standard tab of the Form Generator Options

dialog, shown next, to specify the location of the template form. The way to specify the location of the template form depends on how the form is stored.

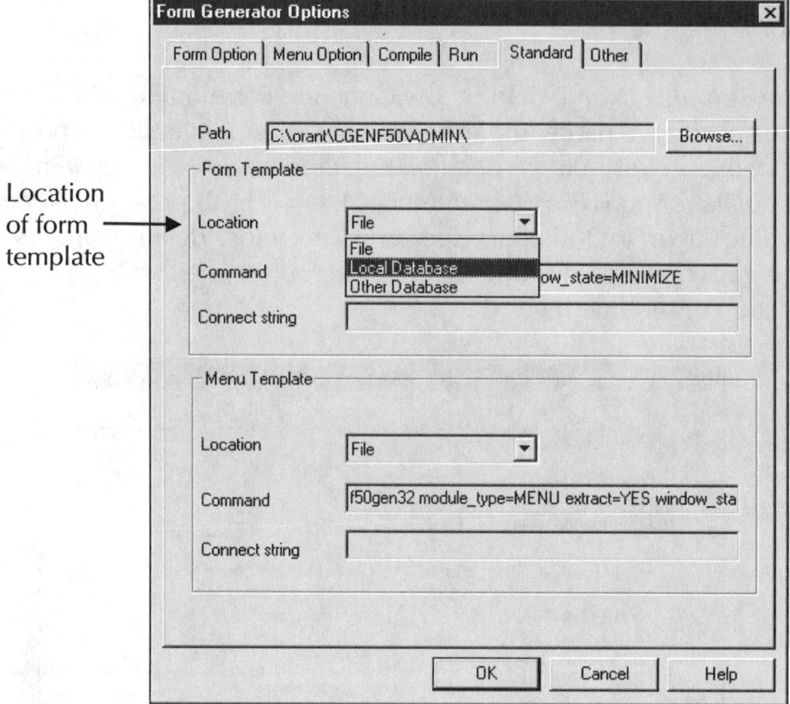

If the Template Form Is Stored as an Operating System File

1. On the Standard tab of the Form Generator Options dialog, set Form Template Location to **File**.
2. If the template form is not in the current working directory, specify the location of the template form:

- Include the full path to the template form in the Template Name field on the Generate Form dialog.
- On the Standard tab of the Form Generator Options dialog, enter a path in the Path field (use a semicolon to separate multiple entries).

If the Template Form Is Stored in the Same Database as the Repository

1. On the Standard tab of the Form Generator Options dialog, set Form Template Location to **Local Database**.
2. Specify a command to extract the template form from the database in the Command field. For example:

   f50gen32 extract=YES window_state=MINIMIZE
3. Specify the full connect string (username/password@database) in the Connect String field.

If the Template Form Is Stored in a Different Database from the Repository

1. On the Standard tab of the Form Generator Options dialog, set Form Template Location to **Other Database**.
2. Specify a command to extract the template form from the database in the Command field. For example:

   f50gen32 extract=YES window_state=MINIMIZE
3. Specify the full connect string (username/password@database) in the Connect String field.

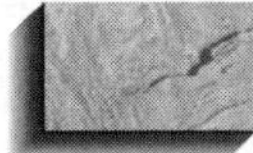

NOTE
If the template form is held in a database, and you do not own the template module, you must specify who owns the template. Use the Standards → Owner of the template form (STFOWN) *preference to specify the owner. The owner must also grant access on the template to you.*

Template Menus

Similar to form templates, menu templates can be used to tailor the menu generation process. Menu templates are more basic, easy to use, and offer less features than form templates. Menu templates allow you to easily generate and maintain the menu items that are common to many menus.

What Are Template Menus?

Template menus provide a basis for Form Generator to build new menu modules. Template menus are regular Oracle Developer menu modules. The purpose of menu templates is to define menu items that are common to several menu modules generated from Oracle Designer. When Form Generator generates a menu module, it simply merges the generated menu items with the menu items from the template menu. The generated menu items can be placed *before* or *after* the template menu items, but they cannot be placed between them. The location of the generated menu items is specified in the *Menu Preferences – Generation Options → Sequence generated menu items after template items (MNUSGA)* preference.

Unlike template forms, there are no special generator items available for template menus. For example, there are no special CG$ menu items. Menu items in template menus can invoke regular form built-ins or user-defined PL/SQL routines. User-defined PL/SQL routines can be stored either in the menu module or a PL/SQL library. Template menu items can also be subclassed from an object library (or referenced from a reference menu).

Template menus do not have as big of an impact on your application as template forms or object libraries do. Form Generator does not support the *Template/Library Object* feature for menu item generation.

Template Menu Shipped with Oracle Designer

Oracle Designer is shipped with a standard template menu module called OFGMNUT.MMB. This template menu module contains items and associated PL/SQL procedures very similar to the Form Builder default form menu. Figure 22-11 shows menu items included in the standard menu template.

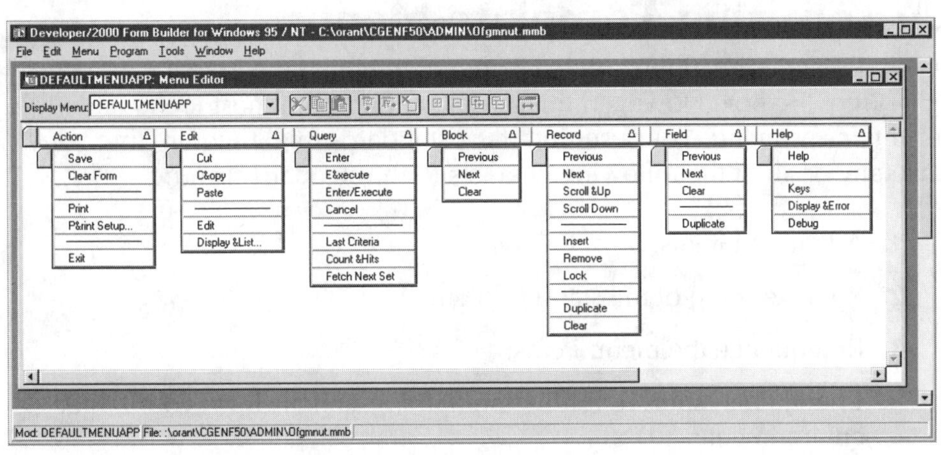

FIGURE 22-11. *Standard menu template (OFGMNUT.MMB) items*

Some of the standard template menu items are defined to be visible on a horizontal menu toolbar. A menu toolbar is a toolbar of iconic buttons corresponding to the menu items. Each menu item can be assigned to a horizontal or a vertical toolbar, or even to both of them. For a menu item to be visible on the menu toolbar there must be an icon associated with it. The menu toolbars and the icons for the corresponding menu options are automatically attached and displayed in forms. The following illustration shows the standard menu toolbar.

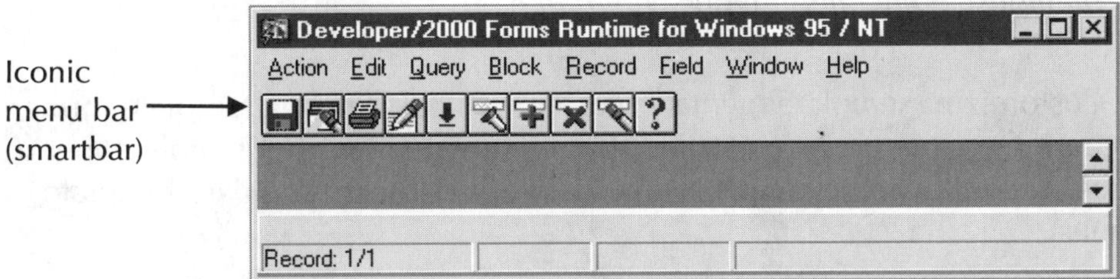

Customizing Template Menus

Oracle Designer is shipped with a standard template menu that can be used right out of the box. However, this template menu is almost identical to the default Forms menu. Your user interface standards might require that you make any or all of the following changes to the standard menu:

1. Add menu items.
2. Remove some of the standard items.
3. Resequence the menu items.
4. Change the labels to follow the naming standards for your target environment.

For example, you may want to add a new menu called *Options* to allow your users to customize their work environment, or you may want to modify the Help menu by adding another menu item called *About this form* and removing the *Debug* menu item from it.

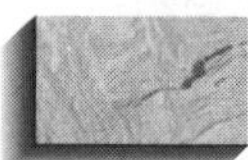

TIP

Remember the benefits of subclassing or referencing when you are creating your menu templates. When template menu items are subclassed from object libraries, it is a lot easier to change them without impacting the previously generated menus very much.

Customizing template menus is easier than customizing template forms, because there are no special rules about template menus or template menu items. The following examples show how to customize standard template menus.

NOTE
When customizing, always make a copy of a standard template menu and modify the copy rather than modifying a standard template menu directly.

Example 1: Adding an Options Menu

Typically, many user-friendly applications allow users to customize their work environment by providing them with a list of options, or preferences. For example, some users want to defer validations, some don't; some users don't like to see confirmation messages such as *2 records committed*, but some do. The best way to handle these situations is to allow each user to set their own preferences from an Options menu. In order to include an Options menu to generated menus, add the Options menu to the template menu.

1. Make a copy of the standard template menu, if you have not done so yet.
2. Open the template menu in Form Builder.
3. Add the new Option menu, menu items, and the PL/SQL code as desired. Remember the guidelines for adding PL/SQL code in templates, and place the code in PLL libraries. Optionally, set the *Visible in Horizontal Menu Toolbar* to **True**, and specify an icon filename for the Option menu item.
4. Document your changes, and save the template menu module.

Example 2: Changing Horizontal Menu Toolbar to Vertical Menu Toolbar

The default template menu assigns menu items to a horizontal menu bar; however, you may wish to use the smartbar in conjunction with your iconic toolbar. Rather than having two horizontal bars, you may wish to display the smartbar as a vertical bar.

1. Make a copy of the standard template menu, if you have not done so yet.
2. Open the template menu in Form Builder.

3. Find all of the menu items assigned to the horizontal menu bar (i.e., those for which the *Visible in Horizontal Menu Toolbar* property is set to **True**) and change this property to **False**. Set the *Visible in Vertical Menu Toolbar* property to **True**.
4. Document your changes, and save the template menu module.

How to Create a New Menu Template

Template menus are regular Oracle Forms Modules and can be easily created using Form Builder. In order to create a new template menu:

1. Use Form Builder either to open the standard template menu module (OFGMNUT.MMB) shipped with Oracle Designer or to create a new menu module manually.
2. Add menus and menu items as desired.
3. Document your changes, and save the template menu module.

How to Specify the Template Menu to Use During Generation

In order to specify which template menu module Form Generator should use during menu generation, follow these steps:

1. Use the *Template Name* field on the Generate Form dialog to specify the name of the template menu module Form Generator should use during generation. The default value in this field is specified by *Standards → The name of the template menu (STMMMB)* preference. The STMMMB preference can hold values of up to 240 characters, and there is no factory default value. The STMMMB preference can be set at either application or module level.
2. If a path to locate the templates is not specified in the Template Name field, use the Standard tab of the Form Generator Options dialog to specify the template's location. The way to specify the location of the template menu depends on how the menu is stored.

If the Template Menu Is Stored as an Operating System File

1. On the Standard tab of the Form Generator Options dialog, set Menu Template Location to **File**.
2. If the template menu is not in the current working directory, specify the location of the template menu:
   - Include the full path to the template menu in the Template Name field on the Generate Form dialog.
   - On the Standard tab of the Form Generator Options dialog, enter a path in the Path field (use a semicolon to separate multiple entries).

If the Template Menu Is Stored in the Same Database as the Repository

1. On the Standard tab of the Form Generator Options dialog, set Menu Template Location to **Local Database**.
2. Specify a command to extract the template menu from the database in the Command field. For example:

   f50gen32 module_type=MENU extract=YES window_state=MINIMIZE
3. Specify the full connect string (username/password@database) in the Connect String field.

If the Template Menu Is Stored in a Different Database than the Repository

1. On the Standard tab of the Form Generator Options dialog, set Menu Template Location to **Other Database**.
2. Specify a command to extract the template menu from the database in the Command field. For example:

   f50gen32 module_type=MENU extract=YES window_state=MINIMIZE

3. Specify the full connect string (username/password@database) in the Connect String field.

NOTE
If the template form is held in a database, and you do not own the template module, you must specify who owns the template. Use the Standards → Owner of the template form (STFOWN) *preference to specify the owner. The owner must also grant access on the template to you.*

Customizing Object Libraries

Oracle Designer is shipped with a standard object library (OFGSTND1.OLB) that is ready to use right out of the box. This object library is actually a very good example of how object libraries should be designed for generating forms with Oracle Designer. It contains almost all the standard source and implementation objects, including some hierarchy of these objects. For example, it includes a standard source object CGSO$DEFAULT_ITEM for all types of items, a standard source object CGSO$CHAR for text items with character data type, and four other variations of this object: CGSO$CHAR_CT for character text items in control blocks, CGSO$CHAR_MR for character text items in multirecord blocks, CGSO$CHAR_MD for mandatory character text items, and CGSO$CHAR_DO for display-only character items.

The objects in the object library are grouped based on their usage and organized into object library tabs. Figure 22-12 shows library tabs defined in the standard object library.

Although the standard object library is a very good example, it may not meet some or all of your requirements. For example, your user interface standards may require different fonts with different sizes, colors, and patterns than the standard library objects. If this is the case, you will need to customize the standard object library or develop new object libraries from scratch. It is impossible to design a universally accepted object library that would satisfy every single requirement asked from thousands of systems generated. Therefore, the standard object library shipped with Oracle Designer should be regarded as a good example, not as a complete solution.

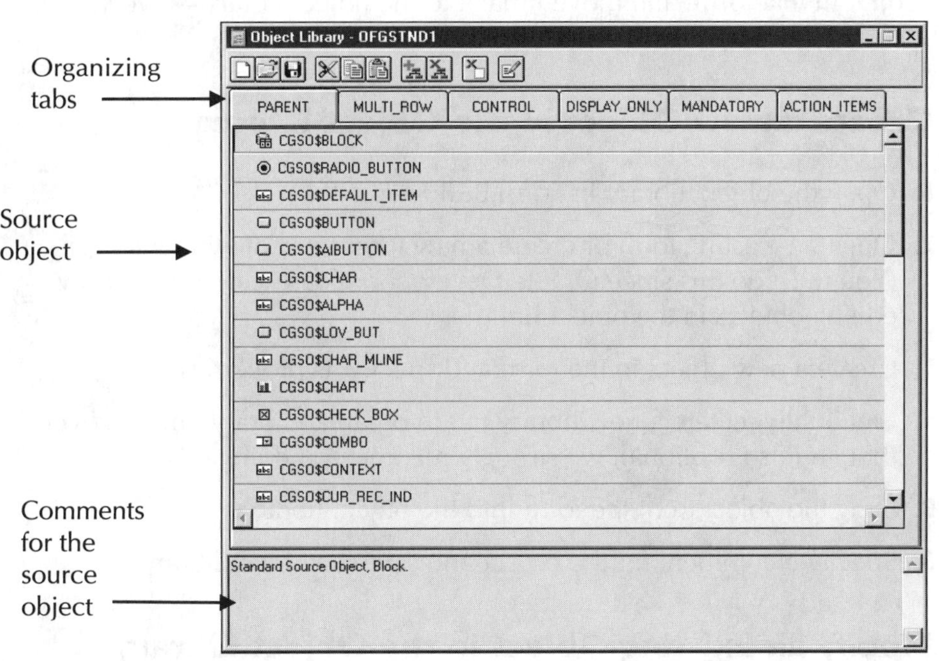

FIGURE 22-12. *Organization of Objects in the Standard Object Library (OFGSTND1.OLB)*

Usually, customizing the standard object library is the easiest, because developing new object libraries requires an in-depth understanding of standard source and implementation objects and the hierarchy among these, along with experience with both Form Builder and object libraries. Note: When customizing, always make a copy of the standard library and modify the copy rather than modifying a standard object library directly.

Editing Object Libraries

Customizing object libraries is a little bit more complicated than customizing templates, because Form Builder in Oracle Developer release 2 does not allow editing objects in object libraries. Library objects need to be created or edited in a form module first before they are included in the object libraries. In order to modify a library object, we have to move it to a form, edit it in that form, and move it back to the object library—a very cumbersome process.

To Create a New Object in the Object Library

1. Open the object library in Form Builder.
2. Open an existing form or create a new form to create the object(s). (You must do this since Oracle Developer release 2 does not allow editing objects in the object libraries.)
3. Create a new object in the form and specify its properties.
4. Optionally, create a new library tab to organize library objects. Even though this is optional, we strongly recommend doing this.
5. Drag the object from the form into the object library.
6. Specify a comment for the object and save the object library.

To Modify an Existing Object in the Object Library

1. Open the object library in Form Builder.
2. Open an existing form or create a new form. (You must do this since Oracle Developer release 2 does not allow editing objects in the object libraries.)
3. In the Object Library, press the CTRL key and drag the desired object to the desired node in the Object Navigator. For example, a canvas object needs to be dragged to the canvases node.
4. Form Builder will display the Copy/Subclass dialog. Click Copy to create an editable copy of the object.
5. Modify the object as needed.
6. Drag the object back to the Object Library. When Form Builder displays the Replace Existing Object dialog, click Yes to replace the existing object with the modified object.
7. Add any comments to the modified object, and save the object library.

Nested Subclassing

When creating new objects, check to see if the new object can be subclassed from a parent object in an object library. For example, you may have a standard button object defined in an object library that you can subclass from the standard object instead of creating from scratch. This will drastically reduce the maintenance work down the road.

If you want to fully exploit the advantages of subclassing, try this: subclass objects from other subclassed objects. For example, the whole hierarchy of CGSO$ objects for items can be started from a parent item, CGSO$DEFAULT_ITEM. Once CGSO$DEFAULT_ITEM is created, CGSO$CHECKBOX, CGSO$CHAR, CGSO$RADIO, etc., can be subclassed from it. Similarly, CGSO$CHAR_MR, CGSO$CHAR_CT, etc., can be subclassed from CGSO$CHAR. Nesting and subclassing gives you a very flexible architecture.

FORM2LIB Utility

The method specified above for modifying an object in the object library can be an inefficient and error-prone way of making massive changes to the objects in the object library. The fact that Form Builder in Oracle Developer release 2 does not allow editing objects in object libraries makes this process very cumbersome. But there is another alternative: a utility called FORM2LIB. This utility is shipped with Oracle Designer release 2, and it enables you to create and maintain source objects in a regular form module instead of an object library. The FORM2LIB utility simply converts a form into an object library (as its name implies).

The FORM2LIB utility is used to build the standard object library OFGSTND1.OLB shipped with Oracle Designer from a source form called OFGSTND1.FMB (placed in the <ORACLE_HOME>\CGENF50 directory).

Besides eliminating the need for dragging objects between a form and the object library, this utility helps with another major problem: when objects are dragged from an object library into a form module for editing purposes, any subclassing information they might have is lost. For example, if the CGSO$CHAR_MD object (source object for mandatory text items with character data type) is subclassed from the CGSO$CHAR object (source object for all text items with character data type), dragging it into a form module for editing causes it to lose its link to the CGSO$CHAR object. This additional subclassing information is not lost if the FORM2LIB utility is used.

However, this utility needs some setup work in the Windows95/NT registry. For more information about using the FORM2LIB utility, refer to the file FORM2LIB.TXT in the <ORACLE_HOME>\CGENF50 directory.

How to Specify the Object Library to Use During Generation

In order to specify the object library Form Generator is to use during generation, follow these steps:

1. Use the *Object Library Name* field on the Generate Form dialog to specify the name and extension of the object library to use during generation. The default value in this field is the object library currently specified by *Standards → Name of the object library (STOOLB)* preference. The value of this preference is used as the default in the Object Library Name field on the Generate Form dialog box. The Object Library Name field initially defaults to this preference. However, Form Generator ignores this preference if you subsequently change or remove the value in the Object Library Name field. If you change the name in the field, the name you enter is used instead of STOOLB. When you restart Oracle Designer, the name is restored to the value of STOOLB.
2. If you do not specify a path to locate the object library in the Object Library name field, use the Path field on the Standard tab of the Form Generator Options dialog box to specify the object library's location. If you do not specify a path in the Object Library Name field or the object library is not in the path you specify in the field, Form Generator first searches for the specified object library in the current working directory. If the object library is not in the current working directory, Form Generator searches in the locations specified in the Path field (working from left to right) until it finds the specified object library.

Object Libraries and Earlier Versions of Oracle Designer

In Oracle Designer release 2, support for object libraries and subclassing objects from object libraries supercedes most of the functionality previously provided by template forms and user preferences. The use of object libraries has a big impact on the following areas:

- Obsolete preferences
- CG$ template objects
- CG$ visual attributes

Object Libraries and Obsolete Preferences

In earlier versions of Oracle Designer, user preferences were used to set some of the object properties. However, in Oracle Designer release 2, Form Generator uses source objects in the object library to subclass or to copy the properties of generated objects. For example, whether the hint for an item is automatically displayed or not used to be controlled by the *End User Interface → Set automatic help for all fields (AUTOHP)* preference; in release 2, it is controlled by the *Display Hint Automatically* property of the source object.

Subclassing the object properties from object libraries is more obvious than using preferences. It also offers more flexibility, because changes in object properties can be easily propagated to subclassed objects in generated forms simply by recompiling the forms instead of having to generate them from Oracle Designer again. Given the flexibility provided by the object libraries, there is no reason to use some of these user preferences anymore, and that is why a number of preferences have become obsolete. Table 22-3 shows a list of obsolete preferences and the equivalent form object properties.

Even though these preferences have become obsolete, to ensure backward compatibility, Oracle Designer release 2 allows us to use them by setting the *Standards → Object library keep old preferences (OLBOLD)* preference. When this preference is set to **Yes**, Form Generator ignores the object library and uses user preferences to set the properties of generated objects. However, we strongly recommend you do not use the obsolete preferences, because the obsolete preferences will be totally removed from Oracle Designer in future releases.

Obsolete Preference	Equivalent Form Object Property
AUTOHP	Display Hint Automatically
BLKVSB	Show Vertical Scroll Bar
COLSEC	Enforce Column Security
IMGBEV	Image Item – Bevel
IMGCMP	Image Item – Compression Quality
IMGDHT	Image Item – Height
IMGDWD	Image Item – Width
IMGHSB	Image Item – Show Horizontal Scroll Bar
IMGQLT	Image Item – Display Quality
IMGSZS	Image Item – Sizing Style
IMGVSB	Image Item – Show Vertical Scroll Bar
LOVNAV	Push Button – Keyboard Navigable
TXTBEV	Text Item – Bevel
WINCLO	Window – Close Allowed
WINDLG	Window – Window Style
WINFHT	Window – Height
WINFIX	Window – Resize Allowed
WINFWD	Window – Width
WINFXP	Window – X Position
WINFYP	Window – Y Position
WINHSB	Window – Show Horizontal Scrollbar
WINICN	Window – Icon Filename
WINICO	Window – Minimize Allowed
WINICT	Window – Minimized Title
WINMOV	Window – Move Allowed
WINVSB	Window – Show Vertical Scrollbar
WINZOO	Window – Maximize Allowed

TABLE 22-3. *Obsolete Preferences and Their Equivalent Form Object Properties*

Object Libraries and CG$ Template Button Items

In earlier versions, Form Generator could use a number of CG$ template button items from the template form to provide default Form Builder functionality. In Oracle Designer release 2, this functionality can also be implemented by the use of shipped implementation source objects in the object library. Table 22-4 shows a list of the shipped implementation source objects and the equivalent CG$ template button items.

CG$ Template Button Item	Default Oracle Developer Functionality	Shipped Implementation Source Object
CG$CQ	Cancel Query	CGAI$CANCEL_QUERY
CG$CB	Clear Block	CGAI$CLEAR_BLOCK
CG$CF	Clear Item	CGAI$CLEAR_ITEM
CG$CR	Clear Record	CGAI$CLEAR_RECORD
CG$CM	Commit	CGAI$COMMIT
CG$CP	Copy	CGAI$COPY
CG$CH	Count Query Hits	CGAI$COUNT_HITS
CG$CT	Cut	CGAI$CUT
CG$DE	Display Error	CGAI$DISPLAY_ERROR
CG$DF	Duplicate Item	CGAI$DUPL_ITEM
CG$DR	Duplicate Record	CGAI$DUPLICATE_RECORD
CG$ED	Edit Item	CGAI$EDIT
CG$EQ	Enter Query Mode	CGAI$ENTER_QUERY
CG$XQ	Execute Query	CGAI$EXECUTE_QUERY
CG$EX	Exit	CGAI$EXIT
CG$FN	Fetch Next Set	CGAI$FETCH_NEXT_SET
CG$HP	Help	CGAI$HELP
CG$IR	Insert Record	CGAI$INSERT_RECORD

TABLE 22-4. *Shipped Implementation Objects and CG$ Button Items*

CG$ Template Button Item	Default Oracle Developer Functionality	Shipped Implementation Source Object
CG$KY	Keys	CGAI$KEYS
CG$LQ	Last Criteria	CGAI$LAST_CRITERIA
CG$LR	Lock Record	CGAI$LOCK_RECORD
CG$LV	List of Values	CGAI$LOV
CG$NB	Next Block	CGAI$NEXT_BLOCK
CG$NF	Next Item	CGAI$NEXT_ITEM
CG$NP	Next Page	CGAI$NEXT_PAGE
CG$NR	Next Record	CGAI$NEXT_RECORD
CG$PA	Paste	CGAI$PASTE
CG$PB	Previous Block	CGAI$PREV_BLOCK
CG$PF	Previous Item	CGAI$PREV_ITEM
CG$PP	Previous Page	CGAI$PREV_PAGE
CG$PR	Previous Record	CGAI$PREV_RECORD
CG$OP	Print	CGAI$PRINT
CG$RF	Refresh	CGAI$REFRESH
CG$RR	Remove Record	CGAI$REMOVE_RECORD
CG$RB	Rollback	CGAI$ROLLBACK
CG$SD	Scroll Down	CGAI$SCROLL_DOWN
CG$SU	Scroll Up	CGAI$SCROLL_UP

TABLE 22-4. *Shipped Implementation Objects and CG$ Button Items* (continued)

There is a slight difference in how Form Generator uses CG$ template buttons and how it uses CGAI$ implementation objects. CG$ template buttons in template forms are generated into every form without any additional setup work. For example, you don't have to specify them in every module; Form Generator generates them from the template forms. However, CGAI$ objects need to be explicitly defined in module definitions. This can be done either by specifying implementation source objects in every module, or by using the better approach of creating a reusable module component with these CGAI$ objects and then including it in every module that is to include the buttons.

Object Libraries and Generator-Named Visual Attributes

In earlier versions, Form Generator could use a number of CG$ visual attributes from the template form to set the font and pattern properties of generated objects. In Oracle Designer release 2, this functionality is superceded by the support for object libraries and copying or subclassing objects and their properties from the objects in an object library. In release 2, Form Generator uses objects in an object library to set the properties of generated objects. Subclassing objects from object libraries is more flexible since changes made to object properties in the object library are automatically inherited by the subclassed objects in generated forms simply by recompiling the forms.

CG$ named visual attributes should not be used anymore with the exception of the ones that are used for decorations and titles that do not have any corresponding object in the object library (for example, CG$BLOCK_TITLE and CG$RADIO_TITLE).

Object Libraries and Generated Items' Widths, Lengths, and Formats

In earlier versions of Designer, Form Generator used some of the user preferences *(Layout – Text Item)* to determine an item's width or height or format if this information was not defined in the repository. In Oracle Designer release 2, Form Generator uses source objects in the object library to set these properties. However, Form Generator still uses the *Layout – Text Item* preferences if it cannot derive this information from the source objects.

Defining an Architecture for Template Forms and Object Libraries

Generating forms from Oracle Designer is a complicated process, especially with the vast array of options available in Oracle Designer release 2. There are many decisions and choices that you will need to make when you set up your form generation environment that will impact the development of your systems in many ways. Your goal should be to build highly generated, easy-to-maintain systems. Therefore, the architecture (usage of template forms, object libraries, and PL/SQL libraries) you choose for forms generation is very important.

Form Generation Architectures

Since the early days of Oracle Designer when it was called Oracle Design Dictionary or Oracle CASE, there have been quite a few different approaches to the architecture to use in a form generation environment. With each new release of the product and the introduction of new features in Oracle Designer and Oracle Developer, you are forced to reconsider the architecture you are using for generating forms. Naturally, you would like to take advantage of the latest features, achieve higher levels of generation, and generate easy-to-maintain systems. As a result, the architecture you use is constantly evolving. Table 22-5 shows a brief summary of the evolution of such architectures.

Template Form–Only Architecture

First, all we had was template forms. Everything, including user objects and the application logic (PL/SQL code) had to be defined in the template forms. These were the fat templates. One big drawback with these template forms was that once a form was generated, objects were copied from the template

Form Generation Architecture	Description
Templates	All of the template code is placed directly in the templates. Simplest architecture, but inherits maintenance problems due to copied objects from templates.
Templates + Reference forms	Most of the objects in the templates are referenced from reference forms. Drastically improved application maintenance.
Templates + Reference forms + libraries	PL/SQL code moved to PLL libraries. Shared code. Improved code maintenance.
Templates + Reference forms + Nested libraries	Hierarchies in PLL libraries. Suitable for enterprise-wide application development.
Templates + Object libraries + Nested libraries	Very Thin Templates. Subclassing from object libraries (less rigid referencing). More flexible.
Templates + Object libraries + Nested libraries + Application logic	Well balanced, distributed objects.

TABLE 22-5. *Evolution of Form Generation Architectures*

into the generated forms. When a change had to be made in the template form, the previously generated forms had to be generated again or manually brought up to synch with the template form. The result was a maintenance nightmare, because no matter how stable the templates were, there was always a need for a small change. This would cause a domino effect in hundreds of forms—some with post-generation changes—generated. Figure 22-13 shows how the template-based architecture works.

Template Form + Reference Form Architecture

The next generation of form generation architectures made use of referencing. Template form objects that are not generated or overridden by the Form Generator were moved to reference forms and then referenced back into the template forms. When a form was generated, these objects kept their referencing information and automatically picked up changes in

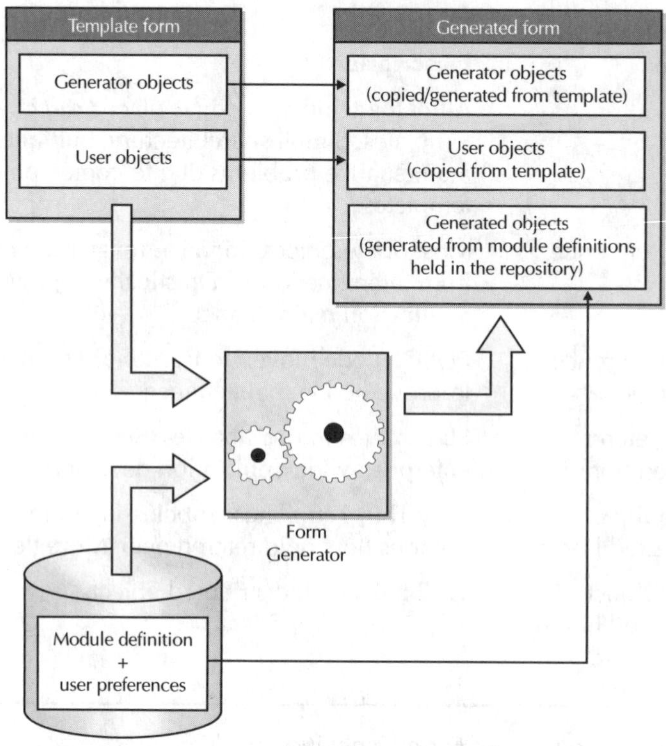

FIGURE 22-13. *Template form architecture*

source objects when the form was recompiled. This approach helped reduce the tremendous maintenance problems experienced with fat templates. The downside was that referenced objects could not be modified. Among the referenced objects were all of the user objects, CG$ visual attributes, and form-level triggers that were not generated by Form Generator. Form-level triggers were used to trap events without interfering with what Form Generator generated. Figure 22-14 shows how the reference form and template-based architecture works.

Template Form + Reference Form + PLL Library Architecture

Even though referencing form objects did help with some of the maintenance problems, there was still a lot of PL/SQL code (program units

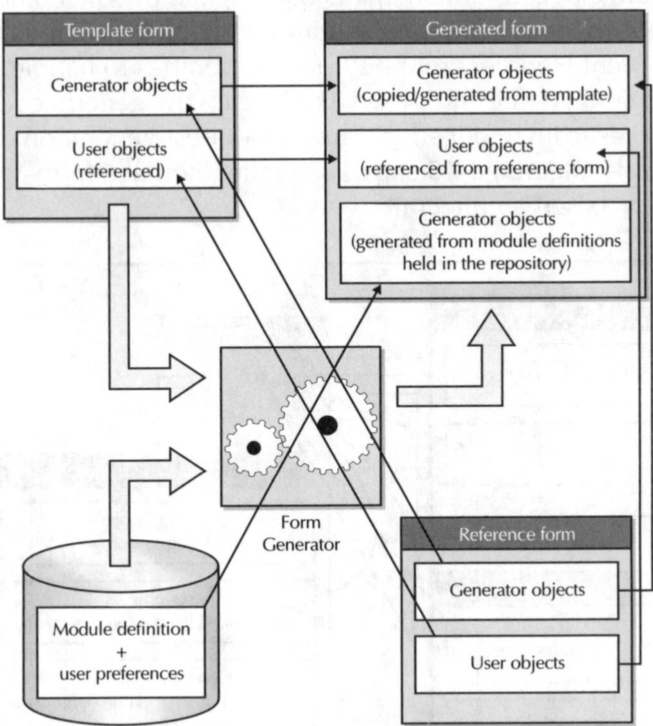

FIGURE 22-14. *Template form + reference form architecture*

implementing functionality) in templates that could not be referenced from reference forms. The solution was to move the PL/SQL code into PLL libraries that could be shared among many forms. These libraries could then be attached to generated forms either via a *Form - Library Attachment → Module specific library attachment (MODLIB)* user preference or indirectly through the library attachments of the template forms. Using the user preference only, one library could be attached to a generated form. Sharing the code helped with the application maintenance, but the PL/SQL code had to be very generic and written with a different style. Direct referencing of form objects (a.k.a. **:** notation) could not be used in PLL libraries; NAME_IN and COPY built-ins had to be used. It did not take long for many of us to adopt this change because the benefits outweighed the difficulties. The logic in triggers converted to PLL library routines and triggers started calling a centralized "Event-Handler" routine from the libraries to handle form events such as WHEN-NEW-RECORD-INSTANCE, etc. The generic code and event trapping has drastically reduced the amount of post-generation changes in the PL/SQL code. Figure 22-15 shows how the reference form– , template- , and PLL library–based architecture works.

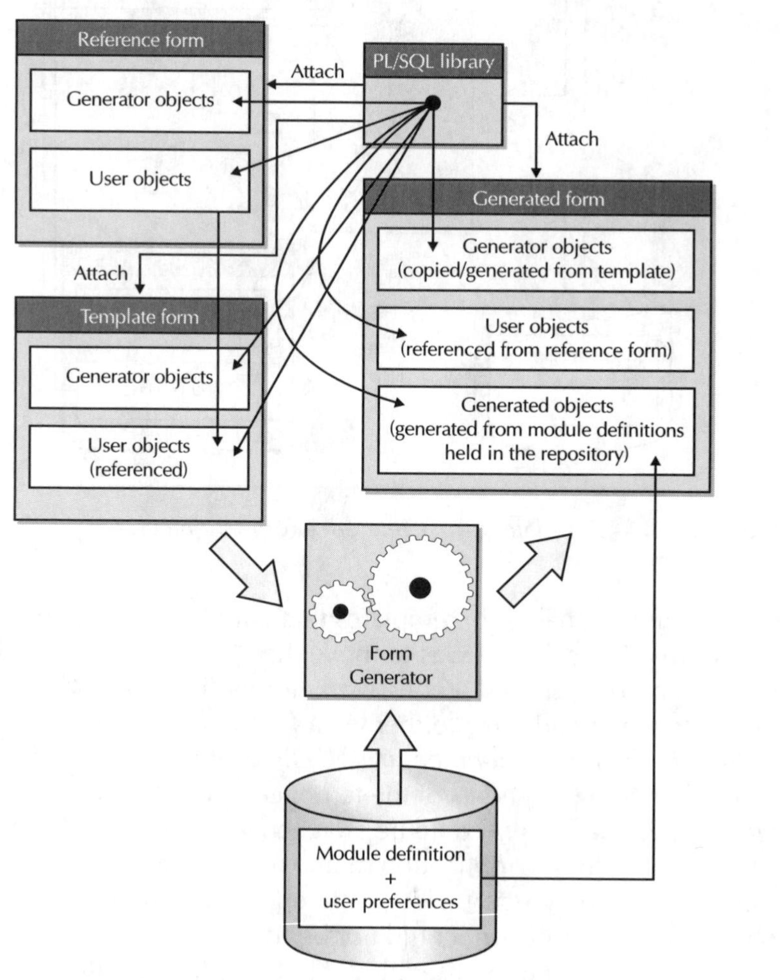

FIGURE 22-15. *Template form + reference form + PLL library architecture*

Template Form + Reference Form + Nested and Event-Driven PLL Library Architecture

After the benefits of using PLL libraries were realized, the use of PLL libraries was often exploited to its fullest extent. There was a real need for this: generic libraries were too generic at times, and we needed to override some of the code for a single or a set of modules. This forced us to add two more layers: business area or application-specific and module-specific library layers. This library architecture is conveniently named as *Event-Driven Nested Library* architecture by Ken Atkins, one of the authors of this book. Up at the top of the hierarchy is the standard library; followed by the application library; and, finally, the module library, a daisy chain of PLL libraries. The standard library contained standards for the entire applications for an organization. At a level below, application libraries attached the standard library and were used to add/remove certain features that were specific to one application from the standard library. Similarly, module libraries attached the application library and were used to add/remove module-specific features from the application and/or standard library. This hierarchy yielded the desired flexibility with increased code sharing. However, additional layers of libraries presented a steeper learning curve for the developers. This is the architecture used by all three of the commercial template packages that we know about, at least for their release 1 versions. Figure 22-16 shows how the reference form– , template- , and nested PLL library–based architecture works.

Template Form + Object Library + Nested and Event Driven PLL Library Architecture

In Oracle Designer release 2, Form Generator introduced the use of object libraries in form generation. Oracle must have realized the benefits of referencing in Oracle Developer Forms, because they extended the referencing feature and came up with the concept of subclassing objects from other objects in object libraries. Different from referencing, subclassed objects can override some or all of the properties they inherit from the source object, and the rest of the properties will still be subclassed. This is a very powerful object inheritance mechanism. In Oracle Designer release 2, Form Generator can subclass objects from the object libraries. It is also possible to specify that the Form Generator use a specific source object in an object library when generating a specific object. The object properties that we could

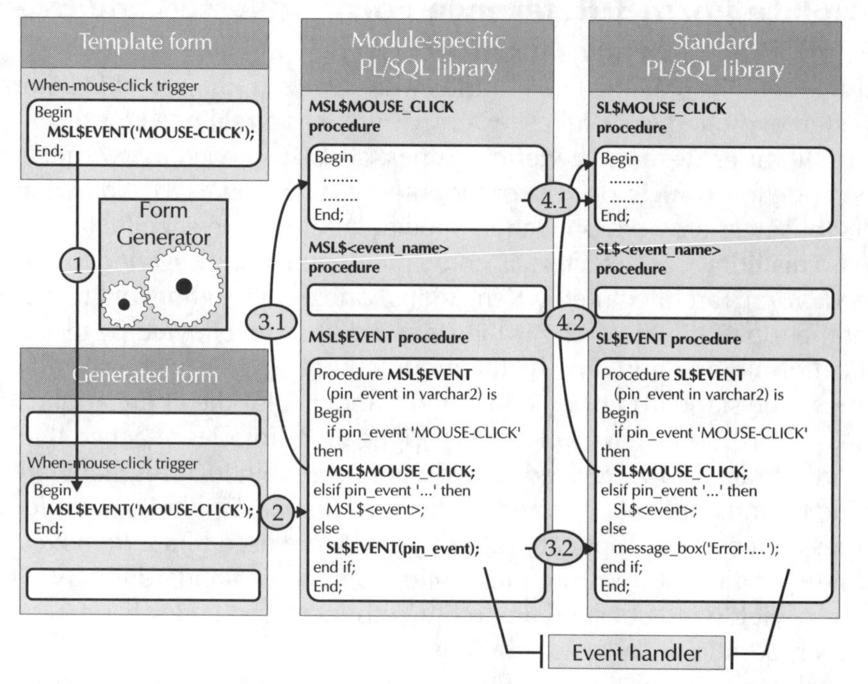

FIGURE 22-16. *Template form + reference form + nested and event-driven PLL library architecture*

not control through the repository now can be controlled via source objects in the object libraries. Subclassing objects from an object library now supercedes referencing objects from a reference form. This means the objects in reference forms need to be moved to object libraries for this more flexible approach to generation. The PL/SQL code can still be kept in nested event-driven PLL libraries. Figure 22-17 shows how the object library, template, and nested event-driven PLL library–based architecture works.

Template Form + Object Library + Nested and Event-Driven PLL Library + Application Logic Architecture

In addition to subclassing objects from object libraries, Oracle Designer release 2 offers an option to define the application logic right in the repository. For example, we can define new triggers for items, blocks, and even forms that are not generated by Form Generator, or we can customize

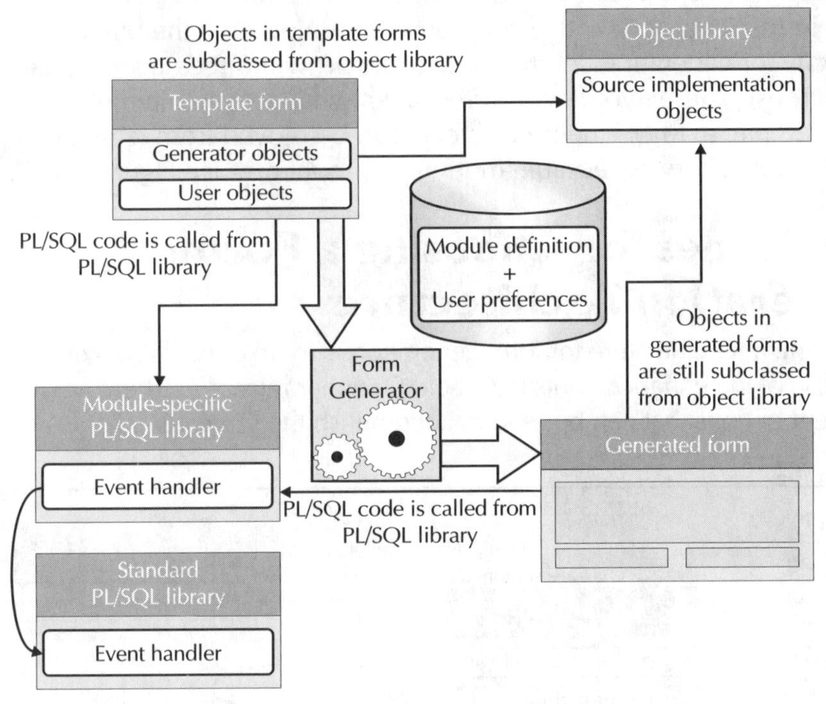

FIGURE 22-17. *Template form + reference form + nested and event-driven PLL library architecture*

the code Form Generator will generate by adding and sequencing our own custom code segments in between the code to be generated. This alone is a great enhancement that may eliminate the need for module-specific libraries. The whole purpose of module-specific libraries is to meet module-specific requirements. Since we can do this by adding the application logic needed to meet these requirements right in the repository, module-specific libraries may no longer be needed. The capacity for defining the application logic in the repository may seem like it should replace nested, event-driven PLL libraries. However, this may not be practical after all, depending on how the application logic is used. Moreover, we don't have to choose one or the other; instead, we could build hybrid architectures that use the best features of each and provide a better overall solution.

To make things more complicated, there are also two new features in Oracle Designer release 2 that will greatly affect how architecture is selected. One is reusable module components (blocks that can be defined once in the repository and used in other modules), and the other one is the capacity for generating control blocks (blocks without data source/target definitions). These two new features affect what goes into template forms. For example, many of the user objects can be moved from template forms into the repository as reusable module components. See Figure 22-18.

Guidelines for Choosing a Forms Generation Architecture

Choosing an architecture for form generation is more difficult than ever because of the enhancements in Oracle Designer release 2. There are many different options that can be used to accomplish the same goal. For example,

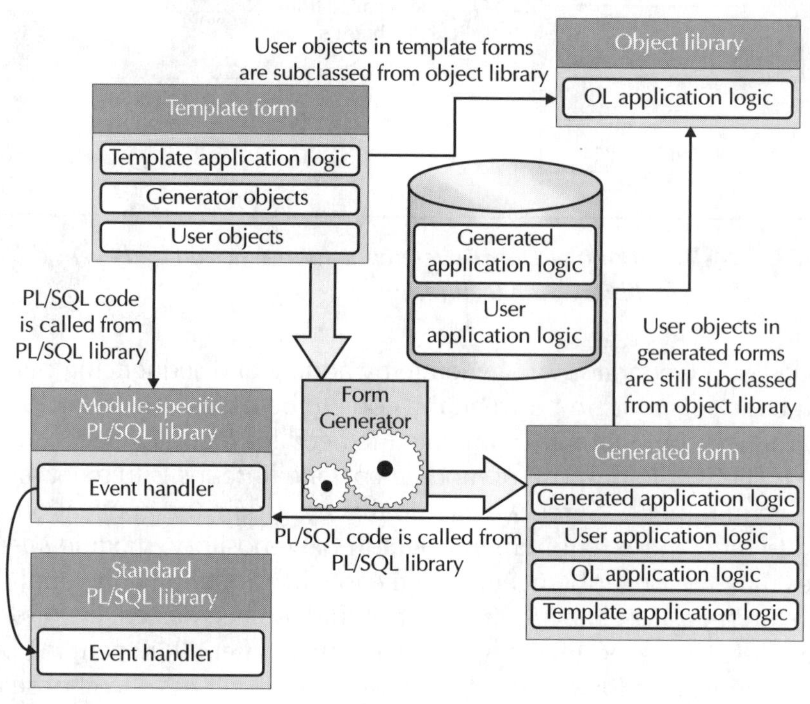

FIGURE 22-18. *Template form + reference form + nested and event-driven PLL library + application logic architecture*

the application logic can either be held in the repository or in the libraries. Having more options is definitely good, but along with the additional possibilities are additional decisions you have to make. In order to make the right decision for your environment, you have to understand the ramifications of each decision. In order to choose the right architecture successfully from many different combinations, you need to consider which of the following factors are important to you: ease of use, ease of maintenance, repository integration, and better documentation.

In this section, we will help you decide when you should choose one of these options.

Reusable Module Components Versus User Objects in Template Forms

Reusable module components can be used to build user objects. However, not all user objects should be defined as reusable module components. It is best to use reusable module components when a specific feature is needed in only a few modules and when it is possible to do so in the repository. The benefit of defining user objects in the repository is better documentation and more complete impact analysis. However, there are some features (like complex layouts) that can be developed more easily in the template forms than in the reusable module components. Also, when user objects are defined as reusable module components, there may still be some need to build source objects in object libraries. Reusable module components should not be used to replace those user objects that are common to many or most of the forms in your application. For example, a common toolbar that is to be placed in every form in your system should not be defined as a reusable module component. This is because if you end up having to change the toolbar, you will have to generate all of the forms in your system again. This defeats the main reason you are using reference forms and object libraries in the first place.

Application Logic Versus PLL Library Code

Application logic can be used to add/modify PL/SQL code generated into the modules. Application logic gives us better control over the custom PL/SQL code generated into the modules. However, as with reusable module components, the application logic should not be used to implement every possible customization. For example, form-level triggers in template forms and object libraries could be placed into the repository if you wanted to. However, if you did this, an identical set of triggers would need to be defined as event codes for each module. This would be very inefficient, and it would conflict with the goal of code reuse and sharing. The best use for application logic is to eliminate post-generation changes in the PL/SQL code. While this has some benefits, such as better documentation and impact analysis, there are some problems with storing application logic in the repository:

1. Application logic cannot be compiled in the repository before the module is generated. The workaround is to create, test, and debug the code in Form Builder; and, once it's finalized, use Designer's *design recovery* feature to pull the code back into the repository. Then you can generate the module from Oracle Designer again.
2. If you delete and re-create the bound item, table usage, or module component that has the application logic, you will lose all of the PL/SQL you have entered. In the best case, you will just have to reenter it. In the worse case, you will have forgotten it was there and will end up introducing defects into your system.

One way to avoid both of these problems is to develop the functionality of the code in a procedure or function in a PL/SQL library attached to the form. Then the application logic will only be one line, a call to the relevant procedure in the library. This allows you to compile the code (in the library) and easily reapply the application logic, since it is only one line. The drawback of this solution is that you will have to develop your PL/SQL using the indirect item references (NAME_IN & COPY).

Storing and Generating Libraries from the Repository

Oracle Designer release 2 allows us to define libraries in the repository. Libraries can be defined in two ways:

- The source code for the library is defined in the repository. Better documentation, better impact analysis, but poor syntax checking.
- The source code for the library is held in a file on the file system. Minimal documentation.

Regardless of which method you choose, defining libraries in the repository allows you to attach (using module networks) more than one library to form modules. This will be covered in more detail in Chapter 23.

Template Form and Object Library Troubleshooting Guide

Problem	Resolution
I have changed the value of the STOOLB preference, but the Generate Form dialog still shows the old value.	If you change the value of this preference, the change will not be reflected on the Generate Form dialog until you either press the reset button on this dialog or restart Oracle Designer.
Form Generator cannot find the template during generation. OR I have created a new template, but the Form Generator did not use it.	Try the following: 1. Make sure that the Path field in the Standard tab of the Form Generator Options dialog includes the correct path. 2. Make sure that you are specifying the template name correctly.
Form Generator cannot find the object library during generation.	Try the following: 1. Make sure the object library is available in the working directory or in one of the paths specified in the FORMS50_PATH registry entry. 2. Make sure that you are naming the object library correctly. The Object Library Name field in the Generate Form dialog must specify a valid object library name.
The colors in my generated form are wrong.	Modify the template form and set the color palette properly.
I have used a generator item in my block, but Form Generator did not generate it.	Generator items can only be generated as part of a header or footer. Make sure that the generator item is defined in a generator control block and is displayed in a header or footer canvas.

Problem	Resolution
I wanted to show page numbers on my stacked header or footers, but I could not get it to work.	Page numbers (CG$PN, CG$PM, and CG$PT) cannot be displayed on stacked header or footers.
I have added a user item in my template, but Form Generator did not copy it into my generated form.	User items can only be generated as part of user blocks. Make sure that the item is defined in a user block.
The user item that I have added to CG$Stacked_Header canvas is not showing up in my stacked header for the second page.	User items are copied only once. If you want this user item to show on all stacked canvases, either include mirror items or put it onto a separate canvas.
I have defined a new user item but the Form Generator did not copy it into my form.	Form Generator ignores any generator item placed either partially or totally off its template canvas.
I received the message, "CGEN-01077 WARNING Implementation source object not found in Object Library."	Make sure that the implementation source object specified in this message is defined in the object library. Also, make sure that the right object library is being used.
I received the message, "CGEN-01076 WARNING Implementation source object specified, but no Object Library loaded."	Make sure that an object library is specified and can be found in the search path.
I added a generator object to my template, but its corresponding object is not being generated into the form.	Make sure you have entered the name of the object correctly. If you mistype the keyword name for the generator object, the generator will ignore the object and will not give you any errors or warnings.
Form Generator is not appending its code into my form-level triggers.	Make sure that these triggers are not referenced. Form Generator ignores referenced triggers defined at form level, since a referenced object cannot be modified.

CHAPTER 23

Application Logic and Code Reuse

In recent years, there has been a paradigm shift in software development toward object-oriented or component-based methods. The benefits of component-based development are obvious: increased efficiency, increased productivity, and reduced maintenance. Realizing the huge benefits of object-oriented or component-based development methods, many software development tools, including Oracle Designer and Developer, added features to support these methods.

Release 2 of Oracle Designer contains major enhancements that increase productivity and usability by a significant amount. The new object library and reusable module components features of Oracle Developer/Designer allow you to design, build, and generate systems much faster and with more code reuse.

Another major improvement in release 2 is the support for application logic. Application logic is the custom code needed by the generated applications to support business rule implementation. You can store custom application logic code in the Designer Repository in two methods:

- By defining event code (code that executes in response to particular events such as WHEN-NEW-BLOCK-INSTANCE, etc.)
- By using named routines (packages, procedures, functions etc.)

The greatest benefit of storing application logic in the repository is that you don't have to resort to post-generation changes or complex library code to handle your complex business rules. The custom code can be added to the module modified before it is generated. This eliminates many of the post-generation changes that had to be made to the modules in the previous versions of Oracle Designer.

Storing the application code in the repository would not be complete if Oracle Designer did not support generation of Oracle Developer libraries. Release 2 of Oracle Designer allows you to create library modules in the repository, generate them from the repository, and attach them to other modules (including other libraries) in the repository.

The support for reusable module components, storing application logic in the repository, library generation from the repository, and the support for object libraries represent big changes in the capabilities of Oracle Designer. These changes force us reevaluate our generation methodology and template/library architecture.

In this chapter, we will review the application and code reusability in release 2 of Oracle Designer. We will highlight the advantages and disadvantages of each option. Wherever applicable, a troubleshooting section will help you solve some of the most common problems. The following topics will be discussed in this chapter:

- Reusable module components
- Application logic
- Library generation

Reusable Module Components

If you have already built systems using previous releases of Oracle Designer, you have probably noticed many similarities among some of your modules. For example, you might have had three of four modules that had the similar query-only block for querying a customer first before drilling into the detailed information regarding that customer. Figure 23-1 shows five different modules, all including the same common block. If you discovered these similarities before you built the second or the third module, you might have taken the time to split the first module into two, one that has the query-only block and the other that has the rest of the module. Then, you could have the query-only module call out the other detail modules, to avoid repeating functionality. Alternatively, if you were under tight time constraints, you might have copied one of your existing modules first and then modified it to build other modules. You can also create a new template and include this common block in the template form.

Release 2 of Oracle Designer offers another option to approach this common problem in system design: *reusable module components*. As mentioned earlier, module components are the building blocks that are used for client-side application (forms, reports, Web server modules) design. A module definition in the repository is composed of at least one or more module components, which are used to define discrete groups of information within the module. When a module is generated, each module component becomes a block in the generated form or a group in the generated report. Module components may or may not contain table usages (module components without data usages generate control blocks).

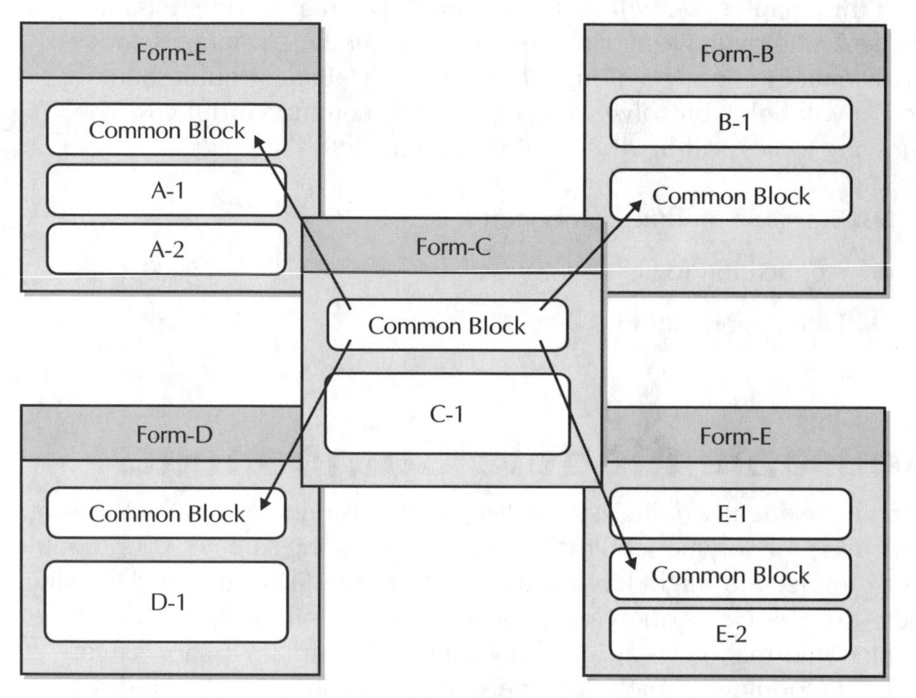

FIGURE 23-1. *The same block in more than one generated form*

Reusable module components are a special type of module component. While regular module components are part of a specific module (you have to create a module first, and then create a module component), reusable module components are not specific to any single module. You don't have to create a module before creating a reusable module component. Reusable module components are common to more than one module, and they can be shared across all modules in an application system and even in different application systems. In order to distinguish a reusable module component from a specific module component, different icons are used.

How to Create Reusable Module Components

There are two ways to create reusable module components:

- Creating a reusable module component from existing module components
- Creating new reusable module components

Creating a Reusable Module Component from Existing Module Components

In the Design Editor only, there is a special utility for module component creation. This utility allows you to create a reusable module component from an existing module component. You can use the following procedure to use this utility.

1. Right-click on the module component (either on the module diagram or in the navigator) that you wish to share with other modules to bring up the context-sensitive pop-up menu.
2. From the pop-up menu, select *Make Reusable* to create a reusable module component, as shown here. The utility will create a reusable module component and link the source module component to the newly created reusable module component. The source module component will become an instance of the reusable module component included in that specific module.

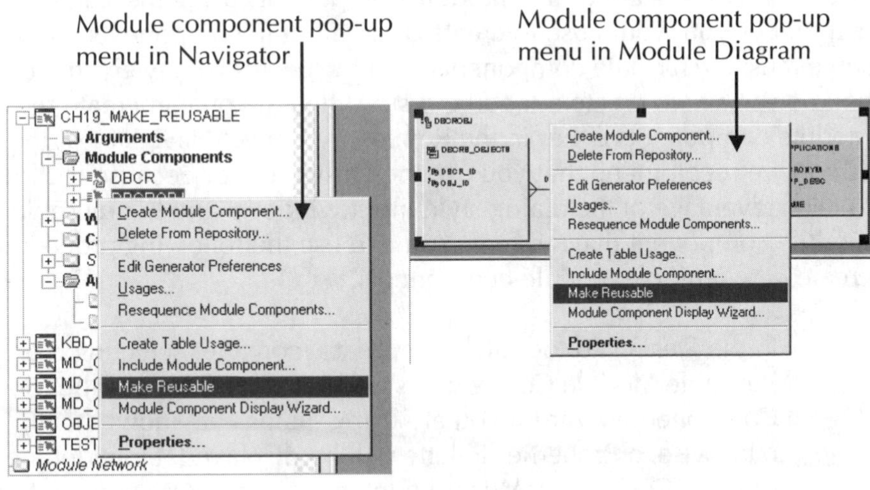

3. Alternatively, you could use the Property Palette to change the *Module Component Type* property of the module component from **Specific** to **Re-usable**, as shown here:

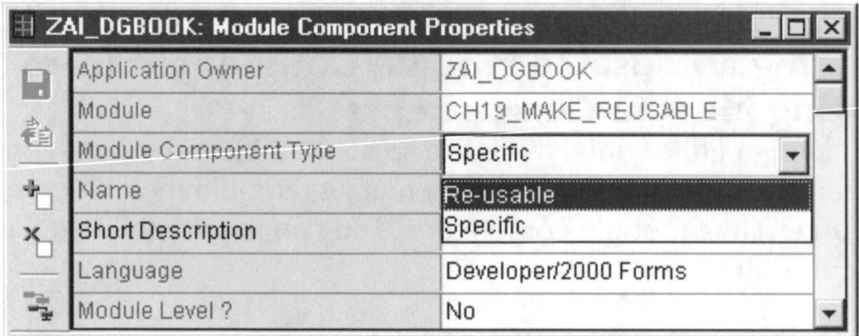

TIP

You can also make a private copy of a reusable module component. Right-click on the reusable module component that you have already included in your module. From the pop-up menu, select ***Make Private Copy****.*

Creating New Reusable Module Components

You can also create reusable module components using the same techniques you would use to create other module components. However, since reusable module components are not specific to any given module, you don't have to create a module first. Although you can create reusable module components either in the Repository Object Navigator or the Design Editor, we recommend that you use the Design Editor because it allows you to take advantage of the dialog-style input windows and the reusable module component diagrammer. You can use the following procedure to create new reusable module components.

1. In the Design Editor, click the Create icon after selecting the Reusable Module Components node. This will invoke the Module Component Wizard if you are using dialogs (as shown next); otherwise, a Properties Palette will be displayed. Don't let the Module Component Wizard confuse you (because you are trying to create a *reusable* component): the window title will indicate that you are about to create a reusable module component.

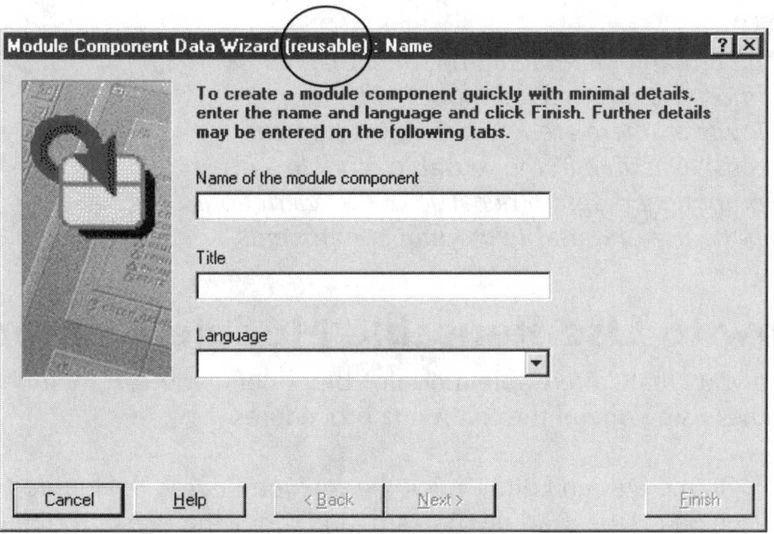

2. Add the table and item usages as necessary. Use the reusable module component diagram, shown here, (simply drag the reusable module component onto an open space in Design Editor) to finish editing reusable module components. Create item groups, specify Forms Generator preferences, etc.

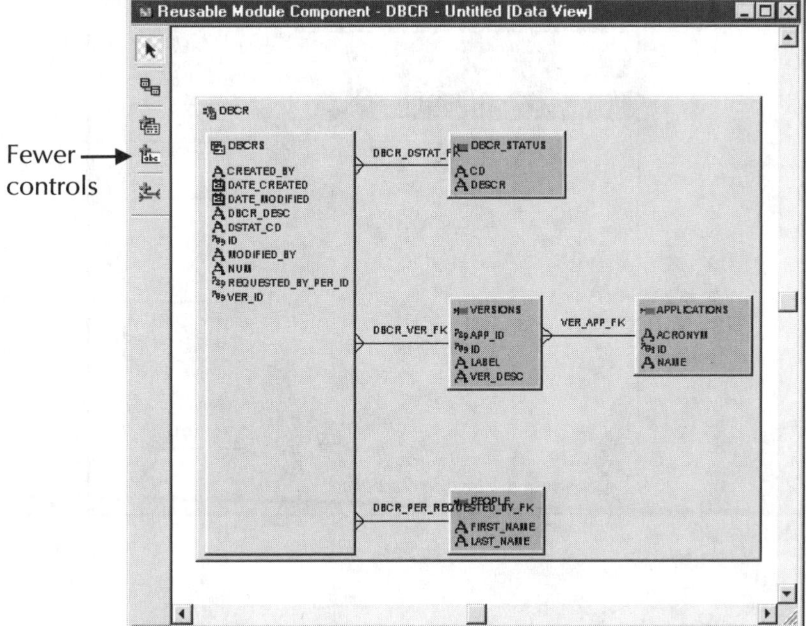

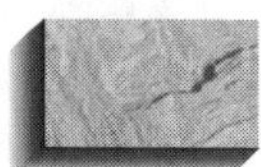

TIP
The reusable module component diagram is almost the same as the module diagram. However, there are fewer controls (toolbar icons) available in the reusable module component diagram because of the restrictions on the use of reusable module components.

How to Use Reusable Module Components

Once you create a reusable module component, you can include it in other modules using one of the following procedures.

1. In the Design Editor, click the *Include Reusable Module Component* icon on the module diagram, and move the cursor to the position where you want it to be included. From the Include Module Component window, shown here, select the one you wish to include from the list of all reusable module components.

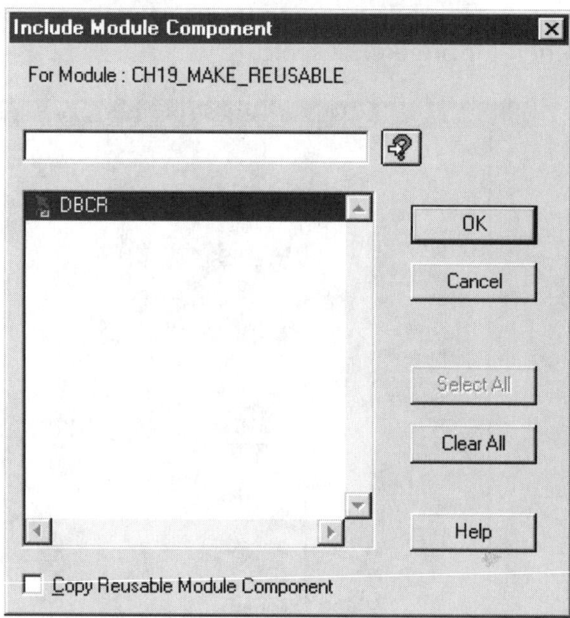

2. In the Design Editor, right-click on the module component branch of the module on the navigator. From the Include Module Component window that pops up, select the one you wish to include from the list of all reusable module components.

After including a reusable module component, you can create key-based links to connect it to the other module component that might exist in your module. Figure 23-2 shows a data view of a module that contains a reusable and a specific module component that are linked together.

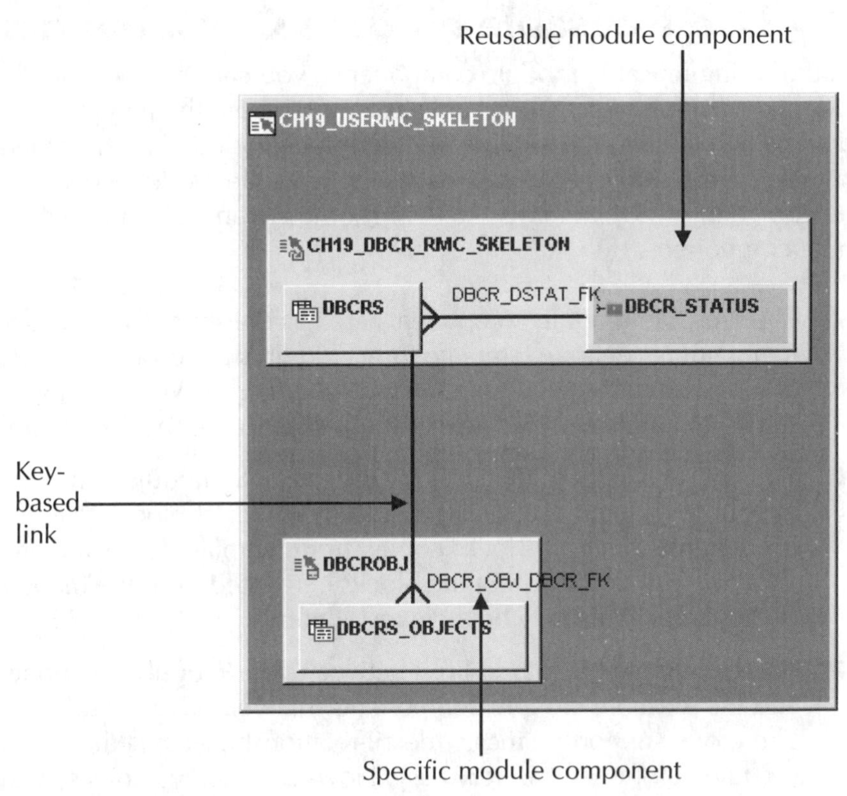

FIGURE 23-2. *Linking a specific module component with a reusable module component*

TIP

Reusable module components have a Language property, just as modules do (Developer/2000 Forms). In most cases, the language of a module component must be the same as the module that uses it. The exceptions to this rule are Developer/2000 graphics components. These can be included in modules of language Developer/2000 Forms, Reports, and Graphics.

Why Use Reusable Module Components?

Instead of using reusable module components, you can include common blocks as part of a template form and easily implement them in many modules. For example, the toolbar is a user block included in the generated forms using this method. So, what makes the reusable module components a better choice in some situations? Here are some advantages of reusable module components:

- The reusable module components are easier to use. Creating and maintaining separate template forms requires a thorough knowledge of template design and Oracle Developer Forms. When using separate templates, you have to make sure to use the right template.
- You can explicitly select and include reusable module components in your form in any order. However, the order of blocks in templates is pretty much static. Blocks copied from template forms are ordered either before or after all of the blocks generated from the module components. This may be a big restriction.
- You can create key-based links between your module components and the reusable module components that you have included. Therefore, supporting master/detail relationships using the reusable module components is very easy. However, there is no easy way to link a module component to a block copied from a template form.

- Reusable module components are better documented, and they provide more accurate impact analysis information. It is also possible to document templates and template usages in the repository, but this is never as simple and clean as using a reusable module component.

Restrictions on the Use of Reusable Module Components

Nothing is perfect. Reusable module components have the following restrictions in release 2.1.2 of Oracle Designer.

- The properties and structure of a reusable module component cannot be modified within the module that references it. In other words, reusable module component implementation, as of this release, does not support subclassing (i.e., inherited properties cannot be overridden, and they will be grayed out in the dialog windows or the Property Palette). Only the *Placement* properties (window, placement, *x* and *y* position) can be modified. When a reusable module component is included within another module, only a link to that reusable module component (nothing else) is created in the including module.

You will often (if not always) need to override some of the inherited properties of the reusable module components, which is not possible in release 2.1.2. Depending on what is needed, there may be a way to work around this limitation. For example, if the Where clause of a table usage in a reusable module component needs to be dynamic, you could add some application logic to the reusable module component to allow for dynamic queries. You just have to be more creative to find a generic solution that eliminates the need for modifying the reusable module component in the including module. Another option is to copy the original reusable module component, modify the copy as needed, and link it back to the including module. After all, there may be other modules that use this slightly different version. If you choose to make a copy, you will have to maintain two (or more) versions by hand.

- Reusable module components cannot have action items. However, you can either create push-button type unbound items to simulate action items or create action items in the including module after including the reusable component (even in the included reusable module component itself).
- Reusability is limited to module components only. Objects at lower levels cannot be marked as reusable. For example, a complex lookup table usage and its chained lookups would be a good candidate for a reusable object. In fact, lookups are among those objects that are used repeatedly. It would make the most sense to define these as reusable objects. However, this is not possible in release 2.
- If you are using multiple object libraries, you have to make sure that the template/source objects specified in the reusable module component exist in the object library specified for the module. Otherwise, template/source objects will be ignored, and standard source objects will be used.

Reusable Module Components Troubleshooting Guideline

Problem	**Resolution**
When trying to make a specific module component reusable, I got the following message: "CDA-02000: Module Component '<component>': Uniqueness conflict."	There must be another reusable module component with the same name. Reusable module component names must be unique within an application system, whereas specific module component names are unique within a module. Change the name of module component before making it reusable.
I identified a source object for an item in the reusable module component, but the generated form that used the component still used the standard source object for the item.	Make sure that all of the source objects you use in the reusable component exist in the object library that is defined for the module.

Problem	Resolution
I cannot change the properties of a reusable module component that I have included in my module.	Oracle Designer does not allow reusable module components to be edited in place (i.e., in the module where they are included). You can only change the *Placement* properties in here; you have to edit the reusable module component itself for all other changes!

Application Logic

Application logic is one of the most important enhancements in release 2 of Oracle Designer because it eliminates the need for making post-generation changes in the generated forms to implement those business rules that cannot be generated by the Forms Generator.

Application logic is the code created in the generated client-side applications to implement functionality that cannot be declaritivly generated. For Oracle Developer Forms, application logic is PL/SQL code that becomes triggers and program units. Figure 23-3 shows a list of different types of application logic.

Starting with release 2, Oracle opened the code generation component of the Forms Generator to allow you add your own code and/or modify the standard code to be generated before it is generated. This was one of the major enhancement requests for Oracle Designer. It is impossible for the Oracle Designer Generators to generate all possible types of business requirements. Instead, Oracle Designer provided us with means to merge our own custom code with the generated code.

Application logic can be defined for all types of modules, including Oracle Developer Forms/Reports applications, Web Server applications, Visual Basic applications, etc. In this section, we will focus on how application logic can be used in Oracle Developer Forms generation.

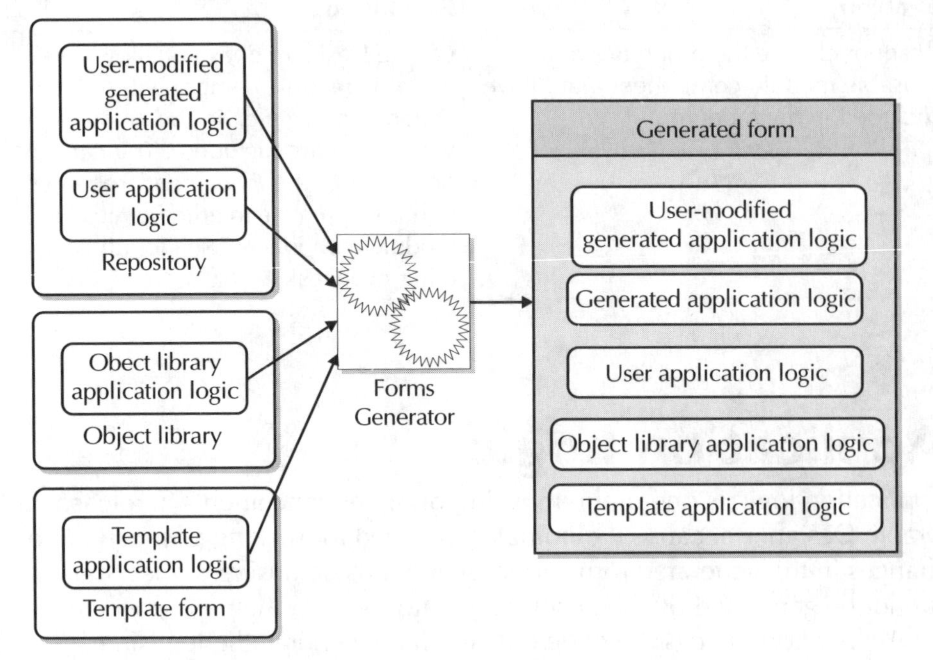

FIGURE 23-3. *Application logic types*

Application Logic Types

Application logic is generated into a form as form triggers and program units. However, depending on the nature of the code generated, application logic can be any of the following types:

- Generated application logic
- Generated but user-modified application logic
- User application logic

Generated Application Logic

Generated application logic is the standard PL/SQL code generated by the Forms Generator. When a form is generated, the Forms Generator creates the code as needed, based on the module definition and the definitions of data sources used in the module definitions. For example, code to initialize a form, code to synchronize blocks in different pages, and code to implement referential integrity rules in the client are all examples of standard generated application logic.

The generated code is created on the fly from the *Standard Code Groups* as the Forms Generator analyzes the requirements and builds the form. The generated application logic is never held in the repository; there is no need for this since the Forms Generator creates it from scratch every single time a form is generated.

The Forms Generator creates the following PL/SQL elements as part of the generated application logic in the generated forms.

- **Generated Code Groups** The blocks of PL/SQL code, marked by unique comments for easy identification, generated in the form triggers, and program units. For example the CGLY$MANAGE_CANVASES code group in the WHEN-NEW-FORM-INSTANCE trigger ensures that correct canvases are visible (see Figure 23-4). For a complete list of the Forms Generator code groups (both grouped by functionality, such as unique key implementation, etc., and grouped alphabetically), please refer to Oracle Designer Online Help and search for "code groups."
- **Generated Named Routines** The PL/SQL program units created by the Forms Generator that are called from the code groups generated in the form triggers, for example the CGLY$MANAGE_CANVASES code group in a WHEN-NEW-FORM-INSTANCE trigger on a block calls a program unit named CGLY$CANVAS_MANAGEMENT.

Generated But User-Modified Application Logic

After a form is generated, you can modify the generated PL/SQL code to add/remove code to implement the functionality you need. By default, generated application is re-created each time a form is generated. Therefore, if you modify the generated application logic, it will be lost next time you generate the form. However, if you want to prevent your changes from being overwritten by the Forms Generator, you can capture the application logic back into the repository.

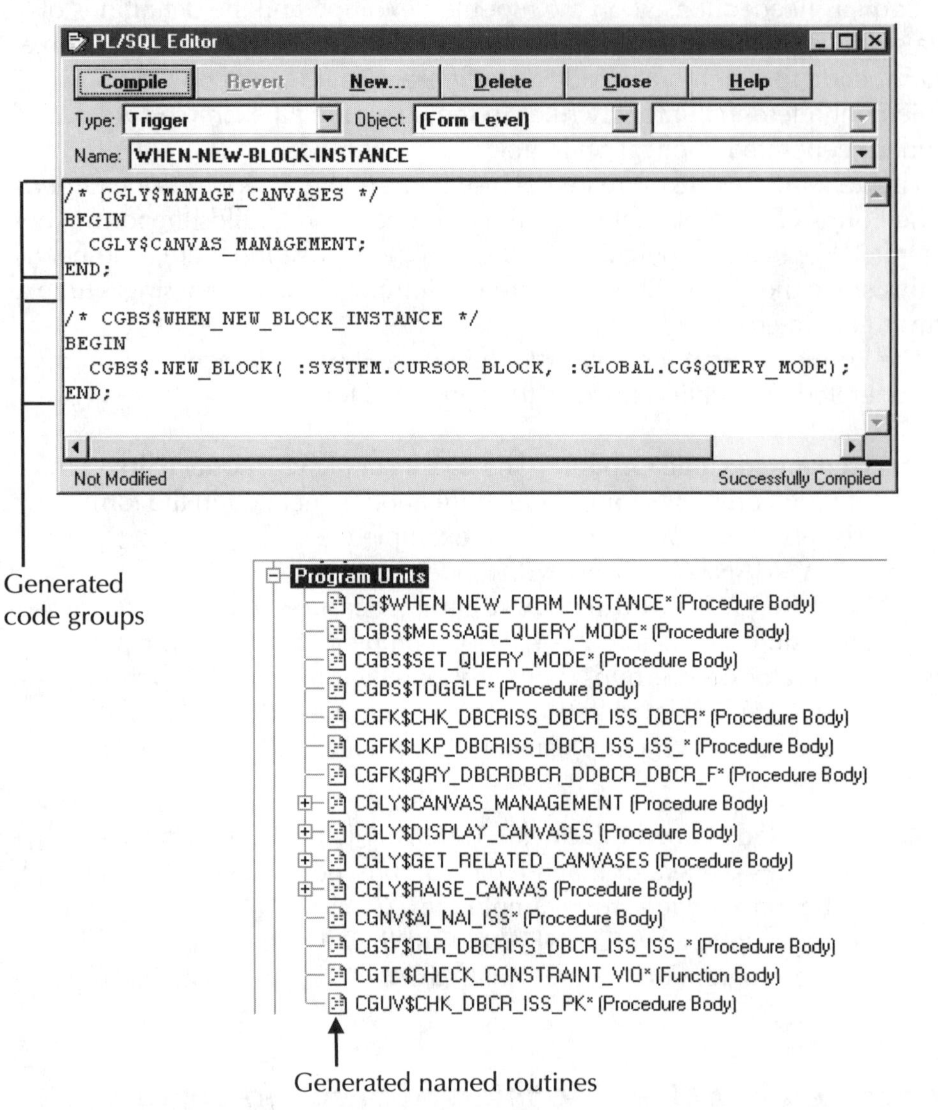

FIGURE 23-4. *Generated application logic*

In order to capture the changes made to the generated application logic, you need to append text to the comment mark generated by the Forms Generator. This is needed to identify the parts of generated application logic that have been modified, so that only those that have changed can be captured into the repository. For example, if you have modified the "/* CGRI$CASCADE_UPDATE */" generated code group (part of the application logic), you might change the comment text to "/* CGRI$CASCADE_UPDATE_customized */" and capture the form into the repository. Once the *user-modified* generated application logic is captured into repository, you can edit it using the Logic Editor.

NOTE

Design Capture *Formerly known as reverse engineering, Design capture is the process of taking an existing form or a report, and importing it into the repository. If the form or report module does not exist in the repository, a new module is created, otherwise the existing module definition is updated. For more information about design capture, please refer to Oracle Designer Online Help.*

User Application Logic

User application logic is the PL/SQL code you create in the repository or in the generated form by hand. This is needed to add functionality that cannot be generated by the Forms Generator. Similar to the generated application logic, user application logic might include the following PL/SQL elements as part of the user application logic in the generated forms:

- *Events* The form triggers generated into forms. *Event Code Segments* are the logically and functionally grouped code statements (PL/SQL blocks) in the events (triggers). If you are following object-oriented coding principles, event code segments will include calls to the user named routines (program units) where the actual code is written. As you can see in the following illustration, a given trigger may have quite a few event code segments. Many of these code segments are standard, and some are user defined, such as the "UDECS Change MDI Window Title" event code segment shown in the illustration. Each segment has a label that helps us identify the function it performs, or its purpose. The sequence of user-defined event code segments (with respect to the event segments that are part of the generated application code) can also be controlled by simply dragging and dropping in the navigator (or via the up and down buttons in the Application Logic dialog box).

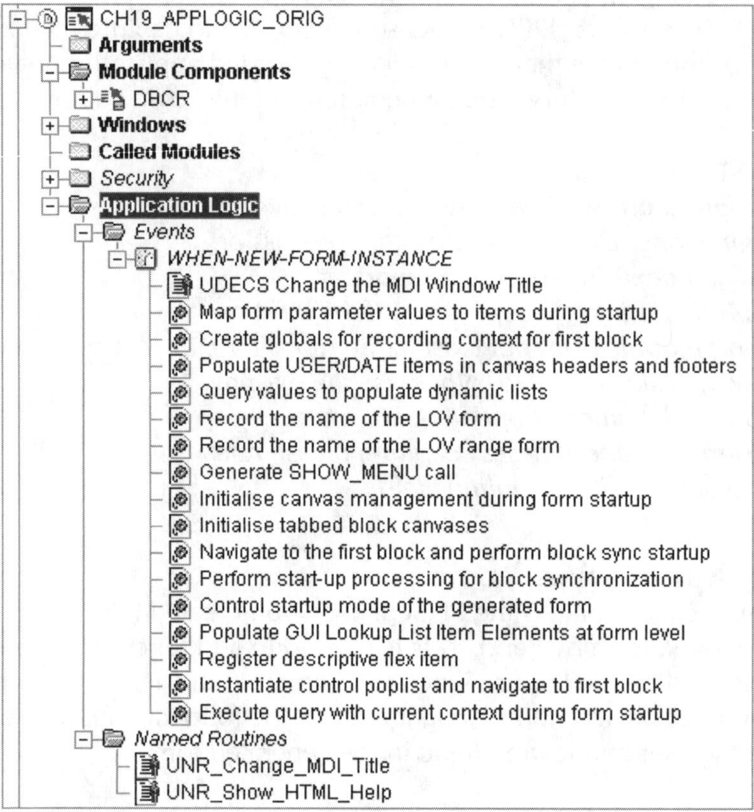

- *User-named routines* The PL/SQL program units (packages, procedures, and functions) that contain the actual PL/SQL code generated into forms. User-named routines need to be called from the event code segments (form triggers). You do not have to create user-named routines in order to create event code segments. However, if you are following object-oriented coding principles, this is how you add user application logic into the generated forms in a structured manner. The previous illustration shows an example of two user-named routines:

- UNR_Change_MDI_Title (changes the MDI window title, called from the "UDECS Change MDI Window Title" event code segment in WHEN-NEW-FORM-INSTANCE event code)
- UNR_Show_HTML_Help (shows online help in HTML format)

Where Can the Application Logic Be Entered?

Oracle Designer allows us to enter the application logic in different locations:

- Template forms
- Object libraries
- Events in the repository (modules, module components, and items)
- PL/SQL libraries attached to the generated forms (in the repository, in the file)
- Database server

In order to answer the question of "Where should I store the application logic?" you need to understand what all the options are and how they work. We think it is worthwhile to review all of your choices one by one before discussing this controversial question.

How to Define Application Logic in Template Forms

You might want to create application logic in template forms to perform common functions in all the forms generated. However, you should never place the actual PL/SQL code in the template forms. If you do, you will have to either generate forms again or apply the changes to each generated form by hand when you need to change the template code. Instead of placing the code directly into the templates, you should place calls to PL/SQL procedures in libraries or, better yet, use the nested event handler library architecture that is used by many commercial template packages. For more information, please refer to Chapter 22.

User named routines (program units) created in the template forms are copied into the generated forms without a change. Forms Generator also copies the form level triggers from the template into the generated form. When copying form level triggers, the forms Generator scans the comments in the template trigger code to determine how to sequence the code found in the template and the standard generated code.

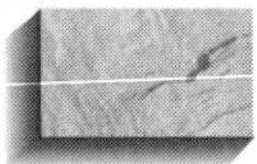

CAUTION

You cannot use subclassing for the form-level triggers in template forms. If a form-level trigger is subclassed from another form or object library, the Forms Generator will not create the code in the generated form.

How to Define Named Routines (Program Units) in Template Application Logic

1. Using the Form Builder, open your template form.
2. Create a new named routine (program unit). This could be a function, procedure, or package.
3. Add a comment such as /* CGAP$TEMPLATE_NAMED_ROUTINE */ to indicate that the program unit is part of template application logic, so that it is not captured into the repository when a generated form is captured into the repository. The comment text does not have to be exactly like this, as long as it is prefixed with CG$AP. For example, CGAP$TNR_TOOLBAR_ACTIONS is also valid.

   We don't want to capture the user named program units in the template forms because we maintain them in the template form at a single location, not in every module in the repository. You can also get an error message if you attempt to generate a program unit that exists in the template forms.
4. Finish entering the code for the program unit.
5. Save the changes you have made to the template form.

6. Generate a form, and try to capture it back to the repository. Check to see if your template named routine(s) is captured or not. If it is captured, make sure that you have entered the proper comments (as described in step 3) in your program units.

How to Define Event Code Segments (Triggers) in Template Application Logic

1. Using the Form Builder, open your template form.
2. Create a trigger at the form level, and enter the required code for your trigger.
3. Add one of the following comments above the code you have entered to specify how your template application logic code should be sequenced among with other generated code groups, user code groups, and the object library code groups:
   - /* CGAP$TES_SEQUENCE_BEFORE */ (if you want your code to execute *before* any other code groups that might be generated into the same trigger).
   - /* CGAP$TES_SEQUENCE_AFTER */ (if you want your code to execute *after* any other code groups that might be generated into the same trigger).

   If you forget to add one of these comments, the Forms Generator will assume that you want your code to be executed before and will add the /* CGAP$TES_SEQUENCE_BEFORE */ comment to your code.
4. Save the changes you have made to the template form.
5. Generate a form, and try to capture it back to the repository. Check to see if your template event segment(s) is captured or not. If it is captured, make sure that you have entered the proper comments (as described in step 3).

How to Define Application Logic in Object Libraries

If you need to associate some PL/SQL code with specific objects in the object library, you can define these against the objects stored in the object library. The Forms Generator will copy any code associated with the source/template object in the generated form when it uses that object.

1. Using the Form Builder, open your source form for your object library, if you have one. Refer to Chapter 22 for more information about maintaining the object libraries. If you are not using a source form for your object library, create a new form module as a temporary placeholder for the objects you want to edit from the object library.
2. Create a new object, or find the object to which you want to add event code segments (triggers). If you are not using a source library and want to edit one of the existing objects in the object library, drag the object from the object library into the temporary placeholder form.
3. Enter the required code for your trigger.
4. Add one of the following comments above the code you have entered to specify how your object library application logic code should be sequenced among with other generated code groups, user code groups, and the template application logic code groups:
   - /* CGAP$OLES_SEQUENCE_BEFORE */ (if you want your code to execute *before* any other code groups that might be generated into the same trigger).
   - /* CGAP$OLES_SEQUENCE_AFTER */ (if you want your code to execute *after* any other code groups that might be generated into the same trigger).

   If you forget to add one of these comments, the Forms Generator will assume that you want your code to be executed before and will add /* CGAP$OLES_SEQUENCE_BEFORE */ to your code.
5. If you are using a source form for your object library, save the changes you have made to the source form. Run the FORM2LIB utility to re-create your object library.
6. If you are *not* using a source form for your object library, drag the object back to the object library.

7. Generate a form, and try to capture it back to the repository. Check to see if your object library event segment(s) is captured or not. If it is captured, make sure that you have entered the proper comments (as described in step 4).

How to Define Application Logic in Generated Forms

One the most important features in release 2 is that you can directly enter PL/SQL code against a module in the repository before it is generated. If there is some special processing requirement that cannot be generated by the Forms Generator or cannot be placed in a library (because it is unique to a given form) then the application logic can be entered against the repository module elements.

How to Define a Named Routine in User Application Logic

1. In the Design Editor, switch to dialogs mode if you are not using the dialogs already.
2. Select the *Application Logic* node for the module, module component, or item (bound/unbound/action) that you wish to add the named routine.
3. Right-click, and from the pop-up menu, select *Create Named Routine.*
4. Once the Create Application Logic dialog box is displayed, enter the name and the type of routine (procedure, function, package specification, package body, or user-named trigger). The name you specify must be unique within the module, less than 30 characters long, and should not conflict with names reserved for generated routines (CG??$ routines).
5. Finish the dialog by choosing the *Create the definition and open the Logic Editor to enter the logic code* option.
6. Enter the code for the named routine in the Logic Editor.

CAUTION

When you enter application logic using the Logic Editor, the code you enter might cause the form not to compile during generation. Although the Logic Editor has a syntax checker, this does not compile the code against the PL/SQL engine in the Form Builder. If you are not entirely sure, generate the form first. Then enter the code in the Form Builder, compile it, debug it, and test it. Make sure that the code works and only then copy the code in the repository. Alternatively, you could use the Design Capture (formerly known as Reverse Engineering) features of the Forms Generator to capture the code in the repository. Figure 23-5 outlines the process of adding application logic into the repository.

How to Define an Event Code Segment in User Application Logic

1. In the Design Editor, switch to dialogs mode if you are not using the dialogs already.
2. Expand the *Application Logic* node for the module, module component, or item (bound/unbound/action) that you wish to add the event code segment.
3. Expand the *Events* node.
4. If the event for which you want to add code already exists, select the event, right-click and select *Add Logic* from the pop-up menu. Skip to step 8 in this procedure.
5. If the event for which you want to add code does not exist already, right-click and select *Create Event* from the pop-up menu.
6. Once the Create Application Logic dialog box is displayed, select the event type you want to create.

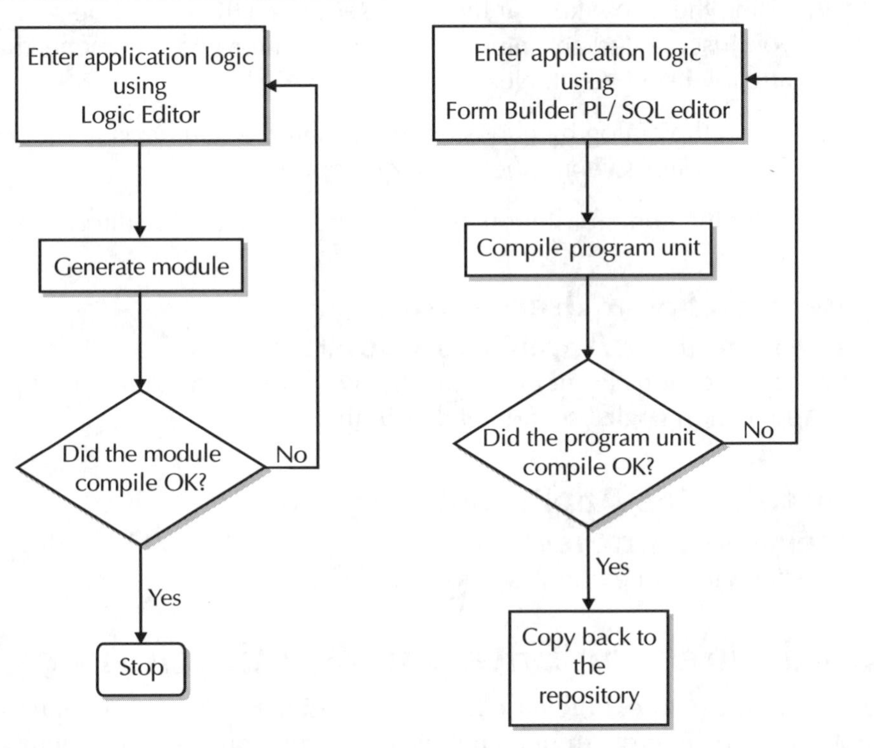

FIGURE 23-5. *Adding application logic in the repository*

7. Specify the *Execution Style* property:

   - **Override** To have the current trigger fire instead of any trigger by the same name at any higher scope
   - **Before** To have the current trigger fire before firing the same trigger at the next-higher scope
   - **After** To have the current trigger fire after firing the same trigger at the next-higher scope

   Then click Next.

8. Enter a description for the event code logic you want to create. You should enter a useful description of the functionality you are about to enter.

9. Using the arrow keys at the right, sequence the user code segment you just created among the Forms Generator code segments that are already listed. Click Next.
10. Finish the dialog by choosing the *Create the definition and open the Logic Editor to enter the logic code* option.
11. Enter the code for your named routine in the Logic Editor.

How to Define a User-Named Trigger in User Application Logic

Follow the directions listed under the "How to Define a Named Routine in User Application Logic" section earlier in this chapter.

How to Define Application Logic in Generated Libraries

See the "Library Generation" section later in this chapter.

Guidelines for Entering Application Logic

As mentioned before, in release 2, Oracle Designer allows us to enter the application logic in different locations. In the previous releases, there were only two places to enter application code: templates and libraries. Under these constraints, we developed some complex and flexible template/library architectures (such as the event-driven nested library architecture mentioned in Chapter 22) that optimized the use of templates and libraries and minimized the maintenance impact.

Now, we have many more options to juggle with than we had before, and we have to figure out the best strategy to take advantage of the new features. When deciding where to enter the application logic, you should consider the following:

- **Ease of Maintenance** One of your main goals should be to generate systems that are easy to maintain. No system is ever perfect, and every system needs maintenance. It is much easier to maintain the code if it is in named routines stored in PL/SQL libraries or the database server because when the code changes, the form does not need to be generated again. Therefore, you should avoid putting the actual PL/SQL code in the event code segments that are generated into the forms. Instead, place calls to named routines that are placed in PL/SQL libraries or the database server.

- **Performance** The generated systems should perform at an acceptable level. In client/server applications, network traffic between the client form and the database server is crucial to the system's performance. In order to minimize the network traffic, data oriented routines, which access database to read and write data, should be placed in the database server.
- **Feasibility** Sometimes it may not be feasible to enter a particular piece of code in some of the possible locations listed here. For example, it is not possible to enter block-level event codes in the template form.
- **Documentation and impact analysis** This is also very crucial for system maintenance. Ideally, if the entire application could be stored in the same place, performing an impact analysis would be very easy. However, we all know that this is not practical. Some may argue that if the application logic is stored in the repository, it is better documented. Some may argue otherwise. We believe in a repository-based development environment, with the preferred method being to store as much as possible in the repository.

Keeping these goals in mind, Figure 23-6 shows where the application logic should be entered. As you can see from the figure:

- Events (triggers) should only call named routines in the database server or in PL/SQL libraries attached to the generated form through the either template form, module network, or MODLIB preference. A good architecture for library design is the *Event Driven Nested Library Architecture* used by many commercial template packages. For more information about how to design your library architecture, refer to Chapter 22.
- User-named routines should be included in PL/SQL libraries or database server. If a routine accesses a database, it should be created in the database to minimize the network traffic.

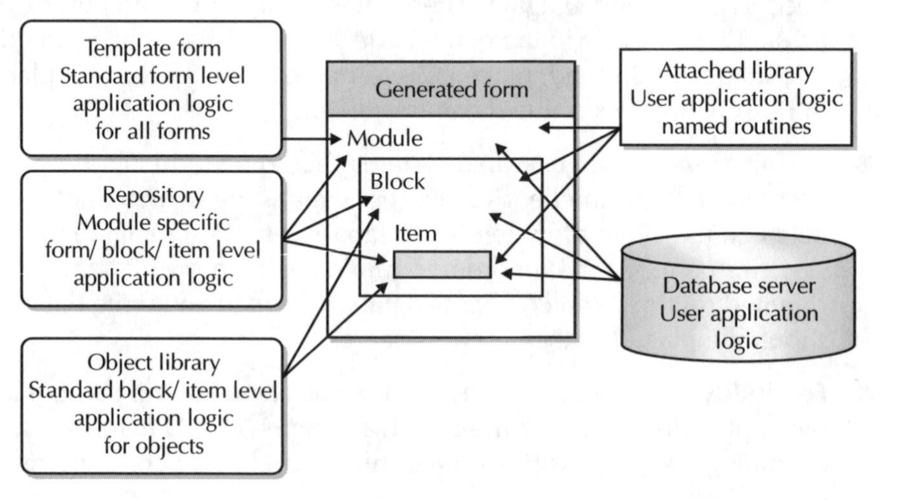

FIGURE 23-6. *Where to enter application logic*

- If the event code is going to be included in every form:
  - **Form-level events** These should be entered in the template form instead of entered against every module. Note that form-level code cannot be subclassed from an object library, because form itself cannot be subclassed.
  - **Block- and item-level events** These should be entered in the object library instead of entered against module components and items in every module.
- If the event code is going to be included only in some of the forms:
  - **Form-, block-, and item-level events** These need to be entered against modules, module components, and items.

Table 23-1 summarizes the advantages and disadvantages of each option. The best solution will probably be a hybrid solution.

Application Logic Defined In	Advantages	Disadvantages
Template forms	Standard form-level triggers; common to all generated forms; can be easily defined.	Only code stubs should be created in templates. Actual code needs to be placed in libraries.
Object libraries	Standard logic for a specific object (the object can be one of the standard source objects as well).	Code is scattered around. Difficult to maintain and to do an impact analysis.
Repository module definitions	Module-specific logic. Documented in the repository, support for better impact analysis.	
Attached PL/SQL libraries	User application logic common to more than one module. Code is in a single location. Easier to review and modify.	Cannot use ":" notation to reference form objects. If the code in libraries is not stored in repository, difficult to do an impact analysis.
Database	Perfect for routines accessing the database.	

TABLE 23-1. *Where to Enter the Application Logic*

Library Generation

One of the new features in release 2 of Oracle Designer is the ability to generate PL/SQL libraries. Similar to the Forms Generator, the Library Generator can generate Oracle Developer Library modules from the module definitions in the repository. The Library Generator can also capture existing Oracle Developer PL/SQL Library modules into the repository.

PL/SQL library modules are collections of PL/SQL program units such as functions, procedures, and packages. They can be used to store client-side application logic and to share them among multiple applications. Libraries can be attached to modules or to other libraries. Once a library is attached to a module, that module can reference the program units in the library.

All Oracle Developer modules can use a generated Oracle Developer Library module, unless it contains forms-, reports-, or graphics-specific built-in programs. The *Language* property of a library module can be used to specify whether a library is common or specific to forms, for example. The Library Generator uses this property to determine the proper compiler to use (for example, Form Builder compiler versus Report Builder compiler).

How to Create Library Modules

1. Create a new repository module of type *Library.*
2. Set the *Language* property of the module to
   - **Forms**, if the library will contain calls to Form Builder built-ins
   - **Reports**, if the library will contain calls to Report Builder built-ins
   - **Common Library**, if the library will not contain any calls to either Form Builder or Report Builder built-ins
3. Specify whether the code for the library module is recorded in the repository or outside the repository.
4. If the library code will be stored in the repository you will need to do the following:
   a. Set the *Source Code for the Library* property to **Repository** (as illustrated next), if you are using the dialogs.

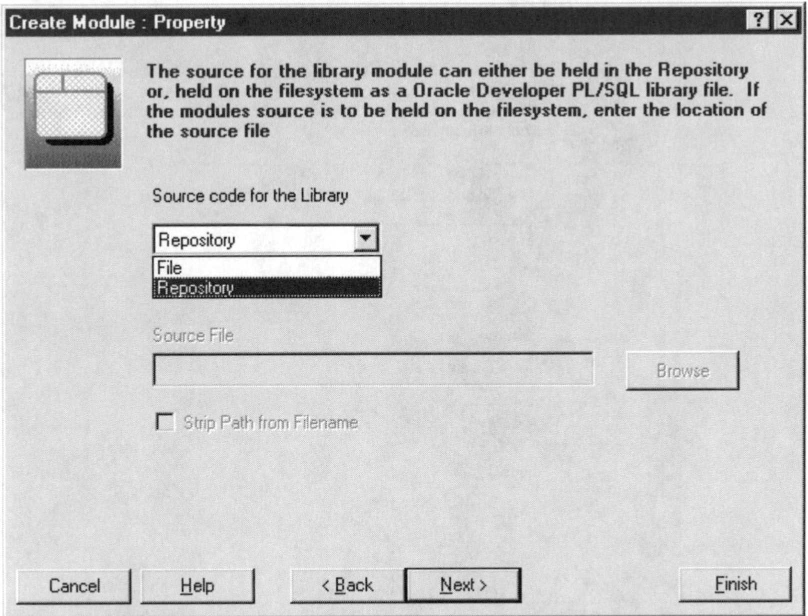

b. Leave the *Source File* property of the library module blank, if you are using the Property Palette.

c. Enter and edit the code required using the Logic Editor.

5. If the code is stored outside of the repository on the file system, you will need to do the following:

   a. Set the *Source Code for the Library* property to **File** if you are using the dialogs, as shown in the next illustration:

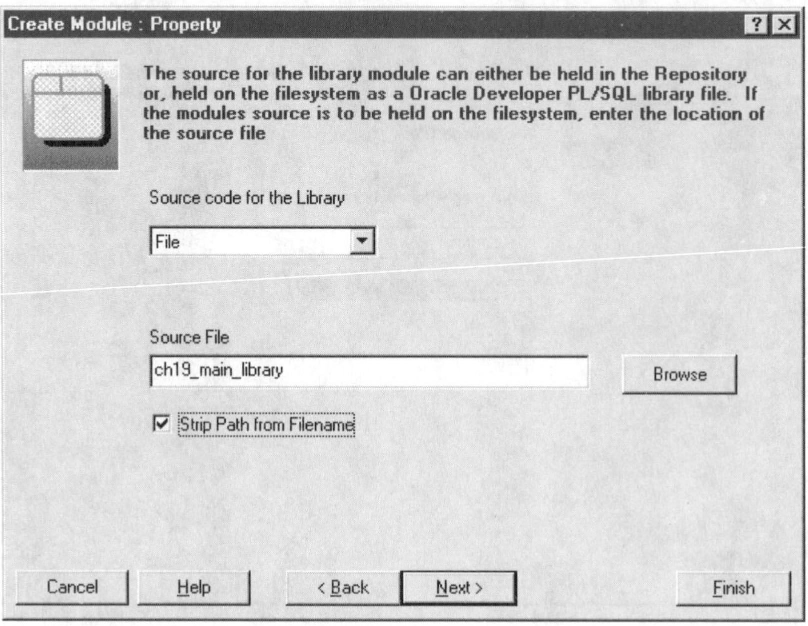

b. Set the *Source File* property of the library module to the name of the Oracle Developer file. When entering the source path, enter only the filename, and, to avoid hard coding of the path information, do not include any directory information. Use the registry variables (FORMS50_PATH, REPORTS30_PATH, and ORACLE_PATH) to locate the file.

c. Enter and edit the code required in the library using the Form Builder.

How to Attach Library Modules to Other Modules

There are a few different ways to attach libraries to other modules:

- Use the module network to link one or more library module(s) to another module. Make sure that the library language is proper for the attaching module. For example, do not attach a Reports Library to a Forms Module. Also, remember libraries can be attached to other libraries as well.
- Attach the libraries to a template form to inherit the library attachments from the template form. All of the libraries attached to a template form will be attached to generated forms that use the same template.
- Use the *Form Library Attachment → Module specific library attachment (MODLIB)* preference to attach a *single* library module. This is not the recommended way because this preference will be obsolete in future releases. In addition, the Forms Generator will attach the libraries specified in a module network or attached to a form before attaching the library specified by this module.

How to Generate Library Modules

There are two ways to generate Oracle Developer Library modules:

- Run the Library Generator to generate specific library modules.
- Run the Form or Report Generator and run the Library Generator to generate any attached libraries. In order to generate attached libraries, check the *Generate Attached Libraries* checkbox before you generate a module, as illustrated next. The attached libraries will be generated if they have the same language as the module being generated or if they are Oracle Developer Common Libraries.

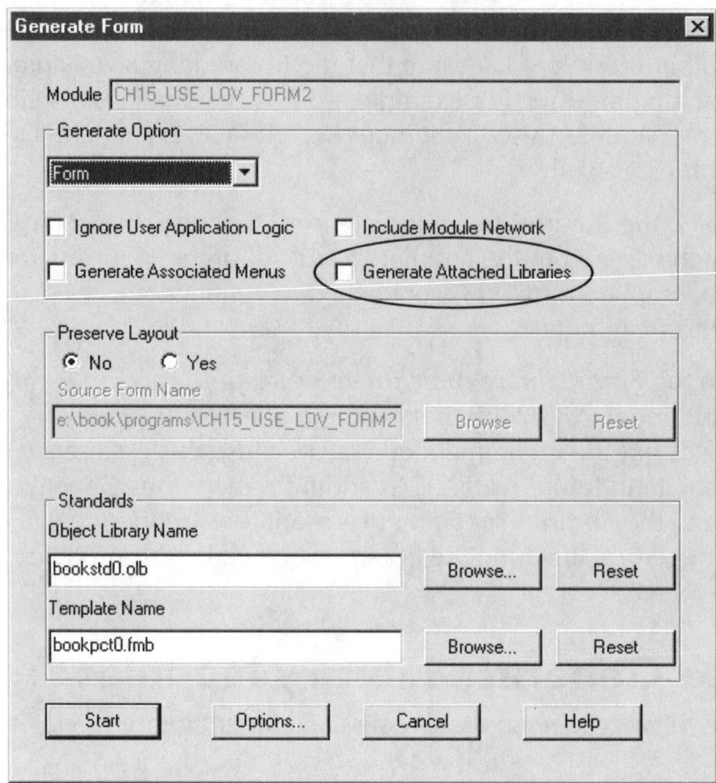

Before you generate libraries, make sure to customize the following options by selecting Options → Generate Options → Library from the menu as shown next, and filling in the following:

1. The destination of generated PLL files (portable library source files).
2. Whether a PLD file (text version of the generated library file) needs to be created, and where it should be placed.
3. Whether the generated library needs to be compiled to create a PLX file for distribution. PLX files are platform specific (much like FMX or MMX files) and only contain the executable code; hence, they are smaller.
4. A connect string.

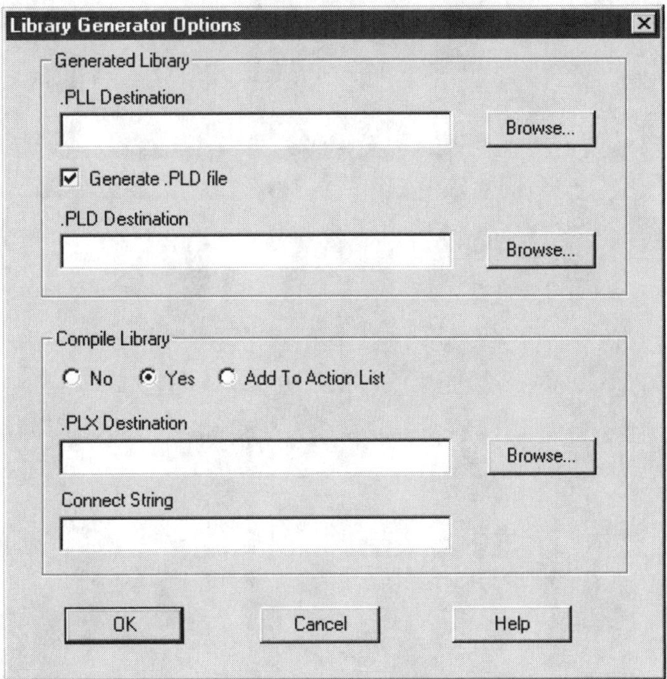

Library Generation Troubleshooting Guideline

Problem	Resolution
I cannot generate a library module—the system hangs.	Make sure to specify the correct connect string in the following format: <username>/<password>@<data-base_alias>.

CHAPTER 24

Help Generation

nline help is a very important part of all applications. The design, content, and quality of the help system can have a significant impact on the acceptance of an application. In this chapter, we will discuss the two types of help systems that Oracle Designer supports, including

- MS Help system generation
  - What is the MS Help generator?
  - The repository sources of help information
  - The procedure for defining and generating the MS Help system
  - A "how to" guide to additional help features
  - MS Help generation troubleshooting and tips guide
- Form-based Help system generation
  - What is the Form-based Help system?
  - Form-based Help design decisions
  - Form-based Help generation tasks
  - The structure of the help table
  - Repository Information that affects Form-based Help system
  - Form-based Help generation troubleshooting guide

Introduction to Oracle Designer Help Generation

Oracle Designer Help generation is the creation of context-sensitive online help. The two types of help are hint text and multiline help text.

Hint text is the item-level information that is displayed on the status line of the root window. The actual text is generated from the *Hint* property of bound or unbound items. Refer to the "Column Properties Used as Bound Item Defaults" section in Chapter 11 for more information on hint text.

Multiline help text is much more detailed than hint text in both content and scope. In this type of help system, you can include help for modules, module components, item groups, and items. The MS Help system and the form-based help system are examples of multi-line help text.

The MS Help system uses application help text files stored in MS Help format. The MS Help generator creates these files for you. Calls to these files are then integrated into the generated forms by the Form Generator. This is the best type of help to use when you are implementing the application on MS platforms.

The form-based help system uses a table stored in the database that contains all of the help for the application. The generator inserts information into this table based on repository definitions. The Form Generator then builds select statements against this table to derive the help for the application. This type of help system can be used when you are implementing systems on non-MS platforms such as Motif or on Internet browsers.

Microsoft(MS) Help System Generation

The first type of help system we will cover is the Microsoft (MS) Help system.

What Is the MS Help Generator?

The MS Help generator creates MS Help files used by the Windows Help system based on repository definitions. This generator is quite simple to use once the design of the help system has been determined. We will address this topic later in this chapter. The remainder of this section will provide you with an overview of the MS Help system and design alternatives for using it.

Description and Overview of the Windows Help System

The Windows Help system is the standard, online help provided with most Windows-compatible products. It is comprised of one or more help files (.HLP) that are accessible by many different products or applications. The help system is organized into different categories for easier and faster access to the information. You can start up the Windows Help system as a stand-alone system by searching for .HLP files in Windows Explorer and double-clicking on one of the files. You will then see the standard Help window for the information you selected.

Windows Help System Features

The MS Help system has a number of features that a developer can choose to implement. In the remainder of this section, we will present a brief definition of each of these features.

TOPIC A topic is text and/or graphic information contained in one page. The Windows Help system is comprised of a hierarchy of topics. Each topic can have hypertext links to related topics as well. Topics are accessible from the Index button in the Help Topics window within the help system.

POP-UP WINDOWS A pop-up window is a separate window containing additional information (usually definitions) that is activated via a hypertext link from within a window of topic information.

CONTENTS TOPIC The Contents Topic is a nested structure linked to all of the topics in the help system, very similar to a table of contents of a book. The Contents Topic is accessible from the Contents button in the Help Topics window within the help system.

KEYWORDS Keywords provide an index of words similar to the index of a book. Selecting a keyword brings up all the topics that contain that keyword. The Find button in the Help Topics window within the help system is where you specify a keyword and navigate to a topic.

GLOSSARY The glossary is a listing of words, terms, and associated definitions. The glossary is usually accessible from a button from within a topic window.

BROWSE BUTTONS Browse buttons allow you navigate forward and backward within a topic window. These buttons will navigate you to the next or previous topic page in the order of information allowing you to page through topics as you would with a book. The sequence of topics is the same sequence you will find in the Contents Topic window.

OPENING WINDOWS HELP There are several ways to open the Windows Help system. The Help menu option and a Help icon, if available, will start the Windows Help system and bring you to the Help Topics window. The F1 key will bring up content-sensitive help pertaining to the object where the cursor is currently located.

Example Screen from Generated MS Help System

The following illustration is an example screen from a generated MS Help system.

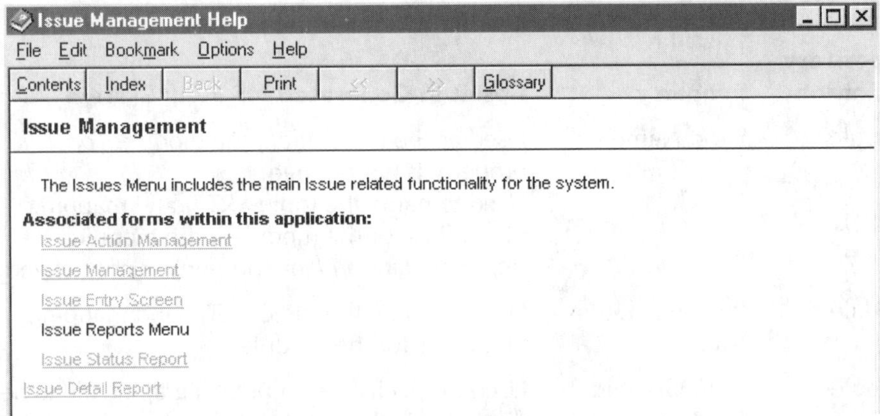

Source of Help Information

The source of information in the generated help systems comes directly from repository properties. Table 24-1 is a listing of the all of the repository items that will be used by the MS Help generator to create the help system.

Repository Definition	Property	Result in Generated MS Help System
Module	Help File Name	The name of a project file (<file_name>.hpj) and the compiled help file (<file_name>.hlp).
Module	Help Context ID Prefix	Used in context-sensitive help to map the module to the correct textual description.
Module	Top Title	If this is the top-level module of the help system, the property sets The help file title in the generated help file The content topics title at the top of the Contents Topic page The title beneath the Help icon on the windows desktop If this is not the top-level module, this property sets The hypertext link from the Contents Topic page

TABLE 24-1. *Repository Definitions Used in the MS Help System*

Repository Definition	Property	Result in Generated MS Help System
Module	Short Name	Used as the topic title if the module *Top Title* property is not defined. Used to name the topic (.RTF) and mapping (.HM) files for the module if the module *Implementation Name* property is not defined.
Module	Implementation Name	Used to name the topic (.RTF) and mapping (.hm) files for the module.
Module	Help Graphic File Name	Used to specify the name of a graphic file to be displayed in the nonscrolling area at the top of the Content and Module Topic pages, depending on the level of the module.
Module	User/Help Text	Used as topic text and generated keywords. If this is a top-level module, the text appears as the help file introduction on the Contents Topic page.
Module Component	Title	Used for the topic title or heading for module component help text and generated keywords. If this property is not defined, the module component *Name* property is used.
Module Component	Name	Used as the topic title or heading for module component help text and generated keywords if the module component *Title* property is not defined.
Module Component	Help Context ID Prefix	Used in context-sensitive help to map the module component to the correct textual description.
Module Component	User/Help Text	Used as topic text and generated keywords.
Item Group	Prompt	Used for the topic title or the heading for item group help text and generated keywords.

TABLE 24-1. *Repository Definitions Used in the MS Help System* (continued)

Repository Definition	Property	Result in Generated MS Help System
Item Group	Name	Used for the topic title or the heading of the item group help text and generated keywords if the item group *Prompt* property is not defined.
Item Group	User/Help Text	Used as topic text and generated keywords.
Item Group	Stacked ?	If the item group is set as a stacked item group, then a topic help page can be created for the Item Group, depending on *New topic for each item group* (IGPLCT) preference.
Item	Prompt	Used as the topic heading for item help text and generated keywords.
Item	Name	Used as the topic heading for item help text and generated keywords if item *Prompt* Property is not defined.
Item	User/Help Text	Used for topic text and generated keywords.

TABLE 24-1. *Repository Definitions Used in the MS Help System* (continued)

Procedure for Defining and Generating MS Help

Creating MS Help for an application is simply a matter of performing the correct tasks at the appropriate time. In this section, we define a high-level procedure for completing this task. This procedure is based on a procedure available in the online help, which covers MS Help generation very well. We have also included a detailed example so that you can see how these steps can be applied to an application system.

1. Tell Designer to Generate an MS Help Type Help System.

You will need to tell Designer to generate an MS Help type help system (as opposed to a Forms-based Help system). Do this by setting the *End User Interface* → *Type of Help System Used (HLPTYP)* preference to **MS Help**.

This is the default setting, but you should probably make sure it is set correctly before you begin.

2. Generate Your Application System First.

Generate your application system prior to generating the help system. By doing this, you will have a much better understanding of what information will be in the help system. However, you should still enter help information into the system as it is gathered throughout the lifecycle of project. This is important, because you will have to regenerate your application system to implement MS Help. If you wait too long to define your help system, it may cause your project to be delayed.

3. Set the MS Help Generator Options.

The MS Help generator requires some information to function properly. Specifically, it needs to know

- Where to put the generated help files
- The name of the help compiler
- The name of the help executable (viewer)

You can specify this information by navigating to *Options → Generation Options → Help System*. The dialog that you will use to collect this information is shown here. The settings used to create the help system in this example are shown on this dialog.

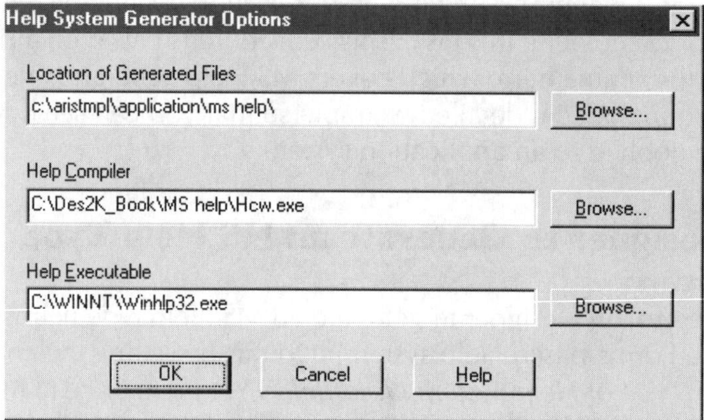

LOCATION OF GENERATED FILES It is important to specify where you would like the generated output to be placed, because the default is Designer's working directory, which is determined by the directory specified on the start-in property of the Designer icon. If you have not changed it, its value is <oracle_home>\bin, which is probably not a good place to generate your help files. You can use the *Location of Generated Files* property to control where the help files will be created. In our example, we set the *Location of Generated Files* property to **c:\aristmpl\application\ms help**.

HELP COMPILER The MS Help generator doesn't create the executable help file (.HLP). It generates three source files that are used to create the executable help file. The names of these three files are the mapping (.HM) file, the help topic (.RTF) file, and the project (.HPJ) file. The most important file to the help compiler is the project file. It contains the name of the mapping and help topic files along with options, configuration, and Windows-specific information.

You will need to specify which help compiler you would like to use to create the help executable from the generated files. The name of the help compiler will vary, depending on the operating system you are using. Some of the compilers for Windows NT and Windows 95 are HCP.EXE, HC31.EXE, HC.EXE and HCW.EXE. To make sure you choose the correct compiler, use Windows Explorer to determine which executables exist on your operating system. If you don't find one, you can download one from Microsoft's Web site. In this example, we set the *Help Compiler* property to **c:\Des2k_Book\MS help\Hcw.exe**.

CAUTION
Most compilers will require one or more DLL to work properly. A commonly used DLL is HWDLL.DLL. If you are downloading a help compiler, be sure that you also get the appropriate DLL(s).

HELP EXECUTABLE (VIEWER) The name of the help executable that you specify will determine the application that will be used to view the generated help system. Typically you will use WINHELP.EXE or WINHLP32.EXE. To make sure you choose the correct viewer, use Windows Explorer to determine which executables exist on your operating system. In this example, we set the *Help Executable* property to **C:\WINNT\Winhlp32.exe**.

4. Plan the Help System.

You can design your help system to use one of the following architectures:

- One help file for the entire application
- One help file for each subsystem in the application
- One help file per module

To determine which architecture is best for your application, you will need to spend some time analyzing the module network of your application. Looking at the module network, you will be able to determine the hierarchy of your application modules, which should direct you toward one of the architectures. The module hierarchy in our sample application is shown in the following illustration. Based on this hierarchy, we decided to use one help file for each subsystem in the application.

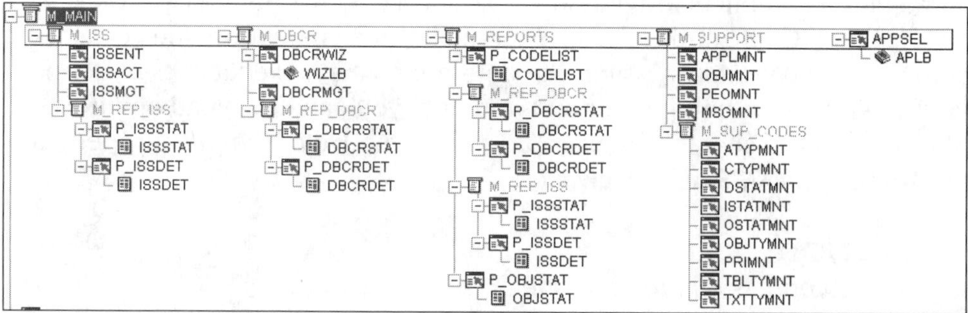

5. Name the Help Files.

Once you have determined the architecture of your help system, you need to specify a name for your help files. Help files will be created for each module in the network that has a value in the *Help File Name* property, unless there is a higher level module in the hierarchy with the same *Help File Name.* Any subordinate modules in that hierarchy will be included in the help file of the next highest level module if the *Help File Name* property is either set to the same value as the parent or is null.

In our example, we created five separate help files, one for each subsystem in the application. Table 24-2 shows the top-level modules and the names used for the help files.

6. Define the Content of the Help System.

Populate the *User/Help Text* property of each module definition, module component, item group, and item in your application for which you want to make help available. You can do this by using the Properties Palette or the Module Diagrammer. It might be useful to refer to Table 24-1 when completing this task to gain a better understanding of which repository properties will be used in the generated help system. A sample of the help text entered for a module is shown here:

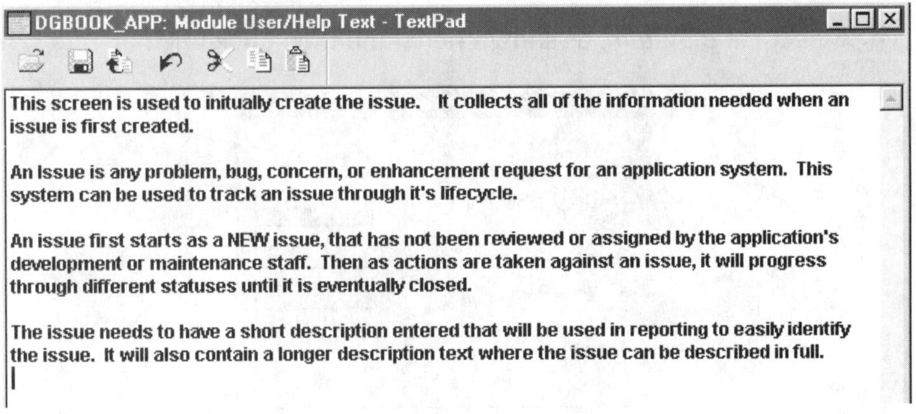

Module Name	Help Filename
M_ISS	ISSUE
M_DBCR	DBCR
M_REPORTS	REPORTS
M_SUPPORT	SUPPORT
M_SUP_CODES	CODE

TABLE 24-2. *Help Filenames*

7. Generate MS Help Source Files.

In order to generate the MS Help source files, perform the following steps:

1. Determine the scope of your generation. Are you generating the help system for your entire application, a subsystem, or a module? This step is important because it will determine which module you should navigate to and how many times you will need to repeat this process to generate all of the content of the help system.
2. Navigate to the top module that will be used to create a project file (.HPJ). This should correspond to the module(s) that you defined the *Help File Name* property for in step 4, "Plan the Help System."
3. Select *Generate* → *Generate Module As* from the main menu.
4. Select *Help System*, as shown here, and then click OK.

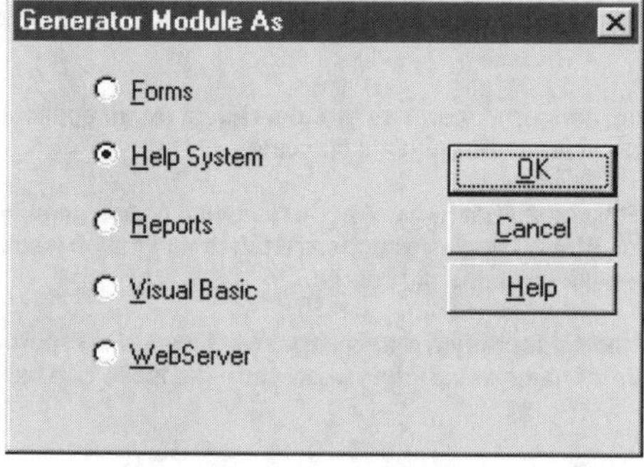

5. Set the scope of the generation. Using this dialog, shown next, you can generate the source files for the module specified by selecting the *Generate all the MS Help source files* radio button. You can also choose to generate the source files for each of the modules that are subordinate to this module in the application hierarchy by selecting the *Include the module network in this help system* checkbox. You have one other option. You can choose to only update the project file for this module by selecting the *Only generate the topic (.RTF) file and the mapping (.HM) files* radio button. MS Help generator does not use the other options on this dialog.

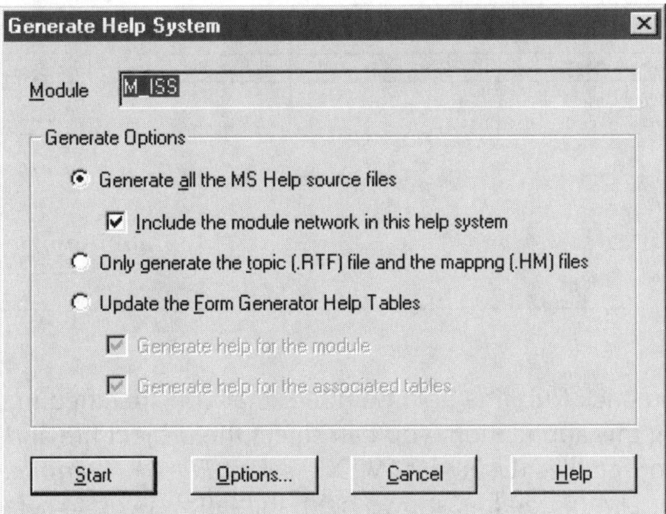

6. Generate. Numerous topic, mapping, and glossary files will be created during this process. However, there should only be one project file per generation.

8. Compile MS Help Source Files.

The MS Help generator does not create a compiled help system. It creates three different types of files that need to be compiled after generation. These files include.

- Project file (.HPJ) Only one per generation
- Topic file (.RTF) One per module
- Mapping file (.HM) One per module

You can, however, compile the source files immediately following generation. Right after you have generated the help source files but before you have dismissed Message Window, select *Messages → Build Actions.* This will launch the Build Action dialog, shown next, that can be used to compile the source files and then run the compiled help file.

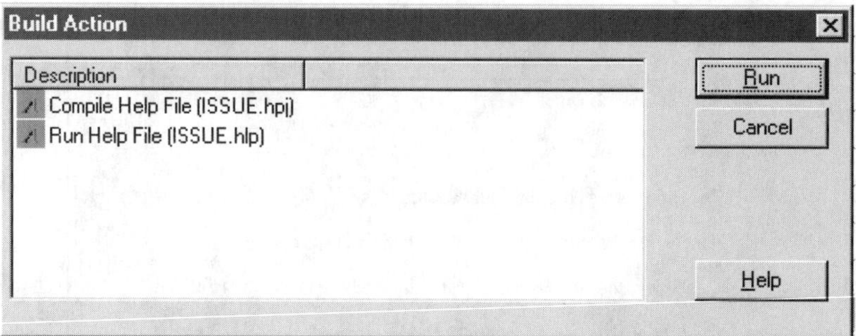

When you click Run, the help compiler that you specified in step 2 will be run. Using this application, you can select the project file and then select the project source files. Using HCW.EXE, select *File → Compile*. You are then presented with a dialog, shown next, that allows you to select a project file to compile. Select the project file and then click Compile. This will create a help file (.HLP) with the same name as the project file.

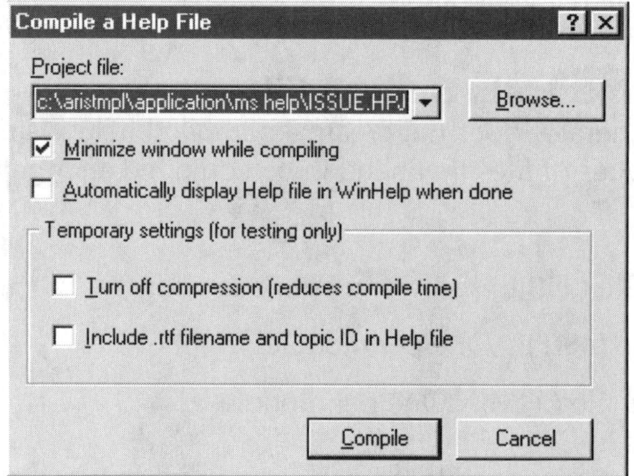

You also have the option of compiling the help source files outside of Designer. To do this, run the help compiler application and compile the project files as just described.

9. Run and Check Generated Help.

After you have created the help file, run it. Review its contents, checking for completeness and accuracy. There are many ways you can do this. Some of your choices include running the help file from the build actions dialog, running the help file from the Windows Help viewer executable, or simply running the help file directly.

10. Integrate the Help System into Your Application.

Once you have tested the help system, the last step is to integrate it into your application. For a Forms application, do the following:

1. Make sure the *End User Interface →Type of Help System Used (HLPTYP)* is set to **MSHELP**. It is best to set this preference at the application level.
2. Make sure that the HELPFILE_PATH environment variable is set to the location of the help files.
3. Generate each form module in your application system.

Enhancing the Help System

This section explains how to add some features that can enhance your help system. Each feature is defined, and a procedure for how to implement each feature is included.

Add Glossary Terms

Glossary terms add additional reference information to your help system. When a glossary term is selected, the definition of the term is displayed in a pop-up window. To add glossary terms, follow these steps:

1. Open the Repository Object Navigator (RON)
2. Navigate to the *Reference Data Definition → Business Terminology* node. Create a new business terminology definition by clicking the Create icon.

3. The value you specify for the *Name* property will be the name of the glossary item in the help file. The text that you enter into the *Comment* property will be the text displayed in the pop-up window when the glossary item is selected.

4. Generate all of the help source files.

Add Extra Keywords

You can add extra keywords to any repository item that has help text, including module definitions, module components, item groups, and items. These extra keywords can enhance the overall search capabilities of your help system. To add extra keywords, follow these steps:

1. Open the Design Editor.

2. Navigate to the repository item that requires keywords.

3. View the contents of the *User/Help Text* property in an editor.

4. Immediately following the help text, add extra keywords. Each additional keyword must by prefixed with @@. An example is shown here:

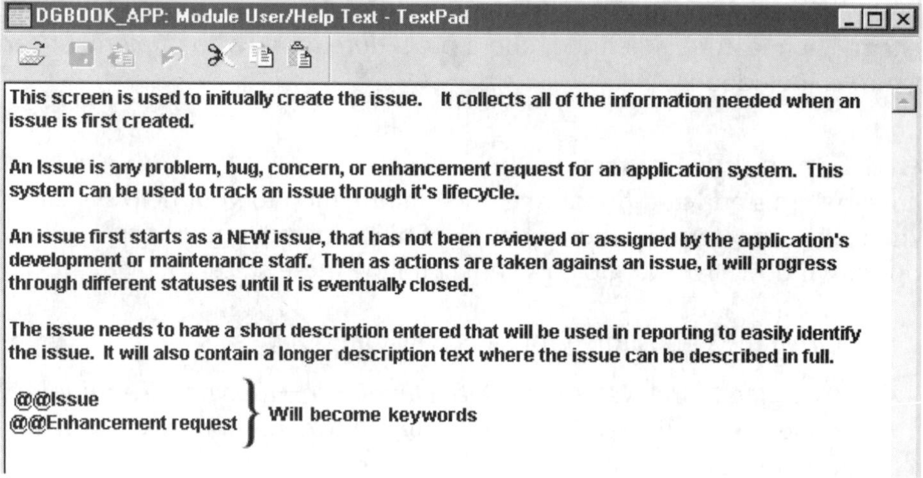

5. Generate the modules topic and mapping files.

Add Graphics to the Help Systems (Illustrate Module Topics)

You can illustrate each module topic with a graphic by simply specifying the graphic name and location. You can incorporate three different types of graphics in your help system: bitmaps (.BMP), Windows metafiles (.WMF), or multiresolution bitmaps (.MRB). To add a graphic to a module topic, follow these steps:

1. Open Design Editor.
2. Navigate to the module definition that requires the graphic.
3. Using the Properties Palette, populate the *Help Graphic File Name* property with the name of the graphic to be used. Do not include the location of the graphic.
4. Edit the Generator Preferences. Be sure to choose the Help Generator as the product.
5. Set the *General → Graphics Locations (GRHLOC)* preference to the location where the graphics for the help system are located. This preference can only be set at the application level, so you will need to put all of the graphics files that are to be included in the help system in the same location.
6. Generate the modules topic and mapping files.

Add a Unique Context ID Prefix

If you plan on sharing modules or module components between application systems, you should consider adding a unique context ID prefix to the items that will be shared between systems. The MS Help generator creates context IDs when creating the help source files. Each item is assigned a context ID that will be used to link the application item to their help file descriptions. When a module or reusable module component is used in more than one application, it is possible that it will not be assigned a unique context ID for each application. By adding the context prefix, you can be sure that item will be uniquely identified and will be displayed correctly in the context sensitive help. To add a context ID prefix, follow these steps:

1. Open the Design Editor.

2. Navigate to the module or reusable module component that requires the context-sensitive help.
3. Using the Properties Palette, populate the *Help Context ID Prefix* property with a unique value of up to three digits. There is no validation on this property that will tell you that the number you have entered is already in use, so there may be some trial and error.
4. Generate the modules topic and mapping files.

Customize Topic Structure (*LCT Preferences)

Depending on the size and complexity of the modules in your application, you may want to consider customizing the topic structure used in your help system. By default, each module and module component is contained in its own topic file. In instances where you have very small, simple modules, you might want to consider placing all of the module components in the same topic as the module. Likewise, when you have large, complex modules, you may want to break out each module component and item group for clarity.

There are two preferences that can help you make these decisions. The first preference controls the topic structure for module components, *Topic Structure → New Topic for each Module Component (TUPLCT).* The settings for this preference are described in Table 24-3.

The second preference controls the topic structure for item groups, *Topic Structure → New Topic for each Item Group (IGPLCT).* The settings for this preference are described in Table 24-4.

Setting	Description
Always	A new topic is created for each module component.
More than One (Default Setting)	If there is more than one module component, a new topic is created for each module component. If there is only one module component, it will be described in the module topic.
Never	A single topic is created for the module and all of the module components.

TABLE 24-3. *Settings of the TUPLCT Preference*

Setting	Description
Always	A new topic is created for each item group.
More than One	A new topic is created for each stacked item group. Item groups that are not stacked will be described in the module component topic.
Never (Default Setting)	Each item group is described in the module component topic.

TABLE 24-4. *Settings of the IGPLCT Preference*

Customize Hyperlink Titles (*LTL Preferences)

You can customize the titles above the hypertext links in your help system. This allows you to tailor descriptions that will be meaningful to the users of the application system. The default values of these preferences are shown in Table 24-5. If you chose to change the default value, you can enter a descriptive title of up to 240 characters.

Level	Preference Name	Default Value
Module	Hyperlink Titles → Title for Module Hyperlinks (MODLTL)	Associated forms/reports within this application:
Module Component	Hyperlink Titles → Title for Module Component Hyperlinks (DTULTL)	This form consists of the following components:
Item Group	Hyperlink Titles → Title for Item Group Hyperlinks (GRPLTL)	This form consists of the following groups:
Item	Hyperlink Titles → Title for Item Hyperlinks (DCULTL)	This component consists of the following items:

TABLE 24-5. *LTL Preferences*

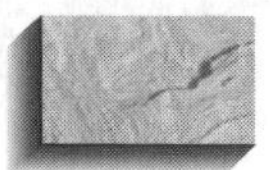

NOTE
*The LTL preference value in the repository is actually **DEFAULT**. The text in this column is what will appear in the generated help system.*

MS Help Generation Troubleshooting and Tips Guide

Problem	Solution
The graphics I have included are causing problems in my scrolling area.	The graphics will be displayed in the nonscrolling area of the module topic window. Try to keep the graphic small to leave plenty of room for the scrolling area.
I included some graphics to illustrate my help system and now it won't compile.	The size of a help text and graphic is limited to 64K. The larger the graphic, the less text will fit in this limit. If the 64K limit is exceeded, you will have problems with the compilation of the help file.
Each time I compile the help system, it does not appear in the location that I specified on the Help System Generation Option dialog.	If you compile the help system within Designer, the compiled help file is created in the start-in directory specified on the property sheet of the Oracle Designer icon, even if you've specified a location in the help system generation option dialog box.

Form-Based Help System Generation

Another option you have for generating a help system for your application is the Form-based Help system.

What Is the Form-Based Help System?

The Form-based Help system is just that: It is a help system that is based on forms alone. It does not use the MS Help system at all, and therefore can be used on platforms that cannot run the MS Help system.

This system is based on the following components:

- **A Help Table (CG_FORM_HELP)** The system uses a help table to store the context information from the *User/Help Text* property of the applications' Tables, Columns, Modules, Module Components, and Items.
- **A Help Display Form (OLGHLPF)** A help display form is provided with Designer that is used to display the help information.
- **Code Generated into the Forms to Call the Help Module** Code will be generated into the KEY-HELP trigger to call the help display form, passing it the context information needed to display the correct help.

This illustration is an example of the help display form:

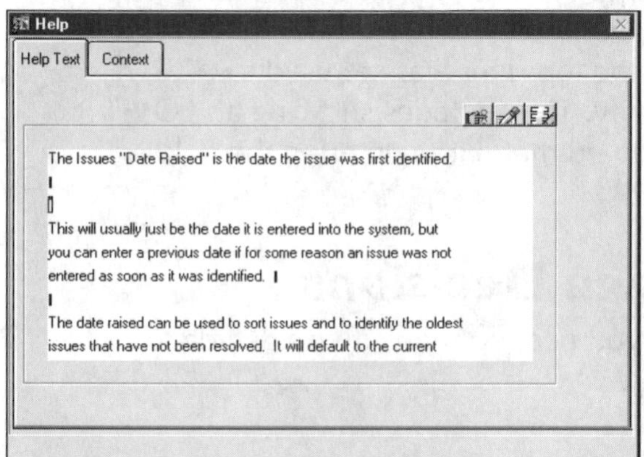

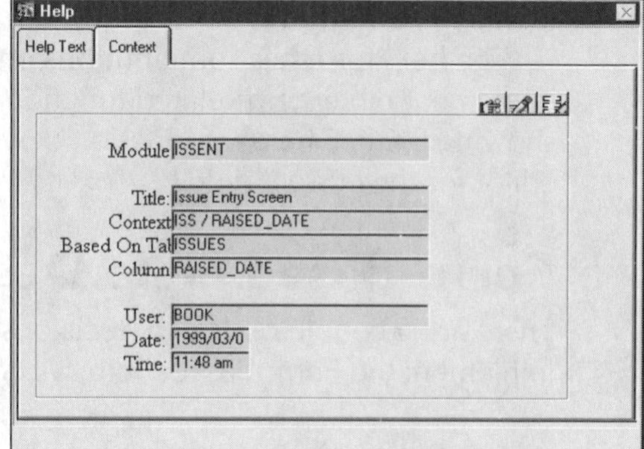

The help form has two tabs, as shown here. The first tab has the actual text of the help for the current context. The second tab displays some information about the context that the help was called for, including the item name, module name, module title, base column, and table.

The Functionality of the Form-Based Help System

In the generated application, when the user presses the Help key (usually F1), the help form illustrated above is displayed. The user's current context (block and item name) is passed to the help form. The help form uses this information to display the help for the closest context. For example, if there is *User/Help Text* recorded in the module definition for the item that the help form is called from, that text is displayed. If there is no *User/Help Text* entered for the bottom context level, the help at the next higher level is displayed. The hierarchy of help levels is

1. Module Help
2. Table Help
3. Module Component (Block) Help
4. Column Help
5. Item (Field) Help

The user can move through the hierarchy by pressing the Help key. For example, if the help form starts at the item level, the column help will be displayed when the user presses the Help key. If any levels do not have help defined, the form will show the next higher level.

The help form has some buttons on the top right that are used to implement other help-related functionality. This includes showing an LOV, showing the key help information (keyboard map), and entering the field editor for the current field.

Form-Based Help Design Decisions

There are a couple of design decisions you need to make if you decide to implement the Form-based Help system.

Scope of Help Table

You need to specify the scope of the help table that is used to store the context help. This is done by setting the *DBA → Scope of on-line help table (HPTABL)* preference. It can be set to one of the following values:

- **Single Table (GENERIC)** (Default) Will use a single table called CG_FORM_HELP, which is created to hold online help text for forms generated from all the application systems.
- **Application System Wide Table (APPSYS)** Will use a separate table for each application system named <application_system_name>_FORM_HELP.

The standard help form that is provided with Designer (OFGHLPF) assumes that this preference is set to **Single Table** and uses the CG_FORM_HELP table. If you decide to use a table for each application, you will have to modify this form and change every reference to CG_FORM_HELP to the correct name for the application system. If you are implementing help for multiple application systems, you will have to create a modified version of the form for each application system.

Modifications to Help Form

The help display form that is provided with Designer (OFGHLPF) can be used to display the context help. However, the design of this form may not fit into the overall design of your application, so you have the option of modifying this form to fit into your application better. Some of the modifications you might want to make are

- Change the colors and fonts to match your application standard.
- Change the window size, making it larger or smaller.
- Suppress the context tab (which is not really very useful).
- Enable the context level display (which is disabled in the default form).
- Remove the other help functionality buttons (LOV, Edit, etc.).

Form-Based Help Generation Tasks

This section details some tasks that you need to perform in order to generate and use the Form-based Help system.

Selecting Form-Based Help System Generation

In order to generate the Form-based Help system, you will need to set the *End User Interface → Type of Help System used* (HLPTYP) preference to **Forms popup (HELPFORM).** This tells the generator to populate the help table and to add a KEY-HELP trigger to the generated forms to call the help form. This preference should be set at the application level before any of the modules are generated. If modules have already been generated before this preference is set, you will need to generate them again.

Creating and Populating the Help Table

If you have set up your application to use the Form-based Help system (as we just detailed), then whenever you generate a module for the first time, the help information for that module will be generated into the help table. On subsequent generations, the help information is not updated.

NOTE
The generator uses the Module Generation History text to determine whether it should create the help text for a module. If there are any values in this property, the module help text is not generated.

In order to update the help information for your system, you will have to perform the following procedure for each module:

1. In the Design Editor, select the module for which you want to generate help.
2. Select *Generate → Generate Module As* from the Design Editor menu. You will see the following dialog:

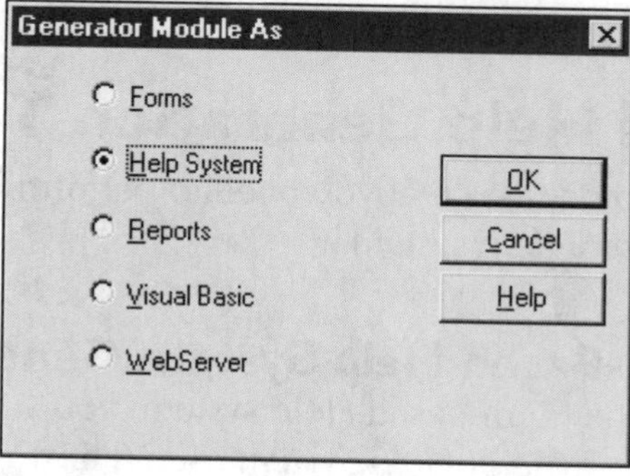

3. Select *Help System* and click the OK button. You will see the following dialog:

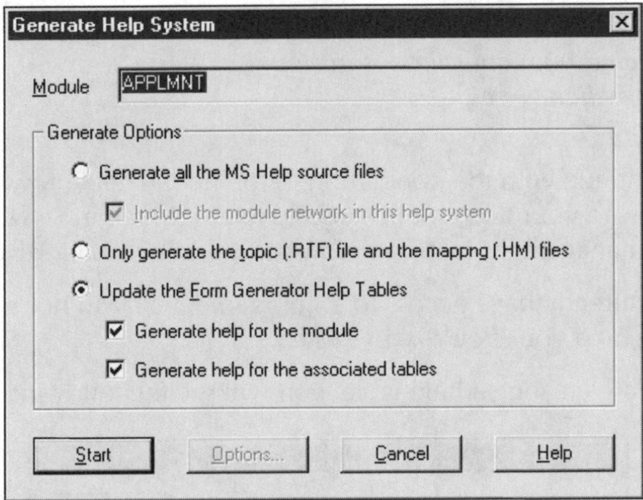

4. Select *Update the Form Generator Help Tables* and select one or both of the following options:

   - *Generate help for the module*   Generates the help information for the selected module.
   - *Generate help for the associated tables*   Generates help related to the tables that are used by the selected module.

5. Click the Start button. If the account you are using does not have access to a help table, you will see the following dialog:

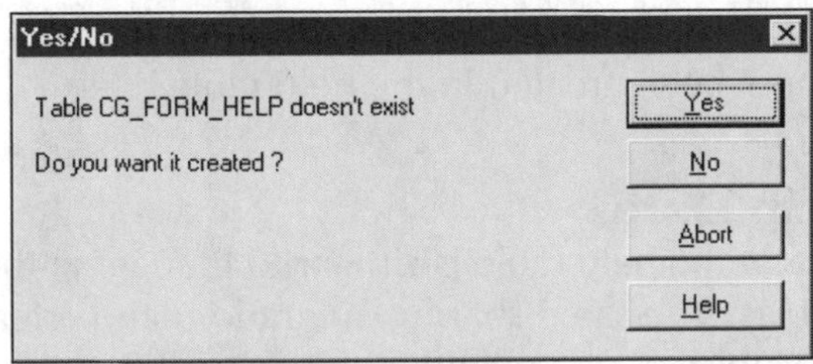

If you want to create a help table at this time, click Yes. If not, you can click No, and the help table generation and population will stop.

NOTE
If you selected both checkboxes in step 4, you will have to click No twice!

To continue with the population of the help data, you will have to make sure your account has access to a help table. See the help table management section below for more information about this.

If you already have access to a help table, you will not see this dialog, and you should skip to step 7.

6. If you are creating a help table, you will see the following dialog next:

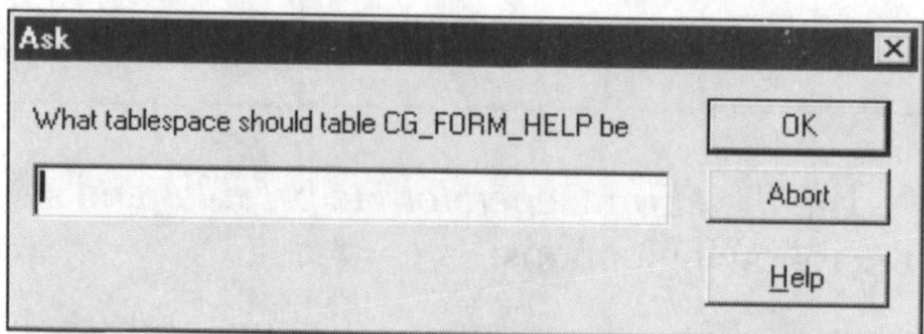

Enter the tablespace you want the help table to be created in. If you leave it blank, it will use the default tablespace of the Oracle user account you are connected to Designer with.

7. You should see messages like the following:

```
0 rows deleted / 7 rows added from/to table CG_FORM_HELP for table APPLICATIONS
0 rows deleted / 5 rows added from/to table CG_FORM_HELP for module APPLMNT
```

The help has now been created in the help table.

Managing Help Data

Managing the data in the help table is similar to managing the data in the reference code tables. The same sharing, migration, and release issues that apply to reference tables apply to help tables as well. Refer to the "Managing Reference Code Data" section in Chapter 26 for information and suggestions about how to manage this data.

Changing the Help Table Name in the Help Form

If you decide to implement application system–specific help tables, you will have to modify the help form to use the correct table name. To do this, you will have to open the form up in form builder and change each occurrence of CG_FORM_HELP to <AppName>_FORM_HELP. Make the following changes to the standard help form in order to make it work with a different table name:

Object Type	**Object Name**	**Property / Procedure**
Data Block	HELP_TEXT	Change the *DML Data Target Name* from **CG_FORM_HELP** to the correct table name.
Program Unit	NUM_ROWS	Edit the *Program Unit Text* and replace the occurrence of **CG_FORM_HELP** with the correct table name.
Items	HELP_TEXT.HLP_TEXT	Set the *Primary Key* property to **Yes**.

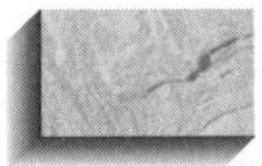

NOTE
We found that we had to make the Primary Key change identified in this table to compile the modified help form.

Structure of the Help Table

You may never need to work directly with the help table, but just in case you do, here is some information about the table structure and how the help information is retrieved into the help form. Table 24-6 lists the tables' columns and describes their purposes.

Design of Help Index

The HLP_INDEX column in the help table is the key to how the table is used. It is the column that is used by the help form to retrieve the appropriate help index for the context it is called for. It consists of one or more Designer component names concatenated together, separated by periods ("."). These component names can be the item name, module component name, module name, table name, and column name. These components are put together slightly differently, depending on the type of help that is being displayed (as determined by the HLP_TYPE column). See Table 24-7 for a list of the help types and the corresponding help index formats.

Column Name	Type	Purpose
HLP_APPLN	VARCHAR2(30)	The application name of the application the help is for.
HLP_INDEX	VARCHAR2(100)	The index that is used by the help form to locate the correct help text by context. See the "Design of Help Index" section.
HLP_MODTAB _NAME	VARCHAR2(30)	Either the name of the table or module the help is defined for.
HLP_GENERATED	VARCHAR2(1)	A flag that indicates if the help records were insert by Oracle Designer or not.
HLP_SEQ	NUMBER(5)	The sequence of the text line within its group (same index).
HLP_TEXT	VARCHAR2(2000)	The actual help text.
HLP_TYPE	VARCHAR2(1)	The help type. See Table 24-7 for possible values and meanings.

TABLE 24-6. *Structure of the Help Table*

HLP_TYPE	Help Type	HLP_INDEX Format
F	Field (or item) help	<Item>.<Module>.<Module Component>
B	Block-level help	<Module>.<Module Component>
M	Module-level help	<Module>
C	Column help	<Column>.<Table>
T	Table help	<Table>

TABLE 24-7. *Help Types and Help Index Formats*

Adding Your Own Help Records

The HLP_GENERATED column is a flag that indicates if the help records were generated out of Designer. It can have one of the two following values:

Y = Generated
N = Not generated

Designer will only manage (add or delete) the records with this flag set to **Y**. You can add your own help records by adding records directly to this table with this flag set to **N** (or anything else, for that matter). If you do this, Designer will ignore the records, but you will have to manage them yourself.

Repository Information that Affects Form Help Generation

Table 24-8 is a list of the various data components of the generated help system, and their source in the Designer Repository. Table 24-9 is a list of the generator preferences that affect the form help system generation and their purpose.

Target in Form Help System	Source in Designer Repository
Help Text	*User/Help Text* property for that level
Module	Current module's *Name*
Title	Current module's *Top Title*
Context	Module component *Name* / item *Name*
Based on Table	Bound item's *Table Usage*
Column	Bound item's *Column*

TABLE 24-8. *Designer Sources of Help Information*

Preference	Purpose
DBA →Scope of on-line help table (HPTABL)	See the "Scope of Help Table" section earlier in this chapter.
End User Interface → Name of form that displays user help (HLPFRM)	Specifies the name of the form used to display the help information. If you modify the help form and save it under a different name, you need to specify that name here. Should be set at the application level.
End User Interface → Type of Help System used (HLPTYP)	Must be set to **Forms Popup (HELPFORM)** in order to implement the forms based help system. Should be set at the application level

TABLE 24-9. *Preferences Used for Form Help System Generation*

Form-Based Help System Generation Troubleshooting Guide

Problem	Solution
I generated the help into the help table, but it does not appear when I run the application.	Make sure the application is running against the same help table as the generator used. Users sometimes accidentally create a private help table in their Designer account, which is populated during help generation. The application is then run using a different test user who cannot see the help information.
I generated help with the scope of online help table set to **Application System,** and I get errors when I try to run the help form.	You need to modify the help form to point to the application-specific help table you generated.

Problem	Solution
When I try to run the help form, I get the message, "trigger raised unhandled exception ORA-00942"	The help form does not have access to the CG_FORM_HELP (or <App>_FORM_HELP) table. Make sure that the table was created and installed in the instance you are running your application in.
When I try to compile the help form after I modified it, I get the error, "identifier 'CG_FORM_HELP' must be declared"	You need to create the help table before you can modify and compile the help form. Then connect to a schema that has access to the table before you compile the form. Also, if you are using application-specific help tables, make sure to replace all occurrences of CG_FORM_HELP with the correct name of the help table for your application.
When I try to generate the table help information for a module, I get the message, "ORA-06502: PL/SQL: numeric or value error" and no data is added to CG_REF_CODES.	This is a bug in Release 2.1.2. Previous to release 2, all of the Designer text was stored in multiple 80-character records. In release 2, the text is now stored in up to 2,000-character records. This means that each record may contain many lines of text. However, the code that converts the *User/Help* text to the CG_REF_CODES table still requires that each line be less than 80 characters. The only way we know to fix this at this time is to use the Designer API to chop the text into 80-character lines.
I get the error, "Block must have at least one primary key item" when I try to compile the help form after changing the help table name.	Set the *Primary Key* property of the HELP_TEXT.HLP_TEXT item to **Yes.**

CHAPTER 25

Deployment Options

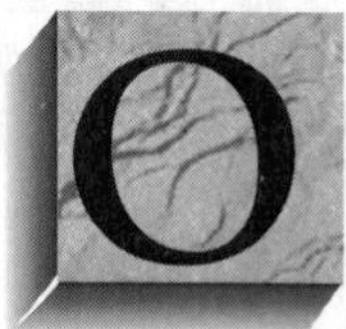
ne of the big advantages of Oracle Developer applications is that they can be designed and built on one platform and easily deployed on other platforms. The platforms supported by Oracle Developer include

- Character-mode (for example, a VT terminal)
- MS Windows (both 16- and 32-bit environments)
- Motif in X-Windows environments
- Macintosh
- Web browsers

The same applications can be deployed on any of these platforms by simply recompiling the common source code (FMB, MMB, PLL, OLB, and RDF files) on the target platform. An exception to this is deploying forms on the Web, which does not even require forms to be recompiled as long as the applet viewer is run on the same platform on which the forms were initially compiled.

When an application is deployed on a platform different than the one it was designed and built under, Oracle Developer automatically takes care of translating standard user interface objects (text items, checkboxes, radio buttons, etc.) to the native format supported by the deployment platform. For example, a checkbox looks different on Motif than it does on MS Windows; and checkboxes on a MS Windows 32-bit and 16-bit (same platform, different versions) environment do not look the same. Figures 25-1 through 25-3 show a sample form running on three different platforms: MS Windows, Motif, and Web Forms on MS Windows.

Oracle Designer is only available on MS Windows platforms, and the applications generated via Forms and Reports Generators (Graphics Generator is obsolete in release 2!) are MS Windows applications. However, you might have to install and run the generated applications on a different platform or in multiple different platforms.

Of course, it is not really as simple as that. There are differences in the capabilities and architectures of the different platforms that will have an effect on how the forms function. You need to take these differences into account when you are designing an application that will run on more than one platform.

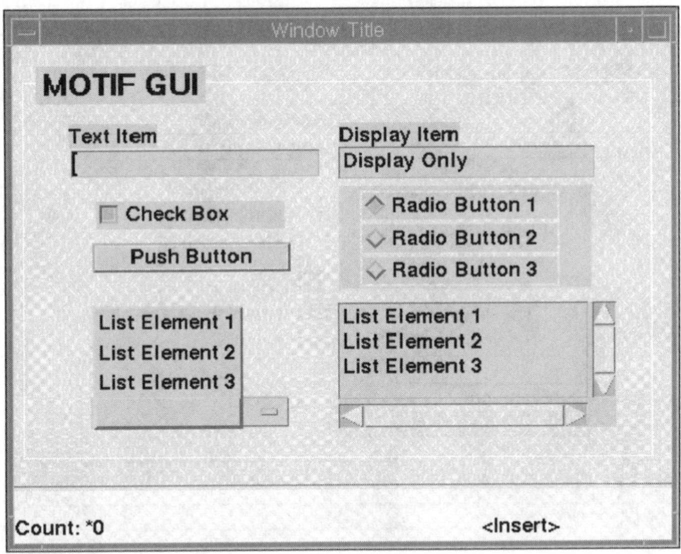

FIGURE 25-1. *Motif GUI*

FIGURE 25-2. *Windows GUI*

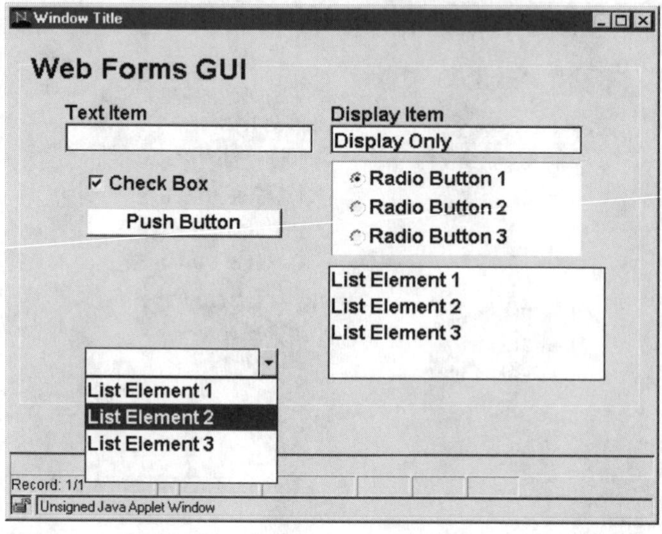

FIGURE 25-3. *Web Forms GUI*

In this chapter, we will review some of the deployment options and portability issues regarding Oracle Developer applications. We will highlight the advantages and disadvantages of each option. At the end of the chapter, a troubleshooting section will help you solve some of the most common problems related to deployment. The following topics will be discussed in this chapter:

- Portability issues
- Development and deployment strategies

Portability Issues

As mentioned before, by simply recompiling an application on a target platform, an Oracle Developer application (form, report, or graphic) can be deployed on that target platform without making any single change in the source code (FMB, MMB, RDF files). However, each platform has its own unique characteristics that need to be considered so that a truly portable application can be built. For example, the MDI window is not supported on either the Motif or Web Forms platform. Therefore, it is very important to think about the target platforms and features supported (or not supported) in these environments.

When an application is deployed on more than one platform, there are some issues that need to be carefully considered:

- File locations
- GUI issues such as fonts, colors, screen sizes, etc.
- Features supported on target platforms
- Code portability (if there are any user exits, or if O/S specific foreign functions are used)

File Locations

The simplest but most important issue in deploying an application on different platforms is the location of files. Avoid hard-coding file locations in your application at all costs; otherwise, you may run into a lot of problems. There are quite a few places where you have the option of storing the file location in the application programs. For example, when you attach a PL/SQL library to a form you have the option to keep the path to that library file or remove it. If you choose to keep the path, and the application is installed under a different directory structure, it may not run. The same applies to icon files, subclassed objects, menus, etc. It is very important that you do not have any hard-coded path or filenames in your applications. Instead, use the environment variables provided with the tools, such as FORMS45_PATH. When needed, create your own environment variables, and read these values at run time using the Form Builder TOOL_ENV package (or any other method that allows you to read these variables). Make sure that your application can adapt itself to the environment on which it is installed.

GUI Concerns

One of the most important issues to consider when designing portable applications is how the application will look on different platforms. Should the application look the same in all platforms? Or should it follow specific GUI styles for each platform? For example, a checkbox in a Motif environment is rendered differently than it is rendered in an MS Windows environment, and it is difficult to tell whether it is checked on or off. If this becomes an issue, you may decide not to use checkboxes on forms that will be deployed in the Motif environment. Some of the most important GUI related issues are

- **Selection of a coordinate system** Unless your application will be ported to character-mode, you should use the Real coordinate systems.
- **Selection of screen sizes** Use the lowest common denominator to determine the screen size of monitors. Design for the smallest size.
- **Selection of fonts** Supported fonts vary from platform to platform. For example, MS Sans Serif (the recommended font for MS Windows) is not available on the Motif platform; Helvetica is the recommended font for Motif instead. In addition, supported sizes and styles may vary from platform to platform. Oracle Developer uses font alias files to map fonts across different platforms. Using consistent font sizes and styles helps reduce the font mapping issues. Generally, you should use the fonts recommended for each platform and provide either proper font-alias files or visual attributes (not available for static graphic text such as block titles, item group titles, etc.). Be sure to test and make sure fonts are mapped correctly, and that they look nice on each target platform.
- **Selection of colors** To conserve system resources, try not to use too many colors. Select consistent colors from the basic color list. For example, the default background color on MS Windows is gray; but it is blue on Motif. If you want your application to look the same on all platforms, use the same background color.
- **Placement of the console** The placement of the console (an area of an application window where the item hint text, and some other indicators such as the LOV indicator, are displayed) varies from platform to platform. On MS Windows, the console is always

displayed at the bottom of the MDI window. However, on Motif or Web Forms the console appears on a user-specified window (because there is no MDI window in these platforms). Use the root window to display the console in Motif or Web Forms. The console can only be displayed on a single window, and the console window assignment cannot be changed programmatically at run time.

- **Placement of the toolbar(s)** The placement of toolbars varies from platform to platform. Just like the console, the toolbars are usually attached to the MDI window in MS Windows applications. However, on other platforms, you may have to attach the toolbars to each window individually or to the root window that is shared by all windows in all forms.
- **Placement of the menu** The placement of menus varies from platform to platform—and even within the same platform. On MS Windows, the menu is usually attached to the MDI window (if running in MDI mode). However, on Motif and Web Forms (as well as on MS Windows when running in SDI mode), each window has a menu attached.
- **Using icons** Icons are platform-specific graphic files. Create separate icon files for each platform, but use the same name. Be sure to set the Forms environment variable TK25_ICON properly. For Web deployment, create proper GIF files.
- **Function key assignments** Function key assignments vary from platform to platform. Try using Resource files to use the same key mapping across all platforms.

TIP

Oracle Developer online documentation contains an excellent source document Developer/2000 Guidelines for Building Applications. *For more information about portability, refer to Chapter 5, "Designing Portable Applications," in this documentation.*

Features Supported on Target Platforms

Features supported by the operating system or other helper applications vary from platform to platform. Try not to use platform-specific functionality:

- **Selection of help system** Remember MS Help is available only for the MS Windows platforms. Try using something that is portable, like the form-based Help system that can be generated from Oracle Designer. While you don't have to use the form that is shipped with Designer, you can still use its architecture to build a portable help system. Oracle Developer Demos also include an alternative Windows style Online Help system that you might consider using. If you are deploying on the Web, you might want to consider developing an HTML-based help system.
- **Using platform-specific controls** VBX controls and OLE containers are specific to MS Windows platforms. ActiveX components cannot be run on a Web browser in a Motif environment. Avoid using these type of components if you are going to port to a non-Windows platform.

Code Portability

Do not use platform-specific code, because it has to be recompiled for each platform. For example, if you are using user exits, they have to be recompiled and relinked on each target platform. If you must use programs written in other programming languages, try using Oracle Foreign Function Interface (FFI) for more portable implementations. For more information about the FFI interface, refer to the Form Builder Online Help, and the demos provided with Oracle Developer.

Be aware of limitations in target platforms. For example, the When-Mouse-Enter trigger does not fire in Web Forms, due to the high network traffic generated. If you have code relying on this trigger, you will have to rewrite it when deploying on Web Forms.

Reconsider using HOST commands, since they are platform-specific. If you must use host commands to execute platform-specific operating system commands, try externalizing these into PLL libraries and check the current platform before executing a HOST command.

Development and Deployment Strategies

When designing and building Oracle Developer applications using Oracle Designer, you need to make a few strategic decisions about the development and deployment options. The most important decision is whether you're going to maintain single or multiple source files for an application. You can maintain a separate application source for each platform you intend to deploy, or you can maintain only a single application source across all platforms. Each has its own advantages and disadvantages.

Multiple Source Files

When using multiple application sources, there is a separate copy of each source file specifically built for a target platform (see Figure 25-4). The product will be totally customized for a specific platform. The main advantage to this is that platform-specific features can be exploited to create the best-looking application with the best of functionality available on that platform. For example, using miscellaneous VBX/OLE/ActiveX components, one can really take advantage of rich features available on MS Windows. The same is true of other platforms, such as Motif, Mac, Web Forms etc.

However, the major disadvantage to multiple source files is the maintenance of many platform-specific copies of application sources, although the maintenance headache can be somewhat relieved if reusability techniques are used during the design.

Single Source File

When using a single application source, there is only a single copy of each source file that is common across all platforms (see Figure 25-5). The product will look and react the same on all platforms. The major advantage to this is that there is only one copy of each source file to maintain.

However, the features included in the application will be limited to those that are available in all of the target platforms. In other words, the lowest common denominator platform will be dictating what can be included in the application for all the platforms. For example, context-sensitive MS Help

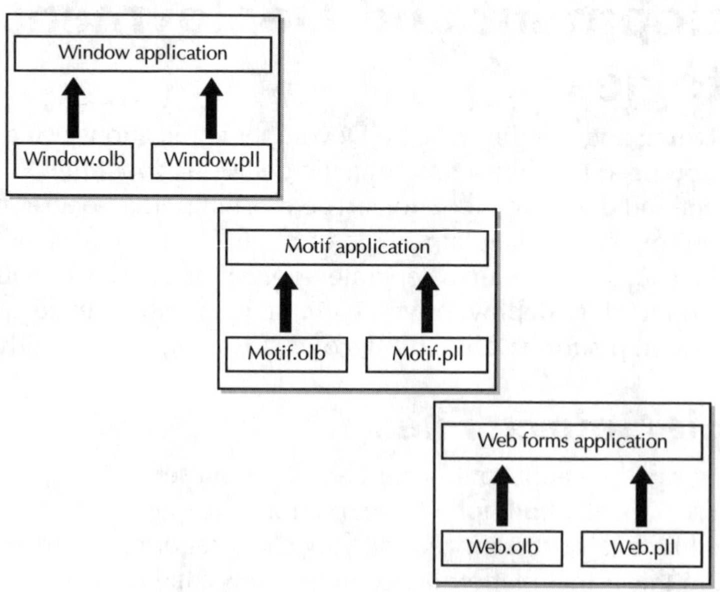

FIGURE 25-4. *Multiple source files*

generated from Oracle Designer cannot be implemented on Motif, and therefore the single source application has to use a different help system. This situation only gets worse if one of the supported platforms is in character-mode!

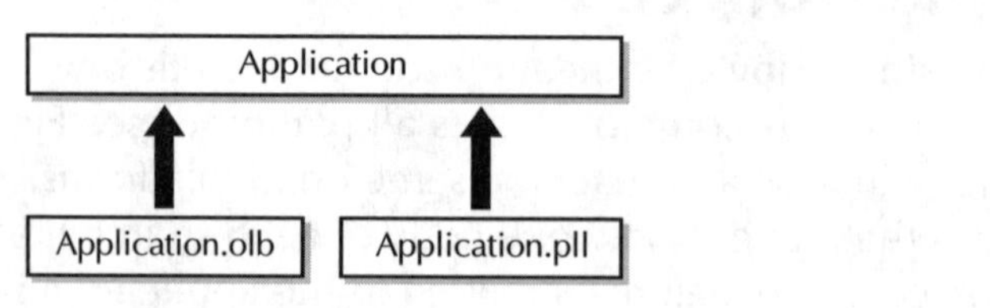

FIGURE 25-5. *Single source files*

Hybrid Method

In the hybrid method, the best features of single and multiple source deployment options are brought together. As you can see from Figure 25-6, there is only one application source file, but there are many platform-specific libraries. It is these application-specific libraries (both object and PL/SQL libraries) that allow us to exploit the features available on each platform.

However, the event code in the generated application may be more complex due to dynamic code that checks the current platform via the GET_APPLICATION_PROPERTY built-in. For example, objects that are not supported on a specific platform need to be dynamically hidden when the application is run on that platform.

In order to deploy applications using the hybrid method, follow these steps:

1. Create a common object library for all standards and objects (PORTING.OLB).
2. Create separate object libraries for each deployment platform (WINDOW.OLB, MOTIF.OLB, WEB.OLB, etc.).
3. Create a common PL/SQL library for all standard code (PORTING.PLL).
4. Create separate PL/SQL libraries for each deployment platform (WINDOW.PLL, MOTIF.PLL, WEB.PLL).
5. In each platform's specific library files (OLB and PLL), develop code to handle the application objects in the manner ideal for that particular platform.
6. Design and build the modules as needed.
7. In order to deploy your application on a particular platform, copy that platform's object library (e.g., WINDOW.OLB) to PORTING.OLB and its PL/SQL library (e.g., WINDOW.PLL) to PORTING.PLL.
8. Compile the source to build the platform-specific application.

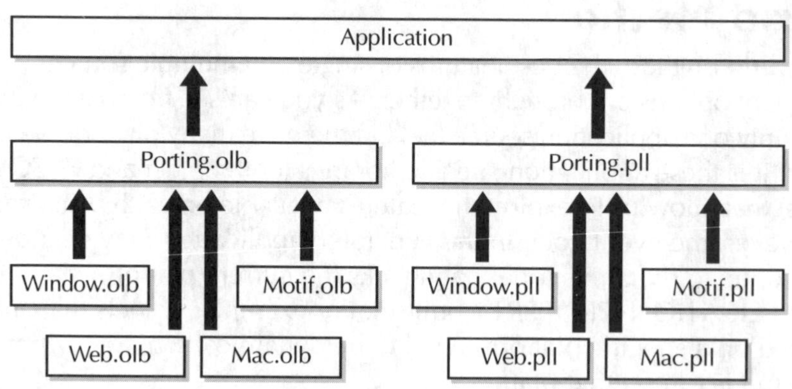

FIGURE 25-6. *Hybrid method*

When using this architecture, there are a few techniques you should consider:

- **Using the GET_APPLICATION_PROPERTY built-in** This built-in returns information about the application, the platform, and the user interface on which the application is running. By querying the platform and the user interface, we can dynamically hide objects that are supported on that platform or change the attributes of these objects, depending on the platform.
- **Using subclassing** Subclassing is the key to successful implementation of the hybrid architecture mentioned above.

Forms Deployment Troubleshooting Guideline

Problem	**Resolution**
I am trying to deploy my application on MOTIF, and my fonts are looking ugly.	Make sure that you have the font alias file UIFONT.ALI with the correct mappings. Also, check your font size and styles.
I am trying to deploy my application on MOTIF, and my icons are black and white.	Use icon files with the XPM extension; icon files with the ICO extension are black and white. Do not specify the extension when entering the icon filename.

Problem	Resolution
On Motif, checkboxes and pop-list items are not intuitive for our end users.	Try using text items with LOVs.
When I run my application through the applet viewer, I am not seeing the toolbar or the messages.	Make sure that the console and toolbar are assigned to a window other than the forms MDI window, because there is no MDI window in Web Forms.
When I run my application through the applet viewer, I am not seeing the icon for the list of values button.	Web Forms use GIF files rather than ICO files. Convert your ICO files to GIF format, and place them in your icons folder.

CHAPTER 26

Managing Reference Code and Code Control Tables

here are two special tables that need to be generated from Oracle Designer and installed into your application schema in order to support some of the generated functionality. These two tables and the functionality they support are

- **Reference Code Table (CG_REF_CODES)** A reference code table contains the values, abbreviations, and meanings for allowable values defined against columns and domains. A reference code table is generated to provide the list of values and field validation for items defined to use allowable values. This table can also be used to validate an item against a range of valid values.
- **Code Control Table (CG_CODE_CONTROL)** A code control table is generated to provide unique and sequential numbers for columns that are defined to use a code control type sequence.

This chapter is a detailed guide to help you generate and maintain these tables. In this chapter we will cover

- When the generators use these tables
- Creating the tables
- Populating the tables
- Managing and migrating the data stored in these tables

Reference Code Tables

Oracle Designer allows you to record a list of *Allowable Values* for column definitions, domains, and unbound items. When you do this, the generators can be directed to use these values to validate any items that are defined using that column or domain. In order for the generator to enforce this validation dynamically, the allowable values must be moved out of the repository and into an Oracle table that you can install in your production instance. This table is called the reference code table, and it contains the *values, abbreviations,* and *meanings* that are defined against the column, domain, or unbound item. The reference code table generated by Oracle Designer is often called the CG_REF_CODES table, because this is the default table name. The following illustration is an example of some *Allowable Values* that are defined for a domain.

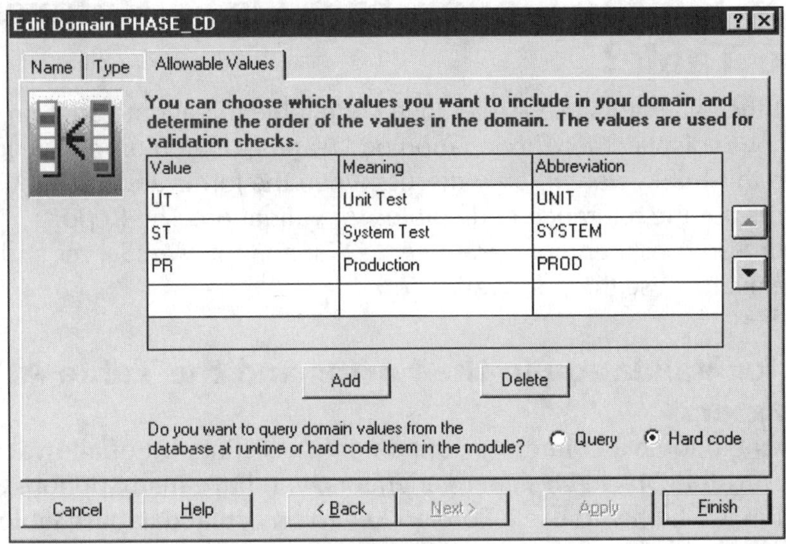

The domain shown here causes the following data to be generated into the CG_REF_CODES table:

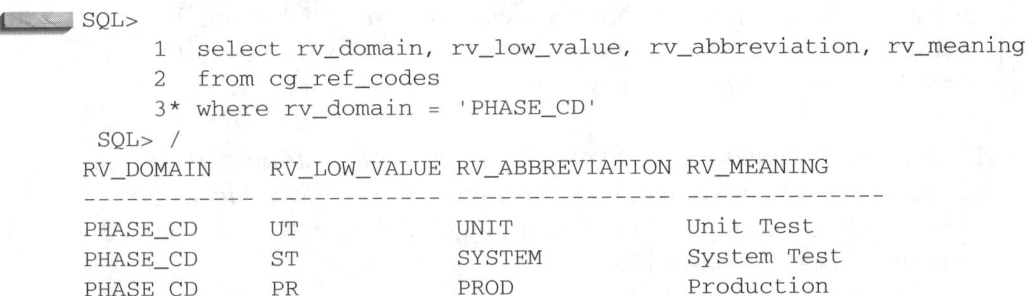

```
SQL>
     1  select rv_domain, rv_low_value, rv_abbreviation, rv_meaning
     2  from cg_ref_codes
     3* where rv_domain = 'PHASE_CD'
 SQL> /
RV_DOMAIN     RV_LOW_VALUE RV_ABBREVIATION RV_MEANING
------------ ------------ --------------- --------------
PHASE_CD      UT           UNIT            Unit Test
PHASE_CD      ST           SYSTEM          System Test
PHASE_CD      PR           PROD            Production
```

As you can see, the reference code table is just a place to store the *Allowable Value* information for use in your production system.

The reference code table can also be used to validate an item against a range of valid values. When this is done, the reference code table is used to store the range of values that is used by the generated programs to perform the validation.

When Do the Generators Use a Reference Code Table?

Many of the generators use a reference code table to validate an item or column or to display the *Abbreviation* or *Meaning* of a column instead of its value. In this book, we will only discuss when the forms and Table API generators use the reference code tables for validation. The Reports generator also uses them for parameter LOVs, and the WebServer and Visual Basic generators use them for validation.

Used for Validation in the Forms and the Table API Generators

If you want to force a column to contain only a distinct list of allowable values using the Oracle Designer generators, you have many options. The first option is whether to use a Foreign Key to an actual database table to enforce the validation or to rely on the *Allowable Values* validation that can be generated by Oracle Designer. If you decide to use the Foreign Key validation, you will not be using a reference code table for validation.

If you decide to use the *Allowable Values* to enforce the validation, you still have a couple of options for how you want to generate the functionality. Depending on the options you choose, the generator may or may not use a reference code table to enforce the validation. Here is a list of your options:

- **Use Check Constraints** If you set the *Dynamic List?* property of the column or domain to **No**, then the values in the *Allowable Values* will be generated as a check constraint, and they will not be placed in the reference code table.
- **Use Client Items Values Only** It is possible to generate items based on the *Allowable Values* of a column or domain when the values are hard-coded into the form, for example, using a checkbox item for yes/no flag columns or a radio group to show all of the possible values on the screen. You can use these types of items to implement the *Allowable Values* without using the reference code tables.

- **Use the Table API** If the column (or the domain used by the column) has the *Dynamic List?* property set to **Yes**, then the reference code table will be used by the Table API to validate the column.
- **Use Client Validation** If the column (or the domain used by the column) has the *Dynamic List?* property set to **Yes**, then the reference code table will be used by the generated client module to validate the column.

As you can see, the method you decide to use to validate the column will determine if the reference code table is used at all. It is also possible to select different validation methods for different columns in your database. If any of the columns or items use the reference code tables, you will have to make sure to create and populate them.

Used for Range Validation

The Oracle Designer Forms Generator can be instructed to implement range validation dynamically using the reference code table. This is done by setting the DVHILO (List of Values → Implement single range using field attributes) preference to **No**. If you design your application to use dynamic range validation, you will need to make sure to create and populate the reference code table for these columns.

Used by the Reports Generator to Validate Parameters

The Oracle Designer Reports generator can also be instructed to generate parameter validation based on the reference code tables. This is done by setting the LOVTYP (Parameters → List of Values Type) preference to include **PV** or **CV** and setting the *Dynamic List* property of the arguments to **Yes.** If you design your reports to use the dynamic LOV validation for the parameters, you will need to make sure to create and populate the reference code table for these report modules.

Creating Reference Code Tables

Before you can implement any validation that uses the reference code table, you need to know how to actually create the table. There are two ways to create the reference code tables from Oracle Designer:

- When the rest of your tables are generated using the *Generate Database from Server Model* menu option
- For specific modules by using the *Generate Reference Code Tables* menu option

Both of these options are available under the *Generate* menu in the Design Editor. If you have allowable values defined against columns in your database, you will likely use the first option. If you are only using allowable values for unbound items, or you created your database tables before you defined allowable values for any of the columns, you will likely use the second option.

Reference Code Table Design Considerations

Before you jump in and generate the table however, there are some design decisions that you need to consider. These are implemented by setting some generation options. Below is a step-by-step procedure detailing the decisions you need to make and showing you how to set these options.

1. To define the options, select *Options* → *Generator Options* → *General* from the Design Navigator pull-down menu:

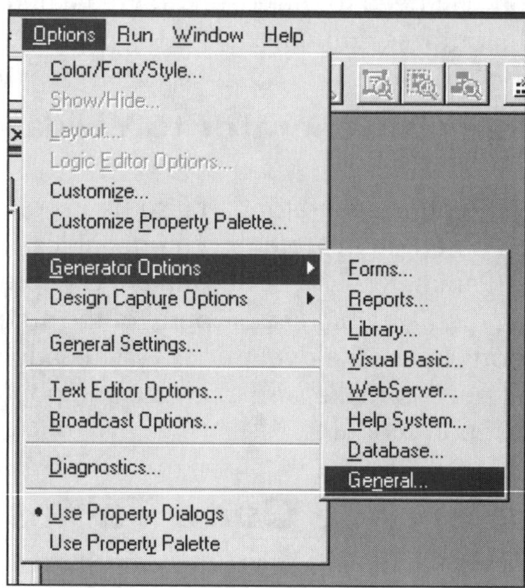

2. When you do this, you will see the *General Generator Options* dialog shown below. This dialog is used to set the scope and tablespace for the reference code and code control tables.

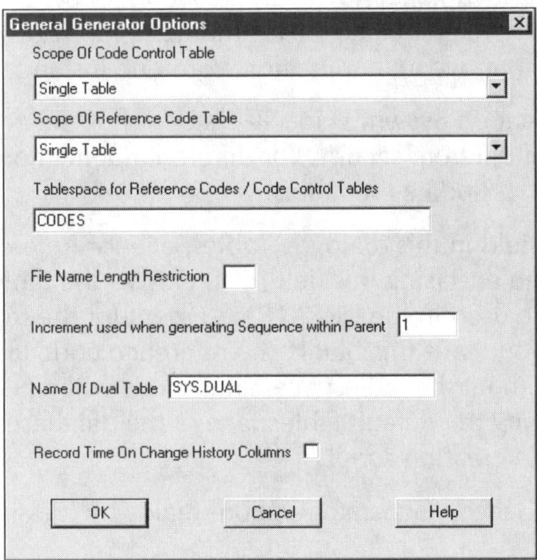

3. The second field in this dialog is called *Scope Of Reference Code Table*. The possible values for this field and their effects on the table generation are

   - **Single Table** This is the default option, and it instructs the generators to use only one reference code table for all of your applications. The name of the reference code table will always be CG_REF_CODES.
   - **Application System Wide Table** If you select this option, there will be one reference code table created for each of your application systems. The name of the table will be <Application System Name>_REF_CODES. For instance, the example application for this book is called DESGENBOOK. Thus, for this application, the reference code table would be called DESGENBOOK_REF_CODES.

   Which of these options you choose depends on how you want to implement and manage your reference code data. The Single Table option has the advantage of having fewer objects to maintain, so it is simpler to implement. It is also the best option if you have multiple tightly integrated applications that share modules between them. Its primary disadvantage, however, is that it can be more difficult to maintain the reference codes for multiple applications, especially if you need to move an application from one instance to another.

The Application System Wide Table option is better if you need to implement different security for different applications relating to who is allowed to update the tables.

4. The third field in this dialog is Tablespace for Reference Code / Code Control Tables. Using this field, you can set the tablespace name that will be used in the CREATE statement for the reference code tables. If you leave this blank, the reference code tables will be created without the tablespace clause; this will cause the tables to be created using the default tablespace of the database schema used to execute the creation script.
5. Close the General Generator Options dialog by pressing the OK button.

Now you are ready to generate the reference code table using one of these two techniques.

Generating the Reference Code Table During Table Generation

The Reference Code tables are generated when you generate any table that uses them. When you generate a table that has *Allowable Values* defined against one of its columns or domains, the CREATE statement for the CG_REF_CODES table will be generated into the .tab file along with the CREATE statement for the tables you selected to be generated.

1. You will need to generate a table that has a column defined to use *Allowable Values*. You can do this either by selecting such a table in the navigator, and then selecting the Generate option in the right mouse menu, or by selecting the Generate Database from Server Model option of the Generate pull-down menu. When you do this, you will see the Generate Database from Server Model dialog:

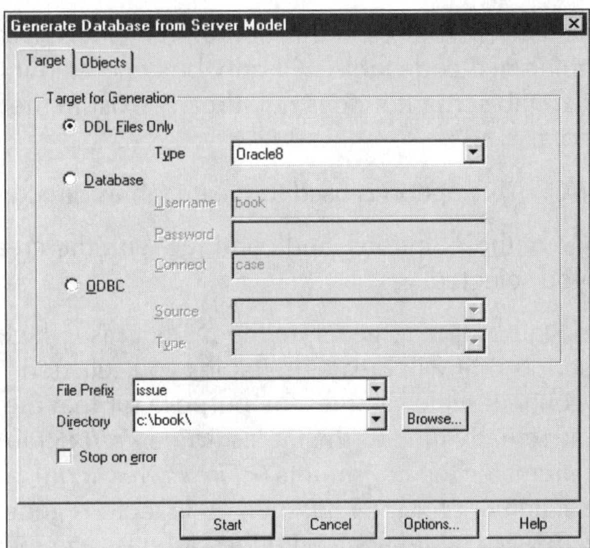

It is not in the scope of this chapter to give a full treatment of the generation of the database using this dialog. However, the options that are important for that reference code table generation are covered in this procedure.

2. First, fill in the *File Prefix* field. When you generate tables from Oracle Designer, the DDL generator will create multiple SQL scripts to create the tables and their associated objects (indexes, constraints, etc.). The filename for all of these files is determined by the value of the *File Prefix* field on this dialog.

3. Fill in the *Directory* field. All of the files created by the DDL generator will be placed in this directory.

4. There are two main methods for creating the scripts needed to build the schema. Which of these options you select affects how the CREATE statements for the reference code tables are generated. These options are determined by selecting the appropriate radio button:

   - **DDL Files Only** If you select this option, the CREATE statement for the reference code table will always be generated into the <*File Prefix*>.tab script.

- **Database** If you select this option, the CREATE statement for the reference code table will only be generated into the <*File Prefix*>.tab script if it does not already exist in the specified schema.
- **ODBC** This option is used to create tables directly using ODBC.

Select one of these options, and continue with the creation of the table(s) you selected.

5. Press the Start button to generate the DDL. This will generate a series of SQL scripts that will create the tables you selected. The extension of each generated file signifies the purpose for that file. There is one script that actually creates the tables (<*File Prefix*>.tab), another script that creates the constraints (<*File Prefix*>.con), and so on. The CREATE statement for the reference code table is generated into the <*File Prefix*>.tab table along with the CREATE statements for the other tables you selected.
6. If you open the <*File Prefix*>.tab script after generation, you will see a CREATE statement that starts with CREATE TABLE CG_REF_CODES... (or <APP>_REF_CODES...) at the top of the file. If you choose the Database option for creation, you have the option of executing the script to create the selected tables, including the reference code table. If you do not see the CREATE statement for the table, or the table is not created in the schema, you should check the following:

   - Make sure you have selected at least one table that uses *Allowable Values* or a domain with *Allowable Values*.
   - Make sure the *Dynamic List* property of the domain or column is set to **Yes**.
   - If you selected the Database option when you created the table, the reference code table may already exist in the schema you specified. When this is the case, the generator does not generate the CREATE statement into the script. If you want to make sure the reference code table is generated, use the DDL Files Only option.

Generating the Reference Code Table for Modules

Some systems may only use the reference code functionality for unbound items in the modules and, therefore, do not have any *Allowable Values* defined for columns in the database. If this is the case, there will be no reference code table generated even when all of the tables for the system are generated. In order to generate the reference code table in this case, you can simply follow the procedure in the upcoming section, "Populating Reference Code Tables for Modules." This procedure will create the reference code table as well as populate it.

Populating Reference Code Tables

Now that you have created the reference code table, you will need to populate it with the data from your domains, columns, and unbound items' *Allowable Values*. There are two methods that can be used to generate the scripts to populate the reference code tables:

- **For Tables** During the schema generation
- **For Modules** Selecting Generate Reference Code Tables from the menu

Both of these methods will generate scripts that will populate the tables. The difference between them is primarily how you plan to implement and use the data in the reference code tables.

Populating Reference Code Tables for Modules

This method allows you to easily populate the reference code table with all of the needed data for all of the modules in your system.

1. Select the modules for which you want to generate reference codes. You can select as many modules as you want (or all of the modules in the system), and the reference codes will be generated for all of the selected modules.
2. From the Generate pull-down menu, select the *Generate Reference Code Tables* option.

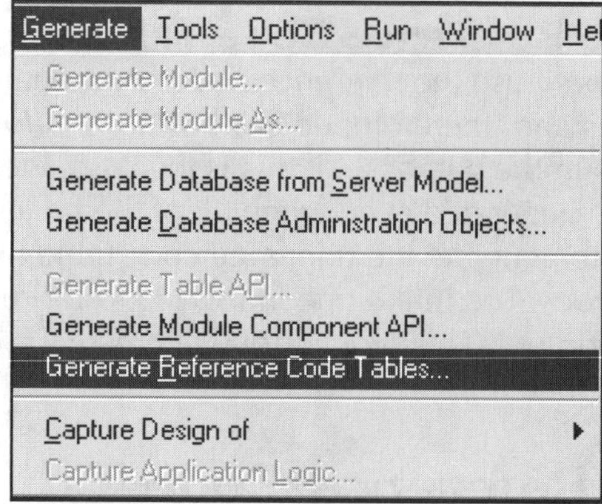

3. When you select this menu item, you will see the Generate Reference Code Tables dialog:

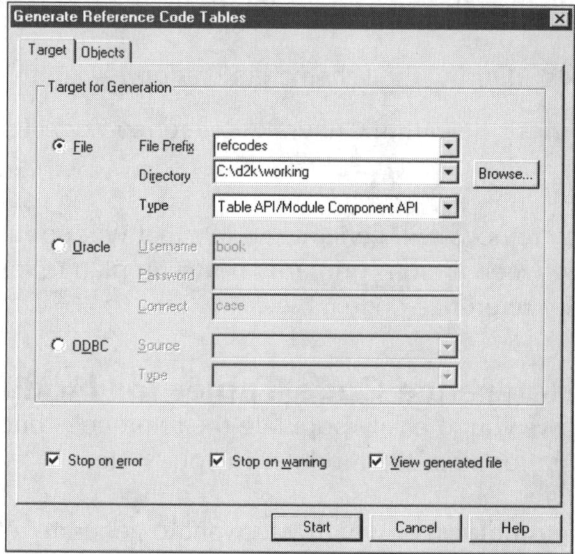

4. This dialog works the same way that the Generate Database from the Server Model dialog does, with similar *Target* options. If you select File, you will be able to generate a SQL script with the specified *File Prefix* that will be located in the specified *Directory*. If you select Oracle, you will be able to install the codes directly into the specified instance.

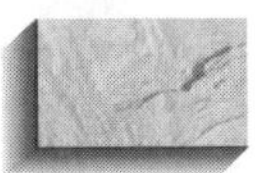

CAUTION
In release 221, the Type field for the File Target option is automatically populated with the only option available, Table API/Module Component API. This field is available in many of the generation dialogs, and is always set to this value. This is probably a minor bug in the system, and it makes this dialog confusing—it would make more sense for the value to be something like Reference Code Values. However, the value of this field is unimportant at this time. Leave this field as it is, and the script will be generated correctly anyway. In a future release, the functionality of this field may change, so be aware of any changes to the values for this field when you upgrade the tool.

5. Press the Start button to generate the codes. The Messages window will pop up and, among other messages, you will see a message that says

   ```
   Generating Module <Module Name> (1 of 1)...
   ```

   The modules are not actually being generated at this time, so this message is misleading. It means that the reference code data needed for that module is being generated.

6. If you selected the Oracle option, the codes are actually generated into the CG_REF_CODES table in the specified schema when the process is complete. You are not given the option of viewing the SQL files before they are executed, as you are when you generate the database. With the Oracle option, the files are always executed immediately. Also, if the reference code table does not already exist, it will be created for you before the values are inserted.

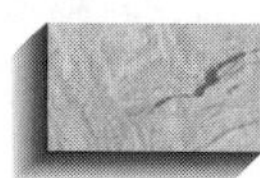

CAUTION

Be careful not to accidentally create a private version of the reference code table when you are populating reference code tables using the Oracle option. Usually, the whole development team will share one central version of the reference code table, and if your private schema is not set up correctly to share the table (using grants and a public synonym), you will create a private version of the table when you select this option. Accidentally creating a reference code table in your own schema instead of in a publicly available version of the table can lead to problems. For example, the reference codes you generate will not be available to anyone else who is working on the system; this may cause problems in the development and testing of the rest of the system. For more information about managing reference code tables, see the section "Managing Reference Code Data," later in this chapter.

7. If you selected the File option, the generator will write a script with the filename specified by the *File Prefix*.

TIP

If you selected the Oracle option to generate and populate the reference codes, a script named cdsddl.sql is written and executed. You can copy and rename this script to migrate the codes into other instances. This is useful for the migration of reference codes for specific modules because you can easily control which modules you want to generate the codes for.

Populating Reference Codes for Tables

The script to populate the reference code tables is generated at the same time as the script to generate the tables themselves. During the normal process of creating your database, you will generate scripts that create the table (<*File Prefix*>.TAB), as well as other scripts that create indexes, constraints, etc. One of the scripts that is automatically created will populate the reference code tables for the domains and columns that are used by the tables you selected. This script uses the extension .AVT (<*File Prefix*>.avt). You will find this script every time you generate a table that needs to use a reference code table. To help you see how this process works, the procedure is outlined here:

1. Select all of the tables for which you would like to generate reference code table data. This will include any tables that have columns with *Allowable Values* defined for them and any columns that are using domains with *Allowable Values.*

2. Generate the scripts to create the tables. You can do this by selecting a table and selecting the *Generate* option in the right mouse menu, or by selecting the *Generate Database from Server Model* option of the Generate pull-down menu. When you do this, you will see the *Generate Database from Server Model* dialog (shown earlier).

3. Follow the standard procedures for generating the database. For a brief discussion of the fields in this dialog, see steps 4 through 6 in the procedure in the section "Creating Reference Code Tables" earlier in this chapter. When you have completed the dialog, press Start to generate the scripts.

4. The generator will create a file called <*File Prefix*>.avt. If you open this file, you will see SQL statements like these:

```
DELETE FROM CG_REF_CODES
WHERE RV_DOMAIN = 'NUMLIST'
/
INSERT INTO CG_REF_CODES (RV_DOMAIN, RV_LOW_VALUE,
                          RV_HIGH_VALUE,
                          RV_ABBREVIATION, RV_MEANING)
VALUES ('NUMLIST', '5', NULL, 'Five', 'Fifth Value')
/
```

   These SQL statements will delete any existing records for each domain or column and will then insert new records for all of the values defined in the repository.

5. When you install the tables using the standard procedures (either by executing the <*File Prefix*>.sql script or by installing them immediately using the Database option), the records will be automatically created because <*File Prefix*>.avt will be executed.

Structure of Reference Code Tables

If you plan to use the standard generated functionality, you may never need to worry about the structure of the reference code tables. All you really need to know is how to create and maintain the data in the tables, which was covered in the previous sections.

However, there are times when you may need to look at the data in the tables in order to troubleshoot a problem with the programs that use the table. You may also want to design utilities to maintain the data in the reference tables directly instead of relying on the generated scripts. To help you with this, we are giving you some basic information, shown in Table 26-1, about the design and use of the reference code tables.

How the Reference Code Tables Are Accessed (RV_DOMAIN)

The key to the reference code tables is the RV_DOMAIN column. Its value is determined by the source of the *Allowable Values* used to create the records. There are four possible values:

- **Domains** The domain *Name*
- **Columns** A concatenation of the following two properties separated by a period (.): <Table Name>.<Column Name>
- **Unbound Items** A concatenation of the following three properties separated by periods: <Module Name>.<Module Component Name>.<Unbound Item Name>
- **Parameters** A concatenation of the following two properties separated by a period: <Module Name>.<Parameter Name>

Column Name	**Null?**	**Type**	**Purpose**
RV_DOMAIN	NOT NULL	VARCHAR2(100)	The main key to the table, which identifies the domain, column, or item for which the data is to be used
RV_LOW_VALUE	NOT NULL	VARCHAR2(240)	The *Value* of the *Allowable Value.*
RV_HIGH_VALUE		VARCHAR2(240)	The *High Value* of the *Allowable Value.*
RV_ABBREVIATION		VARCHAR2(240)	The *Abbreviation* of the *Allowable Value.*
RV_MEANING		VARCHAR2(240)	The *Meaning* of the *Allowable Value.*

TABLE 26-1. *Structure of Reference Code Tables*

The code that is generated by Oracle Designer uses the RV_DOMAIN to access the reference code table. To do this, a predicate selecting the appropriate RV_DOMAIN is always added to the Where clause of any program that accesses the data.

Managing Reference Code Data

Both before and after the reference code tables are created and populated there are some specific data management tasks and options to consider. This includes setting up the tables to be shared effectively by multiple schemas and migrating data between instances.

Sharing the Reference Code Table Across an Instance

Usually, you do not want to create separate reference code tables for each user or schema in your instance. Therefore, you will need to create the table in one schema and then grant access to it to the other users in the instance:

1. Follow the procedure in the section "Creating Reference Code Tables," earlier in this chapter, to generate the script to create the reference code table.
2. Edit the <*File Prefix*>.tab file, cut out the CREATE statement for the reference code table, and save it in another file or execute it in the desired schema to create the table.
3. You can use the following commands to make the table accessible to all of the users in the instance, where <Schema> is the name of the user (or schema) that you installed the reference code table into.

```
GRANT SELECT, INSERT, UPDATE, DELETE ON CG_REF_CODES
TO PUBLIC;
CREATE PUBLIC SYNONYM CG_REF_CODES FOR
<Schema>.CG_REF_CODES;
```

If you selected the Application System Wide Table option to create the table, replace CG_REF_CODES in this code with the appropriate table name. These commands should be executed from an account with DBA privileges.

There are other security designs that can be used for sharing the reference code table, but this is the simplest method to use for development. When you install the table in your production instance, you will grant SELECT only on the reference table.

Migrating Reference Code Data to Test or Production Instances

During the development phase of your project, the reference code tables are usually populated haphazardly as the developers modify and enhance the *Allowable Values* for various columns, domains, and unbound items. When it is time to move the data into your test or production instances, it is usually best to populate all of the reference code data for your application at once. This will hopefully reduce the chances of some of the data being missed.

Populating Reference Code Data When a Database Is First Created

The first time you create the database, the table-related reference code data will automatically be populated by the <*File Prefix*>.avt script that is normally generated during this process. However, any reference code data for unbound items will not automatically be installed. Therefore, you should make sure to select all of the modules in the application and select the Generate Reference Code Tables option in the menu (see the full procedure for this in the previous sections to create a script to populate the rest of the reference code data. This script may repopulate some of the domains that were populated by the initial installation, but that should not be a problem because the source data is the same.

Updating the Reference Code Data in an Existing Database

In subsequent releases of your application, you might add new tables; modify existing tables; or modify the *Allowable Values* for existing columns, domains, or unbound items. In order to make sure that the reference code data is updated in production, it is a good idea to make sure to repopulate the reference code table(s) for all of the tables and modules in the system. To do this, you will have to generate two scripts:

- **For tables** The easiest way to do this is to generate the values for all of the tables in the system. You can do this by selecting all of the tables and using the preceding procedure to generate one *File Prefix*.avt file for all of them. This file can then be used to update the reference code data for the whole system.
- **For modules** Just as with the initial installation of the application system, you will have to generate and execute a separate SQL script for all of the modules in the system to install any changes to Unbound Items reference code data. To do this, select all of the modules in the system and use the procedure detailed in the section "Populating Reference Code Tables for Modules," earlier in this chapter.

Maintaining the Reference Code Data Directly in Your Production Instance

It is possible to implement a utility form that allows you to maintain the data in the CG_REF_CODES table directly in your production instance. The big advantage of doing this is that you can easily maintain the allowable values of the domains and columns without having to regenerate anything from the Oracle Designer repository. The disadvantage to this is that the data you have in the repository will no longer match the data in production. This means that you have less documentation about the system and, more importantly, it may be possible for you to accidentally overwrite the data you maintained directly. Thus, maintaining the data directly in your production instance is probably only worth doing if you design a system that has *Allowable Values* that change frequently. Here is a very rough outline of how you could go about doing this:

1. After you create your reference code table, use the design recovery features to pull it into the Oracle Designer repository.
2. Design a module that uses this definition to maintain the code tables directly. You can use your application's templates and menu structure to integrate this module into your application's structure and security.
3. Generate the module and migrate it to production like any other module in your system.

You may also want to implement a method to get the data back into the repository after it has been updated in production. To do this, you would write a Designer API script that updates the repository. You can use this script to "sync up" the Oracle Designer repository with the production version of the reference code table from time to time.

Reference Code Table Troubleshooting Guide

Problem	Solution
The CG_REF_CODES CREATE statement is not generated into the <*File Prefix*>.tab script even though I generated a table that uses *Allowable Values*.	1. Make sure you have selected at least one table that uses *Allowable Values* or a domain with *Allowable Values*. 2. Make sure *Dynamic List* property of the domain or column is set to **Yes**. 3. If you selected the Database option when you created the table, the CG_REF_CODES table may already exist in the schema you specified. For this option, when the table already exists, the generator does not generate the CREATE statement into the script. If you want to make sure the CG_REF_CODES table is generated, use the DDL Files Only option.
When I try to generate the reference code tables using the Oracle option I get the following errors: CDI-15007 Error: (Oracle error) ORA-00903: invalid table name CDI-15007 Error: (Oracle error) ORA-00928: missing SELECT keyword	This is a bug in version 2.1.2 of Oracle Designer. For some reason, the name of the reference code table is left off of all of the DDL generated using this option. You will have to use the File option until this bug is fixed.

Problem	Solution
When I try to install the reference code values for a module either by using the Oracle option in the dialog, or by executing the generated script, I get the following error: ORA-01031: insufficient privileges	The schema you are generating the codes into has access to the reference code table, but it does not have privilege to update its data. This usually happens when the reference code table is placed in a single location in an instance and shared across all of the applications and schemas in that instance. If you get this error, you have a few options depending on how your organization manages this type of data: 1. You could ask your DBA (or whoever is responsible for maintaining the code table) to grant INSERT, UPDATE, and DELETE rights on the reference code table (usually CG_REF_CODES) to the target schema. 2.You could enter the username/password of the schema that owns the reference code table whenever you need to update its data. Many organizations will only allow one person to maintain tables like this. In that case, you will have to ask them to update the table with the data you need.
When I generate the table, the domain is not generated into the CG_REF_CODES table.	Make sure the *Dynamic List* property is set to **Yes**. If set to **No** (which is the default), the values will not be generated into the table.

Code Control Tables

Oracle Designer has two types of sequence methods that can be used to implement a sequence number populated column. Which type of sequence method is used is determined by the value of its *Code Control?* property. The most widely used method is to use a standard Oracle Sequence, which is the default. This method allows you to easily generate unique sequential numbers to populate a column. However, there are some limitations to

Oracle sequences. While the sequences are guaranteed to be unique, they do not guarantee that the sequence values will be consecutive, and there will be gaps in the sequence of numbers generated this way.

The other option is to implement a code control sequence. This will cause the generator to use a code control table to populate the sequenced column. The main advantage of using code control sequences is that the sequence numbers are guaranteed to be consecutive. These sequences are usually only used when consecutive sequence numbers are required by the system (for instance, when generating invoice numbers). These sequences should not be used for high transaction systems in which there are multiple records being inserted at the same time, because each insert will have to wait for its turn to lock the table before it can be executed.

Code control tables are used much less frequently than reference code tables; therefore, we are not going to cover them in as much detail. For the most part, they are generated and managed in much the same way as are reference code tables, so we will be referring you to the previous procedures in some of the sections that follow.

When Do the Generators Use a Code Control Table?

The *Sequence* property of the column definitions in Oracle Designer determines which sequences are used to populate a sequence-derived column. If you assign a column to a code control sequence definition (one that has its *Code Control?* property set to **Code Control Table**), the generated code will use a code control table in one of the following ways:

- **Table API** If the *Server Derived* property for a column defined to use a sequence is set to **Yes**, the Table API generated for that table will include the code that populates the column based on the code control table.
- **Client Side (Forms)** If the *Server Derived* property for a column defined to use a sequence is set to **No**, the code to populate the column will be generated into the client.

For both methods, you will have to create and install the code control table before you can install the generated system. During generation, the Server Generator creates the code control table and inserts a row in the table to store details about the code control sequence. Each row in the code control table records the sequence name, the next value to be automatically generated during an insert operation, the increment value, and any comment recorded about the sequence in the repository.

Creating and Populating Code Control Tables

The following procedure can be used to create your code control tables:

1. Before you actually generate the code control table, you will need to set some generation options that will affect its generation. To define the options, select *Options → Generator Options → General* from the Design Navigator pull-down menu.

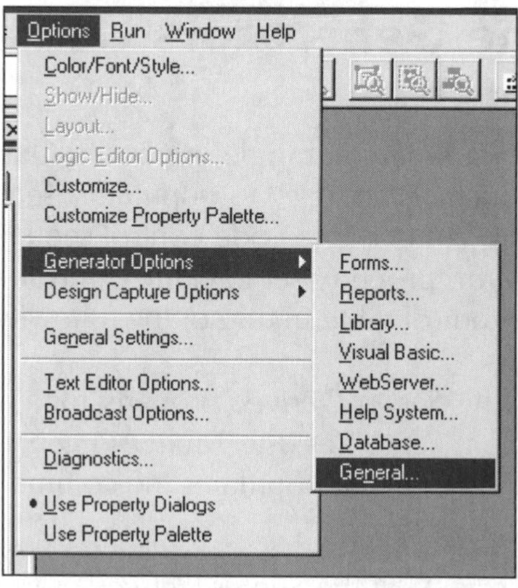

2. When you do this, you will see the *General Generator Options* dialog shown next. This dialog is used to set the scope and tablespace for both the reference code and code control tables.

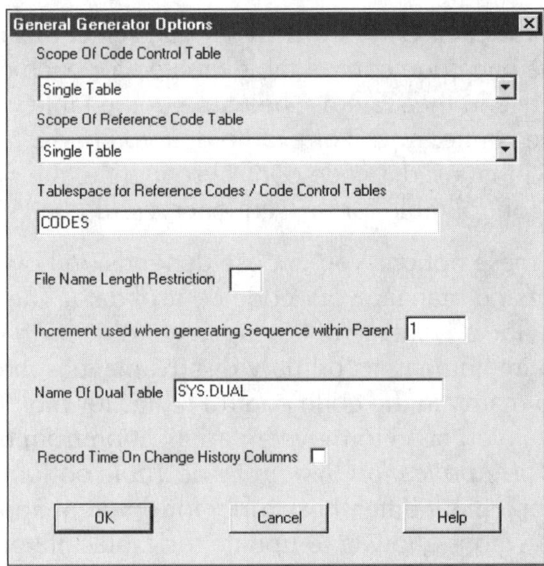

3. The first field in this dialog is *Scope Of Code Control Table*. The possible values for this field and their effects on the table generation are

   - **Single Table** This is the default option, and it instructs the generators to use only one code control table for all of your applications. The name of the code control table will always be CG_CODE_CONTROLS. Each code control sequence will use one row in this table.

   - **Application System Wide Table** If you select this option, there will be one code control table created for each of your application systems. The name of the table will be <Application System Name>_CODE_CONTROLS. For instance, the example application for this book is called DGBOOK. Thus, for this application, the code control table would be called DGBOOK_CODE_CONTROLS. There will still be one row for each code control sequence, but each table will only include the code control sequenced for one application.

- **Table for each Code Control** If you select this option, there will be one code control table created for each code control sequence in the system. The name of the table will be <Table Name>_CC. For example, if you had a table named ISSUES that used a code control sequence, the name of the code control table for the sequence would be ISSUES_CC.

Which of these options you choose depends on how you want to implement and manage your code control data. The *Single Table* option has the advantage of having fewer objects to maintain, so it is simpler to implement. Its primary disadvantage is that it can be more difficult to maintain the code control tables for multiple applications, especially if you need to move an application from one instance to another. The *Application System Wide Table* option is better if you need to implement different security for different applications relating to who is allowed to update the tables. If you have a lot of code control sequences to implement and your transaction rate is fairly high, you probably should select the *Table for each Code Control* option to prevent the bottleneck that occurs when many processes try to access and lock the same table.

4. The third field in this dialog is *Tablespace for Reference Code / Code Control Tables*. Using this field, you can set the tablespace name that will be used in the CREATE statement for the code control tables. If you leave this blank, the code control tables will be created without the tablespace clause, and this will cause the tables to be created using the default tablespace of the database schema used to execute the creation script.
5. Close the *General Generator Options Dialog* by pressing the Close button.
6. Now that you have set the generator options that relate to code control tables, you have two different ways to actually generate the CREATE statement.

- **Creating the Code Control Table Directly** It is possible to generate the code control tables directly by selecting the code control sequence definition and using the *Generate Database* *from Server Model* menu selection. For more information about how this dialog works, look at the procedure in the "Creating Reference Code Tables" section above. If this procedure is followed, the CREATE statement will be generated into the <*File Prefix*>.tab script along with the other CREATE statements.

- **Creating the Code Control Table Along with the Table that Uses It** When you generate a table that has a column assigned to a code control sequence definition, the CREATE statement for the code control table will be generated into the <*File Prefix*>.tab script along with the CREATE statement for the table itself. For more information about how to do this, look at the procedure in the section "Creating Reference Code Tables," earlier in this chapter.

CAUTION

If you select Table for each Code Control *in the Scope of Code Control Table field, you can only generate the code control table along with the table that uses it (i.e., you would be using the second method listed earlier). If you select the sequence definition directly and try to generate it by itself, you will see a "No DDL generated" message, and nothing will be generated.*

7. When the code control table is initially created, it will be populated with the rows needed to implement all of the code control sequences selected at the same time. Since you have to select at least one code control sequence definition or a table that uses one in order to generate the CREATE statement, there will always be at least one INSERT statement generated at the same time. The INSERT statements needed to populate the code control table are generated into a script named <*File Prefix*>.ccs. This script will automatically be executed along with the other scripts during the standard installation procedure.

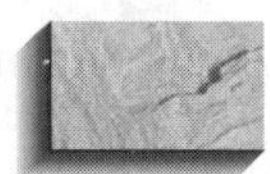

TIP

If you want to create a code control sequence that has an increment other than 1, you will need to create a Sequence Implementation for the sequence definition by using the DB Admin tab. The Sequence Implementation is necessary because the Increment *property can only be set for the implementation, not for the sequence definition itself. You will also have to generate the sequence from the implementation by selecting the desired sequence implementation and choosing Generate Database from Server Model from the DB Admin tab.*

Structure of Code Control Tables

Column Name	Null?	Type	Purpose
CC_DOMAIN	NOT NULL	VARCHAR2(100)	The main key to the table. It is the *Name* of the sequence definition.
CC_COMMENT	NOT NULL	VARCHAR2(240)	The *Comment* of the sequence definition.
CC_NEXT_VALUE		VARCHAR2(240)	Holds the next value to be used by the sequence. Updated by the generated code whenever a new sequence number is derived.
RV_INCREMENT		VARCHAR2(240)	This column is used to specify the amount to increment sequence with every use. It defaults to 1. It is set by the *Increment* property of the sequence definition implementation under the DB Admin tab.

Managing Code Control Tables

There are a few management issues you should consider when you are using code control tables.

Sharing the Code Control Table Across an Instance

Sharing across an instance for code control tables is virtually identical to sharing across an instance for reference code tables. Look at the section "Sharing the Reference Code Table Across an Instance," earlier in this chapter, for help with this. The only difference is that the production instance will need to update privilege for the code control tables where it does not for the reference code tables.

When Should the Code Control Table Be Updated?

The code control definitions are generated into the tables when you first generate any tables that are defined to use them. However, during the course of your development you may make changes that will make it necessary for you to manually generate the definitions. You should make sure to generate code control sequence definitions in the following situations:

- Before generating the server definitions
- Before generating modules containing items that derive values from a code control sequence
- After changing a code control sequence definition that is used by your modules
- When you associate another column with a code control sequence

Code Control Table Troubleshooting Guide

Problem	Solution
When I try to generate a code control sequence directly by selecting the code control sequence and using *Generate Database from Server Model,* I see a "No DDL generated" message, and it does not generate the script.	Check the value of the *Scope of Code ControlTable* in the General Generator Options field. If this is set to Table for each Code Control, then you cannot generate the code control table this way. The create table for the code control table will always be generated into the <*File Prefix*>.tab script along with the CREATE statement of the table using it.
I cannot find where to set the increment for the code control sequence.	The *Increment* property for a sequence is found on the sequence implementation for that sequence. You can view the sequence implementation by navigating to the DB Admin tab in the Design Editor. If there is no implementation created for the sequence definition, you will have to create one before you can set the *Increment* to anything other than its default of 1.

PART V

Reports Generation

Report Templates

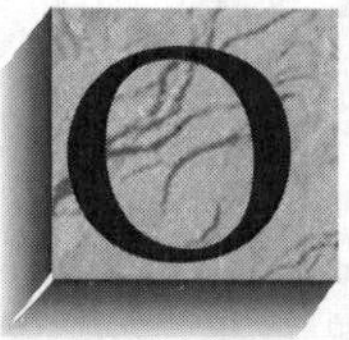

ne of the most important aspects of generating Oracle Developer applications from Oracle Designer is the usage of templates. Templates allow you to specify and enforce standards and tailor the report generation process to meet your specific needs.

Oracle Designer is shipped with some ready-to-use templates. Right out of the box functionality provided with these templates is often sufficient for a good start. However, standard template reports may not meet all of your requirements for sophisticated layouts or business-specific functionality. In these cases, you can either customize the standard templates or create new templates from scratch that meet your development standards and business needs.

This chapter will help you understand the purpose of templates and their role in the report generation process. We will cover the following:

- An overview of the report generation process
- Components of a report template
- The report templates shipped with Oracle Designer
- How to specify a template to use during generation
- How to customize templates
- A troubleshooting guide to assist you with common generation problems

A Brief Overview of the Report Generation Process

The generation of an Oracle Developer report module from Oracle Designer is a complicated process, with many steps, that requires a lot of information from many sources. A major source of this information is the module definition stored in the repository. A module definition defines the structure of a module. This includes information such as the table and columns in the report queries, which columns are to be displayed in what order, the layout style of the report, and arguments (parameters) used.

User preferences are the second source of information the Report Generator uses to generate a Report module. User preferences are basically a set of production directives stored in the repository. They influence the way the module definitions are assembled and placed on the template report. This includes directives such as the spacing to be used between frames, the number of queries to use, and how the SQL is written.

Report templates are the last source of information used by the Report Generator. The primary usage of report templates is to standardize the layout of generated reports. This can include customization of all report pages using generator objects, user-defined objects, and template application logic.

Working very diligently, the Report Generator collects information from different sources and brings many tiny pieces of a giant puzzle together to create the generated report. Figure 27-1 shows the report generation process. For further information about the report generation process, refer to Chapter 1.

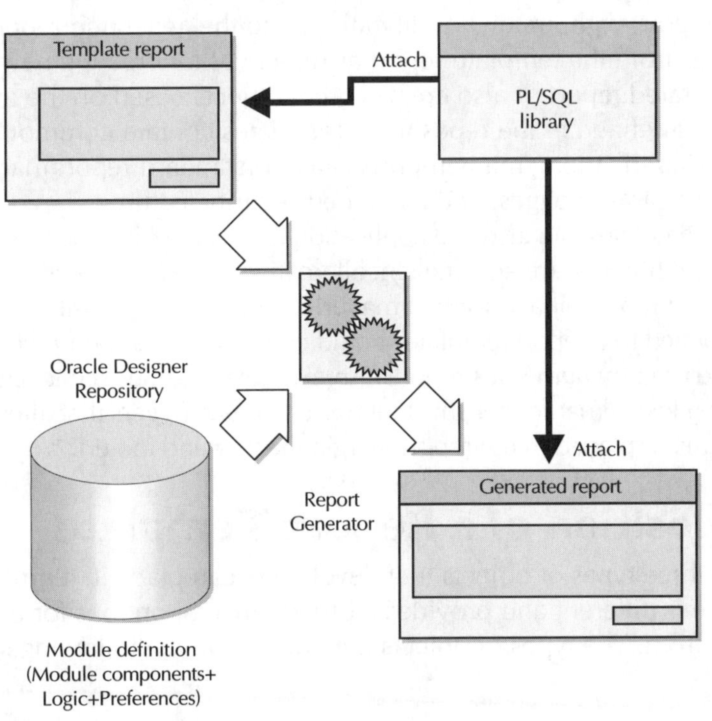

FIGURE 27-1. *The report generation process*

What Is a Report Template?

As we have mentioned, report templates play a major role in the report generation process. A report template is a Report Builder template file (.TDF) that exists outside of the repository. It is created and maintained exclusively using Report Builder. A report template helps the Report Generator do the following:

- Determine the properties of report objects that cannot be derived from the repository
- Provide a standard and consistent user interface for generated reports
- Reuse standards and objects that may be common to many reports

Templates act as a basis for the Report Generator to build new reports. When generating a report, the Report Generator copies objects from the template report, without any modification, into the generated report and uses objects from the template report as directives for creating new objects in the generated report. It also creates other objects based on the module components defined in the repository. Templates contain common objects and code shared among many reports, such as standard report margins, header pages, trailer pages, and advanced security features.

Report templates can also use application logic stored in report libraries (.PLL). Report libraries are an excellent alternative to coding directly in a report template (or a report binary, for that matter!). Logic contained within a report library attached to a report template should consist of common functionality that can be used by numerous reports. An example might be a package for determining lexical parameter substitutions or format triggers that allow you to control items displayed in the report margin (header and footer).

Composition of a Report Template

There are three types of objects that developers can place in templates. Each object type is different and provides a broad range of options for developers to choose from. The types of objects are outlined in the following sections.

1. **Template Application Logic**

   Template application logic consists of Event Code (Triggers) and Named Routines (Program Units) defined in the template report or Named Routines (Program Units) in an attached report library (.PLL). Template application logic should consist of common functionality that will be used by numerous reports. Examples of template application logic include

   - A package for determining lexical substitutions
   - Advanced application security requirements
   - Format triggers on items in the report margin that allow you to dynamically determine the objects displayed in the header and footer

2. **Generator Objects**

   Generator objects are names that the Report Generator recognizes at runtime and replaces with values from the repository. These values are then displayed as boilerplate (static) items in the generated report layout using the location, font, and style indicated in the report template.

NOTE
If a generator object is null in a generated report, check to see if the associated repository property is populated. Problems with generator objects are often caused by insufficient data in the repository.

Generator objects are very useful for placing identifying information on the report, such as the module short name, report title, or project code. Table 27-1 contains a listing of the generator objects supported in release 2 of Oracle Designer. Note that each item is prefixed with CG$. This prefix is reserved for generator objects and should not be used for naming custom objects in the template.

Generator Object Name	Description	Populated By
CG$AN	Displays the application system name	APPLICATION SYSTEM DEFINITION Property: *Name*
CG$AT	Displays the application system display title	APPLICATION SYSTEM DEFINITION Property: *Title*
CG$AV	Displays the application system version number	APPLICATION SYSTEM DEFINITION Property: *Version*
CG$CN	Displays the company name	REPORTS APPLICATION LEVEL PREFERENCE Preference Category: *Field Layout* Preference: *Company Name*
CG$MB	Displays the module bottom title	REPORT MODULE DEFINITION Property: *Bottom Title*
CG$MJ	Displays the module project code	REPORT MODULE DEFINITION Property: *Project*
CG$MK	Displays the module task code	REPORT MODULE DEFINITION Property: *Task*
CG$MN	Displays the module name	REPORT MODULE DEFINITION Property: *Name*
CG$MO	Displays the module owner	APPLICATION SYSTEM DEFINITION Property: *Application Owner*
CG$MP	Displays the module purpose	REPORT MODULE DEFINITION Property: *Purpose*
CG$MS	Displays the module short name	REPORT MODULE DEFINITION Property: *Short Name*
CG$MT	Displays the module top title	REPORT MODULE DEFINITION Property: *Top Title*
CG$PS<*n*>	Displays page-level summary	Specifies the boilerplate object used to display the value of a page-level summary, where *n* is the sequence number of the summary item

TABLE 27-1. *Report Generator Objects*

Generator Object Name	Description	Populated By
CG$US	Displays the current Oracle username	The Oracle username that was used in Designer to generate the report

TABLE 27-1. *Report Generator Objects* (continued)

The list of generator objects recognized by the Report Generator can change with each release. It is good practice to check the online help when evaluating new releases of Oracle Designer. You can verify that objects that you are currently using in your templates will still be supported and determine if there are any new features that you can take advantage of.

3. User-Defined Objects

User-defined objects are objects native to Oracle Reports. They are not linked to the Designer repository in any way. They are created and exist within the template and are simply passed on by the Report Generator into the generated report. User-defined objects can consist of static items displayed in boilerplate items and dynamic items displayed in fields. Typical examples of user-defined objects include

- Boilerplate objects (text and graphic)
- Images
- Fields that use the setting of the *Source* property to determine their values

Fields that use the setting of the *Source* property to determine their values are the most typical user-defined objects included in report templates. The *Source* field layout property is a mandatory property that contains a listing all the possible objects that can be displayed in the field. Items that can be included in a report template include

- System parameters (DESNAME, DESTYPE, etc.)
- Built-in functions

The built-in functions are standard modifications to most templates. In fact, the templates shipped with Oracle Designer contain many of these objects. Table 27-2 contains a list of these built-in functions and descriptions of their use.

User-defined objects give you the capability to customize the layout of your templates to meet your specific business needs. As opposed to generation objects, support for user-defined objects rarely changes with new releases of Oracle Designer. Support for user-defined objects is most directly tied to new

Built-In Functions	**Definition**
Current Date	Operating system date when the report runs, after the Runtime Parameter Form is finished
Page Number	Current page number based upon numbering the output by logical pages
Panel Number	Current panel number within the logical page
Physical Page Number	Current page number based upon numbering the output by physical pages
Total Pages	Total number of pages based upon numbering the output by logical pages
Total Panels	Total number of panels within a logical page
Total Physical Pages	Total number of pages based upon numbering the output by physical pages

TABLE 27-2. *Built-In Functions in the* Source *Field Layout Property*

releases of Oracle Developer. However, it is still good practice to check the online help of Oracle Developer when evaluating new releases of Oracle Designer. That way, you can verify that objects that you are currently using in your templates will still be supported and determine if there are any new features that you can take advantage of.

Report Templates Shipped with Oracle Designer

The report templates shipped with Oracle Designer are very useful when you are first starting to use the Reports Generator. They are a generic set of templates that enforce typical layout standards and functionality. The features common to each template include

- A header page that displays the following objects:
  - Company Name (Generator Object CG$CN)
  - Application Title (Generator Object CG$AT)
  - Report Name (Generator Object CG$MN)
  - File Name (User-Defined Object DESNAME System Parameter)
  - User Name (Generator Object CG$US)
  - Report Date (User-Defined Object Current Date Built-In)
  - Boilerplate text objects (User-Defined Objects that display prompts)
- A customized margin of each page of the body that contains the following objects:
  - User Name (Generator Object CG$US)
  - Module Top Title (Generator Object CG$MT)
  - Company Name (Generator Object CG$CN)
  - Page Number (User-Defined Object Page Number Built-In)
  - Total Pages (User-Defined Object Total Pages Built-In)
  - Module Bottom Title (Generator Object CG$MB)

- A trailer page that contains the following objects:
  - Company Name (Generator Object CG$CN)
  - Application Title (Generator Object CG$AT)
  - Report Name (Generator Object CG$MN)
  - Boilerplate text objects (User-Defined Objects that display prompts)

NOTE
Each of the detail report templates do not include the header and trailer pages. Reports generated using these templates will not have these pages.

Table 27-3 contains a list of these templates and descriptions that can help you decide which one to use.

Template Filename	Long Name	Description
CGBMDT	**C**ase **G**enerated **B**it**M**ap **D**e**T**ail	Bitmap drill-down detail template
CGBMLS	**C**ase **G**enerated **B**it**M**ap **L**and**S**cape	Bitmap landscape template
CGBMPT	**C**ase **G**enerated **B**it**M**ap **P**or**T**rait	Bitmap portrait template
CGCHDT	**C**ase **G**enerated **CH**aracter **D**e**T**ail	Character drill-down detail template
CGCHLS	**C**ase **G**enerated **CH**aracter **L**and**S**cape	Character landscape template
CGCHPT	**C**ase **G**enerated **CH**aracter **P**or**T**rait	Character portrait template

TABLE 27-3. *Reports Templates Shipped with Oracle Designer*

The location of each of these templates is <oracle_home>\cgenr30\admin. To use one of these templates you will need to do one of two things:

- Set the *Layout Template* preference located in the *Templates* category for the module to the *path\filename* of the template you would like to use. This template that you specify will then be the default template that will be used each time the report definition is generated. For example,

  Templates → Layout Template = **'c:\orant\cgen30\admin\cgbmls.tdf**

NOTE
You could also set this preference at the application level. This would make the template the default template for all report definitions in the application.

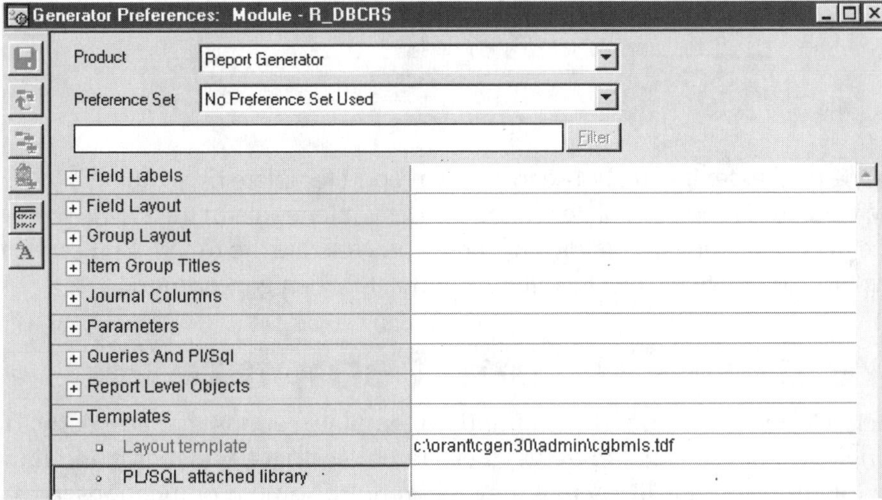

- Set the *Name* property in the Report Generation dialog to the *path\filename* of the report you desire. For example,

  Name = **c:\orant\cgen30\admin\cgbmls.tdf**

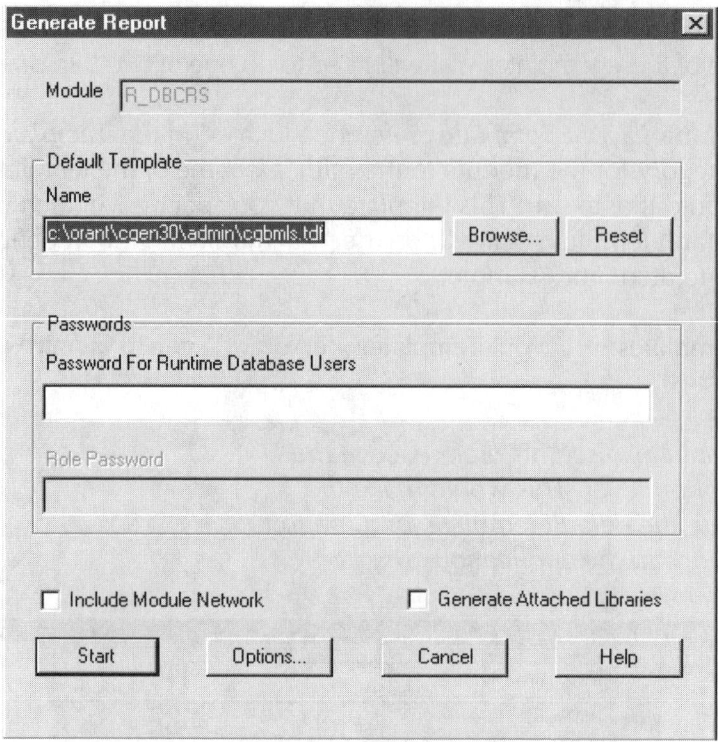

One final note: if you choose to select a report template by setting the preference, this report template will be the default template in the *Name* property of the Report Generation dialog each time you generate the report. You can either accept this template or select a different template when generating.

Creating Custom Templates

Oracle Designer is shipped with standard template reports that are ready to use right out of the box. However, these templates have very basic and limited functionality, and it is likely that they will require some modifications to comply with your reporting standards. For example, all of the templates shipped with Oracle Designer display the Company Name in the margin of each body page, and your reporting standards may not require this.

Another typical reason for customizing templates is the targeted platform of deployment. Report designs normally vary based on how the report will be deployed. For instance, the number of columns to be displayed is typically lower in character-based reports than bitmap reports. Also, Web-based reports are more frequently designed as drill-down reports than bitmap and character reports. Since report designs vary based on deployment, so should the templates used to create them. Templates should be customized to use different font types and sizes, generation objects, user-defined objects, and template application logic to support each deployment alternative. For instance, character-based reports typically encounter truncation problems. Therefore, the size and type of font selected is very important, as is the amount of space allocated for each field and boilerplate object. Web-based reports, however, typically require bookmarks and hypertext links, features not normally attributed to bitmap or character-based reports. While we are not advocating creating dozens of templates, we do think it is a good idea to have a couple of different template choices per deployment alternative. The good news is that Oracle has anticipated that not all of their standard templates will meet your needs and has provided us with the ability to create new templates from scratch, as well as to customize the existing templates. In most cases, customizing an existing template is the quickest and easiest method of creating a new template. The standard templates have many useful features that can be easily modified, added to, or simply removed. The process of customizing templates also requires far less knowledge of how the Report Generator uses templates than creating a template from scratch.

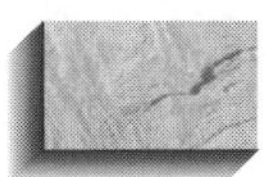

NOTE

Do not customize a template shipped with Oracle Designer directly. Always make a copy of the template and modify the copy. Not only is this a good development practice, it will save you valuable time in upgrades and support.

All custom templates should be in a common location that can be referenced by more than one application development project. Quite often templates customized by one development team within an organization are shared with other development teams and become the de facto standard. However, you may want to consider limiting write access to the directory in which the templates are stored. This will ensure that only your more experienced developers will have access to create and modify these templates.

The following examples show how to customize the standard templates shipped with Oracle Designer. For the sake of simplicity, these examples all use CGBMLS.TDF as the base template.

Example 1: Adding Template Application Logic

A common usage of template application logic is to process values for lexical parameters. You can define a function to process the generic states of most lexical parameters in one simple, easy-to-use function. This includes single values, multiple values, or null values. You can also modify the function to add specific business processing based on values passed, such as determining how to process a value passed as "OTHER". The function returns an evaluated string that can then be passed directly into the appropriate query. The listing below presents a sample function that completes this evaluation.

```
FUNCTION TM$LIST (p_list in varchar2 ,p_column in varchar2)
 RETURN VARCHAR2 IS
l_list varchar2(240);
  BEGIN
  -- Handles All and NULL values for a parameter
  IF instr(p_list,'ALL') > 0 OR p_list is null THEN
    l_list := ' 1 = 1 ';

  -- Handles multiple values for given parameter
  ELSIF       instr(p_list, ',',1,1) > 0 THEN
    l_list := p_column||'
in('''||REPLACE(p_list,',',''',''')||''')';

  -- Handles one value for given parameter
  ELSE
    l_list := p_column||' = '''||p_list||'''';
  END IF;
  RETURN(l_list);
END;
```

Note that the TM$LIST function handles the generic evaluation of all lexical parameters. The function requires two arguments:

- **p_list** The string of values to be evaluated for a given lexical parameter
- **p_column** The table_alias.column_name of the column that the values in p_list will be evaluated against in the report query

Each of these arguments is evaluated by the function, and an evaluated string is returned to the report. The evaluated string is then ready to be passed directly to a query in the report. For example,

If p_list = ('value1','value2','value3')

and

p_column = emp.dept_type_cd

then the evaluated string returned by the function would be

Emp.dept_type_cd in('value1','value2','value3');

To make use of the function in this example, follow these steps:

1. Make a copy of the standard report form, if you have not done so yet.
2. Create a new PL/SQL library in Report Builder.
3. Create a new function in the PL/SQL library like the one defined in the listing above.
4. Save the PL/SQL library.
5. Open the Template Report in Report Builder.
6. Attach the newly created PL/SQL library to the Template Report.
7. Document and save your changes.

Example 2: Adding Generator Objects

Another common template modification is adding/removing generator objects. For example, you may want to display the module short name in the margin of each body page and remove the company name from the margin of each body page. These are very simple modifications that can be implemented by following these steps:

1. Make a copy of the standard template form, if you have not done so yet.
2. Open the template report in Report Builder.
3. Create a new boilerplate text object in the margin named CG$MS.
4. Delete the CG$CN boilerplate text item in the margin.
5. Document and save your changes.

Example 3: User-Defined Objects

Another common template modification is adding/removing user-defined objects. For example, you may want to display the current date in the margin of each body page or remove the DESNAME system parameter from the header page. These are very simple modifications that can be implemented by following these steps:

1. Make a copy of the standard template form, if you have not done so yet.
2. Open the template report in Report Builder.
3. Create a new field in the margin layout and set the *Source* property to **Current Date**.
4. Delete the field that displays the DESNAME parameter and the boilerplate text item that displays its prompt from the header page.
5. Document and save your changes.

 Generation Troubleshooting Guide

Problem	Solution
When generating, I keep getting the message, "CGEN 02007 – Error: Module: Failed to parse generated SQL statement"	If you look in the help, it tells you to check two things: 1. That the object exists in the database 2. That the account that you are using in Designer has access to the object A good way to debug this is to open the generated report in Report Builder. Open a query, add a space, and then click OK. You will likely get a much more specific error message, such as "Table or view does not exist," or "Invalid column" Another thing to note if both the above conditions are met is that if a relational table definition in the repository does not match the definition in the database, you will also get this error. Make sure that the repository table definitions and the database are synchronized.
The changes I made to my template are not working. They do not show up in the generated reports.	Make sure that you are specifying to use the customized template when generating. You can do this in one of two ways: 1. Set the *Name* property on the Report Generation dialog to the path\filename of your template. 2. Set the *Layout Template* preference in the *Template* category for the report definition or application system to ensure that the correct template is always defaulted.

Problem	Solution
When I open a template, I keep losing library attachments. The following error is always displayed, "REP 0756: Unable to find PL/SQL library '<name>'"	You need to ensure that the directory path of the library is located in one of two places: 1. The working directory of the application (Report Builder) 2. The REPORT30_PATH environment variable set in the registry
I have modified the REPORTS30_PATH variable, but it seems to be ignoring my entry. I still keep losing library attachments and receive the following error, "REP 0756: Unable to find PL/SQL library '<name>' "	Check the length of the string in the REPORTS30_PATH variable. When installing Oracle Developer, there are many entries written to this variable, which makes the string quite long. We have seen that there is an operating system limitation when evaluating long strings. Entries at the end of the string are simply ignored. To avoid this problem, you can do one of two things: 1. Remove unnecessary entries such as Report Demos from the string. 2. Place your entry at the beginning of the string to ensure that it is evaluated first. Note that this should only be a problem encountered by developers. End user machines should be configured without all of the Oracle product entries in this variable.
The generator object I added to my template is null.	The repository property used to populate this generator item is likely also null. Check the corresponding repository property and make sure it has a value, and then regenerate the report.

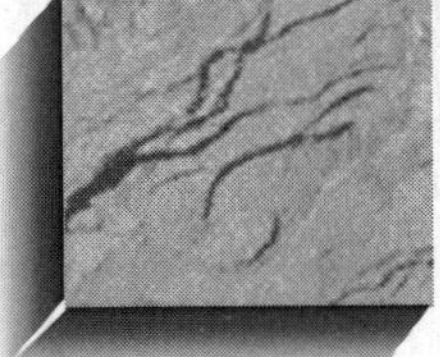

CHAPTER 28

Defining a Report Definition

The Report Generator has taken a big step forward in release 2 of Oracle Designer, and developers will be able to take advantage of its many new features to generate complicated reports easily. Since so much has changed, we designed this chapter to walk you through the process of defining and generating a report definition. As we progress through this, we will discuss important concepts and provide examples that demonstrate how each concept can be defined and generated. In this chapter, we will cover the following concepts:

- Base table usages
- Lookup table usages
- Displayed items
- Item groups

We will conclude the chapter by defining and generating a sample report that will show how to apply these concepts using the dialogs. We will also include a troubleshooting guide to assist you with common generation problems.

Creating the Base Report

The process you go through to initially create the report definition and the module components is called creating the base report. The first thing to do when developing a report is to determine where the data is located. Most people do not think much about user parameters, Where clause conditions, or the format of the layout until they have confirmed that they can indeed select the values required by the report specification. This concept is well supported by the three sets of dialogs that will be presented to you when you first create your report definition. You will use these to

- Define the report definition. The first set of dialogs gathers identifying information about the report definition.
- Select the module component data. The second set of dialogs gathers information that will be used to generate the SELECT statement.
- Generate the module component display. The third set of dialogs gathers information that will be used to generate the body of the report layout.

Using the three sets of dialogs, you can quickly and easily create the foundation for your report. After you have completed the dialogs, you will be ready to refine the report by adding functionality like Where clause restrictions, user parameters (arguments), and function columns (unbound items).

We will cover these topics and more in detail in the remainder of the chapters in Part V. Right now, let's turn our attention to the concepts you will need to know when first creating your report definition.

Data Selection

When first creating your report definition, you will need to have a good understanding of base and lookup table usages. These two types of table usages typically make up the majority of the generated SELECT statement for the report. Figure 28-1 shows the repository definitions used to create the generated SELECT statement. Notice how many times base and lookup table usages are mentioned.

Base Table Usage

The base table usage is the foundation or main building block of each module component. This is because each module component must have one and only one base table usage. A base table usage can be defined using a table, view, or snapshot. Your choice of which to use will vary greatly based on the layout you are trying to generate. In Chapter 31, we will discuss layout implications of module component designs. You will use the base table usage for three main purposes:

- To determine the columns selected directly from the base table. These columns will be stored as *Bound Items* in the repository.
- To relate other table usages to make the selection criteria for that module component more complete. These relationships will be stored as *Constraint Usages* in the repository.
- To relate to other module components (for reports that require more than one module component) to complete the generated reports SELECT statement. These relationships will be stored as *Key Based Links* in the repository.

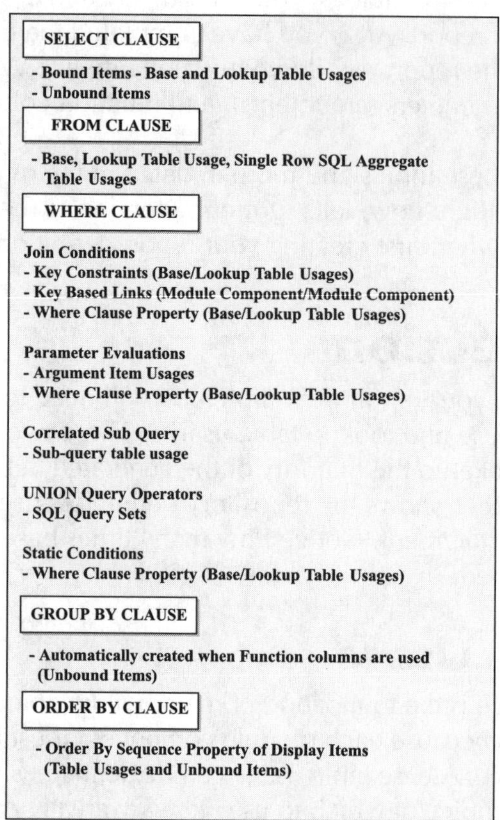

FIGURE 28-1. *Repository definitions used to create the generated SELECT statement*

Typically, you will specify the base table usage when you are initially creating each module component. This is because you really cannot do anything with a module component (such as create other types of table usages or define many types of unbound items) until the base table usage has been defined.

Lookup Table Usage

A lookup table usage has a 1:M relationship with the base table usage. A lookup table usage is used primarily for descriptive columns, in which you "look up" the descriptive name of a code column used in the foreign key relationship. Another common usage of the lookup table is to define the base table using an associative table between two fundamental tables. You can add each fundamental table as lookup table usages. This allows you to have all three tables in the same module component.

Similar to a base table usage, a lookup table usage can be defined using a table, view, or snapshot. Your choice of which to use will vary greatly, based on the layout you are trying to generate. In Chapter 31 we will discuss layout implications of module component designs.

Layout Design

The layout of the items selected by the base and lookup table usages is also important to consider at this time. This is because once you have determined what is to be selected from where, you will have the opportunity to create an initial layout for the report. The two key components in this discussion are displayed items and item groups.

Displayed Items

Displayed items are definitions that are created when you specify which of the columns in the SELECT statement you wish to display. This can include information selected from bound items in table usages or unbound items. Displayed items have the same set of repository properties as the bound or unbound items. The only difference is that the *Display* property for these items has been set to **TRUE**.

Typically, the most important properties that you will set for displayed items are

- *Prompt* The title of the displayed item in the generated report
- *Display Datatype* The datatype that will be used to define the layout field in the generated report
- *Width* The length of the display field

Displayed items also take into account how the report is to be formatted. For instance, the order in which the displayed items are to be displayed is based on the value of each displayed item's *Usage Sequence* property. When the Report Generator creates the layout of the report, the displayed items are placed on the report starting with the lowest *Usage Sequence* and ascending through the displayed items until they are all placed in the body of the generated report.

Item Groups

Item groups are used in report definition for two main purposes:

- To define break groups in the report layout
- To group associated displayed items

The difference between these two types of item groups is based on the *Break Group* property of the item group. If this property is set to **Yes**, then the Report Generator will create a break group for that item group. By default, each item group you define will have an associated displayed item based on that item group. You can then assign additional displayed items based on bound or unbound items to the item group. The Report Generator will use this information to determine which columns to display in the generated break group.

Sample Report

To show you how all of the material we have covered thus far works in the real world, let's walk through the following sample report. Figure 28-2 is a server model diagram of the data used to generate this example report.

We are going to create a report that displays a listing of Database Change Requests (DBCRS), the person who requested each, and the person assigned to resolve it. We will display these records breaking first on the application system name and second on the status of the DBCR.

Follow the steps listed next to create the sample report. Since there is more than one way to accomplish this task, we focused on defining steps that minimized the amount of time required to create the definition, while still taking advantage of the new features of release 2. We have chosen to use the dialogs for all the steps in this example. The completed version of this report module is available in the sample application, CH28_DBCRS.

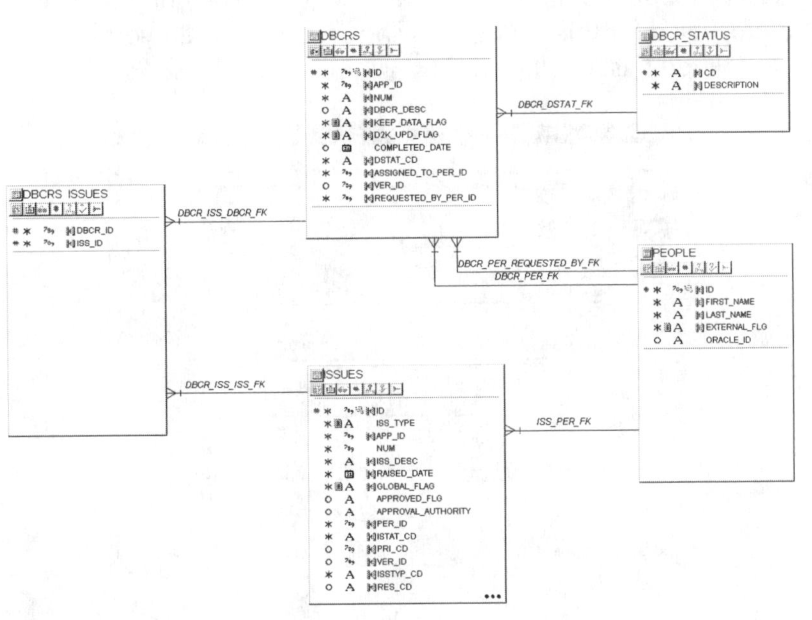

FIGURE 28-2. *Server model diagram*

To create the sample report:

1. In the Design Editor (DE), click on the Modules tab.
2. Create a new report definition. Do this by pressing the Create icon in the Design Editor toolbar. This will launch the first of three sets of dialogs that we will use to define this report definition.
3. The first set of dialogs is the report definition dialogs; the Name dialog is the first that will be displayed. Use this to specify identifying information for this report definition. First, specify the name that will be used to name generated files (*Short Name* = **CH28_DBCRS**). Next, specify a unique name for the report definition that will be used to identify the report definition in the repository (*Module Name* = **CH28_DBCRS**); then fill in the purpose or a short description of the report definition (*Purpose* = **Report that lists DBCRS by Application and Status**). Finally, specify the language that will be used to define and generate this module (*Language* = **Developer/2000 Reports**). This is the property that determines what

type of module definition you are creating. The completed Name dialog used for this example is shown here. When you have completed this, click Next.

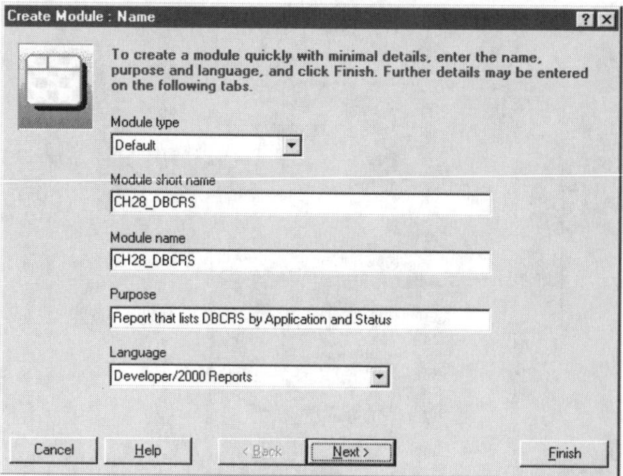

4. The Titles dialog is the second that will be displayed. Use it to specify the titles that you would like to have displayed and the overall layout style of the generated report. Specify the main title or top title of the report (*Report Title* = **Database Change Requests (DBCRS)**). Next, specify the layout style of the report (*Layout format* = **Master Detail**). The completed Titles dialog used for this example is shown here. When you have completed it, click Next.

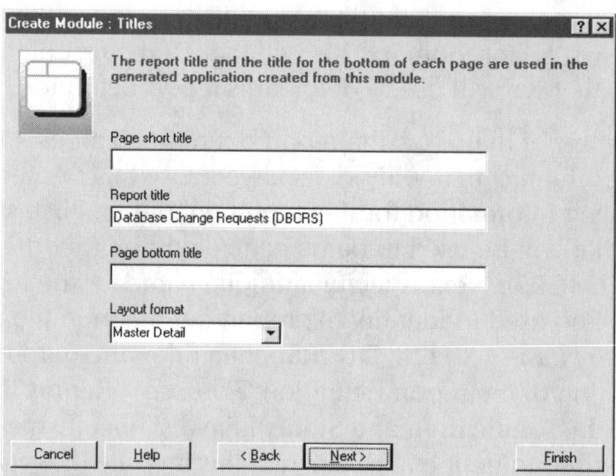

5. The Arguments dialog is the third that will be displayed. You can use this to specify user parameters; we will address this topic in Chapter 30. For now, click Next to skip this dialog.

6. The Files dialog is the fourth that will be displayed. You can use it to specify a name that will be used for all generated files. However, if you choose to supply a value here, it will supersede the name you just supplied for the *Short Name* on the Name dialog. Click Next to skip this dialog.

7. The Module Network is the fifth dialog that will be displayed. This is used to create module networks. Click Next to skip.

8. The Goodbye dialog is the last report definition dialog that will be displayed. Use it to choose how you would like to have the report definition created and what to do next. Select option 2 (*Invoke the Module Component Data Wizard to create a module component*) and then click Finish. The completed Goodbye dialog used for this example is shown here:

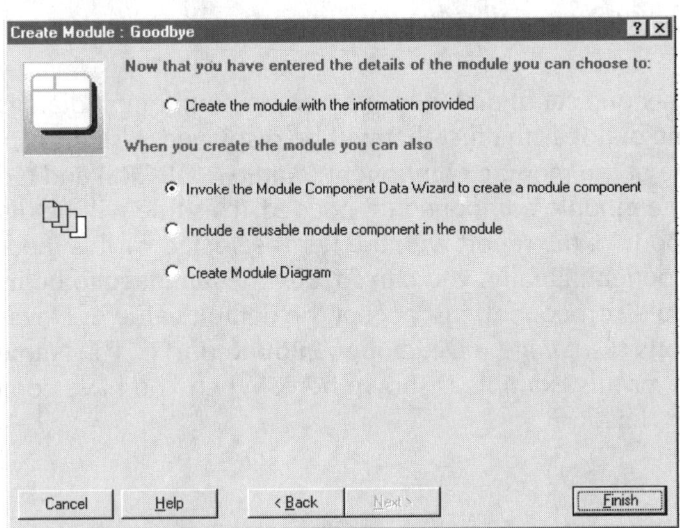

NOTE
You could select one of the other three options, but they are not specifically tailored for new report definitions. Option 1, Create the module with the information provided, is a good choice if you are simply creating report definitions for an application system but are not ready to define module components. Option 3, Include a reusable module component in the module, is a good choice once you have already created some report definitions and have identified module components that can be reused. Option 4, Create Module Diagram will use a diagram to accomplish the same result as option 2. However, to use this option, you must already understand how to create a module diagram because you will not be lead through the process. Thus, option 2 is generally the best alternative when initially creating a report.

9. The second set of dialog is the module component dialogs; the Name dialog is the first that will be displayed. Use it to specify the name of the module component (*Name* = **DBCRS**) and a display title for the module component, if needed. This title will be displayed in the body of the report with the items selected by this module component. Finally, you can specify the language to be used for this module component; just accept the default value of Developer/2000 Reports (*Language* = **Developer/2000 Reports**). The Name dialog used for this example is shown here. When you have completed it, click Next.

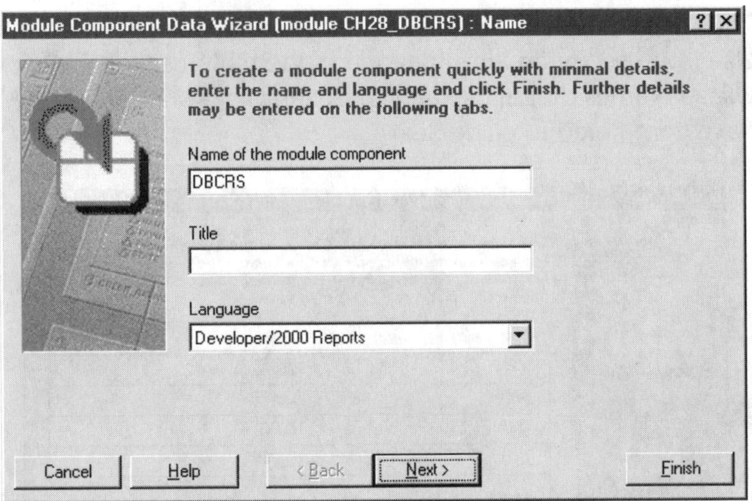

10. The Table Usage Selection dialog is the second that will be displayed. Use it to specify the base table usage for this module component (*Base Table* = **DBCRS**). You can also specify lookup table usages for the module component (*Lookup table usages* = **PEOPLE**, **APPLICATIONS**, **DBCR_STATUS**). The completed Table Usage Selection dialog used for this example is shown here. When you have completed it, click Next.

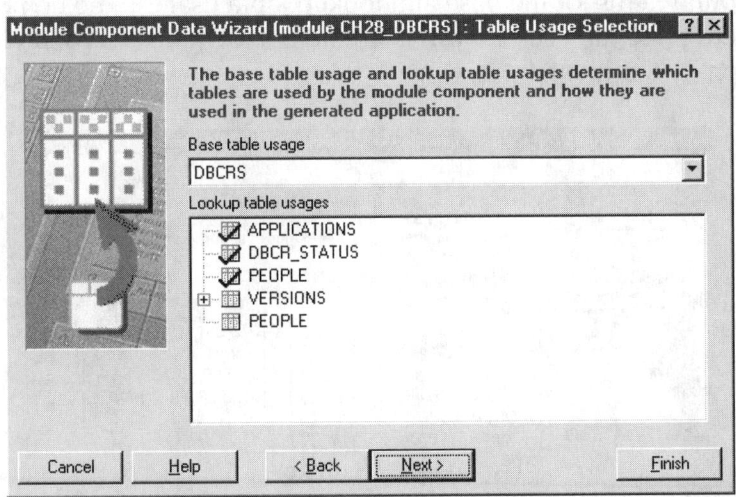

11. The Usage Names dialog is the third dialog that will be displayed. Use it to specify an alias for each of the table usages. The completed Usage Names dialog used for this example is shown here. When you have completed it, click Next.

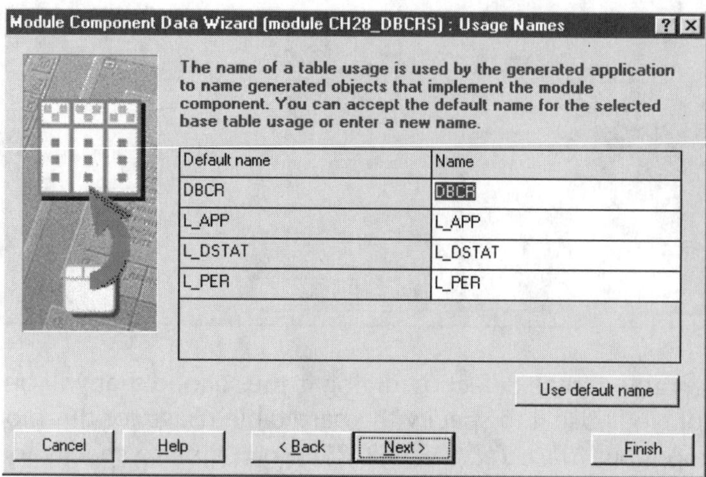

12. The Item Selection dialog is the fourth dialog that will be displayed. Use it to specify the columns to be selected by the query based on this module component. All of the selected items will be stored as bound items for the base and lookup table usages. The completed item selection used for this example is shown here. When you have completed it, click Next.

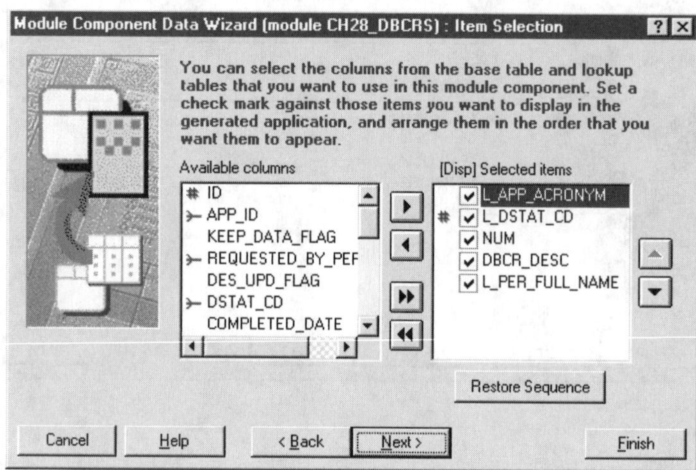

TIP

The [Disp] checkbox column in front of the selected items allows you to specify whether you would like the selected item to be displayed in the generated report layout. If you check the checkbox, a displayed item definition will be created for the bound items. You will also have the opportunity to specify displayed items using the Module Component Display Wizard.

13. The Item Names dialog is the fifth dialog that will be displayed. Use it to specify an alias for each selected column. These will be used in the generated query. Default values are normally okay. In this example, we removed all of the **L_** prefixes from the lookup bound items. The completed Item Names dialog used for this example is shown here. When you have completed it, click Next.

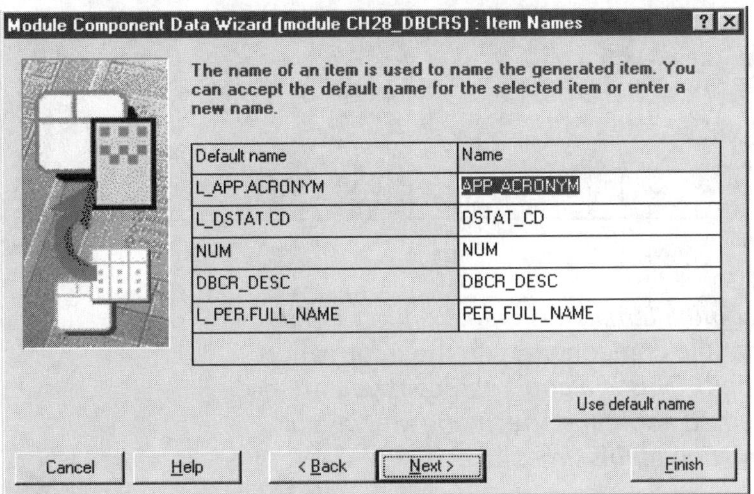

14. The Links dialog is the sixth dialog that will be displayed. Since we do not have any other module components in this example, this will appear blank. Click Next to skip it.

15. The Options dialog is the last module component data dialog that will be displayed. Use this to choose how you would like to create the module component. Select option 2 (*Create the module component and then invoke the Module Component Display Wizard to define display details for the component*). Just as the option describes, a module component will be created, and then another set of dialogs will be launched to gather information that will be used to display the selected items. The completed Options dialog used for this example is shown here. When you have completed it, click Finish.

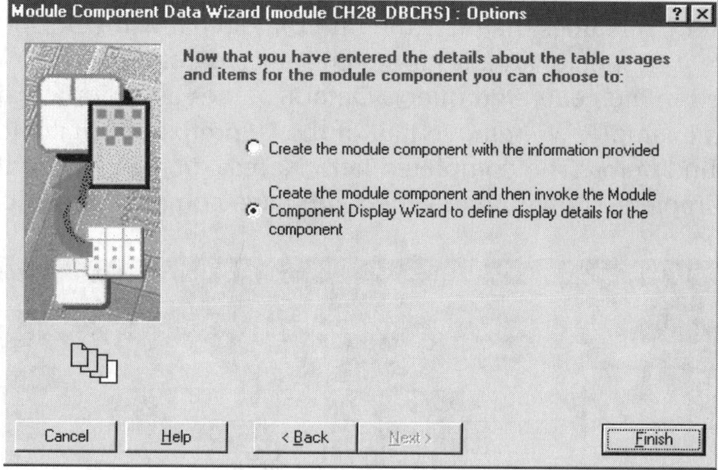

NOTE
*You could alternatively select option 1 (*Create the module component with the information provided*). This is a good choice if you are not concerned about the specifying any layout information at this time.*

16. The third and last set of dialogs is the module component display dialogs. The Display dialog is the first that will be displayed. Use it to select the overall layout style for the module component (*Layout*

Style = **Tabular**). Leave the *Number of rows to be displayed* property blank because it will be automatically populated with **0** when you leave this dialog. Shown here is the completed Display dialog used for this example. When you have completed this it, click Next.

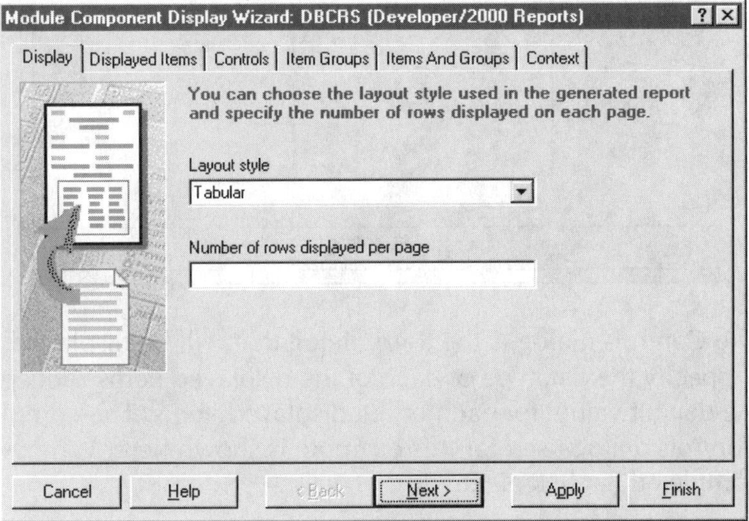

17. The Displayed Items dialog is the second that will be displayed. Use it to choose which columns from the total list of selected columns you would like displayed. Based on the results of step 12, all of the selected items that had the [Disp] checkbox checked were defaulted into the displayed items column. To display all of the columns we are selecting in the report layout, make sure all of the columns are included as displayed items. The completed Displayed Items dialog used for this example is shown here. When you have completed it, click Next.

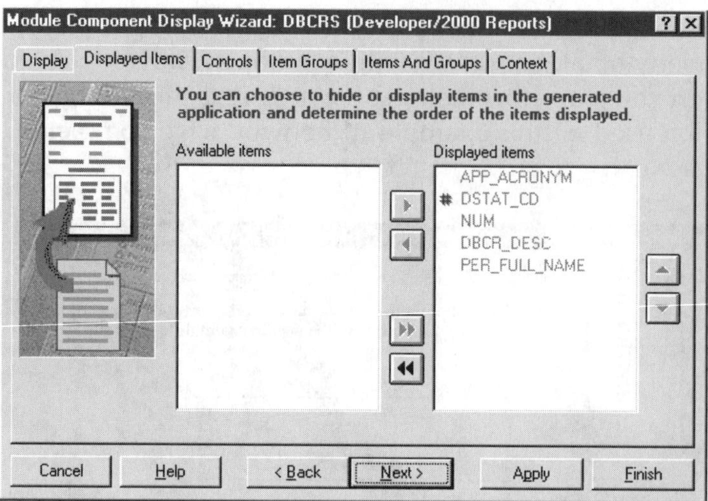

18. The Controls dialog is the third dialog that will be displayed. Use it to specify the datatype of each of the displayed items. Accept **Text**, the default value, for each of the displayed items. The completed Controls dialog used for this example is shown here. When you have completed it, click Next.

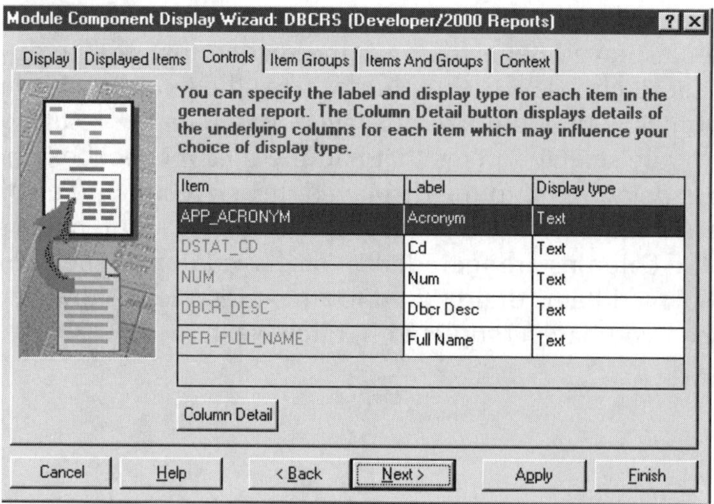

19. The Item Groups dialog is the fourth dialog that will be displayed. Use it to create the break groups needed by this report. In this example, we created three item groups, **Application**, **Status**, and **Body**, and designated them as break groups by setting the *Break Group?* property to **Yes**. The completed Item Groups dialog used for this example is shown here. When you have completed it, click Next.

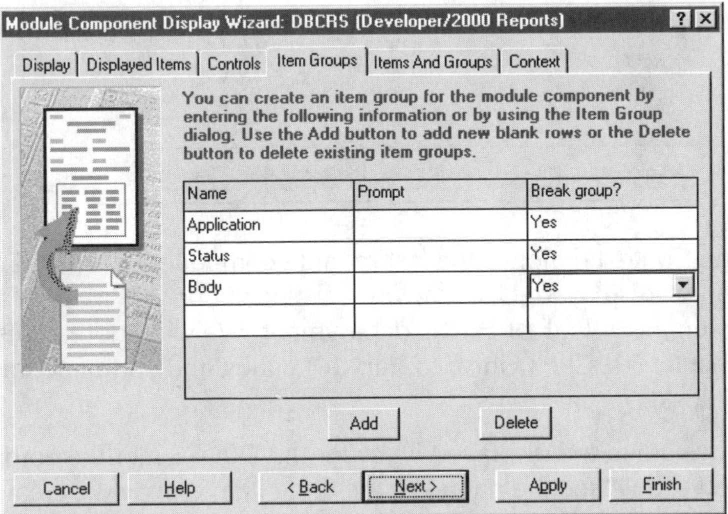

20. The Items and Groups dialog is the fifth that will be displayed. Use it to specify the relationship between displayed items and item groups and the display order of display items and break groups. In this example, we assigned the **APP_ACRONYM** displayed item to the **APPLICATION** item group, the **DSTAT_CD** displayed item to the **STATUS** item group, and all of the other displayed items to the **BODY** item group. We then sequenced the columns to be in the order in which we wanted to have them displayed. The completed Items and Groups dialog used for this example is shown here. When you have completed it, click Next.

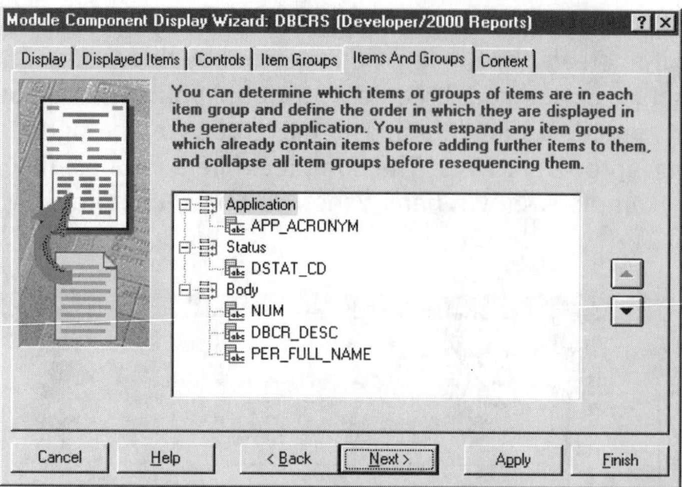

21. The Context dialog is the last module component display dialog that will be displayed. Using it, you can specify bookmark display columns for PDF or HTML deployment. We will address this topic in Chapter 31. Click Finish to skip this dialog and complete this set of dialogs.

22. Navigate to the displayed items for the DBCRS module component. You should see the names of the three item groups we created for this report. Select the **APPLICATION** item group and launch the properties dialogs. We will use these to set the layout style of each item group and ensure that the report break groups are related correctly.

23. The Name dialog is first dialog that will be displayed. This will display the values you specified in step 18. Click Next to skip it.

24. The Report Break Group is the second dialog that will be displayed. Use it to specify the break direction for the item group (*Break Group Direction* = **Down**) and the layout style for the item group (*Break Group Style* = **Form**). The complete Report Break Group dialog used for this example is shown here. When you have completed it, click Next.

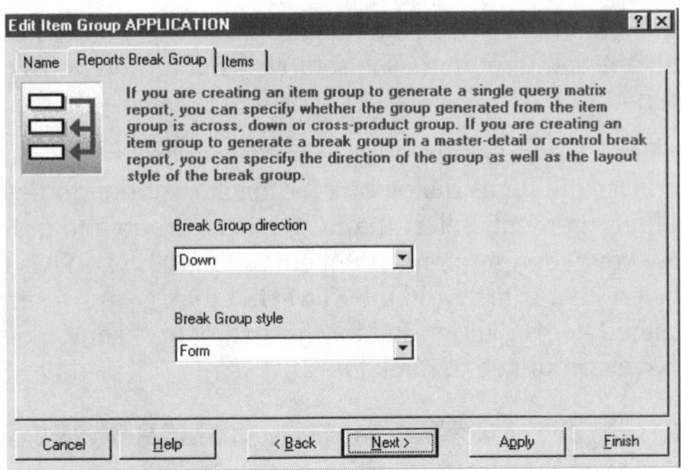

25. The Items dialog is the last that will be displayed. Use it to specify the relationship between the application item group, its displayed item, and the other two item groups. Since we want the report to break first by application, each of the other two item groups should be subordinate to this item group. Select both the **STATUS** and **BODY** item groups and press the RIGHT ARROW key. Then sequence the items so that the **APP_ACRONYM** displayed item is first, the **STATUS** break group is second, and the **BODY** break group is third. The completed Items dialog used for this example is shown here. When you have completed it, click Finish.

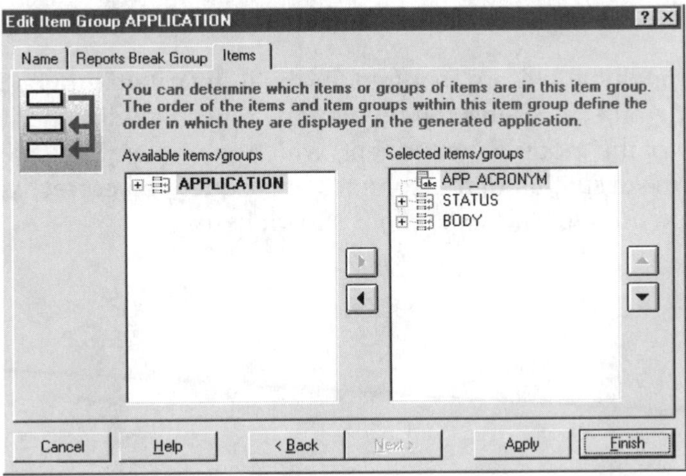

26. Next, click on the **STATUS** item group and repeat steps 21–23, using exactly the same settings. The settings used for the Items dialog are defined in step 27.

27. The **STATUS** item group represents the second break group for this report. Use the Items dialog box for this item group to define this layout requirement. Select the **BODY** item group and press the RIGHT ARROW key. Then sequence the items so that the **DSTAT_CD** displayed item is first, and the **STATUS** break group is second. The completed Items dialog used for this example is shown here. When you have completed it, click Finish.

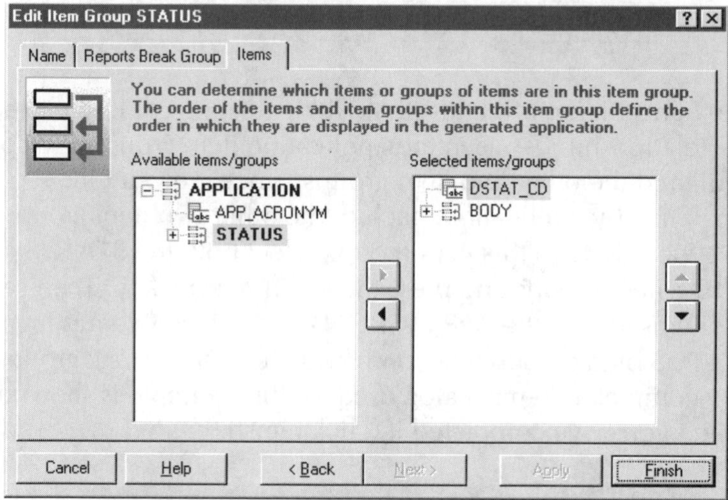

28. No modifications are required for the **BODY** item group. Since this item group represents the body of the report, it will inherit the layout style of the module component, which is tabular. However, so you can make sure all of the columns are sequenced correctly, the Items dialog used for this example is shown here.

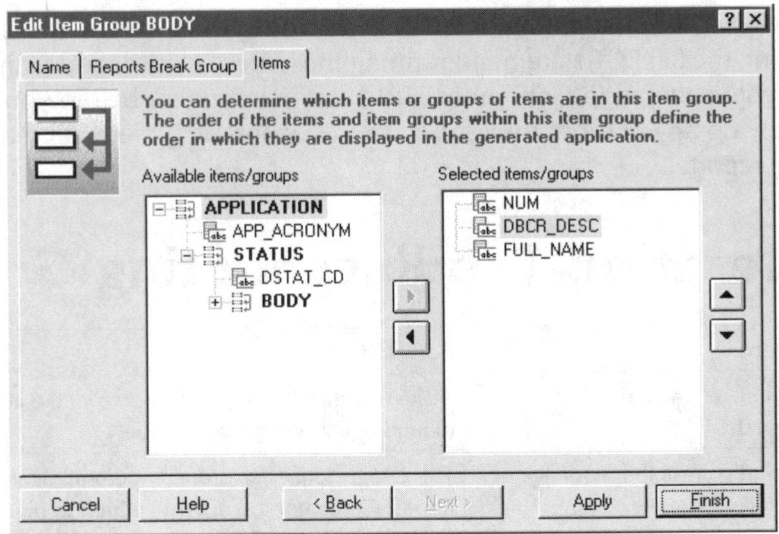

29. Generate the report definition. The body of the generated report layout is shown here:

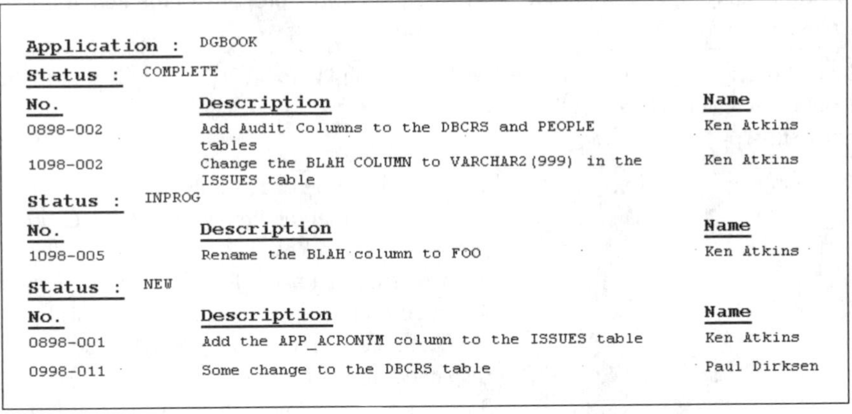

Application : DGBOOK

Status : COMPLETE

No.	Description	Name
0898-002	Add Audit Columns to the DBCRS and PEOPLE tables	Ken Atkins
1098-002	Change the BLAH COLUMN to VARCHAR2(999) in the ISSUES table	Ken Atkins

Status : INPROG

No.	Description	Name
1098-005	Rename the BLAH column to FOO	Ken Atkins

Status : NEW

No.	Description	Name
0898-001	Add the APP_ACRONYM column to the ISSUES table	Ken Atkins
0998-011	Some change to the DBCRS table	Paul Dirksen

In the chapters that follow, we will show you how to enhance this report by refining the SELECT statement, refining the Where clause, and using some layout generation techniques. Just keep in mind that before you can effectively do any of those things, you must become proficient at creating the base report.

Generation Troubleshooting Guide

Problem	**Solution**
How do I get an item to be displayed?	Make sure that the *Display?* property of the item (bound or unbound) is set to **True**.
How do I control the sequence of the displayed items?	The *Usage Sequence* property communicates to the Report Generator the order in which to place the items in the report layout. The first column you would like to have displayed should have the lowest number and the last item should have the highest number.
How do I change the prompt of a displayed item?	Modify the *Prompt* property of the item (bound or unbound).
The text of some of the items in the layout is truncated. How can I change this?	Make sure the *Wrap Style* property is set to **Wrap**.
My report is not breaking correctly.	This could be one of a couple things. 1. Make sure that the item group *Break Group?* property is set to **Yes**. 2. Make sure that each displayed item is assigned to the correct item group. You can do this by checking the *Item Group* property of each displayed item. 3. If you are using more than one item group as a break group, make sure that the relationship between each break group has been established. You can do this by checking the *Parent Item Group* property of each item group.

Problem	**Solution**
I have extra titles appearing in my report body. How do I suppress them?	These titles are coming from your module components. To remove them, delete each of the values from each module component's *Title* property.
The body of my report did not generate when I used the **Across** break group style for my item group.	Use the **Form** break group style.

CHAPTER 29

Refining Data Selection

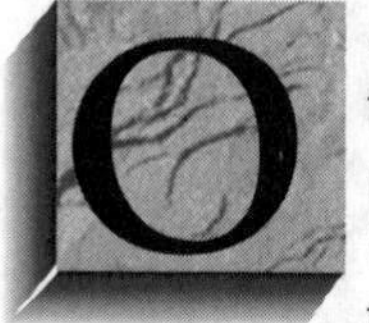

Once you have created the basic report definition, you can then focus on refining the data selected by the generated report. This is primarily accomplished by using unbound items. This is a new feature to release 2 of Oracle Designer that is really useful. In this chapter, we will cover each of the following types of unbound items:

- SQL expression
- Single row SQL aggregate
- Client-function
- Server-function
- Computed

We will also provide step-by-step examples of how to implement each type of feature and a generation troubleshooting guide to assist you with common generation problems. As a common point of reference, we will be referring to the server model diagram shown in Figure 29-1 for all of the examples shown in this chapter.

SQL Expression

A SQL expression unbound item allows you to specify any SQL expression you like, as long as it references a column of a table usage included in the module component, whether a bound item has been created for it or not. This expression will then be placed into the select clause of the generated query. Typical uses of SQL expression unbound items include

- Decode statements
- Concatenation of column values
- Functions (sum, average, count, etc.)

You can also call server-side functions, although you really should use the server-side function unbound item type to implement that functionality. We will explain how to implement a server-side function call later in this

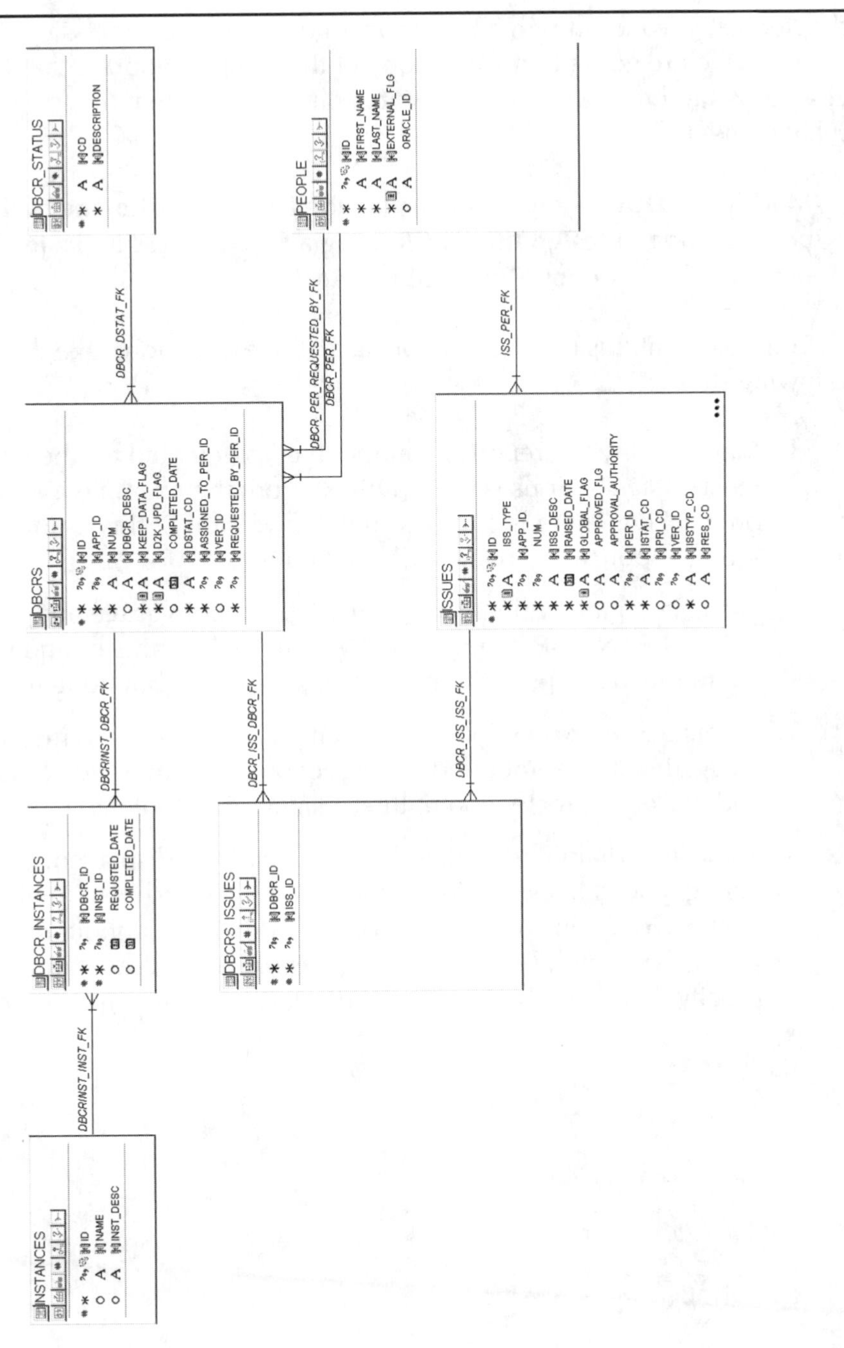

FIGURE 29-1. *Server model diagram*

chapter. Let's work through an example of using a SQL expression. In this example, we are going to make a copy of the sample report created in Chapter 28 and refine the SELECT statement to implement the following enhancement:

> **Modify the DBCRS report to display the first and last name of the person who requested the DBCR using a SQL expression instead of the denormalized column (PER_FULL_NAME).**

To implement this requirement using a SQL expression, take the following steps.

1. Make a copy the report definition that you created for the example in Chapter 28 (or use CH28_DBCRS from the example application on the CD). There is also a completed version of this example in the sample application named CH29_SQL
2. Navigate to the bound items of the L_PER table usage and delete the PER_FULL_NAME bound item. We will replace this bound item in the following steps with one SQL expression unbound item.
3. Create a SQL expression unbound item definition. Do this by navigating to the unbound items section of the module component and click the Create icon in the Design Editor toolbar.
4. The Name dialog is the first dialog that will be displayed. Using this dialog, you can specify the name of the unbound item (*Item Name* = **NAME**). You can specify that you would like the unbound item to be a SQL expression (*Item Type* = **SQL Expression**). You can also specify that the unbound item is displayed in the generated report

layout (*Is this item displayed?* = **Yes**). The illustration below shows the completed Name dialog used for this example. When you have completed this dialog, click Next.

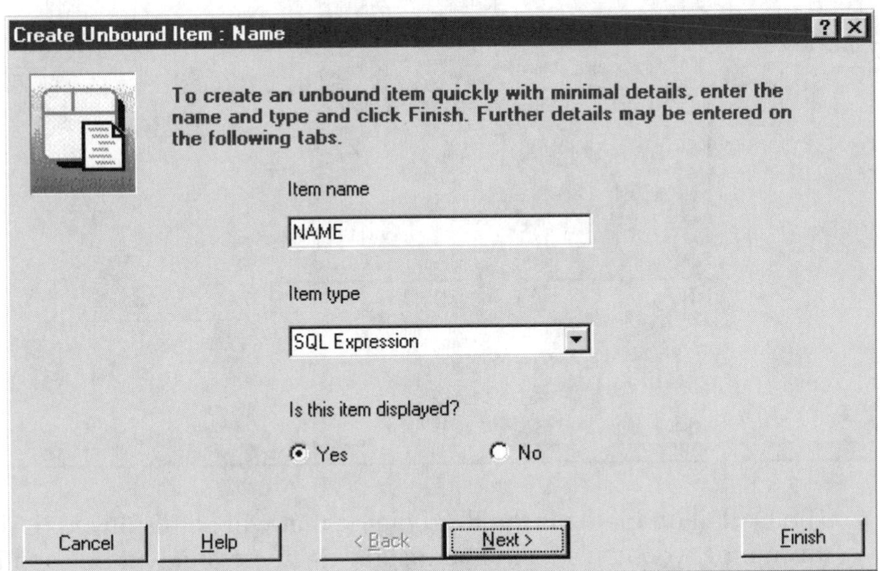

5. The SQL Expression dialog is the second dialog that will be displayed. Using this dialog, you can specify the SQL expression you would like to add to the select clause of the generated query. In this example, you are specifying a SQL expression that will not use any of the bound items in the report definition. Because of that, you need to be sure to include the table alias of the columns to be included in the SQL expression. (*SQL expression* = **L_PER.FIRST_NAME||' '||L_PER.LAST_NAME**). The following illustration shows the completed SQL Expression dialog used in this example. When you have completed this dialog, click Next.

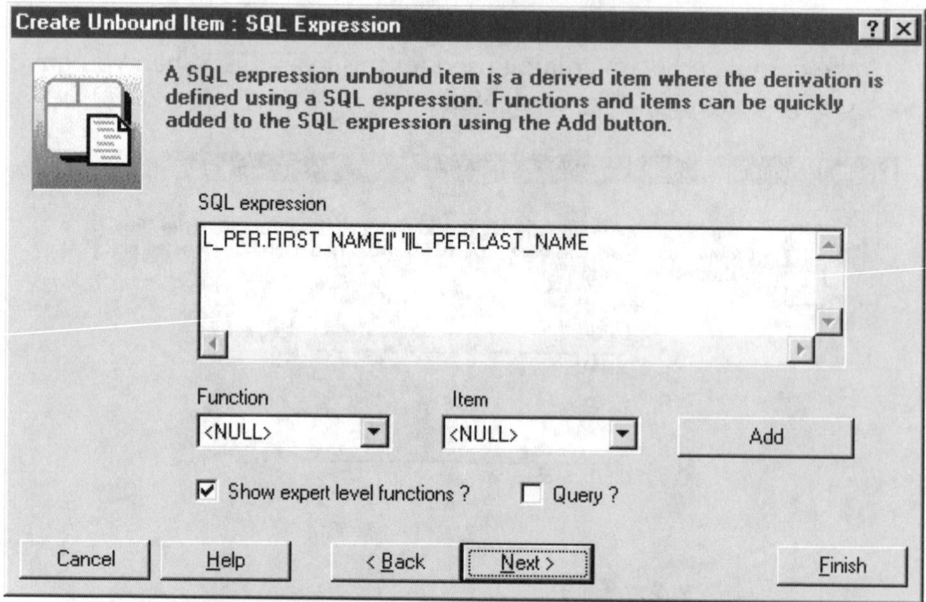

6. The Definition dialog is the third dialog that will be displayed. Using this dialog, you can specify the display datatype that will be used in the report layout (*Datatype* = **CHAR**). The illustration below shows the completed Datatype dialog used for the example. When you have completed this dialog, click Next.

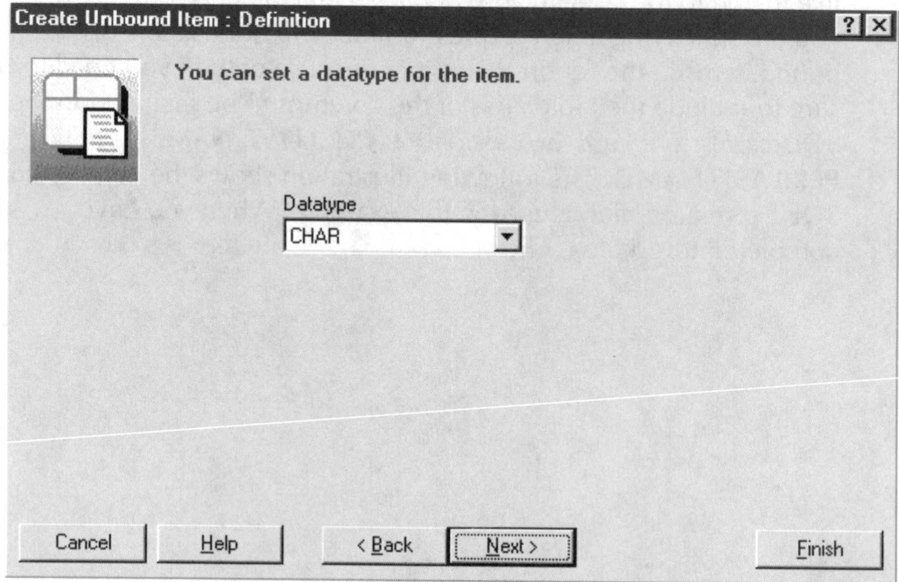

7. The Allowable Values dialog is the fourth dialog that will be displayed. This dialog allows you to specify allowable values for this unbound item. Click Next to skip this dialog.

8. The Controls dialog is the last dialog that will be displayed. Using this dialog, you can specify many different display characteristics for this item. The illustration below shows the completed Controls dialog used for this example. When you have completed this dialog, click Finish.

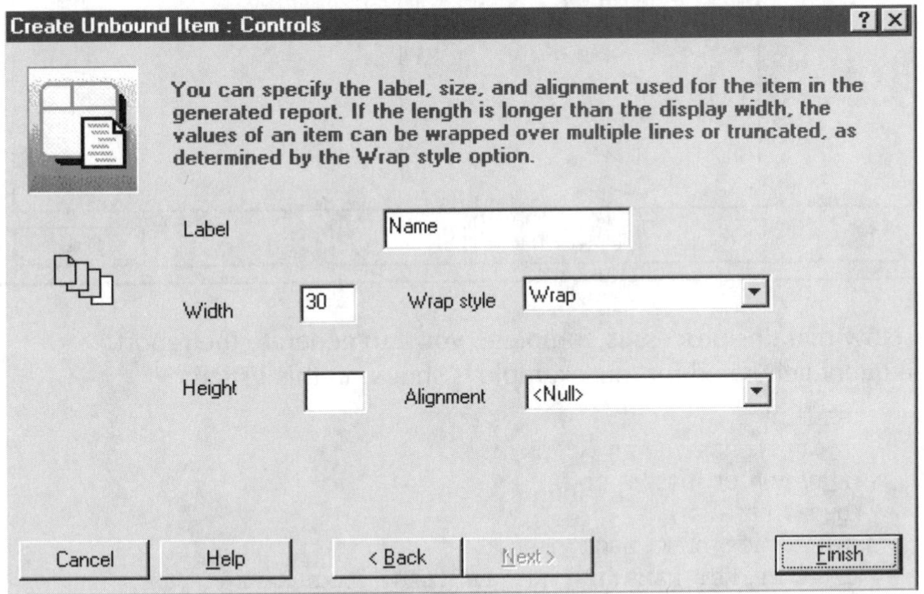

9. Navigate to the BODY item group in the Displayed Items and Groups section of the DBCRS module component and launch the Properties dialogs. Click on the Items tab and assign the NAME unbound item to the BODY item group. The next illustration shows the completed Items dialogs used for this example. When you have completed this dialog, click Finish.

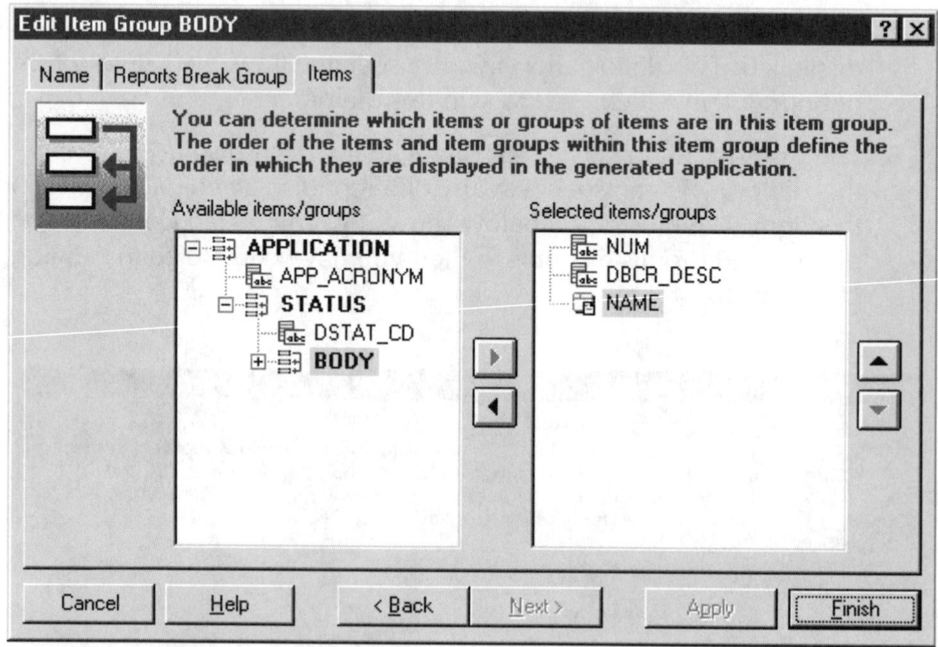

Now that this process is complete, you can generate the report. The query generated for this example is shown in this listing:

```
SELECT
L_APP.ACRONYM APP_ACRONYM,
L_DSTAT.CD DSTAT_CD,
DBCR.NUM NUM,
DBCR.DBCR_DESC DBCR_DESC,
L_PER.FIRST_NAME||' '||L_PER.LAST_NAME NAME
FROM
PEOPLE L_PER,
DBCR_STATUS L_DSTAT,
APPLICATIONS L_APP,
DBCRS DBCR
WHERE
DBCR.APP_ID = L_APP.ID AND
DBCR.DSTAT_CD = L_DSTAT.CD AND
DBCR.REQUESTED_BY_PER_ID = L_PER.ID
```

You can see by looking at the generated query that the SQL expression was placed in the select clause.

Single Row SQL Aggregate

A single row SQL aggregate (SRSA) unbound item allows you to add a function column (count, average, sum, etc.) into the select clause of the generated query. You can define an SRSA unbound item using any of the bound items in the module definition, including base and lookup table usages and SQL query sets.

You also have the option of including a new table as a SRSA table usage. A table that can be used as an SRSA table usage is a child to the base table usage in the module component. The SRSA table usage will then be added to the from clause of the generated query, and a predicate will be added to the where clause that joins this table usage to the base table usage. These table usages do not have bound items, but you can specify SRSA unbound items to use column definitions contained within the table. An SRSA table usage cannot be defined until you have created the base table usage for the module component. This type of table usage is valid only for the Report generator. Let's work through an example of using a single row SQL aggregate. In this example, we are going to make a copy of the sample report created in Chapter 28 and refine the SELECT statement to implement the following enhancement:

> **Modify the DBCRS report to include a count of issues that the DBCR is associated with.**

To implement this requirement using a single row SQL aggregate, take the following steps.

1. Make a copy the report definition that you created for the example in Chapter 28 (or use CH28_DBCRS from the example application on the CD). There is also a completed version of this example in the sample application named CH29_SRSA
2. Create an SRSA table usage for the module component. Do this by navigating to the table definition in the DBCRS module component and pressing the Create icon in the Design Editor toolbar.
3. The Optional dialog is the first dialog that will be displayed. Using this dialog, you can specify that the type of table usage you are

creating is a single row SQL aggregate (*Which type of table usage would you like to create?* = **Single Row Summary**). The illustration below shows the completed Optional dialog used for this example. When you have completed this dialog, click Next.

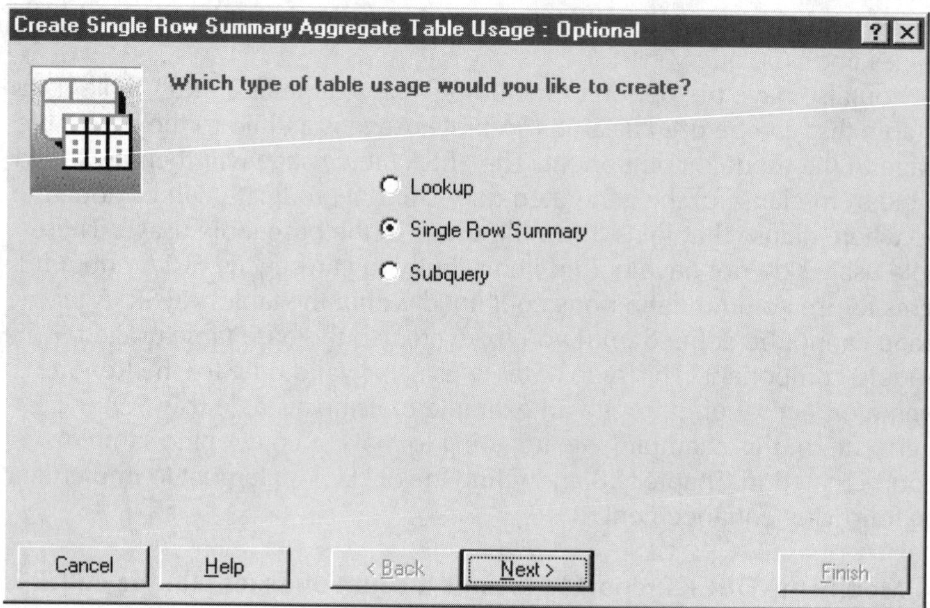

4. The Table Usage dialog is the second dialog that will be displayed. Using this dialog, you can specify the table that you would like to include in the query (*Table* = **DBCRS_ISSUES**). A column of this table will later be used in a single row SQL aggregate unbound item. You can also specify an alias for this table usage and whether or not this table usage should be joined to the base table using an outer join. In this example, we accepted the default table alias and chose to use an outer join. The following illustration shows the completed

Table Usage dialog used in this example. When you have completed this dialog, click Next.

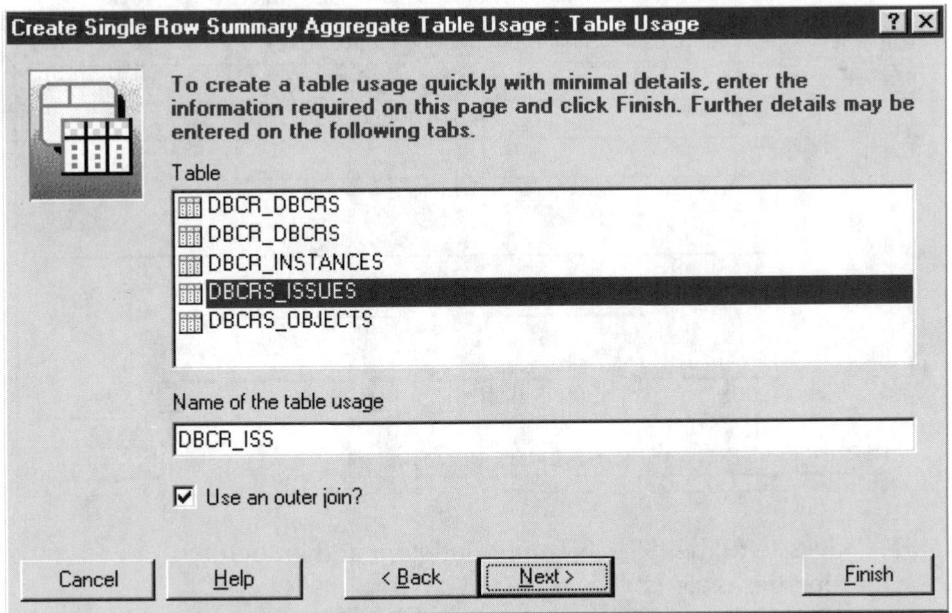

5. The Where dialog is the third dialog that will be displayed. This dialog is used to specify predicates that will be generated into the where clause of the SELECT statement. Click Next to skip this dialog.

6. The Aggregates dialog is the last dialog that will be displayed. This dialog will create the single row SQL aggregate unbound item based on the information provided. In this example, you can specify that you want to count the number of issues in the DBCRS_ISSUES table. The next illustration shows the completed Aggregates dialog used for this example. When you have completed this dialog, click Finish.

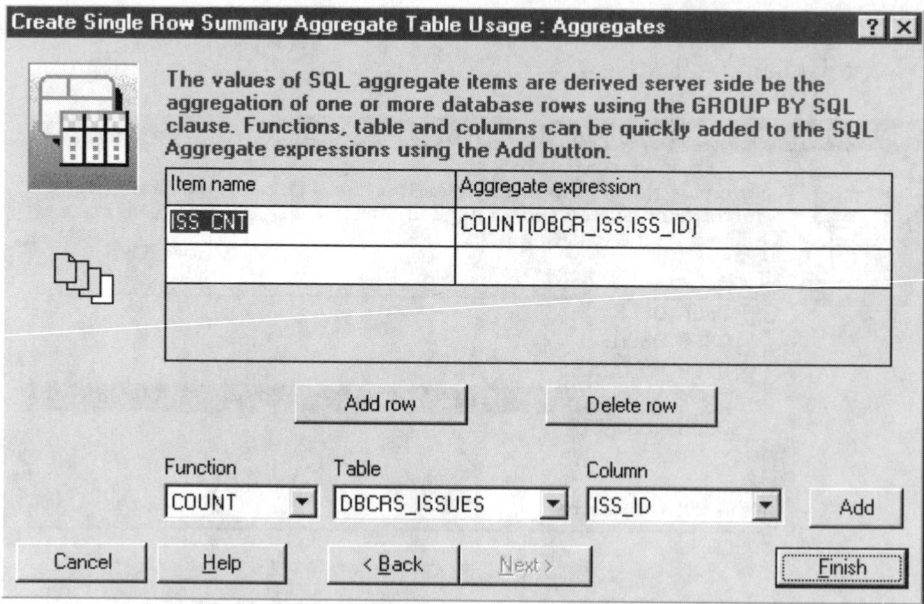

7. Navigate to the ISS_CNT unbound item and launch the Properties dialogs.

8. The Name dialog is the first dialog that will be displayed. Click Next to skip this dialog.

9. The SQL Aggregate dialog is the second dialog that will be displayed. This dialog will display the aggregate function that you specified in step 6. Click Next to skip this dialog.

10. The Definition dialog is the third dialog that will be displayed. This dialog allows you to specify the display datatype that will be used in the report layout (*Datatype* = **NUMBER**). The next illustration shows the completed Definition dialog used for the example. When you have completed this dialog, click Next.

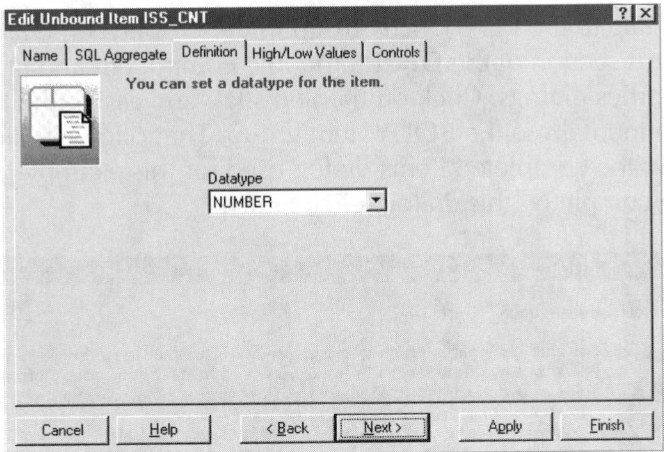

11. The Controls dialog is the last dialog that will be displayed. This dialog allows you to specify many different display characteristics for this item. The following illustration shows the completed Controls dialog used for this example. When you have completed this dialog, click Finish.

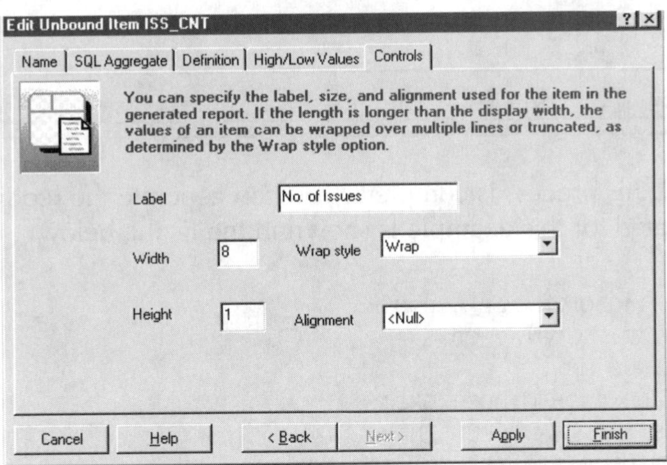

12. Navigate to the BODY item group in the Displayed Items and Groups section of the DBCRS module component and launch the Properties dialogs. Click on the Items tab and assign the ISS_CNT unbound item to the BODY item group. The following illustration shows the completed Items dialog used for this example. When you have completed this dialog, click Finish.

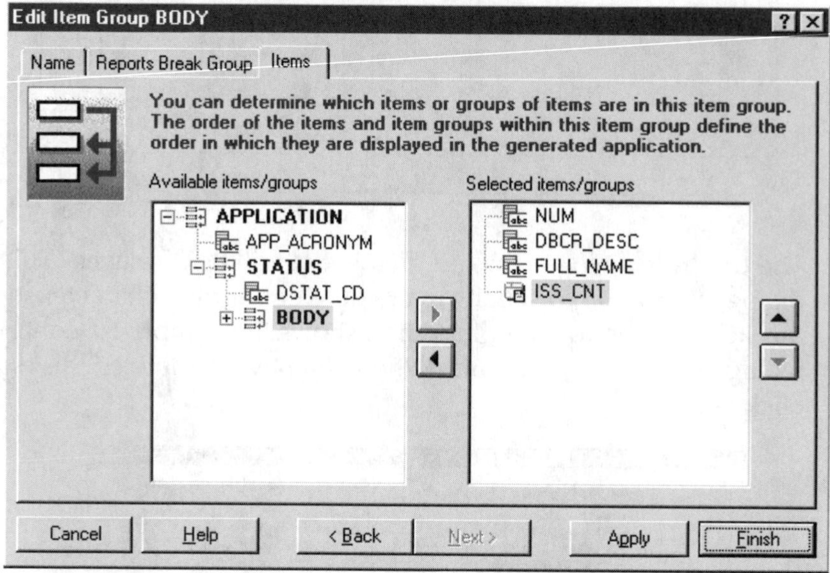

Now that this process is complete, you can generate the report. The query generated for this example is shown in the listing below:

```
SELECT
L_APP.ACRONYM APP_ACRONYM,
L_DSTAT.CD DSTAT_CD,
DBCR.NUM NUM,
DBCR.DBCR_DESC DBCR_DESC,
L_PER.FULL_NAME FULL_NAME,
COUNT(DBCR_ISS.ISS_ID) ISS CNT
FROM
PEOPLE L_PER,
DBCR_STATUS L_DSTAT,
APPLICATIONS L_APP,
DBCRS DBCR,
DBCRS_ISSUES DBCR_ISS
```

```
WHERE
DBCR.APP_ID = L_APP.ID AND
DBCR.DSTAT_CD = L_DSTAT.CD AND
DBCR.ASSIGNED_TO_PER_ID = L_PER.ID AND
DBCR_ISS.DBCR_ID (+) = DBCR.ID
GROUP BY
L_APP.ACRONYM,
L_DSTAT.CD,
DBCR.NUM,
DBCR.DBCR_DESC,
L_PER.FIRST_NAME,
L_PER.LAST_NAME
```

You can see by looking at the generated query that using a single row SQL aggregate had many effects. The single row SQL aggregate unbound item was generated into the select clause. This also caused the group by clause to be created. The single row SQL aggregate table usage was added to the from clause, and a predicate was added joining this table to the based table of the module component in the where clause.

Server-Side Function

A server-side function unbound item allows you to call a function stored in the database from the select clause of the generated query. Some typical uses of server-side function unbound items include

- **SQL aggregations** Summarizing child information based on parent column values in the report query
- **SQL expressions** Concatenating column values, decoding column values, etc.

When using server-side functions, be sure to work with your DBA to define a strategy for developing and maintaining these objects. If you are going to use several functions in an application, consider putting the functions in a package. This reduces the total number of objects in the database without negatively impacting any generated applications.

Let's work through an example of how to use a server-side function unbound item. In this example, we are going to make a copy of the sample report created in Chapter 28 and refine the SELECT statement. This example implements the same enhancement as the previous single row SQL aggregate example.

Modify the DBCRS report to include a count of issues that the DBCR is associated with.

To implement this requirement using a server-side function, take the following steps.

1. Make a copy the report definition that you created for the example in Chapter 28 (or use CH28_DBCRS from the example application on the CD). There is also a completed version of this example in the sample application named CH29_SERVER.
2. Create a server-side function unbound item definition. Do this by navigating to the unbound items section of the module component and clicking the Create icon in the Design Editor toolbar.
3. The Name dialog is the first dialog that will be displayed. Using this dialog, you can specify the name of the unbound item (*Item Name* = **ISS_CNT**). You can specify that you would like the unbound item to be a server-side function (*Item Type* = **Server Side Function**). You can also specify that the unbound item is displayed in the generated report layout (*Is this item displayed?* = **Yes**). The illustration below shows the completed Name dialog used for this example. When you have completed this dialog, click Next.

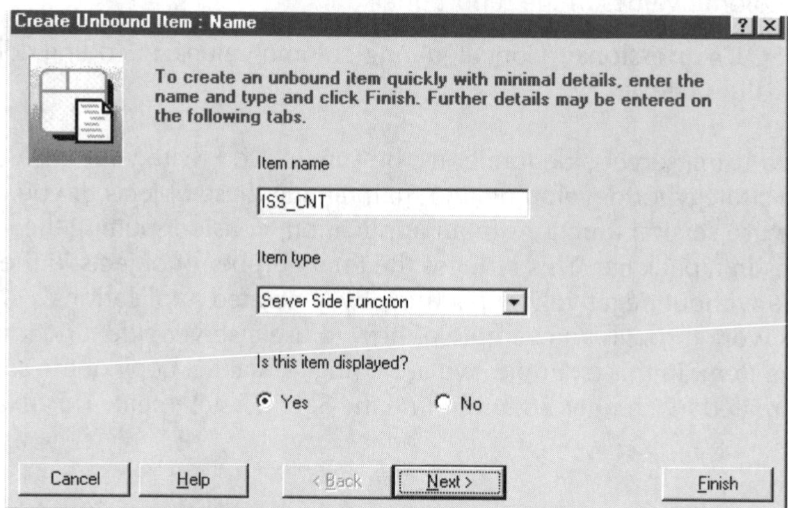

4. The Server Side Function dialog is the second dialog that will be displayed. Using this dialog, you can specify the server-side function you would like to add to the select clause of the generated query (*SQL expression* = **CH29_ISS_CNT(DBCR.ID)**). The illustration below shows the completed Server Side Function dialog used in this example. When you have completed this dialog, click Next.

NOTE
The PL/SQL definition you use does not have to exist in the repository. It must, however, exist in the database and the appropriate permissions need to be granted to the Oracle user account that will be used to generate the report definition.

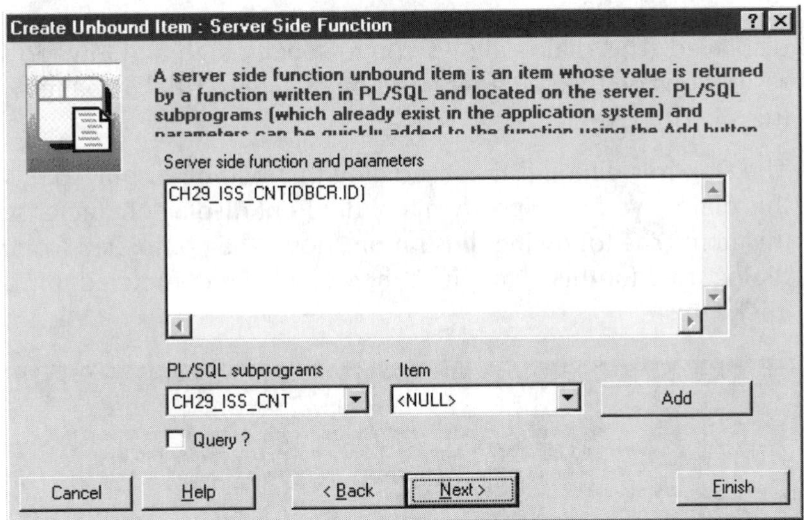

5. The Definition dialog is the third dialog that will be displayed. Using this dialog, you can specify the display datatype that will be used in the report layout (*Datatype* = **NUMBER**). The next illustration shows the completed Datatype dialog used for the example. When you have completed this dialog, click Next.

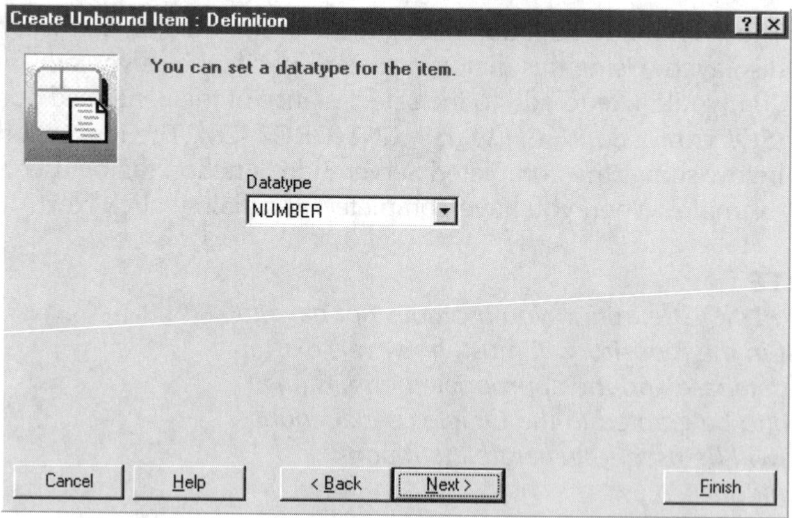

6. The High/Low Values dialog is the fourth dialog that will be displayed. This dialog allows you to specify high and low range restrictions on the value returned by this item. Click Next to skip this dialog.

7. The Controls dialog is the last dialog that will be displayed. Using this dialog, you can specify many different display characteristics for this item. The following illustration shows the completed Controls dialog used for this example. When you have completed this dialog, click Finish.

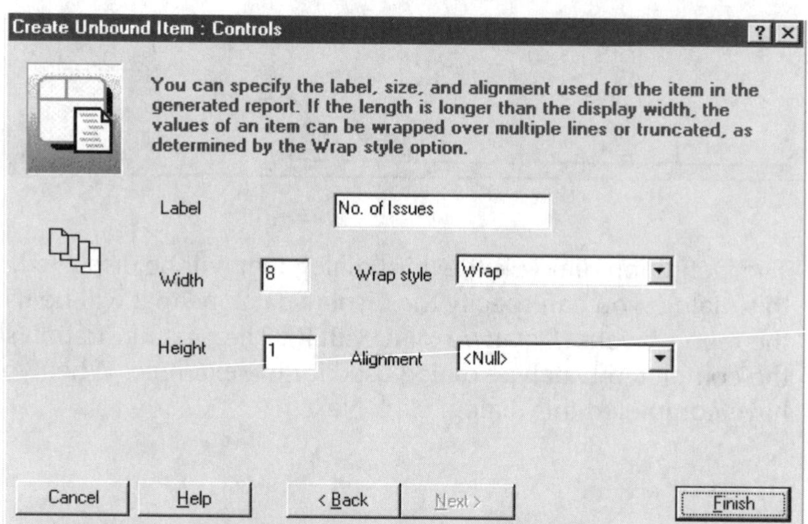

8. Navigate to the BODY item group in the Displayed Items and Groups section of the DBCRS module component and launch the Properties dialogs. Click on the Items tab and assign the ISS_CNT unbound item to the BODY item group. The illustration below shows the completed Items dialogs used for this example. When you have completed this dialog, click Finish.

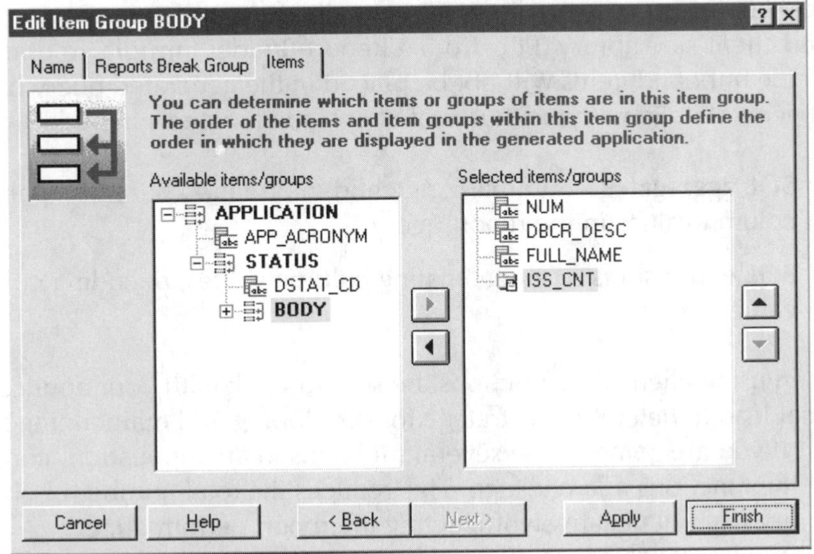

Now that this process is complete, you can generate the report. The query generated for this example is shown in the listing below:

```
SELECT
L_APP.ACRONYM APP_ACRONYM,
L_DSTAT.CD DSTAT_CD,
DBCR.NUM NUM,
DBCR.DBCR_DESC DBCR_DESC,
L_PER.FULL_NAME FULL_NAME,
CH29_ISS_CNT(DBCR.ID) ISS_CNT
FROM
PEOPLE L_PER,
DBCR_STATUS L_DSTAT,
APPLICATIONS L_APP,
DBCRS DBCR
WHERE
DBCR.APP_ID = L_APP.ID AND
DBCR.DSTAT_CD = L_DSTAT.CD AND
DBCR.REQUESTED_BY_PER_ID = L_PER.ID
```

You can see by looking at the generated query that the server-side function was placed in the select clause. An advantage of using a server-side function call is that you can avoid adding a group by clause to the report query, which can improve the performance of the report.

Client-Side Function

A client-side unbound item allows you to call a function stored in an attached client-side library (PLL) from a Report Builder formula column. Client-side unbound items will not be placed in the generated query by the Report generator. Some typical uses of client-side functions include

- **SQL aggregates** Summarizing child information based on parent column values in the report query
- **SQL expressions** Concatenating column values, decoding column values, etc.

When using client-side functions, be sure to work with your application technical lead to determine a strategy for developing and maintaining these objects. If you are going to use several functions in an application, consider putting the functions in a package. This reduces the total number of objects in a library without negatively impacting the report performance.

Let's work through an example of how to use a client-side function unbound item. In this example, we are going to make a copy of the sample report created in Chapter 28 and refine the SELECT statement. This example implements the same enhancement as the single row SQL aggregate and previous server-side function examples.

Modify the DBCRS report to include a count of issues that the DBCR is associated with.

To implement this requirement using a client-side function, take the following steps.

1. Make a copy the report definition that you created for the example in Chapter 28 (or use CH28_DBCRS from the example application on the CD). There is also a completed version of this example in the sample application named CH29_CLIENT.

2. Create a client-side function unbound item definition. Do this by navigating to the unbound items section of the module component and clicking the Create icon in the Design Editor toolbar.

3. The Name dialog is the first dialog that will be displayed. Using this dialog, you can specify the name of the unbound item (*Item Name* = **ISS_CNT**). You can specify that you would like the unbound item to be a client-side function (*Item Type* = **Client Side Function**). You can also specify that the unbound item is displayed in the generated report layout (*Is this item displayed?* = **Yes**). The illustration below shows the completed Name dialog used for this example. When you have completed this dialog, click Next.

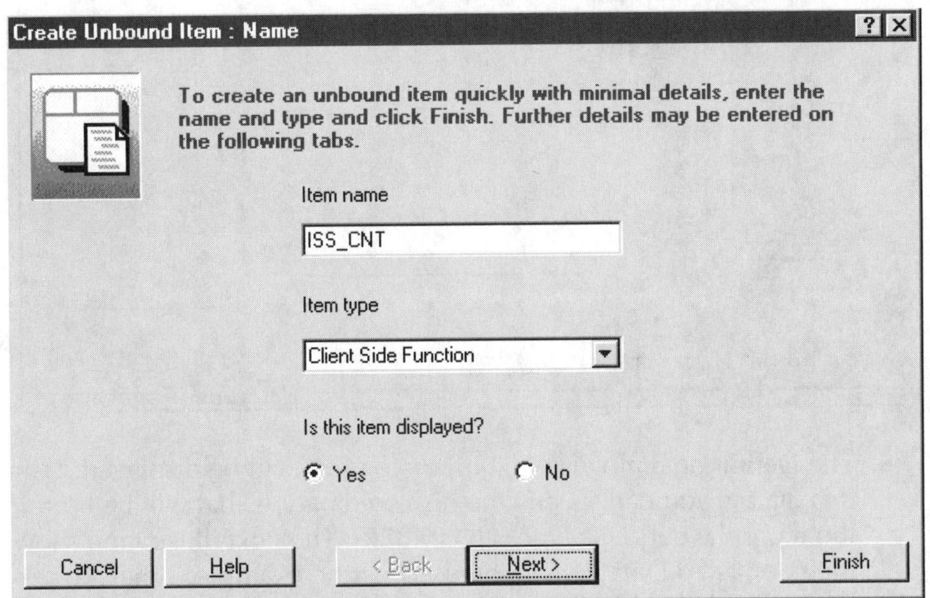

4. The Client Side Function dialog is the second dialog that will be displayed. Using this dialog, you can specify the client-side function you would like to use to create a formula column in the generated report (*SQL expression* = **TMLB$ISS_CNT(:ID)**). The next illustration shows the completed Client Side Function dialog used in this example. When you have completed this dialog, click Next.

CAUTION
You can only pass literal values and/or column values included in the query to the client-side function. You cannot pass a table_alias.column_name argument to the function, because it is not part of the SELECT statement.

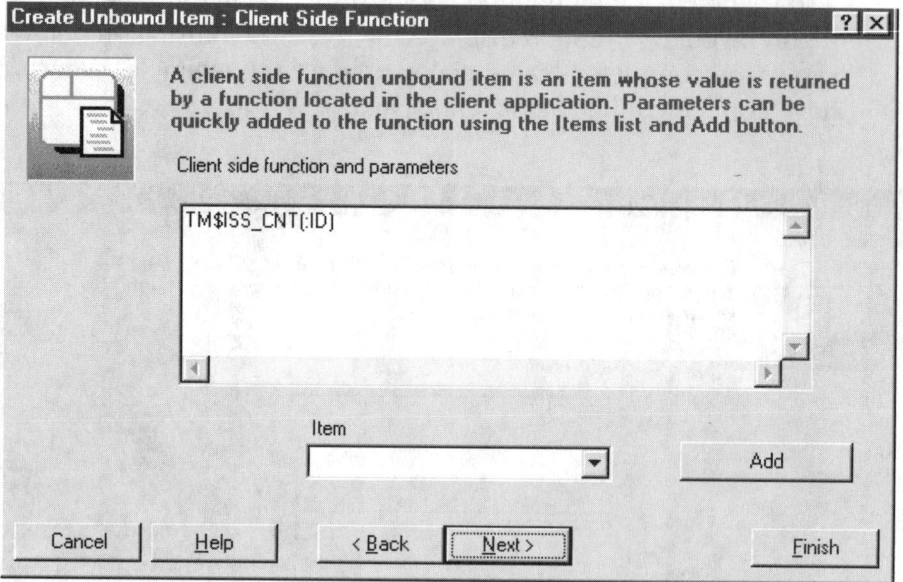

5. The Definition dialog is the third dialog that will be displayed. Using this dialog, you can specify the display datatype that will be used in the report layout (*Datatype* = **NUMBER**). The next illustration shows the completed Datatype dialog used for the example. When you have completed this dialog, click Next.

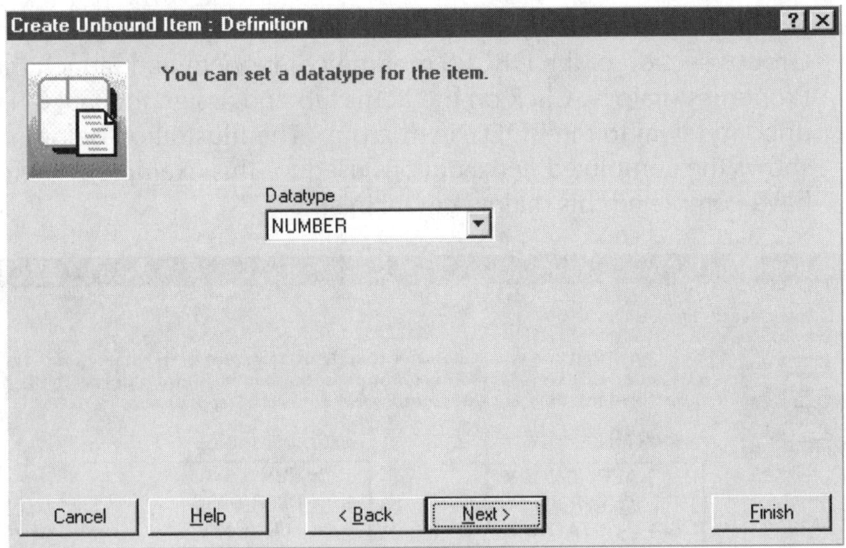

6. The High/Low Values dialog is the fourth dialog that will be displayed. This dialog allows you to specify high and low range restrictions on the value returned by this item. Click Next to skip this dialog.
7. The Controls dialog is the last dialog that will be displayed. Using this dialog, you can specify many different display characteristics for this item. The illustration below shows the completed Controls dialog used for this example. When you have completed this dialog, click Finish.

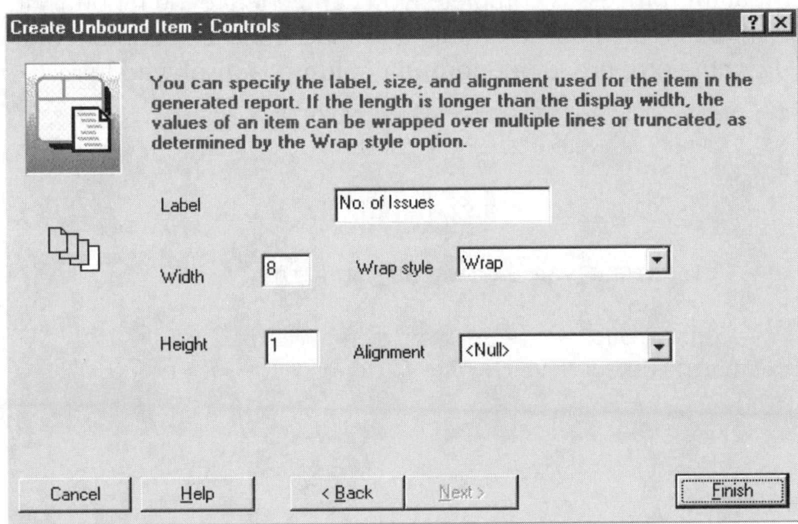

8. Navigate to the BODY item group in the Displayed Items and Groups section of the DBCRS module component and launch the Properties dialogs. Click on the Items tab and assign the ISS_CNT unbound item to the BODY item group. The illustration below shows the completed Items dialogs used for this example. When you have completed this dialog, click Finish.

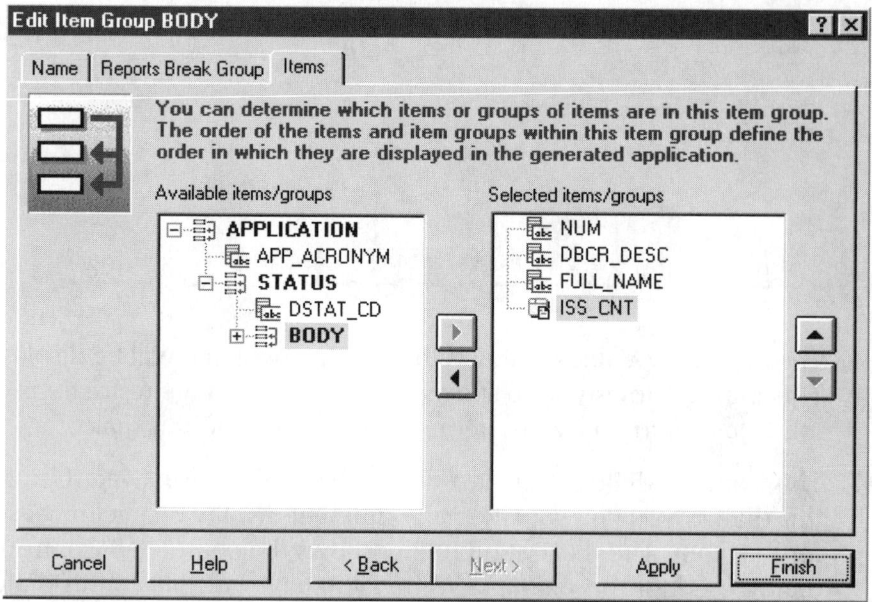

Now that this process is complete, you can generate the report. A function column will be created based on this unbound item. The content of the *PL/SQL Formula* property of the formula column is displayed here:

```
function CG$CF_ISS_CNT return NUMBER is
CS_RETURN_VAR NUMBER ;
begin
  -- CG$CS0001.DC.DBCRS.ISS_CNT
BEGIN
     CS_RETURN_VAR := TM$ISS_CNT(:ID);
END;
  -- CG$CS0001.DC.DBCRS.ISS_CNT
return CS_RETURN_VAR;
end;
```

You can see by looking at the generated function body that a call was made to the client-side function that will determine how many issues the current DBCR is associated with. An advantage of using a client-side function is that you can avoid adding a group by clause to the report query, which can improve the performance of the report.

Computed

A computed unbound item allows you to create a computed summary of another column's data. Computed unbound items will not be placed in the generated query by the Report generator. Rather, a summary column will be created at the reset level specified in the unbound item definition. Unbound item types require three pieces of information to work correctly:

- **Item** The name of the item whose values will be used in the computation
- **Function** The mathematical function to be applied (sum, average, count, etc.)
- **Reset level** The level of summary to create (Current Group, Parent Group, Module, Page, Named Group)

Let's work through an example of how to use a computed unbound item. In this example, we are going to make a copy of the sample report created for the previous server-side example in this chapter.

Modify the DBCRS report to include a total number of associated issues for each status.

To implement this requirement using a computed unbound item, take the following steps:

1. Make a copy the report definition that you created for the server-side function example in this chapter (or use CH29_SERVER from the example application on the CD). There is also a completed version of this example in the sample application named CH29_COMPUTED.

2. Create a computed unbound item definition. Do this by navigating to the unbound items section of the module component and clicking the Create icon in the Design Editor toolbar.

3. The Name dialog is the first dialog that will be displayed. Using this dialog, you can specify the name of the unbound item (*Item Name* = **STAT_TOT**). You can specify that you would like the unbound item to be computed (*Item Type* = **Computed**). You can also specify that the unbound item is displayed in the generated report layout (*Is this item displayed?* = **Yes**). The illustration below shows the completed Name dialog used for this example. When you have completed this dialog, click Next.

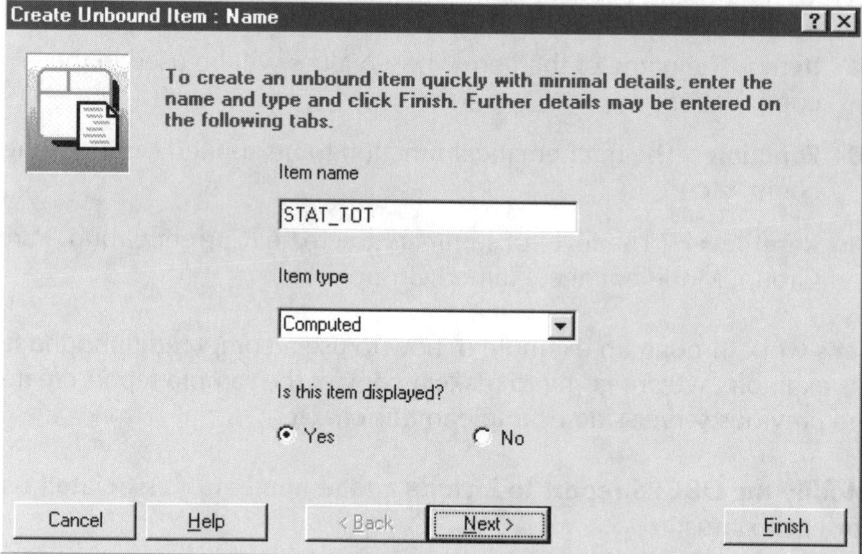

4. The Computed dialog is the second dialog that will be displayed. Using this dialog, you can specify function (*Function* = **SUM**) and item (*Item Used* = **ISS_CNT**) to be used in the computation. Note that the item used in the computation is a server-side function unbound item. The next illustration shows the completed Computed dialog used in this example. When you have completed this dialog, click Next.

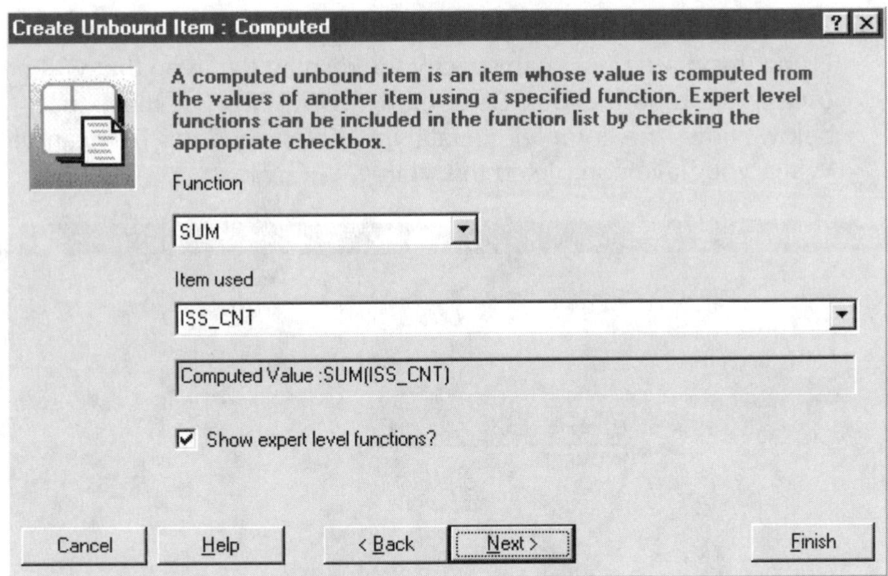

5. The Reset Level dialog is the third dialog that will be displayed. Using this dialog, you can specify the level that the summary column will be reset (*Reset level* = **Current Group**). In this report, this means that the summary column will be reset for each status. The illustration below shows the completed Reset Level dialog used for this example. When you have completed this dialog, click Next.

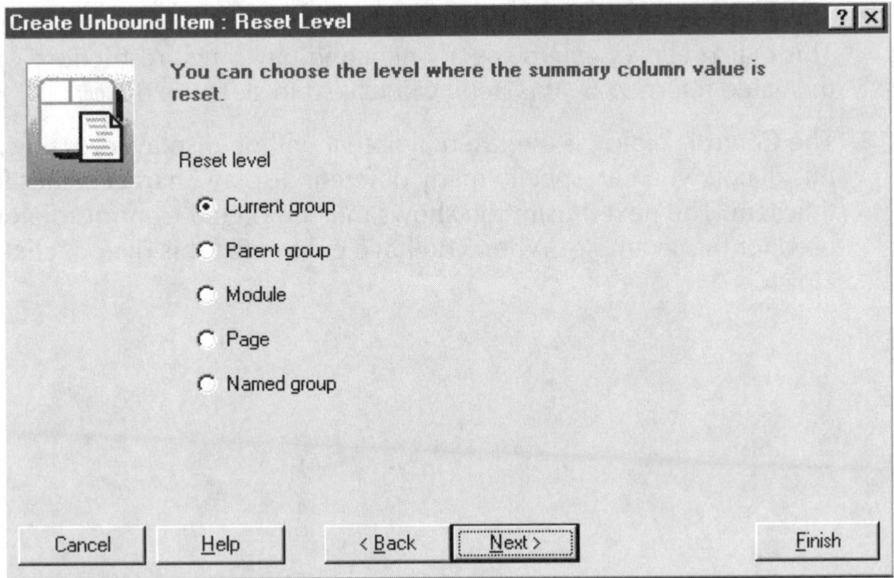

6. The Definition dialog is the fourth dialog that will be displayed. Using this dialog, you can specify the display datatype that will be used in the report layout (*Datatype* = **NUMBER**). The illustration below shows the completed Datatype dialog used for this example. When you have completed this dialog, click Next.

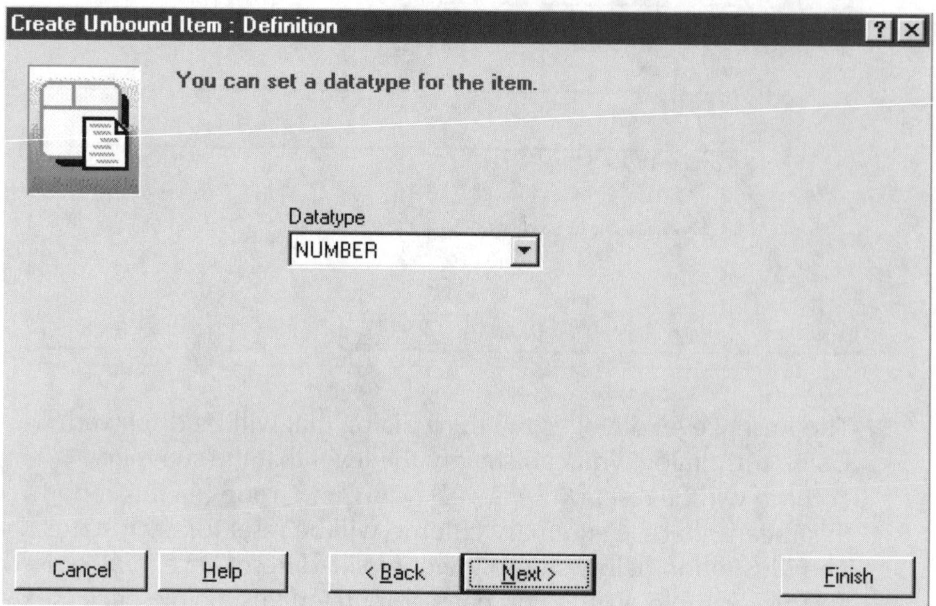

7. The High/Low Values dialog is the fifth dialog that will be displayed. This dialog allows you to specify high and low range restrictions on the value returned by this item. Click Next to skip this dialog.

8. The Controls dialog is the last dialog that will be displayed. Using this dialog, you can specify many different display characteristics for this item. The next illustration shows the completed Controls dialog used for this example. When you have completed this dialog, click Finish.

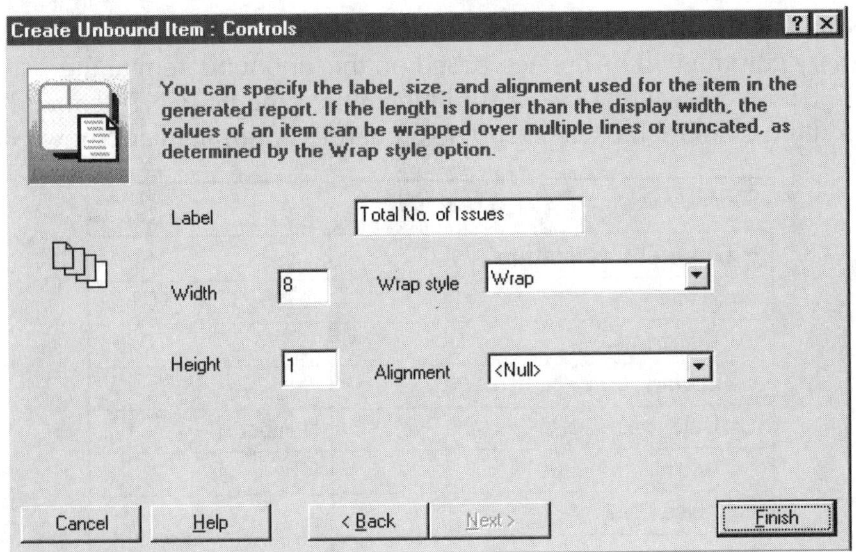

9. Navigate to the STATUS item group in the Displayed Items and Groups section of the DBCRS module component and launch the Properties dialogs. Click on the Items tab and assign the STAT_TOT unbound item to STATUS item group. The illustration below shows the completed Items dialogs used for this example. When you have completed this dialog, click Finish.

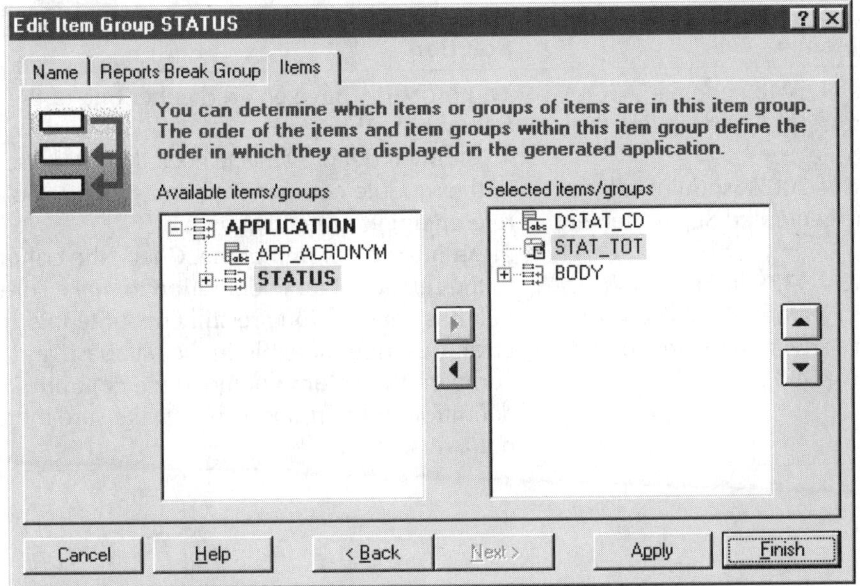

Now that this process is complete, you can generate the report. A summary column will be created based on this unbound item at the CG$C_STATUS level that uses a sum function on the ISS_CNT item and resets at the CG$G_STATUS level. The properties of this item are shown here:

Summary Column: CG$S_STAT_TOT	
General Information	
Name	CG$S_STAT_TOT
Comments	
Column	
Datatype	Number
Width	38
Value if Null	
Summary	
Function	Sum
Source	ISS_CNT
Reset At	CG$G_STATUS

Generation Troubleshooting Guide

Problem	Solution
When I try to generate a SQL expression, I keep getting the messages, "CGEN-2007 Module: failed to parse generated SQL statement" and, "CGEN-3379 Item <item_name>: Syntax error in item derivation expression text 'ORA-00904:"	You probably have entered either one of the following: 1. An invalid table alias. Check the table usage in the module component to make sure you are referencing it correctly. 2. An invalid column name. Check the column in the relational table definition to make sure that it is valid. If you are still encountering this error, describe the table in the database and compare the column name to the column definition in the repository to make sure there is not a mismatch.

Problem	Solution
When I try to generate a sever-side function I keep getting the messages, "CGEN-2007 Module: failed to parse generated SQL statement" and, "CGEN-3379 Item <item_name>: Syntax error in item derivation expression text 'ORA-00904: invalid column name'"	You have done one of two things incorrectly: 1. You used an invalid function name. Check the database to ensure that the function exists in the database, a synonym has been created on the object, and the user account that you are using has the appropriate permissions granted on the object. 2. You passed in an invalid argument to the function. Normally, this means that you have passed the wrong table_alias.column_name to the function.
When trying to generate a client-side function, I keep getting the message, "CGEN-2030 Warning: Module failed to compile PL/SQL"	This means that the call to the client-side function is invalid. 1. Check to ensure that the client-side library contains the function you are calling is attached to the generated report. 2. Check to make sure that you are correctly referencing the function, including spelling of the function name and the number and types of arguments. Remember that client-side functions can reference the columns included in the SELECT statement. These types of references must be made using a ':' and then the column alias.

CHAPTER 30

Refining the Where Clause

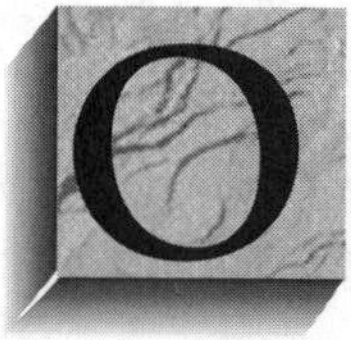

nce you have created the basic report definition, you can focus on adding conditions to the Where clause of the generated query. Depending on what you are trying to accomplish, you have a number of options to choose from, including

- Sub-query table usage
- SQL query sets
- User parameters (arguments)
- The *Where Clause of Query* property

Each of these methods for adding conditions to the Where clause serves a different purpose. In this chapter, we will discuss each of these methods and provide a step-by-step example for each. We will also provide a generation troubleshooting guide to assist you with common generation problems. As a point of reference, we will be referring to the server model diagram shown in Figure 30-1 for all of the examples shown in this chapter.

Sub-Query Table Usage

A sub-query table usage can be used to create a correlated sub-query. The correlated sub-query is created in the Where clause of the query based on the base table usage of the module component using either an Exists or Not Exists operator. A sub-query table usage can be used to implement selection criteria from a child table that has a many-to-one relationship to the base table without causing records to be duplicated in the base query. This is often done to ensure that specific reporting conditions are met.

A sub-query table usage cannot be defined until you have created the base table usage for the module component. Sub-query table usages are valid for report generation only. To show you how sub-query table usages work, we will work through an example report that refines the Where clause of the sample report created in Chapter 28. For our example, we will implement the following modification to the existing report:

Modify the DBCRS report to display DBCRS that have been implemented in the production database.

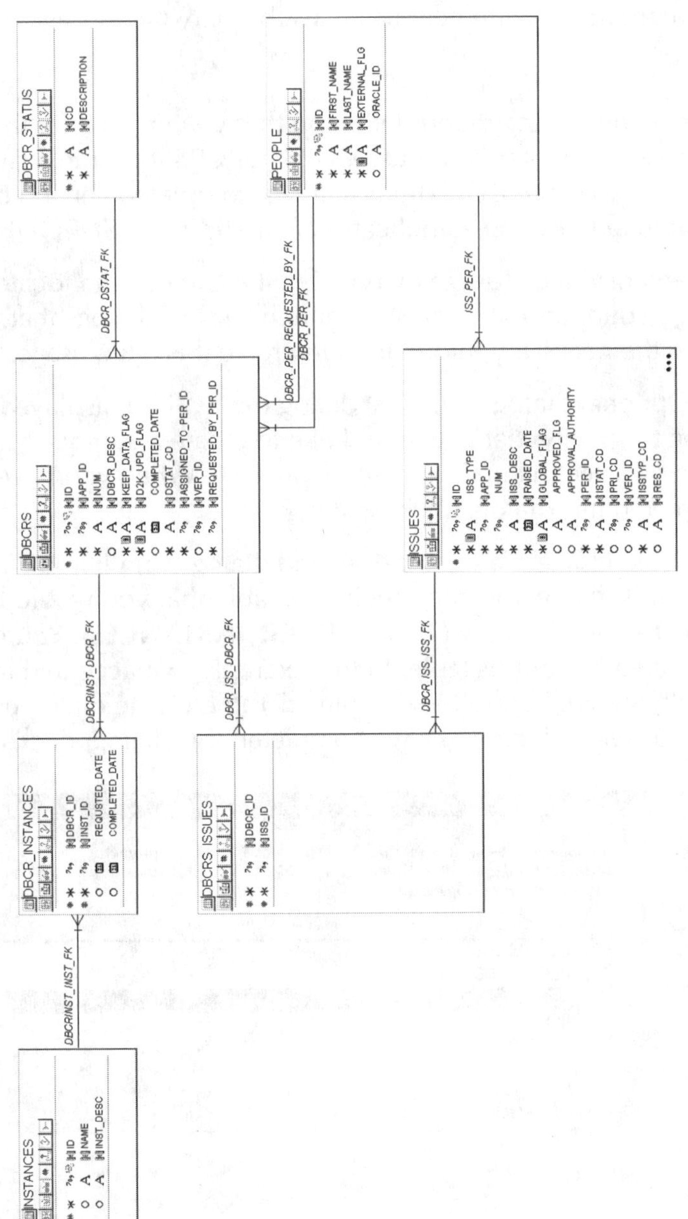

FIGURE 30-1. *Server model diagram*

To implement this requirement using a sub-query table usage, take the following steps:

1. Make a copy of the report definition that you created for the example in Chapter 28 (or use CH28_DBCRS from the example application on the CD). There is also a completed version of this example in the sample application named CH30_SUBQUERY.
2. Create a new table usage by pressing the Create icon located on the Design Editor toolbar. This will launch a set of dialogs that will gather the necessary information to create this table usage.
3. The Optional dialog is the first dialog that will be displayed. Use this dialog to specify that you would like to create a sub-query table usage by selecting option three (*Subquery*). When you have completed this dialog, click Next.
4. The Table Usage dialog is the second dialog that will be displayed. Using this dialog you can specify the table that you would like to use to create the sub-query (*Table* = **DBCR_INSTANCES**). You can also select an alias for this table. In this example, we accepted the default. Shown here is the completed Table Usage dialog used for this example. When you have completed this dialog, click Next.

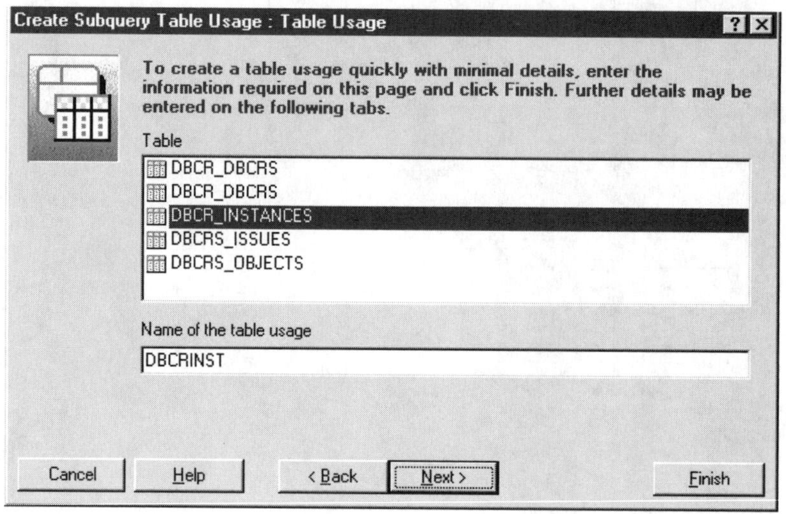

5. The Where dialog is the third dialog that will be displayed. Use this dialog to specify Where clause conditions that the sub-query must meet in order to return True and specify whether the sub-query will use an Exists or Not Exists query operator. In this example, enter a condition to exclude DBCRS that have been implemented in the production database instance (*WHERE restriction* = **INST_CD = 'PROD'**). We also left the *Implement as a 'NOT EXISTS' clause?* property blank. The completed Where dialog used for this example is shown here. When you have completed this dialog, click Finish.

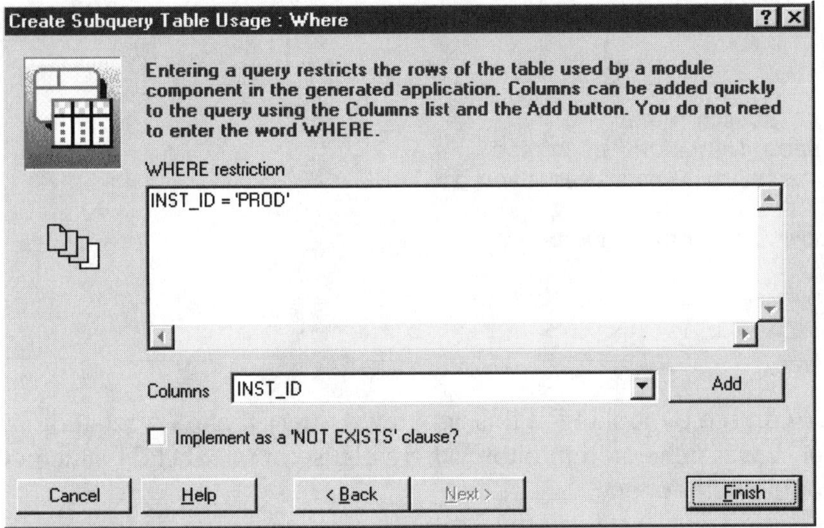

CAUTION

Do not enter the predicate that joins the sub-query to the base table usage. The Report Generator will create this predicate for you. If you specify the predicate as well, there will be two similar join predicates generated in the Where clause of the sub-query.

Now that this process is complete, you can generate the report. The query generated for this example is shown in this listing:

```
SELECT
L_APP.ACRONYM APP_ACRONYM,
L_DSTAT.CD DSTAT_CD,
DBCR.NUM NUM,
DBCR.DBCR_DESC DBCR_DESC,
L_PER.FULL_NAME PER_FULL_NAME
FROM
APPLICATIONS L_APP,
PEOPLE L_PER,
DBCR_STATUS L_DSTAT,
DBCRS DBCR
WHERE
EXISTS (SELECT NULL
FROM DBCR_INSTANCES DBCRINST
WHERE DBCR.ID = DBCRINST.DBCR_ID
AND
DBCRINST.INST_CD = 'PROD'
) AND
DBCR.DSTAT_CD = L_DSTAT.CD AND
DBCR.ASSIGNED_TO_PER_ID = L_PER.ID AND
DBCR.APP_ID = L_APP.ID
```

You can see by looking at this generated query that a correlated sub-query was generated into the Where clause of the SELECT statement for the module component.

SQL Query Sets

A SQL query set gives you the ability to merge two SELECT statements using a Union query operator. The SELECT statement that you define as a SQL query set will be merged with the SELECT statement based on the base table usage for the module component. Currently, you can only use a Union operator with SQL query sets. You cannot specify an Intersect or Minus operator.

REMEMBER
When using a Union operator to merge two SELECT statements, each query must have the same number of columns selected, and the columns selected must be of the same datatype.

Let's work through an example of using a SQL query set by creating a new report based on the following requirement:

Create a report that displays a consolidated listing of Issues and DBCRS.

To implement this requirement using a SQL query set, take the following steps:

1. Create a new report definition. Specify DBCRS as the base table usage and select DBCR_ID and DBCR_DESC as displayed columns. See Chapter 28 for assistance in completing this step. There is also a completed version of this example in the sample application named CH30_UNION.
2. Set the *Datasource Type* property for the module component that you defined in step 1 to **QUERY**. This will allow you to create a SQL query set for the module component. If you leave this properties value set to **TABLE**, you will receive an error when you try to define the SQL query set.
3. Create a SQL query set for the module component by navigating to the SQL query set definitions for the module component and pressing the Create icon located on the Design Editor toolbar. The properties sheet for the SQL query set will appear. You cannot complete this step using dialogs. Enter the name of the SQL query set (*Name* = **ISSUE**) and enter a usage sequence for this SQL query set (*Usage Sequence* = **1**). The properties sheet used for this example is shown here.

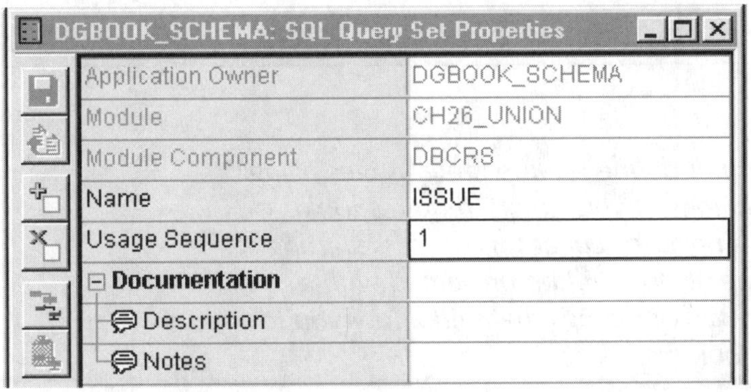

DGBOOK_SCHEMA: SQL Query Set Properties

Application Owner	DGBOOK_SCHEMA
Module	CH26_UNION
Module Component	DBCRS
Name	ISSUE
Usage Sequence	1
Documentation	
Description	
Notes	

4. Next, create the SELECT statement of the SQL query set. Navigate to the Table Usages of the SQL query set and then press the Create icon in the Design Editor toolbar. This will launch a set of dialogs that will gather the necessary information to build the SELECT statement that will be merged with the SELECT statement based on the module components base table usage.

5. The Table Usage dialog is the first dialog that will be displayed. Use this dialog to specify the table that you would like to select from (*Base Table* = **ISSUES**). You can also define an alias for this table usage. In this example, we accepted the default. The completed Table Usage dialog used for this example is shown here. When you have completed this dialog, click Next.

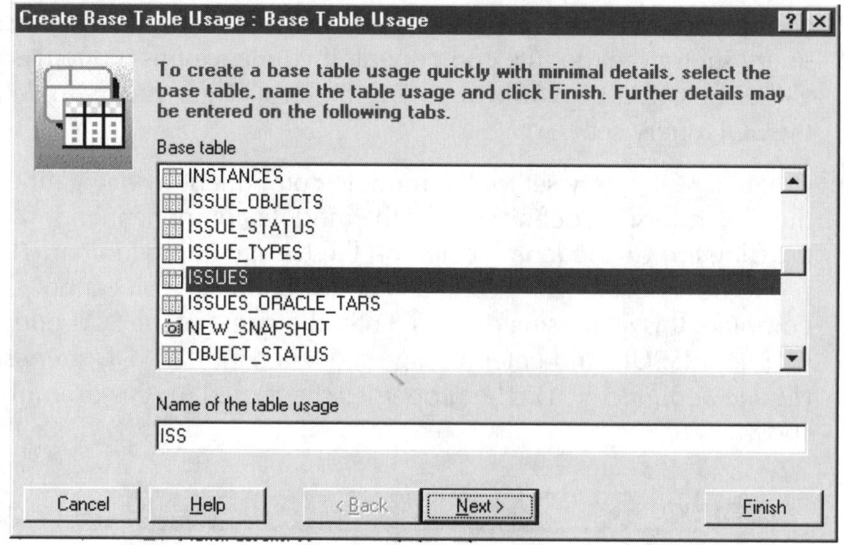

NOTE

You cannot define lookup table usages using these dialogs. If your query requires lookups, you will need to repeat this process starting with step 3. You will be presented with a different set of dialogs that will allow you to define lookups.

6. The Where dialog is the second dialog that will be displayed. You can use this dialog to specify conditions that will be placed in the Where clause. In this example, we did not have any special requirements. Click Next to skip this dialog.

7. The Items dialog is the third dialog that will be displayed. Use this dialog to specify which columns will be selected. Each of the items that you specify will be stored as bound items for this SQL Query Set. In this example, we selected the ID and description columns (*[Disp] Selected Items* = **ID**, **ISS_DESC**). The completed Items dialog used for this example is shown here. When you have completed this dialog, click Next.

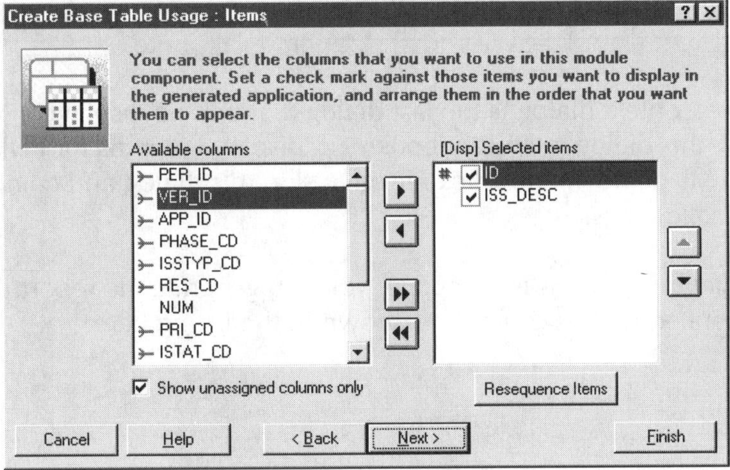

8. The Item Names dialog is the fourth dialog that will be displayed. You can use this dialog to specify aliases for the selected columns. In this example, we accepted the default values. Click Next to skip this dialog.

9. The Display dialog is the fifth dialog that will be displayed. Use this dialog to specify display characteristics of the selected items. In this example, we modified the default values of ISS_DESC to set the display title to **Description** and display width to **50**. The completed Display dialog used for this example is shown here. When you have completed this dialog, click Next.

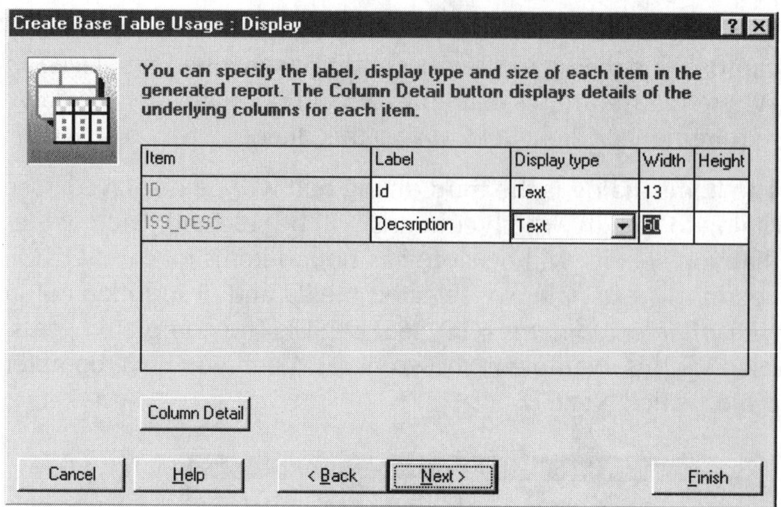

10. The Context dialog is the last dialog that will be displayed. You can use this dialog to specify bookmark display columns for PDF or HTML deployment. Click Finish to skip this dialog and complete this set of dialogs.

Now that this process is complete, you can generate the report. The query generated for this example is shown in the listing here:

```
(SELECT
DBCR.ID ID,
DBCR.DBCR_DESC DBCR_DESC
FROM
DBCRS DBCR
UNION
SELECT
ISS.ID ID2,
ISS.ISS_DESC ISS_DESC
FROM
ISSUES ISS
)
ORDER BY
ID
```

You can see by looking at this generated query that the query based on the SQL query set was merged with the base table usage using a Union query operator.

User Parameters (Arguments)

Oracle Designer provides you with the ability to define and generate bind parameters to limit the rows returned by a generated report query. It also provides you with lexical parameters to allow for more dynamic query predicates. These parameters are defined in the repository as arguments for a report definition. In the sections that follow, we will explain the process for creating bind parameters and lexical parameters.

Bind Parameters

Bind parameters allow you to do simple, single-value substitutions in either a report query, trigger, or program unit. The value of the bind parameter will be replaced at runtime by either a user-supplied value or a default value.

Creating a bind parameter in Oracle Designer involves two components. First, you need to create an argument definition for each bind parameter that you need in the report. Second, you need to define an evaluation statement for the argument, which you can do either by creating an argument item usage (simple evaluations only) or by defining the condition in the *Where Clause of Query* property of the appropriate module component table usage.

Let's work through an example of using bind parameters by refining the Where clause of the sample report created in Chapter 28. The example report will be modified to implement the following enhancement:

Modify the DBCRS report to display DBCRS that have been completed during a user-specified date range and that have a user-specified status.

To implement this requirement using bind parameters, take the following steps:

1. Make a copy of the report definition that you created for the example in Chapter 28 (or use CH28_DBCRS from the example application on the CD). There is also a completed version of this example in the sample application named CH30_BIND.

2. Launch the properties dialogs and select the Arguments tab. This dialog allows you to define the arguments used by this report. The following table shows the properties and settings used for this example:

Name	Defined By	Datatype	Length
Start_date	Datatype	Date	<null>
End_date	Datatype	Date	<null>
Stat_cd	Datatype	Varchar2	12

TIP

Do not specify a prefix for your argument definitions. When the report definition is generated, the Report Generator will assign a prefix of CG$P_ for each argument definition.

The Arguments dialog used in this example is shown here. When you have completed this dialog, click Finish.

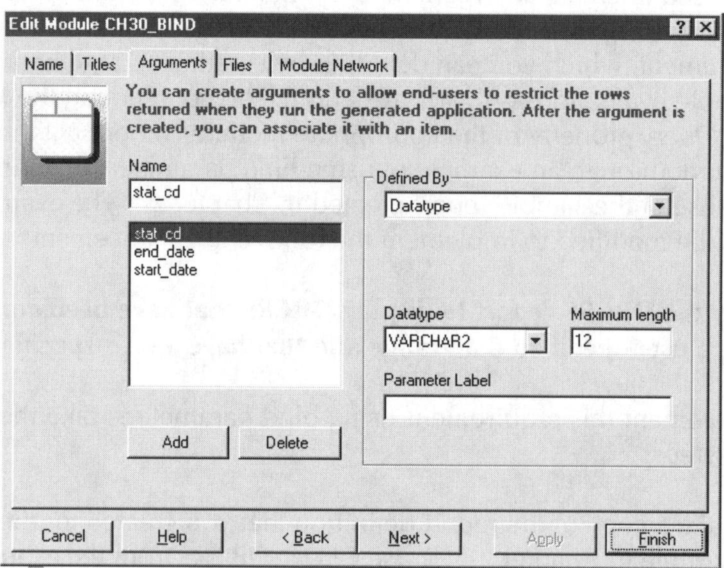

3. Create an argument item usage for the STAT_CD argument by navigating to the argument item usages for the STAT_CD argument and pressing the Create icon in the Design Editor toolbar. This will launch a dialog that allows you to select the column that you would like to have evaluated by the STAT_CD parameter (*Argument Item Usages* = **DBCRS.DSTAT_CD**). The Argument Item Usages dialog used for this example is shown here. When you have completed this dialog, click OK.

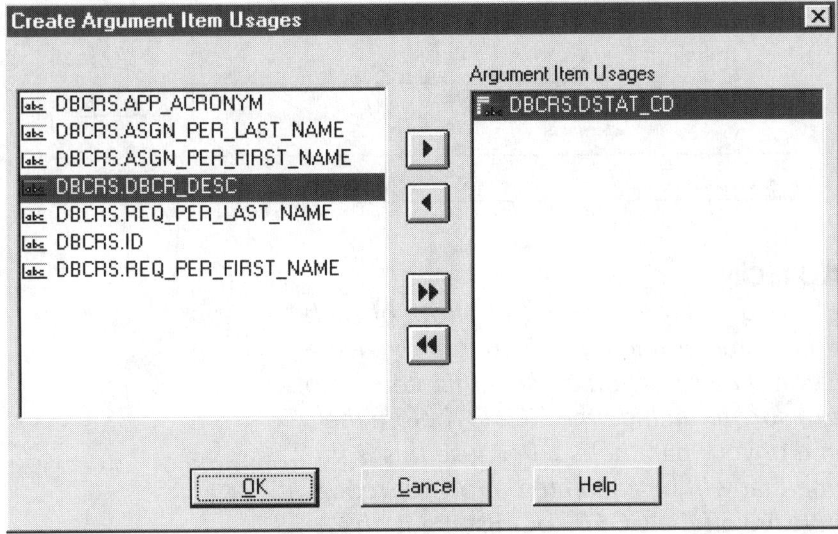

4. Navigate to the DBCR base table usage of the DBCRS module component and launch the properties dialogs.

5. Select the Where tab. Use this dialog to enter the Where condition so that only DBCRS that have been completed between a user-supplied data range will be reported (*Where restriction* = **COMPLETED_DATE between :cg$p_start_date and :cg$p_end_date**). The completed Where dialog used in this example is shown here. When you have completed this dialog, click Finish.

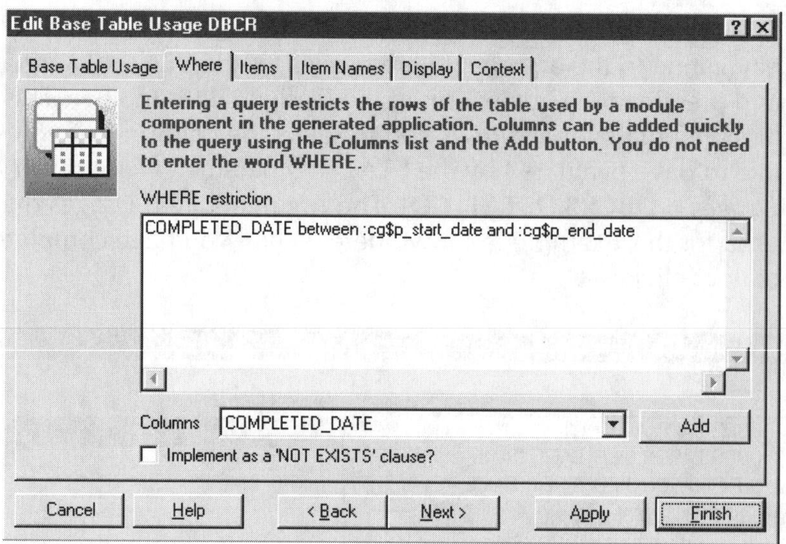

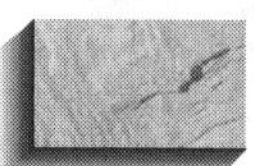

CAUTION

Be sure to include a colon (:) in front of each bind parameter reference. You will receive a generation error if you neglect this step. Also, make sure to include the CG$P_ before the name of your parameters, because this is the name that will be generated into your report. If you leave off the CG$P_ or mistype it, the report will generate, but the parameter passing will not work.

Now that this process is complete, you can generate the report. The query generated for this example is shown in this listing:

```
SELECT
L_APP.ACRONYM APP_ACRONYM,
L_DSTAT.CD DSTAT_CD,
DBCR.NUM NUM,
DBCR.DBCR_DESC DBCR_DESC,
L_PER.FULL_NAME PER_FULL_NAME
FROM
APPLICATIONS L_APP,
PEOPLE L_PER,
DBCR_STATUS L_DSTAT,
```

```
DBCRS DBCR
WHERE
DBCR.COMPLETED_DATE between :cg$p_start_date and :cg$p_end_date AND
DBCR.DSTAT_CD = L_DSTAT.CD AND
DBCR.ASSIGNED_TO_PER_ID = L_PER.ID AND
DBCR.APP_ID = L_APP.ID AND
L_DSTAT.CD = :CG$P_stat_cd
```

You can see by looking at the generated query that the bind parameter predicates were generated into the Where clause.

Lexical Parameters

Lexical parameters allow you to do string substitutions in a report query. The value of the lexical parameter will be replaced at runtime by either a user-supplied value or a default value.

Since lexical parameters allow you to do string substitutions, you can use lexical parameters anywhere in the SELECT statement. Lexical parameters are often used to avoid unnecessary table joins and Where conditions in order to increase report performance. However, not all of the methods of using lexical parameters are practical to use in generated reports. You can spend a lot of time trying to define and generate lexical parameters into the select and from clauses of reports, You will often have to use generation techniques that are difficult to understand and hard to support. Defining these directly in Report Builder and documenting what you have created in the report definitions' release notes is usually a better option for these requirements.

The most practical usage of lexical parameters in generated reports is in the Where clause. Lexical parameters are particularly useful in situations in which a user can specify 0 to *n* values for a given parameter.

NOTE
To implement this type of example in an application, you must use Oracle Forms to accept the values entered by the user using text fields or a GUI widget, such as check boxes. Once the user has finished entering the criteria for the report, you will need to call the report passing the user parameters in a string that will be evaluated using logic in the After Parameter Form trigger.

Creating a lexical parameter to implement this type of requirement involves three components. First, you will need to create two argument definitions for each lexical parameter. One argument will be used to accept the string of values passed by the form and will be evaluated in the After Parameter Form trigger. The second argument will be used as the lexical reference in the query, and its value will be set based on the value of the first argument.

Next, you will need to define an evaluation statement for the argument. Unlike bind parameters, lexical parameter evaluation statements can only be made using the *Where Clause of Query* property of the appropriate module component table usage.

The last thing you will need to do is add some application logic to the After Parameter Form trigger. You can do this by creating an After Parameter Form application logic event for the Window definition.

Let's work through an example using lexical parameters by refining the Where clause of the sample report created in Chapter 28. The example report will be modified to implement the following enhancement:

Modify the DBCRS report to display DBCRS that have a user-specified status. The user may enter none, one, or more values for this parameter. If no status is specified, the report should run for all statuses.

To implement this requirement using lexical parameters, take the following steps:

1. Make a copy of the report definition that you created for the example in Chapter 28 (or use CH28_DBCRS from the example application on the CD). There is also a completed version of this example in the sample application named CH30_LEXICAL.
2. Launch the properties dialogs and select the Arguments tab. This dialog allows you to define the arguments used by this report. The following table shows the properties and settings used for this example.

Name	Defined By	Datatype	Length
Stat_eval	Datatype	Varchar2	100
Stat_real	Datatype	Varchar2	100

TIP
Do not specify a prefix for your argument definitions. When the report definition is generated, the Report Generator will assign a prefix of CG$P_ for each argument definition.

The Arguments dialog used in this example is shown here. When you have completed this dialog, click Finish.

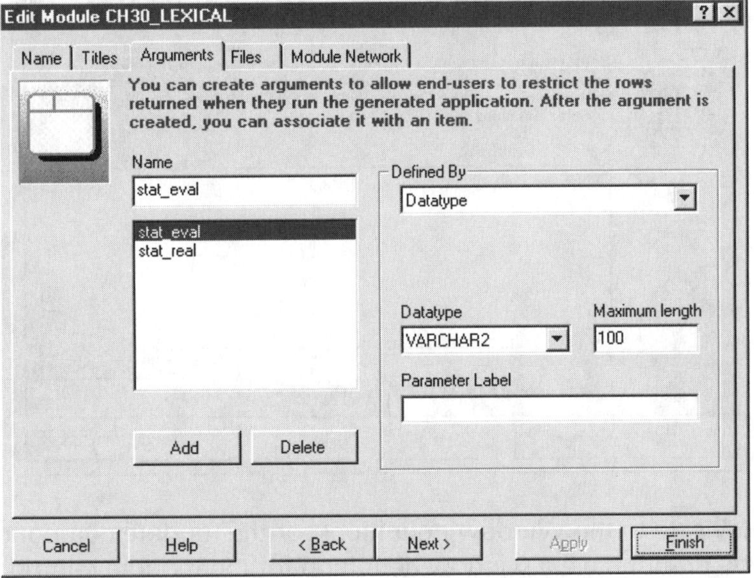

3. Switch to the Properties Palette and navigate to the STAT_REAL argument definition you created in the previous step. Set the *Default* property to **1=1**. This is important, because you will use this argument as the lexical reference in the generated query, and all lexical references must have an initial value. If an initial value is not defined, the Report Generator will not generate the report.
4. Navigate to the DBCR base table usage of the DBCRS module component and launch the properties dialogs.

5. Select the Where tab. Use this dialog to define a predicate for the lexical parameter by placing the full name of the parameter in the *Where restriction* property. Be sure to include an ampersand (&) in front of the lexical parameter reference. If you don't, you will receive a generation error. Also, remember to include the CG$P_ prefix for the parameter name. The completed Where dialog used in this example is shown here. When you have completed this dialog, click Finish.

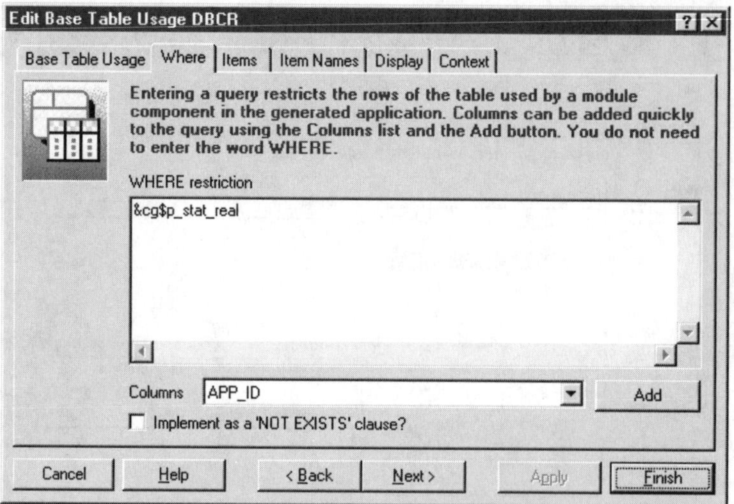

6. Navigate to the Window definitions for the module component. If you do not have a window definition for the module component, create a new one by clicking the Create icon in the Design Editor toolbar. Windows are generally used in report generation for drill-down reports, but they can also be used to allow you to define report-level triggers, which is what we are doing here.

7. The Name dialog is the first and only dialog that will be displayed. Use this dialog to specify a name (*Window name* = **DBCRS**) and a title (*Report title* = **Database Change Requests (DBCRS)**) for the window. The completed Name dialog used in this example is shown here. When you have completed this dialog, click Finish.

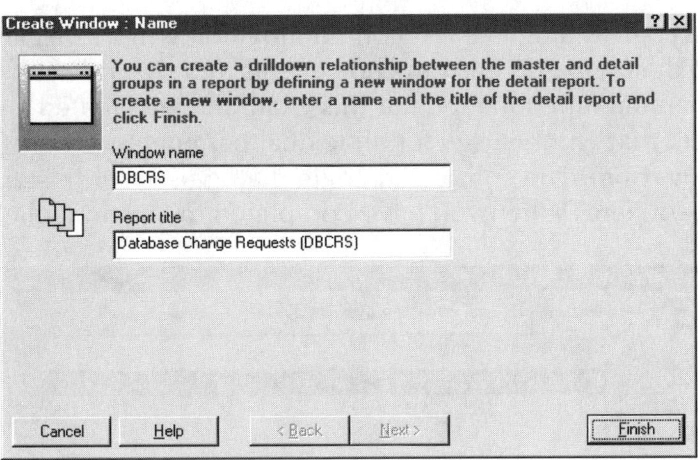

8. Create an application logic event for the window definition by navigating to application logic events definitions for the window and pressing the Create icon in the Design Editor toolbar. This will launch a set of dialogs that you can use to define the application logic to validate the lexical parameter.

9. The Events dialog is the first dialog that will be displayed. Use this dialog to specify that you would like to add logic to the generated reports After Parameter Form trigger (*Events* = **AfterParameterForm**). The complete dialog used for this example is shown here. When you have completed this dialog, click Next.

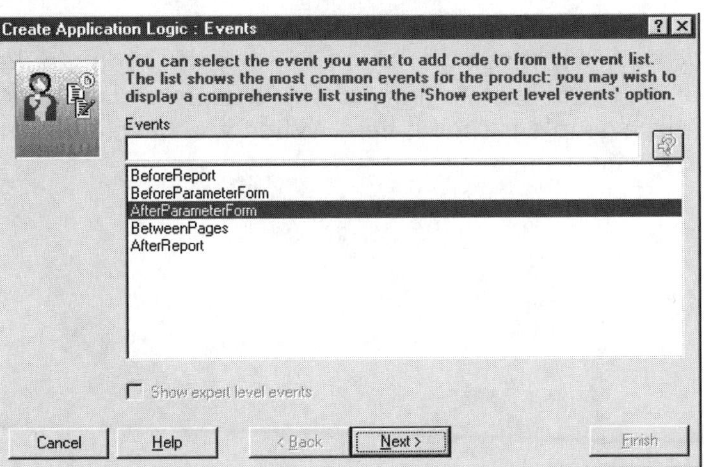

10. The Logic dialog is the second dialog that will be displayed. Use this dialog to add custom code events and override standard generated functionality. For this example, we created a new code event that will be used for all lexical parameters (*Name* = **Lexical Evaluation**). The completed Logic dialog used for this example is shown here. When you have completed this dialog, click Next.

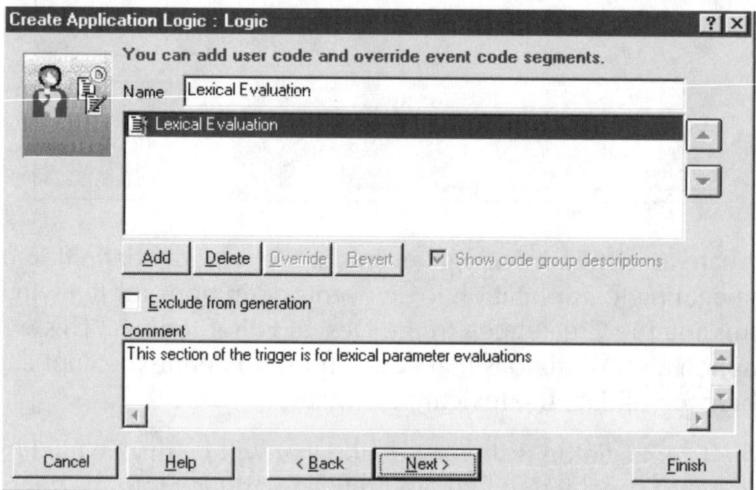

11. The Last dialog is, naturally, the last dialog that will be displayed. Use this dialog to choose how you would like to create the application logic event you just defined. Select option two (*Create the definition and then open the Logic Editor to enter the logic code*). This will allow you to enter the code required to evaluate the lexical parameter. The completed Last dialog used for this example is shown here. When you have completed this dialog, click Finish.

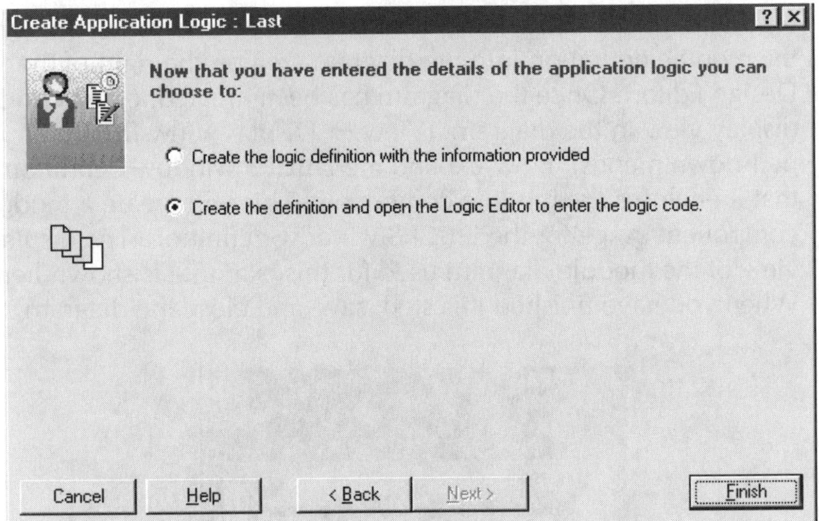

12. Use the Logic Editor to enter the evaluation condition for the lexical parameter. Below is the code entered for this example.

```
BEGIN
:cg$p_stat_real := TM$LIST(:cg$p_stat_eval,'dbcr.dstat_cd');
END;
```

The TM$LIST function is included in the L_STDRPT library that is attached to the T_RPTLND template. This function will build the predicate that will be used to replace the lexical parameter in the Where clause. An overview of the TM$LIST procedure is provided in Chapter 27.

13. You will need to assign the module DBCRS module component definition to the DBCRS window definition. If you do not, two report binary files will be created when this report definition is generated. This best way to do this is to use a module diagram. Highlight the

report definition and select File → New → Module Diagram (or drag the module definition into the diagram area on the right of the Design Editor). Once the diagram has been created, change to the display view in the diagram. (View → Display View from the pull-down menus). Now expand the DBCRS window definition so that it encloses the module component. This will create a module component usage for the DBCRS window definition. The display view of the module diagram used for this example is shown here. When you have finished this step, save and close the diagram.

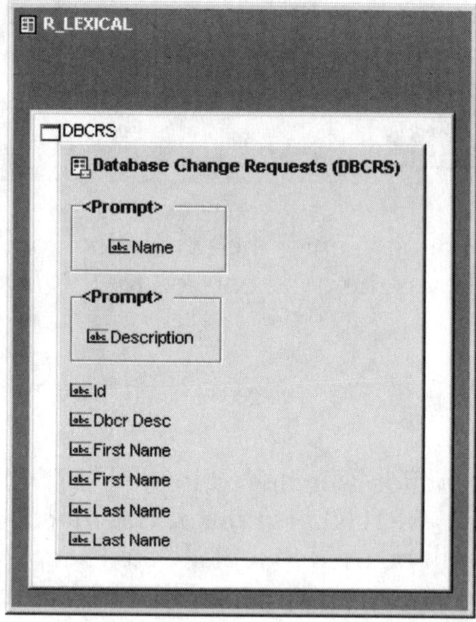

Now that this process is complete, you can generate the report. The query generated for this example is shown in the following listing:

```
SELECT
L_APP.ACRONYM APP_ACRONYM,
L_DSTAT.CD DSTAT_CD,
DBCR.NUM NUM,
DBCR.DBCR_DESC DBCR_DESC,
```

```
L_PER.FULL_NAME PER_FULL_NAME
FROM
PEOPLE L_PER,
DBCR_STATUS L_DSTAT,
APPLICATIONS L_APP,
DBCRS DBCR
WHERE
&cg$p_stat_real  AND
DBCR.APP_ID = L_APP.ID AND
DBCR.DSTAT_CD = L_DSTAT.CD AND
DBCR.ASSIGNED_TO_PER_ID = L_PER.ID
```

You can see by looking at the generated query that the lexical parameter reference was generated into the Where clause. The After Parameter Form trigger also contains the logic specified to build the predicate that will replace the lexical parameter reference. The After Parameter Form trigger is as follows.

```
function AfterParameterForm return boolean is
begin

--  USER ENTERED APPLICATION LOGIC
-- Lexical Evaluation
--
--
BEGIN
:cg$p_stat_real := TM$LIST(:cg$p_stat_eval,'dbcr.dstat_cd');
END;
   --  USER ENTERED APPLICATION LOGIC

return(TRUE);
end;
```

Where Clause of Query Property

The most commonly used option for generating conditions into the Where clause is the *Where Clause of Query* property. This property allows you to enter any condition or set of conditions for any of the table usages or SQL query sets defined for a module component. The only restriction of this property is that each condition added must be a valid SQL expression and must relate to a table usage in the generated query. In the sections that follow, we will explain how this property can be used for each type of table usage and SQL query sets.

Base and Lookup Table Usages

Using the *Where Clause of Query* property of either the base or lookup table usage will generate conditions into the Where clause of the query based on the base table usage of the module component. You can use either type of table usage. The only difference between placing the conditions in either the base or a lookup table is where the generated predicates will be placed in the Where clause. In most cases, this will not affect the functionality of the generated SELECT statement. However, it is generally good practice to place the conditions that apply to a lookup usage in its Where clause.

Some of the types of conditions you could add for base and lookup table usages using this property include

- Hard-coded query restrictions (such as DSTAT_CD = 'NEW')
- User parameters predicates (Bind and Lexical)
- Correlated sub-queries (Exists, Not Exists)
- Using set operators (Union, Intersect, Minus)
- More complex logic operators (In, Not In, Between, Not Between, Like, etc.)

Let's work through an example of using the *Where Clause of Query* property for base and lookup table usages by refining the Where clause of the sample report created in Chapter 28.

Modify the DBCRS report to display DBCRS records that

- Have a user-supplied status. (The user may enter none, one, or more values for this parameter. If no status is specified, then the report should run for all statuses.)
- Have been completed during a user-specified date range.
- Have been implemented in the production database.

To implement these requirements using the *Where Clause of Query* property of the base table usage, take the following steps:

1. Make a copy the report definition that you created for the example in Chapter 28 (or use CH28_DBCRS from the example application on the CD). There is also a completed version of this example in the sample application named CH30_DBCR_WHERE.
2. Create the Arguments needed for this example. For assistance with this step, please refer to the "User Parameters (Arguments), " section, earlier in this chapter.
3. Navigate to the base table usage of the DBCRS module component and launch the properties dialogs.
4. Select the Where tab. Use this dialog to enter the Where condition needed to implement the Where clause conditions listed earlier. The completed Where dialog used in this example is shown here. When you have completed this dialog, click Finish.

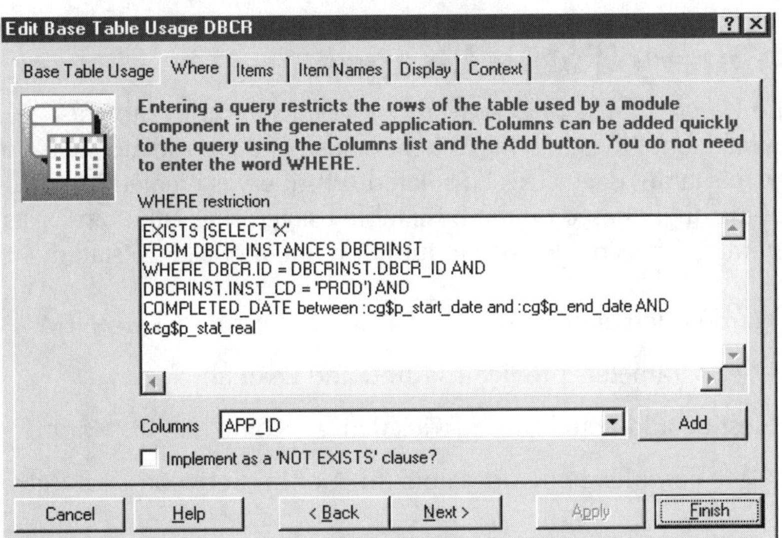

Now that this process is complete, you can generate the report. The query generated for this example is shown in the following listing:

```
SELECT
L_APP.ACRONYM APP_ACRONYM,
L_DSTAT.CD DSTAT_CD,
```

```
DBCR.NUM NUM,
DBCR.DBCR_DESC DBCR_DESC,
L_PER.FULL_NAME PER_FULL_NAME
FROM
DBCR_STATUS L_DSTAT,
PEOPLE L_PER,
APPLICATIONS L_APP,
DBCRS DBCR
WHERE
EXISTS (SELECT 'X'
FROM DBCR_INSTANCES DBCRINST
WHERE DBCR.ID = DBCRINST.DBCR_ID
AND DBCRINST.INST_CD = 'PROD') AND
DBCR.COMPLETED_DATE between :cg$p_start_date and :cg$p_end_date AND
&cg$p_stat_real  AND
DBCR.APP_ID = L_APP.ID AND
DBCR.ASSIGNED_TO_PER_ID = L_PER.ID AND
DBCR.DSTAT_CD = L_DSTAT.CD
```

You can see by looking at the generated query that all of the predicates we specified were included in the Where clause.

Sub-Query Table Usages

Using the *Where Clause of Query* property of a sub-query table usage, you can generate conditions into the Where clause of the correlated sub-query based on this table usage. This correlated sub-query is created in the Where clause of the query based on the base table usage using either an Exists or Not Exists operator. This enables you to further refine the SELECT statement by

- Hard-coded query restrictions (such as DSTAT_CD = 'NEW')
- User parameters predicates (Bind and Lexical)
- Nesting additional sub-queries (Exists, Not Exists, In, Not In)
- More complex logic operators (In, Not In, Between, Not Between, Like, etc.)

The example shown in the section "Sub-Query Table Usage,"earlier in this chapter, includes usage of this property. Refer to that example for assistance on how to use this property for a sub-query table usage.

SQL Query Sets

Using the *Where Clause of Query* property of a SQL query set will generate conditions into the Where clause of the query merged with the query based on the base table usage of the module component. This enables you to further refine the SELECT statement of the SQL query set by

- Hard-coded query restrictions (such as DSTAT_CD = 'NEW')
- User parameters predicates (Bind and Lexical)
- Nesting additional sub-queries (Exists, Not Exists)
- More complex logic operators (In, Not In, Between, Not Between, Like, etc.)

Let's work through an example of using the *Where Clause of Query* property for a SQL query set by modifying the Where clause of the SQL query set created earlier in this chapter to implement the following enhancement.

Create a report that displays a consolidated listing of Issues and DBCRS. Display all DBCRS, but only include Issues that have a status of 'New'.

To implement this requirement using the *Where Clause of Query* property of the SQL query set, take the following steps:

1. Make a copy of the report definition that you created for the SQL query set example in this chapter (or use CH30_UNION from the example application on the CD). There is also a completed version of this example in the sample application named CH30_UNION_WHERE.
2. Navigate to the ISS table usage of the SQL query set and launch the properties dialogs.
3. Select the Where tab. Use this dialog to enter the Where condition needed to implement the Where clause condition listed above. The completed Where dialog used in this example is shown here. When you have completed this dialog, click Finish.

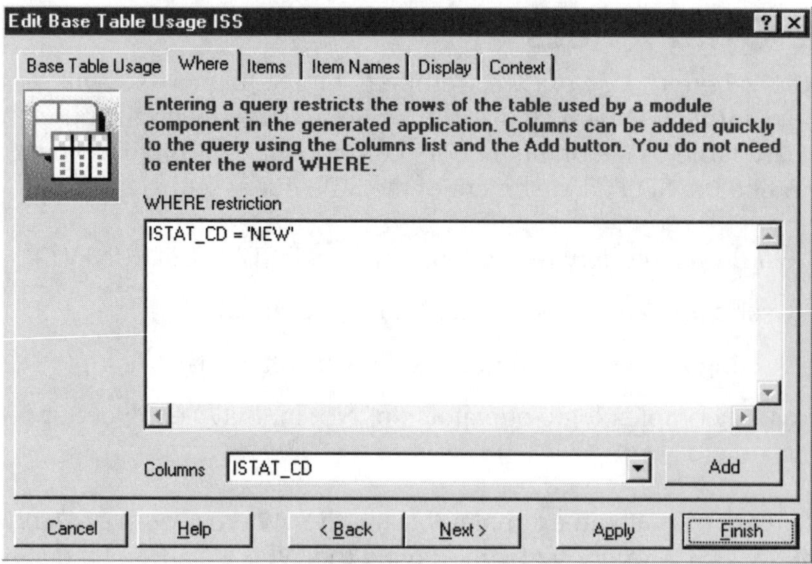

Now that this process is complete, you can generate the report. The query generated for this example is shown in this listing:

```
(SELECT
DBCR.ID ID,
DBCR.DBCR_DESC DBCR_DESC
FROM
DBCRS DBCR
UNION
SELECT
ISS.ID ID2,
ISS.ISS_DESC ISS_DESC
FROM
ISSUES ISS
WHERE
ISTAT_CD = 'NEW'
)
ORDER BY
ID
```

You can see by looking at this generated query that the predicate was added into the Where clause of the query based on the SQL query set.

Generation Troubleshooting Guide

Problem	Solution
When adding a sub-query table usage, I keep getting a message that says: "CGEN-02007 ERROR: Module: Failed to parse generated SQL statement error."	This is probably because the Where clause you entered was invalid. You may have typed a column name wrong or left out a quote or parentheses. One easy way to troubleshoot complex Where clauses is to cut the whole SQL statement out of the Messages window and execute it directly in SQL*Plus. This will give you a more detailed error message.
When I try to define a SQL Query Set, I keep getting a message that says: "CDA: SQL Query Set <*name*> Cannot be based on Module Component with DATASOURCE_TYPE = 'TABLE'"	Set the *Datasource type* property of the module component to **QUERY**. You will then be able to define a SQL Query set for the module component.
When trying to generate a report using a SQL query set, I keep getting a message that says: "CGEN-03485 ERROR: SQL_QUERY_SET.ISSUE: Inconsistent item datatypes or wrong number of items in query set"	You need to make sure that each query in your report (from the table usage or query sets) has the exact same number of columns and that each column has the same data types as its corresponding column in the other queries.
The user parameters created by the Report Generator do not match the names I defined for the arguments.	This is because the Report Generator prefixes each user parameter with CG$P_. Be sure to include this prefix if you plan to generate application logic that references a parameter.
When I try to generate a bind parameter reference into the Where clause, I keep getting a message that says: "CGEN-02030 WARNING: Module: Failed to compile PLSQL."	This is probably because you forgot to prefix the bind parameter with a colon (:).

Problem	**Solution**
When I try to generate a lexical parameter reference into the Where clause, I keep getting a message that says: "CGEN-02030 WARNING: Module: Failed to compile PLSQL."	This probably is either because 1. You forgot to prefix the lexical reference with an ampersand (&), or 2. You forgot to enter an initial value for the argument in the *Default* property. This can only be done using the Properties Palette.
When I add application logic to the report level triggers, two reports are generated. One report contains the report level trigger. The other report contains the SELECT statement and layout for the report.	This is because you have not assigned the module components to the window definition. The best way to do this is by using a module diagram. 1. Create the diagram by choosing File → New → Module Diagram from the Design Editor menu. 2. Once the diagram has been created, switch to the display view by choosing View → Display View from the Module Diagram menu. 3. Enclose the module component(s) in the window definition. 4. Save and close the diagram. If you then navigate back to the window definition for the report, you will see module component definition(s) for those you included using the module diagram.
I can't add an existing module component to a window definition. The dialogs that are displayed are prompting me to create a new module component, not to add an existing module component.	This is a bug. Currently, the best way to do this is by using a module diagram. Please see the solution in the preceding table entry for instructions on how to do this.

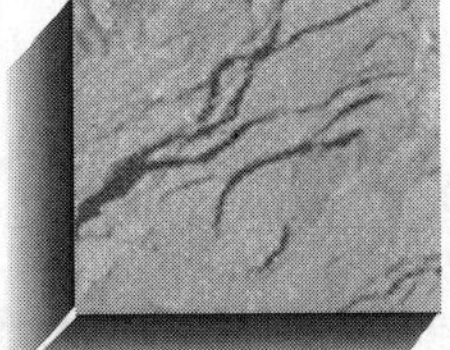

CHAPTER 31

Layout Features and Techniques

nce you have created the basic report definition, you can begin refining the layout of the report. With release 2, there are some new features and enhanced functionality that have the potential to really increase the quality of generated report layouts and boost the productivity of developers and support staff. In this chapter, we will present generation techniques that we believe will help you generate better report layouts in less time. Specifically, we will cover

- How to design reports for generation
- How to define and generate item format triggers
- How to design and generate Web-specific functionality
- A troubleshooting guide to assist you with common generation problems

Designing Report Definitions for Better Layout Control

Report layout design is one of the most important aspects of generating reports. As a rule of thumb, the closer the report design follows the relationships in the application data model, the less time and money report development and support will cost. However, this will not mean much to the user of the report if the report does not present the data in a usable format.

In the remainder of this section, we will discuss why it is important to follow the relationships in your application database and give you alternatives to use when you have report requirements that do not follow the relationships.

How Repeating Frames Are Created

In order to ensure that a report design can be generated, you will need to understand how the Report Generator creates repeating frames. Since errors related to frame frequency are typical, a good understanding of this topic will help you identify problem report design early. This will help you avoid unnecessary development time.

The Report Generator creates a repeating frame for each module component in a report definition. Each module component consists of one base table usage and may also include one or more other table usages (lookup, single-row SQL aggregate, or sub-query). It does not matter how many of the other table usages you include in a module component; there can only be one base table usage in the module component, and the Report Generator will create one repeating frame for that module component.

Generation preferences do not affect this process. The most common preference used to avoid this problem is the *Queries and PL/SQL → Merge Queries (DOJOIN)* preference. By default, the Report Generator creates one query per module component. However, when this preference is set to YES (*DOJOIN* = **YES**), the Report Generator merges the queries of module components that are related using key-based links. While this preference may positively impact the performance of the report, it does not change the report layout in any way. Even though the Report Generator creates one merged query in the report, it will still create a break group to separate the items of each module component usage. This effectively creates one repeating frame for each module component usage.

What to Do with Difficult Report Designs

If you are having difficulty generating a report design, there are alternatives. The best option is to work with your user community to develop a new layout design for the report that follows the relationships of the data model more closely. You can also work with your DBA(s) to refine the relationships in the application when real problems are identified. If neither of these is an option, there are a couple of other alternatives.

Using Views or Snapshots

A simple way to avoid reporting problems is to consider using views or snapshots. The benefits of using either of these in report development are almost identical (which is why we're presenting them in the same section). The main difference is how current the data is and how well the queries perform.

Views are stored select statements. Each time a client query accesses a view, it executes its stored select statement. An advantage of using views is that the data in the view is always current. A disadvantage is that the SQL is executed each time the view is accessed by a query.

Snapshots are static tables. Like views, they use a stored select statement when they are built and then again when refreshed. Unlike views, the data is actually stored in a separate table and is then refreshed on a scheduled basis. Selecting from a snapshot returns data just like selecting from any other table. An advantage of using snapshots is that it is just like hitting a table. It can be indexed, and constraints can be built to other tables in the application system. A disadvantage is that the data is static and will not change until the snapshot is refreshed.

Both of these types of objects will add to the number of objects that must be maintained in the database, so you should work with your DBA to work out a strategy for their development and support. They do, however, have a number of benefits that we believe are worth considering. Some of these benefits are

1. **Support for denormalized report designs**

   The select statement of a view or snapshot can merge data from many "base" tables, which allows you to create a report definition using one module component. This one module component will create one repeating frame when generated. You then have the ability to decide how many repeating frames you wish to generate, instead of having the Report Generator decide for you. You can do this by creating an item group and setting the *Break Group* property to **YES**. Then you can assign the displayed items to the item group, or break group, by setting the *Item Group* property of each displayed item to the name of the appropriate item that represents a break level within the report.

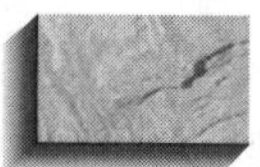

CAUTION
When you design the select statement that will be used by a view or snapshot, be careful not to accidentally replicate the data (Cartesian Join). Make sure your joins correctly return the rows you desire, or add GROUP BY or DISTINCT to the selects to return the correct number of rows.

2. **Simplified select statements**

   The select statement of a view or snapshot can include SQL functions such as decode statements, concatenations, and datatype conversions (to_char, or to_number, for example). This is a major benefit if you have to use these functions to display data commonly requested by the end users on more than one module. You can preformat the columns in the select statement of the view or snapshot and then use that object to develop the modules. Doing this means you will only have to format this information once. If the format changes, simply change the select statement of the view or snapshot, and all of the modules that reference that object will inherit the change.

3. **Join to table, view or snapshot definitions in the repository**

   A view can be joined to other table, view, and snapshot definitions in the repository by defining pseudo-PK/FK relationships. These relationships are not valid in the database and, therefore, would never be physically created in the schema.

TIP
Set the Create? property of PK/FK definitions created for views to ***NO****. This will ensure that these constraints are not generated by mistake.*

A snapshot can also be joined to other table, view, and snapshot definitions in the repository. Unlike views, constraint relationships for snapshots are valid. The obvious exception is a relationship defined with a view.
The advantage of defining these relationships is that developers can use views and snapshots along with tables in module development. This also allows developers to focus on designing views and snapshots that are targeted for specific purposes. This practice helps preserve the performance of the view or snapshot by not overpopulating it with every column in a report definition. It also contributes to the reuse of the object by other modules in the application.

Using Server-Side Application Logic

Server-side application logic is another way to help you avoid a number of report related issues. However, this approach will also create objects in the database that will need to be maintained. Work with your DBA and application technical lead to develop a strategy for developing and maintaining these objects. You also should consider putting related functions and procedures into a package. This will reduce the number of objects in the database and the associated support effort.

- **Support for denormalized report designs**

Server-side application logic can be used to denormalize individual column values. Specifically, server-side application logic is useful for aggregating child values into a parent record. This includes operational denormalization such as averaging the number of days it takes to fill all the lines of an order, or business rule denormalization, where all child records are searched for a particular status. If that status is found, it will be displayed on the parent record to represent all child records in that query. This can be done with a server-side function and defining a server-side function unbound item in the report. See Chapter 29 for more information about how to do this.

Server-side application logic can also be used for more complex denormalization. Package procedures and functions are also very useful for creating a presentation layer of data in decisions support systems and data warehouses. In these instances, the server-side application logic is usually not selected directly by the generated report, but it is used to populate snapshots or tables.

Item Format Triggers

A new feature of the Report Generator in release 2 is the ability to define and generate format triggers. Each displayed item in the layout of the generated report has a *Format Trigger* property, which contains a PL/SQL function that is executed each time that item is formatted and displayed. This function must return a Boolean value (True or False). If it returns False, the item will not be displayed on the report, even if it has data. Because of this design, a format trigger is best used to simply repress the display of fields under certain conditions. For instance, if you are reporting sensitive information and the report is distributed publicly, you may want to suppress the printing of certain information. If the report is distributed to a restricted audience, you may want to display all of the information. You can do both of these without having to maintain two separate reports by using format triggers. You can also use format triggers to add Web-specific functionality to a generated report. Using Report Builder SRW built-in function calls, you can change the visual display of a displayed item for Web-specific deployment. This topic will be covered in more detail later in this chapter.

To show how to generate a format trigger, let's work through an example. Although this example may be a little nonsensical, it will show you how to define and generate format triggers. In this example, we are going to make a copy of the sample report created in Chapter 28 and implement the following enhancement:

Modify the DBCRS report to suppress first name field if the status is complete.

To implement this requirement using a format trigger, follow these steps:

1. Make a copy the report definition that you created for the example in Chapter 28 (or use CH28_DBCRS from the example application on the CD). There is also a completed version of this example in the sample application named CH31_FMT.
2. Create a new application logic event for the PER_FIRST_NAME bound item in the L_PER lookup table. Do this by navigating to the application logic events for that bound item and pressing the Create icon in the Design Editor toolbar.
3. The Events dialog is the first dialog that will be displayed. Using this dialog, you can specify that you want to create a format trigger (*Events* = **FormatTrigger**). The completed Events dialog used in this example is shown here. When you have completed this dialog, click Next.

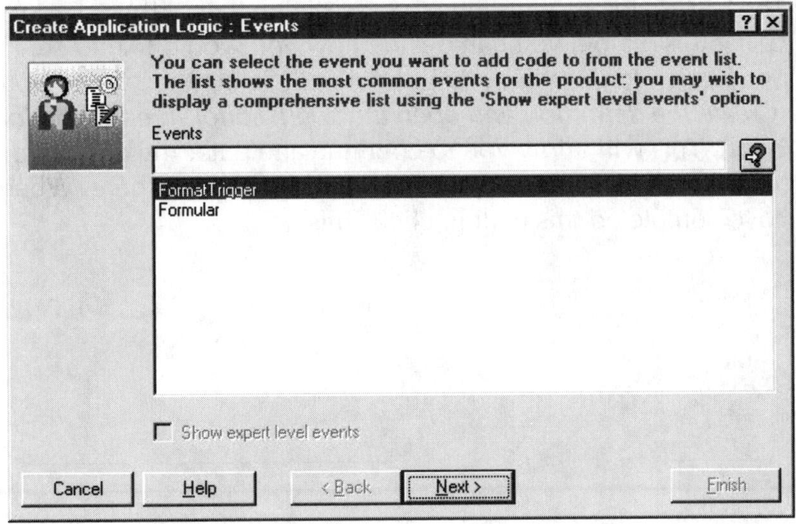

4. The Logic dialog is the second dialog that will be displayed. Using this dialog, you can add custom code events and override standard generated functionality. For this example, we created a new code event, which will be used for display rules (*Name* = **Display**). The completed Logic dialog used for this example is shown here. When you have completed this dialog, click Next.

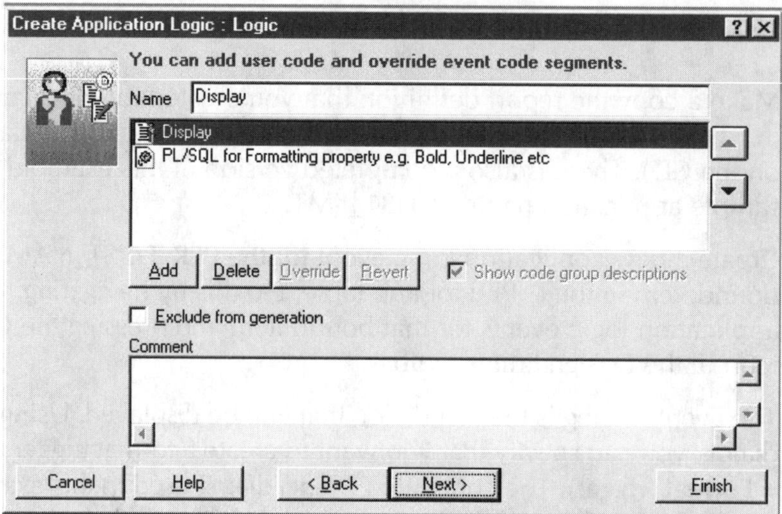

5. The Last dialog is, naturally, the last dialog that will be displayed. Using this dialog, you can decide how you would like to create the application logic event you just defined. Select the second option (*Create the definition and open the Logic Editor to enter the logic code*). This will allow you to continue and enter the code into the format trigger. The completed Last dialog is shown here. When you have completed this dialog, click Finish.

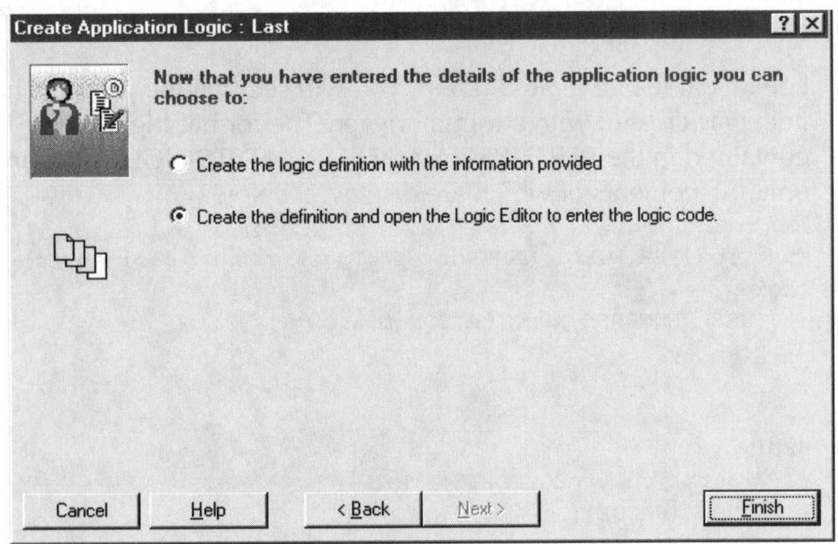

6. Using the Logic Editor, enter the code to be executed by the format trigger. The code entered for this example is shown here:

```
BEGIN
 IF :dstat_cd = 'COMPLETE' THEN
  RETURN (FALSE);
 ELSE RETURN (TRUE);
 END IF;
END;
```

TIP

Be sure to use the correct item name and prefix it with a colon(:). This will ensure that the PL/SQL will compile when it is generated.

7. Generate the report.

   Looking at the generated report, you will see that the per_first_name item was created with a format trigger. The format trigger logic is contained in the PER_FIRST_NAMEFORMAT_TRIGGER program unit, the contents of which are displayed below.

```
function PER_FIRST_NAMEFormatTrigger return boolean is
begin
--  USER ENTERED APPLICATION LOGIC
-- Display
--
--
BEGIN
 IF :dstat_cd = 'COMPLETE' THEN
  RETURN (FALSE);
 ELSE RETURN (TRUE);
 END IF;
END;
--  USER ENTERED APPLICATION LOGIC
return(TRUE);
end;
```

Web-Specific Functionality

There are some types of Web-specific functionality that can be added to generated reports that will be deployed using hypertext markup language (HTML) or portable document format (PDF). The topic of Web deployment of reports is much greater in scope and complexity than what will be covered in this section, but the intent of this section is to communicate the Web-specific functionality that can be generated based on repository definitions. There are three types of features that can be generated into HTML and PDF reports, bookmarks, hypertext links, and tags, as well as one that is specific to PDF only, command line. These are discussed next.

BOOKMARKS Bookmarks are a method that can be used to navigate around the report output. If you implement bookmarks, the report will have an area on the left side of the screen with tags that identify sections on the report. If you click one of these tags, the report viewer will navigate to that section. Bookmarks are often used to navigate to specific break groups in the report easily.

HYPERTEXT LINKS Hypertext links allow you to link a specific item in the report output to another location in the same report, another report output, or any other document available on the Web. They can be used for drilldown reports or to provide definitions and other static information that may be useful for the report.

TAGS Tags are locations in your report output that can be referenced by other hypertext links. You can connect a set of interrelated reports together using tags and hypertext links.

COMMAND LINE (PDF ONLY) The PDF report output gives you the capability to add a link that executes any other program or operating system command. You can use this capability to link reports together or integrate the report with other tools.

When choosing to add Web-specific functionality into a generated report, you need to be aware of how the Report Generator will create the generated report. The Report Generator will always create an .RDF file for each generated report. The Web-specific functionality that you generate will not be visible until you deploy in either HTML or PDF format. This can be done by opening the generated report in Report Builder, viewing the report in the Live Previewer, and then selecting View → Web Preview → Generate to Web Browser. You will then see the Web-specific functionality that you generated.

There is also one significant preference that will assist you in generating Web-specific functionality. The *Report Level Objects → Report Output Type (DSPFMT)* preference communicates to the Report Generator what type of output the report is targeted for. If the report should support output types such as HTML or PDF, you should specify that with this preference. Using this parameter you have four options, as shown in Table 31-1.

By using this preference, you can increase the layout quality of Web reports. For instance, if you are planning on using bookmarks in an HTML report, you should set this preference to **HTMLCSS**. When you create the .HTM version of this report, it will be presented with bookmarks on the left and a data view on the right. If you do not set this preference, the bookmarks will not function properly.

Setting	Description
RDF	Generate the report for RDF output.
HTML	Generate the report for HTML output.
HTMLCSS	Generate the report for HTML with support for cascading style sheets.
PDF	Generate the report for PDF.

TABLE 31-1. *Settings of the DSPFMT Preference*

Implementing Web Features

There are three different features that are implemented in a very similar way: hypertext links, tags, and PDF command line. These features are implemented by defining an item format trigger on a bound or unbound item and calling a Report Builder SRW built-in function. This functionality is only visible when the report is deployed on the in HTML or PDF format. At run time, the SRW built-in functions change the visual display of the items implementing the type of web functionality you specified. This table shows the feature types and the SRW functions that are needed to implement them:

Type of Functionality	SRW Call	Example
Hypertext link	SRW.SET_HYPERLINK('target')	SRW.SET_HYPERLINK('www.aris.com')
Tag	SRW.SET_LINKTAG(:item_name)	SRW.SET_LINKTAG(:per_first_name)
PDF Command Line	SRW.SET_ACTION('command')	SRW.SET_ACTION('C:\orant\bin\r30run\ ch28_dbcrs.rdf')

The item format trigger section in this chapter has a detailed step-by-step example of how to define and generate an item format trigger. You simply need to replace the trigger text in step 6 with the appropriate SRW built-in function call. After you generate the report, run it in HTML or PDF format and you will see the Web functionality that you generated.

Implementing a bookmark is different than the other types of Web functionality. This feature is implemented by setting the *Context* property of the desired bound or unbound item to **YES**. Just as with the other types of Web functionality previously described, this feature is only visible when the report is deployed on the in HTML or PDF format.

Generation Troubleshooting Guide

Problem	**Solution**
When I try to generate a format trigger for a displayed item, I keep getting the message, "CGEN-02030 WARNING: Module: Failed to compile PLSQL."	This is probably because of one of two things: 1. You forgot to prefix the item name with a colon (:). 2. You entered the wrong item name. Verify that the item name you entered to be evaluated by the format trigger matches the *Name* property of the bound item.
When I try to generate a hypertext link for a displayed item, I keep getting the message, "CGEN-02030 WARNING: Module: Failed to compile PLSQL."	If you're targeting a document or a www address: 1. You forgot to enclose the target with single quotes. If you're targeting a field in the report: 1. You forgot to prefix the item name with a colon (:), or, 2. You entered the wrong item name. Verify that the item name you entered to be evaluated by the format trigger matches the *Name* property of the bound item.
When I try to generate a tag for a displayed item, I keep getting the message, "CGEN-02030 WARNING: Module: Failed to compile PLSQL."	This is probably because of one of two things: 1. You forgot to prefix the item name with a colon (:). 2. You entered the wrong item name. Verify that the item name you entered to be evaluated by the format trigger matches the *Name* property of the bound item.
When I try to generate a PDF command line for a displayed item, I keep getting the message,"CGEN-02030 WARNING: Module: Failed to compile PLSQL."	This is probably because you forgot to enclose the target with single quotes.

CHAPTER 32

Report Layout Standards

In this chapter, we will present a number of standard report designs that you can use as a baseline for your report development. The information in this chapter is presented in a high-level, cookbook style approach. We are assuming that you are already familiar with the Report Generator. If not, please refer to the other chapters in Part V or to the online help for assistance. In this chapter, we will cover significant layout properties. In addition, we will go over the layout design standards of the following reports:

- A tabular report
- A form report
- An address (mailing label) report
- A control break report
- A master detail report
- A matrix report

Each of the above report layout standards will include the following information:

- A screenshot of the generated report layout
- General characteristics of each report layout
- A table showing the layout property settings used to produce the report layout
- A procedure to help you create the report layout
- Layout generation tips that will include some techniques and warnings about the generated report layout

Significant Layout Properties

There are four layout properties of a report definition that significantly influence the layout of generated reports. These properties exist in a relationship hierarchy and are used by the Report Generator to determine how the layout of the generated report will look. The layout of the report can be modified in many ways by mixing and matching the settings of these properties. Once these properties are set, you can use generation preferences to refine the appearance of the report. The name and level of each of the four properties is shown in Table 32-1.

Level One—Report Module

The first level in the hierarchy is the report module level. At this level, the *Layout Format* property of the report module determines the overall layout format or structure for the report. The settings of this property are shown in Table 32-2.

Level Two—Module Component

The second level in the hierarchy is the module component. At this level, the *Layout Style* property of the module component communicates to the Report Generator which layout style to apply to the module component when creating it within the format or structure defined at the report module level. The settings for this property are shown in Table 32-3.

The layout of simple reports will be defined at this level. This includes tabular, form, and address reports. These types of reports have one module component and do not use item (break) groups.

Level	**Repository Definition**	**Property**
One	Report Module	Layout Format
Two	Module Component	Layout Style
Three	Item Group	Layout
Three	Item Group	Break Style*

*This property is only valid when the Item Group *Break Group?* property is set to **Yes**.

TABLE 32-1. *Significant Layout Properties*

Setting	Description
Label	All groups will be created using the address layout style.
Master Detail	Multiple group (parent-child) reports: parent groups will be generated using the form layout style; the last child group will be generated using the tabular layout style. Single group (parent only) reports: the layout will be created for the single group using the tabular layout style.
Control Break	All groups will be created using the tabular layout style.
Matrix	The across layout style will be used for groups in the Across master hierarchy. The tabular layout style will be used for groups in the Down master hierarchy.
<null>	The layout of the report will be determined by the settings of the module component *Layout Style* property.

TABLE 32-2. *Settings of the Report Module Layout Format Property*

Setting	Description
Tabular	Multifield, multiple rows per page. The prompts of the items in the report body are displayed above. Records are ordered vertically down the page.
Form	One record is displayed per page. The prompts of the items in the report body are displayed to the left.
Address	Multifield, multiple rows per page. Items are displayed without prompts. Records are ordered horizontally across the page.
Across	Used primarily in matrix reports. Displays prompts above and data below.
<null>	The layout style will be inherited from the setting of the *Layout Format* property of the report module, or the *Layout Style* property of the module component.

TABLE 32-3. *Settings of the Module Component Layout Style Property*

Level Three—Item (Break) Group

The third level in the hierarchy is the item group. There are two properties that significantly influence the layout of the report at this level, the Item Group *Layout Style* property and the Item Group *Break Style* property. The *Break Style* property is only significant when the *Break Group?* property is set to **Yes**.

For all reports that use item groups, the Item Group *Layout Style* property functions very similarly to the *Layout Style* property of the module component. This property determines how the displayed items assigned to the item group will be displayed within the module component. The settings for this property are shown in Table 32-4.

For break reports (master detail and control break), the Item Group *Break Style* property communicates to the Report Generator how to create the print direction for the repeating frames created by each item (break) group. This property also influences the number of records displayed per page. The settings for this property are shown in Table 32-5.

Setting	Description
Tabular	Multifield, multiple rows per page. The prompts of the items in the report body are displayed above. Records are ordered vertically down the page.
Form	One record is displayed per page. The prompts of the items in the report body are displayed to the left.
Address	Multifield, multiple rows per page. Items are displayed without prompts. Records are ordered horizontally across the page.
Across	Used primarily in matrix reports. Displays prompts above and data below.
Standard	The layout style will be inherited from the setting of the *Layout Format* property of the report module.

TABLE 32-4. *Settings of the Item Group Layout Style Property*

Setting	Description
Down	Multifield, multiple rows per page. The prompts of the items in the report body are normally displayed above. Records are ordered vertically down the page.
Across	One record is displayed per page. The prompts of the items in the report body are normally displayed to the left.
Intersect	Multifield, multiple rows per page. Items are displayed without prompts. Records are ordered horizontally across the page. This style is designed to be used in matrix reports, but can be used in other style reports. When used in nonmatrix reports, layouts will generally mimic either the Down or Across Break group styles, depending on the Report Format.
<null>	The layout style will be inherited from the setting of the *Layout Style* property of the item group.

TABLE 32-5. *Settings of the Item Group Break Style Property*

By mixing and matching the two item group properties discussed, you can generate many different variations in break reports, whether you wish to break the above (master-detail) or to the left (control-break).

Tabular Report

Prompts above items →

Multiple records per page

No.	Description	Requested By
0898-001	Add the APP_ACRONYM column to the ISSUES table	Ken Atkins
0898-002	Add Audit Columns to the DBCRS and PEOPLE tables	Ken Atkins
0998-011	Some change to the DBCRS table	Paul Dirksen
0998-012	Another change to the DBCRS table	Paul Dirksen
0998-013	Yet Another change to the DBCRS table	Paul Dirksen
0998-014	What, another change?	Paul Dirksen
0998-015	Enough with the changes to Issues already!	Paul Dirksen

General Characteristics

- **One Module Component—No Item (Break) Groups**

  A simple tabular report normally consists of one module component and no item groups. This is because all of the data that will be displayed is at the same frequency.

- **Multiple fields, multiple rows per page**

  Fields are aligned horizontally across the page with prompts above. The data returned by the report is displayed vertically down the report.

Layout Property Settings

The layout properties used to produce the sample report are shown here:

Level	Property	Setting
Report Module	Layout Format	<Null>
Module Component	Layout Style	Tabular

Procedure to Create the Sample Report

The following steps provide you with a high-level procedure for creating this report. We are assuming that you are already familiar with defining and generating reports. If you would like more detailed information on how to create a report or how to implement a particular feature, please refer to the other chapters in this section or to the online help.

1. Create a report definition. Be sure to set the *Layout Format* property to **<null>**. The completed version of this example is available in the sample application named CH32_TABULAR.
2. Create one module component. Be sure to set the *Layout Style* property to **Tabular**. Do not create any item (break) groups for this module component. The following table shows the tables and columns that should be included in this module component.

Table	Type	Column
DBCRS	BASE	Bound Item: NUM Bound Item: DBCR_DESC
PEOPLE	LOOKUP	Bound Item: FULL_NAME

3. Generate the report.

Layout Generation Tips

- **Setting the Layout Format Property**

  There is only one compatible setting of the report module *Layout Format* property for a tabular report, **<Null>**. This means that the other four settings are incompatible for tabular reports. If you choose to use an incompatible setting, you will receive the following generation warning:

  ```
  CGEN-02201 WARNING: Module layout style of <style name> is
  incompatible with structure of report
  ```

  Don't let this warning alarm you. The report will still generate successfully, creating the layout using the tabular layout style. This message simply states that the layout format specified is invalid for this type of report. The layout format is ignored and the report layout is created based on the setting of the module component *Layout Style* property.

Form Report

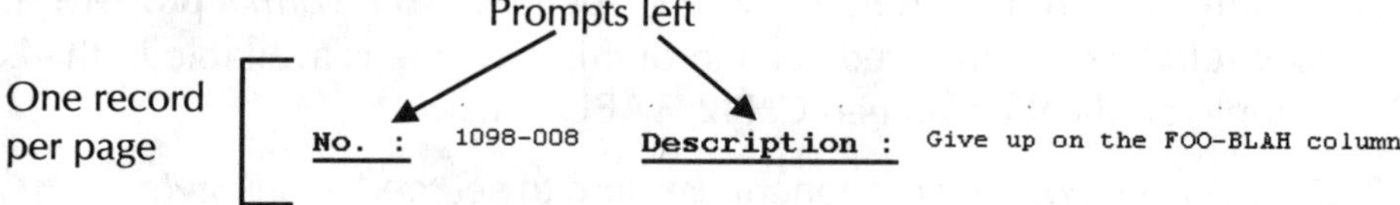

General Characteristics

- **One Module Component**
  A simple form report normally consists of one module component. This is because all of the data that will be displayed is at the same frequency.

- **One Break Group**

  Form reports require one break group. All of the displayed items should be assigned to this break group. If you do not create the break group, the Report Generator will create an implicit break group when generating the report. This break group will not be visible in the Design Editor. Also, you can not change the property settings of the default break group.

- **One record per page**

  Form reports typically display one record per page. The fields are displayed horizontally across the page with prompts aligned to the left.

Layout Property Settings

The layout properties used to produce the sample report are shown here:

Level	Property	Setting
Report Module	Report Format	<Null>
Module Component	Layout Style	Form
Item Group	Layout Style	Standard
Item Group	Break Group?	Yes
Item Group	Break Style	<Null>

Procedure to Create the Sample Report

The following steps provide you with a high-level procedure for creating this report. We are assuming that you are already familiar with defining and generating reports. If you would like more detailed information on how to create a report or how to implement a particular feature, please refer to the other chapters in this section or to the online help.

1. Create a report definition. Be sure to set the *Layout Format* property to **<null>**. The completed version of this example is available in the sample application named CH32_FORM.

2. Create one module component. Be sure to set the *Layout Style* property to **Form**. The following table shows the tables and columns that should be included in this module component.

Table	Type	Column
DBCRS	BASE	Bound Item: NUM Bound Item: DBCR_DESC
PEOPLE	LOOKUP	Bound Item: FULL_NAME

3. Create one item group. Be sure to set the *Layout Style* property to **Standard**, the *Break Group?* property to **Yes,** and the *Break Style* property to **<null>**.
4. Assign all of the displayed items to the item group.
5. Generate the report.

Layout Generation Tips

- **Implicit Break Groups**

  If you do not create an item group for a form layout style report you will receive the following generation warning the first time the report is generated.

  ```
  CGEN-02201 WARNING: Module layout style of <style name> is
  incompatible with structure of report
  ```

  Don't let this warning alarm you. The report will still generate successfully, creating the layout using the form layout style. The Report Generator will create an implicit break group for the report, which will not be visible to you in the Design Editor. You will only receive this message the first time the report is generated.

Address (Mailing Label) Report

Vertically stacked fields with no prompts

```
Ken Atkins         Paul Dirksen       Askin Ince         Ian Fisher
1234 Some Street   1234 Some Street   1234 Some Street   1234 Some Street
Some City          Some City          Some City          Some City
Somewhere          Somewhere          Somewhere          Somewhere
US                 US                 US                 UK
```

General Characteristics

- **One Module Component—No Break Groups**

  An address report normally consists of one module component and no item (break) groups. This is because all of the data that will be displayed is at the same frequency.

- **Vertically stacked, no prompts**

  Records are displayed vertically stacked, ordered across the page without prompts.

Layout Property Settings

You have three different sets of layout properties that can be used to create the sample report layout. The alternatives are shown in Tables 32-6, 32-7, and 32-8.

Procedure to Create the Sample Report

The following steps provide you with a high-level procedure for creating this report. We are assuming that you are already familiar with defining and generating reports. If you would like more detailed information on how to create a report or how to implement a particular feature, please refer to the other chapters in this section or to the online help.

1. Create a report definition. Be sure to set the *Layout Format* property to **Label**. The completed version of this example is available in the sample application named CH32_ADDRESS.
2. Create one module component. Be sure to set the *Layout Style* property to **<null>**. The following table shows the tables and columns that should be included in this module component.

Table	Type	Column
ADDRESS	BASE	Bound Item: ADDRESS_LINE_1 Bound Item: CITY Bound Item: STATE Bound Item: COUNTRY
PEOPLE	LOOKUP	Bound Item: FULL_NAME

3. Generate the report.

Level	Property	Setting
Report Module	Report Format	Label
Module Component	Layout Style	<Null>

TABLE 32-6. *Address Report Layout Properties, First Alternative*

Level	Property	Setting
Report Module	Report Format	<Null>
Module Component	Layout Style	Address

TABLE 32-7. *Address Report Layout Properties, Second Alternatives*

Control Break Report

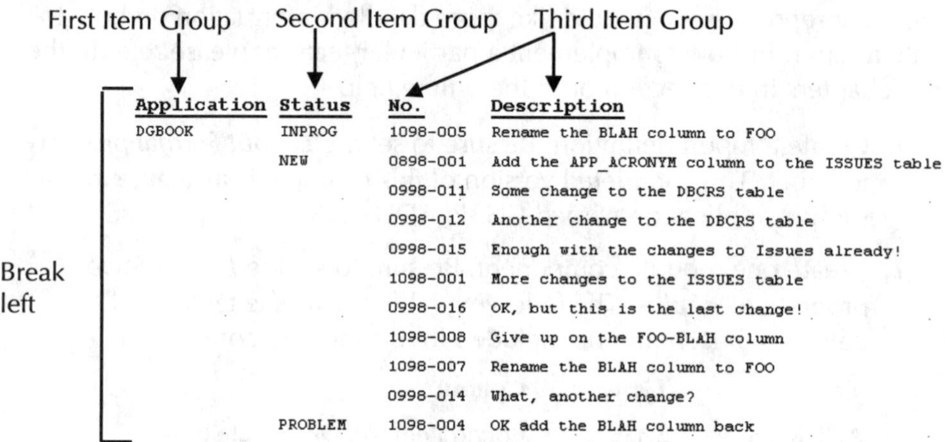

First Item Group
Second Item Group
Third Item Group
Break left
Application Status No. Description
DGBOOK INPROG 1098-005 Rename the BLAH column to FOO
NEW 0898-001 Add the APP_ACRONYM column to the ISSUES table
0998-011 Some change to the DBCRS table
0998-012 Another change to the DBCRS table
0998-015 Enough with the changes to Issues already!
1098-001 More changes to the ISSUES table
0998-016 OK, but this is the last change!
1098-008 Give up on the FOO-BLAH column
1098-007 Rename the BLAH column to FOO
0998-014 What, another change?
PROBLEM 1098-004 OK add the BLAH column back

General Characteristics

- **One module component with break groups**

  A control break report consists of one module component with one or more break groups. You cannot use the control break layout style if you have more than one module component in the report definition.

Level	Property	Setting
Report Module	Report Format	Label
Module Component	Layout Style	Address

TABLE 32-8. *Address Report Layout Properties, Third Alternative*

- **Break left, prompts above**

  Control break reports break left. The general layout style is similar to the tabular layout style, with prompts displayed above.

Layout Property Settings

The layout properties used to produce the sample report are shown in Table 32-9.

Procedure to Create the Sample Report

The following steps provide you with a high-level procedure for creating this report. We are assuming that you are already familiar with defining and generating reports. If you would like more detailed information on how to create a report or how to implement a particular feature, please refer to the other chapters in this section or to the online help.

1. Create a report definition. Be sure to set the *Layout Format* property to **Control Break**. The completed version of this example is available in the sample application named CH32_CONTROL_BREAK.

Level	**Property**	**Setting**
Report Module	Report Format	Control Break
Module Component	Layout Style	<null>
First Item Group	Layout Style	Standard
First Item Group	Break Group?	Yes
First Item Group	Break Style	Down
Second Item Group	Layout Style	Standard
Second Item Group	Break Group?	Yes
Second Item Group	Break Style	Down
Third Item Group	Layout Style	Standard
Third Item Group	Break Group?	Yes
Third Item Group	Break Style	Down

TABLE 32-9. *Control Break Report Layout Properties*

2. Create one module component. Be sure to set the *Layout Style* property to **<null>**. The following table shows the tables and columns that should be included in this module component.

Table	Type	Column
DBCRS	BASE	Bound Item: NUM Bound Item: DBCRS_DESC
APPLICATIONS	LOOKUP	Bound Item: ACRONOYM
DBCRS_STATUS	LOOKUP	Bound Item: DSTAT_CD

3. Create three item groups. See Table 32-9 for the layout property settings. The names used for each item group are shown here:

Item Group Level	Name
First	Application
Second	Status
Third	Body

4. Specify the hierarchy of item groups. This table shows the hierarchy used for the report:

Item Group	Parent Item Group
Application	<null>
Status	Application
Body	Status

5. Assign the columns to the item groups. The following table shows the item group assignments used in this report:

Item Group	Item
Application (First Item Group)	Bound Item: ACRONYM
Status (Second Item Group)	Bound Item: DSTAT_CD
Body (Third Item Group)	Bound Item: NUM Bound Item: DBCR_DESC

6. Generate the report.

Layout Generation Tips

- **Item Group Break Style**

  You cannot mix and match the settings of the *Break Style* property on each item (break) group in a control break report. The Report Generator will use the setting of the *Break Style* property in the first item group and apply it to all of the item groups in the report.

  If the *Break Style* property is set to **<null>**, the Report Generator will use **Down** as the default value. When you generate the report, you will receive the following generation warning informing you of this action.

  ```
  CGEN-02202 WARNING:  Break group direction for all groups
  has been defaulted to DOWN
  ```

  Don't let this warning alarm you. The report will still generate successfully, creating the layout using the control break layout style. You will only receive this message each time the report is generated until the *Break Style* property is set to a value other than null.

Master Detail Report

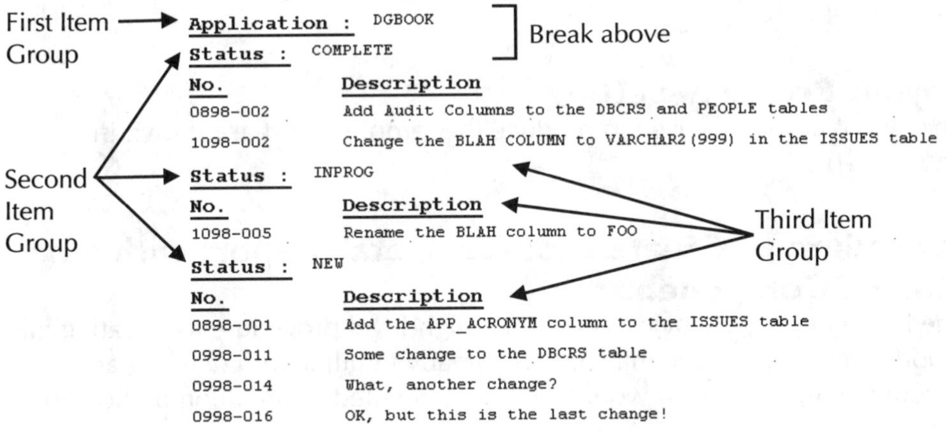

General Characteristics

- **One module component with break groups, or many module components**

  A master detail report can be defined using one module component with break groups. It can also be defined using many module components, which may also use break groups. If only one module component is used, then one or more item (break) groups are required. If more than one module component is used, a break will be generated into the report layout for each module component. Often times, item (break) groups are used to provide additional breaks.

- **Break above, form and tabular layout styles**

  Master detail reports typically break above. Each of the breaks is displayed using the form layout style except the last break group, which is displayed using the tabular layout style.

Alternative One—One Module Component

The first alternative for creating the sample report is to use one module component.

Layout Property Settings

The layout properties used to produce the sample report are shown in Table 32-10.

Procedure to Create a Master Detail Report with One Module Component

The following steps provide you with a high-level procedure for creating this report. We are assuming that you are already familiar with defining and generating reports. If you would like more detailed information on how to

Level	Property	Setting
Report Module	Report Format	Master Detail
Module Component	Layout Style	Tabular
First Item Group	Layout Style	Form
First Item Group	Break Group?	Yes
First Item Group	Break Style	Down
Second Item Group	Layout Style	Form
Second Item Group	Break Group?	Yes
Second Item Group	Break Style	Down
Third Item Group	Layout Style	Standard
Third Item Group	Break Group?	Yes
Third Item Group	Break Style	<null>

TABLE 32-10. *Master Detail Report Layout Properties*

create a report or how to implement a particular feature, please refer to the other chapters in this section or to the online help.

1. Create a report definition. Be sure to set the *Layout Format* property to **Master Detail**. The completed version of this example is available in the sample application named CH32_MD.
2. Create one module component. Be sure to set the *Layout Style* property to **Tabular**. The following table shows the tables and columns that should be included in this module component.

Table	Type	Column
DBCRS	BASE	Bound Item: NUM Bound Item: DBCRS_DESC
APPLICATIONS	LOOKUP	Bound Item: ACRONOYM
DBCRS_STATUS	LOOKUP	Bound Item: DSTAT_CD

3. Create three item groups. See Table 32-10 for the property settings. The names used for each item group are shown in the following table:

Item Group Level	Name
First	Application
Second	Status
Third	Body

4. Specify the hierarchy of item groups. The following table shows the hierarchy used for this report:

Item Group	Parent Item Group
Application	<null>
Status	Application
Body	Status

5. Assign the columns to the item groups. The following table shows the item group assignments used in this report:

Item Group	Item
Application (First Item Group)	Bound Item: ACRONYM
Status (Second Item Group)	Bound Item: DSTAT_CD
Body (Third Item Group)	Bound Item: NUM Bound Item: DBCR_DESC

6. Generate the report.

Layout Generation Tips

- **Item Group Layout Style Defaults**

  For master detail reports that have only one module component, the Report Generator will use the form layout style for all break levels in the report except the last one. The tabular layout style will be applied to that break group. You can override these defaults by changing the *Layout Style* property of each of the item groups.

Alternative Two—More than One Module Component

The second alternative for creating the sample report is to use more than one module component, as shown here:

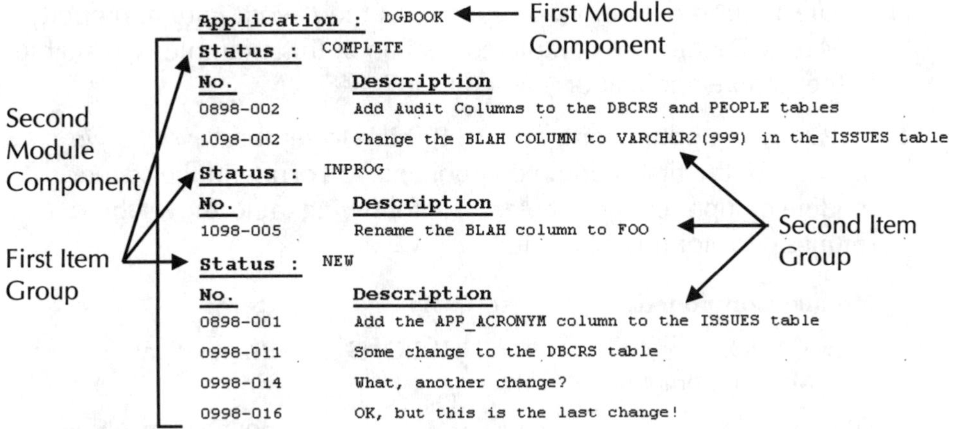

Layout Property Settings

The layout properties used to produce the sample report are shown in Table 32-11.

Level	Property	Setting
Report Module	Report Format	Master Detail
First Module Component	Layout Style	Form
Second Module Component	Layout Style	Tabular
First Item Group	Layout Style	Form
First Item Group	Break Group?	Yes
First Item Group	Break Style	Down
Second Item Group	Layout Style	Standard
Second Item Group	Break Group?	Yes
Second Item Group	Break Style	<null>

TABLE 32-11. *Master Detail Report Layout Properties*

Procedure to Create the Sample Report with More Than One Module Component

The following steps provide you with a high-level procedure for creating this report. We are assuming that you are already familiar with defining and generating reports. If you would like more detailed information on how to create a report or how to implement a particular feature, please refer to the other chapters in this section or to the online help.

1. Create a report definition. Be sure to set the *Layout Format* property to **Master Detail**. The completed version of this example is available in the sample application named CH32_MD_2MC.

2. Create two module components. Be sure to set the *Layout Style* property of the first module components to **Form** and the second module component to **Tabular**. The following table shows the settings used for this example:

Module Component	Base Table	Items
APPLICATIONS (First Module Component)	APPPLICATIONS	Bound Item: Acronym
DBCRS (Second Module Component)	DBCRS *Also include DBCR_STATUS as a lookup table usage	Bound Item: NUM Bound Item: DBCR_DESC Bound Item: DSTAT_CD from DBCR_STATUS

3. Create a key-based link between the two module components. The following table shows the settings used for this example:

Module Component	From Base Table	To Base Table
OBJECT_TYPES (First Module Component)	APPLICATIONS	DBCRS

4. Create two item groups in the second module component. See Table 32-11 for the property settings. The names used for each item group are shown in the following table:

Item Group Level	Name
First	Status
Second	Body

5. Specify the hierarchy of item groups. The following table shows the hierarchy used for this report:

Item Group	Parent Item Group
Status	<null>
Body	Status

6. Assign the displayed items to the item groups. The following table shows the item group assignments used in this report:

Item Group	Item
Status (First Item Group)	Bound Item: DSTAT_CD
Body (Second Item Group)	Bound Item: NUM Bound Item: DBCR_DESC

7. Generate the report.

Layout Generation Tips

- **Module Component Layout Style Defaults**

The Report Generator will apply the form layout to all module components except the last in master detail reports that have more than one module component. The tabular layout style will be applied to that module component. When you generate the report, you will receive the following generation warning informing you of this action.

```
CGEN-02203 WARNING: Layout style for master group default
to FORM in Master Detail report
```

These defaults will occur regardless of the settings of the module component *Layout Style* property. The only way to override them is to create item groups and use the *Layout Style* property of the item groups.

Matrix Report

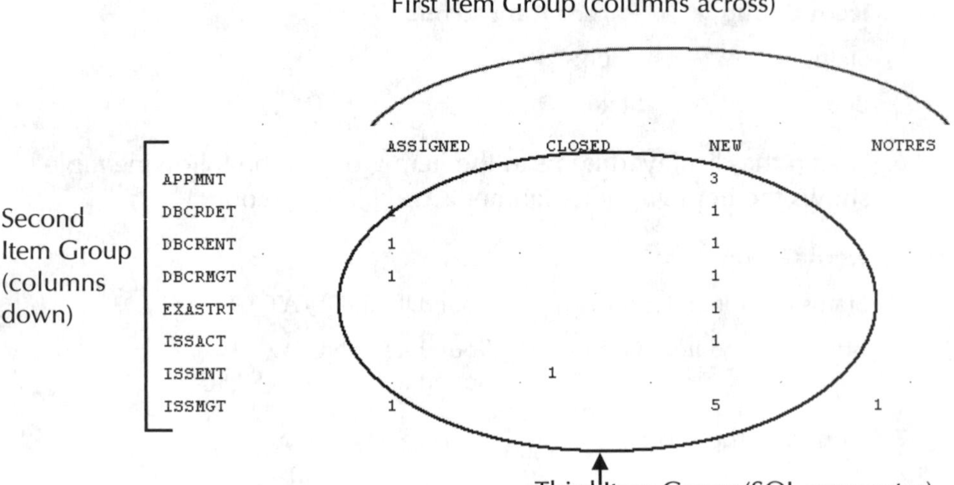

General Characteristics

- **Spreadsheet layout**

  Matrix reports display data in a spreadsheet-type layout. The prompts above and to the left are selected from database columns. The data in the middle is typically a SQL aggregate such as count(*).

- **Two parents, one common child**

  To use the matrix layout style, you must have a data model that has two parents and one common child. This could be a fundamental table with two code tables or an associative table that splits a many-to-many relationship of two fundamental tables.

- **Two different approaches to defining a matrix report**

  A matrix report can be defined using one module component that has three item (break) groups, or using three different module components.

Alternative One— One Module Component

The first alternative for creating the sample report is to use one module component.

Layout Property Settings

The layout properties used to produce the sample report are shown in Table 32-12.

Procedure to Create the Sample Report with One Module Component

The following steps provide you with a high-level procedure for creating this report. We are assuming that you are already familiar with defining and

Level	Property	Setting
Report Module	Report Format	Matrix
Module Component	Layout Style	<Null>
First Item Group	Layout Style	Standard
First Item Group	Break Group?	Yes
First Item Group	Break Style	Across
Second Item Group	Layout Style	Standard
Second Item Group	Break Group?	Yes
Second Item Group	Break Style	Down
Third Item Group	Layout Style	Standard
Third Item Group	Break Group?	Yes
Third Item Group	Break Style	Intersection

TABLE 32-12. *Matrix Report—One Module Component*

generating reports. If you would like more detailed information on how to create a report or how to implement a particular feature, please refer to the other chapters in this section or to the online help.

1. Create a report definition. Be sure to set the *Layout Format* property to **Matrix**. The completed version of this example is available in the sample application named CH32_MATRIX.

2. Create one module component. Be sure to set the *Layout Style* property to **<Null>**. The following table shows the tables and columns that should be included in this module component.

Table	**Type**	**Column**
ISSUES_OBJECTS	BASE	SQL Aggregate Unbound Item: COUNT(*)
OBJECTS	LOOKUP	Bound Item: NAME
ISSUES	LOOKUP	Bound Item: ISTAT_CD

3. Create three item groups. See Table 32-12 for the property settings. The names used for each item group are shown in this table:

Item Group	**Name**
First	Issues
Second	Objects
Third	Body

4. Assign the columns to the item groups. The following table shows the item group assignments used in this report:

Item Group	**Item**
Issues (First Item Group)	Bound Item: ISTAT_CD
Objects (Second Item Group)	Bound Item: NAME
Body (Third Item Group)	Unbound Item COUNT(*)

5. Generate the report.

Alternative Two—Three Module Components

To create a matrix report using three module components, use the following layout property settings and procedure specified in this section. The sample report layout is shown here:

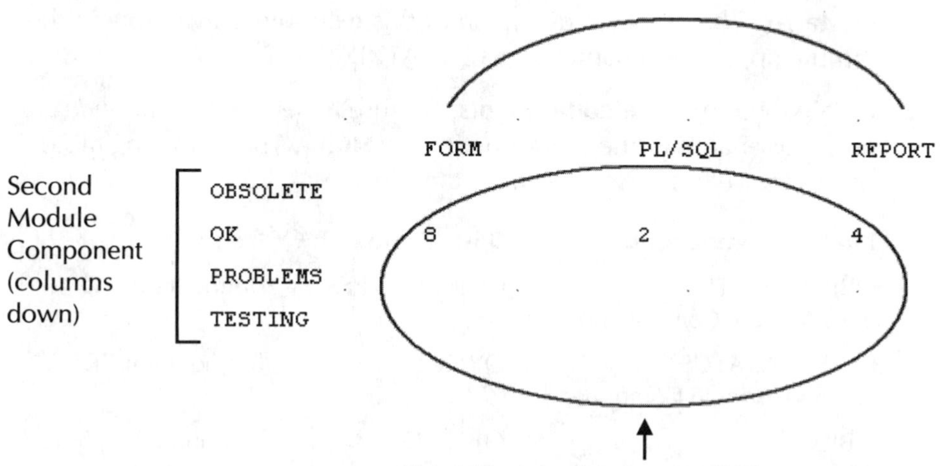

Layout Property Settings

The layout properties used to create the sample report are shown in this table:

Level	**Property**	**Setting**
Report Module	Report Format	Matrix
First Module Component	Layout Style	<Null>
Second Module Component	Layout Style	<Null>
Third Module Component	Layout Style	<Null>

Procedure to Create the Sample Report with Three Module Components

The following steps below provide you with a high-level procedure for creating this report. We are assuming that you are already familiar with defining and generating reports. If you would like more detailed information on how to create a report or how to implement a particular feature, please refer to the other chapters in this section or to the online help.

1. Create a report definition. Be sure to set the *Layout Format* property to **Matrix**. The completed version of this example is available in the sample application named CH32_MATRIX_3MC

2. Create three module components. Be sure to set the *Layout Style* property of all module components to **<Null>**. The following table shows the settings used for this example:

Module Component	Base Table	Items
OBJECT_TYPES (First Module Component)	OBJECT_TYPES	Bound Item: CD
OBJECT_STATUS (Second Module Component)	OBJECT_STATUS	Bound Item: CD
OBJECTS (Third Module Component)	OBJECTS	Unbound Item SQL Aggregate: Count(*)

3. Create key-based links for the first two module components to the third module component. The following table shows the settings used for this example:

Module Component	From Base Table	To Base Table
OBJECT_TYPES (First Module Component)	OBJECT_TYPES	OBJECTS
OBJECT_STATUS (Second Module Component)	OBJECT_STATUS	OBJECTS

4. Generate the report.

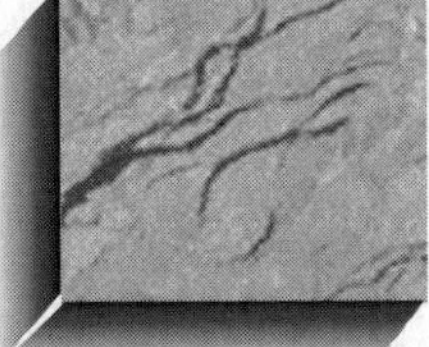

APPENDIX A

Example Application

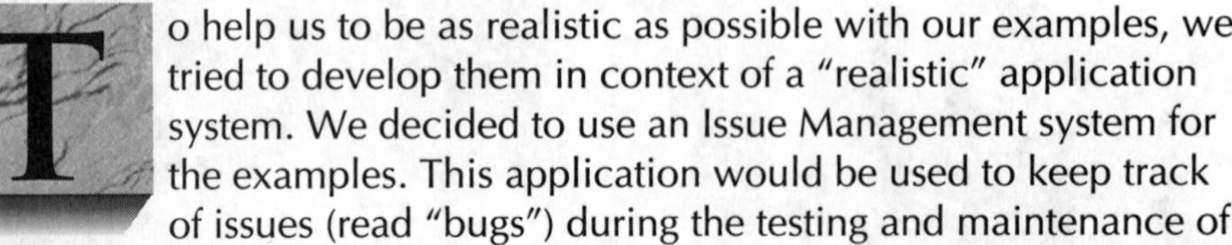

To help us to be as realistic as possible with our examples, we tried to develop them in context of a "realistic" application system. We decided to use an Issue Management system for the examples. This application would be used to keep track of issues (read "bugs") during the testing and maintenance of application systems. We developed a fairly robust data structure that allowed us to generate fairly complex examples. The data model includes the following features:

- Tracks issues for multiple application systems
- Keeps track of an issue's creation date, status, type, priority, and person who encountered it
- Allows issues to be related to the modules or tables (or any other application object) that they were encountered for
- Assigns issues to developers and application versions for resolution
- Keeps track of actions taken on issues
- Keeps track of Database Change Requests (DBCRs) for an application
- Maps the DBCRs to application objects (tables and modules)
- Maps the DBCRs to issues
- Assigns DBCRs to people, have status, create dates, etc.
- Keeps track of when the DBCR was implemented on multiple instances
- Keeps track of Oracle TARs and how they map to modules and DBCRs

To help you place the examples in the context of the whole application, we are providing a schema diagram of the whole data model here (see Figures A-1 through A-3). You can also access the full description of the application, including the diagrams and descriptions of the tables in the example Designer application that is included on the CD.

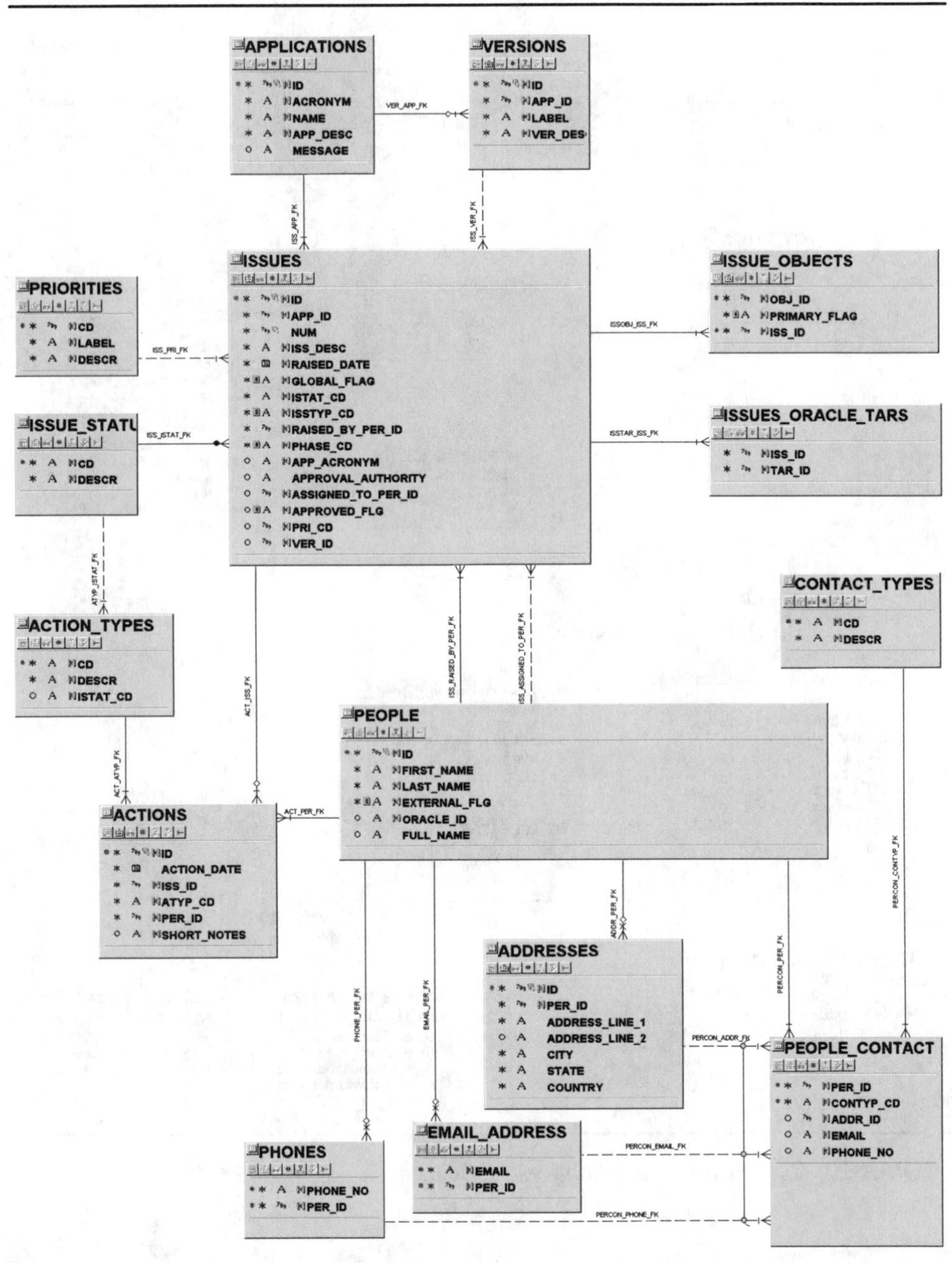

FIGURE A-1. *Example application—Issues area*

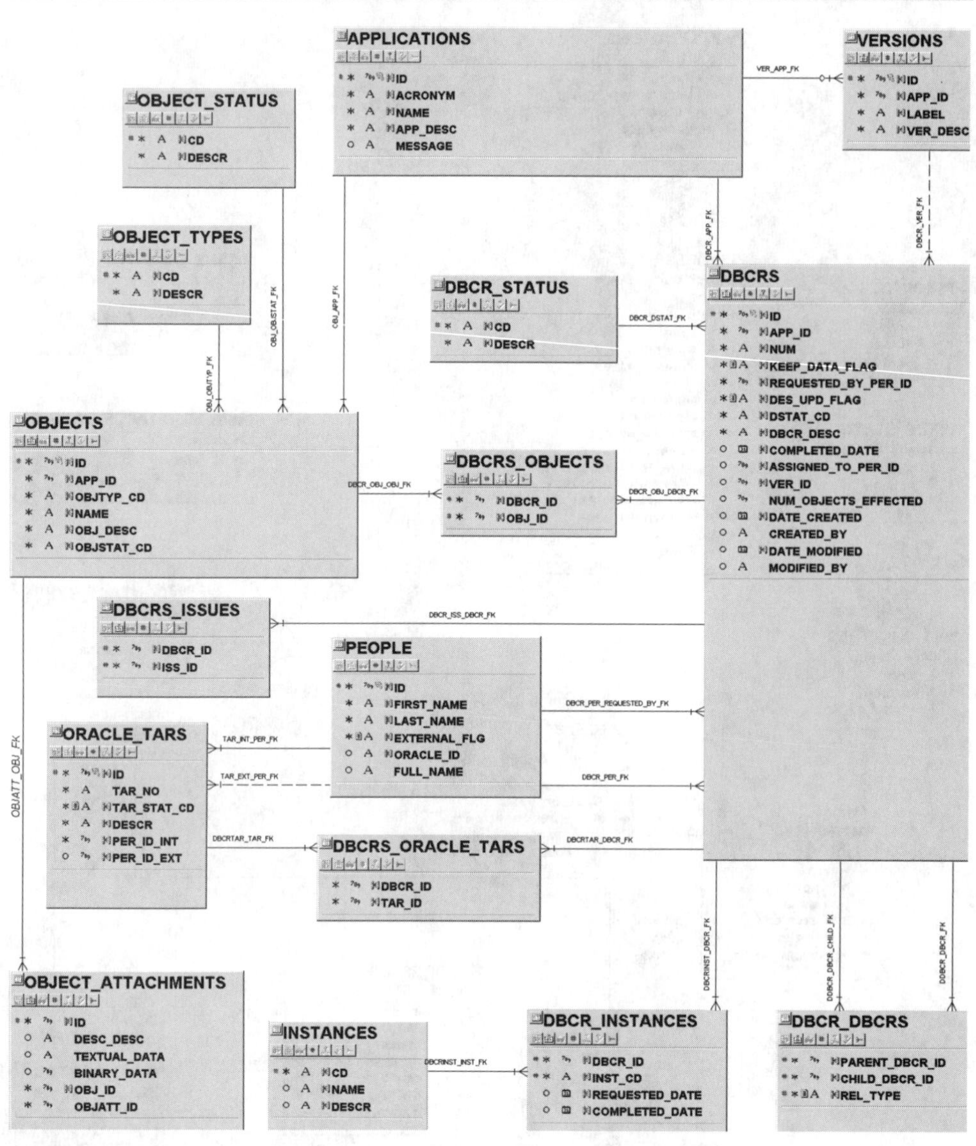

FIGURE A-2. *Example application—DBCRs area*

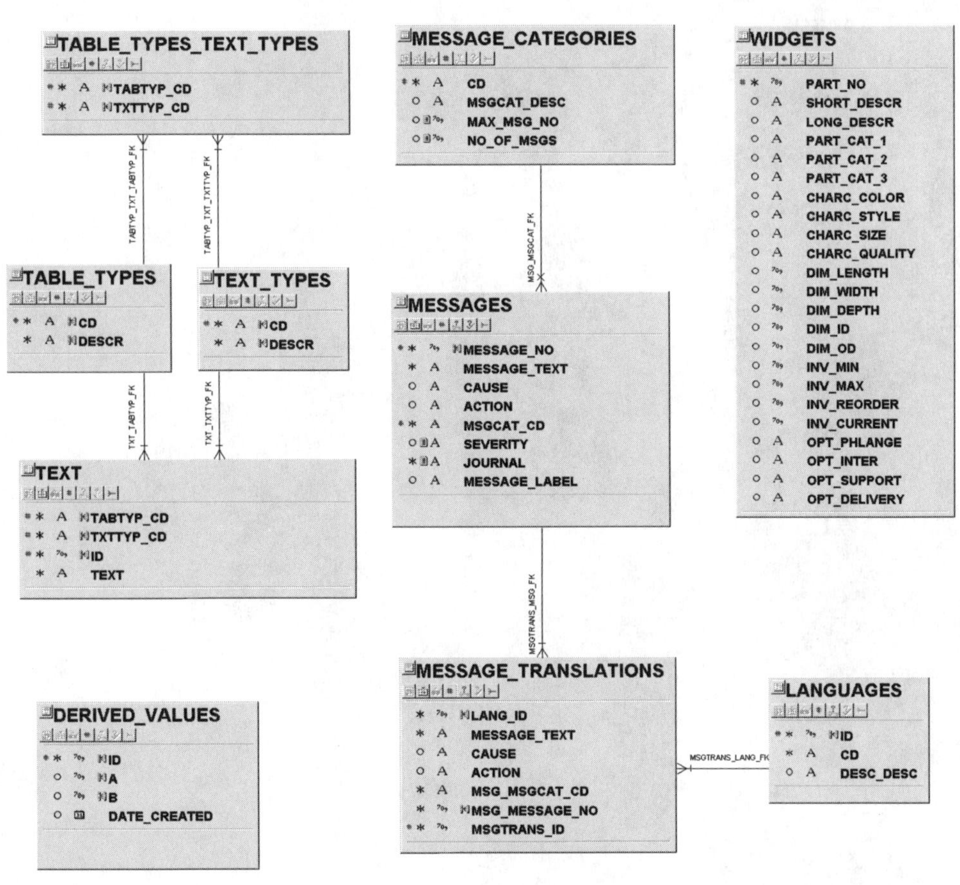

FIGURE A-3. *Example application—Miscellaneous area*

The examples did not implement every aspect of the model; we just wanted enough complexity to work with. This is not necessarily a production-worthy data model. Some of the modeling was done to implement specific examples, not in a way we would ever really do it in a production system. We used an issues-tracking system because the purpose and functionality of such an application should be understandable to most Oracle developers.

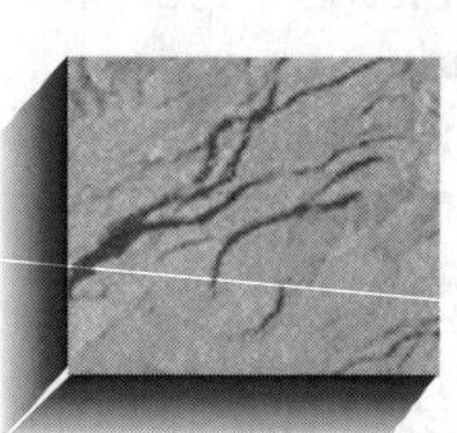

Index

A

B

C

D

G

H

I

K

L

M

N

Q

R

S

U

V

W

Z

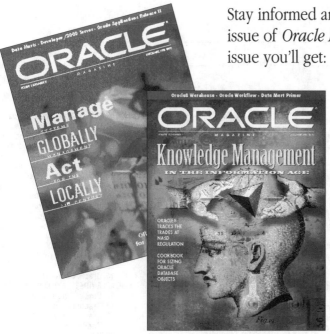